European Marketing Data and Statistics

European Marketing Data and Statistics

2009

44th edition

Euromonitor International Plc, 60-61 Britton Street, London EC1M 5UX

European Marketing Data and Statistics 2009

First published 1964
Forty-fourth edition
ISBN 978-1-84264-484-3
Published by:

Western Europe
Euromonitor International Plc
60-61 Britton Street
London EC1M 5UX
United Kingdom
Tel: +44 207-251-8024
Fax: +44 207-608-3149
email: info@euromonitor.com

North and Latin America
Euromonitor International Inc
224 South Michigan Avenue
Suite 1500
Chicago
IL 60604, USA
Tel: + 1 312 922 1115
Fax: +1 312 922 1157
email: insight@euromonitorintl.com

Asia Pacific and Australasia
Euromonitor International (Asia) Pte Ltd
3 Lim Teck Kim Road
#08-01 Singapore Technologies Building
Singapore 088934
Tel: + 65 6429 0590
Fax: + 65 6324 1855
email: info@euromonitor.com.sg

China
Euromonitor International (Shanghai) Co., Ltd
Level 21 Unit 06, Tian An Center
No. 338 Nanjing Road (West)
Shanghai 200003, China
Tel: 86 21 6372 6288
Fax: 86 21 6372 6289
email: info@euromonitor.com.cn

Middle East
Euromonitor International (Middle East)
Building 5E, Block A, office 321,
Dubai Airport Free Zone,
P.O. Box 54709 Dubai,
U.A.E.
Tel: +971 4 609 1340
Fax: +971 4 609 1343
email: info-mena@euromonitor.com

Africa
Euromonitor International
The Forum, Unit GS04
6473 Northbank Lane
Century City
Cape Town, 7441
Republic of South Africa
Tel: +27 21 552 0037
Fax: +27 21 552 7071

Central and Eastern Europe
Euromonitor International (Eastern Europe) UAB
Jogailos Street 4,
Vilnius
LT-01116
Lithuania
Tel: +370 5 243 1577
Fax: +370 5 243 1599
email: info@euromonitor.lt

Website: http://www.euromonitor.com

British Library Cataloguing in Publication Data.

A CIP catalogue record for this book is available from the British Library

Euromonitor International is a member of the Data Publishers Association and the European Association of Directory Publishers

Disclaimer
This edition of European Marketing Data and Statistics has been prepared with painstaking care but the editors cannot accept responsibility for any errors which may have occurred during its compilation. We would welcome comments and feedback about the contents to assist in the compilation of subsequent editions.

Printed in the United Kingdom

Summary of contents

Table of contents

Section Eleven
Energy Resources and Output **327**

Section Twelve
Environmental Data **349**

Section Thirteen
Foreign Trade **359**

Section Fourteen
Health **389**

Foreword and Guide

Foreword

European Marketing Data and Statistics 2009 is a compendium of statistical information on the countries of Western and Eastern Europe. Published annually, it provides a wealth of detailed and up-to-date statistical information relevant to pan-European market planning. The information is regularly updated and held on an international database of market information comprising 23 subject areas.

Published annually since the late 1960s, **European Marketing Data and Statistics**, or EMDAS, is now in its 44th edition. All data sections have been thoroughly revised for this new edition.

The data are presented in table form and a number of extrapolated tables have been included. The data coverage includes a considerable number of long-term time-series (dating back to 1980 as available) which permit the analysis of socio-economic trends over a longer time span as a basis for forecasting. The inclusion of figures from the most recent complete year (in this edition 2007) for key parameters ensures that up-to-date information is available for analysis. Quarterly datasets cover 2006, 2007 and the first half of 2008 where avialable, whilst monthly datasets cover the latest 12 months available.

In addition to reporting on major European countries, the country coverage also includes smaller European countries and principalities. Although the availability of statistical information on these countries is limited and they are minor markets, it assists in building up a more comprehensive picture of the total European market and will be of interest to academic users.

The handbook contains a full alphabetical index, and we have included a section summarising the major sources of pan-regional and international information which have been used in the compilation of data. Readers requiring detailed guidance on sources of information are referred to the World Directory of Business Information Web Sites (Euromonitor International, 2007), the World Directory of Trade and Business Journals (Euromonitor International, 2007), the World Directory of Trade and Business Associations (Euromonitor International, 2007), the World Directory of Non-Official Statistical Sources (Euromonitor International, 2007), and the World Directory of Business Information Libraries (Euromonitor International, 2007) for more comprehensive listings.

A companion volume of marketing data, International Marketing Data and Statistics (IMDAS) is also available. Country coverage in IMDAS 2009 provides a comprehensive worldwide context, and data are provided in the same format for ease of comparison with the European figures presented here. The data included in both volumes are also accessible as part of the Global Marketing Information Database (GMID) on the web.

User comments are welcomed concerning the databases in **European Marketing Data and Statistics**. Also, whilst the editors have made every effort to ensure accuracy Euromonitor International cannot accept responsibility for any errors which may have occurred.

Guide to Using the Handbook

Scope of the Handbook

European Marketing Data and Statistics (EMDAS) is a statistical yearbook of business and marketing information, featuring over 500 pages of up-to-date and detailed marketing statistics on 23 principal subject areas. These statistics are stored on a database of international marketing information and are regularly updated by Euromonitor International's research team.

The sections of EMDAS cover a wide variety of marketing topics, ranging from socio-economic trends and background information through to key consumer marketing parameters. Data covering international trade, transport, industrial output and agricultural resources are included, as well as sections on service industries such as tourism and retailing.

In EMDAS 2009, each statistical tabulation presents pan-European comparative information, either in the form of time-series from 1980 to 2007 or 2008, or with single-year data for the latest year available. All the countries are listed down the left-hand column, presented in two geographical entities (Western and Eastern Europe). Where appropriate, regional subtotals are included.

Where data is in value form, units have been generally left in national currencies. However the spreadsheets on which the data is stored facilitate calculations in US dollars. These are calculated only for the latest year available (usually 2007) as fluctuations in exchange rates and contrasts in rates of inflation render year-on-year conversions meaningless.

In addition, calculations have been made where deemed appropriate to show growth rates over a defined period, and per capita data. These permit easy cross-comparisons between countries, regions and markets.

Using EMDAS 2009 is easy. Whatever topic is of interest, you simply look up the tables (using the contents or index) and the table will show the relevant data for all countries. The heading shows the relevant section, title summary and title of the table, and unit. A guide to the sources used in the compilation of the data appears at the foot of the table, while any relevant notes are gathered together at the end of each section.

The aim of EMDAS is to locate in one handbook the essential statistical information relevant to European market planning. The handbook will save the busy marketeer or researcher hours of time trawling through statistics from many sources and provides a wealth of hard-to-get information drawn from the many reports and studies compiled by Euromonitor International over the last 2-3 years - many based on trade interviews and original extrapolations. Business users and librarians will find the handbook especially useful.

Subject Coverage

EMDAS 2009 is presented in 23 separate sections or "databases" which have all been specially compiled by Euromonitor International. The subjects have been selected as those most appropriate for strategic planning and European market analysis, covering both background marketing parameters and detailed consumer market information. The 23 databases are discussed below.

1 Marketing Geography

This database includes a summary of data (population, area, currency, location, language, religion, main industries, economic and political structure, energy resources, heads of state and of government and last election results) for each country covered.

2 Advertising

This section includes a range of data on advertising expenditure trends, organised into seven tables.

3 Agricultural Resources

This section presents key data on land use and output of various agricultural and forestry products. There are 11 tables on the database, mostly including figures for 2007.

4 Automotives and Transport

This 31-table database covers the circulation, manufacture and sales of cars, commercial vehicles and two-wheelers, including tables on automotive fuel prices; it also covers major movements in terms of the road, rail, air and shipping transport sectors. Quarterly and/or monthly datasets are included in this edition for four indicators.

5 Banking and Finance

This section features tabulations mainly showing data from 1980-2007 and covering bank assets, liabilities, claims and interest rates, as well as information on credit card holders and accepting outlets. Quarterly datasets are newly available for four indicators.

6 Consumer Expenditure

The presentation of this section comprises total consumer spending, a consolidated breakdown by product sector, and a series of tables analysing each major consumer sector. New 2007 data have been included and all the data are presented in 18-year trends with growth rates and 2007 dollar comparisons.

7 Consumer Market Sizes

Per capita consumption and retail market sizes are included in 17 tables for 2007. The information is drawn from Euromonitor International's market information database, which forms the basis for the publication Consumer Western Europe (24th edition, Euromonitor International, 2008), and its companion title Consumer Eastern Europe (16th edition, Euromonitor International, 2008).

8 Consumer Prices and Costs

Trends in consumer prices and selected European living costs are included in 16 tables of data. Quarterly and monthly consumer price indices are included in EMDAS 2009.

9 Cultural Indicators

This section includes 12 tables covering available data on museums and film.

10 Economic Indicators

This database features tables of key economic data, again with the emphasis on time-series data. All the main economic indicators are covered, including GDP, GNP, inflation, money supply, public and private consumption, government finance and exchange rates. Quarterly and/or monthly datasets are included for 13 economic indicators.

11 Energy Resources and Output

This section consists of 21 tables on energy supply and demand. Coverage extends to household energy consumption with several tables containing data for more than 20 years. Quarterly and monthly datasets are available for three indicators.

12 Environmental Data

This section includes tables covering various environmental factors. Coverage includes pollution, recycling, waste generation, protected areas and threatened species.

13 Foreign Trade

This section includes 17 tables which give a cohesive and structured trade overview covering total imports and exports and external trade breakdowns by origin, destination and commodity. Quarterly and monthly datasets feature for total imports, total exports and trade balance.

14 Health

This database comprises six tables covering major health indicators (including a table on the number of reported AIDS cases).

15 Household Profiles

This section comprises tables of comparative statistics on households. Data on housing stock and household composition are included, as well as possession of household durables.

16 Income and Deductions

This section includes four tables covering gross and disposable income parameters.

17 Industrial Markets
This section provides key industrial indices for a 27-year period and includes output tables covering major industrial materials. Quarterly and monthly datasets are now included for general industrial production, manufacturing production and mining production indices.

18 IT and Telecommunications
This section features information on a number of communications and information technology topics including Internet statistics.

19 Labour
This database covers the key employment indicators including numbers employed, unemployed and hours of work. The structure of the economically active population by age group and status is included for latest years available, along with a breakdown of the total workforce into industry sectors. Quarterly and/or monthly datasets are included for eight indicators.

20 Education
A range of educational statistics are included in this four-table section.

21 Population
This database features statistical compilations covering population trends, vital statistics, urbanisation, demographic analysis by age and sex, and population forecasts. Much of the data included are from 1980 to the latest year, forming a basis for forecasting and projections. Quarterly and monthly datasets are available for birth rates and death rates.

22 Retailing
This section has drawn on Euromonitor International's extensive European retail research in recent years, with tables covering retail sales and channels and breakdowns for different retail sectors.

23 Travel and Tourism
This database consists of 12 tabulations covering tourism values and movements, tourist accommodation and its usage, reflecting holidaying habits across Europe.

Data Coverage
Each of the statistical compilations is presented in one of five data periods:

(1) A 27-year trend table from 1980-2007, with data for each country drawn from the same consistent source. Some intermediary years have been excluded for reasons of space.

(2) A different period trend, eg 1990-2007 (18-year trend) or a recent period.

(3) Latest year available, with the years differing between countries. These are used where the information is drawn from occasional studies, eg a census, or where statistical offices vary in the speed of publishing statistics.

(4) A single year, eg 2007, where space does not permit trends or where an interactive range of information is provided (eg imports by origin, usage of GDP, etc).

(5) Quarterly datasets cover 2006, 2007 and the first half of 2008 where available, whilst monthly datasets are for the latest 12 months available.

The statistics in this volume are as available during the compilation period (June-October 2008). Figures for 2007 (in some cases provisional or estimated) have been included where possible. Various one-off surveys cover earlier years only.

Country Coverage
This edition of EMDAS includes a total of 44 countries in both Western and Eastern Europe. These are grouped into two geographic entities, as follows:

Western Europe

Austria	Belgium
Cyprus	Denmark
Finland	France
Germany	Gibraltar
Greece	Iceland
Ireland	Italy
Liechtenstein	Luxembourg
Malta	Monaco
Netherlands	Norway
Portugal	Spain
Sweden	Switzerland
Turkey	United Kingdom

Eastern Europe
Albania	Belarus
Bosnia-Herzegovina	Bulgaria
Croatia	Czech Republic
Estonia	Georgia
Hungary	Latvia
Lithuania	Macedonia
Moldova	Poland
Romania	Russia
Serbia and Montenegro	Slovakia
Slovenia	Ukraine

Country Note

Data for Germany prior to 1991 refer to the former East and West Germany, for the Czech Republic data prior to 1993 refer to the former Czechoslovakia, and for Serbia and Montenegro data prior to 1992 refer to the former Yugoslavia.

Sources

European Marketing Data and Statistics is based on an extensive and on-going programme of research into European markets and industries. A Europe-wide network of market analysts and researchers work to pull together available data on socio-economic patterns, market conditions and trends, living standards and background information relevant to business, export and market planning.

The principal sources used in the compilation of EMDAS are as follows:

— International and European organisations, such as the United Nations, OECD, and the International Monetary Fund.

— National statistical offices and central banks in each country.

— Pan-European and national trade and industry associations.

— Industry study groups and unofficial research publishers.

— Euromonitor International's own research publications, including one-off reports and statistical compilations.

— Original research specially commissioned for the handbook, including consumer research, trade interviews and retail surveys.

A guide to the main sources used in the compilation of each table is included at the foot of each table. For reasons of space the main sources are only briefly cited; in some cases, many different reports and publications are used in the preparation of just one table. For example, we may have extracted data from publications by the national statistical offices for all the countries covered in order to compile one table. In other cases, statistical compilations are from secondary sources, which have in turn used many different sources.

A brief guide to the main sources used in each of the databases follows.

1 Marketing Geography
Information mainly drawn from the business press, data from the yearbooks of the national statistical offices and various informal studies on the countries covered.

2 Advertising
Drawn from data published by the World Association of Newspapers and various other media study groups, advertising associations and agents in various countries.

3 Agricultural Resources
Mainly based on the publications and databases of the Food and Agricultural Organisation of the United Nations (FAO).

4 Automotives and Transport
Automotives data are drawn from national statistics, and the publications of various motor trades organisations. Transport statistics are based on national statistics and on various UN publications; the International Civil Aviation Organisation; the International Road Federation and Lloyd's Register of Shipping.

5 Banking and Finance
The major source of comparative financial data is the IMF's International Financial Statistics.

6 Consumer Expenditure
Drawn from the OECD and the national accounts of each country (generally published by the national statistical offices). Euromonitor International estimates have been used to reach levels of consolidation.

7 Consumer Market Sizes
Drawn from Euromonitor International's consumer market database; primary sources include trade associations and interviews with industry leaders in all countries.

8 Consumer Prices and Costs
Mainly from national statistics, the International Monetary Fund and the OECD; living costs from the International Labour Organisation.

9 Cultural Indicators
Mainly drawn from the UN, UNESCO, the Council of Europe and national statistical offices.

10 Economic Indicators
The principal international sources are the OECD and the International Monetary Fund (IMF). National statistical offices (yearbooks, national accounts) and economic bulletins by leading banks are also used.

11 Energy Resources and Output
This compilation draws mainly on data from BP, the UN and the OECD/IEA, national statistics and various industry publications.

12 Environmental Data
Drawn largely from the OECD, United Nations, and the World Resources Institute, as well as national statistics.

13 Foreign Trade
The IMF, UN and OECD track external trade flows in some detail. National statistical yearbooks are also utilised.

14 Health
Compiled from various publications from national statistical offices, OECD and UN publications and incorporating Euromonitor International estimates and calculations.

15 Household Profiles
Compiled from various publications from national statistical offices, and from Eurostat and UN publications, and incorporating Euromonitor International estimates and calculations.

16 Income and Deductions
Data from national statistical offices of each country. Specific sources include Household Budget Surveys and National Accounts. Euromonitor International estimates have been used.

17 Industrial Markets
Mainly drawn from UN and OECD publications, and from national statistics. Various industry sectors are covered by associations as stated.

18 IT and Telecommunications
Mainly based on national statistics and UN data, particularly the publications of the International Telecommunications Union (ITU), and incorporating some data from the World Bank.

19 Labour
In addition to national statistics, the primary international source is the International Labour Organisation, which publishes both a statistical yearbook and quarterly bulletins.

20 Education
The main source is UNESCO with data from national statistical offices incorporated as available.

21 Population
Drawn mainly from the statistical yearbooks of the national statistical offices supplemented with population data and forecasts from the UN, Eurostat and the Council of Europe.

22 Retailing
Drawn from a wide number of Euromonitor International's own surveys and market reports on European retailing, including Retail Trade International (Euromonitor International 2007), and also original research. Primary sources include retail trade censuses (various countries) by national statistical offices, retail trade associations, major retailers etc.

23 Travel and Tourism
A compilation sourced from the World Tourism Organisation and Euromonitor International's own research.

List of Abbreviations

BLEU	Belgo-Luxembourg Economic Union
EFMA	European Financial Management and Marketing Association
EFTA	European Free Trade Association
EU	European Union
FAO	Food and Agriculture Organisation of the United Nations
FT	Financial Times
IAA	International Advertising Association
IATA	International Air Transport Association
IBRD	International Bank for Reconstruction and Development (World Bank)
ICAO	International Civil Aviation Organisation
IEA	International Energy Authority
ILO	International Labour Organisation
IMF	International Monetary Fund
IMMA	International Motorcycle Manufacturers' Association
IRF	International Road Federation
ITU	International Telecommunication Union (a UN agency)
OECD	Organisation for Economic Co-operation and Development
SMMT	Society of Motor Manufacturers and Traders
UN	United Nations
UN ECE	United Nations Economic Commission for Europe
UNESCO	United Nations Educational, Scientific and Cultural Organisation
WHO	World Health Organisation
WTO	World Tourism Organisation
EAP	Economically active population
GDP	Gross domestic product
GNP	Gross national product
LPG	Liquefied petroleum gases
NGL	Natural gas liquids
SITC	Standard International Trade Classification
'000	thousand
gWh	gigawatt-hours
ha	hectare
hl	hectolitre
kg	kilogramme
km	kilometre
km2	square kilometre
kWh	kilowatt-hours
m2	square metre
m3	cubic metre
mn	million
MTOE	million tonnes of oil equivalent
MW	megawatts
R/P	reserves/production
TJ	terajoules
0	denotes less than 0.5 where no fraction given

Map of Europe

1   SLOVENIA
2   CROATIA
3   BOSNIA-HERZEGOVINA
4   SERBIA
4a Vojvodina
4b Kosovo
5   MONTENEGRO
6   MACEDONIA

Key European Marketing Information Sources

Sources introduction

This section identifies the major European sources for researching the European market. The listings are not intended to be exhaustive: rather we aim to list some of the main international and national organisations publishing statistics.

Readers are referred to several other currently available and forthcoming Euromonitor International publications for further information on European sources:

Source: Euromonitor
(1st edition, Euromonitor International 2008)

The directory has full contact details for more than 7,000 market information providers, together with details of their activities and publications. These include: official organisations; trade development bodies; business information libraries; leading market research companies; private research publishers; trade associations; major trade and business journals; and on-line database sources.

World Directory of Trade and Business Associations
(5th edition, Euromonitor International 2007)

This directory lists some 5,000 trade associations throughout the world from a broad range of sectors, with details of membership, key personnel, structure, aims and objectives, activities and publications.

World Directory of Business Information Web Sites
(7th edition, Euromonitor International 2007)

Comprehensive coverage of over 2,500 web sites from all over the world. Web sites included offer access to the following types of information: socio-economic statistics; consumer market statistics; industrial market statistics; market research surveys and reports; company information; and business news sources.

World Directory of Business Information Libraries
(6th edition, Euromonitor International, 2007)

This directory details around 1,500 of the world's major libraries that provide public access to business information, including libraries belonging to national statistical offices, chambers of commerce, academic bodies, private companies, etc.

World Directory of Non-Official Statistical Sources
(5th edition, Euromonitor International, 2007)

This directory provides details of over 7,000 regularly produced statistical information publications from non-official organisations throughout the world, with special emphasis on the major industrialised nations including the USA, Canada, and Japan.

Consumer Western Europe 2008/2009
(24th edition, Euromonitor International, 2008)

Primarily a handbook of consumer market data, this annual publication includes a sources section listing the major trade associations and trade journals publishing information on consumer markets across Western Europe.

Consumer Eastern Europe 2008/2009
(16th edition, Euromonitor International, 2008)

As for Consumer Western Europe, this annual publication includes a sources section listing the major trade associations and trade journals publishing information on consumer markets across Eastern Europe.

International Official Sources

Agence Internationale de l'Energie (AIE)
International Energy Agency (IEA)

Address: 9 rue de la Fédération, Paris Cédex 15, 75739, France
Telephone: +33 1 4057 6500
Fax: +33 1 4057 6559
E-mail: info@iea.org
Website: www.iea.org

Guides: web catalogue and online bookshop. The Studies and Country Reviews are available in paper and in PDF format and most statistical publications in paper, PDF or on CD-Rom

Activity: acts as energy policy advisor for its 26 member countries, conducts a broad programme of energy research, data compilation, publications and public dissemination of the latest energy policy analysis and recommendations on good practices.

Website(s) information:
International Energy Agency — url: www.iea.org **Description:** compilation of news and articles on the latest developments and issues affecting the world's energy resources sector. Access to oil market reports, and samples of country studies; environmental briefings and essays; and various statistics on world energy resources **Coverage:** by entering the "Statistics Section", online access is provided to a series of annually and monthly updated publications: Key World Statistics; Monthly Electricity Survey; Monthly Price Statistics; Monthly Natural Gas Survey; and Monthly Oil Survey. Access is also provided to IEA Energy Technology R&D Statistics database, 1974-1998, and to Energy Indicators per country

Publication(s):
CO2 Emissions from Fuel Combustion — **Language:** English/French **Frequency:** irregular **Content:** study of emissions of CO_2 from 1971 to 2004 for more than 140 countries and regions by sector and by fuel. Emissions were calculated using IEA energy databases and the default methods and emission factors from the Revised 1996 IPCC Guidelines for National Greenhouse Gas Inventories

Coal Information — **Language:** English/French **Frequency:** annual **Content:** Part I provides a statistical overview of developments in the world coal market. It covers world coal production and coal reserves, coal demand by type (hard, steam, coking), hard coal trade and hard coal prices.
Part II provides, in tabular and graphic form, a more detailed and comprehensive statistical picture of historical and current coal developments in the 30 OECD Member countries, by region and individually

Electricity Information — **Language:** English/Russian **Frequency:** monthly **Content:** Part I provides a statistical overview of developments in the electricity and heat market.
Part II provides, in tabular form, detailed and comprehensive statistical coverage of the power and heat industry developments for each of the 30 OECD Member countries and for OECD and IEA regional aggregates

Energy Balances of Non-OECD Countries — **Content:** Contains data on the supply and consumption of coal, oil, gas, electricity, heat, renewables and waste presented as comprehensive energy balances, expressed in tonnes of oil equivalent for over 100 non-OECD countries. Historical tables summarise production, trade and final consumption data as well as key energy and economic indicators **Edition:** 2007

Energy Balances of OECD Countries — **Language:** English/French **Frequency:** annual **Content:** Contains data on the supply and consumption of coal, oil, gas, electricity, heat, renewables and waste presented as comprehensive energy balances expressed in million tonnes of oil equivalent. Historical tables summarise production, trade and final consumption data as well as key energy and economic indicators

Energy Prices and Taxes — **Language:** English **Frequency:** quarterly **Content:** International compilation of energy prices at all market levels: import prices, industry prices and consumer prices. The statistics cover main petroleum products, gas, coal and electricity, giving for imported products an average price both for importing country and country of origin

Energy Statistics of Non-OECD Countries — **Language:** English/French **Frequency:** annual **Content:** contains data on energy supply and consumption in original units for coal, oil, gas, electricity, heat, renewables and waste for over 100 non-OECD countries. Historical tables summarise data on production, trade and final consumption. The book includes definition of products and flows and explanatory notes on the individual country data **Edition:** 2007

Key World Energy Statistics — **Frequency:** annual **Content:** contains statistics on the supply, transformation and consumption of all major energy sources

Natural Gas Information — **Language:** English **Frequency:** annual **Content:** information on LNG and pipeline trade, gas reserves, storage capacity and prices. The main part of the book, concentrates on OECD countries, showing a detailed supply and demand balance for each country and for the three OECD regions: North America, Europe and Pacific, as well as a breakdown of gas consumption by end-user. Import and export data are reported by source and destination

Oil Information — **Frequency:** annual **Content:** Gives current developments in oil supply and demand. The first part of this publication contains key data on world production, trade, prices and consumption of major oil product groups, with time series back to the early 1970s.
The second part gives a more detailed and comprehensive picture of oil supply, demand, trade, production and consumption by end-user for each OECD country individually and for the OECD regions

Renewables Information — **Language:** English/Spanish **Content:** Part I provides a statistical overview of developments in the markets for renewables and waste in the OECD Member countries. It also provides selected renewables indicators for non-OECD countries.
Part II provides, in tabular form, a more detailed and comprehensive picture, including preliminary data, of developments for renewable and waste energy sources for each of the 30 OECD Member countries. It encompasses economic and energy indicators, generating capacity, electricity and heat production **Edition:** 2007

World Energy Outlook — **Language:** English **Frequency:** monthly **Content:** Covers energy market reform, energy policy and projections. Projects the impact that targeted policies and more robust deployment of energy technologies could have on sustainability through to 2030

World Energy Statistics — **Language:** English **Frequency:** annual **Content:** Provides annual historical energy data extracted from four IEA/OECD data bases: energy statistics and energy balances, which contain data for most of the OECD countries from 1960 and energy statistics and balances for more than 100 non-OECD countries from 1971

Bank for International Settlements
Address: Centralbahnplatz 2, Basel, 4002, Switzerland
Telephone: +41 61 280 8080
Fax: +41 61 280 9100
E-mail: email@bis.org
Website: www.bis.org

Guides: annual and quarterly reports on financial markets, reports on current issues regarding business

Activity: fosters international monetary and financial cooperation and serves as a bank for central banks

Website(s) information:
Bank for International Settlements — url: www.bis.org **Description:** contains a series of detailed reports covering economic, banking and financial markets **Coverage:** statistics on the world banking industry and regulations: international banking statistics; consolidated banking statistics; securities statistics; derivatives statistics; triennial foreign exchange and derivatives survey; joint BIS-IMF-OECD-World Bank Statistics on External Debt; guide to the international banking statistics; the BIS statistics on international banking and financial market activity

Publication(s):
Annual Report — **Language:** English/German/Spanish/French/Italian **Frequency:** annual **Content:** annual survey of the global economy, monetary policy in the advanced industrial economies, foreign exchange markets, financial markets, etc

BIS Quarterly Review — **Language:** English/German/Spanish/French/Italian **Frequency:** quarterly **Content:** overview of the international banking market, the international debt securities market, the derivatives market, and special features

---

Common Fund for Commodities
Address: PO Box 74656, Amsterdam, 1070 BR, Netherlands
Telephone: +31 20 575 4949
Fax: +31 20 676 0231
Website: www.common-fund.org

Guides: reports based on project and country can be downloaded free

Activity: intergovernmental financial institution established within the framework of the UN. The Fund's specific mandate is to support developing countries that are commodity dependent to improve and diversify commodities production and trade

Website(s) information:

Common Fund for Commodities — **url:** www.common-fund.org **Description:** Common Fund for Commodities is a partnership of 106 Member States. The European Community (EC), the African Union (AU), the Common Market for Eastern and Southern Africa (COMESA) are institutional members. Membership is also open to Members States of the United Nations, its specialised agencies; and the International Atomic Energy Agency, in addition to intergovernmental and regional economic integration organisations. Projects can be selected by country and commodity and downloaded from the website

Food and Agricultural Organisation of the United Nations (FAO)

Address: Viale delle Terme di Caracalla, Rome, 00100, Italy
Telephone: +39 06 57051
Fax: +39 06 5705 3152
E-mail: FAO-HQ@fao.org
Website: www.fao.org

Guides: FAO Books in Print (annual catalogue of FAO publications in English, free of charge); list of documents (listing of publications in all languages)

Activity: the FAO leads international efforts to defeat hunger; helps developing countries and countries in transition to modernise and improve agriculture, forestry and fisheries practices and ensure good nutrition for all

Website(s) information:

FAOSTAT — **url:** www.fao.org **Description:** FAOSTAT is a statistical database of FAO that currently contains more than 3 million time-series records. FAOSTAT-ON LINE can be accessed on the FAO Web site at http://faostat.fao.org. Incorporates statistical information as available on-line at the end of May 2005, covering more than 300 countries and territories and 3000 items in many areas of agriculture, fisheries, forestry and nutrition **Coverage:** access to worldwide databases on food related sectors: agriculture; nutrition; fisheries; forestry; food quality control; innternational statistics cover production; trade; fertiliser and pesticides; land use and irrigation; forest products; fishery products; population; agricultural machinery; and food aid shipments

Publication(s):

FAO Statistical Yearbook — **Language:** English/French/Spanish/Arabic/Chinese **Frequency:** annual **Content:** indicators by topic for all countries of the world

Key Statistics of Food and Agriculture External Trade — **Content:** statistics on commodities imported and exported by country

Major Food and Agricultural Commodities and Producers — **Language:** English **Content:** agricultural production statistics for the 20 most important food and agricultural commodities (ranked by value) in a given country for the year indicated

State of Agricultural Commodity Markets — **Language:** English **Frequency:** irregular **Content:** coverage of the development and food security needs of developing countries

State of Food and Agricultural — **Language:** English/French/Spanish/Arabic/Chinese **Frequency:** annual **Content:** provides a set of indicators for the food and agricultural sector for the various countries in the world

State of the World's Forests 2007 — **Language:** English **Frequency:** biennial **Content:** offers a global perspective on the forest sector, including its environmental, economic and social dimensions. Part I reviews progress region by region. Each regional report is structured according to the seven thematic elements of sustainable forest management. Part II presents selected issues in the forest sector, probing the state of knowledge or recent activities in 18 topics of interest to forestry. Climate change, forest landscape restoration, forest tenure, invasive species, wildlife management and **Edition:** 7th Edition

State of World Fisheries and Aquaculture — **Language:** English **Frequency:** annual **Content:** recognition of the many failures in management have now led FAO member countries and other relevant stakeholders to broaden the approach and governance used to manage fisheries and aquaculture in a sustainable manner

Summary of World Food and Agricultural Statistics — **Language:** English **Content:** broad range of statistics pertaining to world food and agriculture; presents the differences between developed and developing countries, continents and regions. The figures given refer to the most recent period for which data are available and, where relevant, for selected benchmark periods to allow analysis of trends over time

Yearbook of Forest Products — **Language:** English/French.Spanish.Arabic/Chinese **Content:** compilation of statistical data on basic forest products for all countries and territories of the world. Contains annual data on the production and trade of forest products and also contains historic information

International Atomic Energy Agency

Address: PO Box 100, Wagramer Strasse 5, Vienna, A-1400, Austria
Telephone: +43 1 2600-0
Fax: +43 1 2600-7
E-mail: info@iaea.org
Website: www.iaea.org

Activity: works for the safe, secure and peaceful uses of nuclear science and technology. Its key roles contribute to international peace and security, and to the World's Millennium Goals for social, economic and environmental development

Publication(s):

IAEA Annual Report — **Language:** English/Arabic/Chinese/French/Spanish/Russian **Content:** summarises and highlights developments over the past year in major areas of the Agency's work. It includes a summary of major issues, activities, and achievements, and status tables and graphs related to safeguards, safety, and science and technology

International Civil Aviation Organisation (ICAO)

Address: 999 University Street, Montreal, H3C 5H7, QUE, Canada
Telephone: +1 514 954 8219
Fax: +1 514 954 6077
E-mail: sta@icao.int
Website: www.icao.int

Activity: ICAO works in close co-operation with other members of the United Nations family such as the World Meteorological Organisation, the International Telecommunication Union, the Universal Postal Union, the World Health Organization and the International Maritime Organization. Non-governmental organizations which also participate in ICAO's work include the International Air Transport Association, the Airports Council International, the International Federation of Air Line Pilots' Associations, and the International Council of Aircraft Owner and Pilot Associations.

Website(s) information:

ICAOData — **url:** www.icaodata.com/ **Description:** The database contains detailed financial, traffic, personnel and fleet information for commercial air carriers. It also holds Traffic by Flight Stage (TFS) information and On-flight Origin/Destination statistics for air carriers. Financial and traffic data for airports and air navigation service providers also available **Coverage:** Coverage includes commercial air carriers (traffic, on-flight origin and destination, traffic by flight stage, fleet-personnel and financial data), airports (airport traffic and financial data), air navigation service providers (financial and traffic data), as well as data on civil aircraft on register

International Coffee Organisation

Address: 22 Berners Street, London, W1T 3DD, United Kingdom
Telephone: +44 20 7612 0600
Fax: +44 20 7612 0630
E-mail: info@ico.org
Website: www.ico.org

Guides: unrestricted free access is provided to Coffee Prices and Trade Statistics on this site. For the users who require more detailed information the ICO offers a subscription service to its statistical and economic data, including monthly exports, quarterly and annual statistics with comprehensive data which include statistics supply, exports/imports, indicator prices, prices paid to growers and retail prices.

Activity: intergovernmental organisation for coffee, bringing together producing and consuming countries to tackle the challenges facing the world coffee sector through international cooperation

Website(s) information:
International Coffee Organisation — **url:** www.ico.org **Description:** Unrestricted free access is provided to coffee prices and trade statistics on this site. For the users who require more detailed information the ICO offers a subscription service to its statistical and economic data, including monthly exports, quarterly and annual statistics with comprehensive data which include statistics supply, exports/imports, indicator prices, prices paid to growers and retail prices **Coverage:** exports, imports, market prices, prices to growers, production, stocks and inventories

International Copper Study Group (ICSG)

Address: 6th Floor, Rue Almirante Barroso, Lisbon, 1000-013, Portugal
Telephone: +351 21 351 3870
Fax: +351 21 352 4035
E-mail: mail@icsg.org
Website: www.icsg.org

Activity: intergovernmental organisation that serves to increase copper market transparency and promote international discussions and cooperation on issues related to copper

Website(s) information:
International Copper Study Group (ICSG) — **url:** www.icsg.org **Coverage:** trends in world refined copper stocks and prices; world refined copper production and usage trends; copper mine, smelter, refinery production, and refined copper usage by geographical area

Publication(s):
Copper Bulletin — **Frequency:** monthly **Content:** Includes statistics on copper and copper products, their production, consumption and trade by country, providing a global view of supply and demand

Copper Bulletin Yearbook — **Frequency:** annual **Content:** Includes annual statistics on copper and copper products, their production, usage and trade by country, as well as stocks and exchange prices, providing a global view of supply and demand for the past 10 years. Subscribers to the Copper Bulletin receive the Yearbook as part of their annual subscription

Directory of Copper and Copper Alloy Fabricators (First Use) — **Frequency:** annual **Content:** covers wire rod plants, ingot makers (for castings), master alloy plants, brass mills, and electrodeposited copper foil mills. Powder and chemical plants are not included. Encompasses data to the end of the year for over 75 countries and over 1200 existing, developing and planned first use plants, with anticipated changes in the coming year

Directory of Copper Mines and Plants — **Frequency:** quarterly **Content:** Highlights current capacity and provides a five year outlook of forecasted capacity for over 700 existing and planned copper mines, plants and refineries on a country by country basis

International Cotton Advisory Committee (ICAC)

Address: 1629 - K Street NW, Suite 702, Washington, DC 20006-1636, USA
Telephone: +1 202 463 6660
Fax: +1 202 463 6950
E-mail: secretariat@icac.org
Website: www.icac.org

Guides: online publications catalogue
Activity: provides statistics on world cotton production, consumption, trade and stocks and to identify emerging changes in the structure of the world cotton market

Website(s) information:
International Cotton Advisory Committee (ICAC) — **url:** www.icac.org **Coverage:** Cotton supply and demand, production, prices, forecasts

Publication(s):
Cotton This Month — **Language:** English/French/Russian/Spanish **Frequency:** monthly **Content:** Supply, demand and price projections.

Cotton: Review of the World Situation — **Language:** English/French/Spanish **Frequency:** bi-monthly **Content:** Examination of the world cotton market. Provides projections of world supply and demand by country and international cotton prices

Cotton: World Statistics — **Language:** English/French/Spanish **Content:** World cotton supply/demand statistics since 1940/41 Data by country since 1980/81 with 5-year projections. Tables updated twice a year

World Cotton Trade — **Frequency:** annual **Content:** Trade developments in raw cotton since 1980

International Fund for Agricultural Development (IFAD)

Address: Via del Serafico 107, Rome, 00142, Italy
Telephone: +39 6 545 91
Fax: +39 6 504 3463
E-mail: ifad@ifad.org
Website: www.ifad.org

Guides: publications available in English, Spanish, Arabic and French
Activity: specialist agency of the United Nations dedicated to eradicating rural poverty in developing countries

Website(s) information:
International Fund for Agricultural Development — **url:** www.ifad.org **Coverage:** statistical information on rural poverty, rural finance, food security and nutrition, livestock and agricultural land areas

Publication(s):
IFAD Annual Report — **Language:** English/French/German **Frequency:** annual **Content:** provides statistical information on countries' performance in the areas of science, technology, globalisation and industry

International Grains Council

Address: 1 Canada Square, Canary Wharf, London, E14 5AE, United Kingdom
Telephone: +44 20 7513 1122
Fax: +44 20 7513 0630
E-mail: igc-fac@igc.org.uk
Website: www.igc.org.uk

Activity: intergovernmental organisation concerned with the grain trade. It administers the Grains Trade Convention 1995

Website(s) information:
International Grains Council — **url:** www.igc.org.uk **Coverage:** Grain Market Report subscribers can take advantage of a weekly electronic service designed to provide updates on the latest grain market developments. In addition to the current monthly report GMRPlus will have two elements. Grain Market Indicators, to be issued each Wednesday, will provide the latest export price and US futures quotations and carry short market commentaries on wheat, maize (corn), other grains (barley, sorghum, oats, rye and soyabeans) and ocean freight rates. GMR Statistics Update will allow subscribers to access weekly updates of some key GMR statistical tables, as well as a weekly diary of main grain market events

Publication(s):
Grain Market Report — **Language:** English/French/Russian/Spanish **Frequency:** monthly **Content:** review of the current situation and outlook for wheat (including durum) and coarse grains (including maize (corn), barley, sorghum, oats and rye). Separate chapters cover production, trade, consumption, stocks, prices, ocean freight rates and national policy developments. The analysis is supported by some 30 statistical tables with periodic features on trade in wheat flour and barley malt.
Subscribers can take advantage of a weekly electronic service designed to provide updates on the latest grain market

Wheat and Coarse Grain Shipments — **Content:** Provides 50 pages of tables, detailed statistics on commercial and non-commercial world trade in wheat (including wheat flour, durum and semolina) and coarse grains (including maize (corn), barley, sorghum, oats and rye) in the crop year **Edition:** 2004/2005

World Grain Statistics — **Frequency:** annual **Content:** tables on production, trade, consumption, stocks and prices for wheat (including durum and wheat flour) and coarse grains. Additional tables deal with ocean freight rates. Most tables cover a 10-year period **Edition:** 2005

International Jute Study Group (IJSG)

Address: 145 Monipuripara, Near Farmgate Tejgaon, Dhaka, 1215, Bangladesh
Telephone: +880 2 912 4887
Fax: +880 2 912 5248
E-mail: info@jute.org
Website: www.jute.org

Activity: intergovernmental body set up under the aegis of UNCTAD to function as the International Commodity Body (ICB) for jute, kenaf and other allied fibres

Website(s) information:
International Jute Study Group (IJSG) — url: www.jute.org **Description:** Online statistical search by country and by year **Coverage:** production, imports, exports and consumption of jute and jute products

International Labour Organisation (ILO)

Address: 4 route des Morillons, Geneva 22, 1211, Switzerland
Telephone: +41 22 799 7912
Fax: +41 22 799 8577
E-mail: communication@ilo.org
Website: www.ilo.org

Guides: online catalogue in PDF format
Labordoc, the ILO Library catalogue, contains over 350,000 references
Activity: UN specialised agency which seeks the promotion of social justice and internationally recognised human and labour rights

Website(s) information:
International Labour Migration Database (ILM) — url: www.ilo.org **Coverage:** contains basic data on stocks and flows of migrant labour

LABORDOC — url: www.ilo.org **Description:** Labordoc, the ILO Library's database, contains references and full text access to the world's literature on the world of work. It covers all aspects of work and sustainable livelihoods and the work-related aspects of economic and social development, human rights and technological change **Coverage:** databases covering a wide variety of topics and areas within the labour market sector: CISDOC; ILOLEX; LABORDOC; LABORSTA; NATLEX, etc.

LABORSTA — url: http//laborsta.ilo.org **Description:** LABORSTA is the main ILO database on labour statistics covering economically active population, employment, unemployment, employment by sex for detailed occupational group, public sector employment, statistical sources and methods, hours of work, wages, etc **Coverage:** yearly and periodical data of total and economically active population, employment, unemployment, hours of work, wages, labour costs, consumer price indices, occupational injuries, strikes and lockouts

Publication(s):
Bulletin of Labour Statistics — **Language:** English/French/Spanish **Frequency:** bi-annual **Content:** statistics on general level of employment; employment in non-agricultural activities and employment in manufacturing; data on unemployment rates; average number of hours worked; average earnings or wage rates; consumer prices; general indices and food indices **Readership:** international organisation; labour statisticians

Decent Working Time. New trends, new issues — **Language:** English **Frequency:** irregular **Content:** covers the problems relating to increasing employment insecurity and instability, time-related social inequalities, particularly in relation to gender, workers' ability to balance their paid work with their personal lives, and even the synchronisation of working hours with social times, such as community activities. In addition, the book offers valuable insights on how policy-makers, academics, and the social partners can together help further develop and refine an effective policy framework for advancing

Occupational Wages and Hours of Work and Retail Food Prices, Statistics from the ILO October Inquiry — **Edition:** 2005

Yearbook of Labour Statistics — **Language:** English/French/Spanish **Frequency:** annual **Content:** development of labour, living and working conditions throughout the world; includes statistical information on more than 190 countries, areas and territories, from the last ten years; information is on total and economically active population, employment, unemployment, hours of work, wages, labour costs, consumer prices, occupational injuries, and strikes and lockouts **Edition:** 65th Edition

International Lead and Zinc Study Group

Address: 5th Floor, Rua Almirante Barroso 38, Lisbon, 1000-013, Portugal
Telephone: +351 21 359 2420
Fax: +351 21 359 2429
E-mail: root@ilzsg.org
Website: www.ilzsg.org/ilzsgframe.htm

Activity: works to ensure transparency in the markets for lead and zinc worldwide; tracks world developments in the market

Website(s) information:
International Lead and Zinc Study Group — url: www.ilzsg.org **Description:** Includes subscription to electronic statistical database with data back to 1960. Statistical overview is free
Coverage: Detailed figures on mine production, metal production, metal consumption, principal imports and exports of concentrates and refined metal, secondary recovery, prices and stocks

Publication(s):
Lead & Zinc: End Use Industry Statistical Supplement — **Language:** English **Content:** This report covers the ten-year period 1994-2003, with information from 79 countries. Included are data on the world automotive industry, battery shipments in major markets, the construction sector, the galvanizing of steel sheet worldwide, general galvanizing in Europe, the production of kitchen appliances and brass production. Economic and social data by country and industrial production indices, for both total and metal products industries and historic oil price levels are also presented

Monthly Bulletin — **Language:** English **Content:** Detailed figures on mine production, metal production, metal consumption, principal imports and exports of concentrates and refined metal, secondary recovery, prices and stocks. Includes subscription to electronic statistical database with data back to 1960.

World Directory 2006: Primary and Secondary Lead Plants — **Language:** English **Content:** An overview and full detailed listing of primary and secondary lead smelters and refineries in 55 countries showing addresses, telephone and fax numbers, e-mail, web addresses types of plant operated and current capacities. Also includes summary tables and graphs. 92 pages

International Monetary Fund (IMF)

Address: 700 19th Street NW, Washington, DC 20431, , USA
Telephone: +1 202 623 7000
Fax: +1 202 623 4661
E-mail: publicaffairs@imf.org
Website: www.imf.org

Guides: publications catalogue available online
Activity: fosters global monetary cooperation among 184 member countries, secures financial stability, facilitates international trade, promotes high employment and sustainable economic growth

Website(s) information:
International Monetary Fund — url: www.imf.org **Description:** global view of international monetary and economic affairs. Access to a series of news, fact sheets, briefings and databases on world economic growth, international capital markets and various online publications, including IMF's Annual Report **Coverage:** statistics on different economic, financial and monetary issues can be found in various online publications and fact sheets. The Country Reports section includes individual country statistical appendixes for most IMF member nations

Publication(s):
Balance of Payments Statistics Yearbook — **Language:** English **Frequency:** annual **Content:** balance of payments statistics covering most countries in the world

Direction of Trade Statistics — **Language:** English/French/Spanish **Frequency:** quarterly **Content:** provides data on the country and area distribution of countries' exports and imports. Quarterly issues cover data for the most recent six quarters and the latest year for about 156 countries and ten quarters and five years for the world and area tables

Direction of Trade Statistics Yearbook — **Language:** English/French/Spanish/Arabic **Frequency:** annual **Content:** contains annual data covering 12 years for countries appearing in the monthly issues of IFS

Global Financial Stability Report — **Language:** English/French/German **Frequency:** Semi-annual **Content:** semi-annual publication provides comprehensive coverage of mature and emerging financial markets and seeks to identify potential fault lines in the global financial system that could lead to crises. It is designed to deepen understanding of global capital flows, which play a critical role as an engine of world economic growth

Government Finance Statistics Yearbook — **Language:** English **Frequency:** annual **Content:** contains statistical data on government financial operations for 133 IMF member countries

IMF Survey — **Language:** English **Frequency:** 22 per annum **Content:** macroeconomic research and policy analyses, country analyses, issues in international finance, as well as the latest development in IMF policies and activities

International Financial Statistics — **Language:** English **Frequency:** monthly **Content:** statistics covering international reserves, interest rates, exchange rates, prices, unit values and commodity prices, trade, national accounts

International Financial Statistics Yearbook — **Language:** English **Frequency:** annual **Content:** contains some additional series to the monthly edition

World Economic Outlook — **Language:** English/French/Spanish/Arabic **Frequency:** 2 per annum **Content:** global outlook on the world's economy, analysing latest economic and financial developments in developed and developing countries, as well as emerging markets

International Network for Bamboo and Rattan (INBAR)

Address: PO Box 100102-86, Beijing, 100102, China
Telephone: +86 10 6470 6161
Fax: +86 10 6470 2166
E-mail: info@inbar.int
Website: www.inbar.int

Activity: international organisation dedicated to improving the social, economic, and environmental benefits of bamboo and rattan. INBAR connects a global network of partners from the government, private, and not-for-profit sectors in over 50 countries to define and implement a global agenda for sustainable development through bamboo and rattan

Publication(s):
Journal of Bamboo and Rattan — **Language:** English **Frequency:** irregular **Content:** journal on research and development of bamboo and rattan, including technical properties, socio-economical aspects, environmental aspects and bio-energetics

International Nickel Study Group (INSG)

Address: Scheveningseweg 62, The Hague, 2517 KX, Netherlands
Telephone: +31 70 354 3326
Fax: +31 70 358 4612
E-mail: insg@insg.org
Website: www.insg.org

Activity: autonomous, intergovernmental organisation engaged in publishing statistics on nickel markets, facilities and environmental regulations and provides a forum for discussion on nickel issues

Website(s) information:
International Nickel Study Group (INSG) — **url:** www.insg.org/curstats.htm **Coverage:** world nickel statistics in thousands of tonnes

Publication(s):
World Nickel Statistics — **Frequency:** monthly **Content:** special Issues are published once a year in the November issue and contain annual data for the latest available 11-year period; the other eleven monthly issues focus on the latest available monthly data covering about 22 months plus annual data for the most recent two to three years

International Olive Oil Council (IOOC)

Address: Príncipe de Vergara 154, Madrid, 28002, Spain
Telephone: +34 915 903 638
Fax: +34 915 631 263
E-mail: iooc@internationaloliveoil.org
Website: www.internationaloliveoil.org

Activity: intergovernmental organisation in charge of administering the International Olive Oil Agreement

Website(s) information:
International Olive Council — **url:** www.internationaloliveoil.org **Description:** Every six months the IOOC updates series of world statistics on production, imports, exports and consumption. The series show the world data over the last fifteen table olive crop years, itemised by country. The term table olive crop year means the period from 1 September to 31 August. Downloadable data. The statistics are presented in three separate groups. The first covers the producing countries that are mainly exporters, the second concerns the producing countries that are mainly importers, and the third relates to countries that are importers only. **Coverage:** olive production, import, export and consumption statistics

Publication(s):
EU Producer Prices — **Language:** English **Content:** the IOOC tracks the movements in the producer prices of virgin olive oil, refined olive oil and refined olive-pomace oil on representative markets inside the European Union. As these markets account for a large share of world production, the production prices paid on them have a significant bearing on prices elsewhere. Tables giving weights and prices in Euros up to the current month

International Rubber Study Group

Address: 1st Floor, Heron House, 109/115 Wembley Hill Road, Wembley, HA9 8DA, Middlesex, United Kingdom
Telephone: +44 20 8900 5400
Fax: +44 20 8903 2848
E-mail: irsg@rubberstudy.com
Website: www.rubberstudy.com

Activity: provides a forum for the discussion of matters affecting the supply and demand for both synthetic and natural rubber. It covers all aspects of the world rubber industry, including marketing, shipping, distribution and trade in raw materials and the manufacture and sale of rubber products

Publication(s):
Outlook for Elastomers — **Frequency:** annual **Content:** Provides the Study Group's latest authoritative, in-depth analysis of production and consumption of elastomers for the previous year with estimates and forecasts for the current year, and the following year

Rubber Statistical Bulletin — **Frequency:** bi-monthly **Content:** reports authoritative rubber statistics. Data is reported in monthly format and is available by country

Summary of World Rubber Statistics — **Content:** Provides information on rubber production, consumption, trade and prices in a vastly simplified format, without the wealth of detail in the Group's flagship document, the Rubber Statistical Bulletin, on which it is based. Data is limited to two years - latest year versus last year - with trends over the past five years indicated in graphical format

World Rubber Statistics Handbook 1975-2001 — **Frequency:** irregular **Content:** Covers all aspects of the world elastomer economy and associated rubber products such as tyres, cars and commercial vehicles. It contains authoritative statistics on the production, consumption and trade in natural and synthetic rubber as reported in the bimonthly Rubber Statistical Bulletin, including revisions to data series back to 1975 **Edition:** Volume 6

International Statistical Institute (ISI)

Address: PO Box 950, Prinses Beatrixlaan 428, Voorburg, 2270 AZ, Netherlands
Telephone: +31 70 337 5737
Fax: +31 70 386 0025
E-mail: isi@cbs.nl
Website: www.cbs.nl/isi/

Activity: an autonomous society, which seeks to develop and improve statistical methods and their application through the promotion of international activity and co-operation

Website(s) information:
International Statistical Institute — **url:** www.cbs.nl/isi/ **Coverage:** contains addresses of publishers of statistics, mathematics and probability; a listing of statistical publications, books and statistics online; annual report, economic data

Publication(s):
Directory of Official Statistical Agencies & Societies — **Language:** English **Frequency:** annual **Content:** contact details of official statistical agencies throughout the world

International Telecommunication Union (ITU)

Address: Place des Nations, Geneva 20, 1211, Switzerland
Telephone: +41 22 730 5111
Fax: +41 22 733 7256
E-mail: itumail@itu.int
Website: www.itu.int

Activity: covers all aspects of telecommunication, from setting standards; adopting operational procedures; designing programmes to improve telecommunication infrastructure in the developing world

Website(s) information:
International Telecommunications Union (ITU) — **url:** www.itu.int **Coverage:** overview of the telecommunications industry worldwide; access to several industry related databases and to online publications as well as online statistical documents

Publication(s):
African Telecommunication Indicators — **Language:** English/French/Spanish **Frequency:** annual **Content:** 20 regional tables covering key telecommunication indicators, 55 individual country pages with a five-year profile from 1998-2002, and a directory with names of telecommunication ministries, regulators and operators in the region **Edition:** 7th Edition

Americas Telecommunication Indicators — **Language:** English/Spanish **Frequency:** annual **Content:** comprises an analytical overview, regional and country statistics and a directory of telecommunication organisations **Edition:** 2005

Asia-Pacific Telecommunication Indicators — **Language:** English/Russian **Content:** The publication consists of three parts: an analytical overview, regional statistics and a directory of telecommunication organizations **Edition:** 6th Edition

World Telecommunication Indicators — **Language:** English **Content:** contains time series data for the years 1960, 1965, 1970 and annually from 1975-2004 for around 80 communications statistics covering telephone network size and dimension, other services, quality of service, traffic, staff, tariffs, revenue and investment **Readership:** Telecommunication academics and libraries **Edition:** 9th

World Telecommunication/ICT Development Report — **Language:** English/French/Spanish **Frequency:** annual **Content:** reviews the progress made in measuring the impact of ICT on social and economic development; the report provides the latest telecommunication/ICT indicators for some 180 economies worldwide **Readership:** Telecommunication academics and libraries

Yearbook of Statistics - Telecommunications Services — **Language:** English **Frequency:** annual **Content:** compilation of annual statistical data relating to the development of the telecommunications industry worldwide **Readership:** Telecommunication academics and libraries **Edition:** 33rd Edition

International Trade Centre UNCTAD/WTO (ITC)

Address: Palais des Nations, Geneva 10, 1211, Switzerland
Telephone: +41 22 730 0111
Fax: +41 22 733 4439
E-mail: itcreg@intracen.org
Website: www.intracen.org

Guides: publishes directories and bibliographies, market survey and commodities handbooks, and trade promotion handbooks
Activity: technical cooperation agency of the United Nations Conference on Trade and Development (UNCTAD) and the World Trade Organization (WTO) for operational, enterprise-oriented aspects of trade development.
ITC supports developing and transition economies, and particularly their business sector, in their efforts to realize their full potential for developing exports and improving import operations

Website(s) information:
International Trade Centre (UNCTAD/WTO) — **url:** www.intracen.org **Description:** development and promotion of trade activities between developed and developing countries, as well as emerging economies. Information provided on: product-specific trade, from handicraft products to coffee, leather products, textiles, etc; trade in services; and access to ITC databases on Trade Information Index and Periodicals **Coverage:** country-specific business information, including trade statistics for UN individual member nations: trade performance index; national export performance; national import profile; trade and employment, etc

Publication(s):
International Trade Forum — **Language:** Spanish/French/English **Frequency:** quarterly **Content:** covers trade promotion and development of exporting and importing activities in developing countries and economies in transition

World Directory of Trade Promotion Organisations and Other Foreign Trade Bodies —

International Tropical Timber Organization (ITTO)

Address: International Organizations Center, 5th Floor, Pacifico-Yokohama 1-1-1, Minato-Mirai, Nishi-ku, Yokohama, 220-0012, Japan
Telephone: +81 45 223 1110
Fax: +81 45 223 1111
E-mail: itto@itto.or.jp
Website: www.itto.or.jp

Activity: intergovernmental organisation promoting the conservation and sustainable management, use and trade of tropical forest resources

Website(s) information:
International Tropical Timber Organization (ITTO) — **url:** www.itto.or.jp **Description:** Registered users get free access to the ITTO MIS report, which is updated every two weeks, and access to the MIS archive, which contains reports dating back to 1998 **Coverage:** MIS delivers a twice-monthly report on the international tropical timber market. Provides market trends and trade news from around the world, as well as indicative prices for over 400 tropical timber and added-value products

Publication(s):
Annual Review and Assessment of the World Timber Situation — **Language:** English/French/Spanish **Content:** International statistics available on global production and trade of timber, with an emphasis on the tropics. Includes chapters on the Production and Trade of Timber, over 5 years and Trade in Secondary Processed Wood Products. It also provides information on trends in forest area, forest management and the economies of ITTO member countries. Data tables are available as Excel files

Organisation for Economic Co-operation and Development (OECD)

Address: 2 rue André Pascal, Paris Cédex 16, 75775, France
Telephone: +33 1 4524 8200
Fax: +33 1 4524 8500
E-mail: sales@oecd.org
Website: www.oecd.org

Guides: OECD Statistics Catalogue available online
Activity: discussion, development and fine-tuning of economic and social policies

Website(s) information:
SourceOECD — **url:** www.oecd.org **Description:** Online library of all OECD books, periodicals, working papers and statistical databases from January 1998 to date. Includes 100 indicators for the world's leading economies. **Coverage:** statistical section includes a wide range of data on different socio-economic indicators for OECD member countries. Statistics are sold as hard-copy publications, on CD-ROM format, or online. Some of the data available online (subject to charge) covers: general OECD statistics (from demographic trends to environment and health); economic statistics; agricultural and food statistics (agricultural databases); energy statistics; development co-operation and public management; education, labour and social affairs; science, technology and industry statistics; health statistics; and transport statistics

Publication(s):

Education Trends In Perspective: Analysis of the World Education Indicators — **Language:** English **Frequency:** irregular **Content:** Data on educational attainment, education expectancy, enrolment rates of different age groups, age ranges of universal primary and secondary education, female participation, upper secondary enrolment patterns, entry rates into upper secondary and tertiary education, graduation rates, grade repetition, population and GDP, expenditure on education, teaching staff, class size, teachers salaries, and expenditure per student

Health at a Glance — **Language:** English **Content:** provides the latest comparable data and trends on different aspects of the performance of health systems in OECD countries **Readership:** Health researchers, policy advisors in Governments, private sector and academic communities

Insurance Statistics Yearbook — **Language:** English/French **Frequency:** annual **Content:** Provides annual information on insurance activities including: number of companies, number of employees, premiums by type of insurance, market share by foreign companies in each country, business written abroad, premiums in terms of risk destination (foreign or domestic risks), foreign and domestic investments, gross claims payments, gross operating expenses and commissions, OECD market share, penetration, density, and premiums per employee

International Migration Outlook — **Language:** English/French **Frequency:** annual **Content:** international migration statistics and legislation

International Trade by Commodity Statistics — **Language:** English/French **Frequency:** 5 p.a. **Content:** Provides import and export data in US dollars broken down by commodity and by partner country. Each of the first four volumes of ITCS contains the tables for 7 or 8 OECD countries. The data are published in the volumes as they come in from reporting countries.
The fifth volume includes the OECD main country groupings (OECD-Total, NAFTA, OECD-Asia Pacific, OECD-Europe, EU-15, etc). For each country, this publication shows detailed tables relating to the SITC

Labour Force Statistics — **Language:** English/French **Content:** provides detailed statistics on population, labour force, employment and unemployment over the past 10 years

Main Economic Indicators — **Language:** English/French **Frequency:** monthly **Content:** provides a comprehensive picture of the most recent economic statistics in the 30 OECD countries and a number of non-member countries including Brazil, China, India, Indonesia, the Russian Federation, and South Africa

Monthly Statistics of International Trade — **Language:** English/French **Frequency:** monthly **Content:** source of data on trade flows between OECD countries and their trading partners. Provides detailed insight into the most recent trends in world trading patterns. Available in other formats (Pdf, CD-ROM, Online)

OECD Agricultural Outlook 2006-2015 — **Language:** English/French **Content:** Provides an assessment of agricultural market prospects based on medium-term projections that extend to 2015 for production, consumption, trade and prices of major agricultural commodities **Edition:** 12th Edition

OECD Communications Outlook — **Language:** English/French **Frequency:** irregular **Content:** provides an extensive range of indicators for different types of communications networks and compares performance indicators such as revenue, investment, employment and prices for service throughout the OECD area

OECD Economic Outlook — **Language:** English/French/German **Frequency:** 2 p.a. **Content:** analyses major trends and examines the economic policies required to foster high and sustainable growth in member countries. Developments in major non-OECD economies are also evaluated

OECD Economic Surveys — **Language:** English/French **Frequency:** regular **Content:** national economic survey and prospects for each OECD member country. Most reports are for 2006 and 2007

OECD Employment Outlook — **Language:** English/French **Frequency:** irregular **Content:** overview of labour markets in OECD countries and its comprehensive statistical annex, this edition also includes articles covering trade adjustment costs in OECD labour markets, regional disparities in labour markets, the role of in-work benefits in increasing employment, and evaluating the impact of labour market programmes and public employment services

OECD Factbook 2007 - Economic, Environmental, and Social Statistics — **Language:** English/French **Content:** statistical annual covering all OECD countries and most topics addressed by the OECD. Includes more than 100 indicators with definitions, time-series tables, and graphics showing key messages **Edition:** 3rd Edition

OECD Health Data — **Language:** English/French **Frequency:** annual **Content:** statistics and health indicators for 30 countries

OECD Journal on Development — **Language:** English **Frequency:** 4 per annum **Content:** annual reference document for statistics and analysis on the latest trends in international aid

OECD Science, Technology and Industry Scoreboard — **Language:** English **Frequency:** bi-annual **Content:** explores the growing interaction between knowledge and globalisation. As innovation becomes a key determinant for long-run economic growth and social well-being, the STI Scoreboard provides a comprehensive picture of countries' performance in the areas of science, technology, globalisation and industry **Edition:** 8th Edition

Oil, Gas, Coal and Electricity -Quarterly Statistics — **Language:** English/French **Frequency:** quarterly **Content:** detailed data on production of crude oil, natural gas, liquids and refinery stocks, crude oil and product trades, refinery intake and output, final consumption, stock levels and changes

Review of Fisheries in OECD Countries — **Language:** English/French **Frequency:** annual **Content:** volume 1 covers Policy and Summary Statistics (major developments affecting fisheries in OECD countries, including changes in government policies, trade, and fisheries and aquaculture production. Summary statistics are included for each country); Volume 2 covers Country Statistics (fishing fleet, employment in fisheries, government financial transfers, total allowable catches, landings, aquaculture production, recreational fisheries, and imports and exports)

Trends in the Transport Sector 1970-2006 — **Language:** English/French **Content:** Internationally comparable figures on key transport trends. Analysis of the transport situation in the western and eastern European countries, as well as the Baltic States and the CIS

Organisation Internationale de la Vigne et du Vin (OIV)

International Organisation for Vine and Wine

Address: 18 rue D'Aguesseau, Paris, 75008, France
Telephone: +33 1 4494 8080
Fax: +33 1 4266 9063
E-mail: contact@oiv.int
Website: www.oiv.int

Activity: intergovernmental organisation working with vines, wine, wine-based beverages, table grapes, raisins and other vine-based products

Website(s) information:

Organisation Internationale de la Vigne et du Vin (OIV) *(International Organisation of Vine & Wine)* — **url:** www.oiv.int **Coverage:** statistical figures for raisins, vinegar and wine

Publication(s):

State of the Vitiviniculture World Market — **Frequency:** annual **Content:** Data published in these reports was harmonised with data provided by the Statistics Department of the Food and Agriculture Organisation of the United Nations (FAO)

Organisation of Petroleum Exporting Countries (OPEC)

Address: Obere Donaustraße 93, Vienna, 1020, Austria
Telephone: +43 21 112 279
Fax: +43 21 498 27
E-mail: info@opec.org
Website: www.opec.org

Guides: OPEC produces a variety of publications, including research about the oil and gas industry with a special focus on its Member Countries

Activity: OPEC is made up of 11 developing nations whose economies rely on oil export revenues. The OPEC member countries coordinate their oil production policies in order to help stabilise the oil market and to help oil producers achieve a reasonable rate of return on their investments

Website(s) information:

Organisation of Petroleum Exporting Countries (OPEC) — **url:** www.opec.org **Description:** access to Annual Report, including overview of OPEC in the world economy; macroeconomic figures for member countries; crude production by member country; world supply/demand balance; prices for selected crudes **Coverage:** market indicators

Publication(s):

Annual Report — **Language:** English **Frequency:** Annual **Content:** reviews of OPEC Member Countries' economic performances and the world oil market, activities of the OPEC Secretariat and listings of OPEC officials

Annual Statistical Bulletin — **Language:** English **Frequency:** Annual **Content:** tables, charts and graphs detailing the world's oil and gas reserves, production and refining activities, plus economic and other data. archive available

OPEC Bulletin — **Language:** English **Frequency:** monthly **Content:** organization's monthly flagship magazine, featuring news from Member Countries, incisive forum articles, a review of the oil market

Organización Mundial del Turismo
World Tourism Organisation (WTO)

Address: Capitán Haya, 42, Madrid, 28020, Spain
Telephone: +34 91 567 8100
Fax: +34 91 571 3733
E-mail: ceu@world-tourism.org
Website: www.unwto.org

Guides: all the publications are available for purchase in electronic format in the UNWTOelibrary and in hardcopy format in the UNWTO Infoshop

Activity: agency of the United Nations specialised in the tourism industry

Website(s) information:
World Tourism Organisation — **url:** www.unwto.org **Description:** provides access to global tourism data and trends; news and articles on developments within specific market sectors; information on trade in tourism services, quality of tourism development and sustainable development of tourism **Coverage:** statistics for all the countries around the world. All statistical tables available are displayed and can be accessed individually; available for free as part of any subscription to the WTOelibrary; non-subscribers may purchase the complete set of statistical tables

Publication(s):
City Tourism and Culture — **Language:** English/Spanish/French **Frequency:** annual **Content:** information on cultural city trips, marketing and product development

Compendium of Tourism Statistics — **Language:** English/French/Spanish **Content:** condensed and quick-reference guide on the major tourism statistical indicators in each country. Provides statistical information on tourism in 209 countries and territories around the world over a five year period

Marketing Activities — **Language:** Spanish/English/French **Frequency:** annual **Content:** information on the promotional effectiveness of tourism destinations

Measuring the Importance of the Meetings Industry: Developing and Tourism Satellite Account Extension — **Language:** English **Frequency:** irregular **Content:** Examines the contribution to national economies of the meetings industry. Provides a summary of the demand and supply and examines the use of these data in development a model for evaluating the economic contribution of the industry in macroeconomic terms

Spanish Ecotourism — **Language:** English/Spanish/French **Frequency:** irregular **Content:** information and analysis on nature tourism and ecotourism markets, with data on market volume; characteristics; major trends; development profiles; consumer profiles; the role of the different marketing tactics; product typologies and the main marketing tools used

Tourism 2020 Vision: Global Forecast and Profile of Market Segments — **Language:** English/French/Spanish **Frequency:** irregular **Content:** Examines the development of tourism in the world in the 1990s and the global tourism prospects for the period to the year 2020. Analysis of the ten most dynamic market segments during the next decades

Tourism Highlights — **Language:** English **Frequency:** annual **Content:** statistics and analysis on international tourist arrivals, international tourism receipts, results by region, major regional destinations by arrivals and receipts, and outbound tourism

Tourism Indicators — **Language:** English/French/Spanish **Frequency:** irregular **Content:** international tourist arrivals and receipts; international tourism expenditure and outbound tourism by region of origin

Tourism Market Trends — **Language:** Spanish/English/French **Frequency:** annual **Content:** analysis of tourism flows and earnings in Europe; including data on global and regional trends with special emphasis on the countries of each region; arrivals, receipts, hotel capacity, and major source markets

World Tourism Barometer — **Language:** English/French/Spanish **Frequency:** 3 per annum **Content:** a short-term evolution of tourism; contains three permanent elements: an overview of short-term tourism data from destination countries and air transport, a retrospective and prospective evaluation of tourism performance by the UNWTO Panel of Tourism Experts and selected economic data relevant for tourism

Yearbook of Tourism Statistics — **Language:** English/French/Spanish **Frequency:** annual **Content:** provides data for 206 countries and territories data on total arrivals and overnight stays associates to inbound tourism with breakdown by country of origin

United Nations (UN)
Address: United Nations Publications, Room DC2-853, 2 UN Plaza, New York, NY 10017, USA
Telephone: +1 212 963 8302
Fax: +1 212 963 3489
E-mail: publications@un.org
Website: www.un.org

Guides: catalogue of UN Publications (annual, free); lists all publications currently in print from UN bodies and affiliated agencies whose publications are sold by UN Sales Sections; UNDOC Current Index (United Nations Document Index) is issued 10 times a year, on a subscription basis, and gives a comprehensive coverage of UN documentation

Activity: maintains international peace and security; develops friendly relations among nations; cooperates in solving international economic, social, cultural and humanitarian problems and in promotes respect for human rights and fundamental freedoms

Website(s) information:
United Nations — **url:** www.un.org **Description:** official site of the United Nations. Access to information in the form of online publications, reports and briefings, news, surveys and press releases, covering a wide range of issues in the areas of human rights, socio-economic and human development, environment and poverty reduction. Provides links to UN official bodies and institutions and is available in all UN official languages: English, French, Spanish, Russian, Arabic and Chinese. (For more information on UN Statistics see UN Statistical Division site)

United Nations Statistics Division — **url:** unstats.un.org/unsd/ **Description:** database of statistical data for member states of the United Nations, covering a total of 188 countries. Available in Spanish, French and English **Coverage:** data provided for each country covers: geography, economy, population and social indicators. 1) Geography: area, capital and largest city; official language; urban population; energy consumption; forest area; etc; 2) Economy: currency; GDP (US$); GDP per capita (US$); major export industries; unemployment; tourist arrivals; 3) Population: total population; density; years; female/male ratio; infant mortality; growth; total fertility rate; 4) Social indicators: life expectancy; literacy rate; parliamentary seats (women/men); spending on education; school enrolment; homicides; motor vehicles; telephones; refugees; etc

Publication(s):
Africa Renewal — **Language:** English/French **Frequency:** quarterly **Content:** development of African countries

Demographic Yearbook — **Language:** English **Content:** demographic statistics provided for some 200 countries, covering size, distribution and trends in population, fertility, mortality, marriage and divorce, international migration and population census data

Economic and Social Survey of Asia and the Pacific — **Language:** English **Frequency:** annual **Content:** analyses recent economic and social developments in the region with particular emphasis on economic and social policy issues and broad development strategies

Economic and Social Survey of Latin America and the Caribbean — **Language:** English **Frequency:** irregular **Content:** analyses the economic situation in the region

Economic Survey of Europe — **Language:** English **Frequency:** irregular **Content:** update on the current economic situation in Europe, North America and the Commonwealth of Independent States (CIS), focusing on regional disparities and economic convergence

Industrial Commodity Statistics Yearbook — **Language:** English **Frequency:** annual **Content:** Yearbook consists of two parts. Part one contains annual quantity data on production of industrial commodities by country, geographical region, economic grouping and for the world. For some 200 countries, information has been presented for about 230 commodities over a ten-year period . Part two presents data by country on apparent consumption of about 530 industrial commodities over the same period

International Trade Statistics Yearbook — **Language:** English **Frequency:** annual **Content:** presents the basic information for individual countries' external trade performance in terms of the overall trends in current value, as well as in volume and price; the importance of trading partners and the significance of individual commodities imported and exported

Monthly Bulletin of Statistics — **Language:** English **Frequency:** monthly **Content:** economic and social statistics from more that 200 countries and territories, as well as quarterly statistics on industrial production

Population and Vital Statistics Report — **Language:** English **Frequency:** quarterly **Content:** estimates of world and regional populations as well as estimates for 218 countries. Data is compiled and collected by national statistical offices and related official organisations, based on latest national population census

Statistical Yearbook for Asia and the Pacific — **Language:** English/French **Frequency:** annual **Content:** statistics covering a total of 56 countries, covering a wide range of topics including: population, manpower, national accounts, agriculture, forestry and fishing, industry, energy production and consumption, transportation and communication, internal and external trade, wages, banking, finance and social statistics

Statistical Yearbook for Latin America and the Caribbean — **Language:** English/French **Frequency:** annual **Content:** annual compilation of a wide range of socio-economic statistics for a total of 33 Latin American countries. Data covers topics including: population, national accounts, employment, social conditions, agriculture, industry, import-export goods and services, balance of payments and infrastructure services

UN Statistical Yearbook — **Language:** English **Frequency:** annual **Content:** presents an overall comprehensive description of the world economy, its structure, major trends and recent performance

World Economic and Social Survey — **Language:** English **Frequency:** annual **Content:** assesses the current global economic situation, including a forecast of output, international trade and other key economic variables

World Population Prospects — **Language:** English **Frequency:** irregular **Content:** presents population estimates and projections for the world, the more developed and less developed regions, the least developed countries, 5 major areas, 21 regions and 184 countries or areas

World Statistics Pocketbook — **Language:** English **Frequency:** annual **Content:** international compilation of basic economic, social and environmental indicators for 208 countries and areas worldwide. It covers 57 key indicators in the areas of population, economic activity, agriculture, industry, energy, international trade, transport, communications, gender, education and environment

United Nations Conference on Trade and Development (UNCTAD)

Address: Palais des Nations, 8-14 Avenue de la Paix, Geneva 10, 1211, Switzerland
Telephone: +41 22 917 5634
Fax: +41 22 917 0042
E-mail: sgo@unctad.org
Website: www.unctad.org

Guides: reference service holds a collection of 20,000 items; books, periodicals, CD-ROMs, on international economic relations, trade and development issues. Themes and documentation of UNCSTAD include: World Investment Report (annual), Trade and Development Report (annual), Handbook on Trade and Development Statistics, Least Developed Countries (reports), International trade in goods, services and commodities, investment, technology and enterprise development, services infrastructure for development and trade efficiency

Activity: promotes the development-friendly integration of developing countries into the world economy

Website(s) information:
UNCTAD GlobStat — **url:** globstat.unctad.org **Coverage:** statistics covering the world on countries, population and economic trends; external finance, debt, and foreign direct investment; transnational corporations and foreign affiliates; international trade in merchandise and service; production and international trade of commodities; production and international trade of manufacturers; information and communication technology

Publication(s):
Development and Globalisation: Facts and Figures — **Language:** English **Frequency:** annual **Content:** statistics on countries, population and economic trends; external finance, debt, and foreign direct investment; transnational corporations and foreign affiliates; international trade in merchandise and services; production and international trade of commodities and manufacturers; information and communication technology

Economic Development in Africa Report — **Language:** English **Frequency:** annual **Content:** analyses selected aspects of Africa's development problems and major policy issues confronting African countries. It makes policy recommendations for action by African countries themselves and by the international community to overcome the development challenges that the continent faces **Edition:** 6th

Information Economy Report (IER) and E-commerce and Development Report (ECDR) —

Review of Maritime Transport (RMT) — **Language:** English **Frequency:** annual **Content:** reports on the worldwide evolution of shipping, ports and multimodal transport related to the major traffic of liquid bulk, dry bulk and containers

Trade and Development Report — **Language:** English **Frequency:** annual **Content:** collection of statistical data relevant to the analysis of international trade, investment and development, for individual countries and for economic and trade groupings

UNCTAD Handbook of Statistics —

World Investment Report (WIR) — **Language:** English **Frequency:** annual **Content:** analyses current trends and major international policy issues regarding information and communication technologies and their use for, and effect on, trade and development

United Nations Educational, Scientific and Cultural Organisation (UNESCO)

Address: 7 place de Fontenoy, Paris Cédex 07, 75352, France
Telephone: +33 1 4568 0359
Fax: +33 1 4568 5642
E-mail: publishing.promotion@unesco.org
Website: www.unesco.org

Guides: UNESCO Publishing is the publishing arm. Their website presents titles currently for sale in English, French, Spanish, Russian and Arabic published or co-published by UNESCO. These include books, multimedia (DVDs, CD-Roms, VHS videos), periodicals, and scientific maps for professionals

Activity: specialised agency of the United Nations. Its purpose is to contribute to peace and security by promoting international collaboration through education, science, and culture

Website(s) information:
Unesco Institute for Statistics — **url:** www.uis.unesco.org **Description:** wide range of online documents and databases providing data and statistics on world education, science and technology, and culture. Includes access to the UNESCO database searchable by subject, region, country and year; wide range of country education indicators covering schooling, participation in education, internal efficiency, primary education, indicators on resources, and literacy; and selected tables from the UNESCO yearbook **Coverage:** provides statistical information, fast facts and regional profiles in the following fields: Education, Literacy, Science and Technology, Culture and Communication

United Nations Industrial Development Organisation (UNIDO)

Address: PO Box 300, Vienna International Centre, Wagramerstr. 5, Vienna, 1400, Austria
Telephone: +43 26026 0
Fax: +43 26926 69
E-mail: unido@unido.org
Website: www.unido.org

Guides: publications can be purchased through UNIDO or downloaded for free
Activity: working to improve the living conditions of people and promote global prosperity through offering tailor-made solutions for the sustainable industrial development of developing countries and countries with economies in transition

Website(s) information:
IDSB - Industrial Demand-Supply Database — **url:** www.unido.org **Description:** In addition to offering sets of production-related industrial statistics (i.e. INDSTAT3 and INDSTAT4 Databases), UNIDO is making its Industrial Demand-Supply Balance Databases (IDSB) available to external users **Coverage:** Database covers industrial output, trade and apparent consumption

INDSTAT — **url:** www.unido.org **Description:** INDSTAT data are compiled in collaboration with the Organisation for Economic Cooperation and Development (OECD): Data for non-OECD countries are collected by UNIDO while those for OECD member countries are collected and provided to UNIDO by OECD for inclusion in the database. UNIDO maintains and updates the data annually **Coverage:** Industrial statistics database containing time series data on selected data items for the period 1990 onwards. Information is presented by country, year and industry, covering number of establishments; employment; female employment; wages and salaries; output; value added; gross fixed capital formation

UNIDO — **url:** www.unido.org **Description:** free access to PDF documents, reports, economic research papers and publications **Coverage:** Globalisation and its implications; industrial growth, trade and finance; investment, productivity and export in African manufacturing; competitiveness; environmental resources and their management; enterprise and business development; industrial policy

Publication(s):

International Yearbook of Industrial Statistics — **Language:** English **Frequency:** annual **Content:** worldwide statistics on current performance and trends in the manufacturing sector. Analyses patterns of growth, structural change and industrial performance in individual industries in over 120 countries **Readership:** economists, planners, business people, policy makers

World Directory of Industrial Information Sources — **Language:** English **Content:** Industrial information sources for technology and equipment. Contains profiles of information providers such as information and documentation centres, banks, training institutes, development agencies, manufacturers associations etc

United Nations Population Fund (UNFPA)

Address: 220 East 42nd Street, New York, NY 10017, , USA
Telephone: +1 212 297 5028
Fax: +1 212 297 4908
E-mail: gharzeddine@unfpa.org
Website: www.unfpa.org

Activity: supports countries in using population data for policies and programmes to reduce poverty

Website(s) information:
United Nations Population Fund (UNFPA) — **url:** www.unfpa.org/worldwide/ **Description:** reports on every country and up-to-date demographic, health and economic indicators **Coverage:** provides indicators and policy developments by country; country/territory profiles

Publication(s):
Country Profiles for Population and Reproductive Health — **Frequency:** Every 2 years **Content:** covers the areas of socioeconomic health, adolescent reproductive health, gender equality and reproductive health commodity security. Indicators for ICPD Goals as well as MDGs are identified

Gender, Health and Development in the Americas: Basic Indicators — **Language:** English/Spanish **Frequency:** irregular **Content:** profiles gender differences in health and development in the 48 states and territories in Latin America and the Caribbean, focusing on women's reproductive health, access to key health services, and major causes of death

Maternal Mortality — **Language:** English **Frequency:** annual **Content:** Reports the global, regional, and country estimates of maternal mortality in the past year and the findings of the separate assessments of trends of maternal mortality levels since 1990.

State of World Population 2007 — **Language:** English/Spanish/French/Arabic/Russian **Content:** The 2007 State of World Population report outlines the challenges and opportunities presented by the coming, inevitable urban growth. It also dispels many misconceptions about urbanization and calls on policymakers to take concerted, proactive steps to harness the potential of cities to improve the lives of all

United Nations Statistics Division

Address: Statistics Division, United Nations, New York, NY 10017, USA
Fax: +1 212 963 4116
E-mail: statistics@un.org
Website: www.un.org/Depts/unsd

Guides: publishes data updates, including the Statistical Yearbook and World Statistics Pocketbook, and books and reports on statistics and statistical methods. Many of the Division's databases are also available on their website, as electronic publications and data files in the form of CD-ROMs, diskettes and magnetic tapes, or as printed publications

Activity: global centre for data on international trade, national accounts, energy, industry, environment, transport and demographic and social statistics gathered from many national and international sources

Website(s) information:
UN Statistical Division — **url:** www.un.org/Depts/unsd **Description:** wide range of world statistics, including: world economic statistics; environment statistics; demographic and social data **Coverage:** UNSD statistical databases on-line provide different world socio-economic data including population size and composition, birth, deaths, marriages, disability, education, oil data, national accounts, social indicators family, health, work, politics and human rights

Publication(s):
Bulletin of Statistics — **Language:** English **Frequency:** monthly **Content:** current economic and social statistics for more than 200 countries and territories of the world; contains over 50 tables of monthly and/or annual and quarterly data on a variety of subjects illustrating important economic trends and developments, including population, prices, employment and earnings, energy, manufacturing, transport, construction, international merchandise trade and finance

Energy Statistics Yearbook — **Language:** English/French **Frequency:** annual **Content:** annual compilation of a wide range of economic, social and environmental statistics on over 200 countries and areas of the world, compiled from more than 35 sources including UN agencies and other international, national and specialised organisations. This issue contains the most recent data available to the Statistics Division as of March 2006 and presents them in 76 tables on topics such as: agriculture; balance of payments; culture and communication; development assistance; education; energy; environme

International Trade Statistics Yearbook Vols 1 & 2 — **Language:** English/French **Content:** provides information relevant to the external trade performance of approximately 180 countries or areas and highlights world trade of selected commodities

National Accounts Statistics: Analysis of Main Aggregates — **Language:** English **Frequency:** annual **Content:** Contains detailed national accounts estimates for 169 countries and areas. The national data for each country and area are presented in separate chapters using uniform table headings and classifications recommended in the United Nations System of National Accounts 1993 (SNA 1993). The yearbook publishes integrated accounts for institutional sectors, as well as the cross-classification of value added by institutional sector and economic activity

Population and Vital Statistics Report — **Language:** English **Content:** presents data for countries or areas on population size (total, male, and female) from the latest available census, estimated total population size for latest available year, and the number and rate of vital events (live births, deaths, and infant deaths) for the latest available year since 1980

Statistical Yearbook — **Language:** English/French **Frequency:** annual **Content:** contains data available to the Statistics Division and presents them in 76 tables on topics such as: agriculture; balance of payments; culture and communication; development assistance; education; energy; environment; finance; nutrition; industrial production; international merchandise trade; international tourism; labour force; manufacturing; national accounts; population; prices; research and development; transport; and wages **Edition:** 50th Edition

World's Women: Progress in Statistics — **Language:** English **Frequency:** irregular **Content:** reviews and analyses the current availability of data and assesses progress made in the reporting of national statistics, as opposed to internationally prepared estimates, relevant to gender concerns. Analysing statistics reported by 204 countries during the past 30 years, The World's Women sets out a blueprint for improving the availability of data in the areas of demographics, health, education, work, violence against women, poverty, decision-making and human rights

Universal Postal Union

Address: International Bureau, Case Postale 13, Berne 15, 3000, Switzerland
Telephone: +41 31 350 3111
Fax: +41 31 350 3110
E-mail: info@upu.int
Website: www.upu.int

Activity: 190 member countries; the UPU is the primary forum for cooperation between postal services and helps to ensure a truly universal network of up-to-date products and services. In this way, the organisation fulfils an advisory, mediating and liaison role, and renders technical assistance where needed. It sets the rules for international mail exchanges and makes recommendations to stimulate growth in mail volumes and to improve the quality of service

Website(s) information:
Universal Postal Union — url: www.upu.int **Description:** The UPU's statistical database provides a dynamic overview of postal development in each country. It contains data from over 200 countries or territories and includes approximately 100 indicators of postal development, grouped in 12 chapters. The data is collected annually by the International Bureau from all UPU member postal administrations

Coverage: postal statistics and trends

Publication(s):
Postal Statistics — Language: English **Frequency:** annual **Content:** It contains data from over 200 countries or territories and includes approximately 100 indicators of postal development, grouped in 12 chapters. The data is collected annually by the International Bureau from all UPU member postal administrations.

World Bank

Address: 1818 H Street NW, Washington, DC 20433, , USA
Telephone: +1 202 473 1000
Fax: +1 202 477 6391
E-mail: pic@worldbank.org
Website: www.worldbank.org

Guides: available online under: http://publications.worldbank.org/ecommerce
Activity: provides financial and technical assistance to developing countries

Website(s) information:
World Bank — url: www.worldbank.org **Description:** provides information about the World Bank and its activities; provides access to the World Bank's formal publications, including World Development Report and a range of books that cover the full spectrum of economic and social development; it is also the gateway to the World Development Indicators Online, the premier source for data on the global economy, and to the World Bank e-Library, the comprehensive and fully searchable collection of the Bank's books; holds over 15,000 free, downloadable documents, including operational documents (project documents, analytical and advisory work, and evaluations), formal and informal research papers, and most Bank publications
Coverage: general economic indicators; vital statistics of world countries

World Development Indicators — url: http://publications.worldbank.org/WDI/
Coverage: contains statistical data for over 600 development indicators and time series data from 1960-2003 (selected data for 2004) for over 200 countries and 18 country groups; data includes social, economic, financial, natural resources, and environmental indicators

Publication(s):
Africa Development Indicators — Language: English **Frequency:** annual **Content:** general socio-economic indicators of African countries **Edition:** 2006

Atlas of Global Development: A Visual Guide to the World's Greatest Challenges — Language: English **Frequency:** annual **Content:** Social, economic, and environmental issues that are facing the planet are presented in world maps, tables, graphs, text and photographs. Drawing on data from the World Bank's authoritative World Development Indicators, the book brings to life country comparisons of social indicators like life expectancy, infant mortality, safe water, population, growth, poverty and energy efficiency. Issues that have been hitting the headlines such as AIDS, population living below $1 a day, freshwater, trade are presented

Global Economic Prospects 2007: Managing the Next Wave of Globalization — Language: English **Content:** Over the next 25 years developing countries will move to center stage in the global economy. analyses the opportunities and stresses this will create. While rich and poor countries alike stand to benefit, the integration process will make more acute stresses already apparent today - in income inequality, in labour markets, and in the environment

Global Monitoring Report 2007 — Content: Millennium Development Goals: assesses the contributions of developing countries, developed countries, and international financial institutions toward meeting universally agreed development commitments. Fourth in a series of annual reports leading up to 2015, this year's report reviews key developments of the past year, emerging priorities, and provides a detailed region-by-region picture of performance in the developing regions of the world, drawing on indicators for poverty, education, gender equality,

Sustainable Energy in China: The Closing Window of Opportunity — Content: This title uses historical data from 1980 and alternative scenarios through 2020 to assess China's future energy requirements and the resources to meet them. It calls for a high-level commitment to develop and implement an integrated, coordinated, and comprehensive energy policy

World Bank Annual Report — Language: English/French/Russian/Spanish/Arabic/Chinese/Portuguese/Hindi/German/Japanese **Frequency:** annual **Content:** provides an annual overview of World Bank activities

World Development Indicators — Language: English **Frequency:** annual **Content:** compilation of data about development. This statistical reference allows you to consult over 900 indicators for some 150 economies and 14 country groups in more than 80 tables. It provides a current overview of the most recent data available as well as important regional data and income group analysis.The CD-ROM editions contain 45 years of time series data, covering periods since 1960, and offer mapping, charting, and data export formats

World Development Report: Development and the Next Generation — Language: English/French **Frequency:** annual **Content:** analysis of world development policies, world disparities and inequalities, poverty and sustainable growth, and policies for future global progress **Edition:** 2007

World Conservation Union (IUCN)

Address: Rue Mauverney 28, Gland, 1196, Switzerland
Telephone: +41 22 999 0000
Fax: +41 22 999 0002
E-mail: webmaster@iucn.org
Website: www.iucn.org

Guides: publications produced by the WCU from 1948 to the present. Includes publications of CITES - Convention on International Trade in Endangered Species of Wild Fauna and Flora, the Ramsar Convention on Wetlands, TRAFFIC - the joint wildlife trade monitoring programme of IUCN and WWF, UNEP-World Conservation Monitoring Centre, and a selection of titles from IUCN members or other publishers
Activity: the world's largest environmental network with over 1,000 members including states, government agencies, and non-governmental organisations in 140 countries

World Customs Organisation (WCO)

Address: Rue du Marché 30, Brussels, B-1210, Belgium
Telephone: +32 2 209 9503
Fax: +32 2 209 9490
E-mail: publications@wcoomd.org
Website: www.wcoomd.org

Guides: online publications catalogue
WCO News magazine available for free download
Activity: intergovernmental body that works to enhance the effectiveness and efficiency of Customs administrations

Publication(s):
Customs and Tobacco Report 2007 — Language: English/French **Content:** Global review of legitimate tobacco trading and smuggling. Includes statistical analyses of trends

World Health Organisation (WHO)/Organisation Mondiale de la Santé

Address: Avenue Appia 20, Geneva 27, 1211, Switzerland
Telephone: +41 22 791 2111
Fax: +41 22 791 3111
E-mail: info@who.int
Website: www.who.ch

Guides: access to the online library database WHOLIS on their website

Activity: The WHO is the UN specialised agency for health; its objective is the attainment by all peoples of the highest possible level of health; the WHO is governed by 192 Member States

Website(s) information:

WHO Statistical Information System (WHOSIS) — url: www.who.int/whosis
   Coverage: statistics cover basic health indicators; diseases; numbers of doctors, dentists and nurses; HIV/AIDS data; population estimates and projections; data can be accessed in respect of each member State

World Health Organisation (WHO) — url: www.who.ch **Coverage:** information on WHO and the present state of health services worldwide; includes information on child immunisation; health expenditures; infant mortality; maternal mortality; deaths by type of condition, etc.

Publication(s):

Bulletin of the World Health Organisation — **Language:** English/French/Spanish **Frequency:** monthly **Content:** aims to give public health policy and practice guidance, also encourages closer links between scientific investigation and the art of helping populations to lead healthier lives

World Health Report — **Language:** English **Frequency:** annual **Content:** the report reveals an estimated shortage of almost 4.3 million doctors, midwives, nurses and support workers worldwide. The shortage is most severe in the poorest countries, especially in sub-Saharan Africa, where health workers are most needed **Readership:** donor agencies, international organisations

World Intellectual Property Organisation (WIPO)

Address: 34 Chemin des Colombettes, Geneva, Switzerland
Telephone: +41 22 338 8186
Fax: +41 22 338 8210
E-mail: information.center@wipo.int
Website: www.wipo.int

Activity: WIPO is one of the 16 specialised agencies of the United Nations system of organisations. It administers 23 international treaties dealing with different aspects of intellectual property protection

Website(s) information:

World Intellectual Property Organisation (WIPO) — url:
   http://www.wipo.int/ipstats/en/resources/ **Description:** Access to an online database with statistical information on patent filings, patent grants and patents in force and other free information products such as the WIPO Magazine **Coverage:** WIPO collects and publishes annual statistics on industrial property, by country and in accordance with the relevant international industrial property classification systems administered by WIPO. The statistics relate to patents, utility models, marks, industrial designs, plant varieties and microorganisms and are published in a unique collection of statistical tables which bring together data supplied by Industrial Property Offices in respect of filings under national, regional and international legislations

Publication(s):

WIPO Patent Report - Statistics on Worldwide Patent Activities — **Language:** English/French/Spanish **Content:** presents an overview of worldwide patenting activity based on statistics up to the end of 2004

WPO Industrial Property Statistics — **Frequency:** regular updates **Content:** provides statistical information on the number of applications and registrations regarding patents, utility models, trademarks, industrial designs, as well as related information concerning plant varieties and microorganisms from 1994 to 2000 in PDF and Excel format. Online version provides 1978-2004 statistics

World Meteorological Organization (WMO)

Address: Case Postale No 2300, 7bis avenue de la Paix, Geneva, CH-1211, Switzerland
Telephone: +41 22 730 8111
Fax: +41 22 730 8181
E-mail: wmo@wmo.int
Website: www.wmo.int

Activity: intergovernmental organisation with a membership of 187 Member States and Territories. It originated from the International Meteorological Organization (IMO), which was founded in 1873. WMO became the specialized agency of the United Nations for meteorology (weather and climate), operational hydrology and related geophysical sciences in 1951

Publication(s):

World Climate News — **Language:** English/Spanish/French **Frequency:** 6 monthly **Content:** official magazine of the WMO. Also produces a quarterly journal - The Bulletin

World Trade Organisation (WTO)

Address: Centre William Rappard, 154 rue de Lausanne, Geneva 21, CH-1211, Switzerland
Telephone: +41 22 739 5111
Fax: +41 22 731 4206
E-mail: enquiries@wto.org or publications@wto.org
Website: www.wto.org

Guides: online bookshop at www.onlinebookshop.wto.org

Activity: deals with the rules of trade between nations

Website(s) information:

World Trade Organisation (WTO) — url: www.wto.org **Description:** offers information on global trade and rules defining international commercial activities around the world; a compilation of news on the WTO and international trade; articles and briefings on various trade topics; access to free online publications on trade policies reviews, agreements and statistics **Coverage:** statistics compiled by the WTO, including International Trade Statistics (annual), an Annual Report, and a Historical Series; data covers the main features of trade activities around the world: global trade figures; merchandise trade by product; commercial services trade; trade by world region; trade by economic sector

Publication(s):

International Trade Statistics — **Language:** English/French/Spanish **Frequency:** annual **Content:** provides comprehensive, comparable and up-to-date statistics on trade in merchandise and commercial services for an assessment of world trade flows by country, region and main product groups or service categories

Pan-regional Official Sources

Eastern Europe

Interstate Statistical Committee of the Commonwealth of Independent States

Address: 39 Myasnitskaya Street, Building 1, Moscow, 107450, Russia
Telephone: +7 495 207 4237/207 4802
Fax: +7 495 207 4592
E-mail: statpro@sovam.com
Website: www.cisstat.com/eng/index.htm

Guides: full catalogue is available online
Activity: coordinates the activities of national statistical services, promotes the organisation of information exchange, carries out analysis of socio-economic development of the states and elaborating common recommendations in the field of statistics

Website(s) information:
Web Database Statistics of the CIS — **url:** www.cisstat.com/0base/index-en.htm **Description:** an online portal, which contains data drawn directly from the statistical services of all the CIS states; provides statistical information about society, economics, business, trade, environmental and demographic developments **Coverage:** statistical database covering all the CIS countries and providing data on basic economic indicators, movements of labour and people, environmental, trade, demographic data

Publication(s):
Commonwealth of Independent States — **Language:** Russian/English **Frequency:** annual **Content:** contains generalised comparable statistical materials on the basis of official data of the national statistical services of the countries of the CIS (Armenia, Azerbaijan, Belarus, Georgia, Kazakhstan, Kyrgyzstan, Moldova, Russia, Tajikistan, Ukraine, and Uzbekistan), characterising socio-economic situation in the Commonwealth countries by main indicators of macroeconomics, branch economy, external trade, social sphere. International comparisons are given for some indicators

Ministry of Foreign Affairs of Russia

Address: , 32/34 Smolenskaya-Sennaya pl., Moscow, 119200, Russia
Telephone: +7 95 244 3096
Fax: +7 95 244 1797
E-mail: ac-chair@mid.ru
Website: http://www.arctic-council.org

Guides: Links to publications and reports available on their website
Activity: government ministry

Publication(s):
Economic and Social Development of the Small Indigenous Peoples of the North up to the Year 2011 — **Language:** English **Content:** social development of indigenous populations report

Western Europe

Commonwealth Secretariat

Address: Marlborough House, Pall Mall, London, SW1Y 5HX, United Kingdom
Telephone: +44 20 7747 6500
Fax: +44 20 7930 0827
E-mail: info@thecommonwealth.org
Website: www.thecommonwealth.org

Guides: titles cover policy issues, case studies and best practices in areas of Commonwealth expertise, including globalisation and multilateral trade issues, export and enterprise development, education, gender, public service management and reform, human rights and corporate governance
Activity: active in a number of areas including development, democracy, debt management and trade

Website(s) information:
Commonwealth Network — **url:** www.thecommonwealth.org **Description:** news and articles on the Commonwealth and its 54 member countries, including information on regional and country level programmes on: health; debt management; education; finance; trade; gender equality; etc

Council of Europe

Address: Palais de l'Europe, Avenue de l'Europe, Strasbourg Cédex, 67075, France
Telephone: +33 3 8841 2000
Fax: +33 3 8841 2781
E-mail: infodoc@coe.int
Website: www.coe.int

Activity: acts as a political anchor and human rights watchdog for Europe's post-communist democracies, assists the countries of central and eastern Europe in carrying out and consolidating political, legal and constitutional reform in parallel with economic reform, provides know-how in areas such as human rights, local democracy, education, culture and the environment

Website(s) information:
Council of Europe/Conseil de L'Europe — **url:** www.coe.int **Description:** official web site of the Council of Europe, providing general information on the Council's structure, activities and services: the Committee of Ministers; Parliamentary Assembly; Human Rights Court; Commissioner for Human Rights; Congress of Local and Regional Authorities; and the Secretary General. Online access to different documents on Human Rights Case Law, European Treaties and publications and reports of the Library and Archive Division. A series of different theme files provide information on: human rights; social topics (e.g. population; demographic trends and migrations; health; development; etc); legal matters; and links to other European and international organisations

Publication(s):
Current Trends in International Migration in Europe — **Language:** English **Content:** migration statistics, stocks of foreign population, flows of foreign population, labour migration, the problem of asylum, migration of expertise, irregular migration and recent initiatives in international co-operation

Recent Demographic Development in Europe — **Frequency:** annual **Content:** information on population developments in forty-six European states: the size of the population and its rate of increase, rates of migration, marriage and divorce, fertility and mortality, and the size of foreign population

European Bank for Reconstruction and Development (EBRD)

Address: One Exchange Square, London, EC2A 2JN, United Kingdom
Telephone: +44 20 7338 6000
Fax: +44 20 7338 6100
E-mail: pubsdesk@ebrd.com
Website: www.ebrd.com

Activity: EBRD is the largest single investor in the region and mobilises significant foreign direct investment beyond its own financing. It is owned by 60 countries and two intergovernmental institutions. It provides project financing for banks, industries and businesses, both new ventures and investments in existing companies. It also works with publicly owned companies, to support privatisation, restructuring state-owned firms and improvement of municipal services. The Bank uses its close relationship with governments in the region to promote policies that will bolster the business environment

Website(s) information:
European Bank for Reconstruction and Development (EBRD) — **url:** www.ebrd.com **Description:** offers descriptions of all projects in the region, information on policies and online working papers. The papers are downloadable online and cover major issues of the European financial system and economic development: European financial structure; competition and enterprise performance; taxation; social changes; monetary transaction; legal changes

Publication(s):
EBRD Investments 1991-2004 — **Language:** English/French/German/Russian **Frequency:** annual **Content:** provides a complete list of every project the Bank has signed on a country-by-country basis

Economics of Transition — **Language:** English/French/German/Russian **Frequency:** quarterly **Content:** Publishes articles on the economics of structural transformation, institutional development, and growth in Central and Eastern Europe and the CIS, China and Vietnam, as well as studies of reform and institutional change in other emerging market environments, including India and Latin America

Environments in Transition — **Language:** English/French/German/Russian **Content:** information on the Bank's environmental programme. Includes updates on environmental aspects of newly approved projects in Central and Eastern Europe

Transition Report — **Language:** English/French/German/Russian **Frequency:** annual **Content:** analysis of the global process of transition to a market economy in central and eastern Europe, the Baltic states and the Commonwealth of Independent States. Includes statistical analysis of major macro-economic indicators, covering market liberalisation and competition matters, macroeconomic stabilisation, enterprise restructuring and privatisation, reform of finance and infrastructure and legal reform

European Central Bank

Address: Postfach 160319, Kaiserstrasse 29, Frankfurt am Main, 60066, Germany
Telephone: +49 69 1344 0
Fax: +49 69 1344 6000
E-mail: info@ecb.int
Website: www.ecb.int

Activity: central bank for Europe's single currency

Website(s) information:
European Central Bank — **url:** www.ecb.int **Coverage:** provides key information on the latest financial and monetary developments in Europe, including access to ECB monthly bulletins in all EU official languages; financial statement of the Euro-system; ECB interest rates; monetary policy operations; minimum reserve statistics; banking system's liquidity position; and general economic and financial developments in the Euro area

Publication(s):
Annual Report — **Language:** All official EU languages **Frequency:** annual **Content:** publication which describes the activities of the bank and reports on monetary policy of both the previous and the current year

Convergence Report — **Language:** All official EU languages **Frequency:** every two years **Content:** report on the progress made in the fulfilment by the Member States of their obligations regarding the achievement of economic and monetary union

ECB Statistics: An Overview — **Language:** English **Frequency:** irregular **Content:** statistics relating to monetary financial institutions, interest rates, balance of payments, international role of the Euro, exchange rates, statistical aspects of enlargement

Economic Research Publications — **Language:** English **Frequency:** irregular **Content:** publications of the Working Paper Series" which disseminate findings within the field of monetary and general economic research and "Occasional Paper Series" which deal with economic research topics

Monthly Bulletin — **Language:** all EU official languages **Frequency:** monthly **Content:** news and features on European Union monetary policies, financial and banking systems. Latest on the Euro, providing financial and economic statistical data for the Euro zone

Statistics Pocket Book — **Language:** English **Content:** population and the labour market, macroeconomic indicators, Euro area balance of payments, income, monetary policy, financial market developments, levels of GDP

European Commission Directorate General for Education and Culture

Address: Directorate-General for Education and Culture, Unit B1, Brussels, B-1049, Belgium
Telephone: +32 2299 9335
Fax: +32 2299 4577
E-mail: eac-info@ec.europa.eu
Website: www.europa.eu.int

Guides: a general overview of EU policy on education and training can be found on the SCADplus database

Activity: opportunities by the EU for living, studying and working in other countries; promotes cross-cultural understanding, personal development and the realisation of the EU's full economic potential

Website(s) information:
European Continuous Tracking Survey (Europinion) — **url:** www.europa.eu.int/comm/dg10/epo/ **Description:** series of consumer attitude surveys conducted across the countries of the European Union. Covers issues relating to the European Union and numerous economic and social issues

Information Network on Education in Europe (EURYDICE) — **url:** www.eurydice.org **Coverage:** EURYBASE database of education systems and on national policies in the field of education in Europe; includes information on legislation; educational structure for each European country; political and economic backgrounds of the various educational systems

Market Access Database — **url:** www.mkaccdb.eu.int **Description:** series of international trade information databases searchable by country. The Sectorial and Trade Barriers Database covers the following: general features of trade policy; tariff barriers; non-tariff barriers; investment related measures. Also includes Applied Tariffs Database; WTO Bound Tariffs Database; Exporters' Guide to Import Formalities; GATS Info-Point (some areas are only accessible from European Union member states) **Coverage:** statistics on EU trade flows by partner country

Publication(s):
Defining a Strategy for the direct Assessment of Skills — **Content:** potential and limits of a European initiative; focus of a European skills assessment initiative; methodological issues; data-collection process

Exploring Sources on Funding for Lifelong Learning — **Content:** statistical information; development of statistical indicators; assessment of existing international data sources; inventory and assessment of existing national data source; general review of the key variables; situation report on the key variables; scenarios and methodological basis for possible future data collection

Indicators for Monitoring Active Citizenship — **Content:** active citizenship and citizenship education; identification of indicators; the role of education in political socialisation and active citizenship; input and output indicators

Study on Access to Education and Training — **Content:** relationship between skills and competitiveness at micro and macro-level; analytical framework; data analysis and qualitative reviews

Study on Basic Skills — Explaining Student Performance — **Content:** overall performance; student background and basic skills; student attitudes and behaviour and basic skills; educational environment and basic skills; data collection activities

Study on Early School Leavers — **Content:** analytical framework; key study areas; overview of trends of the rate of early school leavers in each country studied; the influence of wider external factors; influence of socio-economic characteristics on early school leaving

Study on Private Household Spending on Education and Training — **Content:** factors affecting household expenditure on education; overview of expenditure in the European Union; recent trends in household spending education; indirect and opportunity cost in education

European Environment Agency

Address: Kongens Nytorv 6, Copenhagen K, 1050, Denmark
Telephone: +45 33 367 100
Fax: +45 33 367 199
E-mail: webmaster@eea-europa.eu
Website: www.eea.eu.int

Website(s) information:
European Environment Agency — **url:** www.eea.eu.int **Description:** provides reports and indicators on acidification, air quality, biodiversity, climate change, natural resources, ozone depletion and waste. Also contains sector sub-categories on agriculture, fishery, energy, population, economy, tourism and transport and areas sub-categories on coastal, seas and urban issues **Coverage:** contains data on environmental factors, such as pollution, waste and environmental management in agricultural and fishery industry

European Free Trade Association (EFTA)

Address: 9-11 rue de Varembé, Geneva 20, 1211, Switzerland
Telephone: +41 22 332 2626
Fax: +41 22 332 2677
E-mail: mail.gva@efta.int
Website: www.efta.int

Activity: EFTA was founded on the premise of free trade as a means of achieving growth and prosperity amongst its Member States as well as promoting closer economic co-operation between the Western European countries. EFTA members are Iceland, Liechtenstein, Norway and Switzerland

Website(s) information:
European Free Trade Association — **url:** www.efta.int **Coverage:** trade statistics by country, merchandise and commodities

Publication(s):
Annual Report — **Language:** English **Frequency:** annual **Content:** statistics published annually on EFTAs trade activities among itself, and among third countries; data includes products of trade and customs matters

European Investment Bank (EIB)

Address: Information and Communications Department, 100 boulevard Konrad Adenauer, L-2950, Luxembourg
Telephone: +352 43 791
Fax: +352 43 77041
E-mail: info@eib.org
Website: www.eib.org

Activity: European Union's financing institution, its purpose is to contribute towards the integration, balanced development and economic and social cohesion of the Member Countries

Website(s) information:
European Investment Bank — **url:** www.eib.org **Description:** provides information on latest developments on European financial and banking activities. Research reports including statistical data and analysis on: EIB financial resources; loans and borrowing operations; and evolution of the single monetary system

Publication(s):
EIB Information — **Language:** English/French/German/Italian **Frequency:** quarterly **Content:** Journal of the EIB with articles on recent operations and articles

General Fisheries Commission for the Mediterranean

Address: Viale delle Terme di Caracalla, Rome, 00100, Italy
Telephone: +39 6 5705 6441
Fax: +39 6 5705 6500
E-mail: alain.bonzon@fao.org
Website: www.faogfcm.org

Guides: online catalogue
Activity: to promote the development, conservation and management of living marine resources; formulate and recommend conservation measures

Website(s) information:
General Fisheries Commission for the Mediterranean — **url:** www.faogfcm.org **Description:** downloadable PDF format publications covering the Commission's policies governing the marine environment. Analysis of fish stocks **Coverage:** fish stocks, environmental impact data, socio-economic indicators, case studies

General Secretariat of the Benelux Economic Union

Address: Rue de la Regence 39, Brussels, 1000, Belgium
Telephone: +32 2 519 3811
Fax: +32 2 513 4206
E-mail: info@benelux.be

Activity: internal markets, cross-border cooperation; being responsible for justice, police and immigration; developing political cooperation; cooperating in the fields of culture, research, education and training

Publication(s):
Almanac Benelux — **Language:** French / Dutch **Frequency:** annual **Content:** gives an outline of the authorities and the persons who exercise activities in the frontier region or who work with people on the other side of the border
Rapports annuels (Annual Report) — **Language:** French / Dutch **Frequency:** annual **Content:** security policy, transborder workers, regional development, economic cooperation, international relations

Helsinki Commission - Baltic Marine Environment Protection Commission

Address: Katajanokanlaituri 6 B, , Helsinki, 00160, , Finland
Telephone: +358 207 412 649
Fax: +358 207 412 639
Website: www.helcom.fi

Activity: works to protect the marine environment of the Baltic Sea from all sources of pollution through intergovernmental co-operation between Denmark, Estonia, the European Community, Finland, Germany, Latvia, Lithuania, Poland, Russia and Sweden

Website(s) information:
HELCOM — **url:** www.helcom.fi **Description:** website's shipping pages are designed to provide information on: ships' traffic and navigational safety; ship-generated waste, accidental pollution and response; air pollution; releases of alien species in ballast water; annually updated factsheets available on the marine environment in the region

HM Revenue & Customs

Address: Thomas Paine House, Angel Square, Torrens Street, London, EC1V 1TA, United Kingdom
Telephone: +44 20 8929 0152
E-mail: enquiries.lon@hmce.gsi.gov.uk
Website: www.hmce.gov.uk

Activity: HM Revenue & Customs (HMRC) was formed following the merger of Inland Revenue and HM Customs and Excise Departments - it collects and administers direct and indirect taxes and pays and administers child and working benefits

Website(s) information:
HM Customs & Excise — **url:** www.hmce.gov.uk **Coverage:** quarterly regional and national UK trade statistics including exports and imports; and summary of trade with EU and non-EU countries

International Council for the Exploration of the Sea (ICES), The

Address: H C Andersens Blvd 44-46, Copenhagen V, 1553, Denmark
Telephone: +45 33 386 700
Fax: +45 33 934 215
E-mail: info@ices.dk
Website: www.ices.dk

Website(s) information:
The International Council for the Exploration of the Sea (ICES) — **url:** www.ices.dk **Description:** provides bulletins and magazines on the fishing industry, fisheries statistics, co-operative research reports on chemicals used in the fishing industry, study of the ecosystem, measuring of fish stocks and statistics on the annual catch for fisheries. Also provides a listing of ICES member countries **Coverage:** contains data on yearly nominal catches of fish and shellfish officially submitted by 19 ICES member countries in the Northeast Atlantic including over 200 species

Publication(s):
ICES Fisheries Statistics — **Language:** English **Frequency:** annual **Content:** contains data on nominal catch

Nordic Council of Ministers and Nordic Council

Address:　Store Strandstræde 18, Copenhagen K, DK-1255, Denmark
Telephone:　+45 33 960400
Fax:　+45 33 111870
E-mail:　nordisk-rad@norden.org
Website:　www.norden.org

Guides:　online catalogue. Publications are organised by policy area
Activity:　forum for Nordic parliamentary co-operation. The Council has 87 elected members, representing the five countries and three autonomous territories

Website(s) information:
Nordic Council of Ministers and Nordic Council — **url:** www.norden.org
　　Description: downloadable PDF files in Swedish and English
　　Coverage: economic indicators, socio-economic indicators

Publication(s):
Indicators for the Information Society in the Baltic Region — **Language:** English
　　Content: eIndicators: statistics about the information societies in the Baltic Region

Nordic Countries in Figures — **Language:** English **Content:** key figures on environment, population, health and causes of death, consumption, education, labour market, culture, national accounts, prices, foreign trade, research and development **Edition:** 2005

Nordic Statistical Yearbook — **Language:** English/Swedish **Content:** statistics of various aspects of social life in the five Nordic countries, Denmark, Finland, Iceland, Norway and Sweden. In addition data are also presented on the self-governing regions, the Faroe Islands, Greenland and the Åland Islands **Edition:** 43rd Edition

Nordic Social-Statistical Committee (NOSOSCO)

Address:　Islands Brygge 67, Copenhagen S, 2300, Denmark
Telephone:　+45 72 227 625
Fax:　+45 32 955470
E-mail:　mail@nom-nos.dk
Website:　www.nom-nos.dk/nososco.htm

Guides:　statistical data is available to download free of charge on website. Printed publications is available to order
Activity:　coordinates Nordic socio-economic statistics, collaborating with adjacent areas (e.g. the Baltic countries), and following other international collaboration, mainly the social statistical collaboration in EU/EUROSTAT

Website(s) information:
Nordic Social-Statistical Committee (NOSOSCO) — **url:** www.nom-nos.dk/nososco.htm **Description:** provides a compilation of social statistics for Denmark, Finland, Iceland, Norway, and Sweden **Coverage:** contains data on demographic trends, unemployment, illness, housing, social benefits, social security expenditure and financing in the Nordic countries

Publication(s):
Social Protection in the Nordic Countries — **Language:** English/Danish **Frequency:** irregular **Content:** contains data on population, family, children, employment and health

Press and Communication Service of the European Commission

Address:　BERLAYMONT 4/363, 200 rue de la Loi, Brussels, 1049, Belgium
Telephone:　+32 2296 6491
Fax:　+32 2296 2695
E-mail:　press-web@cec.eu.int
Website:　www.europa.eu.int

Guides:　list of all the publications available on the website, all free to download
Activity:　press and communication service for the European Commission

Website(s) information:
Europa — **url:** www.europa.eu.int **Description:** available in all EU official languages, it is the official portal website of the European Union. It combines all information provided by most institutions and bodies of the EU including the European Parliament, the Council of the Union, the Commission, the Court of Justice, the Court of Auditors, the Economic and Social Committee, the Committee of the Regions, the European Central Bank and the European Investment Bank

Statistical Office of the European Commission (EUROSTAT)

Address:　Batiment Joseph Monnet, Rue Alphonse Weicker, Luxembourg, L-2721, Luxembourg
Telephone:　+352 430 134 567
Fax:　+352 430 132 594
E-mail:　estat-infodesk@cec.eu.int
Website:　www.europa.eu.int/comm/eurostat

Guides:　more than 300 million data, from many different domains, are available online, varying from consumer prices, through poverty and environmental indicators, to detailed external trade data by product
Activity:　statistical office of the European Communities; its task is to provide the European Union with statistics at European level that enable comparisons between countries and regions; to supply statistics to other Directorates and supply the Commission and other European Institutions with data so they can define, implement and analyse Community policies. Themes are: General and regional statistics; Economy and finance; Population and social conditions; Industry, trade and services; Agriculture and fisheries; External trade; Transport; Environment and energy; Science and technology

Website(s) information:
Statistical Office of the European Commission (EUROSTAT) — **url:** europa.eu.int/comm/eurostat **Coverage:** each section/sector covered by EUROSTAT includes data for a wide range of socio-economic indicators: general Statistics: exports and imports of goods; harmonised indices of consumer prices; GDP growth rate; total industrial production; unemployment rate; economy and Finance; population and social conditions; industry, trade and services; agriculture, forestry and fisheries; foreign trade; transport; energy and the environment

Publication(s):
Agricultural Statistics — **Language:** English **Frequency:** annual **Content:** chapters include general statistics, crop and animal production, farm structure, and agricultural prices and accounts; presents selected tables and graphs providing an overview on developments and the situation in the agricultural sector of the European Union. The most recent data are presented here (reference years 2006 and 2007, mostly) showing the situation in the 27 Member States and at the European level (EU-27).

Cultural Statistics — **Language:** English **Content:** main cultural statistics comparable at European level. Selected tables and graphs describe different areas of the cultural field for the 27 EU Member States, the candidate countries and the EFTA countries: cultural heritage, cultural employment, enterprises in certain cultural sectors - publishing, architectural activities and cinema, external trade in cultural goods, households cultural expenditure, cultural participation and time spent on cultural activities

EC Economic Data Pocketbook — **Language:** English **Frequency:** quarterly **Content:** collection of economic data from different domains, covering the European Aggregates, EU Member States and its main economic partners. The publication focuses on the structural aspects of the EU economy; consequently, most of the data given are annual, complemented by selected monthly and quarterly indicators

Energy - Yearly Statistics — **Language:** English/German/French **Frequency:** annual **Content:** overall view of the trends for the principal aggregates, taken from the "energy supplied" balance-sheets of the European Union in tonnes of oil equivalent. Also historical series for each energy source for the principal aggregates characterising the structure of energy economics

Energy, Transport and Environment Indicators Pocketbook — **Language:** English/French/German **Content:** comprises a broad set of data collected by Eurostat and the European Environment Agency. Provides an overview of the most relevant indicators on energy, transport and environment

European Business - Facts and Figures — **Language:** English **Frequency:** annual **Content:** structure, development and characteristics of European business and its different activities: from energy and the extractive industries to communications, information services and media. It presents the latest available statistics from a wide selection of statistical sources describing for each activity: production and employment; country specialisation and regional distribution; productivity and profitability; the importance of small and medium sized enterprises (SMEs); work-force characteristics; extern

European Union Foreign Direct Investment Yearbook — **Language:** English **Frequency:** annual **Content:** provides detailed data on EU - Foreign Direct Investment (FDI) for recent years (1999-2006), for both EU FDI abroad and FDI into the EU. It provides an overview of the position of the EU in World FDI and a comparison with the US

Eurostat Yearbook 2008 - A Portal to European Statistics — **Language:** English, German, French **Frequency:** annual **Content:** annual data on a wide range of social, economic, financial and political EU topics, covering: population and demography; education; labour market structure, earnings and working hours; social protection; consumption and spending patterns; housing, culture and leisure; crime; land and environment. Also includes trade and industry statistics covering: agriculture, forestry and fishing; industry and manufacturing activities; energy resources; service industries; transport; and tourism **Edition:** 12th Edition

Eurostatistics - Data for Short-Term Economic Analysis — **Content:** short-term economic analysis designed to monitor the evolution of the economic activity in the European Union, Euro-zone and Member States

Everything on Transport Statistics — **Language:** English/French/German **Frequency:** Annual **Content:** contains all public documents and data related to transport statistics in Europe and main partner countries. It contains about 27 million items of statistical data and more than 900 documents, mostly produced by Eurostat's transport unit. Historic data from 1972 available.

External and intra-European Union Trade - Statistical Yearbook — **Language:** English **Content:** provides data on long-term trends in the trade of the European Union and its Member States, annual statistics on the trade flows of the EU with its main trading partners, and between the Member States. Data from 1958.

External and intra-European Union trade - Statistical Yearbook — **Language:** English **Frequency:** annual **Content:** contains annual time series on trade of the European Union, the Euro-zone and the 25 Member States. In particular, it provides statistics on trade flows between the EU and its main trading partners with a breakdown by major product groups. Data from 1958.

Fishery Statistics - Data 1990-2006 — **Language:** English **Frequency:** annual **Content:** summary tables for EEA and EU-candidate countries on catches by fishing region, aquaculture production, total production, landings in EEA ports, trade in fishery products, supply balance sheets, EEA fishing fleets and the number of fishermen

Food: From Farm to Fork Statistics — **Language:** English/French/German **Frequency:** monthly **Content:** statistical information on how the food chain evolves in Europe; it gives different indicators for each step of the production-consumption chain, including food and feed

Gas and Electricity Market Statistics — **Language:** English **Frequency:** annual **Content:** provides basic quantitative information on gas and electricity prices, as well as on structures for gas and electricity existing in each country. It also includes statistical information on selected indicators. Data from 1990.

Health in Europe — **Language:** English **Frequency:** annual **Content:** provides a selection of figures on health and health determinants over a five-year period.

Science and Technology in Europe — **Language:** English/French/German **Content:** statistical data and indicators based on a number of data sources available at Eurostat (mainly related to science, technology, innovation and regions

Statistics in Focus — **Language:** English/French/German **Frequency:** irregular **Content:** provides summaries of the main results of statistical surveys, studies and analysis

The EU-15's New Economy: A Statistical Portrait — **Language:** English **Content:** statistical portrait of the EU-15 which makes it possible to benchmark the countries involved in terms of how they are managing to achieve the goals set in the Lisbon strategy

Tourism - Statistical Pocketbook — **Language:** English/French/German **Frequency:** annual **Content:** The data covers a five-year period. The figures presented in this publication cover on the one hand the supply of collective tourist accommodation in Europe, giving information on the available capacity in hotels and other types of collective accommodation and the tourist flows they receive.

Statistical, Economic and Social Research and Training Centre for Islamic Countries - SESRTCIC

Address: Attar Sokak 4, Gaziosmanpasa, Ankara, 06700, Turkey
Telephone: +90 312 468 6172
Fax: +90 312 467 3458
E-mail: oicankara@sesrtcic.org
Website: www.sesrtcic.org

Activity: collating socio-economic statistics

Website(s) information:

SESRTCIC Statistical Database — **url:** www.sesrtcic.org **Description:** various statistics and information covering 56 different Islamic countries in Africa and the Middle East, plus Albania and Turkey **Coverage:** data provided for each nation includes: demographic trends; labour force; health and education; economic sectors; communications and tourism; external trade; money and finances; and national accounts

Publication(s):

Statistical Yearbook of the OIC Countries — **Language:** Arabic/English/French **Content:** Presents data collected from various national and international statistical sources. This source provides, indicator wise and countrywise, information on 172 socio-economic indicators in the 57 OIC member countries for the last ten years **Edition:** 2005

UN Economic Commission for Europe (UNECE)

Address: Palais des Nations, Geneva 10, 1211, Switzerland
Telephone: +41 22 917 1234
Fax: +41 22 917 0505
E-mail: info.ece@unece.org
Website: www.unece.org

Guides: provides a list of publications on the website; topics include environment, human settlements, population, information and communications technologies, sustainable energy, and trade development

Activity: The UNECE strives to foster sustainable economic growth among its 56 member states; to that end UNECE provides a forum for communication among States; brokers international legal instruments addressing trade, transport and the environment; and supplies statistics and economic and environmental analysis

Website(s) information:

UN Economic Commission for Europe — **url:** www.unece.org **Description:** information on economic co-operation and development in Europe, environment and human settlement, sustainable energy, trade, industry and enterprise development, timber and transport; access to a series of press releases, articles and online documents, many of these supported by socio-economic statistical data on the region **Coverage:** includes socio-economic statistics for the member countries of Western, Central and Eastern Europe, as well as North America; data is provided on total population; percentage of population in capital city; country's total area; density of population per km2; GDP per capita; life expectancy at birth; and infant mortality rates. Additionally, it also includes statistics on gross industrial output; trade (exports/imports/ranking of major trade partners); unemployment and education; and final energy consumption

Publication(s):

Annual Bulletin of Housing and Building Statistics for Europe and North America — **Language:** English **Frequency:** annual **Content:** data refers to dwelling stock and structure of dwelling construction, dwellings completed by type of investor and by type of material used, energy consumption by household, consumer price and rent indices, etc.

Annual Bulletin of Transport Statistics for Europe and North America — **Language:** English **Frequency:** annual **Content:** covers: rail, road and inland waterway sectors, container transport, goods loaded and unloaded at sea ports, transport by oil pipeline and various international goods transport, sorted by transport and commodity group

Statistical Journal of the United Nations Economic Commission for Europe — **Language:** English **Frequency:** quarterly **Content:** information on new work going on within official statistics, international organisations, government departments, universities and research institutions **Readership:** statisticians, applied economists, social scientists and policy analysts

Trends in Europe and North America - The Statistical Yearbook of the Economic Commission for Europe — **Language:** English **Frequency:** annual **Content:** contains socio-economic data covering the members states

National Official Sources

Albania

Banka e Shqipërisë
Bank of Albania

Address: Scanderbeg Square, Nr 1, Tirana,
Telephone: +355 4 222 152
Fax: +355 4 223 558
E-mail: public@bankofalbania.org
Website: www.bankofalbania.org

Website(s) information:
Bank of Albania — **url:** www.bankofalbania.org

Publication(s):
Balance of Payments Bulletin — **Language:** English/Albanian **Frequency:** quarterly **Content:** provides detailed statistical information on Balance of Payments of the Republic of Albania

Economic Bulletin — **Language:** Albanian/English **Frequency:** quarterly **Content:** covers official statements of the Bank of Albania, financial, economic and legal articles, results of statistical surveys which are carried out by the Bank of Albania, list of commercial banks exercising economic activity in Albania, and a list of foreign exchange bureaux operating within the Republic of Albania

Official Bulletin — **Language:** Albanian/English **Frequency:** monthly **Content:** decisions approved by Bank of Albania Supervisory Council, which are not subject to any restrictions, all regulations approved by the Bank of Albania Supervisory Council which are obligatory for all commercial banks as well as for other operators, as required by the law

Trade Balance Bulletin — **Language:** English/Albanian **Frequency:** quarterly **Content:** provides a detailed information on foreign trade and main trading partners

Instituti i Statistikës (INSTAT)
Albanian Institute of Statistics (INSTAT)

Address: Rr Leke Dukagjini Nr 5, Tirana
Telephone: +355 4 222 411 ext 159
Fax: +355 4 228 300
E-mail: botim_difuzion@instat.gov.al
Website: www.instat.gov.al

Guides: publications cover economic development related production, foreign trade investments, prices, income, employment
Activity: compiles socio-economic statistics on Albania

Website(s) information:
Instituti Statistikes (INSTAT) (Albanian Institute of Statistics) — **url:** www.instat.gov.al **Coverage:** social and economic indicators (agriculture, energy, sales, construction, population, tourism, etc)

Publication(s):
Albania in figures — **Language:** Albanian/English **Frequency:** annual **Content:** statistical data on economic and social development of Albania

Conjuctura — **Language:** Albanian/English **Frequency:** quarterly **Content:** main economic indicators; provides statistical information on developing trends of the economy

Construction Cost Index — **Language:** Albanian/English **Frequency:** quarterly **Content:** statistical information on construction cost changes

Consumer Price Index — **Language:** Albanian/English **Frequency:** monthly **Content:** provides statistical information on consumer price changes

Retail Trade Indices — **Language:** Albanian **Frequency:** quarterly **Content:** information on development of volume indices in retail trade

Situation of Foreign Trade — **Language:** Albanian/English **Frequency:** monthly **Content:** provides statistical information on export, import and trade balance

Social Indicator Yearbooks — **Language:** Albanian/English **Frequency:** annual **Content:** provides statistical information on demography, labour, education, health, household indicators, investment, crimes etc

Statistika — **Language:** Albanian/English **Frequency:** quarterly **Content:** information on social and economic indicators, also included is data on demography, education, health, the labour market, production, foreign trade, transport, construction, tourism and businesses

Austria

Österreichische Nationalbank (OeNB)
National Bank of Austria

Address: Postfach 61, 1011 Vienna, Otto-Wagner Platz 3, Vienna, 1090
Telephone: +43 404 20
Fax: +43 404 20 2398
E-mail: oenb.info@oenb.co.at
Website: www.oenb.at

Guides: publications on the national bank, the economy and financial market, statistics, and European legislation
Activity: central bank of Austria. Cooperates in the forming of the economic development in Austria and other Euro countries, with a focus on a stability orientated monetary policy

Website(s) information:
Österreichische Nationalbank (National Bank of Austria) — **url:** www.oenb.at **Coverage:** online access to series of different financial publications covering the overall business environment and economic & banking system in Austria and other European countries

Publication(s):
Finanzmarktstabilitätsbericht (Financial Market Stability Report) — **Language:** German **Frequency:** 2 per annum **Content:** market report on financial stability and the factors that have and impact on the same

Geldpolitik & Wirtschaft (Money Policy & Economy) — **Language:** German/English **Frequency:** quarterly **Content:** quarterly analysis of the economic cycle, medium term macro economic forecasts, sums up results of economic policy workshops and conferences

Statistiken - Daten & Analysen (Statistics - Data & Analyses) — **Language:** German **Frequency:** quarterly **Content:** reports on the Austrian financial institutions, cash flow, and foreign trade

STATISTIK AUSTRIA - Bundesanstalt Statistik Österreich
Federal Austrian Statistical Agency

Address: Guglgasse 13, Vienna, 1110
Telephone: +43 71128 7070
Fax: +43 715 68 28
E-mail: info@statistik.gv.at
Website: www.statistik.at

Guides: offers a search machine for publications; statistics can either be downloaded from the website or ordered online; publications are categorised into population, business, spatial economics, economics, and general information
Activity: surveys and edits statistical data on politics, the economy, and society in Austria and other EU countries

Website(s) information:
Statistische Übersichten (Statistical Overlook) — **url:** www.statistik.at **Coverage:** statistical overviews in charts. The information is on indicators of the development of the Austrian economy. This includes prices, income, transport, tourism, energy, environment, and agriculture in Austria. Additional information on the economies of EU and OECD (developed) countries

Publication(s):
Der Tourismus in Österreich (Tourism in Austria) — **Language:** German **Frequency:** annual **Content:** tourism statistics containing information on arrivals and departures, and accommodation statistics. Includes regional breakdowns

Einkommen, Armut und Lebensbedingungen Ergebnisse aus EU-SILC (Income, Poverty, and Living Conditions) — **Language:** German **Frequency:** annual **Content:** statistics on Austrian wages, salaries, incomes, and general information on the living conditions

Jahrbuch der Gesundheitsstatistik (Yearbook of Health Statistics) — **Language:** German **Frequency:** annual **Content:** information and statistics on the Austrian health service system; includes the most common diseases and cause of deaths

Österreichischer Zahlenspiegel (Austrian Data Index) — **Language:** German **Frequency:** monthly **Content:** a collection of current issues in form of statistics and an overview chart of the most important economic indicators

Schnellbericht Der Außenhandel Österreichs (Report of Foreign Trade in Austria) — **Language:** German **Frequency:** monthly **Content:** overview of developments in foreign trade

Statistik der Kraftfahrzeuge (Austrian Automotive Industry Statistics) — **Language:** German **Frequency:** annual **Content:** statistics on motor vehicles in Austria: registrations by makes and types of vehicle; statistics on stock and new registrations are separated; publication includes a CD-Rom

Statistik der Landwirtschaft (Agriculture Statistics) — **Language:** German **Frequency:** annual **Content:** statistics on agriculture and forestry, including field crops, wine, cattle, milk and meat production. Includes regional data

Statistische Nachrichten (Statistical News) — **Language:** German **Frequency:** monthly **Content:** monthly figures covering main time series: population, employment, production, retail sales, wages and prices, etc

Statistisches Jahrbuch für die Republik Österreich (Austrian Statistical Yearbook) — **Language:** German/English **Frequency:** annual **Content:** general statistical yearbook - includes a wide range of annual socio-economic, demographic, cultural, and other statistics on the Austrian republic

Wiener Boerse

Vienna Stock Exchange

Address: PO Box 192, Wallnerstraße 8, Vienna, 1014
Telephone: +43 431 531 650
Fax: +43 431 532 97 40
E-mail: webmaster@wienerborse.at
Website: www.wienerborse.at

Guides: publishes brochures on various aspects of the financial market
Activity: the stock exchange comprises an equity market, a bond market, a derivatives market, and a segment for structured products; offers online real-time market prices

Website(s) information:
Wiener Boerse (Vienna Stock Exchange) — **url:** www.wienerborse.at **Coverage:** daily, monthly and yearly statistics on cash markets, capital market, derivatives, mutual funds and exchange rates

Publication(s):
Vienna Stock Exchange and its Issuers — **Language:** English **Frequency:** annual **Content:** the focus of this brochure is on the group of major players in the capital market: the companies whose stocks are traded on Wiener Börse. Facts and figures on the issuers for an overview of the companies listed on the exchange

Belarus

Council of Ministers of Republic of Belarus

Address: 11 Sovetskaya Street, Minsk, 220010
Telephone: +375 17 222 4173
Fax: +375 17 222 6665
E-mail: contact@government.by
Website: www.government.by

Activity: official government website concerning ministries and the government committee

Website(s) information:
Council of Ministers of Republic of Belarus — **url:** www.government.by **Description:** list and contacts of ministries and official governmental bodies

Ministry of Economy of the Belarus Republic

Address: 14 Bersona Street, Minsk, 220086
Telephone: +375 17 222 6048
Fax: +375 17 200 3777
E-mail: gen@plan.minsk.by
Website: www.economy.gov.by

Activity: carry out state policy and accomplish regulation and control of state assets and privatisation, support of enterprise, development of competition

Website(s) information:
Ministry of Economy of the Belarus Republic — **url:** www.economy.gov.by **Description:** provides information about the Ministry, its structure; reviews of the economic and social situation, long term-development strategies and programmes; provides new legal releases requirements and other related information **Coverage:** data on economic development

Ministry of Foreign Affairs of The Republic of Belarus

Address: 29 Myasnikova Street, Minsk, 220050
Telephone: +375 17 220 2635
Fax: +375 17 220 1964
E-mail: mail@mfabelar.gov.by
Website: www.mfa.gov.by

Activity: body of state administration of the Republic of Belarus implementing national policy in the field of foreign relations

Website(s) information:
Ministry of Foreign Affairs of the Republic of Belarus — **url:** www.mfa.gov.by **Description:** information on the ministry and its activities; provides general information about the country; gives access to statistical data and publications **Coverage:** economy and trade; investment climate and foreign trade and foreign policy; statistics on major economic indicators

Publication(s):
Advantages of Trade-Economic Cooperation with the Republic of Belarus — **Language:** English/Russian

Foreigh Trade — **Language:** Russian/English **Content:** tariff and Non-tariff Regulations; Customs Regulations; Foreign Trade Structures

Results of Economic Development of Belarus — **Language:** Russian/English **Frequency:** irregular **Content:** main macro-economic indicators of Belarus Republic

Ministry of Statistics and Analysis of the Republic of Belarus

Address: 12 Partizansky Avenue, Minsk, 220070
Telephone: +375 17 249 4278
Fax: +375 17 249 2204
E-mail: minstat@mail.belpak.by
Website: www.belstat.gov.by

Guides: releases more than 100 publications, of which biggest are annual, bi-annual, quarterly, which are available in Russian and English
Activity: national statistics office

Website(s) information:
Ministry of Statistics and Analysis — **url:** http://belstat.gov.by **Description:** provides information on the ministry and its activities; most of the data is accessible online in English language; site also contains links to other national statistics offices in CIS countries **Coverage:** data covers: population, unemployment, living standards, national accounts, finance, prices and tariffs, domestic and foreign trade, industry, agriculture, construction and transport; information broken down into territories as well as national statistics

Publication(s):
Basic Socio-Demographic Characteristics of Households of the Republic of Belarus — **Language:** English/Russian **Content:** covers indicators characterising the distribution of families by their size and composition, housing conditions, type of dwelling and number of rooms, and availability of land plots **Edition:** 2006

Belarus in Numbers - Statistical Reference Book — **Language:** Russian/English **Frequency:** annual **Content:** brief characteristics of the social and economic position with comparative figures for previous years. Also demographic measures, information about the standard of living of the population and the social sphere; development of key industries of the economy, investment and external economic activity, price behaviour

Industry of the Republic of Belarus — **Language:** English/Russian **Frequency:** annual **Content:** industrial production in the republic; technical and economic characteristics of industrial enterprises; indices on labour **Edition:** 2006

Investments and Building in the Belarus Republic — **Language:** Russian/Ukraine **Frequency:** annual **Content:** dynamics and structure of investments into fixed asset formation; information about foreign investments is given in branches of the economy; production capacities, apartment houses and objects of social sphere

National Accounts of the Republic of Belarus — **Language:** Russian/English **Frequency:** annual **Content:** contains information on production of goods and services, generation and distribution of income, consumption of goods and services, capital accumulation

Retail Trade of the Republic of Belarus — **Language:** English/Russian **Frequency:** annual **Content:** contains data on the development of the retail trade and catering industry; retail commodity turnover in the distribution over the forms of property and channels; commodity structure, volumes of sale of food and non-food items; commodity reserves in the retail outlet network **Edition:** 2006

Statistical Bulletin — **Language:** Russian/English **Frequency:** quarterly **Content:** comprises data on population, employment, wages and salaries, finance, industry, agriculture, capital investments, transport and communications, foreign trade, retail turnover, prices and tariffs, offences

National Academy of Science of Belarus Republic
Address: 66 Nezavisimost Avenue, Minsk, 220072
Telephone: +375 17 284 1801
Fax: +375 17 284 2816
E-mail: academy@mserv.bas-net.by
Website: www.ac.by

Activity: union of scientific institute and communities

National Bank of the Republic of Belarus
Address: 20 Nezavisimost Avenue, Minsk, 220008
Telephone: +375 17 219 2303/74
Fax: +375 17 219 2242
E-mail: email@nbrb.by
Website: www.nbrb.by

Guides: the publications of the Bank of Belarus provide information related to the activities of the Bank of Belarus, monetary and banking policies, balance of payments and financial statistics
Activity: is the central bank of the Republic of Belarus; its principal objective is to maintain price stability

Website(s) information:
National Bank of the Republic of Belarus — **url:** www.nbrb.by **Description:** provides full information about its activities, information on the basic tasks of monetary policy and its implementation, monetary policy operations, credit institutions supervision activities and other responsibilities established by the legislation as well as information on the national macroeconomic situation, such as analysis of the developments in the national economy and financial markets, and on the financial position of the Bank **Coverage:** basic indicators of the Belarussian financial market

Publication(s):
Annual Report of the National Bank of Republic Belarus — **Language:** Russian/English **Frequency:** annual **Content:** macro-economic indicators for the year

Bulletin of Banking Statistics — **Language:** English/Russian **Frequency:** quarterly **Content:** major macroeconomic and monetary indicators; financial markets **Edition:** 2006

Payment Systems in the Republic of Belarus — **Language:** Russian/English **Content:** data on governmental finances **Edition:** 2001

United Nations Information Centre
Address: 6/F 17 Kirov Street, Minsk, 220050
Telephone: +375 17 227 4876/8149
Fax: +375 17 226 0340
E-mail: dpi_unit@undp.org
Website: www.un.by

Website(s) information:
United Nations Information Centre - Belarus — **url:** http://un.by **Coverage:** general information about Belarus, including population and economic indicators

Publication(s):
Status of Achieving Millennium Development Goals — **Language:** English/Russian **Content:** report determines goals and targets in the spheres of poverty eradication, gender equality promotion, improvement of child and maternal health

Belgium

Agentschap voor buitenlandse handel / agence pour le commerce exterieur
Belgian Foreign Trade Agency
Address: 3 Rue Montoyer, Brussels, 1000
Telephone: +32 2206 3511
Fax: +32 2 203 1812
E-mail: info@abh-ace.org
Website: www.abh-ace.org

Guides: covers foreign trade and world economy; material in French, Dutch, English, German, Spanish; books, journals, company and trade directories, Belgian and international statistics
Activity: economic missions; export, statistics, foreign trade, Belgian markets, projects

Website(s) information:
ABH-ACE-FTA — **url:** www.abh-ace.org **Coverage:** Belgian and Luxembourg exporters directory available online; exports and imports statistics, monthly figures; status in world trade markets

Publication(s):
CD-ROM BLUE — **Language:** French / Dutch / English **Content:** extracts from the database updated by the Belgian Agency for Foreign Trade in cooperation with the Belgian Regional Authorities for Foreign trade; contains information on over 14,400 Belgian and Luxembourg companies **Edition:** 11th edition

Banque Nationale de Belgique
National Bank of Belgium
Address: 3 boulevard de Berlaimont, Brussels, 1000
Telephone: +32 2221 2111
Fax: +32 2221 3100
E-mail: info@nbb.be
Website: http://www.nbb.be/pub/index.htm

Guides: a Statistical Bulletin is published on an annual basis in French, Dutch, German and English explaining the methodology of the statistical reports published by the National Bank of Belgium
Activity: Belgium's central bank

Website(s) information:
Banque Nationale de Belgique (National Bank of Belgium) — **url:** www.bnb.be/sg/index.htm **Description:** information provided on NBB's interest rates, exchange rates, allocation of credits and annual accounts. Access to a wide range of publications including key statistics on major economic indicators and latest developments in the national and EU banking and financial sectors **Coverage:** belgostat.be provides a wide range of statistical information available, free to download

Publication(s):
Balance of Payments — **Frequency:** monthly/quarterly and annually **Content:** the National Bank is responsible for balance of payments statistics and international investment position statistics. In this context, it also draws up statistics relating to international trade in services and statistics for direct foreign investment

Belgian Prime News — **Frequency:** quarterly **Content:** each number contains a "Consensus forecast" concerning the anticipated movement of the main macroeconomic figures for Belgium, as well as a description of the most striking recent economic developments

Business Survey — **Frequency:** monthly and bi-annual **Content:** presents the results of company surveys. Gathering opinions of business people on the state of the economy and on developments which can be forecast over the short-term, these surveys provide a general and concise overview. Twice yearly surveys on investment in the manufacturing industry

Consumer Survey — **Frequency:** monthly **Content:** presents the results of household surveys. Gathers the opinions of consumers on the state of the economy and on developments which can be forecast over the short-term, these surveys provide an additional general overview

Economic Indicators — **Language:** French/Dutch/English **Frequency:** weekly **Content:** the National Bank releases an updated collection (the most recent past estimates and the latest available forecasts for the future) of the main Belgian economic and financial variables (gross domestic product and economic activity, prices, employment, public finance, foreign trade, interest rates and exchange rates

Economic Review — **Frequency:** 3 per annum **Content:** publishes articles on macroeconomic developments and the financial markets, transactions with foreign countries and the situation of enterprises. More specific analyses are also published in the Review

Financial Stability Review — **Content:** general overview of recent economic, financial and structural trends which are likely to have an effect on the stability of the financial system. This overview is complemented by thematic articles. The overview and the articles focus on three areas: monitoring of financial stability and prevention and resolution of systemic risks

Foreign Trade — **Language:** French/Dutch **Frequency:** monthly and quarterly **Content:** monthly bulletin published 10 weeks after the month under review which provides some overall macro-economic totals (foreign trade, price and volume growth, totals per partner country and per large product category). Together with this monthly bulletin a press release with the major figures is published online. Four months after the quarter under review a quarterly bulletin is published with additional information on a more detailed level (such as regional figures)

Money and Banking Statistics — **Frequency:** annual **Content:** the statistics on financial institutions and financial markets provides sector-related information and details on market developments. The statistics on the MFIs are complemented with information about interest rates, exchange rates, stock exchanges and payment systems and tools

National Accounts — **Frequency:** annual; and quarterly **Content:** national accounts are published in a number of series. A first estimate of the annual aggregates, based on the quarterly accounts, is published in April (end of March in electronic form). The detailed accounts and tables, with data per branch of industry and institutional sector (the government accounts can be consulted in June in electronic form), are available at the end of October (in electronic form at the end of September), followed by the supply and consumption tables. The annual accounts cycle is closed with the satellite account of non-profit institutions.
The quarterly accounts are published 70 days after the end of the quarter the estimates relate to. A flash estimate of the GDP, based on revised accounts of the previous quarters, is distributed 30 days after the end of each quarter via a press release

Rapport annuel de la Banque nationale *(Annual Report of the National Bank)* — **Language:** French/Dutch **Frequency:** annual **Content:** national bank's major publication. This document provides useful information on the recent economic and financial developments, both in Belgium and abroad. The synthesis presented by the Governor on behalf of the Council of Regency highlights the previous year's main events and delivers important messages with regard to the economic policy

Statistical Bulletin — **Frequency:** quarterly **Content:** statistics produced by the National Bank more frequently than every three months are compiled into a monthly update. The National Bank provides a wider range, with longer series, than in the Statistical bulletin free of charge on its website via 'Belgostat Online'

Statistics — **Language:** French / Dutch **Frequency:** annual **Content:** comprises overall figures, financial ratios and tables of resources

Bureau Fédéral du Plan
Federal Planning Bureau

Address: 47-49 avenue des Arts, Brussels, 1000
Telephone: +32 2 507 7311
Fax: +32 2 507 7373
Website: www.plan.be

Activity: makes studies and projections on economic, socio-economic and environmental policy issues
the FPB collects and analyses data, explores plausible evolutions, identifies alternatives, evaluates the impact of policy measures and formulates proposals

Website(s) information:
Federal Planning Bureau — **url:** www.plan.be **Description:** various bulletins, newsletters, and statistics relating to the Belgian and international economy **Coverage:** "databases" section covers input-output tables; economic forecasts, time series data on employment and National Accounts. "Forecasts" sections provides information on the consumer price index and health index used for calculating rents

Publication(s):
Euren Report — **Language:** French/Dutch **Frequency:** 2 per annum **Content:** the economic outlook in Europe analysed twice a year

Forecasts & Outlook — **Language:** French/Dutch **Frequency:** annual **Content:** macroeconomic analyses; labour market; economics; social welfare sector-based; studies, inter-industrial relations

Planning Paper — **Language:** French/Dutch **Frequency:** irregular **Content:** features different subjects such as administrative charges in Belgium for a full year, public participation in the market sector, budgetary cost of the unemployed, etc

Short Term Update - Newsletter of the Federal Planning Bureau — **Language:** English **Frequency:** quarterly **Content:** contains the main conclusions from the publications of the FPB, as well as information on new publications, together with an analysis of the most recent economic indicators

Working Papers — **Language:** French/Dutch **Frequency:** monthly **Content:** different economic articles every months such as: linking household income to macro data to project poverty indicators; fiscal councils, independent forecasts and the budgetary process; an evaluation of the risks surrounding the 2006-2012 NIME economic outlook : illustrative stochastic simulations

Institut National de Statistique
National Institute of Statistics

Address: 50 rue du progres, Brussels, 1210
Telephone: +32 2277 5504
Fax: +32 2277 5519
E-mail: info@statbel.mineco.fgov.be
Website: www.statbel.fgov.be

Guides: rapport des activités de l'Institut National de Statistique (annual; free); catalogue des Produits et Services de l'Institut National de Statistique (free; includes monthly updates). Statistics include: territory and environment; population; society; economy and finance; agriculture; industry; services, business and transport

Activity: collects data relative to Belgian society

Website(s) information:
EcoDATA — **url:** http: // ecodata.mineco.fgov.be **Description:** socio-economic statistics in Belgium **Coverage:** Belgian macro - economics data, by selection using graphs and tables

Statistics Belgium *(Ministry of Economic Affairs - National Statistical Institute)* — **url:** www.statbel.fgov.be **Description:** general information on the National Statistical Institute and its services; latest press releases; annual socio-economic surveys; list of major publications and studies, etc. Available in four languages **Coverage:** statistical section provides online annual data on Belgium covering different topics: territory and environment (physical and human geography, environment); population (population structure, demographic trends, households); social data (unemployment rate, general standard of living, health and education, justice and politics, etc); economy and finance (general macro-economic and financial indicators); agriculture, horticulture and fisheries; industry; services, commerce and transport

Publication(s):
Accidents de la circulation avec tués et blessés *(Traffic Accidents: Mortality and Injury)* — **Language:** French / Dutch **Frequency:** annual **Content:** traffic accident statistics

Annuaire de statistiques régionales *(Directory of Regional Statistics)* — **Language:** French / Dutch **Frequency:** annual **Content:** coded data reflecting the economic, financial and social life of various regions

Aperçu des statistiques de l'environnement *(Environmental Statistics)* — **Language:** French / Dutch **Frequency:** annual **Content:** environmental statistics in the form of tables, graphs and of cartogram's, and arranged by subject: air, water, waste, radioactivity, incidence of pollution on the environment, landscapes, nature, economic activities, and the right of the environment

Bulletin de statistique (Statistical Bulletin) — **Language:** French / Dutch **Frequency:** monthly **Content:** monthly publication gives an outline of socioeconomic life by presenting a series of indicators selected in most of the sectors covered by statistics. The population, agriculture, industry, foreign trade, prices, salaries, employment and the national product

Calibrage de l'enquête sur les forces de travail (Survey of the Work Force by Grade) — **Language:** French/Dutch **Content:** labour force statistics

Causes de décès (Causes of death) — **Language:** French / Dutch **Frequency:** annual **Content:** medical causes of death; diseases, accidents and murder; according to age, sex and region

Chiffres-clés (Key figures) — **Language:** French / Dutch **Frequency:** annual **Content:** statistical outline of Belgium

Communiqué hebdomadaire (Weekly Info) — **Language:** French / Dutch **Frequency:** weekly **Content:** last available statistics in the following domains: territory and environment; population; company; economy and finances; agriculture; industry; services, business and transport

Compendium commerce intérieur (Compendium of National Trade) — **Language:** French/Dutch **Frequency:** annual **Content:** data on the number of active companies in various sectors of business

Construction et logement (Construction and Housing) — **Language:** French / Dutch **Frequency:** annual **Content:** collects the data on the licences of construction granted, both for residential building and non-residential at the municipal level

Crédit à la consommation (Consumer Credit) — **Language:** French / Dutch **Frequency:** quarterly **Content:** the value and the number of contracts signed for loans or hire purchases, leases or openings of credit. Certain tables about the nature of the goods bought by means of these credits either on the duration or the value of the loans

Démographie des entreprises (Demography of companies) — **Language:** French /Dutch **Frequency:** annual **Content:** statistics of active persons liable for tax; VAT classified by province, activity according to the wordlist NACE-BEL in 2 figures, class of employment

Dépenses environnementales des entreprises en Belgique (Environmental Expenditure in Belgium) — **Language:** French/ Dutch **Content:** reports and assesses environmental investments

Emploi, chômage et grèves (Employment, Unemployment and Strikes) — **Language:** French / Dutch **Frequency:** annual **Content:** administrative data (resulting from the ONSS, from the ONEM) concerning employment, unemployment and strikes. Includes figures of unemployment in the European Union

Enquête structurelle des entreprises (Company Structure Survey) — **Language:** French / Dutch **Frequency:** annual **Content:** branches of industry: mining industries, manufacturing industry, producers and the distributors of electricity, gas and water, construction, business and the main service sectors, such as hotels and restaurants, transport, storing and communications; real-estate, rent and services companies

Enquête sur le budget des ménages (Inquiry into Household Finances) — **Language:** French / Dutch **Frequency:** annual **Content:** household finances analysis and measures the structure of Belgian household expenditure

Enquête sur l'emploi du temps (Employment Survey) — **Language:** French / Dutch **Frequency:** annual **Content:** employment, tasks, care and education of children, care staff, sleep and rest, education and training, social activities, leisure activities, movements

Enquête sur les forces de travail (Survey of the Work Force) — **Language:** French / Dutch **Frequency:** quarterly **Content:** manpower in Belgium according to various criteria: sex, age, place of residence, registry office, academic standard, sector, function, etc

Enquête voyages (Journeys Survey) — **Language:** French / Dutch **Frequency:** annual **Content:** main results of an inquiry on the behaviour of the vacationers; information on the duration and the motive for the journey, destination, type of accommodation, used means of transport and the mode of organisation for the journey; origin of the traveller

Espérance de vie en bonne santé selon le statut socio-économique en Belgique (Healthy Life Expectation by Socioeconomic Status in Belgium) — **Language:** French / Dutch **Content:** level of education and health in Belgium

Faillites (Bankruptcies) — **Language:** French / Dutch **Frequency:** monthly **Content:** contains data on bankruptcies by activity, region and duration

Hôtels, campings et locations touristiques en Belgique (Hotels, Camping and Tourist Costs in Belgium) — **Language:** French / Dutch **Frequency:** annual **Content:** contains data on the capacity of the tourism sector, arrivals, overnight stays according to the motive for the journey, the tourist region, the mode of accommodation and the country of residence of the visitors

Inégalité socio-économique et mortalité à l'âge moyen en Belgique (Socio-economic Disparity and Mortality by Average Age in Belgium) — **Language:** Dutch **Content:** contains data on mortality in Belgium, with socio-economic comparisons to other industrial nations

La conjoncture (Economic situation) — **Language:** French / Dutch **Frequency:** monthly **Content:** contains data on production, turnover and investments by production and distribution companies, prices in consumption and production, bankruptcies, employees, salaries and working hours

Les dépenses courantes de protection de l'environnement par les industries en Belgique (Running Costs of Environmental Protection by Industries in Belgium) — **Language:** French/Dutch **Content:** contains data on the environmental running costs of the Belgian industries

Mariages et divorces (Marriages and Divorce) — **Language:** French / Dutch **Frequency:** annual **Content:** contains data on marriages and divorces by nationality, previous married state, profession, social status, age, region and province

Ménages et noyaux familiaux au 1 janvier (Households on January 1st) — **Language:** Dutch/French **Frequency:** annual **Content:** contains data on private households, including number of persons in the household and number of persons with responsibility according to the age of the children

Mortalité (Mortality) — **Language:** French/Dutch **Frequency:** annual **Content:** contains data on mortality rate and number of deaths by region, province, age, gender and nationality of the deceased

Mouvement de la population et migrations (Movement of the Population and Migration) — **Language:** French / Dutch **Frequency:** annual **Content:** contains data on population, including geographic movements, changes of nationality and migratory movements

Naissances (Births) — **Language:** French / Dutch **Frequency:** annual **Content:** contains data on births by nationality, age of the mother, gender, province and region and fertility rates by age and region

Occupation du sol pour les provinces, les régions et le Royaume (Activity by Province and Region) — **Language:** French/Dutch **Frequency:** annual **Content:** contains data on land use for agricultural purposes

Population totale et belge au 1 janvier (Total Belgian Population on January 1st) — **Language:** French/Dutch **Frequency:** annual **Content:** contains data on population by sex, age and municipality and of population density by age

Prix à la consommation: indices, prix moyens et inflation (Prices: Consumer, Indicators, Averages and Inflation) — **Language:** French / Dutch **Frequency:** annual **Content:** contains data on prices by inflation, product and consumption in comparison to various countries of the European Union

Production industrielle et construction (Industrial Production and Construction) — **Language:** French / Dutch **Frequency:** monthly **Content:** contains data on the industrial production, including the building industry, construction licences, current construction, energy and recovery

Production industrielle PRODCOM et non-PRODCOM (Industrial Production with and without PRODCOM) — **Language:** French / Dutch **Frequency:** annual **Content:** contains data on the performances of big companies in various branches of industry, including deliveries and volume of employment

Recensement agricole (Agricultural Inventory) — **Language:** French / Dutch **Frequency:** annual **Content:** contains data on use of land, mode of exploitation, manpower, farm implements in use, the agricultural regions, provinces and number of animals

Santé et mortalité foeto-infantile (Health and Foetal-child Mortality) — **Frequency:** annual **Content:** contains data on health and foetal-childish mortality by place of residence, age of the mother, nationality of the mother, professional activity of the mother, social and occupational group of the father, born weight, lasted gestation and initial cause of the death

Santé publique (Public Health) — **Language:** French / Dutch **Frequency:** annual **Content:** contains data on number of doctors, hospitals, hospital beds, patients, days of hospitalization, cases of infection with HIV and AIDS and cases of tumours. Also covers household expenditure in care of health by type of expense and region

Singularité des étrangers sur le marché de l'emploi (Foreign Employment Factors) — **Language:** French / Dutch **Content:** contains data on active foreign workers on the Belgian labour market

Statistique fiscale des revenus (Fiscal Statistics of Incomes) — **Language:** French / Dutch **Frequency:** annual **Content:** contains data on income by regions, provinces and districts, distribution of the taxable net total income and its constituents

Statistique fiscale des revenus par déciles (Tax Statistics of Incomes) — **Frequency:** annual **Content:** contains data on taxable net total income and its constituents, by domestic type and age brackets

Statistiques agricoles *(Agricultural Statistics)* — **Language:** French / Dutch **Frequency:** quarterly **Content:** contains data on agricultural activity by production, modifications, outdoor vegetable farming, dairy farming, pig population, slaughter of animals, agricultural price indices and farm rents

Statistiques mensuelles du transport *(Transport Monthly Statistics)* — **Language:** French /Dutch **Frequency:** monthly **Content:** contains data on types of transport, new registrations, traffic accidents, transport of the goods by sea, waterway or by rail and travellers by plane or train

Statistiques sociales et comptes nationaux: vers une approche SAM *(Labour Accounts and Social Accounting Matrices)* — **Language:** French / Dutch **Content:** contains information on the manual production of SAMs per reference year

Structure and Distribution of Earnings Survey — **Language:** English **Content:** contains data on economic and financial factors and on distribution of earnings

Tourisme et hôtellerie *(Tourism and Hotel Business)* — **Language:** French / Dutch **Frequency:** quarterly **Content:** contains data on the hotel and catering industry, including arrivals, purpose and duration of stay and number of overnight stays by types, province and the origin of the visitors

Une analyse sur l'emploi du temps des Belges *(Analysis of the timetable of Belgians)* — **Language:** French / Dutch **Content:** contains data on time use of active and inactive people, including day-to-day progress, weekend activities, general activities of the population, regional differences and differences between men and women

Ventes de biens immobiliers *(Sales of Real Estate)* — **Language:** French / Dutch **Frequency:** annual **Content:** contains data on real estate, including number, surface, selling price and properties by district

Bosnia-Herzegovina

Agencija za bankarstvo Bosne i Hercegovine
Banking Agency of the Federation of Bosnia and Herzegovina

Address: Koševo 3, Sarajevo, 71000
Telephone: +387 33 721 400
Fax: +387 33 668 811
E-mail: agencija@fba.ba
Website: www.fba.ba

Activity: bank licensing, licensing related to changes of banks' organisational structure and payment systems, collecting, processing and recording data submitted by banks in accordance with current regulations

Website(s) information:
Agencija za bankarstvo Bosne i Hercegovine — **url:** www.fba.ba **Description:** reports on the banking system, financial statements and external audit of banks in the Federation of Bosnia and Herzegovina; available online in Bosnian/Croatian; links to websites of banks **Coverage:** banking system, financial statements and external audit of banks

Agencija za promociju stranih nekretnina Bosne i Hercegovine (FIPA)
Foreign Investment Promotion Agency of Bosnia and Herzegovina (FIPA)

Address: Branilaca Sarajeva 21, Sarajevo, 71000
Telephone: +387 33 278 080
Fax: +387 33 278 081
E-mail: fipa@fipa.gov.ba
Website: www.fipa.gov.ba

Activity: generating new investments; promoting foreign investments, servicing potential and existing investors, providing all information related to business environment in Bosnia and Herzegovina, analysing and promoting sectors for foreign investments, promoting investments and at the same time identifying the main legal obstacles for direct foreign investment, preparing presentations and printing promotional material, creating and maintaining database of investment projects and available locations, developing co-operation with other foreign investment agencies in the region

Website(s) information:
Agencija za promociju stranih nekretnina Bosne i Hercegovine (FIPA) — **url:** www.fipa.gov.ba **Description:** statistical information on general economic indicators available online and in English; **Coverage:** general economic indicators

Publication(s):
Investirajte u turizam *(Invest in Tourism)* — **Frequency:** irregular **Content:** profile report on possible investments in tourism in Bosnia and Herzegovina **Readership:** potential investors, research specialists

Sektor auto-dijelova *(Auto Components Industry)* — **Language:** Bosnian/Croatian/Serbian **Frequency:** irregular **Content:** profile report on auto components industry **Readership:** potential investors, reserarch specialists

Agencija za statistiku Bosne i Hercegovine
Statistical Agency of Bosnia and Herzegovina

Address: Zelenih beretki 26, Sarajevo, 71000
Telephone: +387 33 220 622
Fax: +387 33 220 622
E-mail: bhas@bhas.ba
Website: www.bhas.ba

Activity: producing and publishing statistical reports collected by the entity Institutes for Statistics related to all socio-economic sectors in accordance with internationally recognised standards, representing Bosnia and Herzegovina internationally, fostering co-operation between the two entities and their Institutes and facilitating the exchange of information between the Institutes and their branches

Website(s) information:
Agencija za statistiku Bosne i Hercegovine *(Statistical Agency of Bosnia and Herzegovina)* — **url:** www.bhas.ba **Description:** reports (bulletins) on economic and social situation in Bosnia and Herzegovina; narrative part of the reports are written in Bosnian/Croatian/Serbian, whilst statistical information available in English **Coverage:** socio-economic developments

Publication(s):
Bilteni *(Bulletins)* — **Language:** Bosnian/Croatian/Serbian/English **Frequency:** monthly **Content:** socio-economic situation/developments covering a 5-year period **Readership:** academics, statistical specialists, research specialists, governmental organisations, NGOs

Tematski bilteni *(Thematic Bulletins)* — **Language:** Bosnian/Croatian/Serbian and some in English **Frequency:** annual **Content:** annual overview of different industries and social indicators over a two-year period **Readership:** statistical specialists, research specialsts, academics, governmental organisations, NGOs, businesses

Centralna banka Bosne i Hercegovine
Central Bank of Bosnia and Herzegovina

Address: Marsala Tita 25, Sarajevo, 71000
Telephone: +387 33 278 100
Fax: +387 33 278 299
E-mail: contact@cbbh.ba
Website: www.cbbh.gov.ba

Activity: maintaining monetary stability, defining and controlling the implementation of monetary policy of Bosnia and Herzegovina, supporting and maintaining appropriate payment and settlement systems, co-ordinating the activities of the BH Entity Banking Agencies in charge of bank licensing and supervision

Website(s) information:
Centralna banka Bosne i Hercegovine *(Central Bank of Bosnia and Herzegovina)* — **url:** www.cbbh.gov.ba **Description:** offers narrative and statistical banking reports, as well as bulletins and newsletters related to socio-economic situation and developments in Bosnia and Herzegovina; documents are available in English; **Coverage:** advance release, monthly balance, financial statements, main economic indicators, governmental funds, foreign debt, financial and external sectors

Direkcija za civilnu avijaciju Bosne i Hercegovine (BHDCA)
Civil Aviation Directorate of Bosnia and Hercegovina

Address: Fehima ef. Curcica 6, Sarajevo, 71000
Telephone: +387 33 251 350
Fax: +387 33 251 351
E-mail: bhdca@bhdca.gov.ba
Website: www.bhdca.gov.ba

Activity: implementing civil aviation policy, enforcing the relevant legislation, international standards and practice, developing civil aviation strategy, representing the Directorate internationally, managing financial and other civil aviation resources

Website(s) information:
Direkcija za civilnu avijaciju Bosne i Hercegovine (BHDCA) (Civil Aviation Directorate of Bosnia and Herzegovina) — **url:** www.bhdca.gov.ba
Description: local convergence and implementation plans, including various statistical information about the civil aviation system in BIH; available online and in Bosnian, Croatian, Serbian and English
Coverage: civil aviation

Državna regulatorna komisija za elektricnu energiju (DERK)
State Electricity Regulatory Commission (DERK)

Address: Miška Jovanovica 4/II, Tuzla, 75000
Telephone: +387 35 302 070
Fax: +387 35 302 077
E-mail: info@derk.ba
Website: www.derk.ba

Activity: regulating electricity distribution in Bosnia and Herzegovina, distribution system operation and international trade in electricity

Website(s) information:
Državna regulatorna komisija za elektricnu energiju (DERK) — **url:** www.derk.ba
Description: annual reports available online in Bosnian/Croatian/Serbian **Coverage:** energy distribution and consumption

Federalni zavod za statistiku
Federal Office for Statistics

Address: Zelenih beretki 26, Sarajevo, 71000
Telephone: +387 33 664 553
Fax: +387 33 664 553
E-mail: fedstat@fzs.ba
Website: www.fzs.ba

Guides: extensive list of publications is available on the official site
Activity: collection, processing and publication of statistical data, defining uniform statistical research methodology and standards, developing statistical information systems, developing and implementing administrative and statistical registries (population, companies, etc), exchange of statistical information with other countries and international organisations in accordance with relevant national legislation and international agreements

Website(s) information:
Federalni zavod za statistiku (Federal Office of Statistics) — **url:** www.fzs.ba
Description: all monthly and annual data available online **Coverage:** general data: geographical, geological and census data; monthly data: industrial production, foreign trade, tourism - vital statistics, prices and cost of living. Annual data: basic information, register of business entities, industry and foreign trade, tourism, prices and cost of living, GDP, capital investment, employment/unemployment, population and wages

Publication(s):
Bilten (Bulletin) — **Language:** Bosnian/Croatian/English **Frequency:** monthly **Content:** annual publication containing detailed data related to various fields of statistical research and specific overview of each of the fields at Federal, cantonal and municipal level **Readership:** academics and research specialists

Kantoni u brojkama (Canton Statistical Report) — **Language:** Bosnian/Croatian/English **Frequency:** annual **Content:** annual publication of selected statistical information related to Federation BIH cantons **Readership:** academics and research specialists

Statisticki godišnjak/ljetopis Federacije Bosne i Hercegovine (Statistical Annual Report of the Federation of Bosnia and Herzegovina) — **Language:** Bosnian/Croatian/English **Frequency:** annual **Content:** covers detailed statistical data on population, employment/unemployment rate, annual national income, local products, agriculture, industry, transport, tourism, education, culture and social care at Federal, cantonal and municipal level **Readership:** academics and research specialists

Statisticki podaci o privrednim/gospodarskim i drugim kretanjima u Fedaraciji BIH (Statistical Data on Economic and Other Developments in Federation BIH) — **Language:** Bosnian/Croatian/English **Frequency:** monthly **Content:** contains results of monthly research of economic and other developments in Federation BIH (cantons), as well as selected annual reports **Readership:** academics and research specialists

Žene I muškarci (Gender) FBIH (Gender of the Federation BIH) — **Language:** Bosnian/Croatian/English **Frequency:** irregular **Content:** statistical data on gender in the Federation of Bosnia and Herzegovina **Readership:** academic, research specialists, NGOs

Institut za statistiku Republike Srpske
The Institute for Statistics of the Republic of Srpska

Address: Veljka Mladenovica 12d, Banja Luka, 78000
Telephone: +387 51 450 275
Fax: +387 51 450 279
E-mail: stat@rzs.rs.ba
Website: www.rzs.rs.ba

Activity: providing statistical information on all sectors in the Republic of Srpska

Website(s) information:
Institut za statistiku Republike Srpske (Institute for Statistics of the Republic of Srpska) — **url:** www.rzs.rs.ba **Description:** survey and research reports (bulletins) are available online and in English; **Coverage:** socio-economic statistics

Publication(s):
Bilteni (Bulletins) — **Language:** Bosnian/Croatian/Serbian/English **Frequency:** annual **Content:** various industries and social indicators (2004-2006) **Readership:** academics, research specialists, statistical experts, governmental organisations, NGOs, businesses

Statisticki pregled (Statistical Overview) — **Language:** Bosnian/Croatian/Serbian/English **Content:** ontly and quarterly statistical overview of socio-econoimc situation/developments **Readership:** academics, statistical specialists, research specialists, governmental organisations, NGOs, businesses

Investiciona banka Federacije Bosne i Hercegovine
Investment Bank of the Federation of Bosnia and Herzegovina

Address: Igmanska 1, Sarajevo, 71000
Telephone: +387 33 277 900
Fax: +387 33 668 952
E-mail: info@ibf-bih.com
Website: www.ibf-bih.com

Activity: investing in economic development, especially development of small and medium companies, promoting and developing commercial banks, supporting creation and development of strong national capital market, participating in restructuring and privatizing of national industry

Website(s) information:
Investiciona banka Federacije Bosne i Hercegovine (Investment Bank of the Federation of Bosnia and Herzegovina) — **url:** www.ibf-bih.com
Description: balance sheets, income statements, profit/loss statements; available online and in English **Coverage:** assets, liabilities, interest, income, loss, expenditures

Ministarstvo finansija i trezora Bosne i Hercegovine
Ministry of Finance and Treasury of Bosnia and Hercegovina

Address: Trg BIH 1, Sarajevo, 71000
Telephone: +387 33 205 345
Fax: +387 33 219 923
E-mail: trezorbih@trezorbih.gov.ba
Website: www.trezorbih.gov.ba

Activity: developing principles of tax policy and drafting relevant legislation, establishing relations with international and national financial institutions, planning and managing the debt of Bosnia and Herzegovina, proposing policy of new indebting in country and abroad, drafting budget and final balance of accounts of the country, coordinating activities related provision of budgetary resources of the country, executing budget and financing state institutions

management of money and operating the Single Treasury Account (JRT);

establishment of accounting operations of B-H Institutions; developing and operating financial information system; developing and implementing of internal supervision of budget users;

activities on ex-SFRY succession issues; management of property in possession of B-H Institutions; compilation, distribution and publication of consolidated Government's general fiscal data;

preparation of laws, regulations and public procurement procedures, and

management and specialist operations set forth by laws and regulations.

Website(s) information:
Ministarstvo finansija i trezora Bosne i Hercegovine *(Ministry of Finance & Treasury of Bosnia & Herzegovina)* — **url:** www.trezorbih.gov.ba **Description:** narrative and statistical report on debt of Bosnia and Herzegovina; it is available online and in Bosnian/Croatian/Serbian **Coverage:** debt related statistics

Ministarstvo komunikacija i prometa Bosne i Hercegovine
Ministry of Communications and Transport of Bosnia and Herzegovina

Address: Trg BiH 1, Sarajevo, 71000
Telephone: +387 33 284 750
Fax: +387 33 284 751
E-mail: info@mkt.gov.ba
Website: www.mkt.gov.ba

Activity: developing policies relating to and regulating common and international communication devices, international and inter-entity transport and infrastructure producing contract, agreements and other acts relating to international and inter-entity communications and transport, maintaining relations with international organizations dealing with international and inter-entity communications and transport, drafting strategic and planning documents relating to international and inter-entity communications, transport, infrastructure and information technologies, dealing with control of unimpeded transport in international transport, civil aviation and civil transport control

Ministarstvo pravde Bosne i Hercegovine
Ministry of Justice of Bosnia and Herzegovina

Address: Trg BIH 1, Sarajevo, 71000
Telephone: +387 33 223 501
Fax: +387 33 223 504
E-mail: kontakt@mpr.gov.ba
Website: www.mpr.gov.ba

Activity: functioning as an administrative body for legal institutions, establishing and maintaining international judicial relations, drafting relevant laws, ensuring that judicial system of the country is in accordance with international agreements and acting as a central co-ordinating body to ensure approximation of the entities' legislation

Website(s) information:
Ministarstvo pravde Bosne i Hercegovine *(Ministry of Justice of Bosnia and Herzegovina)* — **url:** www.mpr.gov.ba **Description:** annual narrative reports also containing statistical information about the judicial system, including crime rates **Coverage:** crime statistics

Ministarstvo spoljne trgovine i medunarodnih odnosa Bosne i Hercegovine
Ministry of Foreign Affairs and Foreign Trade of Bosnia and Herzegovina

Address: Musala 9, Sarajevo, 71000
Telephone: +387 33 663 863
Website: www.mvteo.gov.ba

Activity: developing and implementing foreign trade and foreign investment policies, establishing and maintaining international trade relations, developing and implementing customs policy, dealing with national resources, energetics and environmental issues

Website(s) information:
Ministarstvo spoljne trgovine i medunarodnih odnosa Bosne i Hercegovine *(Ministry of Foreign Affairs and Foreign Trade of Bosnia and Herzegovina)* — **url:** www.mvteo.gov.ba **Description:** reports on direct foreign investments covering the period from 1994 to 2004 **Coverage:** direct foreign investments

OSCE misija za Bosnu i Hercegovinu
OSCE Mission to Bosnia and Hercegovina

Address: Fra Andela Zvizdovica 1A, Sarajevo, 71000
Telephone: +387 33 752 100
E-mail: press.ba@osce.org
Website: www.oscebih.org

Activity: responsibility for elections, and human rights in Bosnia and Herzegovina and regional military stabilisation, with democracy-building added subsequently; supporting the establishment of institutions and processes that will ensure Bosnia and Herzegovina's survival as an independent state

Website(s) information:
OSCE misija za Bosnu i Hercegovinu *(OSCE Mission to Bosnia and Herzegovina)* — **url:** www.oscebih.org **Description:** reports on trafficking in human beings and illegal immigration in BiH available online and in English **Coverage:** trafficking and illegal immigration, socio-political indicators

Publication(s):
Public Opinion Research - Attitudes Toward Recent Socio-political Situation in BiH — **Language:** English **Frequency:** irregular **Content:** socio-political situation **Readership:** academics, research specialists, governmental organisations, NGOs, humanitarian organisations

Report on Trafficking in Human Beings and Illegal Immigration in BiH — **Language:** English **Frequency:** irregular **Content:** rafficking and illegal immigration **Readership:** research specialists, humanitarian organisations, police

Savez poslodavaca Republike Srpske
Employers Confederation of the Republic of Srpska

Address: Mladena Stojanovica 111, Banja Luka, 51000
Telephone: +387 51 332 616
Fax: +387 51 332 616
E-mail: ecrs@blic.net
Website: www.poslodavci.rs.ba

Activity: business services, legal counselling, information sharing, organising round-table session on topics of concern to employers, representation and advocating for employers interests in the society

Website(s) information:
Savez poslodavaca Republike Srpske *(Employers Confederation of the Republic of Srpska)* — **url:** www.poslodavci.rs.ba **Description:** annual business survey reports; available online and in Serbian/English; **Coverage:** current trends and issues in business environment

Savjet/Vijece ministara
Council of Ministers

Address: Trg BIH 1, Sarajevo, 71000
Telephone: +387 33 211 581
Fax: +387 33 205 347
E-mail: cmpress@smartnet.ba
Website: www.vijeceministara.gov.ba

Activity: carrying out policies and decisions in the fields of foreign policy and foreign trade
customs, monetary issues, finances of the institutions and for the international obligations of Bosnia and Herzegovina; immigration, refugee, and asylum policy and regulation, international and inter-Entity criminal law enforcement, including relations with Interpol establishment and operation of common and international communications facilities, regulation of inter-Entity transportation, air traffic control; facilitation of inter-Entity coordination

Udruzenje/udruga poslodavaca Bosne i Hercegovine
Confederation of Employers of Bosnia and Herzegovina

Address: Zmaja od Bosne 4/XI, Sarajevo, 71000
Telephone: +387 33 264 830
Fax: +387 33 264 831
E-mail: upfbih@bih.net.ba
Website: www.upfbih.org

Activity: protecting rights of employers and entrepreneurs in the fields of labour and social legislation

Zavod za javno zdravstvo Federacije Bosne i Hercegovine
Institute for Public Health of the Federation of Bosnia and Herzegovina

Address: Maršala Tita 9, Sarajevo, 71000
Telephone: +387 33 716 600
Fax: +387 33 220 548
E-mail: zavodzz@bih.net.ba
Website: www.zzjzfbih.ba

Activity: promoting public and environmental health and illness prevention, designing and implementing health projects and conducting research in the field of public health

Bulgaria

Agency for Economic Analysis and Forecasting
Address: 31 Aksakov Street, Sofia, 1000
Telephone: +359 2 9859 5601
E-mail: aeaf@aeaf.minfin.bg
Website: www.aeaf.minfin.bg

Guides: publications in Bulgarian can be accessed free of charge; a paid subscription is required for the printed publications and for some publications in English; a full catalogue is available online
Activity: analyses the current business environment and the economic situation and elaborates assessments on the country's economic development prospects; prepares short-, medium- and long-term forecasts for Bulgaria's economic development trends under different economic policy scenarios

Website(s) information:
Agency for Economic Analysis and Forecasting — url: www.aeaf.minfin.bg
          Description: files are available in PDF format, the site contains business survey series, working paper series, and information on recent developments in the Bulgarian Economy **Coverage:** detailed monthly data about the Bulgarian business climate, industrial sales and prices, CPI, PPI, unemployment, interest rates, main macroeconomic and microeconomic indicators

Publication(s):
Bulgarian Economy: Analysis and Outlook — **Language:** Bulgarian/English
          Frequency: quarterly **Content:** focuses on the latest trends in the Bulgarian economy and provides a detailed forecast for the following 12 months

Bulgarska Narodna Banka
Bulgarian National Bank

Address: 1 Alexander Battenberg Square, Sofia, 1000
Telephone: +359 2 91 459
Fax: +359 2 980 2425/980 6493
E-mail: press_office@bnbank.org
Website: www.bnb.bg

Guides: publications are available for download online - the bank maintains a free subscription policy
Activity: maintains the stability of the national currency, the Lev, through the implementation of adequate policies and of an efficient payment system; exclusive right to issue coins and banknotes in Bulgaria; regulates and supervises the banking sector aiming at the stability of the banking system; administers the Government Securities Depository and monitors the activities of the Central Depository

Website(s) information:
Bulgarian National Bank — url: www.bnb.bg **Description:** The bank maintains a free subscription policy to all its publications, covering fiscal, monetary, financial, and other matters **Coverage:** provides banking and financial statistics including: exchange rates; balance of payments; foreign trade; gross external debt; aggregated balance sheets and income statements of national commercial banks; trade rates; and monetary survey

Publication(s):
Bank Review — **Language:** English/Bulgarian **Frequency:** quarterly **Content:** contains articles covering the banking and finance sectors

Monthly Bulletin — **Language:** English/Bulgarian **Frequency:** monthly

Coordination Centre for Information, Communication, and Management Technologies
Address: 1 Dondoukov Blvd, Sofia, 1000
Telephone: +359 2 940 3643
Fax: +359 2 940 3646
E-mail: gvalchev@ccit.government.bg
Website: www.ccit.government.bg

Activity: implements information, communications and management technologies through support and coordination of state administration, the donor community and the private sector, leading to an overall improvement in the quality of the public-administrative services and the decision-making processes

Council for Electronic Media
Address: 69 Shipchenski Prohod Blvd, Sofia
Telephone: +359 2 970 8810
Fax: +359 2 973 3769
E-mail: cem@cablebg.net
Website: www.cem.bg

Guides: catalogue available online
Activity: regulation of radio and TV broadcasting in the country by registration and licensing of radio and TV operators

Durzhavna Komisija po Stokovite Borsi i Turzhishtata
State Commission on Stock Exchanges and Markets

Address: Izgrev Region, 3A 165th Street, Sofia, 1040
Telephone: +359 2 970 6037
Fax: +359 2 873 5418
E-mail: office@dksbt.bg
Website: www.dksbt.bg

Guides: available online in PDF format; in Bulgarian only
Activity: works for the creation and development of national centres for wholesale trade with food products and for the transparent functioning of stock markets in the country

Website(s) information:
State Commission on Stock Exchanges and Markets — url: www.dksbt.bg
          Description: availability in PDF format - prices are presented according to product and region within Bulgaria **Coverage:** weekly and quarterly analyses of the wholesale prices of different food products

Executive Environmental Agency

Address: PO Box 251, 136 Tzar Boris III blvd, Sofia, 1618
Telephone: +359 2 955 9011
Fax: +359 2 955 9015
E-mail: ncesd@nfp-bg.eionet.eu.int
Website: nfp-bg.eionet.eu.int/ncesd/index.html

Guides: full catalogue is available online
Activity: conducts research of the main environmental indicators on the territory of Bulgaria

Website(s) information:
Executive Environmental Agency — **url:** nfp-bg.eionet.eu.int/ncesd/index.html **Description:** the site provides online access to information bulletins covering environmental data; it is possible to access the online version of the "Annual State of the Environment Report" for 1998-2003 **Coverage:** data on air quality, water pollution, harmful emissions

Invest Bulgaria Agency

Address: 31 Aksakov Street, Sofia, 1000
Telephone: +359 2 985 5500
Fax: +359 2 980 1320
E-mail: iba@investbg.government.bg
Website: www.investbg.government.bg

Guides: publications are available online in PDF format in separate versions in English, Spanish, German, Italian, Japanese and Bulgarian
Activity: works with potential and existing investors in Bulgaria in order to assist and secure the successful realisation of foreign investment in Bulgaria

Website(s) information:
Invest Bulgaria Agency — **url:** www.investbg.government.bg **Description:** data is available in PDF format **Coverage:** foreign investment figures, import and export, reports on particular industries, including industries attractive for investors, macroeconomic data, country profile

Ministry of Agriculture and Forestry

Address: 55 Hristo Botev Blvd, Sofia, 1040
Telephone: +359 2 985 11255
E-mail: press@mzgar.government.bg

Guides: publications are available in PDF/zip format online
Activity: coordinates, monitors, and implements the agricultural and forestry policy of the Republic of Bulgaria

Website(s) information:
Ministry of Agriculture and Forestry — **url:** www.mzgar.government.bg **Description:** the website contains PDF versions of the main publications of the Ministry - a monthly sector bulletin, an agrostatistical bulletin, and an annual industry report, available from 1998 onward; it also contains legal and policy documents and provisions **Coverage:** analyses of production and sales of staple products, livestock, etc; agrostatistical bulletin with production and structure data; annual reports on the condition of the agricultural industry, inlcuding sector specific figures on production, import and export, prices and state policy

Ministry of Economy and Energy

Address: 8 Slavianska Street, Sofia, 1052
Telephone: +359 2 940 7777
Fax: +359 2 940 7313
E-mail: callcentre@mee.government.bg
Website: www.mi.government.bg

Guides: all publications are available online
Activity: coordinates, monitors and implements the economic and energy policy of the Republic of Bulgaria

Website(s) information:
Ministry of Economy and Energy — **url:** www.mi.government.bg **Description:** the site provides information about the state of Bulgarian economy under the headings of Industry, Trade, Entrepreneurship and Eurointegration. Most reports and documents are available in both English and Bulgarian **Coverage:** covers a wide range of macroeconomic indicators in its monthly bulletin and in its issue "Basic Economic Indicators". Tourism statistics - revenue, number and percentage increase of foreign tourists by year and country of origin; international trade statistics - export figures by type of goods and destination of export; report on the condution of small and medium businesses by sector and region - production, sales, revenue; panorama report of the state of Bulgarian industry by sector - sales, production, overview and trends

Ministry of Energy and Energy Resources

Address: 8 Triadiza Street, Sofia, 1040
Telephone: +359 2 926 3636
Fax: +359 2 980 7630/988 1443
Website: www.doe.bg

Guides: full catalogue is available online; most documents are available online in PDF format
Activity: monitors energy policy in the country

Website(s) information:
Ministry of Energy and Energy Resources — **url:** www.doe.bg **Description:** reports and presentations covering the developments in the Bulgarian energy sector; most of the information is available in both English and Bulgarian; information about current projects and media coverage is also available **Coverage:** developments in the energy sector - privatisation, sector growth, investment opportunities, state of the economy by region and by energy source

Ministry of Environment and Water of Bulgaria

Address: 67 William Gladstone Steet, Sofia, 1000
Telephone: +359 2 940 6222/981 1385
Fax: +359 2 986 2533
E-mail: press@moew.government.bg
Website: www.moew.government.bg

Guides: full catalogue available online; full text available in PDF/zip format
Activity: determines and implements state environmental policy; monitors and reports on the environmental indicators in Bulgaria and elaborates guidelines for environmental protection

Publication(s):
National Catalogue of Environmental Data Sources — **Language:** Bulgarian/English **Content:** data about where and what environmental information is available in Bulgaria, in what format and access information

Ministry of Finance

Address: 102 G. S. Rakovski Street, Sofia, 1040
Telephone: +359 2 9859 2024
E-mail: feedback@minfin.bg
Website: www.minfin.government.bg

Guides: full catalogue available online; most reports and statistical information are available free of charge and can be downloaded from the website; a subscription charge applies to the monthly magazine published by the ministry "The Budget"
Activity: coordinates and implements the budgetary and tax policy of the Republic of Bulgaria

Website(s) information:
Ministry of Finance — **url:** www.minfin.government.bg **Description:** the site provides access to official reports and documents published under the heading of Statistics; the monthly bulletin on government debt management is available under the heading "Publications" **Coverage:** net cash flows to treasury single accounts, fiscal reserve account by month, data on the rebublican budget, government debt management (monthly and annual reports), tax policy and revenue breakdown

Publication(s):

Budget, The — **Language:** Bulgarian/English **Frequency:** per month **Content:** regulations and bylaws, orders, instructions, letters, comments of specialists, monthly information about the execution of the consolidated fiscal program, answers to questions in the financial sphere **Readership:** specialists in the field of finance, state and local government, tax administration, banking, statistics, accountants, students, businessmen

Ministry of Labour and Social Policy

Address: 2 Triaditsa Street, Sofia, 1052
Telephone: +359 2 811 9443
Fax: +359 2 988 4405/986 1318
E-mail: mlsp@mlsp.government.bg
Website: www.mlsp.government.bg

Guides: full catalogue is available online
Activity: determines, coordinates and implements labour and social policy of the Republic of Bulgaria; develops programmes for the reduction of unemployment; determines the minimum wage and pension

Website(s) information:

Ministry of Labour and Social Policy — **url:** www.mlsp.government.bg
Description: the site provides online access to various reports and programmes published by the Ministry since 2000 **Coverage:** national employment statistics by gender, age, education, and economic sector

Ministry of Transport and Communications

Address: 9 Djakon Ignatij Street, Sofia, 1000
Telephone: +359 2 987 5750
Fax: +359 2 987 1805
Website: www.mtc.government.bg

Guides: full catalogue available online
Activity: determines, coordinates and implements official policy on transport and communications

National Centre of Health Informatics

Address: 15 Academic Ivan Geshov Street, Sofia, 1431
Telephone: +359 2 951 5302/951 5303
Fax: +359 2 951 5238
Website: www.nchi.government.bg

Guides: full catalogue is available online
Activity: research in the sphere of public health and well-being indicators; works as a specialized agency of the Ministry of Healthcare and provides input for National Health Strategy

Website(s) information:

National Centre of Health Informatics — **url:** www.nchi.government.bg
Description: online access to the annual public health statistics publication is available in English; most data is available under the heading "health statisitcs" and "health indicators database" in Bulgarian **Coverage:** public health statistics, birth and mortality rate, morbidity indicators, trends in these indicators by region and gender; average life expectancy; health institutions' activity; economic indicators of health insitutions

National Employment Agency

Address: 3 Dondoukov Blvd, Sofia, 1000
Telephone: +359 2 980 8719
Fax: +359 986 7802
E-mail: az@az.government.bg
Website: www.nsz.government.bg

Guides: all publications are accessible online
Activity: executive agency to the Minister of Labour and Social Policy for the implementation of the government policy on employment promotion; registration of unemployed actively seeking employment and available vacancies; Implementation, of projects and programs in the field of employment, professional qualification and training, and social integration

Website(s) information:

National Employment Agency - Statistics and Analyses — **url:** www.nsz.government.bg **Description:** links to monthly, periodical and annual reports on labour force dynamics in Bulgaria by region; there is a difference between the English and the Bulgarian versions of the site, the former being more informative **Coverage:** data on employment and unemployment, labour force dynamics, structure by gender, age and education, number of people attending qualification courses, etc

National Statistical Institute (NSI)

Address: 2 Panajot Volov Street, Sofia, 1038
Telephone: +359 2 985 7729/985 7457
Fax: +359 2 985 7799
E-mail: presscentre@nsi.bg
Website: www.nsi.bg

Guides: a full catalogue of printed, online, regional and library-access publications can be found online
Activity: statistical surveys and the publication and dissemination of statistical data

Website(s) information:

National Statistical Institute (NSI) — **url:** www.nsi.bg **Description:** available online both in Bulgarian and in English, NSI's web site provides information on the Institute's main products and services, including latest news and releases, a catalogue of available publications and access to varied online statistical data such as geographical and meteorological data, economic indicators, governmental constitution, population, employment, wages, personal consumption, GDP, money flows, agriculture, industry, communication, economic relations with foreign countries, tourism, education, culture and arts, health and pension insurance, environment **Coverage:** a wide range of socio-economic statistics are provided for both Bulgaria and other countries (Bulgaria and the World in Figures), including data collected by the NSI, as well as by major pan-regional and international official organisations (e.g. Council of Europe; ILO; etc). Data covers: population and demographics; health services; labour market; energy resources; industrial sector; agricultural sector (crops and livestock); external trade (exports and imports); and transports. There are international comparisons and year coverage varies by sector and by indicator

Publication(s):

Main Macro-economic Indicators — **Language:** Bulgarian/English **Frequency:** annual **Content:** statistical overview of the present state of Bulgaria's economy

Prices, Price Indices and Inflation — **Language:** Bulgarian **Frequency:** monthly **Content:** list of annual and monthly consumer price indices by commodities

Statistical News — **Language:** English/Bulgarian **Frequency:** monthly **Content:** monthly and quarterly updated socio-economic data, as well as statistics for all main sectors of the economy: agriculture, industry, transport, communications and trade

Statistical Yearbook of the Republic of Bulgaria — **Language:** English/Bulgarian **Frequency:** annual **Content:** compilation of annually updated statistics collected by the Institute: demographic, social, and economic indicators

United Nations Development Programme - Bulgaria

Address: Box 700, UN House in Bulgaria, 25 Khan Krum Street, Sofia, 1040
Telephone: +359 2 969 6100
Fax: +359 2 981 3184
E-mail: info@undp.bg
Website: www.undp.bg

Guides: full catalogue is available online; publications are available in English and Bulgarian in PDF format
Activity: works for poverty reduction through social inclusion and economic development; works for the improvement of quality of life through good governance for equitable regional development

Website(s) information:
International Trade Centre (UNCTAD/WTO) — url:
http://www.intracen.org/menus/countries.htm **Description:** the webiste provides country profiles of with this statistical coverage, as well as publications on Bulgaria, and a list of selected sources of information **Coverage:** trade performance index, national export performance, national import profile, trade statistics by industry sector and year (2000-2004)

Publication(s):
National Human Development Report — **Language:** English/Bulgarian **Frequency:** annual **Content:** Looks at social and economic indicators and surveys every region of Bulgaria to determine trends, developments and areas in need of reform

Croatia

Agencija za promicanje izvoza i ulaganja Hrvatske
Croatian Trade and Investment Promotion Agency

Address: Andrije Hebranga 34, Zagreb, 10000
Telephone: +385 1 486 6001
Fax: +385 1 486 6008
E-mail: zeljko.kirincic@apiu.hr
Website: www.apiu.hr

Activity: full service to investors on implementation of their investment projects, proposing measures to enhance the investment environment and promoting the country as a good investment location

Website(s) information:
Agencija za promicanje izvoza i ulaganja Hrvatske *(Croatian Trade and Investment Promotion Agency)* — **url:** www.apiu.hr **Description:** general socio-economic indicators and investment information available online **Coverage:** socio-economic indicators

Državni zavod za statistiku
Central Bureau of Statistics

Address: Ilica 3, Zagreb, 10000
Telephone: +385 1 480 6154
Fax: +385 1 480 6148
E-mail: stat.info@dzs.hr
Website: www.dzs.hr

Guides: calendar of statistical data issues (2005 and 2006) available on the website
Activity: collecting and publishing statistical data

Website(s) information:
Državni zavod za statistiku *(Central Bureau of Statistics)* — **url:** www.dzs.hr **Description:** various statistical information available online in Croatian and English including a calendar of statistical issues from 2005 and 2006 **Coverage:** geography, demography, education, general economic indicators, employment, agriculture and forestry, industry and services, transport and construction, tourism and culture

Publication(s):
Statisticke informacije *(Statistical Information)* — **Language:** Croatian/English **Frequency:** annual **Content:** recently introduced statistical information overview covering socio-economic indicators **Readership:** research specialists, analysts, academics, governmental and non-governmental organisations

Statisticki ljetopis *(Statistical Yearbook)* — **Language:** Croatian/English **Frequency:** annual **Content:** socio-economic overview **Readership:** research specialists, analysts, academics, governmental and non-governmental organisations, businesses

Ekonomski institut Zagreb
Institute of Economy Zagreb

Address: Trg J. F. Kennedyja 7, Zagreb, 10000
Telephone: +385 1 2335 700
Fax: +385 1 2335 165
E-mail: eizagreb@eizg.hr
Website: www.eizg.hr

Activity: scientific and development research in the field of economics (regional development, macro economy, innovations and technological development, company organisation and management)

Website(s) information:
Ekonomski institut Zagreb *(Institute of Economy Zagreb)* — **url:** www.eizg.hr **Description:** the site offers abstracts from the publications containing information about the economy of the country **Coverage:** economic indicators

Publication(s):
Croatian Economic Outlook — **Language:** English **Frequency:** quarterly **Content:** analysis of current economic trends as well as economic policies, and gives a short-term forecast of economic trends in Croatia **Readership:** economists, research specialists, analysts, governmental organisations

Privredna kretanja i privredna politka *(Economic Trends and Economic Policy)* — **Language:** Croatian/English (end of the year edition) **Frequency:** quarterly **Content:** economical overview **Readership:** economists, research specialists, analysts, governmental organisations

Energetski institut Hrvoje Požar
The Institute of Energy 'Hrvoje Pozar'

Address: PP 141, Savska cesta 163, Zagreb, 10001
Telephone: +385 1 632 6100
Fax: +385 1 604 0599
E-mail: eihp@eihp.hr
Website: www.eihp.hr

Activity: expert and scientific research in the field of energy for state, regional and local administration and energy companies; expertise and analyses for the Croatian Energy Regulatory Council; management of National Energy Programmes and pilot projects; organising seminars, workshops and courses; publishing editions, periodicals and other forms of communication with experts, scientists and the general public, especially via Internet

Website(s) information:
Energetski institut Hrvoje Požar *(Institute for Energy 'Hrvoje Pozar')* — **url:** www.eihp.hr **Description:** the site offers various statistical information related to the system of energy supply and other relevant matters in Croatian, English and German **Coverage:** energy and energy systems (gas, oil, electricity)

Financijska agencija Hrvatske (FINA)
Croatian Financial Agency (FINA)

Address: Koturaška 43, Zagreb, 10000
Telephone: +385 1 612 7111
E-mail: info@fina.hr
Website: www.fina.hr

Activity: financial mediation, business information dissemination, cash operations, e-business, archiving, electronic signature authority, payment transactions, training

Website(s) information:
Financijska agencija Hrvatske (FINA) *(Croatian Financial Agency (FINA))* — **url:** www.fina.hr **Description:** various finanical and banking information available online **Coverage:** finance, banks, businesses

Publication(s):
Godišnje izviješce *(Annual Report)* — **Language:** Croatian/English **Frequency:** annual **Content:** basic financial indicators, business secors overview, business network, profit and loss balance, cash flow statement **Readership:** finanical experts, research specialists, analysts, governmental organisations

Hrvatska banaka za obnovu i razvitak
Croatian Bank for Reconstruction and Development

Address: Strossmayerov trg 9, Zagreb, 10000
Telephone: +385 1 459 1620
Fax: +385 1 459 1721
E-mail: info@hbor.hr
Website: www.hbor.hr

Activity: financing the reconstruction and development of the Croatian economy

Website(s) information:
Hrvatska banaka za obnovu i razvitak *(Croatian Bank for Reconstruction and Development)* — url: www.hbor.hr **Coverage:** economy and development

Publication(s):
Godišnji izvještaj *(Annual Report)* — **Language:** Croatian/English **Frequency:** annual **Content:** annual activities of the bank and overview of the country's economy (reports covering periods from 1998 are available online) **Readership:** financial and economic experts, research specialists, analysts, governmental organisations, investors

Institut za turizam
The Institute of Tourism

Address: Vrhovec 5, Zagreb, 10000
Telephone: +385 1 390 9666
Fax: +385 1 390 9667
E-mail: biblioteka@iztzg.hr
Website: www.iztzg.hr

Guides: publications available through library catalogue
Activity: research, information and documentation, publishing, education, planning and development

Website(s) information:
Institut za turizam — url: www.iztzg.hr **Description:** the site offers an online catalogue of publications, as well as magazines covering the tourism industry

Publication(s):
Casopis Turizam *(Tourism Magazine)* — **Language:** Croatian/English **Frequency:** quarterly **Content:** travel and tourism **Readership:** research specialists, analysts

Ministarsto vanjskih poslova i europskih integracija Hrvatske
Croatian Ministry of Foreign Affairs and European Integrations

Address: Trg N. Š. Zrinskog 7 -8, Zagreb, 10000
Telephone: +385 1 456 9964
Fax: +385 1 455 1795
E-mail: mvp@mvp.hr
Website: www.mvpei.hr

Activity: implementing national foreign affairs and international integrations policy

Website(s) information:
Mission of the Republic of Croatia to the United Nations, Ministry of Foreign Affairs and European Integrations — url: http://un.mfa.hr **Description:** comprehensive socio-economic overview of Croatia **Coverage:** socio-economic indicators

Ministarstvo Financija Hrvatske
Croatian Ministry of Finance

Address: Katanciceva 5, Zagreb, 10000
Telephone: +385 1 459 1333
Fax: +385 1 492 2583
E-mail: kabinet@mfin.hr
Website: www.mfin.hr

Activity: managing the financial system

Website(s) information:
Ministarstvo financija Hrvatske *(Croatian Ministry of Finance)* — **url:** www.mfin.hr **Description:** statistical information related to the ministry and financial system of the country **Coverage:** financial and economic indicators

Publication(s):
Financijsko izvješće javnih institucija *(Financial Report on State Institutions)* — **Language:** Croatian **Frequency:** quarterly **Content:** finances of public institutions (State Agency for Deposit Insurance, Croatian Development Bank, Privatisation Fund); reports cover the period of 2000 - 2005 **Readership:** research specialists, analysts, financial experts, governmental organisations

Financijsko izvješće javnih poduzeca *(Financial Report on State-owned Companies)* — **Language:** Croatian **Frequency:** irregular **Content:** finances of public companies (Croatia Insurance, Croatian Energy, Croatian Post Service, Croatian Forests, Croatian Oil Company, Jadrolinija, Narodne novine and Plovput); reports cover the period of 2000 - 2005 **Readership:** research specialists, analysts, governmental organisations

Godišnjak *(Yearbook)* — **Language:** Croatian **Frequency:** annual **Content:** overview of state finances and macroeconomic indicators from 1994 **Readership:** research specialists, analysts, governmental organisations

Statisticki prikazi *(Statistical Overview)* — **Language:** Croatian **Frequency:** monthly **Content:** macroeconomic indicators of the country's economy by month (1995-2006) **Readership:** research specialists, analysts, governmental organisations

Ministarstvo gospodarstva, rada i poduzetništva Hrvatske
Croatian Ministry of Economy, Labour and Entrepreneurship

Address: Ulica grada Vukovara 78, Zagreb, 10000
Telephone: +385 1 610 6111
Fax: +385 1 610 9110
E-mail: info@mingorp.hr
Website: www.mingo.hr

Activity: defining and implementing economic and labour policies

Website(s) information:
Ministarstvo gospodarstva, rada i poduzetništva Hrvatske *(Croatian Ministry of Economy, Labour and Entrepreneurship)* — url: www.mingo.hr **Description:** the site contains links to statistical economic and financial information provided by the Statistical Office and National Bank **Coverage:** economic indicators

Ministarstvo mora, turizma, prometa i razvitka Hrvatske
Croatian Ministry of the Sea, Tourism, Transport and Development

Address: Prisavlje 14, Zagreb, 10000
Telephone: +385 1 378 4520
Fax: +385 1 378 4550
E-mail: ministar@ws.mmtpr.hr
Website: www.mmtpr.hr

Activity: implementing the state policies on tourism, transport and development

Website(s) information:
Ministarstvo mora, turizma, prometa i razvitka Hrvatske *(Croatian Ministry of the Sea, Tourism, Transport and Development)* — url: www.mmtpr.hr **Coverage:** tourism related

Publication(s):
Hrvatski turizam *(Croatian Tourism)* — **Language:** Croatian/English **Frequency:** irregular **Content:** data on tourism in Croatia **Readership:** research specialists, analysts, toursit agencies

Turizam u brojkama *(Tourism - Facts and Figures)* — **Language:** Croatian/English **Frequency:** irregular **Content:** statistical reports on the tourism industry (2000 - 2005) **Readership:** research specialists, analysts, tourist organisations

Ministarstvo poljoprivrede, šumarstva i vodnoga gospodarstva Hrvatske
Croatian Ministry of Agriculture, Forestry and Water Management

Address: Ulica grada Vukovara 78, Zagreb, 10000
Telephone: +385 1 610 6600
Fax: +385 1 610 9200
E-mail: office@mps.hr
Website: www.mps.hr

Activity: defining and implementing agricultural policy

Website(s) information:
Ministarstvo poljoprivrede, šumarstva i vodnoga gospodarstva Hrvatske (Croatian Ministry of Agriculture, Forestry and Water Management) — **url:** www.mps.hr **Description:** the site offers various documents containing statistical information about the agricultural system **Coverage:** agriculture, forestry and water resources

Publication(s):
Hrvatska poljoprivreda na raskršcima (Croatian Agriculture at the Crossroads) — **Language:** Croatian/English **Frequency:** irregular **Content:** overview of the country's agricultural system **Readership:** research specialists, analysts, governmental organisations

Izvozne mogucnosti poljoprivrede, ribarstva i prehrambene industrije (Export Capacity in Agriculture, Fishery and Food Industry) — **Language:** Croatian **Frequency:** irregular **Content:** agriculture, fishery and food industry in the light of export **Readership:** analysts, research specialists, governmental institutions, agricultural specialists

Operativni program razvitka govedarske proizvodnje u Republici Hrvatskoj (Livestock Production Development Programme of the Republic of Croatia) — **Language:** Croatian **Frequency:** irregular **Content:** overview of the current livestock production and prospects for its development **Readership:** agricultural specialists, research specialists, analysts, governmental institutions

Studija o potencijalnim tržištima za certificirano drvo i drvne proizvode iz Hrvatske (Study on Prospective Markets for Certified Wood and Forestry Products from Croatia) — **Language:** Croatian **Frequency:** irregular **Content:** overview of the forestry industry for potential investors and markets **Readership:** businesses, investment companies, research specialists, analysts

Ministarstvo pravosuda Hrvatske
Croatian Ministry of Justice

Address: Dežmanova ulica 6, Zagreb, 10000
Telephone: +385 1 371 0666
Fax: +385 1 371 0602
Website: www.pravosudje.hr

Activity: managing the legal system

Publication(s):
Statisticki pregled (Statistical Report) — **Language:** Croatian **Frequency:** annually **Content:** legal system by districts and courts over the previous 5 years **Readership:** legal experts, analysts, research specialists

Narodna banka Hrvatske
Croatian National Bank

Address: Trg hrvatskih velikana 3, Zagreb, 10002
Telephone: +385 1 456 4555
Fax: +385 1 455 0726
E-mail: info@hnb.hr
Website: www.hnb.hr

Activity: formulating and executing monetary and foreign exchange policies, holding and managing the international reserves of the Republic of Croatia, issuing banknotes and coins, issuing and revoking licenses for banks, supervising banks and enacting regulations on banking operations, maintaining the accounts of banks, performing payment transactions across these accounts, granting loans to banks and taking deposits from banks, regulating, improving and supervising payment system, performing legally prescribed operations on behalf of the Republic of Croatia, enacting regulations on operations within its competency, performing other operations, as stipulated by the law

Website(s) information:
Narodna Banka Hrvatske (National Bank of Croatia) — **url:** www.hnb.hr **Description:** various economic and financial data and surveys available online **Coverage:** banking sector, foreign direct investments, economic indicators

Publication(s):
Bilten HNB (CNB Bulletin) — **Language:** Croatian/English **Frequency:** monthly **Content:** monthly information on latest trends and developments in national economy and banking system **Readership:** research specialists, analysts, banking experts, governmental organisations, investors

Bilten o bankama (Banks Bulletin) — **Language:** Croatian/English **Frequency:** monthly **Content:** statistical information about banks operating in the country **Readership:** research specialists, baking experts, analysts

Godišnji izvještaj (Annual Report) — **Language:** Croatian/English **Frequency:** annual **Content:** macroeconomic developments, monetary policy, instruments and international reserves, management, banking sector, payment operations, currency department operations, financial statements **Readership:** banking experts, research specialists, analysts, banks

Makrobonitetna analiza (Macroprudential Analysis) — **Language:** Croatian/English **Frequency:** irregular **Content:** indicators of the country's economy **Readership:** economic experts, research specialists, analysts, banking experts, governmental and non-governmental organisations

Monetarna politika (Monetary Policy) — **Language:** Croatian/English **Frequency:** irregular **Content:** monetary developments, balance sheets, policy interest rates **Readership:** research specialists, analysts, economists, banking experts

Real Sector — **Language:** Croatian/English **Frequency:** irregular **Content:** actual GDP growth rates, gross value added structure, inflation, unemployment rate, nominal and real net wages, monthly labour costs, industry **Readership:** economists, research specialists, analysist, banking experts, governmental organisations

Sektor bankarstva (Banking Sector) — **Language:** Croatian/English **Frequency:** irregular **Content:** statistical overview of banking system **Readership:** research specialists, analysts, banks

USAID Croatia
Address: Thomas Jeffersona 2, Zagreb, 10000
Telephone: +385 1 661 2175
Fax: +385 1 661 2008
E-mail: usaid-zg@zg.htnet.hr
Website: http://zagreb.usembassy.gov

Activity: implementing a comprehensive transition program that includes economic and fiscal reform, strengthening democratic institutions, training activities

Publication(s):
Annual Report — **Language:** English **Frequency:** annual **Content:** Croatian economy and society **Readership:** research specialists, analyists, governmental and non-governmental organisations

Croatia Country Profile — **Language:** English **Frequency:** irregular **Content:** Croatian economy **Readership:** research specialists, analysts, governmental organisations

Vlada Republike Hrvatske
Government of the Republic of Croatia

Address: Trg Svetog Marka 2, Zagreb, 10000
Telephone: +385 1 456 9222
Fax: +385 1 630 3023
E-mail: predsjednik@vlada.hr
Website: www.vlada.hr

Activity: passes decrees, introduces legislation, proposes the state budget and enforces laws and other regulations enacted by the Croatian Sabor

Website(s) information:
Vlada Republike Hrvatske (Government of the Republic of Croatia) — **url:** www.vlada.hr **Description:** presentation of the country through socio-economic indicators; site provides links to individual ministries **Coverage:** socio-economic indicators

World Bank Croatia

Address: Trg. J.F. Kennedya 6b/III, Zagreb, 10000
Telephone: +385 1 235 7274
Fax: +385 1 235 7200
E-mail: mmilic@worldbank.org
Website: www.worldbank.hr

Activity: helping the country with post war reconstruction, improving people's welfare and boosting the country's development agenda

Website(s) information:
World Bank Croatia — url: www.worldbank.hr **Description:** various statistical information available online (information/ communications/ telecommunications, ICT infrastructure and access, expenditures, and ICT business and government environment, gender, basic demographic data, population dynamics, labour force structure, education and health, health and nutrition, and health finance, education statistics, investment climate indicators; the site also offers a link to all World Bank reports since 1946 (including those on Croatia) **Coverage:** socio-economic indicators

Publication(s):
Country Assistance Evaluation — Language: English **Frequency:** irregular **Content:** an assessment on the role of World Bank assistance to Croatia during 1991-2003 (accounting, adjustment lending, allocative efficiency, bank performance, bank regulation, bank restructuring, banking sector, bankruptcy, banks, bidding, budget deficits, capital flows, capital Markets, civil society, corporate governance, debt, decision making, deficits, democracy, economic assistance, education, elections, emerging markets, employment, expenditure programs, financial management, fiscal deficits, fiscal discipline, fiscal reforms, foreign exchange, foreign exchange reserves, health, health care, health indicators, health insurance, health policy, health programs, health sector, income support, incremental costs, inflation, institutional development, insurance, laws, legal framework, legislation, loan commitments, local demand, macroeconomic stabilization, negotiations, nutrition, patients, pensions, physicians, ports, primary health care, private sector, privatisation, public debt, public expenditure, public expenditure review, public expenditure reviews, public expenditures, public finance, public health, public investment, public ownership, public sector wages, public spending, real sector, reform programs, refugees, rehabilitation, roads, sanitation, savings, social issues, structural adjustment, tax, telecommunications, transport, unemployment, unemployment rate, voucher privatisation, wages, water Supply, workers) **Readership:** research specialists, analysts, governmental organisations, non-governmental organisations

Country Financial Accountability Assessment — Language: English **Frequency:** irregular **Content:** legal framework, institutional capacity and practices for the core financial control processes such as budgeting, treasury and cash management, accounting, financial reporting, internal control, internal audit, external audit and parliamentary oversight **Readership:** academics, financial experts, research specialists, analysts, foreign investors

Croatia Health Study — Language: English **Frequency:** irregular **Content:** review of the country's health system with recommendations to budget planning and targeted social protection **Readership:** medical specialists, governmental organisations, health institutes, analysts, research specialists

Cyprus

Statistical Service of Cyprus (CYSTAT)

Address: Michalakis Karaolis Str., Nicosia, 1444
Telephone: +357 22602129
Fax: +357 22661313
E-mail: cyd.sr@cytanet.com.cy
Website:

www.mof.gov.cy/mof/cystat/statistics.nsf/index_en/index _en?OpenDocument

Guides: all publications are available for sale from the premises of the Statistical Service in Nicosia or the Government Printing Office; when available in electronic form, publications can be downloaded free of charge; the library is open 7.30- 14.30 Monday to Friday.

Activity: responsible for the compilation and the publication of most of the official statistical data in Cyprus; CYSTAT is mainly concerned with the initiation, organisation and carrying out of various censuses, surveys and statistical enquiries of an economic, social or environmental content and the publication of the results with the intention of assisting both the government and the private sector in policy-making and the planning of their activities

Website(s) information:
Statistics and Research Department, Ministry of Finance — url: www.pio.gov.cy/dsr/index.html **Description:** key socio-economic data available online; online database with monthly foreign trade data; available in English and Greek **Coverage:** statistical themes includes: national accounts, short-term economic indicators, agriculture, foreign trade, financial sector statistics, industry, distributive trade, energy and environment statistics, transport, community, personal, business, demographics, health and education, labour force, wages, prices

Publication(s):
Construction and Housing Statistics — Language: English/Greek **Frequency:** annual **Content:** data on the construction industry and housing; analysis of sector distribution of output, capital formation, value added labour costs and materials

Cyprus External Trade Statistics — Language: English **Frequency:** quarterly **Content:** detailed quantity and value data on imports/arrivals classified by commodity and by main trading partner

Cyprus in Figures — Language: English **Frequency:** annual **Content:** recent set of data on the main social and economic indicators of Cyprus

Demographic Report — Language: English/Greek **Frequency:** annual **Content:** population estimates by month, end of the year estimates by five-year age groups, births and fertility statistics, deaths and mortality statistics, life tables, marriages, divorces and migration; analysis of recent demographic developments

Hotels and Restaurants Statistics — Language: English/Greek **Frequency:** annual **Content:** data on the basic economic characteristics of the sub-sector of restaurants, hotels and other eating and drinking places, such as employment, sales costs, value added, and investments

Labour Statistics — Language: English/Greek **Frequency:** annual **Content:** annual statistics on employment, unemployment, vacancies, government labour force, port workers, and employment by UK Authorities, UNFICYP and NAAFI, Cypriots working temporarily abroad, industrial disputes and industrial accidents

Transport Statistics — Language: English/Greek **Frequency:** annual **Content:** economic accounts of the broad transport, storage and communication sector; data on the various types and categories of motor vehicles registered and licensed; accidents and casualties; shipping statistics; civil aviation, postal services and telecommunications

Wholesale and Retail Trade Statistics — Language: English/Greek **Frequency:** annual **Content:** annual data on the economic characteristics of all the activities classified as wholesale and retail trade; the data relates to the value of sales, current costs, value added, investments, stocks and employment

Czech Republic

Ceská národní banka
Czech National Bank

Address: Na Príkope 28, Prague 1, 115 03
Telephone: +420 2 2441 1111
Fax: +420 2 2441 2404
E-mail: info@cnb.cz
Website: www.cnb.cz

Activity: acting as a central bank of the country and the supervisor of the financial market

Website(s) information:
Ceska Narodni Banka (CNB) *(Czech National Bank)* **— url:** www.cnb.cz **Description:** the site offers various financial statistical information in both Czech and English **Coverage:** financial indicators

Publication(s):
Bankovní statistika *(Banking Statistics)* **— Language:** Czech/English **Frequency:** monthly **Content:** financial statistics **Readership:** financial experts, economists, banks, research specialists, analysts

CNB Economic Reseach Bulletin — **Language:** English **Frequency:** irregular **Content:** findings of the research and analysis of the economy and financial sector **Readership:** economists, financial experts, governmental institutions, research specialists, analysts

Prímé zahranicní investice *(Foreign Direct Investment)* — **Language:** Czech/English **Frequency:** annual **Content:** foreign investments into the country (reports cover a five year period) **Readership:** economists, investors, businesses, governmental institutions, research specialists, analysts

Výrocná správa *(Annual Report)* — **Language:** Czech/English **Frequency:** annual **Content:** economic development and monetary policy, central bank and activities, monetary stability **Readership:** economists, financial experts, bankers, research specialists, analysts

Zprává o inflaci *(Inflation Report)* — **Language:** Czech/English **Frequency:** annual **Content:** inflation - covering annual and monthly percentage changes (available reports cover the period from 2002 to 2005) **Readership:** financial experts, governmental organisations, research specialists, analysts

Zpráva o stabilite bankovního sektoru *(Banking Sector Stability Report)* — **Language:** Czech/English **Frequency:** irregular **Content:** banking sector in general, macro-economic developments, risk assessment and monitoring **Readership:** economic and financial experts, research specialists, analysts

Zprává o výsledku hospodarení Ceské národní banky *(Czech National Bank Financial Report)* — **Language:** Czech **Frequency:** annual **Content:** financial indicators of the state financial system (available reports cover a period from 1999) **Readership:** financial experts, analysts, research specialists, governmental institutions

Ceský statistický úrad
Czech Statistical Office

Address: Na padesátém 81, Praha 10, 100 82
Telephone: +420 2 7405 1111
Fax: +420 2 7405 2304
E-mail: infoservis@czso.cz
Website: www.czso.cz

Activity: collecting and publishing statistical information

Website(s) information:
Ceský statistický úrad *(Czech Statistical Office)* — **url:** www.czso.cz **Description:** statistical information covering all socio-economic sectors; English version of the site and online catalogue of publications **Coverage:** socio-economic data

Publication(s):
Makroekonomické údaje *(Macroeconomic Indicators)* — **Language:** Czech/English **Frequency:** annual **Content:** macro-economy with statistics over a 10-year period **Readership:** economists, research specialists, analysts, governmental institutions, non-governmental organisations

Prumysl Ceské republiky *(Industry of the Czech Republic)* — **Language:** Czech/English **Frequency:** annual **Content:** industrial production figures **Readership:** investors, research specialists, analysts, businesses

Roèenka zahranièního obchodu Èeské republiky *(Report on External Trade of the Czech Republic)* — **Language:** Czech/English **Frequency:** monthly **Content:** external trade **Readership:** economists, businesses, investors, governmental institutions, research specialists, analysts

Spotreba paliv a energie v CR za rok *(Fuel and Energy Consumption in the CR)* — **Language:** Czech/English **Frequency:** annual **Content:** consumption of fuel and energy **Readership:** economists, governmental institutions, research specialists, analysts

Statistická roèenka Èeské republiky *(Statistical Yearbook of the Czech Republic)* — **Language:** Czech/English **Frequency:** annual **Content:** detailed socio-economic data of the country **Readership:** economists, businesses, investors, governmental institutions, non-governmental organisations, research specialists, analysts

Statistický Bulletin *(Statistical Bulletin)* — **Language:** Czech/English **Frequency:** quarterly **Content:** socio-economic indicators **Readership:** research specialists, analysts, governmental and non-governmental organisations

tatistický údajový mìsìèník Èeské republiky *(Monthly Statistics of the Czech Republic)* — **Language:** Czech/English **Frequency:** monthly **Content:** macro-economic and social indicators **Readership:** research specialists, analysts, governmental and non-governmental organisations

Tržní služby *(Market Services)* — **Language:** Czech/English **Frequency:** quarterly **Content:** services (market services, leisure services, real estate services, health, education, etc) **Readership:** economists, research specialists

Údaje o Ceské republice *(Czech Republic in Figures)* — **Language:** English **Frequency:** annual **Content:** main socio-economic indicators **Readership:** research specialists, analysts, governmental and non-governmental organisations

Vývoj ceské ekonomiky *(Czech Economic Development)* — **Language:** Czech/English **Frequency:** quarterly **Content:** detailed analysis of the country's economy **Readership:** economists, businesses, investors, governmental institutions, research specialists, analysts

Ministerstvo financí Ceské republiky
Ministry of Finance of the Czech Republic

Address: Letenkská 15, Prague 1, 118 10
Telephone: +420 2 5704 1111
Fax: +420 2 5704 2788
E-mail: podatelna@mfcr.cz
Website: www.mfcr.cz

Activity: creating and implementing state financial policy

Website(s) information:
Ministerstvo Financi Ceske Republiky *(Ministry of Finance of the Czech Republic)* — **url:** www.mfcr.cz **Description:** statistical information about the financial sector in the country (only some in English) **Coverage:** financial sector

Publication(s):
Hospodarení pojištoven *(Insurance Sector Development)* — **Frequency:** annual **Content:** insurance sector **Readership:** financial experts, insurance sector, research specialists, analysts

Makroekonomická predikce *(Macroeconomic Forecast)* — **Language:** Czech/English **Frequency:** irregular **Content:** macroeconomic development and analysis **Readership:** economists, governmental institutions, research specialists, analysts

Státní dluh *(State Debt)* — **Language:** Czech/English **Frequency:** irregular **Content:** foreign debt of the country **Readership:** economists, governmental institutions, research specialists, analysts

Ministerstvo Promusly a obchodu Ceske Republiky
Ministry of Industry and Trade of the Czech Republic

Address: Na Frantiku 32, Prague 1, 110 15
Telephone: +420 2 2485 1111
Fax: +420 2 2481 1089
E-mail: posta@mpo.cz
Website: www.mpo.cz

Activity: central body of the government administration responsible for commodity exchange, except issues of the Ministry of Agriculture

Website(s) information:
Ministry of Industry & Trade of the Czech Republic *(Ministry of Industry & Trade of the Czech Republic)* — **url:** www.mpo.cz **Coverage:** coal, electricity and oil statistics, including renewables, solid fuels, electricity and heat, oil and oil products, filling station statistics. Statistical surveys available on most industries

Publication(s):
Czech Construction Industry — **Language:** English **Content:** investment development, construction industry and construction materials. Includes macroeconomic indicators: employment and wages, housing, construction, building materials **Edition:** 2006

Ústav zemedelských a potravinárských informací
Institute of Agricultural and Food Information

Address: Slezská 7, Prague 2, 120 56
Telephone: +420 2 2701 0111
Fax: +420 2 2701 0114
E-mail: info@uzpi.cz
Website: www.uzpi.cz

Activity: providing the full transfer of departmental knowledge information from the sectors of agriculture, food production, nutrition, food safety, consumer protection, forestry and environment

Website(s) information:

Ústav zemedelských a potravinárských informací (Institute of Agricultural and Food Information) — **url:** www.agronavigator.cz **Description:** agricultural web portal offers various information about agriculture and food **Coverage:** agriculture and food

Publication(s):

Napojovy prumysl (Drinks Industry) — **Language:** Czech **Frequency:** irregular **Content:** covers main news on the national and international drinks industry **Readership:** drinks manufacturers, importers, exporters, distributors, analysts, economists

Potravinarske aktuality (Food News) — **Language:** Czech **Frequency:** irregular **Content:** information on the food industry (dairy industry, bakery products, sugar, canned meals and meat production) **Readership:** food manufacturers, importers, exporters, distributors, economists, research specialists, analysts

Denmark

Danmarks Eksportråd
Danish Export Council

Address:	Udenrigsministeriet, Asiatisk Plads 2, Copenhagen K, 1448
Telephone:	+45 33 920 000
Fax:	+45 32 540 533
E-mail:	um@um.dk
Website:	www.um.dk

Guides: reports on sectors and Danish companies abroad are available free online

Activity: promotes export and Danish industries abroad

Website(s) information:

Danmarks Eksportråd (Danish Export Council) — **url:** www.um.dk **Description:** provides downloadable publications on Danish export in a variety of sectors **Coverage:** contains data on turn over and production on Danish exporting companies

Danmarks Nationalbank
National Bank of Denmark

Address:	Havnegade 5, Copenhagen K, 1093
Telephone:	+45 3363 6363
Fax:	+45 3363 7103
E-mail:	info@nationalbanken.dk
Website:	www.nationalbanken.dk

Guides: report and accounts available free of charge in Danish at www.nationalbanken.dk

Activity: ensure efficient and secure production and distribution of currency; contribute to efficiency and stability in the payment and clearing systems and in financial markets; act as banker to the central government; prepare reliable and relevant financial statistics; prepare and communicate credible standpoints on economic and financial issues with relation to Denmark's National bank's objectives

Website(s) information:

Danmarks Nationalbank (National Bank of Denmark) — **url:** www.nationalbanken.dk **Coverage:** includes statistical data on market rates, balance sheets, securities, banking sector, investment, direct debt, etc. Publications offered free on the web site include: Report and Accounts; Monetary Review; Financial Statistics; Working Papers

Publication(s):

Coins and Banknotes of Denmark — **Language:** English/Danish **Content:** coins and banknotes of Denmark and how the coins and banknotes are manufactured **Edition:** 2005

Danish Government Borrowing and Debt — **Language:** English **Frequency:** annual **Content:** publication describes the development during the preceding year and reports on issues of relevance to debt management

Financial Stability — **Language:** English **Frequency:** annual **Content:** Financial Stability assesses financial stability in Denmark, with emphasis on financial institutions, markets and payment systems. The report consists of two parts. The first part starts with an analysis of the development in the financial sector, with emphasis on the banking institutions. This is followed by a chapter on the development in the corporate sector and the households. Next the developments in the financial markets are reviewed and finally follow a chapter about the framework for Financial Sta

Mona — **Language:** English **Content:** Danish economy; Inflation, wages and prices; Balance of payments, foreign trade and external debt; Economic activity and employment; Public finances and fiscal policy; Models **Edition:** 2004

Monetary Policy in Denmark — **Language:** English **Frequency:** irregular **Content:** monetary and foreign-exchange policy; monetary conditions; foreign-exchange policy and cooperation; monetary policy instruments; money and currency markets **Edition:** 2003 Second Ed.

Monetary Review — **Language:** English **Frequency:** quarterly **Content:** recent economic and monetary trends

Nyt (News) — **Language:** English/Danish **Frequency:** monthly **Content:** presents key financial statistics produced by the Nationalbank

Online Statistics Database — **Language:** English **Frequency:** irregular **Content:** Danmarks Nationalbank's statistics database, which contains additional and longer time series compared to the statistics publications. You can e.g. find more detailed breakdowns by sector, instrument, country or maturity. You can search and define tables, which you can download in e.g. excel format or have shown with a graph
Tables for: Balance-sheet statistics for investment associations; External financial payments; Securities statistics; Balance and flow statistics of the consolidated MFI sector; Balance and flow statistics of mortgage-credit institutes; Balance and flow statistics of banks; Foreign direct investments
Quarterly financial accounts for Denmark; Exchange rates; Quarterly flow statistics on direct investments

Payment Systems in Denmark — **Language:** English **Content:** describes various aspects of payment systems: roles of central banks in payment systems; reviews the historical background of payment systems, including the background of the involvement of central banks; general principles and risks in various types of payment and securities settlement systems; Danish payments infrastructure and Danmarks Nationalbank's role regarding these systems **Edition:** 2005

Report and Accounts — **Language:** English **Frequency:** annual **Content:** Danmarks Nationalbank's Report and Accounts comprise a presentation and description of the bank's Accounts during the year, and the Report of the Board of Governors

Danmarks Statistik
Statistics Denmark

Address:	Sejrøgade 11, Copenhagen, 2100
Telephone:	+45 3917 3917
Fax:	+45 3117 3999
E-mail:	dst@dst.dk
Website:	www.dst.dk
	www.statbank.dk

Guides: publications may be purchased from Statistics Denmark or from Danish booksellers. Information about the nearest bookseller is obtainable from Statistics Denmark's Publications Service, phone + 45 3917 3020

Activity: national statistics body; produces and disseminates statistics on social and economic trends in society

Website(s) information:

StatBank Danmark (Statistics Bank of Denmark) — **url:** www.statbank.dk **Description:** information on products and services provided by Statistics Denmark: latest statistical releases; online publications and socio-economics statistics **Coverage:** socio-economic data on Denmark can be found by downloading the annual publication Statistical Yearbook, or by accessing different sections such as: Data on Denmark; key indicators; data on municipalities; key figures for transport; and main indicators (subscription required)

Publication(s):

Agriculture — **Language:** English/Danish **Frequency:** annual **Content:** agricultural and horticultural censuses, production and prices, cereal stocks, fruit and berries, feeding stuff consumption, livestock density, stocks of pigs and cattle, dairy products, commercial fertilizers, greenhouses, factor incomes, capital formation, interest payments and debts, volume and price indices and forest felling

Earnings — **Language:** English **Content:** Indices of average earnings at the level of industries in the private and public sectors; Earnings in the private sector; Earnings in the central government; Earnings in the local government; Total labour costs in the private sector

Education and Culture — **Language:** English/Danish **Content:** Cohort analysis of education; Education and employment; Adult education and continuing training; Number of students

Environment and Energy — **Language:** English **Content:** covers: environmental state of air and water, flora and fauna, environmental effects caused by agriculture, forestry, fishing, manufacturing, mining and quarrying, energy consumption, transport, waste water, refuse dumps and chemical substances. Environmental protection, municipal inspection, nature and environmental monitoring, recycling and environmental economics

External Trade — **Language:** English **Content:** total external trade - incl. latest month; Indices on total external trade - incl. latest month; Imports /exports /trade balance (SITC categories, country); Imports by end-use (BEC) and country

General Economic Statistics — **Language:** Danish/English **Content:** accounts statistics, business units registered for VAT settlement, registration of new business units, turnover in non-agricultural industries, employment in businesses and bankruptcies

Incomes, Consumption and Prices — **Language:** English/Danish **Frequency:** monthly **Content:** covers possession of consumer durables, consumption of alcoholic beverages, consumer price index, index of net retail prices, whole price index and price index for raw materials, sales of property, bankruptcies, incomes and wealth

Labour Market — **Language:** English **Content:** labour force; Labour force survey; Population by level of education and employment; Unemployment, final average figures; Unemployment, in percentage

Manufacturing Industries — **Language:** English **Content:** raw material and industrial services; Manufacturers sale divided among goods and sector of Industry; Industrial production and new orders statistics; Tendency survey for manufacturing industries; Stock changes in manufacturing industries and wholesale; Historical figures - discontinued data series

Money and Capital Market — **Language:** English **Content:** shares and bonds; Interest rates and share prices; Lending and deposits, banks and bond issuing institutions; Accounts; Non-bank consumer credit and leasing; International statistics

National Accounts and Balance of Payments — **Language:** English **Content:** balance of payments; Annual national accounts, ESA95; Quarterly national accounts; Environmental accounts

Population and Elections — **Language:** English **Content:** population size, vital statistics, foreign nationals, births, deaths, internal and external migrations, marriages, divorces, families, households, adoptions, legal abortions, mortality and occupation, fertility surveys and population forecasts

Public Finance — **Language:** English **Content:** government finances; Taxation; Financial accounts;

Retail Trade Index — **Language:** English **Content:** Retail trade index for 2000-2006 **Edition:** 2006

Services sector — **Language:** English/Danish **Content:** index of retail prices, holiday and business trips, nights spent at camping sites, hotels and youth hostels, travellers' currency, rented holiday dwellings, yachting and product statistics for the services sectors; Internet usage in the population; Public sector use of ICT

Social Conditions, Health and Justice — **Language:** English/Danish **Content:** housing benefits; Family allowance and child benefits; Hospitalizations; Justice; Social pensions; Health insurance; Payments of child maintenance

Statistical Yearbook — **Language:** English/Danish **Frequency:** annual **Content:** contains statistics and trends in Denmark, the Faroe Islands and Greenland. There is also a chapter on international statistics. Period coverage is over the previous five years.

Grønlands Statistik
Statistics Greenland

Address:	PO Box 1025, Nuuk, 3900, Greenland
Telephone:	+45 345 564
Fax:	+45 322 954
E-mail:	stat@gh.gl
Website:	www.statgreen.gl

Guides: publications are available on a free database and data can be exported in several file formats

Activity: publish detailed statistical information on the Greenlandic society

Website(s) information:

Grønlands Statistiks *(Statistics Greenland)* — **url:** www.statgreen.gl **Description:** provides a database with socio-economic statistics and downloadable publications **Coverage:** contains data on labour market, population and housing, fishing, exports, national accounts, elections, health, tourism, crime, environment and energy

Publication(s):

Greenland in Figures — **Language:** English **Frequency:** annual **Content:** contains socio-economic data on Greenland

Statistisk Årbog *(Statistical Yearbook)* — **Language:** Danish/Kalaallisut **Frequency:** annual **Content:** contains socio-economic data on Greenland

Økonomiministeriet
Ministry of Economic Affairs

Address:	Slotsholmsgade 10-12, Copenhagen, 1216
Telephone:	+45 33 923 350
Fax:	+45 33 123 778
E-mail:	oem@oem.dk
Website:	www.oem.dk

Guides: publications are downloadable on website

Activity: works to improve the conditions for growth in Denmark, through economic analyses and suggestions for policy initiatives in areas imperative to economic growth

Website(s) information:

Økonomiministeriet *(Ministry of Economic Affairs)* — **url:** www.oem.dk **Description:** provides macro-economic indicators on the Danish economy including key figures and online publications in English **Coverage:** contains macro-economic statistics, including use and supply of goods and services, key figures of the Danish economy, comparison between the present forecast and economic surveys

Estonia

Eesti Pank
Bank of Estonia

Address:	Estonia pst. 13, Tallinn, 15095
Telephone:	+372 668 0719
Fax:	+372 668 0836
E-mail:	info@epbe.ee
Website:	www.eestipank.info/frontpage/en

Guides: publications catalogue available online

Activity: participating in the economic policy of Estonia via pursuing an independent monetary policy, consulting the government, and continuing international cooperation; maintaining financial stability in Estonia by shaping financial sector policy and sustaining reliable and well-functioning payment systems; arranging cash circulation in Estonia; preparing for equal partnership with the other central banks of the Euro area in developing a common economic and single monetary policy

Website(s) information:

Eesti Pank *(Bank of Estonia)* — **url:** www.eestipank.info/frontpage/en **Description:** access to different publications covering the latest developments and trends in Estonia's economy and financial climate. Includes access to statistics and data collected by the bank and other official organisations **Coverage:** participating in the economic policy of Estonia via pursuing an independent monetary policy, consulting the government, and continuing international cooperation; maintaining financial stability in Estonia by shaping financial sector policy and sustaining reliable and well-functioning payment systems; arranging cash circulation in Estonia; preparing for equal partnership with the other central banks of the Euro area in developing a common economic and single monetary policy

Publication(s):

Ajakiri Kroon ja Majandus — **Language:** English/Estonian **Frequency:** quarterly **Content:** quarterly newspaper; banking news; investments; etc

Eesti 2006 aasta I kvartali esialgne maksebilanss *(Estonian Preliminary Balance of Payments for the First Quarter of 2006)* — **Language:** English/Estonian **Frequency:** quarterly **Content:** goods; services; income; current and capital transfers; direct investment; portfolio investment; other investment; reserve assets

Eesti majanduse ülevaade Eesti Panga aastaaruandes *(Estonian Economy)* — **Language:** English/Estonian **Frequency:** annual **Content:** non-financial sector; Inflation; financial sector; institutional development

Eesti Panga aasta finantsaruanne *(Financial Statements of Eesti Bank)* — **Language:** English/Estonian **Frequency:** annual **Content:** financial statements, balance sheet, profit and loss account, statement of changes in equity and the respective appendices

Lähenemisaruanne *(Convergence Report)* — **Language:** English/Estonian **Frequency:** irregular **Content:** country examinations; framework for analysis; country summaries

Rahapoliitiline Ülevaade *(Monetary Developments & Policy Survey)* — **Language:** English/Estonian **Frequency:** annual **Content:** economic policy summary; economic developments; inflation; monetary and financial sector; economic forecast; etc

Tööturu ülevaade *(Labour Market Review)* — **Language:** English/Estonian **Frequency:** annual **Content:** labour supply and demand; employment; vacancies; unemployment; labour costs and price pressures; real unit labour costs; development of labour costs by sectors; Estonian labour market

Eesti Riiklik Autoregistrikeskus
Estonian Motor Vehicle Registration Centre

Address:	Mäepealse 19, Tallinn, 12618
Telephone:	+372 620 1200
Fax:	+372 620 1201
E-mail:	press@ark.ee
Website:	www.ark.ee

Guides: publications are available free of charge
Activity: the registration of motor vehicles and their trailers, maintaining the register and archives

Website(s) information:

Eesti Riiklik Autoregistrikeskus *(Estonian Motor Vehicle Registration Centre)* — **url:** www.ark.ee **Description:** the registration of motor vehicles and their trailers, register and archives **Coverage:** provides information on driving licences and examinations; vehicle registration; certificate of registration; provides overview and free publications; detailed contacts

Publication(s):

ARK Aastaraamat *(ARK Annual Report)* — **Language:** English/Estonian **Frequency:** annual **Content:** statistics; structure; registered cars; motorcycles registered; classification of vehicles by administrative territories

EV Välisministeerium
Estonian Ministry of Foreign Affairs

Address:	Islandi väljak 1, Tallinn, 15049, Estonia
Telephone:	+372 637 7000
Fax:	+372 637 7099
E-mail:	vminfo@vm.ee
Website:	www.vm.ee

Guides: publications are available free online
Activity: foreign relations and diplomacy

Website(s) information:

Estonian Ministry of Foreign Affairs — **url:** www.vm.ee **Description:** access to a series of publications covering the national economy, business environment, political and financial structure, and trade matters with main partners. Regularly updated titles include: "Estonian Review" (weekly); "Estonia Today"; and the "Estonian Economy". Site is available in Estonian, Russian, Finnish, German, Swedish, Spanish, French, and English **Coverage:** provides up-to-date information on foreign relations; free publications and yearbooks; available statistics; detailed information on Estonian embassies

Publication(s):

Economy in Facts and Figures — **Language:** English **Frequency:** irregular **Content:** economic activity; statistics; tables; main export and import

Keskkonnaministeerium
Ministry of the Environment

Address:	Narva mnt 7a, Tallinn, 15172
Telephone:	+372 6262 802
Fax:	+372 626 2801
E-mail:	min@envir.ee
Website:	www.envir.ee

Guides: publications are available online
Activity: to create such preconditions and conditions for preservation of natural biodiversity and a clean environment and to ensure that natural resources are used economically

Website(s) information:

Keskkonnaministeerium *(Ministry of the Environment)* — **url:** www.envir.ee **Coverage:** provides statistics about environment in Estonia

Publication(s):

Aastaraamat Mets *(Forestry Yearbook)* — **Language:** Estonian **Content:** forest reserves; property; deforestation

ISPA Strategy Paper for the Environmental Sector — **Language:** English **Content:** water resources; water supply; wastewater; air quality; waste management; etc

Metsandusliku ja puidutöötlemisalase hariduse hetkeseis ja tulevik *(Forest Management and Wood Processing Industry: Education Now and the Future)* — **Language:** Estonian **Content:** tables; overview; statistics; etc

Konkurentsiamet
Competition Board

Address:	Lõkke 4, Tallinn, 15184
Telephone:	+372 680 3942
Fax:	+372 680 3943
E-mail:	compet@konkurentsiamet.ee
Website:	www.konkurentsiamet.ee

Activity: to examine and analyse the status of competition in different markets for goods and make recommendations for improvements

Website(s) information:

Konkurentsiamet *(Competition Board)* — **url:** www.konkurentsiamet.ee **Coverage:** competition laws and analysis

Publication(s):

Aastaraamat *(Annual Report)* — **Language:** English/Estonian **Frequency:** annual **Content:** age of employees; length of service; level of education; waste and package sector; analysis of prices

Majandus-ja Kommunikatsiooniministeerium
Ministry of Economic Affairs and Communications

Address:	Harju 11, Tallinn, 15072
Telephone:	+372 625 6342
Fax:	+372 631 3660
E-mail:	info@mkm.ee
Website:	www.mkm.ee

Guides: publications are available online

Activity: active in industry, trade, energy, housing, building, transport (including transport infrastructure, carriage, transit, logistics and public transport), traffic management (including traffic on railways, highways, streets, waterways and airways), increasing road safety and reducing environmental hazards; informatics, telecommunications, postal service and tourism; competition surveillance, consumer protection, export promotion and trade safeguards

Website(s) information:
Majandus-ja Kommunikatsiooniministeerium *(Ministry of Economic Affairs and Communications)* — **url:** www.mkm.ee **Coverage:** economic status; transport; energy; communications; foreign trade

Publication(s):
Access of Enterprises to Venture Financing in Estonia — **Language:** English **Content:** government funding; guarantee fund; expansion funds; Investor incentives; tables; etc

Eesti Energeetika (Estonian Energy) — **Language:** English/Estonian **Frequency:** irregular **Content:** gives a review about development of Estonian energy during last five years; tables; statistics; etc

Turism Eestis (Tourism in Estonia) — **Language:** English **Frequency:** irregular **Content:** trends; visitors; tables; statistics; etc

---

Põllumajandusministeerium
Ministry of Agriculture

Address: Lai 39/41, Tallinn, 15056
Telephone: +372 625 6101
Fax: +372 625 6200
E-mail: pm@agri.ee
Website: www.agri.ee

Guides: publications are available online
Activity: to provide conditions for the sustainable and diverse development of Estonian rural development, agriculture, and fishing industry

Website(s) information:
Põllumajandusministeerium *(Ministry of Agriculture)* — **url:** www.agri.ee **Description:** available in English and Estonian **Coverage:** agricultural census; results of selected agricultural holdings; trade; population; wages and salaries, all main social and economic indicators

Publication(s):
Agricultural Market and Trade — **Language:** English **Content:** export and import of agricultural products; foreign trade; tables; statistics

Agriculture and the Development of Rural Life — **Language:** English **Frequency:** irregular **Content:** meat production; alcohol production and market; agricultural research; statistics; tables

Annual report on agriculture — **Language:** English **Frequency:** annual **Content:** overview of the main trends in the agricultural sector

Eesti maaelu arengu strateegia 2007-2013 (Estonian Agriculture Strategy Plan 2007-2013) — **Language:** Estonian **Content:** statistics; tables; income; export; import; etc

Estonian Agriculture, Rural Economy And Food Industry — **Language:** English **Content:** economic results of agriculture; fishing; forest; statistics; tables; etc

Estonian Forestry — **Language:** English **Content:** forestry, wood processing industry, pulp and paper industry and furniture industry; tables; statistics

Estonian Rural Development Plan — **Language:** English **Content:** air pollution; animal production; statistics; tables; water; etc

Kalapüük ja varud (Fishing and supplies) — **Language:** Estonian **Content:** overview about Estonian fishing and supplies; statistics; tables; etc

Tööhõivest maal (Employment in country) — **Language:** Estonian **Content:** overview about employment in country; statistics; tables; etc

---

Rahandusministeerium
Ministry of Finance

Address: Suur-Ameerika 1, Tallinn, 15006
Telephone: +372 611 3558
Fax: +372 696 6810
E-mail: info@fin.ee
Website: www.fin.ee

Guides: free catalogue of publications (English and Estonian) is available from the above address

Activity: plans for and supervises the implementation of the Government's macroeconomic, fiscal and economic reform policies

Website(s) information:
Rahandusministeerium *(Ministry of Finance)* — **url:** www.fin.ee **Description:** access to online publication "Economic Review", providing a general portrait of the present socio-economic, political and business climate in Estonia. Includes analysis and data on: latest GDP growth trends; sales and real growth of the manufacturing industry; growth forecasts for Estonia's main trade partners; balance of trade and services; changes in exports and imports; private consumption; gross fixed capital formation; employment; wages and productivity; price indices; general government deficit; and forecasts for selected indicators **Coverage:** GDP; wages; productivity; forecasts

Publication(s):
2006 aasta kevadine majandusprognoos (Macroeconomic Forecast of the Ministry of Finance of Estonia 2006) — **Language:** English/Estonian **Frequency:** irregular **Content:** economic; unemployment rate; employment; exports and imports; government budget balance; forecast

Eesti Vabariigi Valitsuse poolt võetud laenud (Debt Details of the Central Government of Estonia) — **Language:** English/Estonian **Frequency:** irregular **Content:** base rates and margins; loan balance; interest rates

Estonian Economic Survey — **Language:** English/Estonian **Frequency:** monthly **Content:** external environment; prices; economic sectors; financial sector; state budget

Overview of the Financial Assets and Liabilities of the State Treasury — **Language:** English **Frequency:** irregular **Content:** financial assets, state treasury

Rahandusministeeriumi strateegiline arengukava 2006-2009 (Ministry of Finance Strategic Development Plan 2006-2009) — **Language:** Estonian **Frequency:** irregular **Content:** financial statistics; financial plans; bureau of customs statistics; organisation development

Rahandusministeeriumi strateegiline arengukava 2007-2010 (Ministry of Finance Strategic Development Plan 2007-2010) — **Language:** Estonian **Frequency:** irregular **Content:** financial statistics; financial plans; bureau of customs statistics; organization development

Tagasimakstud laenud ja riigigarantiid (Repaid Loans and Guaranteed Debt) — **Language:** English/Estonian **Frequency:** irregular **Content:** currency; repaid; interest and commitment paid; etc

---

Ravimiamet
State Agency of Medicines

Address: Nooruse 1, Tartu, 50411
Telephone: +372 737 41 40
Fax: +372 737 41 42
E-mail: sam@sam.ee
Website: www.sam.ee

Guides: publications are available free online
Activity: marketing authorisation and quality control of medicinal products including biological products, evaluation and approval of applications for clinical trials, import and export authorisation of medicinal products, control of licit use of psychotropic and narcotic substances, control over precursors, drug information, advertising and promotion control and pharmaceutical inspection

Website(s) information:
Ravimiamet *(State Agency of Medicines)* — **url:** www.sam.ee **Coverage:** provides an overview and statistics (drugs; clinical trials; etc)

Publication(s):
Eesti ravimistatistika aastaraamat (Estonian Statistics on Medicines Yearbook) — **Language:** English/Estonian **Content:** overview; statistics

Ravimiamet (State Agency of Medicines) — **Language:** Estonian **Frequency:** annual **Content:** statistics; tables; overview of the market

---

Sideamet
Estonian National Communications Board

Address: Ädala 2, Tallinn, 10614
Telephone: +372 693 1154
Fax: +372 693 1155
E-mail: sideamet@sa.ee/postbox@sa.ee
Website: www.sa.ee

Guides: publications are available free online

Activity: creates the necessary conditions for the development of electronic communications and postal sectors, promotion of the development of electronic communications networks, publicly available postal and communications services without giving preference to specific technologies and ensuring of the protection of the interests of users of telephone, mobile telephone, data, international telephony, cable distribution and postal services by promoting free competition, quality of service and the purposeful and fair planning, assignment and use of radio frequencies and numbering as well as exercising the supervision in all sectors of its activity

Website(s) information:

Sideamet *(Estonian National Communications Board)* — **url:** www.sa.ee
Description: communications sector industry information also available in English **Coverage:** provides general information about communications sectors in Estonia

Publication(s):

Aastaraamat *(Annual Report)* — **Language:** English/Estonian **Frequency:** annual **Content:** wholesale market; international calls; market overview; connection fees and monthly fees; retail market overview; access to communication networks enabling broadband connection; mobile telephone numbers; overview of Estonia post cost accounting; statistics; tables

Estonian National Communications Board over 10 Years — **Language:** English **Content:** budget; salaries; travel expenses; administrative expenses; investments; etc

Siseministeerium
Ministry of Internal Affairs

Address: Pikk 61, Tallinn, 15065
Telephone: +372 612 5008
Fax: +372 612 5010
E-mail: sisemin@sisemin.gov.ee
Website: www.sisemin.gov.ee

Guides: publications are available online
Activity: internal security; population; local government and regional development

Website(s) information:

Sisministeerium *(Ministry of Internal Affairs)* — **url:** www.sisemin.gov.ee **Coverage:** provides an statistical publications (available free); information about European union; etc

Publication(s):

Analysis of the Development of Estonian Local Government — **Language:** English **Content:** population and number of municipalities; public sector in Estonia; city budgets; etc

Kohalikud Omavalitsused Eestis *(Local Governments in Estonia)* — **Language:** English/Estonian **Frequency:** irregular **Content:** Democracy and participation at local level; international relations in local government area; local government finances; etc

Maareform Eestis *(Territorial reform in Estonia 1998)* — **Language:** English/Estonian **Content:** municipal finances; municipal co-operation; overview; statistics; tables

Siseministeeriumi tutvustav brosüür *(Ministry of the Interior of the Republic of Estonia)* — **Language:** English **Frequency:** irregular **Content:** gives overview what is ministry internal affairs and what they do; etc

Sotsiaalministeerium
Ministry of Social Affairs

Address: Gonsiori 29, Tallinn, 15027
Telephone: +372 626 9301
Fax: +372 699 2209
E-mail: info@sm.ee
Website: www.sm.ee

Guides: publications are available online
Activity: drafting and implementation of plans to resolve state social issues; managing of public health protection and medical care, employment, the labour market and working environment, social security, social insurance and social welfare, promotion of gender equality

Website(s) information:

Sotsiaalministeerium *(Ministry of Social Affairs)* — **url:** www.sm.ee **Coverage:** provides information, statistics, overviews and publications on health; labour market; social insurance; etc

Publication(s):

Eesti täiskasvanud rahvastiku tervisekäitumise *(Health Behavior among the Estonian Adult Population)* — **Language:** Estonian/English **Content:** health status; smoking; dietary habits; consumption of alcohol and drugs; body mass index, physical exercise; quality of water, ambient noise; use of health services and medicines

Haigestumise majanduslikud tagajärjed Eestis *(Economic Consequences of Ill-Health in Estonia)* — **Language:** English **Frequency:** irregular **Content:** population structure; chronic disease prevalence; Distribution of total life years lost (DALY) by gender and diseases; tables, statistics; etc

Haigestumusinfo võrdlev uuring tervishoiu statistilise aastaaruandluse ja Eesti Haigekassa raviarvete andmebaasi põhjal *(Comparative Analysis of Morbidity on the Basis of Annual Statistical Reports and the Database of Estonian Health Insurance Fund)* — **Language:** English/Estonian **Content:** data collection and methods; results; statistics; tables

HIV/AIDS-i temaatikaga seotud teadmised, hoiakud ja käitumine Eesti noorte hulgas *(Knowledge, Additudes and Behaviour Related to HIV/AIDS Among Estonian Youth)* — **Language:** English/Estonian **Content:** socio-demographic data; overview of the implementation of the research; use of contraceptives; major risk groups; sexual activity

Impact of the European Union Common Pension Objectives on the Estonian Pension System — **Language:** English **Content:** pension overview; tables; statistics

Lapsed ja Eesti ühiskond *(Children and Estonian Society)* — **Language:** Estonian **Frequency:** irregular **Content:** government support; pocket money; trends; statistics; tables; etc

Nordic/Baltic Health Statistics — **Language:** English **Frequency:** irregular **Content:** statistics and tables on population and health problems

Potential of Estonia's Working Age Population to Work in the Countries of the European Union — **Language:** English **Content:** number of people wanting to work abroad; a socio-demographic picture of people wanting to work abroad; labour market situation; tables; overview; etc

Prostitutsioon - kas ühiskondlik probleem? *(Prostitution - a social problem?)* — **Language:** English/Estonian **Content:** criminalisation; prohibition; abolition; analysis method and samples; analysis results; statistics; tables; etc

Sotsiaalsektor arvudes *(Social Sector in Figures)* — **Language:** English/Estonian **Frequency:** annual **Content:** population, health care; wages and salaries; working environment; social welfare

Sotsiaaltöö ajakirjad *(Social Work journals)* — **Language:** Estonian **Frequency:** bi-monthly **Content:** overview on social work in Estonia; statistics; tables; articles; contact numbers

Tervishoiustatistika Aastaraamat *(Health Care Statistics Yearbook)* — **Language:** English/Estonian **Frequency:** annual **Content:** hospital discharges; day care; doctors' hourly wage; statistics; tables

Towards a Balanced Society-Women and Men in Estonia 2000 — **Language:** English **Frequency:** irregular **Content:** equal opportunities for men and women; health; income; gendered leisure; wage ratios; etc

Statistikaamet
Statistical Office of Estonia

Address: Endla 15, Tallinn, 15174
Telephone: +372 6259 300
Fax: +372 6259 370
E-mail: stat@stat.ee
Website: www.stat.ee

Guides: free catalogue of publications (English and Estonian) is available from the above address
Activity: collecting data; producing and publishing objective official statistics for public institutions, business and research spheres, international organisations and individuals

Website(s) information:

Statistical Office of Estonia — **url:** www.stat.ee **Description:** information on products and services provided by the institute, including catalogue of publications; latest releases; information service; population census; information centre, request for information, news releases, order for information, the web site, public database, ordering of foreign trade and industrial statistics and statistics on Estonia. Online databases and regional development database which includes environment, economy, population and social life **Coverage:** main socio-economic indicators including statistics on population; gross domestic product; estimated economic growth; consumer price index; producer price index; export/import price index; average monthly gross wages and salaries; environment, social life, unemployment; industrial sales; retail trade sales; trade balance

Publication(s):

Aastaaruanne *(Annual Report)* — **Language:** English/Estonian **Frequency:** annual **Content:** statistics on products and consumers; population; socio-economic; salaries; macroeconomic; general government and financial sector; foreign trade; enterprise; agricultural; environment and sustainable development; regional

Eesti ettevõtja ja tema sissetulek *(Self-Employed in Estonia and their Income)* — **Language:** English/Estonian **Frequency:** irregular **Content:** self-employed and employees by sex, main economic activities of the self-employed, self-employed and employees by region, self-employed and employees by age, self-employed and employees by type of household, self-employed and employees by income quintiles, self-employed and employees by quintiles of earned income

Eesti Põhilised Sotsiaal- ja Majandusnäitajad *(Main Social and Economic Indicators of Estonia)* — **Language:** English/Estonian **Frequency:** monthly **Content:** social and economic indicators

Eesti rahvamajanduse arvepidamine *(National Accounts of Estonia)* — **Language:** English/Estonian **Frequency:** annual **Content:** contains main indicators on the national accounts of Estonia: the gross domestic product (GDP) compiled by production, expenditure and income approach, cost components of the value added of institutional sectors, gross fixed capital formation by institutional sectors and economic activity, structure of private consumption expenditure, accounts of institutional sectors

Eesti statistika aastaraamat *(Statistical Yearbook of Estonia)* — **Language:** English/Estonian **Frequency:** annual **Content:** annual statistics on socio-economic life and environment

Eesti Statistika Kuukiri *(Monthly Bulletin of Estonian Statistics)* — **Language:** English/Estonian **Frequency:** monthly **Content:** provides short-term statistics; environment and socio-economic

Ehitushinnaindeks *(Construction Price Index)* — **Language:** English/Estonian **Frequency:** quarterly **Content:** buildings (detached houses, apartment buildings, industrial and office buildings) and by resources (labour force, building machines and materials); repair and reconstruction work price indices

Energiabilanss *(Energy Balance)* — **Language:** English/Estonian **Frequency:** annual **Content:** statistics on energy production and consumption, exports and imports as well as prices for the year with comparison with previous years

Estonia, Latvia, Lithuania in Figures — **Language:** English **Frequency:** annual **Content:** statistics on economic and social conditions

Ettevõtete majandusnäitajad *(Financial Statistics of Enterprises)* — **Language:** English/Estonian **Frequency:** annual **Content:** enterprises demography; IT use in business; research and development; enterprise groups; foreign-controlled enterprises in Estonia

Ettevõtlus *(Business)* — **Language:** English/Estonian **Frequency:** quarterly **Content:** short-term statistics on the economic situation of enterprises

Ettevõtlus Eestis *(Business in Estonia)* — **Language:** English/Estonian **Frequency:** irregular **Content:** pocket-sized reference book provides data on general indicators of enterprises (number of enterprises, number of persons employed, turnover, balance sheet total, investments, value added, etc

Keskkond *(Environment)* — **Language:** English/Estonian **Frequency:** annual **Content:** analytical overview, emissions into the air, waste generation, wastewater discharge, use and emissions of chemicals and ozone depleting substances

Keskkond arvudes *(Environment in Figures)* — **Language:** English/Estonian **Frequency:** annual **Content:** emission of pollutants, use of natural resources, etc; ph level of precipitation, pollution of air, etc; pollution prevention and control expenditures, includes tables and diagrams

Keskkonnakaitsekulutused *(Environment Protection Expenditures)* — **Language:** English/Estonian **Frequency:** annual **Content:** public sector (Government of the Republic, municipality and city governments and Environmental Investments Centre) environmental investments, current expenditures on environment protection, expenditures on research and development and the receipts from environmental protection

Leibkonna elujärg *(Household Living)* — **Language:** English/Estonian **Frequency:** annual **Content:** analytical overview of households, their economic situation, living conditions and expenditure in the current year and dynamics during the last ten years

Linnad ja vallad arvudes *(Cities and Rural Municipalities in Figures)* — **Language:** English/Estonian **Frequency:** annual **Content:** includes analysis and comparisons reflecting the development of cities and rural municipalities on the basis of several indicators

Monthly Bulletin of Estonian Statistics *(Eesti Statistika Kuukiri)* —

Naised ja mehed *(Women and Men)* — **Language:** English/Estonian **Frequency:** irregular **Content:** demographic aspects, education, time use, income, poverty, lifestyle, labour market

Põllumajandus *(Agriculture)* — **Language:** English/Estonian **Frequency:** annual **Content:** data on economic indicators of agriculture and supply-balance sheets of agricultural products, agricultural land use, areas under and yields of field crops, fruits and berries, number and production of livestock, use of mineral and organic fertilizers

Põllumajandus arvudes *(Agriculture in Figures)* — **Language:** English/Estonian **Frequency:** annual **Content:** financial statistics of agriculture and supply-balance sheets of agricultural products, agricultural land use, areas under and yields of field crops, fruits and berries, number and production of livestock, use of fertilisers

Põllumajanduslikud majapidamised *(Agricultural Holdings)* — **Language:** English/Estonian **Frequency:** annual **Content:** land use, animal husbandry, agricultural machinery and equipment, labour force and other activities of agricultural holdings

Rahvastik *(Population)* — **Language:** English/Estonian **Frequency:** annual **Content:** population and population composition

Sissetulek ja elamistingimused *(Income and Living Conditions)* — **Language:** English/Estonian **Frequency:** annual **Content:** living conditions of households, care of children, safety, social contacts and health of household members

Töötasu *(Earnings)* — **Language:** English/Estonian **Frequency:** annual **Content:** full-time and part-time employees; male and female employees by group of earnings; separate part deals with hourly earnings of male and female employees by major groups of occupations and economic activities; hourly earnings of other occupational groups as a proportion of legislators', senior officials' and managers' hourly earnings and women's hourly earnings as a proportion of men's hourly earnings

Tööturg *(Labour Market)* — **Language:** English/Estonian **Frequency:** annual **Content:** labour market by sex, age, education, place of residence and ethnic nationality

Transport Side *(Transport Communications)* — **Language:** English/Estonian **Frequency:** annual **Content:** statistics on transport and communications; road network, vehicles, aircraft and vessels registered in registers; transport of passengers and goods carried by road, by sea, by inland waterways; railway and air transport enterprises; passenger and shipping traffic and transport of goods through ports; ship accidents, traffic accidents on public railways; road traffic accidents, persons killed and injured; the length of pipelines and the amount of gas transported via pipelines; postal and telecommunication

Turism/Majutus *(Tourism/Accommodation)* — **Language:** English/Estonia **Frequency:** annual **Content:** foreign visitors' motivation and expenditure, tourism of Estonian population, capacity of accommodation establishments, number of tourists in accommodation establishments; sales, exports and imports of tourist services, domestic and international tourism, foreign visitors, outgoing visitors and overnight visitors served by travel agencies and tour operators, etc

Väliskaubandus *(Foreign Trade)* — **Language:** English/Estonian **Frequency:** annual **Content:** detailed reviews of the exports and imports of agricultural products, wood and articles of wood, metal and articles of metal, machinery and equipment, transport vehicles and mineral fuels

Tervishoiuamet
Health Care Board

Address: Gonsori 29, Tallinn, 15157
Telephone: +372 650 9840
Fax: +372 650 9844
E-mail: info@tervishoiuamet.ee
Website: www.tervishoiuamet.ee

Guides: legislation; health care professionals registration documents available free; statistics available in Estonian
Activity: registration of health care professionals; issue of activity licences; exercise state supervision and apply enforcement powers of the state

Website(s) information:
Tervishoiuamet (Health Care Board) — **url:** www.tervishoiuamet.ee **Coverage:** provides health overview in Estonia and free publications and online statistics

Publication(s):
Kiirabikutsed 1998-2005 (Ambulance calls 1998-2005) — **Language:** English/Estonian **Frequency:** irregular **Content:** tables; statistics; etc

Tööinspektsioon
Labour Inspectorate

Address: Gonsiori 29, Tallinn, 10147
Telephone: +372 626 9400
Fax: +372 626 9404
E-mail: ti@ti.ee
Website: www.ti.ee

Guides: publications are available online
Activity: investigates fatal and serious occupational accidents and diseases and analyse their causes; collects statistics on accidents in the work place

Website(s) information:
Tööinspektsioon (Labour Inspectorate) — **url:** www.ti.ee **Coverage:** provides statistics about accidents at work in Estonia; health problems

Publication(s):
Ametialased õnnetused ja haigused Eestis (Occupational Accidents and Diseases in Estonia) — **Language:** English **Frequency:** irregular **Content:** fatal accidents per 100 000 workers; occupational diseases per 100 000 workers; tables; statistics; etc
Enterprises Inspected between 1999-2002 — **Language:** English **Frequency:** irregular **Content:** tables; statistics; etc
Most recent statistical news — **Language:** English **Frequency:** irregular **Content:** economic growth; consumer price index; export and import price index; average monthly gross wages and salaries; etc
Occupational diseases by factors — **Language:** English **Frequency:** irregular **Content:** tables; statistics; etc
Population Aged 15-69 by Sex, Indicator and Year — **Language:** English **Content:** population; tables; statistics
Riik ja selle kodanikud (The country and its people) — **Language:** English/Estonian **Content:** demography; deaths per 1000 population; population; births per 1000 population; etc
Serious and fatal accidents by fields of activity — **Language:** English **Content:** accidents per 1000 employees; tables; field of activity; tables; statistics; etc
Tööjõud Eestis (Labour Force in Estonia) — **Language:** English/Estonian **Frequency:** irregular **Content:** labour force; employed persons; employees; tables; etc

Tööturuamet
Labour Market Board

Address: Gonsiori 29, Tallinn, 15156
Telephone: +372 15 501
Fax: +372 625 7702
E-mail: tta@tta.ee
Website: www.tta.ee

Guides: publications are available online

Activity: to reduce unemployment and provide assistance to those seeking work and to employers by means of an efficient labour market policy

Website(s) information:
Tööturuamet (Labour Market Board) — **url:** www.tta.ee **Description:** statistics available to download for the labour market for 2003 and 2004. Yearbook also available giving statistics for the period 1999-2005 **Coverage:** labour market statistics

Publication(s):
Statistics — **Language:** English **Frequency:** annual **Content:** socio-economic statistics; working age population (15-64 year-olds) by gender and status
Tööturuameti Aastaraamat (Estonian Labour Market Board Yearbook) — **Language:** English/Estonian **Frequency:** annual **Content:** unemployment rates; working-age population; duration of unemployment; active labour market measures; statistics; etc

Veterinaar-ja Toiduamet
Veterinary and Food Board

Address: Väike-Paala 3, Tallinn, 11415
Telephone: +372 605 1710
Fax: +372 621 1441
E-mail: vet@vet.agri.ee
Website: www.vet.agri.ee

Guides: publications are available online
Activity: to ensure the production of safe, healthy and good quality food; to prevent and eradicate infectious animal diseases

Website(s) information:
Veterinaar-ja Toiduamet (Veterinary and Food Board) — **url:** www.vet.agri.ee **Coverage:** animal health; animal welfare; food control; trade, import and export, organic farming

Publication(s):
Veterinaar-ja Toiduameti Aastaraamat (Veterinary and Food Board Yearbook) — **Language:** English/Estonian **Frequency:** annual **Content:** trade; import; export; statistics; tables; etc

Finland

Laakelaitos
National Agency for Medicines

Address: PO Box 55, Mannerheimintie 166, Helsinki, 00301
Telephone: +358 9 473 341
Fax: +358 9 714 469
E-mail: kirjaamo@nam.fi
Website: www.nam.fi

Activity: promotes the health and safety of the citizens by regulatory control of medicinal products, medical devices and blood products

Website(s) information:
Lääkelaitos Läkemedelverket (National Agency for Medicines) — **url:** www.nam.fi **Coverage:** prescriptions, sales and consumption of drugs

Publication(s):
Finnish Statistics on Medicines — **Language:** English/Finnish **Frequency:** annual **Content:** statistics covering drug prescriptions, drug sales, consumption, drug registration, etc

Liikenne- ja viestintäministeriö
Ministry of Transport and Communications

Address: PO Box 31, Eteläesplanadi 16-18, Helsinki, 00023
Telephone: +358 916 002
Fax: +358 9 1602 8596
E-mail: kirjaamo@mintc.fi
Website: www.mintc.fi

Guides: publications are available free
Activity: responsible for two broad government sectors: transport policy and communications policy

Website(s) information:
Liikenne- ja viestintäministeriö *(Ministry of Transport and Communications)* — **url:** www.mintc.fi **Coverage:** provides free publications and statistics data covering telecommunications, mass media, postal services and communication policy in Finland

Publication(s):
Price Level of Finnish Telecommunications Charges — **Language:** English/Finnish **Content:** call prices; long-distance calls; international calls; local calls; monthly charges; etc

Prices of Mobile Calls — **Language:** English/Finnish **Frequency:** irregular **Content:** overview of the market situation; statistics; etc

Matkailun edistämiskeskus
Finnish Tourist Board

Address: PO Box 625, Töölönkatu 11, Helsinki, 00101
Telephone: +358 10 605 8000
Fax: +358 10 605 8333
E-mail: mek@mek.fi
Website: www.mek.fi

Guides: publications are available in three languages: Finnish; English; Swedish
Activity: to promote tourism in Finland

Website(s) information:
Matkailun edistämiskeskus *(Finnish Tourist Board)* — **url:** www.mek.fi **Description:** official site of the Finnish Tourist Board. Includes statistics on the national tourism industry, including balance of payments, travel; foreign passengers visiting Finland; overnight stays in Finland; tourist attractions in Finland **Coverage:** provides online statistics and free publications; also detailed contacts about Finnish tourist board offices all over the world

Publication(s):
Annual Report — **Language:** English/Finnish **Frequency:** annual **Content:** business environment; organisation; research activity international co-operation; statistics; overview; etc

Matkailufaktat *(Travel Facts)* — **Language:** English/Finnish **Content:** statistics on the Finnish tourism sector by bookings for accommodation, etc

Matkailukohteiden Kavijamaarat *(Number of Visitors to Tourist Attractions)* — **Language:** English/Finnish **Content:** statistical information on visitors, basis of calculation and reliability; monthly variation in number of visitors; number of visitors to tourist attractions; current and historic numbers

Rajahaastattelututkimus: Ulkomaiset matkailijat Suomessa vuonna *(Border Interview survey: Foreign Visitors in Finland)* — **Language:** English/Finnish **Frequency:** annual **Content:** main reasons for visiting Finland; length of stay; main destination in Finland; outdoor activities; results by country of residence; visitors by month; age and gender

Suomen Pankki
Bank of Finland

Address: PO Box 160, Snellmaninaukio, Helsinki, 00101
Telephone: +358 10 8311
Fax: +358 9 174 872
E-mail: info@bof.fi
Website: www.bof.fi

Guides: list of publications available online
Activity: to ensure price stability and the stability and efficiency of the payment and financial system

Website(s) information:
Suomen Pankki *(Bank of Finland)* — **url:** www.bof.fi **Description:** economic statistics: inflation; interest rates; exchange rates; monetary aggregates; banking and finance; current account, financial account and international reserves; supply, demand and labour market; central government finances; EMU convergence criteria. Bank of Finland's balance sheet **Coverage:** statistics on Finnish, European and international interest rates, EURIBOR daily and monthly data, currency exchanges, monetary data, bonds and payments balances, public funds, and other main economic indicators

Publication(s):
Balance of Payments and International Investment Position — **Language:** English/Finnish/Swedish **Frequency:** quarterly **Content:** current account; financial account; investment position; export; import

Financial Integration — **Language:** English **Frequency:** irregular **Content:** financial integration; securities markets integration; integration of European banking and insurance; financial stability, regulation and supervision; statistics

Financial Markets *(Statistical Review)* — **Language:** English/Finnish/Swedish **Frequency:** monthly **Content:** daily, weekly, monthly, quarterly and annual series covering key interest rates, money market liquidity, lending, monetary aggregates and deposits, exchange rates and banks´ forex transactions, balance of payments, Bank of Finland balance sheet, and bonds

Financial Stability — **Language:** English **Frequency:** annual **Content:** international developments and provides thorough evaluations on the current state and future prospects of the financial system

Finland´s Balance of Payments — **Language:** English/Finnish **Frequency:** monthly **Content:** Includes data on main items of the balance of payments: goods and services, income, current transfers and financial accounts

Finnish Balance of Payments and International Investment Position Statistics — **Language:** English **Frequency:** irregular **Content:** external stability of the economy in real and financial transactions; financial positions; capital and financial accounts; national income; balance of savings; investments in the economy; etc

International Reserves and Foreign Currency Liquidity — **Language:** English **Frequency:** monthly **Content:** official reserve assets; predetermined short-term net drains on foreign currency assets; contingent short-term net drains on foreign currency assets

Main Indicators for the Finnish Economy — **Language:** English/Finnish **Frequency:** monthly **Content:** financial markets; statistics

Soumen Pankin Vousikertomus *(Bank of Finland Annual Report)* — **Language:** English/Finnish/Swedish **Frequency:** annual **Content:** monetary policy; economic policy; financial markets and statistics; maintenance of currency supply; etc

Studies in Time Series Analysis of Consumption, Asset Prices and Forecasting — **Language:** English **Frequency:** irregular **Content:** statistical models and economic analysis; economic forecasting; recent trends in applied econometrics; asset prices and co integration

Suomen joukkovelkakirjalainat *(Finnish Bond Issues)* — **Language:** English/Finnish/Swedish **Frequency:** annual **Content:** statistical bulletin; comprises loan-specific information on government and private sector bonds issued in Finland; etc

Tilastokeskus
Statistics Centre of Finland

Address: , , Työpajankatu 13, Helsinki, 00022
Telephone: +358 9 1734 2220
Fax: +358 9 1734 2279
E-mail: stat@stat.fi
Website: www.stat.fi

Guides: 200 different statistics and over 700 releases made annually; statistical data can be browsed by 26 topics
Activity: national statistics office

Website(s) information:
Tilastokeskus *(Statistics Finland)* — **url:** www.stat.fi **Description:** information on products and services provided; Statistics Finland, Eurostat and IBS News Service; and various statistical sections providing free online data on Finland and other countries **Coverage:** statistical data can be browsed by 26 topics covering socio-economic development, financial, health, labour and other sectors etc

Publication(s):
Asuntojen hinnat *(House Prices)* — **Language:** Finnish **Frequency:** annual **Content:** statistics on house prices; overview of changes; etc

Asuntojen hinnat neljännesvuosittain *(House Prices Quarterly)* — **Language:** Finnish **Frequency:** 4 per annum **Content:** statistics on quarterly changes on house prices; overview of changes; etc

Asunto-osakeyhtiöiden taloustilasto *(Statistics on the Finances of Housing Corporation)* — **Language:** English/Finnish **Frequency:** annual **Content:** financial statistics; overview; etc

Education in Finland — **Language:** English **Frequency:** annual **Content:** compact book in English with statistical data on education in Finland

***Energiaennakko** (Preliminary Energy Statistics)* — **Language:** English/Finnish **Frequency:** annual **Content:** statistics on energy production in Finland

***Energiatilasto** (Energy Statistics)* — **Language:** English/Finnish **Content:** statistical data on energy production, consumption, import and export, investment on energy, public finance of energy and emissions. National energy statistics and international review

***Energy in Finland** —* **Language:** English **Frequency:** annual **Content:** main Finnish energy statistics, with data compiled since the 1970s

***Finland in Figures** —* **Language:** English **Frequency:** annual **Content:** statistical overview of Finland's main socio-economic indicators

***Finnish Business in Finland** —* **Language:** English **Frequency:** irregular **Content:** statistics and diverse information on companies operating in Finland and their development

***Information Society Statistics** —* **Language:** English **Frequency:** annual **Content:** data on development of information society in Finland and comparisons made with the other European countries

***Internet ja sähköinen kauppa yrityksissä** (Internet Use and E-commerce in Enterprises)* — **Language:** Finnish **Frequency:** annual **Content:** statistical data on number of internet users in Finland; development of the IT sector

***Joukkoviestimet** (Finnish Mass Media)* — **Language:** Finnish **Frequency:** annual **Content:** statistics about Finnish mass media

***Kansantalouden tilinpito** (National Accounts)* — **Language:** English/Finnish **Frequency:** irregular **Content:** comparisons made on changes to national accounts over a 10-year period

***Kansantalouden tilinpito** (National Accounts Quarterly)* — **Language:** English/Finnish **Frequency:** quarterly **Content:** national accounts tables, statistics

***Kansantalouden tilinpito, Ennakkotietoja** (National Accounts, Preliminary Data)* — **Language:** English/Finnish **Frequency:** annual **Content:** national accounts tables; domestic product at market prices; net national income

***Kuluttajabarometri** (Consumer Survey)* — **Language:** English/Finnish **Frequency:** annual **Content:** statistical data and analysis of different surveys on consumption

***Kuntasektorin palkat** (Local Government Workers' Salaries)* — **Language:** Finnish **Frequency:** annual **Content:** local government personnel's wage information based on area, sector, profession, education, gender and age

***Kuolemansyyt** (Causes of Death)* — **Language:** English/Finnish **Frequency:** annual **Content:** causes of death; statistics; etc

***Kymmenvuotiskatsaus** (10 Year Review)* — **Language:** Finnish **Frequency:** annual **Content:** statistical review of the development in Finland during last 10 years. Contains analysed statistical data about the development of Finnish society and economy. The key topic of the publication is business

***Liikennetilastollinen Vuosikirja** (Transport in Finland Yearbook)* — **Language:** Finnish **Frequency:** annual **Content:** data on transport statistics: road, railway, air and sea

***Luonnonvarat ja ymparisto** (Natural Resources and Environment)* — **Language:** English/Finnish/Swedish **Frequency:** annual **Content:** report on development of national resources and state of environment

***Maa-, metsä- ja kalatalous** (Agriculture, Forestry and Fishery)* — **Language:** Finnish/Finnish/Swedish **Frequency:** annual **Content:** series of publications offering key statistics covering the agriculture, forestry and fishery industries in Finland

***Maatilatilastollinen vuosikirja** (Yearbook of Farming Statistics)* — **Language:** English/Finnish **Frequency:** annual **Content:** data on number of farms and livestock by type

***Matkailutilasto** (Tourism Statistics)* — **Language:** English/Finnish **Frequency:** annual **Content:** arrivals, departures, receipts and expenditure; business travel; length of stay; purpose of visit; etc

***Matkailutilasto kuukausittain** (Tourism Statistics Monthly)* — **Language:** English/Finnish **Content:** arrivals, departures, receipts and expenditure; business travel; length of stay; purpose of visit

***Metsätilastollinen vuosikirja** (Finnish Statistical Yearbook of Forestry)* — **Language:** English/Finnish **Frequency:** annual **Content:** data on forestry in Finland

***Moottoriajoneuvot** (Motor Vehicles in Finland)* — **Language:** English/Finnish **Frequency:** annual **Content:** statistical data on automotive sector in Finland

***Oikeustilastollinen vsk** (Annual Legal Statistics)* — **Language:** Finnish **Content:** statistics on legal environment, crime and imprisonment

***Oppilaitostilastot** (Education Statistics)* — **Content:** educational statistics from elementary schools to universities

***Päihdetilastollinen vuosikirja** (Yearbook of Alcohol and Drug Statistics)* — **Language:** English/Finnish **Frequency:** annual **Content:** statistics on drugs and alcohol use in Finland

***Perheet** (Families)* — **Language:** English/Finnish **Frequency:** annual **Content:** statistics on families; family size to education and earnings

***Sosiaali- ja terveyshuollon tilastollinen vuosikirja** (Statistical Yearbook on Social Welfare and Health Care)* — **Language:** English/Finnish **Frequency:** annual **Content:** statistical data on health care and social welfare; etc

***Suomalaisten matkailu** (Finnish Travel)* — **Language:** Finnish **Frequency:** annual **Content:** statistics and overview of Finnish tourism

***Suomen tilastollinen vuosikirja** (Statistical Yearbook of Finland)* — **Language:** English/Finnish **Frequency:** annual **Content:** statistics and overview on general socio-economic indicators

***Suomen Tilastollinen Vuosikirja** (Finnish Statistical Yearbook)* — **Language:** Finnish/Swedish/English **Frequency:** annual **Content:** compilation of annual data covering a wide range of topics, including population, agriculture, fishing, forestry, industry, internal and external trade (including retailing), enterprises, banking and credit, insurance, transport and communications, state finances, income and property, national accounts, consumption and prices, labour market, wages

***Tieto&trendit** (Information and Trends)* — **Language:** Finnish **Frequency:** 8 per annum **Content:** facts and figures, country reports, trends. Replaced former newspapers Economic Trends and Tietoaika.

***Tilastokatsaus taulukkoluettelo** (Bulletin of Statistics)* — **Language:** Finnish/English/Swedish **Frequency:** quarterly **Content:** statistical data on general socio-economic indicators

***Tukku- ja vähittäiskauppa vsk** (Wholesale and Retail Trade)* — **Language:** English/Finnish **Frequency:** irregular **Content:** statistical data on wholesale and retail trade in Finland

***Tulo-ja varallisuustilasto** (Statistics on Income and Wealth)* — **Language:** Finnish **Frequency:** annual **Content:** statistical data and comparisons on wages, wealth and taxation

***Tulonjakotilasto** (Income Distribution Statistics)* — **Language:** English/Finnish **Frequency:** annual **Content:** statistical data on incomes

***Tutkimus- ja kehittamistoiminta** (Research and Development)* — **Language:** Finnish **Content:** information on research and development activity practiced by Finnish public sector, companies and academies

***Tyotapaturmat** (Accidents at Work)* — **Language:** English/Finnish **Frequency:** irregular **Content:** statistics; overview; accident types; etc

***Työtunnin kustannus 1996-2005** (Hourly Wages 1996-2005)* — **Language:** English/Finish **Frequency:** irregular **Content:** comparisons of changes in overall cost of an hourly wage

***Työvoimatilasto** (Labour Force Statistics)* — **Language:** Finnish **Frequency:** annual **Content:** national labour force statistics

***Ulkomaalaiset ja siirtolaisuus** (Foreigners and International Migration)* — **Language:** English/Finnish **Frequency:** annual **Content:** migration statistics; tables; foreigners statistics; etc

***Ulkomaankauppa** (Foreign Trade)* — **Language:** Finnish/English **Frequency:** monthly **Content:** import and export statistics

***Väestönmuutokset** (Vital Statistics)* — **Language:** English/Finnish **Frequency:** annual **Content:** statistics; tables; vital statistics; etc

***Väestörakenne ja väestömuutokset kunnittain** (Population Structure and Vital Statistics by Municipality)* — **Language:** English/Finnish **Frequency:** annual **Content:** statistics, overview on population structure

***Valtion kuukausipalkat** (Government Workers Monthly Wages)* — **Language:** Finnish **Content:** data of government workers' wages based on age, gender, length of service, degree, region

***Vuokratilasto** (Rents)* — **Language:** English/Finnish **Frequency:** annual **Content:** statistical data on house rents in Finland

***Women and Men in Finland** —* **Language:** English **Content:** statistics on equality of men and women in Finland (comparisons of the position, wages, home duties and ect.)

***Yksityisen sektorin kuukausipalkat** (Private sector monthly wages)* — **Language:** Finnish **Frequency:** annual **Content:** private sector workers' wage statistics based on profession and education

***Ympäristötilasto** (Environmental Statistics)* — **Language:** English/Finnish **Frequency:** annual **Content:** environmental statistics

Valtiovarainministerio
Ministry of Finance

Address: PO Box 28, , Helsinki, 00023,
Telephone: +358 9 160 01
Fax: +358 9 1603 4854
E-mail: valtiovarainministerio@vm.fi
Website: www.ministryoffinance.fi

Guides: publications are available free in three languages: Finnish; English; Swedish
Activity: to prepare economic and fiscal policy, drafts the annual Budget and offers experience in tax policy matters

Website(s) information:
Valtiovarainministerio (Ministry of Finance) — url: www.vn.fi **Description:** offers information on the national economy and state finances **Coverage:** provides free graphs and statistics database of economy, budget; general government finances; etc; free publications in English, Finnish, Swedish; detailed overview about the ministry of finance and detailed contact information

Publication(s):
Finnish Public Sector as an Employer — **Language:** English/Finnish/Swedish **Frequency:** annual **Content:** overview of the situation of public sector as an employer in Finland; includes statistics

Taskutilasto (Pocket Statistics) — **Language:** English/Finnish/Swedish **Content:** average total earnings by education; labour costs; labour costs by cost category; etc

France

Banque de France
Bank of France

Address: BP 14001, 48 rue Croix des Petit Champs, Paris, 75001
Telephone: +33 14 292 3908
Fax: +33 14 292 3940
E-mail: infos@banque-france.fr
Website: www.banque-france.fr

Guides: Catalogue des Publications available
Activity: banking and monetary policy

Website(s) information:
Banque de France (Bank of France) — url: www.banque-france.fr **Description:** information and statistics on the French banking and financial system. Data on the main economic and monetary indicators for the EU, USA and Japan, the organisation of financial activities in France, credit institutions, banking and financial regulations, payment instruments, and payment systems and securities settlement systems **Coverage:** statistics coverage include regulation, national financial accounts, statistics of the monthly digest, monetary statistics, balance of payments, international banking statistics, European sectoral references, and links to statistics pages of ESCB websites

Publication(s):
Banque de France Annual Report — **Language:** English/French **Frequency:** annual **Content:** describes the activities of the Banque de France, its balance sheet and income statements and presents the Governor's comments on the economic and monetary situation

Bulletin de la Banque de France (Bank of France' Bulletin) — **Language:** English/French **Frequency:** monthly **Content:** reference work on economic, monetary and financial issues

Financial Stability Review — **Language:** English/French **Frequency:** bi-monthly **Content:** provides information on financial sector players and observers, such as decision makers, academics and market participants; it reviews developments affecting financial institutions, markets and their infrastructures from a cyclical and structural perspective

French Ministry of Foreign Affairs
Address: 244 boulevard Saint-Germain, Paris, 75303
Telephone: +33 1 4317 9000
Website: www.diplomatie.gouv.fr

Guides: offers magazines covering various topics

Publication(s):
Label France — **Language:** English/French **Frequency:** quarterly **Content:** covering topics such as French cinema, tourism, business life, science and technology, humanities, international relations, and sport

Institut National de la Statistique et des Etudes Economiques (INSEE)
National Institute of Statistics and Economic Studies

Address: Tour Gamma A, 195 rue de Bercy, Paris Cédex 12, 75582
Telephone: +33 8 2588 9452
Fax: +33 1 5317 8809
E-mail: insee-contact@insee.fr
Website: www.insee.fr

Guides: annual catalogue of publications (free, available online)
Activity: collects and produces information on the French economy and society

Website(s) information:
Institut National de la Statistique et des Etudes Economiques (INSEE) (National Institute of Statistics and Economic Studies) — url: www.insee.fr **Description:** official site of INSEE, provides information on the Institute's main products and services, including list of publications and latest statistical releases; general profile of 26 French regions; access to SIRENE database (French companies database); and compilation of various online statistics **Coverage:** up-to-date statistics can be found by accessing both section "Les Grands Indicateurs" and "La France en Faits et Chiffres". Main Indicators section includes data on: consumer price index; cost-of-construction index; major economic indicators and analyses; and quarterly and annual accounts. France in Facts and Figures provides general socio-economic statistics covering: geography, population and demographics; labour force; health, education and general living standards; agriculture; industry; retailing and wholesaling; and services

Publication(s):
Annuaire Statistique de la France (Statistical Yearbook of France) — **Language:** French **Frequency:** annual **Content:** detailed demographic, economic and social statistics on France, with technical commentaries, notes on sources of information and bibliographic references; includes section entitled 'commerce interieur' with data on retailing establishments, by region and by type, turnover, employees, investment, etc.

Bulletin Mensuel de Statistique (Monthly Statistical Bulletin) — **Language:** French **Frequency:** monthly **Content:** most up-to-date information on all indices and statistical series which INSEE maintain regularly

Consommation des Menages (Household Consumption) — **Language:** French **Frequency:** annual **Content:** household consumption statistics covering food products, clothing, accommodation, household equipment, healthcare, transport, cultural and leisure activities and other goods and services

Courrier des Statistiques — **Language:** English/French **Frequency:** quarterly **Content:** reports on key events, developments, and debates in official French and international statistics since 1977

Daily Economic Monitor — **Language:** French **Frequency:** daily **Content:** provides information on national accounts, activity in the industrial sector, investment, employment and labour market, financing economy, foreign trade etc

Economie & Statistique — **Language:** French **Frequency:** monthly **Content:** provides information on the transition from education to employment

France in Figures — **Language:** English/French **Frequency:** every 2 years **Content:** provides information on geography, population, living standards, employment, consumer prices, business, production, external transactions, finance and budget in France

France, Social Portrait — **Language:** French **Frequency:** annual **Content:** contains detailed social data on the French population

Les Comptes de l'Agriculture (Agriculture Accounts) — **Language:** French **Frequency:** annual **Content:** statistical portrait of the French agricultural sector

Les Comptes du Commerce (Retail Industry Accounts) — **Language:** French **Frequency:** annual **Content:** results of annual survey of retail trade activities in France

Les Entreprises du Commerce (Retailing Companies) — **Language:** French **Frequency:** annual **Content:** results of survey of retail establishments and enterprises

Les Industries Agro-Alimentaires (Food Industries) — **Language:** French **Frequency:** annual **Content:** annual statistics on French agriculture and food industries

Tableaux de l'Economie Française (French Economy Table) — **Language:** French **Frequency:** annual **Content:** double page format of 80 tables plus commentary and explanation of technical terms, intended to make figures on the main aspects of the economy easily accessible

International Fertilizer Institute

Address: 28 rue Marbeuf, Paris, 75008
Telephone: +33 1 5393 0500
Fax: +33 1 5393 0545
E-mail: ifa@fertilizer.org
Website: www.fertilizer.org

Guides: gives access to database which contains more than 1,300 IFA publications covering all aspects of fertilizer use, manufacture and trade

Activity: main activity is to provide information about the industry worldwide, especially through conferences and meetings of various kinds in different regions, and the exchange of non-commercial information in the form of statistics and publications

Website(s) information:

International Fertilizer Institute Statistics — url: www.fertilizer.org **Description:** news and information on fertilisers **Coverage:** statistics on production, imports, exports and consumption of nitrogen, phosphate and potash fertilisers by country. Also includes Fertiliser Indicators, a collection of graphs and diagrams illustrating the development in different regions of the world of the capacities, production, consumption and trade of nitrogen, phosphate and potash fertilisers, and certain important intermediates and raw materials. The development of world cereal production and stocks and the crops on which fertilisers are used, is also illustrated

Publication(s):

Environmental Aspects of Phosphate and Potash Mining — **Language:** English **Content:** completes a series that looks at environmental aspects of the fertilizer industry throughout the life-cycle of mineral fertilizer products

Le ministère délégué au Tourisme
Ministry of Tourism

Address: Grande-Arche de la Défense, Paris, 92055
Telephone: +33 1 4081 2122
Fax: +33 1 4081 1178
Website: www.tourisme.gouv.fr

Guides: provides statistical data and reports on tourism in France
Activity: promotes and represents the tourism sector

Publication(s):

Tourisme et innovation- bilan et perspectives (Tourism and Innovation- Report and Perspectives) — **Language:** French **Content:** provides information on innovation in the tourist sector regarding new technologies

L'Institut français de l'environnement
French Institute of Environment

Address: 5 route d'Olivet, Orleans Cedex 2
Telephone: +33 2 3879 7878
Fax: +33 2 3879 7870
E-mail: ifen@ifen.fr
Website: www.ifen.fr

Activity: organises and collects data on natural risks and technological innovations; collaborates with the administration to implement necessary elements to the constitution of environmental information; implements national, European and international programmes; provides statistical data on the environment

Website(s) information:

L'Institut français de l'environnement (French Institute of Environment) — url: www.ifen.fr **Coverage:** quality of air and water, evolution of biodiversity, greenhouse gas transmissions, protection of the environment

Publication(s):

Activity Report — **Language:** French **Frequency:** annual **Content:** provides annual review from the activities of institutions, the most important environmental events and publications

Le 4 pages de l'Ifen (The Four Pages of Ifen) — **Language:** French **Frequency:** monthly **Content:** provides information on energy consumption and the greenhouse effect

Les dossiers de l'Ifen (Information of Ifen) — **Language:** French **Frequency:** monthly **Content:** analytical and technical data and news on principal environmental subjects

Ministère de l'Agriculture et de la Pêche
Ministry of Agriculture and Fisheries

Address: 78 rue de Varenne, Paris 07 SP, 75349
Telephone: +33 14 955 4955
E-mail: communication@agriculture.gouv.fr
Website: www.agriculture.gouv.fr

Guides: provides information bulletins, various reports related to the agricultural industry

Activity: monitors the quality and sanitary security of food; preservation of the environment and natural space, responsibility for agricultural teaching, economic development of agricultural sectors and agro-industrials in France and within the EU, development of employment

Website(s) information:

Ministère de l'Agriculture et de la Pêche (Ministry of Agriculture and Fisheries) — url: www.agriculture.gouv.fr **Description:** general statistics on French agricultural and fishing activities: yields and production of various sectors; livestock; labour; forestry; import and export trade figures; agricultural census; and key figures **Coverage:** provides statistical information on agricultural products

Publication(s):

La PAC : un Modèle Équilibré à Mieux Comprendre (Understanding of Better Models) — **Language:** French **Content:** presents nine topics related to the EU, also provides information on the French environment, and quality and security of food

Ministère de l'Économie, des Finances et de l'Industrie
Ministry of the Economy, Finances and Industry

Address: 139 rue de Bercy, Paris Cedex 12, 75572
Telephone: +33 1 4004 0404
Fax: +33 1 5318 3640
E-mail: francetresor@oat.fiances.gouv.fr
Website: www.minefi.gouv.fr

Guides: provides up-to-date information on the financial market and current events; provides reports and statistics, incorporates a Euro Info Centre

Activity: determines fiscal policy and budgetary issues

Website(s) information:

Ministère de l'Économie, des Finances et de l'Industrie (Ministry of the Economy, Finances and Industry) — url: www.minefi.gouv.fr **Coverage:** provides indexes on consumption prices, inflation

Publication(s):

Bulletin officiel de la Concurrence, de la Consommation et de la Répression des fraudes (Official Bulletin of Competition, Consumption and the Repression of Fraud) — **Language:** French

Georgia

Georgian - European Policy and Legal Advice Center (GEPLAC)
Address: 3a Chitadze Street, Tbilisi, 0108
Telephone: +995 32 921 371
Fax: +995 32 931 716
E-mail: office@geplac.ge
Website: www.geplac.org

Activity: to support the legal reform process and economic reform policy

Website(s) information:
Georgian - European Policy and Legal Advice Center (GEPLAC) — url: www.geplac.org **Coverage:** Georgian law and economic development review and legal inventory

Publication(s):
Georgian Economic Trends — **Language:** Georgian/English **Frequency:** quarterly **Content:** national accounts and main trends including agriculture & food processing, production, infrastructure, investment. Also covers government finance, money & finance, international trade, privatisation and employment **Edition:** 2006

Ministry of Economic Development of Georgia
Address: 12 Chanturia Street, Tbilisi, 0108
Telephone: +995 32 996 996
Fax: +995 32 921 845
E-mail: ministry@econom.ge
Website: www.economy.ge

Guides: data available in Georgian and English on their website

Activity: to ensure sustainable economic development based on stable macroeconomic policy and private entrepreneurship development (incorporates Department of Tourism & Resorts; Department of Highways of Georgia; Department of Statistics; State Procurement Agency; Georgian National Investment Agency; Enterprises Management Agency)

Ministry of Energy of Georgia
Address: 10 Lermontov Street, Tbilisi, 1079
Telephone: +995 32 983 194
Fax: +995 32 983 194
Website: www.minenergy.gov.ge

Activity: analyses electricity demand industrial, residential and commercial customers, to achieve economic independence and stability of the power sector and to ensure security (technical, economic and political) by means of the maximum possible utilization of the power sector resources and diversification of the import sources

Website(s) information:
Ministry of Energy of Georgia — url: www.minenergy.gov.ge **Coverage:** energy statistics and forecasts; key players in the energy sector; energy legislation

Publication(s):
Investment Opportunities in the Energy Sector of Georgia — **Language:** English **Content:** main facts and latest developments; market structure and legal framework; privatisation and construction **Edition:** 2006

Natural Gas Strategy for Georgia — **Language:** English **Content:** analysis and proposals; cconomic and geopolitical context **Edition:** 2006

Ministry of Finance of Georgia
Address: 70 Abashidze Street, Tbilisi
Telephone: +995 32 235 013
Fax: +995 32 235 013
E-mail: finabx@mof.ge
Website: www.mof.ge

Activity: central government (state administration) institution in the field of economic policy

Website(s) information:
Ministry of Finance of Georgia — url: www.mof.ge **Description:** provides information on the Ministry and its working areas; publications are available online on a free basis as well as all the current data concerning Georgia's economic development **Coverage:** statistical data on various economic indicators; state budget analysis

Publication(s):
Daily Bulletin — **Language:** Georgian/English **Frequency:** daily **Content:** statistical publications on governmental finances

National Bank of Georgia
Address: 3/5 Leonidze St, Tbilisi, 380005
Telephone: +995 32 996 505
Fax: +995 32 999 885
Website: www.nbg.gov.ge

Publication(s):
Banki — **Frequency:** monthly **Content:** financial news and analysis

State Department of Statistics, Georgia
Address: 4 Gamsakhurdia Avenue, Tbilisi, 1085
Telephone: +995 32 331 450
Fax: +995 32 932 414
E-mail: info@statistics.gov.ge
Website: www.statistics.ge

Guides: collates and publish statistical information on the demographic, social and economic status of the country

Activity: national statistics office

Website(s) information:
State Department of Statistics, Georgia — url: www.statistics.ge **Description:** provides information about the Statistics Office and its activities; provides access to up-to-date statistics online **Coverage:** up-to date statistical data available online in English language on main demographic, socio-economic, industry sector indexes

Publication(s):
Agriculture in Georgia — **Language:** Georgian **Frequency:** annual **Content:** statistical collection contains information on rural population and its employment, data on the share of agriculture in GDP, output of this branch of economy, physical volume indices and other indicators, that describe the real state of agriculture in 1985-2004

Households of Georgia — **Language:** Georgian **Frequency:** irregular **Content:** general survey of households in Georgia

Labour Market in Georgia — **Language:** Georgian **Frequency:** irregular **Content:** trends in Georgia's labour market from 2003-2005

Quarterly Statistical Bulletin — **Language:** Georgian **Frequency:** quarterly **Content:** contains socio-economic and financial data

Statistical Yearbook of Georgia — **Language:** Georgian **Frequency:** annual **Content:** consists of data on population, labour, income, expenditure and consumption of households; education, science and culture; public health and social security; natural resources and environment; national accounts, business activities, prices

United Nations Information Centre
Address: UN House, 9 Eristavi Street, Tbilisi, 0179
Telephone: +995 32 25 1126/28/31
Fax: +995 32 25 02 71/2
E-mail: registry.ge@undp.org
Website: www.undp.org.ge

Guides: available online

Activity: UNDP along with the Georgian government has identified several areas for targeted assistance. The projects are pro-poor, pro-women, and environmentally sustainable

Website(s) information:
United Nations Development Programme — url: www.undp.org.ge **Coverage:** information on human rights, labour force, social security issues

Publication(s):
Millenium Development Goals in Georgia — **Language:** English **Content:** Targets and goals till 2015 **Edition:** 2004

National Human Development Report Georgia — **Language:** English **Frequency:** irregular

Problems and Prospects of Agriculture and Rural Development in Georgia — **Language:** English **Edition:** 1997

Germany

Bundesministerium der Finanzen (BMF)
Ministry of Finance

Address: Wilhelmstraße 97, Berlin, 11016
Telephone: +49 30 186820
Fax: +49 30 186824248
E-mail: Poststelle@bmf.bund.de
Website: www.bundesfinanzministerium.de

Guides: database of publications
Activity: shaping of financial and economic policy in Germany

Website(s) information:
Bundesministerium der Finanzen *(Ministry of Finance)* — **url:** www.bundesfinanzministerium.de **Coverage:** research reports on the latest trends in German public finances; overall recent economic evolution, and outlook for the development of major economic indicators

Publication(s):
Monatsbericht der BMF *(Monthly Report of the BMF)* — **Language:** German **Frequency:** monthly **Content:** monthly update on new legislation and policy

Bundesministerium für Ernährung, Landwirtschaft und Verbraucherschutz (BMELV)
Federal Ministry of Food, Agriculture and Consumer Protection

Address: Postfach 11055, Wilhelmstraße 54, Berlin, 10117
Telephone: +49 30 2006 0
Fax: +49 30 2006 4262
E-mail: poststelle@bmvel.bund.de
Website: www.bmelv.de

Guides: The Agrarpolitischer Bericht is supplemented by the Buchführungsergebnisse der Testbetriebe in which the economic data of over 7000 representative agricultural companies is demonstrated.
Blickpunkt Welternährung can be downloaded from the website whenever a report is issued. The recipients of printed versions are issued with a report every six weeks

Website(s) information:
Bundesministerium für Ernährung, Landwirtschaft und Verbraucherschutz (BMELV) — **url:** www.bmelv-forschung.de **Coverage:** analysis of the implications of recent research and scientific findings on agriculture in Germany and the rest of Europe

Bundesministerium für Ernährung, Landwirtschaft und Verbraucherschutz (BMELV) *(Federal Ministry of Food, Agriculture and Consumer Protection)* — **url:** www.bmelv.de **Coverage:** statistics and analysis of the agricultural sector in Germany including data on: horticulture and viniculture national production; agricultural labour force; forestry and forestry related industries; agricultural export trade; and EU agricultural policy

Publication(s):
Agrarpolitischer Bericht *(Agricultural Politics Report)* — **Language:** German **Frequency:** annual **Content:** includes goals of national agricultural politics, the state of agricultural economics, agricultural and nutritional policy measures, financing of agricultural measures

Berichte über Landwirtschaft *(Report on Agriculture)* — **Language:** German/English **Frequency:** 3 per annum **Content:** publications on current issues of agricultural politics and science in Germany and the rest of Europe **Edition:** 83

Blickpunkt Welternährung *(Focus on World Feeding)* — **Language:** German **Frequency:** irregular **Content:** current topics related to international food and agricultural organisations, world feeding and sustainable development

Forschungs Report *(Research Report)* — **Language:** German **Frequency:** 2 per annum **Content:** reports on current issues of agricultural science which can be used as policy issues on food, agriculture and consumer protection

Statistisches Bundesamt Deutschland
Federal Statistical Office of Germany

Address: Statistisches Bundesamt, Statistischer Informationsservice, Gustav-Stresemann-Ring 11, Wiesbaden, 65189
Telephone: +49 611 752 405
Fax: +49 611 753 330
E-mail: info@destatis.de
Website: www.destatis.de

Guides: library open 9.00-15.00 Monday to Thursday and on Friday 9.00-14.00. Each region has a statistical office, and publishes results for smaller statistical units. Further details of individual titles are given in the Gesamtverzeichnis Statistischer Berichte der Statistischen Landesämter (general list of statistical reports of the regional statistical offices), available free of charge from the regional statistical offices.
The Statistical Office also publishes subject-matter related series including publications on prices, the population, energy and environment, education, the labour market, information society, culture, justice and transport in Germany

Website(s) information:
Genesis Online - Das Statistische Informationssystem *(Federal Statistical Office Germany)* — **url:** www-genesis.destatis.de **Description:** information database from all areas of official statistics. Access to Genesis-online requires registration. Registration as a guest is possible **Coverage:** focuses are on data from population statistics, employment statistics, education and transport statistics, price statistics, foreign trade statistics and national accounts

Statistisches Bundesamt Deutschland *(Federal Statistical Office of Germany)* — **url:** www.destatis.de **Description:** offers information on the Statistisches Bundesamt main products and services: list of major titles and online publications; compilation of press releases; scientific forum; and up-to-date statistical data on the country **Coverage:** includes free online statistics on Germany, covering different socio-economic and financial indicators for the last three years (period coverage may vary according to indicator/topic in question). Also offers basic key data, in the areas of: geography and climate; population and demographics; employment and salaries; finance; social security; industry and agriculture; domestic and foreign trade, etc. Tends to concentrate on data on latest economic indicators, covering: labour market; foreign trade; money and banking; national accounts; industrial production; tourism; etc

Statistisches Bundesamt Online Publications — **url:** www-ec.destatis.de **Description:** offers Statistisches Bundesamt publications which are downloadable online **Coverage:** offers Statistisches Bundesamt publications which are downloadable online. Data covered include: population; employment; education; environment; economy; foreign trade; prices; income and expenditure

Publication(s):
Bevölkerungsstruktur und Wirtschaftskraft der Bundesländer *(Population Structure and Economic Resources of the Länder)* — **Language:** German **Frequency:** biennial **Content:** publication containing selected numerical data from all spheres of official statistics. Its essential part is demographic and economic data

Datenreport *(Data Report)* — **Language:** German **Frequency:** biennial **Content:** publication containing a compilation of current data of official statistics and new results of survey and social research

Die Bundesländer: Strukturen und Entwicklungen *(The Länder: Structures and Trends)* — **Language:** German **Content:** publication presenting the economic and social situation of the Länder

Statistisches Jahrbuch für das Ausland *(Statistical Yearbook for Foreign Countries)* — **Language:** German **Frequency:** annual **Content:** statistical yearbook containing information on structures and trends of most countries of the world

Statistisches Jahrbuch für die Bundesrepublik Deutschland *(Statistical Yearbook of Germany)* — **Language:** German **Frequency:** annual **Content:** statistical yearbook giving data on latest trends in Germany's social, economic and cultural life

Wirtschaft und Statistik *(Economy and Statistics)* — **Language:** German **Frequency:** monthly **Content:** monthly compilation of latest national economic and social statistics

Zahlenkompass - Statistisches Taschenbuch für Deutschland *(Zahlenkompass - Key Statistical Data on Germany)* — **Language:** German **Frequency:** annual **Content:** handbook containing current benchmark data on all areas of German society

Greece

Bank of Greece

Address: PO Box 3105, 21 Eleftheriou Venizelos Avenue, Athens, 102 50
Telephone: +30 210 320 1111
Fax: +30 210 323 2239
E-mail: secretariat@bankofgreece.gr
Website: www.bankofgreece.gr

Guides: the bank publishes an annual report and two monetary policy reports; it also publishes economic and statistical bulletins; the special studies division publishes working papers
Activity: monitoring and analysing economic developments

Publication(s):
Annual Report — **Language:** Greek/English **Frequency:** annual **Content:** information on the Greek economy: developments, policies and prospects

Economic Bulletin — **Language:** English/Greek **Frequency:** bi-annually **Content:** specific topics on Greek economy; includes reports on external financing, growth, and capital structure of companies

Monetary Policy — **Language:** English/Greek **Frequency:** bi-annually **Content:** monetary policy and monetary policy interim reports examine the international economic environment and discuss economic developments, in the Euro area and Greece

Statistical Bulletins — **Language:** English/Greek **Content:** monthly statistical bulletin and a bulletin of regional combined indicators for Macedonia-Thrace which deal with economic indicators

General Secretariat of National Statistical Service of Greece

Address: 46 Pireos & Eponiton Street, Piraeus, 185 10
Telephone: +30 210 4852313 5
Fax: +30 210 4852819
E-mail: nfo@statistics.gr
Website: www.statistics.gr

Guides: publications can be referred to in the library, 09:00-13:00 from Monday to Friday; information on the availability of material can be accessed in the online catalogue
Activity: designs, collects and processes data from studies, censuses and statistical surveys and presents the data in statistical publications

Website(s) information:
National Statistical Service of Greece (NSSG) — **url:** www.statistics.gr **Coverage:** data on socio-economic topics covering: demography, the labour market, national accounts, trade and services, the primary and secondary (industry) sectors

Publication(s):
Concise Statistical Yearbook — **Language:** Greek/English **Frequency:** irregular **Content:** statistical publication on socio-economic indicators of Greece

Monthly Statistical Bulletin — **Language:** Greek/English **Frequency:** monthly **Content:** monthly statistical data covering a wide variety of topics, including: population; employment; labour; salaries and wages; public health; agriculture and fishing; industry; energy; trade; transports and communications; tourism; public finance; prices; and money and banking

Statistical Year Book of Greece — **Language:** Greek/English **Frequency:** annual **Content:** general demographic, economic and social statistics on Greece

Hellenic Marine Environment Protection Association (HELMEPA)

Address: 5, Pergamou Str., Nea Smirni, Athens, 17121
Telephone: +30 210 9343088
Fax: +30 210 9353847
E-mail: helmepa@helmepa.gr
Website: www.helmepa.gr

Guides: an annual report is available as well as information on training
Activity: to eliminate ship-generated marine pollution and enhance safety at sea

Publication(s):
Annual Report — **Language:** Greek/English **Frequency:** annual **Content:** report on the activities of the organisation as well as on education in the field

Hellenic Organisation for Standardisation (ELOT)

Address: Acharnon 313, Athens, 111 45
Telephone: +30 210 2120100
Fax: +30 210 228 30 34
E-mail: elotinfo@elot.gr
Website: www.elot.gr

Guides: publishes catalogues on standardisation in Greek and English
Activity: elaborates Hellenic national standards maintains a central point for testing of materials, assesses management systems and certifies products and services, provides public or on site training and technical information

Ministry of Economy and Finance

Address: 5 Nikis Street, Syntagma Square, Athens, 101 80
Telephone: +30 210 3332492
Fax: +30 210 3332499
E-mail: generalsecra@mnec.gr
Website: www.mof-glk.gr

Guides: summaries of the budget, reports and studies, public debt bulletins
Activity: responsible for the budget of Greece

Publication(s):
Public Debt Bulletin — **Language:** English/Greek **Frequency:** quarterly **Content:** graphs on Greek interest rate and inflation; charts on Government securities and bonds, etc

National Organization for Medicines

Address: 284 Messogion Av., Athens, 155 62
Telephone: +30 210 6507200
Fax: +30 210 6545535
E-mail: relation@eof.gr
Website: www.eof.gr

Activity: ensures public health and safety with regard to medicinal products for human and veterinary use, medicated animal foods and food additives, foodstuffs intended for particular nutritional uses and food supplements, biocides, medical devices, cosmetics

Hungary

Gazdasagi es Kozlekedesi Miniszterium

Ministry of Economy and Transport

Address: V. Honvéd utca 13-15, Budapest, 1055
Telephone: +36 1 374 2700
E-mail: ugyfelszolgalat@gkm.gov.hu
Website: www.ikm.iif.hu

Activity: supports foreign investments, focusing on developing the transport infrastructure, facilitating the spread of information technology, encouraging research and development and strengthening micro, small and medium-sized enterprises

Website(s) information:
Gazdasagi es Kozlekedesi Miniszterium *(Ministry of Economy and Transport)* — **url:** http://en.gkm.gov.hu/ **Coverage:** economic policy; foreign economic affairs (foreign trade); investment promotion; retail industry and energy; infrastructure

Publication(s):
Hungarian Economy — **Language:** English **Frequency:** annual **Content:** Hungarian economic policy, economic trends, external economy, business

Kozponti Statisztikal Hivatal
Hungarian Central Statistical Office

Address: Keleti Károly u. 5-7, Budapest, 1024
Telephone: +36 1 345 6000
Fax: +36 1 345 6788
E-mail: erzsebet.veto@office.ksh.hu
Website: http://portal.ksh.hu/

Activity: designing and conducting surveys, recording, processing and storing data, data analyses and dissemination, protection of individual data. Provides data for the parliament and public administration, social organisations, local authorities, scientific bodies, economic organisations, the general public and the media as well as for international organisations and users abroad. Official data regarding the socio-economic situation as well as the changes in the population of the country are published by the HCSO

Website(s) information:

Kozponti Statisztikal Hivatal (Hungarian Central Statistical Office) — **url:** http://portal.ksh.hu/ **Description:** general information on library and documentation services; professional and scientific institutes; catalogue of publications; news and press releases; and access to series of databases and online statistics **Coverage:** different sections provide statistics on Hungary, including "Hungary in Figures", "Major Annual Figures" and "Agricultural Census". Major Annual Figures section provides data in more detail, covering different socio-economic topics for the last ten years (period coverage varies according to indicator/sector in question). Includes statistics on: population and labour force; earnings, household incomes, consumption and savings; health and education; culture; annual GDP by industry sector; agriculture, industry and construction; investment and finances; external trade; tourism; transports and communications; and balance of energy

Publication(s):

Cestat Statistical Bulletin — **Language:** English/Hungarian **Frequency:** quarterly **Content:** basic economic data in monthly and quarterly time series and annual national economic indicators

Change of Course in Hungary 1990-2004 — **Language:** English **Frequency:** annual **Content:** presents economic and social processes in Hungary between the change of regime and the accession to the European Union **Edition:** 2006

Consumer Price Indices — **Language:** English/Hungarian **Frequency:** annual **Content:** development of consumer prices and price levels **Edition:** 2002

Cultural Statistical Data of Hungary — **Language:** English/Hungarian **Frequency:** annual **Content:** cultural statistics from 1991. The main topics are the following: book production, libraries, cultural institutes, mass communication, theatres, museums, cinemas and film production

Demographic Yearbook — **Language:** English/Hungarian **Frequency:** annual **Content:** population structure and latest demographic trends in Hungary **Edition:** 2005

Environmental Statistical Yearbook of Hungary — **Language:** English/Hungarian **Frequency:** annual **Content:** analyses environmental-economic processes. The main topics are the following: land; mineral resources; energy; water resources; water uses; forestry; emissions of air pollutants; waste water discharge; waste; noise; soil, ambient air quality; water quality; wildlife; environmental health; urban (built) environment; nature conservation; environment industry; environmental protection expenditure; environmental taxes

Foreign Direct Investment in Hungary — **Language:** English/Hungarian **Frequency:** annual **Content:** foreign capital based on its originating country, sectoral and regional development

Monthly Bulletin of Statistics — **Language:** English/Hungarian **Frequency:** monthly **Content:** summarising analyses on most recent economic developments and trends evolving in the course of year concerned

National Accounts Hungary — **Language:** English/Hungarian **Frequency:** annual **Content:** macroeconomic statistics including statistical indicators. Economic cycle of production; income distribution; consumption and capital formation. Data on production and income by institutional sectors and industries; per capita GDP figures in international comparison; gross national income (GNI); income and consumption of households **Edition:** 2006

Population Trends in the East-Central-European Capitals — **Language:** English/Hungarian **Frequency:** irregular **Content:** the analysis deals primarily with the period between 1990 and 2003; main subject matters are the following: changes of the population number and their causes; fertility trends; migration trends; ageing process of the population; households and family types **Edition:** 2005

Population Trends in the East-Central-European Capitals — **Language:** English/Hungarian **Frequency:** annual **Content:** concentrates on East-Central-Europe and analyses the demographic trends of capitals. Main subject matters are: changes of the population number and their causes; fertility trends; migration trends; ageing process of the population; households and family types **Edition:** 2005

Productivity and Competitiveness of the Hungarian Economy — **Language:** English/Hungarian **Frequency:** annual **Content:** publication on productivity disseminated in recent years. Per employee GDP and per hour GDP presented as a productivity measure

Public Utilities — **Language:** English/Hungarian **Frequency:** annual **Content:** provides information on the status of energy supply; public water supply and sewerage; on municipal services (urban green areas; street cleaning; municipal solid waste and liquid waste treatment) and on the length and area of urban roads **Edition:** 2006

Regional Data of Education — **Language:** English/Hungarian **Frequency:** annual **Content:** modified regional data on education and training. Statistical data of the pre-primary level to the post secondary education are included by regions according to new methodology. English tables and summary are supplemented.

Regional Statistical Yearbook — **Language:** English/Hungarian **Frequency:** annual **Content:** data collection on the economic and social conditions in Hungary broken down by territorial units

Research and Development — **Language:** English/Hungarian **Frequency:** annual **Content:** main data of organisations having research and development activities. The number of research personnel by gender and educational attainment sum of expenditure on R&D by financial sources, separated capital expenditure in different sectors of R&D, by legal form of organizations, industries and by branch, sector of science; shows results of R&D activities; main data are detailed by regions **Edition:** 2006

Small and Medium-sized Enterprises and Entrepreneurship — **Language:** English/Hungarian **Frequency:** annual **Content:** provides a comprehensive picture on SMEs and entrepreneurship in the Hungarian economy in international perspective **Edition:** 2006

Statistical Yearbook of Agriculture — **Language:** English/ Hungarian **Frequency:** annual **Content:** status of the agricultural sector. It presents the share of this sector within the national economy and provides data on employment of the agriculture and food-industry, on production, exports, imports and consumption **Edition:** 2005

Statistical Yearbook of External Trade — **Language:** English/Hungarian **Frequency:** annual **Content:** tables demonstrate the foreign trade activity of Hungary **Edition:** 2006

Statistical Yearbook of Hungary — **Language:** English/Hungarian **Frequency:** annual **Content:** annual statistics on major socio-economic indicators **Edition:** 2004

Vineyards in Hungary — **Language:** English/Hungarian **Frequency:** annual **Content:** information on the vineyards located on the 2172 settlements in Hungary. Regional, additionally NUTS 3 and 4 level data on the distribution of the vineyards by age, varieties, size and shortage of vine-stocks

Yearbook of Household Statistics — **Language:** Hungarian/English **Frequency:** annual **Content:** a voluntary data collection based on one month diary keeping period of the responding households and an interview about their incomes and greater purchases at the end of the year **Edition:** 2006

Yearbook of Industrial and Construction Statistics — **Language:** English/Hungarian **Frequency:** annual **Content:** publishes data deriving form the industrial and construction surveys and other special statistics; contains detailed data of industrial products and services **Edition:** 2005

Yearbook of Tourism — **Language:** English/Hungarian **Frequency:** annual **Content:** statistical analysis of the tourism industry in Hungary **Edition:** 2005

Magyar Nemzeti Bank
National Bank of Hungary

Address: Szabadság tér 8/9, Budapest, 1850
Telephone: +36 1 428 2600
Fax: +36 1 428 2500
Website: www.mnb.hu

Guides: publications available online. Occasional papers available through the Library free of charge

Activity: central bank
European monetary policy; achieving financial stability; issuing of notes and coins; research library; influencing and setting exchange rates and interest rates; services to the state, financial sector and the public

Website(s) information:

Magyar Nemzeti Bank (National Bank of Hungary) — **url:** www.mnb.hu
Description: provides both information on the Bank's main activities and services, and an in-depth portrait of latest developments in the Hungarian economy and banking system. Access is provided in both English and Hungarian to the Bank's main publications, such as the "Annual Report", the "Monthly Report", and the "Quarterly Report on Inflation" **Coverage:** online titles such as the monthly updated economic reports cover a wide range of economic and financial topics, providing data on: GDP growth; consumer price index; inflation; industrial output; employment and unemployment; monthly gross earnings; monetary conditions and developments; money and capital markets; financial savings; balance of payments and external trade; and government lending and borrowing

Publication(s):

Annual Report — **Language:** English/Hungarian **Frequency:** annual **Content:** business report and financial statements of the Bank; information on the recent economic and financial developments including interest rates changes and monetary developments; financial achievements over the year **Edition:** 2006

External Accounts Statistics Hungary — **Language:** English/Hungarian **Frequency:** annual **Content:** presents country specific details of the balance of payments and international investment position

Hungarian Banking Sector — **Language:** English **Frequency:** 2 p.a. **Content:** overview of the Hungarian banking system: size and increase of the market, and changes in banking rates and bank's risks

Monetary Policy in Hungary — **Language:** English/Hungarian **Frequency:** irregular **Content:** presents an overview of the monetary policy of the National Bank of Hungary

Occasional Papers — **Language:** English or Hungarian **Frequency:** irregular **Content:** they contain the results of analysis and research work conducted at the NBH. Their purpose is to encourage readers to present their comments, which may be useful for the authors in further research.
Many issues of the NBH Working Papers are published in English/Hungarian, some of them are available only in Hungarian or in English

Report on Convergence — **Language:** English/Hungarian **Frequency:** annual **Content:** overview of the central bank's position regarding the current state of convergence and the challenges expected in the near future. Contains analysis on price stability, long-term interest rates and other factors of convergence **Edition:** 2005

Report on Financial Stability — **Language:** English/Hungarian **Frequency:** annual **Content:** it focuses on the analysis of long-term trends and the foreseeable evaluation of risks. Informs stakeholders on the topical issues related to financial stability; reviews risks which pose a threat to financial stability and identifies the components and trends which increase the vulnerability of the financial system **Edition:** 2006

Report on Inflation — **Language:** English/Hungarian **Frequency:** 2 per annum **Content:** it presents forecasts for the retail price index, underlying inflation, components of GDP and full analyses and forecasts for the financial market, and macro-economic and balance processes; twice a year partial updates of the forecasts are also prepared **Edition:** 2006

Iceland

Statistics Iceland

Address: Borgartúni 21a, Reykjavík, 150
Telephone: +354 528 1000
Fax: +354 528 1099
E-mail: information@statice.is
Website: www.statice.is

Guides: most data is downloadable from the website www.statice.is
Activity: to collect and publish socio-economic statistics on Iceland

Website(s) information:

Statistics Iceland — **url:** www.statice.is **Description:** provides a wide range of online socio-economic statistics, searchable by mulitple indicators and years **Coverage:** provides a wide range of online socio-economic statistics

Publication(s):

Agriculture — **Language:** English **Frequency:** annual **Content:** contains data on fertilisers, livestock and field crops, production and hunting

Culture — **Language:** English **Frequency:** annual **Content:** contains data on advertising, books and libraries, newspapers and periodicals, sound recordings, cinemas, videos, broadcasting, arts and museums

Education — **Language:** English **Frequency:** annual **Content:** contains data on pre-primary institutions, compulsory schools, upper secondary schools and universities

Elections — **Language:** English **Frequency:** annual **Content:** contains data on general, local government and presidential elections

Enterprises and Turnover — **Language:** English **Frequency:** annual **Content:** contains data on enterprises, insolvencies, turnover and financial accounts by industry

External Trade — **Language:** English **Frequency:** annual **Content:** contains data on balance of trade, exports and imports

Fisheries — **Language:** English **Frequency:** annual **Content:** contains data on monthly updates, catch and value, fish processing, imports and exports, fishing vessels, fish products, price indices and financial accounts for the fishing industry

Geography and Environment — **Language:** English **Frequency:** annual **Content:** contains data on geographical areas, temperature and precipitation, gas emissions and waste

Health, Social Affairs and Justice — **Language:** English **Frequency:** annual **Content:** contains data on lifestyle, health services, social protection expenditure, social insurances, municipal social services, courts, prisons and prisoners

Manufacturing and Energy — **Language:** English **Frequency:** annual **Content:** contains data on producer price index, manufacturing, construction and energy

Money and Credit — **Language:** English **Frequency:** annual **Content:** contains data on banking, currencies, stocks, loans and investment credit funds

National Accounts and Public Finance — **Language:** English **Frequency:** annual **Content:** contains data on consumption expenditure, public finances, gross fixed capital formation, production approach and short term indicators

Population — **Language:** English **Frequency:** annual **Content:** contains data on migration, municipalities, citizenship, demography, marriages and divorces, religion and names

Prices and Consumption — **Language:** English **Frequency:** annual **Content:** contains data on the consumer price index, building cost index, wage index, purchasing power parity, consumption and producer price index

Statistical Yearbook of Iceland — **Language:** English **Frequency:** annual **Content:** contains an overview of statistical information in a number of economic and social fields

Tourism, Transport and Information Technology — **Language:** English **Frequency:** annual **Content:** contains data on tourist industry, accommodations, passengers, aviation, ships, vehicles, telecommunication, postal service and IT

Wages, Income, and Labour Market — **Language:** English **Frequency:** annual **Content:** contains data on wages, income and labour market by occupation, gender, age and sector

Ireland

Central Bank of Ireland

Address: PO Box 559, Dame Street, Dublin, 2
Telephone: +353 1 434 4000/671 6666
Fax: +353 1 671 6561
E-mail: enquiries@centralbank.ie
Website: www.centralbank.ie

Guides: publishes annual reports in English and Gaelic
Activity: has responsibility for monetary policy functions, financial stability, economic analysis, currency and payment systems, investment of foreign and domestic assets and the provision of central services

Website(s) information:

Central Bank of Ireland — url: www.centralbank.ie **Description:** provides full information about its activities, information on the basic tasks of monetary policy and its implementation, monetary policy operations, credit institutions supervision activities and other responsibilities established by the legislation as well as information on the national macroeconomic situation, such as analysis of the developments in the national economy and financial markets, and on the financial position of the Bank; The Bank publishes annual reports, monthly and quarterly bulletins where it presents information about its activities as well as a wide range of financial and macroeconomic information **Coverage:** the "Statistics" section offers key exchange rates, euro interest rates, and the latest credit, money, and banking statistics

Publication(s):

Annual Reports — **Language:** English/Gaelic **Frequency:** annual **Content:** global economic development features review of the economy of Ireland; exchange rate and monetary policy; interest rates; foreign reserve management; cash management; payment and securities settlement systems; annual financial statements of the Bank

Financial Stability Report — **Language:** English **Frequency:** annual **Content:** involves monitoring both domestic and international financial developments and highlighting potential areas of concern relevant to the Irish financial system

Monthly Statistics — **Language:** English **Frequency:** monthly **Content:** statistical data on government finances

Quarterly Bulletin — **Language:** English **Frequency:** quarterly **Content:** quarterly analysis of latest developments in the national economy and the banking sector, supported by economic and financial statistics and data

Central Statistics Office

Address: Skehard Road, Cork
Telephone: +353 21 453 5000
Fax: +353 21 453 5555
E-mail: information@cso.ie
Website: www.cso.ie

Guides: releases more than 100 publications; all available online from the year 1993 onward

Activity: national statistics office

Website(s) information:

Central Statistics Office — url: www.cso.ie **Description:** provides information on Ireland's Statistics Office, its activities, surveys and mythology; provides access to all its publications and new up-dates **Coverage:** monthly, quarterly and annual statistical data covering more than 25 topics including statistics, socio-economic development, infrastructure, transport, industry

Publication(s):

Agriculture and Fishing — **Language:** English **Frequency:** monthly **Content:** consists of data on area, yield and production; agricultural labour input; livestock surveys; output, input and income in agriculture; production prices

Balance of Payments — **Frequency:** annual **Content:** consists of data on balance of international payments; external debt; foreign direct investment; service exports and imports and other related indexes

Births Deaths and Marriages — **Language:** English **Frequency:** annual **Content:** statistical data on births, deaths; marriages by age

Census of Population — **Language:** English **Frequency:** annual **Content:** includes detailed statistics covering: population classified by area; ages and marital status; household composition and family units

EU Survey on Income and Living Conditions — **Language:** English **Frequency:** quarterly **Content:** comparisons of different indexes of living conditions in EU countries

Health and Social Conditions — **Language:** English **Frequency:** annual **Content:** consists of survey on income and living conditions disability update; pensions update; module on childcare; module on health

Housing and Households — **Language:** English **Frequency:** annual **Content:** consists of module on housing; planning permissions; data on construction and building

Information Society and Telecommunications — **Language:** English **Frequency:** annual **Content:** data on development of the IT sector and information society

National Employment Survey — **Language:** English **Frequency:** annual **Content:** consists of comparisons of hourly earnings of people working in different sectors of industry

National Household Survey Module on Educational Attainment — **Language:** English **Frequency:** quarterly **Content:** comparisons of changes in educational attainment

National Income and Expenditure — **Language:** English **Frequency:** quarterly **Content:** data on income, prices of products and services, savings

Prices — **Language:** English **Frequency:** quarterly **Content:** consists of wholesale price index; consumer price index; consumer prices: average price analysis - in Dublin and outside Dublin

Quarterly National Household Survey — **Language:** English **Frequency:** quarterly **Content:** data on different household indexes

Statistical Bulletin — **Language:** English **Frequency:** quarterly **Content:** statistical data on more than 25 topics; socio-economic and industry development

Statistical Yearbook of Ireland — **Language:** English **Frequency:** annual **Content:** statistical data on more than 25 topics

Tourism and Travel — **Language:** English **Frequency:** annual **Content:** consists of data on overseas travel; tourism and travel; household travel survey

Trade Statistics — **Language:** English **Frequency:** monthly **Content:** very detailed publication, including imports and exports classified by country for current month and year-to-date

Transport — **Language:** English **Frequency:** annual **Content:** data on vehicles in the country

Department of Finance

Address: Government Buildings, Upper Merrion Street, Dublin, 2
Telephone: +353 1 676 7571
Fax: +353 1 678 9936
E-mail: webmaster@finance.gov.ie
Website: www.irlgov.ie/finance

Guides: publish statistical information and government finance information

Activity: plays a central role in implementing Government policy, in particular the Programme for Government, and in advising and supporting the Minister for Finance and the Government on the economic and financial management of the State and the overall management and development of the public sector

Website(s) information:

Department of Finance — url: www.irlgov.ie/finance **Description:** information on economic and business climate, providing statistical data on socio-economic, banking and finance indicators; national budget and information about taxes is provided; offers economic forecasts **Coverage:** Economic Statistics in the "Finance and Economic Information" section provides data that covers public finances, EU transfers, economic output and growth, balance of payments, external trade, production, earnings, population, prices, employment, consumption and construction

Publication(s):

Economic Bulletins — **Language:** English **Frequency:** monthly **Content:** data on economic development, government and public finances and information and data on sartorial issues like housing, tourism and agriculture

Italy

Instituto Nazionale di Statistica (ISTAT)
National Institute of Statistics

Address: Via Cesare Balbo 16, Rome, 00184
Telephone: +39 06 46731
Fax: +39 06 4673 3107
E-mail: biblio@istat.it
Website: www.istat.it

Guides: Catalogo ISTAT (annual catalogue of publications with summaries of contents)

Activity: main supplier of official statistical information in Italy; collects and produces information on Italian economy and society and makes it available for study and decision-making purposes

Website(s) information:
Istituto Nazionale di Statistica (ISTAT) *(National Institute of Statistics)* — **url:** www.istat.it **Coverage:** statistics on GDP, consumer prices, production prices, industrial production, retail trades, employment and wages

Publication(s):
Annuario Statistico Italiano *(Italian Statistical Yearbook)* — **Language:** Italian **Frequency:** annual **Content:** annual statistical review of Italy's main socioeconomic and financial indicators

Bollettino Mensile di Statistica *(Monthly Statistical Bulletin)* — **Language:** Italian **Frequency:** monthly **Content:** statistics on population and people as well as economic indicators of Italy

I viaggi in Italia e all'estero *(Travelling in Italy and Abroad)* — **Language:** Italian **Frequency:** annual **Content:** travel statistics covering the movement of Italians within the country and trips abroad

Ministero delle Politiche Agricole Alimentari e Forestali
Ministry or Agriculture and Forestry

Address: Via XX Settembre, n. 20, Rome, 00187
Telephone: +39 06 46651
Fax: +39 06 4742314
Website: www.politicheagricole.it

Guides: publications can be downloaded
Activity: is responsible for conducting policy affairs in the field of agriculture and affiliated sectors in Italy

Website(s) information:
Agricoltura Italiana Online *(Italian Agriculture)* — **url:** www.agricolturaitalianaonline.gov.it **Coverage:** information on the different sectors of agriculture; includes statistics on production, occupation, consumption, and foreign trade

Ministero delle Politiche Agricole Alimentari e Forestali *(Ministry of Agriculture and Forestry)* — **url:** www.politicheagricole.it **Coverage:** documents on the development of agriculture in Italy and Europe

Publication(s):
Parametri ex_post 2006 relativi ai prodotti primavera/estate *(Parameter of 2006 Regarding Products of Spring/Summer)* — **Language:** Italian **Content:** information on the development of the country and infrastructure

Ministero dell'Economia e delle Finanze
Ministry of Economy and Finance

Address: Via Pastrengo 22, Rome
E-mail: pubblicazione.sito@tesoro.it
Website: www.mef.gov.it

Guides: publications can be found online; all are downloadable free of charge; includes some documents in English
Activity: responsible for the economic and fiscal development of Italy; regulates policy accordingly

Website(s) information:
Ministero dell'Economia e delle Finanze *(Ministry of Economy and Finance)* — **url:** www.mef.gov.it **Coverage:** information on the development of the economy of Italy; data on public and private finance

World Food Programme (WFP)
Address: Via C G Viola 68, Parco dei Medici, Rome, 00148
Telephone: +39 6 65131
Fax: +39 6 6513 2840
E-mail: wfpinfo@wfp.org
Website: www.wfp.org

Guides: IFPRI identifies and studies policies, which help developing countries meet their food needs. Under the 'Linking Research and Action' initiative, IFPRI and WFP have joined forces to produce a series of briefs studying the linkages between food policy research and food aid programming
Activity: WFP is the food aid arm of the United Nations system

Website(s) information:
World Food Programme (WFP) — **url:** www.wfp.org **Coverage:** Lists data on its operations, including expenditures, food shipments/deliveries, resources, transport and staff. Drawing on a variety of sources, including non-governmental organisations and other UN Agencies, WFP also compiles useful facts and figures on the general state of world hunger; this data covers malnutrition, child hunger, agricultural production and global food aid

Latvia

Latvijas Banka
Bank of Latvia

Address: K. Valdemara iela 2a, Riga, LV-1050
Telephone: +371 702 2300
Fax: +371 702 2420
E-mail: info@bank.lv
Website: www.bank.lv

Guides: publishes Bank's annual reports, the quarterly monetary reviews and Latvia's balance of payments, the monthly Monetary Bulletin and Latvia's Balance of Payments and the newspaper Averss un Reverss
Activity: to regulate currency in circulation by implementing monetary policy and to maintain price stability in Latvia

Website(s) information:
Bank of Latvia — **url:** www.bank.lv **Description:** Latvian monetary system; access to wide range of general macro-economic indicators, financial data, rules and regulations; access to publications available **Coverage:** current data available on banking and monetary statistics; payment systems' statistics; balance of payment statistics; external debt statistics; interest rate statistics; securities statistics

Publication(s):
Averss un Reverss — **Language:** Latvian **Frequency:** monthly **Content:** banking news

Finansu Stabilitates Parskats *(Financial Stability Report)* — **Language:** Latvian/English **Frequency:** annual **Content:** goal of the Report is to analyse and assess the performance of the Latvian financial system, paying particular attention to the banking sector and the operation of leasing companies

Latvijas Bankas gada parskats *(Annual Reports)* — **Language:** Latvian/English **Frequency:** annual **Content:** global economic development features; review of the economy of Latvia; exchange rate and monetary policy; interest rates; foreign reserve management; cash management; payment and securities settlement systems; annual financial statements of the Bank of Lithuania

Latvijas Maksajumu Bilance *(Latvian Balance of Payments)* — **Language:** Latvian/English **Frequency:** quarterly **Content:** summarises economic transactions of Latvia's residents with the ROW; also includes Latvia's international investment position and information on foreign investment stocks in Latvia broken down by activity and country

Latvijas Maksajumu Bilance (Pamatraditaji) *(Latvia's Balance of Payments (Key Items))* — **Language:** Latvian/English **Frequency:** monthly **Content:** monetary policy and to provide a general background of money market trends

Monetarais Apskats *(Monetary Review)* — **Language:** Latvian/English **Frequency:** quarterly **Content:** discusses monetary and fiscal policies, foreign trade and developments in the national economy

Monetarais Biletens *(Monetary Bulletin)* — **Language:** Latvian/English **Frequency:** monthly **Content:** macroeconomic and monetary indicators, money market interest rates and the consolidated balance sheet of credit institutions

Latvijas Republikas Ekonomikas Ministrija
Ministry of Economy of the Republic of Latvia

Address: Brivibas iela 55, Riga, LV-1519
Telephone: +371 728 0882
Fax: +371 728 0882
E-mail: pasts@em.gov.lv
Website: www.em.gov.lv

Guides: publishes reports on the economic development and status of Latvia

Activity: central government (state administration) institution in the field of economic policy; the ministry is the head institution for the subordinated state administration institutions

Website(s) information:

Latvijas Republikas Ekonomikas Ministrija *(Ministry of Economy of the Republic of Latvia)* — **url:** www.em.gov.lv **Description:** provides information on the Ministry and its working areas: industry, tourism, foreign trade and building; publications are available online on a free basis as well as all the current data concerning Latvia's economic development; information about Latvia's EU membership is also given **Coverage:** statistical data on industries (food, wood, light, ect.), tourism, foreign trade and building in Latvia

Publication(s):

Makroekonomiskais apskats *(National Economy of Latvia: Macroeconomic Review)* — **Language:** Latvian/English **Frequency:** quarterly **Content:** review of development of the Latvian economy

Zinojums par Latvijas tautsaimniecibas attistibu *(Report on the Economic Development of Latvia)* — **Language:** Latvian/English **Frequency:** per annum 2 **Content:** evaluates the economic situation in Latvia and progress of reforms as well as offers economic development forecasts

Latvijas Republikas Finansu Ministrija
Ministry of Finance of the Republic of Latvia

Address: Smilsu iela 1, Riga, LV-1919
Telephone: +371 709 5405
Fax: +371 709 5503
E-mail: info@fm.gov.lv
Website: www.fm.gov.lv

Guides: publishes speeches, articles and interviews
Activity: ministry of finance

Website(s) information:

Latvijas Republikas Finansu Ministrija *(Ministry of Finance of the Republic of Latvia)* — **url:** www.fm.gov.lv **Description:** provides information about the Ministry, Latvian taxation and monetary systems, strategies of budget formation, international financial cooperation; information on customs; provides links to press releases, articles and commentaries; all up-to-date economic data available on free basis on-line **Coverage:** up-to-date data on state and pocket budget (monthly and annual data), data on taxes and fees, main economic indicators and forecasts

Publication(s):

Valsts Budzeta Apskats *(National Budget Explanation)* — **Language:** Latvian/English **Frequency:** annual **Content:** contains information about macroeconomic indicators in Latvia and describes its future development; analysis of the external economic environment, its development tendency and possible impact on the state national economy; information about the fiscal review, analysis of revenues, central government budget expenditure and structure of the Central Government Budget law

LR Centrala Statistikas Parvalde
Central Statistical Bureau of Latvia

Address: Lacplesa iela 1, Riga, LV-1301
Telephone: +371 7 366 6850
Fax: +371 7 830 137
E-mail: csb@csb.gov.lv
Website: www.csb.lv

Guides: statistics Latvia releases annual, bi-annual, quarterly, monthly releases on demographic, agricultural, general, industrial, foreign trade, domestic trade, as well as price and labour statistics sections
Activity: national statistical bureau

Website(s) information:

LR Centrala Statistikas Parvalde *(Central Statistical Bureau of Latvia)* — **url:** www.csb.lv **Description:** covers main products and services provided by the Central Bureau, including: a catalogue of publications (Latvian and English); press releases; population census results; and online socio-economic statistics **Coverage:** current data on macroeconomic indicators and finances; population; employment; personal income; price indices; agriculture; industry; investments and construction; transport; foreign and domestic trade; education and health; and tourism

Publication(s):

Buvnieciba Latvija *(Construction in Latvia)* — **Language:** Latvian/English **Frequency:** annual **Content:** data collection on non-financial investment, construction of objects in the social and production sector, as well as construction of private houses, the volume of construction work performed by construction enterprises, sales, exports and imports of the main construction materials, construction cost indices, labour remuneration and occupational injuries, designing, as well as construction permits issued for buildings and civil engineering

Dazada Latvija: pagasti, novadi, pilsetas, rajoni, regioni. Vertejumi, perspektivas, vizijas *(Diverse Latvia: Civil Parishes, Counties, Cities and Towns, Districts, Regions. Evaluations, Forecasts, Visions)* — **Language:** Latvian **Frequency:** irregular **Content:** socio-economic development of all administratively territorial units of Latvia between 1996 and 2003

Demografija *(Demography)* — **Language:** Latvian/English **Frequency:** annual **Content:** number and changes of population, gender, age and ethnic composition, demographic burden, registered marriages and divorces, fertility, mortality, long-term migration, citizenship, granting and loss of citizenship, asylum seekers and refugees are given in this statistical data collection

Environment Indicators in Latvia — **Language:** English **Frequency:** annual **Content:** provides information on harmful atmospheric emissions from stationary sources, water abstraction and utilisation, wastewater discharge and the operation of wastewater treatment equipment, municipal and hazardous waste, management of national parks and other reserves, forestry and hunting

Estonia, Latvia and Lithuania in Figures — **Language:** English **Frequency:** annual **Content:** essential comparable annual statistics on economic and social conditions of contemporary Estonia, Latvia and Lithuania

Estonia, Latvia and Lithuania in Figures — **Language:** English **Frequency:** quarterly **Content:** review illustrate the key principles of the country's economic policy and provide an analysis of the macroeconomic development, including forecasts of the main macroeconomic indicators

Household Budget — **Language:** English **Frequency:** annual **Content:** surveyed households, their incomes and expenditures, living conditions, self-evaluation of the living conditions of the households and other indicators of the country as a whole, in urban and rural areas, as well as in seven major cities on average and Riga separately

Housing Stock — **Language:** English **Frequency:** annual **Content:** data collection on the housing stock, provision of amenities in the country as a whole and with breakdowns by city and town, administrative district and ownership

Informacijas Sabiedriba Latvija *(Information Society in Latvia)* — **Language:** Latvian/English **Frequency:** annual **Content:** presents information on the infrastructure of information society: availability of PCs in households, enterprises, organisations and educational establishments of Latvia; use of Internet; use of information technologies for e-commercial purposes

Komercdarbibas Finansialie Pamatraditaji *(Basic Financial Indicators of Business Activity)* — **Language:** Latvian/English **Frequency:** annual **Content:** financial information on business activity within private and public sectors broken down by the main activity of the enterprise and the number employed. Indicators of financial activity are presented

Latvijas Arteja Tirdznieba *(Foreign Trade of Latvia)* — **Language:** Latvian/English **Frequency:** annual **Content:** presents aggregated data on merchandise exports and imports broken down by country and merchandise group

Latvijas Energobilance *(Energy in Latvia)* — **Language:** Latvian/English **Frequency:** annual **Content:** data collection contains statistical indicators characterising the consumption of major energy resources in Latvia, as well as breakdowns by kind of activity and information on average prices of energy resources purchased in the sector of manufacturing are provided

Latvijas Lauksaimnieciba *(Agriculture of Latvia)* — **Language:** Latvian/English **Frequency:** annual **Content:** the most important statistical indicators over the past five years characterising the situation of agriculture in total, including supply balance sheets of agricultural products, as well as main agricultural sectors; output and productivity indicators of the main agricultural products in the Baltic countries

Latvijas Makroekonomiskie Raditaji *(Macroeconomic Indicators of Latvia 2005)* — **Language:** Latvian/English **Frequency:** quarterly **Content:** the most important macroeconomic indicators such as GDP and the principal items of the balance of payments, foreign trade, government finance and banking statistics

Latvijas Regioni Skaitlos *(Latvia's Regions in Figures)* — **Language:** Latvian/English **Frequency:** annual **Content:** data collection contains information on the gross domestic product, employment and other economic indicators for the country as a whole and breakdowns by regions

Latvijas Statistikas Gadagramata *(Statistical Yearbook of Latvia)* — **Language:** Latvian/English **Frequency:** annual **Content:** statistics on Latvia's main socioeconomic indicators

Latvijas Statistikas Ikmenesa Biletens *(Monthly Bulletin of Latvian Statistics)* — **Language:** Latvian/English **Frequency:** monthly **Content:** statistical overview of the present socioeconomic environment in Latvia

Latvijas Valsts Finanses *(Public Finances of Latvia)* — **Language:** Latvian/English **Frequency:** quarterly **Content:** collection comprises data on the budget of Latvia, banking system, activities of insurance companies, financial leasing companies, Riga Stock Exchange; comparisons of the main indicators for Baltic countries are provided

Latvijas Veselibas Aprupes Statistikas Gadagramata *(Health Care Statistics in Latvia)* — **Language:** Latvian/English **Frequency:** annual **Content:** provides all-round characteristics of health and the system of health care in the country. The statistical data are compared with the data of the previous year, which are specified during the compilation of each edition. The most relevant data are compared with other countries

Paterina Cenas *(Consumer Prices)* — **Language:** Latvian/English **Frequency:** quarterly **Content:** average prices of foods and services for survey quarter in months are published

Turism Latvija *(Tourism in Latvia)* — **Language:** Latvian/English **Frequency:** annual **Content:** data collection contains information drawn from a survey of persons crossing the state border and a survey on the travelling public

Liechtenstein

Amt für Volkswirtschaft
Liechtenstein Department of Economics

Address: Giessenstrasse 3, Vaduz, 9490
Telephone: +4175 236 6876
Fax: +4175 236 6931
E-mail: info.statistik@avw.llv.li
Website: www.llv.li

Guides: data is available on website
Activity: publishes official statistics on socio-economic indicators

Website(s) information:
Amt für Volkswirtschaft *(Liechtenstein Department of Economics)* — **url:** www.llv.li **Description:** provides key statistics on Liechtenstein **Coverage:** contains data on economic indicators, population and tourism

Lithuania

Lietuvos Bankas
Bank of Lithuania

Address: Gedimino pr. 6, Vilnius, LT-01103
Telephone: +370 5 268 0029
Fax: +370 5 262 8124
E-mail: info@lb.lt
Website: www.lb.lt

Guides: the publications of the Bank of Lithuania provide information related to the activities of the Bank of Lithuania, monetary and banking policies, balance of payments and financial statistics
Activity: central bank of the Republic of Lithuania; its principal objective is to maintain price stability

Website(s) information:
Lietuvos Bankas *(Bank of Lithuania)* — **url:** www.lb.lt **Description:** provides full information about its activities, information on the basic tasks of monetary policy and its implementation, monetary policy operations, credit institutions supervision activities and other responsibilities established by the legislation as well as information on the national macroeconomic situation, such as analysis of the developments in the national economy and financial markets, and on the financial position of the Bank; The Bank of Lithuania publishes annual reports, monthly and quarterly bulletins where it presents information about its activities as well as a wide range of financial and macroeconomic information available from 2000; provides all the current information about adoption of the Euro in Lithuania **Coverage:** statistical data on a free basis is available on main economic and financial indicators; official exchange rate statistics; monetary policy; monetary financial institutions balance sheet and monetary statistics; monetary financial institutions interest rates on loans and deposits statistics; money, currencies and financial market statistics; balance of payments and foreign reserves statistics

Publication(s):
Banku statistikos metrastis *(Banking Statistics Yearbook)* — **Language:** Lithuanian/English **Frequency:** annual **Content:** provides general information about main economic indicators; detailed data on money, deposits, loans, inter-bank lending market, interest rate, foreign exchange market turnover, securities market, balance of payments **Edition:** 2006

Ketvircio biuletenis *(Quarterly Bulletin)* — **Language:** Lithuanian/English **Frequency:** quarterly **Content:** development of economy of Lithuania; review of Lithuanian financial markets

Lietuvos Respublikos mokejimu balansai *(Balance of Payments of the Republic of Lithuania)* — **Language:** Lithuanian/English **Frequency:** quarterly **Content:** balance of payments data **Edition:** 2006

Menesinis biuletenis *(Monthly Bulletin)* — **Language:** Lithuanian/English **Frequency:** monthly **Content:** review of general economic indicators: money, deposits, loans, interest rates on deposits and loans, money and foreign exchange markets **Edition:** 2006

Metine ataskaita *(Annual Report)* — **Language:** English/Lithuanian **Frequency:** annual **Content:** global economic development features review of the economy of Lithuania; exchange rate and monetary policy; interest rates; foreign reserve management; cash management; payment and securities settlement systems; annual financial statements of the Bank of Lithuania **Edition:** 2006

Metine Lietuvos Banko finansine ataskaita *(Annual Financial Statements of the Bank of Lithuania)* — **Language:** English/Lithuanian **Frequency:** annual **Content:** independent auditors' report; balance sheet and profit (loss) statement of the Bank of Lithuania; explanatory notes to the financial statements of the Bank of Lithuania

Lietuvos Respublikos Finansu Ministerija
Ministry of Finance of the Republic of Lithuania

Address: J Tumo-Vaizganto 8a/2, Vilnius, LT-01512
Telephone: +370 5 239 0000
Fax: +370 5 279 1481
E-mail: finmin@finmin.lt
Website: www.finmin.lt

Guides: publish statistical information on state debt and government securities
Activity: Ministry of Finance

Website(s) information:
Lietuvos Respublikos Finansu Ministerija *(Ministry of Finance of the Republic of Lithuania)* — **url:** www.finmin.lt **Description:** information on Lithuanian economic and business climate, providing statistical data on socio-economic, banking and finance indicators from the year of 1999; national budget and information about taxes is provided; offers economic forecast; financial aspects of Lithuania's EU membership and current information on the integration in the Euro zone **Coverage:** provides data on fiscal policies, national budget, government finance statistics, government budget deficit, state debt, taxes

Publication(s):
Bendroji valstybes skola *(General Government Debt)* — **Language:** Lithuanian/English **Frequency:** annual **Content:** Lithuania's economic development; credit ratings; debt level, structure, dynamics and limits; borrowing by the government

Lietuvos vyriausybes vertybiniu popieriu apzvalgos (Overview of Lithuanian Government Securities) — **Language:** Lithuanian/English **Frequency:** annual **Content:** review of Government Securities circulation

Lietuvos Respublikos Ukio Ministerija
Ministry of Economy of the Republic of Lithuania

Address: Gedimino pr 48/2, Vilnius, LT-01104
Telephone: +370 5 262 3863
Fax: +370 5 262 3974
E-mail: kanc@ukmin.lt
Website: www.ukmin.lt

Guides: publishes annual reports on development of Lithuanian economy
Activity: Ministry of Economics

Website(s) information:
Lietuvos Respublikos Ukio Ministerija (Ministry of Economy of the Republic of Lithuania) — **url:** www.ukmin.lt **Description:** provides information about the Ministry, its structure; reviews of the economic and social situation of the Republic of Lithuania, long term-development strategies and programmes; detailed information on energy sector, foreign trade, industry and business, innovation and technologies; information on European Union structural funds support to business, energy and public tourism sectors in Lithuania; provider of links to organisations that work under the Ministry of Economy of the Republic of Lithuania **Coverage:** provides all current data on development of the main economic indicators; data on energy sector, foreign trade, industry and business, innovation and technologies

Publication(s):
Energetika Lietuvoje (Energy in Lithuania) — **Language:** Lithuanian/English **Frequency:** annual **Content:** current status of the Lithuanian energy sector (power system, oil refinery, district heat and gas supply), energy balances, economical-financial indicators of the largest energy companies as well as trends of basic comparative indicators

Lietuvos ekonomines ir socialines situacijos pazvalga (Review of Economic and Social Situation of the Republic of Lithuania) — **Language:** Lithuanian/English **Frequency:** annual **Content:** short review of main data on economic development

Metine ataskaita (Annual report) — **Language:** Lithuanian/English **Frequency:** annual **Content:** covers main sectors of economy: energy, small and medium sized business and support, state property privatisation policy and management of the companies, domestic and foreign trade, tourism development; co-ordination of EU matters, management of EU structural funds

Statistikos departamentas prie Lietuvos Respublikos vyriausybes
Department of Statistics to the Government of the Republic of Lithuania

Address: Gedimino pr 29, Vilnius, LT-01500
Telephone: +370 5 236 4822
Fax: +370 5 236 4845
E-mail: statistika@stat.gov.lt
Website: www.std.lt

Guides: statistics Lithuania releases more than 100 publications, of which biggest are annual, bi-annual, quarterly, monthly and approximately 15 press releases per month
Activity: national statistics office

Website(s) information:
Statistikos Departamentas (Department of Statistics to the Government of the Republic of Lithuania) — **url:** www.std.lt **Description:** information is classified into 9 domains: general statistics, economy and finance, population and social statistics, business statistics, agriculture, foreign trade, transport and communication, environment and energy, science and technology, regional statistics; the majority of indicators have been produced since 1995 enables to track changes and make comparisons; registered users have an access to Statistical analytical system; the site has links to all Lithuanian public institutions, embassies, international organizations, national statistical offices **Coverage:** statistics available on a free basis provide a general socio-economic portrait of Lithuania; all information is divided into 9 main domains: general statistics, economy and finance, population and social statistics, business statistics, agriculture, foreign trade, transport and communication, environment and energy, science and technology, regional statistics

Publication(s):
Darbo jega, uzimtumas ir nedarbas (Labour Force, Employment and Unemployment) — **Language:** Lithuanian/English **Frequency:** annual **Content:** information on economic activity of the population based on the Labour Force Survey carried out by Statistics Lithuania; the structure of employed is given by gender, age, economic activity, occupation group and hours worked; the structure of unemployment rate is given by age, methods used for seeking work, duration of unemployment for a five-year period

Darbo jega, uzimtumas ir nedarbas (Labour Force, Employment and Unemployment) — **Language:** Lithuanian/English **Frequency:** quarterly **Content:** information is given on the number of employed, unemployed, unemployment rate and other indices

Darbo statistikos metrastis (Yearbook of Labour Statistics) — **Language:** Lithuanian/English **Frequency:** annual **Content:** data on the number of hired employees, employed, average earnings (hourly and monthly), working time, strikes, labour costs, structural indicators of tax on earnings and other labour statistics indicators of the economy of the country by economic activity, economic sector; minimum rates of earnings approved by the Government are shown

Darbo uzmokestis (Wages and Salaries) — **Language:** Lithuanian/English **Frequency:** quarterly **Content:** quarterly data on the number of the hired employees, average monthly earnings (gross, net, real), average hourly earnings, working time and their changes by economic activity, categories of employees (manual and non-manual) and gender in the national economy and by economic sectors (individual enterprises excluded); also, quarterly labour costs index is given

Demografinis metrastis (Demographic Yearbook) — **Language:** Lithuanian/English **Frequency:** annual **Content:** statistical data characterising demographic development of the country as well as comprehensive data on births, deaths and causes of deaths, marriages, divorces and migration; demographic indicators of foreign countries are presented for comparison with figures on Lithuania

Ekonominis ir socialinis vystymasis Lietuvoje (Economic and Social Development in Lithuania) — **Language:** Lithuanian/English **Frequency:** monthly **Content:** up-to-date information about the country's economic and social development; quarterly data in time-series for gross domestic product, direct foreign investment, budgets, households' disposable income, earnings, agriculture, construction and other indicators is presented; comparable indicators of Latvia and Estonia are published; structural indicators of the EU member states are presented

Ekonominis ir socialinis vystymasis Lietuvoje, Latvijoje ir Estijoje (Economic and Social Development of Lithuania, Latvia and Estonia) — **Language:** Lithuanian English **Frequency:** monthly **Content:** monthly changes in main economic and social development indicators of Lithuania, Latvia and Estonia

Finansu imoniu statistika (Statistics of Financial Enterprises) — **Language:** Lithuanian/English **Frequency:** annual **Content:** indicators of credit institutions, insurance companies, financial leasing companies and other financial intermediation enterprises: indicators of profit (loss) statement, balance sheet, investments

Gamtos istekliai ir aplinkosauga (Natural Resources and Environment Protection) — **Language:** Lithuanian/English **Frequency:** annual **Content:** data on climate, usage of natural resources, protection of atmosphere, management of waste, usage of chemical substances, expenditure related to environment protection

Gyvenamasis fondas ir statyba (Stock of Dwellings and Construction) — **Language:** Lithuanian/English **Frequency:** annual **Content:** data related to existing stock of dwellings and new building construction; number of dwellings, rooms, useful space, conveniences; accounting of the stock of dwellings is accomplished by type of ownership, by location; building construction consists of information on building permits granted, new residential and non-residential buildings completed

Gyventoju pajamos ir pragyvenimo lygis (Income and Living Conditions) — **Language:** Lithuanian/English **Frequency:** annual **Content:** data on disposable income, its structure, housing conditions, employment, health care; indicators are presented by place of residence of the household, age, sex and education of the persons

Gyvuliu skaicius (Number of Livestock) — **Language:** Lithuanian/English **Frequency:** annual **Content:** data on the number of livestock, poultry, beehives at the beginning of year; data on cattle are broken down by age, sex, economic purpose, data on pigs by weight, age and economic purpose

Imoniu bankrotas (Bankruptcy of Enterprises) — **Language:** Lithuanian/English **Frequency:** per annum 2 **Content:** presents analysis of the enterprises undergoing bankruptcy or already bankrupt in the previous year and over a five year period; information about administration of bankruptcy procedures is also included

Imoniu finansiniai rodikliai (Financial Indicators - Enterprises) — **Language:** Lithuanian/English **Frequency:** 2 per annum **Content:** information about quarterly financial indicators: assets, equity, liabilities, income, costs, profits

Informacija apie gamintoju parduotos pramones produkcijos kainu pokycius (Information about Changes in Producer Prices for Industrial Production) — **Language:** Lithuanian/English **Frequency:** monthly **Content:** brief methodology for calculation of the producer price index (PPI) and analysis of data of the reporting month as well as changes in producer prices over a month, over the period from the beginning of the year, over twelve months by main industrial grouping and by economic activity is presented in this publication; also indices in time series and weights used for the PPI calculation are shown

Informacija apie importuotu ir eksportuotu kainu pokycius (Information about Changes in Export/Import Prices) — **Language:** Lithuanian/English **Frequency:** monthly **Content:** short explanations of methodology on calculating export and import price indices (EPI/IPI) and analysis of statistical data of the reporting month as well as changes in export/import prices over a month, comparisons with the base year by economic activity

Informacija apie vartojimo prekiu ir paslaugu kainu pokycius (Information on Changes in Consumer Prices for Goods and Services) — **Language:** Lithuanian/English **Frequency:** monthly **Content:** short explanations of calculation methodologies of the consumer price index (CPI) and the harmonized CPI as well as data analysis of the reporting month are given; also, changes in prices for the group of consumer goods and services per month, period from the beginning of the year, twelve months are given; besides, average annual price changes, and indices in time series and weights used in the calculation of indices are shown; finally, the harmonized CPI of EU member states is presented

Informacines technologijos Lietuvoje (Information Technologies in Lithuania) — **Language:** Lithuanian/English **Frequency:** annual **Content:** statistical data on information technologies (IT) are given: the IT sector production and value added tax evaluation; IT goods production, exports and imports; a review of the information and telecommunication technologies' market; IT usage in households, enterprises, public administration, educational establishments

Ketvirtines nacionalines saskaitos (Quarterly National Accounts) — **Language:** Lithuanian/English **Frequency:** quarterly **Content:** quarterly macroeconomic indicators such as gross value added and gross domestic product by three approaches: production, expenditure and income; gross national income, net savings and net lending / borrowing are published; revenue and expenditure as well as financial assets and liabilities of the General Government are presented

Kuro ir energijos balansas (Energy Balances) — **Language:** Lithuanian/English **Frequency:** annual **Content:** annual balances of energy resources for a five-year period and other balances of fuel and energy

Lietuva Europoje (Lithuania in Europe) — **Language:** Lithuanian/English **Frequency:** annual **Content:** presents main economic and social indicators of Lithuania and other EU member states

Lietuva skaiciais (Lithuania in Figures) — **Language:** Lithuanian/English **Frequency:** annual **Content:** general information about the country, geographical and climate-related indicators, national accounts, finances, population, education, culture, science, health care, labour, industry, agriculture, construction, trade, transport and other statistics is presented in the tables and diagrams of the publication

Lietuvos apskritys (Counties of Lithuania) — **Language:** Lithuanian/English **Frequency:** annual **Content:** statistical information about the population, unemployment rate, sales of industrial production, direct foreign investment

Lietuvos apskritys (Counties of Lithuania) — **Language:** Lithuanian/English **Frequency:** annual **Content:** statistical information about economic and social development, demographic and environmental processes, industrial and commercial processes in the country, its counties and municipalities as well as definitions of the indicators are presented

Lietuvos ekonomikos apzvalga (Survey of the Lithuanian Economy) — **Language:** Lithuanian/English **Frequency:** 2 per annum **Content:** compilation of articles contains a general review of the economy; demographic situation and social status; financial market; economic relations with foreign countries; trends in industrial development; economic reforms and priorities; forecasts of macroeconomic indicators; current issues of economy, discussions

Lietuvos gyventojai pagal amziu (Lithuanian Population by Age) — **Language:** Lithuanian/English **Frequency:** annual **Content:** statistical data on population by gender and age as of 1 January are presented by county, municipality, urban and rural area

Lietuvos gyventojai: struktura ir demografine raida (Population of Lithuania: Pattern and Demographic Development) — **Language:** Lithuanian/English **Frequency:** annual **Content:** dynamics of the population, population by county and municipality, age, gender, ethnicity, religion, education, employment, marital status, structure and size of families and households, number of the children given birth, disability, migration, socio-demographic mortality differentials and innovative census-linked methodology. Publication of statistical analysis based on population censuses (1989, 2001) data

Lietuvos gyventoju mirtingumo sociodemografiniai skirtumai (Socio-demographic Mortality Differentials in Lithuania) — **Language:** Lithuanian/English **Frequency:** annual **Content:** statistical analysis on the relative cause-specific mortality ratios by socio-demographic group. Based on the census-linked methodology using socio-demographic mortality differentials. The major longevity indicators (life expectancy) are presented by urban-rural residence, education, marital status and ethnicity

Lietuvos gyventoju sveikatos tyrimu rezultatai (Health Survey Results of Lithuanian Population) — **Language:** Lithuanian/English **Frequency:** annual **Content:** information about the health status of population, chronic diseases and temporary health problems, use of health care services and use of pharmaceuticals etc. Compiled based on the results of a health population survey

Lietuvos nacionalines saskaitos (National Accounts of Lithuania) — **Language:** Lithuanian/English **Frequency:** annual **Content:** financial and non-financial national accounts are shown in series and in terms of the whole country, separately by institutional sectors and, in addition, by sub-sectors of the General Government; comparisons of GDP with other EU member states are made

Lietuvos regionu portretas (Portrait of the Regions of Lithuania) — **Language:** Lithuanian/English **Frequency:** annual **Content:** economic-social data review of the country by counties; data on: geography (including a review of the region, its advantages and disadvantages, territory and natural resources), population, employment, economy, environment, health and culture

Lietuvos statistikos darbai (Lithuanian Statistics: Articles, Reports and Studies) — **Language:** Lithuanian/English **Frequency:** irregular **Content:** economic and social articles and their abstracts

Lietuvos statistikos metrastis (Statistical Yearbook of Lithuania) — **Language:** Lithuanian/English **Frequency:** annual **Content:** detailed statistics related to different areas (country's economic and social development; demographic and environmental processes; industrial, commercial, financial, and investment activities of natural and legal persons; sustainable development and structural indicators)

Mazmenine ir didmenine prekyba (Retail and Wholesale Trade) — **Language:** Lithuanian/English **Frequency:** annual **Content:** trade and catering enterprises turnover, its changes, composition of turnover of retail trade enterprises by commodity group; turnover, number of shops, sales area in retail trade enterprises, number of seats in restaurants and other catering enterprises; basic wholesale trade indicators such as turnover, number of persons employed, and turnover by type of customer and commodity groups are also given

Metu zemes ukio strukturos tyrimo rezultatai (Results of Farm Structure Survey in Lithuania) — **Language:** Lithuanian/English **Frequency:** annual **Content:** data on the Census of Agriculture and the Farm Structure Survey on land and its usage, number of livestock by kind and age groups, tractors and other agricultural machines, farm holders and their family members, number of hired employees on the farm and duration of their working time, other non-agricultural activities

Mirties priezastys (Causes of Death) — **Language:** Lithuanian/English **Frequency:** annual **Content:** data on mortality and causes of death by age and sex; data are presented by urban and rural area, county and municipality and on national level

Mokslo darbuotojai ir ju darbai *(Research Activities)* — **Language:** Lithuanian/English **Frequency:** annual **Content:** data on employees engaged in research and experimental development and expenditure; personnel data; distribution of personnel by higher education, private and public sectors, field of science, sex, age

Moterys ir vyrai Lietuvoje *(Women and Men in Lithuania)* — **Language:** Lithuanian/English **Frequency:** annual **Content:** gender statistics: the number of men and women, family creation and its stability, education, health care and social protection, employment and unemployment, earnings, participation in public administration

Namu ukio pajamos ir islaidos *(Household Income and Expenditure)* — **Language:** Lithuanian/English **Frequency:** annual **Content:** statistical information about household composition, income and consumer expenditure and their structure, housing conditions, possession of consumer durables and assessment of living conditions; the indicators are presented by place of residence, socio-economic group, age, sex and education of household head as well as type of household

Nusikalstamumas ir teisesaugos instituciju veikla *(Crime and the Law Enforcement Activity)* — **Language:** Lithuanian/English **Frequency:** annual **Content:** information referring to crime situation, sentenced persons, incarcerated persons in imprisonment institutions, juvenile delinquency, conviction and crime prevention, as well as activity of law enforcement institutions is provided

Paslaugos *(Services)* — **Language:** Lithuanian/English **Frequency:** annual **Content:** short-term statistics on turnover of enterprises whose main activity is to provide services; numbers employed in the industry

Pragyvenimo lygis ir skurdas *(Living Standard and Poverty)* — **Language:** Lithuanian/English **Frequency:** annual **Content:** trends of changes observed in the standards of living over a three-year period; the levels of relative poverty in various household groups; indicators of social exclusion and standards of living in the households living in relative poverty

Pramones darbo rezultatai *(Industrial Activity Results)* — **Language:** Lithuanian/English **Frequency:** monthly **Content:** production indices of mining, quarrying, manufacturing, electricity, gas and water supply; comparisons are made to previous period, to corresponding period of previous year

Smulkiu, vidutiniu ir dideliu imoniu pagrindiniai rodikliai *(Main Indicators of Small, Medium and Large Enterprises)* — **Language:** Lithuanian/English **Frequency:** annual **Content:** key financial indicators according to size of enterprises: number of employees, assets, equity, costs, income, value added, debt and liquidity ratio

Socialine apsauga Lietuvoje *(Social Protection in Lithuania)* — **Language:** Lithuanian/English **Frequency:** annual **Content:** number of pensioners and persons entitled to benefits, support for illness, old-age, disability, unemployment and other cases, social benefits for families and children

Svietimas *(Education)* — **Language:** Lithuanian/English **Frequency:** annual **Content:** data on public and private educational establishments, students enrolled and teaching staff; it embraces information about pre-school establishments, general, vocational schools, colleges and universities; the number of pupils and students is shown by age, sex, educational attainment, field of study and continuation of education

Tiesiogines uzsienio investicijos Lietuvoje *(Foreign Direct Investment in Lithuania)* — **Language:** Lithuanian/English **Frequency:** annual **Content:** annual data on foreign direct investment (FDI) positions that reflect the real situation of FDI at the beginning of the year 2002-2006; FDI in Lithuania and Lithuanian direct investment abroad is broken down by country-investor and economic activity

Transportas ir rysiai *(Transport and Communication)* — **Language:** Lithuanian/English **Frequency:** annual **Content:** information about the length of roads, number of motor-vehicles, traffic of goods and passengers by all means of transport as well as about post and telecommunication services

Transporto ir rysiu imoniu rodikliai *(Indicators of Transport and Communication Enterprises)* — **Language:** Lithuanian/English **Frequency:** monthly **Content:** data on passengers and goods carried by road transport and railways as well as goods and passengers carried by water and air transport; information about transportation of oil and oil products by oil pipelines; review of road traffic accidents; work carried out by communication enterprises and post offices

Turizmas Lietuvoje *(Tourism in Lithuania)* — **Language:** Lithuanian/English **Frequency:** annual **Content:** data on occupation of accommodation establishments (hotels, motels, tourist camps, rest and health establishments, etc.), outgoing and incoming tourism organised by travel agencies and tour organizers as well as the survey of local and outgoing tourism

Ukio subjektai. Pagrindiniai duomenys *(Economic Entities. Main Data)* — **Language:** Lithuanian/English **Frequency:** annual **Content:** data on diverse classification of the operating economic entities from the Statistical Register of Economic entities; number of operating entities as well as small and medium sized enterprises nationwide provided by legal forms, economic activity, personnel and income by 1 January of each year

Uzsienio paskolos Lietuvai *(Foreign Loans Extended to Lithuania)* — **Language:** Lithuanian/English **Frequency:** 2 per annum **Content:** data on debt of the entities within the Government sector having the right to undertake borrowings; foreign loans, allocated to the Central Government, use, repayment and debt status by country, main financial institutions and by financing trends, are presented

Uzsienio prekyba *(Foreign Trade)* — **Language:** Lithuanian/English **Frequency:** annual **Content:** data on foreign trade balance, exports and imports by country, commodity group and commodities by country (a six-digit breakdown of the Combined Nomenclature of the European Economic Communities) are presented; also data on exported and imported commodities were grouped by the Standard International Trade Classification, Broad Economic Categories; publication deals with information about commodity distribution by main foreign trade partners, exports and imports indices, foreign trade data

Vartotoju ir gamintoju kainu indeksas *(Consumer and Producer Price Indices)* — **Language:** Lithuanian/English **Frequency:** quarterly **Content:** a short description of the calculation methodology of consumer price indices (CPI), producer price indices of manufactured goods of industry, construction input price indices, producer price indices of agricultural products also export / import price indices is given; current quarterly data are analysed; comparisons with the respective data of EU member countries are presented

Zaliavos ir medziagos *(Raw Materials)* — **Language:** Lithuanian/English **Frequency:** annual **Content:** data on main raw materials, their production, utilisation and stocks are presented; data on basic and non-ferrous scrap and secondary raw materials

Zemes ukio produkcijos supirkimas *(Purchase of Agricultural Production)* — **Language:** Lithuanian/English **Frequency:** annual **Content:** data on purchase of all types of agricultural products, by type of farm, producer prices and price indices for agricultural products

Zemes ukis Lietuvoje *(Agriculture in Lithuania)* — **Language:** Lithuanian/English **Frequency:** annual **Content:** data on total agricultural output, agricultural land area and structure, crop area, harvest and average yield, number of livestock and poultry, productivity and animal products, purchases of agricultural products

Valstybinis turizmo departamentas prie Ukio ministerijos
Lithuanian State Department of Tourism at the Ministry of Economy of the Republic of Lithuania

Address: A. Juozapaviciaus 13, Vilnius, LT-09311
Telephone: +370 5 210 8796
Fax: +370 5 210 8753
E-mail: vtd@tourism.lt
Website: www.tourism.lt

Guides: publishes information on Lithuania and its tourism opportunities
Activity: implements strategic planning of tourist activity and drafts the National Tourism Development Programme; drafts proposals to the Government on tourism policy and implementation

Website(s) information:
Lithuanian Tourism Statistics *(Lithuanian State Department of Tourism at the Ministry of Economy of the Republic of Lithuania)* — **url:** www.tourism.lt **Description:** site provides general information about the organisation, the country, tourism; Lithuanian news, formalities for foreign citizens willing to visit country, tourism statistics; has links to the Official Lithuanian Travel Guide, tourism information centres in Lithuania and abroad **Coverage:** inbound/outbound tourism, regional tourism statistics, activity of Tour operators and Travel agencies, expenditure of tourist, tourist profile; provides Lithuanian border crossing statistics; Lithuanian accommodation statistics

Publication(s):
Lietuvos turizmo statistika *(Lithuanian Tourism Statistics)* — **Language:** Lithuanian/English **Frequency:** annual **Content:** main statistical data on different aspects of tourism: inbound/outbound tourism, regional statistics, accommodation services, activity of Tour operators and Travel agencies, surveys of visitors in Lithuania, visit evaluation

Luxembourg

Service Central de la Statistique et des Etudes Economiques (STATEC)
Central Statistical and Economic Studies Service

Address: Quartier Luxembourg-Kirchberg, 13 rue Erasme, Luxembourg, L-1468
Telephone: +352 4 784 333
E-mail: info@statec.etat.lu
Website: http://www.statistiques.public.lu/fr/

Activity: provides statistical information system on the structure and the activity of the country

Website(s) information:
Service Central de la Statistique et des Etudes Economiques *(Central Statistical and Economic Studies Service (STATEC))* — **url:** statec.gouvernement.lu **Description:** offers information on products and services provided by the Service: catalogue of publications; data banks; national and international statistical programmes; international co-operation; etc **Coverage:** statistics all available online

Publication(s):
Agriculture — **Language:** French **Content:** contains data on agriculture, vine growing, forestry, hunting and fishing

Annuaire Statistique du Luxembourg *(Statistical Yearbook of Luxembourg)* — **Language:** French **Frequency:** annual **Content:** statistical overview of Luxembourg and its regions

Bulletin du Statec *(Statec Bulletin)* — **Language:** French **Frequency:** irregular **Content:** statistics and analysis of latest developments and trends in the national economy

Comptes nationaux *(National Accounts)* — **Language:** French **Content:** statistics on the national economy

Construction — **Language:** French **Content:** building costs, structure of the sector, building authorisations; turn-key projects and real property loans

Environment — **Language:** French **Content:** state of the environment and the measurements taken by the authorities to safeguard the nature and quality of life

Finances publiques *(Public Finance)* — **Language:** French **Content:** national debt; public revenue; national expenditure by government department; taxes of the State recovered during the financial year; customs duties, of excise and other receipts; treasury bills

Horeca et tourisme *(Horeca and tourism)* — **Language:** French **Content:** statistics relating to hotels and tourism

Indicateurs Rapides *(Latest Indicators)* — **Language:** French **Frequency:** monthly **Content:** statistical datasheets issued regularly to provide latest figures for consumer, construction, producer, industrial production and of construction activity; employment; new vehicle registrations; births, deaths and marriages; road traffic accidents; external trade; business prospects; and weather

Industrie *(Industry)* — **Language:** French **Content:** industry statistics including imports and exports; volumes of production and consumption, employment and prices

Le Luxembourg en Chiffres *(Luxembourg in Figures)* — **Language:** French/English/Dutch **Frequency:** annual **Content:** geographic, demographic, social and economic statistics covering Luxembourg

Population et emploi *(Population and employment)* — **Language:** French **Content:** demographic statistics and data on the evolution of employment and unemployment

Relations économiques extérieures *(Foreign Economic Relations)* — **Language:** French **Content:** trade in goods - by products and country

Santé *(Health)* — **Language:** French **Content:** includes data on hospitals, causes of death, diseases and other health statistics

Services financiers *(Financial Services)* — **Language:** French **Content:** credit institutions, Luxembourg stock exchange, undertakings for collective investment, insurances, interest rates

Territoire *(Territory)* — **Language:** French **Content:** provides data on the geographical situation, altitudes, hydrography and on the administrative subdivisions of the country

Transports et communications *(Transport & Communications)* — **Language:** French **Content:** statistical data on railroads, airports and the river ports, road transport people and goods; posts and telecommunications

Macedonia

Agency for Foreign Investments of the Republic of Macedonia
Address: PO Box 114, 7 Nikola Vapcarov Street, Skopje, 1000
Telephone: +389 2 311 7564
Fax: +389 2 312 2098
E-mail: contact@macinvest.org.mk
Website: www.macinvest.org.mk

Guides: catalogue available online - online access
Activity: promotes economic growth in Macedonia through working to attract FDI

Website(s) information:
MacInvest — **url:** www.macinvest.org.mk **Description:** the website provides investment information - information on legal regulations, economic indicators, industry profiles; all information is available in English **Coverage:** basic economic and demographic indicators; international trade volume and structure by trading partner; business climate, industry reports; income statistics

Agency for Promotion of Entrepreneurship of the Republic of Macedonia
Address: PO Box 657, 7 Nikola Vapcarov Street, Skopje, 1000
Telephone: +389 2 312 0132
Fax: +389 2 313 5494
E-mail: apprm@apprm.org.mk
Website: www.apprm.org.mk

Guides: catalogue available online
Activity: supports the establishment and development of small and medium enterprises in Macedonia

Publication(s):
Report of the SME Observatory — **Language:** Macedonian/English **Frequency:** annual **Content:** covers the macroeconomic framework of Macedonia; the size and structure of the SME sector, international trade, balance of trade; employment in SMEs by industry sector and region; financing SMEs - VAT, corporate tax, crediting; net profit and loss by sector

Employment Service Agency of the Republic of Macedonia
Address: 43 Vassil Gorgov Street, Skopje, 1000
Telephone: +389 2 311 1850
Fax: +389 2 311 1856
E-mail: info@zvrm.gov.mk
Website: www.zvrm.gov.mk

Activity: registers and monitors the number of unemployed persons actively seeking employment; works for the reduction of unemployment in Macedonia through projects, professional qualification programmes, maintains job centres all over the country

Website(s) information:
Employment Service Agency of the Republic of Macedonia — **url:** www.zvrm.gov.mk **Description:** the website provides access to the statistical research of the Agency; the site is available in Macedonian only **Coverage:** data on employment and unemployment figures by month; structure of the labour force - by age, gender, education; economically active population; analysis of the flow of unemployment

Ministry of Finance of the Republic of Macedonia
Address: 14 Dame Gruev Street, Skopje
Telephone: +389 2 311 7288
Fax: +389 2 311 7280
E-mail: finance@finance.gov.mk
Website: www.finance.gov.mk

Guides: all publications can be downloaded from the website
Activity: determines and coordinates the monetary and fiscal policy of FYR Macedonia

Website(s) information:

Ministry of Finance of the Republic of Macedonia — **url:** www.finance.gov.mk
Description: the site provides access to the releases of the Bank, including monthly bulletins, brochures, financial reports, etc. Some of the information is available in Macedonian only **Coverage:** macroeconomic indicators, international debt structure and servicing, prices, international trade, short-term economic flows, budget breakdown and allocation by sector, information about ratings, prices and revenue of companies in Macedonia

Publication(s):

Annual Economic Report — **Language:** Macedonian **Frequency:** annual **Content:** surveys basic economic indicators, the real, fiscal, monetary, external and social sectors

National Bank of the Republic of Macedonia

Address: PO Box 401, Kompleks banki b.b., Skopje, 1000
Telephone: +389 2 310 8108
Fax: +389 2 310 8357
E-mail: governorsoffice@nbrm.gov.km
Website: www.nbrm.gov.mk

Guides: full catalogue is available online - most publications can be downloaded from the Bank's website

Activity: establishes and conducts monetary policy; regulates liquidity in international payments; establishes and conducts the Denar exchange rate policy; handles and manages the foreign exchange reserves; regulates the payment system; issues banknotes and coins

Website(s) information:

National Bank of the Republic of Macedonia — **url:** www.nbrm.gov.mk
Description: contains banking and financial information and reports on the macro-economic climate in Macedonia, accompanied by statistical data on key economic and foreign trade indicators. Free online access to some of the Bank's various publications, including: Monthly Bulletin, Quarterly Bulletin, Annual Report **Coverage:** basic economic indicators, data on economic activity, wages and employment, interest rates and deposits in banks, balance of payments, exchange rate information, data on international trade and real growth rates, public debt

Publication(s):

Annual Report — **Language:** Macedonian/English **Frequency:** monthly **Content:** the reports present data on basic economic indicators, trade, investment, information about the competitiveness and liquidity of banks, the management of government debt, etc

Bulletin — **Language:** Macedonian/English **Frequency:** quarterly

Small and Medium Enterprise Development Project at the Ministry of Economy

Address: 15 Jurij Gagarin Street, Office 17, Skopje, 1000
Telephone: +389 2 309 3529
Fax: +389 2 309 3530
E-mail: smedp@economy.gov.mk
Website: www.economy.gov.mk/smedp/mk/index.html

Guides: online catalogue available

Activity: economic analysis and problem identification; strategy and policy development; SME programme and project development; programme and project implementation and management; the monitoring and evaluation of development programmes and projects

Website(s) information:

Small and Medium Enterpise Development Project — **url:** www.economy.gov.mk/smedp/mk/index.html **Description:** online access to reports and surveys of the small and medium enterprise sector in FYR Macedonia **Coverage:** number and structure of small and medium enterprises in Macedonia, competitiveness, technological expertise, profit, trade, employees

State Statistical Office of Macedonia

Address: 4 Dame Gruev Street, Skopje, 1000
Telephone: +389 2 329 5600
Fax: +389 2 311 1336
Website: www.stat.gov.mk

Guides: annually the office releases about 30 publications and 270 releases: full catalogue available online - most publications are available in separate versions in English and Macedonian

Activity: performs regular statistical surveys and monitoring of Macedonia social, economic, and industrial indicators

Website(s) information:

Republic of Macedonia - State Statistical Office — **url:** www.stat.gov.mk
Description: the site provides links to statistical data, charts and graphs by sector and by year **Coverage:** statistical data covering population and labour figures, statistical data by sector - banking and finance, agriculture and forestry, industry and energetics, international trade, transport, tourism and other services

Publication(s):

Monthly Statistical Report — **Language:** Macedonian/English **Frequency:** monthly **Content:** conjectural data for industry, agriculture, forestry, construction, transport, turnover, prices and employment

Statistical Yearbook — **Language:** Macedonian/English **Frequency:** annual **Content:** annual data and time series for population, employment, industry, trade, gross domestic product, education

World Bank Mission in the Republic of Macedonia

Address: 34 Leninova Street, Skopje, 1000
Telephone: +389 2 311 7159
Fax: +389 2 311 7627
E-mail: dboskovski@worldbank.org
Website: www.worldbank.org.mk

Guides: catalogue available online - most publications can be read online, free of charge

Activity: works to assist economic development in Macedonia, for the promotion of civil society and economic growth

Website(s) information:

World Bank - Macedonia — **url:** www.worldbank.org.mk **Description:** the site provides access to online datasheets on Macedonia, World Bank reports on particular aspects of development and particular industries **Coverage:** macroeconomic indicators, external debt - structure and servicing; microeconomic indicators - accessibility of capital, ease of starting up business; data on indicators in particular industries (e.g. IT, energetics) and the social sphere; poverty statistics, etc

Moldova

Departamental Statisticasi Sociologie al Republicii Moldova

National Bureau of Statistics of the Republic of Moldova

Address: 106 Grenoble Street, Chisinau mun, 2019
Telephone: +373 22 40 30 00
Fax: +373 22 22 61 46
Website: www.statistica.md

Guides: e-mail: biblioteca@statistica.md
             tel.: +37322 24 53 73

Activity: compiles and publishes statistical data on socio-economic indicators in Moldova

Website(s) information:

Departamental Statisticasi Sociologie al Republicii Moldova *(Department for Statistics and Sociology of the Republic of Moldova)* — **url:** www.statistica.md **Coverage:** reports on the social and economic developments in Moldova

Publication(s):

Moldova in Figures — **Language:** Moldovan (Romanian)/Russian **Frequency:** irregular **Content:** statistical information regarding the demographic, social and economic situation of the country from 2002-2005; contains data on the 2004 population census results

Prices in the Republic of Moldova — **Language:** Moldovan (Romanian)/Russian **Frequency:** irregular **Content:** statistical data that characterises the price dynamics for 2000-2005; included are analyses of monthly and annual dynamics of indices and consumer price levels for foodstuff and non-foodstuff products, services, prices of industrial products, prices of agricultural products, prices of construction works and prices for exported/imported commodities

Quarterly Statistical Bulletin — **Language:** Moldovan (Romanian)/Russian **Frequency:** quarterly **Content:** contains data on main statistical indicators which characterise the social, economic and demographic situation of the country

Netherlands

Centraal Bureau voor de Statistiek (CBS)
Statistics Netherlands

Address: Kloosterweg 1, Heerlen, 6412 CN
Telephone: +31 4557 06000
Fax: +31 4557 27440
E-mail: infoservice@cbs.nl
Website: www.cbs.nl

Guides: catalogue of publications available online
Activity: collecting, processing and publishing statistics to be used in practice, by policymakers and for scientific research; in addition to its responsibility for (official) national statistics, Statistics Netherlands also has the task of producing European (community) statistics

Website(s) information:
Centraal Bureau voor de Statistiek (CBO) *(Statistics Netherlands)* — **url:** www.cbs.nl
   Description: offers information on the Bureau's latest products and services, including catalogue of publications; access to Statline database and online publications; press releases; links to other national statistical institutes; and various online statistics **Coverage:** online statistics are available both in Dutch and English under "Listing of Key Figures" section. Different socio-economic and financial data is provided, covering the last four to five years (period coverage may vary according to indicator in question): population; standard of living; labour force; industrial resources; income, finance and expenditure; international economic relations; economic demography; prices; energy; information and automation; national accounts; culture; education, health and science; environment

StatLine — **url:** statline.cbs.nl **Coverage:** online database of statistical data drawn from Statistics Netherlands publications. Data covers both national and regional data and comes in the form of either tables or text documents

Publication(s):
Annual Report — **Language:** Dutch/English **Frequency:** annual **Content:** statistics about society, asymmetry project, media, statistics on trade and industry, economic statistics, financial statements, publications guide

Aspects of (un)Healthy Behaviour — **Language:** English/Dutch **Frequency:** irregular **Content:** trend figures on smoking, drinking wherever possible broken down by gender, type of insurance, age and highest level of education

Asylum Requests: Key Figures — **Language:** English/French **Frequency:** annual **Content:** submitted, granted asylum requests and left asylum seekers

Bankruptcies: Monthly Figures — **Language:** English/Dutch **Frequency:** monthly **Content:** pronounced bankruptcies by legal form and economic activities, debt restructuring

Births: Key Figures — **Language:** English/Dutch **Frequency:** annual **Content:** births: key figures by gender, birth order and legitimacy; including figures on stillborn children and multiple births

Business Survey: Manufacturing Industry — **Language:** English/Dutch **Frequency:** monthly **Content:** production and capacity utilisation, orders, sales prices, stocks, final products, competitive position, sales, number of employees for enterprises by activity

Consumer Confidence — **Language:** English/Dutch **Frequency:** monthly **Content:** consumer confidence, economic climate, willingness to buy, consumers' attitudes and expectations

Consumer Price Index (CPI) all Households — **Language:** English/Dutch **Frequency:** monthly **Content:** measure of the average price changes of goods and services purchased by households

Consumption — **Language:** English/Dutch **Frequency:** monthly **Content:** changes, indices, shares, value of consumption of households and of actual individual consumption of household by type of goods and services

Crime Victims by Personal Characteristics — **Language:** English/Dutch **Frequency:** annual **Content:** crime victims by background characteristics: gender, age, highest level of education, number of addresses per km2 of the place of residence, socio-economic bracket

Digital Economy — **Language:** English/Dutch **Content:** domestic ICT sector, share prices of the telecommunication companies, and investments in computers **Edition:** 5th edition

Economic Monitor — **Language:** English/Dutch **Content:** business cycle tracer, economic compass, economic situation, sentiment indicators, monthly indicators, quarterly indicators, focus and tables

Economic Totals per Region — **Language:** English/French **Frequency:** annual **Content:** GDP, GDP per capita, consistency with GDP, total value added, compensation of employees, taxes, subsidies, gross operating surplus by region, COROP area, province and groups of provinces

Emissions into the Atmosphere — **Language:** English/Dutch **Frequency:** 2 per annum **Content:** emissions by stationary and mobile sources, broken down by air polluting substance and combustion emission and other emissions

Financial institutions and markets — **Language:** Dutch/English **Content:** statistics on pension funds, security holdings, insurance companies, loans, insurers, share profits, foreign countries main financiers Dutch public sector, institutional investors, etc

Fixed Capital Formation by Region — **Language:** English/Dutch **Frequency:** annual **Content:** total fixed capital formation (gross), fixed capital formation (gross) by industry, by type of capital good by region, COROP area, province and groups of provinces

History elections: Dutch Lower House — **Language:** English/Dutch **Frequency:** every 4 years **Content:** voters, turnout, total votes, invalid votes, valid votes and distribution of seats by political party in the Dutch Lower House

Households: Key Figures — **Language:** English/Dutch **Frequency:** annual **Content:** households in the Netherlands by size and composition; persons by position in the household on 1 January

Interest Rates on the Money Market — **Language:** English/Dutch **Frequency:** irregular **Content:** official interest, rates short-term deposits unsecured and call money

Investment and Property Investment Funds — **Language:** English/Dutch **Frequency:** irregular **Content:** share index and total return index; investment- and property investment funds (average of the month)

Leisure Activities — **Language:** English/Dutch **Frequency:** annual **Content:** participation; sports, hobbies, culture, recreation, going out, use of the media and holidays by personal characteristics

Marriages: key figures — **Language:** English/Dutch **Frequency:** annual **Content:** marriages between partners of the same and opposite sex, partnership registrations and marriage partners

Monthly Statistics on Retail Trade — **Language:** English/Dutch **Frequency:** monthly **Content:** turnover, price and volume indices, increase and/or decrease in retail trade as a percentage

Mortality: key figures — **Language:** English/Dutch **Frequency:** annual **Content:** mortality: key figures by sex; including figures on infant mortality, perinatal mortality and life expectancy at birth

National Accounts of the Netherlands — **Language:** Dutch/English **Frequency:** annual **Content:** national accounts represent the official statistical review of the national economy

National Government: tax revenue accounts to the ESA — **Language:** English/Dutch **Frequency:** quarterly **Content:** tax on income and property, production and imports and death duty in terms of the ESA categories

National Statistics: Sick Leave — **Language:** English/Dutch **Frequency:** quarterly **Content:** national statistics on sick leave in % excluding pregnancy and maternity leave, by persons characteristics, region and business classification

Population: key figures — **Language:** English/Dutch **Frequency:** annual **Content:** population: key figures by gender, marital status, age, foreign background, households and population growth

Regional Economic Growth — **Language:** English/Dutch **Frequency:** annual **Content:** volume, deflation by region, COROP area, province and part of the country

Regular Educational Institutions — **Language:** English/Dutch **Frequency:** annual **Content:** number of regular educational institutions in the Netherlands; information presented by type of education, denomination and number of pupils/students per institution

Residential Buildings by Region — **Language:** English/Dutch **Frequency:** irregular **Content:** accommodation number, dwelling stock, newly built houses and other changes by region

Trends in the Use of Medical Facilities — **Language:** English/Dutch **Frequency:** annual **Content:** use of medical facilities, visit to the GP, medical specialist, dentist, physiotherapist, alternative healers, hospital admissions, medicines, contraceptive pill, health care centres

Unemployment and the Labour Force — **Language:** English/Dutch **Frequency:** monthly **Content:** employed and unemployed labour force, persons not included in the labour force, seasonally adjusted unemployment rate by gender and age

Urban Waste Water Treatment: Regions — **Language:** English/Dutch **Frequency:** annual **Content:** urban waste water treatment plants: number and capacity per type, influent and effluent; sewage sludge by destination; results by province and river basin district

Value Added Construction — **Language:** English/Dutch **Frequency:** monthly **Content:** volume changes in % compared to the same period of the previous year

Working Population by Gender — **Language:** English/Dutch **Frequency:** annual **Content:** persons employed, labour force, unemployment broken down by personal features (age, level of education, origin) and gender

De Nederlandsche Bank NV
Netherlands Bank

Address: Post Box 98, Amsterdam, 1000 AB
Telephone: +31 20 524 9111
Fax: +31 20 524 2500
E-mail: info@dnb.nl
Website: www.dnb.nl

Activity: DNB and other European central banks jointly pursue a policy designed to safeguard a stable Euro, smooth and secure payments as well as sound and reliable financial institutions

Website(s) information:
De Nederlandsche Bank NV *(Netherlands Bank)* — **url:** www.statistics.dnb.nl **Description:** detailed information about the bank and its publications. Monetary and financial statistical information covering key indicators; monetary and financial developments; balance of payments; capital markets; interest and exchange rates. Also has information about European Economic and Monetary Union **Coverage:** key monetary, financial and economic statistics are available; website contains monetary and financial statistics for the Netherlands compiled by the Nederlandsche Bank (time series starting in 1982) and also published in the DNB Statistical Bulletin

Publication(s):
DNB Statistisch Bulletin *(DNB Statistical Bulletin)* — **Language:** Dutch **Frequency:** quarterly **Content:** monetary and financial statistics

Jaarverslag DNB *(Annual Report)* — **Language:** Dutch **Frequency:** annual **Content:** overview of the activities, global developments, Euro area economy, Dutch economy, financial stability, payment and settlements systems, corporate governance, key economic data

Kwartaalbericht DNB *(Quarterly Journal DNB)* — **Language:** Dutch **Frequency:** quarterly **Content:** information concerning financial-economic developments in the Netherlands. Publishes forecasts for the Dutch economy

Overzicht Financiële Stabiliteit *(Overview of Financial Stability)* — **Language:** Dutch **Content:** overview of the financial system

Ministerie van Economische Zaken
Ministry of Economic Affairs

Address: Bezuidenhoutseweg 30, The Hague, 2594 AV
Telephone: +31 70 308 1986
E-mail: ezinfo@postbus51.nl
Website: www.ez.nl

Activity: stimulates sustainable economic growth; defines, implements, and regulates the enforcement of economic policy

Website(s) information:
Ministerie van Economische Zaken *(Ministry of Economic Affairs)* — **url:** www.ez.nl **Description:** news and detailed data on macro-economic issues in the country such as consumer confidence, prices and business cycles **Coverage:** detailed statistics on key industries and issues including: population; labour; agriculture, forestry and fisheries; mining and manufacturing; construction; trade, hotels, restaurants, cafes and repairs; traffic, transport and communications; business and other services; income, finance and expenditure; international economic relations; prices; economic demography; energy; information and automation; national accounts; politics and government; justice and public safety; culture and recreation; education and science; health and welfare; environment

Publication(s):
Annual Report — **Language:** English/Dutch **Frequency:** annual **Content:** short, concise, and practical overview of the core activities of the Ministry of Economic Affairs; structured account of the Ministry's performance and results

Ministry of Agriculture, Nature Management and Fisheries
Address: Bezuidenhoutseweg 73, The Hague, 2594 AC
Telephone: +31 70 378 6868
Fax: +31 70 378 6100
Website: www.minlnv.nl

Website(s) information:
Ministerie von Landbauw, Natuurbeheer en Visserij *(Ministry of Agriculture, Nature Management and Fisheries)* — **url:** www.minlnv.nl **Description:** provides access to various publications on policy themes about the Dutch agricultural, livestock and fisheries sectors **Coverage:** offers statistical information on animal and crop production, nature management, forestry, trade and industry, fisheries, countryside planning and management, outdoor recreation, quality management, and agricultural research, education and extension

Publication(s):
Feiten en Cijfers van de Nederlandse Agrosector *(Facts and Figures of the Dutch Agriculture Sector)* — **Language:** Dutch **Frequency:** annual **Content:** insight in the developments of the Dutch agro sector

Jaarverslag *(Annual Report)* — **Language:** Dutch **Frequency:** annual **Content:** overview of the activities with a special theme every year, on a specific aspect of the agriculture, livestock, forestry and fishing sectors

Marktrapporten *(Market Report)* — **Language:** Dutch **Content:** market reports on agriculture

Social and Economic Council of the Netherlands
Address: Postbus 90405, Bezuidenhoutseweg 60, Den Haag, 2594 AW
Telephone: +31 70 349 9499
Fax: +31 70 383 2535
E-mail: ser.info@ser.nl
Website: www.ser.nl

Activity: main advisory body to the Dutch government and the parliament on national and international social and economic policy; has an administrative role which consists of monitoring commodity and industrial boards; helps the government to enforce the Works Councils Act, the Establishment of Businesses Act and the Insurance Agencies Act

Publication(s):
Advisory reports — **Language:** English/Dutch **Frequency:** irregular **Content:** diverse reports including co-financing of the common agricultural policy, European small claims procedure and others

Norway

Finansdepartementet
Finance Department

Address: Postboks 8008 Dep, Akersgata 40, Oslo, 0030
Telephone: +47 22 249 090
Fax: +47 22 249 510
E-mail: postmottak@fin.dep.no
Website: odin.dep.no/fin

Guides: budgetry and other information is downloadable from the website

Activity: plans and implements economic policy; co-ordinates the preparation of the budget; ensures government revenues by maintaining and developing the system of taxes and duties

Website(s) information:
Finansdepartementet — **url:** odin.dep.no/fin **Description:** comprehensive information on the Norwegian economy including government budgets; policy; projections; main indicators; government debts; taxes and financial markets

Publication(s):

Statsbudsjettet (State Budget) — **Language:** Norwegian **Frequency:** annual **Content:** contains information on the annual state budget

Mattilsynet
Norwegian Food Safety Authority

Address:	Postboks 8187, Ullevålsveien 76, Oslo, 0454
Telephone:	+47 23 216 800
Fax:	+47 23 217 001
E-mail:	postmottak@mattilsynet.no
Website:	www.mattilsynet.no

Guides: publications are available to download free on the web site, some are available in English

Activity: responsible for food legislation and enforcement; promotes human, plant, fish and animal health, environmentally friendly production, and ethically acceptable farming of animals and fish. It performs duties relating to cosmetics and medicines, and inspects animal health personnel

Website(s) information:

Statens Naeringsmiddeltilsyn (STN) (Norwegian Food Control Authority (SNT)) — **url:** www.snt.no **Description:** provides information on the controls put on food production and import **Coverage:** contains data on animal feed, control and health; plant health, food safety and import and export

Norges Bank
Bank of Norway

Address:	Postboks 1179, Sentrum, Bankplassen 2, Oslo, 0107
Telephone:	+47 22 316 000
Fax:	+47 22 413 105
E-mail:	central.bank@norges-bank.no
Website:	www.norges-bank.no

Guides: annual reports available free of charge in Norwegian and English

Activity: works to achieve a balanced economic developments and a stable financial markets and payment systems

Website(s) information:

Norges Bank (Bank of Norway) — **url:** www.norges-bank.no **Description:** provides information about the bank and contains dowloadable versions of its publications **Coverage:** contains statistical information about interest rates, foreign exchange flows and foreign direct investment rates

Publication(s):

Annual Report — **Language:** Norwegian/English **Frequency:** annual **Content:** contains a summary of the international and domestic fiscal developments

Economic Bulletin — **Language:** Norwegian/English **Frequency:** quarterly **Content:** contains a review of economic trends, with data on the main economic indicators and business statistics

Financial Stability Report — **Language:** Norwegian/English **Frequency:** quarterly **Content:** contains data on developments in households, enterprises, financial institutions, international and macroeconomic

Inflation Report — **Language:** Norwegian/English **Frequency:** quarterly **Content:** contains an overview of price trends and factors which influence price and wage inflation

Investment Management — **Language:** Norwegian/English **Frequency:** quarterly **Content:** contains a review of foreign direct investments; return on the international equity portfolios; international interest rates and bond prices

Statistisk Sentralbyrå
Central Bureau of Statistics

Address:	Postboks 8131 Dep, Sjøfartsbygningen, Kongens gate 6, Oslo, 0033
Telephone:	+47 21 090 000
Fax:	+47 21 094 973
E-mail:	ssb@ssb.no
Website:	www.ssb.no

Guides: publications (free; annual; contains details of main series of publications; English); Veiviser i norsk statistikk/Guide to Norwegian Statistics (free; survey of official Norwegian statistics arranged by subject in Norwegian and English); Catalogue of Norwegian Statistics and Other Publications Published by the Central Bureau of Statistics

Activity: publishes official statistics on Norway

Website(s) information:

Statistisk Sentralbyrå (Statistics Norway) — **url:** www.ssb.no **Description:** provides information on the Sentralbyrå main products and services, including catalogue of publications; Annual Report; and access to series of online publications, most of these provided both in Norwegian and in English **Coverage:** contains monthly and annual statistical data, covering a wide range of socio-economic indicators: population and the environment; health and education; personal economy and housing conditions; labour market; national economy and external trade; industrial activities and financial markets, etc. In the Statistical Yearbook, general data on other Northern European countries is also provided (covering mainly population, employment and consumer price indices)

Publication(s):

Kvinner og menn i Norge (Women and Men in Norway) — **Language:** Norwegian **Frequency:** annual **Content:** data refers to immigration, health, employment, time-use, households and crime

Naturressurser og Miljø (Natural Resources and the Environment) — **Language:** Norwegian **Frequency:** annual **Content:** data refers to growth in consumption and production and its effects on ecosystems

Økonomiske analyser (Economic Survey) — **Language:** Norwegian/English **Frequency:** quarterly **Content:** analysis of latest developments in the Norwegian and international economy, supported by statistical data on major macro-economic indicators

Olje- og gassvirksomhet (Oil and Gas Activity Quarterly) — **Language:** Norwegian **Frequency:** quarterly **Content:** data refers to production, prices, investment costs for exploration, field development, fields on stream and onshore activity

Statistisk Årbok (Statistical Yearbook of Norway) — **Language:** Norwegian/English **Frequency:** annual **Content:** annual socio-economic statistics, covering a wide range of topics, from environment and population, to labour market and financial statistics

Statistisk Månedshefte (Monthly Bulletin of Statistics) — **Language:** Norwegian/English **Frequency:** monthly **Content:** monthly highlights of major socio-economic indicators (population; health and social conditions; labour market; national economy; and public finances)

Poland

Glowny Urzad Statystyczny (GUS)
Central Statistical Office

Address:	al. Niepodleglosci 208, Warsaw, 00925
Telephone:	+48 22 608 3000
Fax:	+48 22 608 3869
E-mail:	SekretariatUSwro@stat.gov.pl, dane@stat.gov.pl
Website:	www.stat.gov.pl

Guides: provides information on socio-economic, demographic, social situation in various regions

Activity: statistical service (regional data bank) and international statistics (UN, EU, OECD)

Website(s) information:

Glowny Urzad Statystyczny (GUS) (Central Statistical Office) — **url:** www.stat.gov.pl **Description:** information on the Polish economy. Statistics covering: socio-economic data; economics; infrastructure; labour and employment; trade; and industry. Only available in Polish **Coverage:** provides data and analysis on demographic, economic and marketing indicators

Publication(s):

Demographic Yearbook — **Language:** English/Polish **Frequency:** annual **Content:** statistical analysis of Poland's population structure and demographic trends

Statistical Bulletin — **Language:** Polish/English **Frequency:** monthly **Content:** monthly update of main economic indicators, covering: GDP; labour market and earnings; money and finance; agricultural and industrial production; etc

Statistical Yearbook of Foreign Trade — **Language:** Polish/English **Frequency:** annual **Content:** foreign trade statistics by country

Statistical Yearbook of Industry — **Language:** Polish/English **Frequency:** annual **Content:** statistical overview of the Polish industrial sector, covering production and manufacturing; price indices; labour costs and productivity; consumption; etc

Statistical Yearbook of Labour — **Language:** Polish/English **Frequency:** annual **Content:** structure of employment and labour market, including statistics of employment and unemployment rates; labour costs, earnings and turnover; etc

Statistical Yearbook of the Republic of Poland — **Language:** Polish/English **Frequency:** annual **Content:** main annual socio-economic statistics for Poland and international comparisons

Instytut Lacznosci
The National Institute of Telecommunications

Address: ul. Szachowa 1, Warsaw, 04894
Telephone: +48 22 512 8100
Fax: +48 22 512 8625
E-mail: info@itl.waw.pl
Website: www.nit.eu

Guides: publishes magazines and specialist scientific and technical books on telecommunications and information technology
Activity: scientific research and development, which covers all areas of telecommunications and statutory works

Website(s) information:
Instytut Lacznosci (National Institute of Telecommunications) — **url:** www.nit.eu
Coverage: provides statistical reports on the use of computers and the internet in Poland in terms of users, purposes, locations etc

Publication(s):
Journal of Telecommunications and Information Technology — **Language:** English/Polish **Frequency:** quarterly **Content:** covers a range of topics including image coding, unequal error protection coding and data encryption, through the problems of mobile ad hoc networks, traffic management in high speed internet, to techniques enabling better bandwidth utilisation and accuracy of hardware

Ministerstwo Rolnictwa i Rozwoju Wsi
Ministry of Agriculture and Rural Development

Address: Wspólna Street No. 30, Warsaw, 00930
Telephone: +48 22 623 1000
Fax: +48 22 629 5599
E-mail: rzecznik.prasowy@minrol.gov.pl or kancelana@minrol.gov.pl
Website: www.minrol.gov.pl

Guides: developments in agriculture in 2007-2013, information on technical infrastructure, food economy in rural areas

Publication(s):
Biuletyn Informacyjny (Information Bulletin) — **Language:** Polish **Frequency:** monthly **Content:** provides current socio-economic and financing information in the agricultural market

Informacje o Rolnictwie na Swiecie (World Agricultural Information) — **Language:** Polish **Frequency:** bi-monthly **Content:** provides current socio-economic and financing information in the agricultural market provides information on organic food, investments, research

Rural Development Programme for Poland 2007-2013 — **Language:** English/Polish **Content:** agricultural policy, plant and animal production, food industry and foreign trade

Ministerstwo Srodowiska
Ministry of the Environment

Address: ul. Wawelska 52/54, Warsaw, 00922
Telephone: +48 22 579 2900
Fax: +48 22 579 2224
Website: www.mos.gov.pl

Guides: publishes documents on environmental technologies and innovations
Activity: representation, promotion and preparation of acts and documents related to the environment

Publication(s):
Enviromental Impact Assessment Procedures in Poland — **Language:** English/Polish **Content:** provides assistance in implementing a new legislation for public administration bodies responsible for carrying out EIA procedures

Roadmap for Implementation Environmental Technology Action Plan in Poland — **Language:** English/Polish **Content:** main direction-elements undertaken in Poland within the scope of environmental technologies and innovations, as well as the establishment of a framework for coordinating these activities

Ministerstwo Transportu i Budownictwa
Ministry of Transport and Construction

Address: ul. Chalubinskiego 4/6, Warsaw, 00928
Telephone: +48 22 630 1000
Fax: +48 22 630 1116
E-mail: info.fe@mtib.gov.pl
Website: www.mtib.gov.pl

Guides: provides directives, ordinances, acts related to road, air and rail transport
Activity: covers the issues related to road, rail, maritime and air transport and telecommunication; also provides development of the domestic road infrastructure network; execution of issues in the scope of construction and architecture, housing policy and management, spatial management and development support and the revitalization of cities as well as state aid in the repayment of housing credits; responsible for the issues related to the provisions of road traffic, road safety and the conditions for the execution of transport

Publication(s):
Directives and Ordinances — **Language:** English/Polish **Frequency:** irregular **Content:** provides directives and ordinances of norms, conditions, perspectives and direction of development in road, train, rail and air transport

Narodowy Bank Polandi
National Bank of Poland

Address: PO Box 1011, Information and Promotion Division, ul. Swietokrzyska 11/21, Warsaw, 00919
Telephone: +48 22 653 1000
Fax: +48 22 620 8518/263 932/269 955
E-mail: npl@nbp.pl
Website: www.nbp.pl

Guides: provides publications which contain information on overall economic and financial performance in Poland; offers various research papers, reports
Activity: maintains price stability, stabilises inflation rates, monetary policy, issue of currency banking supervision, development of payment systems, management of official reserves, education and information, services to the State Treasury

Website(s) information:
Narodowy Bank Polandi (National Bank of Poland) — **url:** www.nbp.pl
Description: offers online access to various Bank of Poland publications including: Official journal of the Bank; information bulletin; annual reports; monetary policy guidelines; inflation report
Coverage: includes statistical reports of exchange rates; interest rates; balance of payments; loans and deposits; assets and liabilities; official reserves; external debt

Publication(s):
Inflation Report — **Language:** English/Polish **Frequency:** quarterly **Content:** inflationary trends, monetary aspects of inflation, and the non-monetary factors, external and internal, inflation

Information Bulletin — **Language:** English/Polish **Frequency:** monthly **Content:** overall economic and financial performance in Poland and on the policies of the Central Bank

Roczny Raport (Annual Report) — **Language:** English/Polish **Frequency:** annual **Content:** contains information on overall economic and financial performance in Poland and on the development of the banking sector, together with the balance sheet of the NBP and the banking system, and the balance of payments of the Republic of Poland

Portugal

Banco de Portugal - Economic Research Department
National Bank of Portugal

Address: Rua do Ouro 27, Lisbon, 1100-150
Telephone: +351 21 321 3200
Fax: +351 21 346 4843
E-mail: info@bportugal.pt
Website: www.bportugal.pt

Activity: maintaining the stability of the domestic financial system

Website(s) information:
Banco de Portugal *(National Bank of Portugal)* — **url:** www.bportugal.pt **Description:** the section statistics includes all kind of economic and financial indicators in pdf or excel format; available in English and Portuguese **Coverage:** main economic indicators, daily reference exchange rates, reference interest rate of the Euro's area money market, monetary and financial, non financial corporation from Central Balance-Sheet database. It aslo includes a list of credit institutions and financial companies registered with the Central Bank of Portugal

Publication(s):
Boletim Económico *(Economic Bulletin)* — **Language:** English/Portuguese **Frequency:** quarterly **Content:** quarterly publication with papers on the policy and economic situation, as well as studies applied to the Portuguese economy

Boletim Estatístico *(Statistical Bulletin)* — **Language:** English/Portuguese **Frequency:** monthly **Content:** monetary and financial statistics, balance of payments and international investment position, and exchange rate statistics. Also includes chapters on main indicators, public finance and general statistics

Evolução das Economias dos PALOP e de Timor-Leste *(Economic Trends of the Portuguese-Speaking African Countries and East-Timor)* — **Language:** English/Portuguese **Frequency:** irregular **Content:** main economic indicators of the Portuguese-Speaking African countries: Angola, Green Cape, Guinea Bissau, Mozambique, São Tomé e Príncipe and Timor-Leste. It also includes economic and financial relations between Portugal and PALOP and East-Timor

Indicadores de Conjuntura *(Monthly Economic Indicators)* — **Language:** English/Portuguese **Frequency:** monthly **Content:** the main economic indicators disclosed throughout the month including tables and graphics

Inquérito aos Bancos sobre o Mercado de Crédito *(Bank Lending Survey)* — **Language:** English/Portuguese **Frequency:** quarterly **Content:** covers loan demands and loan supply factors. Also available from 2003

Relatório Anual *(Annual Report)* — **Language:** English/Portuguese **Frequency:** annual **Content:** presents an integrated analysis on the economic trend in the Euro area and in Portugal. Report and financial statements

Relatório de Estabilidade Financeira *(Financial Stability Report)* — **Language:** English/Portuguese **Frequency:** irregular **Content:** overall assessment, macroeconomic environment, activity, profitability and risk coverage, market Risk, liquidity risk, credit risk

Sistemas de Pagamentos em Portugal *(Payment Systems in Portugal)* — **Language:** English/Portuguese **Frequency:** irregular **Content:** it publishes regularly an extensive report on payments and securities settlements systems (domestic and cross-border) in the European Union Member States

Gabinete de Estratégia e Estudos (GEE)
Economic Planning Secretariat

Address: Rua José Estevão 83A, 1º Esq., Lisbon, 1169-153
Telephone: +351 21 311 0700/0770
Fax: +351 21 311 0773
Website: www.gee.min-economia.pt/site/gepe_home_pt00.asp

Activity: produces economical studies in order to help government decision-making

Website(s) information:
Gabinete de Estrategia e Estudos *(Economic Planning Secretariat)* — **url:** www.gee.min-economia.pt/resources/docs **Description:** Eurostat publications available to download. Business climate indicators for the EU **Coverage:** economic indicators

GEPE-Ministerio de Economia *(Minister of Economy)* — **url:** www.gee.min-economia.pt **Coverage:** fact sheets, foreign trade, energy, companies, economic indicators, balance of payments, investment indicators, labour market, prices.

Publication(s):
Boletin Mensual de Actividad Economica *(Monthly Bulletin of Economic Activity)* — **Language:** Portuguese **Frequency:** monthly **Content:** national and international fact sheet, world economic growth forecast; statistical index of all the economic indicators

Capital de Risco *(Risk Capital)* — **Language:** Portuguese **Frequency:** irregular **Content:** current situation in Portugal, investment evolution in the country. It also contains the investment in R&D in the EU

Dinamica Empresarial - Perspectiva Sectorial e Regional *(Dynamic Enterprises - By Sector and Regional Perspective)* — **Language:** Portuguese **Frequency:** irregular **Content:** sector industry analysis

Indicadores e Medidas *(Indicators and Measures)* — **Language:** Portuguese **Frequency:** irregular **Content:** different indicators about industry, competition, public services, labour markets

Industria de Conteudos. Uma Visao Estrategica *(Audiovisual Industry: A Strategic Vision)* — **Language:** Portuguese **Frequency:** irregular **Content:** contains graphics and tables about the audiovisual industry in Portugal and also includes an analysis of the sector in Europe (GDP, trade balance, commercial structure)

Portugal - Principales Indicadores *(Portugal - Main Indicators)* — **Language:** English **Frequency:** irregular **Content:** main economics indicators of Portugal for last six years. It includes trade account, structure of international trade by group of products, trade with the countries of the enlargement and the main origin and destiny markets of products

Productos Industriales Transformados - Por Grau de Intensidade Tecnologica *(Final Products - Technology Levels)* — **Language:** Portuguese **Frequency:** irregular **Content:** exports and imports of final products (high, medium or low technological level), balance of trade, evolution indicators in volume and price

Projecto Competitividade *(Competition Project)* — **Language:** Portuguese **Frequency:** irregular **Content:** analysis of competitive indicators in 18 sectors of foreign trade from 1998 to 2003

Sector Electrico - Comparaçoes Estatisticas entre Portugal e a Europa *(Electrical Sector - Statistical Comparisons between Portugal and Europe)* — **Language:** Portuguese **Frequency:** irregular **Content:** global production indicators, production of electricity by country

Sector Electrico-Indicadores Comparativos Portugal e Espanha *(Electric Sector-Comparative Indicators between Portugal and Spain)* — **Language:** Portuguese **Frequency:** irregular **Content:** energy and socio-economic indicators, main agents, production of electricity and consumption

Instituto Nacional de Estatística (INE)
National Institute of Statistics

Address: Av. António José de Almeida, Lisbon, 1000-043
Telephone: +351 218 426 100
Fax: +351 218 426 380
E-mail: ine@ine.pt
Website: www.ine.pt

Activity: compilation of national statistics; research studies and publications

Website(s) information:
Instituto Nacional de Estatística Portugal *(National Institute of Statistics of Portugal)* — **url:** www.ine.pt **Description:** online access to the statistical data published by INE; database searchable by area; geographic unit and by word; cost of the service depends on the size of the files downloaded **Coverage:** statistics and major indicators on consumer prices; labour; population; national economic and financial news

Publication(s):
Anuário Estatístico de Portugal *(Statistical Yearbook of Portugal)* — **Language:** Portuguese **Frequency:** annual **Content:** statistics and figures on major demographic; social; economic and industrial indicators

Anuários Estatísticos Regionais *(Regional Statistical Yearbook)* — **Language:** Portuguese **Frequency:** annual **Content:** compilation of regional statistical publications offering a comparison among regions; economic; social and demographic indicators

As Cidades em Números *(Cities in Figures)* — **Language:** Portuguese **Frequency:** irregular **Content:** statistics and figures on demography; construction and companies in 141 Portuguese cities

Boletim Mensal de Estatística (Monthly Bulletin of Statistics) — **Language:** Portuguese **Frequency:** monthly **Content:** monthly update of socio-economic indicators covering population; agriculture and industries; internal and external commerce; services and finances

Boletim Trimestral de Estatística (Statistical Quarterly Bulletin) — **Language:** Portuguese **Frequency:** quarterly **Content:** regional economic conjuncture analysis

Estatísticas Agrícolas (Agriculture Statistics) — **Language:** Portuguese **Frequency:** annual **Content:** statistics and figures on agriculture; livestock; forestry and fishing

Estatísticas da Produção Agro-industrial (Agro-industrial Statistics) — **Language:** Portuguese **Frequency:** irregular **Content:** statistics and figures on agricultural and industrial production

Estatísticas das Comunicações (Communications Statistics) — **Language:** Portuguese **Frequency:** annual **Content:** information on national public and private postal services and telecommunications in Portugal; financial and economic indicators

Estatísticas das Empresas (Companies Statistics) — **Language:** Portuguese **Frequency:** annual **Content:** overview of companies' economic and financial situation

Estatísticas do Ambiente (Environment Statistics) — **Language:** Portuguese **Frequency:** annual **Content:** statistics and figures on the environment

Estatísticas do Comércio Internacional (International Trade Statistics) — **Language:** Portuguese/English **Frequency:** annual **Content:** statistical data on imports and exports by products and by country in Portugal; figures on external trade in Europe

Estatísticas do Turismo (Tourism Statistics) — **Language:** Portuguese **Frequency:** annual **Content:** statistics and figures on domestic trade; tourism and other services

Estatísticas dos Transportes (Transport Statistics) — **Language:** Portuguese **Frequency:** annual **Content:** statistics and figures on maritime; air; road and rail transport

Estatísticas Históricas Portuguesas (Historic Portuguese Statistics) — **Language:** Portuguese/English **Frequency:** irregular **Content:** statistics and figures on population; cities; national accounts; production; currency; prices and wages; finances and foreign trade from 1994 to 2000

Gastos dos Estrangeiros não Residentes em Portugal (Expenses of Foreigners Living in Portugal) — **Language:** Portuguese **Frequency:** irregular **Content:** overview of cost of living in Portugal **Readership:** tourists; future residents

Indicadores Sociais (Social Indicators) — **Language:** Portuguese **Frequency:** annual **Content:** overview of general living conditions in Portugal; covering employment; household incomes and expenditure; social security; health and education services

Índice de Preços no Consumidor (Consumer Prices Index) — **Language:** Portuguese **Frequency:** monthly **Content:** consumer prices indicators

O País em Números (The Country in Figures) — **Language:** Portuguese **Content:** statistics and figures on economy; education; labour; tourism; commerce; environment and other issues from 1991 to 2004; graphs and charts

Península Ibérica em Números (Peninsula in Figures) — **Language:** Portuguese/Spanish **Frequency:** annual **Content:** statistics and figures in Portugal and Spain. Main indicators include economy; labour; technology; transport

Retrato Territorial de Portugal (Portugal's Demographic Profile) — **Language:** Portuguese **Frequency:** annual **Content:** socio-economic description of Portugal region by region

Revista Portuguesa de Estudos Regionais (Portuguese Journal of Regional Studies) — **Language:** Portuguese **Frequency:** quarterly **Content:** statistics and research studies covering major demographic and social indicators; immigration; labour; tourism; etc

Revstat Statistical Journal — **Language:** English **Frequency:** quarterly **Content:** statistics and research studies on economy and demography

Ministério da Agricultura, do Desenvolvimento e das Pescas
Ministry of Agriculture, Rural Development and Fishing

Address: Rua Padre Antonio Vieira 1, Lisboa, 1099-073
Telephone: +351 21 346 3151
Fax: +351 21 347 3798
E-mail: geral@min-agricultura.pt
Website: www.min-agricultura.pt

Activity: responsible for agricultural and fishing policy and the rural economy

Website(s) information:
Ministério da Agricultura, do Desenvolvimento Rural e das Pescas (Ministry of Agriculture, Rural Development and Fisheries) — **url:** www.min-agricultura.pt **Description:** statistical data on agricultural production, imports and exports; forestry; fishing; and EU structural supports. National and EU legislation

Publication(s):
Agricultores, Entidades e Servicios (Farmers, Entities and Services) — **Language:** Portuguese **Frequency:** irregular **Content:** services offered in Portugal to the agricultural producers and managers

Agricultura Portuguesa Principais Indicadores (Portuguese Agriculture Main Indicators) — **Language:** English/Portuguese **Frequency:** annual **Content:** climate, Portuguese agriculture within the EU, territories, agriculture in Portugal: economy, population and employment, environment and structure

Anuario de Campanha - Principais Ajudas Directas (Campaign Yearbook - Main Benefits) — **Language:** Portuguese **Frequency:** annual **Content:** statistical analysis of the main benefits directed to the agricultural sector

Anuario Pecuario (Animal Production Yearbook) — **Language:** English/Portuguese **Frequency:** annual **Content:** cattle, pigs, sheep and goats, poultry and eggs, milk and dairy products: market overview, prices, exchange, consumer prices, foreign trade, supply balance, world market, union market, per capita consumption and degree of self sufficiency of meat and eggs in the EU. Overview of the animal mixed feed industry

Anuario Vegetal (Crop Production Yearbook) — **Language:** English/Portuguese **Frequency:** annual **Content:** fresh fruits and nuts, fresh vegetables, flowers and foliage: Production and marketing characteristics in Portugal, foreign trade, supply balances and consumer prices. Arable crops, olive oil and table olives: Production and foreign trade

Apoios a la Agricultura (Support for Agriculture) — **Language:** Portuguese **Frequency:** annual **Content:** contains tables and figures with all the support programmes available to the agricultural Industry

Envolvente Socio-Economica (Socio-Economic Indicators) — **Language:** Portuguese **Frequency:** annual **Content:** socio-economic indicators

Expectativas dos Empresarios Agricolas 2005-2007 (Farmers Expectations 2005-2007) — **Language:** Portuguese **Frequency:** irregular **Content:** result of a survey after personal interviews involving 928 farmers. Includes expectations from 2004-2006

Romania

Centrul de Informare al Organizatiei Natiunilor Unite pentru Romania
United Nations Information Centre in Romania

Address: Bulevardul Primaverii nr 48A, sector 1, Bucharest, 011975 1
Telephone: +40 21 201 7877
Fax: +40 21 201 7880
E-mail: unic@un.ro
Website: www.onuinfo.ro

Guides: publications can be viewed in the library. Opens from 8.30-13.00 and from 14.45-16.45 (Monday to Friday)
Activity: provides access to documents of the UN

Institutul National de Statistica
National Statistical Institute

Address: 16 Libertatii Avenue, district 5, Bucharest
Telephone: +40 21 318 18 50
Fax: +40 21 312 48 73
E-mail: romstat@insse.ro
Website: www.insse.ro

Activity: compiles statistics on Romania

Website(s) information:

Institutul National de Statistica *(National Statistical Institute)* — **url:** www.insse.ro
Description: online information on the Institute's main products and services; includes both annual and monthly socio-economic indicators **Coverage:** main socio-economic data covering demographics and population trends; industrial production; GDP growth; foreign trade; retail trade; consumer price indices; and income and earnings

Publication(s):

Romania in Figures — **Language:** Romanian/English **Frequency:** annual **Content:** figures on population, labour force, national accounts, agriculture, industry, energy, construction, tourism and other socio-economic data

Romanian Demographic Yearbook — **Language:** Romanian/English **Frequency:** annual **Content:** data on population numbers and demographic and socio-economic structures

Romanian Foreign Trade Yearbook — **Language:** Romanian/English **Frequency:** annual **Content:** Romanian exports and imports, classified by goods

Romanian Statistical Yearbook — **Language:** Romanian/English **Frequency:** annual **Content:** compilation of a wide range of socio-economic indicators for the last five years

Romanian Tourism — **Language:** Romanian/English **Frequency:** annual **Content:** annual statistics on the tourism industry in Romania: structure of the industry; available infrastructures and resources; number of national and international tourists' arrivals; tourists by country of origin; etc

Ministerul Agriculturii, Padurilor si Dezvoltarii Rurale
Ministry of Agriculture, Forestry and Rural Development

Address: B-dul Carol I, nr. 24, sector 3, Bucharest, 020921
Telephone: +40 21 3072300
Fax: +40 21 3078685
E-mail: comunicare@maa.ro;
Website: mapam.ro

Guides: the Ministry disseminates statistics on various areas of agricultural activity in Romania
Activity: regulates policy issues regarding agriculture

Website(s) information:

Ministerul Agriculturii, Padurilor si Dezvoltarii Rurale *(Ministry of Agriculture, Forestry and Rural Development)* — **url:** mapam.ro **Coverage:** statistics of all the main agricultural products in Romania

Ministerul Finantelor Publice
Ministry of Public Finance

Address: 17 Apolodor Street, 5th District, Bucharest, 050741
Telephone: +40 1 4103400
Fax: +40 1 3122509
E-mail: publicinfo@mfinante.gv.ro
Website: www.mfinante.ro

Guides: access to legislation, strategic development plans, financial control and management systems, and a monthly bulletin
Activity: collects and manages public financial resources; ensures the collection of the revenues stipulated in the budget and performs treasury operations

Website(s) information:

Ministerul Finantelor Publice *(Ministry of Public Finance)* — **url:** www.mfinante.ro **Coverage:** online access to various reports on strategies for growth with a focus on new markets and technologies

National Bank of Romania

Address: Strada Lipscani 25, Sector 3, Bucharest, 030031
Telephone: +40 21 3130410
E-mail: Info@bnro.ro
Website: www.bnro.ro/def_en.htm

Guides: periodicals (daily, weekly, monthly, annually) as well as publications on specific issues related to economic and financial developments; all publications can be downloaded online

Activity: the sole institution vested with the power to issue notes and coins; ensures and maintains price stability

Website(s) information:

National Bank of Romania — **url:** www.bnro.ro/def_en.htm **Coverage:** weekly and daily updates of financial development in Romania as well as specific data on foreign direct investment, financial behaviour of households and companies, gross external debt, etc

Publication(s):

Annual Reports — **Language:** Romanian/English **Frequency:** annual **Content:** overview of main economic and financial developments

Financial Stability Report — **Language:** Romanian/English **Frequency:** annual **Content:** report on the financial system and its risks

Monthly Bulletins — **Language:** English/Romanian **Frequency:** monthly **Content:** covers main monthly economic and financial developments. Includes a statistical section

Russia

Central Bank of the Russian Federation

Address: 12 Neglinnaya Street, Moscow, 107016
Telephone: +7 495 771 9100
Fax: +7 495 621 6465
Website: www.cbr.ru

Guides: catalogue available online, as well as links to PDF versions of all documents - access is free of charge
Activity: organisation of money circulation, monetary regulation, foreign economic activity and regulation of the activities of joint-stock and co-operative banks; prints banknotes and coins

Website(s) information:

Central Bank of the Russian Federation — **url:** www.cbr.ru **Description:** detailed information about the bank and the banking system in Russia. Financial market information covering inter-bank credit market; Rouble deposit rate; government securities market; foreign currency market; precious metals market; other information and analytical material. Also has daily information on foreign exchange rates, commodities rates, and Russia's financial reserve rate **Coverage:** major macroeconomic and financial data, which are disseminated by the Bank of Russia in accordance with IMF Special Data Dissemination Standard (SDDS). Monetary statistical data, balance of payment data (1994 - to date) and other types of statistical data relating to the domestic economy and financial markets

Publication(s):

Bulletin of Banking Statistics — **Language:** English/Russian **Frequency:** monthly **Content:** overview of key macroeconomic statistics; financial markets of inter-bank credits, currency exchange markets, government bonds trading, overview of the number, structure and main indicators of crediting institutions; main payments system indicators of the Russian Federation

Ministerstvo Promishlennosti i Energetiki
Ministry of Industry and Energy

Address: 7 Kitaygorodskij Proezd, Moscow, 109074
Telephone: +7 495 710 5500
Fax: +7 495 710 5722
E-mail: info@mte.gov.ru
Website: www.minprom.gov.ru

Guides: list is available online - full guide to publications and publishers details; available in Russian only
Activity: determines Government policy and designs government projects for addressing the problems of light and heavy industry and the energy industry

Website(s) information:

MinPromEnergo - Statistika *(Ministry of Industry and Energy - Statistics)* — **url:** www.minprom.gov.ru/showStatX **Description:** provides links to statistical surveys carried out by the Ministry; contains official data on government projects and policy; surveys are carried out bi-monthly and cover the main trends in the different branches of Russian industry **Coverage:** bi-monthly surveys of the state of the light and heavy industries in Russia - production and consumption figures, trade and prices

Publication(s):

Energija Promishlennogo Posta (Energy of Industrial Growth) — **Language:** Russian **Frequency:** monthly **Content:** mohtly overview and analyses of production figures, growth, exports and consumptions of goods in particular industries; corporate news and data about Russian companies **Readership:** businessmen, producers, government officials, investors

Ministerstvo Transporta Rossijskoj Federatsii
Ministry of Transport of the Russian Federation

Address: 1 Rozhdestvenka Street, Moscow, 109012
Telephone: +7 495 926 1000
Fax: +7 495 926 9128/926 9038
E-mail: info@mintrans.ru
Website: www.mintrans.ru

Guides: a full catalogue and publisher details are provided online
Activity: determines Government policy and the normative-legal regulatory basis for air, road, see and river transport, industrial transport and the naming of geographic sites and cartographic activity on the territory of the Russian Federation

Publication(s):

Transport Rossii (Russia's Transport) — **Language:** Russian **Frequency:** weekly **Content:** articles and analyses on matters in the sphere of transport - government policy, projects, economic developments and news

Ministry of Agriculture of the Russian Federation

Address: 1/11 Orlikov Pereulok, Moscow, 107139
Telephone: +7 495 207 8362
Fax: +7 495 207 8000
E-mail: info@gov.mcx.ru
Website: www.mcx.ru

Guides: available online in PDF format
Activity: determines, coordinates and implements the government's policy for the encouragement of agriculture; sets the minimum standards for agricultural production

Website(s) information:

Ministry of Agriculture of the Russian Federation — url: www.mcx.ru **Description:** the website provides statistsical information under the links "Analyses, Trends, Prognoses" and "Facts and Figures" (about markets of particular goods). The information is available in Russian only **Coverage:** data on the number and kind of agricultural producers by ownership type; production figures, analyses and data on mechanization and the use of artificial fertilisers and other pesticides, data on the number and structure of livestock, crops and others in the RF; financial-economic analysis of the SME sector in agriculture; figures and charts on the markets for crops, meat products, milk and dairy products, sugar, etc.

Ministry of Economic Development and Trade of the Russian Federation

Address: 1st Tverskaya-Yamskaya Street, GSP-3, A-47, Moscow, 125993
Telephone: +7 495 200 0353
Fax: +7 495 251 6965
E-mail: presscenter@economy.gov.ru
Website: www.economy.gov.ru

Guides: catalogue available online
Activity: determines, coordinates and implements the government policy and projects for the promotion of trade and economic development (regional and sectoral)

Website(s) information:

Ministry of Economic Development and Trade — url: www.economy.gov.ru **Description:** links to statistical surveys of the economy carried out by the ministry **Coverage:** provides information about the basic macroeconomic indicators of the Russian economy - quarterly and annual information, monitoring of the average price of sugar

Ministry of Finance of the Russian Federation
Address: 9 Ilinka Street, Moscow, 103097
Telephone: +7 095 298 9101
Website: www.minfin.ru

Guides: catalogue available online - most publications are available online, free of charge
Activity: determines, coordinates and implements the fiscal and monetary policy of the Russian Federation; executes the state budget and services the national public and external debt

Website(s) information:

Special Data Dissemination Standard. National Summary Data Page — url: www2.minfin.ru/sdds/nsdp.htm **Description:** the website provides free access to the data produced by the Ministry of finance, Central bank and Federal State Statistics Service in accordance with the IMF's statistical standards **Coverage:** official data covering the real, fiscal, financial and external sectors and population; data on consumption, employment, investment, foreign trade - by month and year

Publication(s):

Finance — **Language:** Russian **Frequency:** monthly **Content:** banking and finance, foreign investment and Russian enterprises

Ministry of Information Technology and Communications of the Russian Federation

Address: Moscow, 125375
Telephone: +7 495 771 8100
Fax: +7 495 771 8718
Website: www.minsvyaz.ru

Guides: available online in PDF format
Activity: determines, coordinates and implements the government's policy in the sphere of IT and communications; works for the development and growth of this sector and for the implementation of unified standards of quality on the territory of the RF

Website(s) information:

Ministry of Information Technology and Communications of the Russian Federation - Statistics — url: www.minsvyaz.ru **Description:** the website provides links to different statistical studies, conducted by the Ministry uder the heading "Sector Statistics". The link "Library" provides access to an electronic database, which covers a wide range of topics connected to the sector, including economic infornation about particular branches of the sector, foreign investment in the telecommunications market and market dynamics and structure. The website provides an extensive list of IT and telecommunications companies in the RF, sorted by region, specific activity and type of ownership **Coverage:** data on basic indicators of the state of the communications and IT sector - density of services, internet users (by year and region), economic indicators - prices, profit, size of the market and growth; structure of the market and competition

Nauchno Issledovatelskij Finansovij Institut (NIFI)
Institute for Scientific Financial Research

Address: 3 Nastasinskij Pereulok, Corpus II, Moscow, 127006
Telephone: +7 495 299 7414
Fax: +7 495 299 8853
E-mail: savinskiy@nifi.ru
Website: www2.minfin.ru/nifi/index.htm

Guides: online catalogue
Activity: conducts research in the sphere of government finance, monetary and crediting policy, financial markets and other matters in the area of banking and finance

Russian Academy of Sciences, Institute of Economic Forecasting

Address: 47 Nakhimovsky Prospect, Moscow, 117418
Telephone: +7 095 129 3422/129 1800
Fax: +7 095 310 7071
E-mail: office@mail.ecfor.rssi.ru
Website: www.ecfor.rssi.ru

Guides: publishes the journal "Studies on Russian Economic Development", which covers the most important trends and developments in Russian economy and publishes the most significant statistical results of the Institute's research

Activity: carries out short-, medium- and long-term research and forecasting of macroeconomic developments and indicators in Russia

Publication(s):

Studies on Russian Economic Development — **Language:** English/Russian **Frequency:** bi-monthly **Content:** contains information on the key economic and social problems in Russia, presents the most significant results of the research at the Institute, and publishes statistics and methodological materials **Readership:** academics, students, government officials

State Committee of the Russian Federation on Statistics (GOSKOMSTAT)

Address: 39 Myasnitskaya Street, Moscow, 107450
Telephone: +7 095 207 4902
Fax: +7 095 207 4087
E-mail: stat@gks.ru
Website: www.gks.ru

Guides: full catalogue is available online; most annual publications are available in English, and others can be translated at the request of the customer; publications can be obtained in printed, CD-ROM and/or web-access format

Activity: carries out continuous statistical analysis of social and economic activity and trends in the country; the official body for gathering, analysing and disseminating statistical information and analyses on the territory of the Russian Federation

Website(s) information:

Federal Statistics Service — **url:** www.gks.ru **Description:** the official website of the Statistical Survey publishes the most important data from their statistical collections and other publications online **Coverage:** data on population, labour dynamics, economic indicators, health care and status of the population, education, GNP, industrial production, agriculture, transport, trade and services, foreign trade, finance, investment flows

Publication(s):

Agriculture in Russia — **Frequency:** annual **Content:** data on farms, livestock, crops

Demographic Yearbook — **Language:** Russian **Frequency:** annual **Content:** demographics

External Trade of the CIS Countries — **Language:** Russian **Frequency:** annual **Content:** data on foreign trade with post-soviet countries

Incomes, Expenditures and Household Consumption — **Language:** Russian **Frequency:** annual **Content:** data on wages and average expenditure on household products

Information on Socio-economic Situation in Russia — **Language:** Russian **Frequency:** monthly **Content:** monthly overview of data on main so-economic indicators and commentaries

Labour and Employment — **Language:** Russian **Frequency:** annual **Content:** data on available work force in the country and unemployment rates; data is given by regions

Population Size and Migration in Russia — **Language:** Russian **Frequency:** annual **Content:** data on the country's demographic situation

Russia in Figures — **Language:** Russian/English **Frequency:** annual **Content:** general socio-economic overview of the Russian Federation, with statistics covering: population structure and demographic trends; labour market; household expenditure; evolution of major macro-economic indicators; agricultural and industrial production; national accounts and balance of payments; etc

Statistical Insight — **Language:** Russian/English **Frequency:** quarterly **Content:** articles and commentaries on news and trends in statistical science; different types of surveys and data published

Statistical Yearbook — **Language:** Russian **Frequency:** annual **Content:** covers main socio-economic indicators

Serbia and Montenegro

Agencija za promociju investicija i izvoza Srbije (SIEPA)
Serbian Investment and Export Promotion Agency

Address: Vlajkoviceva 3/ V, Belgrade, 11000
Telephone: +38 11 339 8550
Fax: +38 11 339 8814
E-mail: office@siepa.sr.gov.yu
Website: www.siepa.sr.gov.yu

Activity: researching and analysing business environment, publishing information publications to help foreign companies operate in Serbia, assisting businesses and investors obtain permits and licenses, helping Serbian exporters service international markets, linking potential investors, Maintaining an export database

Website(s) information:

Agencija za promociju investicija i izvoza Srbije (SIEPA) *(Serbian Investment and Export Promotion Agency)* — **url:** www.siepa.sr.gov.yu

Publication(s):

Brošure po sektorima *(Sectoral Brochure)* — **Language:** Serbian/English **Frequency:** annual **Content:** automotives, tourism, pharmaceuticals, forestry, IT, fruit and vegetables, agribusiness **Readership:** academics, research specialsts, governmental organisations

SIEPA Newsleter — **Language:** Serbian/English **Frequency:** monthly **Content:** economic developments and investment indicators **Readership:** research specialists, investors

Centralna banka Crne Gore
Central Bank of Montenegro

Address: Bulevar Svetog Petra Cetinjskog 7, Podgorica
Telephone: +38 81 403 191
Fax: +38 81 664 140
E-mail: info@cb-cg.org
Website: www.cb-cg.org

Activity: implementing monetary policy, supervising domestic monetary systems, conducting research related to monetary system, managing national payment system

Website(s) information:

Centralna banka Crne Gore *(Central Bank of Montenegro)* — **url:** www.cb-cg.org **Description:** wide range of financial and banking statistical data available online and in English **Coverage:** banking, finance, economic indicators

Publication(s):

Finansijski izveštaj i izveštaj revizora *(Financial and Audit Report)* — **Language:** Serbian/English **Frequency:** irregular **Content:** bank performance and financial statements **Readership:** research specialists

Godišnji izveštaj *(Annual Report)* — **Language:** Serbian/English **Frequency:** annual **Content:** microeconomic environment, banking system **Readership:** banking experts, research specialists, governmental institutions

Godišnji izveštaj 2003 *(Annual Report 2003)* — **Language:** Serbian/English **Frequency:** annual **Content:** micro-economic environment, banking system **Readership:** banking experts, research specialists, governmental organisations

Godišnji izvještaj o radu sektora za kontrolu banaka za 2004. godinu *(Report on Banking Sector Control for 2004)* — **Language:** Serbian/English **Frequency:** annual **Content:** assessment of compliance, banking system of the country, performance of banks, risks in banking system **Readership:** financial experts, research specialists, governmental institutions

Izveštaj glavnog ekonomiste *(Senior Economic Expert's Third Quarterly Report 2005)* — **Language:** Serbian/English **Frequency:** quarterly **Content:** macro-economic developments, sector developments, monetary system, financial market, international economy **Readership:** financial experts, research specialists, governmental institutions

Ministarstvo finansija i ekonomije Republike Srbije
Ministry of Finance and Economy of the Republic of Serbia

Address: Kneza Miloša 20, Belgrade, 11000
Telephone: +38 11 361 4972
Fax: +38 11 361 8914
E-mail: informacije@mfin.sr.gov.yu
Website: www.mfin.sr.gov.yu

Activity: developing economic and financial policy

Website(s) information:
Ministarstvo finansija i ekonomije Republike Srbije (Ministry of Finance and Economy of the Republic of Serbia) — **url:** www.mfin.sr.gov.yu **Description:** reports available online **Coverage:** budget, revenue, banking

Publication(s):
Bilten javnih finansija (Public Finance Bulletin) — **Language:** Serbian **Frequency:** monthly **Content:** financial market, public debt, general financial and economic information **Readership:** research specialists, academics

Casopis Finansije (Finance Magazine) — **Language:** Serbian **Frequency:** monthly **Content:** national economy, property taxation, international capital investment **Readership:** academics, research specialists, governmental organisations

Ministarstvo poljoprivrede, šumarstva i vodoprivrede Republike Srbije
Ministry of Agriculture, Forestry and Water Management

Address: Nemanjina 22-26, Belgrade, 11000
Telephone: +38 11 306 5038
Fax: +38 11 361 6272
E-mail: office@minpolj.sr.gov.yu
Website: www.minpolj.sr.gov.yu

Activity: developing and implementing agricultural policy

Website(s) information:
Ministarstvo poljoprivrede, šumarstva i vodoprivrede Republike Srbije (Ministry of Agriculture, Forestry and Water Management of the Republic of Serbia) — **url:** www.minpolj.sr.gov.yu **Description:** online statistics **Coverage:** production of berry fruit in 2004

Publication(s):
Bilanski poljoprivrednih proizvoda (Balance of Agricultural Products) — **Language:** Serbian **Frequency:** irregular **Content:** otal production of diddferent agricultural products (both animals and crops) **Readership:** agricultural experts, research specialists, governmental organisations

Glasnik (Journal) — **Language:** Serbian **Frequency:** monthly **Content:** general agriculatural developments and information **Readership:** agricultural experts, research specialists, governmental organisation

Konkurentnos poljoprivrede Srbije (Current Status of Serbian Agriculture) — **Language:** Serbian **Frequency:** irregular **Content:** gricultural overview in light of international agri market **Readership:** academics, research specialists

Ministarstvo privrede Republike Srbije
Ministry of Economy of the Republic of Serbia

Address: Kralja Milana 16, Belgrade, 11000
Telephone: +38 11 361 7599
Fax: +38 11 361 7640
Website: www.mpriv.sr.gov.yu

Activity: development of the economy through recovery and change of economic structure, predominant private ownership, creation of new, profit-generating jobs

Website(s) information:
Ministarstvo privrede Republike Srbije (Ministry of Economy of the Republic of Serbia) — **url:** www.mpriv.sr.gov.yu **Coverage:** economic indicators

Publication(s):
Godišnji izveštaj (Annual Report) — **Language:** Serbian/English **Frequency:** annual **Content:** economic indicators **Readership:** academics, research specialists, governmental organisations

Izveštaj 2004-2006 (Report 2004-2006) — **Language:** Serbian/English **Frequency:** irregular **Content:** activities in 2004 - 2006, statistical data for 2005-2006, industrial development, privatization and restructuring, development of capital market, development of small and medium enterprises and entrepreneurship, competitiveness and co-operation with international institutions, plans for 2006 **Readership:** academics, research specialists, governmental organisations, businesses

Ministarstvo trgovine, turizma i usluga Republike Srbije
Ministry of Trade, Tourism and Services of the Republic of Serbia

Address: Nemanjina 22-26, Belgrade, 11000
Telephone: +38 11 361 3404
E-mail: kabinet@minttu.sr.gov.yu
Website: www.minttu.sr.gov.yu

Activity: developing and enforcing state policies of trade and tourism

Website(s) information:
Ministarstvo trgovine, turizma i usluga Republike Srbije (Ministry of Trade, Tourism and Services of the Republic of Serbia) — **url:** www.minttu.sr.gov.yu **Coverage:** socio-economic indicators, tourism

Publication(s):
Bilten turisticke inspekcije (Tourist Inspection Bulletin) — **Language:** Serbian **Content:** regulations, statistics, surevey results and work of tourist inspection **Readership:** research specialists, toursit organisations

Turisticki pregled (Tourism Overview) — **Language:** Serbian/English **Frequency:** quarterly **Content:** narrative and statistical overview of the country's toursim **Readership:** research specialisits, tourist organisations/institutions

Narodna banka Srbije
National Bank of Serbia

Address: Kralja Petra 12, Belgrade, 11000
Telephone: +38 11 302 7194
Fax: +38 11 302 7394
E-mail: kabinet@nbs.yu
Website: www.nbs.yu

Activity: determination of monetary policy, regulation of money in circulation, domestic and external payment operations and issue of banknotes and coins

Website(s) information:
Narodna banka Srbije (National Bank of Serbia) — **url:** www.nbs.yu **Description:** statistical information on banking system and general socio-economic indicators accessible online in Serbian and English **Coverage:** real sector (GDP, industrial production, prices movements, average monthly earnings, Serbian budget, employment/unemployment rate), monetary sector (selected monetary and forex indicators, banks' loans and investments, monetary aggregates, benchmark interest rates), external sector (balance of payments, external debt, foreign exchange reserves)

Publication(s):
Bilten Narodne banke (National Bank Bulletin) — **Language:** Serbian/English **Frequency:** monthly **Content:** banking system **Readership:** banks, research speciialists, governmental organisations

Ekonometricka analiza potražnje za novcem u Srbiji (Econometric Analysis of Money Demand in Serbia) — **Language:** Serbian/English **Content:** stability of money demands and influencing factors

Ekonomski pregled (Economic Review) — **Language:** Serbian/English **Frequency:** quarterly **Content:** covers prices, international economic developments, external environments **Readership:** banks, research specialists, governmental bodies

Održivost Stranog Duga Srbije (Serbia's External Debt Sustainability) — **Language:** Serbian/English **Content:** preliminary results of the analysis based on outstanding debts as of September 2004 **Readership:** research specialists, investment companies, academics, governmental organisations

Sektor bankarstva (Banking Sector) — **Language:** Serbian/English **Frequency:** quarterly **Content:** banking sector **Readership:** research specialists, governmental organisations, academics, foreign investment banks

Statisticki bilten (Statistical Bulletin) — **Language:** Serbian/English **Frequency:** monthly **Content:** banking and socio-economic developments **Readership:** banks, research specialists, governmental organisations

Republicki zavod za statistiku
Statistical Office of the Republic of Serbia

Address: Milana Rakica 5, Belgrade, 11000
Telephone: +38 11 412 922
Fax: +38 11 411 260
E-mail: stat@statserb.sr.gov.yu
Website: www.statserb.sr.gov.yu

Activity: collecting and publishing statistical information

Website(s) information:
Republicki zavod za statistiku (Statistical Office of the Republic of Serbia) — **url:** www.statserb.sr.gov.yu **Description:** reports, thematic cards, graphics **Coverage:** demographics, population age, gender, birth and death rate, economic trends and indicators

Publication(s):
Društveno-ekonomski trendovi (Socio-Economic Trends) — **Language:** Serbian/English **Frequency:** annual **Content:** socio-economic trends in the country **Readership:** academics, research specialists, governmental and non-governmental organisations

Mesecni statisticki pregled (Monthly Statistical Survey) — **Language:** Serbian/English **Frequency:** monthly **Content:** socio-economic indicators **Readership:** academics, research specialists, governmental and non-governmental organisations

Statisticki godišnjak (Statistical Yearbook) — **Language:** Serbian/English **Frequency:** annual **Content:** socio-economic indicators by municipalities (1949 - present) **Readership:** academics, research specialists

Udruženje za zaštitu potrošaca Vojvodine
Consumer Protection Association of Vojvodina

Address: Vase Stajica 22b, Novi Sad, 21000
Telephone: +38 64 112 4726
Fax: +38 064 112 4726
E-mail: office@consumer.org.yu
Website: www.consumer.org.yu

Activity: protection of consumers' interests

Website(s) information:
Udruženje za zaštitu potrošaca Vojvodine (Consumer Protection Association of Vojvodina) — **url:** www.consumer.org.yu **Description:** extensive statistical information available online in Serbian (English version of site is under construction and should be available soon) **Coverage:** consumer expenditure, consumer prices and costs, consumer basket, household expenditure

Vlada Republike Crne Gore
Government of the Republic of Montenegro

Address: Jovana Tomaševica bb, Podgorica, 81000
Telephone: +38 81 242 530
Fax: +38 81 242329
E-mail: kabinet.premijera@mn.yu
Website: www.vlada.cg.yu

Activity: government office

Website(s) information:
Vlada Republike Crne Gore (Government of the Republic of Montenegro) — **url:** www.vlada.cg.yu **Description:** socio-economic statistical data available online and in English **Coverage:** socio-economic indicators

Publication(s):
Agenda ekonomskih reformi u Crnoj Gori 2002-2007 (Economic Reform Agenda for Montenegro 2002-2007) — **Language:** Serbian/English **Frequency:** irregular **Content:** economic development and indicators from previous years and those planned/expected **Readership:** academics, research specialists, governmental organisations, economic experts

Restrukturianje preduzeca (Restructuring of Companies) — **Language:** Serbian/English **Frequency:** irregular **Content:** verview of companies and plans for their restructuring **Readership:** academics, research specialists, governmental organisations, investors

Vlada Republike Srbije
Government of the Republic of Serbia

Address: Nemanjina 11, Belgrade, 11000
Telephone: +38 11 361 7709
Fax: +38 11 361 7697
E-mail: omr@srbija.sr.gov.yu
Website: www.srbija.sr.gov.yu

Activity: government organisation

Website(s) information:
Vlada Republike Srbije (Government of the Republic of Serbia) — **url:** www.srbija.sr.gov.yu **Description:** statistics by different sections available online and in English **Coverage:** basic facts, provinces, climate, population, language, religion, refugees, energy and mining, industry, transport, agriculture, employment, wages

Zavod za statistiku Crne Gore
Statistical Office of Montenegro

Address: IV proleterske brigade 26, Podgorica, 81000
Telephone: +38 81 241 206
Fax: +38 81 241 270
E-mail: statistika@cg.yu
Website: www.monstat.cg.yu

Activity: collates and publishes statistical data

Website(s) information:
Zavod za statistiku Crne Gore (Statistical Office of Montenegro) — **url:** www.monstat.cg.yu **Description:** montly and annual online statistics **Coverage:** population, employment, wages, gross domestic products, investments, prices, agriculture, forestry, industry, construction, environment, foreign economic relations, tourism, transport and communication, education and culture

Publication(s):
Mjesecni statisticki pregled (Bulletin) — **Language:** Serbian **Frequency:** monthly **Content:** socio-economic developments in the Republic of Montenegro

Statisticki godišnjak (Statistical Yearbook) — **Language:** Serbian/English **Frequency:** annual **Content:** socio-economic situation in the Republic of Montenegro **Readership:** academics, research specialists, governmental and non-governmental organisations

Zavod za statistiku Srbije i Crne Gore
Statistical Office of Serbia and Montenegro

Address: Kneza Miloša 20, Belgrade, 11000
Telephone: +38 11 361 3245
Fax: +38 11 361 7295
E-mail: ranko@szs.sv.gov.yu
Website: www.szs.sv.gov.yu

Activity: collation and publishing of statistical data

Website(s) information:
Zavod za statistiku Srbije i Crne Gore (Statistical Office of Serbia and Montenegro) — **url:** www.szs.sv.gov.yu **Description:** information on the office's main products and services in both English and Serbian. Access to some online statistics on main socio-economic indicators; online catalogue of publications and documents **Coverage:** socio-economic data

Publication(s):
Mesecni pregled privredne statistike (Monthly Economic Overview) — **Language:** Serbian/English **Frequency:** monthly **Content:** economic indicators **Readership:** academics, research specialists, governmental organisations, businesses

Statisticki godišnjak Srbije i Crne Gore (Statistical Yearbook of Serbia and Montenegro) — **Language:** Serbian/English **Frequency:** annual **Content:** socio-economic statistical information **Readership:** academics, research specialists, governmental organisations

Statisticki kalendar (Statistical Pocket Book) — **Language:** Serbian/English **Frequency:** annual **Content:** socio-economic developments **Readership:** academics, research specialists, governmental organisations, NGOs

Slovakia

INFOSTAT, Inštitút informatiky a štatistiky
INFOSTAT, Institute of Information Technology and Statistics

Address: Dúbravská 3, Bratislava, 842 21
Telephone: +421 2 5937 9111
Fax: +421 2 5479 1463
E-mail: infostat@infostat.sk
Website: www.infostat.sk

Activity: developing projects relating to information technology and statistics

Website(s) information:
Inštitút Informatiky a Statistiky *(Institute of Information Technology and Statistics)* — url: www.infostat.sk **Description:** statistical socio-economic data **Coverage:** socio-economic indicators

Publication(s):
Makroekonomické analýzy a prognózy *(Macroeconomic Analysis and Prognosis)* — **Language:** Slovak **Frequency:** irregular **Content:** macroeconomic environment and developments in the country **Readership:** economists, research specialists, analysts

Letové prevádzkové služby Slovenskej republiky
Air Traffic Control Administration of the Slovak Republic

Address: Letisko M. R. Štefánika, Bratislava 21, 823 07
Telephone: +421 2 4857 1111
E-mail: info@lps.sk
Website: www.rlp.sk

Activity: managing air traffic and related services

Publication(s):
Výrocná správa *(Annual Report)* — **Language:** Slovak/English **Frequency:** annual **Content:** air traffic services (economic developments, audit report, balance sheet, profit and loss, cash flow) **Readership:** air traffic specialists, research specialists, analysts

Ministerstvo dopravy, pôst a telekomunikácií SR
Ministry of Transport, Postal Services and Telecommunications of the Slovak Republic

Address: Námestie slobody c. 6, Bratislava, 810 05
Telephone: +421 2 5949 4111
Fax: +421 2 5249 4794
E-mail: info@telecom.gov.sk
Website: www.telecom.gov.sk

Activity: creating and implementing the country's policy on transport, postal services and telecommunications

Website(s) information:
Ministerstvo dopravy, pôst a telekomunikácií SR *(Ministry of Transport, Postal Services and Telecommunications of the Slovak Republic)* — url: www.telecom.gov.sk **Description:** the site offers detailed statistical information about the three sectors **Coverage:** transport, postal services and telecommunications

Publication(s):
Intermodálna doprava v Slovenskey republiky *(Intermodal Transport in The Slovak Republic)* — **Language:** Slovak/English **Frequency:** annual **Content:** intermodal transport (volume of goods in tons transported by intermodal transport and development of transport in general) **Readership:** transport specialists, research specialists, analysts, governmental institutions

Štatistické údaje *(Statistical Data)* — **Language:** Slovak/English **Frequency:** irregular **Content:** infrastructure and volume of all types of transport **Readership:** transport specialists, research specialists, analysts, governmental institutions

Štatistické údaje pôšt *(Statistivcal Data on the Postal Services in SR)* — **Language:** Slovak/English **Frequency:** irregular **Content:** postal services (service indicators) **Readership:** research specialists, analysts

Vybrané štatistické údaje za odvetvie telekomunikácií v SR *(Statistic Data on Telecommunications Sector in SR)* — **Language:** Slovak/English **Frequency:** irregular **Content:** telecommunications sector (infrastructure, revenue, quality, traffic, services) **Readership:** telecommunication specialists, research specialists, analysts, governmental institutions

Výrocna správa *(Annual Report)* — **Language:** Slovak/English **Frequency:** annual **Content:** activities of the Ministry, road, rail and water transport, civil aviation, postal services, telecommunications **Readership:** transport specialists, governmental institutions, research specialists, analysts

Ministerstvo hospodárstva Slovenskej republiky
Ministry of Economy of the Slovak Republic

Address: Mierová 19, Bratislava 212, 827 15
Telephone: +421 2 4854 1111
E-mail: info@economy.gov.sk
Website: www.economy.gov.sk

Activity: central body for the industry (with the exception of food industry, construction products and manufacture of construction materials)

Website(s) information:
Ministerstvo hospodárstva Slovenskej republiky *(Ministry of Economy of the Slovak Republic)* — url: www.economy.gov.sk **Description:** the site offers statistical information about the country's trade and industry **Coverage:** economic indicators

Publication(s):
Statistical Data on Tourism in Slovakia — **Language:** English **Frequency:** quarterly **Content:** tourism arrivals, number of foreign tourists, departures **Readership:** research specialists, analysts

Trade Statistics — **Language:** English **Frequency:** annual **Content:** trade indicators **Readership:** economists, research specialists, analysts, governmental institutions

Ministerstvo pôdohospodárstva Slovenskey republiky
Ministry of Agriculture of the Slovak Republic

Address: Dobrovicova 12, Bratislava, 812 66
Telephone: +421 2 5926 6301
Fax: +421 2 5926 6311
E-mail: tlacove@land.gov.sk
Website: www.mpsr.sk

Activity: creating and implementing the country's agricultural policy

Website(s) information:
Ministerstvo pôdohospodárstva Slovenskey republiky *(Ministry of Agriculture of the Slovak Republic)* — url: www.radela.sk **Description:** presents statistical information about the development in agricultural and food sectors; it offers an extensive overview of branches within the sector **Coverage:** agriculture and food

Publication(s):
Lesné hospodárstvo *(Forestry)* — **Language:** Slovak **Frequency:** irregular **Content:** forestry industry of the country **Readership:** research specialists, analysts, governmental institutions, non-governmental organisations

Vodné hospodárstvo *(Water Industry)* — **Language:** Slovak **Frequency:** irregular **Content:** water industry data **Readership:** research specialists, analysts, governmental organisations

Zelená správa *(Green Report)* — **Language:** Slovak/English **Frequency:** annual **Content:** report on agriculture and food industry **Readership:** agricultural and food experts, governmental institutions, research specialists, analysts

Ministerstvo spravodlivosti SR
Ministry of Justice of the Slovak Republic

Address: Župné námestie 13, Bratislava, 813 11
Telephone: +421 2 5935 3111
E-mail: tlacove@justice.sk
Website: www.justice.gov.sk

Activity: creating and implementing the legal policy of the country

Website(s) information:
Ministerstvo spravodlivosti SR *(Ministry of Justice of the Slovak Republic)* — **url:** www.justice.gov.sk **Description:** the site offers information about the work of legal bodies and crime rate in the country and bay areas **Coverage:** legal system and crime

Ministerstvo zahranicných vecí SR
Ministry of Foreign Affairs of the Slovak Republic

Address: Hlboká cesta 2, Bratislava 37, 833 36
Telephone: +421 2 5978 1111
E-mail: informacie@foreign.gov.sk
Website: www.mzv.sk

Activity: creating and implementing foreign policy of the country

Website(s) information:
Ministerstvo zahranicných vecí SR *(Ministry of Foreign Affairs of the Slovak Republic)* — **url:** www.mzv.sk **Description:** the site offers social and economic indicators **Coverage:** society and economy

Publication(s):
Slovakia, Krajina v ktorej žijeme *(Slovakia, The Country Where We Live)* — **Language:** Slovakian/English/German/French/Russian **Frequency:** irregular **Content:** detailed socio-economic presentation of the country **Readership:** research specialists, analysts, governmental and non-governmental organisations

Ministerstvo zdravotníctva SR
Ministry of Health of the Slovak Republic

Address: 52, Limbová 2, Bratislava 37, 837 52
Telephone: +421 2 5937 3111
Fax: +421 2 5477 7983
E-mail: office@health.gov.sk
Website: www.health.gov.sk

Activity: making and implementing the health policy of the country

Website(s) information:
Ministerstvo zdravotníctva SR *(Ministry of Health of the Slovak Republic)* — **url:** www.health.gov.sk **Description:** the site offers statistical information about the sector **Coverage:** health system

Publication(s):
Výrocná správa Ministerstva zdravotníctva Slovenskej republiky *(Annual Report of the Ministry of Health of the Slovak Republic)* — **Language:** Slovak **Frequency:** annual **Content:** health system of the country and relevant activities of the Ministry **Readership:** health experts, governmental institutions. Research specialists, analysts

Výskyt prenosných ochorení v Slovenskej republike *(Occurrence of Infectious Diseases in the Slovak Republic)* — **Language:** Slovak/English (summary only) **Frequency:** monthly **Content:** infectious diseases data **Readership:** health experts, governmental and non-governmental organisations, research specialists, analysts

Národná banka Slovenska
National Bank of Slovakia

Address: Imricha Karvaša 1, Bratislava, 813 25
Telephone: +421 2 5787 1111
Fax: +421 2 5865 1100
E-mail: info@nbs.sk
Website: www.nbs.sk

Guides: the bank has its own library where all publications can be obtained
Activity: formulating and implementing the country's monetary policy, issuing banknotes and coins, controlling, co-ordinating and providing for the circulation of money, supervising development of the banking sector

Website(s) information:
Národná banka Slovenska *(National Bank of Slovakia)* — **url:** www.nbs.sk **Description:** the site offers detailed information about the country's banking system **Coverage:** facts and figures about the country's banking system

Publication(s):
Analýza bankového sektora *(Analysis of Banking Sector)* — **Language:** Slovak **Frequency:** irregular **Content:** banking sector **Readership:** bankers, investment banks, research specialists, analysts

BIATEC- odborný bankový casopis *(BIATEC - Banking Journal)* — **Language:** Slovenian **Frequency:** irregular **Content:** news from and development of the country's financial system **Readership:** bankers, financial experts, analysts, research specialists

Menový prehlad *(Monetary Survey)* — **Language:** Slovak/English **Frequency:** monthly **Content:** review of economic and financial trends with statistical data covering key economic and financial indicators **Readership:** finanical experts, bankers, governmental institutions, research specialists, analysts

Výrocná správa *(Report on Monetary Development)* — **Language:** Slovenian/English **Frequency:** annual **Content:** monetary system and its development **Readership:** financial experts, bankers, research specialists, analysts

Slovenská agentúra životného prostredia
Slovak Environmental Agency

Address: Tajovskeho 28, Banská Bystrica, 975 90
Telephone: +421 48 437 4111
Fax: +421 48 423 0409
E-mail: sazp@sazp.sk
Website: www.sazp.sk

Activity: ensuring that international requirements regarding environmental protection are complied with, conducting monitoring, implementing waste management policy, assessing risks, implementing project relating to environmental protection

Website(s) information:
Slovenská agentúra životného prostredia *(Slovak Environmental Agency)* — **url:** www.sazp.sk **Coverage:** pollution and waste management

Štatistický úrad SR
Statistical Office of the Slovak Republic

Address: Mileticova 3, Bratislava, 824 67
Telephone: +421 2 5023 6335
Fax: +421 2 5556 1361
Website: www.statistics.sk

Activity: collation and publishing of official statistics

Website(s) information:
Štatistický úrad SR *(Statistical Office of the Slovak Republic)* — **url:** www.statistics.sk **Description:** the site offers the information about products and services, including publications catalogue **Coverage:** detailed socio-economic statistical information

Publication(s):
Aktualizovaná prognóza vývoja vybraných ukazovatelov na rok *(Revised Development Prognosis by Selected Indicators)* — **Language:** Slovak/English **Frequency:** annual **Content:** development trends (findings of a survey on the sectors of industry, construction, trade and market services) **Readership:** economists, research specialists, analysts, governmental organisations, investors

Bulletin SÚ SR *(Bulletin of the Statistical Office of the Slovak Republic)* — **Language:** Slovak/English **Frequency:** monthly **Content:** statistical and narrative report on the latest developments in the Slovak national economy and society **Readership:** economists, research specialists, analysts, governmental organisations, non-governmental organisations

Hospodársky ukazovatel *(Monitor of the Economy)* — **Language:** Slovak/English **Frequency:** monthly **Content:** compilation of monthly and quarterly statistics of the country's economy **Readership:** economists, research specialists, analysts, businesses, governmental institutions

Priemyselná produkcia *(Industrial Production)* — **Language:** Slovak/English **Frequency:** monthly **Content:** industrial production figures **Readership:** statistical and research specialist, analysts, governmental institutions, industrial sector

Rocenka zahranicného obchodu *(Yearbook of Foreign Trade of the Slovak Republic)* — **Language:** Slovak/English **Frequency:** annual **Content:** annual statistical report on the country's foreign trade **Readership:** economists, research specialists, analysts, investors, businessmen

Sociálny vývoj (Social Development Trends in the Slovak Republic) — **Language:** Slovak/English **Frequency:** irregular **Content:** indicators of the country's social development **Readership:** research specialists, analysts, governmental institutions and non-governmental organisations

Statistická rocenka SR (Statistical Yearbook of the Slovak Republic) — **Language:** Slovak/English **Frequency:** annual **Content:** a wide range of detailed socio-economic statistics **Readership:** economists, research specialists, analysts, governmental institutions, non-governmental organisations

Štatistický prehlad o SR (Statistical Review of the Slovak Republic) — **Language:** Slovak/English **Frequency:** quarterly **Content:** latest macro-economic indicators and findings of the most recent surveys and analyses **Readership:** research specialists, analysts, governmental and non-governmental organisations, business and industrial sector

Stavebná produkcia (Construction Industry) — **Language:** Slovak/English **Frequency:** monthly **Content:** construction industry **Readership:** civil engineers, construction industry, research specialists, analysts, investors

Štrukturálny census fariem (Structural Farm Analysis) — **Language:** Slovak/English **Frequency:** irregular **Content:** farming in light of accession to the EU **Readership:** agricultural experts, research specialists, relevant governmental institutions

Vývoj harmonizovaných indexov spotrebitelských cien (Consumer Price Indices) — **Language:** Slovak/English **Frequency:** monthly **Content:** prices and consumers' habits covering certain period and comparison with the previous **Readership:** consumer experts, research specialists, analysts, consumer organisations, businesses

Zamestnanost a priemerná mesacná mzda vo vybraných odvetviach (Employment and Average Monthly Wages by Industries) — **Language:** Slovak/English **Frequency:** monthly **Content:** employment and wages by industries **Readership:** economists, businesses, research specialists, analysts

Výskumné demografické centrum INFOSTAT
Demographic Research Centre INFOSTAT

Address: Dúbravská 3, Bratislava 45, 845 24
Telephone: +421 2 5937 9245
Fax: +421 2 5479 1463
E-mail: vdc@infostat.sk
Website: www.infostat.sk/vdc

Activity: conducting and co-ordinating demographic research in the Slovak Republic

Website(s) information:
Výskumné demografické centrum INFOSTAT (Demographic Research Centre INFOSTAT) — **url:** www.infostat.sk/vdc **Description:** the site offers detailed statistical information about the demographic trends and situation in the country **Coverage:** demographics

Publication(s):
Populacný vývoj v Slovenskej republike (Population in Slovakia) — **Language:** Slovak/English **Frequency:** annual **Content:** demographic indicators **Readership:** research specialists, analysts, governmental and non-governmental organisations

Prognóza vývoja obyvatelov v okresoch SR do roku 2025 (Population Projection of Districts in Slovakia until 2025) — **Language:** Slovak/English **Frequency:** irregular **Content:** analysis of the current and prognosis of the future demographic developments **Readership:** research specialists, analysts, governmental and non-governmental organisations

Reprodukcné správanie obyvatelstva v obciach s nízkym životným štandardom (The Reproductive Behaviour in Municipalities with Low Living Standard) — **Language:** Slovak/English **Frequency:** irregular **Content:** general birth rate and trends in the areas with low living standards **Readership:** research specialists, analysts, governmental and non-governmental organisations

Výskumný ústav dopravný
Transport Research Institute

Address: Velký Diel 3323, Žilina, 010 08
Telephone: +421 41 565 2819
Fax: +421 41 565 2883
E-mail: info@vud.sk
Website: www.vud.sk

Activity: advising on national transport policy making and implementation, conducting research in the fields of engineering and technology, operation, economy, legislation, management and organisation, informatics and automation, ecology, power system, transport infrastructure safety and quality, transport services and tourism management, transport policy, certification and testing in transport

Publication(s):
Horizonty dopravy (Transport Horizons) — **Language:** Slovak **Frequency:** quarterly **Content:** developments in the transport sector **Readership:** transport specialists, analysts, governmental institutions

Výrocná správa za rok (Annual Report) — **Language:** Slovak/English **Frequency:** annual **Content:** information about implemented transport projects and their impact **Readership:** economists, research specialists, analysts

Výskumný ústav ekonomiky polnohospodárstva a potravinárstva
Research Institute of Agricultural and Food Economics

Address: Trencianska 55, Bratislava 3, 821 80
Telephone: +421 2 5341 7428
Fax: +421 2 5341 6408
E-mail: vuz@vuz.sk
Website: www.vuepp.sk

Guides: publications can be obtained from the Institute's library
Activity: conducting research in the fields of agriculture and food (economic analysis, structural development)

Publication(s):
Ekonomický polnohospodársky úcet SR (Economical Overview of Slovak Agriculture) — **Language:** Slovak **Frequency:** irregular **Content:** economic aspect of the agricultural sector **Readership:** agricultural experts, economists, governmental institutions, research specialists, analysts

Slovenské polnohospodárstvo v rokoch 2001-2005 (Slovak Agriculture 2001-2005) — **Language:** Slovak **Frequency:** irregular **Content:** development of agricultural sector of the country **Readership:** agricultural experts, governmental and non-governmental organisations, research specialists, analysts

Vedecký casopis - Ekonomika polnohospodárstva (Economy in Agriculture - Magazine) — **Language:** Slovak **Frequency:** quarterly **Content:** agriculture and economy in the sector **Readership:** agricultural experts, farmers, research specialists, analysts

Slovenia

Agencija Republike Slovenije za kmetijske trge in razvoj podeželja (ARSKTRP)
Agency of the Republic of Slovenia for Agricultural Markets and Rural Development

Address: Dunajska 160, Ljubljana, 1000
Telephone: +386 1 580 7660
Fax: +386 1 478 9206
E-mail: aktrp@gov.si
Website: www.arsktrp.gov.si

Activity: technical implementation of agricultural policy measures; promoting the maintenance and development of Slovenian rural areas and strengthening of agricultural markets

Website(s) information:
Agencija Republike Slovenije za kmetijske trge in razvoj podeželja (ARSKTRP) (Agency of the Republic of Slovenia for Agricultural Markets and Rural Development) — **url:** www.arsktrp.gov.si **Description:** the site offers information about agricultural system **Coverage:** agriculture

Agencija za zavarovalni nadzor Slovenije
Insurance Supervision Agency of Slovenia

Address: Trg republike 3, Ljubljana, 1000
Telephone: +386 1 252 8600
Fax: +386 1 252 8630
E-mail: agencija@a-zn.si
Website: www.a-zn.si

Activity: supervising the country's insurance sector

Website(s) information:
Agencija za zavarovalni nadzor Slovenije (Insurance Supervision Agency of Slovenia)
— url: www.a-zn.si **Description:** the site offers various information about the insurance industry **Coverage:** insurance

Publication(s):
Letno porocilo (Annual Report) — **Language:** Slovenian/English **Frequency:** annual **Content:** developments in the insurance sector and the achievements of the agency itself **Readership:** financial experts, research specialists, analysts

Porocilo o stanju na podrocju zavarovalništva (Report on Business Performance of the Insurance Industry) — **Language:** Slovenian/English **Frequency:** annual **Content:** developments in the insurance sector, structure of the insurance market and performance indicators (reports cover period from 2000 to 2004) **Readership:** financial experts, research specialists, analysts

Register zavarovalnih zastopniških in posredniških družb (Directory of Insurance Agencies and Insurance Brokerage Companies) — **Language:** Slovenian **Frequency:** irregular **Content:** insurance companies operating in the country **Readership:** businessmen, investors, research specialists

Banka Slovenije
The Bank of Slovenia

Address: Slovenska 35, Ljubljana, 1505
Telephone: +386 1 471 9000
Fax: +386 1 251 5516
E-mail: bsl@bsi.si
Website: www.bsi.si

Guides: all publications can be obtained in the library of the bank
Activity: the bank of issue and the central bank of the Republic of Slovenia

Website(s) information:
Banka Slovenije (Bank of Slovenia) — url: www.bsi.si **Description:** various statistical information about the bank's operation and national monetary and banking system available online **Coverage:** monetary and banking sector

Publication(s):
Bilten Banke Slovenije (Monthly Bulletin) — **Language:** Slovenian/English (summary only) **Frequency:** monthly **Content:** monetary and banking system **Readership:** financial experts, research specialists, analysts, academics, governmental institutions

Denarni pregled (Monetary Review) — **Language:** Slovenian/English (summary only) **Frequency:** monthly **Content:** monetary system information **Readership:** financial and monetary experts, research specialists, analysts, governmental institutions

Ekonomski indikatorji mednarodnega okolja (Evaluation of Economic Trends) — **Language:** Slovenian/English **Frequency:** monthly **Content:** real sector, public sector, inflation, balance of payments, international financial transactions, monetary overview and policy, exchange and interest rates **Readership:** economic and financial experts, research specialists, analysts, investors, banks

Letno porocilo (Annual Report) — **Language:** Slovenian/English **Frequency:** annual **Content:** economic indicators, monetary policy, banking system, financial statements **Readership:** financial experts, research specialists, analysts, governmental organisations, investors

Porocilo o naložbah (Investment Report) — **Language:** Slovenian/English (summary only) **Frequency:** irregular **Content:** investments (reports cover the period from 1994 to 2004) **Readership:** financial experts, research specialists, analysts, investors, governmental institutions

Inštitut za ekonomska raziskovanja Slovenije
Slovenian Institute for Economic Research

Address: Kardeljeva plo?cad 17, Ljubljana, 1000
Telephone: +386 1 530 3800
Fax: +386 1 530 3874
E-mail: ier@ier.si
Website: www.ier.si

Guides: publications can be ordered through the library
Activity: conducting macroeconomic and microeconomic research and analysis

Website(s) information:
Inštitut za ekonomska raziskovanja Slovenije (Slovenian Institute for Economic Research) — url: www.ier.si **Description:** the site offers summaries of various publications; the catalogue of all publications can be accessed via the Co-operative Online Bibliographic System & Services (COBISS) at www.izum.si **Coverage:** economy

Publication(s):
An Analysis of the Slovenian Economy with a Quarterly Econometric Model — **Language:** English **Frequency:** irregular **Content:** overview of the economy **Readership:** analysts, research specialists, economists, governmental organisations, trade development bodies

Analysis of Slovenian Households (Income and Quality of Living) — **Language:** English **Frequency:** irregular **Content:** homes and households in the country, standards of living **Readership:** research specialists, analysts

Emerging Economic Geography in Slovenia — **Language:** English **Frequency:** irregular **Content:** economic growth by geographical areas **Readership:** research specialists, analysts, investors

Sector Performance in the Slovene Economy: Winners and Losers of the EU Integrations — **Language:** English **Frequency:** irregular **Content:** economy by sectors with a view to the country's integration in the EU **Readership:** economists, research specialists, analysts, investors

Javna agencija Republike Slovenije za energijo
Energy Agency of the Republic of Slovenia

Address: PO Box 1579, Strossmayerjeva ulica 30, Maribor, 2000
Telephone: +386 2 234 03 00
Fax: +386 2 234 03 20
E-mail: info@agen-rs.si
Website: www.agen-rs.si

Activity: performing regulatory, development and expert tasks in the energy area with the purpose of ensuring transparent and non-discriminatory operation of the energy markets

Website(s) information:
Javna agencija Republike Slovenije za energijo (Energy Agency of the Republic of Slovenia) — url: www.agen-rs.si **Description:** the site offers various information about the energy supply and market in the country **Coverage:** energy

Publication(s):
Letno porocilo Javne agencije RS za energijo (Report on the Energy Sector in Slovenia) — **Language:** Slovenian/English **Frequency:** annual **Content:** performance of the agency, energy sector and relevant legislation **Readership:** economists, research specialists, analysts, governmental organisations

Porocilo o morebitnem prevladujocem položaju na trgu z elektricno energijo, okoriščanju in zatiranju (Report on Market Dominance, Predatory and Anti-competitive Behaviour) — **Language:** Slovenian **Frequency:** annual **Content:** energy market data, companies operating in the market, energy production **Readership:** research specialists, analysts, governmental institutions

Porocilo o stanju na podrocju energetike (Report on the Energy Sector) — **Language:** Slovenian/English **Frequency:** annual **Content:** all available sources of energy in the country **Readership:** research specialists, analysts, governmental institutions

Javna agencija Republike Slovenije za podjetništvo in tuje investicije (JAPTI)

Public Agency of the Republic of Slovenia for Entrepreneurship and Foreign Investments

Address: Dunajska 156, Ljubljana, 1000
Telephone: +386 1 589 1870
Fax: +386 1 589 1877
E-mail: japti@japti.si
Website: www.japti.si

Activity: supporting development of entrepreneurship and promoting the country for foreign investments

Website(s) information:
Javna agencija Republike Slovenije za podjetništvo in tuje investicije (JAPTI)
(Public Agency of the Republic of Slovenia for Entrepreneurship and Foreign Investments) — **url:** www.japti.si **Description:** the site offers numerous information about small and medium entrepreneurship sector and economy **Coverage:** business sector and economy in general

Publication(s):
Business Offer from Slovenia — **Language:** Slovenian/English **Frequency:** irregular **Content:** list of companies with a short description of their business and products they offer to potential international partners **Readership:** businessmen, investors, analysts

Slovenian Country Profile — **Language:** English **Frequency:** irregular **Content:** general socio-economic indicators **Readership:** research specialists, analysts, governmental and non-governmental organisations

Javna agencija za raziskovalno dejavnost RS

Slovenian Research Agency

Address: Tivolska cesta 30, Ljubljana, 1000
Telephone: +386 1 400 5910
Fax: +386 1 400 5957
E-mail: info@arrs.si
Website: www.arrs.gov.si

Activity: selecting and financing research and infrastructure development programmes
managing research projects and other projects assigned to the Agency as part of the National Research and Development Programme and the annual plan of the ministry responsible for science; monitoring the performance, innovation, efficiency, quality, competitiveness and professionalism of funded research organisations; promoting international cooperation ensuring the acquisition of the additional funding for the National Research and Development Programme;
evaluating and analysing the implementation of research and development work; participating in national research and development policy making

Publication(s):
Letna porocilo o financiranju raziskovalne dejavnosti (Annual Report on Research Programme Funding) — **Language:** Slovenian **Frequency:** annually **Content:** research programmes in the country and funding **Readership:** research specialists, analysts

Kmetijski inštitut Slovenije

Agricultural Institute of Slovenia

Address: Hacquetova 17, Ljubljana, 1000
Telephone: +386 1 280 5262
Fax: +386 1 280 5255
E-mail: info@kis.si
Website: www.kis.si

Guides: all publications can be obtained in the Institute's library; in addition to numerous publications relating to agriculture, the library also contains a great number of local and international agricultural journals

Activity: conducting basic and applied research in the field of agriculture; supervising and verification of quality of agricultural products

Website(s) information:
Biotehniška fakulteta, Ljubljana (Biotechnical Faculty, Ljubljana) — **url:** www.agroweb.bf.uni-lj.si **Description:** the site offers numerous information starting from country's profile to detailed agricultural sector overview **Coverage:** agriculture

Kmetijski inštitut Slovenije (Agricultural Institute of Slovenia) — **url:** www.kis.si **Description:** the site offers information about the country's agriculture **Coverage:** agricultural production and sector in general

Mednarodni inštitut za turizem Slovenije

International Tourism Institute Slovenia

Address: Vošnjakova 5, Ljubljana, 1000
Telephone: +386 1 433 9440
Fax: +386 1 433 8659
E-mail: info@turizem-institut.si
Website: www.turizem-institut.si

Activity: research short-term forecasts, implementing educational and training seminars in the field of tourism, designing tourist development and marketing strategies, qualitative research regarding the development of high-quality tourist trademarks

Website(s) information:
Mednarodni inštitut za turizem Slovenije (International Tourism Institute Slovenia) — **url:** www.turizem-institut.si **Description:** the site offers general information about travel and tourism; publications can be ordered via the site **Coverage:** tourism

Ministrstvo za finance RS

Slovenian Ministry of Finance

Address: Županciceva 3, Ljubljana, 1502
Telephone: +386 1 369 5200
Fax: +386 1 369 6659
E-mail: gp.mf@gov.si
Website: www.gov.si/mf

Activity: developing and implementing the country's financial policy

Website(s) information:
Ministrstvo za finance RS (Slovenian Ministry of Finance) — **url:** www.gov.si/mf **Description:** offers numerous documents relating to the state budget and finance **Coverage:** economic and financial indicators

Publication(s):
Bilten javnih financ (Public Finance Bulletin) — **Language:** Slovenian **Frequency:** monthly **Content:** public finance **Readership:** financial experts, research specialists, analysts, governmental organisations

Konvergencni program (Convergence Programme) — **Language:** Slovenian/English **Frequency:** annual **Content:** economic outlook, general government balance and debt, analysis and comparison of the previous and current economic developments and budgetary projections (reports covering the period 2001-2005 available) **Readership:** research specialists, analysts, financial experts, governmental institutions

Porocilo o primanjkljaju in dolgu sektorja država (Report on Deficit and Debts) — **Language:** Slovenian/English **Frequency:** irregular **Content:** deficit and debt **Readership:** financial experts, governmental organisations, research specialists, analysts

Ministrstvo za gospodarstvo Republike Slovenije

Ministry of Economy of the Republic of Slovenia

Address: Kotnikova 5, Ljubljana, 1000
Telephone: +386 1 478 3311
Fax: +386 1 433 1031
E-mail: gp.mg@gov.si
Website: www.mg.gov.si

Activity: supporting further strengthening of international competitiveness of Slovenian companies and the adjustment of the structure of Slovenia's economy

Website(s) information:
Ministrstvo za gospodarstvo Republike Slovenije (Ministry of Economy of the Republic of Slovenia) — **url:** www.mg.gov.si **Description:** various statistical information about the economy in general and by sectors available online **Coverage:** economic indicators

Publication(s):

Analiza programa za pospeševanje razvoja podjetniškega sektora in konkurencnosti (Analysis of the Entrepreneurship and Concurrency Development Programme) — **Language:** Slovenian **Frequency:** irregular **Content:** analysis of various economic programmes by sectors based on the allocated funding **Readership:** economists, financial experts, research specialists, analysts

Energetska bilanca RS (Report on Energy in the Republic of Slovenia) — **Language:** Slovenian **Frequency:** annual **Content:** production, import and consumption of sources of energy **Readership:** research specialists, analysts

Ministrstvo za kmetijstvo, gozdarstvo in prehrano RS
Ministry of Agriculture, Forestry and Food of the Republic of Slovenia

Address: Dunajska 58, Ljubljana, 1000
Telephone: +386 1 478 9000
Fax: +386 1 478 9021
E-mail: gp.mkgp@gov.si
Website: www.mkgp.gov.si

Activity: developing and implementing agricultural and food policy

Website(s) information:

Ministrstvo za kmetijstvo, gozdarstvo in prehrano RS (Ministry of Agriculture, Forestry and Food of the Republic of Slovenia) — **url:** www.mkgp.gov.si **Description:** the site offers general information about agriculture, forestry and food **Coverage:** agriculture, forestry and food

Publication(s):

Reforma skupne kmetijske politike EU (EU Agricultural Reform) — **Language:** Slovenian **Frequency:** irregular **Content:** Slovenian agriculture with a view to the general reform of EU agriculture **Readership:** agricultural experts, governmental organisations, research specialists, analysts

Ministrstvo za okolje, prostor in energijo Republike Slovenije
Ministry of Environment, Spatial Planning and Energy of the Republic of Slovenia

Address: PO Box 653, Dunajska c. 48, Ljubljana, 1000
Telephone: +386 1 478 7300
Fax: +386 1 478 7427
E-mail: gp.mop@gov.si
Website: www.sigov.si/mop

Activity: ensuring a healthy living environment for all the inhabitants of Slovenia and encouraging and co-ordinating efforts towards a sustainable development base

Website(s) information:

Ministrstvo za okolje, prostor in energijo Republike Slovenije (Ministry of Environment, Spatial Planning and Energy of the Republic of Slovenia) — **url:** www.sigov.si/mop **Coverage:** environmental issues, water and energy resources

Publication(s):

Bilten Okolje in prostor (Environment and Planning Information Bulletin) — **Language:** Slovenian/English **Frequency:** monthly **Content:** general information on environment, spatial planning and natural resources **Readership:** environmental experts, research specialists, analysts, governmental organisations

Kazalci okolja (Environmental Indicators) — **Language:** Slovenian/English **Frequency:** annual **Content:** environmental indicators in respect of agriculture, air, climate change, energy, nature and land use, tourism and transport **Readership:** environmental experts, research specialists, analysts, governmental and non-governmental organisations

Vodni svet Slovenije (Slovenian Waters) — **Language:** Slovenian **Frequency:** irregular **Content:** water resources in Slovenia **Readership:** environmental experts, research specialists, analysts, governmental and non-governmental organisations **Edition:** 2004

Ministrstvo za promet Republike Slovenije
Ministry of Transport of the Republic of Slovenia

Address: Langusova 4, Ljubljana, 1000
Telephone: +386 1 478 8000
Fax: +386 1 478 8139
E-mail: gp.mzp@gov.si
Website: www.mzp.gov.si

Activity: performing tasks in the field of railway transport, air transport, maritime and inland waterway transport and road transport (with the exception of road transport safety control), as well as tasks in the field of transport infrastructure and cableway installations

Website(s) information:

Ministrstvo za promet Republike Slovenije (Ministry of Transport of the Republic of Slovenia) — **url:** www.mzp.gov.si **Description:** the site offers information about the road transport system **Coverage:** road transport

Ministrstvo za zdravje Republike Slovenije
Ministry of Health of the Republic of Slovenia

Address: Štefanova 5, Ljubljana, 1000
Telephone: +386 1 478 6001
Fax: +386 1 478 6058
E-mail: gp.mz@gov.si
Website: www.mz.gov.si

Activity: creating and implementing the country's health policy

Website(s) information:

Ministrstvo za zdravje Republike Slovenije (Ministry of Health of the Republic of Slovenia) — **url:** www.mz.gov.si **Description:** the site offers general information about the health care system of the country **Coverage:** health care

Statisticni urad Republike Slovenije
Statistical Office of the Republic of Slovenia

Address: Vožarski pot 12, Ljubljana, 1000
Telephone: +386 1 241 5104
Fax: +386 1 241 5344
E-mail: info.stat@gov.si
Website: www.stat.si

Activity: collecting and publishing statistical information

Website(s) information:

Statisticni urad Republike Slovenije (Statistical Office of the Republic of Slovenia) — **url:** www.sigov.si/zrs/ **Description:** various statistical information and reports available online **Coverage:** demography and social statistics, economy, environment and natural resources, general

Publication(s):

Mesecni statisticni pregled Republike Slovenije (Monthly Statistical Review of the Republic of Slovenia) — **Language:** Slovenian **Frequency:** monthly **Content:** monthly and quarterly updated statistics on main socio-economic indicators **Readership:** research specialists, analysts, governmental and non-governmental organisations

Pomembnejši statistični podatki o Sloveniji (Some Important Statistics on Slovenia) — **Language:** Slovenian/English **Frequency:** monthly **Content:** designed for users who want to obtain the annual (for the last five years), quarterly (for the last eight quarters) or monthly (for the last twelve months) series of statistics regarding different fields; the data about a particular statistical field are selected according to the demand of the users (e.g. consumer price indices, gross and net earnings by activity, natural and migration changes) **Readership:** research specialists, analysts

Slovenija v številkah (Slovenia in Figures) — **Language:** Slovenian/English **Frequency:** annual **Content:** socio-economic indicators **Readership:** research specialists, analysts, governmental and non-governmental organisations, academics

***Statisticni letopis** (Statistical Yearbook)* — **Language:** Slovenian/English **Frequency:** annual **Content:** socio-economic structure (covering a wide range of topics, such as population, labour market, agricultural and industrial sectors, national accounts, foreign trade, etc. The data provided cover both national and regional level and are compared against international trends) **Readership:** research specialists, analysts, governmental and non-governmental institutions, investors, businesses

***Statisticni portret Slovenije v Evropski Uniji** (Statistical Portrait of Slovenia in the EU)* — **Language:** Slovenian/English **Frequency:** irregular **Content:** socio-economic overview of the country comparing to the EU **Readership:** research specialists, analysts, governmental and non-governmental organisations

Svet za varstvo okolja
The Council for Environmental Protection

Address: Slovenska cesta 56, Ljubljana, 1000
Telephone: +386 1 430 60 70
Fax: +386 1 430 60 75
E-mail: svo@svo-rs.si
Website: www.gov.si/svo

Activity: monitoring the quality and the protection of the environment in Slovenia

Website(s) information:
***Svet za varstvo okolja** (Council for Environmental Protection)* — **url:** www.gov.si/svo **Description:** the site offers various information about the environment in Slovenian and English **Coverage:** environmental data

Publication(s):
***Okolje in uravnoteženi razvoj Slovenije** (Environment and Sustainable Development of Slovenia)* — **Language:** Slovenian **Frequency:** irregular **Content:** environmental issues in light of technological development of the country **Readership:** ecologists, research specialists, analysts, governmental institutions, non-governmental organisations

***Promet in okolje** (Traffic and Environment)* — **Language:** Slovenian **Frequency:** irregular **Content:** traffic in Slovenia and its influence on the environment **Readership:** ecologists, research specialists, analysts, governmental institutions, non-governmental organisations

***Turizem in okolje** (Tourism and Environment)* — **Language:** Slovenian **Frequency:** irregular **Content:** report on the impact of tourism on the environment **Readership:** ecologists, research specialists, analysts, governmental institutions, non-governmental organisations

Uprava Republike Slovenije za civilno letalstvo
Civil Aviation Authority of the Republic of Slovenia

Address: Kotnikova 19a, Ljubljana, 1000
Telephone: +386 1 473 4600
Fax: +386 1 431 6035
E-mail: urscl@caa-rs.si
Website: www.caa-rs.si

Activity: maintaining a safe environment for air traffic

Website(s) information:
***Uprava Republike Slovenije za civilno letalstvo** (Civil Aviation Authority of the Republic of Slovenia)* — **url:** www.caa-rs.si **Description:** statistics on civil aviation **Coverage:** civil aviation

Urad Vlade za informiranje
Slovenian Government Public Information and Media Office

Address: Gregorciceva 25, Ljubljana, 1000
Telephone: +386 1 478 2600
Fax: +386 1 251 2312
Website: www.uvi.gov.si

Activity: providing assistance to foreign media in carrying out their work

Website(s) information:
Slovenia.si - Your Gateway to Information on Slovenia — **url:** www.slovenia.si **Description:** the site is intended to present Slovenia through various socio-economic statistical and other types of information **Coverage:** socio-economic

***Urad Vlade za informiranje** (Slovenian Government Public Information and Media Office)* — **url:** www.uvi.gov.si **Description:** the site offers various statistical and other types of information about the country, developments and events **Coverage:** socio-economic indicators

Publication(s):
Facts about Slovenia — **Language:** English **Frequency:** irregular **Content:** short and concise 4-page fact-sheets (general information, international relations, tourism, agriculture and forestry, food, sports) **Readership:** research specialists, analysts, governmental and non-governmental organisations, investors, businessmen, tourists

Facts about Slovenia - Booklet — **Language:** English/German/Russian **Frequency:** irregular **Content:** introduction to the country's social and economic indicators (116 pages **Readership:** analysts, research specialists, governmental and non-governmental organisations, economists, businessmen

***Sinfo** (Sinfo - Promotional Monthly Magazine on Slovenia)* — **Language:** English **Frequency:** monthly **Content:** news on politics, environment, culture, business and sports **Readership:** analysts, research specialists, governmental and non-governmental organisations, economists, businessmen

Slovenia in Brief — **Language:** English **Frequency:** irregular **Content:** culture, economy, education and science, geography, social and health care, history, holidays, media, country and people, sport, state, tourism and international relations **Readership:** research specialists, analysts, governmental and non-governmental organisations

Slovenia News — **Language:** English **Frequency:** weekly **Content:** weekly newsletter on politics, environment, culture, business, science, sports **Readership:** governmental and non-governmental organisations, research specialists, analysts, businessmen, investors, economists

Urad za makroekonomske analize in razvoj Slovenije
Slovenian Office for Macroeconomic Analysis and Development

Address: Gregorciceva 27, Ljubljana, 1000
Telephone: +386 1 478 1012
Fax: +386 1 478 1070
E-mail: gp.umar@gov.si
Website: www.sigov.si/zmar

Activity: monitoring, analysing and forecasting economic developments, participating in drawing up main strategic documents and formulating government policies, research and international co-operation

Website(s) information:
***Urad za makroekonomske analize in razvoj Slovenije** (Slovenian Office for Macroeconomic Analysis and Development)* — **url:** www.sigov.si/zmar **Description:** the site offers various documents containing statistical information about the country's economy and developments **Coverage:** economy and development

Publication(s):
***Ekonomsko ogledalo** (Slovenian Economic Mirror)* — **Language:** Slovenian/English **Frequency:** monthly **Content:** indicators of the country's economy by sectors and topics **Readership:** economists, research specialists, analysts, investors, governmental and non-governmental organisations

***Pomladanska napoved gospodarskih gibanj** (Spring Forecasts of Economic Trends)* — **Language:** Slovenian/English **Frequency:** irregular **Content:** economic developments and trends **Readership:** research specialists, analysts, economists, investors, governmental organisations

***Pomladansko porocilo** (Autumn Report)* — **Language:** Slovenian/English **Frequency:** annual **Content:** autumn economic forecast including the scenario of economic trends beyond 2007 **Readership:** research specialists, analysts, economists, governmental organisations

***Slovenija: Porocilo o razvoju** (Slovenia: Development Report)* — **Language:** Slovenian/English **Frequency:** annual **Content:** economic development in association with EU and international agreements **Readership:** research specialists, analysts, governmental organisations

Vlada Republike Slovenije
Government of the Republic of Slovenia

Address: Slovenska cesta 29, Ljubljana, 1000
Telephone: +386 1 478 2600
Fax: +386 1 251 2312
Website: www.vlada.si

Activity: implementing state policy

Website(s) information:
Vlada Republike Slovenije, Urad za informiranje *(Government of the Republic of Slovenia, Public Relations and Media Office)* — **url:** www.uvi.si
Description: the site offers general socio-economic information in a form of presentation available in English; the site also provides links to economic periodicals published by the Chamber of Commerce and other trade development bodies **Coverage:** culture, economy, education and science, geography, social security and health care, history, holidays, media, people, sport, state, tourism

World Bank Group Slovenia
Address: Ljubljana
Website: www.worldbank.org/si

Activity: helping developing countries and their people alleviate poverty, building the climate for investment, jobs and sustainable growth, investing in and empowering poor people to participate in development

Website(s) information:
World Bank Group Slovenia — **url:** www.worldbank.org/si **Description:** the site offers extensive statistical and other types of information about the country **Coverage:** economic indicators

Publication(s):
Gender Statistics — **Language:** English **Frequency:** irregular **Content:** gender indicators, basic demographic data, population dynamics, labour force structure, and education and health statistics **Readership:** research specialists, analysts, governmental institutions and non-governmental organisations

Governance Indicators — **Language:** English **Frequency:** irregular **Content:** indicators of the cost of doing business by identifying specific regulations that enhance or constrain the business investment, productivity, and growth **Readership:** businessmen, investors, research specialists, analysts, governmental institutions

Health Nutrition Population Statistics — **Language:** English **Frequency:** irregular **Content:** summary indicators for health status, health determinants and health finance **Readership:** health experts, research specialists, analysts, governmental institutions and non-governmental organisations

Information/ Communications/ Telecommunications — **Language:** English **Frequency:** irregular **Content:** ICT infrastructure and access, computers and the internet, ICT expenditures, and ICT business and government environment **Readership:** ICT specialists, research specialists, analysts

Slovenia Country Data Profile — **Language:** English **Frequency:** irregular **Content:** socio-economic profile of the country **Readership:** research specialists, analysts, governmental institutions

Spain

Banco de España
Bank of Spain

Address: Alcalá, 48, Madrid, 28014
Telephone: +34 91 338 50 00
Fax: +34 91 531 00 59
E-mail: be-estad@bde.es
Website: www.bde.es

Website(s) information:
Banco de España *(Bank of Spain)* — **url:** www.bde.es **Description:** provides access to statistical publications **Coverage:** data on various socio-economic and financial issues

Publication(s):
Boletín de Operaciones *(Operations Bulletin)* — **Language:** Spanish **Frequency:** daily **Content:** exchange rates; interbank deposits and issues of public debt

Boletín del Mercado de Deuda Pública *(Public Debt Market Bulletin)* — **Language:** Spanish **Frequency:** daily **Content:** data on government and public debt

Boletín Económico *(Economic Bulletin)* — **Language:** Spanish/English **Frequency:** monthly **Content:** data on the Spanish economy with economic indicators; financial regulation and non-financial corporations

Boletín Estadístico *(Statistical Bulletin)* — **Language:** Spanish/English **Frequency:** irregular **Content:** data on credit system; other financial systems; financial markets; general government agencies and balance of payments

Indicadores Económicos *(Economic Indicators)* — **Language:** Spanish/English **Content:** data on national demand and activity; prices; general government; labour market; balance of payments and financial variables

Informe de Estabilidad Financiera *(Financial Stability Report)* — **Language:** Spanish/English **Frequency:** half-yearly **Content:** financial data on credit and market risks

Tipos de Cambio *(Exchange Rates)* — **Language:** Spanish/English **Frequency:** daily/monthly **Content:** data on exchange rates on the Euro

Tipos de Interés *(Interest Rates)* — **Language:** Spanish/English **Frequency:** daily **Content:** data on Eurosystem monetary operations; interests rates; stock exchange and debt return indexes

Instituto Nacional de Estadística (INE)
National Institute of Statistics

Address: Paseo de la Castellana 183, Madrid, 28071
Telephone: +34 91 583 9100
Fax: +34 91 583 9158
E-mail: indice@ine.es
Website: www.ine.es

Guides: Catálogo de Publicaciones - INE (Publications Catalogue)
Activity: national statistic office

Website(s) information:
Instituto Nacional de Estadística (INE) *(National Institute of Statistics (INE))* — **url:** www.ine.es **Description:** provides free access to statistics, surveys and reports **Coverage:** statistics on main socio-economic indicators such as geography and population; labour market and wages; prices; health and education services; agriculture; transport and communications; tourism; and national accounts

Publication(s):
Anuario Estadístico de España *(Statistical Yearbook of Spain)* — **Language:** Spanish **Frequency:** annual **Content:** annual socio-economic portrait of Spain, covering demography; agriculture; forestry; fishing; industry; production; transport and communications; retailing and distribution; external trade; balance of payments; employment and tourism

Boletín Mensual de Estadística *(Monthly Statistical Bulletin)* — **Language:** Spanish **Frequency:** monthly **Content:** data on a range of socio-economic indicators

Cifras de Poblacion *(Population Figures)* — **Language:** Spanish **Content:** population figures of every municipality grouped by provinces and summaries for autonomous communities; provinces; capitals of provinces and islands

Educacion y Cultura *(Education and Culture)* — **Language:** Spanish **Content:** data on public and private educational institutions; libraries and universities

Encuesta Continua de Presupuestos Familiares *(Household Budget Survey)* — **Language:** Spanish **Frequency:** annual **Content:** data on household expenditure by various socio-demographic characteristics

Encuesta de Servicios *(Services Survey)* — **Language:** Spanish **Frequency:** annual **Content:** data on activities relating to tourism; transport; information; society; real estate and rent; corporate services; recreational, cultural and sports activities and personal services

Encuesta Industrial de Empresas *(Industrial Survey of Companies)* — **Language:** Spanish **Content:** statistics on the industrial sector

Encuesta Industrial de Productos *(Industrial Survey of Products)* — **Language:** Spanish **Frequency:** annual **Content:** data on the value of principal Spanish industrial products

Estadística de Hipotecas (Mortgage Statistics) — **Language:** Spanish **Frequency:** monthly **Content:** statistics of mortgaged goods and total quantity of loans

Indicadores de Ciencia y Tecnología (Indicators of Science and Technology) — **Language:** Spanish **Content:** information on technological innovation and high technology products

Indicadores Sociales (Social Statistics) — **Language:** Spanish **Frequency:** annual **Content:** data on the aging population; pensions; poverty; science and technology

Medio Ambiente (Environment) — **Language:** Spanish **Content:** statistics on water; waste; recycling and treatment

Salud y Servicios Sanitarios (Health and Health Care Services) — **Language:** Spanish **Content:** data on the national health; hospital indicators; causes of death; surveys on disabilities, impairments and health status

Spain in Figures — **Language:** English/Spanish **Frequency:** annual **Content:** data on the demographic, social and economic environment of Spain

Ministerio de Agricultura, Pesca y Alimentación (MAPA)
Ministry of Agriculture, Fisheries and Food

Address: Paseo de la Infanta Isabel 1, Madrid, 28014
Telephone: +34 91 347 55 51
Fax: +34 91 347 57 22
E-mail: mllopisj@mapya.es
Website: www.mapa.es

Activity: publishes statistics on the agriculture and fishing industry

Website(s) information:
Ministerio de Agricultura, Pesca y Alimentación (Ministry of Agriculture, Fisheries and Food) — **url:** www.mapa.es **Description:** provides access to a wide range of information on agriculture, farming, rural development, fishing and food and information on EU legislation and the Common Agricultural Policy **Coverage:** data on the Spanish agricultural, farming and fishing industry, including: annual production; exports and imports; number of livestock and meat production; organic farming; agricultural area and production; socio-economic structure of rural areas; food consumption patterns and food trends

Publication(s):
Anuario de Estadística Agroalimentaria (Agricultural and Food Statistics Yearbook) — **Language:** Spanish **Frequency:** annual **Content:** general agricultural and food statistics

Boletín de Estadística (Bulletin of Statistics) — **Language:** Spanish **Frequency:** monthly **Content:** information on agricultural and cattle sector; production and agrarian economy

Estadística láctea (Lacteal statistics) — **Language:** Spanish **Frequency:** monthly/annual **Content:** statistics on the dairy industry

Estadísticas de Ganadería (Cattle Statistics) — **Language:** Spanish **Content:** data on cattle production and population

Fishing in Spain — **Language:** English **Content:** information about fisheries, fishing fleets and fishing trade

Indicadores de precios y salarios agrarios (Agrarian Price and Salary Indicators) — **Language:** Spanish **Frequency:** monthly **Content:** agrarian salaries and prices paid by the farmers

Informe Semanal de Coyuntura (Weekly Status Report) — **Language:** Spanish **Frequency:** weekly **Content:** information on national food prices including wines; rice; meat; cereals and olive oil

Maquinaria agrícola (Agricultural Machinery) — **Language:** Spanish **Frequency:** monthly **Content:** index of agricultural machinery

Precios de la tierra (Land Prices) — **Language:** Spanish **Frequency:** annual **Content:** growth of average prices of agricultural land

Ministerio de Economía
Ministry of Economy

Address: Subsecretaría de Economía, Alcalá, 5 - 2ª Planta, Madrid, 28071
Telephone: +34 91 595 8000
Fax: +34 91 595 84 77
E-mail: informacion.alcala@meh.es
Website: www.mineco.es

Activity: government ministry

Website(s) information:
Ministerio de Economía (Ministry of Economy) — **url:** www.mineco.es **Description:** provides access to statistical publications **Coverage:** statistics on major socio-economic indicators, with monthly updated analysis on GDP evolution, inflation rates, industrial production indices, consumer price indices and external trade

Publication(s):
Estadísticas Territoriales (Territorial Funding Statistics) — **Language:** Spanish **Frequency:** annual **Content:** data on budgets and liquidation of budgets

Fondos Europeos (European Funds) — **Language:** Spanish **Frequency:** irregular **Content:** data on European funds

Impuestos (Taxes) — **Language:** Spanish **Frequency:** annual **Content:** data on taxes collection and information about VAT; economic results

Indicadores Económicos (Economic Indicators) — **Frequency:** monthly **Content:** data on the Spanish economy, macro-economic forecasts and principal economic indicators

Juegos y Apuestas del Estado (State Lotteries and Gaming) — **Language:** Spanish **Frequency:** weekly **Content:** data on sales of state lotteries and gaming

Presupuesto y Cuentas Públicas (Budget and Public Expenditure) — **Language:** Spanish **Frequency:** annual **Content:** statistical information about the budgets

Tabaco (Tobacco) — **Language:** Spanish **Frequency:** annual **Content:** figures and information about the tobacco market

Tesoro (Treasury) — **Language:** Spanish/English **Frequency:** monthly **Content:** statistics about central government outstanding debt and financing

Ministerio de Educación y Ciencia
Ministry of Education and Science

Address: , Alcalá 36, Madrid, 28071
Telephone: +34 91 701 80 00
E-mail: informacion@mec.es
Website: www.mec.es

Website(s) information:
Ministerio de Educación, Cultura y Deporte (Ministry of Education, Culture and Sport) — **url:** www.mec.es **Description:** provides access to publications catalogue, press release archive and statistical data on education **Coverage:** statistical indicators on education in Spain, including primary and secondary education, university education and government expenditure on education. Data available for 1991-2001

Publication(s):
Estadística Universitaria (University Statistics) — **Language:** Spanish **Frequency:** irregular **Content:** information and figures of the university system; university surveys and reports

Estadísticas Deportivas (Sports Statistics) — **Frequency:** irregular **Content:** statistics of federated sport; public sports installations and doping controls

Estadísticas e Indicadores de Ciencia y Tecnología (Science and Technology Statistics and Indicators) — **Frequency:** annual **Content:** statistics on budgetary public credits; science and technology indicators

Estadísticas Educativas (Educational Statistics) — **Language:** Spanish **Content:** statistics on public expenditure in education and scholarships

Ministerio de Fomento
Ministry of Economic and Industrial Development

Address: Paseo de la Castellana 67, Madrid, 28071
Telephone: +34 91 597 87 87
Fax: +34 91 597 85 73
E-mail: atencionciudadano@fomento.es; portal@administracion.es
Website: www.mfom.es

Website(s) information:

Ministerio de Fomento *(Ministry of Economic and Industrial Development)* — **url:** www.mfom.es **Description:** provides access to press release archive, publication catalogue and statistical information on population, housing and information on budget and investment, grouped by geographical area **Coverage:** socio-economic and housing indicators, with data on population trends, population by age groups, number of households grouped by number of occupants, number of occupants per household, population density, number and distribution of buildings by type of owner and type of building, and dwellings by number of rooms and liveable area

Publication(s):

Anuario Estadístico *(Statistical Yearbook)* — **Language:** Spanish **Frequency:** annual **Content:** statistical information at national; regional and provincial level on liquidation of the ministry budget, transport and communications

Boletín Estadístico *(Statistical Bulletin)* — **Language:** Spanish **Frequency:** monthly **Content:** information referring to construction and housing; transport; communications and ministerial management

Cifras *(Figures)* — **Language:** Spanish **Frequency:** annual **Content:** data on construction and housing; transport; communications and economic management of the department

Estructura Coyuntural de la Construcción *(Construction Structure)* — **Language:** Spanish **Frequency:** annual **Content:** key information and indicators of the construction sector

Indice de Precios de la Vivienda *(Index of Housing Prices)* — **Language:** Spanish **Frequency:** irregular **Content:** statistics of housing prices

Sweden

Konjunkturinstitutet
National Institute of Economic Research

Address: PO Box 3116, Kungsgatan 12-14, 6th floor, Stockholm, 10362
Telephone: +46 8 453 5900
Fax: +46 8 453 5980
E-mail: ki@konj.se
Website: www.konj.se

Guides: reports are published in their entirety on the website and some are available in print
Activity: performs analyses and forecasts of the Swedish and international economy and conducts related research

Website(s) information:

Konjunkturinstitutet *(National Institute of Economic Research)* — **url:** www.konj.se **Description:** detailed information about the institute and its publications. Latest economic forecast; business tendency survey; main economic indicators; forecast comparisons; press releases **Coverage:** economic analyses and forecasts covers wages; supply and demand; public finance; profits, cost of output and prices; public consumption; foreign trade; international economy. Business tendency survey includes data about manufacturing, durables and non-durables goods trade, and construction

Publication(s):

Hushållens Inköpsplaner *(Household Consumer Survey)* — **Language:** Swedish/English **Frequency:** monthly **Content:** data refers to household expectations about the Swedish economy, unemployment and personal finances

Konjunkturbarometern *(Business Tendency Survey)* — **Language:** Swedish/English **Frequency:** monthly **Content:** performs analyses and forecasts on the outcomes and expectations of firms in manufacturing; construction; retail trade; and the private service sector

Konjunkturläget *(Swedish Economy)* — **Language:** Swedish/English **Frequency:** quarterly **Content:** report provides forecasts and analyses on the Swedish and international economy; financial markets, household and government consumption; foreign trade; labour market; and public finances

Lönebildningsrapport *(Wage Formation)* — **Language:** Swedish/English **Frequency:** annual **Content:** analyses the labour market; wage forming and negotiations

Regeringskansliet-Finansdepartementet
Ministry of Finance

Address: Drottninggatan 21, Stockholm, 10333
Telephone: +46 8 405 10 00
Fax: +46 8 21 73 86
E-mail: registrator@finance.ministry.se
Website: finans.regeringen.se

Activity: work to fulfil the economic political goals of the government

Website(s) information:

Regeringskansliet-Finansdepartementet *(Ministry of Finance)* — **url:** finans.regeringen.se **Description:** updates and releases on monetary, budget and macro-economic issues **Coverage:** the Swedish Money Report provides statistics on: GDP, central government debt, expenditure areas, public sector expenditure (available online)

Publication(s):

Internationella Kasinon i Sverige *(International Casinos in Sweden)* — **Language:** Swedish **Frequency:** irregular **Content:** analyses the turnover and the development in international casino activity in Sweden

Sociala broar - Att möta globaliseringens utmaningar *(Social Bridges - Meeting the Challenges of Globalisation)* — **Language:** Swedish/English **Frequency:** irregular **Content:** analyses the economic trends of globalisation and the suggests policies that can reinforce the strength of the global market of goods, services and investments

Svenska vindkraftspolitik *(Swedish Wind Power Politics)* — **Language:** Swedish **Frequency:** irregular **Content:** rapport analyses socio-economical and energy political trends in relation to wind power

Sveriges handlingsplan för sysselsättning *(Sweden's Action Plan for Employment)* — **Language:** Swedish/English **Frequency:** irregular **Content:** analysis and forecasts of employment and unemployment trends; actions to promote employment growth in Sweden; analysis of the labour market in the EU

Statistiska Centralbyrån
Statistics Sweden

Address: SCB Box 24 300, Karlavägen 100, Stockholm, 10451
Telephone: +46 8 5069 4000
Fax: +46 8 661 5261
E-mail: swestat@scb.se
Website: www.scb.se

Guides: catalogue available on website
Activity: produces, supports and coordinates the Swedish system for official statistics

Website(s) information:

Statistiska Centralbyrån *(Statistics Sweden)* — **url:** www.scb.se **Description:** offers information on products and services provided by Statistics Sweden. Includes major publications; statistical databases; latest press releases; and various online statistics, both in Swedish and English **Coverage:** data can be accessed by downloading publications, or by accessing the databases (where registration is required when requesting more than 1000 data cells). National socio-economic statistics on population; housing; labour market; trade; national accounts; education etc are presented in annual publications. In addition, miscellaneous data exists for citizen political and social influence; juridical system; social insurance and service; transport etc

Publication(s):

Arbetskraftsundersökningen *(Labour Force Survey)* — **Language:** Swedish/English **Frequency:** quarterly **Content:** data refers to employment and unemployment rates by gender, age, main activity, sector and by birth country. Aspects of the data are available in English and is also available monthly and annually

Befolkningsstatistik *(Population Statistics)* — **Language:** Swedish/English **Frequency:** annual **Content:** data refers to the population by gender, age, civil status, country of birth and residency in different Swedish regions. The publication also includes data on the changes in population by births, deaths, immigration, migration, marriages, divorces, registered partnership, residency transfers and adoptions. Aspects of the data are available in English

Bostads- och Byggnadsstatistisk Årsbok *(Housing and Building Statistical Yearbook)* — **Language:** Swedish/English **Frequency:** annual **Content:** data refers to housing, building, housing stock, heating and energy usage

***Finansiella Företag** (Financial Enterprises)* — **Language:** Swedish/English **Frequency:** annual **Content:** data refers to industry turnover and performance of banks and other financial institutes and investments enterprises. The data does not include insurance companies for which separate data can be found on the website. Some aspects of the data are available in English

***Hushållens utgifter** (Household Budget Survey)* — **Language:** Swedish/English **Frequency:** annual **Content:** data refers to expenditure on goods and services in households where at least one of the members is aged 0-79. The data also contains expenditure by gender. Aspects of the data are available in English

***Jordbruksekonomiska undersökningen** (Farm Economic Survey)* — **Language:** Swedish/English **Frequency:** annual **Content:** data refers to agricultural income and expenditure, by type of production and size. Aspects of the data are available in English

***Konsumentprisindex** (Consumer Price Index)* — **Language:** Swedish/English **Frequency:** monthly **Content:** data refers to the consumption of the entire population of the country. Prices used in the index are regular prices paid by the public. Aspects of the data are available in English

***Miljöskyddskostnader i Industrin** (Environmental Protection Expenditure in Industry)* — **Language:** Swedish/English **Frequency:** annual **Content:** data refers to investments and expenditure in environmental protection by types of costs, environmental domains, industry activities, and numbers of employees

***På tal om Kvinnor och Män** (Men and Women in Sweden)* — **Language:** Swedish/English **Frequency:** annual **Content:** data refers to education, health, employment, time use, child care, crime and political influence in relation to gender

***Privatpersoners Användning av Datorer och Internet** (Use of Computers and the Internet by the Private Sector)* — **Language:** Swedish/English **Frequency:** annual **Content:** data refers to how often and in what way households are using computers and the internet. It also contains information about IT literacy and access to IT equipment

***Statistisk årsbok för Sverige** (Statistical Yearbook of Sweden)* — **Language:** Swedish/English **Frequency:** annual **Content:** compilation of socio-economic statistics. Aspects of the data are available in English

***Sveriges Ekonomi - Statistiskt Perspektiv** (Swedish Economy - Statistical Perspective)* — **Language:** Swedish/English **Frequency:** quarterly **Content:** data refers to social and economic indicators with emphasis on economic changes and the consistency and inconsistency between different statistical outcomes

***Utbildningsstatistisk Årsbok** (Statistical Yearbook for Education)* — **Language:** Swedish/English **Frequency:** annual **Content:** data refers to all levels of education, including Swedish education abroad, adult education for people with learning difficulties and Swedish for immigrants, by age and gender

***Utrikeshandel med varor** (Foreign Trade in Goods)* — **Language:** Swedish/English **Frequency:** monthly **Content:** data is reported in tables with monthly figures (quarterly data for volume indexes) and annual figures. Collected data on goods, countries and the combination of goods/countries; selected data available in English

Sveriges Riksbank
Swedish Central Bank

Address:　　Brunkebergstorg 11, Stockholm, 10337
Telephone: +46 8 787 0000
Fax:　　　　+46 8 210 531
E-mail:　　registratorn@riksbank.se or info@riksbank.se
Website:　　www.riksbank.se

Guides: Riksbank publications information online
Activity: to maintain price stability, with low stable inflation, promote a safe and efficient payment system, where the consumer price index, CPI, aimed to be maintained at around 2 per cent

Website(s) information:
***Sveriges Riksbank** (Swedish Central Bank)* — **url:** www.riksbank.se **Description:** detailed information about the bank, its policies and its publications. Weekly statistical report covering balance of payments; interest rates; exchange rates **Coverage:** provides downloadable statistics on interest rates; currencies; national, private and public finances etc. in the real; fiscal; financial; and external sector. The website also provides links to relevant statistics at other organisations

Publication(s):
Årsredovisning (Annual Report) —

***Direktinvesteringar** (Direct Investment)* — **Language:** Swedish/English **Frequency:** annual **Content:** data refers to direct investments in and outside Sweden, by country, business activity and geographical zones

***Finansiell stabilitet Rapport** (Financial Stability Report)* — **Language:** Swedish/English **Frequency:** 2 per annum **Content:** contains the Riksbank's analyses and assessments of the stability of the financial system in Sweden, as well as articles discussing particular fields or the Riksbank's policy on financial stability

***Inflationsrapport** (Inflation Report)* — **Language:** Swedish/English **Frequency:** annual **Content:** the report aims to provide background material for monetary policy decisions and spread knowledge about the Riksbank's assessments. It also contains a three year forecast and a risk assessment

***Penning- och Oligationsmarknadens Omsättningen** (Money and Bond Markets' Turnover)* — **Language:** Swedish/English **Frequency:** monthly **Content:** data refers to turnover in the Swedish government and mortgage securities market, by bonds, consumer, broker and market

***Penning- och valutapolitik** (Economic Review)* — **Language:** Swedish/English **Frequency:** quarterly **Content:** report contains articles on topics relevant to the Riksbank's field of operation, as well as a monetary and exchange rate calendar, tables and diagrams depicting statistics concerning central banks and financial markets balances of payment

***Svenska Finansmarknaden** (Swedish Financial Market)* — **Language:** Swedish/English **Frequency:** annual **Content:** the report contains a description of the financial market in Sweden and presents statistics on the financial sector's different components, and aims to explain how these markets, institutions and systems work and what their main functions are in the economy

Tillgångar och Skulder (Assets and Liabilities) —

Switzerland

Banque Nationale Suisse
Swiss National Bank

Address:　　Börsenstraße 15, Zurich, 8022
Telephone: +41 631 3111
Fax:　　　　+41 631 3911
E-mail:　　snb@snb.ch
Website:　　www.snb.ch

Guides: list of publications obtainable online; publications are on price stability, foreign investments, monetary policy of Switzerland
Activity: marshals the money and currency policy in Switzerland; it's primary duty is to guarantee price stability with regard to the economic cycle

Website(s) information:
***Banque Nationale Suisse** (Swiss National Bank)* — **url:** www.snb.ch **Description:** contains economic information on monetary policy concepts, press releases, federal bond issues and debt register claims, current interest rates and exchange rates **Coverage:** various economic, banking and monetary statistics

Publication(s):
***Bankenstatistisches Monatsheft** (Monthly Booklet on Bank Statistics)* — **Language:** German/French/English **Frequency:** monthly **Content:** bank statistics; includes data on credit volume, dividends, trust transactions, etc.

***Die Banken in der Schweiz** (Banks in Switzerland)* — **Language:** German/French **Frequency:** annual **Content:** commented statistics on the development of the banking sector in Switzerland

Statistisches Monatsheft — **Language:** German/French/English **Frequency:** monthly **Content:** key data on Swiss and international economies **Edition:** 81

Bundesamt für Landwirtschaft (BLW)
Swiss Federal Office for Agriculture

Address:　　Mattenhofstraße 5, Bern, 3003
Telephone: +41 31 322 2511
Fax:　　　　+41 31 322 2634
E-mail:　　info@blw.admin.ch
Website:　　www.blw.admin.ch

Guides: periodically publishes market reports

Activity: responsible for legislation in the field of agriculture as well as various aspects of policy concerning trade in agricultural products and rural development

Website(s) information:
Bundesamt für Landwirtschaft *(Swiss Federal Office for Agriculture)* — **url:** www.blw.admin.ch **Coverage:** market reports (regarding prices, turnover, etc) on fruit and vegetables, meat, milk, cereals and eggs, retailers and markets; forecasts of the agricultural sector; imports and exports

Publication(s):
Agrarbeircht *(Agricultural Report)* — **Language:** German/French/English/Italian **Frequency:** annual **Content:** annual survey of the agricultural market in Switzerland; includes general state of agriculture, policy measures and international aspects

---

Bundesamt für Statistik/Office Fédéral de la Statistique
Swiss Federal Statistical Office

Address: Information Service, 10, Espace de l'Europe, Neuchâtel, 2010
Telephone: +41 32 713 6011
Fax: +41 32 713 6012
E-mail: info@bfs.admin.ch
Website: www.statistik.admin.ch

Guides: the website provides a databank of publications
Activity: provides statistics on population and people, the environment, the economy, prices, industry and services, tourism, transport

Website(s) information:
Bundesamt für Statistik/Office Fédéral de la Statistique *(Statistics Switzerland)* — **url:** www.statistik.admin.ch **Description:** general information on the Institutes' main products and services, including latest press releases and news and series of socio-economic online statistics. Also includes news on events, admission, official notices and press releases **Coverage:** statistical data is provided under different sections, covering socio-economic indicators at both national and regional (Cantons) levels. "Key Data for the Whole of Switzerland" provides annual figures for: national consumer price index; index of producer and import prices; industry - production and sales; retail trade; labour market; and GDP growth rates. "Economic and Financial Data for Switzerland" covers the real sector; fiscal and financial sector; external sector; and population

Publication(s):
Arbeitsmarkt Indikatoren *(Employment Market Indicators)* — **Language:** French/German **Frequency:** annual **Content:** labour market structure and unemployment rates statistics

Demos. Informationen aus der Demografie *(Demos. Information of Demography)* — **Language:** German **Frequency:** quarterly **Content:** population statistics; concentrates on one issue related to demography

Landesindex der Konsumentenpreise/L'indice suisse des prix à la consommation *(Consumer Price Index)* — **Language:** German/French **Frequency:** monthly **Content:** average prices of products and services, analyses the prices of essential products and determines the state of the Swiss economy

Mémento statistique de la Suisse/Taschenstatistik der Schweiz/Prontuario statistico della Svizzera/Survista statistica da la Svizra *(Statistical Data on Switzerland 2006)* — **Language:** German/French/Italian/English **Frequency:** annual **Content:** statistics on every stage in a Swiss national's life, from birth rates to education, careers and pensions

Schweizer Tourismus in Zahlen *(Swiss Tourism in Figures)* — **Language:** German/French **Frequency:** annual **Content:** figures on Swiss tourism such as the number of people travelling to and from Switzerland, preferred destinations

Statistisches Jahrbuch der Schweiz/Annuaire Statistique de la Suisse *(Swiss Statistical Yearbook)* — **Language:** French/German **Frequency:** annual **Content:** data covering demographic, economic, social, cultural and political aspects of Swiss life; sections in Italian and English

---

Eidgenössische Finanzdepartement (EFV)
Federal Department of Finance

Address: Bundesgasse 3, Bern, 3003
Telephone: +41 31 322 21 11
Fax: +41 31 323 3852
E-mail: info@gs-efd.admin.ch
Website: www.efd.admin.ch

Guides: publishes information on financial policy, taxes, economy and currency, management, excise and customs
Activity: the EFV plans and decides on the allocation of resources within the State regarding finances, construction, human resources, and IT

Website(s) information:
Eidg. Finanzverwaltung (EFV) *(Federal Department of Finance)* — **url:** www.efd.admin.ch **Description:** news, press releases and reports concerning all aspects of governmental finances such as budget and public expenditure; information available in English, French, Italian, and German **Coverage:** statistics regarding Swiss public financing; includes an international comparison

Publication(s):
Öffentliche Finanzen *(Public Finance)* — **Language:** German/French **Frequency:** annual **Content:** overview of the financial policy of the government, as well as balances of regional entities

---

Staatssekretariat für Wirtschaft/Secrétariat d'Etat á l'économie
State Secretariat for Economic Affairs (SECO)

Address: Effingerstrasse 1, Bern, 3003
Telephone: +41 31 322 56 56
Fax: +41 31 322 56 00
E-mail: biblio@seco.admin.ch
Website: www.seco-admin.ch

Guides: publications on various economic indicators, can be obtained it German, French, English, and Italian
Activity: official organisation for economic policy issues; object of the organisation is to create a common standard for economic policy issues for the purpose of promoting the development of the general economy; prevents and fights unemployment

Website(s) information:
Staatssekretariat für Wirtschaft/Secrétariat d'Etat á l'économie *(State Secretariat for Economic Affairs)* — **url:** www.seco-admin.ch **Coverage:** data on economic development and forecasts, quarterly estimated GDP, figures on unemployment, consumer moods, economic cycle policy instruments, and economic growth

Publication(s):
Die Lage auf dem Arbeitsmarkt *(The State of the Labour Market)* — **Language:** German/French/Italian **Frequency:** monthly **Content:** reports and statistics on the development of the Swiss labour market

Die Volkswirtschaft *(The Economy)* — **Language:** German/French **Frequency:** 10 per annum **Content:** reports and statistical data covering specific issues related to the Swiss economy **Edition:** 78

Prognosen für den Schweizer Tourismus *(Prognoses of Swiss Tourism)* — **Language:** German/French **Frequency:** biannually **Content:** forecasts regarding the tourism industry in Switzerland as well as reports on industry developments such as the number of Swiss nationals and foreign nationals in comparison, the number of beds occupied in hotels, etc

---

Turkey

Basin Yayin ve Enformasyon Genel Mudurlugu
Directorate General of Press and Information

Address: 203 Ataturk Bulvari, Kavaklidere, Ankara, 06688
Telephone: +90 312 455 9000
Fax: +90 312 426 6617
E-mail: newspot@byegm.gov.tr, webadmin@byegm.gov.tr
Website: www.byegm.gov.tr

Activity: contribute to the promotion policy of the state and to the strategies implemented by the government

---

Website(s) information:

Turk Basini *(Turkish Press)* — **url:**
www.byegm.gov.tr/turkbasini/turkbasini/internetbasini.htm
Coverage: directory of all media types (paper, online, radio and television)

Publication(s):

NewSpot — **Language:** English/French/German **Frequency:** 2 per month **Content:** political and economic news

Turkey — **Language:** Turkish/English/French/German/Russian **Frequency:** irregular **Content:** country and people; geographical regions; history; state order, constitution, legal system; developments in the economic sector; macroeconomic developments; work life and social policies; education and science; life in society; cultural life

Baskanlik Dis Ticaret Mustesarligi

Under secretariat of Prime Ministry for Foreign Trade

Address: Inönü Bulvari No 36, Emek, Ankara, 06510
Telephone: +90 312 204 7500
Fax: +90 312 212 3784
E-mail: www@foreigntrade.gov.tr
Website: www.foreigntrade.gov.tr

Website(s) information:

Undersecretariat of Foreign Trade — **url:** www.foreigntrade.gov.tr **Description:** information on the Turkish economy and foreign trade matters. Access to database of Turkish exporters, searchable by exporter's name, product type, or country of destination. Provides various statistics on Turkey's economy and trade **Coverage:** statistics on macro-economic indicators; public sector; monetary developments; and balance of payments. Statistics on foreign trade are included, providing data on US$ value exports and imports by month for each year, as well as ranking of countries of origin and destination

Publication(s):

Export Regime of Turkey — **Language:** English **Content:** objectives, recent developments/strategy

Foreign Investment in Turkey — **Language:** English **Content:** reports; foreign investment legislation; foreign investment statistics; investment in Turkey and improving the investment climate

Free Trade Zones in Turkey — **Language:** English **Content:** Turkish free trade zones (statistics, bulletins, incentives, international membership)

Trade Policies and Measures — **Language:** English **Content:** imports, exports, technical regulations and standardisation for Foreign Trade

Turkey - European Union Relations — **Language:** English **Content:** Turkey-EU customs union; recent developments in Turkey-EU relations; Turkey-EU trade statistics; Turkey-EU financial cooperation

Turkish Economy — **Language:** English **Content:** economic and social indicators of Turkey; foreign trade (1990-2004); foreign trade statistics

Ministry of Foreign Affairs

Address: Disisleri Bakanligi, Balgat, Ankara, 06100
Telephone: +90 312 292 1000
E-mail: webmaster@mfa.gov.tr
Website: www.mfa.gov.tr

Activity: conducts and further promotes international political, economic and cultural relations in the bilateral and multilateral context as well as to contribute to peace, stability and prosperity

Website(s) information:

Ministry of Foreign Affairs — **url:** www.mfa.gov.tr **Description:** general historic and socio-geographic portrait of Turkey, accompanied by an overview of the present state of the economy and latest developments in the national business and financial climate. Includes latest annual data on foreign trade and other selected economic indicators

Publication(s):

Perceptions - Journal of International Affairs — **Language:** English **Frequency:** quarterly **Content:** review of international affairs with Turkey and beyond

T.C. Baskanlik Hazine Mustesarligi

Ministry of Treasury of Turkey

Address: Inönü Bulvari No:36, Emek, Ankara, 06510
Telephone: +90 312 204 6000
Fax: +90 312 212 8764
E-mail: bilgiedinme@hazine.gov.tr
Website: www.hazine.gov.tr

Activity: government treasury body

Website(s) information:

T.C. Baskanlik Hazine Mustesarligi *(Ministry of the Treasury)* — **url:** www.hazine.gov.tr **Coverage:** statistical publications, monthly bulletins and annual reports on foreign direct investment, economic development, insurance

Publication(s):

Dogrudan Yabanci Yatirim Verileri Bülteni *(Foreign Direct Investment Information Bulletin)* — **Language:** English/Turkish **Frequency:** monthly **Content:** number of companies with foreign captial; breakdown of companies with foreign capital by type of establishment, by sector, and by amount of equity

Economic Indicators Bulletin — **Language:** Turkish/English **Frequency:** monthly **Content:** production, investment, employment, productivity and wages; expectations; foreign trade and balance of payments; public finance; prices and financial markets

Hazine Istatistikleri 1980-2003 *(Treasury Statistics 1980-2003)* — **Language:** Turkish/English **Content:** results of main economic policy implementations

Türkiye Cumhuriyet Merkez Bankasi

Central Bank of the Republic of Turkey

Address: Istiklal Caddesi 10 Ulus, Ankara, 06100
Telephone: +90 312 310 3646
Fax: +90 312 310 7434
E-mail: info@tcmb.gov.tr or iletisimbilgi@tcmb.gov.tr
Website: www.tcmb.gov.tr

Activity: carry out open market operations; take necessary measures in order to protect the domestic and international value of Turkish Lira and to establish the exchange rate policy in determining the parity of Turkish Lira against gold and foreign currencies

Website(s) information:

Central Bank of the Republic of Turkey — **url:** www.tcmb.gov.tr **Description:** all main national economic and financial indicators. Also includes weekly, monthly and quarterly bulletins, publications, central bank data, link to other banks in Turkey, and information about the departments within the bank **Coverage:** statistics and data exists on the following subjects: exchange rates, Fixed Bank deposits, financial markets and other types of banking data in a time series format

Publication(s):

Annual Report — **Language:** English **Frequency:** annual **Content:** main macro economic indicators; monetary policy and markets, financial markets, central bank balance sheet

Balance of Payments Report — **Language:** English **Frequency:** quarterly **Content:** external economic developments; goods exports and imports; trade and current account; capital movements

Banks' Loans Tendency Survey — **Language:** English **Frequency:** quarterly **Content:** monitor changes which have already been observed in the supply of loans, as well as those foreseen in the future; identify the factors that are believed to be effective on these changes, and demand for credit

Business Tendency Survey and Real Sector Confidence Index — **Language:** English **Content:** results of a survey conducted with private sector enterprises that are ranked among the "First 500 Industrial Enterprises of Turkey" and the "Next 500 Major Industrial Enterprises of Turkey" lists prepared by the Istanbul Industrial Chamber. BTS aims to find out the senior managers' tendencies and expectations

CBRT Quarterly Bulletin — **Language:** Turkish/English **Frequency:** quarterly **Content:** statistics on economic and business trends in Turkey with data for the latest quarter and some previous quarters **Edition:** 2006

Financial Stability Report — **Language:** Turkish/English **Frequency:** annual **Content:** developments related to banking, public finance, households, corporate and the external sector are discussed. Additionally, the implications of these developments on the financial system and the resilience of the system against shocks are assessed.

Independent Audit Report for Year — **Language:** Turkish/English **Frequency:** annual **Content:** financial report

Türkiye Istatistik Kurumu
State Institute of Statistics

Address: Necatibey Caddesi No 114, Bakanliklar, Ankara, 06100
Telephone: +90 312 410 0410
Fax: +90 312 425 3387
E-mail: bilgi@tuik.gov.tr
Website: www.tuik.gov.tr

Activity: state statistics committee

Website(s) information:
Latest Figures — **url:** www.die.gov.tr/english/SONIST/sonist.html **Description:** statistical information database **Coverage:** statistics covering major industry, economy, and social indicators

SDDS - TURKEY, National Summary Data Page — **url:** www.tuik.gov.tr/english/turcat/turcat.html **Coverage:** economic and financial data

SIS World Wide Web Service — **url:** www.turkstat.gov.tr **Coverage:** recent releases of statistical information on major industrial/social/economic sector

Publication(s):
Agricultural Structure; Production, Price and Value — **Language:** English/Turkish **Frequency:** annual **Content:** includes statistical data on field crops, fruits, vegetables, agricultural equipment and machinery, number of livestock, animal products, poultry, apiculture, sericulture, prices and the marketing ratios of agricultural products

Fishery Statistics — **Language:** English/Turkish **Frequency:** annually **Content:** includes Turkey and region information on fisheries. Breeding information on culture and freshwater fish are included on the basis of provinces **Edition:** 2003

Foreign Trade Statistics — **Language:** Turkish/English **Frequency:** annual **Content:** detailed statistics on Turkish foreign trade activities: imports and exports by commodity, sector and country of origin and destination (accompanied by Excel spreadsheets) **Edition:** 2006

Labour Force — **Language:** Turkish/English **Content:** data represented in excel spreadsheet **Edition:** 2006

Statistical Indicators — **Content:** provides historical perspective on a number of key statistical indicators, including population, demography, health, education, culture, social security and public assistance, agriculture, mining, energy and power, manufacturing, construction, transportation, communication, tourism, domestic and foreign trade, prices and indexes, money and banking, finance, and national accounts. Data from 1923

Statistical Yearbook of Turkey — **Language:** Turkish/English **Frequency:** annual **Content:** annual geographical, socio-economic, and financial statistical portrait of Turkey **Edition:** 2005

Ukraine

National Bank of the Ukraine
Address: 9 Institutska Street, Kyiv, 01601
Telephone: +380 44 253 0180
Fax: +380 44 230 2033/253 7750
E-mail: info@bank.gov.ua
Website: www.bank.gov.ua

Activity: determine and pursue monetary policy in accordance with the general principles developed by the Council of the National Bank of Ukraine

Website(s) information:
National Bank of Ukraine — **url:** www.bank.gov.ua **Description:** detailed economic and financial statistics including: balance sheet of National Bank of Ukraine; interest rates; credit and deposit statistics; GDP; industrial production; consumer goods production; retail turnover; employment; wages; consumer expenditure; imports and exports. Free publications include: Bulletin and Visnyk of the National Bank of Ukraine **Coverage:** statistical data on a free basis is available on main economic and financial indicators; official exchange rate statistics; monetary policy; monetary financial institutions balance sheet and monetary statistics; monetary financial institutions interest rates on loans and deposits statistics; money, currencies and financial market statistics; balance of payments and foreign reserves statistics

Publication(s):
Annual Report of the National Bank of Ukraine — **Language:** English/Russian/Ukrainian **Frequency:** annual **Content:** financial economic indicators for the year

Balance of Payments — **Language:** English/Russian/Ukrainian **Frequency:** quarterly **Content:** general current balance of payments, current account, capital and financial transactions account; balance of payments and trends in Ukrainian balance of payments, trade structure of export and import of goods

Monthly Bulletin of the National Bank of Ukraine — **Language:** English/Russian/Ukrainian **Frequency:** monthly **Content:** general economic, analytical and statistical data; banking and development of banking system (money supply, crediting of economy, refinancing of commercial banks, interest rates, foreign exchange market, government securities market)

National Institute for Strategic Studies
Address: 7A Pirogova Street, Kyiv, 010010
Telephone: +380 44 234 5007
Fax: +380 44 235 2060
Website: www.niss.gov.ua

Activity: divisions of the institution: political strategies; humanitarian policy; social relations and civic community; economic and social strategy; military policy; strategic prognostication; regional policy; sociological studies

Publication(s):
Competitive Economy of the Ukraine under the Conditions of Globalization — **Language:** Ukrainian **Content:** competition and national economy of the Ukraine **Edition:** 2005

Regions of Ukraine: Problem & Priorities of Social & Economic Development — **Language:** Ukrainian **Frequency:** irregular **Content:** contemporary state and trends of economic and social development in the Ukraine

Strategic Panorama — **Language:** Ukrainian/Russian **Frequency:** quarterly **Content:** articles on national security and defence, problems of the national and global safety, regional-economic policy, humanitarian problems, information -communication technologies

State Committee of Statistics of Ukraine
Address: 3 Shota Rustavely street, Kiev, 01023
Telephone: +380 44 287 2433
Fax: +380 44 235 3739
E-mail: office@ukrstat.gov.ua
Website: www.ukrstat.gov.ua

Activity: government statistics committee

Website(s) information:
State Committee of Statistics of Ukraine — **url:** www.ukrstat.gov.ua **Description:** Government statistics department **Coverage:** consolidated statistical analysis, National accounts, finance statistics, industrial statistics, investment and construction statistics, agriculture and environment statistics, transport and communications statistics, Population statistics, Science and innovation statistics

Publication(s):

Agriculture of Ukraine — **Language:** Ukrainian/English **Frequency:** regular
Content: presents key data on the social and economic development of agriculture in Ukraine and its regions from 1990 up to the current year. It also includes data on share of agriculture in the total country's output, number of employees at agricultural enterprises, value of fixed assets, amounts of domestic and foreign investment. Statistics on resource capacities of agriculture, amounts of output, sales and consumption of agricultural products

Capital Investment in Ukraine — **Language:** Ukrainian/English **Content:** contains information about the implemented capital investment and investment into fixed capital (capital formation). Data are given by region, economic activity, technological structure and sources for financing

Consumer Price Indices — **Language:** Ukrainian/English **Frequency:** annual
Content: contains information about producer price indices for industrial output, construction and assembly operations; indices of tariffs for communication services for enterprises, departments, organizations; indices of tariffs for shipment of cargo by rail and pipeline, international comparisons, methodological explanations

Household Expenditures and Resources in Ukraine — **Language:** Ukrainian/English **Frequency:** annual **Content:** publication provides analysis of annual data from household living condition survey. It reports information about subsistence level of the population, its characteristics by structure of income, expenditures and resources; consumption of foodstuffs and durables and services by households depending on level of well-being; composition of household by number of children and employees, by sex and age of the head of household, etc

Industry of Ukraine — **Language:** Ukrainian/Russian **Frequency:** annual
Content: publication provides data that characterize the development of industrial production over the last five years; it has information about structural changes, investment, labour and prices in industry, innovation activity of enterprises, and international comparisons. For most indicators, information is broken down by basic economic activity and regions of Ukraine

Investment of Foreign Trade Activities — **Language:** Ukrainian/English **Frequency:** annual **Content:** contains information about the direct and portfolio investment that had been invested into the Ukraine's economy and abroad, by country, type of economic activity, region, type of currency for the last ten years

Key Financial Indicators of Enterprises of Different Forms of Ownership, by Selected Type of Activity — **Language:** Ukrainian/English **Frequency:** quarterly **Content:** the bulletin gives statistical indicators that characterize financial and economic activity of enterprises. Indicators are presented by type of ownership, region and type of economic activity (960 pages)

National Accounts of Ukraine — **Language:** Ukrainian/English **Frequency:** annual **Content:** contains final data on volumes and changes in GDP, basic accounts of the country's economic activity and Input/Output Table which give the general characteristics of the processes that took place in the country's economy

Population of Ukraine — **Language:** Ukrainian/English **Frequency:** annual
Content: provides population statistics by region, urban and rural areas; sex and age composition of the population, its distribution within the country's area. It also shows data on births by sex and age of mother; deaths by cause of death; marriages by length of marriage and divorces by duration of marriage; annual migration and international comparisons

Statistical Yearbook of the Ukraine — **Language:** Ukrainian/English **Frequency:** annual **Content:** reports wide range of data on social and economic situation in Ukraine. The publication is compiled by the following sections: prices and tariffs, business register, industry, agriculture, hunting, forestry and fishery, investment and construction, transport and communications, external economic activity, wholesale and retail trade, restaurants, services, science, innovations and information, population, employment, population income, expenditure and housing conditions, education, health care, social assi

Statistics of the Ukraine — **Language:** Ukrainian **Frequency:** quarterly **Content:** analysis and statistical publication of issues of social-economic development of the country

Ukraine in Figures — **Language:** Ukrainian/English **Frequency:** annual **Content:** provides a wide range of statistics highlighting social and economic situation in Ukraine for the past year with comparative data. Statistics are compiled according to types of economic or industrial activity, some indicators are presented by region. The sections of the publication cover such topics as national accounts, prices, Unified State Register of Enterprises and Organizations of Ukraine (Business register), industry, agriculture, hunting, forestry and fishery, investment and construction activity,

United Kingdom

Bank of England

Address: Threadneedle Street, London, EC2R 8AH
Telephone: +44 20 7601 4878
Fax: +44 20 7601 5460
E-mail: enquiries@bankofengland.co.uk
Website: www.bankofengland.co.uk

Guides: online catalogue of past and current publications
Activity: determines the monetary policy of the UK, with the core purposes of maintaining monetary and financial stability

Website(s) information:

Bank of England — **url:** www.bankofengland.co.uk **Description:** complete document or a summary of the contents of all the publications of the bank. Searchable by subject (general; monetary analyses and policy; supervision; markets; small business; European Matters) or by format (regular and ad-hoc reports; speeches; fact sheets; press releases; Monetary Policy committee minutes; working papers; consultative papers; CCBS Training Handbooks). Recent highlights such as current inflation reports are also available. Financial markets information is accessible in under the following headings: Open Market Operations, Foreign Exchange Market, Payment and Settlement Systems, Relevant Material, Relevant News Releases, Registrars Brokerage Service, Registrars Main Page, Bank of England Legislation **Coverage:** the statistical section of the web site contains statistical series and supporting material compiled and produced by the Bank of England, consisting mainly of the Bank of England's monetary and financial statistics. Also includes the Bank of England/NOP Inflation Attitudes Survey

Publication(s):

Financial Stability Report — **Language:** English **Frequency:** 2 per annum
Content: shocks to the UK financial system - assessing how macroeconomic and financial developments over the past six months have affected risks to the UK financial system; structure of the UK financial system - looks at changes in the structure of the system over this period; prospects for the UK financial system - provides the Bank's assessment of key vulnerabilities in the light of those developments;
mitigating risks to the UK financial system - links this risk assessment to the mitigating actions that might be undertaken **Readership:** professionals and managers in the financial sector, government officials

Inflation Report — **Language:** English **Frequency:** quarterly **Content:** sets out the detailed economic analysis and inflation projections on which the Bank's Monetary Policy Committee bases its interest rate decisions, and presents an assessment of the prospects for UK inflation over the following two years; contains analysis of money and asset prices; analysis of demand; analysis of output and supply; analysis of costs and prices; assessment of the medium-term inflation prospects and risks

Monetary and Financial Statistics — **Language:** English **Frequency:** monthly **Content:** statistical publication which contains data on money and lending; monetary financial institutions' balance sheets; further analyses of deposits and lending; external business of banks operating in the UK, public sector debt and the money markets (including gilt repo and stock lending); sterling commercial paper, other debt securities, capital issues; financial derivatives, interest and exchange rates and occasional background articles.

Quarterly Bulletin — **Language:** English **Frequency:** quarterly **Content:** provides regular commentary on market developments and UK monetary policy operations; contains research and analysis and reports on a wide range of topical economic and financial issues, both domestic and international **Readership:** profesionals and executives in the financial services sector

Department for Environment, Food & Rural Affairs (Defra)
Address: Nobel House, 17 Smith Square, London, SW1P 3JR
Telephone: +44 8459 335 577
Fax: +44 20 7238 2188
E-mail: helpline@defra.gsi.goc.uk
Website: www.defra.gov.uk

Guides: online catalogue
Activity: works for sustainable development in the UK; develops environmental projects and programmes and works for the implementation of sustainable energy, agricultural and food policies

Website(s) information:
Department for Environment, Food and Rural Affairs — url: statistics.defra.gov.uk/esg **Description:** all statistical releases of DEFRA are made available on this site concerning the status and developments in the agricultural sector **Coverage:** broad statistical coverage including: farming and food; environmental matters and latest development (greenhouse); beverages; fisheries; development indicators; external trade; rural statistics; price indices of agricultural production; agricultural census data

Publication(s):
UK Agricultural Statistics — **Language:** English **Frequency:** annual **Content:** a statistical publication which contains data on key indicators in the agricultural sector such as production, export, import, use of fertilizers, share of organic production, price indices, regional data

Food Standards Agency
Address: Aviation House, 125 Kingsway, London, WC2B 6NH
Telephone: +44 20 7276 8000
E-mail: paul.boyle@foodstandards.gsi.gov.uk
Website: www.foodstandards.gov.uk

Guides: list of available publications is available online
Activity: sets and monitors food quality standards in the UK

Website(s) information:
Food Standards Agency — url: www.foodstandards.gov.uk **Description:** offers press releases, news and regulations information on the food industry. It also provides summaries of market and scientific research projects **Coverage:** statistics on number and type of inspections carried out and infringements established and results of the inspections searchable by region

Publication(s):
Annual Consumer Survey — **Language:** English **Frequency:** annual **Content:** annual investigation into consumer attitudes to food, covering issues such as safety and hygiene, nutrition, diet and shopping

HM Treasury
Address: 1 Horse Guards Road, London, SW1A 2HQ
Telephone: +44 20 7270 4558
Fax: +44 20 7270 4861
E-mail: public.enquiries@hm-treasury.gsi.gov.uk
Website: www.hm-treasury.gov.uk

Guides: available online, free of charge; publications can be found under the relevant headings of different policy areas
Activity: responsible for formulating and implementing the Government's financial and economic policy

Website(s) information:
HM Treasury — url: www.hm-treasury.gov.uk **Description:** monthly economic forecasts for the UK economy; debt management reports; report on the overall economic strategy; recent economic developments report; economic indicators; archive of previous economic indicators; latest press releases **Coverage:** data covers a wide range of macroeconomic statistics and the results of various policies, undertaken by the Treasury

Publication(s):
Annual Budget — **Language:** English **Frequency:** annual **Content:** contains an economic and fiscal strategy report and the financial statement and budget report; surveys the macroeconomic situation in the country, trends in productivity, employment and job creation

National Assembly of Wales
Address: Cardiff Bay, Cardiff, CF99 1NA
Telephone: +44 29 2089 8200
E-mail: assembly.info@wales.gsi.gov.uk
Website: www.wales.gov.uk

Guides: full list available online; publications are available in both English and Welsh, and sometimes in minority languages
Activity: allocates funds made available to it by the UK treasury; develops projects and approves legislation that benefit the population of Wales

Website(s) information:
National Assembly of Wales — url: www.wales.gov.uk **Description:** some of the publications released by the Assembly can be downloaded directly from the webpage; publications cover a wide range of socio-economic issues and provide comprehensive statistical and legal data on the region **Coverage:** varies in different publications

Publication(s):
Annual Population Survey — **Language:** English **Frequency:** annual **Content:** surveys labour markets in Wales and presents statistical data on the characteristics of the labour force

Index of Production and Index of Construction for Wales — **Language:** English/Welsh **Frequency:** quarterly **Content:** statistical information about production in key industry sectors, monitoring of production figures, construction indicators

Welsh Exports — **Language:** English/Welsh **Frequency:** quarterly **Content:** statistical data covering the volume and value of Welsh and UK exports; exports by destination and product type, top export destinations

Welsh Transport Statistics — **Language:** English **Frequency:** annual **Content:** covers a wide range of statistical data, regarding road length and quality, licensing and vehicle ownership, road safety, road traffic, sea, air and river transport, motoring offences

Office for National Statistics (ONS)
Address: Cardiff Road, Newport, NP10 8XG
Telephone: +44 845 601 3034
Fax: +44 1633 652 747
E-mail: info@statistics.gov.uk
Website: www.statistics.gov.uk

Guides: publications are sorted by subject area and can be viewed online free of charge
Activity: the government department that provides UK statistical and registration services. Provides a wide range of economic and social statistics for the use of the government and public, business statistics for corporate users

Website(s) information:
Statistics — url: www.statistics.gov.uk **Description:** The datasets cover most macro-economic time series data compiled by the Office for National Statistics, other government departments and the Bank of England. Monthly datasets include: index of production; financial statistics; producer price indices; retail prices indices; retail sales; labour market; monthly digest of statistics; employment and earnings; economic trends; consumer price indices; retail sales indices. Quarterly datasets include: mergers and acquisitions; UK output, income and expenditure; trade by industry; GDP; consumer trends; economic accounts; public sector accounts. Annual datasets include: balance of payments; UK national accounts; economic trends annual supplement **Coverage:** access to statistical surveys carried out by the Office and grouped in categories covering economics, population, agriculture, consumer trends, etc.

Publication(s):
Agriculture in the United Kingdom — **Language:** English **Frequency:** annual **Content:** general overview of the national agricultural sector. Includes agricultural statistics; information on the impact of agriculture and the food industry in the national economy; structure of the sector and its present economic conditions; output prices and input costs; commodities; incomes; rent; land prices; etc

Consumer Price Indices — **Language:** English **Frequency:** monthly **Content:** information on price indices, including historical series and international indices, as well as average prices of selected products

Consumer Trends — **Language:** English **Frequency:** quarterly **Content:** consumers' expenditure data with description and analysis of underlying factors affecting household consumption trends

Economic Trends — **Language:** English **Frequency:** monthly **Content:** latest statistics on major economic indicators. Includes data for the last five years for national economic accounts; prices, labour market, output and demand, etc. Data is often accompanied by a commentary and analysis of recent developments in the regional, national and international economy

Family Spending — **Language:** English **Frequency:** annual **Content:** analysis of household expenditure and income in the UK. Includes data and information on expenditure on goods and services by household income, structure and location

Key Population and Vital Statistics — **Language:** English **Frequency:** annual **Content:** statistical data on population and demographic trends by health areas in the United Kingdom. Includes data on population estimates; birth and death rates; and internal movements

Labour Market Trends — **Language:** English **Frequency:** annual **Content:** monthly analysis of the UK labour market, providing statistics and information on employment and unemployment rates; training opportunities; vacancies; etc

Living in Britain: Results from the General Household Survey — **Language:** English **Frequency:** annual **Content:** annual statistics compiled from the General Household Survey. The survey covers the following topics; demography, household accommodation, consumer durables, employment, pensions, education, health, smoking, drinking, income

Monthly Digest of Statistics — **Language:** English **Frequency:** monthly **Content:** monthly and quarterly statistics on different social, economic and financial topics

Motor Vehicle Production and New Registrations — **Language:** English **Frequency:** monthly **Content:** monthly statistical data on national vehicle production and registrations, and export production of commercial vehicles by vehicle type and cylinder capacity size

National Food Survey — **Language:** English **Frequency:** annual **Content:** annual report covering household food expenditure, consumption and nutrient intakes. Contains data for the preceding ten years

Overseas Trade Statistics — **Language:** English **Frequency:** annual **Content:** series of five different titles providing data on Great Britain's international trade activities. Data covered includes figures on the UK trade with the EU, with non-EU countries, and the whole world

Social Trends — **Language:** English **Frequency:** annual **Content:** compilation of data and information collected and produced by different official organisations and bodies, providing a general portrait of the present British society and lifestyles in the United Kingdom

Transport Statistics Great Britain — **Language:** English **Frequency:** annual **Content:** annual statistics on the UK's transports' sector, covering road, rail and air travel

Travel Trends - A Report on the International Passenger Survey — **Language:** English **Frequency:** annual **Content:** information and data on patterns of travel to and from the United Kingdom - number of travellers; transports used; accommodation and expenditure; etc

United Kingdom in Figures — **Language:** English **Frequency:** annual **Content:** general overview of a wide range of social and economic topics in the UK

United Kingdom National Accounts: The Blue Book — **Language:** English **Frequency:** annual **Content:** contains estimates of the domestic and national product, income and expenditure. Includes figures for the last 18 years

OSPAR Commission for the Protection of the Marine Environment of the North-East Atlantic

Address: New Court, 48 Carey Street, London, WC2A 2JQ
Telephone: +44 20 7430 5200
Fax: +44 20 7430 5225
E-mail: secretariat@ospar.org
Website: www.ospar.org

Guides: online catalogue with publications covering biological diversity and ecosystems, hazardous substances, offshore oil and gas industry, radioactive substances, monitoring and assessment, available to download

Activity: protection of the marine environment of the North-East Atlantic

Marketing Geography

Albania

Capital city	Tiranë
Capital population	388,000 *(2005)*
Population ('000)	3,207.64 *(2008)*
Urban population (%)	47.64 *(2008)*
Land area (sq km)	28,750
Languages	Albanian (dialects: Gheg, Tosk)
Religion	Religious activities were banned until 1990
Currency	Lek (ALL)
Head of state	Bamir Topi (2007)
Head of government	Sali Berisha (2005)
Ruling party	The Democratic Party of Albania leads the government.

Main urban areas	Population *(Year)*
Tiranë (capital)	388,000 *(2005)*
Dürres	99,546 *(2001)*

Location Albania is situated on the eastern Adriatic coast, with the former Yugoslavian provinces of Montenegro, Serbia and Macedonia marking its northern and eastern boundaries and with Greece to the south. Southern Albania faces the Greek island of Corfu across the Straits of Corfu. The climate is temperate and warm in summer with little rainfall. The capital is Tirana.

Political structure Albania is run under an executive Presidency answerable to a 140-member People's Assembly elected by popular vote. The president is elected for a five-year term by parliament. The president appoints the prime minister. The Assembly of the Republic of Albania has 140 members, elected for a four-year term, with 100 members in single-seat constituencies and 40 members elected through proportional representation.

Last elections Parliamentary elections were last held in July 2005. The right-of-centre Democratic Party claimed 56 seats in the 140-member parliament while the Socialist Party won 42 seats. Minor parties took the remainder. Ex-Prime Minister, Sali Berisha, was returned to the office, replacing Fatos Nano. Bamir Topi was elected President for a 5-year term, taking over from Alfred Moisiu, following the July 2007 Presidential elections. He was finally sworn in after opposition lawmakers ended their coalition's boycott and supported his appointment.

Economy Albania was Europe's poorest country for many years, but has now been replaced by Moldova. In the past four years, the economy has averaged growth of around 5.5% per year. Levels of per capita income have doubled and are now near those of Romania. Despite these achievements, the economy remains vulnerable on several fronts because of a culture of tax evasion, significant amounts of long and short-term domestic public debt, and weak anti-money laundering laws. The informal economy still accounts for nearly one-third of GDP. Poverty is widespread with 12% of the population living on less than €2 per day in 2002. Poverty is worst in the north and in rural areas, with 30% of the rural population living below the poverty line. Per capita GDP is no more than 13% of the level in neighbouring Greece.

Main industries Agriculture is geared to meet domestic needs, with wheat, maize, potatoes and fruit being the main crops. Farm land has been almost completely privatised. Output fell in 2007 and the early part of 2008 owing to a drought. With about one million Albanians working outside the country (mostly in Greece and Italy), the flow of remittances is estimated to be US$600-$750 million per year. This underpins consumer spending, purchases of new homes and cars, and investment in small businesses. The share of the underground "black" economy in GDP is falling as the administration of tax revenues is improved. Albania's infrastructure is inadequate and there is little money for improvements. The country also inherited a very poor highway system from the Communist period. However, a major road-building project costing more than €70 million is underway. Electricity production has dropped sharply owing to a prolonged drought. Albania possesses significant mineral resources, which include some of the world's richest deposits of chrome, molybdenum and copper, as well as nickel and limestone. Start-up operations have been recently launched for both copper and chrome.

Energy Albania has the second largest amount of oil reserves in the Balkans after Romania (approximately 198 million barrels). The country also produces about one billion cubic feet of natural gas to fulfil its domestic demand. Exploration is active, but has yielded no positive results so far. Albania presently imports more than half its modest energy needs.

Austria

Capital city	Vienna
Capital population	1,668,548 *(2007)*
Population ('000)	8,351.79 *(2008)*
Urban population (%)	67.27 *(2008)*
Land area (sq km)	83,855
Languages	German (minorities speak Slovene and Croat)
Religion	Roman Catholic
Currency	Euro (€)
Head of state	President Heinz Fischer (2004)
Head of government	Alfred Gusenbauer (2007)
Ruling party	A governing coalition is under negotiation.

Main urban areas	Population *(Year)*
Vienna (capital)	1,668,548 *(2007)*
Graz	247,698 *(2007)*
Linz.	188,894 *(2007)*
Salzburg	149,018 *(2007)*
Innsbruck	117,693 *(2007)*
Klagenfurt.	92,397 *(2007)*
Wels	58,623 *(2007)*
Villach	58,480 *(2007)*
Sankt Poelten	51,360 *(2007)*
Dornbirn	44,243 *(2007)*

Location Austria occupies a strategic position in the centre of Western Europe, bordering on Germany and the Czech and Slovak Republics in the north, Hungary in the east, Italy and Slovenia in the south, and Switzerland in the west. The climate is temperate, but becomes very cold in winter because of the high altitude. The capital is Vienna.

Political structure The Republic of Austria was formed in 1955 following the end of the post-war administration by the Western allies. It consists of nine provinces, which have little autonomy. The country has a non-executive president who is elected every six years by popular vote, and a bicameral Federal Assembly with a 183-member Nationalrat and a 64-member Bundesrat, or Upper House. Both bodies are elected for four years at a time.

Last elections Parliamentary elections were held in September 2008. The Austrian People's Party (ÖVP) won 51 seats while the Social-Democratic Party took 57 seats and the Freedom Party received 34 seats. The Green Party won 20 seats and the Alliance for the Future of Austria (the Jorg Haider List) won 21 seats. Heinz Fischer of the Social Democratic Party won election as president in April 2004. He defeated Benita Ferrero-Waldner with 52.4% of the vote.

Economy The Austrian economy has consistently performed better than the EU average over the past ten years. Growth has been broadly based, driven by both consumer spending and investment. The country's export-oriented manufacturing sector has flourished and the current account is solidly in surplus. The opening up of the economies of Central and Eastern Europe and their increasing integration with the West continues to provide a boost to Austrian business, which can take advantage of geographic proximity and historic links to capture market share. Wage moderation as a result of a close social partnership helps to maintain competitiveness.

Fundamental long-term challenges must still be addressed. The ageing population will depress potential growth and put increasing pressure on the country's pension system. Greater competition within the enlarged EU will likely make Austria's high tax rates unsustainable. Continued success in the global knowledge-economy will also require more flexible institutions and attitudes.

Main industries Agriculture makes up just 1.5% of GDP. Farms are relatively inefficient and fragmented. Industrial growth was solid in the first quarter of 2008 but has weakened abruptly since then. In manufacturing, the development of multinational pharmaceuticals and electronics companies has replaced "rust-belt" industries such as steel and heavy engineering. There are few multinationals and only a handful of internationally recognised corporations, but many highly specialised and successful small and medium-sized companies. Most of these companies are family-owned; they make high-quality products and export them around the world. Industry leaders in energy, finance and construction materials have invested heavily in Central Europe in recent years. Exporters and manufacturers are now expected to see a prolonged period of slower growth as a result of the weakening global environment. Tourism remains the country's largest single industry and biggest foreign-exchange earner. However, the sector has been in decline as tourists become richer and seek out more exotic locations. An influx of visitors from Eastern Europe helps to offset the loss of tourists from Germany and other Western European countries. Austria's financial sector has close ties with Central and Eastern Europe, a market many times bigger than the domestic one, and faster growing. This region presently accounts for just 10% of the assets of Austrian banks but one-third of their profits. The financial sector's expansion in Eastern Europe has created additional exposure as well as higher profits. At home, the service sector remains relatively inefficient and sheltered from foreign competition.

Energy Austria's liberalisation of the electricity and gas markets is virtually complete. Utilities, however, will face enormous challenges if they are to fend off the interest of competitors. Both the oil and gas and the electricity sectors are too small to survive on their own in an open European market. The fear in Austria is that the local energy sector will be taken over by powerful German neighbours.

Belarus

Capital city	Minsk
Capital population	1,741,000 *(2006)*
Population ('000)	9,718.85 *(2008)*
Urban population (%)	73.31 *(2008)*
Land area (sq km)	207,595
Languages	Belarussian
Religion	Belarussian Orthodox, Roman Catholic
Currency	Belorussian Roubles (BRb)
Head of state	President Aleksandr Lukashenko (1994)
Head of government	Sjarhej Sidorski (2003)
Ruling party	The government is formed by non-partisans, loyal to the president.

Main urban areas	Population *(Year)*
Minsk (capital)	1,741,000 *(2006)*
Gomel	481,500 *(2006)*
Mogilev	369,000 *(2007)*
Vitebsk	343,600 *(2006)*
Grodno	322,000 *(2007)*
Brest	303,000 *(2007)*
Bobrujsk	218,000 *(2007)*
Baranovichi	168,000 *(2007)*
Borisov	150,000 *(2007)*
Pinsk	130,000 *(2007)*

Location Belarus (Byelorussia, or White Russia), borders Poland in the west, Lithuania and Latvia in the north, and Ukraine in the south. The country is a large and swampy plain that is served by several major rivers. The capital is Minsk.

Political structure Belarus declared its independence from the old USSR in August 1990. The National Assembly has two chambers. The House of Representatives has 110 members chosen in single-seat constituencies and elected for four-year terms. The Council of the Republic has 64 members, 56 members indirectly elected and eight members appointed by the president.

Last elections Parliamentary elections were held in September 2008. Supporters of the president won all 110 seats. The result was controversial and poses problems for western countries which had hoped to maintain a dialogue with Belarus. In October 2004, voters approved a referendum allowing Lukashenko to run for a third term. Lukashenko was re-elected as president in March 2006 with 80% of the vote. Charges of voter fraud were widespread.

Economy Belarus's state-dominated economy has been thriving since 2004. Output grew rapidly thanks to ample spare capacity. A new energy agreement with Russia slowed the pace of growth after 2006. Extensive state controls over the economy – notably on prices – complicate economic developments and reduce the efficacy of policy actions. Income distribution is much more equitable than in most countries. Fiscal policy is tight, due mainly to a decline in sources of available financing, such as privatisation proceeds. Structural reforms have progressed very little and the private sector controls only about 20% of GDP.

Main industries Agriculture accounts for 7.4% of GDP. About 60% of agricultural enterprises are loss-making. Forestry and agriculture, notably potatoes, grain, peat and cattle, are important sources of income and employment. Most of the country's industries are dependent on imports for their raw materials and intermediate supplies. Industry accounts for about a third of GDP and the government claims that output is rising by 7-8% per year. However, many analysts doubt the figure. Engineering, machine tools, agricultural equipment, chemicals, motor vehicles and some consumer durables such as watches, televisions and radios are all prominent state-run industries. Many of the products they produce are out of date and inferior to Western versions. The financial situation of the industrial sector continues to be difficult, as indicated by high inventory levels and the fact that one-third of all industrial enterprises report losses. The country's banking system is dominated by the state and is rather weak. Lending practices are extensively influenced by government decisions with loans going for designated purposes, mostly at controlled and subsidised interest rates. Over 80% of domestic assets in the banking system are controlled by just four state-owned banks. An overwhelming portion of the republic's raw materials are imported from Russia, a situation which has given rise to frequent difficulties.

Energy Belarus has a small oil industry which produces around 37,000 barrels per day (bbl/d) of oil each year. The country has 198 million barrels of oil in proven reserves, but the absence of any legitimate reform programme discourages foreign investors from entering the industry. The state-owned oil production monopoly estimates that active oil deposits may last for another 17 years. The country must import nearly 75% of its oil from Russia. Belarus serves as a transit country for Russian oil exports. Although it does not transit nearly as much Russian natural gas as does Ukraine, its importance as a transit state is growing. In 2007, the country agreed to a new 5-year deal that doubles the price of gas during the year and will bring gas prices in line with European countries by 2011.

Belgium

Capital city	Brussels
Capital population	145,917 *(2007)*
Population ('000)	10,618.42 *(2008)*
Urban population (%)	97.36 *(2008)*
Land area (sq km)	30,520
Languages	Dutch (Flemish) and French (Walloon), with German minority
Religion	Mainly Roman Catholic
Currency	Euro (€)
Head of state	HM King Albert II (1993)
Head of government	Vacant
Ruling party	The Christian Democrats lead a multiparty coalition.

Main urban areas	Population *(Year)*
Anvers	466,203 *(2007)*
Gand	235,143 *(2007)*
Charleroi	201,550 *(2007)*
Liege	188,907 *(2007)*
Brussels (capital)	145,917 *(2007)*
Bruges	116,982 *(2007)*
Schaerbeek	113,493 *(2007)*
Namur	107,653 *(2007)*
Anderlecht	97,601 *(2007)*
Mons	91,196 *(2007)*

Location Belgium lies on the north-western coast of continental Europe, facing the North Sea some distance north of the English Channel. Belgium's excellent road and rail communications make it an obvious choice for the administrative centre of the EU. The climate is moderate with mild winters. The capital is Brussels.

Political structure Belgium is a constitutional monarchy in which the monarch has often been required to mediate and to propose governments. There is a 150-seat Chamber of Representatives, normally elected for four years, and a Senate of 71 members. In the Senate, 40 members are directly elected, 21 are appointed and 10 are co-opted from already-elected officials. Four reforms since the 1970s have transformed Belgium from a unitary into a federal state. The result is a federation of three "regions": Flanders, Wallonia and Brussels-Capital, overlaid with three languages – Flemish, French and German. Each has its own parliament.

Last elections General elections were held in June 2007. In the Chamber of Representatives the Socialist party received 20 seats and the Reformist Movement won 23 seats, while the Christian Democrats and Flemish Alliance took 30 seats. The Flemish Interest Party received 17 seats and the Open VLD Party gained 18 seats. Smaller parties received the remaining seats. In the Senate, the Christian Democrats and Flemish Alliance won 9 seats, the Open Flemish Liberals took 5 seats as did the Flemish Interest Party, while the Reformist Movement gained 6 seats. Seven additional parties divided the remaining Senate seats. In July 2008, Yves Leterme resigned as prime minster.

Economy An economic recovery that began in 2005 continued through 2007. Structural reforms improved economic efficiency while household income rose. Similarly, greater business confidence supported investment. The government managed to balance the budget throughout most of this decade, leading to a steady fall in public debt. The economy weakened significantly in 2008, however. Policy makers have begun to tackle the serious problem of early retirement. However, more needs to be done to reduce retirement incentives and increase the demand for older workers if the objective of doubling the employment rate for the older working-age population – which would also boost Belgium's currently low overall employment rate – is to be met.

Main industries Belgium's manufacturing sector accounts for 16.5% of GDP. Food processing industries are especially important with some of the world's largest producers including Kraft, Nestlé, Danone and Campina operating in the country. The pharmaceuticals sector employs nearly 30,000 workers and accounts for around 10% of total

exports. Long the country's industrial powerhouse, French-speaking Wallonia is now struggling with large pockets of unemployment and many obsolete industries. The financial sector, which has never experienced a systemic crisis, has seen its performance improve. Profitability has risen, mainly in the banking sector. A wave of mergers and takeovers has left about four-fifths of the Belgian market in the hands of just a few banks. Meanwhile, the country's small private banking industry is growing at a double-digit pace.

Energy Competition among energy suppliers is gathering pace. The country's consumption of nuclear energy is among the highest in Europe, accounting for almost a tenth of all primary use. Nevertheless, the government has decided to phase out its seven reactors by 2025. There is strong opposition from industry, which argues that closure leaves no clear alternative. Crude oil accounts for almost half of the total energy consumption.

Bosnia-Herzegovina

Capital city	Sarajevo
Capital population	304,065 *(2007)*
Population ('000)	3,940.40 *(2008)*
Urban population (%)	47.43 *(2008)*
Land area (sq km)	51,129
Languages	Serbo-Croat
Religion	Mainly Islam
Currency	Marka (BAK)
Head of state	Haris Silajdžic, Nebojša Radmanovic and Željko Komšic (2006)
Head of government	Nikola Spiric (2007)
Ruling party	The government is formed by a coalition of several parties.

Main urban areas	Population *(Year)*
Sarajevo (capital)	304,065 *(2007)*
Banja Luka	165,100 *(2005)*

Location Bosnia-Herzegovina lies in the centre of the former territory of Yugoslavia, with its eastern borders alongside Serbia and Montenegro and the western edge against Croatia. The mountainous interior gives way to a stretch of coastline in the southwest running down to the city of Dubrovnik. The capital is Sarajevo.

Political structure The country has a rotating collective presidency of three. The candidate with the most votes in an ethnic group is elected. Together, they serve one four-year term, rotating the presidency every eight months. There is a bicameral parliament consisting of the House of Representatives (42 members) and the House of Peoples (15 members), two thirds of whose members are elected from the Muslim-Croat Federation and one third from the Serbian Republic. A valid majority requires at least one third of the members representing each entity. The Federation and the Serbian Republic have their own parliaments. Western governments have a "high representative" who can dismiss officials he deems to be impeding the peace process.

Last elections Presidential elections were held in October 2006. Haris Silajdžic took the Bosniak office with 62.1% of the vote. Nebojša Radmanovic won the Serbian office with 54.8% of the vote while Željko Komšic won the Croatian presidency with 40.8% of the vote. Elections to the House of Representatives of the Federation were held in October 2006. The Party of Democratic Action won 8 seats, the Party for Bosnia and Herzegovina took 7, the Alliance of Independent Social Democrats also took 7, the Social Democratic Party received 5 and the Serb Democratic Party captured 3. Seven other parties are represented in the House.

Economy Fifteen years ago, Bosnia-Herzegovina's economy was twice as big as it is today. After the collapse of a socialist-built economy wracked by war and the deterioration of heavy industry, a remarkable recovery has taken place. Real GDP has tripled since 1995, exports have risen many-fold and the fiscal deficit has been sharply reduced. However, macroeconomic policies are sometimes chaotic and often poorly designed. Bosnia is still the poorest country in Europe. Around 20% of the population live in poverty and another 30% (including many state employees) are only slightly better off. Unemployment is believed to be around 50%. Much economic activity is thought to take place in the informal economy. Growth in the formal economy remains partially dependent on the international aid going to the country but these funds are now being supplied in smaller amounts and with conditions.

Main industries Bosnia-Herzegovina's economy relied almost exclusively on agriculture before the war and this sector is even more dominant today. However, large tracts of land remain in dispute between the different ethnic groups and between different families. The industrial sector is expanding briskly. Output in the Republika Srpska rose by 19.5% in 2006 and 11.9% in the first half of 2007. Most of the country's larger foreign investors are now reporting profits after encountering obstacles in the first few years. The most dynamic industries are chemicals, furniture, rubber and plastics. Industrial output in Bosnia increased by 7.5% in 2006 but rose by just 1.6% in the first half of 2007. Bosnia's main exports are wood, paper, metals and metal products. World prices for metals have surged, helping to boost exports of these industries. The fragmentation of bank supervision among different agencies is a serious weakness. Foreign banks dominate the banking industry.

Energy The country has no energy resources of its own and relies on imports.

Bulgaria

Capital city	Sofia
Capital population	1,156,796 (2008)
Population ('000)	7,571.37 (2008)
Urban population (%)	71.81 (2008)
Land area (sq km)	110,910
Languages	Bulgarian
Religion	Bulgarian Orthodox
Currency	Lev (Lev)
Head of state	Georgi Parvanov (2002)
Head of government	Sergey Stanishev (2005)
Ruling party	The Socialist Party leads a three-party coalition.

Main urban areas	Population *(Year)*
Sofia (capital)	1,156,796 *(2008)*
Plovdiv	345,249 *(2008)*
Varna	313,983 *(2008)*
Bourgas	187,514 *(2008)*
Rousse	156,761 *(2008)*
Stara Zagora	140,303 *(2008)*
Pleven	112,570 *(2008)*
Sliven	94,717 *(2008)*
Dobrich	93,300 *(2008)*
Shoumen	86,735 *(2008)*

Location With its southern borders meeting Turkey, Greece, Macedonia and Serbia, and its northern border meeting Romania, Bulgaria has been exposed to a wide range of cultures. The climate is equable, with low rainfall especially along the popular Black Sea coast. The capital is Sofia.

Political structure The constitution provides for a unicameral 240-seat parliament which is elected according to a proportional system for a four-year term. The president is directly elected for a five-year term but most power rests with the Prime Minister who is generally leader of the dominant party.

Last elections Presidential elections were held in October 2006. Georgi Parvanov of the Bulgarian Socialist Party was re-elected in the second round of voting. He received 75.9% of the vote. In parliamentary elections occurring in June 2005, the Socialists took 82 seats while the National Movement won 53 seats. The Movement for Rights and Freedom, a party of ethic Turks, garnered 34 seats and

the Ataka, a new nationalist party, received 21 seats. The remainder were scattered among several smaller parties.

Economy Bulgaria became a member of the EU in 2007. The economy has performed well in recent years with GDP growth averaging 6.1% in 2003-2007. However, with a per capita income that is about a third of the EU average, Bulgaria will probably be the poorest member-state for years to come. Recent projections suggest that it will take more than 20 years to realise a per capita income that is two-thirds of the EU average. Low wage levels together with the prospect of EU membership pulled in investment over the past three years but productivity growth was slow. As a result, Bulgarian firms lost ground just at the time when EU membership exposed them to greater competition. The confidence inspired by Bulgaria's economic performance, and expectations for convergence with the EU, have been reflected in strong growth of domestic demand, fuelled by bank credit and investment flows from abroad. Rapid growth of imports has led to a rapidly rising current account deficit. Following many years of decline, the gross external debt ratio has started to rise again, and remains at a high level.

Main industries Agriculture presently accounts for 13.4% of GDP. Bulgaria has the potential to become a major agricultural supplier for all of Central Europe, but its farms are inefficient and underfinanced. Output fell in the second half of 2007. EU subsidies equivalent to 1.7% of GDP will go to agriculture in the first three years of membership. The banking system is well-capitalised and profitable but there are risks in an environment of rapid credit growth. Nonetheless, Bulgaria still lags well behind the Central European lending average. The country's real estate market is booming despite the mortgage crisis and credit problems in many other parts of the world. Russians and other Eastern Europeans have become buyers of holiday homes near the Black Sea. Tourism holds promise, especially sites along the Black Sea coast. The number of visitors is also growing and reached 7.9 million in 2007, up from 5.0 million in 2000. The country's roadway system is in very poor condition. Few repairs have been made over the past two decades owing to a shortage of funds. The EU Regional Development Fund will provide €300 million, most of it for this purpose, between 2007 and 2013. The EU has also earmarked €25 million for the technological modernisation of small and medium-sized enterprises.

Energy Bulgaria had 15 million barrels of proven oil reserves. It produces around 3,000 barrels per day (bbl/d) and consumes about 106,000 bbl/d. There is one oil refinery with a capacity of 115,000 bbl/d. The country also has a small amount of natural gas. A pipeline connecting the Bulgarian Black Sea port of Burgas with the Albanian Adriatic port of Vlore is under construction and should be finished by 2008. The project is estimated to cost US$1.2 billion. Bulgaria is also increasing its natural gas transit capacity. Presently, Russian gas passes through the country but the country could become a transit base for Iranian gas in the future. The government is pressing ahead with plans for a €6 billion nuclear power plant on the Danube to replace capacity lost by EU-ordered closures of reactors from the communist era.

Croatia

Capital city	Zagreb
Capital population	689,000 *(2005)*
Population ('000)	4,434.96 *(2008)*
Urban population (%)	61.29 *(2008)*
Land area (sq km)	56,538
Languages	Serbo-Croat
Religion	Mainly Roman Catholic
Currency	Kuna (HRK)
Head of state	President Stipe Mesic (2000)
Head of government	Ivo Sanader (2003)
Ruling party	Croatian Democratic Union (HDZ)

Main urban areas	Population *(Year)*
Zagreb (capital)	689,000 *(2005)*
Split	175,140 *(2001)*
Rijeka	143,800 *(2001)*
Osijek	90,411 *(2001)*
Zadar	69,556 *(2001)*
Slavonski Brod.	58,642 *(2001)*
Pula	58,594 *(2001)*
Karlovac.	49,082 *(2001)*
Sisak	36,785 *(2001)*
Dubrovnik.	31,756 *(2001)*

Location Croatia lies in the north of the old Yugoslavia, with its western edge straddling the Adriatic coast and sharing an eastern border with Hungary. To the north is Slovenia, with Bosnia-Herzegovina and Serbia to the east. The capital is Zagreb.

Political structure The president is elected for a five-year term by the people. Legislative authority is vested in the House of Representatives with up to 160 members, directly elected for a four-year term. Since 1999, the constitution has been changed to shift power away from the president to the parliament.

Last elections Parliamentary elections were held in November 2007. The HDZ took 66 seats in the 153-member parliament while the Social Democratic Party won 56 seats. The remainder were scattered among eight other parties and independents. In January 2005, Mesic won a second five-year term as president.

Economy Based on most economic indicators, Croatia is already performing better than Romania or Bulgaria, which joined the EU in 2007. The economy is open to trade and capital flows, and privatisation is well advanced, although uneven. The private sector accounts for 60% of the economy, including virtually the entire banking system, and foreign direct investment has been strong. Several reform programmes have been implemented and public spending has been cut back. However, an unanticipated jump in private borrowing has led to a continued rise in the external debt-to-GDP ratio. The current account deficit has also risen. The public sector is still very large and imposes a drag on growth. Public agencies and enterprises are not subject to strict financial discipline, and state aid in various forms exceeds that in other Central and Eastern European countries. Rapid growth of commercial credit has created problems for the government. Unemployment is high but is now lower than at any time since 2000. However, the incomes of many workers have yet to reach the levels they enjoyed in 1990. Savings rates are lower than in neighbouring countries and have fallen further in the past few years.

Main industries Agriculture accounts for more than 8% of GDP but remains very inefficient and untouched by any reforms. Despite a mild climate and fertile land, the country is a net importer of food. Up to a fifth of the work force in the central and eastern regions is employed in agriculture but only 4-5% in the rest of the country. Farming output has contracted in recent years. The share of manufacturing in GDP has declined sharply since 1990. Private industry is the main source of job creation and enjoys a healthy rate of investment along with buoyant exports. Industrial output rose by nearly 4% in 2007. Croatia has a number of large and successful companies in comparison with other countries in Central Europe. The service sector is the backbone of the economy, accounting for

around 65% of GDP. Tourism is one of the main sources of income, contributing almost half of all foreign exchange earnings and generating more than a quarter of GDP. The country has thousands of kilometres of coastline but poor infrastructure. A shortage of good hotels also limits growth but foreign investors aim to fill the luxury gap along the coast. There is strong demand from other European counties, particularly Germany and Italy. The financial system is adequate but faces some risks owing to rapid credit expansion. More than 90% of the banking system is controlled by foreign banks.

Energy Croatia has proven oil reserves of only 74 million barrels and produces about 23,000 barrels per day. The country also contains 1.05 trillion cubic feet of natural gas. Croatia is the largest consumer of natural gas in the Balkans and imports most of this from Russia. The country hopes to assume more importance as a transit centre for energy supplies moving to the West.

Cyprus

Capital city	Nicosia (Greek sector only)
Capital population	47,832 *(2001)*
Population ('000)	863.62 *(2008)*
Urban population (%)	69.86 *(2008)*
Land area (sq km)	9,250
Languages	Greek (78%), Turkish (18%), Armenian
Religion	Greek Orthodox (78%); Islamic (18%)
Currency	Euro (€)
Head of state	President Demetris Christofias (2008) (Northern Cyprus: Mehmet Ali Talat – 2005)
Head of government	President Demetris Christofias (2008) (Northern Cyprus: Ferdi Sabit Soyer – 2005)
Ruling party	The Democratic Rally leads a coalition with the Democratic Party. In Northern Cyprus, the Democratic Party and the Republican Turkish Party form a coalition.

Main urban areas	Population *(Year)*
Limassol	94,250 *(2001)*
Nicosia (Greek sector only) (capital).	47,832 *(2001)*

Location Cyprus is located in the eastern Mediterranean, barely 150km south of Turkey and much closer to Syria than to Greece, whose descendants represent by far the largest percentage of the population. The climate is warm and dry. The capital is Nicosia.

Political structure For international purposes, Cyprus is represented by the south of the island, where a Greek majority elects an executive president and a 56-seat House of Representatives. A further 24 unoccupied seats and the vice-presidency are reserved for Turkish-Cypriots but have not been filled since 1963. There are eight observer seats reserved for the Armenian, Maronite and Roman Catholic minorities. The so-called "Turkish Republic of Northern Cyprus", which was declared after the Turkish invasion of 1974, has an executive president and a 50-seat parliament. The two sides have long discussed UN proposals for a federal union, where each group would live in separate self-governing areas with separate parliaments.

Last elections In February 2008, Christofias became president of Greek-controlled Cyprus, defeating Yiannakis Kassoulides. Christofias won 53.5% of the vote. Elections to the House of Representatives took place in May 2006. The Progressive Party of the Working People took 18 seats, the Democratic Rally also received 18 seats and the Democratic Party claimed 11 seats. The remaining seats were dispersed among three smaller parties. Parliamentary elections in northern Cyprus were held in January 2005. The Republican Turkish Party won 24 seats, the Democratic Party took six seats, the Party of National Unity received 19 seats and the Peace and Democracy Movement won one seat. Presidential elections were held in the

Turkish sector in April 2005. Talat was elected president with nearly 55.8% of the vote.

Economy After a period of relatively weak growth, the Cypriot economy has rebounded. Economic growth has recovered despite high oil prices and shocks to the tourism sector. The tax system is being modernised and a uniform corporate tax rate of 10% has been introduced, which implies a reduction in the taxation of profits. Growth is expected to outpace that of the EU in the near future, meaning that income convergence will continue. There is still a large income gap between the Greek and Turkish sectors of the country. Per capita income in the Greek zone is around US$20,000 but it is about half of that in the Turkish area. Many of the Turkish-Cypriots have left for a better life in Britain. In their place, Turks from the mainland have flooded in, mostly poor and uneducated. In the Turkish north, unemployment is high. Foreign remittances from the 200,000 Turkish-Cypriots abroad help to keep the Turkish part of the economy afloat. In recent years, gains in productivity have lagged behind real wage increases, undermining the island's competitiveness in many of its manufacturing industries.

Main industries Agriculture (along with mining) accounts for only 3% of GDP. The manufacturing sector accounts for 9% and its share has been falling over time. The most important sectors in terms of value added are food and beverages, clothing, furniture and metal products. Other industrial sectors, which continue to expand, include printing and publishing, plastics, chemical and pharmaceutical products. The manufacturing sector has been going through difficult times, experiencing a fall in the growth of production, exports and employment as a result of an erosion in competitiveness. Reasons for the manufacturing slump include rising labour costs and low productivity. Cyprus is rich in human capital, with large numbers of Greek-Cypriots having advanced degrees from foreign universities. The country also has the fourth largest ship register in the world. Within the service sector, the most important areas are tourism, finance, insurance and real estate. The larger Greek Cypriot banks are profitable; they compete aggressively in the home market and are working to expand into Eastern Europe. Tourism accounted for about 20% of GDP in recent years though its share has been falling. Tourism revenues in the Greek zone fell by 5.7% in the first half of 2008 (compared to the corresponding period in 2007), even though the number of visitors rose by 2.7% in the same time period. Competition from low cost destinations has intensified. In the north, tourism suffers from the international boycott but several large investments have been made in the past two years. Cyprus' thriving offshore sector is a valuable source of foreign exchange. The island has more than 32,000 registered offshore companies and approximately half of them are active. Initiatives are underway to strengthen financial sector regulation and supervision, and align them to EU standards – including for insurance and the stock market. While structural reform has proceeded, competition continues to be limited and inefficiency prevalent in sectors such as air travel, electricity and telecommunications.

Energy Crude oil, all of which has to be imported, is the primary source of energy in Cyprus. Thermal plants are used to meet the island's electricity requirements.

Czech Republic

Capital city	Prague
Capital population	1,188,126 *(2007)*
Population ('000)	10,316.65 *(2008)*
Urban population (%)	74.95 *(2008)*
Land area (sq km)	78,864
Languages	Czech
Religion	Catholic (70%); Protestant (15%)
Currency	Czech Koruny (CK)
Head of state	Vaclav Klaus (2003)
Head of government	Mirek Topolanek (2006)
Ruling party	The Civic Democratic party leads a three-party coalition.

Main urban areas	Population *(Year)*
Prague (capital)	1,188,126 *(2007)*
Brno	366,680 *(2007)*
Ostrava	309,098 *(2007)*
Plzen	163,392 *(2007)*
Olomouc	100,168 *(2007)*
Liberec	98,781 *(2007)*
Ceske Budejovice	94,747 *(2007)*
Usti nad Labem	94,565 *(2007)*
Hradec Kralove	94,255 *(2007)*

Location The Czech Republic formed part of a federation with Slovakia until January 1993, when the two parted. The country is located in central Europe, southeast of Germany, with Poland to the north, Austria to the south and Slovakia to the east. The climate is temperate with harsh winters. The capital is Prague.

Political structure Until the end of 1992, Czechoslovakia was a federation of two ethnically distinct states, the Czech and Slovak republics, which had been forged in 1919. In 1993, the two states declared their independence. The Czech parliament has two chambers. The Chamber of Deputies has 200 members, elected for a four-year term by proportional representation with a 5% barrier. The Senate has 81 members, elected for a six-year term in single-seat constituencies, in which one third is renewed every two years. The president is elected for a five-year term by the parliament.

Last elections Elections to the Senate were held in October 2006. The Civic Democratic Alliance took 14 seats, the Czech Social Democratic Party took 6 six seats, the Christian-Democratic Union won 4 seats, and the remainder were divided up among smaller parties. Elections to the Chamber of Deputies took place in June 2006. The Civic Democratic Party claimed 81 seats. The Czech Social Democratic Party won 74 seats, the Communist Party of Bohemia and Moravia received 26 seats, the Christian Democratic Union won 13 seats and the Green Party took 6 seats. After lengthy negotiations, Topolanek emerged as the prime minister. Vaclav Klaus of the Civic Democratic Alliance won re-election as president in February 2008. He defeated Jan Švejnar.

Economy Economic growth continues, leading to further strides toward convergence with the EU-15. Past reforms, the accession to the EU and expanding capacity in the automotive industry have driven these gains. Trade performance is good with double-digit growth in exports in recent years. Entry to the eurozone is expected in 2010 and should provide an additional boost to growth. Inflation remains low but upward pressures on prices are emerging. Increases in indirect taxes, which are triggered in part by EU harmonisation, are one reason for the upward pressure on prices. A government deficit of around 3% of GDP reflects strong growth and new budgetary rules. The gradual shift in taxation from income to consumption should boost savings and investment in the medium term.

Main industries The Czech Republic's agricultural sector is not large but productivity is high by Eastern European standards. Farmers have taken advantage of membership of the EU to sell pork and milk to Germany for higher prices than they can fetch in the domestic market. Food processors, however, have suffered, cutting jobs and production. Czech farmers also face increased competition from

Poland, where the agricultural sector is larger and costs are lower. The country is self-sufficient in wheat, barley, vegetables, potatoes and fruit. There are extensive forests offering substantial scope for timber development. Foreign-owned companies account for roughly half of industrial output and 70% of exports. These firms are the foundation of the country's industrial progress. In 2007, Hyundai announced plans for a €1 billion investment in order to supply its car-making plants in Slovakia. In the future, the government hopes to attract more FDI into service-sector projects. Services and research are seen as vital because some manufacturing investors are bound to move further east as Czech wages rise. The banking industry is in good health, but faces challenges. Lending to households (mortgages, and more recently consumer loans) has expanded at rapid rates in recent years, raising household debt and credit risks. Foreign banks control over 90% of assets. The tourist industry is competitive and strong, attracting close to seven million visitors each year.

Energy The Czech Republic has proven oil reserves of only 15 million barrels and produces just 13,530 barrels per day (bbl/d). Exploration is taking place in the Western Carpathians, an area bordering Austria and Slovakia. There are two refineries having a combined capacity of 178,000 bbl/d. Reserves of natural gas are also minimal – only 140 billion cubic feet. With nearly 32,000 miles of natural gas pipelines, the Czech Republic is a major transit centre for Russian gas.

Denmark

Capital city	Copenhagen
Capital population	509,861 *(2008)*
Population ('000)	5,461.53 *(2008)*
Urban population (%)	85.79 *(2008)*
Land area (sq km)	43,075
Languages	Danish
Religion	Mainly Protestant
Currency	Danish krone (DKr)
Head of state	HM Queen Margrethe II (1972)
Head of government	Anders Fogh Rasmussen (2001)
Ruling party	The government is led by a liberal-conservative coalition.

Main urban areas	Population *(Year)*
Copenhagen (capital)	509,861 *(2008)*
Arhus.	298,538 *(2008)*
Aalborg.	195,145 *(2008)*
Odense	186,932 *(2008)*
Esbjerg	114,244 *(2008)*
Vejle	104,933 *(2008)*
Randers	93,644 *(2008)*
Frederiksberg	93,444 *(2008)*
Viborg	92,084 *(2008)*

Location Denmark is an archipelago of low-lying islands which control the straits between the Baltic Sea and the North Sea. The country borders Germany to the south, but is close to Sweden (no more than 50km across the Oresund strait). Denmark controls the Faroe Islands in the North Sea and Greenland, which lies off the coast of Canada. The capital is Copenhagen.

Political structure The Kingdom of Denmark is a constitutional monarchy in which executive authority lies with a Prime Minister who answers to a 179-member unicameral Parliament, with 175 members elected for a four-year term (135 of them by proportional representation in 17 districts and 40 others allotted in proportion to their total vote). There are two representatives each from the Faroe Islands and Greenland.

Last elections Parliamentary elections were held in November 2007. The Liberal Party won 46 seats while the Social Democratic party gained 45 seats, the Danish People's Party took 25 seats, the Socialist People's Party received 23 seats and the Conservative People's Party gained 18 seats. The remainder were scattered amongst minor parties.

Economy Denmark's economy has performed surprisingly well throughout most of this decade. The country enjoys some of the highest living standards of all Western European countries and has one of the most equal distributions of income, thanks in large part to its comprehensive welfare system. Labour market reforms are producing a rise in employment, while careful fiscal policy has yielded budget surpluses and a drop in government debt as a share of GDP. Inflation has been low but pressures are mounting owing to labour shortages and rapid growth in credit. Investment in housing is declining owing to stagnating house prices and the rising costs of construction.

Main industries Agriculture accounts for just 1.2% of GDP but the sector is important in terms of its net foreign currency earning capacity, its effect on employment in related industries and its importance in supplying foodstuffs domestically. Agriculture consists of thousands of mainly small farms supplying pig meat products, dairy goods and cereals such as wheat and barley. In general, farming is so intensive that it has recurrently threatened serious environmental consequences in Denmark's low-lying and often marshy landscape. Farmers are bound by special legislation requiring safe storage and treatment of wastes. Manufacturing presently contributes 12.8% of GDP and that proportion has changed very little in recent years. Engineering, food processing, pharmaceuticals and brewing are among Denmark's most successful industries. Biotechnology is also making strides but even more important is the country's elaborate infrastructure for information technology. Improvements in the subway systems in major cities during 2008-2012 are expected to cost US$2.4 billion. Services account for the bulk of GDP. Housing prices continue to rise but the gains are less than in some other countries and do not appear to be inflationary. The government plans to boost spending on infrastructure.

Energy Denmark's total oil production is about 313,000 barrels per day. New fields have helped bolster output. The country maintains an "open door" policy towards oil companies. Under this policy, oil companies are invited to bid for licences in specified acreage and are not required to commit to drilling wells before seismic work has been completed. As part of EU efforts to create a single market for energy, Denmark has completely liberalised its market for electricity.

Estonia

Capital city	Tallinn
Capital population	396,852 *(2007)*
Population ('000)	1,335.14 *(2008)*
Urban population (%)	69.43 *(2008)*
Land area (sq km)	45,226
Languages	Estonian
Religion	Mainly Christian
Currency	Estonian Kroon (EEK)
Head of state	Toomas Hendrik Ilves (2006)
Head of government	Andrus Ansip (2005)
Ruling party	The government is formed by the Reform Party and the Centre Party.

Main urban areas	Population *(Year)*
Tallinn (capital)	396,852 *(2007)*
Tartu	101,965 *(2007)*
Narva	66,712 *(2007)*
Kohtla-Järve	45,399 *(2007)*
Pärnu	44,074 *(2007)*
Viljandi	20,190 *(2007)*

Location Estonia, the smallest of the three Baltic republics, faces Finland across the Gulf of Finland, with Latvia to the south and Russia dominating its entire eastern frontier. Like Latvia, its land is mainly low-lying and marshy, and its territory includes some 800 islands in the Baltic. The capital is Tallinn.

Political structure Estonia was one of the first Soviet states to declare its formal secession from the USSR, in the summer of 1991. It was recognised in September 1991. The Riigikogu (Parliament) has 101 members. The president is elected for a five-year term by parliament (1st-3rd round) or an electoral college (4th and further rounds).

Last elections In parliamentary elections held in March 2007, the Reform Party won 31 seats, the Centre Party took 29 seats and the Res Publica Party received 19 seats. The Social Democrats gained 10 seats, while the Green Party and the Peoples' Party both received 6 seats. Presidential elections were held in 2006 when Ilves came to office. Adrus Ansip was chosen by the President and took his office on 12 April 2005.

Economy Estonia's economy grew at a brisk pace for more than a decade before beginning to slow in the second half of 2007. Incomes are about half the average in Western Europe but the real living standard now surpasses those in most new member states of the EU. The economy has been driven by both strong domestic investment and consumption demand. Labour market developments are also positive with higher employment and lower unemployment. Real wages have increased substantially, exceeding gains in productivity. Euro adoption remains a key objective but the authorities have limited tools to reduce inflation below the Maastricht threshold.

Main industries Agriculture accounts for just over 5% of GDP and employs around 4% of the work force. The sector is based mainly on livestock rearing, although dairy farming is also important. Manufacturing contributes more than a quarter of GDP. It depends on well-established engineering, machine-building and textile industries, along with consumer goods and food-processing industries. Estonia's close ties with Scandinavian countries provide ready-made markets for some of its products, as well as a source of capital and technological know-how. Export-oriented manufacturing investment is becoming increasingly important, with Finnish companies using Estonia as a low-cost production base. Services accounts for more than two-thirds of GDP and employs almost 60% of the work force. Estonia's banking system is financially sound but profitability is falling as households struggle to reduce indebtedness. More than three million tourists visit the country each year, a majority of them from Finland. Estonia has substantial deposits of minerals (including phosphate and oil shale) as well as extensive forest resources. The latter benefit greatly from Scandinavian investment and should soon provide a substantial resource base for development of competitive industries in the fields of timber, paper and paper products.

Energy Estonia produces about 7,000 barrels per day, most of it from oil shale, which is abundant in the north-eastern part of the country. There are no domestic natural gas reserves. A substantial amount of electricity is produced by Estonia's oil shale-fired power plants and the country is a net exporter. Oil shale production is heavily polluting, however, and Estonia is under heavy pressure from the EU to cut back its output significantly. The government expects the oil shale industry to continue for another 40 years, but no new mines are scheduled to be built. There are no refineries, so the country must import all petroleum products, either by rail or by pipeline. Meanwhile, Estonia is positioning itself as a major transit centre for oil exports from Russia and the newly independent states to Europe. The country's ports at Tallinn and Muuga have become major terminals for the export of petroleum products from the former Soviet Union.

Finland

Capital city	Helsinki
Capital population	571,354 *(2008)*
Population ('000)	5,297.20 *(2008)*
Urban population (%)	62.55 *(2008)*
Land area (sq km)	337,030
Languages	Finnish (93%), Swedish (6.3%), Lapp (0.2%)
Religion	Lutheran (90%); Greek Orthodox
Currency	Euro (€)
Head of state	Tarja Halonen (2000)
Head of government	Matti Vanhanen (2003)
Ruling party	The Centre Party leads a coalition with the Social Democrats and the Swedish People's Party in Finland.

Main urban areas	Population *(Year)*
Helsinki (capital)	571,354 *(2008)*
Espoo	239,741 *(2008)*
Tampere	207,864 *(2008)*
Vantaa	193,946 *(2008)*
Turku	174,757 *(2008)*
Oulu	131,950 *(2008)*
Lahti	99,571 *(2008)*
Kuopio	91,115 *(2008)*
Jyvaskyla	84,739 *(2007)*
Pori	76,185 *(2007)*

Location Finland lies on the Baltic coast with its western border bridging Sweden, with Norway to the north, and the entire eastern flank meeting Russia. Most of the territory is forested, with the main habitation centres to the south. The climate ranges from sub-Arctic in the north to temperate in the south. The capital is Helsinki.

Political structure Finland has a semi-executive president who exercises extensive political powers even though the main executive functions are vested in the prime minister. Elected by universal suffrage for a six-year term, the president may appoint any prime minister and cabinet which can secure the approval of the 200-member Eduskunta (Parliament). Members of parliament are also elected for four-year terms. In January 1995, Finland became a full member of the EU.

Last elections In January 2006, Tarja Halonen was re-elected as president, defeating Sauli Niinisto. Parliamentary elections were held in March 2007. The Centre Party won 51 seats, while the National Coalition Party received 50 seats. The Social Democrats took 45 seats, the Left Alliance secured 17 seats and the Green League won 15 seats. The remaining seats were divided among several smaller parties. Anneli Jaatteenmaki of the Centre Party assumed the office of prime minister after the election but was forced to resign only two months later, being succeeded by Vanhanen.

Economy Finland enjoyed an economic boom in 2006-2007. The country also ranks high in innovation performance and educational attainment, both of which are key drivers of productivity. However, the pace of growth is slowing now. The contribution of high-tech industries has waned and gains in employment have been meagre, though the number of working elderly has been increasing rapidly from a low level. Cuts in labour taxes are welcome, but an increase in public spending is risky, making it difficult to cope with the future fiscal implications of ageing. Population ageing in Finland will occur sooner and more rapidly than in most other OECD countries. Fiscal policy will therefore need to be stringent to ensure the long-run sustainability of public finances. The government's target of raising the employment rate to 70% by 2007 was met in 2006. But it will be difficult to meet the 75% goal for 2011 in view of the continuing shift of investment abroad. Employment continues to rise but a tighter labour market will make future increases increasingly difficult.

Main industries Agriculture accounts for 2.8% of GDP. Farm production, however, is on the increase as many farms are being consolidated and reorganised. These changes are driven by greater investment in agriculture, and are being encouraged by public aid. In manufacturing, forestry accounts for almost 30% of exports and a sizeable portion of GDP. Finland claims around a third of Western Europe's total capacity in the forestry industry and is the world's second largest exporter of paper products behind Canada. The electronics industry is dominated by Nokia which contributes more than a quarter of all exports and a significant portion of GDP. The metal and engineering industries are both growing strongly. The country is a major producer of luxury liners, oil-drilling platforms and a variety of metal products. Tourism is an underdeveloped part of the service sector. The government, however, plans to channel resources into this industry over the next several years with the goal of developing a year-around appeal. Overnight stays by foreign tourists are projected to rise by 5% per year between now and 2013 and the sector's share of GDP is expected to increase by 3%.

Energy Finland relies totally on imports of oil and gas, which it once obtained from the Soviet Union. Plans for a substantial expansion of Finnish gas drilling projects in Russia have been considered but never implemented. Nuclear energy accounts for about a sixth of the country's total energy needs. Finland is currently the only EU member that is expanding its nuclear capacity. It hopes to bring a new 1,600-MW reactor online by 2009 but the project is behind schedule. The Nordic area has a common power market, and any shortage in one country may push up prices throughout the region.

France

Capital city	Paris
Capital population	2,168,000 *(2006)*
Population ('000)	61,766.80 *(2008)*
Urban population (%)	77.35 *(2008)*
Land area (sq km)	543,965
Languages	French
Religion	Roman Catholic
Currency	Euro (€)
Head of state	President Nicolas Sarkozy (2007)
Head of government	François Fillon (2007)
Ruling party	The Union for a Popular Movement (UMP) leads a coalition.

Main urban areas	Population *(Year)*
Paris (capital)	2,168,000 *(2006)*
Marseilles	826,700 *(2005)*
Lyon	467,400 *(2005)*
Toulouse	437,100 *(2005)*
Nice	346,900 *(2005)*
Nantes	281,800 *(2005)*
Strasbourg	272,500 *(2005)*
Montpellier	248,000 *(2005)*
Bordeaux	229,500 *(2005)*
Lille	224,900 *(2005)*

Location France, the largest country in Western Europe, also lies at the heart of the continent. It meets Spain and Andorra in the south across the Pyrenees, and Italy in the southeast. Switzerland and Germany lie to the east and Belgium and Luxembourg in the north. The capital is Paris.

Political structure France has a semi-executive presidency in which the head of state, elected by universal suffrage for a five-year term, appoints a prime minister in accordance with the bicameral Parliament. The 577-seat National Assembly is elected every five years, and one third of the Senate's 321 members come up for re-election every three years, for a nine-year term. France has an unusually centralised decision-making process.

Last elections Presidential elections were held in May 2007. Sarkozy received 53% of the vote, defeating Ségolene Royal of the Socialist Party. Parliamentary elections were held in June 2007. The UMP and its allies took 345 seats. The Socialist Party and its allies (including the Green Party and the French Communist Party) won 227 seats. The remaining seats were scattered among several minor parties. In May 2005, French voters rejected the proposed EU constitution by 54.7%.

Economy Disposable income rose at a brisk rate throughout much of this decade but too much of the additional demand spilled over into imports. Consumption also plays a more important role than in other large Eurozone countries. Gains in employment and increases in minimum wages supported household income. The lacklustre performance in the past two years has strained public finances. Over the medium-term a comprehensive reform of the healthcare system should help contain overall government spending. With the retirement age at only 60 years (compared to 65 years for most EU member states), reforms in the pension system are needed. Further fiscal consolidation and policies to lower structural unemployment are expected to absorb the remaining costs, while five-yearly reviews of the pension system will allow for further modifications. To strengthen labour market performance, subsidies are now offered to employers who hire people on protracted income support. However, many critics argue that existing programmes are insufficient.

Main industries Agriculture accounts for just over 2% of GDP but plays an important role in French politics. Together, agriculture and the agro-food industries account for a larger share of economic activity than in many other Western European countries – about 6% of total value added in the economy and around 10% of total exports. France is the EU's largest producer of cereals. Farms are small, and even though the soil quality is usually excellent, they remain inefficient and require massive financial support. France grows soft fruits, cereals, maize, root vegetables, sugar beet, cattle and poultry, and is famed for its wine production. The manufacturing sector's greatest strengths are in motor vehicles, pharmaceuticals, transport equipment and aerospace (civil and military). The country's two major carmakers, Peugeot and Renault, face growing competition, higher component prices and ageing product lines but analysts expect them to bounce back over the next few years. Manufacturing contributes about three-quarters of total exports of goods and services but the sector's share in world markets is falling. A sharp drop in labour productivity is the main culprit. There are fears that the slowdown could eventually lead to a flood of low-cost imports. Industrial production contracted in the first half of 2008 and business confidence has weakened. France's services sector is large even by EU standards, accounting for the bulk of GDP. A significant portion of this sector consists of government services. In banking, housing credit expanded strongly, bank profitability increased, and nonperforming loans declined.

Energy France has 122 million barrels of proven oil reserves. Despite the lack of significant resources, France is the tenth-largest consumer of oil in the world, consuming 1.97 million bbl/d. The country's crude oil refining capacity is 1.96 million bbl/d. Strict EU environmental regulations have been forcing refineries in France, as well as in all EU member states, to upgrade their facilities not only to reduce their emissions but also to meet new fuel specifications. France has about 341 billion cubic feet (Bcf) of proven natural gas reserves. The country is also the world's largest nuclear power generator on a per capita basis, and ranks second in total installed nuclear capacity (behind the USA). Due to the lack of domestic oil sources, the French government has encouraged the use of nuclear power as an alternative energy source to oil where possible.

Georgia

Capital city	Tblisi
Capital population	1,092,800 *(2007)*
Population ('000)	4,360.80 *(2008)*
Urban population (%)	52.44 *(2008)*
Land area (sq km)	70,000
Languages	Georgian
Religion	Mainly Christian (Georgian Orthodox)
Currency	Lari (Lari)
Head of state	Mikheil Saakashvili (2004)
Head of government	Lado Gurgenidze (2007)
Ruling party	United National Movement (UNM)

Main urban areas	Population *(Year)*
Tblisi (capital)	1,092,800 *(2007)*
Kutaisi	189,700 *(2007)*
Batumi	122,200 *(2007)*
Rustavi	117,900 *(2007)*

Location Georgia is one of the smallest but most influential states to have emerged from the former USSR. Located on the Black Sea, it borders on Turkey in the south, Armenia and Azerbaijan in the east and the Russian Federation in the north. Its mainly mountainous terrain includes the Greater Caucasus in the north and the Lesser Caucasus in the south. The capital is Tbilisi.

Political structure Georgia's independent stance is underlined by the fact that it was the last of the former Soviet states (apart from the Baltic States) to join the Confederation of Independent States. Georgia has an executive president who is elected for a five-year term by the people. The unicameral Parliament has 150 members who serve four-year terms.

Last elections Parliamentary elections held in May 2008. The UNM took 119 seats and the Joint Opposition Bloc received 17 seats. The remaining seats were divided among several smaller parties. Saakashvili, the leader of the UNM, was re-elected as president in January 2008. He received 52.8% of the vote, defeating his nearest rival, Levan Gachechiladze who took 25% of the vote. Lado Gurgenidze was named prime minister prior to the latest presidential election.

Economy Driven by a surge in foreign investment, Georgia's economy has performed impressively for several years. The government has significantly improved its fiscal performance and pushed ahead with structural reforms, including the privatisation of state-owned enterprises and further legal, fiscal, and financial reforms. Success has brought not only foreign investment but a widening current account deficit. Georgia has one of the lowest tax-to-GDP ratios in the region but an overhaul of the tax code in 2004 (to simplify the tax structure, broaden the tax base, and eliminate exemptions and low-yield taxes) significantly improved tax administration. As a result, tax revenues were about 25% of GDP in 2007, and are expected to rise above 27% by 2010. The tariff regime has also been liberalised; 88.7% of all imports now enter duty free. Corruption remains a problem. According to the EBRD, Georgian enterprises are reported to pay the highest proportion of revenue in bribes in Central Asia. The government has made progress, however, launching several initiatives to combat the problem.

Main industries Georgia has a fertile agricultural sector that accounts for 20% of GDP. Economic growth exceeded 12% in 2007 and the forecast for 2008 is for growth of 9%. An increase in farming output and private capital inflows are the main reasons for the country's strong rate of growth. A wide range of crops are produced, including tea, tobacco, citrus fruits and flowers. Wine production (and quality) has risen dramatically and presently amounts to around 50 million bottles per year. Industry contributes 25% of GDP. The sector, which is very capital-intensive, grew by about 10% in 2007. The more important industries are based mainly on mineral resources. Metallurgy, construction materials and machine building represent the core of the sector, though many of these enterprises are badly in need of modernisation and additional capital investment. Tourism revenues rose significantly in 2007. The

government has strengthened the physical and financial viability of the energy sector, though more is needed to ensure reliable power supplies. A building programme is designed to provide new hospitals, schools and highways in 2008, though this might be slowed by the recent hostilities. Investment from Kazakhstan is coming into the tourist industry. The Supsa oil pipeline brings in US$8 million a year in transit fees. As the Caspian oil and gas industry moves into the production phase, the volume of equipment and other imports into the region will grow. Georgia also has deposits of manganese and coal, and a number of oil refineries. Planners have high hopes for the tourist industry. The number of visitors was just 250,000 in 2006 but they expect at least 1 million by 2009. At least 20 new hotels are expected to open before the end of the decade.

Energy Georgia's proven reserves are estimated at 0.35 billion barrels, from which the country produced just under 1,000 barrels per day (bbl/d) of crude oil in 2007. Foreign oil companies are involved in oil exploration both on and offshore. Natural gas, which is imported from Russia, represents 50% of domestic consumption. In 2005, the price was US$110 per thousand cubic meters but by 2007 the price was raised to US$235 per thousand cubic meters. Roughly 150 miles of the pipeline corridor extending from Baku, Azerbaijan, to Turkey will pass through Georgia. This corridor will include both the Baku-Tbilisi-Ceyhan oil pipeline and the Baku-Tbilisi-Erzurum natural gas pipeline, which was completed in July 2007. Analysts expect these pipelines to become two of the primary conduits for Caspian Sea region oil and natural gas exports over the next decade. Georgia will be paid transit tariffs by the pipeline's operators and will receive a small percentage of fuel passing through the Republic.

Germany

Capital city	Berlin
Capital population	3,404,037 *(2007)*
Population ('000)	82,216.00 *(2008)*
Urban population (%)	88.98 *(2008)*
Land area (sq km)	356,840
Languages	German
Religion	Roman Catholic (35%); Protestant (40%)
Currency	Euro (€)
Head of state	Horst Kohler (2004)
Head of government	Angela Merkel (2005)
Ruling party	The Christian Democratic Union leads a grand coalition with the Social Democrats.

Main urban areas	Population *(Year)*
Berlin (capital)	3,404,037 *(2007)*
Hamburg	1,754,182 *(2007)*
Munich	1,294,608 *(2007)*
Cologne	989,766 *(2007)*
Frankfurt	652,610 *(2007)*
Stuttgart	593,923 *(2007)*
Dortmund	587,624 *(2007)*
Essen	583,198 *(2007)*
Duesseldorf	577,505 *(2007)*
Bremen	547,934 *(2007)*

Location Germany occupies a central position in Western Europe bordering no less than six other Western European countries. The country's terrain ranges from the marshes of the Danish border in the north, to the Bavarian Alps in the south. The five eastern Länder, together with the eastern sector of Berlin, formed the German Democratic Republic until unification in 1990. The capital is Berlin.

Political structure The Federal Republic consists of 16 states, of which 11 are in western Germany and five in the east. Germany has an extensively devolved political structure. At the federal level the non-executive president appoints a Chancellor as leader, in accordance with a 603-member Parliament elected for four years. There are circumstances in which in which some candidates win so-called "overhang mandates", resulting in a larger parliament. The Federal Council is indirectly elected. The Council has 69 members representing the governments of the states. Each state has its own Parliament and Premier.

Last elections Elections to the Bundestag were held in September 2005. The Social Democrats took 222 seats in the new parliament, while the Green Party has 51 seats. The Christian Democratic Union (in alliance with the Christian Social Union in Bavaria) has 226 seats; the Free Democratic Party has 61 and the Democratic Socialists have 54 seats. Of these, 9 SPD and 7 CDU members hold overhang mandates, bringing the size of the 16th German Bundestag to 614 members. After lengthy negotiations, Merkel became Chancellor. Presidential elections were held in May 2004 when Kohler scored a narrow victory.

Economy Germany's economy struggled in the first half of this decade and even experienced a brief recession (the first decline since 1993). Growth has steadily picked up since then, bolstered by strong exports, which reflects improvements in external competitiveness and gains in consumer and business confidence. However, with the global downturn, the economy (and its exporters) is struggling once again. Wage moderation, while strengthening competitiveness, has held back consumer spending. Germans are cautious consumers and hold less debt than most Europeans. This has helped them to avoid the worst effects of a US-style credit card crisis. Stronger investment helped to compensate but business confidence deteriorated in 2008. The economy performed well through most of 2007 but its future is uncertain.

Main industries Agriculture makes up less than 1% of GDP. Farms are small (although larger in the east), and crops include wheat, barley, potatoes, apples and grapes for wine making. Germany's manufacturing sector accounts for 23.5% of GDP and is dominated by many large companies producing motor vehicles, precision engineering, brewing, chemicals, pharmaceuticals and heavy metal products. Automotive producers employ one in every seven workers but are shedding workers as their export markets contract. The main impetus for growth in manufacturing comes from the country's many small and medium-sized companies. A surge of investment in machinery and equipment has helped to raise productivity and keep wages from rising rapidly. Germany's service sector expects to create around 200,000 new jobs in 2008. Many firms, however, are concerned over possible falls in domestic demand and the threat of higher energy prices. A failure to implement structural reforms has forced some firms to move abroad. Another problem is corporate tax reform which has been a stop-start process, leaving companies uncertain about future tax bills and benefits. Productivity growth in the service sector is nil. The financial sector is recovering, but progress in market-driven restructuring is slow. A new law passed in August 2008 gives the government the ability to more tightly regulate investment vehicles such as hedge funds.

Energy Germany has 367 million barrels of proven oil reserves, most of it in northern and northeastern Germany. Over one-half of all crude oil production comes from a single field. Germany is the fifth-largest consumer of oil in the world, with consumption reaching 2.7 million barrels per day. The country relies on imports to meet most of its energy needs. Germany is a world leader in developing renewable energy. In 2000, the government set a goal to double the proportion of renewable energy sources by 2010. By 2050, half of Germany's entire energy demand should be met by solar, wind, biomass, hydro, and geothermic sources, according the German government. The country also has 9.0 trillion cubic feet of proven natural gas reserves, the third largest in the EU, after the Netherlands and the UK. Germany is the EU's second largest consumer of natural gas after the UK, and consumption is expected to rise in the future.

Gibraltar

Capital city	Gibraltar
Capital population	28,875 *(2006)*
Population ('000)	29.29 *(2008)*
Urban population (%)	100 *(2008)*
Land area (sq km)	5
Languages	English
Religion	Mainly Roman Catholic
Currency	Gibraltar pound (Gib£)
Head of state	HM Queen Elizabeth II (1952)
Head of government	Peter Caruana (1996)
Ruling party	Gibraltar Social Democrats (GSD)

Main urban areas	Population *(Year)*
Gibraltar (capital)	28,875 *(2006)*

Location Located on the southern tip of Spain, Gibraltar faces the coast of North Africa across a narrow strip of water that controls western access to the Mediterranean Sea. Hence the immense strategic importance attached over the centuries to its ownership, both as a defensive position and as a centre for the trans-shipment of sea cargoes. The capital is Gibraltar.

Political structure Gibraltar, a British dependent territory, is technically ruled from London, though in practice most decisions are taken not by the UK-appointed governor, but by the locally elected chief minister and his cabinet. They are answerable to a House of Assembly (parliament) comprising 17 elected members, an independent Speaker, the Attorney-General and the Financial & Development Secretary. Spain controls the border, which was reopened in 1985.

Last elections Parliamentary elections were held in October 2007. The GSD received 10 seats while a coalition of the Socialist Labour Party and the Gibraltar Liberal Party won the remaining seven seats.

Economy Gibraltar's GDP of about US$955 million means a per capita GDP of about US$33,058. The economy used to be substantially dominated by the British naval dockyard and military presence, but major cuts have reduced its share to about 8% of the local economy. Tourism contributes up to half of all economic activity in one form or another. Local authorities have also had some success in developing a centre for financial services. Foreign investment in Gibraltar is actively promoted by the government, largely to create job opportunities. Tax concessions are available to light manufacturers who intend to export from Gibraltar. Any corporation with a development aid license – granted by the governor for a project that will benefit Gibraltar's economy – is exempt from paying income tax on profit earned from the development, until the total gains from the development exceed the percentage of approved capital expenditure. Many businessmen now believe that some accommodation with Spain is essential if the economy is to show further progress. This goal would receive a substantial boost if Gibraltar's status could one day be renegotiated to resemble that of Andorra.

Main industries The economy used to be substantially dominated by the British naval dockyard and military presence, but major cuts over the last 20 years have reduced the share of these expenditures to a small fraction of the local economy. In recent years, Gibraltar has seen major structural change from a public to a private sector economy, but changes in government spending still have a major impact on the level of employment. In 2004, the European Commission ruled that companies in Gibraltar must pay the same rate of corporate taxation as in Britain. Impressive port facilities exist, so that shipping and tourism are the mainstays of the economy. The colony's proximity to the North African coast is only one reason for the 3,000-4,000 merchant vessels that dock every year. More than five million people visit Gibraltar in a typical year, many of them arriving via cruise liners. Spanish visitors often arrive for shopping or for short breaks, though others may be motivated more by tax evasion than duty-free shopping. In recent years, Gibraltar has built up a respectable finance centre that now accounts for one-fifth of the economy. The government pins its hopes for the future on the financial services sector, which has been growing rapidly. Growth in the technology sector is also promising, with a number of large betting and gaming companies taking advantage of the low-tax regime and good telecommunications facilities.

Energy Gibraltar depends completely on imports for all its fuel needs – primarily from Spain. Thermal power stations provide all domestic electricity.

Greece

Capital city	Athens
Capital population	731,806 (2007)
Population ('000)	11,211.47 (2008)
Urban population (%)	62.39 (2008)
Land area (sq km)	131,985
Languages	Greek
Religion	Mainly Roman Catholic
Currency	Euro (€)
Head of state	President Karolos Papoulias (2005)
Head of government	Costas Karamanlis (2004)
Ruling party	The New Democracy Party (ND) leads the government.

Main urban areas	Population (Year)
Athens (capital)	731,806 (2007)
Thessaloniki	353,335 (2007)
Patra	172,002 (2007)
Iraklio	165,413 (2007)
Larissa	142,184 (2007)
Volos	138,383 (2007)
Chania	131,120 (2007)
Ioannina	107,184 (2007)
Chalkida	96,155 (2007)
Acharnae	90,841 (2007)

Location Greece comprises the mainland and the archipelago, which lies in the Mediterranean between the Adriatic and the Aegean and includes the larger islands of Corfu and Crete to the southeast. The capital is Athens.

Political structure Greece's modern political system dates back to 1975. The country has a non-executive president elected by parliament for a five-year term. The president's main function is to guarantee its political system and supervise its proper functioning. The president appoints his own cabinet, and is answerable to a 300-member Parliament which is also elected for a five-year term. Members are elected for a four-year term by a system of reinforced proportional representation in 51 multi-seat constituencies and five single-seat constituencies.

Last elections Parliamentary elections were held in September 2007. New Democracy received 152 seats in the 300-seat parliament with 102 seats going to the Panhellenic Socialist Movement. The Communist Party gained 22 seats, the Coalition of the Radical Left won 14 seats and the Popular Orthodox Rally took 10 seats. Karamanlis, the leader of New Democracy, will retain his position as prime minister. In February 2005, parliament elected Karolos Papoulias as president.

Economy The Greek economy has outperformed that of most other industrialised countries during this decade. Per capita income is now around 90% of the EU-15 average. Rising incomes, along with a sharp rise in credit, drive private consumption, while increased profitability spurs investment spending. Spending for the Athens Olympics was a major factor behind this strong performance, amounting to almost €7 billion. Grants from the EU also helped; structural aid has amounted to more than 1.5% of GDP in every year since 2001. Finally, economists calculate that Greece's expanding relations with southeastern Europe add about 0.6% to growth each year. In the long-term, population ageing threatens fiscal sustainability. On current estimates, pension and health-care costs will rise by more than in any other EU country between now and 2040, while high

public debt and the weak budget position leave little room for fiscal manoeuvre.

Main industries Agriculture employs a quarter of the population but accounts for 5.0% of GDP, producing tree fruits, vegetables, olives, tobacco, sugar, rice and some wheat. Nursery products, frozen fish, tree nuts and wood products are among the fastest growing industries in this sector. The country's main agricultural exports are fresh and processed fruits and vegetables, especially canned peaches and tomato products, olive oil, durum wheat and tobacco. The manufacturing sector has performed poorly in the past couple of years. The poor performance is partly due to a drop in textile production following the liberalisation of trade in textiles and clothing. Greek companies have substantially increased their investments in Bulgaria and Romania as a result of these countries' accession to the EU. Tourism, Greece's most important industry, is improving. In 2006, the government finally opened the sector to foreign investment by approving a €1.2 billion investment by a British company which plans an integrated resort on Crete. Tourist bookings reached a ten-year high in 2007, thanks mainly to the recovery in Germany. Growth may lag in 2008, however, owing to the slowdown in other European economies. The growth of imports and transit trade with new EU members has prompted Athens to begin expanding the ports of Piraeus and Thessaloniki. Total investment will be about €759 million, much of it from Chinese firms. Funds from the EU will help upgrade the highway network. Greek banks are moving quickly to internationalise their operations. The banking industry's aim is to make at least 30% of revenues and 20% of profits outside Greece by 2009. Banks are investing €3 billion per year in neighbouring countries.

Energy Greece presently has oil reserves of just 5 million barrels and produces around 6,400 barrels per day. This makes the country highly reliant on imports. Oil's market share is slowly declining, as natural gas becomes more important in the Greek energy market. By 2025, oil is expected to account for 57% of Greece's energy demand.

Hungary

Capital city	Budapest
Capital population	1,702,297 (2008)
Population ('000)	10,038.92 (2008)
Urban population (%)	67.05 (2008)
Land area (sq km)	93,030
Languages	Magyar
Religion	Mainly Roman Catholic
Currency	Forint (HuF)
Head of state	László Sólyom (2005)
Head of government	Ferenc Gyurcsany (2004)
Ruling party	The governing coalition between the Hungarian Socialist Party (MSzP) and the Alliance of Free Democrats (SzDSz) parted ways in April 2008. The MSzP now leads a minority government.

Main urban areas	Population (Year)
Budapest (capital)	1,702,297 (2008)
Debrecen	205,084 (2008)
Miskolc	171,096 (2008)
Szeged	167,039 (2008)
Pecs	156,664 (2008)
Gyor	128,808 (2008)
Nyíregyháza	116,874 (2008)
Kecskemet	110,316 (2008)
Szekesfehervar	101,755 (2008)
Szombathely	79,300 (2008)

Location Hungary has long-standing ties with Austria to the west. Bordering on Serbia, Croatia and Slovenia to the south, Romania and Ukraine to the east and the Slovak Republic to the north, it is an important gateway to western Europe. The capital is Budapest.

Political structure Hungary has a non-executive president and a prime minister who is elected by popular mandate for a term of five years. The National Assembly has 386 members, elected for a four-year term: 176 members in single-seat constituencies, 152 by proportional representation in multi-seat constituencies and 58 members elected to realise proportional representation. Since 1995, the country's Romany have had their own 53-seat parliament.

Last elections Parliamentary elections to the unicameral National Assembly were held in April 2006. The MSzP won 186 seats while their coalition partners, the SzDSz, took 18 seats. Another 6 seats were taken by joint candidates of the two parties. The Hungarian Citizens' Party (Fidesz) took 164 seats while the Hungarian Democratic Forum captured 11 seats. The Association for Somogy County won the remaining seat. In 2004, voters approved a controversial plan to extend citizenship to 2.5 million ethnic Hungarians living abroad. However, not enough voters turned out for the referendum to pass. In June 2005, parliament elected Sólyom as president.

Economy The record of the Hungarian economy is impressive. GDP per capita was 69% of the EU average in 2006 (measured in purchasing power parity terms), up from 59% in 2000. However, the pace of growth has slowed since 2005 and the economy has lost ground relative to its neighbours. In the past decade, export strength has been the result of a steady move from low- to medium-skilled export products, counteracting the appreciation of the forint. Competitive pressures also rose however. Low-wage Asian economies made substantial inroads in export markets at the low end of the technology spectrum. Reforms during the first half of the decade were terribly slow and marred by political considerations. The result has been budget problems driven by populist spending on everything from family benefits to energy subsidies. Real wages in the public sector rose by 43% in 2000-2006, with the effects spilling over into the private sector and weakening external competitiveness. As a result, Hungary's fiscal deficit soared to more than 9% of GDP in 2006, forcing sharp cuts in public spending. Policy makers have now set a goal of reducing the deficit to 4% in 2008 and have a good chance of meeting that target.

Main industries The agricultural sector accounts for just over 4% of GDP and is performing well but lacks adequate infrastructure. The government subsidises low-quality food products but has devoted little to modernisation. The wine industry, with the help of foreign investors, has made real progress and gained market share in Western Europe. Agricultural exports have been rising and presently amount to well over €3 billion. However, sectors such as vegetable and fruit production as well as pork have been negatively affected by competition from other EU member states. The manufacturing sector makes up 22.2% of GDP. Growth of industrial output had slowed to less than 2% on an annual basis in the first half of 2008. More than 70% of the country's manufactured exports come from foreign-owned plants set up by IBM, Philips and others. In the automotive industry, major companies including Ford, General Motors, Audi, and Suzuki have established multi-million dollar plants. Electronics is the second largest industry within manufacturing. Though business profitability is sound overall, about two-fifths of small and medium-sized enterprises are reported to be unprofitable. The country's system of urban transport remains very rudimentary, hindering labour mobility and development of the retail sector. High levels of home ownership and regional disparities in purchasing power also discourage labour mobility. The banking system remains sound but there are worrying signs. More aggressive bank lending activities and practices have raised credit risks. Bankruptcies and liquidations are on the rise, putting major parts of the banking system under strain. Taxes on interest were raised in 2007. Officials are trying to convert Hungary into a regional hub for transportation, informatics and finance. Services, including financial services, advertising and retailing, are all becoming more competitive and customer friendly.

Energy Hungary is the largest producer of crude oil in Central Europe, though still a small producer by international standards. Presently, the country is producing about 45,000 barrels per day (bbl/d). Most of this comes from small fields in amounts less than 2,000 bbl/d. Oil reserves are approximately 127 million barrels. Oil companies have increased domestic exploration, estimating that only 60% of the country has been thoroughly explored. The government intends to invest US$40-US$50 million annually on exploration activities. Hungarian natural gas production has been declining for

many years, though domestic production still accounts for a significant share of consumption. Hungary has several Soviet-designed nuclear power plants, although the EU regards these as unsafe by Western standards. The government intends to liberalise the energy sector and adjust prices of electricity and natural gas prices to cost-recovery levels.

Iceland

Capital city	Reykjavik
Capital population	116,642 *(2007)*
Population ('000)	303.49 *(2008)*
Urban population (%)	93.04 *(2008)*
Land area (sq km)	102,820
Languages	Icelandic
Religion	Mainly Evangelical Lutheran Church (93%)
Currency	Icelandic króna (ISK)
Head of state	Ólafur Ragnar Grímsson (1996)
Head of government	Geir Haarde (2006)
Ruling party	The conservative/centrist Independence Party (SSF) leads a coalition with the Progressive Party (PP).

Main urban areas	Population *(Year)*
Reykjavik (capital)	116,642 *(2007)*

Location Located in the North Atlantic, Iceland is a large volcanic island and enjoys generally clear summers. Recurrent volcanic eruptions in the 13th-17th centuries almost depopulated the island, but they have not been serious in recent times. Rich fishing grounds and geothermal energy are important to the economy. The capital is Reykjavik.

Political structure The president is elected for a four-year term by the people. A cabinet is appointed by the 63-member parliament (Althing) elected for a four-year term by proportional representation.

Last elections Grímsson was re-elected as president in June 2004 with 86% of the vote. Parliamentary elections were held in May 2007. The IP won 25 seats while the Progressive Party received 7 seats. The Social Democratic Alliance won 18 seats and the Left Greens gained 9 seats. The remaining seats were scattered among smaller parties. In June 2006, Halldór Ásgrímsson resigned as prime minister. He was replaced by Haarde. Presidential elections scheduled for June 2008 were cancelled after no one had registered by the 24th May deadline to challenge incumbent President Grimsson.

Economy Iceland is one of Europe's most wealthy economies. The economy was growing strongly until 2006 when the pace of growth slowed sharply. Unemployment fell to a very low level, pushing up the rate of inflation. A series of structural reforms, privatisations and fiscal consolidation, as well as large investment projects in the aluminium-smelting sector, also served to boost growth. As the pace of growth accelerated, the available slack in the economy disappeared. Iceland's per capita income exceeds that of most industrialised countries and the gap has been growing in recent years. The country has also made headway in diversifying its exports, though it remains exposed to destabilising external shocks. In the longer term, the government will face pressure to consider some form of linkage with the euro. This is particularly important for the tourist industry which has suffered from the relatively high level of the krona in recent years.

Main industries Rapid growth has changed the structure of the economy. Before the latest boom, the fishing industry accounted for 17% of GDP but that share has now fallen to less than 13%. Fishing still accounts for more than 80% of export earnings. The agricultural sector (including fishing) presently accounts for around 19% of GDP. Sheep are reared in large numbers, but otherwise agricultural activity tends to be restrained by the poor weather conditions. The industrial sector contributes 21% of GDP and is dominated by a few industries such as aluminium and computer software. At present, economic growth is mainly being driven by major investments in aluminium-related projects. Other expanding industries include software production and biotechnology. To finance the country's growing current account deficit, major banks have been borrowing aggressively abroad. This has stretched them far in excess of their depositor base. The increased debt level of the mining industry is also raising concerns.

Energy Iceland has vast geothermal potential in its volcanic rock structure, of which only a small part is currently exploited. With sufficient capital investment, it could easily become a major exporter of electricity.

Ireland

Capital city	Dublin
Capital population	506,211 (2006)
Population ('000)	4,378.35 (2008)
Urban population (%)	61.31 (2008)
Land area (sq km)	68,895
Languages	Irish, English
Religion	Catholic (93%); Church of Ireland (3%); Presbyterian (0.4%)
Currency	Euro (€)
Head of state	President Mary Patricia McAleese (1997)
Head of government	Brian Cowen (2008)
Ruling party	The government is formed by the Fianna Fáil (FF), the Green Party and the Progressive Democrats (PD).

Main urban areas	Population (Year)
Dublin (capital)	506,211 (2006)
Cork	119,418 (2006)
Galway	72,414 (2006)
Tallaght	63,978 (2006)
Blanchardstown	62,976 (2006)
Limerick	52,539 (2006)
Waterford	45,748 (2006)
Clondalkin	43,879 (2006)
Lucan	37,424 (2006)
Swords	33,998 (2006)

Location The Republic of Ireland (Eire) comprises the greater part of an island off the western coast of Great Britain, the remaining northern part of the island forming part of the UK. With little mountainous terrain but considerable areas of hills and down, Ireland's mild climate contributes to good agricultural conditions. The capital is Dublin.

Political structure Ireland's president is elected for a seven-year term by universal suffrage, but most executive powers are exercised by a prime minister and cabinet appointed from among the National Parliament (Oireachtas). The House of Representatives (Dail Eireann), or Lower House, has 166 members elected by universal suffrage for five years, and the Senate (Seanad Eireann), or Upper House, has 60. Eleven senators are appointed by the prime minister while the remainder are elected by several different methods.

Last elections McAleese was re-elected as president in November 2004. Elections to the House of Representatives took place in May 2007. The conservative Fianna Fáil Party won 78 seats. The Christian-Democratic Fine Gael took 51 seats and the Labour Party received 20 seats. The remainder were scattered amongst smaller parties. Elections to the Senate were held in July 2002 when the Fianna Fáil won 30 seats and the Fine Gael won 15 seats. The remainder was spread among several smaller parties. Bertie Ahern resigned as prime minister in April 2008 and was replaced by Cowen.

Economy The economy has performed better than any other OECD country throughout most of this decade, but the pace of growth has finally begun to slow. After years of rising prices, a weakening property market and turbulence in international financial markets is causing concerns. The country's infrastructure has come under severe pressure due to significant gains in population and rapid economic growth in previous years. Other bottlenecks have also emerged that are imposing costs and will act as a brake on growth. The country is also going through a transition period during which it is upgrading many of its social services.

Main industries The structure of Ireland's economy is different from that of other EU countries. Industry accounts for more than a third of GDP (a much higher level than in other member states) and the share of construction is one of the highest in Europe. The construction industry is in the midst of a deep slump as the economy weakens. Growth in industry has also recorded a sharp slump. Agriculture has contracted in both relative and absolute terms in recent years. Farming, however, is still relatively more important than in other economies in Western Europe. The cornerstone of the country's industrial success was an economic strategy focused on inward foreign investment in export-oriented industries such as semiconductors, development of computer software and pharmaceuticals. More recently, Ireland has also become a key location for pharmaceuticals, with nine of the top ten companies operating there. Meanwhile, traditional indigenous industries, including clothing and footwear production, have suffered an almost continuous decline in the face of intense competition from Asia and Central and Eastern Europe. In the past, economic growth led to bottlenecks in infrastructure which prompted the government to launch an expensive, seven-year programme to improve facilities. Although the economy is slowing today, the government plans large-scale investment in infrastructure throughout the remainder of this decade.

Energy Ireland has large reserves of coal and peat, but its oil and gas requirements are met through imports. Some oil reserves have been located in the Irish Sea.

Italy

Capital city	Rome
Capital population	2,705,603 (2007)
Population ('000)	58,975.64 (2008)
Urban population (%)	67.93 (2008)
Land area (sq km)	301,245
Languages	Italian
Religion	Roman Catholic (90%)
Currency	Euro (€)
Head of state	President Giorgio Napolitano (2006)
Head of government	Silvio Berlusconi (2008)
Ruling party	The government is led by a centre-right coalition.

Main urban areas	Population (Year)
Rome (capital)	2,705,603 (2007)
Milan	1,303,437 (2007)
Naples	975,139 (2007)
Turin	900,569 (2007)
Palermo	666,552 (2007)
Genova	615,686 (2007)
Bologna	373,026 (2007)
Firenze	365,966 (2007)
Bari	325,052 (2007)
Catania	301,564 (2007)

Location In the north, Italy meets with France, Switzerland, Austria and Slovenia. In the south, it divides into two peninsulas, the lower of which almost connects with the island of Sicily. The capital is Rome.

Political structure Italy has been a republic since 1946, when it abolished the monarchy. The president is elected by parliament and 58 regional representatives for a seven-year term and exercises only semi-executive functions. The prime minister is appointed by the president. The 630-member Chamber of Deputies (Lower House) is elected for five years by universal suffrage through a system of proportional representation, as are all but seven of the 315-member Senate.

Last elections Napolitano was elected president by Parliament in May 2006. Parliamentary elections were held in April 2008. Berlusconi's centre-right coalition claimed a majority in both houses. In the Chamber of Deputies (lower house) the coalition won 344 seats. These consist of the People of Freedom Party (275 seats), the Northern League (61) and Movement for Autonomy (8). The centre-left coalition has 246 seats of which the Democratic Party has 217 and Italy of Values has 29. Other opposition parties include the Catholic Union of Christian and Centre Democrats (UDC) which took 36 seats. The remainder were scattered among several smaller parties. In the Senate, the centre-right coalition holds 171 seats. Included are the People of Freedom (144 seats), the Northern League (25 seats) and the MPA (2 seats). The centre-left coalition has 133 seats in the Senate made up of the Democratic Party (119 seats) and Italy of Values (14 seats). The Catholic UDC received 3 seats and the remainder were scattered among smaller parties and independents.

Economy Italy's economic performance has lagged behind that of other EU members for most of this decade. There has also been a decline in potential growth and costs are rising as productivity growth stagnates. These problems are rooted in country-specific factors such as the vulnerability of small, family-owned Italian firms and their patterns of product specialisation. Italy also faces increasing competition (in both domestic and international markets) from eastern European and Asian suppliers. The country's share of world exports (in volume terms) has fallen steadily during this decade. Hardest hit have been traditional exporters such as textiles, leather and apparel. Growth of overseas demand in these markets has been weak but the gains recorded by Italy's exports have been even lower.

Main industries The agricultural sector is small but well diversified, producing soft fruits and vegetables, as well as wheat, olives and citrus products for export. The most fertile areas are in the north; in the south, agriculture is mainly for subsistence purposes. Agriculture accounts for 2.1% of GDP. Manufacturing output is rising very slowly. There are relatively few large private companies, but those that exist play a major role in the economy. Examples are Fiat, which is controlled by the Agnelli family; Pirelli, controlled by the Pirelli family; and Fininvest, controlled by the former Prime Minister, Berlusconi. The strongest component of the Italian economy consists of clusters of small and medium-sized family-owned companies in so-called "industrial districts", mostly in the north-east and the centre of the country. In order to compete, these companies require a low-cost base that has proved difficult to maintain. Problems are compounded by a failure to invest in product innovation and research, leaving many small firms exposed to competition from China, Indonesia, Turkey and Eastern Europe. The service industry began to struggle in 2007 and contracted during the first three months of 2008. Italy's tourist industry remains important but has lost much ground relative to other destinations. Thirty years ago, the country was the world's leading tourist destination but it presently ranks fifth.

Energy Italy has proven crude oil reserves of 600 million barrels, the third largest in the EU. The country produces an estimated 151,000 barrels of oil per day, sufficient to meet less than 10% of consumption. Italy is Europe's third largest oil importer. There are three main oil-producing fields in southern Italy and other fields located offshore in the Adriatic and in Sicily (both onshore and offshore). Within the EU, Italy has the greatest crude oil refining capacity, at 2.3 million barrels per day. There are large oil refining facilities along the Mediterranean coast and on Mediterranean islands, capable of processing a wide range of crude oils from North Africa and the Persian Gulf.

Latvia

Capital city	Riga
Capital population	722,485 *(2007)*
Population ('000)	2,266.74 *(2008)*
Urban population (%)	68.3 *(2008)*
Land area (sq km)	64,589
Languages	Latvian
Religion	Mainly Christian
Currency	Lat (Lats)
Head of state	President Valdis Zatlers (2007)
Head of government	Ivars Godmanis (2007)
Ruling party	The government is formed by a coalition of four parties.

Main urban areas	Population *(Year)*
Riga (capital)	722,485 *(2007)*
Daugavpils	108,091 *(2007)*
Liepaja	85,477 *(2007)*
Jelgava	66,051 *(2007)*
Jurmala	55,408 *(2007)*
Ventspils	43,544 *(2007)*
Rezekne	36,345 *(2007)*

Location Latvia, the second smallest of the three Baltic republics, lies between Lithuania in the south and Estonia in the north, with Russia dominating its eastern border, and with the Baltic Sea and the Gulf of Finland extending to the west. The land is mainly flat and low-lying, although chains of hills run through it. The capital is Riga.

Political structure Latvia's independence was officially recognised in September 1991, some six months after its original declaration. The country has a semi-executive president, who is the de facto Chairman of the Supreme Council (or Parliament). He is elected for a four-year term by the parliament. The Diet has 100 members, elected for a four-year term by proportional representation.

Last elections Parliamentary elections were held in October 2006. The New Era, a centrist party, obtained 18 seats, the Union of Greens and Farmers also won 18 seats, the Harmony Centre Party took 17 seats and the Peoples' Party won 23 seats. Other representation was scattered among smaller parties. Valdis Zatlers won the May 2007 presidential election, defeating Aivars Endzins with 58% of the votes versus 39%. In December 2007, Aigars Kalvitis, the prime minister resigned and was replaced by Godmanis.

Economy In the past few years, the growth of GDP in Latvia has exceeded that of other accession countries. Per capita income (in purchasing power parities) has risen by 16% since the mid 1990s. This has reflected strong growth in productivity, supplemented in recent years by rapid investment and solid growth in employment. But at only 43%, relative per capita income in terms of purchasing power parities remains the lowest in the EU. The economy began to weaken in 2008 but prices and wages have continued to rise. Inflation is likely to remain above the Maastricht threshold. Recent price rises have forced the government to abandon its goal of adopting the euro in 2008. The target for euro adoption has been pushed back to 2011-2013. The national unemployment rate continues to fall despite a weakening economy. Unemployment rates in some eastern districts are more than five times higher than in Riga. The standard of living around Riga is high but in some rural inland areas per capita incomes are much lower. Income convergence with the EU-15 still remains a long-term objective. Roughly 69% of GDP is produced in the private sector today, up from 62% in 1997. In terms of employment, the percentage is slightly higher.

Main industries Agriculture accounts for just 4.0% of GDP but 15% of total employment. Agriculture is centred on the cultivation of crops such as potatoes, cereals and fodder crops, along with dairy farming. The share of manufacturing makes up 12.8% of GDP, down from 30.9% in 1990. The bulk of industrial activity is in heavy industries such as chemicals and petrochemicals, metalworking and machine building. Growth of output in several of these industries began to slow in 2008 and the manufacturing sector in general weakened. In the financial sector, real estate now accounts for nearly half of total loans. This leaves banks dangerously exposed to the real property market. Furthermore, with half of all loans extended in foreign currency, banks face large indirect exchange rate risks. Some three-quarters of Latvian banking assets are owned by foreign banks, mainly Scandinavian. Latvia has a good resource base and transport system but investors are hesitating between many rival projects in Estonia, Lithuania, Poland and Germany. In the longer term, the government believes that banking, information technology, tourism and other services will provide plenty of opportunities for growth.

Energy Latvia produces no oil domestically and is entirely dependent on imports. Until 2002, Latvia's port, Ventspils, was Russia's primary northern crude oil export terminal. Russia stopped deliveries following the completion of its own port of Primorsk. Having been left starved of oil, authorities at Ventspils undertook an effort to increase shipments of crude oil and petroleum products delivered by rail. Ventspils has, however, lost significant market share, and has exposed its balance sheet to greater risk as petroleum products and rail-borne crude oil are more expensive than crude delivered via pipeline, and carry slimmer profits. The future of the port is uncertain.

Liechtenstein

Capital city	Vaduz
Capital population	5,091 *(2007)*
Population ('000)	35.48 *('2008)*
Urban population (%)	14.45 *(2008)*
Land area (sq km)	160
Languages	German
Religion	Mainly Roman Catholic
Currency	Swiss franc (CHF)
Head of state	Prince Hans-Adam II (1989)
Head of government	Otmar Hasler (2001)
Ruling party	The government is formed by the Progressive Citizens' Party (FBP).

Main urban areas	Population *(Year)*
Schaan	5,764 *(2007)*
Vaduz (capital)	5,091 *(2007)*

Location Liechtenstein lies in Alpine territory to the east of Switzerland, bordering on the Austrian province of Vorarlberg. Thanks in part to an excellent communications system, the country's prominence is mainly to due to its activities as a tax haven and banking centre. Swiss authorities represent the country abroad. The capital is Vaduz.

Political structure Liechtenstein is a constitutional monarchy in which executive power is exercised by the prime minister – though the constitution gives the monarchy considerable powers. The Landtag (Parliament) is elected by popular mandate for a four-year term and has 25 members. Only a few of the residents are eligible to vote, since the great majority of the population comprises foreign nationals. Prince Hans-Adam persuaded the conservative legislators to join the European Economic Area in 1995.

Last elections Elections to the 25-seat Landtag were held in March 2005, when the FBP won 48.7% of the vote and 12 seats. The Fatherland Union (VU) captured 10 seats. The Free Voters' List took the remaining three seats. Women were allowed to vote for the first time in 1989, but a proposal to lower the voting age from 20 to 18 years of age was rejected in a national referendum in 1992. In March 2003, voters approved a referendum on constitutional changes that gives the Prince the right to sack the government, veto legislation and nominate judges.

Economy Growth has not been impressive in recent years but it is more than 20 years since there was a recession in Liechtenstein. GDP per head is very high, while inflation is low and unemployment remains low at 2.6%. The country has substantial financial reserves and there is no national debt. Despite its small size and limited natural resources, Liechtenstein has developed into a prosperous,

highly industrialised, free-enterprise economy with a vital financial service sector and living standards on a par with the urban areas of its larger European neighbours. Low business taxes – the maximum tax rate is 18% – and easy incorporation rules have induced about 74,000 holding or so-called "letter box companies" to establish nominal offices in Liechtenstein, providing 30% of state revenues. Per capita exports are roughly four times greater than Switzerland's. The country participates in a customs union with Switzerland and is a member of the European Economic Area. Liechtenstein's main challenge is to balance the need for integration in a European framework with the implementation of steps to safeguard its independence.

Main industries Liechtenstein's principal activity is the provision of financial services. The financial sector accounts for 30% of GDP, but only about 14% of employment. Services offered include, in particular, private asset management, international asset structuring, investment funds and insurance solutions. Approximately 90% of Liechtenstein's financial services business is provided to non-residents. The country is under pressure to agree to EU rules on interest payments taxation. Industry is limited in scale but of a specialist nature and the largest source of employment in the country. The sector accounts for about 47% of GDP. Industry is heavily export oriented. The most important activities are mechanical engineering, plant construction, manufacturing of precision instruments, dental technology and food-processing. Many firms operate in highly specialised market niches. The emphasis is less on the production of mass and inexpensive goods, and more on the development of high quality, high-tech products. The average business in Liechtenstein has less than ten employees. Liechtenstein is also one of the world's biggest producers of false teeth. Farming is important despite the relative lack of available land, with wheat, barley, corn, potatoes, livestock and dairy products being grown mainly on small plots of land. The labour force numbers about 31,000, of which 19,000 are foreigners. Most of these workers commute from Austria, Germany or Switzerland on a daily basis. In addition to feed production for animal husbandry, the cultivation of vegetables has gained importance in recent years.

Energy Liechtenstein imports more than 90% of its energy requirements.

Lithuania

Capital city	Vilnius
Capital population	544,206 *(2008)*
Population ('000)	3,366.33 *(2008)*
Urban population (%)	67.21 *(2008)*
Land area (sq km)	65,300
Languages	Lithuanian
Religion	Mainly Roman Catholic
Currency	Lita (Litai)
Head of state	President Valdas Adamkus (2004)
Head of government	Gediminas Kirkilas (2006)
Ruling party	A centre-leftist minority coalition leads the government.

Main urban areas	Population *(Year)*
Vilnius (capital)	544,206 *(2008)*
Kaunas	355,586 *(2008)*
Klaipeda	184,657 *(2008)*
Siauliai	127,059 *(2008)*
Panevezys	113,653 *(2008)*
Alytus	68,304 *(2008)*
Marijampole	47,010 *(2008)*
Mazeikiai	40,572 *(2008)*
Jonava	34,446 *(2008)*
Utena	32,572 *(2008)*

Location Lithuania, the most southerly of the three Baltic republics, lies on the Baltic coast with Latvia to its north, Poland to the south, and Belarus to the east. There is also a small Russian enclave on the Baltic coast, around Zelenogradsk. The capital is Vilnius.

Political structure The country has an executive president who is elected directly for a five-year term and appoints the prime minister. The 141-seat Seimas (parliament) has 71 members elected in single-seat constituencies and 70 members elected by proportional representation. All members serve a four-year term.

Last elections In presidential elections in June 2004, Adamkus was elected with 53% of the vote, defeating Kazimira Prunskiene. Parliamentary elections were held in October 2004. The Labour Party received 39 seats, the Alliance for a Working Lithuania took 31 seats, the Homeland Union won 25 seats and the Liberal and Centre Union captured 18 seats. The remainder were divided among several smaller parties. Kirkilas was appointed prime minister after Zigmantas Balcytis, the interim prime minister, failed to gather the necessary support from the Seimas.

Economy The country has enjoyed strong growth and macroeconomic stability over the past decade. There has been considerable structural change which has produced substantial gains in productivity, though wages are rising even faster. The fiscal deficit has widened, driven by spending related to EU membership. The country's direction of trade has shifted drastically away from the market of the Commonwealth of Independent States towards the EU and North America. The potential for sustained economic growth exists if macroeconomic policies and structural reforms are continued. The unemployment rate continues to fall. Though unemployment is declining, problems such as skills mismatches, a lack of labour mobility and insufficient job creation in the private sector mean that it will continue to be a problem over the medium term. The pace of growth is slowing as the government struggles to contain inflation.

Main industries Lithuania inherited the disproportionate weight of several enormous Soviet-era industrial projects. These included the Ignalina nuclear power complex and the Mazeikiu Nafta oil refinery, both geared to the needs of the integrated Soviet economy. The EU has spent millions of euros upgrading Ignalina, which generates four-fifths of the country's electricity, but the returns from these investments have been marginal. Now, the EU must spend more to close it by 2009. The agricultural sector accounts for 5.4% of GDP with meat, dairy and fish products being major exports. EU funds are expected to provide resources to help restructure the agricultural sector. Traditional Lithuanian exporters of textiles, furniture and foodstuffs have made the most successful transition to Western markets. Other important manufacturing industries are machine-building and metal-working which concentrate on the production of agricultural machinery, food processing equipment, shipbuilding and maintenance equipment. In the service sector, retailing activities are showing robust growth. The banking system is sound but rapid growth of credit poses inflationary dangers.

Energy Lithuania has 12 million barrels of proven reserves and produces about 9,000 barrels per day. The port of Butinge exports slightly more oil than the country's larger port of Ventspils. This is because Butinge has enjoyed considerably better relations with its Russian suppliers than has Ventspils. Several onshore drilling projects are under way in western Lithuania. Russia is the main supplier of crude oil. The country recently completed a US$120 million upgrade of the port at Klaipeda, expanding petroleum product export capacity to 160,000 bbl/d. Lithuania's 263,000-bbl/d Mazeikiai refinery is the only refinery in the Baltic region, and the country's largest revenue generator.

Luxembourg

Capital city	Luxembourg-Ville
Capital population	85,467 *(2008)*
Population ('000)	472.06 *(2008)*
Urban population (%)	82.42 *(2008)*
Land area (sq km)	2,585
Languages	French (official); Letzeburgesch is the local French dialect, and German is also widely spoken as a first language
Religion	Mainly Roman Catholic (95%)
Currency	Euro (€)
Head of state	Grand Duke Henri (2000)
Head of government	Jean-Claude Juncker (1995)
Ruling party	The government is formed by the Christian Social Peoples' Party (CSV) and the Democratic Party (DP).

Main urban areas	Population *(Year)*
Luxembourg-Ville (capital)	85,467 *(2008)*

Location The Duchy of Luxembourg is situated in northwestern Europe, on the coalfields which extend from Lille in northern France through Belgium and into the Ruhr valley. With Germany to its east, Belgium to the northwest and France to the south, its excellent communications have helped to make it one of the most important trade and transport centres in the EU. Its climate is temperate, with generally mild winters. The capital is Luxembourg-Ville.

Political structure As a constitutional monarchy, Luxembourg vests all legislative authority in the unicameral Chamber of Deputies and in the cabinet. The Chamber of Deputies has 60 seats and its members are elected by popular mandate for a term of five years.

Last elections Elections to the Chamber of Deputies were held in June 2004. The CSV received 24 seats, the Socialist Workers' Party took 14 seats and the DP won 10 seats. Minor parties, including the Green Alternative, received the remaining seats. Juncker was re-elected as prime minister. In July 2005, the country voted in favour of the EU constitution with 56.5% of the votes. The vote went ahead despite rejections in France and the Netherlands.

Economy Although the pace of growth has slowed, performance remains well above the euro area average. External demand for financial services strengthened during recent years, underpinning a large increase in the net exports' contribution to growth. Relatively generous wage settlements and falling productivity have led to a significant increase in labour costs that reduced corporate profitability and competitiveness, which has also been weakened by the appreciation of the euro. To forestall a larger deterioration, the rate of public spending has been cut from the near double-digit growth rates of previous years. Nonetheless, upward pressures on the general government deficit persist. Luxembourg is in the unique position of being able to draw on a reservoir of well-educated labour from neighbouring regions in Germany, France and Belgium. As a consequence, the country's pace of growth can change for prolonged periods of time without triggering wage and price pressures.

Main industries The agricultural sector is very small, accounting for just 1% of GDP. However, production is adequate to allow for self-sufficiency in food products, mainly wheat, potatoes and other vegetables. The tourist sector attracts about one million visitors per year. The country refrains from encouraging mass tourism but earns substantial income from the visitors it receives. The industrial sector, initially dominated by steel, has become increasingly diversified to include chemicals, rubber and other products. Several multinationals including Goodyear, Dupont and Delphi Automotive Systems maintain manufacturing operations and distribution centres in the country. In other parts of the industrial sector, Luxembourg's largest businesses have successfully crossed borders to forge global concerns. The service sector is the biggest part of the economy, accounting for 65% of GDP. Services are led by the country's thriving financial institutions, reflecting Luxembourg's success in diversifying its economy. The financial sector, which itself now accounts for about 28% of GDP, remains sound and resilient to potential adverse shocks. Financial sector soundness is also helped by an increasing diversification of income sources, as the shift to investment fund services has boosted commission income. The country has become one of Europe's leading centres for the investment fund industry with net assets of more than US$900 billion. There are ambitious plans to develop a pan-European market in securitised assets and to make the Grand Duchy a centre for electronic commerce and banking.

Energy Luxembourg has large coal stocks, but it relies on oil and gas imports from abroad for the majority of its energy needs.

Macedonia

Capital city	Skopje
Capital population	475,000 *(2005)*
Population ('000)	2,039.96 *(2008)*
Urban population (%)	70.97 *(2008)*
Land area (sq km)	25,713
Languages	Macedonian
Religion	Mainly Christian
Currency	Denar (MKD)
Head of state	Branko Crvenkovski (2004)
Head of government	Nikola Gruevski (2006)
Ruling party	The Coalition for a Better Macedonia (VMRO-DPMNE) leads the government.

Main urban areas	Population *(Year)*
Skopje (capital)	475,000 *(2005)*

Location Macedonia is south of Serbia and borders Bulgaria in the east, Albania in the west and Greece to the south. The geography is mainly mountainous with a river valley running north to south through the centre of the country. The capital is Skopje.

Political structure The country has a non-executive president and an elected cabinet that answers to a unicameral parliament. The president is elected for a five-year term by popular vote. Parliament has 120 members elected for four-year terms by proportional representation.

Last elections Early presidential elections were called in April 2004 following the death of former president Bois Trajkovski in February 2004. Branko Crvenkovski was elected president, receiving 42.5% of the vote. His main rival was Sashko Kedev who took 34.1% of the vote. Early parliamentary elections were held in June 2008. The VMRO-DPMNE won 63 seats, the Coalition for a Better Europe took 27 seats and the Democratic Union for Integration secured 18 seats. Minor parties and Albanians representatives took the remainder.

Economy The economy has been improving since 2004 with average growth of 4%. Officials are anxious to attract more foreign investment but have had little success. They have managed to boost the growth of credit to small and medium businesses. The country's ambitious programmes to improve roads, power, water and other infrastructure (mainly through internationally-funded projects), could lay the basis for sustainable future growth. Economic performance since independence has been marked by notable achievements in macroeconomic management, offset by disappointments in the area of structural reforms. Inflation was brought down from the hyperinflationary levels of the mid-1990s to the current low single digits.

Main industries Agriculture accounts for about 11% of GDP. Macedonia's 180,000 private farmers produce about three-quarters of agricultural output on fragmented holdings with an average size of only 2.8 hectares. Important agricultural products include wheat, corn, maize, barley, tobacco, fruits and vegetables. Dairy farming is also significant. Farming is expected to grow in importance as the transition to a market economy gains momentum. Growth suffered in 2007 as a result of droughts. Industry makes up 28% of GDP. Industrial output was rising at a double-digit pace during the early part of 2008. The sector consists mainly of factories that date back to the first years after the Second World War. Business confidence indicators have improved and credit rose sharply. Manufactured

exports have increased, owing to a brisk growth in steel and other metals exports. The government plans to increase spending on infrastructure to improve roads, electricity and irrigation networks. Rail transport will be privatised in 2008.

Energy Macedonia has only small amounts of oil and natural gas. The country experiences perennial fuel shortages. In 2008, large electricity users will be required to make their purchases at market prices thus eliminating the need for government subsidy.

Malta

Capital city	Valletta
Capital population	7,086 *(2006)*
Population ('000)	408.21 *(2008)*
Urban population (%)	96.07 *(2008)*
Land area (sq km)	316
Languages	Maltese, English
Religion	Roman Catholic
Currency	Euro (€)
Head of state	Eddie Fenech Adami (2004)
Head of government	Lawrence Gonzi (2004)
Ruling party	Nationalist Party (PN)

Main urban areas	Population *(Year)*
Birkirkara	21,858 *(2005)*
Valletta (capital)	7,086 *(2006)*

Location Malta lies in the southern half of the central Mediterranean, some 100km south of Sicily. Its close proximity to North Africa (Algeria, Tunisia and Libya) has left its mark on the country's character, as has its traditional activity in the world of shipping. The climate is warm and generally dry. The capital is Valletta.

Political structure Malta, an independent member of the Commonwealth, has a House of Representatives whose minimum 65 members are elected for a five-year term through the Single Transferable Vote (STV) system of proportional representation. Additional seats are given to the party with the largest popular vote to ensure a legislative majority. The House in turn appoints the president for five years, and he then appoints the prime minister and his cabinet.

Last elections In parliamentary elections held in March 2008, the Nationalist Party narrowly won a majority of votes – though not of seats – and accordingly was granted four extra seats in parliament, retaining its majority in the House of Representatives with 35 seats. The Labour Party holds the other 34 seats.

Economy Malta's economy has been growing slowly throughout most of this decade. However, the pace began to pick up in the second half of this decade as a result of a boom in public investment financed mainly by EU grants. The country's exporters face increased competition from Asia, while export markets remain weak. The balance of trade has deteriorated throughout most of this decade. Domestically, low rates of employment and a lack of skills have held back output and restricted employment growth. Malta's main hopes for a healthier economy are continued strong growth in Western Europe (which boosts tourism) and realisation of its goal of converting the island into a centre for trans-shipment throughout the Mediterranean.

Main industries The Maltese economy is primarily based on services, which accounts for almost 70% of GDP. Manufacturing makes up another quarter, while agriculture accounts for less than 5% of GDP. The semi-conductor industry is the most important part of manufacturing, typically accounting for about three-quarters of the sector's exports. Exports of semi-conductors are forecast to rise in 2008 while some expansion of the pharmaceutical industry is planned. The island has lost much of its textile industry to Asia but other manufacturers are moving up-market. The production and export of high-quality wooden furniture, for example, is thriving. The country's main earner of foreign exchange is tourism. In most years the sector accounts for 20-30% of GDP. About one million people visit the island each year and an estimated 35,000 people – one-tenth of the island's total population – are directly or indirectly employed in tourism. Agriculture is the second most important foreign exchange earner with exports of fruits, vegetables, wheat, grapes and horticultural products (especially cut flowers). Malta has high hopes for its financial sector. Authorities hope to attract more international business and have offered tax relief for foreign investors. By 2008, more than 150 hedge funds had located on the island (up from none in 2000). The number of retail funds is also on the rise. With this success comes more pressure to combat money laundering and eliminate the financing of terrorism.

Energy Malta has no domestic energy sources and relies entirely on imports for its fuel requirements.

Moldova

Capital city	Kishinev
Capital population	593,800 *(2006)*
Population ('000)	3,759.60 *(2008)*
Urban population (%)	47.35 *(2008)*
Land area (sq km)	33,700
Languages	Romanian
Religion	Mainly Christian (Eastern Orthodox, Russian Orthodox)
Currency	Moldovan Lei (MDL)
Head of state	President Vladimir Voronin (2001)
Head of government	Zinaida Greceanîi (2008)
Ruling party	The government is dominated by the Party of the Communists of the Republic of Moldova (PCRM).

Main urban areas	Population *(Year)*
Kishinev (capital)	593,800 *(2006)*
Tiraspol	157,000 *(2006)*
Balti	122,700 *(2006)*
Tighina	96,000 *(2006)*

Location Located in the western part of the former Soviet Union, Moldova is sandwiched between Romania and Ukraine. It includes a substantial part of the territory to the east of the Pruth River, once known as Bessarabia, and also a predominantly Russian area to the east. The climate is warm and pleasant, and agriculture flourishes. The capital is Chisinau.

Political structure Moldova comprises the bulk of the former Moldavian SSR within the former Soviet Union. The president is elected by parliament for a four-year term. Parliament has 101 members, elected for four-year terms by proportional representation. At least 50% of registered voters must participate in the election for the poll to be deemed valid.

Last elections Parliamentary elections in March 2005 gave the Communist Party a reduced majority with 56 seats. The Democratic Electoral Bloc took 34 seats and the Christian Democratic People's Party received 11 seats. In April 2005, parliament overwhelmingly re-elected Voronin as president. In March 2008, Vasile Tarlev unexpectedly resigned as prime minister. Greceanîi was approved with 56 votes out of the 101-seat parliament, and is the country's first female prime minister.

Economy Moldova has become the poorest country in Europe (replacing Albania for that dubious distinction). In recent years, the economy has been growing but disputes with Moscow have slowed progress. The growth of exports slowed, hurt by the rise in energy prices. More recently, however, exports have begun to pick up. Growth is being driven by strong consumer spending, which in turn is underpinned by large gains in real wages and workers' remittances. Remittances, which are several times greater than FDI, are the highest of any country in central Europe. Private sector investment has risen but remains too low to support strong medium-term growth. Moldavans continue to emigrate at a rapid pace. The government estimates that more than 500,000 have left the country to work abroad, either in western Europe or Russia. They send home about US$200 million per year. Most of the rich Moldavans are those who smuggle their compatriots into the EU for a hefty price and then take a slice of their wages.

Main industries The economy depends heavily on agriculture, featuring fruits, vegetables, wine and tobacco. Farm output slumped in 2007 owing to a severe drought. Half the country's population depends on subsistence farming. The agricultural sector is still largely in government hands. Moscow's decision to ban imports of Moldavan wine was a serious blow. Traditionally, almost all wine exports went to Russia. Wine exports should recover now that the embargo has been lifted. Light industry consists mainly of textiles and consumer goods. In addition, there is a modest chemical industry. There is some evidence of a shift of resources and employment into manufacturing (mainly textiles) where low labour costs offer a competitive advantage. So far, the banking industry has managed to deal with the effects of the wine ban, though around 12% of all bank loans are to wineries.

Energy Moldova's reserves are estimated at just 15 million barrels. It has no natural gas resources, and is entirely dependent on Russia to meet its consumption. In January 2006, Russia's Gazprom stopped natural gas supplies due to a lack of agreement over prices. An agreement was later reached whereby Moldova would pay US$170 per thousand cubic metres with the price rising to near-European levels over the next five years.

Monaco

Capital city	Monaco-Ville
Capital population	1,034 *(2000)*
Population ('000)	32.82 *(2008)*
Urban population (%)	100 *(2008)*
Land area (sq km)	2
Languages	French
Religion	Mainly Roman Catholic (90%)
Currency	Euro (€)
Head of state	HSH Prince Albert II (2005)
Head of government	Jean-Paul Proust (2005)
Ruling party	Union for Monaco (UPM)

Main urban areas	Population *(Year)*
Monte-Carlo	15,507 *(2000)*
Monaco-Ville (capital)	1,034 *(2000)*

Location Monaco, one of the smallest states in Europe, is a Mediterranean principality that is surrounded on all its land borders by France, though the Italian coastline is within easy reach. The country is entirely urban, having no undeveloped land whatever, apart from parks and gardens. The capital is Monte Carlo.

Political structure The Principality of Monaco is a hereditary monarchy, which has enjoyed French protection since 1861. Legislative power is vested jointly in the Prince and in the 24-member unicameral National Council, which is elected for a five-year term by universal suffrage. Executive power is exercised by the Prince in collaboration with a four-member Council of Government. The judicial code of France applies. Prince Rainier III died in April 2005. He was automatically succeeded by Albert in accordance with long-standing tradition.

Last elections National Council elections took place in February 2008. The distribution of seats remained unchanged from the previous election. The UPM won 21 seats and the National and Democratic Union, also known as the Rally for Monaco, took three seats. Although the principality has 30,000 residents, only the 5,000 Monegasques are eligible to vote.

Economy In an area of less than 200 hectares Monaco still manages to generate billions of dollars in business. The state carries no debts and possesses a large (unpublished) amount of liquid reserves. Although Monaco is not a member of the EU, it adopted the euro in 2002 and received permission to issue its own coins. Monaco has no equal along the Mediterranean coast for per capita wealth, provision of public services and sheer scale of development in such a confined space. Unemployment is estimated to be around 3%. The principality's special protected status, under the control of France, gives it a high degree of security. Authorities are reluctant to admit it, but one of the reasons for the principality's success is its privileged fiscal status. Residents pay no personal income tax. Nor are they subject to a capital gains tax when they sell assets such as shares or property. In theory, corporate profits are taxed at the same rate as in France, but in practice professional firms pay no taxes. Nor do local firms that conduct 75% of their operations within the principality. Some Monaco-based companies conduct business between themselves, in order to raise the proportion of activity in their country and therefore obtain eligibility for tax exemption.

Main industries The government has presided over a successful transformation of Monaco's economy into services and small, non-polluting industries producing high value products. The country has no income tax, low business taxes and thrives as a tax haven both for individuals who have established residence and for foreign companies that have set up businesses and offices. More than half of Monaco's annual revenue is generated from VAT levied on hotels, banks and the industrial sector. Industry employs about a quarter of the work force. Producers of chemicals, pharmaceuticals and cosmetics are prominent. The state retains monopolies in a number of sectors, including tobacco, the telephone network and the postal service. Another quarter of all revenue is derived from tourism. Approximately 40% of all tourism is business related. Monaco is also a popular location for international companies that employ close to 20% of the workforce. The principality has invested heavily in telecommunications in an effort to carve out a role as a carrier of transit traffic. Monaco also plays host to over 40 financial institutions. The financial industry employs almost a quarter of the work force.

Energy The country depends on imports for all its energy needs.

Netherlands

Capital city	Amsterdam
Capital population	747,584 *(2008)*
Population ('000)	16,383.16 *(2008)*
Urban population (%)	66.66 *(2008)*
Land area (sq km)	41,160
Languages	Dutch
Religion	Roman Catholic (38%); Protestant (30%)
Currency	Euro (€)
Head of state	HM Queen Beatrix (1980)
Head of government	Jan Peter Balkenende (2002)
Ruling party	The Christian Democratic Appeal Party (CDA) leads a coalition.

Main urban areas	Population *(Year)*
Amsterdam (capital)	747,584 *(2008)*
Rotterdam	580,952 *(2008)*
Haag	475,932 *(2008)*
Utrecht	294,810 *(2008)*
Eindhoven	210,456 *(2008)*
Tilburg	201,931 *(2008)*
Almere	183,299 *(2008)*
Groningen	182,954 *(2008)*
Breda	170,985 *(2008)*
Nijmegen	161,226 *(2008)*

Location The Netherlands occupies some 250km of the North Sea coast between Belgium in the south and Germany in the north and east. About a third of the country is below water level, having been reclaimed from the sea by an extensive reclamation programme. The capital is Amsterdam.

Political structure The Netherlands is a constitutional monarchy in which the monarch rules through a Council of Ministers. Parliament consists of a 150-member Lower House, whose members are elected through a system of proportional representation for four-year terms, and a 75-seat First Chamber which is appointed by the provincial legislatures for a term of four years. The Netherlands rules over the Netherlands Antilles and Aruba, but wide autonomy prevails.

Last elections Elections to the Lower House were held in November 2006. The CDA took 41 seats while the Socialist Party received 25 seats. The opposition Labour Party won 33 seats while the Peoples' Party for Freedom and Democracy gained 22 seats and Democrats 66 received 3 seats. The Party for Freedom took 9 seats and the remaining seats were spread amongst several smaller parties including some new parties. In June 2005, Dutch voters rejected the proposed EU constitution, with 62% opposing it.

Economy Average annual growth in 2001-2003 was only 0.7%, but a recovery began in 2004 and has continued through 2007. The acceleration of economic activity after a prolonged downturn was instrumental in restoring consumer confidence. Private consumption, which grew annually at only half a percentage point on average in 2001-2005, has strengthened. In part, the recent gains in consumer spending represent a catching-up process after several years of anaemic growth. Business confidence has also strengthened and employment started to rise for the first time since 2001. Modest wage increases have helped to reverse the decline in competitiveness - a positive development for export prospects. Growing employment bodes well for private consumption. Further improvements in competitiveness could be undermined as labour shortages emerge. Stronger corporate balance sheets alongside export growth are among the factors supporting higher investment.

Main industries The agricultural sector, which accounts for 2.1% of GDP, is larger than in most West European countries. Farms are efficient and farmers benefit from the low-lying and well-irrigated character of the landscape. The Netherlands has a leading position in the world market for horticultural products and is a major exporter of meat and dairy products. The manufacturing sector makes up 13.9% of GDP. Manufacturing is dominated by industries such as engineering, vehicle manufacture, electrical and electronic products, chemicals, aerospace and petrochemicals, all of international importance. Investment initiatives have attracted a wide variety of foreign firms in recent years, including Polaroid, Esso, Dow Chemical, Fuji, Nissan, Engelhardt, Amsco, Thorn EMI and Rank Xerox. The services sector is comparatively large, providing over 70% of GDP. Commercial services account for nearly half of GDP (48%), with public-sector and personal services making up almost a quarter. The financial sector is performing well, though credit quality has deteriorated with the continued expansion of mortgages. The ratio of mortgage debt-to-GDP is high. At the same time, other indicators for banks have been improving. As exports and imports of goods and services each account for well over 65% of nominal GDP, the Dutch economy depends crucially on foreign trade. Rotterdam is Europe's largest port, handling more than twice as much cargo as its nearest European rival, Antwerp. The port's industrial and distribution activities generate annual added value equivalent to around 10% of Dutch GDP. There are also a large number of coastal and international vessels providing cargo services, and an important ship servicing and repair industry exists around Rotterdam.

Energy The Netherlands has experienced a decline in offshore oil production over the past three years. Proved reserves are at 100 million barrels. Many oil fields are nearing the decommissioning stage. The Dutch gas sector is much larger than its oil sector. For years, the Netherlands, along with Russia, has been one of the top natural gas suppliers for Western Europe. Proved reserves are 62 trillion cubic feet. Most of the country's natural gas reserves are located onshore. By law, natural gas production is limited to an estimated 2.68 trillion cubic feet (Tcf) per year, with this ceiling dropping to 2.47 Tcf between 2008 and 2013. The law is intended to maintain reserves for future use.

Norway

Capital city	Oslo
Capital population	560,484 *(2008)*
Population ('000)	4,701.29 *(2008)*
Urban population (%)	82.56 *(2008)*
Land area (sq km)	323,895
Languages	Norwegian
Religion	Evangelical Lutheran church (92%)
Currency	Norwegian krone (NKr)
Head of state	HM King Harald V (1991)
Head of government	Jens Stoltenberg (2005)
Ruling party	The Labour Party leads a three-party coalition.

Main urban areas	Population *(Year)*
Oslo (capital)	560,484 *(2008)*
Bergen	247,746 *(2008)*
Trondheim	165,191 *(2008)*
Stavanger	119,586 *(2008)*
Bærum	108,144 *(2008)*
Kristiansand	77,840 *(2007)*
Fredrikstad	71,297 *(2007)*
Tromso	64,492 *(2007)*
Sandnes	60,507 *(2007)*
Drammen	58,730 *(2007)*

Location Norway occupies almost the entire western half of the peninsula which it shares with Sweden, running southwest from the Arctic Circle to meet up with Denmark across the Skagerrak straits which form the entry from the North Sea to the Baltic Sea. With an almost entirely mountainous geography, and with most of its western coastline characterised by deep-sea inlets (fjords), most of its population live in the southern coastal lowlands. The capital is Oslo.

Political structure The Kingdom of Norway is a constitutional monarchy with executive power vested in a prime minister and cabinet, and legislative authority in a unicameral parliament (the Storting). Parliament's 169 members are elected by proportional representation for a four-year term. For legislative purposes they divide themselves into an Upper and Lower Chamber.

Last elections Parliamentary elections were held in September 2005. The Norwegian Labour Party won 61 seats. Its coalition allies, the Socialists and the Centre Party won 15 and 11 seats respectively. The opposition Progressive Party captured 38 seats. The remaining seats were divided among several parties including the Christian Democrats, the Conservatives and the Liberal Party. Stoltenberg of the Labour Party took over as prime minister.

Economy The Norwegian economy has been one of the world's strongest in recent decades. Growth has been well-balanced with almost all demand components making a solid contribution. Mounting oil wealth has resulted in Norway's per capita income being on a par with that of the US, but this good performance is also due to effective macroeconomic policies. An influx of labour from the new EU member states has helped to slow the rise in wages. These inflows help to contain wage gains but additional wage moderation will crucial to avoid inflationary pressures. The country also enjoys a strong work ethic, as reflected in unusually high participation rates for men and women. Higher oil prices have stimulated a sharp acceleration in investment, boosting demand for goods and services in the mainland economy. Officials have acknowledged that the assets of the general pension fund will not be sufficient to cover future pension obligations.

Main industries Oil has transformed the Norwegian economy, moving ahead of fishing, timber and agriculture as the country's leading industry. Norway's oil and natural gas extraction sector represents about 20% of the country's GDP and employs a similar proportion of the workforce, either directly or indirectly. Agriculture accounts for just over 1.6% of GDP and its share is falling. The sector provides employment for 4% of the work force. Farms tend to be small in size, and have required consistent government aid to survive. Norway is under pressure to reduce the amount of financial aid it provides to its farmers. Agriculture and food processing also enjoy extensive protection from foreign competition. A wave of acquisitions and mergers in the past has led to economies of scale but also a highly concentrated and vertically-integrated retail sector, notably in food. Fishing provides 10% of total exports and is an integral part of the country's political and social culture. Norway brings in around 2.5 million tonnes of fish each year and is the largest supplier in Europe. Manufacturing makes up 9.5% of GDP and contributes about a third of all exports in a typical year. The sector is strongest in engineering, chemicals and timber products as well as oil products. The banking industry is healthy but prolonged rises in credit and house prices pose a risk.

Energy Norway has 7.8 billion barrels of proven oil reserves, the largest in Western Europe. All of Norway's oil reserves are located offshore. Oil production is expected to rise until 2011 and then fall gradually, while gas production should grow rapidly until 2013 before stabilising. The country consumes little of the oil it produces and is the world's third largest exporter. The Norwegian oil fields are in a region that is not readily accessible for smaller independent companies. Project development requires large upfront costs, and high tax rates favour larger fields which produce more, and therefore compensate for Norway's high tax rates (a 28% tax on corporations and a 50% tax on petroleum production). Investment levels reflect expectations that Norway's oil production will remain roughly constant for several years, and then begin a gradual decline. As fields mature, the government has become involved in finding new resources for its companies to develop outside the North Sea region. The country also has 84.3 trillion cubic feet (Tcf) of proven natural gas reserves. The North Sea holds the majority of these reserves, but there are also significant quantities in the Norwegian and Barents Seas. Norway is the eighth-largest natural gas producer in the world.

Poland

Capital city	Warsaw
Capital population	1,704,717 *(2007)*
Population ('000)	38,045.55 *(2008)*
Urban population (%)	61.94 *(2008)*
Land area (sq km)	312,685
Languages	Polish
Religion	Mainly Roman Catholic
Currency	New zloty (PLN)
Head of state	Lech Kaczynski (2005)
Head of government	Donald Tusk (2007)
Ruling party	The Civic Platform Party leads a coalition.

Main urban areas	Population *(Year)*
Warsaw (capital)	1,704,717 *(2007)*
Lódz	756,666 *(2007)*
Kraków	756,336 *(2007)*
Wroclaw	633,950 *(2007)*
Poznan	564,035 *(2007)*
Gdansk	456,103 *(2007)*
Szczecin	408,583 *(2007)*
Bydgoszcz	362,397 *(2007)*
Lublin	352,786 *(2007)*
Katowice	313,461 *(2007)*

Location Poland, one of the largest states in central Europe, extends from the 400-km Baltic coast, bordering Russia and Lithuania in the north, to the Czech and Slovak borders, some 1,200km to the south, and from Germany in the west to Russia, Belarus and Ukraine in the east. The country's terrain is of mixed and mainly agricultural quality. The capital is Warsaw.

Political structure The 1997 constitution provides for executive powers to be shared between the prime minister and the president. The president is elected by popular vote for a five-year term. The National Assembly has two chambers. The Diet (or Sejm) has 460 members, elected for a four-year term. Of these, 391 members are elected by proportional representation in multi-seat constituencies and 69 are selected in a national constituency by proportional representation among parties obtaining more than 7% of the popular vote. The Senate has 100 members elected for a four-year term in 40 multiple-seat constituencies.

Last elections Parliamentary elections were held in October 2007. In the Sejm, the Civic Platform Party took 209 seats, Law and Justice received 166 seats, the Democratic Left Alliance won 53 seats and the Polish Peoples' Party received 31 seats. One seat went to the German Minority. In the Senate, Civic Platform won 60 seats, Law and Justice took 39 seats and one went to an independent. Elections for president were held in October 2005. Lech Kaczynski received 54% of the vote, defeating Donald Tusk.

Economy The economy's record was disappointing during the first half of this decade. The poor performance can be attributed to a combination of factors including a wave of restructuring, particularly in the export-oriented firms, lagging openness to trade, an obsolete infrastructure, and a large government sector. However, a cyclical recovery is now driving the economy. For the first time in years, Poland is enjoying a pattern of balanced growth, rising employment, and a small current account deficit. Large transfers from the EU and greater integration with EU trading partners help to boost investment. Employment is rising strongly and exporters are moving into higher-technology products. Continued growth will require additional increases in investment to raise employment and productivity. In turn, this means that domestic savings and foreign investment inflows must exceed current levels. Meanwhile, the competition for investment and export market shares will be intense. The country's lax fiscal policies have been tightened. Growing labour shortages have been exacerbated by continued emigration to Western Europe.

Main industries The agricultural sector accounts for 4.6% of GDP. A vast majority of farms are uneconomically small, which explains why the rural population has become dependent on government transfers that, on average, represent one third of their income. Under existing laws for land ownership rules, small holders are unwilling to sell their farms – preventing the consolidation that will be essential if agricultural productivity levels are to improve. Inward investment is changing the landscape of the manufacturing sector. Since 2000, Poland has become a major producer of high-end consumer electronics. The country already produces about 20% of Europe's flat-screen monitors and the government estimates that by 2010 around 75% of Europe's television sets will be Polish-made. In 2007, the first cars produced by a joint venture between General Motors and a Ukrainian industrial group rolled of the line. The company intends to add to both its output and workforce through 2010. Poland's location in the centre of Europe gives it ready access to the rest of the continent. Multinational companies dominate exports, particularly in industries such as electronics and automobile production. Car makers, however, export more than 95% of output, making them vulnerable to a downturn in foreign markets. Investment in services, by both foreign and domestic firms, is booming. Poland's transportation system is abysmal with just 3% of all roads meeting EU standards. The number of cars on the road has more than doubled between 1991 and 2007 but the country has only 340 kilometres of expressway. With EU aid set to rise from 2% of GDP to 4%, the government has ambitious plans for improvements in transportation. The energy sector is equally obsolete. Up to 60% of all power generating facilities are more than 30 years old and badly in need of replacement.

Energy With proven oil reserves of only 96 million barrels, Poland produces about 37,600 barrels per day (bbl/d). The country's oil demand is expected to increase by as much as 50% by 2020. Poland has 350,000-bbl/d in refining capacity, the largest in Central Europe. Several of these refineries, however, were built in the 1960s and 1970s and are badly in need of modernisation. There is an estimated 5.8 trillion cubic feet of natural gas reserves and more exploration is actively being conducted. Natural gas, however, is uneconomical for power generation in Poland compared with coal. Poland has the largest coal reserves in the EU. The EU accession treaty requires Poland to liberalise its natural gas market. Along with divesting and unbundling state-owned natural gas companies, the government is required to open the natural gas market to outside competition, thus allowing customers to choose their own supplier. Poland's national supplier relinquished its monopolist position in the natural gas market in 2004.

Portugal

Capital city	Lisbon
Capital population	517,618 *(2007)*
Population ('000)	10,642.64 *(2008)*
Urban population (%)	57.3 *(2008)*
Land area (sq km)	91,630
Languages	Portuguese
Religion	Mainly Roman Catholic
Currency	Euro (€)
Head of state	Anibal Cavaco Silva (2006)
Head of government	José Socrates (2005)
Ruling party	The government is formed by the Socialist Party.

Main urban areas	Population *(Year)*
Lisbon (capital)	517,618 *(2007)*
Vila Nova de Gaia	308,440 *(2007)*
Porto	234,703 *(2007)*
Amadora	177,549 *(2007)*
Braga	175,051 *(2007)*
Coimbra	147,210 *(2007)*
Setúbal	122,256 *(2007)*
Funchal	99,111 *(2007)*

Location Portugal occupies about half of the Atlantic coast on the Iberian peninsula, and more than three quarters of the west-facing section, with Spain, its only immediate neighbour, accounting for the rest. The country extends only a maximum of 200km inland but about 600km from north to south. The Atlantic archipelagos of the Azores and Madeira also belong to Portugal. The terrain is largely mountainous inland, but there are innumerable fertile valleys. The climate is Mediterranean. The capital is Lisbon.

Political structure The Republic of Portugal has an executive president who is elected by universal suffrage for a renewable term of five years and appoints the prime minister. Legislative authority is vested in the unicameral Assembly of the Republic, whose 230 members are elected by universal suffrage to serve four-year terms.

Last elections Presidential elections took place in January 2006. Cavaco Silva, a former prime minister, received 51% of the vote, defeating two other contenders. Elections to the Assembly of the Republic were held in February 2005. The Socialist Party won a majority, taking 120 seats. The Social Democrats received 72 seats, the Portuguese Communists won 14 seats and the Peoples' Party gained 12 seats. The remaining seats were scattered amongst smaller parties.

Economy The economy grew steadily from mid 2005 through 2007 but a slowdown emerged in 2008. Rising investment and an improved export performance were the main supports. Portugal depends on other EU countries for 85% of its export sales and its traditional low-cost, cheap-labour industries have fallen substantially as a percentage of total exports. Their place has been taken by higher value-added, more technologically sophisticated sectors such as car components, electronics and chemicals. These trends are encouraging, but Portuguese exporters also face growing competition from other economies – including new members of the EU – which are following a similar path. Potential output growth is believed to be about half what it was in the second half of the 1990s. Some of the economy's problems include: low levels of labour productivity in most sectors; a misallocation of capital equipment in the business sector and a reluctance to adopt new technologies.

Main industries Portugal has developed an increasingly service-based economy. Agriculture accounts for 2.8% of GDP, a large drop from the 24% it claimed in 1960. However, farming still provides employment for more than 12% of the work force. This reflects the low productivity of the agricultural sector. The main agricultural products include citrus fruits, olives, wines and vegetables. Cork is grown for export, and the country has an important fishery industry. Yet Portugal's farmers are the poorest in the EU. They benefit least from the Common Agricultural Policy because these funds are channelled mainly to meat, dairy and cereal production, which is limited in the country. Tourism is an especially important sector, accounting for 10% of employment. Tourism receipts are rising rapidly and experts predict that Portugal could become the world's 10th largest market by 2020, pulling in 44 million visitors a year. According to these forecasts, tourism will account for nearly 23% of employment in ten years. To achieve this goal, the industry is planning to diversify into new regions and create new attractions. In the past, the country's manufacturing sector has survived on account of low wages. Cheap labour, combined with unrestricted access to the EU market, attracted foreign investment, particularly in the automotive and electronics sectors. The situation may now be changing as investment moves into more sophisticated activities such as computer software and other high-tech operations. Business services have now become more important than exports of cheap textiles and footwear.

Energy Portugal has extremely limited domestic energy resources, and must import about 90% of its energy needs, much of which is oil. The government has been working with Spain towards integrating the two countries' electricity markets in order to create a regional market. Despite decades of exploration activity, Portugal has yet to discover a commercially viable oil deposit. Portugal has two refineries with a combined capacity of 304,000 barrels per day. The natural gas sector has grown considerably in the last few years, although there are no commercially viable reserves. Privatisation in the Portuguese oil sector (nationalised in 1975) began in 1992, but the state retains a controlling share in the country's oil company.

Romania

Capital city	Bucharest
Capital population	1,931,838 *(2007)*
Population ('000)	21,496.61 *(2008)*
Urban population (%)	54.96 *(2008)*
Land area (sq km)	237,500
Languages	Romanian
Religion	Romanian Orthodox, Roman Catholic
Currency	Romanian New Leu (RON)
Head of state	Traian Basescu (2004)
Head of government	Calin Tariceanu (2004)
Ruling party	The government is formed by a minority coalition between the National Liberal Party (PNL) and the Democratic Union of Hungarians in Romania.

Main urban areas	Population *(Year)*
Bucharest (capital)	1,931,838 *(2007)*
Iasi	315,214 *(2007)*
Cluj-Napoca	310,243 *(2007)*
Timisoara	307,347 *(2007)*
Constanta	304,279 *(2007)*
Craiova	299,429 *(2007)*
Galati	293,523 *(2007)*
Brasov	277,945 *(2007)*
Ploiesti	230,240 *(2007)*
Braila	215,316 *(2007)*

Location Romania borders on the Black Sea in the east and Ukraine and Moldova in the north, with Bulgaria in the south and Hungary and Serbia in the west. The capital is Bucharest.

Political structure The country's president is non-executive and answerable to a parliament. Nevertheless, he exercises considerable influence. The president is elected for a four-year term by the people. Parliament has two chambers. The Chamber of Deputies has 332 members, elected for four-year terms on the basis of a list system and independent candidatures by the principle of proportional representation. The Senate has 137 members, elected for four-year terms by proportional representation.

Last elections Presidential elections were held in November 2004 when Traian Basescu defeated Adrian Nastase, the prime minister.

Basescu received 51.2% of the vote. Elections to the Chamber of Deputies took place in November 2004. A coalition made from the former Social Democratic Party and the Humanist Party of Romania won 132 seats. The Justice and Truth Alliance (formed from the National Liberal Party in alliance with the Democratic Party) won 112 seats, the Democratic Union of Hungarians in Romania took 22 seats, and the Great Romanian Party 48 seats. The remaining seats were scattered amongst smaller parties. Elections to the Senate were held at the same time. The Social Democratic Party in combination with the Romanian Humanist Party took 57 seats while the Justice & Truth Alliance was awarded 49 seats. The remainder were taken by several smaller parties.

Economy Romania's approach to its transition to a market economy was initially hesitant and piecemeal. However, the country has made considerable progress in recent years, culminating in EU membership in 2007. Foreign and domestic investment surged after entry in the EU. Fiscal tightening and a reduction in the losses of state-owned enterprises brought down the annual inflation rate in the first half of this decade. Upward pressures on prices are mounting again, however, and inflation should be higher in 2008. The economy still has a long way to go. Romania has the lowest income per capita in central Europe, the worst environmental standards, the largest tax arrears, the most pervasive corruption and the lowest education spending. Unreported, untaxed economic activity is estimated to represent nearly half of real GDP.

Main industries The share of the agricultural sector has contracted significantly since the end of the Cold War but the sector still provides employment for a third of the workforce. Private ownership of farmland makes up almost three quarters of the total. There are several million subsistence and semi-subsistence farms. Most will disappear as funds from the EU begin to modernise the sector. Agricultural output fell in 2007 owing to drought and no significant recovery is expected in 2008. The manufacturing sector's share of GDP has also fallen from 39% in 1990 to less than 23% today. The share of traditional industries such as textiles and shoes is declining while that of automakers, car parts and engineering products is rising. Dacia, owned by Renault, has experienced unexpected success. Altogether, the company has invested more than €650 million in the country. Other foreign investors, including Hewlett-Packard, are investing. A shortage of skilled and semi-skilled workers has forced some companies to recruit and import workers from elsewhere. Industrial activity should remain buoyant 2008. The mining sector is of special concern because it is the source of most resistance to economic reform. Mines producing copper, lead, zinc, gold, silver and coal require substantial subsidies. Tourism accounts for just 1% of GDP (compared to 5% in Hungary) but the number of visitors is rising very fast. At present, Romania is not ready for the influx, though many new, up-market facilities are being planned. The transportation infrastructure (particularly roadways) remains in poor shape.

Energy With proven reserves of 600 million barrels, Romania is largest oil producer in Central and Eastern Europe. However, production has fallen precipitously over the past two decades. Romania dominates South-eastern Europe's downstream petroleum industry. Several of its refineries were privatised in 2005 and 2006. Capacity far exceeds domestic demand for refined petroleum products, allowing the country to export a wide range of oil products and petrochemicals. However, years of low investment have left the country's refining industry in poor health, requiring massive amounts of capital to modernise and improve efficiency. Romania is central and eastern Europe's largest producer of natural gas. The country has natural gas reserves of 2.2 trillion cubic feet and a sizeable domestic market. A number of pipeline projects are planned to increase natural gas transport capacity.

Russia

Capital city	Moscow
Capital population	10,470,318 (2008)
Population ('000)	141,386.12 (2008)
Urban population (%)	73.97 (2008)
Land area (sq km)	17,075,400
Languages	Russian
Religion	Mainly Christian (Russian Orthodox)
Currency	Russian Roubles (Rb)
Head of state	Dmitry Medvedev (2008)
Head of government	Vladimir Putin (2008)
Ruling party	The government is formed by the United Russia Party and non-partisan technocrats.

Main urban areas	Population (Year)
Moscow (capital)	10,470,318 (2008)
St Petersburg	4,568,047 (2008)
Novosibirsk	1,391,900 (2008)
Ekaterinburg	1,315,100 (2008)
Nishniy Novgorod	1,278,300 (2008)
Samara	1,139,000 (2008)
Omsk	1,134,700 (2008)
Kazan	1,116,000 (2008)
Chelyabinsk	1,091,500 (2008)
Rostov-na-Donu	1,051,600 (2008)

Location Russia, the largest state in Asia, extends nearly 9,000km from the Finnish border in the west to the Bering Straits in the east. The vast terrain ranges from the Arctic wastes of the north to the Caspian Sea in the south. The capital is Moscow.

Political structure The executive president is elected by universal suffrage to a four year term, and answers to a Federal Assembly comprising two chambers: the 168-member Federation Council which includes two members from each administrative unit within the federation, and the 450-member State Duma, elected for a four-year terms. There is also a prime minister, who is appointed by the president on the Duma's recommendations.

Last elections In March 2008, Medvedev was elected president with 70.2% of the vote. His nearest rival was Gennady Zyuganov who received 17.7%. There were charges of vote rigging. Elections to the Duma took place in December 2007. The United Russia Party won 315 of the 450 seats, while the Communist Party took 57 seats. The Liberal Democratic Party won 40 seats and the Fair Russia Party gained 38 seats. Vladimir Putin, the previous president, was appointed as prime minister in May 2008.

Economy The average rate of growth has exceeded 5% since 2000 and is currently close to economic potential. A combination of rising incomes and higher consumption drives the economy. Productivity is improving as labour moves to more productive sectors. In addition to oil, Russia has the world's fifth largest gold reserves and is one of the ten largest economies. The number living below the official poverty line is still high at 22 million but has fallen by 20 million since 2000. Although the middle-income class has grown substantially, the number is still matched by those living in poverty. Russia has become much more integrated into the global economy but its many critics refer to it as a "petro-state". Policy makers pay lip service to reforms such as removing barriers to competition and reducing administration pressures on the economy, but more and more strategic assets are being returned to state control.

Main industries Agriculture contributes just under 5% to GDP and is nominally privatised. Output has been rising but farm production is still below the levels it was a decade ago. Farmers have suffered greatly because of the debt write-offs provided to state farms. Manufacturing accounts for almost 19% of GDP. Manufacturers have been hurt by rapid wage growth, capacity constraints and expansion of the state sector. Many firms, however, began to recover in 2007 when important new markets emerged in China, India and the former Soviet republics. Moscow expects car makers to invest more than US$2 billion by 2010 with new companies capturing more than

50% of the market. There are massive mineral and forest resources with iron ore, copper, aluminium, manganese, salt and precious metals all being produced, though facilities are in need of modernisation. Oil and gas account for 25% of GDP and 65% of exports but employ less than 1% of the population. Raw materials, such as oil, natural gas, and metals, make up more than two-thirds of all export revenues. However, the state has gained direct control over most natural resources (and especially energy) and will only allow foreign minority partners in on a selective basis. Russia's retail sector is exploding. The banking system is still tumultuous and murky but attracts foreign investors because the country is regarded as severely "underbanked". Banks have no sub-prime exposure and appear to be weathering the present international crisis successfully. Credit is growing at more than 40% per year. With average incomes rising, more than 100,000 families become "bankable" every year.

Energy Russia is the world's 8th largest exporter of oil. It has proven oil reserves of 60 billion barrels. Oil production was just over 9.8 million barrels per day (bbl/d) in 2008. New fields will produce almost all of Russia's annual oil growth in the next five years and will likely produce more than half of the country's oil in 2020. Russia holds the world's largest natural gas reserves, with 1,680 trillion cubic feet – nearly twice the reserves in the next largest country, Iran. The country is the world's largest natural gas producer, as well as the world's largest exporter. But unlike the Russian oil industry, the natural gas industry is not growing. Both production and consumption have remained relatively flat since independence. Output of natural gas is projected to grow slowly through 2009 and then begin a steep decline.

Serbia and Montenegro

Capital city	Belgrade
Capital population	1,106,000 (2005)
Population ('000)	10,477.45 (2008)
Urban population (%)	73.97 (2008)
Land area (sq km)	102,173
Languages	Serbo-Croat
Religion	Mainly Christian (Serbian Orthodox)
Currency	Dinar (YUD)
Head of state	President of Serbia Boris Tadic (2008); President of Montenegro Filip Vujanovic (2002); President of Kosovo Fatmir Sejdiu (2006)
Head of government	Prime Minister of Serbia Mirko Cvetkovic (2008); Prime Minister of Montenegro Milo Djukanovic (2008); Prime Minister of Kosovo Hashim Thaci (2008)
Ruling party	Serbia: The Democratic Party for a European Serbia leads a coalition with the Socialist Party and several ethnic minority representatives. Montenegro: the ruling Coalition for European Montenegro coalition includes the Democratic Party of Socialists (DPS), the Social Democratic Party (SDP) and others. Kosovo: a frequently changing coalition leads the government.

Main urban areas	Population (Year)
Belgrade (capital)	1,106,000 (2005)
Novi Sad	243,232 (2003)
Niš	174,092 (2003)
Priština	165,844 (2004)
Kragujevac	146,568 (2003)
Podgorica	139,724 (2004)
Subotica	108,714 (2003)
Prizren	107,614 (2004)

Location Serbia's northern border is with Hungary and on its eastern side are Romania and Bulgaria, and Croatia is to its northwest. In the centre of the region is Belgrade, the capital. Kosovo is bordered by Macedonia and Albania in the south, Montenegro in the west and by Serbia in the north and east. In addition to its shared border with Serbia, Montenegro borders on Bosnia-Herzegovina to the north and Albania to the south. Podgorica is the capital of Montenegro.

Political structure The Union of Serbia and Montenegro was created in 2003. Both states functioned as parliamentary democratic republics until 2006 when Montenegro voted for independence from Serbia by a narrow margin. Serbia's National Assembly has 250 members, elected to four-year terms. Montenegro's Assembly of the Republic has 82 members who serve four-year terms. The president of Montenegro is elected for a period of five years. The Assembly of Kosovo has 120 members elected for a four-year term. It includes ten seats reserved for Kosovo Serbs and ten reserved for non-Serb minorities.

Last elections Voters elected Boris Tadic as president of Serbia in February 2008. He defeated Tomislav Nikolic, receiving 50.3% of the vote. Elections to the Serbian parliament were held in May 2008. The Democratic Party for a European Serbia won 102 seats, the Serbian Radical Party won 78 seats, the Democratic Party took 30 seats, the Socialist Party received 20 seats, and the Liberal Democratic Party took 13 seats. The remainder were scattered among several smaller parties. Presidential elections in Montenegro were held in April 2008. Filip Vujanovic was returned to office with 52% of the vote. The first legislative elections since Montenegro became independent were held in September 2006. The Coalition for European Montenegro won 41 seats. Another 12 seats went to the Serb List while the Movement for Change took 11 seats as did the coalition of the Socialist Peoples' Party, the Peoples Party and the Democratic Serbian Party. The remaining seats were taken by the Liberals and the Bosnian Party. Željko Šturanovic resigned as prime minister due to health reasons in January 2008. He was replaced by Milo Djukanovic, who had previously served as prime minister.

Economy Serbia's economy has seen growth of 6% or more over the past four years. The Belgrade area has won some of the largest greenfield investments by foreign companies in south-eastern Europe. Unemployment remains high and is reportedly rising. Fixed investment is increasing but is still less than 20% of GDP. The share of the private sector has risen significantly. Montenegro's economic growth has been strong and the level of international reserves is comfortable but there are inflationary pressures and the current account deficit (over 32.7% of GDP in 2008) is large. The deficit is mainly due to the rapid inflow of FDI and low savings rates.

Main industries Agriculture is the largest sector of both economies, with fruits, vegetables and tobacco of particular importance. Serbia's farmers expect a much better harvest in 2008 than in recent years. Industrial output in Serbia rose by 4-5% in 2007. The most dynamic industries in Montenegro are machinery and chemicals. Producers of food, textiles and wood products have all contracted. Serbia's textile industry – without an association agreement – is also doing poorly. The Serbian government intends to increase its investments in the railway and road system significantly beginning in 2009. In Montenegro, tourism is expanding rapidly with strong investor support. The industry already accounts for around 15% of Montenegro's GDP and employs 22,000. Investment of €60 million is underway and revenues are expected to triple in the next decade. Arrivals have risen in recent years and the length of stay has increased. The entry of foreign banks is transforming Serbia's financial sector. As confidence grows, cash is finding its way back into the financial system. Montenegro's banking industry has been radically restructured.

Energy Serbia has 78 million barrels of oil reserves and produces small amounts each year. The country's oil company was privatised in 2003. The Serbian region near Pozarevac is believed to contain hydrocarbons. However, most oil is imported, primarily via the Adria pipeline. These facilities were all damaged during the war. In Montenegro, energy shortages slow economic growth.

Slovakia

Capital city	Bratislava
Capital population	426,091 *(2007)*
Population ('000)	5,393.60 *(2008)*
Urban population (%)	56.49 *(2008)*
Land area (sq km)	49,035
Languages	Czech, Slovak
Religion	Predominately Catholic
Currency	Slovak Koruny (SKK)
Head of state	Ivan Gašparovic (2004)
Head of government	Robert Fico (2006)
Ruling party	The Direction – Social Democracy Party (Smer) leads a three-party coalition.

Main urban areas	Population *(Year)*
Bratislava (capital)	426,091 *(2007)*
Kosice	234,596 *(2007)*
Presov	91,650 *(2007)*
Zilina	85,425 *(2006)*
Nitra	85,172 *(2006)*
Banska Bystrica	81,281 *(2006)*
Trnava	68,828 *(2006)*
Martin	59,257 *(2006)*
Trencin	56,750 *(2006)*
Poprad	55,158 *(2006)*

Location Slovakia, which was linked until January 1993 in a federation with the Czech Republic, is located in central Europe, south east of Germany and south of Poland, but to the north of Austria and Hungary. The Czech Republic lies to the west. The climate is temperate, with occasionally harsh winters. The capital is Bratislava.

Political structure From 1919 until the end of 1992 Slovakia was part of a federation with the Czech Republic. At the start of 1993 the two countries began an independent existence. The president is elected for a five-year term by the people. The National Council of the Slovak Republic has 150 members, elected for four-year terms by proportional representation.

Last elections In presidential elections held in April 2004, Gašparovic defeated the ex-prime minister, Vladimir Meciar, garnering 59.9% of the vote. Parliamentary elections were held in June 2006. The Direction – Social Democracy Party won 50 seats, the Slovak Democratic and Christian Union took 31 seats, the Slovak National Party received 20 seats as did the Party of the Hungarian Coalition, the Peoples Party gained 15 seats and the Christian Democratic Movement took 14 seats.

Economy Over the past few years, Slovakia has been one of central Europe's strongest economic performers. Per capita income is still only 70% of the EU average but a speedy catch-up is still possible. In November 2005, Slovakia joined the ERM II, the preparatory stage for adoption of the euro. The government hopes to make this move in 2009. There is an obvious need to push for smaller and more effective government, against a strong constituency in favour of maintaining the status quo which includes a large share of general government jobs in total employment. The Slovak economy suffers one of the lowest employment rates in the OECD area. Unemployment is concentrated among the low-skilled, the young and the elderly in the eastern part of the country. The number of jobless remains high but is falling. However, the long-term unemployment rate is the highest of all OECD countries.

Main industries The country's agricultural sector is comparatively small. Major crops are grains (wheat, barley and corn), oilseeds, potatoes, sugar beets, fruits and vegetables. One bright spot for Slovakia has been the recent inflow of foreign direct investment, much of it from carmakers. Peugeot will invest €1.1 billion in a plant that will begin production in 2009 while Kia plans investments of €835 million. Already, Volkswagen alone accounts for one-fifth of Slovakia's exports. By 2008, Slovakia is forecast to be producing a million cars per year in a country with just 5.4 million people. The automobile makers' exports should account for about 30% of the country's total in 2007. The main attraction for investors is the combination of low wage rates and guaranteed access to the EU. Slovakian wages are just a fifth of those in Western Europe. Tourism receipts presently contribute around 2% to GDP but lack the necessary infrastructure. There is no tourism ministry and transportation links are poor. Banks continue to lend vigorously, showing no effects from the credit crunch in many countries. More than 90% of the banking industry is foreign-owned.

Energy Slovakia's oil reserves amount to only 9 million barrels. Production is equally miniscule, only about 8,850 barrels per day. Slovakia has limited amounts of natural gas but is very important as a transit country. It is estimated that about 25% of the natural gas consumed in West Europe transits through the country. This represents about 70% of the Russian natural gas exported to Western Europe. Slovakia's natural gas market is being liberalised in stages. The country has two nuclear power plants, which generate about 60% of its electricity. The two oldest reactors are due to be decommissioned as part of the energy chapter of Slovakia's accession agreement with the EU. However, some government officials oppose that decision. A reversal of the agreement would be strongly opposed by neighbouring Austria. Slovakia is self-sufficient in coal and lignite. These two fuels account for two-thirds of the country's total energy requirements.

Slovenia

Capital city	Ljubljana
Capital population	260,183 *(2008)*
Population ('000)	2,016.50 *(2008)*
Urban population (%)	51.07 *(2008)*
Land area (sq km)	20,254
Languages	Slovenian
Religion	Mainly Roman Catholic
Currency	Euro (€)
Head of state	Danilo Turk (2007)
Head of government	Janez Jansa (2004)
Ruling party	The Slovenian Democrats (SD) lead a four-party coalition.

Main urban areas	Population *(Year)*
Ljubljana (capital)	260,183 *(2008)*
Maribor	93,584 *(2008)*
Celje	38,408 *(2008)*
Kranj	36,071 *(2008)*
Velenje	26,826 *(2008)*
Koper-Capodistria	24,568 *(2008)*
Novo Mesto	22,849 *(2008)*
Ptuj	18,338 *(2008)*
Trbovlje	15,732 *(2008)*
Nova Gorica	13,290 *(2008)*

Location Slovenia lies in the far north of the former Yugoslav Federation. Austria lies to the north of the country, Italy to the west, Hungary to the east and Croatia to the south. The capital is Ljubljana.

Political structure Slovenia declared its independence in June 1991. The president, who has a mainly ceremonial function, is elected by universal suffrage for a five-year once-renewable period. He proposes a prime minister. The State Chamber has 90 members, elected for a four year term; 40 seats are directly elected, and 50 selected by proportional representation. Two seats of the 90 seats are set aside for ethnic minorities. The State Council has 40 members: 18 members representing local councillors and 22 members representing commercial and non-commercial interests.

Last elections Elections to the National Assembly were held in September 2008. The Slovenian Democrats gained 29 seats, the Slovenian Democratic Party took 28 seats, the New Politics Party won 9 and the Democratic Party of Pensioners received 7 seats. Smaller parties accounted for the remainder. Turk was elected as president in November 2007 with 68% of the vote.

Economy Before accession, Slovenia's per capita GDP (at purchasing power parities) reached about 50% of the EU average. But in the 25-country group that includes so many poorer countries, that figure has risen to about 85%. At this level, Slovenia is not eligible for structural funds given to the EU's poorest regions. The economy grew at a rate above economic potential from 2005 until mid-2007, raising concerns about inflation. However, most observers agree that the country must attract more foreign investment to support the growth of domestic companies. The relatively slow growth in productivity suggests that Slovenia is not moving up the technology ladder fast enough. While there is evidence of increasing specialisation into high-tech sectors, the pace of export-quality upgrading lags behind other countries in the region. Although wages are high, the quality of production and firms' export successes attest to Slovenia's competitiveness. Unemployment is low compared with most members of the EU. Labour costs are estimated to be 53% of the EU average, the highest among the accession countries.

Main industries Slovenia's economic profile resembles those of Western countries to a much greater extent than is true in other parts of Eastern Europe. Agriculture accounts for only 2.5% of GDP, the smallest share among the central European countries. The country's farmers are very productive, with large surpluses of maize, wheat, sugar beet and potatoes being produced. Manufacturing makes up 24.6% of GDP, down from 33.0% in 1990. Slovenia's manufacturers have an impressive record in exploiting niche markets abroad and their exports are very important to the overall health of the economy. EU membership has accelerated the decline of textiles, furniture-making and food processing but the elimination of customs checks at borders has helped other companies prosper. The country has not done well in attracting FDI, however. Slovenia missed the 1990s wave of investment in manufacturing. The banking system is sound, but still largely state-owned and comparatively inefficient. Profits are under pressure in an increasingly competitive environment. The rapid growth of credit to enterprises is increasing risk.

Energy Slovenia has some coal, but must import most of its primary energy. It is for this reason that the country usually runs a trade deficit.

Spain

Capital city	Madrid
Capital population	3,132,463 *(2007)*
Population ('000)	45,056.37 *(2008)*
Urban population (%)	77.05 *(2008)*
Land area (sq km)	504,880
Languages	Spanish (Castilian, Catalan, Galician), Basque
Religion	Mainly Roman Catholic
Currency	Euro (€)
Head of state	HM King Juan Carlos (1975)
Head of government	José Luis Rodriguez Zapatero (2004)
Ruling party	Spanish Socialist Workers Party (PSOE)

Main urban areas	Population *(Year)*
Madrid (capital)	3,132,463 *(2007)*
Barcelona	1,595,110 *(2007)*
Valencia	797,654 *(2007)*
Sevilla	699,145 *(2007)*
Zaragoza	654,390 *(2007)*
Malaga	561,250 *(2007)*
Murcia	422,861 *(2007)*
Palma de Mallorca	383,107 *(2007)*
Palmas de las Gran Canaria	377,203 *(2007)*
Bilbao	353,168 *(2007)*

Location Spain occupies the greater part of the Iberian Peninsula with coastal orientations in all four directions. Its only neighbours are Portugal, which it surrounds on both its land borders, and France. It is a co-administrator of Andorra. The territory also includes the Balearic Islands (in the Mediterranean), the Canary Islands and the Moroccan enclaves of Ceuta and Melilla. The capital is Madrid.

Political structure Spain is a constitutional monarchy in which the King plays a relatively modest political role. There is a 350-member Congress of Deputies (Lower House) elected for four years, and a Senate with 248 members. In the Senate, 208 members are elected for a four year term in four-member constituencies, with 40 members designated by the regional legislatures. The administrative regions have been extensively reorganised to create 17 autonomous regions, including Andalusia, Catalonia and the Basque country.

Last elections Parliamentary elections were held in March 2008. In the Senate, the People's Party won 100 seats, the Spanish Socialist Workers Party took 88 seats and the remainder was divided among small parties and regional interests. In the Congress of Deputies the Spanish Socialist Workers Party received 169 seats whilst the People's Party and its allies won 153 seats. Catalan nationalists took 11 seats, Basque nationalists received 6 seats and the reformed communists won 2 seats. Remaining seats were divided among minor parties. The PSOE rules without the aid of a coalition, but often requires the cooperation of smaller parties to pass legislation.

Economy Before the present downturn, the Spanish economy grew steadily for ten consecutive years, making it one of the best-performing economies in the EU. Spain was a major exporter of people in the 1960s and 1970s but during the present decade it has emerged as the largest recipient of immigrants in the EU. The Spanish economy has generated more than half of all new jobs in the Eurozone in recent years but as the economy slumps unemployment has reached double digits. More than €100 billion in FDI has poured into Spain since the mid-1990s. Spanish multinationals have also become foreign investors in their own right. The country became a net exporter of capital as well as a net importer of immigrant labour in recent years. In 2008, however, foreign investment plummeted. Over the last few years, however, economic growth became increasingly lopsided and imbalances have worsened. The current account deficit has risen to unsustainable levels. The rising deficit reflects in part higher oil prices, weakening demand in traditional export markets, and Spain's rising investment.

Main industries Agriculture continues to be a very important sector, but water shortages plague many farmers. Fruits, nuts, olives, tomatoes and peppers are the main export products. Growth of industrial output stagnated in 2008 after rising in 2006 and 2007. Major industries include electronics, steel, chemicals, fertilisers, food, wine and tobacco products, leather goods and timber products. Most important, however, is the car industry – Spanish carmakers manufacture around two million cars per year. Production is now being cut back as the market for automobiles weakens. Recent increases in labour costs have eroded the competitiveness of some other manufacturers. Spain's construction and real estate groups are among the largest in Europe following a 10-year building boom but both started to contract in 2008. Approximately 300,000 construction workers lost their jobs in 2008. Tourism, which accounts for 5% of GDP, is a key economic sector though growth has slowed owing in part to the strength of the euro. Nevertheless, Spain remains the second most popular tourist destination in the world. The industry employs roughly one in 10 of the workforce. Around 80% of the visitors to Spain are Europeans. The banking sector has been hurt by the international credit crisis and growing uncertainty at home, but the system is sound.

Energy Spain has a limited amount of proven domestic crude oil reserves – 150 million barrels in 2006. Its crude oil production is also marginal, averaging just 3,000 barrels per day. Exploration is underway for oil and natural gas in two offshore regions, though preliminary results are disappointing. The government's 10-year energy plan depends heavily on natural gas and renewable energy. These two sources are projected to account for 22.5% and 12.0%, respectively, of Spain's primary energy consumption by 2011. Spain has only 90 billion cubic feet of proven natural gas reserves and natural gas production is insignificant.

Sweden

Capital city	Stockholm
Capital population	795,163 *(2008)*
Population ('000)	9,157.12 *(2008)*
Urban population (%)	83.64 *(2008)*
Land area (sq km)	449,790
Languages	Swedish
Religion	Evangelical Lutheran Church (95%)
Currency	Swedish krona (SEK)
Head of state	HM King Carl Gustaf XVI (1973)
Head of government	Fredrik Reinfeldt (2006)
Ruling party	A four-party coalition, the Alliance for Sweden, leads the government.

Main urban areas	Population *(Year)*
Stockholm (capital)	795,163 *(2008)*
Gothenburg	493,502 *(2008)*
Malmo	280,801 *(2008)*
Uppsala	187,541 *(2008)*
Linkoping	140,367 *(2008)*
Vasteras	133,728 *(2008)*
Orebro	130,429 *(2008)*
Norrkoping	126,680 *(2008)*
Helsingborg	124,986 *(2008)*
Jonkoping	123,709 *(2008)*

Location Sweden occupies the eastern and southern section of the Scandinavian Peninsula which runs southwest from the Arctic Circle to meet with Denmark across the narrow sea channel which gives access to the Baltic from the North Sea. The terrain is predominantly hilly and mountainous. The main population centres are in the south and east. The capital is Stockholm.

Political structure Sweden is a constitutional monarchy in which the King appoints the prime minister on the basis of parliamentary advice. Legislative authority is vested in a unicameral 349-seat Parliament (Riksdag), which is elected by universal suffrage for a term of four years. Sweden became a full member of the EU in January 1995 after having been in the European Monetary System for many years.

Last elections General elections were held in September 2006. The Workers' Party-Social Democrats won 130 seats, the Moderate Coalition Party received 97 seats and the Liberal People's Party took 28 seats. The remainder were scattered amongst several other parties. Altogether, the centre-right coalition known as the Alliance for Sweden will have a majority of seats. In September 2003, voters rejected the government's plan to adopt the euro.

Economy A strong economic upswing occurred during 2004-2007, outpacing the eurozone by a wide margin. Since then, the pace of growth has slowed owing to global uncertainties and capacity constraints at home. Private consumption is weakening but should continue to be the main driving force for growth. The share of household consumption in GDP has been steadily falling for the past several decades while the share of trade (both exports and imports) has been rising. These secular trends are a reflection of the increasing globalisation of the economy. By some measures, the degree of Sweden's globalisation is second only to that of the US. Economists estimate that more than a fifth of the working-age population is economically inactive. It is this problem that has prompted the current government's ambitious reform of labour market policies.

Main industries Agriculture accounts for 1.6% of GDP, while manufacturing makes up 19.5%. The public sector accounts for around 30% of all services in Sweden. Farming is the main livelihood in large parts of the country, especially in the north, though elsewhere forestry and related products are the mainstays of the local economy. Sweden is a leader in mobile phone usage and development of the mobile internet. Biotechnology is another important emerging industry. The country's automotive trio (Volvo, Saab and Scania) have reorganised, consolidated some operations and sold off others in order to better compete in international markets. A weakening of foreign demand in pharmaceuticals and telecoms has put pressure on these industries. Growth of industrial output has been slowing in 2008, in part owing to the sector's heavy dependence on exports. The service sector is the fastest-growing in the economy but retail sales are slumping. Household debt has been rising in recent years and, at around 120% of disposable income, is relatively high. Swedish banks have little exposure to the sub-prime crisis but are highly vulnerable to the problems in the Baltic States.

Energy Sweden has no indigenous fuels except for its hydroelectric energy. The country is one of four in the EU that have proclaimed the intention to phase out its nuclear plants by the year 2010. One reactor was shut in 1999 but with no economic alternatives the government decided to postpone the closing of a second reactor. Sweden is one of seven EU countries to have completely opened its electricity market to competition in compliance with EU rules. In a normal year, about half of the country's electric power is produced by 12 commercial nuclear reactors.

Switzerland

Capital city	Berne
Capital population	122,422 *(2007)*
Population ('000)	7,530.08 *(2008)*
Urban population (%)	68.28 *(2008)*
Land area (sq km)	41,285
Languages	German, French, Italian, Romansch
Religion	Roman Catholic (47.6%); Protestant (44.3%)
Currency	Swiss franc (CHF)
Head of state	Pascal Couchepin (2008)
Head of government	Pascal Couchepin (2008)
Ruling party	A four-party coalition agreed by formula leads the government.

Main urban areas	Population *(Year)*
Zurich	350,125 *(2007)*
Geneva	178,603 *(2007)*
Basel	163,081 *(2007)*
Berne (capital)	122,422 *(2007)*
Lausanne	118,049 *(2007)*
Winterthur	94,709 *(2007)*
St Gallen	70,375 *(2007)*
Lucerne	57,890 *(2007)*
Lugano	49,719 *(2007)*
Biel	49,038 *(2007)*

Location Centrally located in southern Europe, Switzerland's three official languages (French, German and Italian) reflect its three most important neighbours. Switzerland represents Liechtenstein at diplomatic level. The capital is Bern.

Political structure Switzerland is a federation of 20 cantons and six half-cantons which include German, French, Italian and Romansch speakers. The first three of these are official languages, while Romansch is a "semi-official" language. There is a high degree of political devolution. There is a 200-member National Council elected by a system of proportional representation and a 46-member Council of States elected by simple majority in the cantons. Members of both bodies serve four-year terms. At the federal level, the executive president is elected every year by the National Council from among the seven-member Cabinet.

Last elections Elections to the National Council took place in October 2007. The Swiss People's Party received 62 seats, the SPS took 43 seats and the Radical Free Democratic Party gained 31 seats as did the Christian Democratic People's Party. The Green Party won 20 seats and the remainder were scattered amongst several minor parties. Elections to the Council of States were held at the same time. The Christian Democratic People's Party received 14 seats, the Radical Free Democratic Party won 11 seats, the Social Democratic Party gained 9 seats and the Swiss People's Party took 7 seats. The remainder went to the Green Party. Members of both the National

Council and the Council of States elected Couchepin as president in January 2008.

Economy The economy has outperformed the average for Eurozone countries since 2004. GDP per capita is one of the highest in the western world. The financial sector accounts for almost half of all growth. Analysts see the country's slow gains in productivity as the main source of problems. In the longer term, the main challenge is to increase the economy's potential rate of growth, mainly by raising productivity. Substantial efforts are needed to deal with the serious shortcomings in the functioning of the product markets, which are reflected in the very high level of prices compared with other countries.

Main industries Switzerland's agricultural sector is small and relatively inefficient. Since the mid-1990s, the level of support to agriculture has been one of the highest among industrialised countries. A lack of foreign competition leads to higher food prices than abroad and funnels resources into low-productivity activities. The country's 73,000 farmers derive 75% of their farming income from subsidies. Tourism, especially winter sports, is one of the most important parts of the economy but faces intense competition from other tourist-based countries. Financial services account for about 12% of GDP. Banks are well capitalised but have been hard-hit by the global crisis. The country's leading banks reported huge losses in 2008. In 2005, the country began to voluntarily levy a withholding tax on EU residents' savings and transfer the proceeds to their home tax authorities in return for the preservation of client confidentiality. The move has pushed up costs in the Swiss private banking market. The number of banks in Switzerland could fall in the coming few years as pressures increase. The large insurance sector has a good track record, but strains are emerging. Several Swiss multinationals (particularly in pharmaceutical and precision engineering) are among the world's leaders but generate the bulk of their profits outside the country. The overseas investments of these huge companies exceed the size of the domestic economy and are an important reason for the country's high standard of living. These companies are already well entrenched in the EU and the fact that Switzerland is not an EU member presents no problem for them as it does for small and medium-sized companies.

Energy Switzerland has no indigenous fuel sources apart from its hydroelectric potential and is forced to rely on nuclear power to an unusual degree. All other fuels are imported.

Turkey

Capital city	Ankara
Capital population	3,763,591 *(2008)*
Population ('000)	74,357.78 *(2008)*
Urban population (%)	68.82 *(2008)*
Land area (sq km)	779,450
Languages	Turkish
Religion	Islam (99%)
Currency	Turkish new lira (YTL)
Head of state	Abdullah Gul (2007)
Head of government	Recep Tayyip Erdogan (2002)
Ruling party	The Justice and Development Party (AKP) leads the government.

Main urban areas	Population *(Year)*
Istanbul	10,757,327 *(2008)*
Ankara (capital)	3,763,591 *(2008)*
Izmir	2,606,294 *(2008)*
Bursa	1,431,172 *(2008)*
Adana	1,366,027 *(2008)*
Gaziantep	1,175,042 *(2008)*
Konya	967,055 *(2008)*
Antalya	775,157 *(2008)*
Mersin	623,861 *(2008)*

Location With control over both banks of the Bosporus, Turkey controls access to the Black Sea. The country has a land border with

Greece and Bulgaria to the west. In the southeast it meets with Syria and Iraq, while the eastern border meets with Iran and in the northeast it borders Georgia and Armenia. The capital is Ankara.

Political structure Turkey's president is elected by popular vote for seven years by parliament. The country has a unicameral Grand National Assembly with 550 members, elected for a five-year term by mitigated proportional representation with a barrier of 10%. Although Islam is dominant, the country has been secular since 1919. The Kurdish Democracy Party was banned in 1994 after a series of terrorist attacks.

Last elections Parliamentary elections were held in July 2007. The AKP, led by Erdogan won 341 seats while the Republican Peoples Party took 112 seats and the Nationalist Movement Party received 71 seats. The remaining seats are held by independents.

Economy In 2001, Turkey suffered perhaps the worst economic crisis in its history. Since then, the economy has averaged growth of well over 6% per year, raising output by a third. The boom was supported by strong growth in emerging markets. Many jobs were created in both industry and services while labourers left the agricultural sector. Annual growth in productivity has surged from 3.8% in the 1990s to an annual rate of more than 10%. Today, there is also a better balance in terms of the sources of growth. Modern industries have flourished but traditional industries which rely on the country's plentiful supply of unskilled labour have suffered. Net job creation is woefully inadequate given the many new entrants to the job market each year. These consequences were accentuated when the economy's performance began to deteriorate in the latter part of 2007and 2008.

Main industries Agriculture accounts for about 10.6% of GDP. Much of the population works in agriculture, cultivating grapes, fruit, barley, cotton and other products. Farmers suffered in 2007 and 2008 owing to the effects of a drought. Manufacturing makes up more than 22% of GDP and output and exports are steadily rising. The textile industry is often referred to as the country's "economic engine". The industry is dominated by clothes manufactures and accounts for nearly 40% of total exports (most of it to the EU). Textile exports have slumped as demand in foreign markets has weakened. Turkey has become a production hub for the automobile industry with new investments being implemented by Renault, Fiat, Hyundai and Toyota. Most of the new production is destined for the EU. However, there is an ever-present threat from cheaper competitors based in India and China. The government's goal is to establish the country as a centre for product design and research and development in the car industry. The tourist industry is thriving after exceptional profits in the past few years. The growth of credit has slowed but still remains high. Meanwhile, there have been important reforms to the banking system. Ankara continues to push its privatisation programme.

Energy Turkey has 300 million barrels of proven oil reserves and is currently producing around 43,000 barrels per day (bbl/d), down from 90,000 in the 1990s. Many oil fields are old and inefficient. However, there are oil prospects in Turkey's European provinces, in the Black Sea shelf region, and in other oil basins in southern and southeastern Turkey. Turkey also has 300 billion cubic feet of proven natural gas reserves. The country is in the midst of a large-scale exploration for oil and gas in the Black Sea and Mediterranean. Oil provides over 40% of Turkey's total energy requirements, but its share is declining as the usage of natural gas rises. Oil and gas transportation is a crucial and contentious issue in the Caspian Sea/Central Asia regions. Turkey and the United States have pushed for a "Western route" pipeline that will carry oil from Baku, through Azerbaijan and Georgia, and then across Turkey to Ceyhan. In 2005, construction of the 1-million-bbl/d capacity, US$4 billion pipeline was completed and oil began to flow in 2006.

Ukraine

Capital city	Kiev
Capital population	2,698,900 *(2008)*
Population ('000)	46,192.31 *(2008)*
Urban population (%)	67.91 *(2008)*
Land area (sq km)	603,700
Languages	Ukrainian
Religion	Mainly Christian
Currency	Hryvnia (Hr)
Head of state	Viktor Yushchenko (2005)
Head of government	Yulia Tymoshenko (2007)
Ruling party	A coalition of Yuliya Tymoshenko Bloc and Our Ukraine-People's Self Defence lead the government.

Main urban areas	Population *(Year)*
Kiev (capital)	2,698,900 *(2008)*
Kharkov	1,461,000 *(2006)*
Dnepropetrovsk	1,039,000 *(2006)*
Odessa	1,001,000 *(2006)*
Donezk	999,975 *(2005)*
Zaporozzie	799,348 *(2005)*
L'vov	733,728 *(2005)*
Krivoy Rog	696,667 *(2005)*
Mikolaev	509,011 *(2005)*
Mariupol	482,440 *(2005)*

Location Ukraine borders on Poland, Slovakia, Hungary, Moldova and northern Romania in the west, on Belarus in the north and on Russia in the east and south, where it meets the Black Sea. There are innumerable rivers, including the Dnepr and its tributaries. The capital is Kiev.

Political structure The country has an executive president who is elected by universal suffrage for a five-year term. Parliament has 450 members elected for five-year terms by proportional representation.

Last elections Parliamentary elections were held in September 2007. The Party of Regions won 175 seats, the coalition led by Yulia Tymoshenko took 156 seats, Our Ukraine-People's Self-Defence Bloc received 72 seats, the Communist Party gained 27 seats and the Lytvyn Bloc took 20 seats. Presidential elections were held in November 2004. Viktor Yanukovich, the prime minister, won a narrow victory over Viktor Yushchenko but the Supreme Court later threw out the results. The election was rerun in December 2004 and Yushchenko emerged as victor with 54.1% of the vote. In December 2007, parliament elected Tymoshenko as prime minister (for the second time). Tymoshenko replaces Viktor Yanukovych, the Orange Revolution antagonist, as prime minister.

Economy After several years of robust growth, the pace slowed temporarily in the middle of this decade. A strong recovery began in 2006, however. Once an agricultural leader, Ukraine's heavy industries are now driving growth. Inflationary pressures have been rising as Moscow pushes up energy prices. Reorienting trade towards Europe and Asia has resulted in an improved macroeconomic environment and an increased level of public trust in market institutions. Privatised companies have greatly contributed to the broad-based improvements in manufacturing, retail trade, agriculture and construction. Non-cash transactions in the economy have also fallen, reflecting the ban on these types of transactions. Recently approved tax reforms have reduced rates, while broadening the tax base. The economy nevertheless remains vulnerable to economic shocks over the long run.

Main industries The agricultural sector has strengthened in recent years. Ukraine is the world's sixth largest grain exporter. Large foreign investors have spent nearly US$1 billion in Ukraine grain production. The government has tightened export quotas on grain with the increasing shortages in world markets. Another complication is the country's unorthodox policies. Small export quotas on most grains and a ban on wheat exports have resulted in huge losses for farmers. Production in 2007 was disappointing. Industries such as food processing (where the government has minimised its intervention) are thriving. Steelmakers have also benefited thanks to high world prices but steel export prices are expected to soften over the medium term. Foreign investment, notably Mittal Steel's US$4.8 billion acquisition of the Kryvorizhstal mill, is pouring in. Exporters' profits have fuelled an investment and construction boom. Kiev also plans to build a large refinery near Odessa that would process Caspian oil. The move will reduce the importance of Russian supplies. Financial sector reforms have boosted public confidence in the banking sector, prompting rapid growth in banking deposits. The banking industry is under stress as a result of growing liquidity risks. Minerals are as important to Ukraine as oil is to Russia. The country has the world's largest supply of titanium, the third largest deposit of iron ore and 30% of the world's manganese ore. The metals industry accounts for two-fifth of all exports and output has more than doubled during this decade. Most of these gains were due to higher world prices but now the industry is facing increased competition from China, India and others.

Energy Energy is Ukraine's greatest challenge. Most industries are very energy-inefficient, making the country one of the largest energy consumers in Europe. The country has 395 million barrels of proven oil reserves and has had no success in its exploration efforts. Ukraine remains highly dependent on imported oil, most of which comes from Russia. The price of gas imported from Russia has risen dramatically. Ukraine's geographic location provides a useful corridor for oil and natural gas to transit from Russia and the Caspian Sea to European markets. More than a fifth of Russia's oil exports go through the Ukraine or are consumed there. Up to 1.6 million bbl/d could eventually be exported through the country after a 15-year intergovernmental oil transit improvement agreement comes to fruition. The country has 39.6 trillion cubic feet of natural gas but imports large amounts from Russia.

United Kingdom

Capital city	London
Capital population	7,512,400 *(2006)*
Population ('000)	61,015.07 *(2008)*
Urban population (%)	89.47 *(2008)*
Land area (sq km)	244,755
Languages	English
Religion	Protestant
Currency	Pound sterling (£)
Head of state	HM Queen Elizabeth II (1952)
Head of government	Gordon Brown (2007)
Ruling party	Labour Party

Main urban areas	Population *(Year)*
London (capital)	7,512,400 *(2006)*
Birmingham	1,006,500 *(2006)*
Leeds	750,200 *(2006)*
Glasgow	580,690 *(2006)*
Sheffield	525,800 *(2006)*
Bradford	493,100 *(2006)*
Edinburgh	463,510 *(2006)*
Manchester	452,000 *(2006)*
Liverpool	436,100 *(2006)*
Bristol	410,500 *(2006)*
Kirklees	398,200 *(2006)*

Location Lying off the coast of western continental Europe between the Atlantic Ocean and the North Sea, the UK consists mainly of two distinct land masses. The larger incorporates England, Scotland and the Principality of Wales, and the smaller consists of Northern Ireland – actually, the northeastern part of the island of Ireland. The capital is London.

Political structure The UK is considered to be a constitutional monarchy even though it has no written constitution. The non-executive monarch rules through an elected House of Commons (the lower House of Parliament), and this is supplemented in an advisory capacity by a House of Lords (Upper House). Devolved power returned to Northern Ireland in 2007, bringing an end to direct rule from London. In 1997, Scotland voted in favour of a referendum creating a Scottish parliament of 129 members. England and Scotland have shared the same monarch since 1603.

Last elections Elections to the House of Commons took place in May 2005. Labour took 356 seats while the Conservatives captured 197 seats. The Liberal Democrats claimed 62 seats with minor parties taking the remainder. Elections to the Scottish parliament were held in May 2007. The Labour Party won 46 seats while the Scottish National Party took 46 seats. The Scottish Conservatives received 17 seats while the Liberal Democrats won 16 seats. The remainder were divided amongst smaller parties. Tony Blair resigned as prime minister in June 2007 and was replaced by Gordon Brown.

Economy The economy was growing faster than the average for the Eurozone throughout most of this decade. The pace picked up in 2006 but an abrupt slowdown occurred in 2008. Unemployment has edged upward. Consumer spending is supported by an increase in employment, but is weakening as a result of problems in the housing market. Consumer borrowing has reached a level roughly equal to annual economic output. The cost of debt servicing could pose a serious problem in the future. The fiscal position has deteriorated over the past several years. The widening of the deficit reflected an increase in government spending in response to the perceived demand for better public services. The deficit was cut in 2006 but remains high by international standards. Labour productivity per hour worked remains lower than in other advanced countries. On average, workers in the UK must work nine hours to produce the same output that Germans achieve in eight and workers in France in seven. Growth of productivity has also slowed, reflecting a low capital-labour ratio, low efficiency in the use of capital and labour inputs, and a lack of innovation. The UK's public capital is low compared with major economies, especially in continental Europe. The country's infrastructure is also regarded as decrepit and hinders gains in productivity.

Main industries Agriculture is of limited importance, despite the fact that the country is fully self-sufficient in most basic products. Farms tend to be larger than the European average. Manufacturing output rose sharply in 2007 but the pace will slow markedly in 2008. Although a number of UK businesses tend to contract out non-core activities, output in others is flourishing. The decision by several large companies to relocate their headquarters elsewhere has added to concerns about the government's policy on corporate taxes. The services sector has expanded and now accounts for two-thirds of GDP. Financial services lead the way. Government consumption has been contained in recent years by strict controls on public spending, but is set to rise again as the government strives to improve deficient public services. The rate of overall fixed capital formation in the UK is depressed by the very low level of public investment. The UK is by far the largest petroleum producer and exporter in the EU (which does not include Norway). It also is the largest producer and an important exporter of natural gas in the EU. The government hopes to have 5% of all transport running on biofuels by 2010.

Energy The UK has 3.9 billion barrels of proven crude oil reserves, the most of any EU member country. The importance of oil has declined slightly over the past two decades; over 2006-2007, total oil consumption dropped by 4%. Total oil production was 1.7 million bbl/d in 2007, more than three-quarters less than the peak of production in 1999. The government expects oil production in the country to continue to decline, reaching 1.38 million bbl/d by 2009. Analysts predict that the country will become a net importer of these fuels by the end of the decade. Unlike non-EU member Norway, the UK has some onshore oil production and is one of the world's largest oil consumers, ranking in the top 15. Waters in the central North Sea off the east coast of Scotland contain nearly half of the UK's remaining oil reserves, with about a quarter of reserves located in the northern North Sea near the Shetland Islands. There is still some unexplored territory west of the Shetlands.

Section Two

Advertising

Advertising

Table 2.1

Advertising Expenditure by Medium 2007
US$ million

	Television	Radio	Print	Cinema	Outdoor	Online	Total
Western Europe							
Austria	781.1	231.8	1,884.4	21.8	246.3	61.9	3,227.3
Belgium	1,539.9	488.9	1,833.9	42.3	323.2	121.1	4,349.3
Cyprus	580.1	30.6	60.5				671.1
Denmark	484.2	52.7	1,323.4	10.0	77.7	429.7	2,377.7
Finland	348.0	64.3	1,212.7	1.0	48.6	76.9	1,751.4
France	5,902.0	1,303.5	6,025.3	189.1	1,957.3	1,014.3	16,391.5
Germany	5,811.8	947.4	15,059.5	142.1	1,102.1	841.0	23,904.0
Gibraltar							
Greece	981.6	136.2	1,864.9	23.1	456.0		3,461.7
Iceland	55.8		151.8	0.3	4.0		211.8
Ireland	489.6	185.3	1,704.0	14.3	202.5	43.9	2,639.7
Italy	6,368.2	822.2	4,033.7	92.2	425.1	331.4	12,072.8
Liechtenstein							
Luxembourg	14.3	28.8	133.4	1.7	5.0		183.2
Malta							
Monaco							
Netherlands	1,136.8	366.2	3,123.8	106.7	244.0	228.1	5,205.5
Norway	1,040.6	186.9	2,130.2	31.1	169.0	676.5	4,234.3
Portugal	690.2	69.4	295.1	7.8	158.4	10.8	1,231.8
Spain	4,623.2	905.8	3,500.5	54.5	769.5	522.5	10,376.0
Sweden	649.0	83.8	1,637.4	11.9	164.1	316.0	2,862.3
Switzerland	790.0	114.1	1,845.3	41.9	365.6	51.0	3,207.9
Turkey	1,280.6	87.0	865.1	28.8	149.6	29.1	2,440.2
United Kingdom	6,500.9	923.1	10,905.6	316.6	1,633.4	4,290.0	24,569.5
Eastern Europe							
Albania							
Belarus							
Bosnia-Herzegovina							
Bulgaria	379.6	14.7	124.4		63.9	9.1	591.8
Croatia	599.9	37.6	245.1		58.0	2.2	942.8
Czech Republic	1,268.6	137.1	1,024.2	11.1	135.7	125.0	2,701.7
Estonia	35.2	9.8	70.5		8.2	7.2	130.9
Georgia							
Hungary	1,937.6	213.3	623.6	6.9	236.2	68.2	3,085.7
Latvia	60.2	19.1	64.7	1.1	16.0	8.5	169.6
Lithuania	347.9	10.5	95.8	0.4	23.1	6.2	484.0
Macedonia							
Moldova							
Poland	1,159.5	183.5	596.2	24.0	193.7	95.7	2,252.5
Romania	357.7	39.9	108.2	4.1	50.0	8.2	568.1
Russia	3,924.6	412.6	1,931.8	77.1	1,442.4	131.0	7,919.4
Serbia and Montenegro	66.6	4.3	32.5		7.7		111.1
Slovakia	1,307.6	77.4	191.4	0.9	53.6	14.1	1,644.9
Slovenia	270.5	27.4	188.5	1.4	47.9	12.5	548.2
Ukraine	449.6	39.3	217.1	9.3	186.1	11.4	912.7

Source: *Euromonitor International from World Association of Newspapers*

Table 2.2

TV Adspend 1985-2007

Million units of national currency

	1985	1990	1995	2000	2002	2003	2004	2005	2006	2007	US$ million 2007
Western Europe											
Austria	152	240	270	479	456	463	497	508	545	570	781.1
Belgium	150	234	393	782	865	945	1,004	982	1,071	1,124	1,539.9
Cyprus	2	3	16	131	205	238	256	305	349	423	580.1
Denmark	240	612	1,510	1,823	1,675	1,927	2,125	2,254	2,471	2,636	484.2
Finland	75	127	161	213	201	207	227	231	243	254	348.0
France	1,773	1,958	2,111	3,046	3,635	3,744	3,998	4,028	4,209	4,306	5,902.0
Germany	814	1,642	3,420	4,709	3,956	3,811	3,860	3,930	4,114	4,240	5,811.8
Gibraltar											
Greece	53	200	837	676	718	638	684	693	705	716	981.6
Iceland				2,823	2,556	2,972	3,220	3,346	3,485	3,575	55.8
Ireland	33	51	112	200	207	195	236	287	326	357	489.6
Italy	2,360	2,864	2,595	4,134	4,028	4,224	4,647	4,808	4,736	4,646	6,368.2
Liechtenstein											
Luxembourg	3	4	6	8	8	9	11	11	11	10	14.3
Malta											
Monaco											
Netherlands	142	271	483	783	792	746	757	779	810	829	1,136.8
Norway	9	137	2,333	4,630	4,458	4,916	5,196	5,696	5,923	6,100	1,040.6
Portugal	45	100	216	519	445	464	504	517	512	504	690.2
Spain	1,833	1,696	1,323	2,311	2,185	2,317	2,675	2,951	3,181	3,373	4,623.2
Sweden	25	324	2,373	3,959	3,519	3,749	4,143	4,546	4,466	4,386	649.0
Switzerland	88	220	339	520	527	533	737	810	889	948	790.0
Turkey	0	1	12	285	525	693	957	1,140	1,442	1,669	1,280.6
United Kingdom	1,088	1,548	2,267	3,327	3,144	3,173	3,392	3,455	3,282	3,249	6,500.9
Eastern Europe											
Albania											
Belarus											
Bosnia-Herzegovina											
Bulgaria	2	2	2	108	200	261	325	413	477	542	379.6
Croatia						1,801	1,842	2,046	2,810	3,218	599.9
Czech Republic	876	1,382	3,772	14,516	15,529	16,869	18,153	21,350	23,681	25,745	1,268.6
Estonia	3	22	65	155	195	232	254	310	363	403	35.2
Georgia											
Hungary	557	3,719	18,826	129,605	204,058	242,570	286,106	331,203	347,080	355,789	1,937.6
Latvia	2	1	5	10	14	14	17	22	27	31	60.2
Lithuania		2	16	74	578	606	606	777	837	878	347.9
Macedonia											
Moldova											
Poland	32	150	808	4,452	6,375	6,600	6,861	2,603	3,010	3,209	1,159.5
Romania			8	165	256	341	428	554	749	872	357.7
Russia			938	7,595	28,879	38,068	48,994	65,900	85,900	100,395	3,924.6
Serbia and Montenegro				1,505	2,459	2,803	3,353	3,794	4,198	4,621	66.6
Slovakia			2,265	5,789	10,074	11,881	17,808	22,491	27,543	32,289	1,307.6
Slovenia	3	9	29	144	161	159	191	193	195	197	270.5
Ukraine				444	679	851	1,279	1,827	2,271		449.6

Source: Euromonitor International from World Association of Newspapers

Radio Adspend

Table 2.3

Radio Adspend 1985-2007
Million units of national currency

	1985	1990	1995	2000	2002	2003	2004	2005	2006	2007	US$ million 2007
Western Europe											
Austria	94	126	136	158	147	154	171	172	170	169	231.8
Belgium	21	48	100	186	208	229	253	290	327	357	488.9
Cyprus	2	2	6	7	12	14	14	17	19	22	30.6
Denmark	34	81	165	213	222	216	211	280	283	287	52.7
Finland	55	43	28	38	44	48	48	47	47	47	64.3
France	304	422	579	715	883	921	971	986	1,001	951	1,303.5
Germany	295	425	608	733	595	579	619	664	680	691	947.4
Gibraltar											
Greece	5	20	70	71	90	76	91	94	96	99	136.2
Iceland											
Ireland	13	20	33	55	65	87	91	106	124	135	185.3
Italy	238	217	201	454	387	440	529	534	576	600	822.2
Liechtenstein											
Luxembourg	5	7	9	12	16	18	20	20	21	21	28.8
Malta											
Monaco											
Netherlands	16	45	111	235	229	245	250	253	262	267	366.2
Norway	177	177	403	604	649	698	941	1,141	1,124	1,096	186.9
Portugal	96	43	25	62	54	54	57	56	52	51	69.4
Spain	2,139	899	346	502	485	508	540	610	637	661	905.8
Sweden		3	234	592	448	491	515	606	576	567	83.8
Switzerland	38	59	100	139	129	127	129	135	136	137	114.1
Turkey	0	0	2	47	54	60	75	80	101	113	87.0
United Kingdom	26	78	230	455	419	447	463	443	458	461	923.1
Eastern Europe											
Albania											
Belarus											
Bosnia-Herzegovina											
Bulgaria	1	1	3	6	7	8	20	25	22	21	14.7
Croatia						183	185	187	194	202	37.6
Czech Republic	262	413	635	1,050	1,693	2,169	2,157	2,398	2,640	2,783	137.1
Estonia		2	22	76	79	81	87	90	105	112	9.8
Georgia											
Hungary	140	774	4,187	12,042	14,429	15,929	26,514	26,819	33,764	39,169	213.3
Latvia			1	5	5	5	6	7	9	10	19.1
Lithuania			4	10	19	20	20	24	26	27	10.5
Macedonia											
Moldova											
Poland	6	22	123	544	704	872	1,043	435	482	508	183.5
Romania			1	10	20	22	40	59	80	97	39.9
Russia			151	1,266	3,610	4,759	5,764	8,500	9,500	10,554	412.6
Serbia and Montenegro				124	171	196	224	251	275	299	4.3
Slovakia			334	612	969	1,104	1,494	1,737	1,831	1,912	77.4
Slovenia	9	10	13	21	12	10	9	18	19	20	27.4
Ukraine					42	42	73	104	141	198	39.3

Source: *Euromonitor International from World Association of Newspapers*

Print Adspend 1985-2007

Million units of national currency

	1985	1990	1995	2000	2002	2003	2004	2005	2006	2007	US$ million 2007
Western Europe											
Austria	180	403	671	1,134	1,113	1,139	1,186	1,255	1,320	1,375	1,884.4
Belgium	319	399	479	652	655	743	813	872	1,163	1,338	1,833.9
Cyprus	2	3	6	23	24	27	30	33	37	44	60.5
Denmark	5,481	4,967	5,478	5,965	5,127	5,325	5,667	6,180	6,767	7,204	1,323.4
Finland	447	583	556	828	759	774	817	837	859	885	1,212.7
France	3,629	2,695	3,274	4,587	4,348	4,291	4,381	4,430	4,506	4,396	6,025.3
Germany	8,756	9,920	12,037	13,476	11,154	10,473	10,573	10,550	10,836	10,987	15,059.5
Gibraltar											
Greece	87	148	292	823	909	855	1,013	1,139	1,243	1,361	1,864.9
Iceland				5,395	5,496	7,006	8,080	8,696	9,229	9,724	151.8
Ireland	99	108	175	446	652	763	927	926	1,102	1,243	1,704.0
Italy	3,108	2,069	1,792	2,976	2,678	2,681	2,711	2,783	2,882	2,943	4,033.7
Liechtenstein											
Luxembourg	27	34	46	57	86	87	89	92	95	97	133.4
Malta											
Monaco											
Netherlands	1,313	1,475	1,793	2,721	2,486	2,293	2,211	2,212	2,273	2,279	3,123.8
Norway	2,777	2,777	4,757	7,105	7,531	8,705	9,962	11,104	11,922	12,486	2,130.2
Portugal	221	150	134	280	216	214	217	218	215	215	295.1
Spain	4,302	2,940	1,677	2,427	2,228	2,097	2,248	2,341	2,479	2,554	3,500.5
Sweden	9,040	8,788	9,751	11,952	9,945	10,008	10,556	11,263	11,199	11,067	1,637.4
Switzerland	2,653	2,600	2,569	3,033	2,546	2,302	1,901	1,952	2,136	2,215	1,845.3
Turkey	0	0	13	272	410	472	682	890	1,020	1,127	865.1
United Kingdom	2,595	3,163	4,103	5,987	5,684	5,692	5,957	5,778	5,547	5,450	10,905.6
Eastern Europe											
Albania											
Belarus											
Bosnia-Herzegovina											
Bulgaria		1	1	54	100	97	108	138	159	178	124.4
Croatia						810	779	930	1,031	1,315	245.1
Czech Republic	199	973	3,698	11,309	12,962	13,760	15,535	16,855	19,151	20,785	1,024.2
Estonia	2	17	180	400	476	510	556	638	737	806	70.5
Georgia											
Hungary	2,169	6,626	21,732	64,682	78,428	88,104	98,050	106,208	110,735	114,507	623.6
Latvia	1	1	8	13	19	20	22	25	30	33	64.7
Lithuania		2	22	87	181	211	210	222	235	242	95.8
Macedonia											
Moldova											
Poland	19	80	428	2,247	2,322	2,964	3,646	1,543	1,593	1,650	596.2
Romania			2	67	109	123	202	198	231	264	108.2
Russia			1,364	9,564	23,700	28,705	34,584	39,300	44,600	49,417	1,931.8
Serbia and Montenegro				165	410	782	1,267	1,561	1,910	2,252	32.5
Slovakia			823	1,740	2,681	3,220	3,877	4,320	4,575	4,726	191.4
Slovenia	16	23	36	70	75	79	97	107	124	138	188.5
Ukraine					151	318	418	684	924	1,096	217.1

Source: *Euromonitor International from World Association of Newspapers*

Cinema Adspend

Table 2.5

Cinema Adspend 1985-2007

Million units of national currency

	1985	1990	1995	2000	2002	2003	2004	2005	2006	2007	US$ million 2007
Western Europe											
Austria	3	4	6	11	9	11	10	14	15	16	21.8
Belgium	10	10	17	25	23	25	25	29	30	31	42.3
Cyprus											
Denmark	4	23	57	46	70	55	51	57	55	55	10.0
Finland	2	1	1	2	2	2	2	2	1	1	1.0
France	67	58	46	81	115	100	103	120	126	138	189.1
Germany	65	102	160	175	161	161	147	132	117	104	142.1
Gibraltar											
Greece	2	2	2	13	14	14	14	15	16	17	23.1
Iceland				100	35	31	27	23	21	19	0.3
Ireland	1	1	4	6	9	9	10	9	10	10	14.3
Italy	12	16	17	50	61	70	76	76	70	67	92.2
Liechtenstein											
Luxembourg			1	1	1	1	1	1	1	1	1.7
Malta											
Monaco											
Netherlands	9	9	11	13	7	7	6	7	55	78	106.7
Norway	60	60	73	124	120	143	147	162	173	182	31.1
Portugal				6	6	7	7	7	6	6	7.8
Spain	91	57	29	55	45	48	41	43	41	40	54.5
Sweden	68	70	81	78	70	59	68	74	78	81	11.9
Switzerland	47	30	34	45	38	38	50	50	50	50	41.9
Turkey	0	0	1	8	9	18	23	28	33	38	28.8
United Kingdom	20	32	59	109	154	151	162	158	158	158	316.6
Eastern Europe											
Albania											
Belarus											
Bosnia-Herzegovina											
Bulgaria											
Croatia											
Czech Republic					63	111	167	154	199	226	11.1
Estonia											
Georgia											
Hungary	1	11	122	1,076	1,089	1,328	1,265	1,323	1,280	1,265	6.9
Latvia					0	0	0	0	1	1	1.1
Lithuania					0	0	0	1	1	1	0.4
Macedonia											
Moldova											
Poland	1	2	3	27	44	99	128	53	64	66	24.0
Romania		0	0	2	2	6	7	8	10		4.1
Russia				84	283	368	432	1,100	1,600	1,973	77.1
Serbia and Montenegro											
Slovakia			0	4	13	12	12	21	22	23	0.9
Slovenia								1	1	1	1.4
Ukraine							16	26	37	47	9.3

Source: *Euromonitor International from World Association of Newspapers*

Table 2.6

Outdoor Adspend 1985-2007

Million units of national currency

	1985	1990	1995	2000	2002	2003	2004	2005	2006	2007	US$ million 2007
Western Europe											
Austria	29	54	79	112	136	138	139	157	170	180	246.3
Belgium	183	138	129	162	182	198	205	215	227	236	323.2
Cyprus											
Denmark			153	338	336	345	359	370	405	423	77.7
Finland	14	21	24	35	32	31	33	37	36	35	48.6
France	1,036	1,009	1,060	1,383	1,418	1,379	1,414	1,411	1,414	1,428	1,957.3
Germany	288	377	540	746	713	710	720	769	787	804	1,102.1
Gibraltar											
Greece	4	13	67	240	324	290	248	265	306	333	456.0
Iceland				279	307	270	264	259	256	253	4.0
Ireland	4	13	20	70	98	101	106	117	134	148	202.5
Italy	596	296	171	318	294	306	312	315	312	310	425.1
Liechtenstein											
Luxembourg							3	4	4	4	5.0
Malta											
Monaco											
Netherlands	71	72	84	139	137	122	139	151	165	178	244.0
Norway	176	176	258	263	375	575	658	759	894	991	169.0
Portugal	38	35	48	99	103	105	117	114	114	116	158.4
Spain	876	400	160	308	409	422	442	494	529	561	769.5
Sweden	343	446	573	848	826	925	1,000	1,065	1,091	1,109	164.1
Switzerland	427	386	446	592	571	566	392	402	423	439	365.6
Turkey	0	0	2	57	83	76	95	110	160	195	149.6
United Kingdom	124	191	349	592	587	668	721	762	792	816	1,633.4
Eastern Europe											
Albania											
Belarus											
Bosnia-Herzegovina											
Bulgaria				17	42	46	24	49	78	91	63.9
Croatia						218	223	234	272	311	58.0
Czech Republic				1,190	1,934	1,674	1,938	1,943	2,502	2,753	135.7
Estonia			14	31	44	57	66	67	84	94	8.2
Georgia											
Hungary	1	85	3,307	16,680	21,233	22,382	28,327	31,797	38,484	43,363	236.2
Latvia			1	2	2	2	3	4	7	8	16.0
Lithuania	1	1	5	17	26	32	40	46	52	58	23.1
Macedonia											
Moldova											
Poland	3	15	101	685	543	566	678	474	523	536	193.7
Romania			4	35	41	34	67	81	102	122	50.0
Russia			447	4,641	12,556	16,271	20,462	25,700	32,100	36,897	1,442.4
Serbia and Montenegro				268	376	521	522	525	529	532	7.7
Slovakia			130	370	556	492	612	875	1,130	1,323	53.6
Slovenia	0	1	3	11	13	14	15	24	30	35	47.9
Ukraine					198	313	454	606	731	940	186.1

Source: *Euromonitor International from World Association of Newspapers*

Online Adspend

Table 2.7

Online Adspend 1999-2007
Million units of national currency

	1999	2000	2001	2002	2003	2004	2005	2006	2007	US$ million 2007
Western Europe										
Austria			10	22	10	22	28	37	45	61.9
Belgium	7	13	11	11	18	32	44	72	88	121.1
Cyprus										
Denmark			310	418	486	582	742	1,794	2,339	429.7
Finland	6	11	15	15	17	23	36	47	56	76.9
France	79	144	115	99	131	179	382	542	740	1,014.3
Germany	77	153	185	227	246	271	332	495	614	841.0
Gibraltar										
Greece			2	5						
Iceland			8							
Ireland		2	3	4	6	9	16	26	32	43.9
Italy	29	139	107	99	103	107	138	197	242	331.4
Liechtenstein										
Luxembourg										
Malta										
Monaco										
Netherlands	21	38	34	32	40	66	97	137	166	228.1
Norway		300	235	250	325	455	2,119	3,119	3,966	676.5
Portugal	4	5	5	5	4	4	5	7	8	10.8
Spain	15	53	52	72	75	94	162	310	381	522.5
Sweden	497	1,037	895	1,139	1,325	1,974	2,996	2,237	2,136	316.0
Switzerland	12	25	19	20	30	29	36	52	61	51.0
Turkey			1	2	4	8	18	30	38	29.1
United Kingdom	43	132	141	162	295	700	1,162	1,714	2,144	4,290.0
Eastern Europe										
Albania										
Belarus										
Bosnia-Herzegovina										
Bulgaria						3	5	10	13	9.1
Croatia								9	12	2.2
Czech Republic	55	100	200	240	348	664	830	2,028	2,537	125.0
Estonia	4	13	19	20	28	29	40	66	82	7.2
Georgia										
Hungary						2,460	5,637	9,610	12,522	68.2
Latvia		0	0	1	1	1	2	3	4	8.5
Lithuania	0	1	0	1	5	5	10	14	16	6.2
Macedonia										
Moldova										
Poland			24	33	50	87	148	215	265	95.7
Romania					2	5	8	16	20	8.2
Russia	25	84	175	345	553	865	1,700	2,700	3,351	131.0
Serbia and Montenegro										
Slovakia			100	120	175	230	273	307	347	14.1
Slovenia						3	4	7	9	12.5
Ukraine				5	5	10	10	31	57	11.4

Source: *Euromonitor International from World Association of Newspapers / Jupiter research*

Agricultural Resources

Indices of Agricultural Output | Table 3.1

Indices of Agricultural Output 1985-2007
1999-2001 = 100

	1985	1990	1995	2000	2002	2003	2004	2005	2006	2007
Western Europe										
Austria	92.9	96.4	93.8	98.1	99.7	93.2	98.6	95.7	95.1	94.8
Belgium	73.6	77.8	93.4	102.1	101.6	99.2	104.0	98.8	94.4	92.0
Cyprus	87.3	94.0	103.4	99.5	101.1	98.9	102.2	91.6	87.6	85.2
Denmark	89.2	96.6	97.6	100.1	99.8	101.0	102.4	101.2	98.0	96.5
Finland	109.0	113.4	99.0	102.5	105.0	102.8	102.4	106.3	103.8	103.1
France	95.7	96.0	95.7	100.9	101.7	93.2	101.3	95.6	92.0	87.3
Germany	100.8	102.5	91.9	100.2	96.7	92.0	101.7	98.2	96.0	95.0
Gibraltar										
Greece	88.3	80.3	98.0	101.0	93.3	85.5	92.8	95.7	92.0	90.7
Iceland	114.7	93.4	90.8	101.2	103.5	104.4	105.3	104.7	104.7	104.5
Ireland	88.1	92.4	91.9	98.0	96.2	97.2	100.8	97.3	98.9	99.8
Italy	95.8	91.3	95.2	100.1	95.1	91.6	101.6	99.3	96.1	94.5
Liechtenstein		110.3	100.0	100.0	100.0	100.0	100.0	100.0	100.0	100.0
Luxembourg				104.8	109.6	104.3	97.6	95.7	94.9	94.2
Malta	73.9	79.6	92.3	99.5	95.4	95.2	95.0	92.8	93.5	92.7
Monaco			64.4	57.3	58.6	59.4	59.7	60.3	60.9	61.5
Netherlands	91.7	97.1	100.4	101.8	94.3	89.1	94.8	92.0	90.1	88.9
Norway	101.7	107.7	101.9	98.2	97.4	96.9	101.1	98.7	99.2	99.5
Portugal	76.6	95.2	95.2	100.2	100.6	92.1	97.5	93.6	92.7	91.5
Spain	76.9	87.6	73.2	102.4	104.0	112.8	107.7	97.6	101.9	104.8
Sweden	110.2	110.2	97.0	101.1	99.6	98.0	101.3	97.7	92.9	90.7
Switzerland	105.3	106.4	102.5	102.4	101.2	97.1	101.5	99.4	99.1	98.7
Turkey	75.0	88.7	91.9	104.1	102.2	103.5	104.8	110.3	110.7	111.3
United Kingdom	102.0	103.3	104.3	101.8	100.6	98.2	98.7	99.2	98.1	97.5
Eastern Europe										
Albania	79.9	84.5	98.5	100.7	103.8	102.6	106.3	106.9	109.9	112.6
Belarus			109.5	101.3	103.3	105.4	120.6	119.5	125.8	128.3
Bosnia-Herzegovina			83.9	91.5	103.9	95.2	121.6	121.1	123.9	125.0
Bulgaria	156.3	158.9	116.8	95.9	102.1	80.3	99.3	83.3	84.8	87.2
Croatia			91.7	93.8	112.4	88.8	100.1	91.3	95.2	97.6
Czech Republic			102.6	97.7	95.0	84.7	101.8	94.6	89.0	86.5
Estonia			111.2	103.8	95.2	94.0	97.0	104.7	98.4	96.3
Georgia			111.2	92.0	94.4	107.1	97.2	110.9	97.0	96.9
Hungary	124.5	128.3	94.4	94.0	96.6	87.4	114.2	103.9	98.8	94.9
Latvia		107.2	122.2	100.6	108.0	106.8	107.8	119.9	114.3	115.4
Lithuania		99.5	99.9	106.7	101.6	104.5	103.7	105.5	89.2	85.5
Macedonia		99.7	96.0	103.0	86.7	93.7	105.0	105.6	104.7	104.1
Moldova		101.6	143.5	100.0	109.5	103.2	113.8	109.5	103.0	97.6
Poland	117.5	123.4	101.7	99.5	97.0	95.6	102.5	96.5	93.4	91.1
Romania	137.9	110.6	112.9	89.2	98.9	106.6	127.9	113.4	111.2	108.4
Russia		95.4	112.0	99.5	110.1	106.8	111.5	112.5	115.1	116.9
Serbia and Montenegro			110.9	99.8	103.4	101.1	112.0	114.2	118.6	121.9
Slovakia		99.6	110.3	90.2	100.5	91.1	96.0	92.5	85.1	79.7
Slovenia		104.9	99.3	101.3	104.8	95.1	105.4	103.3	99.9	98.1
Ukraine		94.0	122.6	99.7	111.3	100.1	119.6	119.8	117.1	115.8

Source: UN Food and Agriculture Organisation, FAOSTAT

Table 3.2

Indices of Food Output 1985-2007

1999-2001 = 100

	1985	1990	1995	2000	2002	2003	2004	2005	2006	2007
Western Europe										
Austria	92.9	96.4	93.8	98.1	99.7	93.2	98.6	95.7	96.9	96.1
Belgium	73.5	77.8	93.4	102.1	101.5	99.0	103.9	98.8	94.4	89.6
Cyprus	87.2	94.0	103.4	99.5	101.1	98.9	102.2	91.5	87.5	80.2
Denmark	89.2	96.6	97.6	100.1	99.8	101.0	102.4	101.2	98.0	96.5
Finland	109.0	113.3	99.0	102.5	105.0	102.8	102.4	106.3	103.8	102.6
France	95.6	96.0	95.7	100.9	101.7	93.2	101.3	95.6	91.9	87.2
Germany	100.7	102.4	91.9	100.2	96.7	92.0	101.7	98.2	96.0	94.5
Gibraltar		90.7	107.4	96.4	94.8	94.0	93.6	93.1	92.9	92.7
Greece	92.5	82.7	97.4	100.9	93.8	85.8	92.8	96.1	91.9	90.5
Iceland	109.6	93.3	91.2	100.9	104.6	105.6	106.1	105.7	105.7	105.5
Ireland	88.1	92.1	91.8	98.0	96.2	97.2	100.8	97.3	98.9	99.8
Italy	95.6	90.6	95.2	100.1	95.1	91.6	101.7	99.4	96.2	94.8
Liechtenstein		109.2	100.0	100.0	100.0	100.0	100.0	100.0	100.0	100.0
Luxembourg				104.8	109.6	104.3	97.6	95.7	94.9	93.6
Malta	73.8	79.6	92.2	99.5	95.4	95.2	94.9	92.8	93.5	93.8
Monaco		95.6	79.7	95.1	99.6	102.1	104.2	105.9	107.1	108.6
Netherlands	91.7	96.9	100.4	101.8	94.3	89.1	94.8	92.0	90.1	88.5
Norway	101.7	107.7	101.9	98.2	97.3	96.9	101.1	98.7	99.3	99.6
Portugal	76.4	95.2	95.2	100.2	100.6	92.1	97.6	93.6	92.8	91.9
Spain	76.8	87.7	73.4	102.6	104.1	113.1	107.9	97.7	102.4	104.3
Sweden	110.2	110.2	97.0	101.1	99.6	98.0	101.3	97.7	92.9	88.6
Switzerland	105.2	106.4	102.4	102.4	101.2	97.1	101.5	99.4	99.1	98.8
Turkey	75.3	88.3	91.4	104.4	102.0	104.3	105.1	111.3	111.6	114.9
United Kingdom	102.3	103.2	104.3	101.7	100.6	98.2	98.8	99.2	98.1	97.8
Eastern Europe										
Albania	74.2	81.5	98.4	100.5	104.6	103.7	107.3	108.0	111.0	112.8
Belarus			109.2	101.3	103.4	105.3	120.4	119.3	125.9	128.6
Bosnia-Herzegovina			84.2	91.5	103.6	95.3	121.6	121.0	123.9	125.1
Bulgaria	149.6	157.1	118.7	96.5	100.9	78.5	97.5	81.8	84.4	87.7
Croatia			91.8	93.8	112.5	88.7	100.0	91.2	95.2	97.6
Czech Republic			102.3	97.7	95.0	84.7	101.8	94.7	89.1	82.8
Estonia			111.2	103.8	95.2	94.0	97.0	104.7	98.4	95.6
Georgia			111.4	93.1	95.6	109.0	99.1	113.4	97.9	97.3
Hungary	128.9	128.3	94.4	94.0	96.6	87.3	114.3	103.9	98.8	94.9
Latvia			122.2	100.7	108.0	106.8	107.8	119.9	114.3	111.1
Lithuania			99.7	106.6	101.5	104.4	103.7	105.6	89.3	82.1
Macedonia			98.5	104.2	86.4	94.3	106.3	105.2	104.3	103.2
Moldova			144.0	99.4	111.2	105.5	116.3	112.0	105.6	102.0
Poland	116.2	123.0	101.6	99.5	97.1	95.7	102.6	96.5	93.3	88.7
Romania	136.9	110.1	112.8	89.1	98.8	106.7	128.2	113.7	111.6	108.8
Russia		104.7	111.7	99.5	110.1	106.8	111.5	112.5	115.1	116.9
Serbia and Montenegro			111.0	99.9	103.2	101.4	112.2	114.4	116.9	119.3
Slovakia			109.5	90.2	100.5	91.0	96.0	92.6	85.2	79.8
Slovenia			99.3	101.3	104.8	95.1	105.4	103.2	99.9	98.0
Ukraine			122.4	99.7	111.4	100.2	119.6	119.8	117.1	115.8

Source: UN Food and Agriculture Organisation, FAOSTAT

Total Surface Area (Land and Water)

Table 3.3

Land Use and Irrigation 2007
'000 hectares

	Total Area	Land Area	Arable Land	Permanent Crops	Permanent Pasture	Irrigated Land	Irrigated as % of Land Area
Western Europe							
Austria	8,387	8,245	1,388	66	1,810	4	0.05
Belgium	3,053	3,023	846	23	511	67	2.23
Cyprus	925	924	127	41	4	40	4.33
Denmark	4,309	4,243	2,219	7	336	450	10.60
Finland	33,815	30,459	2,245	5	26	64	0.21
France	55,150	55,010	18,531	1,125	9,891	2,579	4.69
Germany	35,705	34,877	11,930	194	4,893	485	1.39
Gibraltar	1	1					
Greece	13,196	12,890	2,590	1,133	4,585	1,469	11.40
Iceland	10,300	10,025	7		2,274		
Ireland	7,027	6,889	1,225	2	2,933		
Italy	30,134	29,411	7,518	2,525	4,429	2,775	9.43
Liechtenstein	16	16	4		5		
Luxembourg	259	259	59	3	68		
Malta	32	32	9	1		2	6.25
Monaco	0						
Netherlands	4,153	3,388	909	33	978	565	16.68
Norway	32,380	30,428	859		174	127	0.42
Portugal	9,212	9,150	1,001	628	1,884	650	7.10
Spain	50,549	49,944	13,910	4,913	10,027	3,809	7.63
Sweden	45,029	41,033	2,706	3	538	115	0.28
Switzerland	4,128	4,000	412	24	1,089	25	0.63
Turkey	78,356	76,963	23,810	2,823	14,617	5,770	7.50
United Kingdom	24,361	24,193	5,760	45	11,157	170	0.70
Eastern Europe							
Albania	2,875	2,740	578	122	423	360	13.13
Belarus	20,760	20,748	5,417	114	3,342	131	0.63
Bosnia-Herzegovina	5,121	5,120	996	97	1,052	3	0.06
Bulgaria	11,099	10,797	3,060	185	1,927	558	5.16
Croatia	5,654	5,592	1,023	112	1,435	16	0.29
Czech Republic	7,887	7,726	3,041	239	975	24	0.31
Estonia	4,523	4,239	624	10	305	4	0.09
Georgia	6,970	6,949	802	264	1,940	469	6.75
Hungary	9,303	8,961	4,602	208	1,055	236	2.64
Latvia	6,459	6,229	1,137	13	636	20	0.32
Lithuania	6,530	6,268	2,032	39	821	7	0.11
Macedonia	2,571	2,543	566	46	630	55	2.16
Moldova	3,384	3,287	1,846	295	371	297	9.05
Poland	31,269	30,697	11,786	395	3,218	100	0.33
Romania	23,839	23,009	9,259	564	4,591	3,074	13.36
Russia	1,709,824	1,638,151	121,540	1,791	92,496	4,600	0.28
Serbia and Montenegro	10,217	10,200	3,549	314	1,732	43	0.42
Slovakia	4,903	4,810	1,371	25	457	185	3.84
Slovenia	2,027	2,014	176	26	308	4	0.18
Ukraine	60,355	57,939	32,434	897	7,936	2,191	3.78

Source: UN Food and Agriculture Organisation, FAOSTAT

Table 3.4

Livestock

Number of Livestock 2007
'000 head

	Asses	Cattle	Goats	Horses	Pigs	Sheep
Western Europe						
Austria		1,970.0	54.2	85.0	3,160.4	325.5
Belgium	0.0	2,669.1	26.2	34.8	6,294.9	154.7
Cyprus	6.7	54.9	344.9	0.7	469.0	275.0
Denmark		1,572.0		52.9	12,880.0	233.7
Finland		949.3	6.6	66.7	1,455.0	125.6
France	32.3	19,417.9	1,229.6	422.9	14,730.0	8,796.1
Germany		12,630.0	171.7	500.4	26,521.3	2,516.6
Gibraltar						
Greece	96.0	630.0	5,351.9	29.0	1,000.0	8,723.1
Iceland		63.4	0.4	75.5	41.2	447.8
Ireland	6.5	6,800.0	7.7	70.0	1,616.0	6,475.1
Italy	33.0	6,255.0	939.9	300.0	9,200.0	7,956.0
Liechtenstein		6.0	0.3		3.0	2.9
Luxembourg		182.9	2.0	4.4	84.2	9.5
Malta	0.8	20.4	6.6	1.0	73.0	14.6
Monaco						
Netherlands		3,680.0	323.3	128.5	11,300.0	1,961.5
Norway		918.5	72.5	31.3	827.5	2,316.0
Portugal	165.0	1,440.8	556.9	17.0	2,344.0	3,166.7
Spain	252.0	6,464.0	2,595.5	240.0	25,400.0	22,360.0
Sweden		1,590.4		95.7	1,640.0	485.8
Switzerland	6.0	1,554.7	80.5	57.2	1,667.0	450.8
Turkey	404.0	10,800.0	6,369.3	200.0	1.1	25,348.7
United Kingdom		10,070.0		184.0	4,933.0	34,356.2
Eastern Europe						
Albania	127.0	624.0	916.8	53.0	154.9	1,816.5
Belarus	9.0	4,050.0	68.7	160.0	3,620.0	47.8
Bosnia-Herzegovina		549.0	73.5	25.5	738.0	1,070.6
Bulgaria	215.0	593.0	567.6	150.0	943.0	1,565.1
Croatia	4.0	482.9	112.3	9.9	1,488.5	722.3
Czech Republic		1,373.6	14.4	23.6	2,810.0	167.8
Estonia		249.5	2.5	4.6	346.5	59.0
Georgia	10.1	1,260.4	99.4	42.8	444.0	760.4
Hungary	3.7	708.0	78.2	73.3	3,640.0	1,526.1
Latvia		385.2	15.5	13.9	427.9	45.9
Lithuania		800.3	22.3	61.8	1,128.0	37.7
Macedonia		248.2		57.1	155.8	1,254.1
Moldova	2.0	295.0	117.2	66.7	460.7	814.5
Poland		5,700.0	123.8	307.0	18,880.6	289.5
Romania	29.0	2,862.0	691.1	834.0	6,622.0	7,713.9
Russia	16.1	20,800.0	2,286.5	1,270.0	13,200.0	16,943.6
Serbia and Montenegro		1,213.0	155.9	41.7	3,223.7	1,875.0
Slovakia		527.9	40.6	8.3	1,108.3	318.8
Slovenia		452.8	22.1	20.0	547.4	140.1
Ukraine	12.0	6,230.0	834.0	590.9	7,052.8	871.0

Source: *UN Food and Agriculture Organisation, FAOSTAT*

Food Production

Table 3.5

Production of Selected Crops 2007
'000 tonnes

	Apples	Bananas	Grapes	Hops	Potatoes	Rapeseed	Sugar Beet	Tomatoes
Western Europe								
Austria	477.9		329.8	0.3	613.5	142.1	2,651.2	46.9
Belgium	330.0		0.6	0.4	2,877.7	38.5	5,746.9	245.0
Cyprus	10.8	6.9	45.5		135.0			35.0
Denmark	30.0				1,625.6	596.3	2,255.3	20.0
Finland	3.0				701.6	114.0	673.1	38.2
France	1,800.0		6,500.0	1.4	6,271.0	4,554.0	32,338.0	750.0
Germany	911.9		1,300.0	28.6	11,604.5	5,320.0	26,114.0	57.0
Gibraltar								
Greece	270.0	6.0	950.0		830.0	6.0	862.3	1,450.0
Iceland					13.0			1.6
Ireland	16.0			0.0	454.8	20.0	45.0	12.0
Italy	2,072.5	0.4	8,519.4		1,837.8	15.0	4,629.9	6,025.6
Liechtenstein			0.2					0.2
Luxembourg	4.0		16.9		20.2	18.4		0.1
Malta	0.1		5.0		25.0			16.6
Monaco								
Netherlands	370.0		0.1		7,200.0	14.0	5,400.0	690.0
Norway	15.0				380.0	12.0		12.0
Portugal	198.2	34.0	1,050.0	0.1	638.9		320.0	1,000.0
Spain	672.4	365.2	6,013.0	1.5	2,502.3	37.8	5,141.0	3,615.0
Sweden	20.1				790.1	223.0	2,000.0	18.0
Switzerland	250.0		130.0	0.0	490.0	67.7	1,584.0	27.0
Turkey	2,266.4	186.6	3,923.0		4,280.7	25.5	14,800.0	9,919.7
United Kingdom	230.0		1.0	1.5	5,635.0	2,108.0	6,500.0	85.6
Eastern Europe								
Albania	17.5		105.0	1.0	154.9		40.0	156.0
Belarus	275.2				8,744.0	240.0	3,624.0	239.5
Bosnia-Herzegovina	61.0		21.3		387.2	3.9		33.3
Bulgaria	25.0		376.7	0.6	290.6	93.0	16.3	133.2
Croatia	78.7		180.0		215.3	38.0	1,582.6	28.9
Czech Republic	250.0		55.0	5.6	784.7	1,038.4	2,598.7	35.0
Estonia	3.6		1.4		173.7	132.4		4.5
Georgia	42.5		93.0	0.1	174.5			56.2
Hungary	538.0		543.4		531.3	498.2	2,000.0	205.0
Latvia	25.2				642.0	211.7	10.8	8.0
Lithuania	40.6		13.6		576.1	311.9	799.9	1.5
Macedonia	78.0		225.0		192.5	2.0	5.9	120.0
Moldova	172.0		598.0		199.0	7.0	612.0	48.5
Poland	1,039.1			3.1	11,221.1	2,112.6	11,057.8	652.0
Romania	374.8		821.3	0.2	3,498.4	348.2	698.6	555.4
Russia	2,211.0		326.8	0.3	36,784.2	600.0	29,000.0	2,393.0
Serbia and Montenegro	249.7		394.3	0.4	572.8	2.2	3,590.4	3,590.4
Slovakia	18.0		50.7	0.3	381.6	336.4	855.3	60.0
Slovenia	114.5		122.5	2.2	131.1	14.7	260.0	4.4
Ukraine	707.0		415.0	0.7	19,102.3	1,060.0	16,978.0	1,520.0

Source: UN Food and Agriculture Organisation, FAOSTAT

Table 3.6

Production of Dairy Products and Eggs 2007

'000 tonnes

	Butter and Ghee	Cheese	Fresh Cows' Milk	Hens' Eggs
Western Europe				
Austria	29.8	190.4	3,145.0	90.0
Belgium	112.7	59.8	3,000.0	223.6
Cyprus		5.9	153.0	9.5
Denmark	42.1	375.0	4,600.0	78.0
Finland	61.8	90.4	2,300.0	57.0
France	414.5	1,814.8	23,705.0	765.0
Germany	454.1	2,066.5	27,900.0	800.0
Gibraltar				
Greece	4.3	232.5	780.0	100.0
Iceland	1.9	7.1	115.0	2.8
Ireland	146.6	124.0	5,200.0	33.0
Italy	125.7	1,111.5	11,000.0	670.0
Liechtenstein			11.5	
Luxembourg	0.5		312.5	1.2
Malta		0.2	41.0	7.0
Monaco				
Netherlands	136.7	671.4	10,750.0	610.0
Norway	14.4	80.1	1,550.0	50.5
Portugal	27.0	72.8	1,924.7	119.1
Spain	63.1	143.6	6,716.7	883.6
Sweden	40.9	122.3	3,000.0	102.0
Switzerland	37.1	189.2	4,000.0	39.0
Turkey	132.0	145.0	11,000.0	744.0
United Kingdom	133.3	414.0	14,450.0	590.0
Eastern Europe				
Albania	0.8	14.1	917.0	26.7
Belarus	89.1	118.8	5,882.0	179.0
Bosnia-Herzegovina	0.4	10.9	587.0	16.1
Bulgaria	1.4	77.9	1,148.3	99.0
Croatia	2.4	22.2	860.1	48.2
Czech Republic	47.1	129.1	2,700.0	87.0
Estonia	6.7	17.7	605.9	10.8
Georgia	0.5	0.0	734.0	15.6
Hungary	8.7	97.8	1,800.0	164.0
Latvia	7.4	20.9	838.6	39.0
Lithuania	16.7	83.6	1,997.0	52.9
Macedonia	8.7	3.9	385.3	18.0
Moldova	3.1	8.6	573.2	39.3
Poland	206.7	615.7	11,800.0	537.5
Romania	8.8	71.5	5,441.1	320.9
Russia	241.3	567.5	31,950.0	2,093.1
Serbia and Montenegro	2.7	16.9	1,880.0	75.1
Slovakia	5.7	82.7	1,000.0	70.0
Slovenia	5.4	20.5	654.0	17.1
Ukraine	144.3	371.2	12,300.0	779.6

Source: UN Food and Agriculture Organisation, FAOSTAT

Food Production

Table 3.7

Production of Meat 2007
'000 tonnes

	Beef and Veal	Goat Meat	Horse Meat	Mutton and Lamb	Pig Meat	Poultry	Total (including others)
Western Europe							
Austria	210.0	0.6	0.2	7.0	515.0	113.8	854.0
Belgium	262.0	0.0	3.8	2.4	1,000.1	453.6	1,721.8
Cyprus	4.0	4.3		2.8	50.4	23.8	86.3
Denmark	130.0		0.7	1.8	1,750.0	175.2	2,060.7
Finland	90.0		0.2	0.7	210.0	100.0	400.9
France	1,449.6	7.3	5.6	95.0	1,982.0	1,472.9	5,064.2
Germany	1,190.0	0.4	2.7	46.5	4,670.0	1,026.2	7,052.8
Gibraltar							0.0
Greece	73.1	58.0	2.7	95.0	110.0	147.5	494.4
Iceland	3.2		0.8	8.8	5.4	5.7	23.9
Ireland	560.0		1.6	72.0	210.0	138.7	982.3
Italy	1,101.0	2.7	37.0	59.0	1,600.0	946.8	3,976.5
Liechtenstein							0.0
Luxembourg	17.7		0.3	0.1	9.0	0.1	27.3
Malta	1.4	0.0	0.1	0.1	8.5	4.2	15.9
Monaco							0.0
Netherlands	382.0	0.2	0.4	15.3	1,295.6	666.2	2,359.8
Norway	88.0	0.3	0.4	26.0	120.0	62.3	300.4
Portugal	106.1	0.9	0.2	23.3	331.7	251.8	718.3
Spain	705.0	11.9	5.6	224.5	3,221.7	1,086.9	5,362.1
Sweden	140.0		1.0	4.1	270.0	99.0	533.1
Switzerland	135.0	0.5	0.9	6.0	250.0	53.5	449.4
Turkey	352.7	45.0	2.0	272.0	0.3	914.8	1,586.5
United Kingdom	850.0		3.1	330.0	700.0	1,523.1	3,411.2
Eastern Europe							
Albania	42.0	7.3	0.2	13.0	10.0	8.4	80.7
Belarus	290.0		2.7	1.1	368.4	154.6	817.5
Bosnia-Herzegovina	24.8		0.0	2.2	10.9	24.5	62.4
Bulgaria	22.9	5.5	0.0	18.0	75.0	104.9	226.3
Croatia	32.0	0.2	3.0	2.0	56.0	46.2	139.4
Czech Republic	80.0	0.1	0.1	1.5	360.0	236.0	718.7
Estonia	14.5	0.0	0.0	0.5	35.1	12.0	62.1
Georgia	49.0	0.0	0.2	8.9	34.6	15.1	108.0
Hungary	33.5	0.3	0.0	0.8	490.0	379.2	914.3
Latvia	22.8		0.1	0.5	40.4	20.6	84.4
Lithuania	60.0	0.4	0.0	0.3	114.0	72.6	247.4
Macedonia	7.1			6.5	8.9	3.5	26.0
Moldova	16.8		0.1	2.6	53.8	34.9	109.1
Poland	355.0		10.0	1.4	2,100.0	878.3	3,353.2
Romania	186.0	3.9	9.4	56.8	525.6	317.6	1,103.9
Russia	1,828.0	20.0	47.0	140.0	1,788.0	1,769.0	5,601.8
Serbia and Montenegro	150.2	1.8	0.7	21.2	562.2	90.3	759.9
Slovakia	25.0	0.3	0.0	1.0	130.0	87.1	247.4
Slovenia	35.6	0.3	0.3	1.9	57.0	54.1	149.2
Ukraine	563.0	7.2	13.3	7.6	650.0	670.0	1,923.8

Source: *UN Food and Agriculture Organisation, FAOSTAT*

Table 3.8

Production of Cereals 2007

'000 tonnes

	Barley	Maize	Millet	Oats	Rice	Rye	Sorghum	Wheat	Total (including others)
Western Europe									
Austria	811.0	1,555.9	9.0	98.9		188.6		1,399.3	4,594.7
Belgium	365.0	602.6		23.9		3.3		1,480.7	2,519.4
Cyprus	60.5			0.5				9.0	70.0
Denmark	3,104.2			311.6		135.3		4,519.2	8,220.2
Finland	1,984.4			1,265.9		86.7		796.8	4,181.2
France	9,472.0	13,107.0	25.5	443.0	93.0	117.0	318.0	33,219.0	58,707.1
Germany	11,034.2	3,480.6		800.0		3,319.0		21,366.8	42,294.6
Gibraltar									
Greece	264.5	1,767.5		130.0	200.7	37.9	0.1	1,403.2	3,807.5
Iceland									
Ireland	1,130.2			144.1		0.4		684.9	1,969.2
Italy	1,205.6	9,891.4		407.3	1,493.2	7.7	200.3	7,260.3	20,499.3
Liechtenstein									
Luxembourg	44.6	1.9		5.6		6.8		70.4	150.8
Malta	1.6							9.2	10.8
Monaco									
Netherlands	260.0	217.0		8.0		11.0		990.0	1,506.0
Norway	580.0			260.0		30.0		380.0	1,250.0
Portugal	73.9	646.5		47.9	154.6	23.8		135.8	1,102.5
Spain	11,684.0	3,647.9	0.8	1,274.2	701.3	258.0	26.0	6,376.9	24,134.8
Sweden	1,439.0			892.3		137.5		2,254.7	5,058.9
Switzerland	218.1	186.0		10.6		10.4		562.2	1,048.6
Turkey	7,423.0	3,875.0	6.1	202.2	685.0	263.8	0.2	17,678.0	30,211.9
United Kingdom	5,149.0			740.0		38.0		13,362.0	19,368.5
Eastern Europe									
Albania	3.5	215.9		21.4		3.3		249.5	493.6
Belarus	1,911.0	541.0		580.0		1,305.0		1,397.0	7,016.0
Bosnia-Herzegovina	60.7	635.3		38.5		8.9		257.1	1,000.6
Bulgaria	419.8	312.9	2.5	22.5	3.1	8.5	1.8	2,390.6	3,180.5
Croatia	149.0	1,424.6	0.0	55.0		6.0	0.5	950.0	2,606.6
Czech Republic	1,919.7	608.2	1.7	171.6		176.9		3,955.4	7,065.8
Estonia	372.8			81.5		60.5		322.0	859.6
Georgia	45.0	86.2		2.7		0.0		92.3	226.3
Hungary	1,041.4	8,400.0	10.0	122.2	9.7	77.3	14.0	3,988.2	14,047.0
Latvia	363.2			130.2		181.1		807.3	1,535.1
Lithuania	1,013.7	26.0		119.5		165.2		1,390.7	3,017.0
Macedonia	83.2	99.7	0.0	3.5	12.9	7.4	0.0	157.4	364.2
Moldova	115.0	363.0	0.0	3.1		0.4	0.1	402.0	884.6
Poland	4,065.8	1,639.7	8.0	1,486.5		3,194.1		8,378.6	27,365.2
Romania	503.7	3,686.5	1.7	240.0	23.4	30.9	1.5	2,866.2	7,461.4
Russia	15,663.1	3,953.2	420.9	5,407.0	708.6	3,910.3	32.5	49,389.9	80,495.5
Serbia and Montenegro	261.0	3,913.8	0.3	77.3		11.3	11.3	3,593.1	6,139.5
Slovakia	695.0	675.2	2.5	40.3		56.8	0.4	1,440.6	2,949.8
Slovenia	67.9	308.3	0.5	5.5		2.5		133.3	531.9
Ukraine	6,000.0	6,700.0	75.0	600.0	98.0	550.0	40.0	13,800.0	28,035.0

Source: UN Food and Agriculture Organisation, FAOSTAT

Forestry Production

Table 3.9

Production of Forestry and Paper Products 2007
as stated

	Fuelwood and Charcoal ('000 cu m)	Household and Sanitary Paper ('000 tonnes)	Paper and Paperboard ('000 tonnes)	Printing and Writing Paper ('000 tonnes)	Roundwood ('000 cu m)	Sawnwood and Sleepers ('000 cu m)	Wood Pulp ('000 tonnes)
Western Europe							
Austria	5,403	117	5,394	2,677	20,461	10,194	1,925
Belgium	690	101	1,867	1,119	5,188	1,663	509
Cyprus	3				6	3	
Denmark	1,116		433	156	1,937	196	
Finland	5,377	184	15,276	9,649	49,018	11,568	13,294
France	2,439	727	9,882	3,048	69,639	10,038	2,361
Germany	9,512	1,341	23,787	8,462	66,183	26,861	3,011
Gibraltar							
Greece	1,004	155	510	0	1,437	191	
Iceland							
Ireland	14		45		2,689	1,172	
Italy	5,553	1,394	10,179	3,084	8,539	1,886	497
Liechtenstein	4				22		
Luxembourg	13				281	133	
Malta							
Monaco							
Netherlands	290	100	3,321	1,054	1,107	258	104
Norway	1,051	19	2,017	948	8,312	2,469	2,191
Portugal	600	74	1,674	1,053	10,837	1,010	2,123
Spain	1,383	655	6,768	1,761	15,812	3,882	2,158
Sweden	5,900	322	12,305	3,605	59,350	18,550	12,374
Switzerland	1,552	92	1,639	656	5,986	1,750	223
Turkey	4,189	146	1,643	217	17,123	7,511	225
United Kingdom	317	806	5,466	1,326	8,377	2,956	259
Eastern Europe							
Albania	168		15		296	97	
Belarus	1,170	8	298	7	8,763	2,637	61
Bosnia-Herzegovina	1,436		81		3,783	1,319	20
Bulgaria	3,131	28	326	3	5,995	569	135
Croatia	922	1	514	286	4,758	713	117
Czech Republic	1,458	65	1,096	201	18,717	5,650	770
Estonia	1,200		76	0	6,300	2,030	170
Georgia	459				652	69	
Hungary	3,533	28	540	157	5,881	177	
Latvia	993		67	1	12,860	4,403	
Lithuania	1,305	19	129		5,745	1,474	
Macedonia	775		21		933	16	
Moldova	269				57	5	
Poland	3,728	255	2,968	954	32,559	3,743	1,070
Romania	2,429	71	408	23	12,854	4,529	139
Russia	45,100	165	7,762	621	196,700	22,691	7,059
Serbia and Montenegro	1,733	26	264	25	3,170	484	26
Slovakia	312	133	933	538	7,240	2,289	644
Slovenia	1,027	33	729	249	3,493	613	92
Ukraine	8,787	96	825	19	15,822	2,092	27

Source: UN Food and Agriculture Organisation, FAOSTAT

Organic Farming

Table 3.10

Land Used in Organic Farming 1985-2007

Hectares

	1985	1990	1995	2000	2002	2003	2004	2005	2006	2007
Western Europe										
Austria			335,865	271,950	297,000	328,803	344,916	360,972	361,487	372,382
Belgium	500	1,300	3,385	20,263	20,241	24,163	23,728	22,996	29,308	31,023
Cyprus		-		52	166	393	960	1,698	1,979	2,508
Denmark	4,500	11,581	40,884	165,258	178,360	165,148	154,921	145,636	138,079	133,568
Finland	1,000	6,726	44,695	147,423	156,692	159,987	162,024	147,587	144,558	142,844
France	45,000	72,000	118,393	371,000	509,000	550,000	534,037	560,838	552,824	568,000
Germany	24,940	90,021	309,487	546,023	696,978	734,027	767,891	807,406	825,539	856,043
Gibraltar										
Greece		150	2,401	24,800	28,944	244,455	246,488	288,255	302,256	307,073
Iceland			717	3,400	6,000	6,000	4,910	4,684	5,512	5,670
Ireland	1,000	3,800	12,634	32,355	29,850	28,514	30,670	35,266	39,947	43,758
Italy	5,000	13,218	204,494	1,040,377	1,168,212	1,052,002	954,361	1,067,102	1,148,162	1,180,215
Liechtenstein			410	690	984	984	984	1,040	1,027	1,041
Luxembourg	350	600	571	1,030	2,004	3,002	3,158	3,243	3,630	3,839
Malta						14	13	14	20	22
Monaco										
Netherlands	2,450	7,469	12,909	27,820	42,610	41,865	48,152	48,765	48,424	50,610
Norway	90	1,578	5,768	20,523	32,546	38,176	41,035	43,033	44,624	46,773
Portugal	50	1,000	10,719	50,002	85,912	120,729	206,524	233,458	269,374	318,922
Spain	2,140	3,650	24,079	380,838	665,055	717,204	733,182	807,569	926,390	996,119
Sweden	1,500	28,500	83,490	171,682	187,000	207,488	219,423	200,010	225,385	231,351
Switzerland			31,815	95,000	107,000	110,000	121,387	117,117	125,596	130,795
Turkey		1,037	10,000	21,000	80,096	103,190	108,597	93,133	100,275	99,303
United Kingdom	6,000	31,000	48,448	527,323	724,523	695,619	657,736	619,852	604,571	574,222
Eastern Europe										
Albania						192	804	987	1,170	1,496
Belarus										
Bosnia-Herzegovina					1,113	712	310	363	416	469
Bulgaria				500	458	437	12,284	14,320	4,692	4,340
Croatia			120	120	1,957	3,530	3,357	3,184	6,204	7,095
Czech Republic		3,480	14,127	165,699	235,136	254,995	260,120	254,982	281,535	290,382
Estonia				9,872	30,552	40,890	46,016	59,862	72,886	83,551
Georgia			100	100	100	100	100	130	247	364
Hungary				47,221	103,672	113,816	128,690	123,569	122,765	125,748
Latvia			1,147	20,000	16,934	48,000	57,333	118,612	135,558	150,151
Lithuania			582	4,709	8,780	23,289	41,869	69,430	96,718	121,194
Macedonia								249	509	639
Moldova								11,075	11,405	11,735
Poland		550	6,855	22,000	53,515	49,928	82,730	167,740	228,009	257,689
Romania				20,500	57,500	75,500	75,000	87,916	107,582	118,276
Russia			20,000	5,276	30,059	6,900	31,003	40,000	3,192	
Serbia and Montenegro			350	758	16,981	18,761	20,542	22,322	25,957	28,356
Slovakia		15,140	18,813	48,120	49,999	54,478	73,335	92,191	121,461	143,789
Slovenia			200	5,200	15,000	23,280	23,032	23,499	26,831	28,015
Ukraine					239,542	239,771	240,000	241,980	260,034	266,788

Source: Euromonitor International from Organic Centre Wales, University of Wales

Organic Farming

Table 3.11

Number of Organic Farms 1985-2007
Number

	1985	1990	1995	2000	2002	2003	2004	2005	2006	2007
Western Europe										
Austria	420	1,539	18,542	19,031	18,576	19,056	19,826	20,310	20,162	20,531
Belgium	50	160	193	628	700	688	712	693	783	815
Cyprus				15	45	48	103	305	305	391
Denmark	130	523	1,050	3,466	3,714	3,510	3,166	2,892	2,794	2,675
Finland	60	671	2,793	5,225	5,071	4,983	4,887	4,296	3,966	3,853
France	2,500	2,700	3,538	9,283	11,177	11,377	11,059	11,402	11,640	11,728
Germany	1,610	3,438	6,642	12,732	15,628	16,476	16,603	17,020	17,557	17,917
Gibraltar										
Greece		25	568	5,270	6,047	6,028	8,269	14,614	23,900	25,389
Iceland		12	30		20	20	25	23	27	29
Ireland	8	150	378	1,014	923	889	897	978	1,104	1,176
Italy	600	1,500	10,630	51,120	49,489	44,043	36,639	44,733	45,115	45,472
Liechtenstein			22	33	41	43	42	35	41	40
Luxembourg	10	10	19	51	48	59	66	72	72	76
Malta						20	20	6	10	11
Monaco										
Netherlands	215	399	561	1,391	1,560	1,522	1,469	1,377	1,448	1,463
Norway	15	263	728	1,823	2,303	2,466	2,484	2,496	2,583	2,622
Portugal	1	50	349	763	1,059	1,455	1,302	1,577	1,696	1,776
Spain	264	350	1,042	13,424	17,751	18,747	16,013	15,693	17,214	17,610
Sweden	150	1,588	2,473	3,329	3,530	3,363	3,374	2,951	2,380	2,216
Switzerland	322	803	2,121	5,852	6,466	6,445	6,373	6,420	6,563	6,602
Turkey		313	2,000	10,000	16,215	13,044	12,806	14,401	14,256	14,660
United Kingdom	300	700	828	3,563	4,057	4,017	4,151	4,285	4,485	4,641
Eastern Europe										
Albania						60	57	75	93	104
Belarus										
Bosnia-Herzegovina					92	107	122	74	26	21
Bulgaria				50	55	58	351	351	218	203
Croatia			18	18	103	130	200	269	368	447
Czech Republic		30	176	563	654	810	836	829	963	1,014
Estonia				231	583	746	810	1,013	1,173	1,315
Georgia			5	5	5	5	5	38	47	56
Hungary				471	1,116	1,255	1,583	1,553	1,553	1,652
Latvia			90	225	350	1,200	1,525	2,873	4,095	4,578
Lithuania				230	393	700	1,170	1,811	2,284	2,812
Macedonia							50	50	101	127
Moldova								121	121	121
Poland		49	236	1,419	1,977	2,304	3,760	7,183	9,187	10,334
Romania				650	1,200	1,200	1,200	2,920	3,033	3,644
Russia			15	19	16	15	15	40	8	
Serbia and Montenegro							3,000		50	50
Slovakia		36	34	100	84	100	148	196	279	339
Slovenia			40	620	1,150	1,429	1,568	1,718	1,953	2,128
Ukraine					69	70	70	72	80	84

Source: *Euromonitor International from Organic Centre Wales, University of Wales*

Automotives and Transport

Automotives

Table 4.1

Commercial Vehicles in Use 1980-2007
'000

	1980	1985	1990	1995	2000	2002	2003	2004	2005	2006	2007	Number in use /'000 persons 2007
Western Europe												
Austria	208.2	237.3	295.0	347.8	395.9	386.4	396.9	405.0	410.3	417.1	428.2	51.5
Belgium	354.5	340.2	423.6	487.3	593.3	627.8	644.6	668.4	691.4	706.3	726.9	68.8
Cyprus	25.2	45.0	76.6	103.9	117.6	120.8	122.9	121.0	121.6	118.9	119.5	139.8
Denmark	259.2	267.4	300.8	342.3	393.7	411.2	422.4	482.4	479.4	518.7	544.4	100.0
Finland	166.9	200.5	294.2	280.4	327.8	341.8	348.9	376.8	370.8	383.5	396.4	75.1
France	2,570.5	3,980.0	4,910.0	5,195.0	5,753.0	5,984.0	6,068.0	6,139.0	6,198.0	6,261.0	6,429.3	104.7
Germany			1,989.4	3,061.9	3,533.9	3,567.5	3,541.2	3,539.7	3,133.2	3,172.0	3,231.9	39.3
Gibraltar	0.7	1.0	2.5	1.1	2.3	1.4	2.0	2.6	2.1	2.3	2.3	80.1
Greece	418.7	565.0	776.7	847.5	1,055.0	1,136.4	1,158.2	1,185.9	1,213.3	1,246.8	1,283.0	114.9
Iceland	9.0	12.7	14.4	16.1	21.1	22.0	22.9	24.8	27.4	30.0	33.0	109.8
Ireland	70.2	101.0	152.2	155.2	226.3	258.7	278.7	296.7	316.1	349.9	374.4	87.1
Italy	1,428.8	1,910.1	2,494.5	2,863.4	3,581.5	3,976.0	4,166.0	4,250.9	4,274.1	4,579.6	4,765.9	80.9
Liechtenstein	1.2	1.5	2.0	2.3	2.5	2.7	2.6	2.6	2.6	2.5	2.6	73.9
Luxembourg	15.5	14.0	18.1	27.1	31.4	35.1	35.9	35.6	36.1	36.1	36.1	77.5
Malta	14.2	17.5	21.2	50.9	44.3	45.0	45.4	45.7	45.5	46.7	47.8	117.5
Monaco				2.7	2.9	3.0	3.1	3.2	3.2	3.3	3.4	103.3
Netherlands	376.0	428.0	560.0	658.0	883.0	996.0	1,039.0	1,069.0	1,070.0	1,063.0	1,059.2	64.7
Norway	164.5	249.7	329.5	382.0	451.0	464.8	470.3	480.1	493.9	514.5	532.4	114.0
Portugal	264.0	356.0	568.0	824.0	1,157.0	1,253.0	1,275.1	1,305.7	1,323.3	1,335.0	1,355.0	127.7
Spain	1,380.9	1,570.9	2,378.7	3,071.6	3,977.9	4,315.8	4,419.4	4,660.4	4,907.9	5,146.4	5,388.8	121.1
Sweden	194.4	231.4	324.1	322.3	388.6	423.0	435.3	453.3	474.6	493.4	509.7	55.9
Switzerland	169.4	200.5	283.4	299.3	318.8	332.5	336.0	343.0	352.9	360.5	372.2	49.6
Turkey	428.2	553.1	709.9	982.4	1,543.1	1,636.2	1,747.4	2,379.0	2,653.9	2,938.6	3,181.4	43.3
United Kingdom	1,912.8	1,650.0	2,861.0	3,208.7	3,463.5	3,501.3	3,694.2	3,819.4	3,943.2	4,144.7	4,346.2	71.6
Eastern Europe												
Albania				48.4	67.6	82.0	85.2	79.8	82.8	83.6	84.0	26.3
Belarus			70.8	96.5	118.9	122.5	131.9	134.6	141.6	147.7	152.5	15.6
Bosnia-Herzegovina					77.5	88.2	94.5	98.2	106.3	109.0	110.9	28.2
Bulgaria			240.2	257.1	283.0	293.0	297.7	303.2	307.2	312.3	314.8	41.3
Croatia			52.4	77.4	127.2	143.5	153.1	159.7	157.5	164.1	170.8	38.5
Czech Republic			162.7	222.7	293.9	344.8	360.7	391.4	435.2	488.6	528.8	51.4
Estonia	57.5	66.4	75.6	72.6	88.2	85.5	88.8	91.0	91.4	92.8	93.9	70.1
Georgia						45.5	42.9	68.6	68.6	71.8	74.4	16.9
Hungary	190.0	216.0	272.5	324.6	384.3	414.0	424.7	427.9	445.1	463.1	474.0	47.1
Latvia			71.7	85.2	108.6	113.9	115.6	118.3	123.8	131.7	140.2	61.5
Lithuania			98.2	118.5	114.2	121.4	126.5	130.5	137.8	142.5	147.7	43.6
Macedonia			20.6	15.1	45.9	50.1	50.1	50.1	50.2	50.2	50.3	24.7
Moldova			83.4	67.4	68.5	70.5	70.6	68.5	71.7	74.5	77.0	20.3
Poland	1,373.4	1,722.0	2,329.0	2,651.0	1,865.4	2,518.5	2,518.5	2,632.2	2,494.3	2,476.0	2,609.0	68.5
Romania			287.0	385.1	467.9	487.9	505.0	525.6	532.6	614.3	692.7	32.1
Russia							3,200.0	5,536.0	5,642.3	5,642.3	5,695.5	40.1
Serbia and Montenegro						132.7	188.8	256.2	283.0	292.7	301.0	28.8
Slovakia				160.2	169.6	168.7	166.8	162.7	183.3	198.1	208.6	38.7
Slovenia			49.1	60.9	59.2	63.1	65.1	68.7	72.1	75.9	83.8	41.7
Ukraine			59.7	175.7	349.9	500.0	703.0	985.7	1,050.0	1,108.6	1,163.5	25.0

Source: *Euromonitor International from SMMT/national statistics*
Notes: *There may be wide variations from year to year in SMMT estimates and in other figures due to interpretation of definitions*

Table 4.2

Passenger Cars in Use 1980-2007
'000

	1980	1985	1990	1995	2000	2002	2003	2004	2005	2006	2007	Number in use /'000 persons 2007
Western Europe												
Austria	2,247.0	2,530.8	2,991.3	3,593.6	4,097.1	3,987.1	4,054.3	4,109.1	4,156.7	4,205.0	4,256.2	511.9
Belgium	3,158.7	3,278.8	3,833.3	4,239.1	4,628.9	4,724.9	4,772.6	4,818.6	4,861.4	4,929.3	4,973.7	470.5
Cyprus	92.0	120.0	178.6	219.7	267.6	287.6	302.5	335.6	355.1	372.9	389.6	455.8
Denmark	1,389.5	1,500.9	1,590.6	1,684.8	1,842.9	1,890.0	1,894.2	1,914.4	1,961.2	2,013.9	2,016.2	370.2
Finland	1,225.9	1,546.1	1,938.9	1,900.9	2,120.7	2,180.0	2,259.4	2,331.2	2,414.5	2,489.3	2,501.6	474.1
France	19,150.0	21,090.0	23,550.0	25,100.0	28,060.0	29,160.0	29,560.0	29,900.0	30,100.0	30,400.0	31,247.4	508.8
Germany			30,695.1	40,499.4	43,772.3	44,657.3	45,022.9	45,375.5	46,090.3	46,559.7	46,837.7	569.0
Gibraltar	6.5	10.6	19.8	18.4	25.8	12.9	12.8	13.9	14.6	14.7	15.0	512.5
Greece	879.8	1,188.0	1,735.5	2,204.8	3,150.0	3,646.1	3,839.5	4,073.5	4,303.1	4,543.0	4,798.5	429.6
Iceland	80.0	100.0	119.7	119.2	158.9	161.7	166.9	175.4	187.4	197.3	207.5	689.4
Ireland	734.4	709.5	796.4	990.4	1,319.3	1,447.9	1,507.1	1,582.8	1,662.2	1,778.9	1,849.3	430.2
Italy	17,686.2	22,494.6	27,416.0	30,301.4	32,583.8	33,706.2	34,310.4	33,973.1	34,667.5	35,297.3	35,560.7	603.9
Liechtenstein	12.6	14.8	16.9	18.8	21.8	23.3	23.5	23.9	24.4	24.3	24.7	703.1
Luxembourg	147.4	152.0	183.4	229.0	257.8	282.4	287.2	293.4	299.8	304.5	314.3	673.6
Malta	66.2	75.0	104.7	147.6	189.1	201.9	208.8	211.4	212.6	218.2	223.7	550.3
Monaco				20.7	22.9	22.6	22.7	22.9	23.0	23.1	23.2	710.1
Netherlands	4,515.0	4,901.0	5,196.0	5,633.0	6,343.0	6,710.0	6,855.0	7,151.0	7,299.0	7,256.0	7,234.6	442.3
Norway	1,233.6	1,514.0	1,613.0	1,684.7	1,851.9	1,899.7	1,933.6	1,977.9	2,028.8	2,084.8	2,153.7	461.1
Portugal	941.0	1,185.0	1,630.0	2,611.0	3,593.0	3,885.0	3,966.0	4,100.0	4,200.0	4,290.0	4,363.8	411.3
Spain	7,556.5	9,273.7	11,995.6	14,212.3	17,449.2	18,732.6	18,688.3	19,541.9	20,250.4	20,908.7	21,648.9	486.7
Sweden	2,883.0	3,151.2	3,601.0	3,630.8	3,998.6	4,042.8	4,075.4	4,113.4	4,153.7	4,202.5	4,258.5	467.3
Switzerland	2,246.8	2,617.2	2,985.4	3,229.2	3,545.2	3,701.0	3,753.9	3,811.4	3,861.4	3,900.0	3,955.8	527.6
Turkey	742.3	983.4	1,649.9	3,058.5	4,422.2	4,600.1	4,700.3	5,400.4	5,772.7	6,141.0	6,472.2	88.1
United Kingdom	15,437.7	19,458.2	21,989.0	24,428.6	27,959.7	29,320.9	29,895.8	30,267.2	30,650.4	30,994.8	31,339.2	516.2
Eastern Europe												
Albania			5.3	58.7	114.5	148.5	174.8	190.0	209.6	228.6	247.6	77.6
Belarus			604.5	939.6	1,385.9	1,515.9	1,620.1	1,671.3	1,737.1	1,814.8	1,873.3	192.1
Bosnia-Herzegovina			450.3		289.2	321.7	335.0	348.0	357.2	361.9	366.7	93.2
Bulgaria	500.0	600.0	1,276.8	1,647.6	1,809.4	1,951.0	1,990.0	2,041.0	2,063.6	2,072.4	2,109.9	276.8
Croatia			795.4	710.9	1,124.8	1,244.3	1,293.4	1,337.5	1,384.7	1,435.8	1,491.1	335.8
Czech Republic			2,520.4	3,043.3	3,438.9	3,647.1	3,706.0	3,815.5	3,958.7	4,108.6	4,154.6	403.9
Estonia	126.5	177.0	240.9	383.4	463.9	400.7	434.0	471.2	493.8	501.7	506.8	378.3
Georgia			485.0	360.6	247.9	252.0	255.2	255.2	269.7	273.9	278.3	63.3
Hungary	925.0	1,435.9	1,856.7	2,044.9	2,364.7	2,629.5	2,777.2	2,828.4	2,888.7	2,953.7	3,012.2	299.5
Latvia				331.8	556.8	619.1	648.9	686.1	742.4	822.0	904.9	396.8
Lithuania			493.0	718.5	1,172.4	1,180.9	1,256.9	1,315.9	1,455.3	1,529.8	1,597.6	472.0
Macedonia			230.8	285.9	299.0	308.0	300.0	312.5	299.8	303.5	305.6	149.9
Moldova			209.0	165.9	231.0	260.8	257.1	270.6	279.8	287.6	293.9	77.5
Poland	2,269.9	3,450.0	5,261.0	7,517.0	9,991.3	11,243.8	11,243.8	11,975.2	12,339.4	13,384.2	14,589.0	382.9
Romania			1,292.3	2,197.5	2,777.6	2,973.4	3,087.6	3,225.4	3,363.8	3,225.4	3,518.4	163.2
Russia			8,986.3	14,195.3	17,050.0	21,152.0	23,383.0	24,208.0	25,569.7	25,569.7	27,092.5	190.7
Serbia and Montenegro						1,359.2	1,381.7	1,404.2	1,497.4	1,511.8	1,539.6	147.2
Slovakia			860.0	1,015.8	1,247.0	1,326.9	1,356.0	1,388.2	1,303.7	1,333.7	1,361.9	252.6
Slovenia			578.3	698.2	866.1	894.5	910.4	933.9	960.2	980.3	1,014.1	504.5
Ukraine			3,272.0	4,468.7	5,372.0	5,529.0	5,585.0	5,603.8	5,800.0	5,986.0	6,071.0	130.7

Source: Euromonitor International from SMMT/national statistics
Notes: There may be wide variations from year to year in SMMT estimates and in other figures due to interpretation of definitions

Automotives

Table 4.3

Two-Wheelers in Use 1980-2007
'000

	1980	1985	1990	1995	2000	2002	2003	2004	2005	2006	2007	Number in use /'000 persons 2007
Western Europe												
Austria	574.1	648.4	548.0	546.4	628.0	596.8	606.9	612.2	621.0	629.9	638.2	76.8
Belgium	445.7	466.1	481.8	548.5	626.9	651.2	665.4	628.6	642.3	653.0	660.1	62.4
Cyprus		40.0	51.0	50.4	43.3	40.3	41.5	41.4	41.3	41.5	41.5	48.5
Denmark				58.0	138.3	151.3	155.7	162.1	175.0	183.6	190.5	35.0
Finland				159.0	192.6	222.7	244.4	270.6	284.2	298.1	310.2	58.8
France				2,289.0	2,410.0	2,441.0	2,448.0	2,462.0	2,471.7	2,485.7	2,495.3	40.6
Germany				3,920.2	5,062.8	5,256.9	5,306.0	5,462.5	5,535.4	5,606.1	5,666.2	68.8
Gibraltar		1.6	2.8	6.6	8.5	5.7	5.6	6.2	6.6	7.0	7.2	246.0
Greece	749.0	1,254.3	1,222.6	1,821.5	2,438.9	2,524.6	2,586.5	2,600.7	2,631.7	2,655.5	2,670.8	239.1
Iceland		0.9	1.1	1.9	2.3	2.6	2.7	3.1	3.2	3.4	3.5	11.5
Ireland		26.0	22.7	23.5	30.6	32.9	35.1	35.8	36.5	37.1	37.5	8.7
Italy				7,905.8	9,773.1	10,149.5	10,295.4	10,224.6	9,996.5	9,784.1	9,632.0	163.6
Liechtenstein	1.2	1.5	2.0	2.3	2.5	2.7	2.6	2.6	2.6	2.5	2.5	71.0
Luxembourg		24.7	25.4	28.5	32.8	34.7	36.0	36.9	37.9	38.3	38.8	83.2
Malta				8.0	12.4	13.3	13.7	12.8	13.0	13.1	13.2	32.5
Monaco		4.0	4.7	5.3	6.6	6.9	7.0	7.2	7.3	7.5	7.6	231.7
Netherlands		728.0	612.0	848.0	970.8	1,002.5	1,015.6	1,019.1	1,030.6	1,035.1	1,039.5	63.5
Norway		186.6	203.5	197.8	249.9	277.0	292.3	301.7	310.6	318.1	323.8	69.3
Portugal	1,069.1	1,091.2	968.6	838.5	734.0	604.0	633.0	611.0	555.1	550.5	544.1	51.3
Spain		2,350.3	3,073.6	3,402.0	3,648.2	3,561.4	3,657.1	3,854.1	4,066.3	4,176.3	4,211.2	94.7
Sweden				258.9	313.3	351.5	367.0	385.1	406.2	421.6	431.4	47.3
Switzerland	808.8	862.1	763.9	721.6	732.6	745.1	762.9	770.6	770.6	783.5	787.8	105.1
Turkey	137.9	289.1	531.9	819.9	1,011.3	1,046.9	1,073.4	1,218.7	1,441.1	1,508.0	1,534.4	20.9
United Kingdom	1,457.0	1,148.0	879.8	900.2	1,157.7	1,256.4	1,314.0	1,338.3	1,382.9	1,427.8	1,456.0	24.0
Eastern Europe												
Albania		8.6	6.9	3.8	3.4	3.9	4.9	5.4	5.8	6.1		1.9
Belarus		404.1	504.2	523.6	525.0	506.4	454.6	436.5	416.9	397.0		40.7
Bosnia-Herzegovina												
Bulgaria		481.7	519.3	519.2	530.3	535.7	541.9	546.2	550.1	554.0		72.7
Croatia				65.3	85.3	99.2	113.0	124.9	134.4	143.6		32.4
Czech Republic			1,172.7	1,125.3	737.1	759.4	751.6	756.6	794.0	803.9	818.8	79.6
Estonia			2.7	3.3	6.7	7.3	8.1	9.1	9.6	10.1	10.6	7.9
Georgia			29.7	27.9	4.6	2.8	3.3	5.2	5.5	5.7	5.9	1.3
Hungary			169.8	157.0	91.2	97.6	103.5	106.2	109.1	111.7	113.5	11.3
Latvia				15.7	20.7	22.2	22.9	29.9	30.7	31.4	32.0	14.1
Lithuania				20.0	19.8	21.0	21.9	22.9	24.0	24.6	25.2	7.4
Macedonia			1.9	1.6	2.3	2.5	2.6	2.7	2.8	2.8	2.9	1.4
Moldova			196.4	144.7	45.5	13.4	14.4	15.7	16.7	17.4	18.1	4.8
Poland		1,546.5	1,356.6	929.3	802.6	824.1	845.5	835.8	753.6	717.0	688.5	18.1
Romania		297.5	311.6	327.7	315.7	238.5	235.8	234.7	225.3	218.3	214.4	9.9
Russia				7,735.0	7,841.2	8,177.4	8,275.7	8,399.5	8,523.6	8,600.5		60.5
Serbia and Montenegro				13.7	13.4	13.3	14.8	15.1	15.5	16.0		1.5
Slovakia				45.6	47.9	48.7	52.0	53.2	54.3	55.6		10.3
Slovenia			50.4	45.9	49.4	50.8	42.5	40.4	49.4	51.8	53.8	26.8
Ukraine				3,253.4	3,102.6	2,156.4	1,744.4	1,369.0	1,145.4	951.6	786.1	677.1	14.6

Source: Euromonitor International from SMMT/national statistics
Notes: Two-wheelers consist of motorcycles and mopeds

Table 4.4

Production of Commercial Vehicles 1980-2007

'000

	1980	1985	1990	1995	2000	2002	2003	2004	2005	2006	2007
Western Europe											
Austria	8.5	11.2	11.0	9.2	25.0	19.9	21.0	21.5	22.7	26.9	28.1
Belgium	47.0	48.7	90.0	103.6	121.1	120.3	112.7	43.2	33.2	36.1	44.7
Cyprus			22.0	5.0	4.0	4.0	3.9	3.8	3.8	3.7	3.7
Denmark											
Finland	1.1	0.8	0.9	0.4	0.4	0.4	0.4	0.5	0.4	0.4	0.3
France	439.9	383.7	474.2	423.8	468.6	309.1	399.7	438.6	436.0	446.0	465.0
Germany	357.6	279.2	315.9	307.1	394.7	346.1	361.2	377.9	407.5	421.1	504.3
Gibraltar											
Greece			1.4	0.4	0.1	0.1	0.1	0.1	0.1	0.1	0.1
Iceland											
Ireland	2.6										
Italy	165.1	183.8	246.2	244.9	316.0	301.3	295.2	308.4	312.8	319.1	373.5
Liechtenstein											
Luxembourg											
Malta											
Monaco											
Netherlands	32.1	14.3	17.3	17.6	30.5	48.9	52.2	59.9	65.6	72.1	76.7
Norway											
Portugal	58.4	26.5	77.5	85.7	68.2	68.3	73.8	75.9	81.5	83.8	42.2
Spain	152.8	187.5	374.0	375.0	666.5	588.3	630.5	609.7	654.3	698.8	693.9
Sweden	63.1	60.3	74.4	102.5	35.7	38.2	42.6	49.9	49.9	44.6	49.2
Switzerland	1.2										
Turkey	19.4	37.3	62.8	49.0	133.5	142.4	239.2	376.3	425.4	442.1	464.5
United Kingdom	389.2	266.0	270.3	233.0	172.4	193.1	188.9	209.3	206.8	206.3	215.7
Eastern Europe											
Albania											
Belarus			43.0	13.0	14.6	16.9	18.4	21.7	23.0	25.3	26.9
Bosnia-Herzegovina											
Bulgaria			8.9	0.5	0.2	0.2	0.2	0.2	0.2	0.2	0.2
Croatia			129.0	31.0	45.7	48.3	49.2	50.1	50.7	51.3	51.5
Czech Republic					29.8	7.2	6.9	6.9	8.0	8.2	12.7
Estonia											
Georgia											
Hungary	15.2	14.0	8.1	1.2	3.4	3.3	3.8	4.1	3.5	3.2	4.0
Latvia			17.1	4.3	1.0	0.9	0.9	0.9	0.9	0.9	0.9
Lithuania											
Macedonia			14.6	1.8							
Moldova											
Poland	116.0	57.1	42.8	10.6	42.6	23.6	15.2	78.0	85.4	82.3	89.7
Romania	49.1	19.8	17.6	21.2	14.0	14.2	19.5	23.2	20.6	11.9	7.6
Russia			716.9	214.9	244.6	239.7	268.4	276.0	283.1	330.4	371.5
Serbia and Montenegro						1.7	907.0	1.9	1.6	1.4	1.7
Slovakia			0.9	0.2	0.4	276.0	187.0	0.0	0.0	0.0	0.0
Slovenia					367.0	0.0	7.6	15.0	39.6	35.3	24.2
Ukraine		45.2	40.3	8.7	2.5	3.4	4.9	7.8	19.0	20.4	22.5

Source: Euromonitor International from SMMT/national statistics

Automotives

Table 4.5

Production of Passenger Cars 1980-2007
'000

	1980	1985	1990	1995	2000	2002	2003	2004	2005	2006	2007
Western Europe											
Austria	7.5	7.1	12.7	59.2	116.0	132.8	118.7	227.2	230.5	248.1	200.0
Belgium	281.7	248.5	311.8	385.9	912.2	936.9	791.7	852.4	895.1	881.9	789.7
Cyprus											
Denmark											
Finland	21.5	38.7	30.2	34.6	38.3	41.1	19.2	10.1	21.2	32.4	24.0
France	2,938.6	2,632.4	3,294.8	3,050.9	2,879.8	3,292.8	3,220.3	3,227.4	3,113.0	2,723.2	2,550.9
Germany	3,520.9	4,166.7	4,660.7	4,360.2	5,131.9	5,123.2	5,145.4	5,192.1	5,350.2	5,398.5	5,709.1
Gibraltar											
Greece			12.6	3.2	2.9	2.8	2.6	2.4	2.3	2.2	2.1
Iceland											
Ireland	44.6										
Italy	1,445.2	1,389.2	1,874.7	1,422.4	1,422.3	1,125.8	1,026.5	833.6	725.5	892.5	910.9
Liechtenstein											
Luxembourg											
Malta											
Monaco											
Netherlands	80.8	108.1	121.3	100.4	215.1	182.4	163.1	187.6	115.1	87.3	61.9
Norway											
Portugal	45.5	61.0	60.2	73.2	178.5	182.6	165.6	150.8	137.6	143.5	134.0
Spain	1,028.8	1,230.1	1,679.3	1,958.8	2,366.4	2,266.9	2,399.4	2,402.5	2,098.2	2,078.6	2,195.8
Sweden	235.3	400.7	335.9	387.7	279.0	238.0	280.4	290.4	288.7	288.6	316.9
Switzerland											
Turkey	31.5	60.4	167.6	233.4	297.5	204.2	294.1	447.2	453.7	545.7	634.9
United Kingdom	923.7	1,048.0	1,295.6	1,532.1	1,641.5	1,629.9	1,657.6	1,647.2	1,596.3	1,442.1	1,534.6
Eastern Europe											
Albania											
Belarus								0.0	0.0	0.0	
Bosnia-Herzegovina											
Bulgaria		15.0	14.6	1.1	1.8	2.0	2.1	2.2	2.3	2.3	2.3
Croatia					1.2	1.4	1.4	1.5	1.6	1.6	1.6
Czech Republic				213.0	428.2	441.3	436.3	443.1	596.8	848.8	925.8
Estonia											
Georgia											
Hungary				36.5	77.3	138.2	122.3	118.6	148.5	187.6	288.0
Latvia											
Lithuania											
Macedonia											
Moldova											
Poland	364.5	283.0	266.4	391.9	532.0	287.5	306.8	523.0	540.0	632.3	695.0
Romania	79.3	114.4	99.9	71.0	64.2	65.3	75.7	99.0	174.5	201.7	234.1
Russia	1,166.0	1,165.0	1,103.0	893.6	969.2	980.1	1,010.4	1,110.1	1,068.1	1,177.9	1,288.7
Serbia and Montenegro						10.3	13.0	13.3	12.6	9.8	8.2
Slovakia				22.3	181.3	225.4	281.2	223.5	218.3	295.4	571.1
Slovenia			74.7	63.5	122.9	126.7	110.6	116.6	138.4	115.0	174.2
Ukraine		167.5	103.4	58.7	11.7	50.4	103.0	179.1	196.7	274.9	380.1

Source: *Euromonitor International from SMMT/national statistics*

Automotives

Table 4.6

Production of Two-Wheelers 1985-2007

'000

	1985	1990	1995	2000	2002	2003	2004	2005	2006	2007
Western Europe										
Austria	160.8	20.9	13.2	29.2	53.4	56.0	56.7	59.8	61.7	63.3
Belgium	58.3	61.3	8.2	6.4	5.8	5.4	4.8	4.6	4.4	4.2
Cyprus										
Denmark										
Finland	14.8	5.2	0.3	0.2	0.1	0.1	0.1	0.1	0.1	0.2
France			394.6	451.4	158.6	154.8	255.7	259.2	268.5	273.7
Germany	85.8	55.3	44.6	112.6	121.7	109.1	102.8	105.9	107.9	109.2
Gibraltar										
Greece										
Iceland										
Ireland										
Italy	808.3	894.9	1,101.1	1,048.2	736.5	697.0	685.5	695.0	699.8	704.5
Liechtenstein										
Luxembourg										
Malta										
Monaco										
Netherlands				9.6	10.8	11.2	12.4	12.9	13.1	13.3
Norway										
Portugal			19.4	21.3	22.2	21.5	20.6	20.2	19.8	19.4
Spain	173.5	384.6	279.9	284.8	223.7	209.0	230.9	249.5	271.3	285.6
Sweden		1.3	0.1	0.1	0.3	0.3	0.3	0.4	0.5	0.5
Switzerland	11.7	0.8								
Turkey				217.2	199.6	216.0	229.5	236.7	243.7	245.3
United Kingdom	2.0	1.9	11.2	25.6	30.0	31.5	26.2	34.6	35.0	35.1
Eastern Europe										
Albania										
Belarus				36.6	37.6	38.1	38.7	38.9	39.2	39.5
Bosnia-Herzegovina										
Bulgaria										
Croatia										
Czech Republic				3.9	7.9	2.2	1.8	2.1	2.5	3.1
Estonia										
Georgia										
Hungary				0.3	0.2	0.2	0.2	0.2	0.2	0.2
Latvia				1.0	1.0	1.0	1.0	1.0	1.0	1.0
Lithuania				0.0	0.0	0.0	0.0	0.0	0.0	0.0
Macedonia										
Moldova										
Poland				0.0	0.0	0.0	0.0	0.0	0.0	0.0
Romania	2.0	4.1	0.1	0.2	0.2	0.2	0.3	0.3	0.3	0.3
Russia	818.0			32.8	26.0	25.8	25.3	25.1	24.9	24.7
Serbia and Montenegro										
Slovakia			17.2							
Slovenia		57.5	56.2	59.9	65.1	64.0	60.8	59.5	58.2	56.9
Ukraine				0.2	0.3	0.3	0.2	0.2	0.2	0.2

Source: Euromonitor International from SMMT/national statistics

Automotives

Table 4.7

Price of Automotive Diesel 1980-2007
Units of national currency per 10 litres (inc. tax)

	1980	1985	1990	1995	2000	2002	2003	2004	2005	2006	2007	US$ per litre 2007
Western Europe												
Austria	6.21	7.81	5.98	6.25	7.78	7.19	7.27	8.09	9.48	10.09	10.03	1.37
Belgium	3.46	4.51	5.28	6.07	8.10	7.26	7.56	8.81	10.40	10.79	11.19	1.53
Cyprus								7.31	8.64	8.98	9.61	1.32
Denmark	20.00	28.14			70.91	67.93	67.84	68.20	76.62	81.80	81.88	1.50
Finland	3.29	4.70	5.19	5.91	8.50	7.84	8.08	8.48	9.69	10.22	10.53	1.44
France		5.82	4.94	5.87	8.45	7.71	7.93	8.83	10.23	10.79	10.79	1.48
Germany			4.89	5.73	8.01	8.40	8.87	9.38	10.68	11.16	11.87	1.63
Gibraltar												
Greece	0.43	1.04	1.94	4.10	6.65	6.22	6.37	7.40	8.27	9.64	10.64	1.46
Iceland												
Ireland	3.20	7.06	6.95	6.79	8.42	7.74	8.04	8.82	10.36	10.95	11.35	1.56
Italy	2.33	4.16	6.39	6.93	8.92	8.56	8.77	9.38	11.08	11.65	11.54	1.58
Liechtenstein												
Luxembourg	3.01	4.97	3.11	4.96	6.89	6.32	6.38	6.90	8.43	9.17	9.63	1.32
Malta								7.24	8.76	9.87	10.02	1.37
Monaco												
Netherlands	4.38	5.70	4.74	7.02	8.45	7.90	7.95	8.89	10.23	10.87	11.23	1.54
Norway	18.42	23.50			98.98	81.98	83.88	86.80	98.30	106.48	114.81	1.96
Portugal	0.82	3.29	4.96	5.22	6.54	6.45	7.10	7.87	9.37	10.61	11.35	1.56
Spain	3.51	4.51	4.81	4.93	6.95	6.89	6.94	7.54	8.93	9.47	9.59	1.31
Sweden	14.65	30.73	49.22	63.46	84.46	83.38	81.14	85.47	103.53	111.33	114.62	1.70
Switzerland	12.72	14.18	11.23	11.94	14.36	13.35	13.58	14.46	16.38	17.40	18.05	1.50
Turkey				0.19	4.35	10.96	13.94	15.39	19.56	22.24	27.40	2.10
United Kingdom	2.78	3.65	3.98	5.43	8.13	7.55	7.79	8.19	9.09	9.52	9.98	2.00
Eastern Europe												
Albania												
Belarus												
Bosnia-Herzegovina												
Bulgaria	88.00											
Croatia												
Czech Republic	158.10	55.00	98.00	156.50	247.00	217.30	218.95	248.68	278.73	289.57	304.76	1.50
Estonia								107.97	130.93	135.82	145.12	1.27
Georgia												
Hungary	65.50	93.00	300.00	834.10	2,150.80	2,013.35	2,098.85	2,185.63	2,500.93	2,709.10	2,915.44	1.59
Latvia							4.50	5.60	6.03	6.08	7.17	1.40
Lithuania								24.60	28.44	30.65	32.32	1.28
Macedonia												
Moldova												
Poland	7.15			10.01	25.55	25.80	28.36	31.68	36.82	38.17	39.69	1.43
Romania	0.19			0.42	8.48	15.90	18.87	24.67	30.32	32.85	35.01	1.44
Russia					57.83				140.16	167.83	208.93	0.82
Serbia and Montenegro				24.00								
Slovakia		55.00	98.00	176.30	317.10	281.30	299.27	338.43	376.35	398.07	400.01	1.62
Slovenia								8.08	9.46	9.62	9.89	1.36
Ukraine												

Source: Institute of Petroleum, OECD Energy Prices and Taxes/Euromonitor International

Table 4.8

Price of Automotive Diesel by Quarter 2006-2008

Units of national currency per 10 litres (inc. tax)

	2006 1st Quarter	2006 2nd Quarter	2006 3rd Quarter	2006 4th Quarter	2007 1st Quarter	2007 2nd Quarter	2007 3rd Quarter	2007 4th Quarter	2008 1st Quarter	2008 2nd Quarter
Western Europe										
Austria	9.85	10.41	10.41	9.67	9.45	9.86	10.60	11.49	11.55	13.04
Belgium	10.73	11.11	10.93	10.40	10.17	10.73	11.00	11.85	12.02	
Cyprus	8.54	9.07	9.21	8.52	8.23	8.78	9.16	9.83	10.20	11.12
Denmark	80.96	84.19	83.46	78.60	76.71	80.98	83.23	89.40	92.17	
Finland	10.11	10.36	10.39	10.03	9.74	9.87	10.12	11.01	12.25	
France	10.65	11.10	11.05	10.34	10.25	10.70	10.98	11.73	12.26	13.23
Germany	11.03	11.37	11.44	10.82	10.83	11.48	11.72	12.70	12.94	
Gibraltar										
Greece	9.21	9.74	9.96							
Iceland										
Ireland	10.79	11.05	11.29	10.65	10.24	10.65	11.02	11.28	11.85	
Italy	11.54	11.98	11.92	11.17	10.96	11.32	11.71	12.48	12.94	
Liechtenstein										
Luxembourg	8.98	9.49	9.45	8.77	8.66	9.15	9.42	10.16	10.61	
Malta	9.64	10.10	10.23	9.36	9.05	9.09	9.73	10.05	10.19	10.91
Monaco										
Netherlands	10.87	11.10	11.10	10.41	10.28	10.77	11.06	11.79	12.24	
Norway	100.90	103.50	113.40	108.13	99.15	101.00	103.70	110.00	117.00	
Portugal	10.14	10.66	10.84	10.81	10.11	10.60	10.91	11.61	12.09	
Spain	9.30	9.76	9.78	9.03	8.89	9.43	9.69	10.27	10.81	11.80
Sweden	110.88	114.56	113.46	106.44	105.66	108.50	108.20	116.05	126.39	
Switzerland	17.10	17.47	17.83	17.20	16.87	17.33	17.63	18.87	19.37	
Turkey	20.60	22.44	23.58	22.33	21.79	22.70	22.95	24.65	26.14	
United Kingdom	9.35	9.79	9.75	9.19	9.13	9.61	9.65	10.36	11.02	
Eastern Europe										
Albania										
Belarus										
Bosnia-Herzegovina										
Bulgaria										
Croatia										
Czech Republic	279.51	297.73	299.09	281.97	269.70	281.00	287.33	310.55	313.22	
Estonia	134.81	138.97	138.82	130.69	129.29	129.33	134.99	149.04	173.44	184.66
Georgia										
Hungary	2,589.89	2,749.42	2,860.46	2,636.64	2,478.57	2,574.10	2,648.33	2,820.77	3,030.03	
Latvia	5.92	6.33	6.23	5.84	5.96	6.11	6.24	6.87	7.34	7.92
Lithuania	30.58	31.50	31.34	29.19	28.56	29.87	30.47	32.29	36.12	39.40
Macedonia										
Moldova										
Poland	36.73	38.81	39.65	37.51	35.68	36.77	37.55	40.63	40.78	
Romania	32.40	33.10	34.00	31.90	30.40	30.90	31.20	33.60	37.80	
Russia	165.09	165.54	169.22	171.48	170.63	169.84	170.75	178.93	202.02	
Serbia and Montenegro										
Slovakia	392.30	408.10	411.00	380.90	360.70	371.30	378.20	401.30	414.30	
Slovenia	9.32	9.78	9.95	9.44	9.09	9.57	9.90	10.34	10.60	11.59
Ukraine										

Source: *Institute of Petroleum, OECD Energy Prices and Taxes/Euromonitor International*

Automotives

Table 4.9

Price of Leaded Petrol 1980-2007
Units of national currency per 10 litres (inc. tax)

	1980	1985	1990	1995	2000	2002	2003	2004	2005	2006	2007	US$ per litre 2007
Western Europe												
Austria	6.30	8.65	7.12	8.57	8.30	8.71	8.76	9.07	9.93	10.44	10.51	1.44
Belgium	5.73	8.38	7.18	8.41	11.02	10.48	10.14	9.99	11.00	11.78	12.31	1.69
Cyprus												
Denmark	45.30	61.35	62.82	60.89								
Finland	4.85	6.50	8.57									
France	5.15	8.52	7.71	8.94	11.67	10.95	10.97	11.43	12.69	13.57	14.20	1.95
Germany	5.96	7.37	6.25	8.65	10.43	11.45	11.83	12.38	13.20	13.81	14.67	2.01
Gibraltar												
Greece	1.02	2.01	3.37	5.99	8.11	7.84	7.88	8.69	9.44	10.85	11.86	1.63
Iceland												
Ireland	4.06	8.43	8.18	7.69	10.37	11.75	12.60	13.42	13.97	14.40	14.68	2.01
Italy	3.62	6.82	7.61	9.46	11.27	11.53	11.67	12.07	12.98	13.55	13.71	1.88
Liechtenstein												
Luxembourg	4.42	6.76	5.38	6.95	7.52	7.88	8.15	8.39	9.34	10.00	10.57	1.45
Malta									9.48	9.90	11.64	12.12	1.66
Monaco												
Netherlands	6.51	8.77	7.76	9.35								
Norway	37.15	51.28	65.44	87.74	111.76	95.70	99.83	106.70	114.02	120.01	122.68	2.09
Portugal	2.17	5.44	6.82	7.77	8.61	9.55	9.97	10.92	12.05	13.80	14.74	2.02
Spain	3.25	5.59	4.97	6.78	8.75	8.71	8.86	9.39	10.39	11.13	11.29	1.55
Sweden	29.47	46.63	64.66	78.88	98.13	106.45	112.23	119.18	126.30	129.50	132.08	1.95
Switzerland	11.60	12.60	10.80	12.30	13.09	13.37	13.48	13.65	14.46	15.44	15.81	1.32
Turkey				0.29	5.82	14.79	18.10	19.66	25.20	27.45	32.74	2.51
United Kingdom	3.29	4.31	4.86	5.97	8.49	7.70	7.99	8.45	9.10	9.40	9.84	1.97
Eastern Europe												
Albania												
Belarus												
Bosnia-Herzegovina												
Bulgaria	250.00											
Croatia	45.00											
Czech Republic	65.00	80.00	141.90	195.80	289.80	307.84	312.26	317.31	319.40	320.00	336.71	1.66
Estonia												
Georgia												
Hungary	110.00	200.00	500.00	1,010.00								
Latvia								4.85	5.81	6.36	7.70	1.50
Lithuania												
Macedonia												
Moldova												
Poland	9.10	20.70	2.78	12.25	31.48	45.00	48.00	52.00	54.70	55.70	56.92	2.06
Romania	0.25			0.57	10.93	20.70	25.15	28.36	32.70	34.50	39.48	1.62
Russia												
Serbia and Montenegro				31.50								
Slovakia	65.00	80.00	103.80	188.71	331.20	300.40	314.40	310.73	328.00	349.00	350.22	1.42
Slovenia												
Ukraine	806.20											

Source: Institute of Petroleum, OECD Energy Prices and Taxes/Euromonitor International

Table 4.10

Automotives

Price of Premium Unleaded Petrol 1980-2007

Units of national currency per 10 litres (inc. tax)

	1980	1985	1990	1995	2000	2002	2003	2004	2005	2006	2007	US$ per litre 2007
Western Europe												
Austria			6.84	8.21	9.42	8.74	8.80	9.50	10.30	10.91	10.94	1.50
Belgium			6.74	7.78	11.08	10.53	10.20	11.40	12.80	13.53	14.12	1.94
Cyprus				5.50	6.46	6.95	6.07	7.90	8.66	9.35	10.23	1.40
Denmark				60.58	83.59	83.82	82.15	83.94	90.29	95.83	97.50	1.79
Finland	6.60	6.68	6.48	8.38	11.58	11.00	10.90	11.40	12.10	12.88	13.15	1.80
France			7.53	8.62	11.12	10.37	10.20	10.60	11.60	12.37	12.81	1.76
Germany			5.77	7.93	10.15	10.48	10.92	11.40	12.20	12.89	13.72	1.88
Gibraltar												
Greece			3.18	5.59	7.69	7.35	7.40	8.12	8.82	9.87	10.91	1.49
Iceland												
Ireland			7.70	7.10	8.90	8.55	8.71	9.50	10.50	11.17	11.50	1.58
Italy			9.56	8.89	10.81	10.48	10.59	11.30	12.20	12.86	13.00	1.78
Liechtenstein												
Luxembourg			5.14	6.15	8.28	7.73	7.78	9.00	10.20	10.82	11.43	1.57
Malta								8.78	9.53	11.09	11.00	1.51
Monaco												
Netherlands		8.49	7.43	8.85	12.08	12.10	11.59	12.53	13.52	14.15	14.96	2.05
Norway			59.44	81.08	105.66	92.70	93.72	99.85	108.16	114.57	116.64	1.99
Portugal			6.53	7.82	9.02	9.20	9.65	10.33	11.47	13.10	13.92	1.91
Spain			6.92	6.42	8.19	8.14	8.17	8.70	9.50	10.21	10.48	1.44
Sweden			64.70	75.04	95.12	96.83	94.03	99.64	109.55	114.55	118.51	1.75
Switzerland			10.20	11.83	14.48	13.55	13.12	14.01	15.27	16.43	16.82	1.40
Turkey			0.02	0.29	5.83	14.76	18.04	19.59	25.35	27.77	34.04	2.61
United Kingdom			4.20	5.86	8.73	7.98	7.60	8.02	8.67	9.12	9.58	1.92
Eastern Europe												
Albania												
Belarus												
Bosnia-Herzegovina												
Bulgaria	104.00											
Croatia	43.00											
Czech Republic	191.00		124.00	192.90	287.10	245.89	248.05	266.80	284.80	295.99	308.87	1.52
Estonia								113.20	124.60	135.46	148.98	1.30
Georgia												
Hungary	755.00	1,580.00		971.30	2,324.10	2,228.60	2,327.90	2,396.20	2,601.00	2,771.57	3,066.54	1.67
Latvia								4.74	5.70	6.11	7.27	1.41
Lithuania								26.90	28.60	31.11	33.32	1.32
Macedonia												
Moldova												
Poland	11.90			11.75	31.37	31.92	33.53	37.36	39.91	39.81	42.69	1.54
Romania	0.26			0.59	11.21	20.22	24.29	27.20	32.40	33.48	35.55	1.46
Russia					73.92	70.06	87.71	121.03	152.84	177.22	230.13	0.90
Serbia and Montenegro				32.00								
Slovakia	217.00		123.80	194.80	334.80	300.80	314.40	351.80	372.80	395.20	396.92	1.61
Slovenia								8.91	9.52	9.95	10.71	1.47
Ukraine												

Source: Institute of Petroleum, OECD Energy Prices and Taxes/Euromonitor International

Automotives   **Table 4.11**

Price of Premium Unleaded Petrol by Quarter 2006-2008
Units of national currency per 10 litres (inc. tax)

	2006 1st Quarter	2006 2nd Quarter	2006 3rd Quarter	2006 4th Quarter	2007 1st Quarter	2007 2nd Quarter	2007 3rd Quarter	2007 4th Quarter	2008 1st Quarter	2008 2nd Quarter
Western Europe										
Austria	10.60	11.36	11.47	10.20	10.10	11.09	11.62	12.03	12.09	12.74
Belgium	13.21	14.13	13.98	12.80	12.93	14.06	13.88	14.50	14.69	
Cyprus	8.84	9.49	9.80	8.63	8.55	9.68	9.75	9.84	10.09	10.50
Denmark	92.29	100.89	99.58	90.58	89.92	100.88	98.54	100.38	102.06	
Finland	12.47	13.40	13.41	12.24	12.11	13.31	13.32	13.18	14.16	
France	12.12	12.93	12.84	11.60	11.92	12.99	12.91	13.09	13.54	14.01
Germany	12.62	13.50	13.28	12.14	12.55	13.66	13.66	13.77	14.00	
Gibraltar										
Greece	9.25	10.07	10.30							
Iceland										
Ireland	10.81	11.25	11.85	10.77	10.28	11.06	11.75	11.57	11.83	
Italy	12.51	13.31	13.39	12.21	12.15	13.11	13.26	13.41	13.71	
Liechtenstein										
Luxembourg	10.56	11.39	11.24	10.10	10.40	11.58	11.36	11.53	11.75	
Malta	11.12	11.30	11.51	10.26	9.92	10.15	10.77	10.77	10.85	10.90
Monaco										
Netherlands	13.85	14.75	14.56	13.42	13.77	14.94	14.77	14.87	15.23	
Norway	111.40	118.13	119.80	108.93	110.00	119.40	119.20	118.70	123.20	
Portugal	12.24	13.24	13.50	13.42	12.46	13.53	13.41	13.49	13.81	
Spain	9.87	10.69	10.77	9.49	9.53	10.56	10.59	10.70	10.92	11.49
Sweden	111.86	120.55	118.85	106.93	109.11	119.90	116.45	118.93	124.61	
Switzerland	15.90	16.87	17.30	15.63	15.53	17.13	17.20	17.50	17.67	
Turkey	26.03	28.34	29.48	27.23	27.27	29.42	28.72	29.76	31.16	
United Kingdom	8.89	9.52	9.46	8.62	8.72	9.45	9.54	10.00	10.46	
Eastern Europe										
Albania										
Belarus										
Bosnia-Herzegovina										
Bulgaria										
Croatia										
Czech Republic	281.80	306.42	313.68	282.07	270.04	297.20	305.87	307.05	308.08	
Estonia	132.72	143.16	142.24	123.70	126.25	141.44	141.02	141.11	159.29	167.85
Georgia										
Hungary	2,626.24	2,859.26	2,985.95	2,614.85	2,557.04	2,790.26	2,840.42	2,858.54	2,955.93	
Latvia	5.86	6.45	6.51	5.60	5.83	6.49	6.54	6.65	7.09	7.34
Lithuania	30.50	32.91	32.52	28.53	28.29	32.14	32.01	31.81	35.02	36.97
Macedonia										
Moldova										
Poland	37.24	41.43	42.91	37.66	38.14	43.16	43.54	43.55	42.73	
Romania	32.70	33.90	35.00	32.30	31.00	33.20	33.40	34.20	36.30	
Russia	169.45	171.19	180.30	187.95	186.30	186.77	190.02	195.19	206.52	
Serbia and Montenegro										
Slovakia	387.00	410.90	414.30	368.60	358.70	385.40	388.20	388.90	394.50	
Slovenia	9.40	10.11	10.62	9.66	9.62	10.70	10.64	10.24	10.41	10.86
Ukraine										

Source: *Institute of Petroleum, OECD Energy Prices and Taxes/Euromonitor International*

Table 4.12

New Registrations of Commercial Vehicles 1980-2007

'000

	1980	1985	1990	1995	2000	2002	2003	2004	2005	2006	2007
Western Europe											
Austria	21.8	22.3	30.9	29.2	38.0	31.3	35.6	40.9	39.0	38.8	41.5
Belgium	32.5	31.9	49.5	45.8	68.7	60.2	62.2	70.0	74.9	72.1	81.7
Cyprus		5.4	10.6	9.2	6.2	9.5	9.2	3.8	5.1	6.1	6.5
Denmark	19.4	38.5	23.3	30.7	37.0	36.2	36.7	50.0	62.4	69.5	63.7
Finland	17.9	18.7	32.2	10.6	18.7	19.4	18.8	22.1	20.0	20.9	22.2
France	323.3	342.2	447.0	357.8	477.2	460.9	431.4	459.9	480.1	498.4	519.5
Germany	175.5	134.6	203.4	260.5	314.8	270.6	264.7	283.4	272.8	304.4	334.1
Gibraltar		0.1	0.3	0.2	0.3	0.2	0.3	1.2	0.6	0.3	0.6
Greece		19.0	44.6	11.6	25.0	20.3	20.7	27.2	25.5	26.4	27.1
Iceland		0.8	2.0	0.8	2.0	0.9	1.4	2.0	2.8	3.1	3.4
Ireland	12.2	16.2	28.4	16.4	33.6	28.4	30.5	31.2	38.4	43.6	46.0
Italy	122.3	100.7	159.5	148.1	226.4	320.2	242.3	255.1	251.4	272.0	281.2
Liechtenstein					0.2	0.2	0.2	0.2	0.2	0.2	0.2
Luxembourg		3.4	6.1	2.9	4.7	5.0	4.8	3.9	4.6	4.7	5.3
Malta		0.6	1.4		2.0	0.4	0.6	0.4	0.7	0.6	0.9
Monaco											
Netherlands	48.0	63.1	69.0	65.1	114.4	95.5	91.0	109.4	80.8	84.7	97.3
Norway	15.1	42.5	23.0	38.0	35.7	28.5	31.3	38.4	42.7	49.2	53.0
Portugal	47.0	23.1	75.8	63.0	161.0	84.7	73.4	76.6	75.1	70.5	74.8
Spain	104.5	122.0	267.7	191.4	336.8	305.9	250.2	275.3	329.2	351.1	324.5
Sweden	19.7	22.9	33.1	14.8	39.3	35.7	36.0	39.5	44.6	48.3	53.5
Switzerland	22.4	20.5	28.9	20.1	29.1	26.6	23.7	25.3	25.6	28.9	30.7
Turkey			62.1	54.7	144.3	80.3	164.6	285.2	310.2	313.7	274.0
United Kingdom	272.0	286.7	293.5	249.9	298.0	322.3	363.7	389.9	386.0	389.5	395.6
Eastern Europe											
Albania											
Belarus			12.9	5.3	8.1	7.9	7.3	7.2	7.5	7.5	7.6
Bosnia-Herzegovina											
Bulgaria			14.6	10.7	4.2	4.3	4.9	6.5	9.0	10.0	10.7
Croatia			3.0	17.0	7.2	13.3	9.1	8.2	9.1	10.3	11.2
Czech Republic					33.9	21.7	25.7	35.5	48.5	60.7	32.6
Estonia			1.3	0.7	1.8	2.5	6.3	6.2	7.9	8.2	8.5
Georgia											
Hungary		27.0	23.4	31.2	32.7	35.1	31.1	30.1	26.5	21.6	21.9
Latvia				4.1	6.0	3.2	2.0	2.5	3.0	4.9	6.9
Lithuania						1.7	2.8	4.1	5.5	6.7	10.5
Macedonia			1.8	0.9							
Moldova					4.7	4.3		12.5			
Poland		39.0	65.2	56.3	41.3	20.2	40.1	50.0	36.2	41.0	34.0
Romania			9.0	37.9	17.9	23.2	28.5	35.8	40.9	40.8	51.2
Russia					262.6	247.3	273.0	281.0	286.3	331.1	374.1
Serbia and Montenegro							1.1	1.7	3.2	3.8	4.2
Slovakia						8.2	12.7	13.3	18.1	24.4	29.4
Slovenia			2.9	6.2	5.1	6.0	6.4	7.7	8.0	10.4	12.7
Ukraine											

Source: Euromonitor International from SMMT/national statistics

Automotives

Table 4.13

New Registrations of Diesel Cars 1985-2007
'000

	1985	1990	1995	2000	2002	2003	2004	2005	2006	2007
Western Europe										
Austria	32.2	66.3	119.1	182.8	194.6	214.6	220.3	199.9	191.8	175.8
Belgium	95.0	155.4	168.0	290.3	300.4	312.9	339.3	348.6	392.3	404.4
Cyprus									1.1	
Denmark	10.4	3.6	3.9	14.9	22.5	21.8	29.2	34.9	40.2	60.4
Finland	14.4	7.2	5.5	26.3	18.2	22.4	22.1	25.1	29.5	35.7
France	264.8	762.1	897.7	1,046.5	1,354.9	1,354.2	1,392.9	1,429.0	1,427.7	1,525.7
Germany	530.7	337.6	483.5	1,026.0	1,236.2	1,291.5	1,437.3	1,425.6	1,535.9	1,504.8
Gibraltar										
Greece				2.0	2.4	3.9	8.4	4.0	5.9	8.1
Iceland	0.4		0.5	2.3	0.8	1.7	1.6	3.6	4.3	4.8
Ireland	8.6	12.2	13.1	23.4	25.6	25.0	29.5	38.0	49.0	50.6
Italy	438.7	171.0	178.8	805.2	987.0	1,093.9	1,318.2	1,300.8	1,350.9	1,389.7
Liechtenstein								0.6	0.7	
Luxembourg	3.5	6.4	8.0	21.1	26.9	30.4	35.0	36.6	39.3	40.3
Malta										
Monaco										
Netherlands	71.3	54.8	61.8	134.4	110.1	110.5	118.8	123.9	130.0	143.1
Norway	1.7	2.2	5.5	8.8	15.5	21.0	32.5	43.1	52.8	96.1
Portugal	2.3	10.3	21.3	62.4	77.8	85.2	111.7	127.8	126.4	139.9
Spain	125.2	136.2	274.2	735.4	762.7	842.3	1,068.9	1,036.8	1,022.3	1,144.9
Sweden	5.7	1.4	4.7	18.2	17.7	20.1	21.1	26.6	55.8	106.5
Switzerland	9.3	9.0	10.7	29.0	52.1	58.7	69.3	72.2	80.1	91.7
Turkey										
United Kingdom	66.2	128.6	405.1	313.2	602.6	704.1	835.3	897.9	898.5	964.0
Eastern Europe										
Albania										
Belarus										
Bosnia-Herzegovina										
Bulgaria										
Croatia										
Czech Republic								35.3	34.9	34.6
Estonia										
Georgia										
Hungary										
Latvia		4.2	22.0	28.2	30.8	32.7	34.7	35.6	36.3	
Lithuania										
Macedonia										
Moldova										
Poland										
Romania									86.3	
Russia								61.2	103.2	
Serbia and Montenegro										
Slovakia										
Slovenia										
Ukraine										

Source: *Euromonitor International from SMMT/national statistics*

Table 4.14

Automotives

New Registrations of Passenger Cars 1980-2007

'000

	1980	1985	1990	1995	2000	2002	2003	2004	2005	2006	2007
Western Europe											
Austria	227.5	242.7	288.6	279.6	309.4	279.5	300.1	311.3	307.9	308.5	298.2
Belgium	407.2	378.2	473.5	358.9	515.2	467.6	458.8	484.8	480.1	526.1	524.8
Cyprus		12.2	19.5	13.1	19.9	28.1	30.0	43.8	38.7	37.2	36.1
Denmark	74.0	157.5	80.9	135.7	113.6	111.6	96.5	122.5	148.6	156.7	162.5
Finland	103.8	139.0	139.1	79.9	134.8	124.1	147.4	142.6	148.2	145.7	125.3
France	1,873.2	1,766.3	2,309.1	1,930.5	2,133.9	2,145.1	2,009.2	2,013.7	2,067.8	2,000.5	2,064.5
Germany	2,426.2	2,379.3	3,040.8	3,314.1	3,378.3	3,252.9	3,236.9	3,266.8	3,342.1	3,468.0	3,148.2
Gibraltar		2.0	2.1	1.7	1.7	2.0	1.8	1.4	1.2	1.3	1.3
Greece		109.4	132.5	125.4	290.2	268.5	257.3	289.8	269.7	267.7	279.7
Iceland		5.7	6.8	6.4	13.6	6.9	9.9	12.0	18.1	17.2	15.9
Ireland	91.7	60.4	81.2	86.9	225.3	150.5	143.0	149.6	166.3	173.3	180.8
Italy	1,530.5	1,745.9	2,348.2	1,720.0	2,412.0	2,302.9	2,254.3	2,272.4	2,244.4	2,329.9	2,493.0
Liechtenstein				1.7	1.8	2.1	1.8	1.8	1.9	1.9	2.0
Luxembourg		26.9	34.6	28.0	41.9	43.4	43.6	48.2	48.5	50.8	51.3
Malta		4.1	8.9		11.3	10.3	10.8	6.2	6.6	6.7	7.0
Monaco											
Netherlands	450.1	495.7	502.7	446.4	597.6	510.7	489.0	483.9	465.2	484.0	505.5
Norway	95.6	159.1	61.9	90.5	97.4	88.7	89.9	115.6	109.9	109.2	129.2
Portugal	58.4	104.2	212.7	229.9	257.8	226.1	189.8	197.6	206.5	194.7	201.8
Spain	574.1	575.1	1,007.0	870.5	1,381.4	1,331.9	1,466.0	1,616.2	1,649.3	1,634.6	1,614.8
Sweden	192.6	263.0	229.9	169.8	354.6	293.9	307.1	311.5	311.8	313.8	338.5
Switzerland	280.5	265.5	323.0	268.0	314.5	293.0	269.7	267.5	257.5	267.5	284.7
Turkey		63.9	267.8	196.9	256.9	117.6	289.0	451.3	406.8	396.5	353.5
United Kingdom	1,513.8	1,832.0	2,008.9	1,945.4	2,221.6	2,563.6	2,579.1	2,567.3	2,439.7	2,344.9	2,404.0
Eastern Europe											
Albania											
Belarus		45.3	82.4	65.2	74.1	89.8	86.8	84.8	83.8	83.1	
Bosnia-Herzegovina											
Bulgaria		48.0	33.4	74.4	63.5	55.0	45.0	54.0	26.0	36.7	41.0
Croatia			66.2	67.6	92.4	95.2	75.0	69.6	70.5	78.8	84.9
Czech Republic				148.7	147.8	149.6	133.0	127.4	124.0	174.5	
Estonia			3.1	10.2	14.7	15.8	16.5	19.6	21.3	23.1	
Georgia											
Hungary		101.3	83.9	127.8	149.1	239.1	274.4	255.8	239.7	203.1	195.6
Latvia			49.3	35.7	7.8	8.7	11.3	16.7	25.6	32.8	
Lithuania				7.3	7.5	9.4	10.7	14.6	21.3		
Macedonia			13.8	9.0							
Moldova				12.1	11.0		32.3				
Poland		259.9	358.1	311.1	478.7	308.3	353.6	318.1	235.5	238.8	221.5
Romania			82.0	87.1	66.3	88.8	106.8	145.1	215.5	256.4	315.6
Russia					821.3	1,053.2	1,223.6	1,453.3	1,578.1	2,080.9	2,570.8
Serbia and Montenegro							8.6	11.9	21.6	28.5	35.2
Slovakia						65.3	57.5	57.4	56.9	59.1	59.7
Slovenia			69.3	63.5	63.5	61.3	71.6	78.8	79.4	81.5	94.4
Ukraine											

Source: Euromonitor International from SMMT/national statistics

Automotives

Table 4.15

New Registrations of Two-Wheelers 1985-2007
'000

	1985	1990	1995	2000	2002	2003	2004	2005	2006	2007
Western Europe										
Austria	49.2	20.1	29.4	45.1	33.0	37.8	40.5	46.8	49.4	50.7
Belgium	47.1	54.5	42.1	58.5	48.2	41.6	42.8	42.3	39.7	36.4
Cyprus	4.3	8.3	5.7	5.4	4.5	4.9	6.2	6.6	7.3	8.1
Denmark	2.6	1.7	13.1	13.1	7.7	6.6	7.8	10.7	13.2	16.1
Finland			95.4	11.6	13.8	19.0	25.6	30.1	24.9	28.1
France			302.4	371.8	334.9	342.1	349.8	351.5	355.7	358.8
Germany	214.7	171.2	342.7	361.3	298.7	284.3	254.8	266.0	271.6	277.2
Gibraltar	0.2	0.6	0.7	1.1	0.9	0.8	0.7	0.8	0.8	0.9
Greece				107.7	91.2	97.0	93.5	87.1	85.7	82.0
Iceland		0.1	0.1	0.2	0.1	0.2	0.4	0.4	0.5	0.5
Ireland	4.1	3.1	2.3	6.9	7.9	5.0	3.8	3.2	2.9	2.6
Italy			655.3	836.5	559.5	570.5	551.8	549.6	547.5	546.4
Liechtenstein			0.1	0.2	0.2	0.2	0.2	0.3	0.3	0.3
Luxembourg	0.5		1.3	1.7	1.8	2.1	1.9	2.0	2.2	2.3
Malta				0.8	0.8	0.8	0.9	0.9	0.9	0.9
Monaco			1.1							
Netherlands	47.7	74.4	77.0	86.6	70.7	62.6	56.7	57.7	58.3	58.7
Norway	23.6	8.8	10.1	17.3	17.7	18.2	18.9	19.2	19.5	19.8
Portugal	1.4	7.3	54.1	32.7	20.9	11.2	11.6	11.2	11.3	10.9
Spain			189.9	320.7	177.1	187.9	241.3	321.2	316.0	320.3
Sweden	11.3	7.6	10.1	28.4	44.3	43.5	53.7	40.7	48.2	51.0
Switzerland	54.2	51.1	47.1	50.8	47.4	48.9	47.9	45.2	45.7	46.3
Turkey		65.2	35.7	35.7	17.3	15.3	14.6	14.0	13.3	13.3
United Kingdom	123.6	94.4	68.9	170.1	159.7	155.7	133.9	132.8	137.5	138.3
Eastern Europe										
Albania			13.9							
Belarus		5.3	9.9	5.1	3.8	3.4	3.3	3.3	3.1	3.1
Bosnia-Herzegovina										
Bulgaria	16.0	6.0	2.8	3.5	3.5	3.6	3.6	3.6	3.7	3.7
Croatia		9.5	8.6	9.0	13.4	14.6	14.7	14.3	14.2	13.9
Czech Republic				10.6	9.8	9.8	9.5	14.9	11.8	14.8
Estonia		0.3	0.2	0.2	0.2	0.2	0.2	0.2	0.2	0.2
Georgia										
Hungary				1.3	3.5	4.3	7.3	8.5	9.6	10.8
Latvia				0.5	0.8	1.0	1.0	1.1	1.2	1.2
Lithuania				0.4	0.8	0.9	1.1	1.6	1.7	1.8
Macedonia		0.2	0.1							
Moldova										
Poland	50.0	31.4	5.3	7.2	13.8	7.3	10.8	11.7	11.0	12.3
Romania		5.0	2.0	0.1	0.1	0.1	0.1	0.1	0.2	0.2
Russia				5,745.3	4,640.0	3,950.0	3,274.0	2,994.4	2,628.8	2,335.2
Serbia and Montenegro										
Slovakia				1.1	2.2	4.0	4.0	4.8	5.7	6.2
Slovenia		0.8	0.7	1.2	6.0	3.0	3.7	5.0	3.4	3.7
Ukraine		2.0	2.1	0.5	0.7	0.7	0.8	0.8	0.9	0.9

Source: Euromonitor International from SMMT/national statistics

Table 4.16

New Registrations of All Vehicles by Quarter 2006-2008

'000

	2006 1st Quarter	2006 2nd Quarter	2006 3rd Quarter	2006 4th Quarter	2007 1st Quarter	2007 2nd Quarter	2007 3rd Quarter	2007 4th Quarter	2008 1st Quarter	2008 2nd Quarter
Western Europe										
Austria	87.2	102.5	82.0	75.6	85.5	100.3	77.5	76.4	74.1	94.5
Belgium										
Cyprus	11.1	12.1	10.9	9.3	10.8	11.9	10.7	9.2	10.2	10.9
Denmark	53.0	63.9	52.6	56.7	54.7	60.1	54.2	57.1	56.4	64.3
Finland	44.6	50.0	39.9	32.0	45.9	42.8	37.4	21.3	37.2	34.1
France	700.0	729.3	520.7	624.1	650.2	641.8				
Germany	868.2	1,045.8	882.8	975.7	800.8	960.8	848.1	872.5	773.8	956.1
Gibraltar										
Greece	70.3	79.6	70.7		87.6	85.6	75.2	58.4	76.5	75.2
Iceland	6.0	6.1	4.9	3.3					5.3	5.2
Ireland	94.8	68.3	41.2	12.7	102.5	71.6	40.7	12.0	60.5	
Italy										
Liechtenstein										
Luxembourg	13.8	18.3	11.5	11.9	17.1	17.0	12.5	13.1	13.0	16.1
Malta										
Monaco										
Netherlands	185.3	147.7	129.9	105.8	190.1	159.0	144.5	109.3	169.8	139.3
Norway	35.6	39.5	40.0	43.3	44.4	44.8	45.6	47.4	49.0	46.8
Portugal	71.2	75.1	57.2	61.6	67.8	82.9	60.5	65.4	67.1	71.6
Spain										
Sweden	78.6	106.6	84.4	92.5	88.4	108.7	87.6	107.4	89.8	113.1
Switzerland	72.2	123.4	89.1	11.7	70.5	97.7	74.6	72.6	80.7	
Turkey	172.9	224.4	174.6	138.3	137.3	154.5	172.7	163.0	151.1	144.5
United Kingdom	755.4	679.6	766.0	533.4	722.8	643.7	733.2			
Eastern Europe										
Albania										
Belarus										
Bosnia-Herzegovina										
Bulgaria										
Croatia	19.7	26.6	22.7	20.2	25.4	28.8	23.5	18.4	25.4	
Czech Republic	49.3	50.4	41.5	43.5	44.4	60.0	50.3	52.4		53.8
Estonia	5.6	8.4	8.3	7.2	7.4	8.9	7.4	7.5	8.3	8.7
Georgia										
Hungary	53.3	63.5	51.7							
Latvia	5.6	8.1	7.0	9.7	9.9	11.5	9.3	9.0	12.4	11.8
Lithuania	4.1	6.1	5.6	5.5	7.8	11.9	5.7	6.5	10.0	11.6
Macedonia										
Moldova	6.4	5.6	5.7	6.8	5.7	6.3				
Poland										
Romania										
Russia										
Serbia and Montenegro										
Slovakia										
Slovenia	22.6	27.8	21.5	20.0	25.3	32.1	26.0	23.5	25.9	31.1
Ukraine										

Source: *Euromonitor International from SMMT/national statistics*

Civil Aviation

Table 4.17

Airline Freight Traffic 1980-2007
Million tonne-kilometres

	1980	1985	1990	1995	2000	2002	2003	2004	2005	2006	2007
Western Europe											
Austria	21.7	35.3	53.9	173.5	443.9	396.0	427.6	502.3	537.5	572.0	630.9
Belgium			656.4	415.2	1,016.4	782.9	873.2	901.0	959.1	1,026.8	1,083.9
Cyprus	24.4	24.3	34.3	36.2	43.1	40.4	43.1	47.5	46.6	47.0	48.5
Denmark	159.7	154.5	147.7	144.7	196.4	180.0	181.0	183.0	184.1	185.5	187.0
Finland			134.9	211.1	280.7	215.6	255.7	325.2	353.6	408.8	479.0
France	1,956.0	2,786.6	4,017.2	4,479.5	4,973.7	4,873.7	4,879.3	5,352.8	5,526.3	5,855.2	6,224.0
Germany			7,983.0	11,667.0	14,225.1	14,323.7	14,517.8	16,048.8	15,360.8	16,179.9	16,805.1
Gibraltar											
Greece	83.1	92.5	112.7	117.0	127.5	80.9	56.5	53.6	58.5	62.9	65.3
Iceland		29.8	35.5	45.1	99.6	92.1	75.4	117.3	121.5	128.6	140.0
Ireland			128.3	105.0	167.6	170.8	184.3	190.6	202.5	214.4	225.6
Italy	484.0	692.6	1,171.3	1,469.6	1,748.4	1,923.5	1,998.5	2,089.6	2,185.1	2,280.0	2,334.8
Liechtenstein											
Luxembourg			2,229.1	2,247.0	3,523.1	3,884.6	3,945.7	4,126.2	4,288.7	4,432.8	4,608.3
Malta	3.5	2.5	4.8	13.7	14.3	14.8	16.3	17.0	18.3	19.6	20.9
Monaco											
Netherlands		1,513.2	2,125.2	3,635.2	4,165.2	3,990.9	4,111.8	4,535.1	4,650.5	4,703.4	4,922.5
Norway	168.8	160.5	152.7	148.1	200.4	157.4	142.7	135.7	129.4	121.3	114.9
Portugal	124.8	127.8	166.6	192.8	223.7	194.1	203.5	234.5	233.3	292.4	331.5
Spain	470.7	601.4	751.9	688.0	845.1	798.8	862.6	1,030.6	1,008.0	1,056.5	1,134.3
Sweden	252.7	245.5	232.4	209.3	289.3	250.9	230.7	209.1	189.7	172.8	156.9
Switzerland	452.9	695.1	927.3	1,487.0	1,966.9	1,758.3	1,726.0	1,654.3	1,620.2	1,576.7	1,529.9
Turkey			73.3	177.3	374.8	364.8	353.1	346.4	340.4	332.6	326.0
United Kingdom			2,389.5	3,568.2	5,163.7	4,951.6	5,163.3	5,701.8	6,010.4	6,214.2	6,612.6
Eastern Europe											
Albania											
Belarus			3.4	5.9	1.6	2.5	2.6	2.7	2.8	2.9	3.0
Bosnia-Herzegovina											
Bulgaria			4.0	24.4	5.9	6.1	6.2	6.3	6.4	6.5	6.6
Croatia			1.0	2.4	2.5	2.7	2.6	2.4	2.4	2.1	1.9
Czech Republic				25.6	32.2	27.3	36.0	40.1	38.8	39.4	40.6
Estonia			0.1	0.4	1.3	1.2	1.5	1.3	1.3	1.1	1.0
Georgia					2.0	2.1	2.3	2.3	2.3		
Hungary	8.5	9.3	6.3	19.2	50.8	55.1	56.2	58.0	59.6	61.2	63.0
Latvia			5.0	1.1	0.4	0.4	0.4	0.9	1.9	2.3	4.2
Lithuania			4.2	1.5	1.6	1.5	1.3	1.2	1.3	1.3	1.3
Macedonia			0.4	0.6	1.4	2.0	2.2	2.5	2.7	3.0	3.3
Moldova											
Poland	20.8	10.5	42.5	66.2	77.8	66.7	70.9	77.1	71.3	79.9	83.4
Romania	10.4	10.0	12.8	17.9	12.4	8.7	6.8	4.9	5.3	4.9	4.5
Russia			2,545.3	642.2	686.6	781.3	852.1	1,237.6	1,408.1	1,619.1	2,018.6
Serbia and Montenegro											
Slovakia			0.0	0.0	0.0	0.6	0.3	0.2	0.2	0.1	0.1
Slovenia			1.1	4.1	3.9	4.5	3.6	3.2	2.6	2.3	2.0
Ukraine			0.0	2.0	10.0	10.0	15.9	35.0	36.1	29.1	39.3

Source: *Euromonitor International from International Civil Aviation Authority/national statistics*

Table 4.18

Airline Passenger Traffic 1980-2007

Million passenger-kilometres

	1980	1985	1990	1995	2000	2002	2003	2004	2005	2006	2007
Western Europe											
Austria	1,120.0	1,426.4	4,735.8	8,114.0	15,864.0	16,548.0	14,556.0	17,520.0	18,828.0	19,920.0	17,929.3
Belgium	4,966.2	5,818.6	7,641.6	8,620.1	16,660.1	20,314.7	21,903.6	22,940.0	24,081.4	25,028.2	25,936.2
Cyprus	797.6	1,580.1	2,405.8	2,734.9	3,336.0	3,924.0	3,348.0	3,408.0	3,180.0	3,272.5	3,363.0
Denmark	2,963.5	2,975.1	4,173.1	4,950.8	5,436.0	6,012.0	5,784.0	6,132.0	5,940.0	6,012.0	6,068.7
Finland	3,472.0	5,010.1	9,361.2	10,348.3	7,428.0	8,472.0	8,640.0	10,476.0	11,160.0	12,636.0	15,649.0
France	34,099.2	40,015.4	52,427.7	66,629.6	91,800.0	96,768.0	97,644.0	105,254.0	115,116.0	123,336.1	129,655.2
Germany	21,102.1	24,569.9	45,550.3	64,232.0	95,208.0	93,636.0	105,732.0	123,576.0	137,364.0	143,568.0	152,081.0
Gibraltar											
Greece	4,792.3	5,878.4	7,764.4	7,945.0	10,632.0	9,060.0	6,084.0	6,780.0	7,332.0	7,044.0	7,478.0
Iceland	1,377.5	2,586.6	1,795.5	2,581.6	4,716.0	3,816.0	2,988.0	3,624.0	4,308.0	4,260.0	4,146.9
Ireland	2,550.3	2,522.8	4,561.8	5,640.0	22,015.6	30,716.6	35,067.1	39,417.6	43,768.2	53,163.9	60,599.9
Italy	13,220.8	15,194.1	20,332.8	40,385.9	20,397.7	30,493.3	46,916.5	36,890.2	49,109.3	50,791.5	52,410.3
Liechtenstein											
Luxembourg	128.0	331.2	526.4	390.8	774.0	1,094.0	1,026.7	951.6	890.5	831.5	781.8
Malta	665.9	642.8	903.0	1,722.8	2,383.8	2,304.0	2,302.9	2,281.0	2,259.8	2,249.7	2,236.7
Monaco					3.5	7.7	7.1	7.9	11.3	9.1	10.9
Netherlands	15,003.0	18,479.0	31,138.5	44,679.7	72,864.0	70,308.0	59,460.0	63,012.0	68,316.0	71,770.9	74,496.4
Norway			2,422.8	3,078.5	9,876.0	10,464.0	10,512.0	9,132.0	7,500.0	6,780.0	6,840.0
Portugal	4,519.9	4,911.1	6,835.8	7,770.0	13,452.0	14,520.0	12,804.0	14,736.0	16,356.0	18,744.0	20,781.6
Spain	17,264.9	22,363.7	22,112.2	42,952.7	67,444.8	54,048.0	54,672.0	61,680.0	66,084.0	77,100.0	81,021.0
Sweden				3,217.5	5,964.0	4,516.0	3,749.2	3,496.6	5,875.9	5,755.0	5,726.8
Switzerland	10,886.6	12,776.9	16,199.2	21,503.8	41,835.1	26,246.5	23,016.0	23,952.0	28,488.0	22,788.0	25,020.0
Turkey			4,829.3	9,475.4	16,488.0	15,720.0	15,036.0	17,388.0	20,328.0	23,301.1	24,994.9
United Kingdom	59,253.5	66,195.7	112,777.9	186,341.6	204,456.0	187,908.0	166,500.0	181,464.0	196,488.0	128,004.0	228,042.0
Eastern Europe											
Albania					12.0	16.0	17.7	19.3	20.7	22.0	23.2
Belarus				2,651.0	356.7	468.4	477.6	501.0	522.0	541.3	558.8
Bosnia-Herzegovina											
Bulgaria			1,349.9	2,084.4	1,703.8	340.2	722.5	1,206.2	1,617.1	1,949.5	1,816.0
Croatia				413.9	648.0	936.0	864.0	936.0	972.0	1,008.0	1,114.9
Czech Republic	1,773.6	2,121.9	2,288.1	2,640.0	3,972.0	4,608.0	4,740.0	5,904.0	6,552.0	6,648.0	6,403.0
Estonia	990.0	1,130.0	1,244.0	129.1	276.0	336.0	408.0	540.0	648.0	684.0	772.3
Georgia				308.3	240.3	296.0	393.5	480.3	557.1	636.0	697.2
Hungary	1,076.2	1,333.0	1,635.8	1,768.8	2,893.9	3,460.7	3,908.3	4,293.7	4,325.0	4,482.7	4,807.3
Latvia				237.7	258.3	336.2	422.9	819.6	1,445.3	2,046.8	2,874.5
Lithuania				370.8	324.0	420.0	420.0	396.0	540.0	696.0	564.0
Macedonia					740.3	235.6	280.2	275.6	293.0	298.6	308.5
Moldova				227.6	127.8	161.1	237.7	277.0	346.7	382.7	465.9
Poland	2,009.5	1,482.7	2,505.7	4,241.8	5,700.0	6,132.0	5,433.8	5,860.7	6,216.0	6,730.0	6,965.4
Romania	1,209.3	1,462.0	1,833.9	2,861.4	2,508.0	1,908.0	1,656.0	1,452.0	1,956.0	2,436.0	3,645.3
Russia				33,177.2	25,906.3	36,804.0	39,636.0	46,248.0	48,828.0	54,252.0	68,172.0
Serbia and Montenegro								1,285.7	1,251.7	1,092.0	1,185.3
Slovakia				185.9	268.8	422.6	583.4	1,570.2	2,462.3	2,913.9	2,986.1
Slovenia				325.6	857.5	791.2	835.6	895.7	1,019.4	1,043.1	1,185.5
Ukraine				3,125.8	1,656.0	1,884.0	2,340.0	3,288.0	4,080.0	4,392.0	4,611.8

Source: Euromonitor International from International Civil Aviation Authority/national statistics

Civil Aviation

Table 4.19

Airline Passenger Traffic by Quarter 2006-2008

Million passenger-kilometres

	2006 1st Quarter	2006 2nd Quarter	2006 3rd Quarter	2006 4th Quarter	2007 1st Quarter	2007 2nd Quarter	2007 3rd Quarter	2007 4th Quarter	2008 1st Quarter	2008 2nd Quarter
Western Europe										
Austria	4,499.0	5,012.0	5,585.0	4,824.0	4,686.0	4,369.8	4,793.1	4,080.4	3,835.3	
Belgium										
Cyprus	560.4	902.7	1,041.8	767.6	618.5	866.7				
Denmark	1,309.9	1,630.6	1,658.6	1,412.8	1,328.9	1,630.7	1,713.6	1,395.4	1,346.3	
Finland	2,828.2	3,130.2	3,664.3	3,013.2	3,424.0	3,787.1	4,592.5	3,845.4	3,942.9	
France	28,806.2	30,881.3	33,375.3	30,273.3	30,289.7	32,396.9	36,025.1	30,943.4	31,186.2	
Germany	31,209.1	37,264.0	40,434.9	34,660.0	33,611.3	39,624.9	41,692.0	37,152.8	35,265.4	
Gibraltar										
Greece	1,329.6	1,894.8	2,277.0	1,542.7	1,378.3	1,959.5	2,449.6	1,690.6		
Iceland	674.8	1,196.4	1,521.8	867.0						
Ireland										
Italy										
Liechtenstein										
Luxembourg										
Malta										
Monaco										
Netherlands	16,345.2	18,081.2	19,578.2	17,766.2	16,826.3	19,105.5	20,380.7	18,183.9	17,399.3	
Norway	1,424.6	1,853.9	1,953.0	1,548.5	1,442.9	1,857.6	1,946.6	1,592.8	1,539.9	
Portugal	3,714.2	4,738.0	5,684.8	4,607.0	4,276.2	5,025.3	6,277.1	5,203.0		
Spain	16,586.6	19,623.5	21,790.4	19,099.5	18,587.2	20,580.1	23,205.1	18,648.5		
Sweden	1,338.5	1,573.6	1,335.9	1,507.0	1,306.2	1,506.3	1,439.6	1,474.7	1,396.3	
Switzerland	5,017.8	6,034.9			5,664.5	6,163.8	6,724.9	6,466.8	6,295.4	
Turkey										
United Kingdom	28,153.9	33,519.8	35,625.2	30,705.1	49,671.8	58,481.7	65,000.2	54,888.2		
Eastern Europe										
Albania										
Belarus										
Bosnia-Herzegovina										
Bulgaria										
Croatia	133.7	296.5	376.9	201.0	159.3	315.5	400.7	239.4	195.2	
Czech Republic	1,255.2	1,794.9	2,094.7	1,503.1	1,246.4	1,666.9	2,014.2	1,475.5	1,223.0	
Estonia	132.4	201.6	209.6	140.4	138.5	211.3	252.3	170.3	147.7	
Georgia										
Hungary										
Latvia										
Lithuania	133.3	187.6	212.3	162.9	145.8	141.5	142.6	134.0	190.9	
Macedonia										
Moldova										
Poland	1,153.9	1,812.0	2,316.8	1,447.4	1,247.2	1,900.0	2,360.7	1,457.5		
Romania	458.9	619.3	717.5	640.3	676.8	928.3	1,117.8	922.4	848.4	
Russia	10,056.2	13,538.2	18,026.3	12,631.2	12,558.5	14,405.8	25,888.2	15,319.6	15,382.6	
Serbia and Montenegro										
Slovakia	751.2	751.2	417.3							
Slovenia	212.5	269.2			221.4	314.9	365.8	283.3	272.3	
Ukraine	1,014.8	1,219.7	1,452.7	704.8	2,088.8	572.4	1,099.4	851.1		

Source: *Euromonitor International from International Civil Aviation Authority/national statistics*

Table 4.20

Airline Passenger Traffic by Month 2007

Million passenger-kilometres

	January	February	March	April	May	June	July	August	September	October	November	December
Western Europe												
Austria	1,572.6	1,474.8	1,638.5	1,439.8	1,403.7	1,526.3	1,635.5	1,593.2	1,564.4	1,508.8	1,331.6	1,240.0
Belgium												
Cyprus	211.2	-179.1	228.2	304.2	273.2	289.2	362.3	396.3				
Denmark	405.1	402.1	521.8	477.8	561.7	591.3	605.6	556.5	551.4	564.7	453.2	377.5
Finland	1,095.1	1,058.9	1,270.1	1,178.6	1,201.7	1,406.8	1,549.6	1,558.7	1,484.3	1,424.9	1,196.7	1,223.8
France	10,266.1	9,121.9	10,901.7	10,714.4	10,491.8	11,190.8	12,609.0	12,233.3	11,182.7	10,120.1	10,185.5	10,637.8
Germany	11,021.3	10,201.3	12,388.6	12,454.3	13,396.5	13,774.1	14,723.4	14,580.0	12,388.6	12,454.3	13,396.5	11,302.1
Gibraltar												
Greece	465.3	381.6	531.5	635.9	631.8	691.8	824.1	859.3	766.2	656.6	477.7	556.3
Iceland												
Ireland												
Italy												
Liechtenstein												
Luxembourg												
Malta												
Monaco												
Netherlands	5,664.7	5,116.5	6,045.1	6,072.9	6,136.4	6,896.2	6,939.9	6,896.2	6,544.6	6,580.4	5,782.9	5,820.6
Norway	415.7	443.7	583.6	564.6	615.6	677.5	672.5	635.5	638.5	651.5	534.6	406.7
Portugal	1,452.7	1,276.0	1,547.6	1,734.3	1,627.3	1,663.7	2,072.5	2,159.3	2,045.3	1,903.9	1,582.9	1,716.2
Spain	6,124.4	5,800.8	6,662.1	6,775.6	6,611.8	7,192.7	7,864.0	7,917.3	7,423.8	7,444.9	4,822.9	6,380.7
Sweden	378.0	412.0	516.2	491.6	469.3	545.4	422.5	456.5	560.6	563.0	504.4	407.3
Switzerland	1,884.5	1,716.1	2,063.9	2,039.0	2,034.0	2,090.8	2,278.2	2,295.1	2,151.6	2,250.3	2,052.9	2,163.6
Turkey												
United Kingdom	16,206.4	15,033.7	18,431.7	18,639.2	19,076.3	20,766.3	21,895.9	22,340.0	20,764.3	20,082.6	17,346.2	17,459.4
Eastern Europe												
Albania												
Belarus												
Bosnia-Herzegovina												
Bulgaria												
Croatia	51.4	47.3	60.6	86.3	109.9	119.2	133.6	136.7	130.5	102.8	71.9	64.7
Czech Republic	413.4	348.3	484.7	526.5	544.8	595.7	656.8	697.5	659.9	599.8	450.1	425.6
Estonia	42.1	42.1	54.4	61.5	68.7	81.0	87.2	87.2	77.9	70.8	53.3	46.2
Georgia												
Hungary												
Latvia												
Lithuania	49.3	45.0	51.5	44.0	50.4	47.2	50.4	50.4	41.8	38.6	46.1	49.3
Macedonia												
Moldova												
Poland	414.8	354.6	477.9	506.5	612.6	780.8	829.6	814.3	716.8	568.7	438.7	450.2
Romania	221.0	209.1	246.6	295.0	298.9	334.4	374.9	389.7	353.2	339.4	270.3	312.7
Russia	4,342.6	3,870.2	4,345.7	4,407.7	4,480.1	5,517.9	6,734.6	7,020.9	12,132.6	5,238.8	5,059.0	5,021.8
Serbia and Montenegro												
Slovakia										1,927.0			
Slovenia	75.6	67.4	78.4	92.1	104.5	118.3	121.0	119.7	125.2	110.0	88.0	85.3
Ukraine	743.0	600.9	744.9	240.7	41.7	290.0	358.3	392.4	348.8	305.2	273.0	273.0

Source: Euromonitor International from International Civil Aviation Authority/national statistics

Civil Aviation

Table 4.21

Distance Flown on Scheduled Flights 1980-2007

Million kilometres

	1980	1985	1990	1995	2000	2002	2003	2004	2005	2006	2007
Western Europe											
Austria	22.0	23.1	47.4	103.7	113.2	158.5	156.1	176.4	185.8	192.8	179.4
Belgium	71.8	65.6	77.9	103.4	191.0	267.5	286.0	303.2	310.3	320.9	328.6
Cyprus	9.5	12.0	16.8	20.7	21.0	24.2	25.5	26.1	24.0	24.2	17.1
Denmark	65.9	66.0	68.0	69.4	73.9	73.2	72.9	72.5	78.2	75.4	77.5
Finland	42.8	46.1	79.7	84.5	116.9	104.8	106.9	115.3	116.0	122.9	142.5
France	345.3	335.4	402.8	484.7	874.6	746.7	757.8	742.7	757.3	783.0	803.6
Germany	196.7	229.3	414.6	879.3	1,148.7	715.7	948.1	1,040.1	1,196.7	1,430.6	1,528.1
Gibraltar											
Greece	40.5	46.4	55.6	62.0	79.9	67.2	59.0	66.1	65.8	66.3	67.2
Iceland	11.5	19.2	18.5	22.5	35.1	29.6	28.7	34.9	36.9	38.5	39.5
Ireland	31.8	27.4	45.3	51.0	147.0	198.3	224.0	249.7	275.4	331.6	380.7
Italy	122.7	109.8	156.7	302.6	185.3	290.3	439.3	315.7	412.3	407.2	402.5
Liechtenstein											
Luxembourg	2.6	5.2	8.4	5.6	28.0	21.9	22.0	21.5	18.9	18.1	17.1
Malta	7.8	7.5	9.4	20.5	26.0	25.8	25.8	26.0	26.1	26.2	26.3
Monaco					0.6	0.9	0.8	1.2	1.4	1.6	1.8
Netherlands	110.3	115.9	180.6	270.3	363.0	342.4	341.3	362.8	378.5	393.4	401.8
Norway			30.6	52.7	67.1	66.7	70.6	87.6	104.6	90.7	88.7
Portugal	43.3	40.8	55.1	76.6	106.4	117.7	121.0	165.3	161.0	180.0	193.3
Spain	182.1	189.0	175.4	354.6	537.7	553.7	597.6	637.1	666.7	522.8	688.3
Sweden				31.3	35.5	23.6	20.4	43.8	65.9	60.5	59.4
Switzerland	98.5	107.2	149.8	197.2	351.9	254.6	242.7	211.4	214.2	212.8	210.7
Turkey	25.2	27.9	44.4	94.0	148.9	140.5	141.5	151.4	166.6	177.5	188.8
United Kingdom	456.1	470.3	744.1	1,058.8	1,483.4	1,497.0	1,480.6	1,573.5	1,767.8	1,829.1	1,865.4
Eastern Europe											
Albania					0.8	1.1	1.3	1.4	1.5	1.7	1.8
Belarus					8.0	11.9	12.1	13.1	13.5	14.1	14.6
Bosnia-Herzegovina											
Bulgaria	10.7	22.0	27.3	22.0	22.0	6.1	9.7	14.8	19.4	25.0	22.2
Croatia				8.1	10.5	13.6	14.0	14.5	15.9	15.4	15.7
Czech Republic	28.5	27.0	27.3	30.1	58.8	47.0	54.4	83.7	95.9	97.9	100.8
Estonia				5.3	9.1	9.2	8.9	10.5	12.8	12.2	11.8
Georgia				4.3	4.0	4.8	6.3	7.4	8.8	9.9	10.9
Hungary	20.6	22.3	25.8	27.4	37.5	42.0	49.2	57.9	57.5	59.9	61.4
Latvia				7.1	8.6	9.6	12.2	17.5	25.8	32.5	38.9
Lithuania				9.9	11.6	10.7	10.9	13.9	16.2	16.3	16.4
Macedonia					9.6	2.8	3.1	3.1	3.2	3.2	3.2
Moldova				4.5	4.2	4.6	5.3	5.8	5.7	5.5	6.1
Poland	34.6	22.8	35.1	41.5	55.4	65.6	67.9	72.9	87.6	91.7	102.6
Romania	19.7	20.3	22.9	37.2	32.8	26.9	29.3	30.4	39.1	45.2	56.2
Russia				362.3	268.9	410.7	429.8	526.2	537.8	588.2	705.2
Serbia and Montenegro								19.7	18.9	11.6	19.2
Slovakia				2.8	3.6	5.5	8.0	18.0	25.0	27.5	24.1
Slovenia				6.5	13.7	13.5	14.6	15.8	17.8	18.3	21.9
Ukraine				65.0	36.7	38.5	57.7	77.4	87.4	88.8	93.9

Source: *Euromonitor International from International Civil Aviation Authority/national statistics*

Scheduled Airlines: Departures, Load Factor and Passengers Carried 2007

As stated

	Aircraft Departures ('000)	Passengers Carried ('000)	Passenger Load Factor (%)
Western Europe			
Austria	164.0	10,490	75.5
Belgium	342.9	15,555	59.3
Cyprus	10.5	1,127	71.1
Denmark	104.0	8,720	73.3
Finland	92.7	8,170	76.0
France	570.5	50,459	80.1
Germany	1,139.7	110,557	75.4
Gibraltar			
Greece	90.2	5,957	67.2
Iceland	18.2	1,648	74.5
Ireland	382.1	54,305	78.5
Italy	362.6	31,923	66.6
Liechtenstein			
Luxembourg	18.3	847	50.2
Malta	16.0	1,519	74.9
Monaco	19.0	123	85.8
Netherlands	218.1	23,215	69.5
Norway	128.4	10,208	70.8
Portugal	124.4	10,013	68.7
Spain	675.7	60,395	71.7
Sweden	73.3	6,547	72.8
Switzerland	176.8	13,102	59.4
Turkey	145.2	15,559	76.4
United Kingdom	1,240.5	126,008	66.8
Eastern Europe			
Albania	10.9	220	62.8
Belarus	7.6	260	42.4
Bosnia-Herzegovina	6.3	111	
Bulgaria	15.2	1,122	72.5
Croatia	24.3	1,715	64.8
Czech Republic	91.5	6,847	74.3
Estonia	10.1	746	67.7
Georgia	6.1	326	63.5
Hungary	52.8	3,290	69.6
Latvia	44.3	2,074	58.5
Lithuania	10.5	591	55.4
Macedonia	2.9	257	68.7
Moldova	4.9	341	57.2
Poland	95.9	4,980	75.0
Romania	56.3	3,298	61.9
Russia	328.3	29,162	72.6
Serbia and Montenegro	21.8	1,285	60.5
Slovakia	20.1	2,405	79.8
Slovenia	25.6	1,136	67.1
Ukraine	65.8	3,826	48.5

Source: Euromonitor International from International Civil Aviation Authority/national statistics

Merchant Shipping

Table 4.23

Size of Merchant Shipping Fleet 1980-2007
'000 gross tons

	1980	1985	1990	1995	2000	2002	2003	2004	2005	2006	2007
Western Europe											
Austria	88.8	134.2	139.3	91.9	51.2	29.9	32.0	34.1	34.1	34.1	14.0
Belgium	1,809.8	2,400.3	1,954.5	72.0	137.2	186.7	1,392.9	3,973.3	4,058.4	4,312.7	4,091.3
Cyprus	2,091.1	8,196.1	18,335.9	24,652.5	23,206.4	22,997.0	22,054.2	21,283.4	19,019.1	19,032.2	18,954.3
Denmark	5,390.4	4,942.2	5,188.1	5,747.2	6,357.8	7,602.9	7,726.7	7,763.1	8,290.4	8,799.6	9,476.3
Finland	2,346.2	1,649.7	1,093.6	1,581.4	1,620.4	1,545.2	1,452.1	1,428.9	1,475.2	1,422.6	1,570.1
France	11,924.6	8,237.4	3,832.4	4,194.3	4,681.2	4,731.5	4,859.2	4,974.9	5,611.1	6,164.8	6,350.2
Germany	9,887.8	7,611.4	5,737.8	5,626.2	6,552.2	6,545.8	6,111.8	8,246.4	11,497.2	11,364.3	12,934.2
Gibraltar	2.3	583.3	2,008.5	307.1	722.0	960.9	993.0	1,142.4	1,156.6	1,297.4	1,515.4
Greece	39,471.7	31,031.5	20,521.6	29,434.7	26,401.7	28,782.8	32,203.1	32,040.7	30,744.7	32,048.1	35,704.5
Iceland	188.2	180.3	176.6	190.2	185.8	187.3	187.4	194.1	188.5	184.2	180.0
Ireland	209.0	194.0	180.8	213.4	254.0	279.6	471.0	496.8	309.8	193.3	187.2
Italy	11,095.7	8,843.2	7,991.4	6,905.0	9,048.7	9,595.9	10,245.8	10,956.0	11,616.0	12,571.2	12,971.7
Liechtenstein											
Luxembourg			3.3	880.8	1,754.2	1,493.8	1,006.0	689.7	570.0	779.9	883.5
Malta	132.9	1,855.8	4,518.7	17,678.3	28,170.0	26,331.4	25,134.3	22,352.6	23,015.6	24,849.8	27,754.4
Monaco											
Netherlands	5,723.8	4,301.3	3,784.8	2,903.0	5,167.7	5,664.3	5,702.6	5,622.9	5,669.4	5,818.8	6,139.8
Norway						22,194.5	20,509.3	18,936.2	17,531.9	18,222.3	18,156.0
Portugal						1,099.7	1,156.3	1,136.5	1,239.6	1,223.6	1,070.1
Spain	8,112.2	6,256.2	3,807.1	1,618.6	1,552.6	2,371.2	2,651.0	2,869.1	2,901.7	3,004.6	3,061.8
Sweden	4,234.0	2,620.0	2,782.0	2,880.0	2,887.0	3,177.5	3,579.3	3,666.9	3,765.7	3,876.5	4,044.9
Switzerland	310.8	342.0	287.5	381.0	495.0	559.1	588.7	487.5	479.6	510.0	588.6
Turkey	1,454.8	3,684.4	3,718.6	6,267.6	5,832.7	5,658.8	4,950.6	4,678.9	5,044.7	4,848.8	4,995.1
United Kingdom	27,135.2	14,343.5	9,836.0	8,935.0	9,702.5	13,773.0	17,314.2	18,344.3	19,652.0	20,835.7	21,947.2
Eastern Europe											
Albania	56.1	56.1	55.8	63.0	23.6	48.7	70.0	72.8	74.8	74.7	67.5
Belarus											
Bosnia-Herzegovina											
Bulgaria	1,233.3	1,322.2	1,360.5	1,166.1	989.6	889.3	747.9	789.5	894.2	875.5	911.1
Croatia					841.4	834.7	847.7	1,016.1	1,135.2	1,157.2	1,373.5
Czech Republic	155.3	184.3	325.8	140.3							
Estonia				597.7	383.4	357.4	358.2	334.9	292.5	416.7	389.8
Georgia				282.0	160.6	569.3	814.9	974.3	1,091.9	1,129.3	1,048.4
Hungary	75.0	77.2	98.3	45.1	8.4	3.8	7.6				
Latvia				798.1	118.2	88.7	90.9	294.3	304.8	333.3	261.8
Lithuania				610.2	401.6	435.3	442.1	453.4	476.7	448.6	425.8
Macedonia											
Moldova								3.7	11.4	15.7	50.1
Poland	3,639.1	3,315.3	3,369.2	2,358.0	1,119.2	585.6	282.4	162.7	190.1	193.4	193.3
Romania	1,856.3	3,023.8	4,004.6	2,536.4	766.9	622.0	563.1	426.7	336.5	272.1	269.5
Russia				10,818.0	10,485.9	10,380.0	10,430.8	8,638.9	8,334.5	8,046.0	7,587.3
Serbia and Montenegro							1.1	6.1	12.3	10.5	13.1
Slovakia				19.3	15.2	7.4	29.2	126.4	211.2	232.7	233.3
Slovenia				2.1	1.7	2.3	1.7	1.5	1.1	1.6	1.6
Ukraine				4,613.0	1,546.3	1,349.9	1,378.8	1,144.8	1,154.0	1,136.5	1,144.6

Source: *Euromonitor International from Lloyd's Register/national statistics*
Notes: *Ships of 100 gross tons or more. Gross tonnage (gt) is a measure of the total volume within the hull, and above deck, available for cargo, passengers, crew, fuel, stores etc. 1gt = 100 cu ft*

Table 4.24

Length of Public Railway Network 1980-2007

Kilometres at end-year

	1980	1985	1990	1995	2000	2002	2003	2004	2005	2006	2007
Western Europe											
Austria			5,624	5,672	5,563	5,642	5,656	5,670	5,680	5,689	5,699
Belgium	3,978	3,712	3,479	3,368	3,471	3,518	3,521	3,536	3,543	3,552	3,559
Cyprus											
Denmark	2,461	2,471	2,344		2,768	2,779	2,785	2,791	2,798	2,805	2,811
Finland			5,846	5,859	5,854	5,850	5,851	5,741	5,742	5,742	5,743
France	34,382	34,678	34,260	31,940	31,397	31,320	30,990	30,880	30,798	30,724	30,650
Germany	28,517	27,634	26,950	41,718	36,588	35,804	35,593	35,372	35,235	35,109	35,002
Gibraltar											
Greece	2,461	2,461	2,484	2,474	2,385	2,383	2,414	2,419	2,424	2,427	2,430
Iceland											
Ireland	1,987	1,944	1,944	1,945	1,919	1,921	1,922	1,922	1,923	1,923	1,924
Italy	16,133	16,183		16,005	16,147	15,985	15,974	15,967	15,960	15,951	15,944
Liechtenstein											
Luxembourg	270	270	271		271	274	275	275	275	275	275
Malta											
Monaco											
Netherlands	2,760	2,794	2,780	2,813	2,802	2,806	2,811	2,811	2,812	2,813	2,814
Norway			4,044	4,023	4,179	4,077	4,077	4,077	4,087	4,087	4,087
Portugal	3,588	3,607	3,126	3,065	2,814	2,801	2,797	2,791	2,783	2,777	2,771
Spain	13,542	12,710	12,560	12,280	12,310	12,312	12,575	12,837	12,894	12,933	12,980
Sweden			10,801	9,782	9,877	11,095	11,037	11,120	11,145	11,173	11,182
Switzerland			2,978	2,987	5,062	5,049	5,028	5,024	5,017	5,009	5,004
Turkey	8,193	8,169	8,429	8,549	8,671	8,671	8,697	8,697	8,704	8,711	8,716
United Kingdom	18,028	17,122	16,924	16,999	16,994	17,020	16,950	16,458	16,446	16,431	16,421
Eastern Europe											
Albania				447	400	428	428	428	428	428	428
Belarus	5,512	5,540	5,569	5,543	5,512	5,502	5,496	5,492	5,487	5,482	5,478
Bosnia-Herzegovina						608	608	608	608	608	608
Bulgaria	4,267	4,297	4,299	4,293	4,320	4,318	4,318	4,317	4,317	4,316	4,316
Croatia		2,441		2,296	2,726	2,726	2,726	2,726	2,726	2,726	2,726
Czech Republic			9,451	9,327	9,444	9,600	9,602	9,613	9,621	9,626	9,633
Estonia	993	1,009	1,026	1,021	968	967	959	959	958	958	957
Georgia		1,465	1,583	1,575	1,575	1,575	1,575	1,575	1,575	1,575	1,575
Hungary	7,826	7,406	7,772	7,632	7,668	7,676	7,681	7,685	7,687	7,689	7,692
Latvia	2,384	2,384	2,397	2,413	2,331	2,270	2,270	2,270	2,270	2,270	2,270
Lithuania	2,008	2,014	2,007	2,002	1,905	1,775	1,774	1,782	1,771	1,770	1,768
Macedonia			696	699	699	699	699	699	699	699	699
Moldova			1,150		1,139	1,121	1,111	1,111	1,111	1,111	1,111
Poland	27,181	25,848	26,228	23,986	22,560	21,073	20,665	20,250	20,253	19,980	19,751
Romania	11,110	11,269	11,348	11,376	11,015	11,002	11,077	11,081	11,084	11,091	11,094
Russia			87,000	87,000	86,075	85,542	85,394	85,000	85,000	85,000	85,000
Serbia and Montenegro			3,959			4,058	4,058	4,058	4,058	4,058	4,058
Slovakia			3,660	3,665	3,662	3,657	3,657	3,660	3,658	3,658	3,658
Slovenia	1,229	1,228	1,196	1,201	1,201	1,229	1,229	1,229	1,228	1,228	1,228
Ukraine	22,553	22,698	22,799	22,756	22,301	22,078	22,051	21,990	21,954	21,920	21,898

Source: Euromonitor International from national statistics

Rail Transport   **Table 4.25**

Railway Statistics of Major National Carriers 2007
As stated

	Locomotives (number)	Rail motor vehicles (number)	Passengers carried (million)	Average journey length (km)	Total goods carried (million tonnes)
Western Europe					
Austria	1,360	355.0	238.5	40.3	107.5
Belgium	733	1,497.0	177.4	50.1	54.1
Cyprus					
Denmark	154	667.0	176.8	34.8	7.9
Finland	634		65.5	51.8	41.5
France	4,467		1,008.3	75.0	102.2
Germany	5,195	5,200.0	2,197.7	34.3	326.8
Gibraltar					
Greece	147		10.5	179.8	3.3
Iceland					
Ireland	101		39.2	46.5	1.6
Italy	3,097		809.6	63.0	95.1
Liechtenstein			1.0	1.0	
Luxembourg					9.7
Malta					
Monaco					
Netherlands	194		660.8	22.8	30.4
Norway	160	186.0	53.2	51.8	8.7
Portugal	176	313.0	147.1	24.3	10.2
Spain	778	1,989.0	517.9	38.5	24.9
Sweden	634		153.0	59.2	65.9
Switzerland	2,011		337.7	46.3	65.6
Turkey	689		75.6	63.3	20.6
United Kingdom	1,681		1,145.2	38.7	124.3
Eastern Europe					
Albania	58		1.9	38.5	0.4
Belarus	1,076		142.3	68.3	88.6
Bosnia-Herzegovina	186		0.3	47.7	7.6
Bulgaria	579	76.0	26.5	81.9	16.8
Croatia	271	196.0	41.2	32.3	15.5
Czech Republic	2,337		183.4	36.8	82.8
Estonia	317		5.0	54.0	70.1
Georgia					17.7
Hungary	1,004	262.0	150.6	63.8	52.3
Latvia	211	389.0	27.7	35.5	64.4
Lithuania	243	59.0	6.5	62.3	52.5
Macedonia	50		0.7	400.7	2.7
Moldova	158		5.4	74.1	16.2
Poland	4,612	989.0	231.5	73.0	292.8
Romania	1,898		75.1	92.8	74.1
Russia	22,653		1,347.1	133.5	1,355.4
Serbia and Montenegro					
Slovakia	1,025		51.5	38.6	48.9
Slovenia	143	110.0	16.4	48.1	16.5
Ukraine	4,240		430.7	105.9	434.6

Source: *Euromonitor International from International Road Federation/national statistics*

Table 4.26

Railway Freight Traffic 1980-2007

Million net tonne-kilometres

	1980	1985	1990	1995	2000	2002	2003	2004	2005	2006	2007
Western Europe											
Austria	11,200	11,292	12,158	13,714	16,602	17,132	16,869	17,099	17,303	17,491	17,662
Belgium	8,037	8,277	8,354	7,304	7,694	7,297	7,293	7,247	7,197	7,147	7,098
Cyprus	-										
Denmark	1,619	1,749	1,801	1,998	2,025	1,906	1,997	2,169	1,976	2,042	2,101
Finland	8,300	8,066	8,400	9,559	10,107	9,664	10,047	10,066	10,133	10,199	10,266
France	68,815	55,121	50,670	48,136	55,448	50,036	46,835	45,878	45,376	44,858	44,639
Germany				69,483	75,884	76,300	79,800	86,400	95,400	98,767	101,367
Gibraltar											
Greece	814	733	647	306	426	327	456	572	646	681	706
Iceland											
Ireland	624	601	589	602	491	426	373	346	336	326	316
Italy	18,384	16,853	13,259	24,050	19,259	20,680	21,393	22,044	22,695	23,346	23,997
Liechtenstein											
Luxembourg	660	648	615	715	632	617	568	560	553	547	540
Malta											
Monaco											
Netherlands	3,468	3,269	3,070	3,097	3,819	4,323	4,962	5,038	5,107	5,176	5,244
Norway	3,084	2,928	2,559	2,715	2,399	2,191	2,158	2,128	2,104	2,081	2,058
Portugal	1,001	1,196	1,444	2,020	2,183	2,583	2,438	2,509	2,563	2,617	2,670
Spain	10,528	11,415	10,142	10,074	11,620	11,894	11,867	11,460	11,071	10,842	10,558
Sweden	15,914	17,331	19,102	19,391	15,422	19,197	20,141	20,531	20,769	21,006	21,243
Switzerland	7,799	7,434	8,958	8,686	9,937	9,639	9,534	10,245	10,328	10,454	10,580
Turkey	5,029	7,747	8,031	8,632	9,895	7,224	8,669	9,417	9,681	9,938	10,195
United Kingdom	17,640	16,047	16,778	13,000	18,200	18,700	18,900	18,900	18,962	19,013	19,063
Eastern Europe											
Albania				53	28	21	31	32	34	36	38
Belarus	66,264	73,243	75,373	25,510	31,425	34,169	38,402	40,331	43,559	45,723	46,943
Bosnia-Herzegovina							212	445	745	786	829
Bulgaria		18,172	14,132	8,595	5,538	4,628	5,274	5,101	4,939	4,776	4,613
Croatia	7,561	8,674	6,535	1,974	1,928	2,206	2,487	2,493	2,835	2,945	3,049
Czech Republic			41,150	22,634	17,496	15,810	15,862	15,499	15,191	15,054	14,874
Estonia			6,977	3,851	7,788	9,330	9,283	9,505	9,659	9,814	9,968
Georgia	14,656	13,487	12,354		3,900	5,075	5,448	5,706	5,910	6,049	6,150
Hungary	24,041	21,929	16,593	8,132	8,093	7,751	8,028	8,071	8,136	8,201	8,266
Latvia		19,933	18,538	9,757	13,310	15,020	17,955	18,490	18,918	19,193	19,474
Lithuania			19,258	7,220	8,919	9,767	11,457	11,637	12,457	12,713	13,004
Macedonia	712	992	769	169	509	334	373	379	386	394	402
Moldova	15,200		15,007	3,134	1,538	2,715	3,000	3,195	3,348	3,432	3,490
Poland	132,576	118,863	83,530	69,116	54,448	47,756	49,595	52,332	49,972	50,589	51,144
Romania	78,390	64,090	57,253	27,179	16,354	15,218	15,039	17,022	17,445	18,013	18,581
Russia	2,316,000	2,506,000	2,523,000	1,214,000	1,373,178	1,510,203	1,668,921	1,802,000	1,858,000	1,928,029	1,978,441
Serbia and Montenegro	8,500		7,700		1,969	2,319	2,656				
Slovakia			23,176	13,764	11,234	10,383	10,113	9,702	9,463	9,259	9,069
Slovenia	3,851	4,292	4,209	3,076	2,596	2,834	3,018	3,149	3,245	3,336	3,407
Ukraine			488,243	195,762	172,840	193,141	225,288	236,943	250,160	262,831	271,174

Source: Euromonitor International from national statistics

Rail Transport

Table 4.27

Railway Passenger Traffic 1980-2007
Million passenger-kilometres

	1980	1985	1990	1995	2000	2002	2003	2004	2005	2006	2007
Western Europe											
Austria	7,600	7,290	8,575	9,628	8,206	8,300	8,484	8,668	9,236	9,414	9,621
Belgium	6,963	6,572	6,540	6,757	7,755	8,260	8,265	8,675	8,778	8,827	8,897
Cyprus											
Denmark	3,803	4,546	4,851	4,784	5,327	5,479	5,700	5,921	5,957	6,063	6,144
Finland	3,200	3,224	3,300	3,184	3,405	3,318	3,300	3,352	3,366	3,381	3,395
France	54,660	62,070	63,740	55,560	69,571	73,227	73,793	74,359	74,959	75,289	75,574
Germany				60,514	74,015	69,848	71,364	72,879	73,889	74,731	75,348
Gibraltar											
Greece	1,464	1,732	1,978	1,568	1,886	1,836	1,752	1,668	1,854	1,868	1,886
Iceland											
Ireland	1,032	1,023	1,226	1,291	1,389	1,537	1,560	1,582	1,781	1,803	1,826
Italy	39,492	37,401	45,512	43,859	43,752	45,957	47,606	49,254	49,731	50,449	50,991
Liechtenstein								1	1	1	1
Luxembourg	300	288	264	304	332	268	272	274	276	278	280
Malta											
Monaco											
Netherlands	8,916	9,007	11,060	13,977	14,666	14,288	14,193	14,097	14,730	14,904	15,092
Norway	2,400	2,232	2,430	2,676	2,635	2,679	2,681	2,683	2,723	2,736	2,753
Portugal	6,077	5,725	5,664	4,809	3,834	3,926	3,810	3,693	3,809	3,693	3,576
Spain	13,527	15,979	15,476	15,318	18,547	19,781	19,333	19,022	19,806	19,865	19,949
Sweden	6,787	6,586	6,353	6,345	8,301	8,739	8,686	8,634	8,910	8,979	9,055
Switzerland	9,964	10,163	12,678	13,408	12,620	14,147	14,509	14,914	15,177	15,403	15,630
Turkey	6,011	6,489	6,410	5,797	5,833	5,204	5,878	5,237	5,036	4,927	4,787
United Kingdom	30,300	30,400	33,200	30,000	38,200	39,728	40,900	42,400	43,120	43,792	44,349
Eastern Europe											
Albania				197	125	123	105	89	81	77	72
Belarus	10,922	13,761	16,852	12,505	17,722	14,349	13,308	13,893	10,351	9,968	9,721
Bosnia-Herzegovina							19	19	15	15	14
Bulgaria	7,056	7,785	7,793	4,693	3,472	2,598	2,471	2,396	2,321	2,246	2,172
Croatia	3,619	4,063	3,429	943	1,252	1,195	1,163	1,213	1,266	1,296	1,329
Czech Republic			13,313	8,023	7,300	6,597	6,518	6,589	6,667	6,690	6,748
Estonia			1,510	421	261	177	185	193	248	260	272
Georgia		4,214	2,497	371	378	401	410	416	419	422	424
Hungary	12,372	10,464	11,400	5,880	9,693	10,531	10,348	10,165	9,851	9,725	9,600
Latvia			5,364	1,373	715	744	778	811	894	937	984
Lithuania			3,640	1,130	611	498	432	443	428	409	403
Macedonia	358	417	354	65	170	98	176	253	263	277	285
Moldova			1,464	1,019	315	355	367	380	387	394	398
Poland	46,300	51,978	50,373	26,635	19,706	20,749	19,638	18,690	18,157	17,466	16,887
Romania	23,220	31,082	30,582	18,879	11,632	8,502	7,990	7,605	7,325	7,117	6,964
Russia	227,300		274,400	192,117	167,054	152,900	157,600	164,300	171,600	175,756	179,790
Serbia and Montenegro					1,436	1,146					
Slovakia			6,381	4,202	2,870	2,682	2,455	2,228	2,182	2,071	1,986
Slovenia	1,436	1,667	1,429	595	705	750	777	764	777	784	790
Ukraine	60,160		81,998	63,752	51,767	49,231	48,503	47,775	47,046	46,318	45,590

Source: *Euromonitor International from national statistics*

Road Transport

Table 4.28

Car Traffic Volume 1980-2007
Million car-kilometres

	1980	1985	1990	1995	2000	2002	2003	2004	2005	2006	2007
Western Europe											
Austria	25,840	27,500					37,000	37,000	37,000	37,000	37,000
Belgium	40,861	42,101	50,467	85,200	88,719	81,780	78,310	79,550	80,203	80,547	80,728
Cyprus								6,384			
Denmark	21,800	24,200	29,504	33,200	38,186	38,854	36,491	34,128	33,086	32,445	32,276
Finland	26,800	25,970	39,800	35,800	39,815	41,676	42,566	28,480	44,192	44,863	45,476
France	240,000	262,000	314,000	351,000	402,000	422,000	425,000	425,000	420,000	418,000	416,833
Germany				514,900	555,800	583,600	577,800	590,400	578,200	573,700	571,613
Gibraltar											
Greece	9,392				48,573	54,465	59,241	65,236	69,057	71,489	72,850
Iceland	986					2,062					
Ireland	14,798	20,540	24,800		26,204	28,463	29,342	29,776	29,955	30,287	30,497
Italy					46,864	43,144	42,782	42,479	42,354	42,178	42,044
Liechtenstein											
Luxembourg	1,382	2,191	2,971	2,954	3,408	3,548	3,532	3,524	3,518	3,515	3,513
Malta					1,507						
Monaco				1							
Netherlands	61,400	65,000	76,960	89,094	93,185	98,812	101,151	103,709	104,767	106,090	107,188
Norway	22,743	22,565			28,113	28,507	29,162	29,395	29,543	29,607	29,642
Portugal		22,500	30,300	44,250	52,339	55,072	56,278	57,066	57,392	57,907	58,269
Spain	52,780	56,300	81,344	107,994	180,908	197,597	204,211	209,389	213,883	217,503	220,456
Sweden		52,900		57,400	56,400	44,092	60,000	60,500	63,000	64,200	65,320
Switzerland	32,071	36,468	42,649	43,794	49,585	51,758	52,000	53,768	54,338	55,030	55,704
Turkey	7,444	9,415	14,755	28,837	36,224	33,204	33,802	38,403	40,490	42,433	43,872
United Kingdom	201,100	228,000	329,700	353,200	376,798	392,926	393,049	398,056	401,456	403,352	405,641
Eastern Europe											
Albania				2							
Belarus				935	966	760	861	731	716	704	694
Bosnia-Herzegovina											
Bulgaria			10,597	11,230	13,189	13,897	14,698	15,033	15,368	15,694	15,916
Croatia					11,158	13,432	14,600	15,365	16,038	16,617	17,065
Czech Republic				24,540	28,400	33,445	34,298	35,013	35,309	35,705	36,017
Estonia					5,116	5,431	5,898	6,263	6,373	6,420	6,446
Georgia				17		252					
Hungary			17,155		16,000	15,800	15,800	16,200	16,365	16,491	16,606
Latvia			1,660			6,268	6,809	7,486	7,979	8,435	8,869
Lithuania							6,472	7,051	6,753	6,604	6,559
Macedonia			2,400	2,621							
Moldova				180	143	191	198	202	204	206	208
Poland	20,494	20,193	34,194	75,150	94,600	95,000	95,120	95,320	95,658	95,893	96,098
Romania			19,681	24,019	27,545	30,593	42,969	55,344	62,361	68,590	72,860
Russia				14,711	17,099	18,086	18,479	18,786	19,073	19,292	19,473
Serbia and Montenegro											
Slovakia				8,251	9,754	9,854	9,862	9,891	9,911	9,926	9,943
Slovenia			4,749	5,640	8,130	8,762	8,918	9,334	9,490	9,771	9,960
Ukraine				44,687	3,347	3,786	4,241	4,697	4,788	4,861	4,919

Source: Euromonitor International from International Road Federation/national statistics

Road Transport

Table 4.29

Goods Transported by Road 1980-2007
Million car-kilometres

	1980	1985	1990	1995	2000	2002	2003	2004	2005	2006	2007
Western Europe											
Austria	7,931	9,099	15,317		26,300	26,374	26,411	26,436	26,458	26,476	26,491
Belgium	16,738	19,124	25,979	27,500	32,450	44,915	51,147	54,856	58,450	61,458	63,749
Cyprus								1,100			
Denmark	9,600	9,500	10,664	10,786	11,696	11,810	11,174	10,538	11,058	11,318	11,448
Finland	17,900	20,800	25,400	23,200	27,500	29,000	27,800	28,100	27,800	27,667	27,632
France	115,500	112,000	145,000	154,379	266,500	214,833	189,000	197,000	193,000	191,400	189,160
Germany				199,196	226,477	225,467	227,197	232,296	237,609	240,847	242,364
Gibraltar											
Greece			12,485	16,700	18,360	19,241	19,362	19,452	19,489	19,544	19,585
Iceland						800	800				
Ireland					6,500	14,448	15,900	17,298	18,603	19,711	20,727
Italy	119,629	144,129	177,945	174,432	184,756	192,700	195,887	197,742	199,614	200,766	201,579
Liechtenstein											
Luxembourg	278	431			6,797	9,142	9,493	9,692	9,829	9,913	9,968
Malta											
Monaco											
Netherlands	17,663	19,249	23,300	23,491	45,700	66,634	77,100	82,333	86,694	90,037	92,193
Norway	5,252	6,418	7,692	10,395	12,483	13,614	14,115	14,966	15,414	15,894	16,191
Portugal	11,800		11,712	11,457	20,470	23,187	24,274	25,288	25,875	26,592	27,210
Spain	94,800	108,100	102,544	74,034	133,078	124,472	132,868	132,821	133,721	135,776	136,422
Sweden	21,362	21,177	26,519	29,324	32,419	36,620	37,048	37,677	39,373	40,303	41,353
Switzerland	7,287	8,640	11,214	12,868	21,949	24,500	14,582	15,000	15,753	15,770	16,033
Turkey	39,233	62,480	97,843	152,210	161,552	150,912	152,163	156,853	166,831	171,076	174,394
United Kingdom	95,900	102,100	136,300	149,600	165,827	161,276	159,000	160,000	163,000	164,600	165,533
Eastern Europe											
Albania					2,200	2,200	2,200	2,200	2,200	2,200	2,200
Belarus			22,361	9,539	9,745	11,400	12,710	13,969	15,055	15,816	16,463
Bosnia-Herzegovina					300						
Bulgaria						6,840	9,015	11,843	12,760	13,250
Croatia			2,458	1,251	1,090	7,413	8,241	8,819	9,328	9,839	10,265
Czech Republic				31,267	39,036	45,059	46,600	46,862	47,106	47,561	47,848
Estonia			2,097	1,549	3,689	4,387	6,364	6,837	7,641	8,183	8,486
Georgia				98	475	543	562	570	581	590	596
Hungary					13,329	12,000	12,505	12,771	12,964	13,071	13,134
Latvia			5,853	1,100	4,789	1,930	2,324	2,330	2,767	2,990	3,168
Lithuania			7,336	5,160	7,769	10,709	11,462	12,279	15,908	17,294	18,266
Macedonia			3,510	1,178	800	2,693	4,100	4,650	5,040	5,431	5,653
Moldova			6,305	1,121	1,001	1,153	1,577	1,673	1,791	1,880	1,931
Poland	44,546	36,593	49,800	71,600	72,843	74,679	85,989	110,481	119,740	124,747	127,977
Romania	11,756	5,388	28,994	22,400	14,288	25,350	30,854	37,220	40,333	42,830	44,826
Russia					23,300	23,200	25,200	25,707	26,117	26,441	26,648
Serbia and Montenegro					2,500	2,900	3,100	3,200	3,283	3,347	3,388
Slovakia				5,158	14,340	14,929	16,859	18,517	19,565	20,596	21,426
Slovenia					5,252	6,609	7,040	9,007	11,033	12,212	13,074
Ukraine			79,668	34,478	16,811	20,593	24,387	19,726	23,895	25,885	26,912

Source: *Euromonitor International from International Road Federation/national statistics*

Table 4.30

Average Annual Distance Travelled by Car 1980-2007

Kilometres

	1980	1985	1990	1995	2000	2002	2003	2004	2005	2006	2007
Western Europe											
Austria	11,500	10,866					9,126	9,004	8,901	8,799	8,693
Belgium	12,936	12,840	13,165	20,099	19,166	17,308	16,408	16,509	16,498	16,341	16,231
Cyprus								19,021			
Denmark	15,689	16,123	18,549	19,706	20,720	20,558	19,265	17,827	16,871	16,111	16,008
Finland	21,861	16,797	20,528	18,834	18,774	19,117	18,840	12,217	18,303	18,022	18,179
France	12,533	12,423	13,333	13,984	14,326	14,472	14,378	14,214	13,953	13,750	13,340
Germany					12,714	12,698	13,068	12,833	13,011	12,545	12,322	12,204
Gibraltar											
Greece	10,675				15,420	14,938	15,429	16,015	16,048	15,736	15,182
Iceland	12,325					12,750					
Ireland	20,151	28,948	31,140		19,863	19,658	19,469	18,812	18,022	17,026	16,491
Italy					1,438	1,280	1,247	1,250	1,222	1,195	1,182
Liechtenstein											
Luxembourg	9,376	14,414	16,199	12,897	13,218	12,562	12,296	12,011	11,736	11,544	11,178
Malta					7,968						
Monaco				48							
Netherlands	13,599	13,263	14,811	15,816	14,691	14,726	14,756	14,503	14,354	14,621	14,816
Norway	18,436	14,904			15,180	15,006	15,082	14,862	14,561	14,201	13,763
Portugal		18,987	18,589	16,948	14,567	14,176	14,190	13,919	13,665	13,498	13,353
Spain	6,985	6,071	6,781	7,599	10,368	10,548	10,927	10,715	10,562	10,402	10,183
Sweden		16,787		15,809	14,105	10,906	14,722	14,708	15,167	15,277	15,339
Switzerland	14,274	13,934	14,286	13,562	13,986	13,985	13,852	14,107	14,072	14,110	14,082
Turkey	10,029	9,573	8,943	9,428	8,191	7,218	7,191	7,111	7,014	6,910	6,779
United Kingdom	13,027	11,717	14,994	14,458	13,476	13,401	13,147	13,151	13,098	13,014	12,944
Eastern Europe											
Albania					34						
Belarus				995	697	501	531	437	412	388	370
Bosnia-Herzegovina											
Bulgaria			8,300	6,816	7,289	7,123	7,386	7,366	7,447	7,573	7,543
Croatia					9,920	10,795	11,288	11,488	11,582	11,573	11,444
Czech Republic				8,064	8,259	9,170	9,255	9,176	8,919	8,690	8,669
Estonia					11,028	13,553	13,591	13,292	12,906	12,796	12,719
Georgia				47		1,000					
Hungary			9,239		6,766	6,009	5,689	5,728	5,665	5,583	5,513
Latvia						10,125	10,493	10,911	10,747	10,262	9,801
Lithuania							5,149	5,358	4,640	4,317	4,106
Macedonia			10,400	9,167							
Moldova				1,085	619	732	770	747	729	716	708
Poland	9,029	5,853	6,500	9,997	9,468	8,449	8,460	7,960	7,752	7,165	6,587
Romania			15,230	10,930	9,917	10,289	13,917	17,159	18,539	21,266	20,708
Russia				1,036	1,003	855	790	776	746	754	719
Serbia and Montenegro											
Slovakia				8,123	7,822	7,426	7,273	7,125	7,602	7,442	7,301
Slovenia			8,212	8,078	9,387	9,795	9,795	9,994	9,883	9,968	9,821
Ukraine				10,000	623	685	759	838	826	812	810

Source: Euromonitor International from national statistics

Road Network

Table 4.31

Road Network 2007
Kilometres

	Total	Motorway	National Highway	Secondary Regional	Other Local	% Paved	Density (km per sq km of land)
Western Europe							
Austria	134,518	2,831	10,107	23,580	98,000	100.00	1.60
Belgium	151,508	1,754	12,531	1,349	135,874	78.00	5.01
Cyprus	12,293	270	2,749	3,222	6,052		1.33
Denmark	72,382	1,035	637	9,695	61,015	100.00	1.71
Finland	79,222	681	13,663	13,486	51,392	65.32	0.26
France	950,852	11,024	24,828	365,000	550,000	100.00	1.73
Germany	231,480	12,363	40,983	86,553	91,581	100.00	0.66
Gibraltar							
Greece	118,499	880	10,548	31,471	75,600	91.80	0.92
Iceland	13,052		4,260	3,976	4,816	37.35	0.13
Ireland	97,451	245	5,310	11,662	80,234	100.00	1.41
Italy	487,379	6,621	46,009	122,600	312,149	100.00	1.66
Liechtenstein							
Luxembourg	5,231	147	842	1,892	2,350	100.00	2.02
Malta	2,254		185		2,069	87.53	7.04
Monaco	50					100.00	25.64
Netherlands	130,714	2,771	6,960	59,443	61,540	90.00	3.86
Norway	93,337	269	27,502	27,249	38,318	81.06	0.31
Portugal	79,291	2,178	7,923	5,310	63,880	86.00	0.87
Spain	667,741	11,959	25,054	140,029	490,700		1.33
Sweden	425,792	1,792	15,360	82,980	325,660	31.73	1.04
Switzerland	71,335	1,770	18,116	51,449		100.00	1.78
Turkey	426,925	1,666	31,272	30,787	363,200	37.22	0.55
United Kingdom	406,880	3,730	9,250	41,900	352,000	100.00	1.61
Eastern Europe							
Albania	18,000		3,220	4,300	10,480	39.00	0.66
Belarus	95,629		15,420	68,370	11,839	89.46	0.46
Bosnia-Herzegovina	21,846		3,722	4,104	14,020	52.30	0.43
Bulgaria	46,341	333	2,933	4,155	38,921	99.00	0.43
Croatia	28,483	734	6,819	10,550	10,380	84.00	0.51
Czech Republic	127,851	697	20,720	34,134	72,300	100.00	1.65
Estonia	57,188	99	3,945	12,439	40,705	23.43	1.35
Georgia	20,258		1,474	3,326	15,458	39.38	0.29
Hungary	160,295	533	30,460	71,848	57,454	44.08	1.79
Latvia	70,257		6,959	13,248	50,050	100.00	1.13
Lithuania	79,774	417	1,336	19,581	58,440	89.34	1.27
Macedonia	14,864	280	1,088	4,048	9,448	63.80	0.58
Moldova	12,742		3,332	6,139	3,271	86.28	0.39
Poland	475,812	575	17,953	28,422	428,862	70.89	1.55
Romania	198,918	228	14,817	36,028	147,845	50.70	0.83
Russia	858,000		717,344	140,656		69.51	0.05
Serbia and Montenegro	16,010	457	4,976	10,577		97.00	0.16
Slovakia	43,031	327	3,377	3,673	35,654	87.42	0.89
Slovenia	38,545	621	927	4,879	32,118	100.00	1.91
Ukraine	169,222	15	16,331	113,931	38,960	97.65	0.29

Source: *Euromonitor International from International Road Federation/national statistics*

Banking and Finance

Bank Claims on the Private Sector

Table 5.1

Bank Claims on the Private Sector 1980-2007
Billion units of national currency

	1980	1985	1990	1995	2000	2002	2003	2004	2005	2006	2007
Western Europe											
Austria	54.8	83.7	122.3	162.0	213.0	229.5	234.9	247.7	276.8	292.4	309.0
Belgium	25.2	31.6	60.0	151.2	196.6	198.9	203.8	207.4	223.8	261.5	305.2
Cyprus	0.5	0.9	2.5	5.1	9.4	10.6	11.2	12.1	13.0	14.9	18.7
Denmark	94.0	190.4	429.2	312.9	1,749.3	1,996.8	2,123.2	2,318.4	2,654.0	3,031.5	3,432.3
Finland	15.2	34.2	75.7	58.9	70.1	83.8	93.4	102.9	118.1	130.6	146.6
France	321.2	555.8	969.3	1,028.3	1,225.2	1,325.9	1,407.6	1,499.8	1,591.8	1,769.2	1,991.3
Germany	649.8	889.9	1,250.7	1,856.4	2,445.7	2,505.8	2,497.4	2,479.7	2,504.6	2,536.1	2,556.0
Gibraltar											
Greece	2.6	7.0	14.2	26.8	63.9	94.5	110.4	129.7	153.4	177.5	209.3
Iceland	4.3	46.9	157.1	209.0	663.6	858.9	1,097.2	1,531.3	2,542.8	3,733.2	5,205.1
Ireland	5.5	10.4	17.3	37.0	110.7	142.4	160.2	200.3	260.7	321.8	377.7
Italy	111.2	212.5	385.2	530.8	896.8	1,030.8	1,110.8	1,178.9	1,271.5	1,403.1	1,555.9
Liechtenstein											
Luxembourg	4.0	5.6	11.1	13.0	22.5	24.9	26.5	29.1	39.1	52.5	69.3
Malta	0.1	0.2	0.4	0.9	1.3	1.4	1.4	1.5	1.6	1.9	2.0
Monaco											
Netherlands	102.0	122.9	193.8	284.4	560.8	656.6	705.8	775.2	868.0	929.2	1,092.7
Norway	96.8	241.3	461.7	527.5	969.6	1,144.6	1,232.5	1,354.1	1,583.5	1,879.2	2,027.1
Portugal	5.4	14.3	24.9	55.6	160.5	190.8	194.0	202.7	216.9	244.2	275.0
Spain	71.5	118.8	250.3	323.1	615.9	770.9	886.2	1,050.4	1,321.0	1,634.5	1,918.0
Sweden	219.2	340.6	791.2	596.7	958.7	2,421.7	2,540.3	2,696.3	2,986.9	3,321.5	3,797.3
Switzerland	195.8	335.2	532.8	611.7	668.9	662.9	687.0	716.8	762.3	831.6	904.8
Turkey			0.1	1.4	29.6	50.9	66.2	96.6	144.4	196.7	248.7
United Kingdom	63.7	167.4	645.3	829.1	1,254.3	1,479.4	1,624.6	1,807.6	1,994.9	2,256.2	2,625.9
Eastern Europe											
Albania				8.3	24.4	39.5	51.9	71.1	123.6	194.7	288.9
Belarus				7.4	802.5	2,364.1	4,283.5	6,928.0	10,063.7	15,437.8	22,988.5
Bosnia-Herzegovina					4.4	4.2	5.1	5.9	7.5	9.2	11.8
Bulgaria				0.4	3.4	6.3	9.4	14.0	18.6	23.2	37.7
Croatia				30.7	56.8	91.0	104.7	119.9	140.1	172.2	198.2
Czech Republic				1,036.6	1,029.9	720.6	782.5	886.8	1,076.9	1,312.9	1,686.4
Estonia				7.0	34.8	54.3	69.0	92.1	121.9	173.4	229.6
Georgia				0.1	0.4	0.6	0.7	1.0	1.7	2.7	4.8
Hungary		208.6	971.3	1,263.2	4,247.6	5,989.2	7,988.9	9,480.0	11,271.3	13,152.2	15,624.5
Latvia				0.2	0.9	1.9	2.6	3.8	6.2	9.8	13.1
Lithuania				3.9	6.0	8.4	13.0	18.0	29.5	41.4	59.2
Macedonia				39.2	42.2	43.1	47.2	58.6	70.9	92.7	129.0
Moldova				0.4	2.0	3.9	5.6	6.8	8.9	12.3	19.7
Poland		0.6	11.8	56.9	197.8	221.8	236.7	260.1	284.4	352.8	464.0
Romania			0.1		5.8	15.4	27.1	38.6	57.5	89.1	144.7
Russia				133.8	969.4	1,915.1	2,772.5	4,108.9	5,557.6	8,312.0	12,539.9
Serbia and Montenegro											
Slovakia				211.8	479.2	435.1	379.0	406.3	521.4	640.6	784.0
Slovenia				4.1	7.8	9.5	10.7	13.1	16.2	20.5	22.6
Ukraine				0.8	18.8	39.8	65.6	86.7	142.0	241.2	419.0

Source: International Monetary Fund (IMF), International Financial Statistics

Table 5.2

Personal Finance

Expenditure by Credit Card Holders 1998-2007

US$ million

	1998	1999	2000	2001	2002	2003	2004	2005	2006	2007
Western Europe										
Austria	132.5	129.8	123.9	143.6	164.3	203.1	264.6	298.8	325.2	352.1
Belgium	56.2	56.6	55.7	61.9	72.4	90.1	103.8	113.5	125.7	132.4
Cyprus										
Denmark	289.7	142.5	141.7	157.4	152.3	170.5	215.8	278.0	329.3	426.0
Finland	815.5	916.9	1,060.3	1,075.2	1,084.6	1,297.8	1,424.7	1,399.9	1,421.7	1,565.1
France	4,065.9	4,546.0	4,471.2	5,160.6	5,872.7	7,440.6	8,767.6	9,459.7	10,363.2	10,966.9
Germany	3,628.9	3,559.8	3,241.2	3,700.5	4,204.9	5,418.3	6,307.4	6,693.7	6,988.1	7,349.9
Gibraltar										
Greece	982.4	1,590.3	2,049.3	1,897.1	2,061.1	4,841.8	6,742.3	7,946.6	8,311.3	8,575.3
Iceland										
Ireland	6,320.4	7,267.0	7,681.1	8,002.0	9,508.5	11,755.8	14,670.3	14,864.5	14,997.6	15,122.2
Italy	2,463.9	2,696.1	2,743.7	3,299.6	3,760.3	5,828.8	7,273.1	8,924.2	10,811.3	12,912.5
Liechtenstein										
Luxembourg										
Malta										
Monaco										
Netherlands	3,544.5	3,390.5	2,958.6	2,906.9	3,088.0	3,768.4	4,258.2	4,389.3	4,542.6	4,595.5
Norway	649.4	859.1	988.4	1,290.1	1,828.7	2,655.3	3,664.2	4,656.6	5,238.3	5,862.8
Portugal	5,268.7	6,392.3	7,094.1	7,056.9	8,643.7	11,034.7	13,737.4	15,414.6	17,298.0	19,858.3
Spain	3,740.1	4,198.3	3,870.0	4,377.6	7,155.8	10,282.2	14,285.4	17,453.7	19,731.9	22,029.1
Sweden	1,401.8	1,573.4	1,816.9	1,843.4	1,860.0	2,228.5	2,448.7	2,406.6	2,443.7	2,532.8
Switzerland	8,268.7	9,059.0	8,441.3	9,071.4	10,030.1	11,428.4	12,897.5	13,725.7	14,994.0	16,357.1
Turkey	15,725.4	12,739.5	16,790.9	12,343.4	16,993.4	26,260.4	45,335.1	63,473.0	78,476.0	85,700.6
United Kingdom	99,770.8	113,869.7	119,236.4	123,278.5	144,409.0	176,254.9	217,127.5	216,326.4	213,773.3	211,332.6
Eastern Europe										
Albania										
Belarus										
Bosnia-Herzegovina										
Bulgaria	7.4	11.0	23.4	42.4	77.3	129.8	191.1	264.1	378.6	563.5
Croatia	7.1	10.7	21.1	36.3	66.0	111.0	161.4	222.5	317.9	476.0
Czech Republic	28.0	60.2	121.8	205.6	452.7	989.8	1,740.4	2,520.4	3,655.8	5,270.9
Estonia										
Georgia										
Hungary	12.8	19.0	42.2	75.8	142.6	236.9	349.9	485.2	698.2	1,098.7
Latvia										
Lithuania										
Macedonia										
Moldova										
Poland	230.8	332.7	425.7	546.2	1,065.4	1,417.6	1,957.8	3,063.2	4,177.2	5,255.3
Romania	16.1	24.0	42.5	82.7	146.5	243.4	412.1	561.4	776.7	1,161.0
Russia						394.7	759.0	1,630.8	3,195.9	4,963.1
Serbia and Montenegro										
Slovakia	6.3	9.4	19.8	36.0	64.1	109.2	158.0	219.5	324.0	485.1
Slovenia	1,086.2	1,218.7	1,351.2	1,483.7	1,616.2	1,748.7	1,873.0	2,030.0	2,138.0	2,428.6
Ukraine										

Source: Euromonitor International from trade sources

Personal Finance

Table 5.3

Expenditure by Charge Card Holders 1998-2007

US$ million

	1998	1999	2000	2001	2002	2003	2004	2005	2006	2007
Western Europe										
Austria	3,006.3	3,002.4	2,907.3	3,480.6	4,004.9	4,785.5	6,333.1	6,821.4	7,427.8	8,037.4
Belgium	5,086.2	5,548.6	5,434.3	6,262.1	6,289.2	11,732.3	10,671.5	11,382.9	12,378.9	13,598.2
Cyprus										
Denmark	6,292.1	3,576.6	3,571.7	3,705.0	4,101.5	4,922.5	6,245.5	6,610.4	6,948.0	7,430.9
Finland	2,958.3	2,962.1	3,256.3	2,936.4	2,957.9	4,254.0	4,770.3	5,106.2	5,526.1	6,636.2
France	40,140.2	47,376.3	48,436.6	55,169.8	67,396.5	93,153.2	115,744.1	128,797.2	142,797.7	156,799.6
Germany	28,651.1	21,272.1	20,839.7	23,454.9	27,579.7	36,488.4	44,558.4	47,324.7	49,186.8	51,373.6
Gibraltar										
Greece	383.6	613.8	824.4	600.3	678.5	917.6	433.4	439.6	300.9	233.6
Iceland										
Ireland	1,578.9	1,828.5	2,064.7	2,328.6	2,459.6	2,734.8	3,251.0	3,417.3	4,035.2	4,234.9
Italy	23,099.3	25,047.2	25,546.3	28,438.3	33,343.4	40,931.4	52,971.3	55,784.1	59,830.0	62,652.4
Liechtenstein										
Luxembourg										
Malta										
Monaco										
Netherlands	3,463.3	4,441.2	3,753.1	3,735.1	3,880.4	4,360.9	5,158.4	5,377.4	5,196.2	5,352.1
Norway	1,895.3	1,961.7	1,954.1	2,013.0	2,191.9	2,386.9	2,685.1	3,383.8	4,631.0	6,237.0
Portugal	807.1	863.0	843.0	877.0	947.0	1,185.1	1,426.3	1,554.4	1,649.5	1,767.8
Spain	8,691.8	9,566.5	8,613.9	9,519.4	15,346.7	21,849.7	29,669.8	35,436.4	39,169.4	42,762.3
Sweden	5,085.0	5,083.3	5,580.0	5,034.3	5,072.6	7,304.8	8,198.5	8,778.2	9,498.2	12,204.1
Switzerland	1,939.6	2,124.9	1,980.1	2,127.9	2,352.7	2,680.7	3,025.3	3,219.6	3,517.1	3,836.9
Turkey										
United Kingdom	24,923.4	28,651.0	32,051.6	35,873.9	37,355.6	41,003.2	48,116.7	49,733.0	57,517.7	60,393.6
Eastern Europe										
Albania										
Belarus										
Bosnia-Herzegovina										
Bulgaria	3.8	4.0	4.7	4.6	3.6	8.1	17.9	23.8	38.4	58.7
Croatia	3.6	3.9	4.3	3.9	3.1	7.0	15.2	20.0	32.2	49.6
Czech Republic	133.5	160.0	203.2	245.7	322.1	433.0	514.5	594.1	684.8	735.3
Estonia										
Georgia										
Hungary	6.5	7.0	8.6	8.2	6.6	14.9	32.9	43.7	70.8	107.5
Latvia										
Lithuania										
Macedonia										
Moldova										
Poland	310.8	534.4	568.3	577.2	827.4	786.8	455.3	507.0	524.3	516.0
Romania										
Russia							8.1	15.5	33.3	65.2	101.3
Serbia and Montenegro										
Slovakia	3.2	3.4	4.0	3.9	3.0	6.8	14.8	19.8	32.9	50.5
Slovenia										
Ukraine										

Source: *Euromonitor International from trade sources*

Table 5.4

Number of Credit Cards in Circulation 1998-2007

'000

	1998	1999	2000	2001	2002	2003	2004	2005	2006	2007
Western Europe										
Austria	69.7	74.7	80.4	85.7	92.7	94.2	92.8	95.8	115.5	122.5
Belgium	188.0	200.0	217.0	221.0	227.0	232.0	234.0	239.0	242.0	256.0
Cyprus										
Denmark	4,120.0	4,373.0	4,778.0	4,674.8	5,252.0	5,365.0	5,509.0	6,149.0	7,372.0	7,128.0
Finland										
France	2,597.5	2,808.0	3,055.0	3,247.5	3,314.2	3,903.2	4,320.8	4,812.8	5,232.0	5,739.5
Germany	170.0	222.0	315.0	444.0	495.0	952.0	1,285.0	2,186.0	3,517.0	3,605.0
Gibraltar										
Greece	1,513.0	2,014.0	3,030.1	4,144.1	5,157.1	5,579.9	5,641.9	6,045.5	6,335.7	6,537.0
Iceland										
Ireland										
Italy	1,456.8	1,542.0	1,696.9	1,999.6	3,265.0	5,500.0	8,500.0	9,600.0	10,482.4	11,372.5
Liechtenstein										
Luxembourg										
Malta										
Monaco										
Netherlands	1,788.0	2,193.0	2,230.0	2,304.0	2,365.0	2,410.0	2,444.0	2,500.0	2,682.4	2,736.0
Norway	880.0	1,158.0	1,221.0	1,638.0	1,925.0	2,271.0	2,502.0	2,891.0	3,553.0	4,366.0
Portugal	1,848.3	1,953.2	2,140.4	2,406.3	2,783.0	3,267.3	3,820.0	4,415.9	5,060.6	7,040.6
Spain	2,584.4	3,312.0	3,564.7	4,259.0	5,174.2	6,680.0	8,978.2	11,304.0	14,250.0	17,400.0
Sweden	3,130.0	3,175.0	3,215.0	3,247.0	3,300.0	3,325.0	3,390.0	3,454.0	3,610.0	3,810.0
Switzerland	2,470.0	2,844.0	2,945.8	3,109.2	3,158.2	3,179.4	3,202.8	3,249.9	3,530.6	3,902.4
Turkey	7,200.0	10,046.0	13,409.0	13,997.0	15,706.0	19,863.0	26,681.0	29,978.0	32,433.0	34,352.1
United Kingdom	38,308.1	41,424.0	47,096.6	51,706.8	58,802.1	66,854.0	70,380.6	70,405.7	70,145.7	66,669.3
Eastern Europe										
Albania										
Belarus										
Bosnia-Herzegovina										
Bulgaria										
Croatia										
Czech Republic	62.0	117.1	196.0	328.0	555.0	652.0	1,051.0	1,604.0	2,150.0	2,908.9
Estonia										
Georgia										
Hungary	22.8	96.0	245.8	447.4	641.6	933.6	506.8	1,027.8	1,560.0	1,916.2
Latvia										
Lithuania										
Macedonia										
Moldova										
Poland	90.9	179.8	371.7	600.1	806.4	1,172.6	1,996.3	3,386.8	5,124.0	7,710.9
Romania										
Russia						577.2	1,273.3	2,463.1	5,695.4	12,002.2
Serbia and Montenegro										
Slovakia										
Slovenia										
Ukraine										

Source: Euromonitor International from trade sources

Personal Finance

Table 5.5

Number of Charge Cards in Circulation 1998-2007
'000

	1998	1999	2000	2001	2002	2003	2004	2005	2006	2007
Western Europe										
Austria	1,607.0	1,673.0	1,874.0	2,049.0	2,113.1	2,145.9	2,131.7	2,174.9	2,283.9	2,384.0
Belgium	1,973.6	2,854.2	2,940.3	3,045.0	3,039.0	3,097.2	3,176.0	3,259.7	3,323.8	3,582.0
Cyprus										
Denmark	122.5	128.6	137.6	154.1	172.6	198.5	240.2	264.2	319.7	334.9
Finland										
France	10,068.6	10,614.4	11,218.6	11,909.9	12,742.6	13,718.9	14,661.3	15,726.7	16,936.5	18,246.3
Germany	16,037.0	17,198.0	19,061.0	20,212.9	21,811.1	22,214.2	22,443.3	23,347.7	23,746.7	24,100.1
Gibraltar										
Greece	275.0	315.0	342.0	305.6	306.3	297.9	76.5	69.5	57.7	51.3
Iceland										
Ireland										
Italy	13,111.2	13,878.0	16,969.0	19,996.0	21,757.0	25,645.0	27,020.0	28,802.0	30,962.2	32,964.0
Liechtenstein										
Luxembourg										
Malta										
Monaco										
Netherlands	2,312.0	2,307.0	2,770.0	2,700.0	2,625.0	3,300.0	3,350.0	3,200.0	3,276.2	3,342.8
Norway	369.0	76.5	416.0	445.0	439.0	451.0	470.0	402.0	484.0	504.0
Portugal	195.0	250.0	298.0	315.0	345.0	400.0	468.7	524.9	595.8	676.3
Spain	10,338.0	12,461.8	12,493.0	13,487.0	15,773.8	17,177.0	19,989.8	21,943.0	24,237.0	26,100.0
Sweden	657.0	706.0	756.0	711.0	771.0	838.0	890.0	982.0	1,005.0	1,032.0
Switzerland	184.0	197.0	185.3	172.0	174.8	179.6	188.2	204.1	224.6	252.7
Turkey										
United Kingdom	3,270.0	3,446.0	3,773.0	4,426.0	4,311.0	4,431.0	4,423.1	4,724.0	4,931.0	5,177.6
Eastern Europe										
Albania										
Belarus										
Bosnia-Herzegovina										
Bulgaria										
Croatia										
Czech Republic	20.0	22.0	24.0	29.0	33.0	40.0	42.0	44.0	46.0	48.7
Estonia										
Georgia										
Hungary	5.2	6.0	6.4	6.2	5.3	10.7	17.2	18.2	20.0	23.3
Latvia										
Lithuania										
Macedonia										
Moldova										
Poland	442.0	828.3	1,001.0	1,037.1	1,016.1	641.7	632.2	617.5	550.2	523.3
Romania										
Russia						26.3	37.5	51.5	75.0	100.0
Serbia and Montenegro										
Slovakia										
Slovenia										
Ukraine										

Source: *Euromonitor International from trade sources*

Table 5.6

Number of Credit Card Transactions 1998-2007

million

	1998	1999	2000	2001	2002	2003	2004	2005	2006	2007
Western Europe										
Austria	2.6	2.6	2.8	3.4	3.8	3.8	5.2	5.5	5.9	6.4
Belgium	0.7	0.8	0.8	0.9	1.0	1.0	1.0	1.0	1.1	1.2
Cyprus										
Denmark	2.8	2.6	2.6	2.8	2.9	3.1	3.5	4.1	4.9	5.8
Finland										
France	8.2	10.8	13.0	15.3	17.6	19.8	22.5	26.9	28.3	31.7
Germany	24.2	26.4	28.9	31.8	36.3	40.3	44.1	47.9	52.5	56.1
Gibraltar										
Greece	24.9	37.6	50.4	41.9	39.3	50.5	59.9	60.7	61.1	61.8
Iceland										
Ireland										
Italy	23.3	24.6	25.6	34.3	42.5	54.8	68.7	74.9	82.4	91.0
Liechtenstein										
Luxembourg										
Malta										
Monaco										
Netherlands	26.3	26.6	26.8	27.0	27.7	28.6	29.9	31.0	31.7	33.6
Norway	4.9	6.7	8.7	11.6	14.7	18.8	24.7	30.0	35.2	24.5
Portugal	84.0	118.5	157.7	223.5	247.9	266.1	286.4	308.7	336.9	364.5
Spain	36.5	40.3	41.5	48.7	75.8	88.3	115.0	135.0	168.1	203.2
Sweden	16.2	17.0	20.0	26.0	30.0	35.0	38.1	42.3	47.3	54.2
Switzerland	63.1	77.0	80.1	87.1	90.1	88.8	90.7	94.8	103.8	112.2
Turkey	300.0	360.0	465.1	512.0	636.0	829.4	1,133.4	1,300.0	1,348.3	1,395.0
United Kingdom	1,184.5	1,312.2	1,412.7	1,503.5	1,647.2	1,782.8	1,940.6	1,888.7	1,859.6	1,837.9
Eastern Europe										
Albania										
Belarus										
Bosnia-Herzegovina										
Bulgaria										
Croatia										
Czech Republic	0.1	0.3	0.6	0.8	1.4	2.7	4.1	5.1	6.4	8.6
Estonia										
Georgia										
Hungary	0.3	0.4	1.2	2.0	3.2	4.7	6.9	9.4	15.1	20.4
Latvia										
Lithuania										
Macedonia										
Moldova										
Poland	2.0	5.5	9.6	12.9	27.3	34.1	45.1	67.5	94.0	125.0
Romania										
Russia						11.0	20.0	38.0	66.2	106.8
Serbia and Montenegro										
Slovakia										
Slovenia										
Ukraine										

Source: Euromonitor International from trade sources

Personal Finance
Table 5.7

Number of Charge Card Transactions 1998-2007
million

	1998	1999	2000	2001	2002	2003	2004	2005	2006	2007
Western Europe										
Austria	23.6	23.7	25.1	30.7	34.0	33.9	46.6	49.9	53.3	57.2
Belgium	64.1	65.3	66.9	69.4	70.5	70.4	74.2	79.7	93.7	96.6
Cyprus										
Denmark	48.0	54.0	60.4	63.5	70.0	72.1	77.0	81.0	87.0	92.4
Finland										
France	246.2	399.5	476.4	666.6	778.2	920.7	996.1	1,291.3	1,691.2	2,093.7
Germany	252.8	278.6	271.3	289.0	299.0	346.0	366.4	369.5	377.0	382.5
Gibraltar										
Greece	3.6	5.7	8.4	5.9	6.0	6.5	1.8	1.5	1.1	0.8
Iceland										
Ireland										
Italy	196.7	219.3	264.5	306.2	317.6	361.4	446.3	517.7	580.8	636.0
Liechtenstein										
Luxembourg										
Malta										
Monaco										
Netherlands	29.0	30.0	31.1	33.0	35.2	37.4	38.6	37.9	38.7	41.1
Norway	11.7	12.8	14.0	15.1	14.3	15.2	17.2	21.9	25.5	35.4
Portugal	33.3	41.1	45.5	50.1	50.2	56.5	63.4	68.6	73.8	79.5
Spain	152.5	178.7	180.5	210.3	325.2	376.6	463.0	540.0	651.9	764.4
Sweden	36.5	40.0	47.0	50.0	56.5	63.1	66.9	70.6	73.5	80.6
Switzerland	6.6	9.4	10.0	11.2	11.6	11.6	11.9	12.6	14.3	15.8
Turkey										
United Kingdom	175.0	189.0	205.8	242.0	236.0	244.0	241.0	268.0	292.0	306.6
Eastern Europe										
Albania										
Belarus										
Bosnia-Herzegovina										
Bulgaria										
Croatia										
Czech Republic	0.8	1.2	1.2	1.3	1.4	1.6	1.6	1.7	1.8	1.9
Estonia										
Georgia										
Hungary	0.1	0.1	0.1	0.1	0.1	0.1	0.2	0.3	0.4	0.5
Latvia										
Lithuania										
Macedonia										
Moldova										
Poland	4.7	9.6	13.4	17.4	16.7	18.4	9.1	9.6	9.2	8.8
Romania										
Russia						0.2	0.4	0.8	1.3	2.2
Serbia and Montenegro										
Slovakia										
Slovenia										
Ukraine										

Source: *Euromonitor International from trade sources*

Table 5.8

Average Expenditure per Credit Card 1998-2007

US$ per card

	1998	1999	2000	2001	2002	2003	2004	2005	2006	2007
Western Europe										
Austria	1,901.6	1,737.9	1,540.8	1,675.1	1,772.2	2,155.7	2,851.1	3,118.7	2,815.4	2,874.6
Belgium	298.7	283.2	256.8	280.0	319.0	388.3	443.4	474.8	519.5	517.2
Cyprus										
Denmark	70.3	32.6	29.6	33.7	29.0	31.8	39.2	45.2	44.7	59.8
Finland										
France	1,565.3	1,618.9	1,463.6	1,589.1	1,772.0	1,906.3	2,029.2	1,965.5	1,980.7	1,910.8
Germany	21,346.5	16,035.0	10,289.5	8,334.4	8,494.7	5,691.5	4,908.4	3,062.1	1,986.9	2,038.8
Gibraltar										
Greece	649.3	789.6	676.3	457.8	399.7	867.7	1,195.0	1,314.5	1,311.8	1,311.8
Iceland										
Ireland										
Italy	1,691.3	1,748.4	1,616.9	1,650.1	1,151.7	1,059.8	855.7	929.6	1,031.4	1,135.4
Liechtenstein										
Luxembourg										
Malta										
Monaco										
Netherlands	1,982.4	1,546.1	1,326.7	1,261.7	1,305.7	1,563.6	1,742.3	1,755.7	1,693.5	1,679.6
Norway	738.0	741.9	809.5	787.6	950.0	1,169.2	1,464.5	1,610.7	1,474.3	1,342.8
Portugal	2,850.6	3,272.7	3,314.4	2,932.7	3,105.9	3,377.3	3,596.2	3,490.7	3,418.2	2,820.5
Spain	1,447.2	1,267.6	1,085.6	1,027.8	1,383.0	1,539.3	1,591.1	1,544.0	1,384.7	1,266.0
Sweden	447.9	495.6	565.1	567.7	563.6	670.2	722.3	696.8	676.9	664.8
Switzerland	3,347.6	3,185.3	2,865.6	2,917.6	3,175.9	3,594.4	4,027.0	4,223.5	4,246.8	4,191.6
Turkey	2,184.1	1,268.1	1,252.2	881.9	1,082.0	1,322.1	1,699.2	2,117.3	2,419.6	2,494.8
United Kingdom	2,604.4	2,748.9	2,531.7	2,384.2	2,455.8	2,636.4	3,085.0	3,072.6	3,047.6	3,169.9
Eastern Europe										
Albania										
Belarus										
Bosnia-Herzegovina										
Bulgaria										
Croatia										
Czech Republic	451.4	514.3	621.2	626.8	815.6	1,518.0	1,655.9	1,571.3	1,700.4	1,812.0
Estonia										
Georgia										
Hungary	559.6	197.9	171.8	169.4	222.3	253.7	690.3	472.1	447.6	573.3
Latvia										
Lithuania										
Macedonia										
Moldova										
Poland	2,538.7	1,850.6	1,145.2	910.1	1,321.2	1,208.9	980.7	904.4	815.2	681.5
Romania										
Russia							683.9	596.1	662.1	561.1	413.5
Serbia and Montenegro										
Slovakia										
Slovenia										
Ukraine										

Source: Euromonitor International from trade sources

Personal Finance

Table 5.9

Average Expenditure per Charge Card 1998-2007
US$ per card

	1998	1999	2000	2001	2002	2003	2004	2005	2006	2007
Western Europe										
Austria	1,870.7	1,794.6	1,551.4	1,698.7	1,895.3	2,230.0	2,970.9	3,136.4	3,252.3	3,371.4
Belgium	2,577.1	1,944.0	1,848.2	2,056.5	2,069.5	3,788.0	3,360.0	3,492.0	3,724.3	3,796.3
Cyprus										
Denmark	51,364.5	27,811.8	25,957.0	24,042.8	23,763.0	24,798.7	26,001.3	25,020.3	21,732.8	22,188.5
Finland										
France	3,986.7	4,463.4	4,317.5	4,632.3	5,289.1	6,790.1	7,894.5	8,189.7	8,431.4	8,593.5
Germany	1,786.6	1,236.9	1,093.3	1,160.4	1,264.5	1,642.6	1,985.4	2,027.0	2,071.3	2,131.7
Gibraltar										
Greece	1,394.9	1,948.5	2,410.7	1,964.0	2,215.1	3,080.5	5,664.5	6,324.1	5,211.1	4,557.0
Iceland										
Ireland										
Italy	1,761.8	1,804.8	1,505.5	1,422.2	1,532.5	1,596.1	1,960.4	1,936.8	1,932.4	1,900.6
Liechtenstein										
Luxembourg										
Malta										
Monaco										
Netherlands	1,498.0	1,925.1	1,354.9	1,383.4	1,478.2	1,321.5	1,539.8	1,680.4	1,586.0	1,601.1
Norway	5,136.2	25,643.8	4,697.4	4,523.5	4,993.0	5,292.5	5,713.0	8,417.4	9,568.1	12,375.0
Portugal	4,139.1	3,451.9	2,828.9	2,784.0	2,744.8	2,962.6	3,043.1	2,961.3	2,768.6	2,613.9
Spain	840.8	767.7	689.5	705.8	972.9	1,272.0	1,484.2	1,614.9	1,616.1	1,638.4
Sweden	7,739.7	7,200.1	7,380.9	7,080.6	6,579.3	8,717.0	9,211.8	8,939.1	9,450.9	11,825.7
Switzerland	10,541.1	10,786.5	10,688.6	12,371.3	13,459.6	14,930.2	16,071.7	15,772.4	15,662.3	15,181.0
Turkey										
United Kingdom	7,621.8	8,314.3	8,495.0	8,105.3	8,665.2	9,253.7	10,878.5	10,527.7	11,664.5	11,664.5
Eastern Europe										
Albania										
Belarus										
Bosnia-Herzegovina										
Bulgaria										
Croatia										
Czech Republic	6,675.2	7,273.3	8,467.2	8,473.3	9,760.4	10,823.9	12,250.0	13,502.9	14,886.1	15,094.6
Estonia										
Georgia										
Hungary	1,247.4	1,162.6	1,332.0	1,311.6	1,255.1	1,381.5	1,910.1	2,404.1	3,538.9	4,619.0
Latvia										
Lithuania										
Macedonia										
Moldova										
Poland	703.1	645.2	567.8	556.6	814.3	1,226.1	720.2	821.1	953.0	986.1
Romania										
Russia						306.7	413.0	646.2	869.6	1,012.9
Serbia and Montenegro										
Slovakia										
Slovenia										
Ukraine										

Source: Euromonitor International from trade sources

Table 5.10

Average Expenditure per Credit Card Transaction 1998-2007

US$ per transaction

	1998	1999	2000	2001	2002	2003	2004	2005	2006	2007
Western Europe										
Austria	50.6	49.1	44.1	42.1	43.5	53.2	51.2	54.1	54.7	55.3
Belgium	84.8	70.8	69.7	68.7	70.3	86.6	101.7	110.2	111.2	110.3
Cyprus										
Denmark	103.5	54.4	54.7	56.3	52.0	55.5	61.8	67.3	67.9	73.0
Finland										
France	495.8	420.9	343.9	337.3	333.7	375.8	389.7	351.7	366.2	346.0
Germany	150.0	134.7	112.2	116.5	116.0	134.5	143.1	139.7	133.1	131.0
Gibraltar										
Greece	39.5	42.2	40.7	45.3	52.4	95.9	112.6	131.0	136.1	138.7
Iceland										
Ireland										
Italy	105.7	109.6	107.3	96.2	88.5	106.4	105.9	119.2	131.2	141.8
Liechtenstein										
Luxembourg										
Malta										
Monaco										
Netherlands	134.7	127.4	110.3	107.6	111.5	131.9	142.4	141.7	143.4	136.7
Norway	132.5	128.2	113.6	111.2	124.6	141.2	148.3	155.2	148.8	239.3
Portugal	62.7	53.9	45.0	31.6	34.9	41.5	48.0	49.9	51.3	54.5
Spain	102.5	104.1	93.3	89.9	94.4	116.4	124.2	129.3	117.4	108.4
Sweden	86.7	92.6	90.8	70.9	62.0	63.7	64.2	56.9	51.6	46.7
Switzerland	131.1	117.6	105.3	104.2	111.3	128.6	142.2	144.9	144.5	145.8
Turkey	52.4	35.4	36.1	24.1	26.7	31.7	40.0	48.8	58.2	61.4
United Kingdom	84.2	86.8	84.4	82.0	87.7	98.9	111.9	114.5	115.0	115.0
Eastern Europe										
Albania										
Belarus										
Bosnia-Herzegovina										
Bulgaria										
Croatia										
Czech Republic	215.3	223.1	221.4	257.0	323.3	366.6	424.5	494.2	571.2	612.9
Estonia										
Georgia										
Hungary	37.0	42.5	35.8	37.7	44.1	50.7	50.8	51.4	46.1	53.7
Latvia										
Lithuania										
Macedonia										
Moldova										
Poland	115.4	60.5	44.3	42.3	39.0	41.6	43.4	45.4	44.4	42.0
Romania										
Russia						35.9	38.0	42.9	48.3	46.5
Serbia and Montenegro										
Slovakia										
Slovenia										
Ukraine										

Source: Euromonitor International from trade sources

Personal Finance

Table 5.11

Average Expenditure per Charge Card Transaction 1998-2007
US$ per transaction

	1998	1999	2000	2001	2002	2003	2004	2005	2006	2007
Western Europe										
Austria	127.5	126.4	115.7	113.4	117.9	141.0	136.0	136.8	139.3	140.4
Belgium	79.3	85.0	81.2	90.2	89.2	166.7	143.8	142.8	132.1	140.8
Cyprus										
Denmark	131.1	66.2	59.1	58.3	58.6	68.3	81.1	81.6	79.9	80.4
Finland										
France	163.0	118.6	101.7	82.8	86.6	101.2	116.2	99.7	84.4	74.9
Germany	113.3	76.4	76.8	81.2	92.2	105.5	121.6	128.1	130.5	134.3
Gibraltar										
Greece	108.0	107.7	98.4	101.4	112.6	142.3	235.5	286.4	273.5	292.1
Iceland										
Ireland										
Italy	117.4	114.2	96.6	92.9	105.0	113.2	118.7	107.7	103.0	98.5
Liechtenstein										
Luxembourg										
Malta										
Monaco										
Netherlands	119.4	148.1	120.5	113.1	110.4	116.7	133.6	141.8	134.2	130.3
Norway	162.0	153.9	139.6	133.2	153.1	157.5	156.1	154.6	181.6	176.2
Portugal	24.2	21.0	18.5	17.5	18.9	21.0	22.5	22.7	22.4	22.2
Spain	57.0	53.5	47.7	45.3	47.2	58.0	64.1	65.6	60.1	55.9
Sweden	139.3	127.1	118.7	100.7	89.7	115.8	122.5	124.3	129.2	151.4
Switzerland	292.8	226.3	198.7	189.4	202.7	231.9	254.2	254.6	245.8	242.2
Turkey										
United Kingdom	142.4	151.6	155.7	148.2	158.3	168.0	199.7	185.6	197.0	197.0
Eastern Europe										
Albania										
Belarus										
Bosnia-Herzegovina										
Bulgaria										
Croatia										
Czech Republic	166.9	138.3	166.5	196.1	231.0	267.5	319.9	349.2	387.6	387.0
Estonia										
Georgia										
Hungary	106.6	101.0	103.2	99.5	77.9	174.7	193.3	174.8	194.6	209.2
Latvia										
Lithuania										
Macedonia										
Moldova										
Poland	66.1	55.7	42.4	33.2	49.5	42.8	50.0	52.8	57.0	58.6
Romania										
Russia							36.6	36.9	43.8	48.7	45.2
Serbia and Montenegro										
Slovakia										
Slovenia										
Ukraine										

Source: Euromonitor International from trade sources

Table 5.12

Assets of Deposit Money Banks 1980-2007

Billion current US$

	1980	1985	1990	1995	2000	2002	2003	2004	2005	2006	2007
Western Europe											
Austria	21.71	36.75	65.99	92.04	69.68	91.22	122.77	157.55	167.08	228.71	296.07
Belgium	60.77	92.67	192.03	273.06	108.17	164.25	194.31	236.40	274.52	314.10	399.43
Cyprus	0.05	0.12	2.53	5.34	15.96	14.49	17.72	23.85	33.10	49.06	69.22
Denmark	4.83	14.16	45.55	56.59	70.56	71.59	103.13	128.50	134.38	178.48	252.74
Finland	2.76	7.67	27.00	24.17	19.91	41.88	51.76	66.70	61.33	82.53	98.95
France	160.21	184.38	455.78	705.08	435.49	538.48	635.90	829.48	1,003.06	1,268.93	1,478.58
Germany	85.17	112.93	395.49	578.20	579.53	774.43	1,018.88	1,223.06	1,172.69	1,544.88	1,972.33
Gibraltar											
Greece	1.19	1.98	3.46	8.96	12.63	21.77	32.37	39.51	41.06	62.81	94.20
Iceland	0.03	0.06	0.13	0.09	0.27	0.57	1.59	2.86	8.55	18.58	16.61
Ireland	8.78	3.21	13.45	46.68	135.34	236.53	324.81	433.63	509.69	747.61	991.46
Italy	35.09	50.44	102.73	145.84	85.89	94.26	117.86	122.63	110.30	140.81	156.31
Liechtenstein											
Luxembourg	104.83	130.95	355.12	504.84	174.95	237.00	301.44	332.05	355.16	471.20	594.55
Malta	0.16	0.21	0.96	2.24	8.60	9.42	12.94	16.75	20.74	27.95	40.34
Monaco											
Netherlands	62.63	72.88	185.92	234.14	163.90	256.24	308.25	376.87	409.01	566.33	740.97
Norway	0.63	3.64	7.82	7.47	15.28	17.64	28.59	25.18	34.06	63.11	77.63
Portugal	1.13	1.43	6.16	35.92	29.90	28.93	34.88	37.67	36.83	46.10	49.47
Spain	12.79	20.04	39.11	146.06	77.37	95.10	101.13	153.24	167.65	226.89	293.58
Sweden	8.04	8.94	34.92	36.16	67.36	72.53	102.26	157.44	160.90	229.17	303.92
Switzerland	66.45	85.24	153.25	212.37	465.83	557.85	616.29	680.72	709.24	803.01	1,116.56
Turkey	0.55	2.01	5.51	10.97	18.18	13.59	14.55	21.01	23.47	37.47	43.99
United Kingdom	356.32	590.07	1,068.96	1,350.86	2,059.96	2,477.29	3,023.60	3,643.33	3,937.75	4,914.15	5,539.19
Eastern Europe											
Albania											
Belarus				0.29	0.33	0.26	0.33	0.46	0.69	0.43	1.24
Bosnia-Herzegovina											
Bulgaria				1.06	1.94	2.02	1.94	3.13	3.27	5.57	5.91
Croatia				1.75	2.42	3.64	5.78	7.78	5.77	7.19	9.41
Czech Republic				3.78	13.26	14.64	15.32	20.53	24.10	27.07	38.31
Estonia				0.32	0.62	1.10	1.38	2.49	3.47	3.66	5.93
Georgia				0.03	0.05	0.09	0.11	0.16	0.16	0.22	0.39
Hungary		0.34	1.16	0.92	2.74	4.36	5.94	7.20	6.97	12.43	17.04
Latvia				0.60	2.11	3.02	4.04	5.78	5.63	6.68	11.17
Lithuania				0.12	0.69	0.72	0.93	1.86	2.54	3.75	5.03
Macedonia				0.25	0.43	0.56	0.67	0.82	0.73	0.86	0.92
Moldova				0.17							
Poland	1.48	2.30	6.09	7.15	11.32	13.71	14.92	24.96	25.51	29.54	30.18
Romania	0.26	1.00	0.68	0.07	0.10	1.19	1.08	1.81	1.45	1.81	2.47
Russia				9.95	17.44	19.03	20.66	25.48	37.97	62.49	93.44
Serbia and Montenegro	1.81	2.68	1.69								
Slovakia				1.82	2.35	2.05	2.33	2.87	3.03	3.94	5.93
Slovenia				2.40	2.01	2.26	2.58	2.89	4.19	6.51	6.12
Ukraine				1.04	0.92	0.85	1.36	2.30	2.83	4.07	6.06

Source: International Monetary Fund (IMF), International Financial Statistics

International Liquidity

Table 5.13

Assets of Deposit Money Banks by Quarter 2006-2008
US$ million

	2006 1st Quarter	2006 2nd Quarter	2006 3rd Quarter	2006 4th Quarter	2007 1st Quarter	2007 2nd Quarter	2007 3rd Quarter	2007 4th Quarter	2008 1st Quarter	2008 2nd Quarter
Western Europe										
Austria	193,329.0	202,838.0	212,827.0	228,713.0	244,830.0	264,668.0	275,301.0	296,067.0	319,755.0	346,234.0
Belgium	249,117.0	245,259.0	248,796.0	314,101.0	331,434.0	371,131.0	383,256.0	399,425.0	419,595.0	429,241.0
Cyprus	16,398.6	17,276.4	20,006.4	24,398.1	52,352.0	58,774.5	66,392.4	69,223.2	41,263.0	41,607.5
Denmark	147,275.0	155,273.0	164,607.0	178,477.0	198,607.0	208,912.0	232,846.0	252,743.0	267,414.0	286,832.0
Finland	69,610.1	72,300.1	68,903.3	82,525.9	89,231.9	78,608.6	90,189.8	98,951.6	119,294.0	130,417.0
France	1,059,240.0	1,084,830.0	1,152,790.0	1,268,930.0	1,400,740.0	1,482,290.0	1,427,980.0	1,478,580.0	1,621,320.0	1,521,330.0
Germany	1,277,570.0	1,395,220.0	1,422,500.0	1,544,880.0	1,637,790.0	1,732,850.0	1,892,370.0	1,972,330.0	2,098,900.0	2,055,590.0
Gibraltar										
Greece	45,135.8	49,562.9	55,444.5	62,810.4	77,018.0	76,775.9	85,025.8	94,202.6	99,312.0	111,109.0
Iceland	9,955.0	12,676.1	14,127.2	18,583.9						
Ireland	527,040.0	578,056.0	636,325.0	747,608.0	821,986.0	909,556.0	942,280.0	991,461.0	1,105,490.0	1,092,620.0
Italy	115,899.0	123,724.0	132,826.0	140,814.0	154,281.0	155,553.0	157,302.0	156,306.0	163,169.0	152,685.0
Liechtenstein										
Luxembourg	387,768.0	410,269.0	441,068.0	471,201.0	489,143.0	522,137.0	567,443.0	594,548.0	661,639.0	662,012.0
Malta	22,692.1	26,913.7	26,992.5	27,945.3	31,110.1	35,494.9	38,671.3	40,336.5	35,235.5	39,712.7
Monaco										
Netherlands	488,799.9	491,237.2	535,716.7	566,331.0	667,570.0	698,244.0	754,389.0	740,973.0	799,159.0	739,606.0
Norway	43,280.7	52,256.5	48,832.2	63,105.3						
Portugal	39,422.7	42,959.8	43,542.8	46,101.6	43,822.9	44,081.7	44,981.5	49,469.9	50,435.5	53,279.2
Spain	175,463.0	195,405.0	199,882.0	226,887.0	258,927.0	254,360.0	288,846.0	293,578.0	323,866.0	334,695.0
Sweden	196,191.0	203,330.0	212,443.0	229,174.0	273,311.0	268,491.0	284,829.0	303,915.0	333,852.0	345,255.0
Switzerland	787,125.0	818,382.0	822,753.0	803,014.0	1,007,050.0	981,035.0	1,013,960.0	1,116,560.0	1,146,490.0	948,525.0
Turkey	27,147.4	33,077.1	37,467.9	37,467.9	37,048.1	44,994.9	43,322.5	43,993.9	47,110.1	
United Kingdom	4,351,178.0	4,558,034.6	4,734,677.6	4,914,150.0						
Eastern Europe										
Albania										
Belarus	512.4	732.6	894.5	429.1	965.7	1,247.4	1,245.4	1,240.6	1,756.0	1,123.2
Bosnia-Herzegovina										
Bulgaria	3,836.4	3,912.9	5,091.5	5,567.3	4,859.7	4,765.2	4,429.5	5,915.0	5,006.1	5,878.1
Croatia	4,537.8	4,578.1	5,613.7	7,190.9	6,563.1	7,007.5	8,377.0	9,411.4	9,170.8	8,302.7
Czech Republic	23,374.4	25,671.6	25,751.2	27,070.1	28,527.2	32,434.9	33,703.9	38,313.4	43,760.7	50,390.4
Estonia	3,920.9	3,879.9	3,249.0	3,660.6	3,720.9	4,976.9	4,983.2	5,926.5	6,128.9	5,677.4
Georgia	186.3	211.7	224.2	215.7	306.8	343.5	372.5	393.7	372.9	413.5
Hungary	8,494.4	7,841.4	9,042.4	12,434.1	13,436.2	14,283.8	15,043.3	17,041.4	19,892.5	21,535.4
Latvia	5,596.1	6,184.4	6,418.4	6,675.4	7,577.6	7,833.3	9,418.5	11,169.4	10,076.4	11,004.5
Lithuania	2,652.8	2,865.0	2,965.2	3,745.8	3,760.9	3,667.4	4,238.6	5,025.0	5,393.5	5,021.9
Macedonia	725.2	727.6	762.7	854.8	863.0	861.7	885.2	923.7	866.2	834.6
Moldova										
Poland	28,903.2	28,775.5	30,383.7	29,537.5	30,001.7	27,215.0	29,389.0	30,179.5	34,011.7	32,498.8
Romania	812.3	1,009.6	1,000.9	1,805.3	1,918.6	2,588.9	1,488.8	2,470.5	1,905.2	2,407.4
Russia	48,327.8	48,003.5	50,205.2	62,488.8	79,296.3	65,586.7	87,188.8	93,440.1	111,645.0	110,085.0
Serbia and Montenegro										
Slovakia	2,866.7	3,992.4	4,257.1	3,939.3	3,805.5	4,232.2	4,599.3	5,925.1	5,667.2	7,091.7
Slovenia	4,380.0	5,099.9	5,670.4	6,510.6	3,689.1	4,451.3	5,271.8	6,116.6	6,720.1	6,975.6
Ukraine	3,310.3	3,567.4	4,032.8	4,073.4	4,941.4	4,932.0	5,562.1	6,061.4	6,355.3	8,206.6

Source: *International Monetary Fund (IMF), International Financial Statistics*

Table 5.14

Liabilities of Deposit Money Banks 1980-2007

Billion current US$

	1980	1985	1990	1995	2000	2002	2003	2004	2005	2006	2007
Western Europe											
Austria	24.95	38.03	74.31	99.15	49.93	56.53	70.38	81.78	85.74	103.95	114.25
Belgium	72.95	112.93	239.79	302.86	163.88	199.01	236.31	274.68	328.34	350.61	477.40
Cyprus	0.18	0.41	3.24	6.00	17.14	16.76	19.37	25.24	33.77	48.15	67.17
Denmark	4.88	14.85	44.80	33.25	62.55	75.60	110.65	129.57	128.29	165.90	238.64
Finland	4.57	12.81	59.91	29.27	15.47	26.34	25.27	34.95	39.52	48.61	69.02
France	146.68	197.18	519.81	662.47	384.58	464.83	547.13	701.86	899.66	1,237.77	1,611.18
Germany	72.09	75.77	226.37	482.24	559.07	629.90	719.20	787.91	740.01	842.36	974.61
Gibraltar											
Greece	5.15	7.59	16.46	34.29	39.65	18.56	27.72	44.53	53.22	76.86	115.46
Iceland	0.18	0.42	0.71	0.42	2.65	2.81	3.05	3.66	5.34	9.50	12.83
Ireland	10.72	6.32	17.74	49.10	141.51	255.23	338.47	428.83	487.80	696.75	918.17
Italy	51.41	72.83	205.38	216.81	146.78	153.43	201.52	214.47	212.37	253.35	310.24
Liechtenstein											
Luxembourg	98.45	117.21	308.09	434.11	159.29	173.27	198.97	221.67	235.53	284.00	332.35
Malta	0.02	0.07	0.49	1.58	7.91	8.36	10.92	14.27	18.40	24.70	35.82
Monaco											
Netherlands	64.35	65.68	153.43	220.96	206.13	305.75	328.22	392.49	418.03	562.87	709.32
Norway	2.74	9.16	22.17	9.62	37.02	52.76	69.46	76.04	93.24	140.23	163.73
Portugal	0.81	1.64	5.78	32.43	47.62	62.15	84.36	93.12	86.53	120.58	135.47
Spain	24.50	20.94	63.99	109.25	147.33	176.27	231.74	244.31	241.05	257.68	311.49
Sweden	12.52	17.20	99.36	55.10	102.35	91.64	109.49	157.60	139.93	184.51	196.71
Switzerland	47.95	63.40	133.57	184.87	440.01	498.61	546.82	608.31	634.71	717.63	1,044.11
Turkey	0.70	3.06	4.46	6.11	25.17	11.17	15.58	21.34	36.19	46.13	55.82
United Kingdom	377.71	625.74	1,201.03	1,429.20	2,160.04	2,684.13	3,276.43	4,033.35	4,251.40	5,254.85	5,959.07
Eastern Europe											
Albania											
Belarus				0.12	0.11	0.27	0.40	0.62	0.85	1.38	2.48
Bosnia-Herzegovina											
Bulgaria				0.58	0.26	0.47	0.96	3.38	3.22	4.25	8.87
Croatia				2.85	2.18	4.90	8.16	10.99	10.88	13.74	13.21
Czech Republic				6.43	8.42	7.66	10.09	10.27	9.79	12.05	19.69
Estonia				0.14	0.98	1.58	2.81	3.07	4.50	7.08	12.72
Georgia				0.05	0.06	0.09	0.10	0.12	0.29	0.52	1.20
Hungary		1.20	1.69	2.88	5.51	7.43	12.50	16.39	19.00	25.80	34.60
Latvia				0.45	2.14	3.74	5.30	8.06	10.00	15.68	25.66
Lithuania				0.09	0.52	0.85	1.88	2.81	5.07	8.14	13.83
Macedonia				0.08	0.23	0.21	0.20	0.24	0.28	0.37	0.57
Moldova				0.06							
Poland	25.32	26.68	1.92	2.07	6.61	9.07	12.64	13.72	12.65	19.68	38.07
Romania	8.38	6.05	1.72	0.82	0.51	1.00	2.22	4.98	8.15	16.42	29.90
Russia				6.46	10.11	12.89	23.16	32.17	51.45	105.26	167.99
Serbia and Montenegro	8.26	9.62	9.64								
Slovakia				0.98	0.64	1.50	3.15	5.83	10.01	7.09	13.23
Slovenia				1.48	1.57	2.79	4.59	6.26	9.75	14.02	4.54
Ukraine				0.30	0.46	0.74	1.63	2.25	5.24	12.83	28.61

Source: International Monetary Fund (IMF), International Financial Statistics

International Liquidity

Table 5.15

Liabilities of Deposit Money Banks by Quarter 2006-2008

US$ million

	2006 1st Quarter	2006 2nd Quarter	2006 3rd Quarter	2006 4th Quarter	2007 1st Quarter	2007 2nd Quarter	2007 3rd Quarter	2007 4th Quarter	2008 1st Quarter	2008 2nd Quarter
Western Europe										
Austria	97,300.4	96,836.2	102,113.0	103,953.0	101,953.0	109,565.0	114,952.0	114,247.0	128,914.0	139,876.0
Belgium	322,668.0	325,950.0	323,445.0	350,606.0	376,899.0	439,632.0	453,434.0	477,404.0	496,979.0	531,501.0
Cyprus	17,063.2	18,592.0	20,912.1	23,489.3	51,019.1	57,159.8	64,448.5	67,174.3	37,944.1	38,602.9
Denmark	133,919.8	148,704.2	155,528.3	165,902.0	182,337.0	187,854.0	210,050.0	238,639.0	265,525.0	282,156.0
Finland	44,307.9	46,152.0	42,470.5	48,610.5	60,491.7	46,430.2	53,593.8	69,016.5	80,378.7	88,086.1
France	1,006,640.0	1,055,880.0	1,168,440.0	1,237,770.0	1,381,930.0	1,494,530.0	1,542,070.0	1,611,180.0	1,725,860.0	1,661,990.0
Germany	809,304.0	830,202.0	843,208.0	842,357.0	908,811.0	927,803.0	999,190.0	974,610.0	1,113,320.0	1,072,210.0
Gibraltar										
Greece	58,801.2	66,454.7	69,174.2	76,858.8	87,376.7	94,728.1	101,159.0	115,458.0	125,038.0	128,398.0
Iceland	7,277.9	8,304.2	8,307.7	9,502.2						
Ireland	514,497.0	568,321.0	603,830.0	696,748.0	762,673.0	816,773.0	873,707.0	918,172.0	1,054,100.0	1,053,390.0
Italy	223,251.0	229,048.0	243,683.0	253,346.0	268,707.0	280,634.0	292,551.0	310,242.0	340,559.0	349,576.0
Liechtenstein										
Luxembourg	265,293.0	269,837.0	276,778.0	284,001.0	280,792.0	291,535.0	314,858.0	332,345.0	343,494.0	345,057.0
Malta	20,186.4	23,799.8	23,842.0	24,700.4	27,190.0	30,981.2	33,475.2	35,820.4	24,244.5	26,838.2
Monaco										
Netherlands	485,516.0	490,858.0	523,482.0	562,866.0	600,301.0	619,435.0	703,052.0	709,315.0	828,859.0	811,167.0
Norway	113,598.0	126,546.0	134,112.0	140,232.0						
Portugal	94,673.9	102,640.0	109,742.0	120,578.0	118,849.0	122,209.0	129,595.0	135,474.0	139,549.0	140,525.0
Spain	248,246.0	252,963.0	246,380.0	257,679.0	273,169.0	274,481.0	294,529.0	311,490.0	417,008.0	422,155.0
Sweden	165,638.0	170,196.0	177,192.0	184,505.0	197,777.0	188,405.0	194,468.0	196,713.0	270,422.0	258,260.0
Switzerland	724,541.0	754,203.0	758,809.0	717,630.0	935,072.0	908,470.0	937,628.0	1,044,110.0	1,066,880.0	870,468.0
Turkey	42,019.1	46,488.3	46,127.0	46,127.0	46,103.0	50,647.4	51,722.5	55,818.7	60,441.2	
United Kingdom	4,710,931.0	4,955,294.4	5,079,491.6	5,254,850.0						
Eastern Europe										
Albania										
Belarus	807.0	860.2	1,199.1	1,377.4	1,851.6	2,250.1	2,547.0	2,481.6	3,199.0	3,353.4
Bosnia-Herzegovina										
Bulgaria	3,486.8	3,533.6	3,761.4	4,249.6	4,723.6	5,129.1	6,416.6	8,874.0	9,596.6	13,036.2
Croatia	12,194.5	13,149.9	11,568.6	13,736.2	14,025.9	13,502.4	12,089.5	13,209.0	15,288.7	14,139.7
Czech Republic	8,427.5	9,957.0	11,078.3	12,046.4	12,516.5	15,061.6	17,661.1	19,690.6	24,591.4	28,393.2
Estonia	5,801.4	6,457.6	5,980.4	7,078.0	7,950.4	9,384.3	11,282.4	12,722.4	14,030.9	14,434.7
Georgia	340.8	399.9	465.3	517.1	676.0	812.4	1,030.4	1,195.5	1,317.7	1,642.2
Hungary	19,868.2	22,840.9	23,588.5	25,804.2	26,493.8	29,289.1	31,947.3	34,601.9	40,348.6	44,372.4
Latvia	10,652.9	12,075.7	13,755.2	15,681.0	17,619.3	19,350.6	22,257.5	25,657.0	26,683.1	28,503.4
Lithuania	5,530.2	6,475.7	6,601.4	8,144.8	8,976.9	9,629.5	11,615.8	13,826.6	15,354.7	16,465.9
Macedonia	236.6	255.9	275.4	325.1	362.5	439.2	502.8	572.2	561.7	571.3
Moldova										
Poland	18,901.2	18,810.5	18,434.9	19,683.9	22,165.7	27,194.6	33,551.6	38,065.3	45,228.4	53,353.3
Romania	10,673.6	12,425.3	13,305.6	16,417.8	17,444.5	20,313.0	26,072.7	29,904.8	33,164.1	37,288.7
Russia	59,902.8	70,475.4	83,205.0	105,260.0	113,927.0	134,017.0	150,850.0	167,993.0	176,087.0	198,139.0
Serbia and Montenegro										
Slovakia	9,450.6	9,937.1	6,979.0	7,086.8	10,052.0	9,898.3	10,889.7	13,234.1	13,837.3	16,888.9
Slovenia	10,889.8	12,217.3	12,446.2	14,016.7	2,431.9	3,754.4	4,248.0	4,537.0	4,653.5	4,817.5
Ukraine	5,649.0	6,743.6	8,796.4	12,825.7	15,153.5	19,222.4	23,530.6	28,612.2	31,211.4	35,693.4

Source: *International Monetary Fund (IMF), International Financial Statistics*

Table 5.16

Lending Rates 1980-2007

% per annum

	1980	1985	1990	1995	2000	2002	2003	2004	2005	2006	2007
Western Europe											
Austria					6.33						
Belgium		12.54	13.00	8.42	7.98	7.71	6.89	6.70	6.72	7.49	8.57
Cyprus	9.00	9.00	9.00	8.50	8.00	7.15	6.95	7.57	7.09	6.69	6.74
Denmark	17.20	14.65	14.10	10.32	8.07	7.10					
Finland	9.77	10.41	11.62	7.75	5.61	4.82	4.13	3.69	3.56	3.39	3.35
France	12.54	11.09	10.57	8.12	6.70	6.60	6.60	6.60			
Germany	12.04	9.53	11.59	10.94	9.63	9.70	9.62				
Gibraltar											
Greece	21.25	20.50	27.62	23.05	12.32	7.41	6.79				
Iceland	45.00	32.60	16.18	11.58	16.80	15.37	11.95	12.02	14.78	17.91	19.29
Ireland	15.96	12.44	11.29	6.56	4.77	3.83	2.85	2.57	2.65	2.97	3.20
Italy	19.03	18.06	14.85	13.24	7.02	6.54	5.83	5.51	5.31	5.62	6.33
Liechtenstein											
Luxembourg	9.25	8.75	8.23	6.50							
Malta	8.00	8.00	8.50	7.38	7.28	6.04	5.85	5.32	5.51	5.65	6.24
Monaco											
Netherlands	13.50	9.25	11.75	7.21	4.79	3.96	3.00	2.75	2.77	3.54	4.60
Norway	13.00	13.41	14.15	7.60	8.93	8.71	4.73	4.04	4.04	4.23	6.65
Portugal	18.75	27.29	21.77	13.80	5.45						
Spain	16.85	13.52	16.00	10.05	5.18	4.31	3.88				
Sweden	15.18	16.89	16.69	11.11	5.83	5.64	4.79	4.00	3.31	3.72	4.00
Switzerland		5.49	7.42	5.48	4.29	3.93	3.27	3.19	3.12	3.03	3.15
Turkey	25.67	53.50		88.00	33.00						
United Kingdom	16.17	12.33	14.75	6.69	5.98	4.00	3.69	4.40	4.65	4.65	5.52
Eastern Europe											
Albania				19.65	22.10	15.30	14.27	11.76	13.07	12.94	14.10
Belarus				175.00	67.67	36.88	23.98	16.91	11.36	8.84	8.57
Bosnia-Herzegovina					30.50	12.70	10.87	10.28	9.61	8.01	7.17
Bulgaria				79.36	11.34	9.21	8.54	8.87	8.66	8.89	10.00
Croatia				20.24	12.07	12.84	11.58	11.75	11.19	9.93	9.33
Czech Republic				12.80	7.16	6.72	5.95	6.03	5.78	5.59	5.79
Estonia				19.01	7.43	6.70	5.51	5.66	4.93	5.03	6.46
Georgia				85.62	32.75	31.83	32.27	31.23	21.63	18.75	20.41
Hungary			28.77	32.61	12.60	10.17	9.60	12.82	8.54	8.08	9.09
Latvia				34.56	11.87	7.97	5.38	7.45	6.11	7.29	10.91
Lithuania				27.08	12.14	6.84	5.84	5.74	5.27	5.11	6.86
Macedonia				45.95	18.93	18.36	16.00	12.44	12.13	11.29	10.23
Moldova				39.60	33.78	23.52	19.29	20.94	19.26	18.13	18.82
Poland	10.23	15.34	644.50	33.45	20.00	12.03	7.30	7.56	6.83	5.48	6.16
Romania				41.30	53.80						
Russia				320.31	24.43	15.70	12.98	11.44	10.68	10.43	10.03
Serbia and Montenegro	11.50	71.50	49.30		18.90						
Slovakia				16.84	14.89	10.25	8.46	9.07	6.67	7.67	7.99
Slovenia				23.36	15.77	13.17	10.75	8.65	7.80	7.41	5.91
Ukraine				122.70	41.53	25.35	17.89	17.40	16.17	15.17	13.90

Source: International Monetary Fund (IMF), International Financial Statistics

Lending Rates

Table 5.17

Lending Rates by Quarter 2006-2008
% per annum

	2006 1st Quarter	2006 2nd Quarter	2006 3rd Quarter	2006 4th Quarter	2007 1st Quarter	2007 2nd Quarter	2007 3rd Quarter	2007 4th Quarter	2008 1st Quarter	2008 2nd Quarter
Western Europe										
Austria										
Belgium	7.1	7.3	7.7	7.9	8.2	8.4	8.8	8.8	8.8	
Cyprus	6.7	6.6	6.7	6.8	6.8	6.8	6.8	6.6	6.4	
Denmark										
Finland	3.4	3.4	3.3							
France										
Germany										
Gibraltar										
Greece										
Iceland	16.1	17.3	18.8	19.4	19.3	19.2	19.3	19.4	19.5	
Ireland	3.0	3.0	2.9	3.0						
Italy	5.4	5.5	5.7	5.9	6.1	6.2	6.4	6.7	6.7	6.8
Liechtenstein										
Luxembourg										
Malta	5.5	5.6	5.7	5.8	6.1	6.2	6.3	6.3	6.0	5.9
Monaco										
Netherlands	3.1	3.3	3.7	4.1	4.3	4.6	4.8	4.8	4.8	4.8
Norway	4.1	4.3	4.5	4.3						
Portugal										
Spain										
Sweden	3.4	3.6	3.5	3.5						
Switzerland	3.0	3.0	3.0	3.0	3.0	3.1	3.2	3.2	3.3	3.4
Turkey										
United Kingdom	4.5	4.5	4.7	4.9	5.2	5.4	5.7	5.7	5.3	5.0
Eastern Europe										
Albania	13.0	11.8	12.7	14.3	14.5	14.6	13.7	13.7	14.4	12.8
Belarus	9.3	8.9	8.7	8.5	8.7	8.8	8.4	8.4	8.5	8.3
Bosnia-Herzegovina	8.4	8.2	7.8	7.7	7.5	7.1	7.1	7.0	6.9	
Bulgaria	9.2	9.2	8.7	8.5	9.9	9.9	9.9	10.2	10.6	10.8
Croatia	10.5	10.0	9.8	9.4	9.4	9.3	9.4	9.3	9.8	9.7
Czech Republic	5.6	5.5	5.6	5.7	5.7	5.7	5.8	6.0	6.2	6.3
Estonia	4.9	4.8	5.0	5.4	5.9	6.4	6.5	7.1	7.6	
Georgia	19.4	18.6	18.0	19.0	19.7	20.8	21.3	19.8	19.3	21.4
Hungary	7.3	7.6	8.3	9.2	9.2	9.3	9.0	8.8	8.9	9.7
Latvia	6.7	7.0	7.8	7.7	7.7	11.3	11.6	13.1	11.8	10.4
Lithuania	4.7	5.0	5.3	5.5	5.7	6.4	7.2	8.1	8.1	
Macedonia	12.3	12.5	12.5	12.5	10.6	10.3	10.1	9.9	9.7	9.6
Moldova	18.1	17.7	18.2	18.5	18.6	18.8	18.9	19.0	19.1	20.3
Poland	5.6	5.4	5.4	5.5						
Romania										
Russia	10.4	10.8	10.3	10.4	10.0	9.6	9.8	10.7	10.9	11.2
Serbia and Montenegro										
Slovakia	6.7	7.4	8.2	8.4	7.8	7.8	8.6	7.8	5.7	5.8
Slovenia	7.6	7.4	7.4	7.2	5.6	5.7	6.1	6.3	6.2	6.6
Ukraine	15.9	15.5	14.7	14.6	14.0	13.9	13.7	14.0	14.6	17.2

Source: *International Monetary Fund (IMF), International Financial Statistics*

Table 5.18

Reserves of Deposit Money Banks 1980-2007

Billion units of national currency

	1980	1985	1990	1995	2000	2002	2003	2004	2005	2006	2007
Western Europe											
Austria	3.15	4.02	4.49	5.37	3.88	3.73	4.86	3.82	4.82	5.07	8.40
Belgium	0.52	0.55	0.63	0.94	7.13	4.48	8.32	5.42	6.79	7.93	17.79
Cyprus	0.10	0.24	0.51	0.57	0.78	1.48	1.13	1.18	1.42	1.98	1.53
Denmark	1.14	25.80	8.70	39.57	23.82	32.47	18.91	27.70	25.79	22.54	18.07
Finland	0.67	2.04	3.77	7.73	2.48	3.76	2.15	3.16	3.54	3.77	5.91
France	7.15	17.10	13.93	7.15	28.08	33.29	26.00	26.38	25.69	26.32	49.18
Germany	36.01	40.01	60.17	44.50	51.00	45.59	46.86	41.25	47.94	49.50	64.99
Gibraltar											
Greece	0.39	2.09	4.35	14.67	20.65	4.84	2.48	5.39	4.35	4.63	7.25
Iceland	1.04	7.37	15.04	10.33	25.73	25.29	13.29	29.41	36.91	47.36	100.51
Ireland	0.98	1.05	1.45	1.82		4.91	4.30	4.76	8.72	13.47	22.43
Italy	20.18	43.24	67.13	40.96	8.16	10.34	10.38	13.13	11.62	14.72	41.92
Liechtenstein											
Luxembourg	0.03	0.05	0.08	0.09	4.91	4.64	6.77	5.06	6.81	9.74	10.78
Malta	0.23	0.35	0.14	0.21	0.38	0.72	0.61	0.40	0.38	0.46	0.42
Monaco											
Netherlands	0.47	0.95	1.30	1.40	9.24	8.37	12.54	11.22	15.42	12.47	19.66
Norway	2.65	4.31	3.00	5.15	27.82	65.87	39.49	47.70	53.37	30.45	41.91
Portugal	0.85	5.29	11.11	10.43	3.45	1.88	0.96				
Spain	3.78	23.54	31.03	22.39	8.39	9.29	14.41	13.09	16.53	20.56	52.32
Sweden	5.65	7.71	24.91	9.42	9.80	12.09	20.56	15.82	10.70	11.76	15.01
Switzerland	16.50	15.78	8.27	8.27	12.51	13.62	14.33	13.17	13.60	15.32	19.50
Turkey	0.00	0.00	0.01	0.17	3.27	19.55	21.77	23.10	35.19	38.65	43.94
United Kingdom	2.39	2.88	5.97	7.56	9.75	8.92	9.73	13.00	13.38	29.73	32.24
Eastern Europe											
Albania				10.30	30.16	32.18	35.25	40.63	49.97	60.30	72.66
Belarus				2.84	158.12	438.92	772.81	1,134.53	1,810.24	2,349.29	2,410.68
Bosnia-Herzegovina					0.29	0.60	1.00	1.57	2.23	3.06	4.02
Bulgaria				0.07	0.60	1.07	1.39	2.43	2.96	4.24	6.73
Croatia				3.51	10.59	20.37	26.78	33.74	41.79	48.40	50.20
Czech Republic				160.93	310.93	60.20	56.56	49.99	45.56	60.21	66.67
Estonia				1.29	6.79	4.68	6.24	8.88	13.33	18.78	19.41
Georgia				0.04	0.08	0.13	0.15	0.22	0.27	0.44	0.63
Hungary		117.70	118.37	273.72	646.93	464.06	406.81	677.32	599.14	595.81	723.77
Latvia				0.06	0.14	0.21	0.21	0.31	0.59	1.32	1.56
Lithuania				0.52	1.28	1.39	1.90	1.87	2.82	3.42	4.79
Macedonia				1.84	6.19	6.36	7.09	7.19	11.45	15.25	19.91
Moldova				0.05	0.47	0.98	1.16	2.84	3.53	2.41	4.67
Poland	0.11	0.13	3.91	8.81	14.66	19.86	16.90	18.40	13.58	18.30	25.74
Romania	0.01	0.00	0.00	0.33	5.10	14.40	16.91	26.85	34.07	55.52	68.55
Russia				36.71	310.78	471.56	768.91	837.43	873.09	1,236.50	1,717.00
Serbia and Montenegro											
Slovakia				7.61	51.14	48.68	37.38	30.29	40.62	49.80	79.17
Slovenia				0.95	2.21	4.64	4.95	4.42	4.94	3.73	4.34
Ukraine				0.96	4.75	4.52	7.13	11.63	22.56	22.43	30.47

Source: *International Monetary Fund (IMF), International Financial Statistics*

Reserves of Deposit Money Banks

Table 5.19

Reserves of Deposit Money Banks by Quarter 2006-2008

Million units of national currency

	2006 1st Quarter	2006 2nd Quarter	2006 3rd Quarter	2006 4th Quarter	2007 1st Quarter	2007 2nd Quarter	2007 3rd Quarter	2007 4th Quarter	2008 1st Quarter	2008 2nd Quarter
Western Europe										
Austria	4,859.0	4,706.0	3,697.0	5,068.0	4,779.0	5,017.0	7,730.0	8,398.0	6,329.0	6,781.0
Belgium	9,927.0	8,985.0	7,737.0	7,928.0	9,893.0	8,774.0	9,357.0	17,789.0	13,534.0	6,834.0
Cyprus	1,155.0	1,587.7	1,661.9	1,983.3	1,170.7	1,402.2	1,370.2	1,531.2		
Denmark	29,850.0	19,332.0	20,882.0	22,539.0	18,961.0	18,644.0	14,904.0	18,067.0	36,619.0	29,392.0
Finland	4,956.0	3,911.0	5,402.0	3,766.0	3,439.0	3,755.0	2,049.0	5,910.0	2,760.0	2,263.0
France	26,718.0	33,378.0	35,007.0	26,321.0	29,006.0	36,697.0	41,407.0	49,179.0	43,307.0	40,770.0
Germany	39,025.0	43,353.0	47,303.0	49,495.0	49,424.0	41,314.0	42,330.0	64,986.0	69,763.0	54,702.0
Gibraltar										
Greece	4,058.0	4,895.0	4,756.0	4,625.0	4,344.0	5,239.0	4,826.0	7,248.0	6,418.0	3,317.0
Iceland	46,142.3	33,765.2	25,001.1	47,358.8						
Ireland	7,510.0	11,258.0	11,222.0	13,473.0	16,350.0	15,744.0	12,042.0	22,428.0	14,702.0	12,557.0
Italy	13,086.0	10,275.0	10,221.0	14,716.0	13,611.0	14,198.0	14,878.0	41,918.0	24,355.0	19,638.0
Liechtenstein										
Luxembourg	6,623.7	10,161.2	7,726.4	9,741.9	7,735.9	5,720.1	10,293.4	10,779.7	10,475.8	9,159.0
Malta	174.0	162.0	156.0	196.0	612.4	513.1	303.4	421.1		
Monaco										
Netherlands	17,863.0	12,136.0	12,110.0	12,471.0	16,632.0	14,868.0	11,783.0	19,662.0	14,816.0	42,925.0
Norway	44,604.5	37,635.1	40,875.0	30,448.8						
Portugal										
Spain	17,961.0	15,233.0	13,927.0	20,559.0	19,789.0	24,161.0	24,948.0	52,321.0	21,751.0	21,009.0
Sweden	11,803.0	10,863.0	12,199.0	11,762.0	12,349.0	13,926.0	13,098.0	15,012.0	10,517.0	11,718.0
Switzerland	12,299.0	12,469.0	13,171.0	15,320.0	13,385.0	16,028.0	14,512.0	19,505.0	20,109.0	17,295.0
Turkey	29,884.3	34,741.8	33,457.4	38,653.7	36,881.1	41,246.6	41,195.5	43,938.2	45,815.1	
United Kingdom	11,978.0	28,314.0	26,026.0	29,734.0	25,871.0	24,583.0	33,157.0	32,243.0		
Eastern Europe										
Albania	50,168.4	53,896.8	59,624.9	59,624.9	60,563.9	61,890.0	69,220.0	72,660.0	68,121.4	74,812.0
Belarus	1,325,350.0	1,317,400.0	1,438,930.0	2,349,290.0	1,671,560.0	1,832,250.0	1,958,630.0	2,410,680.0	2,586,720.0	3,314,610.0
Bosnia-Herzegovina	2,401.8	2,434.4	2,887.6	3,061.9	1,653.2	1,859.8	3,923.7	4,022.3	3,906.1	3,953.1
Bulgaria	3,223.3	3,823.0	3,629.8	4,244.0	4,419.0	3,697.0	5,741.0	6,733.0	6,392.0	6,654.0
Croatia	43,046.5	47,475.8	42,893.8	48,402.7	52,817.1	51,062.6	49,990.3	50,201.5	51,660.4	51,121.4
Czech Republic	43,626.0	53,462.0	31,060.0	60,208.0	54,315.0	58,229.0	68,596.0	66,673.0	62,049.0	44,278.0
Estonia	12,197.2	12,873.7	15,783.4	18,782.0	17,356.0	16,055.0	20,605.0	19,411.0	21,373.0	25,511.0
Georgia	269.2	316.2	333.3	442.3	391.0	551.0	613.0	627.6	596.4	660.2
Hungary	478,638.1	524,578.1	611,222.3	595,805.0	701,275.0	930,430.0	668,678.0	723,774.0	554,807.0	588,076.0
Latvia	673.8	924.6	1,040.7	1,317.0	1,244.0	1,360.0	1,500.0	1,557.0	1,582.0	1,556.0
Lithuania	2,850.3	2,874.3	2,927.3	3,419.0	3,269.0	3,571.0	3,213.0	4,789.0	3,887.0	4,272.0
Macedonia	14,462.0	13,500.0	14,020.0	18,195.0	14,597.0	16,245.0	15,991.0	19,912.0	18,697.0	22,896.0
Moldova	3,211.5	2,815.2	2,493.2	2,411.8	3,266.7	2,533.6	2,749.3	4,673.7	4,977.4	5,176.4
Poland	23,006.4	23,591.1	23,083.4	18,302.0	19,732.0	21,123.0	19,134.0	25,737.0	24,770.0	32,261.0
Romania	46,512.1	46,973.9	47,747.4	55,519.2	51,428.7	50,211.8	56,333.7	68,545.6	68,002.7	67,431.3
Russia	678,367.5	887,892.2	925,174.5	1,236,500.0	1,175,200.0	1,761,500.0	1,217,000.0	1,717,000.0	1,378,900.0	1,676,600.0
Serbia and Montenegro										
Slovakia	33,554.6	36,572.1	21,653.9	49,801.0	210,873.0	44,250.0	55,837.0	79,165.0	47,537.0	26,489.0
Slovenia	5,049.5	4,732.5	3,976.4	3,732.4						
Ukraine	16,850.9	15,765.3	16,044.8	22,429.7	22,111.8	26,564.0	30,747.4	30,471.7	26,252.4	29,147.0

Source: International Monetary Fund (IMF), International Financial Statistics

Section Six

Consumer Expenditure

Consumer Expenditure

Table 6.1

Consumer Expenditure 1980-2007

Million units of national currency / as stated

	1980	1985	1990	1995	1996	1997	1998	1999	2000
Western Europe									
Austria			81,193	100,567	105,428	106,869	109,475	112,526	117,808
Belgium			90,549	108,628	111,047	114,702	119,143	122,229	129,580
Cyprus	1,053	2,296	3,330	5,375	5,591	5,927	6,404	7,201	8,018
Denmark			419,184	515,752	535,160	560,603	580,505	589,505	608,142
Finland			43,386	48,025	50,229	53,046	56,472	57,977	61,941
France			587,568	669,053	689,763	699,655	728,683	751,860	797,958
Germany			790,448	1,013,340	1,039,580	1,062,500	1,081,860	1,113,840	1,149,690
Gibraltar	45	55	71	148	159	149	151	148	153
Greece			34,153	71,707	79,163	87,336	94,532	98,809	105,097
Iceland	8,900	73,747	202,035	241,065	257,937	286,139	320,711	354,499	386,592
Ireland			21,189	27,750	30,586	33,814	37,984	42,423	49,017
Italy			404,844	564,871	592,371	624,969	657,392	685,715	727,205
Liechtenstein	563	809	1,126	1,750	1,910	2,058	2,207	2,475	2,554
Luxembourg	2,351	3,554	4,943	6,541	6,825	7,477	7,785	8,150	8,883
Malta	682	992	1,322	2,012	2,122	2,376	2,523	2,876	3,161
Monaco									
Netherlands			121,604	150,920	160,242	169,088	181,430	194,600	209,020
Norway			343,344	446,191	480,563	507,070	533,151	564,422	604,646
Portugal			35,884	55,891	59,172	63,275	68,574	73,597	79,042
Spain			198,340	280,748	296,920	316,311	339,069	366,095	397,750
Sweden			673,082	874,597	894,755	930,179	961,686	1,016,264	1,064,371
Switzerland			182,479	216,079	221,345	226,470	231,278	237,606	245,264
Turkey			270	5,458	9,938	19,619	46,669	71,641	117,499
United Kingdom			335,837	440,632	472,372	500,385	531,784	562,616	593,885
Eastern Europe									
Albania	8,755	9,667	11,890	196,517	335,516	329,856	373,070	408,175	406,499
Belarus			2	70,254	114,185	207,159	403,784	1,773,389	5,211,536
Bosnia-Herzegovina					4,032	5,290	6,558	7,723	9,577
Bulgaria			30	638	1,340	12,929	15,866	17,623	19,533
Croatia			166	62,679	65,615	77,351	81,496	82,086	90,309
Czech Republic			309,121	759,693	896,017	1,002,251	1,092,484	1,137,893	1,193,313
Estonia				25,465	36,666	44,690	49,922	51,904	56,913
Georgia				2,804	4,074	4,481	3,939	4,402	5,257
Hungary			1,309,987	3,777,015	4,556,800	5,513,210	6,590,956	7,589,218	8,883,152
Latvia			49	1,640	2,038	2,335	2,466	2,601	2,884
Lithuania				17,053	21,803	25,038	28,157	29,233	30,221
Macedonia				118,692	126,323	134,791	140,164	142,815	172,523
Moldova			8	3,594	5,120	5,916	6,707	8,727	13,404
Poland			27,674	205,751	265,144	325,160	375,347	419,854	474,779
Romania			55	4,778	7,410	18,374	27,729	39,895	55,731
Russia			315	743,118	1,066,393	1,316,916	1,569,090	2,702,237	3,513,249
Serbia and Montenegro				33,678	60,239	75,722	109,777	144,386	283,126
Slovakia				311,593	348,556	385,960	428,102	474,935	519,687
Slovenia			2,818	9,670	10,078	10,604	11,172	11,936	12,310
Ukraine			2	28,022	55,512	65,773	74,438	90,997	116,019

Source: *National statistical offices/OECD/Eurostat/Euromonitor International*

Consumer Expenditure 1980-2007 *(continued)*

Million units of national currency / as stated

	2001	2002	2003	2004	2005	2006	2007	Total US$ million 2007	US$ per capita 2007
Western Europe									
Austria	122,185	124,895	128,790	134,371	140,246	145,875	151,353	207,450.8	24,950.5
Belgium	133,819	136,393	141,128	146,812	152,831	159,841	166,720	228,513.3	21,618.1
Cyprus	8,524	8,502	8,644	9,077	9,745	10,373	11,669	15,994.2	18,713.9
Denmark	624,005	643,124	655,919	694,854	750,354	795,167	830,928	152,640.3	28,023.2
Finland	65,307	68,486	72,016	74,961	77,899	82,262	86,681	118,808.8	22,514.6
France	831,026	857,970	889,899	927,008	967,558	1,011,153	1,038,741	1,423,737.5	23,184.2
Germany	1,194,030	1,198,080	1,214,846	1,239,260	1,261,177	1,294,076	1,311,103	1,797,047.2	21,832.1
Gibraltar	160	160	158	154	154	159	160	259.9	8,868.5
Greece	112,816	122,367	130,941	138,475	148,042	159,634	169,317	232,072.3	20,778.1
Iceland	407,746	427,765	452,761	494,161	561,435	620,428	679,220	10,603.7	35,227.5
Ireland	53,291	57,495	61,191	64,482	69,933	76,287	83,348	114,239.7	26,575.2
Italy	750,250	771,278	798,455	826,718	851,630	883,404	914,937	1,254,047.8	21,295.6
Liechtenstein	2,567	2,546	2,534	2,620	2,777	2,859	2,945	2,453.2	69,755.5
Luxembourg	9,410	10,046	10,591	11,191	11,823	12,226	12,649	17,336.7	37,158.5
Malta	3,240	3,251	3,247	3,326	3,414	3,506	3,617	4,957.4	12,192.9
Monaco									
Netherlands	222,408	230,830	235,707	239,763	246,943	251,295	260,310	356,791.2	21,811.4
Norway	631,581	659,620	694,859	734,566	768,735	820,636	878,914	149,942.6	32,099.8
Portugal	83,024	86,555	88,839	93,448	97,526	101,979	106,132	145,469.0	13,711.9
Spain	424,597	446,068	473,257	508,494	546,476	584,602	618,521	847,768.4	19,057.7
Sweden	1,100,595	1,149,317	1,191,899	1,230,648	1,284,637	1,329,808	1,388,292	205,406.1	22,539.1
Switzerland	252,132	254,099	257,214	263,314	270,244	278,157	286,356	238,556.2	31,819.7
Turkey	164,319	238,897	324,692	399,390	452,847	523,207	591,555	453,897.0	6,180.3
United Kingdom	622,972	653,999	685,002	720,490	749,781	782,828	827,108	1,654,971.6	27,261.6
Eastern Europe									
Albania	429,667	473,513	511,939	584,035	617,864	687,492	737,428	8,154.9	2,556.4
Belarus	9,917,949	15,647,102	21,049,739	27,001,692	34,170,019	41,158,150	50,766,774	23,655.6	2,426.1
Bosnia-Herzegovina	10,233	11,395	13,030	14,331	15,766	17,338	19,391	13,569.4	3,448.5
Bulgaria	21,929	23,738	25,334	28,081	31,606	36,822	41,579	29,095.3	3,816.4
Croatia	98,861	108,975	116,162	124,323	133,072	141,829	153,623	28,636.8	6,449.9
Czech Republic	1,270,502	1,292,541	1,364,730	1,450,980	1,499,200	1,603,005	1,740,435	85,762.3	8,336.8
Estonia	64,412	72,547	79,344	87,032	98,347	117,032	133,961	11,716.1	8,744.4
Georgia	5,188	5,581	6,085	7,191	7,961	10,838	13,822	8,274.1	1,882.4
Hungary	10,099,598	11,554,448	12,968,788	13,789,361	14,743,156	15,554,791	16,303,632	88,787.2	8,827.6
Latvia	3,176	3,517	3,906	4,550	5,463	6,972	8,907	17,335.3	7,601.8
Lithuania	32,191	34,167	37,158	41,357	47,030	53,976	64,103	25,400.1	7,504.2
Macedonia	161,493	184,760	187,761	204,733	218,734	237,537	255,513	5,712.4	2,802.3
Moldova	15,596	17,738	23,765	27,432	33,134	39,542	46,196	3,805.3	1,003.1
Poland	502,457	535,745	548,799	589,329	613,396	652,589	703,607	254,197.8	6,671.6
Romania	80,614	102,525	128,641	167,944	196,965	235,626	277,875	113,965.0	5,287.0
Russia	4,557,139	5,642,234	6,727,868	8,549,773	10,661,621	12,952,328	15,845,143	619,415.4	4,360.4
Serbia and Montenegro	617,001	779,300	870,283	968,108	1,174,770	1,383,693	1,565,857	26,788.1	2,561.9
Slovakia	590,046	620,795	675,118	753,796	862,701	958,484	1,052,292	42,612.7	7,903.6
Slovenia	12,833	13,510	14,238	14,850	15,617	16,723	18,392	25,208.8	12,540.1
Ukraine	140,147	153,121	179,430	220,861	304,715	382,979	507,205	100,436.6	2,161.5

Source: National statistical offices/OECD/Eurostat/Euromonitor International

Consumer Expenditure

Table 6.2

Consumer Expenditure by Object 2007

US$ million

	Food and Non-alcoholic Beverages	Alcoholic Beverages and Tobacco	Clothing and Footwear	Housing	Household Goods and Services	Health Goods and Medical Services
Western Europe						
Austria	21,393.8	5,092.7	13,196.2	44,609.3	14,466.3	6,585.2
Belgium	30,360.3	8,569.1	11,954.9	53,027.8	12,333.2	9,944.1
Denmark	16,329.0	5,335.6	7,088.0	39,841.4	9,226.7	3,893.4
Finland	14,515.1	5,774.9	5,756.3	29,958.4	6,843.2	5,141.7
France	195,028.9	43,308.1	67,337.4	350,081.9	81,334.3	50,031.6
Germany	205,554.6	64,004.4	93,574.7	442,413.6	121,665.8	83,987.3
Greece	33,683.0	11,136.9	22,220.1	35,454.7	14,687.5	14,419.5
Ireland	8,971.1	5,617.1	5,009.0	23,866.9	7,944.1	4,636.3
Italy	181,859.7	34,508.9	92,036.7	271,146.7	94,023.9	38,509.2
Netherlands	36,577.1	10,509.4	18,416.2	81,404.1	21,124.4	19,625.9
Norway	19,906.1	6,556.1	8,663.0	31,297.9	9,658.0	4,758.4
Portugal	23,899.6	4,718.2	7,224.7	22,696.1	9,370.3	8,333.4
Spain	115,415.5	26,459.2	42,014.0	140,877.8	42,570.6	31,238.4
Sweden	24,087.1	7,200.8	11,066.6	57,343.3	11,197.0	5,759.8
Switzerland	24,604.6	8,546.1	9,184.2	58,155.4	10,833.0	38,082.1
Turkey	112,372.4	18,697.3	26,796.6	122,358.0	27,813.3	9,814.6
United Kingdom	142,694.1	59,756.0	95,333.3	336,247.3	95,606.4	26,696.6
Eastern Europe						
Belarus	10,551.7	1,385.6	1,920.0	2,952.5	1,073.5	552.2
Bulgaria	5,815.1	1,144.8	875.9	5,412.6	1,280.2	1,176.4
Croatia	7,526.9	825.6	1,849.4	8,537.0	1,180.3	609.9
Czech Republic	13,894.2	6,514.8	4,040.6	19,112.3	4,188.3	1,754.6
Estonia	1,884.5	947.6	872.8	2,236.5	637.9	359.8
Hungary	15,167.2	7,108.9	3,355.6	17,350.5	6,802.8	3,515.6
Latvia	3,336.1	1,089.3	1,195.1	3,473.4	608.2	994.8
Lithuania	6,034.3	1,550.4	1,654.0	3,295.5	1,409.9	1,351.3
Poland	52,347.1	16,666.4	11,491.9	60,951.3	11,082.4	10,277.6
Romania	39,098.0	5,653.2	3,910.0	27,087.3	5,913.4	3,910.1
Russia	177,570.9	14,504.0	59,362.1	79,295.5	50,597.3	17,103.2
Slovakia	7,624.4	1,933.0	1,690.3	11,242.6	2,199.3	1,109.3
Slovenia	3,756.9	1,035.8	1,559.8	4,776.2	1,541.3	842.7
Ukraine	42,468.4	6,330.5	15,338.4	9,107.3	3,794.7	4,424.9

Source: National statistical offices/OECD/Eurostat/Euromonitor International

Consumer Expenditure by Object 2007 *(continued)*

US$ million

	Transport	Communi-cations	Leisure and Recreation	Education	Hotels and Catering	Miscellaneous Goods and Services	Total
Western Europe							
Austria	26,187.5	5,303.0	24,310.4	1,350.0	26,006.8	18,949.5	207,450.8
Belgium	34,801.4	5,486.7	21,365.1	1,297.9	11,406.5	27,966.4	228,513.3
Denmark	22,239.4	3,336.5	16,132.4	1,119.2	8,096.1	20,002.7	152,640.3
Finland	15,487.9	3,237.8	13,633.0	531.9	7,683.8	10,244.6	118,808.8
France	210,516.0	41,071.1	130,753.7	9,900.5	87,597.4	156,776.7	1,423,737.5
Germany	241,608.4	51,673.6	170,279.1	12,316.1	93,241.1	216,728.5	1,797,047.2
Greece	17,893.6	6,451.8	14,248.9	4,452.9	43,216.3	14,207.1	232,072.3
Ireland	12,793.7	4,828.4	8,645.1	1,627.4	15,185.4	15,115.2	114,239.7
Italy	171,396.8	35,413.6	88,163.9	9,724.3	122,875.1	114,389.0	1,254,047.8
Netherlands	40,443.9	16,728.1	37,682.3	1,885.6	17,524.1	54,870.0	356,791.2
Norway	22,009.4	4,840.4	20,317.6	829.4	8,732.0	12,374.5	149,942.6
Portugal	19,824.3	3,842.2	9,952.6	1,729.1	15,417.3	18,461.2	145,469.0
Spain	102,118.2	23,630.5	80,298.6	11,525.6	163,443.6	68,176.5	847,768.4
Sweden	27,362.3	6,443.9	24,374.0	589.7	10,609.2	19,372.5	205,406.1
Switzerland	19,326.0	5,813.3	19,593.2	1,328.0	17,505.2	25,585.1	238,556.2
Turkey	61,043.9	19,125.0	9,796.6	9,396.3	18,599.8	18,083.4	453,897.0
United Kingdom	249,188.6	37,584.6	210,019.5	22,704.5	198,015.4	181,125.2	1,654,971.6
Eastern Europe							
Belarus	1,736.5	903.9	803.1	320.4	585.0	871.3	23,655.6
Bulgaria	5,643.9	1,806.0	1,742.0	215.3	2,680.3	1,303.1	29,095.3
Croatia	2,667.6	1,207.5	1,454.6	158.3	801.4	1,818.4	28,636.8
Czech Republic	9,318.2	3,430.8	10,111.5	773.4	5,169.2	7,454.4	85,762.3
Estonia	1,439.3	370.7	971.4	127.5	959.3	908.8	11,716.1
Hungary	14,183.7	4,334.8	7,105.2	1,131.6	4,591.1	4,140.0	88,787.2
Latvia	2,006.0	910.8	1,708.9	650.8	737.6	624.3	17,335.3
Lithuania	4,394.0	807.5	2,011.9	210.0	755.7	1,925.5	25,400.1
Poland	21,505.6	8,575.2	18,470.6	3,290.1	7,171.2	32,368.3	254,197.8
Romania	12,931.5	2,503.5	4,881.2	1,486.6	3,887.3	2,702.9	113,965.0
Russia	74,333.5	26,195.8	44,841.8	16,907.7	25,519.9	33,183.9	619,415.4
Slovakia	3,821.9	1,689.4	3,925.6	681.3	2,650.4	4,045.1	42,612.7
Slovenia	3,683.6	930.9	2,621.7	280.3	1,830.5	2,349.0	25,208.8
Ukraine	4,780.0	2,978.7	3,849.7	2,092.9	2,611.5	2,659.7	100,436.6

Source: National statistical offices/OECD/Eurostat/Euromonitor International

Food and Non-alcoholic Beverages

Table 6.3

Consumer Expenditure on Food and Non-alcoholic Beverages 1990-2007

Million units of national currency / as stated

	1990	1995	1996	1997	1998	1999	2000	2001	2002
Western Europe									
Austria	11,517	12,785	12,967	13,058	13,050	13,096	13,030	13,429	13,813
Belgium	14,465	15,243	15,379	15,767	15,970	15,641	15,929	17,008	18,132
Denmark	59,706	68,186	69,386	72,033	73,139	71,953	74,403	77,075	78,437
Finland	7,095	7,411	7,068	7,191	7,335	7,569	7,808	8,321	8,596
France	91,454	99,680	100,474	102,947	105,939	107,962	112,679	119,301	123,769
Germany	109,485	124,900	125,340	125,130	126,670	128,480	132,140	137,930	138,180
Greece	7,354	12,922	13,981	15,044	15,921	16,416	17,112	17,954	19,297
Ireland	3,876	4,248	4,523	4,561	4,757	4,914	5,394	5,696	5,772
Italy	76,483	94,327	98,268	100,888	103,451	104,927	109,549	112,272	115,867
Netherlands	17,225	19,667	20,262	21,043	21,994	22,699	23,298	24,830	25,877
Norway	59,277	72,466	74,197	77,714	82,188	86,560	90,821	92,796	95,057
Portugal	6,651	10,114	10,583	10,915	11,922	12,502	12,947	14,075	14,562
Spain	39,366	48,226	50,166	51,454	52,535	54,643	56,813	61,171	65,928
Sweden	101,434	122,377	116,748	118,979	121,213	124,579	127,531	133,575	143,826
Switzerland	22,089	24,161	24,240	24,559	24,972	25,516	26,028	27,349	27,467
Turkey	97	2,014	3,322	6,278	16,128	24,320	37,606	50,948	63,715
United Kingdom	42,285	49,700	53,025	53,787	55,162	57,040	58,628	59,804	61,310
Eastern Europe									
Belarus	1	35,395	61,069	116,376	213,036	1,011,114	3,060,851	5,316,413	7,906,477
Bulgaria	8	192	404	4,936	5,237	5,196	5,560	6,069	6,014
Croatia	59	20,104	20,587	23,737	24,507	23,601	22,600	26,289	28,071
Czech Republic	61,643	147,982	170,392	185,987	202,846	213,691	221,837	238,903	234,453
Estonia		8,741	10,831	12,839	12,915	12,460	11,715	12,912	14,296
Hungary	283,587	913,839	1,029,716	1,226,075	1,434,423	1,517,644	1,694,730	1,924,631	2,158,161
Latvia	15	605	718	736	732	696	725	785	880
Lithuania		6,715	8,466	8,795	9,057	9,152	9,204	9,406	9,582
Poland	9,306	56,518	69,900	79,991	85,015	87,926	108,404	115,254	116,608
Romania	19	1,677	2,644	6,568	9,798	13,811	19,341	30,671	36,779
Russia	99	361,155	503,337	566,274	804,943	1,405,163	1,672,306	2,088,174	2,348,566
Slovakia		83,609	93,416	107,507	114,179	119,349	122,759	131,955	139,141
Slovenia	642	1,743	1,760	1,847	2,006	2,064	2,093	2,189	2,275
Ukraine	1	11,769	23,343	27,855	32,009	39,663	53,949	66,570	70,436

Source: National statistical offices/OECD/Eurostat/Euromonitor International

Consumer Expenditure on Food and Non-alcoholic Beverages 1990-2007*(continued)*

Million units of national currency / as stated

	2003	2004	2005	2006	2007	Total US$ million 2007	US$ per capita 2007
Western Europe							
Austria	14,052	14,466	14,913	15,299	15,609	21,394	2,573.1
Belgium	19,382	20,129	20,519	21,523	22,151	30,360	2,872.2
Denmark	78,740	79,979	83,842	86,126	88,890	16,329	2,997.8
Finland	9,116	9,382	9,687	10,164	10,590	14,515	2,750.7
France	128,306	130,986	133,526	139,520	142,291	195,029	3,175.9
Germany	137,935	140,272	144,241	148,529	149,970	205,555	2,497.3
Greece	20,176	20,949	22,015	23,609	24,575	33,683	3,015.7
Ireland	5,652	5,783	6,057	6,273	6,545	8,971	2,086.9
Italy	120,353	122,584	125,745	129,601	132,683	181,860	3,088.3
Netherlands	26,338	26,213	26,169	26,104	26,686	36,577	2,236.0
Norway	99,536	101,988	103,979	109,832	116,683	19,906	4,261.5
Portugal	15,135	15,603	15,785	16,350	17,437	23,900	2,252.8
Spain	69,040	72,112	77,055	81,102	84,206	115,415	2,594.5
Sweden	147,982	150,782	154,494	157,739	162,799	24,087	2,643.1
Switzerland	28,021	28,117	28,300	28,809	29,535	24,605	3,281.9
Turkey	89,241	105,531	112,666	129,709	146,453	112,372	1,530.1
United Kingdom	63,174	65,521	67,077	68,918	71,315	142,694	2,350.5
Eastern Europe							
Belarus	9,751,699	12,284,901	15,546,259	18,725,634	22,644,790	10,552	1,082.2
Bulgaria	6,023	6,579	6,890	7,664	8,310	5,815	762.8
Croatia	31,027	32,212	36,019	37,730	40,378	7,527	1,695.3
Czech Republic	231,873	247,080	250,583	263,767	281,964	13,894	1,350.6
Estonia	15,049	16,194	17,893	19,995	21,547	1,884	1,406.5
Hungary	2,355,456	2,452,647	2,578,503	2,730,899	2,785,085	15,167	1,508.0
Latvia	921	1,010	1,143	1,354	1,714	3,336	1,462.9
Lithuania	10,396	11,683	12,275	13,269	15,229	6,034	1,782.8
Poland	115,744	125,064	129,132	136,289	144,894	52,347	1,373.9
Romania	45,452	58,580	68,077	81,085	95,331	39,098	1,813.8
Russia	2,537,437	3,078,939	3,518,335	3,990,523	4,542,405	177,571	1,250.0
Slovakia	143,717	148,446	164,361	178,214	188,280	7,624	1,414.1
Slovenia	2,369	2,340	2,416	2,535	2,741	3,757	1,868.9
Ukraine	80,539	96,923	130,675	161,940	214,466	42,468	914.0

Source: National statistical offices/OECD/Eurostat/Euromonitor International

Alcoholic Beverages and Tobacco   **Table 6.4**

Consumer Expenditure on Alcoholic Beverages and Tobacco 1990-2007

Million units of national currency / as stated

	1990	1995	1996	1997	1998	1999	2000	2001	2002
Western Europe									
Austria	2,559	2,811	2,808	3,025	3,212	3,341	3,418	3,424	3,743
Belgium	3,877	4,116	4,277	4,549	4,930	5,175	5,347	5,137	5,339
Denmark	24,617	24,726	25,255	25,498	25,403	25,917	26,514	27,214	27,585
Finland	2,850	2,909	3,021	3,178	3,236	3,208	3,416	3,839	3,990
France	16,907	22,192	23,119	23,764	24,866	26,010	27,103	28,354	29,478
Germany	35,267	38,190	38,640	38,740	39,210	40,140	40,240	41,110	43,320
Greece	1,244	3,040	3,412	3,837	4,259	4,572	4,822	5,330	5,785
Ireland	1,296	1,890	2,004	2,176	2,385	2,705	3,153	3,320	3,695
Italy	10,404	13,943	15,001	15,494	16,368	17,317	18,228	18,898	19,827
Netherlands	4,423	5,040	5,224	5,424	5,525	5,827	5,994	6,701	6,867
Norway	17,584	21,169	22,622	25,103	25,975	27,987	29,206	29,892	30,624
Portugal	1,477	2,239	2,354	2,436	2,635	2,811	2,905	3,037	3,214
Spain	4,498	7,471	7,707	8,946	10,185	11,125	12,065	12,885	13,735
Sweden	34,153	38,636	38,352	38,201	37,519	40,064	41,562	43,957	46,481
Switzerland	8,098	8,397	8,492	8,624	8,816	9,052	9,363	9,363	9,448
Turkey	11	255	432	835	2,202	3,412	5,370	7,528	9,697
United Kingdom	14,753	18,776	20,439	21,553	22,459	24,458	24,617	25,158	25,966
Eastern Europe									
Belarus	0	6,756	8,479	17,148	33,263	119,613	350,424	590,215	805,763
Bulgaria	1	17	35	312	421	499	654	751	732
Croatia	6	2,340	2,426	2,830	2,959	2,846	2,726	3,175	3,472
Czech Republic	32,510	73,261	80,709	83,581	91,771	97,372	99,016	101,025	105,265
Estonia		1,909	2,777	3,282	3,815	4,233	4,355	4,654	5,493
Hungary	133,380	311,291	369,655	447,556	561,498	625,073	721,432	827,383	962,929
Latvia	3	126	152	176	179	193	238	240	268
Lithuania		1,605	1,881	2,188	2,263	2,367	2,266	2,324	2,626
Poland	2,632	17,062	22,058	25,757	28,627	30,415	32,993	33,827	35,341
Romania	3	252	396	1,011	1,500	2,311	2,989	3,403	4,263
Russia	19	26,009	37,324	50,043	62,764	102,685	129,990	162,255	181,160
Slovakia		24,079	25,443	26,209	28,189	28,338	30,978	32,818	34,650
Slovenia	106	558	556	548	542	549	602	613	625
Ukraine	0	1,704	3,375	4,100	4,544	5,488	6,960	8,530	9,584

Source: *National statistical offices/OECD/Eurostat/Euromonitor International*

Consumer Expenditure on Alcoholic Beverages and Tobacco 1990-2007*(continued)*

Million units of national currency / as stated

	2003	2004	2005	2006	2007	Total US$ million 2007	US$ per capita 2007
Western Europe							
Austria	3,815	3,756	3,657	3,629	3,716	5,093	612.5
Belgium	5,577	5,785	5,795	5,995	6,252	8,569	810.7
Denmark	28,284	28,729	28,056	28,359	29,045	5,336	979.6
Finland	4,123	3,903	3,906	4,084	4,213	5,775	1,094.4
France	29,378	29,874	29,768	31,098	31,597	43,308	705.2
Germany	43,306	43,493	45,011	46,214	46,697	64,004	777.6
Greece	6,167	6,555	7,072	7,606	8,125	11,137	997.1
Ireland	3,706	3,598	3,743	3,831	4,098	5,617	1,306.7
Italy	20,780	21,826	22,887	24,078	25,177	34,509	586.0
Netherlands	6,986	7,221	7,360	7,485	7,668	10,509	642.5
Norway	31,016	33,243	34,340	36,425	38,430	6,556	1,403.5
Portugal	3,415	3,396	3,438	3,712	3,442	4,718	444.7
Spain	14,710	15,654	16,893	18,086	19,304	26,459	594.8
Sweden	46,737	45,892	46,939	47,062	48,668	7,201	790.1
Switzerland	10,018	9,905	9,808	10,015	10,258	8,546	1,139.9
Turkey	13,453	17,276	18,750	21,291	24,368	18,697	254.6
United Kingdom	27,297	27,713	28,070	28,729	29,864	59,756	984.3
Eastern Europe							
Belarus	1,341,039	1,624,636	2,055,939	2,476,401	2,973,534	1,386	142.1
Bulgaria	903	1,057	1,163	1,418	1,636	1,145	150.2
Croatia	3,993	4,152	4,338	4,241	4,429	826	185.9
Czech Republic	110,213	113,278	115,640	123,170	132,209	6,515	633.3
Estonia	5,829	7,016	7,909	9,393	10,835	948	707.3
Hungary	1,079,727	1,122,211	1,189,337	1,248,390	1,305,385	7,109	706.8
Latvia	292	325	362	448	560	1,089	477.7
Lithuania	2,811	2,908	3,096	3,396	3,913	1,550	458.1
Poland	35,966	38,542	40,541	42,987	46,132	16,666	437.4
Romania	5,959	8,008	9,843	11,810	13,784	5,653	262.3
Russia	214,950	258,280	287,864	314,811	371,023	14,504	102.1
Slovakia	38,432	40,703	41,341	44,999	47,734	1,933	358.5
Slovenia	664	651	666	704	756	1,036	515.3
Ukraine	11,718	14,481	19,605	24,116	31,969	6,331	136.2

Source: *National statistical offices/OECD/Eurostat/Euromonitor International*

Clothing and Footwear

Table 6.5

Consumer Expenditure on Clothing and Footwear 1990-2007

Million units of national currency / as stated

	1990	1995	1996	1997	1998	1999	2000	2001	2002
Western Europe									
Austria	7,821	7,841	8,003	8,070	8,131	8,103	8,280	8,632	8,799
Belgium	6,460	6,699	6,926	6,777	6,899	6,944	7,125	7,231	7,454
Denmark	22,196	26,312	26,960	28,831	29,972	29,678	30,349	30,957	31,559
Finland	2,438	2,218	2,543	2,725	2,851	2,848	2,852	2,999	3,172
France	39,701	38,777	38,980	39,614	40,268	40,798	42,345	42,559	44,195
Germany	64,569	67,310	68,230	68,070	67,820	68,140	69,530	71,840	68,260
Greece	4,167	7,904	8,850	9,568	10,368	10,857	11,370	12,004	12,680
Ireland	1,493	2,006	2,185	2,407	2,704	2,905	3,378	3,535	3,485
Italy	40,269	51,453	52,939	55,979	60,168	62,001	64,471	66,331	67,289
Netherlands	9,252	9,748	10,000	10,468	11,407	12,050	12,659	13,334	13,569
Norway	23,440	27,830	28,665	30,488	31,701	33,511	34,834	37,013	37,938
Portugal	3,246	4,718	4,938	5,251	5,658	5,801	6,079	6,414	6,815
Spain	13,633	18,538	19,501	20,475	21,764	23,599	24,643	26,097	26,555
Sweden	40,893	45,874	45,776	46,849	49,212	53,181	56,325	59,283	59,632
Switzerland	11,344	10,403	10,183	10,382	10,474	10,677	10,691	10,968	10,611
Turkey	18	354	644	1,267	2,996	4,574	7,533	10,468	14,981
United Kingdom	21,259	28,000	29,535	30,901	31,947	33,375	35,479	36,822	39,092
Eastern Europe									
Belarus	0	5,374	9,225	14,119	35,442	179,333	440,577	930,484	1,460,374
Bulgaria	2	40	85	648	811	841	711	840	853
Croatia	4	2,397	2,747	3,528	4,028	4,656	7,085	7,132	7,735
Czech Republic	17,925	40,762	45,566	51,166	55,369	57,915	61,899	65,572	67,492
Estonia		1,569	2,101	2,611	2,914	2,776	3,762	4,300	4,917
Hungary	108,984	194,744	224,657	272,990	320,216	363,800	399,374	454,870	504,938
Latvia	2	106	138	180	219	224	241	238	266
Lithuania		895	1,363	1,537	1,791	1,823	1,847	1,966	2,047
Poland	1,812	11,802	15,024	18,037	19,734	21,334	24,308	24,847	25,836
Romania	3	221	327	784	1,141	1,555	2,027	2,771	3,659
Russia	76	110,725	152,494	197,537	205,551	370,206	481,315	620,742	760,297
Slovakia		22,850	25,987	27,871	28,241	28,166	27,557	26,048	27,096
Slovenia	190	609	599	626	688	722	767	820	850
Ukraine	0	4,355	8,618	10,122	11,340	13,722	16,495	19,469	21,880

Source: *National statistical offices/OECD/Eurostat/Euromonitor International*

Consumer Expenditure on Clothing and Footwear 1990-2007 *(continued)*

Million units of national currency / as stated

	2003	2004	2005	2006	2007	Total US$ million 2007	US$ per capita 2007
Western Europe							
Austria	8,732	8,940	9,274	9,439	9,628	13,196	1,587.1
Belgium	7,618	7,855	8,196	8,514	8,722	11,955	1,131.0
Denmark	32,360	33,795	35,736	37,420	38,585	7,088	1,301.3
Finland	3,386	3,575	3,760	4,012	4,200	5,756	1,090.8
France	45,472	46,228	46,607	48,696	49,129	67,337	1,096.5
Germany	66,487	67,116	67,723	68,824	68,271	93,575	1,136.8
Greece	13,310	13,811	14,485	15,517	16,212	22,220	1,989.4
Ireland	3,280	3,187	3,430	3,474	3,654	5,009	1,165.2
Italy	68,057	68,131	66,306	66,185	67,149	92,037	1,562.9
Netherlands	12,989	12,822	13,338	13,185	13,436	18,416	1,125.8
Norway	39,019	42,168	44,852	47,727	50,780	8,663	1,854.6
Portugal	6,708	6,802	6,912	7,039	5,271	7,225	681.0
Spain	26,781	27,974	28,959	29,788	30,653	42,014	944.5
Sweden	61,454	64,434	68,403	71,365	74,797	11,067	1,214.3
Switzerland	10,321	10,313	10,752	10,887	11,024	9,184	1,225.0
Turkey	20,285	26,032	28,108	30,725	34,923	26,797	364.9
United Kingdom	41,155	42,792	43,792	45,352	47,645	95,333	1,570.4
Eastern Europe							
Belarus	1,737,666	2,133,872	2,700,365	3,252,619	4,120,414	1,920	196.9
Bulgaria	873	916	1,015	1,143	1,252	876	114.9
Croatia	7,930	8,243	8,369	9,248	9,921	1,849	416.5
Czech Republic	68,392	70,834	72,306	76,296	82,000	4,041	392.8
Estonia	5,232	5,846	7,145	8,669	9,979	873	651.4
Hungary	541,619	550,312	571,576	604,600	616,184	3,356	333.6
Latvia	278	312	386	487	614	1,195	524.1
Lithuania	2,184	2,701	3,062	3,476	4,174	1,654	488.7
Poland	26,179	28,065	28,267	29,933	31,809	11,492	301.6
Romania	4,685	6,024	7,031	8,367	9,533	3,910	181.4
Russia	849,310	994,581	1,140,793	1,281,088	1,518,530	59,362	417.9
Slovakia	25,170	25,359	35,195	39,877	41,741	1,690	313.5
Slovenia	901	920	967	1,031	1,138	1,560	775.9
Ukraine	25,222	32,533	45,901	58,529	77,459	15,338	330.1

Source: *National statistical offices/OECD/Eurostat/Euromonitor International*

Table 6.6

Consumer Expenditure on Housing 1990-2007
Million units of national currency / as stated

	1990	1995	1996	1997	1998	1999	2000	2001	2002
Western Europe									
Austria	13,162	18,632	20,074	20,596	21,014	21,530	22,384	23,521	23,967
Belgium	19,578	24,667	26,120	26,944	27,229	27,627	29,291	30,598	31,172
Denmark	109,404	135,538	142,029	145,944	151,319	155,217	162,042	170,925	176,349
Finland	7,870	11,839	12,504	13,486	14,127	14,655	15,319	16,221	17,239
France	117,508	153,213	160,768	164,228	170,945	176,488	183,170	190,773	197,782
Germany	144,046	227,650	239,330	248,030	251,550	257,270	266,460	279,250	281,560
Greece	5,536	12,628	14,159	15,316	16,482	15,857	16,731	17,743	19,159
Ireland	3,188	4,340	4,854	5,686	6,670	7,585	8,941	10,208	11,489
Italy	64,579	103,294	108,461	113,158	119,081	126,915	134,173	140,107	147,176
Netherlands	22,485	32,280	34,848	36,153	37,889	39,886	42,520	45,818	47,359
Norway	83,121	98,477	103,004	105,903	107,640	111,137	118,650	130,446	139,632
Portugal	5,051	7,486	7,922	8,401	8,971	9,524	10,096	10,752	11,511
Spain	27,828	40,084	42,952	45,567	48,263	51,273	60,945	65,590	70,347
Sweden	211,052	273,151	287,133	293,657	294,409	294,732	299,324	310,387	325,605
Switzerland	38,321	50,326	52,394	52,879	53,412	54,684	56,685	59,294	60,027
Turkey	59	1,261	2,461	5,063	11,594	17,843	31,087	42,448	65,285
United Kingdom	58,588	83,126	87,700	91,977	98,114	103,193	108,050	115,905	121,238
Eastern Europe									
Belarus	0	6,373	11,620	17,393	32,844	89,003	290,529	713,836	1,372,582
Bulgaria	9	172	361	3,117	4,131	4,745	4,611	5,085	5,348
Croatia	48	19,122	20,115	23,865	25,164	28,539	29,383	31,237	33,643
Czech Republic	64,563	157,156	177,601	196,198	217,733	228,315	247,479	261,820	280,437
Estonia		5,290	8,237	10,437	12,590	13,483	12,376	13,910	15,268
Hungary	180,946	721,278	921,317	1,118,544	1,294,150	1,485,844	1,679,540	1,850,498	2,102,995
Latvia	19	337	418	473	516	560	619	707	758
Lithuania		3,611	4,204	4,730	4,889	4,914	5,127	5,086	5,486
Poland	4,935	42,500	53,703	70,544	82,430	94,535	97,180	110,439	123,510
Romania	8	837	1,351	3,504	5,389	8,401	12,508	17,624	24,341
Russia	12	44,587	77,847	85,600	103,560	172,943	228,361	325,333	489,859
Slovakia		58,273	65,693	73,483	82,686	100,706	119,187	132,731	144,109
Slovenia	633	1,816	1,929	2,047	2,183	2,330	2,460	2,585	2,669
Ukraine	0	3,084	6,103	7,167	8,030	9,717	11,680	13,786	15,493

Source: *National statistical offices/OECD/Eurostat/Euromonitor International*

Consumer Expenditure on Housing 1990-2007 *(continued)*

Million units of national currency / as stated

	2003	2004	2005	2006	2007	Total US$ million 2007	US$ per capita 2007
Western Europe							
Austria	24,986	26,234	29,075	31,019	32,546	44,609	5,365.3
Belgium	32,494	33,635	35,290	37,018	38,688	53,028	5,016.6
Denmark	180,638	188,521	198,194	207,012	216,885	39,841	7,314.5
Finland	18,324	19,019	19,710	20,780	21,857	29,958	5,677.2
France	209,182	221,049	236,783	247,503	255,415	350,082	5,700.7
Germany	289,841	296,280	306,293	317,062	322,779	442,414	5,374.8
Greece	20,551	21,624	23,034	24,762	25,867	35,455	3,174.4
Ireland	12,673	13,286	14,330	15,721	17,413	23,867	5,552.1
Italy	156,071	166,637	176,318	187,807	197,825	271,147	4,604.5
Netherlands	49,927	51,696	54,764	57,121	59,391	81,404	4,976.4
Norway	149,237	153,377	161,324	171,720	183,458	31,298	6,700.3
Portugal	12,341	13,080	13,873	14,407	16,559	22,696	2,139.3
Spain	76,035	81,608	88,772	95,853	102,783	140,878	3,166.9
Sweden	343,224	352,264	362,629	375,172	387,570	57,343	6,292.2
Switzerland	60,659	62,234	65,135	67,462	69,808	58,155	7,757.0
Turkey	91,840	107,789	117,342	142,136	159,467	122,358	1,666.0
United Kingdom	129,051	138,040	148,182	157,976	168,047	336,247	5,538.8
Eastern Europe							
Belarus	2,466,318	3,321,916	4,203,809	5,063,532	6,336,197	2,952	302.8
Bulgaria	5,627	5,858	6,333	7,132	7,735	5,413	710.0
Croatia	34,095	35,370	39,306	42,014	45,797	8,537	1,922.8
Czech Republic	298,096	316,530	328,877	353,396	387,858	19,112	1,857.9
Estonia	16,294	17,225	18,835	21,848	25,572	2,236	1,669.2
Hungary	2,417,775	2,682,348	2,891,330	3,054,219	3,185,999	17,350	1,725.1
Latvia	836	972	1,117	1,398	1,785	3,473	1,523.1
Lithuania	5,571	5,939	6,474	7,045	8,317	3,295	973.6
Poland	127,380	134,634	145,851	154,657	168,710	60,951	1,599.7
Romania	29,143	38,838	45,860	54,962	66,046	27,087	1,256.6
Russia	708,043	923,886	1,215,425	1,558,487	2,028,442	79,295	558.2
Slovakia	175,738	207,269	227,282	251,127	277,628	11,243	2,085.2
Slovenia	2,747	2,869	2,994	3,179	3,485	4,776	2,375.9
Ukraine	17,681	19,654	27,730	35,360	45,992	9,107	196.0

Source: National statistical offices/OECD/Eurostat/Euromonitor International

Household Goods and Services

Table 6.7

Consumer Expenditure on Household Goods and Services 1990-2007

Million units of national currency / as stated

	1990	1995	1996	1997	1998	1999	2000	2001	2002
Western Europe									
Austria	7,815	9,505	10,011	9,987	9,761	9,968	10,233	10,123	9,743
Belgium	5,667	6,524	6,315	6,700	6,641	6,735	6,658	7,043	7,271
Denmark	24,534	29,896	30,357	32,413	33,703	34,570	35,138	36,040	37,711
Finland	2,335	2,132	2,289	2,500	2,769	2,772	3,006	3,214	3,341
France	39,231	41,057	42,122	42,965	44,649	46,193	48,418	49,610	51,525
Germany	66,001	83,960	84,210	85,800	87,600	86,750	90,530	91,030	87,450
Greece	2,431	4,599	5,008	5,408	5,915	6,284	6,859	7,175	7,840
Ireland	1,552	1,945	2,236	2,457	2,753	3,203	3,621	3,983	4,177
Italy	37,507	49,131	50,844	52,853	55,642	58,684	60,003	60,698	61,467
Netherlands	9,825	10,669	11,228	11,953	13,305	14,223	15,354	16,389	16,343
Norway	21,828	27,969	29,757	32,260	33,911	34,905	38,845	40,535	42,407
Portugal	2,628	3,990	4,350	4,719	5,183	5,509	5,902	6,015	6,293
Spain	12,440	16,956	17,588	18,580	20,253	22,000	23,013	23,958	24,453
Sweden	32,998	39,297	38,772	40,970	43,263	47,199	51,130	53,166	55,895
Switzerland	11,509	11,053	10,867	10,839	11,085	11,452	11,727	11,956	11,902
Turkey	33	506	927	1,770	3,797	5,551	8,681	11,436	17,411
United Kingdom	19,936	26,287	27,758	29,492	31,002	32,846	35,675	37,974	40,448
Eastern Europe									
Belarus	0	2,524	4,174	7,237	15,982	69,014	168,869	388,968	732,465
Bulgaria	1	16	35	272	402	513	678	759	764
Croatia	9	3,274	3,397	3,951	4,052	3,668	3,454	4,406	4,818
Czech Republic	19,513	46,526	55,049	59,485	64,686	66,433	70,998	70,653	69,077
Estonia		1,283	1,912	2,145	2,222	2,285	2,831	3,124	3,577
Hungary	120,555	271,179	306,096	368,899	452,371	511,610	588,930	665,964	769,602
Latvia	1	44	55	64	66	81	91	98	108
Lithuania		603	825	1,204	1,302	1,314	1,289	1,617	1,725
Poland	1,221	9,391	12,606	15,825	18,106	19,976	20,756	21,561	23,639
Romania	4	260	381	897	1,323	1,706	2,305	3,090	3,831
Russia	21	34,927	50,120	80,332	80,024	124,303	189,715	279,210	372,991
Slovakia		16,080	17,479	19,384	22,648	23,927	24,617	30,557	33,037
Slovenia	148	559	556	585	620	686	732	783	827
Ukraine	0	795	1,574	1,849	2,071	2,506	3,012	3,556	3,996

Source: *National statistical offices/OECD/Eurostat/Euromonitor International*

Consumer Expenditure on Household Goods and Services 1990-2007 *(continued)*

Million units of national currency / as stated

	2003	2004	2005	2006	2007	Total US$ million 2007	US$ per capita 2007
Western Europe							
Austria	9,859	10,118	10,286	10,473	10,554	14,466	1,739.9
Belgium	7,649	7,910	8,253	8,665	8,998	12,333	1,166.8
Denmark	38,889	41,590	45,035	48,002	50,227	9,227	1,693.9
Finland	3,617	3,938	4,253	4,648	4,993	6,843	1,296.8
France	53,331	54,999	55,689	58,190	59,340	81,334	1,324.5
Germany	86,281	87,266	87,814	89,206	88,766	121,666	1,478.1
Greece	8,308	8,786	9,339	10,097	10,716	14,687	1,315.0
Ireland	4,453	4,622	4,955	5,347	5,796	7,944	1,848.0
Italy	62,229	64,465	65,494	67,092	68,599	94,024	1,596.7
Netherlands	15,992	15,409	15,382	14,980	15,412	21,124	1,291.4
Norway	43,890	46,853	49,415	52,931	56,612	9,658	2,067.6
Portugal	6,316	6,446	6,665	6,710	6,836	9,370	883.2
Spain	26,084	26,996	28,415	29,851	31,059	42,571	957.0
Sweden	58,496	61,844	67,368	71,488	75,678	11,197	1,228.6
Switzerland	11,919	12,121	12,413	12,688	13,004	10,833	1,445.0
Turkey	18,591	26,455	30,695	32,435	36,249	27,813	378.7
United Kingdom	42,466	44,029	43,792	44,849	47,781	95,606	1,574.9
Eastern Europe							
Belarus	888,400	1,184,118	1,498,474	1,804,928	2,303,846	1,074	110.1
Bulgaria	846	1,044	1,250	1,533	1,829	1,280	167.9
Croatia	5,108	5,470	5,522	5,915	6,332	1,180	265.8
Czech Republic	73,938	75,919	76,211	79,979	84,997	4,188	407.1
Estonia	4,232	4,757	5,545	6,602	7,293	638	476.1
Hungary	874,048	1,020,249	1,122,722	1,187,416	1,249,175	6,803	676.4
Latvia	132	157	186	239	313	608	266.7
Lithuania	1,874	2,149	2,493	2,935	3,558	1,410	416.6
Poland	23,695	25,261	26,722	28,405	30,675	11,082	290.9
Romania	5,950	7,980	9,730	12,267	14,418	5,913	274.3
Russia	487,969	589,296	799,622	1,031,623	1,294,319	50,597	356.2
Slovakia	30,923	37,012	43,516	48,939	54,309	2,199	407.9
Slovenia	864	895	945	1,014	1,125	1,541	766.7
Ukraine	5,465	7,794	10,997	14,022	19,163	3,795	81.7

Source: National statistical offices/OECD/Eurostat/Euromonitor International

Consumer Expenditure on Health Goods and Medical Services 1990-2007
Million units of national currency / as stated

	1990	1995	1996	1997	1998	1999	2000	2001	2002
Western Europe									
Austria	2,231	3,340	3,432	3,442	3,659	3,744	3,808	3,963	4,055
Belgium	2,506	3,688	3,670	4,249	4,581	4,995	5,234	5,242	5,820
Denmark	10,010	12,226	12,936	13,847	14,359	14,790	15,315	16,170	16,768
Finland	1,277	1,631	1,827	1,962	2,046	2,140	2,367	2,530	2,757
France	17,049	22,258	22,873	23,134	23,684	24,466	25,257	26,643	27,927
Germany	21,066	38,820	38,990	43,030	42,780	45,540	47,370	49,470	52,780
Greece	1,508	4,040	4,300	4,704	5,127	5,383	5,635	6,157	6,910
Ireland	600	837	893	968	1,041	1,155	1,302	1,572	1,842
Italy	9,553	18,960	20,384	21,956	23,280	23,735	24,373	23,622	25,155
Netherlands	5,553	6,237	7,374	7,453	7,916	8,497	8,852	9,897	11,104
Norway	8,405	11,521	12,548	13,445	14,418	15,396	16,822	18,090	19,328
Portugal	1,086	2,715	2,818	3,018	3,187	3,424	3,731	3,992	4,229
Spain	6,446	8,989	9,504	9,983	10,754	11,714	12,941	14,047	14,969
Sweden	13,268	18,607	18,773	21,064	22,629	23,838	25,888	28,294	30,332
Switzerland	19,451	27,260	28,825	29,788	31,379	32,416	33,962	35,733	36,396
Turkey	6	114	220	446	1,011	1,547	2,634	3,584	5,557
United Kingdom	4,432	7,000	7,432	7,757	8,306	8,775	9,208	9,976	10,778
Eastern Europe									
Belarus	0	1,574	1,838	2,202	5,812	25,471	81,523	216,440	358,727
Bulgaria	1	15	32	253	260	397	546	722	914
Croatia	2	779	824	986	1,074	1,139	1,473	1,573	1,945
Czech Republic	5,280	12,725	14,906	16,889	18,024	17,709	16,303	22,340	21,209
Estonia		328	502	587	659	843	1,662	1,943	2,203
Hungary	24,405	106,410	130,179	163,387	196,708	249,213	294,487	359,349	422,907
Latvia	1	59	72	93	94	105	125	148	162
Lithuania		460	603	757	989	1,018	1,044	1,073	1,543
Poland	622	6,354	8,667	11,513	14,219	16,641	16,873	18,732	20,734
Romania	1	112	176	448	694	976	1,323	1,933	2,907
Russia	1	8,472	15,702	22,024	30,949	53,299	86,862	94,443	131,705
Slovakia		7,004	7,780	7,500	7,635	9,221	10,123	13,315	13,210
Slovenia	26	214	243	273	296	321	370	404	433
Ukraine	0	1,403	2,778	3,262	3,655	4,422	5,316	6,275	7,052

Source: National statistical offices/OECD/Eurostat/Euromonitor International

Consumer Expenditure on Health Goods and Medical Services 1990-2007 *(continued)*

Million units of national currency / as stated

	2003	2004	2005	2006	2007	Total US$ million 2007	US$ per capita 2007
Western Europe							
Austria	4,244	4,341	4,484	4,636	4,804	6,585	792.0
Belgium	6,115	6,092	6,520	6,818	7,255	9,944	940.7
Denmark	17,086	18,036	19,271	20,280	21,194	3,893	714.8
Finland	2,898	3,076	3,282	3,508	3,751	5,142	974.4
France	29,154	31,429	33,787	35,318	36,502	50,032	814.7
Germany	53,889	56,067	57,391	59,640	61,276	83,987	1,020.4
Greece	7,653	8,242	9,055	9,794	10,520	14,420	1,291.0
Ireland	2,150	2,374	2,626	3,011	3,383	4,636	1,078.5
Italy	25,981	26,580	26,843	27,512	28,096	38,509	653.9
Netherlands	11,726	12,834	13,083	13,738	14,319	19,626	1,199.8
Norway	20,824	22,525	23,617	25,649	27,892	4,758	1,018.7
Portugal	4,729	5,086	5,395	5,717	6,080	8,333	785.5
Spain	16,433	17,792	19,470	21,236	22,791	31,238	702.2
Sweden	31,996	33,758	34,997	36,603	38,929	5,760	632.0
Switzerland	37,740	39,672	41,654	43,912	45,713	38,082	5,079.6
Turkey	7,232	8,942	10,136	11,411	12,791	9,815	133.6
United Kingdom	11,335	11,932	12,115	12,561	13,342	26,697	439.8
Eastern Europe							
Belarus	454,398	587,254	743,156	895,140	1,185,057	552	56.6
Bulgaria	1,004	1,113	1,259	1,482	1,681	1,176	154.3
Croatia	2,014	2,449	2,488	2,894	3,272	610	137.4
Czech Republic	22,706	26,049	29,105	32,069	35,607	1,755	170.6
Estonia	2,592	2,700	2,744	3,576	4,114	360	268.5
Hungary	476,592	512,906	564,941	598,819	645,564	3,516	349.5
Latvia	179	224	302	398	511	995	436.3
Lithuania	1,617	1,723	2,338	2,837	3,410	1,351	399.2
Poland	21,434	24,716	24,575	26,099	28,448	10,278	269.7
Romania	3,910	5,300	6,407	7,835	9,534	3,910	181.4
Russia	149,562	201,366	279,761	342,523	437,513	17,103	120.4
Slovakia	14,200	20,711	20,662	23,946	27,394	1,109	205.8
Slovenia	462	472	504	545	615	843	419.2
Ukraine	7,652	9,489	13,388	17,071	22,346	4,425	95.2

Source: *National statistical offices/OECD/Eurostat/Euromonitor International*

Transport

Table 6.9

Consumer Expenditure on Transport 1990-2007
Million units of national currency / as stated

	1990	1995	1996	1997	1998	1999	2000	2001	2002
Western Europe									
Austria	9,867	11,873	12,957	12,927	13,316	13,805	14,611	14,929	15,391
Belgium	12,993	14,120	14,790	15,227	16,331	17,378	18,616	18,776	19,090
Denmark	48,453	68,181	72,710	76,220	77,892	78,062	73,916	71,524	76,537
Finland	6,294	5,895	6,463	6,888	7,464	7,558	8,046	7,881	8,353
France	90,069	97,962	103,045	100,133	106,247	113,592	120,484	123,849	126,038
Germany	125,841	137,050	145,740	146,330	150,050	156,210	157,680	162,580	165,420
Greece	3,633	6,420	6,908	7,614	8,205	9,046	8,754	9,255	9,790
Ireland	2,492	3,096	3,425	3,949	4,339	4,851	5,961	5,578	5,886
Italy	50,489	72,343	76,573	86,454	91,249	94,441	99,957	101,250	103,266
Netherlands	15,049	17,304	18,045	19,084	20,269	22,467	23,990	24,471	26,096
Norway	46,002	64,066	75,529	78,865	82,527	84,451	93,543	93,047	96,009
Portugal	4,883	7,753	8,433	9,229	10,344	11,645	12,592	12,441	12,437
Spain	18,692	31,569	34,467	38,277	42,137	47,414	49,471	51,346	51,543
Sweden	76,938	107,670	111,622	120,832	126,225	137,732	146,689	144,539	149,035
Switzerland	14,861	16,952	17,239	17,900	18,306	19,298	20,287	20,644	20,330
Turkey	2	147	345	779	1,964	3,615	6,568	11,941	20,773
United Kingdom	51,852	64,087	70,380	77,204	82,506	87,237	93,052	96,435	100,147
Eastern Europe									
Belarus	0	4,351	6,456	12,920	25,693	101,886	318,085	619,768	1,031,869
Bulgaria	4	74	156	1,411	1,584	1,953	2,613	3,154	3,616
Croatia	20	7,127	7,328	8,398	8,619	6,847	8,582	8,974	9,665
Czech Republic	33,094	81,985	99,621	107,817	114,686	118,326	129,855	132,652	126,834
Estonia		2,057	3,828	4,490	4,985	5,169	5,895	6,881	7,722
Hungary	171,623	474,370	589,609	710,829	865,573	1,101,902	1,339,159	1,491,768	1,716,698
Latvia	2	129	173	244	264	256	265	294	323
Lithuania		1,351	1,861	2,428	3,249	3,648	4,275	4,629	4,674
Poland	1,588	15,673	23,188	28,026	34,691	42,064	43,476	45,835	48,668
Romania	9	656	988	2,388	3,506	4,688	6,367	9,083	11,623
Russia	16	43,101	66,116	84,809	102,305	179,429	244,171	350,042	524,738
Slovakia		26,577	28,863	31,468	36,595	42,377	46,138	57,123	58,226
Slovenia	458	1,682	1,744	1,797	1,809	1,951	1,940	1,954	1,971
Ukraine	0	1,403	2,778	3,262	3,655	4,422	5,316	6,275	7,052

Source: National statistical offices/OECD/Eurostat/Euromonitor International

Consumer Expenditure on Transport 1990-2007 *(continued)*

Million units of national currency / as stated

	2003	2004	2005	2006	2007	Total US$ million 2007	US$ per capita 2007
Western Europe							
Austria	15,919	17,218	17,545	18,333	19,106	26,187	3,149.6
Belgium	19,992	21,489	22,815	24,371	25,391	34,801	3,292.3
Denmark	73,596	87,947	104,035	116,226	121,065	22,239	4,082.9
Finland	9,343	9,551	10,008	10,725	11,300	15,488	2,935.0
France	127,489	135,064	142,598	149,025	153,590	210,516	3,428.0
Germany	166,809	171,241	171,089	174,490	176,274	241,608	2,935.3
Greece	10,637	10,932	11,547	12,475	13,055	17,894	1,602.1
Ireland	6,244	6,820	7,736	8,635	9,334	12,794	2,976.2
Italy	107,208	111,506	116,040	120,990	125,049	171,397	2,910.6
Netherlands	26,379	27,113	28,010	28,500	29,507	40,444	2,472.4
Norway	98,087	108,926	113,587	120,364	129,012	22,009	4,711.8
Portugal	12,023	12,994	13,882	14,302	14,464	19,824	1,868.6
Spain	55,112	60,886	65,226	70,508	74,504	102,118	2,295.6
Sweden	153,434	158,600	169,936	177,029	184,935	27,362	3,002.4
Switzerland	20,107	20,696	21,773	22,458	23,198	19,326	2,577.8
Turkey	31,690	37,794	57,087	68,486	79,557	61,044	831.2
United Kingdom	104,569	109,213	113,211	117,593	124,537	249,189	4,104.8
Eastern Europe							
Belarus	1,609,288	1,978,146	2,503,298	3,015,249	3,726,646	1,736	178.1
Bulgaria	4,021	4,526	5,675	6,873	8,065	5,644	740.3
Croatia	10,896	12,121	11,789	13,191	14,310	2,668	600.8
Czech Republic	142,281	156,277	161,723	174,258	189,101	9,318	905.8
Estonia	9,222	10,323	11,901	14,261	16,457	1,439	1,074.2
Hungary	1,990,833	2,139,581	2,305,991	2,433,989	2,604,501	14,184	1,410.2
Latvia	374	488	623	808	1,031	2,006	879.7
Lithuania	5,550	6,262	7,620	9,257	11,089	4,394	1,298.2
Poland	49,980	53,222	53,370	55,888	59,526	21,506	564.4
Romania	14,953	19,488	22,903	27,205	31,530	12,932	599.9
Russia	616,304	872,842	1,172,352	1,527,336	1,901,509	74,333	523.3
Slovakia	63,049	69,306	76,624	84,606	94,379	3,822	708.9
Slovenia	2,078	2,233	2,323	2,484	2,687	3,684	1,832.4
Ukraine	9,018	10,166	14,344	18,290	24,139	4,780	102.9

Source: National statistical offices/OECD/Eurostat/Euromonitor International

Communications

Table 6.10

Consumer Expenditure on Communications 1990-2007

Million units of national currency / as stated

	1990	1995	1996	1997	1998	1999	2000	2001	2002
Western Europe									
Austria	1,482	1,912	2,054	2,332	2,559	2,752	3,051	3,090	3,099
Belgium	1,195	1,586	1,750	1,929	2,149	2,471	2,745	2,950	3,069
Denmark	6,861	9,123	9,323	10,516	10,635	11,393	11,898	12,280	12,283
Finland	625	780	942	1,175	1,429	1,740	1,943	2,158	2,267
France	10,371	12,521	13,089	13,502	14,339	16,284	18,652	20,628	22,706
Germany	13,052	19,910	20,650	22,840	24,140	25,570	28,670	33,360	33,310
Greece	308	1,041	1,353	1,539	1,691	2,610	2,730	3,144	3,488
Ireland	333	511	603	691	732	846	1,130	1,330	1,548
Italy	6,315	10,443	11,697	13,239	15,163	17,223	19,281	20,597	21,476
Netherlands	1,975	3,356	4,157	4,792	5,836	6,889	8,103	9,223	10,360
Norway	7,247	8,329	9,247	9,626	11,451	14,645	16,279	17,637	18,672
Portugal	686	1,175	1,286	1,462	1,541	1,758	1,992	2,417	2,550
Spain	2,601	4,894	5,518	6,056	7,052	8,248	9,397	11,259	12,160
Sweden	11,823	19,624	22,549	25,030	28,337	30,796	31,022	35,302	38,037
Switzerland	3,528	4,664	4,781	4,905	5,039	5,145	5,288	5,639	5,820
Turkey	8	190	385	753	1,676	2,710	4,290	7,174	10,816
United Kingdom	6,510	9,067	9,359	9,984	10,902	12,005	13,356	14,157	14,675
Eastern Europe									
Belarus	0	943	1,579	2,773	5,047	24,267	73,412	209,156	443,309
Bulgaria	0	11	23	232	357	523	848	1,139	1,387
Croatia	0	480	632	929	1,206	1,325	1,942	2,716	4,201
Czech Republic	3,999	11,740	16,936	19,155	20,554	20,861	23,990	30,315	38,167
Estonia		408	670	824	990	1,205	1,723	2,029	2,162
Hungary	8,083	76,283	117,401	164,178	225,619	307,473	376,922	470,037	588,174
Latvia	0	24	31	29	42	70	94	105	129
Lithuania		142	203	421	527	606	795	1,006	1,107
Poland	518	4,674	5,940	5,603	8,015	11,540	12,885	14,806	15,949
Romania	0	26	52	210	630	1,102	1,677	2,244	2,736
Russia	2	7,431	13,863	15,803	18,829	29,725	42,159	62,870	100,471
Slovakia		6,579	7,533	8,452	10,914	14,333	16,965	22,968	24,260
Slovenia	47	179	200	211	224	266	282	320	372
Ukraine	0	608	1,204	1,414	1,584	1,916	2,304	2,719	3,056

Source: *National statistical offices/OECD/Eurostat/Euromonitor International*

Consumer Expenditure on Communications 1990-2007 *(continued)*
Million units of national currency / as stated

	2003	2004	2005	2006	2007	Total US$ million 2007	US$ per capita 2007
Western Europe							
Austria	3,224	3,359	3,517	3,669	3,869	5,303	637.8
Belgium	3,176	3,465	3,505	3,689	4,003	5,487	519.1
Denmark	12,810	14,065	15,731	17,166	18,163	3,336	612.5
Finland	2,331	2,452	2,192	2,190	2,362	3,238	613.6
France	24,380	25,393	26,798	28,010	29,965	41,071	668.8
Germany	34,306	34,772	35,352	36,137	37,700	51,674	627.8
Greece	3,443	3,644	3,918	4,214	4,707	6,452	577.7
Ireland	1,834	2,204	2,518	3,018	3,523	4,828	1,123.2
Italy	22,317	23,230	23,469	24,247	25,837	35,414	601.4
Netherlands	11,028	11,155	11,164	11,378	12,205	16,728	1,022.6
Norway	20,190	21,433	22,464	25,149	28,373	4,840	1,036.2
Portugal	2,602	2,749	2,769	2,769	2,803	3,842	362.2
Spain	12,233	13,642	14,724	15,697	17,240	23,630	531.2
Sweden	39,603	39,814	40,179	40,788	43,553	6,444	707.1
Switzerland	6,120	6,558	6,420	6,692	6,978	5,813	775.4
Turkey	13,946	17,883	19,555	21,873	24,925	19,125	260.4
United Kingdom	15,654	16,448	16,685	17,368	18,784	37,585	619.1
Eastern Europe							
Belarus	696,764	989,951	1,252,760	1,508,963	1,939,821	904	92.7
Bulgaria	1,546	1,695	1,929	2,276	2,581	1,806	236.9
Croatia	4,726	5,470	5,775	5,915	6,478	1,208	272.0
Czech Republic	46,199	49,790	54,606	59,533	69,623	3,431	333.5
Estonia	2,402	2,616	2,816	3,505	4,238	371	276.7
Hungary	615,278	633,399	693,023	735,032	795,982	4,335	431.0
Latvia	165	205	253	365	468	911	399.4
Lithuania	1,170	1,209	1,232	1,594	2,038	807	238.6
Poland	16,894	18,306	20,649	21,618	23,736	8,575	225.1
Romania	3,105	3,933	4,326	5,047	6,104	2,503	116.1
Russia	161,762	251,899	375,289	521,790	670,111	26,196	184.4
Slovakia	26,662	29,351	32,110	35,829	41,718	1,689	313.3
Slovenia	395	454	514	581	679	931	463.1
Ukraine	4,099	6,100	8,606	10,974	15,042	2,979	64.1

Source: National statistical offices/OECD/Eurostat/Euromonitor International

Leisure and Recreation

Table 6.11

Consumer Expenditure on Leisure and Recreation 1990-2007
Million units of national currency / as stated

	1990	1995	1996	1997	1998	1999	2000	2001	2002
Western Europe									
Austria	8,715	11,127	11,721	11,936	12,718	13,645	14,164	14,645	15,078
Belgium	7,762	9,934	10,260	11,010	11,509	12,306	13,033	13,169	12,738
Denmark	41,163	52,489	56,376	59,805	61,322	63,642	66,673	67,955	69,640
Finland	4,848	5,087	5,563	5,830	6,306	6,478	6,994	7,336	7,566
France	49,790	57,828	59,014	60,641	64,951	67,891	72,866	75,942	80,075
Germany	74,857	93,780	96,680	101,340	105,840	110,880	115,940	118,500	116,430
Greece	1,486	3,650	4,179	4,538	4,934	5,523	5,897	6,424	7,111
Ireland	1,776	2,145	2,417	2,510	2,732	2,827	3,607	4,038	4,004
Italy	30,696	40,101	43,100	45,395	47,902	50,260	53,397	54,379	55,401
Netherlands	14,142	16,722	17,821	19,134	20,812	22,804	24,576	26,043	26,948
Norway	29,590	51,714	57,403	61,885	66,897	73,416	78,541	83,416	86,964
Portugal	2,154	3,450	3,746	4,106	4,337	4,665	5,076	5,261	5,607
Spain	16,288	23,170	24,405	25,773	28,330	30,316	36,101	39,041	40,931
Sweden	68,588	90,816	93,370	99,960	108,064	118,305	126,972	132,712	135,703
Switzerland	17,079	19,642	19,768	20,023	20,314	20,798	21,292	21,657	21,745
Turkey	6	114	222	452	1,031	1,592	2,682	3,716	5,890
United Kingdom	35,494	49,274	53,575	58,012	63,246	67,481	70,154	73,452	79,122
Eastern Europe									
Belarus	0	1,216	2,044	3,343	8,335	32,872	82,563	221,851	355,931
Bulgaria	1	22	45	368	538	680	942	850	1,058
Croatia	5	2,265	2,455	2,999	3,300	3,564	4,714	4,567	5,603
Czech Republic	30,443	80,215	98,061	115,539	124,994	129,676	132,569	146,148	148,409
Estonia		1,267	2,257	2,925	3,409	3,553	4,659	5,351	6,167
Hungary	121,255	301,795	358,568	424,001	493,513	565,490	670,447	770,100	889,823
Latvia	1	60	79	104	112	142	192	237	259
Lithuania		512	862	1,104	1,633	1,705	1,729	2,161	2,229
Poland	2,262	16,427	22,772	26,779	32,318	34,187	42,235	38,453	39,034
Romania	3	241	367	890	1,316	1,932	2,778	3,567	4,428
Russia	24	37,407	50,579	72,208	64,716	103,539	157,530	214,418	271,219
Slovakia		23,361	27,445	30,574	34,309	38,765	44,121	54,660	57,441
Slovenia	242	772	849	936	1,020	1,103	1,141	1,209	1,275
Ukraine	0	889	1,759	2,066	2,315	2,801	3,367	3,974	4,466

Source: *National statistical offices/OECD/Eurostat/Euromonitor International*

Consumer Expenditure on Leisure and Recreation 1990-2007 *(continued)*

Million units of national currency / as stated

	2003	2004	2005	2006	2007	Total US$ million 2007	US$ per capita 2007
Western Europe							
Austria	15,365	15,985	16,504	17,009	17,737	24,310	2,923.9
Belgium	13,078	13,614	14,281	14,933	15,588	21,365	2,021.2
Denmark	72,394	75,664	79,714	83,773	87,820	16,132	2,961.7
Finland	7,929	8,426	8,855	9,408	9,946	13,633	2,583.5
France	82,862	86,401	88,758	92,752	95,396	130,754	2,129.2
Germany	115,846	118,125	119,853	122,756	124,233	170,279	2,068.7
Greece	7,655	8,191	8,884	9,654	10,396	14,249	1,275.7
Ireland	4,240	4,764	5,212	5,799	6,307	8,645	2,011.1
Italy	56,225	59,365	60,404	62,361	64,323	88,164	1,497.2
Netherlands	26,520	26,431	26,745	26,511	27,493	37,682	2,303.6
Norway	92,291	98,107	102,633	110,834	119,095	20,318	4,349.6
Portugal	5,690	6,120	6,490	6,897	7,261	9,953	938.1
Spain	43,979	47,181	50,830	54,592	58,585	80,299	1,805.1
Sweden	141,532	145,840	151,165	156,257	164,738	24,374	2,674.5
Switzerland	22,030	22,238	22,544	22,996	23,519	19,593	2,613.4
Turkey	7,135	9,838	11,521	11,380	12,768	9,797	133.4
United Kingdom	84,386	91,057	94,600	100,127	104,962	210,020	3,459.6
Eastern Europe							
Belarus	620,358	904,596	1,144,746	1,378,858	1,723,411	803	82.4
Bulgaria	1,171	1,450	1,710	2,092	2,489	1,742	228.5
Croatia	5,883	6,689	6,746	7,177	7,803	1,455	327.6
Czech Republic	159,258	167,584	175,370	188,974	205,199	10,111	982.9
Estonia	6,670	7,378	7,815	9,491	11,107	971	725.0
Hungary	1,008,041	1,089,473	1,178,986	1,241,358	1,304,705	7,105	706.4
Latvia	303	379	493	679	878	1,709	749.4
Lithuania	2,466	2,784	3,486	4,241	5,078	2,012	594.4
Poland	42,038	46,255	46,475	47,825	51,126	18,471	484.8
Romania	5,859	7,553	8,634	10,156	11,902	4,881	226.4
Russia	401,842	534,935	706,866	921,494	1,147,089	44,842	315.7
Slovakia	57,300	63,407	77,135	86,369	96,941	3,926	728.1
Slovenia	1,352	1,467	1,568	1,714	1,913	2,622	1,304.2
Ukraine	6,285	8,133	11,475	14,632	19,441	3,850	82.9

Source: National statistical offices/OECD/Eurostat/Euromonitor International

Education

Table 6.12

Consumer Expenditure on Education 1990-2007

Million units of national currency / as stated

	1990	1995	1996	1997	1998	1999	2000	2001	2002
Western Europe									
Austria	296	426	454	584	497	526	548	663	783
Belgium	378	445	451	445	534	593	628	732	748
Denmark	2,331	3,718	4,019	4,099	4,600	4,662	4,652	4,641	4,978
Finland	123	228	242	301	314	301	294	303	310
France	3,625	4,122	4,195	4,754	4,858	4,970	4,983	5,158	5,382
Germany	3,820	6,040	6,240	6,900	7,290	7,530	7,890	8,080	8,310
Greece	553	1,467	1,482	1,606	1,641	1,456	1,554	1,570	2,100
Ireland	183	365	441	371	331	364	456	517	687
Italy	4,022	5,702	5,976	6,177	6,311	6,602	6,804	6,994	7,058
Netherlands	979	968	973	1,013	1,068	1,125	1,176	1,233	1,316
Norway	2,058	1,962	2,288	2,438	2,508	2,806	3,049	3,733	3,880
Portugal	369	670	740	752	804	849	922	973	1,034
Spain	2,835	4,602	5,108	5,499	5,895	6,208	6,202	6,605	6,941
Sweden	658	1,229	1,438	1,611	1,706	2,312	2,431	2,544	1,660
Switzerland	696	892	950	976	1,023	1,048	1,079	1,192	1,240
Turkey	2	44	87	179	417	733	1,316	1,889	3,180
United Kingdom	3,222	6,197	6,565	7,440	7,814	8,943	9,534	9,409	9,381
Eastern Europe									
Belarus	0	60	162	1,062	3,288	11,703	34,730	94,484	178,483
Bulgaria	0	3	6	60	142	149	150	197	249
Croatia	1	264	286	356	395	438	517	645	592
Czech Republic	1,764	3,443	4,304	5,153	3,785	4,062	6,264	5,814	6,856
Estonia		198	348	424	546	528	624	712	823
Hungary	9,666	52,316	64,013	70,184	79,368	86,852	95,607	110,952	133,990
Latvia	0	5	9	19	32	41	53	58	65
Lithuania		57	61	133	148	173	182	206	216
Poland	203	2,154	2,654	3,470	4,550	5,871	5,650	6,473	7,197
Romania	1	45	71	131	236	470	497	932	1,413
Russia	7	8,917	13,863	13,169	15,691	40,534	42,159	55,183	83,031
Slovakia		1,818	2,178	2,252	2,481	2,475	3,227	4,703	4,917
Slovenia	48	84	84	90	94	97	107	113	124
Ukraine	0	561	1,111	1,305	1,462	1,769	2,126	2,510	2,821

Source: *National statistical offices/OECD/Eurostat/Euromonitor International*

Consumer Expenditure on Education 1990-2007 *(continued)*

Million units of national currency / as stated

	2003	2004	2005	2006	2007	Total US$ million 2007	US$ per capita 2007
Western Europe							
Austria	823	856	890	929	985	1,350	162.4
Belgium	781	811	834	870	947	1,298	122.8
Denmark	5,048	5,272	5,558	5,792	6,092	1,119	205.5
Finland	320	350	350	367	388	532	100.8
France	5,730	6,252	6,709	7,014	7,223	9,901	161.2
Germany	8,619	8,761	8,715	8,825	8,986	12,316	149.6
Greece	2,241	2,475	2,764	3,041	3,249	4,453	398.7
Ireland	805	806	947	1,071	1,187	1,627	378.6
Italy	7,441	7,844	6,996	7,018	7,095	9,724	165.1
Netherlands	1,427	1,527	1,336	1,340	1,376	1,886	115.3
Norway	3,775	3,939	4,136	4,480	4,862	829	177.6
Portugal	1,054	1,128	1,187	1,219	1,262	1,729	163.0
Spain	7,198	7,445	7,837	8,154	8,409	11,526	259.1
Sweden	2,844	3,188	3,345	3,614	3,986	590	64.7
Switzerland	1,303	1,402	1,427	1,508	1,594	1,328	177.1
Turkey	6,352	8,329	8,466	11,147	12,246	9,396	127.9
United Kingdom	9,610	9,990	10,315	10,616	11,347	22,705	374.0
Eastern Europe							
Belarus	277,878	352,580	446,181	537,430	687,649	320	32.9
Bulgaria	250	251	267	291	308	215	28.2
Croatia	637	758	825	780	849	158	35.7
Czech Republic	7,327	11,629	12,223	13,380	15,695	773	75.2
Estonia	899	927	1,052	1,259	1,458	128	95.2
Hungary	165,742	166,946	184,220	198,237	207,784	1,132	112.5
Latvia	108	105	151	241	334	651	285.4
Lithuania	254	296	332	425	530	210	62.1
Poland	7,508	8,022	7,678	8,447	9,107	3,290	86.4
Romania	1,464	1,947	2,469	2,996	3,625	1,487	69.0
Russia	88,078	146,239	234,556	312,443	432,511	16,908	119.0
Slovakia	5,791	8,331	12,153	14,313	16,825	681	126.4
Slovenia	133	150	164	181	205	280	139.5
Ukraine	3,006	4,405	6,216	7,926	10,569	2,093	45.0

Source: *National statistical offices/OECD/Eurostat/Euromonitor International*

Hotels and Catering

Table 6.13

Consumer Expenditure on Hotels and Catering 1990-2007

Million units of national currency / as stated

	1990	1995	1996	1997	1998	1999	2000	2001	2002
Western Europe									
Austria	8,953	11,210	11,341	11,376	11,920	12,264	13,179	14,001	14,864
Belgium	5,617	5,947	6,004	6,054	6,141	6,474	6,923	7,158	7,378
Denmark	22,077	25,798	25,946	27,514	29,569	29,728	31,118	31,575	31,767
Finland	3,320	3,383	3,588	3,648	3,729	3,766	3,963	4,202	4,246
France	34,361	39,425	39,148	40,615	43,416	45,944	49,559	51,561	53,945
Germany	45,045	57,420	57,650	58,890	59,930	61,890	65,700	66,810	65,770
Greece	4,256	10,513	11,784	14,028	15,271	15,411	17,643	19,507	21,167
Ireland	2,785	4,023	4,412	5,057	5,826	6,501	7,070	7,697	8,372
Italy	33,039	48,724	52,056	54,415	57,837	61,152	68,738	73,148	75,141
Netherlands	6,541	8,511	8,981	9,530	10,205	10,874	11,670	12,252	12,608
Norway	17,297	28,617	30,949	33,781	36,294	38,986	40,320	40,245	41,463
Portugal	3,846	5,934	6,150	6,550	7,220	7,488	8,181	8,753	9,183
Spain	36,674	51,418	53,788	57,587	61,839	67,425	71,984	75,660	80,702
Sweden	26,411	39,042	41,677	43,506	46,908	50,223	53,096	56,302	58,587
Switzerland	14,729	18,251	18,765	19,166	19,272	19,699	19,553	20,386	19,405
Turkey	10	204	398	813	1,859	2,870	4,890	6,781	10,596
United Kingdom	40,603	50,381	55,071	57,164	61,807	64,387	68,557	71,620	76,426
Eastern Europe									
Belarus	0	3,388	4,034	7,394	12,732	55,934	149,944	250,571	381,710
Bulgaria	3	57	119	997	1,540	1,651	1,683	1,849	2,007
Croatia	3	1,425	1,529	1,842	1,956	1,701	2,584	2,326	2,763
Czech Republic	22,272	55,987	65,599	76,622	83,248	80,709	88,664	92,576	86,361
Estonia		1,228	1,629	1,868	2,253	2,484	3,557	4,058	4,567
Hungary	60,358	181,544	222,610	266,746	318,444	367,602	431,244	492,563	560,732
Latvia	2	66	79	101	96	133	143	161	166
Lithuania		514	672	901	961	1,014	969	1,035	1,107
Poland	912	6,634	8,268	9,661	11,773	12,641	14,736	15,076	15,507
Romania	4	346	498	1,151	1,602	2,032	2,714	3,671	4,476
Russia	16	24,940	35,690	41,405	36,747	55,849	77,085	117,504	139,774
Slovakia		23,030	25,509	27,439	32,060	35,895	39,903	46,138	47,063
Slovenia	172	683	701	748	792	793	802	843	885
Ukraine	0	515	1,018	1,196	1,340	1,622	1,949	2,301	2,586

Source: *National statistical offices/OECD/Eurostat/Euromonitor International*

Consumer Expenditure on Hotels and Catering 1990-2007 *(continued)*

Million units of national currency / as stated

	2003	2004	2005	2006	2007	Total US$ million 2007	US$ per capita 2007
Western Europe							
Austria	15,760	16,514	17,268	18,152	18,974	26,007	3,127.9
Belgium	7,572	7,675	7,800	7,997	8,322	11,406	1,079.1
Denmark	31,759	32,767	38,935	41,953	44,073	8,096	1,486.4
Finland	4,502	4,804	5,024	5,357	5,606	7,684	1,456.1
France	56,086	57,124	59,194	61,855	63,910	87,597	1,426.4
Germany	65,385	66,182	66,558	67,620	68,027	93,241	1,132.8
Greece	23,192	25,086	27,095	29,330	31,530	43,216	3,869.3
Ireland	8,830	9,131	9,670	10,343	11,079	15,185	3,532.5
Italy	77,423	79,795	82,679	85,603	89,648	122,875	2,086.6
Netherlands	12,307	12,216	12,579	12,493	12,785	17,524	1,071.3
Norway	42,080	42,930	45,526	48,125	51,184	8,732	1,869.3
Portugal	9,180	9,754	10,140	10,584	11,248	15,417	1,453.2
Spain	86,562	94,807	103,382	112,195	119,246	163,444	3,674.2
Sweden	60,128	61,999	65,823	68,199	71,705	10,609	1,164.1
Switzerland	19,065	19,920	20,232	20,683	21,013	17,505	2,334.9
Turkey	13,457	17,919	19,842	21,719	24,241	18,600	253.3
United Kingdom	78,902	83,595	88,816	93,114	98,963	198,015	3,261.8
Eastern Europe							
Belarus	440,835	688,212	870,917	1,049,029	1,255,552	585	60.0
Bulgaria	2,193	2,507	2,826	3,345	3,830	2,680	351.6
Croatia	2,631	3,493	3,672	3,787	4,299	801	180.5
Czech Republic	87,087	94,394	94,684	99,080	104,903	5,169	502.5
Estonia	4,998	5,756	7,536	9,474	10,969	959	716.0
Hungary	614,616	699,835	757,538	799,798	843,054	4,591	456.5
Latvia	160	189	233	297	379	738	323.4
Lithuania	1,177	1,271	1,440	1,628	1,907	756	223.3
Poland	15,963	17,071	17,529	18,597	19,850	7,171	188.2
Romania	5,236	6,469	7,142	8,348	9,478	3,887	180.3
Russia	206,411	302,432	426,465	516,707	652,821	25,520	179.6
Slovakia	51,300	54,385	55,773	60,047	65,450	2,650	491.6
Slovenia	973	1,047	1,124	1,212	1,336	1,831	910.6
Ukraine	3,826	5,422	7,650	9,755	13,188	2,611	56.2

Source: *National statistical offices/OECD/Eurostat/Euromonitor International*

Miscellaneous Goods and Services

Table 6.14

Consumer Expenditure on Miscellaneous Goods and Services 1990-2007

Million units of national currency / as stated

	1990	1995	1996	1997	1998	1999	2000	2001	2002
Western Europe									
Austria	6,775	9,106	9,606	9,534	9,639	9,752	11,103	11,765	11,559
Belgium	10,050	15,658	15,104	15,052	16,229	15,888	18,050	18,775	18,183
Denmark	47,832	59,560	59,864	63,885	68,594	69,894	76,125	77,646	79,509
Finland	4,311	4,512	4,179	4,162	4,866	4,944	5,933	6,303	6,651
France	77,502	80,018	82,936	83,357	84,523	81,264	92,443	96,650	95,149
Germany	87,400	118,310	117,880	117,400	118,980	125,440	127,540	134,070	137,290
Greece	1,677	3,483	3,748	4,134	4,720	5,394	5,991	6,554	7,039
Ireland	1,616	2,343	2,593	2,981	3,715	4,567	5,004	5,818	6,540
Italy	41,489	56,449	57,069	58,961	60,941	62,456	68,230	71,955	72,155
Netherlands	14,156	20,417	21,329	23,042	25,204	27,258	30,827	32,218	32,385
Norway	27,495	32,072	34,353	35,562	37,642	40,622	43,735	44,730	47,646
Portugal	3,807	5,648	5,853	6,436	6,771	7,621	8,620	8,893	9,120
Spain	17,038	24,831	26,215	28,115	30,062	32,129	34,175	36,939	37,804
Sweden	54,865	78,275	78,545	79,520	82,201	93,304	102,400	100,534	104,524
Switzerland	20,774	24,078	24,840	26,428	27,186	27,820	29,308	27,950	29,709
Turkey	18	253	496	983	1,995	2,875	4,843	6,405	10,994
United Kingdom	36,903	48,737	51,533	55,114	58,519	62,876	67,575	72,260	75,416
Eastern Europe									
Belarus	0	2,299	3,504	5,192	12,311	53,180	160,030	365,763	619,411
Bulgaria	1	19	40	322	442	475	535	515	794
Croatia	8	3,104	3,289	3,930	4,236	3,762	5,250	5,822	6,466
Czech Republic	16,115	47,911	67,273	84,659	94,788	102,824	94,439	102,684	107,980
Estonia		1,189	1,574	2,259	2,622	2,885	3,754	4,538	5,353
Hungary	87,145	171,964	222,978	279,822	349,074	406,715	591,278	681,483	743,498
Latvia	1	77	113	117	115	100	99	105	133
Lithuania		588	802	840	1,347	1,500	1,495	1,682	1,825
Poland	1,662	16,561	20,364	29,954	35,869	42,724	55,283	57,153	63,721
Romania	1	105	160	393	593	911	1,206	1,626	2,068
Russia	22	35,447	49,457	87,712	43,013	64,563	161,595	186,964	238,423
Slovakia		18,332	21,232	23,822	28,165	31,383	34,112	37,029	37,644
Slovenia	106	771	856	894	898	1,056	1,016	1,000	1,203
Ukraine	0	936	1,852	2,175	2,436	2,948	3,544	4,183	4,701

Source: *National statistical offices/OECD/Eurostat/Euromonitor International*

Consumer Expenditure on Miscellaneous Goods and Services 1990-2007 *(continued)*

Million units of national currency / as stated

	2003	2004	2005	2006	2007	Total US$ million 2007	US$ per capita 2007
Western Europe							
Austria	12,012	12,582	12,832	13,287	13,825	18,950	2,279.1
Belgium	17,696	18,352	19,023	19,447	20,404	27,966	2,645.7
Denmark	84,316	88,489	96,247	103,059	108,889	20,003	3,672.3
Finland	6,127	6,487	6,872	7,019	7,474	10,245	1,941.4
France	98,530	102,210	107,339	112,174	114,382	156,777	2,553.0
Germany	146,143	149,685	151,138	154,772	158,122	216,728	2,633.0
Greece	7,609	8,179	8,833	9,537	10,365	14,207	1,272.0
Ireland	7,326	7,906	8,707	9,763	11,028	15,115	3,516.2
Italy	74,370	74,756	78,449	80,910	83,457	114,389	1,942.5
Netherlands	34,089	35,126	37,014	38,459	40,032	54,870	3,354.3
Norway	54,914	59,076	62,862	67,401	72,535	12,374	2,649.1
Portugal	9,647	10,290	10,991	12,273	13,469	18,461	1,740.1
Spain	39,090	42,398	44,913	47,541	49,741	68,177	1,532.6
Sweden	104,467	112,235	119,361	124,493	130,934	19,373	2,125.7
Switzerland	29,911	30,137	29,785	30,046	30,712	25,585	3,412.7
Turkey	11,468	15,603	18,678	20,895	23,568	18,083	246.2
United Kingdom	77,403	80,160	83,128	85,622	90,521	181,125	2,983.6
Eastern Europe							
Belarus	765,095	951,510	1,204,115	1,450,369	1,869,858	871	89.4
Bulgaria	878	1,085	1,289	1,572	1,862	1,303	170.9
Croatia	7,222	7,895	8,223	8,936	9,755	1,818	409.6
Czech Republic	117,359	121,614	127,871	139,103	151,278	7,454	724.6
Estonia	5,925	6,294	7,156	8,958	10,391	909	678.3
Hungary	829,062	719,455	704,991	722,034	760,213	4,140	411.6
Latvia	160	184	215	257	321	624	273.8
Lithuania	2,088	2,432	3,181	3,872	4,860	1,926	568.9
Poland	66,020	70,171	72,608	81,844	89,594	32,368	849.5
Romania	2,923	3,824	4,545	5,546	6,590	2,703	125.4
Russia	306,200	395,076	504,295	633,502	848,869	33,184	233.6
Slovakia	42,836	49,517	76,550	90,218	99,892	4,045	750.3
Slovenia	1,300	1,352	1,433	1,543	1,714	2,349	1,168.5
Ukraine	4,919	5,761	8,128	10,364	13,431	2,660	57.2

Source: National statistical offices/OECD/Eurostat/Euromonitor International

Consumer Market Sizes

Alcoholic Drinks (Off-trade)

Table 7.1

Per Capita Retail Sales of Alcoholic Drinks 2007
Litres per capita

	Alcoholic Drinks	Beer	Wine	Spirits
Western Europe				
Austria	86.98	66.13	16.46	1.98
Belgium	66.22	43.00	20.11	2.62
Denmark	89.30	59.59	26.83	2.39
Finland	97.07	66.61	10.87	5.87
France	55.90	21.19	27.84	4.64
Germany	100.35	68.82	21.49	4.29
Greece	27.07	13.56	11.44	1.93
Ireland	67.71	43.19	12.74	3.25
Italy	46.59	18.35	26.57	1.36
Netherlands	77.54	54.59	19.50	2.50
Norway	57.58	40.93	12.37	2.63
Portugal	58.89	23.65	33.78	1.39
Spain	40.42	25.45	11.56	2.40
Sweden	62.88	38.99	17.25	2.09
Switzerland	60.02	28.09	28.22	2.16
Turkey	9.33	8.43	0.42	0.47
United Kingdom	66.41	37.75	17.67	3.41
Eastern Europe				
Bulgaria	58.82	48.96	4.99	4.86
Czech Republic	98.02	82.13	10.51	5.32
Hungary	74.59	51.49	19.40	3.63
Poland	80.14	64.39	6.41	6.56
Romania	77.11	65.73	9.22	2.16
Russia	88.49	64.96	7.66	13.09
Slovakia	78.93	64.79	9.78	4.16
Ukraine	64.45	49.33	4.67	8.89

Source: *Euromonitor International from industry sources/national statistics*
Notes: *Alcoholic drinks data are off-trade*

Table 7.2

Per Capita Retail Sales of Clothing and Footwear 2007

US$ per capita

	Total Clothing	Men's Outerwear	Women's Outerwear	Footwear
Western Europe				
Austria				
Belgium	798.41	219.11	402.34	64.71
Denmark				
Finland				
France	558.25	137.48	223.38	173.87
Germany	635.92	184.74	308.41	126.79
Greece	937.41	255.50	348.26	150.34
Ireland				
Italy	945.38	252.95	392.94	369.52
Netherlands	801.59	250.70	337.05	186.88
Norway				
Portugal	316.29	93.00	185.18	62.97
Spain	508.79	131.60	195.62	132.56
Sweden	882.15	217.08	341.67	155.29
Switzerland				
Turkey	46.52	15.00	19.63	11.60
United Kingdom	1,079.17	273.79	482.68	167.12
Eastern Europe				
Bulgaria				
Czech Republic				
Hungary	76.90	28.67	34.89	32.14
Poland	108.09	40.14	48.64	65.85
Romania				
Russia	234.25	68.01	91.81	37.81
Slovakia				
Ukraine				

Source: Euromonitor International from industry sources/national statistics

Consumer Electronics

Table 7.3

Per Capita Retail Sales of Consumer Electronics 2007

US$ per capita

	Digital Televisions	DVD Players	Home Audio & Cinema	Personal Computers	Cameras	Camcorders	Portable Media Players	Mobile Phone	In-Car Media Players
Western Europe									
Austria									
Belgium	90.26	17.82	14.83	40.27	15.33	7.25	28.76	66.66	3.20
Denmark									
Finland									
France	65.54	21.90	43.82	54.13	28.57	9.14	39.80	213.48	3.56
Germany	73.68	3.50	18.66	37.34	34.07	5.10	14.94	65.69	10.43
Greece	52.09	7.98	13.10	42.19	13.47	6.31	5.13	97.45	0.91
Ireland									
Italy	98.94	11.38	15.94	14.74	15.08	5.13	10.17	63.07	3.56
Netherlands	105.01	14.99	26.18	44.01	36.81	8.54	17.99	33.37	8.48
Norway									
Portugal	70.90	6.12	17.31	18.67	14.70	4.67	8.67	73.47	5.83
Spain	57.62	13.00	9.43	47.80	24.34	6.27	8.63	100.45	3.91
Sweden	158.19	15.91	20.67	138.50	32.42	8.35	13.78	75.01	3.98
Switzerland									
Turkey	7.55	1.08	3.64	27.43	2.68	0.68	0.78	31.13	0.30
United Kingdom	112.53	22.96	30.91	140.69	50.86	10.00	38.79	34.19	7.52
Eastern Europe									
Bulgaria									
Czech Republic									
Hungary	44.76	6.28	11.83	67.96	17.31	19.11	1.91	39.59	5.34
Poland	19.12	3.96	5.99	63.86	15.60	2.92	4.29	27.00	2.04
Romania	9.43	5.75	4.51	27.56	3.65	1.77	0.68	27.97	0.29
Russia	10.81	2.89	13.75	10.19	9.48	5.09	6.31	48.65	1.70
Slovakia									
Ukraine									

Source: *Euromonitor International from industry sources/national statistics*

Table 7.4

Per Capita Retail Sales of Cosmetics and Toiletries 2007

US$ per capita

	Baby Care	Bath & Shower Products	Deodorants	Hair Care	Colour Cosmetics
Western Europe					
Austria	2.35	16.53	7.52	32.21	22.99
Belgium	2.78	15.82	11.06	29.02	22.15
Denmark	2.61	15.96	13.82	67.76	27.39
Finland	1.64	9.71	7.83	35.46	24.26
France	2.65	15.47	12.16	36.53	23.90
Germany	1.94	11.99	8.97	31.20	19.00
Greece	3.36	10.16	4.26	34.80	14.84
Ireland	5.83	18.81	15.33	39.97	26.00
Italy	3.33	16.91	9.45	25.44	19.78
Netherlands	3.30	17.69	12.26	37.34	23.74
Norway	4.54	31.10	16.37	73.67	49.64
Portugal	2.90	13.44	7.18	30.98	11.37
Spain	3.87	11.91	9.35	33.30	19.42
Sweden	2.35	12.75	7.21	41.63	35.53
Switzerland	2.73	20.77	8.47	31.69	26.72
Turkey	0.62	2.70	1.54	7.81	2.71
United Kingdom	3.64	21.30	23.06	35.62	36.85
Eastern Europe					
Bulgaria	0.68	5.00	2.74	6.92	4.14
Czech Republic	1.57	8.54	7.44	23.73	14.57
Hungary	0.87	11.70	8.17	16.06	7.20
Poland	1.41	6.70	6.74	16.12	8.79
Romania	0.44	5.91	4.55	8.16	7.21
Russia	1.31	4.77	3.38	13.10	8.86
Slovakia	0.90	10.09	5.48	15.30	12.79
Ukraine	0.89	2.21	2.98	8.16	5.84

Source: *Euromonitor International from industry sources/national statistics*

Cosmetics and Toiletries

Per Capita Retail Sales of Cosmetics and Toiletries 2007 *(continued)*
US$ per capita

	Men's Grooming	Oral Hygiene	Fragrances	Skin Care	Sun Care
Western Europe					
Austria	20.13	24.31	21.30	48.63	6.01
Belgium	17.14	15.24	38.65	43.98	4.83
Denmark	20.03	23.51	25.79	32.24	9.97
Finland	10.59	12.82	14.51	50.19	5.11
France	19.08	16.63	37.31	71.13	6.60
Germany	13.04	19.52	29.95	39.35	3.49
Greece	12.34	10.96	16.89	42.13	6.74
Ireland	28.19	23.02	25.43	25.79	6.21
Italy	14.45	22.36	21.64	39.74	7.26
Netherlands	21.73	21.28	37.15	36.99	5.38
Norway	25.74	26.21	17.03	72.18	11.37
Portugal	16.76	19.75	20.84	21.83	6.24
Spain	16.84	16.57	37.56	42.66	10.64
Sweden	11.94	15.91	16.69	36.31	3.48
Switzerland	18.52	22.88	45.85	28.74	9.16
Turkey	3.47	2.73	2.79	4.13	0.36
United Kingdom	22.39	24.07	22.89	48.39	10.27
Eastern Europe					
Bulgaria	2.06	3.49	3.92	6.89	0.92
Czech Republic	6.36	7.97	13.54	18.30	2.70
Hungary	8.99	8.49	9.33	17.38	1.10
Poland	6.69	5.97	13.13	14.19	0.95
Romania	2.19	2.97	12.78	12.24	0.58
Russia	6.99	6.32	13.87	11.60	0.69
Slovakia	6.68	6.23	14.27	21.86	2.06
Ukraine	3.68	3.09	7.19	9.74	0.48

Source: *Euromonitor International from industry sources/national statistics*

Table 7.5

Disposable Paper Products

Per Capita Retail Sales of Disposable Paper Products 2007

US$ per capita

	Sanitary Protection	Nappies, Diapers & Pants	Toilet Paper	Tissues	Kitchen Towels
Western Europe					
Austria	9.58	12.50	20.34	7.95	6.55
Belgium	11.63	19.31	17.30	3.50	7.48
Denmark	16.09	17.21	17.48	1.54	9.45
Finland	11.72	17.46	21.27	1.75	8.76
France	9.78	14.56	16.47	4.55	6.79
Germany	7.94	8.30	13.19	4.47	5.03
Greece	8.78	6.98	15.32	2.43	7.50
Ireland	12.88	23.17	30.01	6.49	9.19
Italy	8.74	13.34	14.73	3.80	6.46
Netherlands	10.42	17.83	20.10	3.23	5.50
Norway	18.18	20.78	36.30	1.83	13.34
Portugal	11.49	10.07	16.03	1.66	4.35
Spain	12.67	11.95	14.56	1.97	4.27
Sweden	9.19	15.73	22.31	3.00	9.35
Switzerland	10.44	12.66	21.61	7.07	6.82
Turkey	3.52	5.21	3.27	0.35	0.27
United Kingdom	9.73	15.13	28.68	5.88	9.42
Eastern Europe					
Bulgaria	3.23	2.30	4.32	3.07	0.60
Czech Republic	7.31	5.32	8.66	3.13	1.16
Hungary	5.68	6.59	7.99	3.42	2.15
Poland	7.67	5.19	5.58	2.05	1.60
Romania	3.52	5.26	5.07	0.39	0.66
Russia	6.37	6.40	2.49	0.22	0.16
Slovakia	6.69	3.26	5.86	2.09	0.59
Ukraine	3.11	2.43	5.34	0.14	0.01

Source: Euromonitor International from industry sources/national statistics

Table 7.6

Per Capita Retail Sales of Large Electrical Appliances 2007

Units per '000 inhabitants

	Refrigeration Appliances	Fridge-freezers	Freezers	Large Cooking Appliances	Microwaves	Home Laundry Appliances	Dishwashers
Western Europe							
Austria	27.81	9.37	6.39	36.82	15.02	28.17	12.85
Belgium	50.02	23.90	17.17	47.63	28.61	44.23	15.66
Denmark	71.10	25.54	20.86	79.62	30.84	48.16	34.88
Finland	49.27	17.35	15.05	52.78	26.05	34.23	18.58
France	52.70	23.30	12.18	64.25	37.49	53.54	21.05
Germany	48.38	17.33	11.42	58.70	23.97	44.14	21.42
Greece	38.72	10.85	5.26	44.66	8.47	29.04	9.84
Ireland	66.73	30.52	17.67	96.89	57.85	98.38	19.72
Italy	45.19	33.08	8.54	48.53	15.10	36.31	14.81
Netherlands	56.20	36.61	15.04	58.14	27.98	60.80	21.30
Norway	89.20	44.18	22.95	111.05	34.76	76.00	45.30
Portugal	44.91	20.28	9.04	69.29	18.85	31.12	14.30
Spain	42.97	33.78	5.21	97.28	28.88	49.02	16.48
Sweden	71.76	24.25	20.85	73.52	38.95	49.43	27.43
Switzerland	36.58	12.36	8.42	48.53	19.81	37.16	16.93
Turkey	32.90	26.99	1.51	26.21	0.79	32.69	12.45
United Kingdom	58.38	29.21	14.28	58.79	54.70	72.18	14.87
Eastern Europe							
Bulgaria	26.80	19.26	4.89	13.53	0.06	24.21	0.01
Czech Republic	40.05	23.10	7.31	46.02	30.62	36.57	10.08
Hungary	41.99	29.95	7.45	28.95	24.06	37.84	7.08
Poland	37.95	31.93	1.45	37.46	14.06	29.12	6.39
Romania	19.55	14.04	3.57	9.87	0.04	17.65	0.01
Russia	24.61	20.31	1.01	18.03	25.61	30.76	0.46
Slovakia	46.71	22.42	6.05	41.87	24.03	32.49	3.83
Ukraine	1.14	0.76	0.02	1.92	0.01	1.04	0.00

Source: *Euromonitor International from industry sources/national statistics*

Table 7.7

Per Capita Retail Sales of Small Electrical Appliances 2007

Units per '000 inhabitants

	Food Preparation Appliances	Small Cooking Appliances	Hair Care Appliances	Irons	Body Shavers	Vacuum Cleaners
Western Europe						
Austria	40.37	119.45	38.81	26.62	24.45	67.71
Belgium	19.84	181.58	54.29	46.52	38.73	75.30
Denmark	120.56	170.38	99.14	36.35	12.67	84.81
Finland	79.79	121.31	44.69	27.17	26.92	34.97
France	69.32	207.26	71.83	55.34	56.95	58.11
Germany	66.96	196.68	85.02	41.39	41.10	74.39
Greece	135.45	58.15	88.75	53.49	9.81	40.60
Ireland	68.21	180.17	199.68	73.16	41.37	93.48
Italy	64.70	79.61	77.04	61.49	24.48	39.33
Netherlands	15.97	124.01	58.71	40.61	24.72	78.91
Norway	55.97	186.25	35.04	27.50	12.32	91.44
Portugal	98.20	118.92	42.87	51.92	35.54	47.67
Spain	94.87	89.46	74.08	68.27	26.59	27.52
Sweden	120.08	169.44	98.76	36.21	12.62	82.74
Switzerland	53.26	157.53	51.20	35.09	32.25	89.30
Turkey	14.28	24.79	7.08	16.74	5.28	10.34
United Kingdom	61.64	164.87	193.00	88.09	39.98	114.47
Eastern Europe						
Bulgaria	4.24	17.68	52.15	32.23	9.34	14.33
Czech Republic	35.59	24.43	39.66	29.36	28.68	60.67
Hungary	12.31	31.57	79.83	44.01	13.71	19.75
Poland	52.37	14.75	58.99	27.75	38.14	28.41
Romania	3.09	12.89	38.03	23.50	6.81	10.45
Russia	58.52	16.91	37.84	39.15	22.17	28.07
Slovakia	37.62	21.81	18.19	7.07	6.74	11.19
Ukraine	3.64	1.61	4.63	4.79	2.10	3.06

Source: *Euromonitor International from industry sources/national statistics*

Fresh Foods

Table 7.8

Per Capita Retail Sales of Fresh Foods 2007
Kg per capita

	Meat	Fish and Seafood	Pulses	Vegetables	Starchy Roots	Fruits	Eggs	Sugar and Sweeteners
Western Europe								
Austria	100.93	14.26	0.29	76.33	63.65	75.45	11.15	52.02
Belgium	64.35	19.99	1.75	145.79	96.27	57.79	12.90	56.31
Denmark	73.69	9.05	0.68	80.31	70.63	95.65	14.06	51.55
Finland	37.68	22.84	1.23	60.52	55.02	52.90	8.20	34.02
France	79.40	24.83	1.18	46.59	34.98	86.99	16.27	16.17
Germany	60.30	4.41	0.21	83.78	31.24	65.41	12.45	43.10
Greece	97.17	23.36	3.55	257.09	57.85	137.37	8.05	32.81
Ireland	80.09	12.60	1.34	74.67	88.68	90.22	6.53	41.73
Italy	66.27	9.36	4.40	63.03	13.11	97.90	12.62	30.91
Netherlands	58.42	24.44	1.41	53.78	66.01	66.80	7.74	39.32
Norway	38.23	35.32	0.81	50.85	53.97	93.11	8.74	48.20
Portugal	101.88	79.38	2.46	200.38	98.30	129.99	11.38	34.19
Spain	56.20	23.70	4.70	59.30	34.87	102.63	12.30	7.40
Sweden	39.30	19.40	1.72	49.43	33.78	70.66	12.59	44.45
Switzerland	54.28	15.36	0.69	79.36	42.48	47.32	10.72	56.04
Turkey	19.27	8.28	11.10	236.77	64.62	86.00	6.23	27.25
United Kingdom	43.85	14.42	0.34	71.35	47.37	65.20	11.37	40.36
Eastern Europe								
Bulgaria	53.53	1.71	3.69	164.25	32.41	36.85	15.65	34.48
Czech Republic	56.63	10.06	1.06	77.15	61.43	41.45	17.77	33.26
Hungary	57.27	3.21	4.09	115.66	63.07	37.09	15.38	62.18
Poland	73.12	7.58	1.87	112.73	119.00	39.37	11.83	42.25
Romania	49.38	2.51	1.35	187.96	103.93	46.58	13.54	27.02
Russia	41.86	11.62	0.84	99.00	118.77	41.01	13.05	25.33
Slovakia	42.76	2.87	3.32	81.70	73.50	48.13	12.02	46.06
Ukraine	23.12	8.57	2.31	118.64	157.67	20.14	9.96	50.84

Source: *Euromonitor International from industry sources/national statistics*

Table 7.9

Per Capita Retail Sales of Hot and Soft Drinks 2007

As stated

	Coffee (Grams)	Tea (Grams)	Bottled Water (Litres)	Carbonates (Litres)
Western Europe				
Austria	3,614.20	208.04	65.11	54.60
Belgium	4,124.72	114.34	113.09	83.39
Denmark	5,012.79	138.65	22.10	54.74
Finland	8,385.91	228.10	16.41	37.09
France	2,957.94	185.56	132.03	31.08
Germany	3,964.01	708.11	133.63	67.65
Greece	1,314.15	19.56	32.09	37.56
Ireland	695.57	2,369.79	37.74	62.82
Italy	2,364.91	102.34	151.24	29.79
Netherlands	4,856.82	585.17	17.70	55.96
Norway	6,617.63	199.61	21.68	115.28
Portugal	1,147.84	54.32	65.98	29.15
Spain	1,422.77	79.89	127.31	64.82
Sweden	6,547.65	291.55	23.57	47.22
Switzerland	4,697.33	355.48	79.80	52.99
Turkey	244.43	1,642.90	66.25	25.18
United Kingdom	872.77	1,952.40	36.84	69.79
Eastern Europe				
Bulgaria	1,499.39	79.50	56.47	44.89
Czech Republic	2,344.08	352.62	81.28	45.86
Hungary	3,356.56	195.98	69.69	49.87
Poland	2,718.69	1,282.02	52.91	45.22
Romania	1,295.03	44.82	46.88	47.06
Russia	694.41	1,136.48	20.83	23.74
Slovakia	2,726.16	322.22	55.27	39.93
Ukraine	812.05	421.63	20.87	32.68

Source: *Euromonitor International from industry sources/national statistics*

247

Household Care Products

Table 7.10

Per Capita Retail Sales of Household Care Products 2007
US$ per capita

	Laundry Care	Fabric Softeners	Hand Dishwashing	Automatic Dishwashing	Surface Care	Air Care
Western Europe						
Austria	36.05	5.06	3.30	5.90	10.59	6.17
Belgium	32.18	7.86	3.04	5.55	12.18	5.78
Denmark	27.55	5.60	4.51	4.92	10.67	0.90
Finland	21.48	4.83	4.06	4.75	10.28	1.27
France	37.69	3.99	3.85	5.03	11.77	8.05
Germany	26.88	4.02	2.90	4.93	11.83	3.10
Greece	39.40	5.52	4.72	2.88	11.55	2.38
Ireland	32.89	6.26	4.64	6.51	11.14	9.08
Italy	40.76	5.79	5.72	3.88	14.73	5.06
Netherlands	26.91	3.63	2.66	5.32	10.84	3.99
Norway	32.35	6.85	5.86	6.46	22.09	1.39
Portugal	28.71	3.51	5.69	2.16	12.22	5.72
Spain	38.77	7.07	4.15	4.36	12.07	6.72
Sweden	21.23	5.20	3.81	4.24	6.68	1.29
Switzerland	47.71	4.33	3.85	7.47	11.19	5.90
Turkey	11.88	0.50	3.05	1.99	1.81	0.26
United Kingdom	43.87	8.25	5.19	5.61	13.39	11.66
Eastern Europe						
Bulgaria	12.91	0.70	1.91	0.45	3.32	1.54
Czech Republic	20.45	2.00	3.69	0.99	4.10	1.61
Hungary	22.11	5.40	3.40	0.88	4.38	1.86
Poland	16.51	2.51	3.58	0.71	5.92	1.80
Romania	18.84	2.39	1.58	0.18	2.28	1.22
Russia	13.53	0.30	2.33	0.09	2.61	0.64
Slovakia	19.93	1.54	2.31	0.13	2.77	0.74
Ukraine	10.21	0.32	1.21	0.45	2.88	0.38

Source: *Euromonitor International from industry sources/national statistics*

Table 7.11

Per Capita Retail Sales of OTC Healthcare Products 2007

US$ per capita

	Analgesics	Cough,Cold and Allergy Remedies	Digestive Remedies	Medicated Skin Care	Vitamins & Dietary Supplements
Western Europe					
Austria	7.61	19.93	5.22	7.93	20.95
Belgium	21.37	23.73	15.66	7.42	31.83
Denmark	15.39	17.71	10.92	6.64	21.89
Finland	16.84	13.78	14.97	9.63	24.39
France	8.61	12.26	6.90	7.79	14.92
Germany	12.55	17.12	8.15	11.58	18.78
Greece	3.79	4.50	1.83	3.61	5.14
Ireland	13.23	20.76	6.06	10.72	15.79
Italy	10.43	12.04	7.30	8.15	28.63
Netherlands	6.67	13.77	4.94	4.30	15.73
Norway	15.01	20.47	10.28	9.52	98.30
Portugal	8.59	6.58	5.44	5.83	8.01
Spain	7.62	10.38	5.71	5.12	6.78
Sweden	16.73	26.23	6.15	7.48	26.27
Switzerland	16.35	30.60	12.30	19.06	19.40
Turkey	5.63	5.33	2.09	1.26	2.66
United Kingdom	14.99	16.84	9.42	13.93	18.94
Eastern Europe					
Bulgaria	6.54	3.60	0.92	1.19	4.77
Czech Republic	10.35	10.69	4.52	3.42	9.26
Hungary	6.36	7.90	4.18	4.28	12.49
Poland	8.43	7.12	3.93	2.56	7.89
Romania	3.80	2.82	1.99	0.96	4.16
Russia	2.40	4.06	2.64	1.44	6.02
Slovakia	6.05	9.46	3.59	2.74	6.26
Ukraine	1.12	4.42	2.14	0.76	3.24

Source: Euromonitor International from industry sources/national statistics

Packaged Food   **Table 7.12**

Per Capita Retail Sales of Dairy Products and Ice Cream 2007
US$ per capita

	Drinking Milk Products	Cheese	Yoghurt and Sour Milk Drinks	Other Dairy Products	Ice Cream
Western Europe					
Austria	52.97	76.47	29.97	41.77	42.19
Belgium	70.52	128.90	46.30	49.09	34.82
Denmark	124.93	177.26	41.76	48.61	78.12
Finland	113.40	153.53	77.96	79.42	89.75
France	47.90	151.04	49.92	60.22	34.22
Germany	50.11	104.91	42.17	53.72	33.76
Greece	60.29	93.08	56.30	30.25	38.70
Ireland	133.97	50.47	69.23	30.86	49.62
Italy	81.79	185.34	35.72	14.22	107.46
Netherlands	52.21	114.18	52.57	56.43	24.96
Norway	196.61	221.38	65.87	80.41	82.43
Portugal	51.65	102.69	47.57	6.82	45.84
Spain	112.41	60.24	55.61	24.31	40.55
Sweden	100.69	138.49	63.18	67.12	57.88
Switzerland	73.55	213.20	81.87	76.77	65.12
Turkey	9.26	12.18	9.62	0.85	7.61
United Kingdom	92.88	64.53	43.69	31.65	46.09
Eastern Europe					
Bulgaria	6.00	42.54	13.20	1.09	6.99
Czech Republic	30.85	71.25	32.91	43.01	17.94
Hungary	54.65	42.79	48.80	37.86	21.33
Poland	29.08	32.97	19.82	28.18	10.16
Romania	9.53	10.72	15.67	13.04	9.41
Russia	17.89	28.65	9.74	12.65	12.14
Slovakia	29.14	51.86	24.22	27.60	12.05
Ukraine	10.16	20.53	7.86	9.71	9.61

Source: *Euromonitor International from industry sources/national statistics*

Table 7.13

Per Capita Retail Sales of Bakery Products 2007

US$ per capita

	Bread	Pastries	Cakes	Biscuits	Breakfast Cereals
Western Europe					
Austria	261.51	33.15	58.90	37.72	9.02
Belgium	147.45	60.12	73.80	65.49	19.56
Denmark	204.88	14.65	35.83	26.77	25.87
Finland	208.79	25.64	40.65	30.54	25.60
France	136.72	55.02	71.32	38.98	13.04
Germany	139.98	17.57	39.68	21.99	9.81
Greece	125.03	106.70	19.30	15.26	7.70
Ireland	132.63	10.79	39.19	51.60	52.39
Italy	124.62	135.84	72.10	35.68	7.69
Netherlands	134.96	5.90	54.30	50.94	6.90
Norway	185.93	27.45	68.87	34.17	19.12
Portugal	66.74	5.50	10.47	42.48	14.31
Spain	123.65	24.62	10.50	21.99	8.18
Sweden	137.92	16.81	46.45	31.34	23.45
Switzerland	210.47	20.97	38.72	68.35	20.55
Turkey	225.29	3.38	13.65	11.87	0.67
United Kingdom	81.11	23.50	59.67	51.32	49.48
Eastern Europe					
Bulgaria	62.42	8.55	3.02	5.14	1.64
Czech Republic	64.73	8.25	4.78	19.88	4.20
Hungary	73.60	3.76	12.49	18.51	7.65
Poland	67.86	1.11	12.04	14.33	5.17
Romania	103.31	3.52	11.81	8.73	3.38
Russia	47.48	2.27	3.45	11.48	2.28
Slovakia	87.46	1.19	4.95	15.12	4.46
Ukraine	13.36	1.52	2.64	14.01	1.38

Source: Euromonitor International from industry sources/national statistics

Table 7.14

Per Capita Retail Sales of Confectionery 2007

US$ per capita

	Total Confectionery	Chocolate Confectionery	Sugar Confectionery	Gum
Western Europe				
Austria	134.66	96.75	31.22	6.68
Belgium	121.84	79.81	31.09	10.94
Denmark	230.70	104.79	110.77	15.15
Finland	175.92	79.21	79.75	16.96
France	104.38	70.63	18.98	14.77
Germany	125.70	85.06	31.41	9.24
Greece	54.31	32.44	5.13	16.73
Ireland	218.20	158.22	44.28	15.71
Italy	86.98	49.75	22.12	15.10
Netherlands	105.38	48.66	43.29	13.43
Norway	285.05	170.32	86.76	27.97
Portugal	45.85	28.58	12.18	5.09
Spain	54.69	25.06	21.18	8.45
Sweden	193.07	90.69	83.25	19.13
Switzerland	212.46	143.31	51.44	17.71
Turkey	22.84	14.33	3.68	4.82
United Kingdom	225.01	159.24	52.83	12.94
Eastern Europe				
Bulgaria	28.74	19.53	3.70	5.51
Czech Republic	57.91	37.15	13.15	7.61
Hungary	66.33	45.61	12.39	8.33
Poland	56.77	37.64	11.46	7.66
Romania	25.78	16.43	3.09	6.26
Russia	63.01	43.48	13.51	6.02
Slovakia	52.62	43.03	4.31	5.28
Ukraine	35.30	21.89	9.45	3.96

Source: *Euromonitor International from industry sources/national statistics*

Table 7.15

Per Capita Retail Sales of Other Selected Packaged Foods 2007

US$ per capita

	Canned Preserved Food	Frozen Processed Food	Dried Processed Food	Chilled Processed Food	Oils and Fats	Sauces, Dressings & Condiments	Sweet and Savoury Snacks
Western Europe							
Austria	23.28	71.11	28.47	96.24	44.79	42.59	27.06
Belgium	70.42	79.41	35.69	174.88	56.46	43.84	18.64
Denmark	61.65	135.64	38.57	253.79	96.52	66.31	42.23
Finland	32.31	80.93	20.41	240.25	74.20	58.46	30.73
France	73.01	53.05	23.81	187.16	48.05	33.58	19.54
Germany	38.74	74.00	28.17	69.23	42.88	43.87	26.33
Greece	27.14	26.31	20.64	43.78	50.76	22.92	77.07
Ireland	35.20	113.89	36.94	127.18	53.18	49.11	107.15
Italy	33.41	40.44	39.30	247.98	47.97	40.86	12.66
Netherlands	34.32	49.55	27.57	140.33	39.38	42.71	42.70
Norway	92.25	204.98	55.78	274.94	77.30	109.06	129.61
Portugal	39.69	21.24	19.44	16.09	57.02	25.27	18.00
Spain	89.66	26.64	16.37	79.64	52.32	29.63	48.57
Sweden	63.29	118.09	33.39	207.06	66.66	77.87	51.07
Switzerland	80.28	115.76	31.45	204.58	66.82	40.44	39.59
Turkey	1.43	1.22	13.92	7.15	46.05	8.36	22.86
United Kingdom	72.37	138.29	27.54	322.44	42.00	70.75	107.74
Eastern Europe							
Bulgaria	9.55	14.91	13.04	47.68	22.08	10.52	4.47
Czech Republic	29.19	41.55	29.31	43.19	64.46	26.87	13.12
Hungary	37.49	26.80	21.23	89.14	36.82	27.90	18.07
Poland	16.73	13.56	19.15	16.43	42.02	29.37	20.26
Romania	9.35	0.79	18.33	40.44	28.59	3.24	11.96
Russia	21.64	37.80	13.79	32.80	37.13	21.83	17.67
Slovakia	34.29	21.50	27.21	59.16	39.52	27.08	16.67
Ukraine	17.41	11.85	8.68	115.27	16.92	18.67	23.68

Source: Euromonitor International from industry sources/national statistics

Tobacco

Table 7.16

Per Capita Retail Sales of Tobacco 2007

US$ per capita

	Total Tobacco	Cigarettes	Cigars	Smoking Tobacco
Western Europe				
Austria	372.42	347.90	20.08	4.44
Belgium	432.91	315.75	30.64	86.51
Denmark	433.03	387.30	15.96	29.76
Finland	271.06	238.03	12.12	20.91
France	309.33	276.75	10.64	21.94
Germany	356.54	306.78	14.72	35.04
Greece	531.47	520.00	9.09	2.39
Ireland	640.15	603.64	19.82	16.69
Italy	369.20	362.31	4.78	2.12
Netherlands	317.74	221.27	15.35	81.11
Norway	430.99	290.06	12.82	128.11
Portugal	321.24	305.74	11.58	3.92
Spain	305.64	284.73	15.51	5.40
Sweden	207.35	188.56	2.82	15.97
Switzerland	484.05	400.34	75.02	8.68
Turkey	171.41	171.27	0.02	0.13
United Kingdom	378.57	333.67	20.86	24.04
Eastern Europe				
Bulgaria	277.66	277.06	0.51	0.09
Czech Republic	302.93	287.25	4.09	11.59
Hungary	214.59	197.51	3.24	13.83
Poland	176.26	169.83	0.34	6.09
Romania	130.38	130.32	0.04	0.02
Russia	93.32	91.46	1.64	0.23
Slovakia	94.92	92.15	2.63	0.14
Ukraine	55.06	54.92	0.11	0.03

Source: *Euromonitor International from industry sources/national statistics*

Table 7.17

Per Capita Retail Sales of Toys and Games 2007

US$ per capita

	Toys and Games	Traditional Toys and Games	Video Games Hardware	Video Games Software
Western Europe				
Austria				
Belgium	96.39	55.65	19.80	20.94
Denmark				
Finland				
France	130.51	62.77	24.77	42.97
Germany	63.96	39.85	9.06	15.05
Greece	38.17	24.46	8.30	5.41
Ireland				
Italy	70.75	46.59	11.19	12.98
Netherlands	121.32	71.13	20.36	29.83
Norway				
Portugal	47.92	26.29	12.40	9.24
Spain	81.00	36.20	22.65	22.15
Sweden	105.24	56.03	12.49	36.72
Switzerland				
Turkey	2.73	2.05	0.31	0.36
United Kingdom	166.22	75.83	33.69	56.69
Eastern Europe				
Bulgaria				
Czech Republic				
Hungary	20.36	15.13	1.30	3.92
Poland	12.98	6.91	0.61	5.46
Romania	5.74	4.96	0.23	0.54
Russia	5.55	4.43	0.39	0.72
Slovakia				
Ukraine				

Source: Euromonitor International from industry sources/national statistics

Consumer Prices and Costs

Index of Consumer Prices

Table 8.1

Index of Consumer Prices 1985-2007

1995 = 100

	1985	1990	1995	2000	2001	2002	2003	2004	2005	2006	2007
Western Europe											
Austria	76.6	85.3	100.0	107.2	110.0	112.0	113.5	115.9	118.5	120.3	122.9
Belgium	79.8	88.6	100.0	108.6	111.3	113.1	114.9	117.3	120.6	122.7	124.9
Cyprus	68.0	79.3	100.0	115.4	117.7	121.0	126.0	128.9	132.2	135.5	138.7
Denmark	74.8	90.7	100.0	112.1	114.7	117.5	120.0	121.4	123.6	125.9	128.1
Finland	70.5	89.8	100.0	108.0	110.7	112.5	113.4	113.7	114.6	116.4	119.4
France	77.0	89.6	100.0	106.2	107.9	110.0	112.3	114.7	116.8	118.6	120.4
Germany	78.7	84.3	100.0	106.5	108.6	110.1	111.2	113.1	115.3	117.2	119.7
Gibraltar	56.7	72.2	100.0	117.3	120.8	122.7	124.8	126.6	127.7	129.2	131.6
Greece	23.5	52.3	100.0	126.7	131.0	135.7	140.5	144.5	149.7	154.5	158.9
Iceland	33.3	83.8	100.0	114.9	122.3	128.6	131.2	134.9	140.5	149.9	157.5
Ireland		88.3	100.0	113.4	118.9	124.4	128.8	131.6	134.8	140.1	146.9
Italy	59.4	78.3	100.0	112.8	115.9	118.8	121.9	124.6	127.1	129.8	132.1
Liechtenstein											
Luxembourg	79.9	87.1	100.0	108.1	111.0	113.3	115.6	118.2	121.1	124.4	127.3
Malta	78.9	84.7	100.0	112.6	115.9	118.5	120.0	123.4	127.1	130.6	132.3
Monaco											
Netherlands	84.3	87.4	100.0	111.4	116.1	119.8	122.4	123.9	126.0	127.4	129.5
Norway	65.7	88.9	100.0	112.0	115.4	116.9	119.8	120.4	122.2	125.0	126.0
Portugal	41.4	70.9	100.0	113.9	118.9	123.1	127.1	130.1	133.1	136.7	140.6
Spain	56.8	77.7	100.0	113.8	117.9	121.5	125.2	129.0	133.3	138.0	141.9
Sweden	60.3	81.4	100.0	102.3	104.8	107.0	109.1	109.5	110.0	111.5	114.0
Switzerland	75.6	85.6	100.0	103.8	104.8	105.5	106.1	107.0	108.3	109.4	110.2
Turkey	0.6	5.5	100.0	1,579.6	2,439.0	3,535.6	4,430.0	4,898.9	5,395.5	5,962.7	6,484.8
United Kingdom	65.5	83.1	100.0	108.3	109.6	111.0	112.5	114.0	116.4	119.1	121.8
Eastern Europe											
Albania		9.2	100.0	181.9	187.6	202.1	203.1	207.8	212.7	217.7	224.1
Belarus			100.0	4,576.7	7,374.6	10,511.6	13,496.7	15,940.7	17,588.8	18,825.8	20,411.2
Bosnia-Herzegovina											
Bulgaria	1.5	2.2	100.0	3,447.1	3,700.8	3,915.9	4,000.3	4,254.2	4,468.6	4,793.1	5,195.8
Croatia			100.0	125.8	130.5	132.7	135.1	137.8	142.4	147.0	151.2
Czech Republic	35.4	39.6	100.0	138.6	145.1	147.7	147.9	152.1	154.9	158.8	163.4
Estonia			100.0	158.2	167.3	173.3	175.6	180.9	188.3	196.7	209.7
Georgia			100.0	191.7	200.6	211.8	221.9	234.6	253.9	277.3	302.9
Hungary	16.2	32.4	100.0	201.7	220.3	231.9	242.7	259.1	268.3	278.7	300.8
Latvia			100.0	140.3	143.7	146.5	150.8	160.2	171.0	182.2	200.5
Lithuania			100.0	145.1	147.0	147.4	145.7	147.4	151.3	157.1	166.1
Macedonia			100.0	109.8	115.5	118.2	119.5	120.8	120.8	124.9	129.3
Moldova			100.0	271.8	298.4	314.2	351.1	395.1	442.3	498.8	560.5
Poland	0.3	16.7	100.0	181.9	191.9	195.5	197.1	204.1	208.4	210.7	215.8
Romania	0.4	0.9	100.0	1,195.1	1,607.0	1,969.2	2,270.0	2,539.6	2,767.9	2,950.1	3,092.8
Russia			100.0	485.6	589.9	683.0	776.4	860.8	969.9	1,063.8	1,159.6
Serbia and Montenegro			100.0								
Slovakia			100.0	148.4	159.2	164.5	178.6	192.1	197.3	206.1	211.8
Slovenia			100.0	148.5	161.0	173.0	182.6	189.2	193.9	198.6	205.8
Ukraine			100.0	363.6	407.1	410.2	431.5	470.6	534.2	582.7	657.5

Source: *National statistical offices/OECD/Eurostat/Euromonitor International*

Table 8.2

Index of Consumer Prices by Quarter 2006-2008

1995 = 100

	2006 1st Quarter	2006 2nd Quarter	2006 3rd Quarter	2006 4th Quarter	2007 1st Quarter	2007 2nd Quarter	2007 3rd Quarter	2007 4th Quarter	2008 1st Quarter	2008 2nd Quarter
Western Europe										
Austria	119.3	120.5	120.6	120.6	121.3	122.7	122.9	124.5	125.0	126.8
Belgium	121.7	122.8	123.3	123.1	123.8	124.5	124.9	126.5	127.3	129.5
Cyprus	133.5	135.9	135.2	137.5	135.5	138.5	138.6	142.2	142.2	145.8
Denmark	124.7	126.2	126.3	126.4	127.1	128.3	127.8	129.1	129.8	131.5
Finland	115.3	116.5	116.7	117.3	117.9	119.3	119.6	120.5	121.8	123.6
France	117.7	118.9	119.1	119.0	119.1	120.3	120.6	121.7	122.4	124.1
Germany	116.4	117.2	117.6	117.7	118.5	119.4	120.0	120.9	122.0	122.9
Gibraltar	127.6	128.9	129.9	130.4	129.7	131.3	132.4	133.0	132.6	134.9
Greece	152.2	155.1	154.1	156.4	156.2	159.2	158.3	162.1	162.7	166.5
Iceland	144.5	149.2	152.4	153.5	154.2	156.2	158.2	161.5	164.2	
Ireland	137.1	139.6	141.3	142.4	143.9	146.6	148.0	149.3	150.0	152.8
Italy	128.7	129.7	130.4	130.3	130.9	131.7	132.5	133.5	134.3	135.9
Liechtenstein										
Luxembourg	123.1	124.6	124.7	125.0	125.8	127.2	127.2	129.0	129.3	131.5
Malta	128.6	131.7	130.9	131.2	129.8	131.5	132.6	135.1	135.4	137.3
Monaco										
Netherlands	126.4	127.7	127.8	127.8	128.4	130.0	129.5	130.0	131.4	133.6
Norway	123.6	125.2	125.2	126.2	124.9	125.5	125.5	128.0	129.6	129.9
Portugal	134.9	137.3	137.1	137.7	138.6	141.2	140.6	141.9	142.7	145.2
Spain	135.8	138.7	138.4	139.2	139.4	142.0	141.5	144.7	145.8	149.3
Sweden	110.3	111.6	111.7	112.3	112.4	113.7	113.9	115.8	116.8	
Switzerland	108.8	109.9	109.3	109.5	108.9	110.5	110.0	111.4	111.5	113.3
Turkey	5,736.1	5,907.1	6,015.3	6,192.2	6,327.9	6,468.8	6,444.9	6,697.5	6,848.4	7,099.0
United Kingdom	116.7	118.7	119.8	121.0	119.7	121.6	122.1	123.7	123.6	126.1
Eastern Europe										
Albania	217.9	218.3	215.6	219.1	224.1	222.1	223.3	226.9	234.5	233.6
Belarus	18,505.3	18,749.5	18,824.3	19,224.2	19,925.1	20,073.2	20,352.5	21,294.2	22,579.2	
Bosnia-Herzegovina										
Bulgaria	4,759.7	4,811.4	4,735.6	4,865.5	5,009.7	5,036.1	5,264.7	5,472.7	5,631.5	5,764.1
Croatia	146.4	147.7	146.6	147.2	148.8	151.0	150.4	154.7	157.5	160.8
Czech Republic	158.1	158.8	159.9	158.4	160.6	162.7	164.1	166.2	172.0	173.2
Estonia	193.0	195.9	198.4	199.4	203.0	206.9	211.3	217.6	225.6	230.7
Georgia	267.5	276.9	280.1	284.6	295.3	297.8	301.9	316.7	330.2	333.8
Hungary	271.0	276.2	280.6	287.0	294.0	299.9	302.0	307.3	318.6	
Latvia	177.9	181.1	183.3	186.4	191.4	196.7	202.2	211.8	225.9	234.6
Lithuania	154.6	156.5	157.5	160.0	161.2	164.0	166.8	172.5	176.5	181.9
Macedonia	124.1	125.4	124.7	125.2	127.1	128.4	129.1	132.6	137.9	
Moldova	479.0	495.1	500.2	521.1	535.7	547.5	566.3	592.6	620.0	
Poland	209.0	210.8	211.3	211.8	213.0	215.8	215.5	218.7	222.3	225.6
Romania	2,911.9	2,943.6	2,954.7	2,990.1	3,023.4	3,055.3	3,102.4	3,190.1	3,273.9	3,327.1
Russia	1,040.0	1,059.5	1,072.0	1,083.7	1,120.4	1,143.7	1,167.2	1,207.2	1,266.7	1,317.2
Serbia and Montenegro										
Slovakia	204.5	206.0	206.6	207.5	210.2	211.1	211.6	214.3	218.3	220.2
Slovenia	195.4	199.2	200.0	200.0	199.9	205.2	207.2	210.9		
Ukraine	568.0	570.0	580.3	612.4	625.7	635.0	662.0	707.5	769.2	834.2

Source: National statistical offices/OECD/Eurostat/Euromonitor International

Index of Consumer Prices

Table 8.3

Index of Consumer Prices by Month 2007-2008
1995 = 100

	July 2007	August 2007	September 2007	October 2007	November 2007	December 2007	January 2008	February 2008	March 2008	April 2008	May 2008	June 2008
Western Europe												
Austria	122.9	122.8	123.0	123.8	124.3	125.3	124.5	124.8	125.8	126.1	126.9	127.3
Belgium	125.0	124.9	125.0	125.6	126.8	127.1	126.4	127.3	128.2	128.5	129.6	130.4
Cyprus	137.5	138.2	140.1	141.4	142.4	142.9	141.3	142.0	143.4	144.9	146.1	146.5
Denmark	127.7	127.5	128.1	128.6	129.5	129.4	128.5	130.1	130.6	131.1	131.5	132.0
Finland	119.4	119.5	120.0	120.4	120.7	120.5	121.1	121.7	122.7	122.9	123.6	
France	120.2	120.7	120.8	121.1	121.8	122.3	122.0	122.2	123.1	123.5	124.2	124.7
Germany	120.1	120.0	120.1	120.3	120.9	121.6	121.4	122.0	122.6	122.4	123.0	123.4
Gibraltar												
Greece	158.0	156.9	159.9	161.0	162.3	162.9	162.3	161.1	164.7	165.8	167.0	166.8
Iceland	157.5	157.5	159.6	160.4	161.4	162.6	161.9	164.1	166.5	172.2		
Ireland	147.4	148.1	148.5	148.6	149.5	149.7	148.3	150.2	151.6	151.8	152.9	153.6
Italy	132.3	132.6	132.6	133.0	133.5	133.9	133.9	134.2	134.9	135.2	136.0	136.6
Liechtenstein												
Luxembourg	126.1	127.7	127.8	128.5	129.0	129.4	128.0	129.4	130.4	130.7	131.6	132.2
Malta	131.8	132.2	133.6	134.9	135.2	135.2	134.8	135.3	136.2	136.7	137.3	137.8
Monaco												
Netherlands	129.1	129.3	130.1	130.1	130.3	129.7	130.4	131.2	132.5	133.0	133.5	
Norway	125.3	125.2	125.9	126.3	128.3	129.4	129.1	129.7	129.8	129.7	129.8	130.1
Portugal	140.8	140.2	140.7	141.5	142.1	142.2	142.0	142.0	144.2	144.5	145.2	
Spain	141.3	141.4	141.9	143.8	144.8	145.4	145.2	145.4	146.7	148.3	149.3	
Sweden	113.6	113.5	114.7	115.3	116.0	116.2	116.1	116.6	117.7	118.3		
Switzerland	110.1	109.9	110.0	110.9	111.5	111.7	111.2	111.4	111.8	112.6	113.6	113.7
Turkey	6,422.1	6,423.5	6,489.2	6,606.5	6,735.2	6,750.9	6,768.1	6,855.7	6,921.5	7,037.6	7,142.6	7,116.8
United Kingdom	121.5	122.2	122.6	123.2	123.6	124.3	122.9	123.8	124.2	125.3	126.0	127.0
Eastern Europe												
Albania	220.0	224.0	225.8	225.6	226.0	229.1	232.3	234.6	236.7	235.8	233.4	231.6
Belarus	20,251.7	20,306.7	20,499.0	20,814.9	21,272.8	21,794.8	22,417.4	22,565.3	22,754.9	23,016.5		
Bosnia-Herzegovina												
Bulgaria	5,136.0	5,294.6	5,363.6	5,398.0	5,480.7	5,539.3	5,574.8	5,636.7	5,682.9	5,731.3	5,757.6	5,803.3
Croatia	149.9	150.7	150.7	153.0	154.5	156.4	157.3	157.2	158.0	159.2	161.0	162.2
Czech Republic	163.9	164.4	163.9	164.9	166.4	167.3	171.8	172.2	172.0	172.6	173.4	173.7
Estonia	210.3	210.6	212.9	214.9	218.1	219.7	224.5	225.3	227.0	229.2	230.7	232.1
Georgia	299.5	301.3	304.9	313.5	317.8	318.7	328.0	331.1	331.4	332.3	334.7	334.4
Hungary	301.5	301.3	303.3	305.7	307.5	308.6	315.6	318.9	321.2			
Latvia	200.6	201.3	204.9	209.4	212.3	213.7	222.8	225.8	229.0	232.6	234.9	236.4
Lithuania	165.7	166.2	168.4	171.0	172.8	173.6	174.6	176.5	178.3	180.5	182.0	183.1
Macedonia	128.2	128.9	130.2	130.9	132.7	134.2	136.8	137.9	139.0	139.6		
Moldova	555.1	567.3	576.6	585.8	593.4	598.6	611.6	620.8	627.6	637.6		
Poland	215.6	214.7	216.3	217.6	219.0	219.6	221.4	222.3	223.3	224.2	226.0	226.5
Romania	3,073.7	3,100.0	3,133.5	3,163.4	3,193.2	3,213.6	3,251.3	3,274.2	3,296.2	3,313.3	3,329.4	3,338.6
Russia	1,163.5	1,164.5	1,173.7	1,192.6	1,207.7	1,221.3	1,251.6	1,266.7	1,281.9	1,300.1	1,317.6	
Serbia and Montenegro												
Slovakia	211.3	211.5	212.1	213.3	214.5	215.1	217.4	218.4	219.0	219.4	220.2	220.9
Slovenia	206.6	207.2	207.9	209.4	211.2	212.2						
Ukraine	654.6	658.6	672.8	692.4	707.7	722.6	746.1	766.2	795.3	820.0	830.7	

Source: *National statistical offices/OECD/Eurostat/Euromonitor International*

Table 8.4

Index of Food and Non-Alcoholic Beverage Prices 1990-2007

1995 = 100

	1990	1995	2000	2001	2002	2003	2004	2005	2006	2007
Western Europe										
Austria	92.0	100.0	103.6	108.2	110.0	111.8	113.8	114.9	115.9	117.0
Belgium	87.2	100.0	107.0	111.9	114.7	117.0	117.6	120.6	122.1	123.6
Cyprus	78.2	100.0	83.2	86.6	90.5	94.0	96.9	100.2		
Denmark	93.8	100.0	107.6	111.7	114.0	115.9	114.4	114.8	113.4	112.7
Finland	109.7	100.0	98.9	102.9	105.2	107.2	107.6	107.9	109.7	111.4
France	93.8	100.0	108.7	114.6	118.8	122.0	122.6	122.6	125.5	126.5
Germany	92.7	100.0	103.4	108.0	109.2	108.8	108.5	109.5	108.9	108.9
Gibraltar	88.0	100.0	110.3	114.1	117.7	119.5	121.9	124.2		
Greece	60.2	100.0	122.9	129.2	136.3	143.2	144.4	145.8	149.3	151.0
Iceland	93.3	100.0	117.4	126.1	130.4	132.9	137.1	140.9		
Ireland	99.3	100.0	110.0	114.9	117.0	115.4	111.9	108.2	105.4	102.5
Italy	82.8	100.0	106.8	110.2	113.3	117.0	118.8	117.4	118.0	118.1
Liechtenstein										
Luxembourg	92.6	100.0	107.7	112.8	117.2	118.1	120.9	123.2		
Malta	87.3	100.0	110.0	116.5	118.0	118.6	120.9	122.8		
Monaco										
Netherlands	93.0	100.0	107.2	113.8	117.1	118.3	113.9	112.4	110.4	108.1
Norway	94.5	100.0	114.8	113.7	111.8	115.0	116.5	118.8	122.0	124.0
Portugal	80.6	100.0	111.6	121.4	125.2	132.2	134.7	132.8	136.5	138.2
Spain	76.4	100.0	111.4	116.3	121.7	126.2	130.2	136.1	140.4	144.5
Sweden	89.6	100.0	92.8	95.8	99.2	99.7	98.3	97.2	96.9	96.1
Switzerland	94.7	100.0	97.3	98.8	100.4	100.9	100.1	98.0	97.3	96.1
Turkey	5.5	100.0	1,455.5	2,079.1	3,146.6	4,024.8	4,468.1	4,460.7	4,914.6	5,170.4
United Kingdom	93.9	100.0	104.8	107.8	108.5	110.9	112.9	114.9	117.5	119.4
Eastern Europe										
Albania		100.0	213.7	221.6	234.3	235.9	241.9	246.7		
Belarus		100.0	5,442.0	7,034.4	10,064.1	11,756.0	13,345.4	15,471.0	16,535.5	17,924.4
Bosnia-Herzegovina										
Bulgaria	2.2	100.0	3,475.2	3,573.5	3,630.1	3,598.4	3,895.2	3,914.0	4,141.8	4,299.4
Croatia		100.0	115.1	116.6	116.7	119.5	121.2	126.9	132.8	136.7
Czech Republic	38.7	100.0	108.0	113.4	111.2	108.9	112.7	112.6	114.1	115.6
Estonia		100.0	126.8	135.7	139.4	138.2	146.9	153.9	157.4	163.0
Georgia		100.0	173.7	185.2	199.1	207.7	217.4	227.1		
Hungary	33.7	100.0	182.9	202.9	210.3	210.7	221.6	221.9	230.2	236.0
Latvia		100.0	115.9	122.1	125.7	129.1	137.8	145.2	151.8	158.4
Lithuania		100.0	98.5	100.2	100.7	101.9	103.6	103.1	104.0	104.5
Macedonia		100.0	101.5	108.2	110.7	111.3	114.1	116.2		
Moldova		100.0	240.8	266.6	278.1	311.4	332.4	356.4		
Poland	21.7	100.0	159.0	166.9	172.1	174.2	180.5	182.7	189.2	196.4
Romania	0.6	100.0	845.9	1,110.8	1,330.8	1,539.6	1,714.4	1,764.3	1,865.3	1,960.5
Russia		100.0	487.4	564.2	612.9	616.5	630.8	679.4	714.2	742.5
Serbia and Montenegro		100.0								
Slovakia		100.0	116.2	121.2	120.8	125.8	133.7	135.0	140.0	144.0
Slovenia		100.0	133.3	145.2	156.1	163.3	163.4	161.6	162.5	162.3
Ukraine		100.0	840.6	1,101.7	1,191.7	1,258.7	1,522.9	1,870.4	1,915.0	2,105.8

Source: National statistical offices/OECD/Eurostat/Euromonitor International

Costs of Goods and Services

Table 8.5

Costs of Selected Food and Drink Items 2007

US$

	Apples (Kg)	Beer (33cl)	Butter (250g)	Flour (Kg)	Fresh Chicken (Kg)	Instant Coffee (250g)
Western Europe						
Austria	2.17	0.69	1.84	1.16	5.46	
Belgium	2.04	0.65	1.79	0.86	5.24	8.02
Cyprus	2.16	0.93	3.31	1.16	5.15	11.68
Denmark	3.01	1.05	2.17	1.00		13.21
Finland	2.51	1.71	1.72	0.47	2.51	10.53
France	3.19	0.66	2.12	1.11	11.82	
Germany	2.55	0.57	1.59	0.64		16.24
Gibraltar	2.10	1.01	1.24	2.22	3.06	11.99
Greece	2.10	0.93	2.07	1.51	3.92	10.16
Iceland	2.39	2.42	1.73	1.00	6.88	23.04
Ireland	5.34	6.02	1.38	1.03	5.96	
Italy	3.38	0.69	2.44	0.73	5.68	
Liechtenstein						
Luxembourg	3.57	0.87	1.78	0.97	7.03	11.58
Malta	1.73	1.19	1.69	0.88	3.25	7.34
Monaco						
Netherlands	2.13	0.73	1.51	0.71	5.48	8.91
Norway	2.44	2.18	1.39	1.20	7.93	18.06
Portugal	1.60	0.61	1.95	1.02	4.00	10.76
Spain	2.33	0.65	2.68	0.84	3.77	7.70
Sweden	2.68	1.45	1.64	0.70	3.41	9.50
Switzerland	3.50	0.93	3.49	1.54	9.46	12.90
Turkey	1.16	1.04	2.34	0.99	2.95	10.86
United Kingdom	2.76	2.75	1.59	0.94	4.24	10.50
Eastern Europe						
Albania	1.40		2.11	0.91	4.21	
Belarus	0.48	0.35	1.05	0.61	2.94	7.34
Bosnia-Herzegovina						
Bulgaria	1.12	0.27	1.20	0.49	2.32	8.94
Croatia	1.18	0.60	1.52	0.84	4.06	12.88
Czech Republic	1.28	0.55	1.24	0.37	2.21	8.52
Estonia	1.76	0.47	1.53	0.52	3.51	6.98
Georgia	0.73	0.46	1.07	0.91	3.65	6.83
Hungary	0.96	0.51	2.60	0.48	3.58	13.95
Latvia	1.19	0.54	1.39	0.64	2.96	7.44
Lithuania	1.62	0.59	1.62	0.67	2.62	8.94
Macedonia	0.67	0.45	1.23	0.47	3.23	19.82
Moldova	0.59	0.60	1.22	0.56	3.98	7.04
Poland	0.33	0.63	1.38	0.59	1.66	10.54
Romania	1.16	0.98	1.75	0.55	3.13	11.85
Russia	1.92	0.49	1.21	0.56	3.16	8.09
Serbia and Montenegro	0.72	0.28	1.59	0.85	2.92	
Slovakia	1.18	0.43	1.92	0.38	2.61	11.62
Slovenia	1.12	0.69	2.06	0.87	3.83	11.76
Ukraine	1.43	0.32	0.96	0.45	2.87	6.55

Source: *Euromonitor International from International Labour Organisation*

Costs of Selected Food and Drink Items 2007 *(continued)*

US$

	Milk (Litre)	Potatoes (Kg)	Red Table Wine (Litre)	Soft Drinks (Cola etc.) (33cl)	Sugar (Kg)	Tea (100g)
Western Europe						
Austria	1.19	1.32	8.22	0.35	1.50	5.17
Belgium	0.99	1.66	9.60	0.39	1.34	
Cyprus	1.61	1.81	6.74	0.53	2.16	1.91
Denmark	1.35	1.74		1.10	1.72	2.79
Finland	1.04	1.04	11.95	0.59	1.43	4.26
France	1.43	2.04	2.28		1.89	
Germany	1.06	0.90	3.67	0.43	1.54	6.05
Gibraltar	1.08	0.63	10.26	0.74	0.70	0.93
Greece	1.69	1.21	5.83		1.19	2.06
Iceland	1.35	1.64	23.77	1.38	2.27	6.62
Ireland	1.25	0.72	18.77		1.58	2.28
Italy	1.84	1.23	3.16	0.40	1.28	4.78
Liechtenstein						
Luxembourg	1.45	2.11	2.17	0.41	1.97	4.11
Malta	0.92	0.77	3.21	0.82	0.89	0.80
Monaco						
Netherlands	1.30	1.06	5.85	0.34	1.22	1.73
Norway	2.01	1.63	21.22	1.82	2.53	5.69
Portugal	1.02	0.86	1.84	0.63	1.40	5.32
Spain	1.26	1.24	1.45	0.33	1.28	4.48
Sweden	1.08	1.34	9.55	0.99	1.50	3.01
Switzerland	1.28	1.93	9.47	0.70	1.57	3.37
Turkey	1.29	0.57	11.03	0.83	2.10	0.77
United Kingdom	1.27	1.52	10.51	0.79	1.52	1.37
Eastern Europe						
Albania	0.67	0.74			1.09	
Belarus	0.44	0.34	5.13	0.22	0.99	1.28
Bosnia-Herzegovina						
Bulgaria	0.93	0.53	4.92	0.21	1.33	1.90
Croatia	0.91	0.68	4.71	0.41	1.23	1.68
Czech Republic	1.21	0.78	3.32	0.10	1.16	1.92
Estonia	0.82	0.87	6.58	0.61	1.53	1.22
Georgia	1.41	0.36	4.07	0.27	0.76	0.97
Hungary	1.08	0.72	1.88	0.77	1.57	1.89
Latvia	0.86	0.81		0.31	1.49	1.05
Lithuania	0.93	0.78	6.63	0.55	1.31	2.69
Macedonia	0.95	0.45	1.69	0.32	1.02	1.86
Moldova	0.69	0.48	5.04	0.46	1.20	1.40
Poland	0.36	0.52	7.40	0.53	1.31	0.82
Romania	0.93	0.55	2.62	0.48	1.40	
Russia	0.82	0.46	5.35	0.24	1.16	0.90
Serbia and Montenegro	1.16	0.34	1.41	0.36	0.65	1.74
Slovakia	0.80	0.74	3.08	0.23	1.37	2.23
Slovenia	0.77	0.99	2.43	0.41	1.15	5.63
Ukraine	0.63	0.64	1.19	0.17	0.99	0.52

Source: Euromonitor International from International Labour Organisation

Index of Consumer Prices

Table 8.6

Index of Alcoholic Beverage and Tobacco Prices 1990-2007
1995 = 100

	1990	1995	2000	2001	2002	2003	2004	2005	2006	2007
Western Europe										
Austria	86.7	100.0	107.4	112.6	117.6	120.8	123.3	130.1	133.8	137.5
Belgium	82.8	100.0	112.9	115.6	118.5	124.5	130.3	132.2	136.5	140.1
Cyprus										
Denmark	96.5	100.0	108.8	110.1	112.9	111.7	106.0	108.3	106.9	105.5
Finland	85.6	100.0	106.4	108.3	109.1	111.7	98.7	97.1	94.3	90.0
France	73.8	100.0	121.2	125.0	132.2	143.2	161.2	161.1	177.9	188.0
Germany	85.3	100.0	109.8	111.7	116.0	120.8	128.1	138.3	146.8	154.4
Gibraltar										
Greece	43.5	100.0	139.9	150.0	160.1	167.1	174.6	178.8	185.6	191.0
Iceland										
Ireland	82.2	100.0	132.2	136.8	145.8	160.5	166.7	169.0	177.4	182.3
Italy	67.4	100.0	119.3	121.7	123.7	132.8	141.9	148.9	157.4	164.3
Liechtenstein										
Luxembourg										
Malta										
Monaco										
Netherlands	82.1	100.0	114.7	121.3	126.2	130.6	139.9	143.8	149.5	154.9
Norway	75.5	100.0	133.5	139.0	139.9	140.9	151.0	154.9	161.3	167.1
Portugal	72.7	100.0	122.1	128.7	137.3	148.2	153.8	159.4	168.8	175.5
Spain	56.4	100.0	138.9	142.2	150.2	154.7	160.3	170.8	177.0	183.5
Sweden	76.4	100.0	110.5	112.2	113.4	115.3	115.0	115.3	116.7	117.1
Switzerland	92.6	100.0	105.8	107.1	108.1	108.6	111.0	114.4	116.9	119.2
Turkey	5.5	100.0	1,982.1	3,055.0	4,702.7	6,866.3	8,362.8	9,122.2	10,050.3	10,968.8
United Kingdom	74.9	100.0	127.2	130.2	132.4	138.3	141.4	144.4	149.1	152.2
Eastern Europe										
Albania										
Belarus		100.0	3,575.4	6,357.3	6,812.3	9,340.3	11,597.5	14,273.2	15,255.3	16,973.1
Bosnia-Herzegovina										
Bulgaria	2.5	100.0	3,762.2	3,654.6	4,716.4	4,902.0	6,304.9	6,544.9	6,925.9	7,512.7
Croatia		100.0	140.4	147.1	149.0	150.5	158.4	168.3	175.0	182.0
Czech Republic	38.7	100.0	150.4	155.2	158.2	159.7	164.5	166.9	171.3	174.7
Estonia		100.0	193.5	205.6	202.1	210.5	206.5	222.8	231.0	237.0
Georgia										
Hungary	41.1	100.0	227.9	246.2	267.3	293.6	326.0	330.1	343.3	357.8
Latvia		100.0	145.0	149.3	153.5	156.3	163.0	164.5	174.5	179.7
Lithuania		100.0	150.2	148.1	165.8	150.7	153.7	151.9	158.8	161.1
Macedonia										
Moldova										
Poland	18.5	100.0	180.9	183.3	182.0	179.5	179.3	178.2	177.1	176.3
Romania	1.7	100.0	1,008.3	1,274.8	1,516.0	1,867.7	2,209.8	2,403.4	2,541.1	2,737.2
Russia		100.0	596.7	708.4	757.3	842.2	897.0	906.0	918.4	940.6
Serbia and Montenegro										
Slovakia		100.0	129.2	132.8	143.7	162.4	178.5	180.3	194.4	203.6
Slovenia		100.0	142.1	151.8	172.6	193.1	203.0	211.2	224.6	233.8
Ukraine		100.0	353.3	420.8	457.4	583.4	714.6	911.5	947.4	1,053.2

Source: *National statistical offices/OECD/Eurostat/Euromonitor International*

Table 8.7

Index of Clothing and Footwear Prices 1990-2007

1995 = 100

	1990	1995	2000	2001	2002	2003	2004	2005	2006	2007
Western Europe										
Austria	84.8	100.0	101.2	102.8	103.9	103.6	103.1	103.1	102.2	101.8
Belgium	90.6	100.0	104.6	105.8	107.4	108.5	108.8	108.8	108.8	108.9
Cyprus	81.2	100.0	113.8	106.2						
Denmark	94.4	100.0	105.1	103.8	106.0	107.4	107.1	106.1	106.3	106.0
Finland	89.1	100.0	97.2	98.0	96.1	97.0	96.8	96.7	97.6	98.7
France	91.5	100.0	102.9	103.4	105.2	105.0	105.3	105.4	107.5	108.3
Germany	89.8	100.0	104.5	105.5	106.3	105.0	104.4	103.1	100.8	99.6
Gibraltar	90.7	100.0	102.1	95.5						
Greece	60.3	100.0	131.8	135.8	140.2	143.2	149.0	156.2	162.1	167.5
Iceland	88.0	100.0	95.0	96.0						
Ireland	100.6	100.0	77.5	74.7	71.3	68.2	65.6	63.6	61.2	59.2
Italy	83.0	100.0	113.6	116.2	118.8	122.7	124.5	124.8	126.1	126.9
Liechtenstein										
Luxembourg	100.0									
Malta	89.7	100.0	95.2	93.0						
Monaco										
Netherlands	99.0	100.0	106.8	107.8	110.6	107.0	104.9	102.0	98.9	96.5
Norway	93.6	100.0	91.7	92.3	87.5	78.6	73.2	70.1	66.8	63.4
Portugal	94.7	100.0	95.7	99.2	103.4	107.9	107.6	105.4	106.9	107.0
Spain	74.7	100.0	113.7	112.1	117.8	121.8	123.2	126.6	128.8	130.8
Sweden	80.3	100.0	102.1	104.7	106.3	106.2	103.3	103.2	102.5	101.5
Switzerland	89.6	100.0	96.8	91.3	88.5	87.6	84.1	82.8	81.1	79.1
Turkey	5.5	100.0	1,315.7	1,886.6	2,871.3	3,626.2	3,988.0	4,001.0	4,408.0	4,632.8
United Kingdom	103.1	100.0	94.1	89.4	85.0	84.4	83.0	81.3	80.4	79.2
Eastern Europe										
Albania										
Belarus		100.0	5,523.0	11,340.9	15,342.0	16,442.5	19,424.2	23,165.0	24,758.9	27,174.8
Bosnia-Herzegovina										
Bulgaria	1.7	100.0	2,883.9	2,792.8	2,831.8	2,771.6	2,824.9	2,752.8	2,913.1	2,954.1
Croatia		100.0	128.1	131.9	135.9	136.2	135.5	136.3	136.1	136.1
Czech Republic	38.7	100.0	112.9	111.1	108.2	102.9	98.7	93.2	89.4	85.5
Estonia		100.0	157.8	163.5	171.6	174.7	175.9	181.4	189.5	193.7
Georgia										
Hungary	38.7	100.0	210.7	217.9	225.6	230.1	236.9	234.4	242.1	245.7
Latvia		100.0	180.7	181.6	180.0	186.8	191.6	214.1	230.3	242.9
Lithuania		100.0	140.5	133.2	130.1	119.2	122.9	138.7	143.6	150.5
Macedonia		100.0	99.4	100.4						
Moldova										
Poland	11.7	100.0	175.2	192.9	195.2	195.9	197.1	198.1	198.4	198.9
Romania	0.9	100.0	990.7	1,222.5	1,431.5	1,616.1	1,769.4	1,798.6	1,901.6	1,985.0
Russia		100.0	524.2	551.2	642.9	687.0	717.0	744.4	787.3	816.4
Serbia and Montenegro										
Slovakia		100.0	127.2	128.7	131.0	135.7	138.3	139.4	142.2	144.0
Slovenia		100.0	127.3	129.1	133.3	141.8	143.9	142.4	144.8	145.6
Ukraine		100.0	415.2	476.4	498.7	542.3	668.0	838.6	861.6	954.5

Source: National statistical offices/OECD/Eurostat/Euromonitor International

Index of Consumer Prices

Table 8.8

Index of Housing Prices 1990-2007
1995 = 100

	1990	1995	2000	2001	2002	2003	2004	2005	2006	2007
Western Europe										
Austria	78.5	100.0	115.8	120.0	122.0	126.1	130.8	138.0	143.0	147.9
Belgium	85.7	100.0	111.4	114.7	116.8	118.7	121.0	128.5	132.1	136.0
Cyprus										
Denmark	88.6	100.0	119.0	123.2	128.2	132.3	135.5	139.6	143.9	147.2
Finland	80.6	100.0	115.6	119.7	123.1	129.5	131.5	135.2	140.6	145.0
France	83.8	100.0	108.8	109.9	113.2	116.4	119.7	124.6	125.8	128.6
Germany	73.8	100.0	112.9	115.5	116.9	118.1	120.0	123.9	126.8	129.3
Gibraltar										
Greece	49.6	100.0	124.6	127.8	132.3	138.5	145.2	158.8	169.0	177.8
Iceland										
Ireland	87.3	100.0	172.2	190.8	211.2	226.9	228.7	234.1	242.2	246.6
Italy	68.6	100.0	123.6	128.1	133.3	139.5	145.8	150.1	155.2	159.4
Liechtenstein										
Luxembourg										
Malta										
Monaco										
Netherlands	80.7	100.0	121.7	128.5	132.9	138.5	142.6	150.8	156.6	161.9
Norway	86.9	100.0	114.9	123.1	129.8	139.8	138.3	140.6	145.3	146.8
Portugal	75.4	100.0	115.6	122.9	128.7	138.3	143.6	148.6	157.1	163.2
Spain	66.7	100.0	122.1	124.5	127.2	130.4	134.1	143.1	147.9	152.9
Sweden	78.7	100.0	103.9	106.7	110.7	115.9	117.6	119.5	123.3	125.4
Switzerland	81.3	100.0	101.2	102.8	102.2	101.9	102.2	103.8	104.4	104.9
Turkey	5.5	100.0	1,858.0	3,027.2	4,320.3	5,306.4	6,020.3	6,424.1	7,077.7	7,588.1
United Kingdom	74.8	100.0	123.1	129.7	134.3	143.0	152.0	163.0	174.3	183.4
Eastern Europe										
Albania										
Belarus		100.0	2,987.0	10,088.0	12,572.3	33,445.4	40,081.2	50,860.3	54,359.7	60,433.9
Bosnia-Herzegovina										
Bulgaria	2.2	100.0	4,495.6	4,662.7	5,435.4	6,070.4	6,628.7	6,752.7	7,145.7	7,457.5
Croatia		100.0	143.2	153.8	157.1	160.7	166.9	174.4	183.9	190.6
Czech Republic	38.7	100.0	167.3	187.4	197.6	199.1	203.8	213.4	220.8	227.1
Estonia		100.0	184.1	202.5	217.8	223.3	232.6	242.5	256.0	265.5
Georgia										
Hungary	31.8	100.0	239.5	259.8	274.9	292.4	328.5	347.0	360.4	380.2
Latvia		100.0	153.4	156.4	163.6	168.3	180.4	186.5	199.2	208.1
Lithuania		100.0	211.2	206.2	201.4	212.6	220.2	231.6	251.5	262.6
Macedonia										
Moldova										
Poland	12.5	100.0	194.1	206.6	211.1	214.4	219.7	224.1	226.8	230.1
Romania	0.9	100.0	1,729.5	2,238.0	3,094.5	3,742.1	4,626.5	5,344.6	5,650.8	6,206.3
Russia		100.0	786.5	901.4	1,352.4	2,102.7	2,494.6	2,844.2	3,371.0	3,738.9
Serbia and Montenegro										
Slovakia		100.0	204.6	237.9	243.3	298.5	350.6	385.7	413.7	446.9
Slovenia		100.0	179.6	198.9	210.4	222.7	237.3	259.0	275.9	291.4
Ukraine		100.0	308.9	378.9	454.5	518.7	578.1	736.8	782.6	859.3

Source: *National statistical offices/OECD/Eurostat/Euromonitor International*

Table 8.9

Index of Household Goods and Services Prices 1990-2007

1995 = 100

	1990	1995	2000	2001	2002	2003	2004	2005	2006	2007
Western Europe										
Austria	87.1	100.0	102.6	104.7	104.0	105.1	105.2	105.9	106.0	106.2
Belgium	90.6	100.0	105.2	108.2	110.9	112.0	112.3	113.9	114.5	115.2
Cyprus										
Denmark	88.8	100.0	112.3	114.9	117.9	119.4	122.2	122.6	124.5	126.0
Finland	91.8	100.0	99.5	101.7	102.1	103.8	103.8	104.9	106.6	108.4
France	90.3	100.0	107.3	109.4	112.1	113.7	115.0	115.1	117.5	118.6
Germany	88.6	100.0	106.0	107.3	108.7	108.8	108.9	109.6	109.0	109.1
Gibraltar										
Greece	55.2	100.0	125.2	128.1	129.8	132.4	134.3	137.2	139.9	142.1
Iceland										
Ireland	99.2	100.0	114.8	118.6	120.7	120.5	119.1	118.2	117.4	116.4
Italy	81.4	100.0	111.0	112.4	114.3	117.2	118.5	119.0	119.8	120.4
Liechtenstein										
Luxembourg										
Malta										
Monaco										
Netherlands	92.9	100.0	107.3	112.0	115.7	117.5	116.3	115.8	115.4	114.7
Norway	93.6	100.0	105.8	108.1	108.9	108.4	107.1	107.3	107.5	107.1
Portugal	78.9	100.0	111.9	117.9	123.5	130.5	133.7	134.2	139.0	142.1
Spain	70.9	100.0	116.8	118.2	120.5	122.5	123.5	127.9	129.5	131.6
Sweden	82.4	100.0	99.9	102.8	104.8	105.8	103.6	101.1	100.3	98.7
Switzerland	90.8	100.0	96.7	96.8	96.4	96.2	95.2	93.8	93.1	92.0
Turkey	5.5	100.0	1,451.9	2,223.2	3,215.7	3,770.7	4,104.8	4,233.1	4,663.7	4,920.6
United Kingdom	94.8	100.0	105.8	106.0	106.7	107.9	110.4	111.4	113.4	115.0
Eastern Europe										
Albania										
Belarus		100.0	3,011.7	6,739.4	11,192.7	11,440.4	14,864.9	18,321.8	19,582.4	21,946.7
Bosnia-Herzegovina										
Bulgaria	2.2	100.0	2,474.5	2,443.2	2,486.7	2,464.8	2,471.2	2,423.3	2,564.3	2,593.3
Croatia		100.0	140.6	141.6	138.8	138.3	137.7	141.1	141.6	142.6
Czech Republic	38.7	100.0	131.3	131.5	131.5	129.4	126.4	123.7	122.2	120.2
Estonia		100.0	126.1	127.0	129.4	128.7	128.2	129.5	131.0	131.6
Georgia										
Hungary	33.0	100.0	185.2	190.3	194.9	194.2	195.1	191.9	195.1	195.4
Latvia		100.0	137.0	137.9	140.5	142.9	144.5	148.0	154.8	158.3
Lithuania		100.0	123.6	119.5	119.5	110.0	110.0	113.1	114.9	116.2
Macedonia										
Moldova										
Poland	19.4	100.0	220.6	236.7	239.9	224.8	218.7	209.0	201.9	195.1
Romania	0.9	100.0	839.1	1,033.4	1,237.7	1,381.7	1,512.1	1,549.4	1,638.1	1,713.1
Russia		100.0	533.3	701.5	859.5	978.0	1,063.4	1,267.2	1,463.2	1,603.9
Serbia and Montenegro										
Slovakia		100.0	123.2	120.8	119.7	121.8	120.8	118.9	118.5	117.5
Slovenia		100.0	115.6	124.4	131.9	138.4	141.7	146.7	151.1	154.8
Ukraine		100.0	326.9	370.8	384.6	472.1	638.2	775.1	775.7	863.9

Source: National statistical offices/OECD/Eurostat/Euromonitor International

Table 8.10

Index of Health Goods and Medical Services Prices 1990-2007
1995 = 100

	1990	1995	2000	2001	2002	2003	2004	2005	2006	2007
Western Europe										
Austria	77.6	100.0	106.8	113.4	116.8	117.7	119.0	125.6	128.0	131.0
Belgium	82.4	100.0	112.6	115.1	117.5	122.6	126.1	123.3	124.9	125.6
Cyprus										
Denmark	94.4	100.0	106.5	105.9	108.2	108.4	108.3	109.5	110.1	110.6
Finland	80.1	100.0	110.7	113.1	117.6	121.5	123.6	126.6	130.8	134.7
France	92.3	100.0	104.7	103.8	105.4	107.5	108.2	108.5	106.8	106.6
Germany	86.3	100.0	109.1	110.3	110.0	109.0	125.5	128.8	139.1	147.9
Gibraltar										
Greece	41.8	100.0	95.4	97.8	102.5	107.4	113.1	118.2	124.1	128.9
Iceland										
Ireland	80.9	100.0	165.0	209.1	269.2	335.2	400.1	478.0	578.7	649.2
Italy	83.3	100.0	119.3	114.1	117.8	121.3	121.4	119.8	119.8	119.1
Liechtenstein										
Luxembourg										
Malta										
Monaco										
Netherlands	86.9	100.0	106.1	112.3	119.0	121.9	133.4	134.9	140.0	145.2
Norway	79.4	100.0	124.1	129.1	134.0	137.9	142.7	147.1	152.7	156.9
Portugal	71.1	100.0	120.9	127.9	136.3	143.9	147.5	147.5	152.6	155.8
Spain	73.5	100.0	117.0	118.1	121.2	123.3	122.9	125.6	126.3	127.2
Sweden	71.5	100.0	121.1	125.8	132.2	136.8	140.2	142.0	146.1	148.7
Switzerland	82.6	100.0	98.8	98.7	98.5	98.7	98.3	97.4	97.2	96.6
Turkey	5.5	100.0	2,197.8	3,127.4	4,347.2	5,542.4	6,304.6	6,357.0	7,003.7	7,424.3
United Kingdom	71.2	100.0	136.2	142.9	150.4	154.6	160.8	164.7	170.2	174.7
Eastern Europe										
Albania										
Belarus		100.0	4,457.9	13,881.0	20,990.2	24,639.3	29,487.6	37,121.7	39,675.9	44,043.1
Bosnia-Herzegovina										
Bulgaria	1.2	100.0	4,621.5	5,750.0	7,509.2	7,906.9	8,076.8	8,504.0	8,998.9	9,315.7
Croatia		100.0	123.9	130.1	146.6	159.1	164.7	170.1	178.5	184.0
Czech Republic	38.7	100.0	78.9	82.1	87.0	91.0	93.1	99.5	104.9	108.9
Estonia		100.0	164.5	180.9	198.4	222.6	229.6	235.5	251.0	259.2
Georgia										
Hungary	18.0	100.0	343.8	376.5	406.0	430.4	458.9	489.4	509.7	532.8
Latvia		100.0	119.9	125.3	129.5	137.4	154.8	182.0	196.0	213.0
Lithuania		100.0	119.7	116.4	117.3	122.2	135.2	142.2	148.7	156.2
Macedonia										
Moldova										
Poland	21.0	100.0	216.0	236.1	242.3	252.8	269.3	283.3	295.2	307.2
Romania	1.3	100.0	1,268.9	1,683.7	2,037.0	2,341.2	2,340.7	2,315.3	2,447.9	2,479.8
Russia		100.0	475.5	521.4	574.9	603.5	683.0	782.4	847.3	918.0
Serbia and Montenegro										
Slovakia		100.0	174.0	177.7	183.4	198.7	228.4	252.7	275.2	297.2
Slovenia		100.0	154.8	173.4	185.2	196.2	199.0	198.4	201.8	203.4
Ukraine		100.0	436.1	544.0	631.2	686.0	820.7	1,076.2	1,149.8	1,284.6

Source: *National statistical offices/OECD/Eurostat/Euromonitor International*

Table 8.11

Index of Transport Prices 1990-2007
1995 = 100

	1990	1995	2000	2001	2002	2003	2004	2005	2006	2007
Western Europe										
Austria	85.1	100.0	110.6	113.2	114.4	115.6	119.6	124.9	127.9	131.4
Belgium	84.1	100.0	116.3	118.9	121.2	123.5	127.5	132.9	136.5	140.3
Cyprus										
Denmark	90.4	100.0	112.5	111.9	115.2	119.3	123.2	127.0	131.5	135.0
Finland	85.4	100.0	108.8	109.7	109.9	110.7	111.1	114.6	117.1	120.0
France	86.9	100.0	111.0	111.1	113.3	116.3	120.7	125.6	129.6	133.4
Germany	80.5	100.0	113.1	114.8	117.2	119.2	121.9	126.8	130.4	133.7
Gibraltar										
Greece	65.6	100.0	120.7	122.4	122.7	126.7	131.1	137.5	142.9	147.6
Iceland										
Ireland	98.5	100.0	119.9	119.1	124.1	128.5	134.6	139.1	144.5	149.1
Italy	78.1	100.0	113.5	114.2	114.4	117.4	120.0	123.4	125.8	128.1
Liechtenstein										
Luxembourg										
Malta										
Monaco										
Netherlands	86.0	100.0	112.9	114.9	116.3	119.4	123.5	128.6	132.3	136.1
Norway	81.0	100.0	116.3	120.6	121.7	123.6	125.7	131.5	135.9	139.3
Portugal	74.0	100.0	120.4	128.9	137.6	148.1	154.7	162.3	172.8	180.7
Spain	74.5	100.0	117.5	117.5	119.8	122.0	126.5	136.5	141.5	147.2
Sweden	83.4	100.0	104.7	106.0	107.6	109.7	112.6	116.5	120.2	123.2
Switzerland	84.2	100.0	100.2	99.7	98.6	98.3	98.4	100.2	101.0	101.6
Turkey	5.5	100.0	1,773.6	2,674.1	4,082.5	5,062.7	5,618.5	6,269.6	6,907.4	7,439.2
United Kingdom	85.6	100.0	118.5	119.2	120.0	122.8	127.4	131.5	135.9	139.8
Eastern Europe										
Albania										
Belarus		100.0	3,933.2	9,203.5	11,303.0	16,282.0	20,554.2	25,266.5	27,005.0	30,119.1
Bosnia-Herzegovina										
Bulgaria	2.2	100.0	3,587.0	3,700.1	3,792.2	3,886.6	4,128.5	4,450.7	4,709.8	4,948.5
Croatia		100.0	143.3	155.7	163.4	167.1	172.1	175.9	183.6	188.3
Czech Republic	38.7	100.0	125.4	126.7	125.0	125.5	128.9	131.6	134.9	137.7
Estonia		100.0	213.0	217.0	218.5	216.8	226.2	241.0	256.5	268.0
Georgia										
Hungary	33.0	100.0	224.3	225.4	227.0	234.0	246.1	255.9	265.4	274.5
Latvia		100.0	166.7	167.3	169.2	174.9	187.0	210.8	228.5	244.0
Lithuania		100.0	163.0	161.8	155.9	155.4	164.0	183.4	196.6	208.3
Macedonia										
Moldova										
Poland	12.9	100.0	189.0	198.8	200.4	202.2	205.2	207.6	209.0	210.7
Romania	0.9	100.0	1,143.6	1,535.8	2,037.9	2,427.1	2,790.0	3,084.6	3,261.3	3,504.3
Russia		100.0	468.7	671.5	813.3	892.2	1,041.9	1,353.3	1,537.2	1,724.2
Serbia and Montenegro										
Slovakia		100.0	139.0	140.2	136.1	148.1	161.7	166.5	172.6	179.7
Slovenia		100.0	161.3	177.5	190.6	199.4	210.6	216.6	224.7	232.1
Ukraine		100.0	291.4	323.1	342.2	393.4	430.0	524.5	542.1	585.4

Source: National statistical offices/OECD/Eurostat/Euromonitor International

Index of Consumer Prices

Table 8.12

Index of Communication Prices 1990-2007
1995 = 100

	1990	1995	2000	2001	2002	2003	2004	2005	2006	2007
Western Europe										
Austria	102.1	100.0	77.5	77.4	77.2	75.4	74.5	68.5	65.4	62.5
Belgium	76.1	100.0	102.4	96.2	96.7	97.3	99.5	100.3	101.3	102.4
Cyprus										
Denmark	101.5	100.0	93.3	90.8	83.1	81.8	79.7	78.5	77.1	75.8
Finland	102.3	100.0	84.4	84.0	83.3	80.2	72.4	61.8	56.5	50.0
France	101.7	100.0	73.5	70.7	69.2	68.6	67.8	66.9	65.1	64.1
Germany	93.0	100.0	78.8	74.4	75.7	75.8	75.0	74.2	73.7	73.1
Gibraltar										
Greece	50.9	100.0	95.7	93.8	89.4	85.4	81.7	81.6	79.2	77.4
Iceland										
Ireland	99.0	100.0	78.1	69.5	69.6	68.6	68.2	66.8	65.9	65.1
Italy	87.9	100.0	94.9	92.5	90.9	89.9	83.7	78.4	74.1	69.4
Liechtenstein										
Luxembourg										
Malta										
Monaco										
Netherlands	84.9	100.0	101.8	98.6	98.2	101.0	100.2	96.3	95.2	93.5
Norway	154.0	100.0	80.3	77.6	79.7	76.7	71.9	71.1	68.9	66.6
Portugal	90.1	100.0	90.2	90.0	92.3	94.1	93.9	92.9	93.9	94.2
Spain	80.2	100.0	101.8	100.2	97.2	94.3	92.7	92.5	90.3	89.2
Sweden	90.6	100.0	90.9	90.0	89.8	89.2	84.8	80.9	78.4	75.3
Switzerland	82.3	100.0	62.7	59.9	59.2	58.6	57.4	53.3	51.6	49.5
Turkey	5.5	100.0	1,967.9	3,283.8	4,590.8	5,728.7	6,219.7	6,122.3	6,745.2	7,037.0
United Kingdom	102.8	100.0	88.5	81.9	82.9	84.4	85.9	84.0	84.6	84.6
Eastern Europe										
Albania										
Belarus		100.0	6,917.2	15,605.2	31,137.2	45,195.4	60,493.3	71,955.8	76,906.8	86,115.5
Bosnia-Herzegovina										
Bulgaria	2.2	100.0	3,040.0	3,381.0	3,792.7	3,775.2	4,004.6	4,067.8	4,304.6	4,458.2
Croatia		100.0	183.2	215.4	260.2	258.9	258.1	257.6	256.2	255.3
Czech Republic	38.7	100.0	38.8	40.7	42.1	40.9	45.3	46.3	48.2	50.4
Estonia		100.0	199.4	196.7	199.0	205.8	204.5	199.9	210.4	211.7
Georgia										
Hungary	33.0	100.0	248.5	256.6	261.9	263.0	261.6	257.9	262.0	261.8
Latvia		100.0	209.6	201.8	194.3	182.0	177.5	176.4	188.8	190.7
Lithuania		100.0	315.0	346.5	370.2	365.7	331.4	313.9	355.5	352.3
Macedonia										
Moldova										
Poland	12.1	100.0	219.2	247.9	261.8	262.9	264.7	266.2	267.5	268.6
Romania	0.9	100.0	3,570.8	4,668.0	5,311.2	6,080.9	6,833.7	6,497.1	6,869.3	7,100.4
Russia		100.0	782.4	981.5	1,255.6	2,079.0	2,889.8	3,998.2	5,272.6	6,198.7
Serbia and Montenegro										
Slovakia		100.0	179.3	214.9	239.3	249.9	254.3	255.8	261.2	264.4
Slovenia		100.0	151.4	167.4	192.7	195.1	194.7	194.3	193.7	193.3
Ukraine		100.0	380.2	485.3	407.2	519.1	745.7	913.5	936.5	1,057.8

Source: *National statistical offices/OECD/Eurostat/Euromonitor International*

Index of Consumer Prices

Table 8.13

Index of Leisure and Recreation Prices 1990-2007

1995 = 100

	1990	1995	2000	2001	2002	2003	2004	2005	2006	2007
Western Europe										
Austria	86.8	100.0	98.9	100.4	103.4	103.7	103.9	104.3	104.0	104.1
Belgium	89.9	100.0	106.2	110.1	113.4	114.1	113.6	115.3	115.5	115.9
Cyprus										
Denmark	91.7	100.0	107.9	111.4	114.6	116.1	116.0	115.1	115.5	115.3
Finland	91.1	100.0	101.5	104.3	105.4	107.6	108.1	107.1	108.6	109.8
France	93.1	100.0	95.7	95.0	95.1	94.3	93.2	91.3	90.4	89.3
Germany	91.2	100.0	100.6	101.2	101.7	99.9	98.7	98.7	97.2	96.4
Gibraltar										
Greece	64.0	100.0	122.6	126.7	129.8	133.2	137.1	139.4	142.8	145.6
Iceland										
Ireland	97.0	100.0	110.7	113.9	119.1	121.9	121.1	119.7	119.9	119.3
Italy	81.6	100.0	105.9	107.8	110.2	111.8	112.3	111.6	111.3	111.0
Liechtenstein										
Luxembourg										
Malta										
Monaco										
Netherlands	93.5	100.0	102.4	106.2	109.6	110.4	109.1	108.3	107.3	106.5
Norway	91.4	100.0	103.7	105.3	106.0	105.2	104.7	105.3	105.8	105.9
Portugal	84.5	100.0	103.8	108.8	113.8	118.9	122.3	123.3	127.6	130.7
Spain	73.4	100.0	114.9	117.0	119.8	120.1	119.4	120.8	120.3	120.3
Sweden	86.7	100.0	95.8	97.5	97.9	97.5	95.0	92.2	90.8	88.9
Switzerland	88.0	100.0	95.9	95.4	94.7	94.0	92.4	90.5	89.3	87.7
Turkey	5.5	100.0	1,352.7	1,968.1	2,711.4	3,202.0	3,747.7	3,816.8	4,205.2	4,494.1
United Kingdom	93.1	100.0	97.8	95.5	96.1	95.1	94.4	92.3	91.3	90.2
Eastern Europe										
Albania										
Belarus		100.0	3,891.9	11,645.7	13,131.6	24,017.5	38,580.9	41,148.7	43,980.0	49,776.1
Bosnia-Herzegovina										
Bulgaria	2.2	100.0	4,003.9	4,195.5	4,379.8	4,455.5	4,604.3	4,549.3	4,814.1	4,918.1
Croatia		100.0	110.3	119.9	122.8	125.5	129.8	133.4	136.8	140.1
Czech Republic	38.7	100.0	166.5	173.9	177.5	177.0	178.6	181.3	184.1	186.2
Estonia		100.0	159.4	165.0	169.4	170.6	170.7	171.0	176.1	177.7
Georgia										
Hungary	33.0	100.0	200.9	212.5	222.3	227.6	237.2	238.6	244.3	249.3
Latvia		100.0	123.3	126.4	127.5	134.6	139.5	146.8	154.0	159.5
Lithuania		100.0	130.3	132.6	131.1	121.2	120.0	120.5	123.1	123.6
Macedonia										
Moldova										
Poland	15.8	100.0	203.4	216.3	218.9	217.7	217.2	216.4	215.5	214.7
Romania	0.9	100.0	1,157.8	1,410.7	1,712.4	1,763.7	1,970.1	2,048.7	2,166.1	2,283.5
Russia		100.0	334.8	461.0	502.7	731.0	1,022.4	1,181.8	1,340.5	1,517.2
Serbia and Montenegro										
Slovakia		100.0	131.8	135.1	135.4	142.2	151.9	157.3	161.9	167.5
Slovenia		100.0	144.3	153.1	165.4	174.1	180.1	182.2	187.1	190.8
Ukraine		100.0	339.8	393.6	434.8	571.6	696.1	859.3	901.3	997.2

Source: National statistical offices/OECD/Eurostat/Euromonitor International

Index of Consumer Prices

Table 8.14

Index of Education Prices 1990-2007
1995 = 100

	1990	1995	2000	2001	2002	2003	2004	2005	2006	2007
Western Europe										
Austria	73.5	100.0	115.9	133.4	160.3	165.4	168.7	172.6	175.9	178.9
Belgium	85.6	100.0	111.3	113.9	117.8	119.4	120.0	122.7	123.9	125.2
Cyprus										
Denmark	91.7	100.0	114.5	117.1	123.0	150.0	154.3	158.1	171.6	177.9
Finland	90.2	100.0	109.7	113.3	116.4	124.9	131.0	136.7	145.4	152.8
France	82.6	100.0	106.8	108.7	111.3	114.8	121.5	127.1	128.2	132.1
Germany	63.2	100.0	122.0	124.3	128.7	130.5	133.2	136.9	141.4	144.6
Gibraltar										
Greece	36.1	100.0	136.5	141.4	146.5	153.3	160.1	166.9	174.4	180.5
Iceland										
Ireland	93.8	100.0	129.1	143.7	148.2	159.7	171.8	183.9	197.6	208.6
Italy	78.3	100.0	111.6	113.2	115.8	120.0	122.9	125.5	128.1	130.2
Liechtenstein										
Luxembourg										
Malta										
Monaco										
Netherlands	79.2	100.0	115.0	117.4	121.8	126.5	129.9	125.0	125.5	125.2
Norway	86.9	100.0	121.8	130.6	138.3	145.9	151.8	154.7	161.6	166.0
Portugal	79.0	100.0	119.2	128.0	137.8	151.5	167.0	177.2	194.2	207.4
Spain	66.7	100.0	124.2	128.3	133.1	139.1	143.7	151.8	157.6	162.9
Sweden	88.0	100.0	123.0	123.4	75.9	67.1	72.7	73.9	60.2	58.2
Switzerland	77.4	100.0	107.4	107.9	108.7	110.0	110.2	109.8	110.4	110.3
Turkey	5.5	100.0	2,175.6	2,985.4	4,685.1	6,444.2	7,961.9	8,646.7	9,526.4	10,415.6
United Kingdom	72.6	100.0	130.5	137.6	145.3	157.7	167.2	176.1	188.2	197.1
Eastern Europe										
Albania										
Belarus		100.0	9,588.5	25,353.9	58,170.2	78,275.9	94,478.5	106,737.9	114,082.1	124,485.3
Bosnia-Herzegovina										
Bulgaria	1.7	100.0	6,332.9	7,732.2	8,362.0	8,843.8	9,406.5	9,652.6	10,214.4	10,611.9
Croatia		100.0	133.5	141.0	142.0	141.9	136.8	142.2	142.1	142.1
Czech Republic	38.7	100.0	169.0	173.9	180.3	186.5	193.1	199.0	207.4	213.5
Estonia		100.0	244.7	261.6	274.3	286.0	305.8	329.1	362.9	385.2
Georgia										
Hungary	28.7	100.0	229.5	242.6	265.6	298.1	333.8	356.2	397.8	426.9
Latvia		100.0	209.1	218.6	220.2	245.2	261.3	267.2	287.4	299.6
Lithuania		100.0	203.9	221.0	224.8	209.3	212.6	210.1	229.2	234.8
Macedonia										
Moldova										
Poland	14.8	100.0	194.0	211.9	219.2	222.4	227.5	231.8	234.3	237.5
Romania	1.7	100.0	3,796.3	5,151.7	6,354.5	7,170.4	8,171.3	8,410.2	8,891.9	9,394.3
Russia		100.0	616.1	799.3	1,030.5	1,269.5	1,669.5	1,891.8	2,250.3	2,534.8
Serbia and Montenegro										
Slovakia		100.0	122.3	127.3	129.9	140.0	158.1	209.2	245.7	276.2
Slovenia		100.0	157.4	172.4	189.8	198.5	214.1	226.3	238.5	250.1
Ukraine		100.0	443.6	546.9	644.9	675.8	971.9	1,223.4	1,216.3	1,373.4

Source: National statistical offices/OECD/Eurostat/Euromonitor International

Table 8.15

Index of Hotel and Catering Prices 1990-2007

1995 = 100

	1990	1995	2000	2001	2002	2003	2004	2005	2006	2007
Western Europe										
Austria	82.2	100.0	109.7	113.2	117.0	120.0	123.3	126.8	129.5	132.3
Belgium	86.0	100.0	110.8	113.6	119.2	123.2	125.8	130.8	134.3	137.6
Cyprus										
Denmark	93.5	100.0	114.7	118.2	122.2	125.2	127.8	130.3	133.4	135.7
Finland	89.4	100.0	109.4	111.9	114.3	118.8	118.9	121.3	124.8	127.7
France	82.7	100.0	111.2	113.8	119.3	122.5	126.0	128.7	132.9	136.0
Germany	81.4	100.0	109.3	111.4	115.8	116.2	117.0	118.9	119.6	120.6
Gibraltar										
Greece	46.4	100.0	142.8	150.0	159.5	167.4	174.6	180.3	188.0	193.9
Iceland										
Ireland	87.2	100.0	124.9	131.8	141.1	150.0	155.4	160.2	167.1	172.0
Italy	75.8	100.0	116.3	120.1	124.8	130.2	133.3	134.7	137.4	139.2
Liechtenstein										
Luxembourg										
Malta										
Monaco										
Netherlands	85.2	100.0	114.8	120.7	128.3	130.6	132.9	135.1	136.8	138.6
Norway	87.2	100.0	117.8	123.4	127.8	131.1	133.3	135.9	139.6	142.0
Portugal	76.9	100.0	116.4	124.1	133.2	144.4	152.8	153.6	162.4	168.2
Spain	70.0	100.0	122.2	126.5	133.4	138.7	143.3	151.4	156.9	162.1
Sweden	81.9	100.0	106.0	109.7	114.3	117.5	118.8	120.9	123.6	125.4
Switzerland	76.5	100.0	100.3	102.0	104.2	104.7	104.4	104.0	104.2	103.8
Turkey	5.5	100.0	1,769.6	2,405.1	3,341.2	4,504.2	5,527.0	6,041.2	6,655.8	7,276.6
United Kingdom	81.5	100.0	121.7	126.1	131.3	135.7	140.4	145.9	151.5	156.1
Eastern Europe										
Albania										
Belarus		100.0	2,778.1	3,720.7	5,576.8	6,711.3	8,652.6	10,991.5	11,747.8	13,210.2
Bosnia-Herzegovina										
Bulgaria	2.2	100.0	4,279.5	4,478.8	4,745.5	4,913.5	5,191.8	5,251.2	5,556.8	5,743.4
Croatia		100.0	115.3	121.4	124.8	129.6	134.4	137.4	141.6	145.1
Czech Republic	38.7	100.0	141.8	146.5	151.8	155.3	163.1	169.4	177.1	183.5
Estonia		100.0	167.2	174.5	184.9	191.6	199.6	209.0	220.4	228.7
Georgia										
Hungary	33.0	100.0	218.5	243.6	266.8	287.1	315.0	328.1	338.2	353.2
Latvia		100.0	132.9	136.0	137.4	141.9	149.5	161.7	169.8	177.8
Lithuania		100.0	139.1	150.5	151.6	151.1	155.6	158.0	166.8	171.2
Macedonia										
Moldova										
Poland	18.5	100.0	164.5	161.6	161.2	162.6	165.0	166.9	168.0	169.4
Romania	0.9	100.0	1,961.1	2,722.0	3,512.0	4,131.9	4,797.7	5,264.7	5,566.2	5,984.2
Russia		100.0	221.6	284.7	328.8	388.2	441.7	458.3	532.5	574.3
Serbia and Montenegro										
Slovakia		100.0	129.8	140.8	145.1	158.8	177.5	190.1	199.4	211.1
Slovenia		100.0	138.5	148.4	161.9	176.0	186.6	195.1	206.4	215.2
Ukraine		100.0	355.6	393.4	423.7	541.2	697.9	861.6	890.7	992.2

Source: National statistical offices/OECD/Eurostat/Euromonitor International

Index of Consumer Prices

Table 8.16

Index of Miscellaneous Goods and Services Prices 1990-2007

1995 = 100

	1990	1995	2000	2001	2002	2003	2004	2005	2006	2007
Western Europe										
Austria	84.0	100.0	111.7	112.1	114.2	113.3	117.4	117.1	117.4	118.5
Belgium	104.2	100.0	100.5	101.7	98.8	98.0	103.1	104.1	105.5	107.7
Cyprus										
Denmark	85.8	100.0	105.2	108.6	108.5	111.5	114.5	117.8	121.3	124.1
Finland	94.5	100.0	118.8	123.0	126.8	108.0	114.9	114.7	111.9	114.0
France	101.1	100.0	101.2	105.2	103.1	104.3	106.6	109.4	111.3	113.4
Germany	86.0	100.0	93.2	96.4	96.4	103.8	106.8	107.9	111.6	113.9
Gibraltar										
Greece	38.0	100.0	135.5	139.9	143.6	147.1	150.0	154.9	158.9	162.4
Iceland										
Ireland	95.2	100.0	123.5	131.2	139.0	144.8	150.6	152.8	157.7	161.4
Italy	79.4	100.0	111.2	113.7	116.1	120.8	121.7	124.8	127.1	128.7
Liechtenstein										
Luxembourg										
Malta										
Monaco										
Netherlands	83.3	100.0	110.3	114.2	118.8	122.9	125.9	128.6	131.5	134.0
Norway	83.8	100.0	97.3	101.2	98.2	101.8	100.1	98.6	99.4	98.7
Portugal	73.6	100.0	120.8	130.0	139.3	149.5	154.6	156.5	164.0	168.9
Spain	67.5	100.0	121.7	124.1	128.4	132.0	134.6	140.3	143.6	146.9
Sweden	75.8	100.0	105.0	104.0	103.4	105.1	109.5	110.6	113.6	116.1
Switzerland	85.8	100.0	98.4	99.8	101.8	102.5	102.3	101.7	101.8	101.5
Turkey	5.5	100.0	1,670.6	2,630.4	3,945.0	4,926.4	5,482.0	5,648.4	6,223.1	6,596.3
United Kingdom	84.8	100.0	122.6	125.4	126.6	128.2	133.3	139.6	144.6	149.4
Eastern Europe										
Albania										
Belarus		100.0	4,647.0	11,327.7	15,823.9	25,047.4	22,313.1	7,598.7	8,121.6	3,216.2
Bosnia-Herzegovina										
Bulgaria	2.2	100.0	3,547.4	3,620.5	3,798.5	3,875.1	3,999.4	3,971.6	4,202.7	4,297.8
Croatia		100.0	142.3	143.5	145.4	146.7	149.6	152.6	154.8	157.1
Czech Republic	38.7	100.0	118.3	124.0	128.9	132.9	138.8	141.2	146.8	150.8
Estonia		100.0	160.7	167.0	176.6	174.3	178.4	183.3	191.1	195.9
Georgia										
Hungary	33.0	100.0	212.0	223.9	235.2	243.2	255.3	258.7	264.2	270.4
Latvia		100.0	171.4	165.0	164.2	168.3	182.7	193.0	202.7	212.6
Lithuania		100.0	147.6	158.9	165.6	154.5	150.0	150.9	157.2	157.8
Macedonia										
Moldova										
Poland	15.7	100.0	165.2	168.3	170.7	172.3	175.0	177.2	178.5	180.1
Romania	0.9	100.0	1,161.9	1,459.8	1,793.3	2,055.7	2,287.3	2,363.7	2,499.1	2,628.6
Russia		100.0	304.7	737.9	858.6	1,121.0	1,373.4	1,402.2	1,547.9	1,671.7
Serbia and Montenegro										
Slovakia		100.0	131.5	136.9	146.0	161.0	170.7	178.8	183.5	189.9
Slovenia		100.0	147.9	160.0	173.2	185.1	193.2	197.4	205.0	210.8
Ukraine		100.0	207.3	226.2	239.1	242.8	248.0	252.8	245.5	246.4

Source: *National statistical offices/OECD/Eurostat/Euromonitor International*

Section Nine

Cultural Indicators

Cinema and Film

Table 9.1

Cinema Statistics 2007
As stated

	Seating Capacity of Fixed Cinemas ('000)	Number of Cinema Screens	Box Office Revenues (US$ million)	Annual cinema trips per capita
Western Europe				
Austria	106.5	584	194.1	2.1
Belgium	123.9	502	196.6	2.3
Cyprus	10.1	25	13.5	0.8
Denmark	59.4	387	211.8	2.3
Finland	56.9	333	76.1	1.2
France	1,059.1	5,434	1,961.3	3.2
Germany	824.8	4,841	1,359.7	1.6
Gibraltar				
Greece		528	109.5	1.1
Iceland	8.1	42	16.4	4.6
Ireland	72.5	440	183.6	4.2
Italy		3,588	1,068.9	1.8
Liechtenstein				1.2
Luxembourg	5.1	23	11.3	2.7
Malta	7.8	42	7.2	2.6
Monaco				
Netherlands	117.8	646	232.5	1.3
Norway	81.6	459	157.4	2.5
Portugal	78.1	464	91.9	1.5
Spain	1,551.3	4,277	1,190.9	2.6
Sweden	201.8	1,174	186.9	1.6
Switzerland	116.4	551	232.6	2.2
Turkey	301.0	1,393	131.9	0.5
United Kingdom	882.8	3,314	1,926.9	2.5
Eastern Europe				
Albania				
Belarus				
Bosnia-Herzegovina				0.0
Bulgaria	12.1	71	11.9	0.3
Croatia	46.7	116	8.1	0.5
Czech Republic	106.8	614	72.7	1.1
Estonia	5.5	63	5.8	1.3
Georgia				
Hungary	82.9	415	85.5	1.1
Latvia	10.0	38	9.5	1.1
Lithuania	18.3	62	7.5	0.5
Macedonia	5.6	19		0.0
Moldova				
Poland	221.2	1,000	226.3	1.0
Romania	55.6	73	14.1	0.1
Russia	245.0	2,729	429.5	0.7
Serbia and Montenegro				
Slovakia	106.3	264	11.6	0.7
Slovenia	30.4	122	16.5	1.3
Ukraine		3,000		0.4

Source: *Euromonitor International from EAO/national statistics*

Table 9.2

Cinema Attendances 1990-2007

Million

	1990	1995	2000	2001	2002	2003	2004	2005	2006	2007
Western Europe										
Austria	10.2	11.5	16.3	18.8	19.3	17.7	19.4	15.7	17.3	17.3
Belgium	17.1	19.2	23.5	24.0	24.4	22.7	24.1	22.1	23.8	24.2
Cyprus	-		0.9	0.9	1.0	1.0	1.0	0.8	0.7	0.7
Denmark	9.6	8.8	10.7	12.0	12.9	12.3	12.8	12.2	12.6	12.7
Finland	6.2	5.3	7.1	6.5	7.7	7.7	6.9	6.1	6.7	6.4
France	121.8	130.2	165.8	187.4	184.4	173.5	195.4	175.4	188.7	194.9
Germany	91.0	123.9	152.5	177.9	163.9	149.0	156.7	127.3	136.7	133.9
Gibraltar										
Greece	13.0	8.2	13.5	14.3	15.0	15.0	12.0	12.7	12.1	11.9
Iceland			1.6	1.5	1.6	1.5	1.5	1.4	1.4	1.4
Ireland	7.5	9.8	14.9	15.9	17.3	17.4	17.3	16.4	17.9	18.0
Italy	90.7	90.7	104.2	113.3	115.6	110.5	116.3	105.6	107.3	106.5
Liechtenstein		0.0	0.0	0.0	0.0	0.0	0.0	0.0	0.0	0.0
Luxembourg	0.6	0.7	1.4	1.4	1.4	1.3	1.4	1.2	1.2	1.2
Malta			1.0	1.0	1.1	1.1	1.0	1.0	1.1	1.0
Monaco										
Netherlands	14.6	17.2	21.5	23.9	24.1	25.0	23.0	20.7	22.5	21.8
Norway	10.8	11.0	11.6	12.5	12.0	13.0	12.0	11.3	11.9	11.6
Portugal (a)	9.6	12.0	17.9	19.5	19.5	18.7	17.1	15.8	16.4	15.7
Spain	78.5	96.7	135.4	146.8	140.7	137.5	143.9	127.7	121.7	117.1
Sweden	15.7	15.2	17.0	18.1	18.3	18.2	16.6	14.6	15.3	14.5
Switzerland	13.6	14.9	15.6	17.1	18.8	16.5	17.2	14.9	16.4	16.4
Turkey	9.4	12.6	25.3	28.2	23.5	24.6	29.7	27.3	34.9	39.5
United Kingdom	97.4	114.9	142.5	155.9	175.9	167.3	171.3	164.7	156.6	153.2
Eastern Europe										
Albania	3.3									
Belarus	115.7	12.4	2.0	1.7	1.3	1.0	0.8	0.6	0.5	0.4
Bosnia-Herzegovina										
Bulgaria	48.2	5.1	2.2	2.0	2.0	3.0	3.1	2.4	2.4	2.2
Croatia	8.7	3.7	2.7	2.9	2.8	2.3	3.0	2.2	2.1	2.0
Czech Republic		9.3	8.7	10.4	10.7	12.1	12.0	9.5	11.5	11.5
Estonia	1.1	1.0	1.1	1.3	1.6	1.3	1.2	1.1	1.6	1.7
Georgia										
Hungary	14.1	14.0	14.3	15.7	15.3	13.7	13.7	12.1	11.7	11.3
Latvia	0.4	1.0	1.5	1.2	1.1	1.1	1.7	1.7	2.1	2.5
Lithuania		0.7	2.1	2.4	1.9	1.4	1.5	1.2	1.7	1.8
Macedonia			0.6	0.4	0.4	0.3	0.3	0.1	0.1	0.1
Moldova										
Poland	16.0	22.0	18.7	26.2	25.9	23.8	33.4	23.6	32.0	37.0
Romania	32.7	17.0	5.1	5.7	5.3	4.5	4.0	2.8	2.8	2.4
Russia	10.3	13.3	42.8	60.0	65.0	68.0	76.5	84.6	89.8	98.5
Serbia and Montenegro										
Slovakia	8.3	5.6	2.6	2.8	3.2	3.0	2.9	2.2	3.4	3.7
Slovenia	4.0	2.9	2.2	2.5	2.8	3.0	3.0	2.4	2.7	2.6
Ukraine	54.9	30.9	4.9	4.9	4.8	4.8	4.7	4.7	4.6	4.5

Source: *Euromonitor International from European Audiovisual Observatory/national statistics*
Notes: *(a) 2004 data is provided through the computerised ticketing system introduced by ICAM in 2004 and is not comparable with 2003 data provided by INE; The corresponding 2004 figure for the INE series is 18,798 million admissions*

Cinema and Film

Table 9.3

Feature Films Released/Produced by Country of Origin 2007
Number

	Feature Films Produced	Of which co-prod- uctions	Total Releases	National Releases
Western Europe				
Austria	31	4	326	29
Belgium	63	11	789	21
Cyprus	4	6	245	1
Denmark	38	14	293	26
Finland	15	8	206	21
France	220	92	598	269
Germany	140	38	477	136
Gibraltar				
Greece	19	3	287	40
Iceland	9	6	164	8
Ireland	14	2	23	23
Italy	160	12	380	111
Liechtenstein				
Luxembourg	18	8	402	
Malta	1			1
Monaco				
Netherlands	25	17	344	27
Norway	23	7	259	22
Portugal	15	4	381	30
Spain	164	19	569	164
Sweden	55	9	292	45
Switzerland	346	25	519	53
Turkey	21	4	255	24
United Kingdom	69	45	515	85
Eastern Europe				
Albania				
Belarus				
Bosnia-Herzegovina				
Bulgaria	9	1	126	2
Croatia	1		579	75
Czech Republic	26	4	216	29
Estonia	4	1	192	15
Georgia				
Hungary	34	4	274	34
Latvia	7	1	230	16
Lithuania	2		149	4
Macedonia	6	1	392	6
Moldova				
Poland	20		248	16
Romania	23	1	210	12
Russia	108	7	431	60
Serbia and Montenegro				
Slovakia	2	9	175	7
Slovenia	7	5	247	7
Ukraine				

Source: *Euromonitor International from EAO/national statistics*

Table 9.4

Cinema and Film

Feature Films Shown by Country of Origin 2007

% long films released

	Imported from USA	Imported from other countries	Produced Nationally
Western Europe			
Austria	41.7	48.2	8.9
Belgium	33.7	61.5	2.7
Cyprus	80.4	11.8	0.4
Denmark	57.3	31.1	8.9
Finland	63.1	25.7	10.2
France	29.4	27.9	45.0
Germany	44.2	28.5	28.5
Gibraltar			
Greece	60.6	24.4	13.9
Iceland	67.1	27.4	4.9
Ireland			100.0
Italy	36.1	36.3	29.2
Liechtenstein			
Luxembourg	43.3	46.0	0.2
Malta			
Monaco			
Netherlands	48.8	43.6	7.8
Norway	53.7	37.5	8.5
Portugal	56.4	37.8	7.9
Spain	38.8	29.3	28.8
Sweden	51.4	31.5	15.4
Switzerland	21.4	61.3	10.2
Turkey	52.2	35.4	9.4
United Kingdom	34.0	48.7	16.5
Eastern Europe			
Albania			
Belarus			
Bosnia-Herzegovina			
Bulgaria	69.8	33.3	1.6
Croatia	89.5	21.8	13.0
Czech Republic	53.2	31.9	13.4
Estonia	56.2	34.4	7.8
Georgia			
Hungary	44.5	41.6	12.4
Latvia	60.0	27.8	7.0
Lithuania	73.8	22.8	2.7
Macedonia	95.7	2.3	1.5
Moldova			
Poland	61.7	34.3	6.5
Romania	62.9	29.5	5.7
Russia	44.1	34.6	13.9
Serbia and Montenegro			
Slovakia	50.9	46.9	4.0
Slovenia	51.8	44.1	2.8
Ukraine			

Source: Euromonitor International from EAO/national statistics

Video and DVD

Table 9.5

Video and DVD Rental Statistics 2007

Number / as stated

	DVD rental transactions (million)	Video rental transactions (million)	DVD rental turnover (US$ million)	Video rental turnover (US$ million)	New DVD rental releases	New video rental releases	Video and DVD rental outlets
Western Europe							
Austria	6.6	0.2	24.65	0.97	450	412	350
Belgium	30.1	0.3	141.21	1.52	1,000	392	700
Denmark	19.9	0.2	127.79	2.46	742	203	1,548
Finland	7.2	2.0	37.66	7.72	895	451	800
France	68.3	0.6	274.66	3.89	271	438	2,000
Germany	153.1	3.2	538.06	15.30	450	417	4,137
Greece	8.9	1.0	18.29	2.97	750	600	530
Ireland	18.5	4.2	101.74	25.89	606	374	1,000
Italy	108.3	8.6	529.43	35.41	410	276	2,721
Netherlands	31.4	2.5	144.67	8.14	1,000	290	1,000
Norway	20.8	0.4	168.50	2.48	912	239	1,657
Portugal	15.1	0.1	43.32	0.16	1,006	124	600
Spain	149.0	11.6	452.44	41.32	537	402	6,120
Sweden	35.8	5.0	216.62	40.69	891	242	805
Switzerland	3.1	0.1	24.32	0.72	450	412	300
Turkey							
United Kingdom	145.0	14.1	785.17	103.34	630	378	3,296
Eastern Europe							
Belarus							
Bulgaria							
Croatia	5.8	0.7	13.46	1.78	699	420	800
Czech Republic	12.9	3.3	26.23	3.94	575	398	810
Estonia							
Hungary	3.5	7.2	14.14	18.90	540	580	957
Latvia							
Lithuania							
Poland	7.4	6.1	14.03	11.86	659	284	1,200
Romania							
Russia	5.5	14.0	11.06				3,000
Slovakia							
Slovenia							
Ukraine							

Source: *Euromonitor International from EAO/national statistics*

Table 9.6

Video and DVD Releases and Sales Outlet Statistics 2007

Number / as stated

	New DVD sales releases	New video sales releases	Video and DVD sales outlets
Western Europe			
Austria	3,000	457	756
Belgium	3,709	206	2,613
Denmark	794	196	2,100
Finland	979	209	1,110
France	7,699	483	5,200
Germany	3,000	356	10,000
Greece	750	150	150
Ireland	10,276	852	1,650
Italy	1,900	986	1,723
Netherlands	5,000	857	3,000
Norway	1,010	200	5,500
Portugal	2,259	202	500
Spain	4,508	275	7,092
Sweden	979	196	5,000
Switzerland	3,000	462	822
Turkey			
United Kingdom	10,758	902	20,000
Eastern Europe			
Belarus			
Bulgaria			
Croatia	1,291		1,125
Czech Republic	900	394	779
Estonia			
Hungary	1,115	122	577
Latvia			
Lithuania			
Poland	820	398	850
Romania			
Russia	2,898	2,618	
Slovakia			
Slovenia			
Ukraine			

Source: *Euromonitor International from EAO/national statistics*

Museums

Table 9.7

Number of Museums by Type, Museum Visitors
As stated

	Year	General	Specialised	Regional	Art
Western Europe					
Austria	2007	34	128	166	63
Belgium	1993	3	5	13	15
Cyprus	1993		4	3	
Denmark	2005	4	5	127	52
Finland	2007		86		65
France	2000				
Germany	2007	233	714	2,291	497
Gibraltar					
Greece	1993	2	16	3	60
Iceland	1995		1	21	14
Ireland					
Italy	1992	38	301	271	
Liechtenstein					
Luxembourg					
Malta	2007	7	21		11
Monaco	1993	1	1	1	
Netherlands	2007	10	234		98
Norway	1997	36			37
Portugal	1995	70	15	53	79
Spain	2007	233	121	39	328
Sweden	1993	16	105	83	27
Switzerland	1996			368	141
Turkey	2007	65			
United Kingdom					
Eastern Europe					
Albania					
Belarus	2007	30			18
Bosnia-Herzegovina					
Bulgaria	1993	47	125		50
Croatia	2007	65	6	21	9
Czech Republic	1993	3			37
Estonia	2007		63	81	15
Georgia	2007		46		12
Hungary	2007	25	285	122	124
Latvia	1993	22	4	9	8
Lithuania	1993	4	4	29	3
Macedonia	1994	16	5		
Moldova	1993		19	10	4
Poland	2007		186	206	81
Romania	2007	67			139
Russia	2007	165	135		297
Serbia and Montenegro	1994	66	93		
Slovakia	1993	2	18	40	
Slovenia	1996				
Ukraine	1993	1	60	101	48

Source: Euromonitor International from UNESCO/national statistics

Number of Museums by Type, Museum Visitors *(continued)*

As stated

	Year	Archae-ology and History	Natural History and Science	Ethno-graphy and Anthro-pology	Total	Visitors (millions)
Western Europe						
Austria	2007	67	32	29	519	11.8
Belgium	1993	19	3	7	65	2.4
Cyprus	1993	9	1	7	24	0.5
Denmark	2005	186	10		257	9.9
Finland	2007	160	18		329	4.2
France	2000				1,300	14.0
Germany	2007	336	823		4,894	103.6
Gibraltar						
Greece	1993	102	19	50	252	2.4
Iceland	1995	54	12		80	0.6
Ireland						
Italy	1992					
Liechtenstein						
Luxembourg						
Malta	2007	11	3	3	56	1.6
Monaco	1993		1	2	6	1.0
Netherlands	2007	414	50	15	821	19.4
Norway	1997	487	15		539	9.0
Portugal	1995	82	27	19	284	5.0
Spain	2007	236	88	207	1,252	50.0
Sweden	1993	8	6	49	231	16.7
Switzerland	1996	75	139	15	862	
Turkey	2007	54		36	155	8.6
United Kingdom						
Eastern Europe						
Albania						
Belarus	2007	34	3	80	165	3.4
Bosnia-Herzegovina						
Bulgaria	1993	49	5	7	221	3.4
Croatia	2007	20	7	7	135	1.3
Czech Republic	1993				181	8.0
Estonia	2007	39	4	7	209	1.8
Georgia	2007	15		37	110	0.3
Hungary	2007	74	127	61	818	11.0
Latvia	1993	51	1	2	97	1.2
Lithuania	1993	14	3	1	58	1.2
Macedonia	1994				21	0.2
Moldova	1993	45		10	78	0.7
Poland	2007	134	41	49	697	18.7
Romania	2007	104	179	76	565	10.6
Russia	2007	487	48	924	2,056	75.0
Serbia and Montenegro	1994				159	1.9
Slovakia	1993				60	2.7
Slovenia	1996		2		85	2.1
Ukraine	1993	72	3	10	295	18.0

Source: *Euromonitor International from UNESCO/national statistics*

Press Trends

Table 9.8

Newspapers 2007
Number / as stated

	Total Number	Dailies	Non-Dailies	Total Circulation ('000)	Daily Circulation ('000)	Non-daily Circulation ('000)
Western Europe						
Austria	268	23	245		3,211	
Belgium	42	29	13		1,628	
Cyprus	33	22	11	150	103	47
Denmark	302	44	258	13,280	3,773	9,507
Finland	338	55	283	3,335	2,416	919
France	128	93	35	14,275	9,998	4,277
Germany	1,769	375	1,394	109,966	20,903	89,063
Gibraltar		1			6	
Greece	60	43	17	1,880	1,510	370
Iceland	27	3	24	327	248	79
Ireland	179	13	166	2,166	1,016	1,150
Italy	531	104	427	12,002	11,466	536
Liechtenstein	2	2		21	21	
Luxembourg	20	6	14	327	114	213
Malta	9	4	5		104	
Monaco			2			
Netherlands	540	32	508	21,039	4,723	16,316
Norway	264	77	187	2,929	2,222	707
Portugal	59	19	40	5,484	1,032	4,452
Spain	376	187	189	16,495	9,917	6,579
Sweden	228	91	137	7,209	4,838	2,371
Switzerland	543	99	444	4,056	3,580	476
Turkey	4,652	83	4,569		5,332	
United Kingdom	1,331	118	1,213	47,638	18,872	28,767
Eastern Europe						
Albania	112	30	82	62		
Belarus	695	17	678	15,760	1,379	14,381
Bosnia-Herzegovina		7			100	
Bulgaria	223	62	161	1,881	429	1,452
Croatia	224	17	207	3,534	893	2,641
Czech Republic	304	96	208	6,687	3,174	3,513
Estonia	149	17	132	630	379	251
Georgia	76	10	66		24	
Hungary	303	30	273		1,752	
Latvia	119	22	97	1,652	407	1,245
Lithuania	309	22	287	2,069		
Macedonia	25	14	11	230	213	17
Moldova	130	7	123	1,065	105	960
Poland	71	48	23	6,676	6,109	567
Romania		72			1,681	
Russia	27,746	573	27,173	8,932,710		
Serbia and Montenegro	625	11	614			
Slovakia	12	11	1	465	459	6
Slovenia	253	8	245		489	
Ukraine						

Source: *Euromonitor International from World Association of Newspapers*

Economic Indicators

GDP

Table 10.1

Total Gross Domestic Product 1980-2007 (national currencies)

Billion units of national currency

	1980	1985	1990	1995	1996	1997	1998	1999	2000
Western Europe									
Austria	75.32	101.48	136.33	175.53	181.87	185.14	192.38	200.03	210.39
Belgium	87.99	121.93	163.41	202.29	211.47	221.07	229.66	237.97	252.00
Cyprus	1.46	3.03	4.16	6.77	7.05	7.51	8.15	9.17	10.08
Denmark	385.81	634.02	840.65	1,019.54	1,069.49	1,125.64	1,163.62	1,213.47	1,293.96
Finland	33.32	57.50	89.75	95.92	99.26	107.63	117.11	122.75	132.27
France	444.67	744.45	1,033.69	1,195.48	1,227.72	1,267.26	1,324.14	1,367.23	1,442.79
Germany	766.60	955.30	1,274.90	1,848.45	1,876.18	1,915.58	1,965.38	2,012.00	2,062.50
Gibraltar				0.37	0.39	0.36	0.38	0.41	0.43
Greece	6.69	18.24	42.85	87.57	96.25	106.53	115.89	123.46	136.28
Iceland	16.14	122.42	365.05	445.11	477.69	526.32	586.80	630.73	683.75
Ireland	13.10	25.00	36.56	53.09	58.71	67.97	78.57	90.50	104.85
Italy	203.38	429.65	701.35	947.34	1,003.78	1,048.77	1,091.36	1,127.09	1,191.06
Liechtenstein	0.90	1.30	1.98	2.87	3.10	3.34	3.60	4.00	4.20
Luxembourg	4.33	6.68	10.50	15.11	15.80	16.42	17.41	19.89	22.00
Malta	0.77	1.27	1.73	2.63	2.77	3.07	3.25	3.67	4.22
Monaco	0.21	0.37	0.54	0.63	0.65	0.67	0.70	0.72	0.76
Netherlands	160.72	199.07	243.56	305.26	319.76	342.24	362.46	386.19	417.96
Norway	314.79	552.38	736.06	943.25	1,032.34	1,118.93	1,140.65	1,240.27	1,480.25
Portugal	7.78	22.10	53.89	85.14	90.51	97.90	106.50	114.19	122.27
Spain	97.39	179.40	319.14	447.20	473.86	503.92	539.49	579.94	630.26
Sweden	548.58	899.75	1,421.42	1,809.76	1,852.09	1,927.00	2,012.09	2,123.97	2,249.99
Switzerland	184.08	244.42	330.93	373.60	376.67	383.99	395.26	402.91	422.06
Turkey	0.01	0.04	0.39	7.76	14.77	28.84	70.20	104.60	166.66
United Kingdom	230.80	355.27	558.16	723.08	768.90	815.88	865.71	911.95	958.93
Eastern Europe									
Albania	15.53	16.86	16.81	229.79	346.40	346.20	409.21	471.58	523.04
Belarus			0.00	121.40	191.84	366.83	702.16	3,026.06	9,133.80
Bosnia-Herzegovina				4.19	6.37	7.24	8.99	10.71
Bulgaria	0.03	0.03	0.05	0.88	1.76	17.43	22.42	23.79	26.75
Croatia	0.04	0.28	0.28	98.38	107.98	123.81	137.60	141.58	152.52
Czech Republic	415.30	473.70	626.19	1,466.52	1,683.29	1,811.09	1,996.48	2,080.80	2,189.17
Estonia				43.18	56.73	69.89	78.43	83.47	95.49
Georgia				3.69	3.87	4.55	5.02	5.67	6.02
Hungary	721.00	1,033.70	2,089.30	5,614.04	6,893.93	8,540.67	10,087.40	11,393.50	13,528.60
Latvia			0.06	2.62	3.13	3.63	3.97	4.26	4.75
Lithuania			0.14	25.96	32.74	40.00	44.70	43.67	45.67
Macedonia				169.52	176.44	186.02	194.98	209.01	236.39
Moldova			0.01	6.48	7.80	8.92	9.12	12.32	16.02
Poland	0.25	1.04	56.03	337.22	422.44	515.35	600.90	665.69	744.38
Romania	0.06	0.08	0.09	7.21	10.89	25.29	37.38	54.57	80.38
Russia			0.64	1,428.52	2,007.83	2,342.51	2,629.62	4,823.23	7,305.65
Serbia and Montenegro				47.14	82.95	108.68	146.30	192.87	381.66
Slovakia			297.51	581.45	647.19	717.67	787.34	845.60	937.96
Slovenia			5.46	15.70	16.34	17.46	18.76	20.24	21.29
Ukraine			0.00	54.52	81.52	93.36	102.59	130.44	170.07

Source: *Euromonitor International from International Monetary Fund (IMF), International Financial Statistics*

Total Gross Domestic Product 1980-2007 (national currencies) *(continued)*

Billion units of national currency

	2001	2002	2003	2004	2005	2006	2007	Total US$ billion 2007	US$ per capita 2007
Western Europe									
Austria	215.88	220.84	226.18	236.15	245.33	257.90	272.82	373.94	44,974.9
Belgium	258.92	267.44	274.57	289.13	301.96	317.12	331.44	454.28	42,976.7
Cyprus	10.80	11.15	11.75	12.69	13.62	14.63	15.56	21.33	24,954.4
Denmark	1,335.61	1,372.74	1,400.69	1,466.18	1,548.15	1,641.52	1,695.52	311.46	57,181.7
Finland	139.87	143.97	145.94	152.35	157.34	167.04	178.76	245.01	46,430.9
France	1,497.54	1,549.79	1,595.82	1,657.79	1,715.80	1,793.58	1,867.93	2,560.26	41,691.3
Germany	2,113.16	2,143.18	2,163.80	2,211.20	2,244.60	2,322.20	2,423.80	3,322.15	40,360.5
Gibraltar	0.45	0.47	0.51	0.56	0.57	0.57	0.58	0.95	32,260.4
Greece	146.26	157.59	171.26	185.22	198.61	213.99	229.54	314.61	28,168.4
Iceland	771.89	816.56	841.48	928.66	1,026.25	1,167.68	1,279.37	19.97	66,354.4
Ireland	116.99	130.19	139.44	148.97	162.17	177.29	190.60	261.25	60,773.2
Italy	1,248.65	1,295.23	1,335.35	1,391.53	1,428.38	1,479.98	1,535.54	2,104.67	35,740.5
Liechtenstein	4.21	4.19	4.13	4.30	4.55	4.78	4.99	4.16	118,276.6
Luxembourg	22.57	23.99	25.73	27.44	30.03	33.85	36.89	50.56	108,373.7
Malta	4.30	4.49	4.42	4.49	4.75	5.08	5.40	7.40	18,199.0
Monaco	0.79	0.81	0.83	0.86	0.89	0.93	0.96	1.31	40,141.6
Netherlands	447.73	465.21	476.94	491.18	508.96	534.32	560.84	768.70	46,992.6
Norway	1,539.33	1,532.63	1,590.49	1,742.95	1,945.60	2,161.81	2,288.78	390.47	83,591.2
Portugal	129.31	135.43	138.58	144.13	149.12	155.28	162.92	223.30	21,048.5
Spain	680.68	729.21	782.93	841.04	908.45	980.95	1,049.85	1,438.96	32,347.6
Sweden	2,326.18	2,420.76	2,515.15	2,624.96	2,735.22	2,899.65	3,073.83	454.79	49,903.9
Switzerland	430.32	434.26	437.73	451.38	463.67	486.18	508.39	423.53	56,492.4
Turkey	240.22	350.48	454.78	559.03	648.93	758.39	859.00	659.11	8,974.4
United Kingdom	1,003.30	1,055.79	1,118.24	1,184.30	1,233.98	1,303.91	1,385.48	2,772.22	45,665.6
Eastern Europe									
Albania	583.37	622.71	694.10	750.78	814.80	891.00	967.02	10.69	3,352.3
Belarus	17,173.20	26,138.30	36,564.80	49,991.80	65,067.10	79,267.00	96,087.20	44.77	4,592.0
Bosnia-Herzegovina	11.60	12.83	14.51	15.79	16.93	19.12	21.11	14.77	3,753.9
Bulgaria	29.71	32.40	34.63	38.82	42.80	49.36	56.52	39.55	5,187.8
Croatia	165.64	181.23	198.42	214.98	231.35	250.59	275.50	51.36	11,566.9
Czech Republic	2,352.21	2,464.43	2,577.11	2,814.76	2,983.86	3,215.64	3,540.11	174.44	16,957.4
Estonia	108.22	121.37	136.01	149.92	175.39	207.06	243.25	21.27	15,878.4
Georgia	6.65	7.46	8.56	9.97	11.62	13.78	17.11	10.24	2,330.3
Hungary	15,270.10	17,180.60	18,940.70	20,718.10	22,042.50	23,795.30	25,414.56	138.40	13,760.7
Latvia	5.22	5.76	6.39	7.43	9.06	11.17	13.93	27.12	11,890.4
Lithuania	48.58	51.97	56.80	62.59	71.38	81.91	96.77	38.35	11,328.7
Macedonia	233.84	243.97	251.49	265.26	286.62	308.77	335.33	7.50	3,677.7
Moldova	19.05	22.56	27.62	32.03	37.65	44.75	52.12	4.29	1,131.7
Poland	779.56	808.58	843.16	924.54	983.30	1,060.19	1,162.79	420.09	11,025.5
Romania	116.77	151.47	197.57	246.47	288.05	342.42	402.23	164.97	7,653.1
Russia	8,943.58	10,830.50	13,243.20	17,048.10	21,625.40	26,879.80	32,984.80	1,289.44	9,077.1
Serbia and Montenegro	771.75	998.28	1,189.15	1,421.44	1,744.83	2,043.62	2,318.75	33.43	3,197.1
Slovakia	1,018.43	1,108.12	1,222.48	1,361.68	1,485.30	1,659.57	1,851.78	74.99	13,908.4
Slovenia	22.50	24.11	25.34	26.76	28.24	30.45	33.62	46.08	22,924.2
Ukraine	204.19	225.81	267.34	345.11	441.45	544.15	718.00	142.18	3,059.9

Source: Euromonitor International from International Monetary Fund (IMF), International Financial Statistics

GDP   **Table 10.2**

Total Gross Domestic Product 1980-2007 (US$)
US$ million

	1980	1985	1990	1995	1996	1997	1998	1999	2000
Western Europe									
Austria	110,867.4	80,960.4	182,661.7	239,945.4	241,350.0	219,421.4	225,391.7	213,129.1	194,050.4
Belgium	129,521.9	97,272.1	218,952.5	276,526.6	280,631.5	261,998.2	269,057.3	253,555.7	232,429.4
Cyprus	2,153.8	2,419.7	5,579.2	9,250.1	9,349.8	8,895.0	9,545.3	9,769.1	9,293.5
Denmark	68,455.0	59,833.3	135,839.0	181,983.7	184,437.1	170,436.3	173,653.1	173,943.3	160,081.4
Finland	49,049.7	45,872.5	120,251.0	131,117.9	131,718.6	127,553.8	137,203.9	130,788.4	121,998.2
France	654,551.4	593,915.5	1,385,026.8	1,634,226.6	1,629,220.2	1,501,904.9	1,551,327.5	1,456,796.2	1,330,729.4
Germany	1,128,427.8	762,134.8	1,708,224.0	2,526,845.9	2,489,751.7	2,270,265.5	2,302,583.8	2,143,810.9	1,902,301.7
Gibraltar				623.5	607.8	583.9	638.8	664.1	649.2
Greece	9,847.6	14,549.4	57,414.2	119,707.5	127,728.2	126,257.3	135,768.8	131,547.1	125,695.8
Iceland	3,363.5	2,949.4	6,263.2	6,880.4	7,183.3	7,423.0	8,269.6	8,719.6	8,697.3
Ireland	19,277.2	19,942.5	48,987.7	72,578.6	77,915.4	80,557.6	92,053.9	96,429.9	96,701.5
Italy	299,377.8	342,772.4	939,733.6	1,295,020.0	1,332,045.9	1,242,954.9	1,278,609.0	1,200,929.4	1,098,545.3
Liechtenstein	534.7	529.1	1,421.7	2,428.8	2,504.0	2,298.6	2,479.6	2,664.2	2,484.0
Luxembourg	6,369.3	5,329.3	14,063.5	20,655.5	20,963.1	19,461.5	20,402.9	21,189.8	20,292.1
Malta	1,134.8	1,014.6	2,311.9	3,599.7	3,671.8	3,633.5	3,809.8	3,908.0	3,893.1
Monaco	310.6	297.6	716.8	862.6	861.2	794.1	818.9	768.2	699.1
Netherlands	236,579.8	158,819.7	326,344.6	417,294.2	424,325.2	405,605.0	424,652.6	411,493.4	385,496.2
Norway	63,732.3	64,251.2	117,587.0	148,890.6	160,057.4	158,188.4	151,177.6	159,025.9	168,175.1
Portugal	11,453.6	17,632.9	72,203.9	116,384.3	120,107.0	116,024.6	124,768.9	121,674.1	112,773.1
Spain	143,349.8	143,126.3	427,618.8	611,332.8	628,820.9	597,226.2	632,054.8	617,935.4	581,309.3
Sweden	129,701.4	104,574.9	240,153.8	253,706.9	276,185.7	252,393.9	253,097.2	257,063.6	245,572.0
Switzerland	109,851.9	99,474.2	238,219.5	315,948.0	304,749.2	264,582.3	272,630.9	268,218.4	249,913.0
Turkey	65,756.5	67,052.0	150,676.2	169,319.3	181,464.5	189,878.5	269,262.5	249,761.8	266,559.8
United Kingdom	536,376.2	455,913.8	991,091.6	1,141,102.3	1,199,618.4	1,335,679.3	1,433,712.5	1,475,503.1	1,450,879.1
Eastern Europe									
Albania	2,218.9	2,408.0	2,170.6	2,479.0	3,314.9	2,324.5	2,716.6	3,424.9	3,639.6
Belarus				10,537.5	14,500.4	14,097.7	15,222.1	12,138.5	10,417.8
Bosnia-Herzegovina						3,671.7	4,116.7	4,897.0	5,046.5
Bulgaria	18,620.1	31,645.6	20,726.0	13,105.7	9,900.4	10,364.9	12,736.7	12,955.1	12,599.8
Croatia				18,808.4	19,870.8	20,097.3	21,624.7	19,907.8	18,425.4
Czech Republic			34,878.7	55,255.5	62,011.3	57,135.1	61,846.5	60,192.3	56,716.6
Estonia				3,766.5	4,712.3	5,034.4	5,572.2	5,687.1	5,627.5
Georgia				2,926.2	3,063.4	3,510.4	3,613.5	2,800.0	3,044.0
Hungary	22,162.6	20,624.7	33,055.5	44,669.0	45,162.6	45,723.6	47,049.0	48,044.2	47,943.3
Latvia				4,956.7	5,681.8	6,252.0	6,732.8	7,288.5	7,833.1
Lithuania				6,489.1	8,184.9	9,999.4	11,174.7	10,916.7	11,418.5
Macedonia				4,475.0	4,413.2	3,720.1	3,580.1	3,673.2	3,586.9
Moldova				1,441.3	1,693.5	1,928.6	1,698.5	1,171.7	1,288.3
Poland	56,788.5	70,985.9	58,975.9	139,061.8	156,684.1	157,153.8	172,901.5	167,801.7	171,276.1
Romania	34,272.7	47,682.6	38,242.1	35,477.4	35,315.2	35,285.7	42,115.3	35,592.3	37,025.4
Russia				313,330.3	392,090.7	404,940.2	270,952.9	195,907.8	259,717.7
Serbia and Montenegro				28,972.4	16,854.9	21,733.4	16,319.2	17,668.4	32,874.9
Slovakia				19,568.7	21,112.9	21,349.0	22,346.5	20,443.4	20,374.9
Slovenia			7,319.5	21,467.5	21,690.3	20,688.1	21,979.9	21,566.0	19,634.5
Ukraine				37,008.7	44,558.8	50,151.5	41,882.6	31,580.7	31,261.5

Source: *Euromonitor International from International Monetary Fund (IMF), International Financial Statistics*

Total Gross Domestic Product 1980-2007 (US$) *(continued)*

US$ million

	2001	2002	2003	2004	2005	2006	2007	US$ per capita 2007
Western Europe								
Austria	193,409.1	208,105.9	255,463.6	293,409.5	305,094.3	323,564.2	373,943.0	44,974.9
Belgium	231,974.8	252,021.5	310,126.7	359,234.6	375,517.3	397,868.2	454,284.3	42,976.7
Cyprus	9,672.2	10,507.5	13,268.9	15,770.0	16,940.5	18,356.3	21,327.8	24,954.4
Denmark	160,475.7	173,881.0	212,623.0	244,728.0	258,158.0	276,035.1	311,464.6	57,181.7
Finland	125,310.3	135,671.6	164,836.3	189,285.0	195,663.0	209,574.0	245,013.9	46,430.9
France	1,341,677.1	1,460,416.6	1,802,468.0	2,059,765.7	2,133,778.6	2,250,274.4	2,560,259.0	41,691.3
Germany	1,893,218.8	2,019,590.9	2,444,002.2	2,747,363.1	2,791,402.1	2,913,492.2	3,322,152.9	40,360.5
Gibraltar	649.3	717.7	819.8	1,028.5	1,036.8	954.7	945.4	32,260.4
Greece	131,037.0	148,498.6	193,435.1	230,137.6	246,991.7	268,471.1	314,614.9	28,168.4
Iceland	7,923.0	8,908.4	10,969.8	13,230.3	16,294.4	16,638.4	19,973.1	66,354.4
Ireland	104,812.6	122,682.4	157,499.1	185,097.9	201,673.4	222,427.6	261,247.8	60,773.2
Italy	1,118,686.6	1,220,535.2	1,508,276.3	1,728,942.7	1,776,338.3	1,856,822.4	2,104,669.8	35,740.5
Liechtenstein	2,491.7	2,688.9	3,070.6	3,454.8	3,658.1	3,809.1	4,159.6	118,276.6
Luxembourg	20,222.7	22,608.5	29,057.4	34,092.3	37,348.0	42,471.6	50,562.8	108,373.7
Malta	3,850.9	4,233.0	4,994.1	5,573.7	5,912.9	6,372.5	7,399.4	18,199.0
Monaco	703.3	762.3	937.5	1,071.0	1,105.6	1,160.5	1,313.1	40,141.6
Netherlands	401,130.4	438,386.9	538,707.2	610,284.4	632,951.6	670,376.7	768,704.6	46,992.6
Norway	171,195.5	191,968.0	224,638.5	258,566.1	301,994.6	337,080.7	390,465.5	83,591.2
Portugal	115,849.4	127,624.0	156,527.7	179,075.6	185,451.8	194,815.8	223,303.0	21,048.5
Spain	609,831.9	687,155.4	884,314.7	1,044,974.6	1,129,755.5	1,230,730.3	1,438,961.8	32,347.6
Sweden	225,206.5	248,611.5	311,038.4	357,191.4	366,009.2	392,999.7	454,791.2	49,903.9
Switzerland	254,988.4	278,618.8	325,051.8	362,990.8	372,374.3	387,751.2	423,530.7	56,492.4
Turkey	196,006.8	232,529.9	303,007.5	392,155.3	482,987.2	530,918.8	659,106.3	8,974.4
United Kingdom	1,444,314.1	1,582,364.5	1,825,781.4	2,168,332.8	2,243,608.2	2,399,155.8	2,772,224.3	45,665.6
Eastern Europe								
Albania	4,065.7	4,443.0	5,695.7	7,304.8	8,158.6	9,082.3	10,693.9	3,352.3
Belarus	12,354.8	14,594.9	17,825.4	23,141.6	30,210.1	36,961.9	44,773.4	4,592.0
Bosnia-Herzegovina	5,306.9	6,173.2	8,370.2	10,021.8	10,763.5	12,264.4	14,770.9	3,753.9
Bulgaria	13,598.7	15,600.3	19,984.7	24,647.5	27,188.0	31,656.4	39,550.7	5,187.8
Croatia	19,857.1	23,023.2	29,593.3	35,626.6	38,887.2	42,925.5	51,355.8	11,566.9
Czech Republic	61,842.8	75,276.2	91,357.7	109,524.6	124,548.6	142,312.7	174,443.7	16,957.4
Estonia	6,191.6	7,306.4	9,815.7	11,902.8	13,937.9	16,610.7	21,274.5	15,878.4
Georgia	3,206.9	3,396.0	3,991.4	5,201.7	6,410.9	7,741.9	10,242.4	2,330.3
Hungary	53,300.6	66,620.7	84,441.0	102,187.5	110,443.3	113,100.9	138,403.9	13,760.7
Latvia	8,313.0	9,314.8	11,186.5	13,761.6	16,041.8	19,934.9	27,115.4	11,890.4
Lithuania	12,146.2	14,134.3	18,558.1	22,508.4	25,731.7	29,759.6	38,345.3	11,328.7
Macedonia	3,437.0	3,791.3	4,629.5	5,368.5	5,815.7	6,327.1	7,496.8	3,677.7
Moldova	1,480.9	1,662.1	1,980.6	2,597.9	2,988.3	3,408.3	4,293.0	1,131.7
Poland	190,420.9	198,179.4	216,800.9	252,769.0	303,912.2	341,648.5	420,090.3	11,025.5
Romania	40,180.9	45,824.6	59,507.4	75,519.2	98,861.6	121,901.2	164,965.9	7,653.1
Russia	306,617.8	345,487.0	431,487.0	591,666.5	764,569.9	988,555.0	1,289,435.7	9,077.1
Serbia and Montenegro	16,055.9	15,708.5	20,617.9	24,109.0	26,025.3	29,450.1	33,430.7	3,197.1
Slovakia	21,061.6	24,447.4	33,244.0	42,213.6	47,884.6	55,882.9	74,988.3	13,908.4
Slovenia	20,162.6	22,717.8	28,625.9	33,253.6	35,124.5	38,207.1	46,083.6	22,924.2
Ukraine	38,008.9	42,392.7	50,133.0	64,880.9	86,141.5	107,753.1	142,178.9	3,059.9

Source: *Euromonitor International from International Monetary Fund (IMF), International Financial Statistics*

GDP

Table 10.3

Total GDP by Quarter 2006-2008
Million units of national currency

	2006 1st Quarter	2006 2nd Quarter	2006 3rd Quarter	2006 4th Quarter	2007 1st Quarter	2007 2nd Quarter	2007 3rd Quarter	2007 4th Quarter	2008 1st Quarter	2008 2nd Quarter
Western Europe										
Austria	60,013	64,008	65,797	68,079	65,121	68,115	69,036	70,553	69,199	
Belgium	77,066	79,271	77,260	83,524	80,847	82,947	80,646	87,000	84,397	
Cyprus	1,918	2,142	2,158	2,144	3,556	3,956	4,039	4,010		
Denmark	389,808	415,337	409,997	426,378	406,216	421,354	423,936	444,014	417,232	
Finland	40,211	41,379	40,937	44,514	42,014	44,627	44,258	47,860	44,523	
France	441,124	447,663	450,211	454,584	458,443	464,210	470,678	474,601	480,511	
Germany	570,408	577,695	584,008	590,089	599,380	603,592	609,291	611,537	623,085	
Gibraltar										
Greece	52,031	52,371	54,393	55,190	56,295	56,881	57,756	58,607	60,213	
Iceland	268,378	282,117	293,655	297,600	302,445	320,055	329,735	327,141	318,353	
Ireland	43,955	43,386	44,874	45,071	48,316	48,106	46,100	48,082	47,259	
Italy	362,947	369,003	371,095	376,936	380,840	383,446	386,053	385,201	387,991	
Liechtenstein										
Luxembourg	7,950	8,228	8,098	8,779	8,787	9,244	8,705	9,859	9,393	
Malta	498	547	576	567	1,236	1,352	1,420	1,391		
Monaco										
Netherlands	131,387	132,830	134,146	135,961	137,618	138,893	141,101	143,225	145,424	
Norway	542,715	524,092	533,720	561,283	549,415	562,223	570,966	606,175	615,199	
Portugal	37,942	38,653	39,069	39,613	40,082	40,624	40,731	41,481	41,335	
Spain	238,256	242,481	247,887	252,330	256,591	260,811	264,101	268,345	271,598	
Sweden	696,694	741,379	693,175	768,402	740,732	779,241	739,453	814,403	771,758	818,018
Switzerland	120,035	121,048	122,160	122,935	124,678	126,340	127,813	129,563	130,898	
Turkey	141,815	176,057	234,109	206,410	189,257	211,118	236,720	221,905		
United Kingdom	317,834	322,514	329,471	334,091	338,604	344,989	349,161	352,727	356,677	
Eastern Europe										
Albania										
Belarus	16,194,373	18,498,308	22,468,791	22,105,528	19,767,300	22,467,000	27,172,200	26,680,700	25,802,500	
Bosnia-Herzegovina										
Bulgaria	10,034	11,708	13,817	13,802	11,288	13,143	15,743	16,346	13,484	
Croatia	56,721	61,911	69,099	62,859	62,463	68,827	74,971	69,240	64,275	
Czech Republic	741,556	815,291	818,917	839,877	819,261	899,778	895,376	925,693	890,372	
Estonia	46,169	52,434	52,608	55,849	54,966	60,873	61,675	65,736	59,476	
Georgia	2,835	3,354	3,625	3,970						
Hungary	5,152,440	5,958,462	6,131,853	6,552,545	5,722,455	6,326,743	6,445,344	6,920,018	6,158,885	
Latvia	2,290	2,672	2,947	3,263	2,872	3,354	3,714	3,992	3,427	
Lithuania	17,018	20,462	21,753	22,672	19,795	23,693	26,051	27,234	24,202	
Macedonia										
Moldova	7,854	9,527	13,673	13,701	10,015	12,405	15,518	14,179	11,935	
Poland	242,914	254,484	262,020	300,771	266,593	280,279	287,218	328,699	292,793	
Romania	60,986	75,967	92,989	112,476						
Russia	5,682,626	6,349,113	7,274,802	7,573,258	6,747,421	7,748,493	8,825,929	9,662,953	8,837,448	
Serbia and Montenegro										
Slovakia	374,089	409,522	430,931	445,028	418,695	453,770	482,466	496,852	472,490	
Slovenia	7,009	7,816	7,772	7,856	7,697	8,558	8,750	8,617	8,517	
Ukraine	106,695	125,613	152,249	159,596	138,625	166,287	198,801	214,291	187,959	

Source: *Euromonitor International from International Monetary Fund (IMF), International Financial Statistics*

Table 10.4

Origin of Gross Domestic Product 2007

US$ million

	Agriculture, Forestry & Fishing	Mining & Quarrying	Manufacturing	Electricity, Gas & Water	Construction
Western Europe					
Austria	5,188.2	1,734.7	65,655.9	8,704.0	25,704.5
Belgium	3,524.6	454.8	66,683.3	8,426.6	20,181.5
Cyprus					
Denmark	2,368.7	11,809.8	34,136.2	4,514.9	15,020.2
Finland	4,785.3	680.0	47,796.6	4,896.2	12,950.9
France	42,614.8	2,629.7	267,033.2	44,969.7	149,253.6
Germany	22,768.8	6,435.8	664,435.3	77,493.6	112,898.8
Gibraltar					
Greece	8,963.0	1,230.4	37,416.3	5,425.8	24,663.5
Iceland					
Ireland	3,311.5	1,022.6	46,542.3	3,043.4	23,256.5
Italy	36,094.0	6,564.2	329,180.6	37,054.7	115,725.8
Liechtenstein					
Luxembourg					
Malta					
Monaco					
Netherlands	13,923.6	25,919.9	87,563.5	10,808.4	35,376.5
Norway	5,004.4	106,163.2	32,699.0	9,920.7	16,421.5
Portugal	4,617.7	625.9	25,525.3	5,001.0	11,889.3
Spain	34,978.1	3,550.1	179,768.1	23,853.3	164,425.4
Sweden	6,272.1	1,641.6	70,083.2	13,263.5	18,292.3
Switzerland	3,738.3	672.4	76,749.0	6,897.2	22,451.3
Turkey	43,805.4	7,773.2	108,346.5	13,945.4	9,041.3
United Kingdom	20,856.0	50,810.2	272,355.4	58,820.2	140,338.6
Eastern Europe					
Albania					
Belarus					
Bosnia-Herzegovina					
Bulgaria	2,290.5	995.6	5,694.1	1,089.9	1,874.2
Croatia	2,345.8	387.0	8,005.7	1,323.6	3,115.7
Czech Republic	3,688.8	2,059.1	40,919.7	5,495.8	9,778.0
Estonia	490.9	161.6	2,818.2	624.7	1,363.7
Georgia					
Hungary	4,831.8	261.8	27,326.9	2,935.9	5,538.1
Latvia	745.1	81.0	2,462.2	489.3	1,549.0
Lithuania	1,820.0	172.2	6,548.0	1,264.4	3,420.4
Macedonia					
Moldova					
Poland	14,917.5	8,795.9	69,356.5	12,083.0	23,116.9
Romania	10,195.5	1,341.8	29,785.0	2,796.1	11,571.8
Russia	24,051.1	50,841.3	53,508.8	19,587.5	28,767.7
Serbia and Montenegro					
Slovakia	2,376.7	339.3	14,786.2	4,113.6	4,461.0
Slovenia	802.7	201.3	9,148.6	1,157.6	2,500.6
Ukraine	4,320.2	2,774.7	14,469.9	2,112.5	2,811.7

Source: Euromonitor International from national statistics

GDP

Origin of Gross Domestic Product 2007 *(continued)*
US$ million

	Wholesale & Retail Trade, Restaurants & Hotels	Transport, Storage & Communications	Finance, Insurance, Real Estate & Business Services	Community, Social & Personal Services	Other	Total GDP
Western Europe						
Austria	41,071.1	20,680.1	78,225.7	48,751.8	12,541.3	330,385.8
Belgium	53,073.3	34,509.7	114,307.1	63,824.3	9,894.1	401,081.0
Cyprus						
Denmark	28,180.6	25,218.5	62,528.2	53,604.8	11,399.2	257,746.3
Finland	21,702.1	20,787.6	43,214.9	35,363.3	7,376.5	205,220.9
France	223,972.0	140,840.5	754,671.9	403,233.8	83,704.8	2,264,144.8
Germany	306,049.1	170,173.2	869,875.6	473,579.4	135,814.1	2,925,596.4
Gibraltar						
Greece	39,935.2	22,464.2	50,511.1	41,205.2	12,694.6	277,979.1
Iceland						
Ireland	21,079.7	11,486.4	61,632.8	36,803.8	6,756.1	223,181.8
Italy	210,510.3	141,961.7	510,763.9	255,341.7	54,374.2	1,860,098.5
Liechtenstein						
Luxembourg						
Malta						
Monaco						
Netherlands	85,332.4	47,346.3	179,812.4	107,832.4	19,730.7	669,445.7
Norway	24,352.2	25,025.5	60,598.9	52,995.7	10,224.3	351,982.5
Portugal	23,786.1	12,902.0	41,019.2	32,281.8	5,228.1	186,234.0
Spain	133,011.7	87,645.5	271,969.3	181,536.0	48,195.7	1,264,161.1
Sweden	41,312.1	29,289.8	91,279.7	82,950.4	16,426.4	380,259.8
Switzerland	51,887.7	25,430.4	96,985.0	62,928.6	37,658.2	401,719.7
Turkey	85,546.0	81,160.9	36,918.7	56,895.9	16,614.2	512,064.3
United Kingdom	271,946.0	162,874.0	789,301.5	421,418.2	115,075.2	2,380,650.8
Eastern Europe						
Albania						
Belarus			1,815.8			
Bosnia-Herzegovina						
Bulgaria	2,925.9	3,637.8	6,243.4	2,435.5	684.6	30,046.3
Croatia	5,899.0	4,469.6	7,160.2	4,356.9	1,137.3	40,236.8
Czech Republic	19,978.0	15,244.7	25,764.4	17,095.6	5,026.9	151,656.5
Estonia	2,817.7	2,100.1	4,098.7	1,863.1	598.0	17,505.7
Georgia						
Hungary	13,623.0	8,962.0	26,978.1	16,856.4	5,033.2	119,314.1
Latvia	4,691.5	2,694.9	4,646.4	2,493.9	884.7	21,636.9
Lithuania	5,894.8	4,474.4	5,055.5	3,524.6	839.3	34,276.8
Macedonia						
Moldova						
Poland	67,195.7	25,556.2	64,730.1	43,349.7	12,781.1	356,007.4
Romania	16,376.5	14,341.5	23,616.6	13,327.8	3,955.8	133,852.5
Russia	60,601.4	30,304.8	114,182.4	57,333.3	13,505.8	445,215.8
Serbia and Montenegro						
Slovakia	10,587.7	6,398.4	12,202.2	6,316.1	1,590.4	65,663.3
Slovenia	4,654.7	3,099.5	8,498.1	5,530.5	1,426.6	38,862.0
Ukraine	8,540.6	6,889.9	11,752.1	6,802.6	1,137.7	63,814.3

Source: *Euromonitor International from national statistics*

Table 10.5

Origin of Gross Domestic Product 2007 (% Analysis)

% of total GDP

	Agriculture, Forestry & Fishing	Mining & Quarrying	Manufacturing	Electricity, Gas & Water	Construction
Western Europe					
Austria	1.57	0.53	19.87	2.63	7.78
Belgium	0.88	0.11	16.63	2.10	5.03
Cyprus					
Denmark	0.92	4.58	13.24	1.75	5.83
Finland	2.33	0.33	23.29	2.39	6.31
France	1.88	0.12	11.79	1.99	6.59
Germany	0.78	0.22	22.71	2.65	3.86
Gibraltar					
Greece	3.22	0.44	13.46	1.95	8.87
Iceland					
Ireland	1.48	0.46	20.85	1.36	10.42
Italy	1.94	0.35	17.70	1.99	6.22
Liechtenstein					
Luxembourg					
Malta					
Monaco					
Netherlands	2.08	3.87	13.08	1.61	5.28
Norway	1.42	30.16	9.29	2.82	4.67
Portugal	2.48	0.34	13.71	2.69	6.38
Spain	2.77	0.28	14.22	1.89	13.01
Sweden	1.65	0.43	18.43	3.49	4.81
Switzerland	0.93	0.17	19.11	1.72	5.59
Turkey	8.55	1.52	21.16	2.72	1.77
United Kingdom	0.88	2.13	11.44	2.47	5.89
Eastern Europe					
Albania					
Belarus					
Bosnia-Herzegovina					
Bulgaria	7.62	3.31	18.95	3.63	6.24
Croatia	5.83	0.96	19.90	3.29	7.74
Czech Republic	2.43	1.36	26.98	3.62	6.45
Estonia	2.80	0.92	16.10	3.57	7.79
Georgia					
Hungary	4.05	0.22	22.90	2.46	4.64
Latvia	3.44	0.37	11.38	2.26	7.16
Lithuania	5.31	0.50	19.10	3.69	9.98
Macedonia					
Moldova					
Poland	4.19	2.47	19.48	3.39	6.49
Romania	7.62	1.00	22.25	2.09	8.65
Russia	5.40	11.42	12.02	4.40	6.46
Serbia and Montenegro					
Slovakia	3.62	0.52	22.52	6.26	6.79
Slovenia	2.07	0.52	23.54	2.98	6.43
Ukraine	6.77	4.35	22.68	3.31	4.41

Source: Euromonitor International from national statistics

GDP

Origin of Gross Domestic Product 2007 (% Analysis) *(continued)*
% of total GDP

	Wholesale & Retail Trade, Restaurants & Hotels	Transport, Storage & Communications	Finance, Insurance, Real Estate & Business Services	Community, Social & Personal Services	Other	Total GDP
Western Europe						
Austria	12.43	6.26	23.68	14.76	3.80	100.00
Belgium	13.23	8.60	28.50	15.91	2.47	100.00
Cyprus						
Denmark	10.93	9.78	24.26	20.80	4.42	100.00
Finland	10.57	10.13	21.06	17.23	3.59	100.00
France	9.89	6.22	33.33	17.81	3.70	100.00
Germany	10.46	5.82	29.73	16.19	4.64	100.00
Gibraltar						
Greece	14.37	8.08	18.17	14.82	4.57	100.00
Iceland						
Ireland	9.45	5.15	27.62	16.49	3.03	100.00
Italy	11.32	7.63	27.46	13.73	2.92	100.00
Liechtenstein						
Luxembourg						
Malta						
Monaco						
Netherlands	12.75	7.07	26.86	16.11	2.95	100.00
Norway	6.92	7.11	17.22	15.06	2.90	100.00
Portugal	12.77	6.93	22.03	17.33	2.81	100.00
Spain	10.52	6.93	21.51	14.36	3.81	100.00
Sweden	10.86	7.70	24.00	21.81	4.32	100.00
Switzerland	12.92	6.33	24.14	15.66	9.37	100.00
Turkey	16.71	15.85	7.21	11.11	3.24	100.00
United Kingdom	11.42	6.84	33.15	17.70	4.83	100.00
Eastern Europe						
Albania						
Belarus						
Bosnia-Herzegovina						
Bulgaria	9.74	12.11	20.78	8.11	2.28	100.00
Croatia	14.66	11.11	17.80	10.83	2.83	100.00
Czech Republic	13.17	10.05	16.99	11.27	3.31	100.00
Estonia	16.10	12.00	23.41	10.64	3.42	100.00
Georgia						
Hungary	11.42	7.51	22.61	14.13	4.22	100.00
Latvia	21.68	12.46	21.47	11.53	4.09	100.00
Lithuania	17.20	13.05	14.75	10.28	2.45	100.00
Macedonia						
Moldova						
Poland	18.87	7.18	18.18	12.18	3.59	100.00
Romania	12.23	10.71	17.64	9.96	2.96	100.00
Russia	13.61	6.81	25.65	12.88	3.03	100.00
Serbia and Montenegro						
Slovakia	16.12	9.74	18.58	9.62	2.42	100.00
Slovenia	11.98	7.98	21.87	14.23	3.67	100.00
Ukraine	13.38	10.80	18.42	10.66	1.78	100.00

Source: *Euromonitor International from national statistics*

Table 10.6

Usage of Gross Domestic Product 2007

US$ million

	Government Final Consumption	Private Final Consumption	Increases in Stocks	Gross Fixed Capital Formation	Exports of Goods & Services	Imports of Goods & Services	Total
Western Europe							
Austria	66,188.0	202,707.8	2,434.3	77,541.8	217,976.7	-192,659.6	373,943.0
Belgium	101,276.5	237,845.5	5,548.3	96,869.9	405,806.2	-393,063.4	454,284.3
Cyprus	3,801.9	14,865.5	97.0	4,320.5	9,833.5	-11,220.3	21,327.8
Denmark	80,379.0	154,759.1	2,124.7	71,197.2	162,756.6	-159,751.8	311,464.6
Finland	51,995.2	123,979.7	4,786.3	49,743.2	109,799.1	-98,362.5	245,013.9
France	598,215.0	1,445,050.2	27,296.4	538,101.6	682,735.5	-731,113.5	2,560,259.0
Germany	597,666.8	1,884,901.7	-7,922.3	618,747.2	1,556,880.5	-1,321,925.7	3,322,152.9
Gibraltar		210.9					945.4
Greece	52,172.0	221,636.3	858.0	80,573.0	69,607.9	-111,040.9	314,614.9
Iceland	4,908.8	11,655.3	46.1	5,489.2	7,052.4	-9,178.7	19,973.1
Ireland	36,685.1	120,784.8	-130.2	68,723.8	207,500.9	-179,579.6	261,247.8
Italy	416,605.5	1,242,379.4	9,352.9	442,834.0	613,294.8	-620,006.8	2,104,669.8
Liechtenstein	448.2	2,426.8	899.7		2,340.1	-1,955.2	4,159.6
Luxembourg	7,638.6	17,405.7		9,583.5	86,980.7	-71,045.7	50,562.8
Malta	615.0	4,637.2	69.4	432.2	2,018.6	-2,065.2	7,399.4
Monaco	309.8	738.8	11.0	274.1	353.6	-374.2	1,313.1
Netherlands	195,289.9	362,321.4	-2,260.2	155,119.2	582,284.1	-515,512.1	768,704.6
Norway	76,648.3	161,404.7	8,847.1	80,712.5	177,887.9	-117,085.7	390,465.5
Portugal	45,191.6	144,273.4	999.3	49,596.0	73,475.4	-89,457.0	223,303.0
Spain	264,174.1	818,413.6	3,051.0	447,421.5	376,958.4	-471,056.8	1,438,961.8
Sweden	117,859.0	212,365.6	3,531.4	86,054.7	238,096.6	-203,442.3	454,791.2
Switzerland	45,645.6	247,014.7	743.0	90,816.2	238,209.1	-198,996.1	423,530.7
Turkey	80,156.2	464,394.7	15,639.0	149,902.3	144,215.4	-177,339.5	659,106.3
United Kingdom	600,025.6	1,752,993.4	15,683.2	500,176.1	718,877.8	-816,248.2	2,772,224.3
Eastern Europe							
Albania	1,034.8	8,386.9	-8.9	3,528.6	2,620.5	-4,961.8	10,693.9
Belarus	8,308.6	23,413.7	1,073.3	13,788.1	27,638.4	-30,377.0	44,773.4
Bosnia-Herzegovina	3,209.2	14,270.1	102.9	3,908.3	4,871.9	-10,427.6	14,770.9
Bulgaria	6,387.6	27,347.4	2,774.7	11,778.8	25,073.1	-33,810.9	39,550.7
Croatia	10,316.6	28,599.1	1,416.0	15,357.5	24,450.4	-28,862.3	51,355.8
Czech Republic	35,138.4	84,113.8	4,788.7	42,228.2	139,285.1	-130,556.3	174,443.7
Estonia	3,628.8	11,291.2	1,133.3	6,779.6	15,479.9	-17,381.1	21,274.5
Georgia	1,297.2	8,287.3	122.1	2,188.3	2,895.7	-5,266.4	10,242.4
Hungary	13,362.1	89,992.7	2,914.5	28,967.4	110,481.6	-107,361.7	138,403.9
Latvia	4,944.8	18,101.3	1,269.0	8,840.3	12,061.5	-17,564.8	27,115.4
Lithuania	6,466.2	25,159.5	1,128.8	10,188.2	21,218.6	-25,829.3	38,345.3
Macedonia	1,326.7	5,824.7	243.8	1,347.9	3,586.8	-4,980.4	7,496.8
Moldova	929.0	4,022.0	214.5	1,463.3	1,991.4	-4,225.2	4,293.0
Poland	71,944.6	256,016.9	5,575.4	93,842.0	173,426.9	-180,674.1	420,090.3
Romania	24,834.9	115,687.9	-931.7	40,132.4	48,242.6	-69,991.8	164,965.9
Russia	227,532.0	625,097.7	44,991.9	271,731.1	393,154.2	-280,940.4	1,289,435.7
Serbia and Montenegro	6,075.9	23,520.2	2,547.2	6,197.2	10,133.8	-16,777.0	33,430.7
Slovakia	13,195.4	41,956.6	1,104.7	19,287.2	64,752.6	-65,103.3	74,988.3
Slovenia	8,338.6	24,548.7	1,079.4	11,742.2	29,954.6	-30,471.1	46,083.6
Ukraine	10,018.8	100,994.7	-672.1	38,711.9	64,001.0	-71,877.0	142,178.9

Source: International Monetary Fund (IMF), International Financial Statistics

GDP

Table 10.7

Usage of Gross Domestic Product 2007 (% Analysis)
% of total GDP

	Government Final Consumption	Private Final Consumption	Increases in Stocks	Gross Fixed Capital Formation	Exports of Goods & Services	Imports of Goods & Services	Total
Western Europe							
Austria	17.70	54.21	0.65	20.74	58.29	-51.52	100.00
Belgium	22.29	52.36	1.22	21.32	89.33	-86.52	100.00
Cyprus	17.83	69.70	0.46	20.26	46.11	-52.61	100.00
Denmark	25.81	49.69	0.68	22.86	52.26	-51.29	100.00
Finland	21.22	50.60	1.95	20.30	44.81	-40.15	100.00
France	23.37	56.44	1.07	21.02	26.67	-28.56	100.00
Germany	17.99	56.74	-0.24	18.62	46.86	-39.79	100.00
Gibraltar		22.31					100.00
Greece	16.58	70.45	0.27	25.61	22.12	-35.29	100.00
Iceland	24.58	58.36	0.23	27.48	35.31	-45.96	100.00
Ireland	14.04	46.23	-0.05	26.31	79.43	-68.74	100.00
Italy	19.79	59.03	0.44	21.04	29.14	-29.46	100.00
Liechtenstein	10.78	58.34	21.63		56.26	-47.01	100.00
Luxembourg	15.11	34.42		18.95	172.02	-140.51	100.00
Malta	8.31	62.67	0.94	5.84	27.28	-27.91	100.00
Monaco	23.59	56.26	0.84	20.88	26.93	-28.50	100.00
Netherlands	25.41	47.13	-0.29	20.18	75.75	-67.06	100.00
Norway	19.63	41.34	2.27	20.67	45.56	-29.99	100.00
Portugal	20.24	64.61	0.45	22.21	32.90	-40.06	100.00
Spain	18.36	56.88	0.21	31.09	26.20	-32.74	100.00
Sweden	25.91	46.70	0.78	18.92	52.35	-44.73	100.00
Switzerland	10.78	58.32	0.18	21.44	56.24	-46.99	100.00
Turkey	12.16	70.46	2.37	22.74	21.88	-26.91	100.00
United Kingdom	21.64	63.23	0.57	18.04	25.93	-29.44	100.00
Eastern Europe							
Albania	9.68	78.43	-0.08	33.00	24.51	-46.40	100.00
Belarus	18.56	52.29	2.40	30.80	61.73	-67.85	100.00
Bosnia-Herzegovina	21.73	96.61	0.70	26.46	32.98	-70.60	100.00
Bulgaria	16.15	69.15	7.02	29.78	63.39	-85.49	100.00
Croatia	20.09	55.69	2.76	29.90	47.61	-56.20	100.00
Czech Republic	20.14	48.22	2.75	24.21	79.85	-74.84	100.00
Estonia	17.06	53.07	5.33	31.87	72.76	-81.70	100.00
Georgia	12.67	80.91	1.19	21.37	28.27	-51.42	100.00
Hungary	9.65	65.02	2.11	20.93	79.83	-77.57	100.00
Latvia	18.24	66.76	4.68	32.60	44.48	-64.78	100.00
Lithuania	16.86	65.61	2.94	26.57	55.34	-67.36	100.00
Macedonia	17.70	77.70	3.25	17.98	47.84	-66.43	100.00
Moldova	21.64	93.69	5.00	34.08	46.39	-98.42	100.00
Poland	17.13	60.94	1.33	22.34	41.28	-43.01	100.00
Romania	15.05	70.13	-0.56	24.33	29.24	-42.43	100.00
Russia	17.65	48.48	3.49	21.07	30.49	-21.79	100.00
Serbia and Montenegro	18.17	70.36	7.62	18.54	30.31	-50.18	100.00
Slovakia	17.60	55.95	1.47	25.72	86.35	-86.82	100.00
Slovenia	18.09	53.27	2.34	25.48	65.00	-66.12	100.00
Ukraine	7.05	71.03	-0.47	27.23	45.01	-50.55	100.00

Source: *International Monetary Fund (IMF), International Financial Statistics*

| **Table 10.8**

Increases in Stocks by Quarter 2006-2008
Million units of national currency

	2006 1st Quarter	2006 2nd Quarter	2006 3rd Quarter	2006 4th Quarter	2007 1st Quarter	2007 2nd Quarter	2007 3rd Quarter	2007 4th Quarter	2008 1st Quarter	2008 2nd Quarter
Western Europe										
Austria	-2,805.9	1,383.2	1,360.8	787.7	7,176.0	10,644.2	5,849.9	-21,894.1	10,458.4	
Belgium	2,514.8	254.7	1,095.8	-37.3	1,986.8	-1,221.1	1,101.2	2,181.1	3,583.8	
Cyprus	59.6	7.2	-174.3	137.5	81.5	102.9	-221.2	107.7		
Denmark	3,309.0	4,758.2	5,330.1	1,923.8	5,598.9	4,105.0	4,807.2	-2,945.1	3,223.6	
Finland	2,284.9	-720.8	705.5	143.4	1,658.0	-62.0	1,726.0	170.0	923.0	
France	749.6	1,939.5	1,439.8	1,739.1	2,371.6	3,353.9	8,332.6	5,857.0	5,018.9	
Germany	5,327.7	5,492.2	3,042.1	-18,532.0	4,157.3	-4,050.0	-2,373.7	-3,513.6	3,822.0	
Gibraltar										
Greece										
Iceland	3,685.7	785.9	6,764.5	2,088.8	1,546.5	1,100.4	2,306.8	-2,001.7	-1,649.6	
Ireland	546.8	640.5	-62.8	217.4	-140.0	-174.0	-433.0	652.0	657.0	
Italy	900.0	-866.5	4,493.9	3,073.0	1,852.0	3,561.6	2,866.7	-1,456.5	-1,923.5	
Liechtenstein										
Luxembourg	-41.9	-173.6	-136.9	185.5	-105.0	-194.1	-176.6	88.2	110.0	
Malta	20.1	44.9	-9.4	-28.1	2.3	27.1	0.0	21.2		
Monaco										
Netherlands	-1,109.2	588.8	1,248.9	-1,067.6	-1,106.0	-78.0	-89.0	-376.0	57.0	
Norway	27,757.5	8,467.0	11,285.1	13,140.5	26,533.0	8,322.0	-713.0	17,717.0	29,147.0	
Portugal					218.7	19.0	227.0	264.4	384.5	
Spain	475.3	522.8	508.3	340.6	493.0	484.0	559.0	690.0	872.0	
Sweden	41,887.9	-24,723.3	-27,014.9	11,179.2	19,131.6	-5,659.1	11,623.1	-1,227.7	12,979.5	1,896.9
Switzerland	1,681.6	1,781.4	-2,435.6	2,858.5	-792.6	-337.3	-501.2	2,523.0	-1,137.9	
Turkey	5,350.5	13,250.1	-4,840.6	2,751.1						
United Kingdom	320.8	1,999.0	1,054.3	-626.1	657.5	1,231.8	3,488.1	2,460.7	-181.6	
Eastern Europe										
Albania										
Belarus	109,132.1	195,176.3	1,297,684.3	398,207.2	-17,600.0	147,700.0	1,581,400.0	591,800.0	441,900.0	
Bosnia-Herzegovina										
Bulgaria	725.6	482.3	918.9	735.4	937.8	907.1	1,123.3	996.9	678.6	
Croatia	6,038.3	3,568.6	-3,637.1	1,389.9	6,092.0	3,864.0	-4,731.0	2,371.0	7,382.0	
Czech Republic	12,594.2	28,657.5	23,150.6	-4,630.3	22,213.0	44,548.0	36,985.0	-6,566.0	33,862.0	
Estonia	2,802.2	2,753.0	1,426.4	1,605.2	3,718.8	3,131.2	4,121.0	1,986.7	2,077.9	
Georgia	16.1	29.6	46.4	64.2						
Hungary	-47,581.1	331,447.4	233,289.1	-186,978.3	162,104.0	308,270.0	194,520.0	-129,725.0	226,686.0	
Latvia	249.7	153.0	325.2	61.9	152.7	211.1	240.0	48.2	1.8	
Lithuania	621.0	643.2	550.1	32.5	888.3	808.2	1,125.6	26.6	1,721.1	
Macedonia										
Moldova	-8.1	578.4	638.3	756.0	994.2	812.5	1,435.8	-638.3	640.4	
Poland	7,973.0	-1,338.6	3,084.3	5,135.3	4,374.7	3,852.4	4,121.5	3,084.0	5,681.8	
Romania	124.7	-892.6	-374.6	-170.3						
Russia	97,940.0	85,232.9	543,176.2	42,035.0	285,323.8	237,455.7	686,424.0	-58,273.5	302,767.9	
Serbia and Montenegro										
Slovakia	8,242.7	11,268.0	11,784.2	-2,826.8	307.0	13,780.0	10,026.0	3,167.0	12,087.0	
Slovenia	303.2	-44.3	118.3	296.9						
Ukraine	337.7	-1,776.0	2,173.0	-79.7	128.0	-5,775.0	5,512.0	-3,259.0	-139.0	

Source: International Monetary Fund (IMF), International Financial Statistics

GDP

Table 10.9

Gross Fixed Capital Formation by Quarter 2006-2008
Million units of national currency

	2006 1st Quarter	2006 2nd Quarter	2006 3rd Quarter	2006 4th Quarter	2007 1st Quarter	2007 2nd Quarter	2007 3rd Quarter	2007 4th Quarter	2008 1st Quarter	2008 2nd Quarter
Western Europe										
Austria	10,116.6	13,333.7	14,373.3	15,242.9	11,703.7	14,106.4	15,177.3	15,586.1	11,998.8	
Belgium	14,903.4	16,123.3	15,243.6	19,414.7	16,103.2	17,388.6	16,582.0	20,601.3	17,380.6	
Cyprus	374.3	417.6	402.8	415.7	754.3	801.0	798.5	798.4		
Denmark	79,080.3	90,095.6	87,499.2	98,124.9	91,772.4	95,679.7	95,275.6	104,848.3	93,253.1	
Finland	8,142.1	7,674.1	7,974.4	8,421.4	7,539.0	8,961.0	9,576.0	10,216.0	8,487.0	
France	91,111.4	93,459.2	94,713.1	96,753.3	95,637.8	97,438.7	98,758.8	100,756.7	102,534.4	
Germany	99,436.4	103,989.8	106,069.6	107,614.3	112,927.5	111,777.5	112,647.5	114,077.5	118,927.4	
Gibraltar										
Greece	13,894.6	13,214.0	13,424.3	14,626.8	14,981.4	14,637.5	15,044.4	14,121.7	14,321.6	
Iceland	83,656.0	90,284.0	94,425.0	97,206.0	77,189.0	92,162.0	99,627.0	82,635.0	78,091.0	
Ireland	12,093.7	11,144.7	12,041.0	12,354.5	14,583.0	12,394.0	11,552.0	11,611.0	11,649.0	
Italy	76,443.8	77,392.1	77,486.9	79,835.2	80,430.1	80,428.5	80,774.5	81,452.8	82,262.5	
Liechtenstein										
Luxembourg	1,375.8	1,637.2	1,363.7	1,673.0	1,658.3	1,990.2	1,755.1	1,890.7	1,831.0	
Malta	122.1	98.9	102.0	104.4	74.7	73.4	73.5	93.8		
Monaco										
Netherlands	25,367.6	26,091.1	27,169.2	27,751.2	27,942.0	27,836.0	28,606.0	28,789.0	30,521.0	
Norway	91,213.2	102,447.3	101,747.1	113,721.4	104,436.0	114,151.0	119,784.0	134,739.0	117,753.0	
Portugal	8,827.1	8,466.8	8,666.8	8,613.6	8,708.5	8,704.2	9,202.4	9,569.5	9,366.1	
Spain	71,722.4	73,932.8	75,495.6	77,038.2	79,250.0	81,314.0	82,322.0	83,547.0	84,063.0	
Sweden	116,503.9	139,389.3	123,432.5	145,366.4	130,522.0	155,348.0	133,478.0	162,276.0	140,966.0	165,225.0
Switzerland	24,838.4	25,873.3	26,325.6	26,711.8	26,854.8	27,749.1	27,138.3	27,270.8	28,029.1	
Turkey	29,834.0	41,721.7	49,786.7	47,702.6						
United Kingdom	55,338.3	57,180.6	58,576.5	60,666.6	61,202.9	61,184.9	62,985.5	64,600.7	63,626.2	
Eastern Europe										
Albania										
Belarus	3,572,331.2	5,397,226.1	6,363,359.3	8,178,283.3	4,628,600.0	6,352,600.0	7,566,000.0	11,043,100.0	6,561,100.0	
Bosnia-Herzegovina										
Bulgaria	2,331.9	2,979.4	3,224.1	4,269.8	3,196.0	3,768.9	4,249.0	5,618.6	4,100.8	
Croatia	17,131.4	19,479.1	19,379.0	18,802.9	19,530.0	21,272.0	21,171.0	20,413.0	22,410.0	
Czech Republic	175,388.1	201,127.3	204,075.1	211,788.5	187,254.0	217,686.0	216,864.0	235,162.0	199,105.0	
Estonia	13,523.4	16,510.5	19,925.6	20,609.9	16,921.0	19,963.7	19,523.3	21,109.9	17,952.2	
Georgia	748.0	800.4	960.2	1,015.7						
Hungary	894,558.6	1,161,849.5	1,344,763.2	1,768,338.7	954,015.1	1,195,391.3	1,328,191.5	1,841,562.1	929,112.0	
Latvia	612.3	814.4	1,015.5	1,202.0	869.5	1,035.0	1,269.3	1,368.2	992.2	
Lithuania	3,499.3	4,902.1	5,700.6	6,188.7	4,642.3	6,331.7	7,141.3	7,597.0	5,490.1	
Macedonia										
Moldova	1,353.8	2,806.2	3,320.7	5,210.9	2,431.5	4,564.2	3,593.4	7,174.7	2,821.6	
Poland	29,586.9	42,881.2	50,073.9	86,322.0	39,405.0	54,574.5	61,504.8	104,265.7	46,413.2	
Romania	9,972.6	17,342.6	26,605.4	30,339.7						
Russia	703,496.5	1,076,166.5	1,346,904.7	1,841,852.4	978,526.6	1,526,540.9	1,843,611.1	2,602,421.5	1,382,550.8	
Serbia and Montenegro										
Slovakia	89,952.3	109,745.1	112,996.6	123,484.0	98,244.0	118,378.0	123,433.0	136,230.0	104,477.0	
Slovenia	1,696.7	1,968.9	2,035.4	2,260.0						
Ukraine	22,352.9	30,895.4	37,956.2	42,880.6	33,017.0	44,823.0	55,258.0	62,397.0	46,899.0	

Source: *International Monetary Fund (IMF), International Financial Statistics*

Table 10.10

Exports of Goods and Services by Quarter 2006-2008

Million units of national currency

	2006 1st Quarter	2006 2nd Quarter	2006 3rd Quarter	2006 4th Quarter	2007 1st Quarter	2007 2nd Quarter	2007 3rd Quarter	2007 4th Quarter	2008 1st Quarter	2008 2nd Quarter
Western Europe										
Austria	35,745	35,566	36,109	37,322	39,543	38,933	39,065	41,492	42,635	
Belgium	69,051	69,399	66,568	72,623	72,369	74,518	72,728	76,455	77,580	
Cyprus	807	1,048	1,271	822	1,370	1,791	2,474	1,540		
Denmark	199,989	212,515	216,782	221,821	210,741	216,826	224,792	233,639	226,426	
Finland	17,500	19,288	18,583	20,118	18,762	20,757	19,861	20,728	19,959	
France	120,024	121,882	120,801	121,837	121,630	124,472	125,909	126,104	131,272	
Germany	249,064	252,613	264,518	280,285	276,889	281,303	287,348	290,341	297,827	
Gibraltar										
Greece	10,510	11,248	12,718	12,392	12,327	12,369	12,448	13,641	13,539	
Iceland	77,196	101,918	102,940	90,134	109,734	106,590	106,521	128,898	114,235	
Ireland	34,310	35,244	35,510	36,598	36,884	38,375	37,036	39,095	36,524	
Italy	99,737	102,381	101,955	107,816	110,898	110,221	113,344	112,989	116,374	
Liechtenstein										
Luxembourg	14,001	14,690	14,414	15,462	14,979	15,624	15,496	16,238	15,535	
Malta	376	452	499	491	328	369	407	369		
Monaco										
Netherlands	96,632	98,227	98,887	100,650	102,858	104,633	107,200	110,136	114,498	
Norway	255,076	245,093	246,780	258,531	253,782	251,279	252,331	285,329	293,100	
Portugal	11,616	11,982	12,424	12,509	13,185	13,364	13,426	13,632	14,029	
Spain	62,228	62,416	64,531	66,139	66,141	67,600	70,608	70,675	71,384	
Sweden	360,582	375,744	355,685	398,858	389,933	405,066	385,962	428,278	425,400	441,145
Switzerland	61,885	62,032	64,407	66,695	69,412	70,620	72,756	73,151	73,474	
Turkey	31,102	41,970	52,619	46,235	41,054	47,184	52,358	47,357		
United Kingdom	97,005	98,118	88,396	87,269	87,085	89,224	90,948	92,018	95,820	
Eastern Europe										
Albania										
Belarus	10,762,987	11,634,865	13,094,614	12,116,334	11,638,600	14,413,000	15,809,600	17,453,000	19,306,100	
Bosnia-Herzegovina										
Bulgaria	6,423	8,066	9,733	7,639	7,147	8,895	10,843	8,946	8,809	
Croatia	20,768	26,257	44,568	28,378	22,360	29,842	48,818	30,145	24,248	
Czech Republic	584,948	608,525	597,696	670,781	677,303	703,805	697,094	748,408	725,136	
Estonia	36,964	42,457	42,151	42,847	39,765	46,438	44,743	46,050	40,986	
Georgia	1,021	1,123	1,192	1,196						
Hungary	4,045,432	4,596,118	4,836,075	5,027,974	4,742,124	4,916,465	5,173,495	5,455,216	5,489,996	
Latvia	1,112	1,273	1,301	1,327	1,386	1,543	1,599	1,669	1,603	
Lithuania	11,190	12,643	12,635	12,424	11,805	13,589	14,483	13,674	14,865	
Macedonia										
Moldova	-3,201	-5,107	-5,001	-7,565	5,044	5,574	6,157	7,400	6,531	
Poland	96,714	105,361	110,181	115,520	113,849	116,912	121,919	127,358	127,727	
Romania	26,228	27,612	28,883	28,181						
Russia	2,061,159	2,285,923	2,372,962	2,359,286	2,088,638	2,408,348	2,564,077	2,996,137	2,928,247	
Serbia and Montenegro										
Slovakia	302,988	341,131	365,231	391,310	372,684	387,134	389,601	449,600	425,277	
Slovenia	4,755	5,140	5,206	5,416						
Ukraine	52,515	61,554	72,322	67,316	67,513	79,664	88,491	87,537	88,537	

Source: *International Monetary Fund (IMF), International Financial Statistics*

GDP

Table 10.11

Imports of Goods and Services by Quarter 2006-2008

Million units of national currency

	2006 1st Quarter	2006 2nd Quarter	2006 3rd Quarter	2006 4th Quarter	2007 1st Quarter	2007 2nd Quarter	2007 3rd Quarter	2007 4th Quarter	2008 1st Quarter	2008 2nd Quarter
Western Europe										
Austria	30,998	32,271	32,918	33,915	34,156	34,315	35,801	36,290	35,823	
Belgium	68,082	66,378	64,132	68,969	69,954	70,943	70,216	75,660	78,410	
Cyprus	1,000	1,043	1,054	1,085	1,875	1,985	2,137	2,188		
Denmark	189,750	199,138	201,133	216,020	210,955	211,928	215,612	231,145	227,077	
Finland	16,081	16,874	16,869	17,371	17,664	18,282	17,243	18,575	18,394	
France	124,318	127,831	127,325	127,831	128,175	132,234	135,818	137,184	140,842	
Germany	224,507	225,703	234,427	235,462	240,020	237,510	243,020	243,910	256,040	
Gibraltar										
Greece	17,215	17,905	18,908	19,725	20,038	19,724	20,426	20,825	20,043	
Iceland	124,476	157,535	152,071	142,428	132,882	148,545	145,069	161,446	150,990	
Ireland	29,688	30,415	29,426	33,098	32,105	31,854	31,742	35,318	32,919	
Italy	102,688	104,484	108,166	108,826	111,133	112,002	114,928	114,287	116,087	
Liechtenstein										
Luxembourg	11,761	12,341	11,889	13,398	12,257	12,741	12,889	13,408	12,708	
Malta	446	496	477	493	334	372	385	416		
Monaco										
Netherlands	85,193	87,475	88,302	90,044	90,788	92,909	95,186	97,227	102,593	
Norway	140,762	149,825	156,901	164,645	161,213	169,863	172,761	182,481	172,430	
Portugal	15,345	15,054	15,518	15,089	15,783	15,951	16,645	16,887	17,568	
Spain	76,895	77,457	79,289	81,950	82,497	84,219	87,341	89,620	91,027	
Sweden	298,246	311,747	303,041	339,956	327,314	339,050	339,066	369,590	360,735	382,031
Switzerland	52,598	53,466	53,536	58,723	57,813	59,245	60,004	61,807	59,726	
Turkey	41,653	55,455	56,991	55,073	51,887	59,382	59,939	59,916		
United Kingdom	108,388	111,879	99,493	97,560	98,680	99,189	104,149	105,919	108,638	
Eastern Europe										
Albania										
Belarus	10,529,199	12,573,982	13,695,816	14,117,204	12,619,200	15,634,000	16,916,100	20,022,200	19,751,300	
Bosnia-Herzegovina										
Bulgaria	8,841	9,946	10,875	11,468	10,409	11,535	12,730	13,644	12,549	
Croatia	32,651	36,017	36,289	37,277	34,692	39,539	39,452	41,151	38,845	
Czech Republic	544,901	580,975	574,636	650,278	618,406	659,463	660,864	710,736	659,821	
Estonia	41,532	47,881	48,244	50,173	47,008	51,232	48,613	51,880	46,730	
Georgia	1,594	1,991	2,186	2,091						
Hungary	4,110,395	4,529,552	4,817,109	4,926,844	4,643,215	4,750,275	5,016,445	5,304,465	5,248,385	
Latvia	1,523	1,745	1,993	2,151	2,066	2,256	2,388	2,314	2,194	
Lithuania	12,814	14,371	15,082	15,130	14,374	16,837	17,037	16,938	18,964	
Macedonia										
Moldova										
Poland	98,450	108,251	114,664	121,033	117,692	123,459	127,317	131,630	132,680	
Romania	32,212	36,771	38,800	44,604						
Russia	1,103,510	1,342,916	1,497,626	1,712,718	1,409,268	1,720,558	1,922,317	2,134,537	1,819,897	
Serbia and Montenegro										
Slovakia	319,082	355,338	377,729	411,992	368,743	388,689	381,091	469,158	418,546	
Slovenia	4,763	5,025	5,253	5,778						
Ukraine	58,242	63,720	71,463	75,775	75,755	85,668	93,516	108,040	109,040	

Source: *International Monetary Fund (IMF), International Financial Statistics*

Table 10.12

Total Gross National Income 1980-2007 (national currencies)
Million units of national currency

	1980	1985	1990	1995	1996	1997	1998	1999	2000
Western Europe									
Austria	75,470	102,016	135,860	172,515	180,033	182,390	189,362	195,800	206,346
Belgium	88,226	121,930	163,654	211,403	215,571	225,777	230,049	242,912	257,435
Cyprus	-1,514	3,086	4,232	6,612	6,894	7,288	8,645	8,850	9,419
Denmark	382,155	615,288	818,974	1,008,640	1,055,830	1,109,710	1,150,470	1,203,240	1,266,610
Finland	32,784	56,430	86,967	94,317	98,098	107,372	116,282	121,129	131,352
France	442,342	725,315	1,006,426	1,198,118	1,235,481	1,278,181	1,335,968	1,388,890	1,461,160
Germany	755,394	937,979	1,251,764	1,834,789	1,866,321	1,901,738	1,945,051	1,990,470	2,043,160
Gibraltar									
Greece	5,543	14,374	41,542	88,102	96,485	106,803	116,077	122,003	136,648
Iceland	15,675	117,211	359,053	441,303	476,310	514,338	574,114	618,343	664,838
Ireland	11,510	20,460	32,396	46,953	51,763	59,359	68,008	77,924	90,359
Italy	199,501	415,559	673,202	909,863	970,707	1,016,867	1,062,682	1,122,160	1,182,140
Liechtenstein									
Luxembourg	3,989	6,535	9,990	14,046	14,815	15,690	16,979	17,868	19,170
Malta	413	394	548	1,002	1,026	1,056	1,091	1,157	1,170
Monaco									
Netherlands	154,449	193,089	233,987	309,796	322,610	346,800	358,704	390,395	426,980
Norway	305,071	542,876	715,315	931,980	1,021,240	1,107,440	1,127,500	1,230,020	1,461,260
Portugal	16,629	24,478	51,002	75,812	80,676	84,503			
Spain	90,627	167,502	298,661	436,695	461,370	489,277	521,558	559,562	603,252
Sweden	549,779	883,312	1,396,300	1,767,370	1,810,800	1,884,950	1,983,610	2,103,000	2,230,660
Switzerland	177,345	241,355	327,585	377,560					
Turkey	4	28	287	7,855	15,064				
United Kingdom	227,681	351,782	550,043	720,317	766,606	816,484	874,620	910,115	959,708
Eastern Europe									
Albania									
Belarus			4	121,351	192,046	366,300	701,810	3,028,910	9,096,100
Bosnia-Herzegovina									
Bulgaria				852	1,692	16,844	21,911	23,464	26,082
Croatia									
Czech Republic				1,463,500	1,660,040	1,782,880	1,959,310	2,031,710	2,139,690
Estonia				43,204	56,962	68,076	77,485	82,320	92,340
Georgia									
Hungary	583,000	842,000	2,080,000						
Latvia				2,631	3,149	3,657	3,994	4,225	4,739
Lithuania				25,928	32,364	39,252	43,685	42,651	44,874
Macedonia									
Moldova				6,480	8,070	9,207	9,279	12,678	16,814
Poland	199	859	50,630						
Romania	62	82	86	7,214	10,839	24,975	38,145		
Russia									
Serbia and Montenegro									
Slovakia									
Slovenia			2,576	15,852	16,469	17,524	18,818	20,313	20,996
Ukraine				53,639	80,472	92,166	100,524	126,934	164,942

Source: *International Monetary Fund (IMF), International Financial Statistics*

GNI

Total Gross National Income 1980-2007 (national currencies) *(continued)*
Million units of national currency

	2001	2002	2003	2004	2005	2006	2007	Total US$ million 2007	US$ per capita 2007
Western Europe									
Austria	210,706	218,110	224,145	233,983	242,807	254,614	269,629	369,563.8	44,448.2
Belgium	262,806	271,036	278,530	292,286	303,643	320,491	335,058	459,243.3	43,445.8
Cyprus	10,209	10,780	11,487	12,182	13,174	14,081	15,606	21,390.2	25,027.4
Denmark	1,316,780	1,356,520	1,392,120	1,472,920	1,569,730	1,671,990	1,727,780	317,390.7	58,269.7
Finland	139,599	144,393	144,052	153,425	158,202	168,730	179,995	246,708.0	46,752.0
France	1,514,920	1,552,790	1,604,810	1,673,350	1,737,220	1,819,980	1,882,720	2,580,528.0	42,021.4
Germany	2,092,150	2,116,640	2,148,670	2,226,270	2,265,000	2,344,370	2,446,410	3,353,143.0	40,737.0
Gibraltar									
Greece	146,470	157,108	169,570	183,086	194,624	210,077	223,439	306,254.0	27,419.8
Iceland	747,638	815,230	828,296	890,912	989,645	1,083,800	1,219,550	19,039.1	63,251.6
Ireland	98,903	108,016	119,150	127,560	139,072	153,765	162,121	222,209.2	51,691.8
Italy	1,240,430	1,285,100	1,324,400	1,383,510	1,423,880	1,477,610	1,527,220	2,093,266.1	35,546.8
Liechtenstein									
Luxembourg	20,050	19,898	19,512	23,834	25,008	27,703	29,051	39,818.5	85,345.0
Malta	1,225	1,312	1,366	1,396	1,454	1,544	1,643	2,252.2	5,539.3
Monaco									
Netherlands	451,110	469,468	482,368	504,333	515,885	557,017	582,295	798,115.8	48,790.6
Norway	1,538,260	1,537,010	1,603,730	1,746,400	1,943,190	2,137,760	2,204,153	376,028.2	80,500.4
Portugal									
Spain	644,093	687,643	735,064	735,072	735,080	735,085	735,091	1,007,543.9	22,649.4
Sweden	2,303,500	2,412,530	2,537,810	2,619,210	2,731,090	2,949,260	3,135,660	463,939.4	50,907.8
Switzerland									
Turkey									
United Kingdom	1,011,620	1,076,860	1,140,890	1,209,840	1,258,190	1,310,400	1,388,320	2,777,906.7	45,759.2
Eastern Europe									
Albania									
Belarus	17,113,100	26,084,300	36,616,300	49,951,600	65,186,600	79,020,900	85,938,050	40,044.2	4,106.9
Bosnia-Herzegovina									
Bulgaria	29,045	33,154	35,125	39,317	43,189	48,130	55,639	38,934.5	5,107.0
Croatia									
Czech Republic	2,273,220	2,352,130	2,466,090	2,660,120	2,841,420	3,057,160	3,339,440	164,555.5	15,996.2
Estonia	103,772	116,369	128,941	142,635	168,609	197,486	236,319	20,668.3	15,426.0
Georgia									
Hungary									
Latvia	5,233	5,775	6,372	7,274	8,945	10,842	13,436	26,149.9	11,467.0
Lithuania	47,943	51,425	55,379	61,251	70,242	80,141	92,813	36,776.0	10,865.1
Macedonia									
Moldova	20,484	24,805	30,838	36,414	42,740	50,026	53,669	4,420.9	1,165.3
Poland									
Romania									
Russia									
Serbia and Montenegro									
Slovakia									
Slovenia	22,156	23,537	24,676	25,941	27,371	30,125	31,502	43,177.2	21,478.5
Ukraine	200,610	222,585	264,247	341,686	436,411	535,459	702,257	139,060.8	2,992.8

Source: *International Monetary Fund (IMF), International Financial Statistics*

Table 10.13

Total Gross National Income 1980-2007 (US$)

US$ million

	1980	1985	1990	1995	1996	1997	1998	1999	2000
Western Europe									
Austria	111,091	81,388	182,038	235,830	238,910	216,160	221,851	208,627	190,319
Belgium	129,867	97,276	219,278	288,989	286,070	267,581	269,519	258,826	237,440
Cyprus	2,229	2,462	5,670	9,039	9,149	8,638	10,129	9,430	8,687
Denmark	67,807	58,066	132,337	180,038	182,081	168,024	171,691	172,477	156,698
Finland	48,258	45,020	116,526	128,932	130,180	127,253	136,232	129,064	121,150
France	651,123	578,654	1,348,498	1,637,838	1,639,524	1,514,847	1,565,182	1,479,879	1,347,669
Germany	1,111,933	748,316	1,677,224	2,508,171	2,476,668	2,253,861	2,278,767	2,120,870	1,884,464
Gibraltar									
Greece	8,159	11,467	55,661	120,436	128,039	126,579	135,993	129,996	126,034
Iceland	3,267	2,824	6,160	6,822	7,163	7,254	8,091	8,548	8,457
Ireland	16,943	16,323	43,407	64,185	68,691	70,349	79,676	83,029	83,341
Italy	293,664	331,531	902,015	1,243,790	1,288,159	1,205,149	1,245,009	1,195,675	1,090,321
Liechtenstein									
Luxembourg	5,872	5,214	13,385	19,201	19,660	18,595	19,893	19,039	17,681
Malta	608	315	734	1,370	1,361	1,251	1,278	1,232	1,079
Monaco									
Netherlands	227,347	154,046	313,517	423,494	428,114	411,013	420,248	415,971	393,816
Norway	61,765	63,145	114,272	147,112	158,336	156,564	149,435	157,712	166,018
Portugal	24,478	19,528	68,337	103,635	107,060	100,150			
Spain	133,402	133,633	400,172	596,966	612,253	579,871	611,042	596,220	556,396
Sweden	129,985	102,664	235,910	247,764	270,028	246,886	249,515	254,526	243,462
Switzerland	105,833	98,226	235,815	319,298					
Turkey	58,326	53,253	110,116	171,335	185,055				
United Kingdom	529,128	451,439	976,679	1,136,742	1,196,032	1,336,666	1,448,468	1,472,542	1,452,055
Eastern Europe									
Albania									
Belarus				10,533	14,516	14,077	15,215	12,150	10,375
Bosnia-Herzegovina									
Bulgaria				12,679	9,511	10,015	12,447	12,777	12,284
Croatia									
Czech Republic				55,142	61,155	56,245	60,695	58,772	55,435
Estonia				3,768	4,732	4,904	5,505	5,609	5,442
Georgia									
Hungary	17,921	16,800	32,908						
Latvia				4,988	5,718	6,295	6,771	7,220	7,814
Lithuania				6,482	8,091	9,813	10,921	10,663	11,219
Macedonia									
Moldova				1,441	1,753	1,991	1,728	1,206	1,352
Poland	45,051	58,352	53,295						
Romania	34,273	47,683	38,242	35,478	35,144	34,843	42,977		
Russia									
Serbia and Montenegro									
Slovakia									
Slovenia			3,452	21,669	21,856	20,769	22,046	21,644	19,365
Ukraine				36,413	43,987	49,507	41,038	30,731	30,319

Source: *International Monetary Fund (IMF), International Financial Statistics*

GNI

Total Gross National Income 1980-2007 (US$) *(continued)*
US$ million

	2001	2002	2003	2004	2005	2006	2007	US$ per capita 2007
Western Europe								
Austria	188,775	205,532	253,171	290,718	301,957	319,445	369,564	44,448.2
Belgium	235,453	255,406	314,598	363,158	377,613	402,096	459,243	43,445.8
Cyprus	9,147	10,158	12,974	15,136	16,383	17,666	21,390	25,027.4
Denmark	158,213	171,826	211,322	245,853	261,756	281,159	317,391	58,269.7
Finland	125,069	136,066	162,706	190,627	196,741	211,693	246,708	46,752.0
France	1,357,245	1,463,246	1,812,626	2,079,097	2,160,420	2,283,394	2,580,528	42,021.4
Germany	1,874,396	1,994,581	2,426,913	2,766,087	2,816,772	2,941,307	3,353,143	40,737.0
Gibraltar								
Greece	131,225	148,048	191,529	227,480	242,036	263,568	306,254	27,419.8
Iceland	7,674	8,894	10,798	12,693	15,713	15,443	19,039	63,251.6
Ireland	88,609	101,787	134,579	158,490	172,951	192,918	222,209	51,691.8
Italy	1,111,324	1,210,993	1,495,904	1,718,978	1,770,748	1,853,848	2,093,266	35,546.8
Liechtenstein								
Luxembourg	17,963	18,750	22,038	29,613	31,100	34,757	39,819	85,345.0
Malta	1,098	1,236	1,543	1,734	1,808	1,937	2,252	5,539.3
Monaco								
Netherlands	404,158	442,396	544,832	626,622	641,559	698,848	798,116	48,790.6
Norway	171,076	192,517	226,508	259,078	301,620	333,331	376,028	80,500.4
Portugal								
Spain	577,055	647,989	830,251	913,309	914,151	922,257	1,007,544	22,649.4
Sweden	223,011	247,766	313,841	356,409	365,457	399,724	463,939	50,907.8
Switzerland								
Turkey								
United Kingdom	1,456,291	1,613,943	1,862,763	2,215,094	2,287,627	2,411,097	2,777,907	45,759.2
Eastern Europe								
Albania								
Belarus	12,312	14,565	17,851	23,123	30,266	36,847	40,044	4,106.9
Bosnia-Herzegovina								
Bulgaria	13,295	15,962	20,272	24,961	27,437	30,867	38,934	5,107.0
Croatia								
Czech Republic	59,766	71,846	87,422	103,507	118,603	135,299	164,556	15,996.2
Estonia	5,937	7,005	9,306	11,324	13,399	15,843	20,668	15,426.0
Georgia								
Hungary								
Latvia	8,333	9,342	11,150	13,465	15,839	19,346	26,150	11,467.0
Lithuania	11,986	13,986	18,093	22,028	25,321	29,119	36,776	10,865.1
Macedonia								
Moldova	1,592	1,828	2,211	2,953	3,392	3,810	4,421	1,165.3
Poland								
Romania								
Russia								
Serbia and Montenegro								
Slovakia								
Slovenia	19,850	22,179	27,871	32,231	34,039	37,795	43,177	21,478.5
Ukraine	37,343	41,787	49,552	64,237	85,158	106,031	139,061	2,992.8

Source: *International Monetary Fund (IMF), International Financial Statistics*

Table 10.14

Total Gross National Income by Quarter 2006-2008

Million units of national currency

	2006 1st Quarter	2006 2nd Quarter	2006 3rd Quarter	2006 4th Quarter	2007 1st Quarter	2007 2nd Quarter	2007 3rd Quarter	2007 4th Quarter	2008 1st Quarter	2008 2nd Quarter
Western Europe										
Austria	58,999.6	63,389.8	64,760.0	67,464.7	64,347.4	67,631.5	67,665.5	69,984.7	67,908.8	
Belgium	77,805.0	82,684.9	76,681.0	83,320.1	81,176.8	86,707.4	80,191.9	86,981.9	84,781.7	
Cyprus										
Denmark	394,136.1	422,513.1	420,487.5	434,853.3	408,424.2	434,817.4	431,663.6	452,874.9	418,017.7	
Finland	40,956.6	40,199.2	41,998.2	45,576.0	42,799.0	42,905.0	45,438.0	48,853.0	45,326.0	
France	447,709.3	454,327.1	456,793.2	461,150.4	462,338.8	467,911.8	474,279.6	478,189.9	484,186.5	
Germany	580,670.7	582,437.8	587,759.2	593,502.2	608,306.3	604,577.8	615,933.3	617,592.6	628,558.2	
Gibraltar										
Greece										
Iceland										
Ireland	38,115.9	37,536.5	38,210.8	39,901.8	41,290.2	40,321.0	39,591.6	40,918.3		
Italy	364,859.2	364,396.7	372,336.0	376,018.2	379,199.0	378,704.0	385,938.0	383,379.0	384,470.0	
Liechtenstein										
Luxembourg										
Malta	479.4	533.6	557.5	563.7	368.5	409.2	432.0	433.5		
Monaco										
Netherlands	137,429.1	141,367.6	133,286.2	144,934.1	143,371.0	146,550.2	140,105.1	152,268.8		
Norway	513,523.8	516,647.8	538,430.7	569,157.7						
Portugal										
Spain										
Sweden	715,060.2	734,713.0	707,033.9	792,452.9	762,928.0	770,347.0	756,453.0	845,932.1	794,793.0	
Switzerland										
Turkey										
United Kingdom	320,594.1	327,559.2	329,982.1	332,264.7	336,250.0	345,967.7	347,268.7	358,833.7	364,818.7	
Eastern Europe										
Albania										
Belarus										
Bosnia-Herzegovina										
Bulgaria	9,801.4	11,480.4	13,409.3	13,439.0	11,205.1	12,920.2	15,148.5	16,365.5	13,531.5	
Croatia										
Czech Republic	722,041.7	765,980.9	768,056.1	801,081.2	796,619.5	834,809.5	830,983.5	877,027.5	861,276.5	
Estonia	43,587.6	49,495.1	50,856.9	53,546.4	52,871.2	60,217.5	59,474.0	63,756.2	56,226.4	
Georgia										
Hungary										
Latvia	2,266.7	2,577.0	2,853.4	3,144.7	2,809.9	3,205.3	3,587.9	3,832.5	3,334.3	
Lithuania	16,595.7	19,772.2	21,216.8	22,556.6	19,123.2	22,599.4	24,577.3	26,513.0	23,338.5	
Macedonia										
Moldova										
Poland										
Romania										
Russia										
Serbia and Montenegro										
Slovakia										
Slovenia	6,945.3	7,754.9	7,657.2	7,767.3						
Ukraine						135,630.0	162,327.0	194,412.0	209,888.0	183,984.0

Source: International Monetary Fund (IMF), International Financial Statistics

Trends in Money Supply

Table 10.15

Money Supply 1980-2007

Billion units of national currency

	1980	1985	1990	1995	2001	2002	2003	2004	2005	2006	2007	Total US$ billion 2007
Western Europe												
Austria	5.8	6.9	9.1	12.3	10.7	11.0	12.3	14.1	14.9	15.4	15.9	21.9
Belgium	9.7	10.1	11.1	11.5	9.1	12.7	14.9	17.2	18.2	18.9	19.6	26.8
Cyprus	0.3	0.6	0.7	1.0	1.8	1.8	2.3	2.5	2.9	3.5	3.9	5.3
Denmark	77.5	156.5	244.5	292.0	414.8	430.8	469.1	536.6	643.6	699.5	755.2	138.7
Finland	0.8	1.4	2.4	2.6	2.7	6.3	7.2	8.6	9.2	9.6	10.2	13.9
France	22.7	33.1	41.1	41.9	34.6	74.2	85.0	97.8	103.2	106.9	111.7	153.2
Germany	46.6	58.7	91.9	134.7	82.8	112.2	125.9	141.3	147.7	152.2	156.9	215.0
Gibraltar												
Greece	0.7	1.6	3.7	6.0	8.7	9.2	10.6	12.8	13.6	14.2	15.0	20.6
Iceland	1.0	6.7	24.6	38.3	70.8	87.8	114.8	141.7	174.0	202.6	294.4	4.6
Ireland	0.9	1.4	2.0	2.7	4.7	4.3	4.7	6.4	7.2	7.7	8.2	11.3
Italy	16.2	29.3	42.7	58.7	65.9	65.5	76.1	86.8	91.2	94.3	98.4	134.8
Liechtenstein												
Luxembourg					0.6	0.7	0.8	1.1	1.2	1.3	1.4	1.9
Malta	0.5	0.9	0.9	1.0	1.6	1.7	3.0	3.7	3.9	3.9	4.2	5.8
Monaco												
Netherlands	10.4	14.0	17.9	18.7	11.4	19.4	21.9	26.4	28.3	29.6	31.0	42.5
Norway	45.6	98.6	237.6	358.7	659.6	713.8	748.0	801.0	842.0	879.1	917.2	156.5
Portugal	0.8	1.6	3.1	4.2	5.9	8.5	9.9	11.8	12.6	13.2	13.8	18.8
Spain	7.6	12.5	27.3	45.3	48.7	40.5	46.4	52.7	55.3	57.1	60.0	82.3
Sweden	33.6	46.8		716.0	731.5	775.9	937.5	1,073.5	1,204.2	1,268.7		187.7
Switzerland	65.2	73.9	84.3	100.6	173.6	191.3	237.4	224.1	238.6	232.6	227.5	189.5
Turkey	0.0	0.0	0.0	0.4	10.7	15.8	23.0	28.6	42.4	67.2	69.4	53.2
United Kingdom	74.8	145.5	523.1	514.6	1,127.1	1,184.0	1,300.3	1,434.7	1,490.3	1,529.2	1,595.5	3,192.5
Eastern Europe												
Albania				59.3	143.0	144.0	139.8	158.8	182.9	214.2	199.1	2.2
Belarus				10.0	889.6	1,259.1	2,002.6	3,111.4	4,945.8	7,023.2	7,155.4	3.3
Bosnia-Herzegovina					2.8	3.2	3.3	3.8	4.4	5.6	6.8	4.8
Bulgaria				0.2	6.0	6.7	8.0	10.3	12.4	16.1	19.2	13.4
Croatia				8.3	23.7	30.9	33.9	34.6	38.9	48.6	57.9	10.8
Czech Republic				431.1	583.5	841.7	964.2	1,026.3	1,162.8	1,325.6	1,453.9	71.6
Estonia				8.2	24.9	27.3	30.8	36.2	48.7	61.9	63.1	5.5
Georgia				0.2	0.4	0.5	0.5	0.8	1.0	1.3	1.8	1.1
Hungary		239.7	517.5	1,011.2	2,779.0	3,298.0	4,027.6	4,169.3	5,188.8	5,835.5	5,859.6	31.9
Latvia				0.4	0.9	1.0	1.6	2.0	2.9	4.1	4.0	7.7
Lithuania				3.5	6.7	8.3	10.5	15.1	20.9	24.8	26.5	10.5
Macedonia				12.2	11.2	27.7	28.3	28.9	31.2	35.7	41.6	0.9
Moldova				0.9	2.4	3.3	4.2	5.6	7.3	8.3	10.9	0.9
Poland	0.1	0.2	9.4	37.4	94.2	112.9	133.6	175.7	220.6	275.8	309.7	111.9
Romania	0.0	0.0	0.0	0.7	6.4	8.8	11.3	15.3	24.6	35.4	41.9	17.2
Russia				150.1	1,170.6	1,469.9	2,150.2	2,812.2	3,815.0	5,539.5	7,528.1	294.3
Serbia and Montenegro					58.1	93.7	99.3	111.3	144.9	200.1	248.8	3.6
Slovakia				149.7	225.6	244.8	354.0	404.7	468.0	529.0	553.2	22.4
Slovenia					1.5	2.4	2.6	5.0	6.2	7.1	7.5	10.3
Ukraine				4.7	29.8	40.4	53.3	67.1	98.6	123.3	181.7	36.0

Source: *International Monetary Fund (IMF), International Financial Statistics*

Table 10.16

Annual Rates of Inflation 1980-2007

% growth

	1980	1985	1990	1995	2001	2002	2003	2004	2005	2006	2007
Western Europe											
Austria	6.33	3.19	3.26	2.25	2.66	1.80	1.36	2.06	2.30	1.45	2.17
Belgium	6.65	4.87	3.45	1.47	2.47	1.64	1.59	2.09	2.78	1.79	1.82
Cyprus	13.52	5.03	4.50	2.62	1.98	2.80	4.14	2.29	2.56	2.50	2.37
Denmark	12.31	4.65	2.65	2.10	2.35	2.43	2.09	1.16	1.81	1.89	1.71
Finland	11.59	5.87	6.10	0.99	2.57	1.56	0.88	0.19	0.86	1.57	2.51
France	13.54	5.83	3.38	1.78	1.66	1.92	2.08	2.13	1.81	1.60	1.52
Germany	5.40	2.10	2.70	1.72	1.98	1.37	1.05	1.67	1.95	1.71	2.11
Gibraltar	11.90	6.00	5.90	4.70	3.00	1.60	1.70	1.45	0.82	1.17	1.87
Greece	24.87	19.30	20.40	8.94	3.40	3.57	3.54	2.89	3.56	3.20	2.90
Iceland	58.55	31.69	15.51	1.65	6.39	5.17	2.06	2.80	4.16	6.69	5.06
Ireland	18.22	5.44	3.27	2.52	4.87	4.65	3.48	2.19	2.43	3.94	4.88
Italy	21.28	9.21	6.50	5.24	2.79	2.47	2.67	2.21	1.99	2.09	1.83
Liechtenstein	4.00	3.40	5.40		1.10	1.00	0.89	0.77	0.56	0.58	0.31
Luxembourg	6.30	4.09	3.70	1.92	2.67	2.07	2.05	2.23	2.49	2.68	2.33
Malta	15.75	-0.24	2.98	4.43	2.93	2.19	1.30	2.79	3.01	2.77	1.25
Monaco					1.01	0.96	0.93	0.90	0.87	0.75	0.94
Netherlands	6.54	2.22	2.45	1.92	4.20	3.26	2.10	1.24	1.70	1.14	1.60
Norway	10.90	5.67	4.11	2.46	3.02	1.29	2.48	0.47	1.52	2.33	0.73
Portugal	16.69	19.65	13.37	4.12	4.39	3.55	3.28	2.36	2.29	2.74	2.81
Spain	15.55	8.82	6.72	4.67	3.59	3.07	3.04	3.04	3.37	3.52	2.79
Sweden	13.70	7.36	10.38	2.46	2.41	2.16	1.93	0.37	0.45	1.36	2.21
Switzerland	4.02	3.43	5.38	1.80	0.99	0.64	0.64	0.80	1.17	1.06	0.73
Turkey	110.17	44.96	60.31	88.11	54.40	44.96	25.30	10.58	10.14	10.51	8.76
United Kingdom	16.80	5.20	7.00	2.60	1.20	1.30	1.40	1.30	2.10	2.30	2.30
Eastern Europe											
Albania			-0.20	7.79	3.11	7.77	0.48	2.28	2.37	2.37	2.93
Belarus				709.35	61.13	42.54	28.40	18.11	10.34	7.03	8.42
Bosnia-Herzegovina				12.90	3.20	0.30	0.50	0.30	3.60	7.50	1.30
Bulgaria		2.80	23.80	62.05	7.36	5.81	2.16	6.35	5.04	7.26	8.40
Croatia				4.04	3.76	1.67	1.77	2.03	3.34	3.21	2.87
Czech Republic	2.90	2.30	9.50	9.47	4.71	1.79	0.11	2.83	1.85	2.53	2.93
Estonia				28.78	5.74	3.57	1.34	3.05	4.09	4.43	6.59
Georgia				162.72	4.65	5.56	4.78	5.70	8.23	9.22	9.25
Hungary	9.29	7.01	28.97	28.30	9.22	5.27	4.64	6.78	3.55	3.88	7.94
Latvia				24.98	2.49	1.94	2.92	6.19	6.76	6.56	10.08
Lithuania				39.66	1.30	0.30	-1.18	1.20	2.66	3.84	5.72
Macedonia				16.37	5.20	2.31	1.10	1.05	0.04	3.34	3.54
Moldova				9.91	9.76	5.30	11.75	12.53	11.96	12.78	12.37
Poland	9.68	11.52	555.38	28.07	5.49	1.90	0.79	3.58	2.11	1.11	2.39
Romania	1.50	-0.20	127.90	32.24	34.47	22.54	15.27	11.88	8.99	6.58	4.84
Russia				197.47	21.46	15.79	13.68	10.86	12.68	9.68	9.01
Serbia and Montenegro				82.66	91.10	21.20	11.30	9.53	16.18	11.82	6.55
Slovakia				9.92	7.33	3.32	8.55	7.55	2.71	4.48	2.76
Slovenia				13.41	8.42	7.47	5.58	3.59	2.48	2.46	3.61
Ukraine				376.75	11.96	0.76	5.20	9.05	13.51	9.09	12.84

Source: Euromonitor International from International Monetary Fund (IMF), International Financial Statistics and World Economic Outlook/UN/national statistics

Rates of Inflation

Table 10.17

Rates of Inflation by Month 2007
% growth

	January	February	March	April	May	June	July	August	September	October	November	December
Western Europe												
Austria	1.59	1.59	1.78	1.77	1.97	1.97	2.07	1.67	2.07	2.76	3.15	3.63
Belgium	1.66	1.77	1.82	1.78	1.28	1.29	1.37	1.12	1.50	2.24	2.94	3.09
Cyprus	1.65	1.45	1.50	1.78	2.21	1.86	2.44	2.48	2.64	3.00	3.54	3.92
Denmark	1.81	1.88	1.97	1.69	1.78	1.42	1.24	1.07	1.24	1.68	2.48	2.30
Finland	2.34	2.17	2.63	2.58	2.35	2.40	2.56	2.32	2.64	2.68	2.86	2.58
France	1.27	1.08	1.22	1.28	1.10	1.22	1.11	1.21	1.53	2.03	2.54	2.66
Germany	1.58	1.71	1.90	2.03	1.84	1.66	1.87	1.87	2.34	2.54	3.12	2.87
Gibraltar												
Greece	2.76	2.72	2.61	2.54	2.67	2.64	2.53	2.56	2.97	3.07	3.93	3.82
Iceland	6.85	7.37	5.87	5.26	4.63	3.94	3.77	3.44	4.17	4.46	5.15	5.81
Ireland	5.08	4.80	5.06	5.06	5.02	4.95	4.89	4.68	4.62	4.72	4.97	4.70
Italy	1.71	1.79	1.71	1.55	1.54	1.69	1.61	1.61	1.69	2.07	2.38	2.61
Liechtenstein												
Luxembourg	2.24	2.04	2.13	2.12	1.95	2.04	1.86	1.94	2.13	2.91	3.20	3.39
Malta	1.41	1.07	0.32	-0.15	-0.41	0.01	0.66	1.35	1.83	2.31	3.29	3.31
Monaco												
Netherlands	1.42	1.41	1.80	1.79	1.79	1.80	1.50	1.10	1.39	1.59	1.99	1.80
Norway	1.21	0.77	1.11	0.25	0.34	0.42	0.42	0.42	-0.33	-0.17	1.51	2.78
Portugal	2.65	2.47	3.18	3.52	3.24	3.24	3.15	2.06	2.14	2.59	2.76	2.67
Spain	2.39	2.40	2.46	2.46	2.39	2.43	2.24	2.14	2.70	3.58	4.12	4.23
Sweden	1.94	1.98	1.92	1.93	1.66	1.85	1.87	1.77	2.19	2.72	3.26	3.46
Switzerland	0.10	-0.01	0.17	0.45	0.48	0.63	0.73	0.43	0.75	1.26	1.77	2.01
Turkey	9.90	10.13	10.83	10.68	9.19	8.57	6.88	7.37	7.10	7.68	8.38	8.36
United Kingdom	2.28	2.47	2.59	2.44	2.31	2.38	2.06	2.19	2.12	2.28	2.30	2.18
Eastern Europe												
Albania	2.84	2.89	2.70	1.89	1.47	1.99	2.06	4.18	4.45	4.19	3.51	3.03
Belarus	7.13	7.81	8.12	6.97	7.06	7.20	7.20	8.21	9.00	9.92	10.34	12.09
Bosnia-Herzegovina												
Bulgaria	7.12	4.47	4.12	4.18	4.31	5.57	8.42	12.02	13.16	12.39	12.58	12.50
Croatia	1.76	1.26	1.75	2.23	2.21	1.93	2.14	2.62	3.89	4.28	4.64	5.79
Czech Republic	1.33	1.58	1.96	2.59	2.45	2.51	2.44	2.56	2.95	4.04	5.11	5.62
Estonia	5.13	4.74	5.72	5.54	5.71	5.82	6.39	5.71	7.20	8.48	9.11	9.59
Georgia	10.46	11.05	9.75	8.12	7.28	7.26	6.57	7.70	8.97	11.22	11.64	10.97
Hungary	7.66	8.82	9.02	8.69	8.46	8.56	8.33	8.23	6.28	6.69	7.09	7.39
Latvia	7.14	7.27	8.51	8.93	8.20	8.80	9.52	10.16	11.39	13.22	13.70	14.11
Lithuania	4.04	4.32	4.59	4.87	4.84	4.83	5.02	5.49	7.05	7.47	7.87	8.22
Macedonia	2.61	2.31	2.51	2.61	2.11	2.72	2.52	3.55	4.69	5.11	5.64	6.16
Moldova	12.78	11.90	10.90	10.90	10.58	10.36	12.03	13.59	14.15	14.14	13.69	13.36
Poland	1.55	1.84	2.44	2.27	2.26	2.56	2.27	1.53	2.11	2.62	3.35	3.86
Romania	4.02	3.82	3.66	3.79	3.83	3.81	4.00	4.97	6.05	6.85	6.69	6.58
Russia	8.20	7.60	7.40	7.61	7.81	8.47	8.73	8.62	9.39	10.85	11.50	11.91
Serbia and Montenegro												
Slovakia	3.04	2.66	2.73	2.72	2.27	2.49	2.27	2.27	2.86	3.22	3.13	3.42
Slovenia	2.66	2.10	2.28	2.57	2.89	3.58	3.85	3.51	3.51	5.06	5.67	5.65
Ukraine	10.89	9.56	10.17	10.59	10.68	13.04	13.60	14.24	14.52	14.83	15.30	16.68

Source: *Euromonitor International from International Monetary Fund (IMF), International Financial Statistics and World Economic Outlook/UN/national statistics*

Table 10.18

Public Consumption 1980-2007

Billion units of national currency

	1980	1985	1990	1995	2001	2002	2003	2004	2005	2006	2007	Total US$ billion 2007
Western Europe												
Austria	13.8	19.8	25.5	35.3	38.9	40.1	41.4	42.8	44.5	46.5	48.3	66.2
Belgium	20.7	28.6	33.6	44.8	56.4	60.3	63.2	66.0	68.7	70.8	73.9	101.3
Cyprus	0.2	0.4	0.7	0.9	1.8	2.0	2.3	2.3	2.5	2.6	2.8	3.8
Denmark	105.3	164.2	211.2	257.2	343.3	360.2	371.2	389.0	401.3	421.2	437.6	80.4
Finland	6.1	11.7	19.4	21.9	28.5	30.3	31.7	33.3	34.9	36.4	37.9	52.0
France	93.8	168.6	224.2	282.3	341.2	362.2	378.4	393.8	408.6	422.6	436.4	598.2
Germany	176.4	220.6	272.3	361.8	400.2	411.8	416.9	415.6	421.5	425.9	436.1	597.7
Gibraltar												
Greece	0.9	3.2	6.7	14.0	25.4	28.7	29.4	31.6	33.0	33.9	38.1	52.2
Iceland	2.5	21.1	73.1	99.0	181.8	207.2	219.3	233.1	252.7	285.4	314.4	4.9
Ireland	2.7	4.8	6.0	8.7	15.4	17.6	19.0	20.5	22.3	24.3	26.8	36.7
Italy	34.4	80.3	141.2	170.2	236.9	248.8	262.9	276.2	290.8	299.1	303.9	416.6
Liechtenstein	0.1	0.1	0.2	0.3	0.5	0.5	0.5	0.5	0.5	0.5	0.5	0.4
Luxembourg	0.7	1.1	1.7	2.4	3.6	4.0	4.2	4.6	5.0	5.2	5.6	7.6
Malta	0.1	0.1	0.1	0.2	0.3	0.4	0.4	0.4	0.4	0.4	0.4	0.6
Monaco	0.0	0.1	0.1	0.1	0.2	0.2	0.2	0.2	0.2	0.2	0.2	0.3
Netherlands	40.4	48.1	56.6	72.7	101.4	110.2	116.8	118.9	121.7	135.5	142.5	195.3
Norway	60.3	102.1	155.9	203.7	317.0	339.4	358.7	373.3	387.2	415.4	449.3	76.6
Portugal	1.0	3.1	8.4	15.3	25.4	27.1	28.1	29.7	32.0	32.2	33.0	45.2
Spain	13.6	28.0	53.2	80.9	116.2	125.4	135.9	149.8	163.7	178.0	192.7	264.2
Sweden	163.6	251.2	389.6	481.7	615.0	658.0	691.7	702.5	722.7	761.9	796.6	117.9
Switzerland	17.9	25.2	37.0	44.2	49.7	50.9	52.3	53.0	53.9	54.0	54.8	45.6
Turkey		0.0	0.0	0.8	29.8	44.6	55.5	66.8	76.5	93.5	104.5	80.2
United Kingdom	50.3	75.5	112.4	142.9	194.5	212.5	232.7	250.7	268.9	286.4	299.9	600.0
Eastern Europe												
Albania	1.4	1.6	1.7	30.7	60.7	69.6	75.6	82.5	88.5	91.9	93.6	1.0
Belarus			0.0	24.9	3,701.3	5,496.7	7,817.3	10,299.9	13,524.4	15,225.1	17,830.9	8.3
Bosnia-Herzegovina					2.8	3.1	3.4	3.5	3.7	4.1	4.6	3.2
Bulgaria	0.0	0.0	0.0	0.1	5.2	5.9	6.6	7.2	7.7	8.2	9.1	6.4
Croatia			0.1	27.8	36.4	39.1	41.6	43.9	45.9	48.9	55.3	10.3
Czech Republic			143.5	306.3	496.7	549.5	603.2	621.6	658.5	684.7	713.1	35.1
Estonia			0.1	11.0	20.5	22.4	25.0	27.0	29.9	33.9	41.5	3.6
Georgia				0.3	0.6	0.7	0.8	1.4	2.0	2.1	2.2	1.3
Hungary	74.2	104.6	221.8	617.7	1,553.7	1,780.3	1,984.0	2,068.1	2,172.1	2,432.1	2,453.6	13.4
Latvia			0.0	0.6	1.1	1.2	1.4	1.5	1.6	1.9	2.5	4.9
Lithuania			0.0	5.6	9.7	10.1	10.4	11.2	12.2	14.8	16.3	6.5
Macedonia				31.5	58.0	54.6	52.0	53.1	54.0	57.6	59.3	1.3
Moldova			0.0	1.8	2.9	4.8	5.7	5.2	6.7	9.6	11.3	0.9
Poland	0.0	0.2	10.5	63.0	139.5	144.7	152.8	162.7	177.8	193.7	199.1	71.9
Romania	0.0	0.0	0.0	1.0	17.7	22.8	38.8	39.8	52.4	61.7	60.6	24.8
Russia			0.1	272.5	1,470.0	1,911.3	2,330.6	2,847.5	3,590.7	4,576.1	5,820.4	227.5
Serbia and Montenegro				10.5	161.5	224.9	273.3	288.9	329.7	361.2	421.4	6.1
Slovakia			69.6	124.9	208.7	224.9	249.6	260.5	272.8	315.3	325.9	13.2
Slovenia			0.5	3.0	4.4	4.7	4.9	5.1	5.4	5.9	6.1	8.3
Ukraine				11.6	16.4	16.7	20.9	23.8	31.1	39.2	50.6	10.0

Source: *International Monetary Fund (IMF), International Financial Statistics*

Public and Private Consumption

Table 10.19

Public Consumption by Quarter 2006-2008
Million units of national currency

	2006 1st Quarter	2006 2nd Quarter	2006 3rd Quarter	2006 4th Quarter	2007 1st Quarter	2007 2nd Quarter	2007 3rd Quarter	2007 4th Quarter	2008 1st Quarter	2008 2nd Quarter
Western Europe										
Austria	11,566.6	11,599.9	11,582.4	11,703.1	11,886.8	11,938.7	12,192.0	12,272.4	12,325.0	
Belgium	17,699.2	17,832.2	16,953.3	18,289.3	18,644.1	18,680.0	17,522.3	19,043.6	19,806.8	
Cyprus	341.2	372.3	358.8	424.5	623.9	608.7	653.1	888.2		
Denmark	102,065.4	104,752.1	105,130.4	109,210.1	106,271.4	108,484.3	108,800.4	114,003.0	109,895.4	
Finland	8,717.9	9,461.7	8,967.2	9,266.1	9,017.0	9,512.0	9,083.0	10,323.0	9,531.0	
France	104,165.4	105,270.7	106,096.0	107,044.9	107,636.3	108,720.2	109,674.6	110,418.8	111,081.3	
Germany	106,906.0	106,455.0	106,114.1	106,404.8	108,722.2	108,882.4	109,382.9	109,062.6	111,645.2	
Gibraltar										
Greece	8,430.9	8,420.2	8,455.2	8,554.2	9,429.9	9,413.1	9,550.0	9,671.0	10,112.1	
Iceland	67,735.8	70,251.7	71,036.7	71,663.7	76,602.8	78,370.8	78,425.8	81,033.7	86,858.7	
Ireland	5,865.0	5,951.8	6,170.1	6,326.1	6,519.0	6,585.0	6,749.0	6,912.0	7,092.0	
Italy	73,469.2	76,626.6	74,925.2	74,053.0	74,964.0	75,698.2	75,911.1	77,376.8	76,073.3	
Liechtenstein										
Luxembourg	1,257.4	1,253.5	1,225.8	1,528.0	1,301.2	1,301.0	1,275.0	1,583.3	1,378.0	
Malta	102.9	104.9	107.2	115.4	105.5	107.7	111.6	123.8		
Monaco										
Netherlands	33,450.4	33,666.1	34,030.5	34,322.0	35,340.8	35,250.8	35,896.7	35,992.7	36,382.7	
Norway	104,451.1	100,933.1	102,696.1	107,295.8	112,050.0	109,472.0	111,427.0	116,338.0	116,893.0	
Portugal	8,047.4	8,055.6	8,049.0	8,055.9	8,134.4	8,220.0	8,279.0	8,337.8	8,380.3	
Spain	42,951.0	43,666.3	44,709.9	46,650.8	47,057.0	47,482.0	48,601.0	49,598.0	51,130.0	
Sweden	179,156.7	194,902.7	185,662.5	202,168.1	186,849.0	201,781.0	191,041.0	216,911.0	197,105.0	211,879.0
Switzerland	13,473.3	13,398.5	13,557.7	13,532.3	13,583.6	13,718.6	13,701.2	13,788.3	13,949.2	
Turkey	19,405.3	22,682.1	23,341.0	28,096.9	22,005.6	24,888.9	25,999.6	31,571.8		
United Kingdom	70,868.9	70,368.7	72,169.8	72,947.6	73,311.7	74,615.2	75,401.3	76,547.7	78,945.3	
Eastern Europe										
Albania										
Belarus	3,425,604.1	3,901,213.9	3,620,973.1	4,277,308.8	4,031,400.0	4,821,500.0	4,078,400.0	4,899,600.0	4,777,700.0	
Bosnia-Herzegovina										
Bulgaria	1,699.9	1,892.3	1,869.5	2,736.9	1,734.0	2,039.1	2,069.3	3,285.7	2,037.1	
Croatia	11,621.5	12,184.1	12,208.5	12,909.2	12,879.9	13,674.2	14,100.6	14,689.3	13,951.0	
Czech Republic	155,915.4	168,348.4	165,480.1	194,940.2	160,537.0	172,534.0	170,129.0	209,889.0	163,744.0	
Estonia	7,377.8	8,889.4	7,259.3	10,348.1	9,103.1	10,737.7	9,096.2	12,553.9	11,034.4	
Georgia	340.9	495.6	535.7	743.8						
Hungary	624,743.9	586,622.4	550,977.7	669,776.0	557,175.8	583,169.8	610,381.8	702,902.7	583,406.8	
Latvia	387.3	435.0	421.9	611.0	537.5	599.4	614.2	789.4	691.7	
Lithuania	2,710.7	3,473.1	3,572.0	5,023.7	3,090.3	4,353.1	3,664.3	5,211.2	3,870.3	
Macedonia										
Moldova	2,421.4	2,413.4	2,331.3	2,446.1	2,586.4	2,966.3	2,502.5	3,222.4	2,992.1	
Poland	46,896.4	49,466.1	47,052.6	50,291.9	48,484.9	51,319.4	48,735.1	50,599.7	49,674.3	
Romania	9,617.0	12,432.5	16,566.2	23,064.5						
Russia	1,103,989.4	1,139,103.7	1,158,048.8	1,174,958.2	1,394,577.6	1,438,697.5	1,463,107.5	1,524,067.4	1,820,096.9	
Serbia and Montenegro										
Slovakia	63,852.5	74,576.2	75,633.2	101,280.0	70,430.0	73,033.0	77,072.0	105,315.0	73,297.0	
Slovenia	1,380.5	1,498.7	1,439.7	1,538.8						
Ukraine	7,981.2	8,827.2	9,582.2	12,834.3	9,210.0	11,712.0	12,720.0	16,953.0	12,057.0	

Source: *International Monetary Fund (IMF), International Financial Statistics*

Table 10.20

Private Consumption 1980-2007

Billion units of national currency

	1980	1985	1990	1995	2001	2002	2003	2004	2005	2006	2007	Total US$ billion 2007
Western Europe												
Austria	43.1	60.1	77.5	100.2	121.6	123.9	127.7	132.8	137.8	142.9	147.9	202.7
Belgium	50.7	73.3	92.9	112.5	138.6	141.5	146.5	152.6	158.9	166.4	173.5	237.8
Cyprus	1.0	1.9	2.5	4.4	7.0	7.2	7.5	8.2	8.9	9.5	10.8	14.9
Denmark	207.2	329.2	423.2	521.8	631.7	652.3	666.9	707.2	759.8	805.2	842.5	154.8
Finland	17.5	30.3	45.5	49.8	67.9	71.1	74.9	78.1	81.2	85.9	90.5	124.0
France	251.8	432.0	592.7	676.7	838.2	866.1	900.0	940.0	981.5	1,025.7	1,054.3	1,445.1
Germany	506.3	639.1	817.5	1,067.2	1,258.6	1,263.5	1,284.6	1,307.5	1,326.4	1,357.5	1,375.2	1,884.9
Gibraltar	0.0	0.1	0.1	0.1	0.1	0.1	0.1	0.1	0.1	0.1	0.1	0.2
Greece	4.6	12.5	32.8	68.4	105.9	113.1	121.9	130.8	140.8	152.0	161.7	221.6
Iceland	8.9	77.2	218.1	258.2	434.0	448.1	481.5	530.3	610.4	685.4	746.6	11.7
Ireland	9.0	15.5	21.8	28.9	55.1	60.2	64.4	67.8	73.8	80.7	88.1	120.8
Italy	120.1	251.7	402.1	553.3	737.7	760.3	789.0	815.8	842.1	874.4	906.4	1,242.4
Liechtenstein	0.5	0.8	1.1	1.7	2.5	2.5	2.5	2.6	2.7	2.8	2.9	2.4
Luxembourg	2.3	3.6	4.9	6.5	9.4	10.1	10.4	10.9	11.6	12.2	12.7	17.4
Malta	0.5	0.9	1.1	1.7	2.9	2.8	2.9	3.0	3.1	3.2	3.4	4.6
Monaco	0.1	0.2	0.3	0.4	0.4	0.5	0.5	0.5	0.5	0.5	0.5	0.7
Netherlands	85.8	103.1	121.9	151.1	224.2	233.0	238.1	242.8	250.3	255.0	264.3	362.3
Norway	149.6	266.5	366.5	470.9	667.6	698.0	738.9	786.0	826.2	883.2	946.1	161.4
Portugal	5.2	15.1	34.7	55.5	81.8	85.4	87.8	92.3	96.7	101.0	105.3	144.3
Spain	62.8	111.7	192.8	268.4	402.3	425.1	451.2	487.1	524.9	563.2	597.1	818.4
Sweden	269.8	440.0	690.1	897.3	1,141.3	1,190.8	1,235.5	1,278.1	1,328.4	1,373.9	1,435.3	212.4
Switzerland	113.8	148.3	188.4	223.0	260.1	262.5	265.9	272.3	279.6	287.9	296.5	247.0
Turkey	0.0	0.0	0.3	5.5	164.3	238.4	324.0	398.6	465.4	534.8	605.2	464.4
United Kingdom	135.3	211.6	347.7	457.5	657.2	690.5	724.3	761.5	792.5	827.6	876.1	1,753.0
Eastern Europe												
Albania	8.8	9.9	12.2	203.1	411.1	466.0	521.9	585.7	635.7	697.9	758.4	8.4
Belarus			0.0	71.7	9,895.9	15,549.9	20,889.6	26,858.8	33,827.0	40,803.1	50,247.6	23.4
Bosnia-Herzegovina					10.8	12.0	13.7	15.1	16.7	18.2	20.4	14.3
Bulgaria	0.0	0.0	0.0	0.6	20.6	23.0	24.4	26.9	30.0	34.8	39.1	27.3
Croatia			0.2	64.0	99.6	109.4	116.6	124.5	133.1	141.8	153.4	28.6
Czech Republic			308.6	746.0	1,220.3	1,262.4	1,332.5	1,416.9	1,464.5	1,567.6	1,707.0	84.1
Estonia			0.5	23.5	60.0	68.6	76.0	82.5	93.8	112.0	129.1	11.3
Georgia				3.4	5.3	5.8	6.2	7.2	7.8	10.9	13.8	8.3
Hungary	441.2	649.3	1,282.5	3,730.3	9,801.8	11,348.2	12,919.7	13,863.1	14,910.7	15,744.4	16,525.0	90.0
Latvia			0.0	1.6	3.3	3.6	4.0	4.7	5.7	7.3	9.3	18.1
Lithuania			0.1	17.1	31.6	33.4	36.5	40.8	46.5	53.5	63.5	25.2
Macedonia				119.4	163.8	188.2	191.9	209.1	222.7	242.0	260.5	5.8
Moldova			0.0	3.6	16.4	18.5	24.7	28.1	34.7	41.4	48.8	4.0
Poland	0.2	0.6	27.2	203.8	506.8	541.0	553.9	594.7	619.4	657.4	708.6	256.0
Romania	0.0	0.0	0.1	4.9	81.8	104.5	130.5	170.4	200.0	239.3	282.1	115.7
Russia			0.3	744.1	4,416.9	5,531.9	6,694.2	8,554.0	10,728.2	13,040.0	15,990.5	625.1
Serbia and Montenegro				34.8	636.2	811.7	906.4	1,008.7	1,223.3	1,441.2	1,631.4	23.5
Slovakia			160.1	301.7	590.4	640.5	694.2	779.4	851.7	943.1	1,036.1	42.0
Slovenia			2.9	9.4	12.5	13.1	13.9	14.4	15.2	16.3	17.9	24.5
Ukraine			0.0	30.1	140.0	153.6	180.7	221.7	306.8	385.7	510.0	101.0

Source: International Monetary Fund (IMF), International Financial Statistics

Public and Private Consumption

Table 10.21

Private Consumption by Quarter 2006-2008
Million units of national currency

	2006 1st Quarter	2006 2nd Quarter	2006 3rd Quarter	2006 4th Quarter	2007 1st Quarter	2007 2nd Quarter	2007 3rd Quarter	2007 4th Quarter	2008 1st Quarter	2008 2nd Quarter
Western Europe										
Austria	34,207.7	35,165.5	36,034.6	37,478.2	35,186.1	36,593.7	37,305.3	38,807.9	36,716.8	
Belgium	40,454.3	42,124.0	41,373.6	42,422.1	41,904.1	44,064.5	42,953.3	44,607.2	44,975.6	
Cyprus	1,335.2	1,340.4	1,354.2	1,429.7	2,636.0	2,639.8	2,681.1	2,888.7		
Denmark	195,321.3	202,500.5	196,638.4	210,715.8	200,772.8	208,234.4	208,735.8	224,719.0	209,424.0	
Finland	20,668.9	21,437.5	21,864.7	21,892.9	21,355.0	22,750.0	22,684.0	23,665.0	22,810.0	
France	253,297.6	256,050.2	258,002.6	258,389.6	258,222.1	261,741.7	265,346.8	268,979.4	271,359.2	
Germany	336,677.3	337,431.5	340,337.9	343,053.2	339,240.0	343,650.0	346,210.0	346,100.0	349,420.0	
Gibraltar										
Greece	36,451.3	37,445.8	38,816.3	39,239.5	39,295.5	39,884.5	40,833.5	41,689.5	41,962.5	
Iceland	160,580.0	176,413.0	170,558.0	178,934.0	170,256.0	190,378.0	187,926.0	198,022.0	191,809.0	
Ireland	19,770.0	19,733.8	19,640.8	21,567.5	21,272.3	21,472.4	21,643.7	23,734.6	22,902.3	
Italy	215,030.2	217,787.3	220,543.4	221,062.1	223,792.0	225,500.0	228,046.0	229,086.0	231,252.0	
Liechtenstein										
Luxembourg	3,118.3	3,163.3	3,120.3	3,326.9	3,100.6	3,147.7	3,135.2	3,343.9	3,131.0	
Malta	323.7	342.9	354.3	377.4	775.9	826.1	867.0	914.2		
Monaco										
Netherlands	63,123.1	63,746.9	64,061.8	64,106.1	65,213.0	65,529.0	66,265.0	67,338.0	67,991.0	
Norway	203,152.1	217,762.3	228,605.5	233,701.0	219,112.0	232,788.0	242,823.0	251,378.0	231,649.0	
Portugal	24,808.0	25,212.7	25,457.0	25,537.3	25,797.5	26,245.8	26,428.4	26,788.2	27,086.0	
Spain	137,750.6	139,362.3	141,906.5	144,196.6	146,147.0	148,150.0	149,352.0	153,455.0	155,176.0	
Sweden	329,655.0	348,021.1	336,776.0	359,407.9	340,940.1	361,311.2	355,834.3	377,244.3	355,414.0	379,358.2
Switzerland	71,083.7	71,778.0	72,305.5	72,717.9	73,132.6	73,654.8	74,498.1	75,223.6	75,913.0	
Turkey	79,294.9	90,721.8	111,254.2	100,690.1						
United Kingdom	202,612.3	205,686.7	208,110.4	211,231.7	214,942.7	217,849.0	220,345.7	222,959.6	227,176.9	
Eastern Europe										
Albania										
Belarus	8,934,780.1	9,735,774.4	11,704,864.8	10,427,680.8	11,339,600.0	11,811,700.0	14,218,000.0	12,878,300.0	14,102,300.0	
Bosnia-Herzegovina										
Bulgaria	7,745.5	8,215.9	8,975.9	9,827.6	8,681.7	9,067.9	10,188.8	11,142.4	10,406.7	
Croatia	33,814.7	36,451.2	32,843.2	38,669.8	36,391.0	39,360.0	35,587.0	42,083.0	40,096.0	
Czech Republic	357,894.5	389,260.4	402,924.8	417,560.4	392,963.1	423,527.0	438,013.0	452,476.9	431,175.0	
Estonia	24,939.9	27,177.3	28,520.6	31,345.2	30,337.5	32,091.5	31,953.6	34,719.4	33,421.2	
Georgia	2,609.7	2,798.9	2,586.6	2,860.8						
Hungary	3,734,407.3	3,846,077.5	3,999,875.9	4,164,039.3	3,948,299.6	4,071,549.9	4,153,000.1	4,352,150.5	4,175,960.1	
Latvia	1,503.4	1,728.1	1,931.5	2,117.5	2,052.2	2,289.2	2,452.9	2,505.9	2,403.3	
Lithuania	11,576.5	13,027.9	14,341.2	14,547.7	13,736.6	15,440.6	16,664.8	17,653.8	17,211.1	
Macedonia										
Moldova	7,523.5	8,835.1	12,249.6	12,752.1	10,248.7	10,729.4	15,659.0	12,189.1	13,168.1	
Poland	162,709.1	163,978.4	165,919.9	164,783.6	177,128.1	176,700.8	178,146.2	176,666.9	194,679.8	
Romania	47,255.2	56,244.3	60,109.9	75,664.6						
Russia	2,814,754.3	3,123,987.1	3,372,471.0	3,728,787.5	3,424,172.1	3,792,472.4	4,136,972.6	4,636,882.9	4,355,102.7	
Serbia and Montenegro										
Slovakia	225,384.6	228,747.2	239,250.5	249,683.7	246,435.5	251,033.5	263,803.5	274,817.5	277,972.5	
Slovenia	3,675.0	4,213.0	4,210.1	4,163.6						
Ukraine	81,360.2	92,474.7	98,928.9	112,917.2	103,535.0	120,360.0	128,935.0	157,193.0	148,321.0	

Source: International Monetary Fund (IMF), International Financial Statistics

Table 10.22

Government Finance and International Liquidity: Latest Year

US$ million / as stated

	Year	Budget Expenditure	Budget Revenue	Budget Surplus/ Deficit	Foreign Debt	Foreign Exchange Reserves	Gold Reserves (million troy oz)
Western Europe							
Austria	1998	120,439.1	58,364.3	-4,656.1	15,908.3	20,918.0	9.64
Belgium	2006	58,720.3	53,635.4	-5,084.9	1,826.7	7,618.9	7.32
Cyprus	2003	5,453.7	4,649.4	-804.3	2,046.9	3,154.5	0.47
Denmark	2000	53,156.8	58,809.5	2,573.8		14,469.0	2.14
Finland	2007	56,364.3	61,952.8	5,588.5	63.0	6,689.2	1.58
France	2003	959,516.5	886,579.4	-72,937.2	10,267.1	23,121.7	97.25
Germany	1999	368,120.7	336,264.0	-31,326.1	218,240.5	52,661.1	111.52
Gibraltar	1992	178.6	178.6	-1.8			
Greece	1996	45,118.6	33,053.6	-12,609.3	5,995.2	17,337.3	3.47
Iceland	2006	4,299.7	5,433.7	790.9	956.8	2,273.2	0.06
Ireland	1996	17,676.5	17,811.8	-63.4	14,580.7	7,714.9	0.36
Italy	2007	744,411.4	691,199.1	-57,213.8	1,005,939.0	27,319.2	78.83
Liechtenstein							
Luxembourg	1997	6,298.5	7,504.9	368.4	184.4	23.9	0.31
Malta	2001	555.0	516.0	-219.4	89.7	1,582.4	0.01
Monaco							
Netherlands	2006	204,034.8	209,250.3	5,215.5		9,327.0	20.61
Norway	2003	94,605.8	96,157.0	6,146.4	50,395.0	35,890.2	1.18
Portugal	1995	41,172.4	37,740.8	-5,504.1	4,067.4	15,315.0	16.07
Spain	2007	192,454.8	203,811.9	11,357.1	221,952.7	10,792.0	9.05
Sweden	2007	112,376.7	127,647.0	15,270.4	36,597.0	26,382.0	4.78
Switzerland	2006	35,897.7	37,774.4	1,876.6		37,364.0	41.48
Turkey	2001	65,295.4	41,877.5	-28,527.5	45,721.5	18,733.0	3.73
United Kingdom	1997	492,716.5	465,507.9	-26,416.3	98,574.7	28,878.0	18.42
Eastern Europe							
Albania	1998	910.3	591.8	-258.7	427.6	323.1	0.12
Belarus	2007	8,048.3	10,170.2	2,121.9		3,952.1	0.27
Bosnia-Herzegovina	2005					2,530.5	0.00
Bulgaria	2006	11,014.9	12,503.2	1,483.9		10,892.1	1.28
Croatia	1997	5,659.0	5,470.7	-188.3	2,963.7	2,391.9	0.00
Czech Republic	2007	47,492.1	47,618.2	126.1	11,639.1	34,445.2	0.43
Estonia	2001	936.2	1,107.5	142.6	137.9	820.2	0.01
Georgia	2005	1,338.3	1,560.6	-4.9	1,401.7	477.6	0.00
Hungary	2007	44,625.3	38,352.5	-8,111.1	27,152.0	23,773.0	0.10
Latvia	1997	1,981.7	2,021.9	40.2	391.3	758.2	0.25
Lithuania	2003	5,124.6	5,077.5	-31.7	2,898.0	3,371.9	0.19
Macedonia	1996	992.7	994.6	4.4		239.5	0.08
Moldova	2001	223.2	224.1	16.2		227.8	0.00
Poland	2007	130,676.7	131,182.5	505.8	75,781.3	62,720.3	3.31
Romania	2005	27,215.3	28,675.3			19,871.5	3.37
Russia	2007	161,136.5	264,823.6	103,687.1	31,672.7	464,004.0	14.48
Serbia and Montenegro							
Slovakia	2006	19,776.2	19,297.7	405.9	2,531.9	12,645.2	1.13
Slovenia	2006	14,939.3	14,706.4	-235.1		6,987.1	0.16
Ukraine	2007	28,605.2	29,138.2	533.0		31,783.2	0.84

Source: Euromonitor International from industry sources/national statistics

Government Finance

Table 10.23

Foreign Exchange Reserves by Quarter 2006-2008

US$ million

	2006 1st Quarter	2006 2nd Quarter	2006 3rd Quarter	2006 4th Quarter	2007 1st Quarter	2007 2nd Quarter	2007 3rd Quarter	2007 4th Quarter	2008 1st Quarter	2008 2nd Quarter
Western Europe										
Austria	7,195.8	7,746.0	6,657.9	6,573.1	7,110.5	7,344.0	9,175.2	10,260.5	10,515.0	10,595.0
Belgium	7,879.7	7,444.7	7,321.3	7,618.9	7,627.2	7,664.1	8,644.9	9,297.8	9,585.2	8,613.5
Cyprus	4,081.9	4,691.8	4,833.7	5,621.5	4,465.5	5,160.2	5,439.5	6,100.1	926.2	830.2
Denmark	28,299.0	29,838.0	29,484.0	29,160.0	30,761.0	30,669.0	33,857.0	32,029.0	36,537.0	32,754.0
Finland	5,696.1	5,755.2	5,867.9	6,134.6	6,006.4	5,822.0	6,598.9	6,689.2	7,075.9	6,732.8
France	26,429.1	29,374.7	34,713.7	40,287.0	41,730.6	40,897.2	47,271.4	43,587.4	47,488.2	43,494.5
Germany	39,010.0	38,500.0	38,120.5	37,718.9	38,189.4	39,664.2	40,968.8	40,768.3	43,707.5	43,817.6
Gibraltar										
Greece	472.1	520.0	533.0	408.3	463.5	355.2	575.7	518.2	270.4	249.1
Iceland	1,065.9	938.5	953.7	2,273.2	2,283.5	2,243.9	2,433.0	2,549.1	2,786.1	2,477.5
Ireland	497.3	548.9	492.4	493.8	568.7	529.1	595.8	590.8	570.8	571.3
Italy	23,819.5	24,170.0	24,250.2	24,413.2	25,940.8	28,395.6	28,599.0	27,319.2	28,491.6	31,457.1
Liechtenstein										
Luxembourg	150.1	151.6	153.4	156.0	158.2	159.7	193.1	93.8	609.0	453.6
Malta	2,390.0	2,717.0	2,794.0	2,865.0	2,704.0	2,635.0	2,874.0	3,662.0	548.8	473.3
Monaco										
Netherlands	7,191.0	8,119.8	8,356.9	9,327.0	8,897.8	8,502.8	8,860.5	8,748.7	10,239.9	9,571.9
Norway	44,853.5	48,963.1	49,663.8	56,181.4	56,342.1	56,084.7	58,951.7	60,294.1	55,033.4	49,885.6
Portugal	2,022.4	1,378.8	1,660.3	1,835.3	1,878.0	1,626.9	932.4	1,044.4	1,349.6	1,368.8
Spain	9,214.8	8,807.6	9,772.3	10,088.2	9,989.8	10,285.4	10,345.0	10,792.0	11,400.5	10,946.5
Sweden	20,710.0	21,628.0	21,702.0	24,074.0	24,717.0	25,436.0	26,652.0	26,382.0	27,116.0	26,040.0
Switzerland	34,898.0	35,667.0	36,188.0	37,364.0	37,175.0	37,389.0	41,588.0	43,867.0	46,494.0	46,089.0
Turkey	58,189.7	57,066.9	58,202.7	60,710.0	67,242.0	68,176.0	71,578.0	73,155.8	76,321.0	75,702.0
United Kingdom	36,274.9	38,235.1	38,527.3	38,888.6	41,848.7	40,874.3	41,620.2	47,497.8	49,205.2	46,751.9
Eastern Europe										
Albania	1,422.0	1,506.1	1,603.4	1,754.8	1,787.2	1,829.3	2,082.9	2,097.0	2,146.7	2,159.2
Belarus	1,068.0	960.7	955.2	1,068.5	1,252.9	2,057.1	1,969.1	3,952.1	4,200.7	4,171.8
Bosnia-Herzegovina	2,746.4	3,015.6	3,147.8	3,371.3	3,492.6	3,753.0	4,345.5	4,524.5	4,546.0	4,026.7
Bulgaria	7,697.0	9,193.7	9,874.3	10,892.1	11,060.1	12,037.5	15,600.6	16,424.2	17,894.1	19,618.9
Croatia	9,765.8	10,957.1	10,304.1	11,487.4	12,678.1	12,349.3	12,465.8	13,674.0	15,543.8	15,675.7
Czech Republic	29,344.7	30,006.4	30,346.9	31,053.7	31,334.6	30,910.8	32,449.4	34,445.2	37,461.6	37,570.6
Estonia	1,883.1	2,105.0	2,370.7	2,781.1	2,784.0	2,805.5	3,449.3	3,262.6	3,694.9	
Georgia	469.3	544.6	616.7	929.9	1,008.1	1,220.1	1,469.8	1,346.3	1,419.8	1,525.8
Hungary	21,296.0	20,825.0	20,649.0	21,316.0	22,374.0	22,569.0	23,090.0	23,773.0	26,310.0	27,051.0
Latvia	2,547.7	3,229.4	3,873.7	4,353.1	4,478.8	4,767.9	5,242.0	5,553.1	6,299.5	6,302.4
Lithuania	3,878.9	4,085.9	4,322.7	5,654.3	5,521.1	6,017.9	6,514.4	7,565.6	6,981.1	7,245.4
Macedonia	1,357.1	1,554.2	1,626.0	1,747.6	1,753.2	1,796.1	2,020.3	2,080.8	2,204.4	2,226.2
Moldova	593.1	632.7	647.9	775.3	785.8	878.5	1,043.3	1,333.5	1,423.1	1,525.8
Poland	42,087.1	44,672.0	46,428.5	46,107.0	48,330.3	52,049.4	55,616.1	62,720.3	73,593.1	79,167.8
Romania	21,971.6	23,110.3	23,735.9	28,065.9	28,671.4	29,661.0	35,739.5	37,193.6	39,668.0	39,268.9
Russia	198,473.0	242,939.0	258,470.0	295,277.0	330,043.0	397,032.0	414,895.0	464,004.0	492,890.0	554,114.0
Serbia and Montenegro										
Slovakia	15,861.1	15,449.9	12,552.2	12,645.2	15,854.0	16,864.5	17,673.6	18,025.8	18,977.0	
Slovenia	8,205.3	8,071.0	7,317.2	6,987.1	1,025.2	1,056.1	1,030.7	942.0	1,087.5	948.0
Ukraine	16,837.5	17,209.1	18,678.0	21,843.2	22,447.7	25,381.9	30,063.5	31,783.2	32,424.8	34,695.0

Source: International Monetary Fund (IMF), International Financial Statistics

Table 10.24

Foreign Exchange Reserves by Month 2007

US$ million

	January	February	March	April	May	June	July	August	September	October	November	December
Western Europe												
Austria	6,495.1	6,894.8	7,110.5	7,022.9	6,974.0	7,344.0	7,578.6	8,280.6	9,175.2	9,637.6	10,050.8	10,260.5
Belgium	7,610.5	7,933.2	7,627.2	7,670.5	7,736.8	7,664.1	8,254.4	7,918.7	8,644.9	8,877.7	9,054.4	9,297.8
Cyprus	4,947.5	4,767.0	4,465.5	4,370.4	4,289.1	5,160.2	5,422.6	4,931.2	5,439.5	5,663.1	5,735.1	6,100.1
Denmark	28,715.0	29,891.0	30,761.0	29,567.0	29,403.0	30,669.0	32,394.0	34,279.0	33,857.0	34,123.0	34,536.0	32,029.0
Finland	6,017.1	6,086.3	6,006.4	5,911.4	5,803.6	5,822.0	6,216.1	6,444.1	6,598.9	6,570.5	6,556.8	6,689.2
France	39,759.7	41,675.4	41,730.6	41,975.5	40,341.5	40,897.2	44,031.0	45,859.7	47,271.4	49,648.6	48,767.4	43,587.4
Germany	38,258.3	38,099.2	38,189.4	39,884.4	40,383.2	39,664.2	39,866.8	40,184.4	40,968.8	40,659.6	40,815.6	40,768.3
Gibraltar												
Greece	246.1	389.7	463.5	468.0	491.0	355.2	535.9	396.1	575.7	540.3	568.3	518.2
Iceland	2,280.1	2,313.2	2,283.5	2,289.9	2,278.4	2,243.9	2,283.6	2,337.6	2,433.0	2,541.6	2,595.7	2,549.1
Ireland	570.3	563.2	568.7	569.5	513.2	529.1	563.0	528.3	595.8	577.6	615.6	590.8
Italy	25,501.2	26,042.8	25,940.8	26,346.1	26,602.0	28,395.6	28,322.8	27,701.9	28,599.0	28,749.5	30,611.4	27,319.2
Liechtenstein												
Luxembourg	156.6	156.9	158.2	158.6	158.9	159.7	167.4	169.4	193.1	164.1	164.3	93.8
Malta	2,734.0	2,746.0	2,704.0	2,751.0	2,764.0	2,635.0	2,666.0	2,695.0	2,874.0	2,850.0	3,743.0	3,662.0
Monaco												
Netherlands	9,395.5	8,649.2	8,897.8	8,592.9	8,269.6	8,502.8	9,501.7	9,239.9	8,860.5	8,590.2	8,087.6	8,748.7
Norway	55,782.2	55,837.8	56,342.1	56,451.9	54,960.4	56,084.7	56,323.3	56,059.8	58,951.7	59,641.3	59,639.9	60,294.1
Portugal	1,904.1	1,832.5	1,878.0	2,216.1	1,920.1	1,626.9	983.0	817.2	932.4	624.2	833.7	1,044.4
Spain	9,856.7	9,978.3	9,989.8	10,002.4	9,878.5	10,285.4	10,509.2	10,662.5	10,345.0	10,653.2	10,759.3	10,792.0
Sweden	23,716.0	24,601.0	24,717.0	25,105.0	23,505.0	25,436.0	25,143.0	26,759.0	26,652.0	27,058.0	27,566.0	26,382.0
Switzerland	37,044.0	36,826.0	37,175.0	36,641.0	36,767.0	37,389.0	37,748.0	38,517.0	41,588.0	41,611.0	42,015.0	43,867.0
Turkey	62,651.0	64,460.0	67,242.0	66,916.0	66,138.0	68,176.0	69,729.0	71,932.0	71,578.0	72,064.5	72,233.1	73,155.8
United Kingdom	38,710.7	40,808.8	41,848.7	43,235.3	42,897.5	40,874.3	41,232.8	41,028.5	41,620.2	45,700.8	48,258.9	47,497.8
Eastern Europe												
Albania	1,742.3	1,772.2	1,787.2	1,807.2	1,791.9	1,829.3	1,881.1	1,899.2	2,082.9	2,100.7	2,119.7	2,097.0
Belarus	1,021.8	988.5	1,252.9	1,296.2	1,463.4	2,057.1	2,069.5	1,669.7	1,969.1	2,171.1	2,520.9	3,952.1
Bosnia-Herzegovina	3,291.6	3,381.5	3,492.6	3,644.6	3,638.7	3,753.0	4,018.4	4,079.5	4,345.5	4,454.0	4,320.6	4,524.5
Bulgaria	10,228.8	10,356.6	11,060.1	11,588.6	11,211.8	12,037.5	12,603.4	13,243.4	15,600.6	16,023.5	16,692.0	16,424.2
Croatia	11,882.1	12,628.9	12,678.1	12,918.3	12,697.7	12,349.3	12,866.3	12,564.2	12,465.8	12,913.9	13,428.3	13,674.0
Czech Republic	30,973.8	31,197.3	31,334.6	31,673.5	31,047.8	30,910.8	31,425.3	31,787.6	32,449.4	32,907.2	34,064.4	34,445.2
Estonia	2,436.7	3,022.8	2,784.0	2,959.6	2,774.7	2,805.5	3,669.8	3,050.5	3,449.3	3,507.2	3,492.6	3,262.6
Georgia	934.6	985.8	1,008.1	1,051.7	1,112.9	1,220.1	1,325.3	1,359.5	1,469.8	1,508.5	1,354.6	1,346.3
Hungary	20,738.0	22,373.0	22,374.0	22,971.0	22,261.0	22,569.0	22,511.0	22,756.0	23,090.0	23,625.0	24,173.0	23,773.0
Latvia	4,356.7	4,539.9	4,478.8	4,466.9	4,711.2	4,767.9	4,944.3	5,128.2	5,242.0	5,296.2	5,436.4	5,553.1
Lithuania	5,774.9	5,737.0	5,521.1	6,007.0	5,605.9	6,017.9	5,770.3	6,525.7	6,514.4	8,009.5	7,679.0	7,565.6
Macedonia	1,690.0	1,704.8	1,753.2	1,856.3	1,846.1	1,796.1	1,856.1	1,898.4	2,020.3	2,087.5	2,130.3	2,080.8
Moldova	772.4	775.7	785.8	826.3	863.0	878.5	977.6	1,002.8	1,043.3	1,155.7	1,290.7	1,333.5
Poland	48,802.2	48,469.1	48,330.3	49,571.8	52,732.3	52,049.4	53,638.4	53,751.8	55,616.1	57,282.4	65,329.8	62,720.3
Romania	28,080.9	28,554.1	28,671.4	29,136.4	29,486.2	29,661.0	30,751.9	33,761.3	35,739.5	36,418.6	37,573.0	37,193.6
Russia	295,273.0	305,579.0	330,043.0	360,116.0	394,384.0	397,032.0	407,132.0	406,747.0	414,895.0	435,634.0	451,785.0	464,004.0
Serbia and Montenegro												
Slovakia	13,274.6	13,226.2	15,854.0	17,057.1	16,828.9	16,864.5	17,125.7	17,059.9	17,673.6	17,940.0	18,213.2	18,025.8
Slovenia	847.0	1,014.4	1,025.2	965.0	1,049.4	1,056.1	883.8	881.6	1,030.7	1,018.6	1,056.2	942.0
Ukraine	21,853.8	22,304.8	22,447.7	22,941.9	24,168.8	25,381.9	26,822.0	28,351.1	30,063.5	31,067.3	32,202.0	31,783.2

Source: *International Monetary Fund (IMF), International Financial Statistics*

Government Finance

Table 10.25

Gold Reserves by Quarter 2006-2008
million troy oz

	2006 1st Quarter	2006 2nd Quarter	2006 3rd Quarter	2006 4th Quarter	2007 1st Quarter	2007 2nd Quarter	2007 3rd Quarter	2007 4th Quarter	2008 1st Quarter	2008 2nd Quarter
Western Europe										
Austria	9.55	9.41	9.28	9.28	9.28	9.15	9.00	9.00	9.00	9.00
Belgium	7.32	7.32	7.32	7.32	7.32	7.32	7.32	7.32	7.32	7.32
Cyprus	0.47	0.47	0.47	0.47	0.47	0.47	0.47	0.47	0.45	0.45
Denmark	2.14	2.14	2.14	2.14	2.14	2.14	2.14	2.14	2.14	2.14
Finland	1.58	1.58	1.58	1.58	1.58	1.58	1.58	1.58	1.58	1.58
France	90.09	89.25	88.66	87.44	86.45	85.75	84.96	83.69	82.58	81.96
Germany	110.21	110.07	110.04	110.04	110.04	109.98	109.87	109.87	109.87	109.74
Gibraltar										
Greece	3.47	3.47	3.48	3.59	3.60	3.60	3.61	3.62	3.63	3.63
Iceland	0.06	0.06	0.06	0.06	0.06	0.06	0.06	0.06	0.06	0.06
Ireland	0.18	0.18	0.18	0.18	0.18	0.18	0.18	0.18	0.18	0.18
Italy	78.83	78.83	78.83	78.83	78.83	78.83	78.83	78.83	78.83	78.83
Liechtenstein										
Luxembourg	0.07	0.07	0.07	0.07	0.07	0.07	0.07	0.07	0.07	0.07
Malta	0.01	0.00	0.01	0.01	0.01	0.01	0.01	0.02	0.01	0.01
Monaco										
Netherlands	21.11	21.06	21.06	20.61	20.61	20.61	20.61	19.98	19.98	19.98
Norway										
Portugal	13.42	13.42	12.30	12.30	12.30	12.30	12.30	12.30	12.30	12.30
Spain	14.72	14.72	13.86	13.40	12.12	9.85	9.05	9.05	9.05	9.05
Sweden	5.31	5.25	5.16	5.10	5.02	4.93	4.85	4.78	4.71	4.63
Switzerland	41.48	41.48	41.48	41.48	41.48	41.03	37.85	36.82	35.79	34.63
Turkey	3.73	3.73	3.73	3.73	3.73	3.73	3.73	3.73	3.73	3.73
United Kingdom	9.98	9.98	9.98	9.97	9.97	9.98	9.98	9.98	9.98	9.98
Eastern Europe										
Albania	0.07	0.07	0.07	0.07	0.07	0.07	0.07	0.07	0.07	0.07
Belarus	0.40	0.30	0.30	0.50	0.43	0.44	0.25	0.27	0.58	0.48
Bosnia-Herzegovina										
Bulgaria	1.28	1.28	1.28	1.28	1.28	1.28	1.28	1.28	1.28	1.27
Croatia										
Czech Republic	0.43	0.43	0.43	0.43	0.43	0.43	0.43	0.43	0.43	0.43
Estonia	0.01	0.01	0.01	0.01	0.01	0.01	0.01	0.01	0.01	
Georgia										
Hungary	0.10	0.10	0.10	0.10	0.10	0.10	0.10	0.10	0.10	0.10
Latvia	0.25	0.25	0.25	0.25	0.25	0.25	0.25	0.25	0.25	0.25
Lithuania	0.19	0.19	0.19	0.19	0.19	0.19	0.19	0.19	0.19	0.19
Macedonia	0.22	0.22	0.22	0.22	0.22	0.22	0.22	0.22	0.22	0.22
Moldova										
Poland	3.31	3.31	3.31	3.31	3.31	3.31	3.31	3.31	3.31	3.31
Romania	3.37	3.37	3.37	3.37	3.37	3.37	3.37	3.33	3.33	3.33
Russia	12.43	12.43	12.51	12.91	12.87	13.08	13.78	14.48	14.69	14.89
Serbia and Montenegro										
Slovakia	1.13	1.13	1.13	1.13	1.13	1.13	1.13	1.13	1.13	
Slovenia	0.16	0.16	0.16	0.16	0.10	0.10	0.10	0.10	0.10	0.10
Ukraine	0.78	0.80	0.81	0.81	0.81	0.82	0.82	0.84	0.84	0.84

Source: *International Monetary Fund (IMF), International Financial Statistics*

Table 10.26

Gold Reserves by Month 2007

million troy oz

	January	February	March	April	May	June	July	August	September	October	November	December
Western Europe												
Austria	9.28	9.28	9.28	9.28	9.27	9.15	9.06	9.04	9.00	9.00	9.00	9.00
Belgium	7.32	7.32	7.32	7.32	7.32	7.32	7.32	7.32	7.32	7.32	7.32	7.32
Cyprus	0.47	0.47	0.47	0.47	0.47	0.47	0.47	0.47	0.47	0.47	0.47	0.47
Denmark	2.14	2.14	2.14	2.14	2.14	2.14	2.14	2.14	2.14	2.14	2.14	2.14
Finland	1.58	1.58	1.58	1.58	1.58	1.58	1.58	1.58	1.58	1.58	1.58	1.58
France	87.12	86.67	86.45	86.18	86.01	85.75	85.47	85.21	84.96	84.31	83.93	83.69
Germany	110.04	110.04	110.04	110.04	109.98	109.98	109.87	109.87	109.87	109.87	109.87	109.87
Gibraltar												
Greece	3.60	3.60	3.60	3.60	3.60	3.60	3.61	3.61	3.61	3.61	3.62	3.62
Iceland	0.06	0.06	0.06	0.06	0.06	0.06	0.06	0.06	0.06	0.06	0.06	0.06
Ireland	0.18	0.18	0.18	0.18	0.18	0.18	0.18	0.18	0.18	0.18	0.18	0.18
Italy	78.83	78.83	78.83	78.83	78.83	78.83	78.83	78.83	78.83	78.83	78.83	78.83
Liechtenstein												
Luxembourg	0.07	0.07	0.07	0.07	0.07	0.07	0.07	0.07	0.07	0.07	0.07	0.07
Malta	0.01	0.01	0.01	0.01	0.01	0.01	0.01	0.01	0.01	0.01	0.01	0.02
Monaco												
Netherlands	20.61	20.61	20.61	20.61	20.61	20.61	20.61	20.61	20.61	20.08	20.00	19.98
Norway												
Portugal	12.30	12.30	12.30	12.30	12.30	12.30	12.30	12.30	12.30	12.30	12.30	12.30
Spain	13.40	13.40	12.12	10.84	9.85	9.85	9.05	9.05	9.05	9.05	9.05	9.05
Sweden	5.08	5.06	5.02	4.99	4.97	4.93	4.91	4.87	4.85	4.83	4.81	4.78
Switzerland	41.48	41.48	41.48	41.48	41.48	41.03	39.93	38.84	37.85	37.50	37.13	36.82
Turkey	3.73	3.73	3.73	3.73	3.73	3.73	3.73	3.73	3.73	3.73	3.73	3.73
United Kingdom	9.97	9.97	9.97	9.97	9.97	9.98	9.98	9.98	9.98	9.98	9.98	9.98
Eastern Europe												
Albania	0.07	0.07	0.07	0.07	0.07	0.07	0.07	0.07	0.07	0.07	0.07	0.07
Belarus	0.47	0.47	0.43	0.40	0.39	0.44	0.44	0.25	0.25	0.25	0.25	0.27
Bosnia-Herzegovina												
Bulgaria	1.28	1.28	1.28	1.28	1.28	1.28	1.28	1.28	1.28	1.28	1.28	1.28
Croatia												
Czech Republic	0.43	0.43	0.43	0.43	0.43	0.43	0.43	0.43	0.43	0.43	0.43	0.43
Estonia	0.01	0.01	0.01	0.01	0.01	0.01	0.01	0.01	0.01	0.01	0.01	0.01
Georgia												
Hungary	0.10	0.10	0.10	0.10	0.10	0.10	0.10	0.10	0.10	0.10	0.10	0.10
Latvia	0.25	0.25	0.25	0.25	0.25	0.25	0.25	0.25	0.25	0.25	0.25	0.25
Lithuania	0.19	0.19	0.19	0.19	0.19	0.19	0.19	0.19	0.19	0.19	0.19	0.19
Macedonia	0.22	0.22	0.22	0.22	0.22	0.22	0.22	0.22	0.22	0.22	0.22	0.22
Moldova												
Poland	3.31	3.31	3.31	3.31	3.31	3.31	3.31	3.31	3.31	3.31	3.31	3.31
Romania	3.37	3.37	3.37	3.37	3.37	3.37	3.37	3.37	3.37	3.33	3.33	3.33
Russia	12.95	12.87	12.87	12.92	12.95	13.08	13.10	13.45	13.78	14.09	14.33	14.48
Serbia and Montenegro												
Slovakia	1.13	1.13	1.13	1.13	1.13	1.13	1.13	1.13	1.13	1.13	1.13	1.13
Slovenia	0.10	0.10	0.10	0.10	0.10	0.10	0.10	0.10	0.10	0.10	0.10	0.10
Ukraine	0.81	0.81	0.81	0.82	0.82	0.82	0.82	0.82	0.82	0.83	0.84	0.84

Source: *International Monetary Fund (IMF), International Financial Statistics*

Government Expenditure by Category

Table 10.27

Government Expenditure by Object 2007

US$ million

	General Public Services	Defence	Education	Health	Social Security & Welfare	Housing/ Amenities	Other Community/ Social	Economic Services	Other
Western Europe									
Austria	22,399	3,350	19,619	25,703	82,587	1,682	1,542	9,419	5,669
Belgium	66,232	4,606	5,736	34,554	89,012	0	378	19,481	5,312
Cyprus	5,104	610	1,928	1,236	5,826	870	402	1,678	670
Denmark	28,842	4,508	12,632	1,151	43,167	996	2,766	5,679	4,125
Finland	12,152	4,051	8,581	9,063	49,139	365	965	7,973	3,296
France	183,917	46,427	109,754	177,918	556,317	6,689	10,942	73,184	30,012
Germany	142,604	34,388	6,200	195,439	697,168	7,762	1,101	45,610	5,558
Gibraltar									
Greece	22,845	7,699	6,111	15,439	68,607	683	839	33,121	4,580
Iceland	1,132		793	1,969	1,526	72	197	920	333
Ireland	11,578	1,756	13,449	21,609	25,796	1,942	689	9,949	3,698
Italy	233,469	33,680	87,476	46,833	466,236	7,057	6,753	30,315	38,814
Liechtenstein									
Luxembourg	2,636	132	1,998	2,318	12,101	154	520	2,218	705
Malta	632	74	422	510	918	51	37	558	223
Monaco									
Netherlands	63,885	9,800	31,456	29,269	147,235	1,910	2,158	16,481	12,516
Norway	20,740	5,064	7,064	21,166	51,172	227	1,696	11,633	3,514
Portugal	25,212	2,891	15,252	15,885	37,562	160	1,098	5,424	4,516
Spain	133,369	15,997	2,461	5,837	173,211	850	4,310	27,327	14,883
Sweden	23,538	7,901	15,706	7,027	77,894	781	1,802	20,880	6,024
Switzerland	17,877	3,652	3,723	189	37,525	386	578	10,056	1,621
Turkey	118,722	8,044	7,023	4,890	7,317	3,786	756	2,941	4,419
United Kingdom	335,229	69,147	58,796	209,863	334,520	5,753	2,536	50,563	43,915
Eastern Europe									
Albania	295	143	336	168	532	125	29	324	64
Belarus	4,576	649	803	627	7,005	73	376	4,282	1,356
Bosnia-Herzegovina									
Bulgaria	2,579	681	752	1,760	4,848	52	190	1,656	980
Croatia	2,225	524	1,665	3,190	7,520	1,272	355	2,502	1,237
Czech Republic	9,292	2,138	6,289	10,668	19,923	1,377	653	10,132	5,270
Estonia	1,018	383	972	286	2,007	609	214	464	2
Georgia	147	597	61	384	375	0	35	329	208
Hungary	17,166	2,503	3,140	4,787	18,968	67	958	16,159	4,494
Latvia	1,814	265	397	736	1,692	192	105	1,806	396
Lithuania	3,999	479	786	586	3,624	0	245	1,271	891
Macedonia									
Moldova	278	16	142	338	592	18	18	240	101
Poland	23,260	5,275	17,484	15,734	63,367	558	782	12,524	7,813
Romania	3,018	2,084	2,284	7,228	19,868	1,291	929	10,615	5,141
Russia	58,199	47,681	13,165	32,721	84,614	349	4,222	17,042	38,047
Serbia and Montenegro									
Slovakia	5,032	964	885	3,696	7,002	112	272	2,516	1,522
Slovenia	3,062	691	2,368	5,118	9,428	12	308	1,526	879
Ukraine	13,356	1,413	3,489	1,416	40,796	354	588	4,026	4,111

Source: *Euromonitor International/International Monetary Fund (IMF), Government Finance Statistics/national statistics*

Table 10.28

Government Expenditure by Object 2007 (% Analysis)

% of total expenditure

	General Public Services	Defence	Education	Health	Social Security & Welfare	Housing/ Amenities	Other Community/ Social	Economic Services	Other
Western Europe									
Austria	13.03	1.95	11.41	14.95	48.02	0.98	0.90	5.48	3.30
Belgium	29.40	2.04	2.55	15.34	39.51	0.00	0.17	8.65	2.36
Cyprus	27.86	3.33	10.52	6.75	31.79	4.75	2.19	9.16	3.65
Denmark	27.77	4.34	12.16	1.11	41.56	0.96	2.66	5.47	3.97
Finland	12.71	4.24	8.98	9.48	51.41	0.38	1.01	8.34	3.45
France	15.39	3.88	9.18	14.89	46.55	0.56	0.92	6.12	2.51
Germany	12.56	3.03	0.55	17.21	61.38	0.68	0.10	4.02	0.49
Gibraltar									
Greece	14.28	4.81	3.82	9.65	42.90	0.43	0.52	20.71	2.86
Iceland	16.31		11.43	28.36	21.98	1.04	2.84	13.25	4.80
Ireland	12.80	1.94	14.87	23.89	28.51	2.15	0.76	11.00	4.09
Italy	24.56	3.54	9.20	4.93	49.04	0.74	0.71	3.19	4.08
Liechtenstein									
Luxembourg	11.57	0.58	8.77	10.18	53.11	0.68	2.28	9.74	3.09
Malta	18.46	2.16	12.31	14.89	26.80	1.49	1.09	16.29	6.51
Monaco									
Netherlands	20.30	3.11	10.00	9.30	46.78	0.61	0.69	5.24	3.98
Norway	16.96	4.14	5.78	17.31	41.85	0.19	1.39	9.51	2.87
Portugal	23.34	2.68	14.12	14.71	34.78	0.15	1.02	5.02	4.18
Spain	35.26	4.23	0.65	1.54	45.79	0.22	1.14	7.22	3.93
Sweden	14.57	4.89	9.72	4.35	48.22	0.48	1.12	12.92	3.73
Switzerland	23.64	4.83	4.92	0.25	49.63	0.51	0.77	13.30	2.14
Turkey	75.19	5.09	4.45	3.10	4.63	2.40	0.48	1.86	2.80
United Kingdom	30.19	6.23	5.30	18.90	30.13	0.52	0.23	4.55	3.96
Eastern Europe									
Albania	14.62	7.08	16.64	8.34	26.40	6.21	1.42	16.09	3.20
Belarus	23.17	3.29	4.07	3.17	35.47	0.37	1.90	21.68	6.87
Bosnia-Herzegovina									
Bulgaria	19.11	5.04	5.57	13.04	35.92	0.38	1.40	12.27	7.26
Croatia	10.86	2.56	8.13	15.57	36.70	6.21	1.73	12.21	6.04
Czech Republic	14.13	3.25	9.57	16.23	30.31	2.09	0.99	15.41	8.02
Estonia	17.10	6.44	16.32	4.81	33.71	10.22	3.59	7.79	0.03
Georgia	6.87	27.93	2.84	17.97	17.58	0.00	1.63	15.42	9.76
Hungary	25.15	3.67	4.60	7.01	27.80	0.10	1.40	23.68	6.59
Latvia	24.50	3.57	5.36	9.94	22.85	2.60	1.42	24.40	5.35
Lithuania	33.66	4.03	6.62	4.93	30.50	0.00	2.06	10.70	7.50
Macedonia									
Moldova	15.93	0.91	8.16	19.36	33.96	1.05	1.05	13.79	5.79
Poland	15.84	3.59	11.91	10.72	43.17	0.38	0.53	8.53	5.32
Romania	5.75	3.97	4.35	13.78	37.87	2.46	1.77	20.24	9.80
Russia	19.66	16.11	4.45	11.05	28.58	0.12	1.43	5.76	12.85
Serbia and Montenegro									
Slovakia	22.87	4.38	4.02	16.80	31.82	0.51	1.24	11.44	6.92
Slovenia	13.09	2.95	10.12	21.88	40.31	0.05	1.32	6.52	3.76
Ukraine	19.20	2.03	5.02	2.04	58.66	0.51	0.85	5.79	5.91

Source: Euromonitor International/International Monetary Fund (IMF), Government Finance Statistics/national statistics

Exchange Rates | | Table 10.29

Exchange Rates Against the US$ 1980-2007

Units of national currency per US$

	1980	1985	1990	1995	1996	1997	1998	1999	2000
Western Europe									
Austria	0.68	1.25	0.75	0.73	0.75	0.84	0.85	0.94	1.08
Belgium	0.68	1.25	0.75	0.73	0.75	0.84	0.85	0.94	1.08
Cyprus	0.68	1.25	0.75	0.73	0.75	0.84	0.85	0.94	1.08
Denmark	5.64	10.60	6.19	5.60	5.80	6.60	6.70	6.98	8.08
Finland	0.68	1.25	0.75	0.73	0.75	0.84	0.85	0.94	1.08
France	0.68	1.25	0.75	0.73	0.75	0.84	0.85	0.94	1.08
Germany	0.68	1.25	0.75	0.73	0.75	0.84	0.85	0.94	1.08
Gibraltar				0.60	0.64	0.62	0.60	0.61	0.66
Greece	0.68	1.25	0.75	0.73	0.75	0.84	0.85	0.94	1.08
Iceland	4.80	41.51	58.28	64.69	66.50	70.90	70.96	72.34	78.62
Ireland	0.68	1.25	0.75	0.73	0.75	0.84	0.85	0.94	1.08
Italy	0.68	1.25	0.75	0.73	0.75	0.84	0.85	0.94	1.08
Liechtenstein	1.68	2.46	1.39	1.18	1.24	1.45	1.45	1.50	1.69
Luxembourg	0.68	1.25	0.75	0.73	0.75	0.84	0.85	0.94	1.08
Malta	0.68	1.25	0.75	0.73	0.75	0.84	0.85	0.94	1.08
Monaco	0.68	1.25	0.75	0.73	0.75	0.84	0.85	0.94	1.08
Netherlands	0.68	1.25	0.75	0.73	0.75	0.84	0.85	0.94	1.08
Norway	4.94	8.60	6.26	6.34	6.45	7.07	7.55	7.80	8.80
Portugal	0.68	1.25	0.75	0.73	0.75	0.84	0.85	0.94	1.08
Spain	0.68	1.25	0.75	0.73	0.75	0.84	0.85	0.94	1.08
Sweden	4.23	8.60	5.92	7.13	6.71	7.63	7.95	8.26	9.16
Switzerland	1.68	2.46	1.39	1.18	1.24	1.45	1.45	1.50	1.69
Turkey	0.00	0.00	0.00	0.05	0.08	0.15	0.26	0.42	0.63
United Kingdom	0.43	0.78	0.56	0.63	0.64	0.61	0.60	0.62	0.66
Eastern Europe									
Albania	7.00	7.00	7.75	92.70	104.50	148.93	150.63	137.69	143.71
Belarus				11.52	13.23	26.02	46.13	249.29	876.75
Bosnia-Herzegovina				1.50	1.73	1.76	1.84	2.12	
Bulgaria	0.00	0.00	0.00	0.07	0.18	1.68	1.76	1.84	2.12
Croatia				5.23	5.43	6.16	6.36	7.11	8.28
Czech Republic			17.95	26.54	27.14	31.70	32.28	34.57	38.60
Estonia				11.46	12.04	13.88	14.07	14.68	16.97
Georgia				1.26	1.26	1.30	1.39	2.02	1.98
Hungary	32.53	50.12	63.21	125.68	152.65	186.79	214.40	237.15	282.18
Latvia				0.53	0.55	0.58	0.59	0.59	0.61
Lithuania				4.00	4.00	4.00	4.00	4.00	4.00
Macedonia				37.88	39.98	50.00	54.46	56.90	65.90
Moldova				4.50	4.60	4.62	5.37	10.52	12.43
Poland	0.00	0.01	0.95	2.42	2.70	3.28	3.48	3.97	4.35
Romania	0.00	0.00	0.00	0.20	0.31	0.72	0.89	1.53	2.17
Russia				4.56	5.12	5.78	9.71	24.62	28.13
Serbia and Montenegro				2.93	4.94	6.66	9.58	18.94	44.02
Slovakia				29.71	30.65	33.62	35.23	41.36	46.04
Slovenia	0.68	1.25	0.75	0.73	0.75	0.84	0.85	0.94	1.08
Ukraine				1.47	1.83	1.86	2.45	4.13	5.44

Source: *International Monetary Fund (IMF)/Euromonitor International research*
Notes: *Annual average market exchange rates*

Exchange Rates Against the US$ 1980-2007 *(continued)*

Units of national currency per US$

	2001	2002	2003	2004	2005	2006	2007
Western Europe							
Austria	1.12	1.06	0.89	0.80	0.80	0.80	0.73
Belgium	1.12	1.06	0.89	0.80	0.80	0.80	0.73
Cyprus	1.12	1.06	0.89	0.80	0.80	0.80	0.73
Denmark	8.32	7.89	6.59	5.99	6.00	5.95	5.44
Finland	1.12	1.06	0.89	0.80	0.80	0.80	0.73
France	1.12	1.06	0.89	0.80	0.80	0.80	0.73
Germany	1.12	1.06	0.89	0.80	0.80	0.80	0.73
Gibraltar	0.69	0.66	0.62	0.55	0.55	0.60	0.62
Greece	1.12	1.06	0.89	0.80	0.80	0.80	0.73
Iceland	97.42	91.66	76.71	70.19	62.98	70.18	64.06
Ireland	1.12	1.06	0.89	0.80	0.80	0.80	0.73
Italy	1.12	1.06	0.89	0.80	0.80	0.80	0.73
Liechtenstein	1.69	1.56	1.35	1.24	1.25	1.25	1.20
Luxembourg	1.12	1.06	0.89	0.80	0.80	0.80	0.73
Malta	1.12	1.06	0.89	0.80	0.80	0.80	0.73
Monaco	1.12	1.06	0.89	0.80	0.80	0.80	0.73
Netherlands	1.12	1.06	0.89	0.80	0.80	0.80	0.73
Norway	8.99	7.98	7.08	6.74	6.44	6.41	5.86
Portugal	1.12	1.06	0.89	0.80	0.80	0.80	0.73
Spain	1.12	1.06	0.89	0.80	0.80	0.80	0.73
Sweden	10.33	9.74	8.09	7.35	7.47	7.38	6.76
Switzerland	1.69	1.56	1.35	1.24	1.25	1.25	1.20
Turkey	1.23	1.51	1.50	1.43	1.34	1.43	1.30
United Kingdom	0.69	0.67	0.61	0.55	0.55	0.54	0.50
Eastern Europe							
Albania	143.49	140.16	121.86	102.78	99.87	98.10	90.43
Belarus	1,390.00	1,790.92	2,051.27	2,160.26	2,153.82	2,144.56	2,146.08
Bosnia-Herzegovina	2.19	2.08	1.73	1.58	1.57	1.56	1.43
Bulgaria	2.18	2.08	1.73	1.58	1.57	1.56	1.43
Croatia	8.34	7.87	6.70	6.03	5.95	5.84	5.36
Czech Republic	38.04	32.74	28.21	25.70	23.96	22.60	20.29
Estonia	17.48	16.61	13.86	12.60	12.58	12.47	11.43
Georgia	2.07	2.20	2.15	1.92	1.81	1.78	1.67
Hungary	286.49	257.89	224.31	202.75	199.58	210.39	183.63
Latvia	0.63	0.62	0.57	0.54	0.56	0.56	0.51
Lithuania	4.00	3.68	3.06	2.78	2.77	2.75	2.52
Macedonia	68.04	64.35	54.32	49.41	49.28	48.80	44.73
Moldova	12.87	13.57	13.94	12.33	12.60	13.13	12.14
Poland	4.09	4.08	3.89	3.66	3.24	3.10	2.77
Romania	2.91	3.31	3.32	3.26	2.91	2.81	2.44
Russia	29.17	31.35	30.69	28.81	28.28	27.19	25.58
Serbia and Montenegro	66.91	64.40	57.59	58.38	66.71	67.15	58.45
Slovakia	48.35	45.33	36.77	32.26	31.02	29.70	24.69
Slovenia	1.12	1.06	0.89	0.80	0.80	0.80	0.73
Ukraine	5.37	5.33	5.33	5.32	5.12	5.05	5.05

Source: *International Monetary Fund (IMF)/Euromonitor International research*
Notes: *Annual average market exchange rates*

Exchange Rates

Table 10.30

Exchange Rates Against the US$ by Month 2007

Units of national currency per US$

	January	February	March	April	May	June	July	August	September	October	November	December
Western Europe												
Austria	0.77	0.76	0.75	0.74	0.74	0.74	0.73	0.73	0.73	0.70	0.68	0.68
Belgium	0.77	0.76	0.75	0.74	0.74	0.74	0.73	0.73	0.73	0.70	0.68	0.68
Cyprus	0.77	0.76	0.75	0.74	0.74	0.74	0.73	0.73	0.73	0.70	0.68	0.68
Denmark	5.73	5.70	5.63	5.51	5.51	5.55	5.43	5.46	5.36	5.24	5.08	5.12
Finland	0.77	0.76	0.75	0.74	0.74	0.74	0.73	0.73	0.73	0.70	0.68	0.68
France	0.77	0.76	0.75	0.74	0.74	0.74	0.73	0.73	0.73	0.70	0.68	0.68
Germany	0.77	0.76	0.75	0.74	0.74	0.74	0.73	0.73	0.73	0.70	0.68	0.68
Gibraltar	0.69	0.69	0.68	0.67	0.67	0.67	0.66	0.66	0.66	0.44	0.44	0.45
Greece	0.77	0.76	0.75	0.74	0.74	0.74	0.73	0.73	0.73	0.70	0.68	0.68
Iceland	70.17	67.45	67.06	65.24	63.08	62.76	60.58	65.00	63.70	60.65	60.74	62.22
Ireland	0.77	0.76	0.75	0.74	0.74	0.74	0.73	0.73	0.73	0.70	0.68	0.68
Italy	0.77	0.76	0.75	0.74	0.74	0.74	0.73	0.73	0.73	0.70	0.68	0.68
Liechtenstein	1.24	1.24	1.22	1.21	1.22	1.23	1.21	1.20	1.18	1.17	1.12	1.14
Luxembourg	0.77	0.76	0.75	0.74	0.74	0.74	0.73	0.73	0.73	0.70	0.68	0.68
Malta	0.77	0.76	0.75	0.74	0.74	0.74	0.73	0.73	0.73	0.70	0.68	0.68
Monaco	0.77	0.76	0.75	0.74	0.74	0.74	0.73	0.73	0.73	0.70	0.68	0.68
Netherlands	0.77	0.76	0.75	0.74	0.74	0.74	0.73	0.73	0.73	0.70	0.68	0.68
Norway	6.37	6.19	6.14	6.00	6.02	6.01	5.79	5.85	5.64	5.41	5.42	5.50
Portugal	0.77	0.76	0.75	0.74	0.74	0.74	0.73	0.73	0.73	0.70	0.68	0.68
Spain	0.77	0.76	0.75	0.74	0.74	0.74	0.73	0.73	0.73	0.70	0.68	0.68
Sweden	6.99	7.03	7.02	6.83	6.81	6.95	6.69	6.84	6.68	6.45	6.33	6.47
Switzerland	1.24	1.24	1.22	1.21	1.22	1.23	1.21	1.20	1.18	1.17	1.12	1.14
Turkey	1.42	1.39	1.40	1.36	1.33	1.32	1.28	1.31	1.26	1.19	1.19	1.18
United Kingdom	0.51	0.51	0.51	0.50	0.50	0.50	0.49	0.50	0.50	0.49	0.48	0.49
Eastern Europe												
Albania	96.04	95.80	95.32	93.36	92.71	91.76	89.18	89.68	89.19	86.05	83.01	83.03
Belarus	2,140.01	2,141.46	2,142.63	2,143.79	2,145.00	2,145.29	2,145.00	2,146.17	2,148.40	2,149.87	2,151.95	2,153.40
Bosnia-Herzegovina	1.50	1.50	1.48	1.45	1.45	1.46	1.43	1.44	1.41	1.37	1.33	1.34
Bulgaria	1.51	1.50	1.48	1.45	1.45	1.46	1.43	1.44	1.41	1.37	1.33	1.34
Croatia	5.66	5.64	5.56	5.48	5.42	5.47	5.32	5.37	5.28	5.15	5.00	5.02
Czech Republic	21.42	21.59	21.19	20.73	20.90	21.27	20.64	20.45	19.87	19.22	18.21	18.04
Estonia	12.03	11.97	11.82	11.58	11.58	11.67	11.41	11.48	11.26	11.00	10.66	10.74
Georgia	1.71	1.71	1.71	1.69	1.68	1.67	1.67	1.66	1.66	1.64	1.62	1.60
Hungary	195.22	193.87	188.74	182.13	183.84	186.69	179.96	187.33	182.44	176.29	173.14	173.86
Latvia	0.54	0.54	0.53	0.52	0.52	0.52	0.51	0.52	0.51	0.49	0.48	0.48
Lithuania	2.65	2.64	2.61	2.56	2.55	2.57	2.52	2.53	2.49	2.43	2.35	2.37
Macedonia	47.06	46.84	46.20	45.33	45.25	45.62	44.66	44.92	44.08	43.04	41.74	42.02
Moldova	12.99	12.83	12.68	12.47	12.37	12.28	12.16	12.01	11.79	11.48	11.33	11.29
Poland	2.98	2.98	2.94	2.83	2.80	2.84	2.75	2.80	2.73	2.60	2.49	2.48
Romania	2.61	2.59	2.54	2.47	2.43	2.41	2.28	2.37	2.41	2.36	2.37	2.42
Russia	26.47	26.34	26.11	25.84	25.82	25.93	25.56	25.63	25.34	24.89	24.47	24.57
Serbia and Montenegro	71.99	72.91	73.45	71.84	72.17	71.37	69.44	69.28	67.49	64.38	63.53	64.47
Slovakia	26.69	26.43	25.58	24.79	24.95	25.35	24.31	24.65	24.38	23.67	22.64	22.88
Slovenia	0.77	0.76	0.75	0.74	0.74	0.74	0.73	0.73	0.73	0.70	0.68	0.68
Ukraine	5.05	5.05	5.05	5.05	5.05	5.05	5.05	5.05	5.05	5.05	5.05	5.05

Source: *International Monetary Fund (IMF)/Euromonitor International research*

Table 10.31

Exchange Rates Against the EUR 1985-2007

Units of national currency per EUR

	1985	1990	1995	1996	1997	1998	1999
Western Europe							
Austria	1.00	1.00	1.00	1.00	1.00	1.00	1.00
Belgium	1.00	1.00	1.00	1.00	1.00	1.00	1.00
Cyprus	1.00	1.00	1.00	1.00	1.00	1.00	1.00
Denmark	8.45	8.29	7.66	7.70	7.83	7.85	7.43
Finland	1.00	1.00	1.00	1.00	1.00	1.00	1.00
France	1.00	1.00	1.00	1.00	1.00	1.00	1.00
Germany	1.00	1.00	1.00	1.00	1.00	1.00	1.00
Gibraltar			0.82	0.85	0.73	0.70	0.65
Greece	1.00	1.00	1.00	1.00	1.00	1.00	1.00
Iceland	33.11	78.09	88.43	88.25	84.03	83.13	77.07
Ireland	1.00	1.00	1.00	1.00	1.00	1.00	1.00
Italy	1.00	1.00	1.00	1.00	1.00	1.00	1.00
Liechtenstein	1.96	1.86	1.62	1.64	1.72	1.70	1.60
Luxembourg	1.00	1.00	1.00	1.00	1.00	1.00	1.00
Malta	1.00	1.00	1.00	1.00	1.00	1.00	1.00
Monaco	1.00	1.00	1.00	1.00	1.00	1.00	1.00
Netherlands	1.00	1.00	1.00	1.00	1.00	1.00	1.00
Norway	6.86	8.39	8.66	8.56	8.38	8.84	8.31
Portugal	1.00	1.00	1.00	1.00	1.00	1.00	1.00
Spain	1.00	1.00	1.00	1.00	1.00	1.00	1.00
Sweden	6.86	7.93	9.75	8.90	9.05	9.31	8.80
Switzerland	1.96	1.86	1.62	1.64	1.72	1.70	1.60
Turkey	0.00	0.00	0.06	0.11	0.18	0.31	0.45
United Kingdom	0.62	0.75	0.87	0.85	0.72	0.71	0.66
Eastern Europe							
Albania	5.58	10.38	126.72	138.67	176.51	176.48	146.71
Belarus			15.75	17.56	30.84	54.04	265.63
Bosnia-Herzegovina			1.99	2.06	2.06	1.96
Bulgaria	0.00	0.00	0.09	0.24	1.99	2.06	1.96
Croatia			7.15	7.21	7.30	7.46	7.58
Czech Republic		24.06	36.28	36.02	37.57	37.82	36.83
Estonia			15.67	15.97	16.45	16.49	15.64
Georgia			1.73	1.68	1.54	1.63	2.16
Hungary	39.99	84.69	171.81	202.57	221.37	251.19	252.68
Latvia			0.72	0.73	0.69	0.69	0.62
Lithuania			5.47	5.31	4.74	4.69	4.26
Macedonia			51.78	53.06	59.26	63.81	60.63
Moldova			6.15	6.11	5.48	6.29	11.20
Poland	0.01	1.27	3.31	3.58	3.89	4.07	4.23
Romania	0.00	0.00	0.28	0.41	0.85	1.04	1.63
Russia			6.23	6.80	6.86	11.37	26.23
Serbia and Montenegro			4.01	6.56	7.89	11.22	20.18
Slovakia			40.62	40.68	39.84	41.28	44.07
Slovenia	1.00	1.00	1.00	1.00	1.00	1.00	1.00
Ukraine			2.01	2.43	2.21	2.87	4.40

Source: *European Central Bank/Euromonitor International research*
Notes: *Annual average market exchange rates*

Exchange Rates

Exchange Rates Against the EUR 1985-2007 *(continued)*
Units of national currency per EUR

	2000	2001	2002	2003	2004	2005	2006	2007
Western Europe								
Austria	1.00	1.00	1.00	1.00	1.00	1.00	1.00	1.00
Belgium	1.00	1.00	1.00	1.00	1.00	1.00	1.00	1.00
Cyprus	1.00	1.00	1.00	1.00	1.00	1.00	1.00	1.00
Denmark	7.46	7.46	7.44	7.44	7.44	7.46	7.46	7.46
Finland	1.00	1.00	1.00	1.00	1.00	1.00	1.00	1.00
France	1.00	1.00	1.00	1.00	1.00	1.00	1.00	1.00
Germany	1.00	1.00	1.00	1.00	1.00	1.00	1.00	1.00
Gibraltar	0.61	0.62	0.62	0.70	0.68	0.68	0.75	0.84
Greece	1.00	1.00	1.00	1.00	1.00	1.00	1.00	1.00
Iceland	72.51	87.28	86.38	86.64	87.21	78.32	88.05	87.80
Ireland	1.00	1.00	1.00	1.00	1.00	1.00	1.00	1.00
Italy	1.00	1.00	1.00	1.00	1.00	1.00	1.00	1.00
Liechtenstein	1.56	1.51	1.47	1.52	1.55	1.55	1.57	1.75
Luxembourg	1.00	1.00	1.00	1.00	1.00	1.00	1.00	1.00
Malta	1.00	1.00	1.00	1.00	1.00	1.00	1.00	1.00
Monaco	1.00	1.00	1.00	1.00	1.00	1.00	1.00	1.00
Netherlands	1.00	1.00	1.00	1.00	1.00	1.00	1.00	1.00
Norway	8.12	8.06	7.52	8.00	8.38	8.01	8.05	8.03
Portugal	1.00	1.00	1.00	1.00	1.00	1.00	1.00	1.00
Spain	1.00	1.00	1.00	1.00	1.00	1.00	1.00	1.00
Sweden	8.45	9.25	9.18	9.13	9.13	9.29	9.26	9.26
Switzerland	1.56	1.51	1.47	1.52	1.55	1.55	1.57	1.65
Turkey	0.58	1.10	1.42	1.70	1.77	1.67	1.79	1.79
United Kingdom	0.61	0.62	0.63	0.69	0.68	0.68	0.68	0.69
Eastern Europe								
Albania	132.55	128.55	132.07	137.64	127.70	124.20	123.08	123.94
Belarus	808.65	1,245.33	1,687.64	2,316.90	2,684.07	2,678.51	2,690.62	2,941.50
Bosnia-Herzegovina	1.96	1.96	1.96	1.96	1.96	1.96	1.96	1.96
Bulgaria	1.96	1.96	1.96	1.96	1.96	1.96	1.96	1.96
Croatia	7.63	7.47	7.42	7.57	7.50	7.40	7.32	7.35
Czech Republic	35.60	34.08	30.85	31.86	31.93	29.79	28.35	27.82
Estonia	15.65	15.66	15.65	15.65	15.65	15.65	15.64	15.67
Georgia	1.82	1.86	2.07	2.42	2.38	2.25	2.23	2.29
Hungary	260.26	256.67	243.02	253.35	251.91	248.20	263.96	251.68
Latvia	0.56	0.56	0.58	0.65	0.67	0.70	0.70	0.70
Lithuania	3.69	3.58	3.46	3.46	3.45	3.45	3.45	3.46
Macedonia	60.79	60.96	60.64	61.36	61.39	61.29	61.23	61.31
Moldova	11.47	11.53	12.79	15.75	15.32	15.67	16.47	16.64
Poland	4.01	3.67	3.84	4.39	4.54	4.02	3.89	3.79
Romania	2.00	2.60	3.11	3.75	4.06	3.62	3.52	3.34
Russia	25.94	26.13	29.54	34.67	35.80	35.17	34.11	35.06
Serbia and Montenegro	40.60	59.95	60.68	65.04	72.54	82.97	84.24	80.12
Slovakia	42.46	43.32	42.71	41.53	40.08	38.57	37.26	33.85
Slovenia	1.00	1.00	1.00	1.00	1.00	1.00	1.00	1.00
Ukraine	5.02	4.81	5.02	6.02	6.61	6.37	6.34	6.92

Source: *European Central Bank/Euromonitor International research*
Notes: *Annual average market exchange rates*

Table 10.32

Exchange Rates Against the EUR by Month 2007

Units of national currency per EUR

	January	February	March	April	May	June	July	August	September	October	November	December
Western Europe												
Austria	1.00	1.00	1.00	1.00	1.00	1.00	1.00	1.00	1.00	1.00	1.00	1.00
Belgium	1.00	1.00	1.00	1.00	1.00	1.00	1.00	1.00	1.00	1.00	1.00	1.00
Cyprus	1.00	1.00	1.00	1.00	1.00	1.00	1.00	1.00	1.00	1.00	1.00	1.00
Denmark	7.48	7.47	7.47	7.46	7.48	7.47	7.46	7.47	7.36	7.48	7.47	7.48
Finland	1.00	1.00	1.00	1.00	1.00	1.00	1.00	1.00	1.00	1.00	1.00	1.00
France	1.00	1.00	1.00	1.00	1.00	1.00	1.00	1.00	1.00	1.00	1.00	1.00
Germany	1.00	1.00	1.00	1.00	1.00	1.00	1.00	1.00	1.00	1.00	1.00	1.00
Gibraltar	0.91	0.91	0.91	0.91	0.91	0.91	0.91	0.91	0.91	0.63	0.64	0.65
Greece	1.00	1.00	1.00	1.00	1.00	1.00	1.00	1.00	1.00	1.00	1.00	1.00
Iceland	91.48	88.40	89.05	88.33	85.56	84.47	83.28	88.87	87.39	86.55	89.36	90.86
Ireland	1.00	1.00	1.00	1.00	1.00	1.00	1.00	1.00	1.00	1.00	1.00	1.00
Italy	1.00	1.00	1.00	1.00	1.00	1.00	1.00	1.00	1.00	1.00	1.00	1.00
Liechtenstein	1.62	1.63	1.62	1.64	1.66	1.66	1.66	1.64	1.62	1.68	1.65	1.66
Luxembourg	1.00	1.00	1.00	1.00	1.00	1.00	1.00	1.00	1.00	1.00	1.00	1.00
Malta	1.00	1.00	1.00	1.00	1.00	1.00	1.00	1.00	1.00	1.00	1.00	1.00
Monaco	1.00	1.00	1.00	1.00	1.00	1.00	1.00	1.00	1.00	1.00	1.00	1.00
Netherlands	1.00	1.00	1.00	1.00	1.00	1.00	1.00	1.00	1.00	1.00	1.00	1.00
Norway	8.31	8.11	8.15	8.12	8.17	8.09	7.96	8.00	7.74	7.72	7.97	8.03
Portugal	1.00	1.00	1.00	1.00	1.00	1.00	1.00	1.00	1.00	1.00	1.00	1.00
Spain	1.00	1.00	1.00	1.00	1.00	1.00	1.00	1.00	1.00	1.00	1.00	1.00
Sweden	9.11	9.21	9.32	9.25	9.24	9.36	9.20	9.36	9.17	9.20	9.31	9.45
Switzerland	1.62	1.63	1.62	1.64	1.66	1.66	1.66	1.64	1.62	1.68	1.65	1.66
Turkey	1.85	1.83	1.86	1.84	1.81	1.77	1.76	1.80	1.73	1.70	1.75	1.72
United Kingdom	0.67	0.67	0.68	0.68	0.68	0.68	0.68	0.68	0.68	0.70	0.71	0.72
Eastern Europe												
Albania	125.22	125.55	126.56	126.40	125.75	123.51	122.60	122.62	122.36	122.79	122.13	121.25
Belarus	2,790.12	2,806.37	2,844.99	2,902.60	2,909.41	2,887.54	2,948.73	2,934.34	2,947.34	3,067.84	3,165.87	3,144.56
Bosnia-Herzegovina	1.96	1.96	1.96	1.96	1.96	1.96	1.96	1.96	1.93	1.96	1.96	1.96
Bulgaria	1.96	1.96	1.96	1.96	1.96	1.96	1.96	1.96	1.93	1.96	1.96	1.96
Croatia	7.38	7.39	7.38	7.42	7.36	7.36	7.32	7.34	7.24	7.35	7.36	7.33
Czech Republic	27.93	28.30	28.13	28.07	28.35	28.63	28.38	27.96	27.25	27.42	26.78	26.34
Estonia	15.69	15.69	15.69	15.69	15.70	15.70	15.68	15.70	15.45	15.69	15.68	15.68
Georgia	2.24	2.25	2.26	2.29	2.28	2.25	2.29	2.28	2.28	2.34	2.39	2.34
Hungary	254.53	254.07	250.61	246.60	249.36	251.28	247.39	256.13	250.29	251.56	254.72	253.88
Latvia	0.70	0.70	0.70	0.71	0.70	0.71	0.71	0.71	0.70	0.71	0.70	0.70
Lithuania	3.46	3.47	3.46	3.47	3.46	3.46	3.46	3.47	3.42	3.47	3.46	3.46
Macedonia	61.36	61.39	61.35	61.38	61.37	61.40	61.39	61.42	60.47	61.42	61.40	61.37
Moldova	16.93	16.81	16.83	16.88	16.77	16.53	16.72	16.42	16.17	16.39	16.67	16.48
Poland	3.89	3.91	3.90	3.83	3.80	3.82	3.78	3.83	3.74	3.72	3.67	3.61
Romania	3.41	3.39	3.38	3.34	3.30	3.24	3.14	3.24	3.30	3.36	3.48	3.54
Russia	34.52	34.51	34.67	34.99	35.02	34.90	35.13	35.04	34.77	35.52	36.00	35.87
Serbia and Montenegro	93.86	95.54	97.52	97.27	97.89	96.07	95.45	94.73	92.59	91.87	93.47	94.14
Slovakia	34.80	34.64	33.97	33.56	33.85	34.13	33.42	33.70	33.44	33.78	33.30	33.41
Slovenia	1.00	1.00	1.00	1.00	1.00	1.00	1.00	1.00	1.00	1.00	1.00	1.00
Ukraine	6.58	6.62	6.71	6.84	6.85	6.80	6.94	6.90	6.93	7.21	7.43	7.37

Source: *European Central Bank/Euromonitor International research*

Energy Resources and Output

Primary Energy Consumption

Table 11.1

Consumption of Refinery Products 2007

'000 metric tonnes

	Motor Gasoline	Liquefied Gases	Aviation Fuels	Diesel/ Gasoil
Western Europe				
Austria	2,011	168	727	8,627
Belgium	1,598	269	1,062	12,291
Cyprus	337	52	286	520
Denmark	1,832	73	1,021	3,872
Finland	1,889	354	584	3,969
France	9,601	3,445	6,768	48,627
Germany	21,347	2,487	8,738	49,131
Gibraltar	26		4	70
Greece	4,116	342	1,138	7,490
Iceland	151	2	153	381
Ireland	1,793	147	846	3,760
Italy	12,739	3,391	3,991	31,865
Liechtenstein				
Luxembourg	449	9	446	2,446
Malta	80	19	91	93
Monaco				
Netherlands	4,047	1,861	3,730	7,750
Norway	1,545	1,333	692	3,678
Portugal	1,702	828	922	5,581
Spain	6,894	2,209	5,668	36,756
Sweden	3,786	1,127	894	4,553
Switzerland	3,518	191	1,145	6,967
Turkey	2,490	4,531	2,121	10,497
United Kingdom	17,961	5,406	13,475	27,979
Eastern Europe				
Albania	204	68	71	750
Belarus	1,082	229		2,266
Bosnia-Herzegovina	446		97	482
Bulgaria	509	404	214	1,839
Croatia	679	197	106	1,900
Czech Republic	2,020	274	357	4,294
Estonia	279	6	50	629
Georgia	340	31	44	245
Hungary	1,505	355	238	3,092
Latvia	339	61	70	725
Lithuania	323	299	59	953
Macedonia	107	44	5	336
Moldova	232	57	16	373
Poland	3,835	2,736	335	10,307
Romania	1,716	752	114	3,050
Russia	26,701	8,094	10,391	23,916
Serbia and Montenegro	1,063	170	40	1,346
Slovakia	675	91	41	1,228
Slovenia	600	86	25	1,595
Ukraine	5,001	372	206	5,263

Source: *Euromonitor International from OECD*

Table 11.2

Consumption of Motor Gasoline 1980-2007

'000 metric tonnes

	1980	1985	1990	1995	2000	2002	2003	2004	2005	2006	2007
Western Europe											
Austria	2,457	2,430	2,552	2,394	1,981	2,145	2,192	2,133	2,071	2,050	2,011
Belgium	2,948	2,502	2,727	2,833	2,245	2,087	2,105	1,932	1,762	1,690	1,598
Cyprus	100	124	163	183	206	228	252	282	303	321	337
Denmark	1,534	1,530	1,581	1,893	1,966	1,944	1,949	1,925	1,868	1,852	1,832
Finland	1,340	1,521	1,986	1,897	1,785	1,840	1,841	1,878	1,876	1,886	1,889
France	17,746	18,006	18,231	15,613	13,803	12,844	12,042	11,447	10,721	10,131	9,601
Germany	26,531	26,212	31,274	30,134	28,806	27,195	25,850	24,993	23,171	22,213	21,347
Gibraltar	4	5	12	16	20	21	22	23	24	25	26
Greece	1,377	1,795	2,423	2,774	3,280	3,543	3,685	3,763	3,918	4,022	4,116
Iceland	90	99	134	136	143	145	145	149	149	150	151
Ireland	1,018	841	885	1,037	1,493	1,585	1,583	1,627	1,712	1,747	1,793
Italy	12,036	11,820	14,055	18,496	16,863	16,458	15,839	14,940	13,936	13,336	12,739
Liechtenstein											
Luxembourg	286	303	412	516	582	557	567	530	486	470	449
Malta	39	20	65	120	61	44	70	58	68	75	80
Monaco											
Netherlands	3,854	3,395	3,445	4,023	4,031	4,169	4,185	4,158	4,097	4,077	4,047
Norway	1,387	1,587	1,785	1,664	1,619	1,664	1,646	1,637	1,580	1,563	1,545
Portugal	751	855	1,369	1,890	2,123	2,067	2,005	1,927	1,808	1,754	1,702
Spain	5,421	5,894	8,145	8,534	8,524	8,094	7,886	7,534	7,260	7,075	6,894
Sweden	3,516	3,750	4,166	4,251	3,977	4,042	4,007	3,926	3,862	3,825	3,786
Switzerland	2,744	3,058	3,724	3,590	3,983	3,795	3,776	3,708	3,595	3,558	3,518
Turkey	1,953	1,916	3,196	4,330	3,619	3,155	2,715	2,415	2,673	2,539	2,490
United Kingdom	19,145	20,403	24,312	21,953	21,603	20,808	19,918	19,484	18,731	18,298	17,961
Eastern Europe											
Albania	175	121	60	133	101	138	145	175	181	192	204
Belarus			2,363	1,154	987	951	960	965	1,033	1,056	1,082
Bosnia-Herzegovina			349	118	240	263	274	320	377	409	446
Bulgaria	1,350	1,213	1,391	1,083	659	610	586	559	544	526	509
Croatia			764	575	784	758	756	723	709	695	679
Czech Republic	1,003	1,069	1,161	1,637	1,858	1,926	2,100	2,092	2,055	2,039	2,020
Estonia			523	247	282	309	306	287	290	285	279
Georgia			894	134	272	323	328	290	334	337	340
Hungary	1,405	1,336	1,790	1,427	1,336	1,425	1,424	1,442	1,477	1,491	1,505
Latvia			608	412	337	346	346	349	342	341	339
Lithuania			980	603	381	362	360	344	338	331	323
Macedonia			161	207	144	138	126	122	117	111	107
Moldova			774	223	117	162	192	210	212	224	232
Poland	3,259	2,944	3,079	4,372	5,001	4,225	4,042	4,095	3,955	3,880	3,835
Romania	2,258	1,405	2,083	1,022	1,326	1,663	1,660	1,715	1,695	1,704	1,716
Russia			30,436	24,836	23,259	25,485	25,662	26,451	26,260	26,475	26,701
Serbia and Montenegro			647	396	340	429	470	972	1,000	1,036	1,063
Slovakia	674	408	438	504	592	722	668	614	643	661	675
Slovenia			565	821	807	767	749	666	655	628	600
Ukraine			10,960	4,355	3,825	4,602	4,069	4,183	4,756	4,799	5,001

Source: Euromonitor International from OECD

Energy Production

Table 11.3

Production of Coal 1985-2007
Million tonnes of oil equivalent

	1985	1990	1995	2000	2002	2003	2004	2005	2006	2007
Western Europe										
Austria	1.0	0.8	0.4							
Belgium										
Cyprus										
Denmark										
Finland			2.0							
France	10.2	8.1	5.3	2.3	1.1	1.3	0.4	0.2	0.2	0.1
Germany	144.8	117.3	74.6	56.5	55.0	54.1	54.7	53.2	50.3	51.5
Gibraltar										
Greece	4.8	7.1	7.5	8.2	9.1	9.5	9.6	9.4	8.6	8.2
Iceland										
Ireland			1.1							
Italy	0.3	0.3	0.1	0.0	0.1	0.2	0.2	0.2	0.2	0.2
Liechtenstein										
Luxembourg										
Malta										
Monaco										
Netherlands										
Norway			0.2							
Portugal										
Spain	13.4	11.9	10.2	8.0	7.2	6.8	6.7	6.4	6.2	6.0
Sweden			0.3							
Switzerland										
Turkey	10.7	12.1	12.1	13.9	11.5	10.5	10.5	12.8	13.4	15.8
United Kingdom	54.9	54.7	31.8	19.0	18.2	17.2	15.3	12.5	11.3	10.4
Eastern Europe										
Albania										
Belarus										
Bosnia-Herzegovina										
Bulgaria	5.3	5.4	5.2	4.4	4.4	4.6	4.5	4.4	4.6	5.1
Croatia										
Czech Republic	43.9	36.7	27.3	25.0	24.3	24.2	23.5	23.5	23.7	23.6
Estonia										
Georgia										
Hungary	5.5	4.0	2.6	2.9	2.7	2.8	2.4	2.0	2.1	2.0
Latvia										
Lithuania										
Macedonia										
Moldova										
Poland	118.0	94.5	91.1	71.3	71.3	71.4	70.5	68.7	67.0	62.3
Romania	10.3	8.7	9.3	6.4	6.6	7.0	6.7	6.5	7.4	7.4
Russia	176.2	176.2	118.5	115.8	114.8	127.1	131.7	139.2	145.1	148.2
Serbia and Montenegro										
Slovakia		1.5	1.1	1.1	1.0	0.9	0.9	0.8	0.8	0.8
Slovenia										
Ukraine	96.5	83.9	44.2	42.2	43.0	41.7	42.2	40.9	41.7	39.6

Source: BP Amoco, BP Statistical Review of World Energy
Notes: Million tonnes of oil equivalent = the amount of oil required to fuel an oil-fired plant in order to generate the same amount of electricity

Table 11.4

Production of Crude Oil 1980-2007

Million tonnes of oil equivalent

	1980	1985	1990	1995	2000	2002	2003	2004	2005	2006	2007
Western Europe											
Austria											
Belgium											
Cyprus											
Denmark		1.0	2.8	4.8	7.3	7.5	7.2	8.5	9.4	9.4	8.3
Finland											
France				2.4	2.0	1.9	1.7	1.5	1.0	0.9	0.8
Germany	16.7	15.7	14.3	14.5	15.2	15.3	15.9	14.7	14.2	14.1	12.9
Gibraltar											
Greece				16.1							
Iceland											
Ireland				16.4							
Italy	10.3	11.5	14.0	16.3	13.7	12.1	11.5	10.7	10.0	9.1	8.0
Liechtenstein											
Luxembourg											
Malta											
Monaco											
Netherlands	68.9	64.4	54.5	60.3	51.6	53.9	52.5	61.9	56.6	58.7	58.0
Norway	22.6	23.6	22.9	25.0	44.8	59.0	65.8	70.6	76.5	78.9	80.7
Portugal											
Spain				0.4							
Sweden											
Switzerland											
Turkey				0.2							
United Kingdom	31.3	35.7	40.9	63.7	97.5	93.2	92.6	86.7	79.4	72.0	65.2
Eastern Europe											
Albania											
Belarus		0.3	0.2	0.2	0.2	0.2	0.2	0.2	0.2	0.2	0.2
Bosnia-Herzegovina											
Bulgaria											
Croatia				1.7	1.4	1.2	1.2	1.2	1.3	1.3	1.3
Czech Republic											
Estonia											
Georgia											
Hungary	4.6	5.8	3.8	3.7	2.4	2.6	2.5	2.4	2.4	2.3	2.3
Latvia											
Lithuania											
Macedonia											
Moldova											
Poland	4.5	4.1	2.4	3.1	3.3	3.6	3.6	3.9	3.9	3.9	3.8
Romania	31.3	31.3	25.5	16.2	12.4	11.9	11.7	11.5	11.2	10.7	10.4
Russia		387.9	538.2	499.9	490.5	499.9	520.8	531.9	538.2	550.9	546.7
Serbia and Montenegro											
Slovakia				3.0	2.8	3.7	3.5	3.3	3.1	2.9	2.7
Slovenia											
Ukraine		36.0	23.6	15.3	15.0	15.7	16.2	17.2	17.4	17.2	17.1

Source: BP Amoco, BP Statistical Review of World Energy
Notes: Million tonnes of oil equivalent = the amount of oil required to fuel an oil-fired plant in order to generate the same amount of electricity

Energy Production

Table 11.5

Production of Crude Oil by Quarter 2006-2008
Million tonnes of oil equivalent

	2006 1st Quarter	2006 2nd Quarter	2006 3rd Quarter	2006 4th Quarter	2007 1st Quarter	2007 2nd Quarter	2007 3rd Quarter	2007 4th Quarter	2008 1st Quarter	2008 2nd Quarter
Western Europe										
Austria										
Belgium										
Cyprus										
Denmark	4.2	4.3	3.9	4.3	3.8	3.8	3.7	3.9	3.5	3.5
Finland										
France										
Germany										
Gibraltar										
Greece										
Iceland										
Ireland										
Italy	1.5	1.5	1.4	1.4	1.5	1.5	1.5	1.4	1.5	
Liechtenstein										
Luxembourg										
Malta										
Monaco										
Netherlands										
Norway	32.9	31.0	32.4	32.4	31.0	28.4	29.3	30.0	27.1	28.4
Portugal										
Spain										
Sweden										
Switzerland										
Turkey										
United Kingdom	20.8	19.0	17.6	19.2	20.0	19.8	17.4	19.6	18.8	
Eastern Europe										
Albania										
Belarus										
Bosnia-Herzegovina										
Bulgaria										
Croatia										
Czech Republic										
Estonia										
Georgia										
Hungary										
Latvia										
Lithuania										
Macedonia										
Moldova										
Poland										
Romania	1.3	1.3	1.3	1.2	1.3	1.3	1.3	1.2	1.2	1.2
Russia	116.4	119.6	122.1	122.4	121.4	121.9	124.2	123.9	125.7	125.4
Serbia and Montenegro										
Slovakia										
Slovenia										
Ukraine										

Source: *BP Amoco, BP Statistical Review of World Energy*
Notes: *Million tonnes of oil equivalent = the amount of oil required to fuel an oil-fired plant in order to generate the same amount of electricity*

Table 11.6

Production of Crude Oil by Month 2007-2008

Million tonnes of oil equivalent

	July 2007	August 2007	September 2007	October 2007	November 2007	December 2007	January 2008	February 2008	March 2008	April 2008	May 2008	June 2008
Western Europe												
Austria												
Belgium												
Cyprus												
Denmark	1.2	1.3	1.2	1.4	1.3	1.2	1.2	1.0	1.2	1.1	1.3	1.1
Finland												
France												
Germany												
Gibraltar												
Greece												
Iceland												
Ireland												
Italy	0.5	0.5	0.5	0.5	0.5	0.5	0.5	0.5	0.5	0.5		
Liechtenstein												
Luxembourg												
Malta												
Monaco												
Netherlands												
Norway	10.5	9.3	9.4	10.2	9.9	10.0	9.9	7.6	9.7	8.4	9.7	
Portugal												
Spain												
Sweden												
Switzerland												
Turkey												
United Kingdom	6.4	5.3	5.8	6.8	6.2	6.6	6.4	5.9	6.5	6.4		
Eastern Europe												
Albania												
Belarus												
Bosnia-Herzegovina												
Bulgaria												
Croatia												
Czech Republic												
Estonia												
Georgia												
Hungary												
Latvia												
Lithuania												
Macedonia												
Moldova												
Poland												
Romania	0.4	0.4	0.4	0.4	0.4	0.4	0.4	0.4	0.4	0.4	0.4	0.4
Russia	41.8	42.0	40.4	41.9	40.3	41.7	42.9	40.0	42.7	41.2	42.6	41.6
Serbia and Montenegro												
Slovakia												
Slovenia												
Ukraine												

Source: BP Amoco, BP Statistical Review of World Energy
Notes: Million tonnes of oil equivalent = the amount of oil required to fuel an oil-fired plant in order to generate the same amount of electricity

Energy Production

Table 11.7

Electricity Production 2007
GWh/% shares

	Net Total Production	% Fossil Fuels	% Combustible Renewables and Waste	% Geothermal	% Hydroelectric	% Nuclear	% Wind Powered
Western Europe							
Austria	68,482	35.54	6.23	0.00	55.52		2.68
Belgium	89,330	40.55	3.64		1.82	53.63	0.36
Cyprus	4,709	99.98					
Denmark	39,227	72.19	9.45		0.06		18.29
Finland	77,949	38.85	13.71		15.87	30.82	0.29
France	583,208	11.28	0.91		9.02	78.46	0.24
Germany	641,179	60.42	4.74		4.29	25.56	4.69
Gibraltar	151	94.78					
Greece	64,201	88.23	0.24		9.14		2.39
Iceland	8,868	0.02	0.01	20.78	79.19		
Ireland	26,660	89.75	0.46		3.72		6.08
Italy	311,878	80.01	2.31	1.76	14.56		1.00
Liechtenstein							
Luxembourg	4,270	74.13	2.41		21.20		1.63
Malta	2,272	107.57					
Monaco							
Netherlands	102,536	88.25	5.19		0.08	4.03	2.28
Norway	144,373	0.46	0.41		98.55		0.54
Portugal	49,724	76.59	4.15	0.12	14.23		4.90
Spain	326,125	63.23	1.57		8.96	17.01	9.08
Sweden	172,108	1.60	5.29		48.72	43.77	0.63
Switzerland	58,356	2.12	4.03		53.64	40.17	0.02
Turkey	182,718	76.18	0.10	0.05	23.64		0.03
United Kingdom	404,249	73.24	3.05		1.98	20.64	1.09
Eastern Europe							
Albania	5,551	1.02			98.98		
Belarus	33,461	99.79	0.09		0.12		0.00
Bosnia-Herzegovina	13,879	60.36			39.64		
Bulgaria	46,355	43.53	0.05		12.75	43.67	0.01
Croatia	12,862	43.95	0.17		55.78		0.10
Czech Republic	88,142	66.10	1.42		2.84	29.61	0.03
Estonia	9,889	98.76	0.41		0.25		0.58
Georgia	7,473	16.80			83.20		
Hungary	37,565	53.26	4.53		0.57	41.60	0.04
Latvia	5,145	31.46	0.86		66.78		0.89
Lithuania	14,868	29.05	0.05		4.74	66.14	0.02
Macedonia	7,234	78.71			21.29		
Moldova	4,328	98.46			1.54		
Poland	162,303	95.74	1.83		2.34		0.09
Romania	63,148	52.67	0.01		38.50	8.82	
Russia	991,362	65.99	0.31	0.04	17.93	15.73	0.00
Serbia and Montenegro	36,574	64.03			35.97		
Slovakia	32,812	24.71	0.93		17.43	56.77	0.02
Slovenia	15,951	37.46	0.72		22.10	39.71	
Ukraine	191,606	44.67			6.92	48.38	0.03

Source: *Euromonitor International from OECD*

Table 11.8

Electricity Production by Quarter 2006-2008

GWh

	2006 1st Quarter	2006 2nd Quarter	2006 3rd Quarter	2006 4th Quarter	2007 1st Quarter	2007 2nd Quarter	2007 3rd Quarter	2007 4th Quarter	2008 1st Quarter	2008 2nd Quarter
Western Europe										
Austria	16,856.4	17,773.9	16,941.3	15,665.4	16,057.9	15,580.8	17,798.4	19,044.7	17,433.3	
Belgium	22,025.3	21,137.3	21,195.9	23,742.5	23,564.5	22,037.5	20,789.8	22,938.1	22,490.0	
Cyprus	1,134.8	1,025.0	1,340.5	1,038.7	1,093.8	1,059.3	1,448.8	1,106.6	1,301.4	1,165.5
Denmark		10,471.2	10,240.8	13,481.3	12,122.6	7,457.0	7,730.3	11,917.0	12,109.6	7,997.7
Finland	21,659.2	17,559.2	17,699.3	21,682.3	22,220.1	16,924.1	16,140.6	22,664.5	21,313.2	17,444.5
France										
Germany	157,447.6	151,309.1	151,603.3	169,430.5	169,130.7	150,624.3	147,464.9	173,959.3	163,312.8	
Gibraltar										
Greece	15,597.4	14,964.3	16,689.9	15,138.2	15,700.2	15,964.4	16,744.2	15,792.6	16,748.3	
Iceland										
Ireland	6,574.1	6,383.1	6,017.9	7,321.4	7,204.2	5,877.3	6,112.5	7,466.2	6,751.3	
Italy	76,947.1	73,352.8	79,727.1	77,761.6	76,845.0	75,358.6	78,620.5	81,054.0	80,333.9	
Liechtenstein										
Luxembourg	1,055.0	1,091.3	994.4	1,079.3	1,240.1	979.8	888.4	1,161.6		
Malta										
Monaco										
Netherlands	25,486.8	23,975.6	24,790.8	27,693.8	27,896.2	22,582.7	23,151.9	28,904.7	25,923.4	
Norway	49,322.0	30,017.3	28,010.7	34,133.1	38,513.2	32,137.4	34,928.5	38,793.9	40,520.9	32,842.6
Portugal	12,116.0	11,328.4	12,135.5	12,884.2	13,978.3	11,688.1	11,574.8	12,482.5		
Spain	77,688.0	73,896.8	80,982.2	78,185.0	82,112.2	77,323.9	81,988.6	84,699.8	86,953.4	
Sweden	48,657.9	41,148.5	31,043.6	46,743.3	50,859.1	42,859.5	34,001.5	44,387.7	48,501.9	39,060.4
Switzerland	13,336.3	15,021.6	15,902.2	14,556.6	12,952.4	15,131.1	16,412.1	13,859.9	14,581.3	
Turkey	41,185.3	41,159.0	45,827.8	44,471.5	43,741.8	44,564.3	47,574.7	46,374.4	49,136.5	47,040.7
United Kingdom	100,596.7	96,633.8	95,184.1	109,972.0	109,122.8	93,530.7	90,354.8	111,240.9	107,537.1	88,357.9
Eastern Europe										
Albania										
Belarus										
Bosnia-Herzegovina										
Bulgaria	12,707.7	10,143.0	10,627.3	12,161.7	11,929.7	10,731.1	10,967.2	12,726.6	12,677.9	10,882.6
Croatia	3,653.9	3,162.2	2,737.8	3,108.1	3,117.0	2,937.3	3,277.7	3,530.0	3,329.9	3,201.1
Czech Republic	22,288.3	19,676.3	19,720.4	22,603.1	23,528.0	20,664.5	20,106.8	23,842.7	24,474.3	19,884.2
Estonia										
Georgia										
Hungary	8,689.3	8,619.2	10,063.4	9,188.8	9,641.1	8,507.8	8,806.1	10,610.4	10,117.1	9,017.9
Latvia	1,257.2	1,366.4	860.0	1,545.2	2,220.8	1,256.8	559.5	1,108.2	5,207.0	
Lithuania	3,597.0	3,546.3	3,551.3	2,728.6	4,487.3	3,893.8	2,130.0	4,356.4	15,013.8	
Macedonia										
Moldova		718.6	493.0	1,579.2	1,800.6	607.6	397.1	1,522.7		
Poland	44,294.2	36,779.1	36,551.1	41,964.1	42,412.3	37,096.7	37,750.8	45,043.4	43,723.6	38,769.8
Romania	16,608.5	14,044.1	14,132.2	16,408.6	17,036.4	14,326.7	14,437.7	17,346.9	17,525.8	14,826.1
Russia	274,178.1	217,688.7	212,420.6	267,242.1	269,007.5	224,903.6	219,495.7	277,954.9	279,108.1	226,134.4
Serbia and Montenegro										
Slovakia	8,837.0	7,722.4	7,154.1	8,481.6	9,340.9	7,815.4	7,260.7	8,394.8	9,015.5	7,647.3
Slovenia										
Ukraine	52,632.2	42,516.4	42,995.7	51,019.1	51,130.9	44,247.1	44,091.0	52,136.8	48,372.4	

Source: Euromonitor International from OECD

Energy Production

Table 11.9

Electricity Production by Month 2007-2008

GWh

	July 2007	August 2007	September 2007	October 2007	November 2007	December 2007	January 2008	February 2008	March 2008	April 2008	May 2008	June 2008
Western Europe												
Austria	6,082.1	5,437.5	6,278.8	6,430.2	6,515.1	6,099.3	5,953.7	5,489.5	5,990.2	5,725.9		
Belgium	6,800.1	7,181.6	6,808.2	7,499.3	7,744.2	7,694.6	7,832.7	7,254.4	7,402.9			
Cyprus	519.3	504.6	424.9	374.8	333.9	397.9	493.5	444.4	363.5	346.3	383.2	
Denmark	2,325.7	2,422.2	2,982.4	3,438.7	4,377.6	4,100.7	4,540.5	3,938.6	3,630.5	2,892.2	2,597.1	2,508.5
Finland	4,901.7	5,386.2	5,852.7	7,124.8	7,723.7	7,816.0	7,521.6	6,781.1	7,010.5	6,337.1	5,631.2	5,476.2
France												
Germany	48,665.6	49,178.3	49,621.0	56,510.2	58,266.5	59,182.7	56,000.6	53,845.6	53,466.5			
Gibraltar												
Greece	5,815.9	5,609.7	5,318.6	5,212.3	5,234.8	5,345.5	6,397.3	5,594.0	4,757.0			
Iceland												
Ireland	1,962.6	2,040.1	2,109.8	2,379.4	2,439.6	2,647.1	2,383.0	2,151.3	2,217.0			
Italy	28,866.0	24,256.2	25,498.4	26,798.4	27,355.6	26,900.0	27,544.8	26,351.4	26,437.8			
Liechtenstein												
Luxembourg	324.8	274.3	289.3	360.3	384.0	417.3						
Malta												
Monaco												
Netherlands	7,641.0	7,537.8	7,973.2	9,464.7	9,696.7	9,743.3	8,890.4	8,129.2	8,903.9			
Norway	10,909.8	11,814.9	12,203.8	12,255.3	12,962.8	13,575.7	13,742.7	13,041.6	13,736.6	11,382.3	10,643.9	10,816.4
Portugal	4,248.0	3,553.8	3,773.1	3,796.3	4,060.6	4,625.6						
Spain	28,570.2	26,366.1	27,052.3	26,694.2	28,130.1	29,875.6	30,393.0	28,804.1	27,756.3	27,096.0		
Sweden	11,937.0	11,381.3	10,683.1	13,258.6	14,907.9	16,221.2	16,706.0	15,560.0	16,235.9	14,695.7	13,606.1	10,758.6
Switzerland	6,254.5	5,216.0	4,941.6	4,932.7	4,452.9	4,474.2	4,996.2	4,700.4	4,884.7	4,824.6		
Turkey	16,936.0	15,381.3	15,257.5	14,627.3	15,511.3	16,235.8	17,297.1	15,975.0	15,864.4	15,248.9	15,740.1	16,051.7
United Kingdom	30,391.0	29,748.8	30,215.0	34,784.5	37,318.7	39,137.6	37,395.5	34,901.9	35,239.7	33,082.8	28,593.4	
Eastern Europe												
Albania												
Belarus												
Bosnia-Herzegovina												
Bulgaria	3,642.9	3,673.9	3,650.4	3,625.8	4,384.3	4,716.5	4,727.0	3,921.1	4,029.8	3,794.2	3,604.4	3,484.0
Croatia	1,330.4	1,003.0	944.3	1,195.5	1,179.1	1,155.4	1,155.0	1,075.4	1,099.5	1,115.2	971.7	1,114.2
Czech Republic	6,596.6	6,889.5	6,620.6	7,653.9	8,052.9	8,135.9	8,610.3	7,932.5	7,931.5		6,476.7	6,257.9
Estonia												
Georgia												
Hungary	2,961.7	3,029.4	2,814.9	3,396.5	3,535.3	3,678.7	3,564.1	3,221.3	3,331.7	3,076.6	2,905.7	3,035.6
Latvia	199.5	180.0	180.0	266.8	368.7	472.8	329.0	330.4	529.3	547.0		
Lithuania	1,210.1	568.9	351.0	1,342.7	1,431.6	1,582.1	1,395.3	1,330.2	1,362.2			
Macedonia												
Moldova	125.1	110.0	162.0	293.6	595.0	634.1						
Poland	11,406.9	13,311.8	13,032.1	14,747.7	14,919.5	15,376.2	15,331.8	14,249.5	14,142.2	13,347.8	12,616.0	12,806.1
Romania	5,285.8	4,681.7	4,470.2	5,144.8	5,978.5	6,223.6	6,118.3	5,747.4	5,660.1	5,084.7	4,928.7	4,812.7
Russia	71,091.9	73,141.2	75,262.7	85,801.4	92,495.1	99,658.5	99,104.6	90,586.7	89,416.8	79,723.1	76,404.7	70,006.7
Serbia and Montenegro												
Slovakia	2,475.2	2,402.7	2,382.8	2,561.7	2,745.3	3,087.8	3,090.9	2,920.9	3,003.7	2,496.8	2,875.6	2,274.9
Slovenia												
Ukraine	14,915.9	14,930.6	14,244.6	16,009.2	17,347.9	18,779.8	17,221.7	15,696.7	15,454.0			

Source: Euromonitor International from OECD

Table 11.10

Production of Natural Gas 1980-2007

Million tonnes of oil equivalent

	1980	1985	1990	1995	2000	2002	2003	2004	2005	2006	2007
Western Europe											
Austria											
Belgium											
Cyprus											
Denmark		1.01	2.82	4.76	7.29	7.54	7.17	8.49	9.40	9.37	8.30
Finland											
France				2.40	1.97	1.92	1.70	1.53	0.97	0.95	0.80
Germany	16.70	15.70	14.30	14.50	15.20	15.30	15.90	14.73	14.22	14.05	12.87
Gibraltar											
Greece				16.11							
Iceland											
Ireland				16.40							
Italy	10.26	11.54	14.03	16.35	13.72	12.06	11.46	10.69	9.96	9.06	8.01
Liechtenstein											
Luxembourg											
Malta											
Monaco											
Netherlands	68.90	64.40	54.50	60.30	51.60	53.90	52.50	61.94	56.59	58.74	58.01
Norway	22.60	23.60	22.90	25.00	44.80	59.00	65.80	70.62	76.47	78.85	80.71
Portugal											
Spain				0.43							
Sweden											
Switzerland											
Turkey				0.20							
United Kingdom	31.31	35.71	40.93	63.73	97.54	93.24	92.58	86.72	79.35	71.97	65.16
Eastern Europe											
Albania											
Belarus			0.25	0.25	0.24	0.23	0.23	0.24	0.24	0.24	0.24
Bosnia-Herzegovina											
Bulgaria											
Croatia				1.68	1.36	1.20	1.24	1.17	1.27	1.29	1.31
Czech Republic											
Estonia											
Georgia											
Hungary	4.60	5.80	3.80	3.70	2.40	2.60	2.46	2.42	2.38	2.30	2.25
Latvia											
Lithuania											
Macedonia											
Moldova											
Poland	4.50	4.10	2.40	3.10	3.30	3.60	3.60	3.92	3.88	3.88	3.85
Romania	31.30	31.30	25.50	16.20	12.40	11.90	11.70	11.51	11.16	10.73	10.40
Russia		387.90	538.20	499.90	490.50	499.90	520.80	531.86	538.17	550.90	546.70
Serbia and Montenegro											
Slovakia				2.99	2.75	3.70	3.50	3.30	3.10	2.90	2.70
Slovenia											
Ukraine		36.00	23.60	15.30	15.00	15.70	16.24	17.15	17.45	17.16	17.11

Source: BP Amoco, BP Statistical Review of World Energy
Notes: Million tonnes of oil equivalent = the amount of oil required to fuel an oil-fired plant in order to generate the same amount of electricity

Energy Production

Table 11.11

Production of Natural Gas by Quarter 2006-2008
Million tonnes of oil equivalent

	2006 1st Quarter	2006 2nd Quarter	2006 3rd Quarter	2006 4th Quarter	2007 1st Quarter	2007 2nd Quarter	2007 3rd Quarter	2007 4th Quarter	2008 1st Quarter	2008 2nd Quarter
Western Europe										
Austria										
Belgium										
Cyprus										
Denmark	2.68	2.45	1.81	2.43	2.18	1.52	2.05	2.54	2.21	1.91
Finland										
France	0.27	0.24	0.22	0.22	0.21	0.17	0.22	0.20	0.14	
Germany	3.77	3.47	3.03	3.79	3.53	3.01	2.84	3.49	3.06	
Gibraltar										
Greece										
Iceland										
Ireland										
Italy	2.31	2.28	2.27	2.20	2.09	2.03	1.95	1.95	1.78	
Liechtenstein										
Luxembourg										
Malta										
Monaco										
Netherlands	26.65	10.50	6.48	15.11	18.39	8.87	8.73	22.02	15.25	
Norway	21.87	17.99	18.05	20.93	20.24	18.60	19.01	22.86		
Portugal										
Spain										
Sweden										
Switzerland										
Turkey										
United Kingdom	22.19	17.55	14.50	17.72	18.45	16.03	12.87	17.80	15.02	13.67
Eastern Europe										
Albania										
Belarus										
Bosnia-Herzegovina										
Bulgaria										
Croatia	0.28	0.32	0.35	0.35	0.34	0.32	0.33	0.33	0.33	0.33
Czech Republic										
Estonia										
Georgia										
Hungary	0.63	0.54	0.54	0.59	0.59	0.51	0.57	0.58	0.60	0.50
Latvia										
Lithuania										
Macedonia										
Moldova										
Poland	1.09	0.95	0.87	0.97	1.08	0.97	0.84	0.96	1.01	0.90
Romania	2.97	2.55	2.46	2.74	2.75	2.64	2.43	2.58	2.60	2.35
Russia	146.39	133.03	126.60	144.88	146.87	133.02	121.28	145.53	154.19	121.63
Serbia and Montenegro										
Slovakia										
Slovenia										
Ukraine	4.35	4.19	4.24	4.38	4.39	4.21	4.21	4.29	4.27	

Source: BP Amoco, BP Statistical Review of World Energy
Notes: Million tonnes of oil equivalent = the amount of oil required to fuel an oil-fired plant in order to generate the same amount of electricity

Table 11.12

Production of Natural Gas by Month 2007-2008

Million tonnes of oil equivalent

	July 2007	August 2007	September 2007	October 2007	November 2007	December 2007	January 2008	February 2008	March 2008	April 2008	May 2008	June 2008
Western Europe												
Austria												
Belgium												
Cyprus												
Denmark	0.59	0.74	0.72	0.81	0.83	0.90	0.77	0.71	0.73	0.70	0.71	0.49
Finland												
France	0.07	0.07	0.07	0.07	0.06	0.06	0.05	0.04	0.05	0.05		
Germany	0.95	0.98	0.90	1.22	1.14	1.14	1.07	0.96	1.03			
Gibraltar												
Greece												
Iceland												
Ireland												
Italy	0.67	0.67	0.61	0.66	0.64	0.65	0.59	0.57	0.62			
Liechtenstein												
Luxembourg												
Malta												
Monaco												
Netherlands	2.61	2.74	3.39	5.14	7.67	9.20	5.41	4.88	4.97	3.65		
Norway	6.31	6.37	6.33	7.30	7.65	7.91						
Portugal												
Spain												
Sweden												
Switzerland												
Turkey												
United Kingdom	4.71	3.99	4.17	5.42	5.98	6.40	5.21	4.70	5.11	4.57	4.57	
Eastern Europe												
Albania												
Belarus												
Bosnia-Herzegovina												
Bulgaria												
Croatia	0.09	0.11	0.13	0.12	0.10	0.10	0.11	0.11	0.11	0.11	0.11	0.11
Czech Republic												
Estonia												
Georgia												
Hungary	0.19	0.20	0.18	0.18	0.19	0.21	0.18	0.16	0.26	0.18	0.16	0.16
Latvia												
Lithuania												
Macedonia												
Moldova												
Poland	0.26	0.28	0.30	0.30	0.33	0.34	0.34	0.34	0.33	0.33	0.29	0.28
Romania	0.82	0.80	0.82	0.84	0.86	0.88	0.93	0.83	0.85	0.80	0.78	
Russia	40.72	39.82	40.74	45.24	48.95	51.34	52.85	49.58	51.76	42.74	40.99	37.91
Serbia and Montenegro												
Slovakia												
Slovenia												
Ukraine	1.41	1.42	1.38	1.44	1.40	1.46	1.46	1.35	1.46			

Source: BP Amoco, BP Statistical Review of World Energy
Notes: Million tonnes of oil equivalent = the amount of oil required to fuel an oil-fired plant in order to generate the same amount of electricity

Energy Production

Table 11.13

Nuclear Energy: Reactor Statistics 2007
As stated

	Operating Reactors: Number	Operating Reactors: Capacity (MW)	Reactors Under Construction: Number	Reactors Under Construction: Capacity (MW)	Electricity Produced by Nuclear Reactors (GWh)
Western Europe					
Austria					
Belgium	7	5,824			47,909
Cyprus					
Denmark					
Finland	4	2,696	1	1,600	24,026
France	59	63,260	1	1,600	457,557
Germany	17	20,430			163,890
Gibraltar					
Greece					
Iceland					
Ireland					
Italy					
Liechtenstein					
Luxembourg					
Malta					
Monaco					
Netherlands	1	482			4,133
Norway					
Portugal					
Spain	8	7,450			55,474
Sweden	10	9,034			75,331
Switzerland	5	3,220			23,439
Turkey					
United Kingdom	19	10,222			83,417
Eastern Europe					
Albania					
Belarus					
Bosnia-Herzegovina					
Bulgaria	2	1,906	2	1,906	20,241
Croatia					
Czech Republic	6	3,619			26,100
Estonia					
Georgia					
Hungary	4	1,829			15,627
Latvia					
Lithuania	1	1,185			9,833
Macedonia					
Moldova					
Poland					
Romania	2	1,305			5,569
Russia	31	21,743	6	3,639	155,896
Serbia and Montenegro					
Slovakia	5	2,034			18,626
Slovenia	1	666			6,334
Ukraine	15	13,107	2	1,900	92,700

Source: *International Atomic Energy Agency/World Energy Council*

Table 11.14

Refinery Output 1990-2007
'000 tonnes of oil per year

	1990	1995	2000	2002	2003	2004	2005	2006	2007
Western Europe									
Austria	8,779	9,271	8,770	9,445	9,157	8,846	9,182	9,406	9,555
Belgium	29,372	29,643	38,092	46,005	45,489	43,233	37,046	35,055	33,664
Cyprus	638	830	1,181	1,083	968	279	0	0	0
Denmark	7,848	9,778	8,231	7,890	8,154	7,954	7,499	7,335	7,199
Finland	10,344	11,533	12,893	13,073	13,028	13,425	12,766	12,905	12,998
France	81,320	83,694	88,576	84,068	87,523	88,406	86,293	85,237	84,708
Germany	3,480	114,414	115,973	114,083	116,165	119,954	122,675	124,107	125,431
Gibraltar									
Greece	16,678	17,651	22,232	21,319	22,113	20,991	21,240	21,406	21,517
Iceland									
Ireland	1,526	2,273	3,286	3,154	3,130	2,895	3,120	3,270	3,370
Italy	91,020	91,171	94,771	96,233	97,840	98,140	100,598	101,288	102,074
Liechtenstein									
Luxembourg									
Malta									
Monaco									
Netherlands	67,905	80,123	80,185	78,664	82,275	83,486	84,900	85,775	86,538
Norway	13,018	13,109	15,196	13,189	14,645	14,093	15,424	16,090	16,422
Portugal	11,144	13,346	12,308	12,393	13,223	13,293	13,563	13,743	13,863
Spain	52,954	55,312	59,830	57,931	57,640	59,483	60,310	60,978	61,351
Sweden	17,239	19,105	22,712	19,519	19,384	20,308	19,800	19,546	19,419
Switzerland	3,047	4,638	4,647	4,915	4,614	5,214	4,855	4,735	4,695
Turkey	22,884	27,140	23,745	26,037	26,461	26,002	25,638	25,572	25,423
United Kingdom	88,120	92,617	86,341	83,998	84,529	89,826	86,003	84,092	83,136
Eastern Europe									
Albania	675	501	311	393	356	399	443	472	496
Belarus	855	12,147	11,662	12,818	13,024	15,926	17,900	19,119	19,917
Bosnia-Herzegovina									
Bulgaria	6,974	7,255	5,181	5,032	5,174	5,769	6,279	6,556	6,786
Croatia		5,234	5,214	5,080	5,358	5,321	5,141	5,069	4,985
Czech Republic		7,260	6,131	6,376	6,710	6,999	8,132	8,425	8,710
Estonia		313							
Georgia		40	19	22	23	24	13	12	10
Hungary	8,316	7,837	7,483	7,233	7,287	7,395	8,380	8,507	8,643
Latvia									
Lithuania		3,269	4,903	6,542	7,106	8,629	9,206	9,650	10,074
Macedonia		111	936	621	972	990	1,008	1,020	1,030
Moldova									
Poland	12,686	13,860	18,480	17,593	18,000	18,564	18,465	18,399	18,355
Romania	22,709	14,559	10,990	13,228	12,040	13,077	14,867	15,809	16,720
Russia		176,047	173,804	184,380	181,275	191,239	203,322	210,671	217,148
Serbia and Montenegro		1,001	2,454	3,438	3,518	3,892	4,044	4,219	
Slovakia		4,954	5,810	6,153	6,156	6,575	6,191	6,199	6,209
Slovenia		593	184	4	8	0	0	0	0
Ukraine		16,554	9,788	20,629	22,018	21,687	18,736	17,642	16,631

Source: Euromonitor International from OECD

Primary Energy Consumption

Table 11.15

Primary Energy Consumption: Selected Materials 2007

Million tonnes of oil equivalent

	Crude Oil	Hydroelectricity	Natural Gas	Nuclear Energy	Coal	Total
Western Europe						
Austria	13.5	7.9	8.0		3.2	32.6
Belgium	41.2	0.6	15.2	10.9	5.6	73.6
Cyprus						
Denmark	9.3		4.1		4.7	18.2
Finland	10.6	3.2	3.7	5.4	4.6	27.4
France	91.3	14.4	37.7	99.7	12.0	255.1
Germany	112.5	6.2	74.5	31.8	86.0	311.0
Gibraltar						
Greece	21.6	0.7	3.6		8.1	34.1
Iceland	1.0	1.9			0.1	3.0
Ireland	9.4	0.3	4.3		1.1	15.0
Italy	83.3	8.8	70.0		17.5	179.6
Liechtenstein						
Luxembourg						
Malta						
Monaco						
Netherlands	48.5		33.4	1.0	8.8	91.8
Norway	10.1	30.6	3.8		0.4	45.0
Portugal	14.4	2.3	3.9		3.3	24.0
Spain	78.7	7.4	31.6	12.5	20.1	150.3
Sweden	16.8	15.0	0.9	15.3	2.2	50.2
Switzerland	11.3	8.3	2.6	6.3	0.4	28.9
Turkey	31.1	8.0	31.6		31.0	101.7
United Kingdom	78.2	2.1	82.3	14.1	39.2	215.9
Eastern Europe						
Albania						
Belarus	7.0		17.5		0.1	24.5
Bosnia-Herzegovina						
Bulgaria	5.4	0.8	2.8	3.3	8.1	20.4
Croatia						
Czech Republic	9.9	0.6	8.0	5.9	18.9	43.3
Estonia						
Georgia						
Hungary	7.6	0.1	10.6	3.3	2.9	24.5
Latvia						
Lithuania	2.9	0.2	3.4	2.2	0.2	9.0
Macedonia						
Moldova						
Poland	24.3	0.7	12.3		57.1	94.4
Romania	10.8	3.6	14.7	1.6	9.0	39.7
Russia	125.9	40.5	394.9	36.2	94.5	692.0
Serbia and Montenegro						
Slovakia	3.8	1.0	5.3	3.5	4.0	17.5
Slovenia						
Ukraine	15.3	2.3	58.2	20.9	39.3	136.0

Source: *BP Amoco, BP Statistical Review of World Energy*

Table 11.16

Consumption of Coal 1980-2007

Million tonnes of oil equivalent

	1980	1985	1990	1995	2000	2002	2003	2004	2005	2006	2007
Western Europe											
Austria	3.3	3.5	3.6	2.4	3.2	3.0	2.9	2.9	2.8	2.8	3.2
Belgium	10.7	10.9	10.4	9.8	7.6	6.7	6.5	6.4	6.1	6.1	5.6
Cyprus	-										
Denmark	5.9	7.1	6.0	6.5	4.0	4.2	5.7	4.6	3.7	5.6	4.7
Finland	3.8	3.5	3.3	3.1	3.5	4.4	5.8	5.3	3.1	5.2	4.6
France	27.7	23.0	19.1	14.5	13.9	12.4	13.3	12.8	13.3	12.1	12.0
Germany	139.6	147.6	129.6	90.6	84.9	84.6	87.2	85.4	82.1	83.5	86.0
Gibraltar											
Greece	4.0	6.0	8.0	8.2	9.2	9.8	9.4	9.0	8.8	8.1	8.1
Iceland		0.1	0.1	0.1	0.1	0.1	0.1	0.1	0.1	0.1	0.1
Ireland	0.7	1.1	2.2	1.9	1.9	1.7	1.8	1.8	1.8	2.0	1.1
Italy	12.6	15.1	14.1	12.5	13.0	14.2	15.3	17.1	17.0	17.1	17.5
Liechtenstein											
Luxembourg											
Malta											
Monaco											
Netherlands	3.9	7.0	9.5	9.8	8.6	8.9	9.1	9.1	8.7	8.5	8.8
Norway	0.4	0.5	0.5	0.7	0.7	0.5	0.5	0.6	0.5	0.4	0.4
Portugal	0.3	0.8	2.8	4.2	4.5	4.1	3.8	3.7	3.8	3.8	3.3
Spain	14.1	19.2	19.0	18.5	21.6	21.9	20.5	21.0	21.2	18.5	20.1
Sweden	1.7	2.9	2.2	2.1	1.9	2.2	2.2	2.3	2.2	2.3	2.2
Switzerland	0.2	0.4	0.3	0.2	0.1	0.1	0.1	0.1	0.1	0.1	0.4
Turkey	7.5	10.6	16.8	17.5	25.5	21.2	21.8	23.0	26.1	28.8	31.0
United Kingdom	71.1	62.9	64.9	47.5	37.5	36.6	39.3	37.8	38.6	42.1	39.2
Eastern Europe											
Albania											
Belarus		1.1	1.1	0.3	0.1	0.1	0.1	0.1	0.1	0.1	0.1
Bosnia-Herzegovina											
Bulgaria	9.1	10.1	8.9	7.8	6.3	6.5	7.1	6.9	6.9	7.1	8.1
Croatia											
Czech Republic	38.5	38.2	33.5	23.5	21.0	20.6	20.8	20.5	19.8	19.4	18.9
Estonia											
Georgia											
Hungary	8.1	7.6	5.6	3.6	3.2	3.1	3.4	3.1	2.7	2.9	2.9
Latvia											
Lithuania		0.6	0.6	0.1	0.1	0.1	0.2	0.2	0.2	0.2	0.2
Macedonia											
Moldova											
Poland	101.6	99.9	80.2	71.7	57.6	56.7	57.7	57.3	55.7	58.0	57.1
Romania	12.9	16.9	11.7	9.7	7.0	7.6	7.8	7.4	7.6	8.5	9.0
Russia		195.6	180.6	119.4	105.2	103.0	104.0	99.5	94.2	96.7	94.5
Serbia and Montenegro											
Slovakia	6.9	7.2	6.9	5.1	4.0	4.0	4.2	4.1	3.9	3.8	4.0
Slovenia											
Ukraine		76.5	74.8	42.1	38.8	38.3	39.0	39.1	37.5	39.8	39.3

Source: BP Amoco, BP Statistical Review of World Energy
Notes: Million tonnes of oil equivalent = the amount of oil required to fuel an oil-fired plant in order to generate the same amount of electricity

Primary Energy Consumption

Table 11.17

Consumption of Crude Oil 1980-2007
Million metric tonnes

	1980	1985	1990	1995	2000	2002	2003	2004	2005	2006	2007
Western Europe											
Austria	12.2	9.8	10.8	11.3	11.8	13.0	14.1	13.8	14.2	14.2	13.5
Belgium	26.6	20.8	24.8	26.4	33.9	33.5	36.4	38.4	39.9	41.1	41.2
Cyprus											
Denmark	13.6	10.7	9.0	10.5	10.4	9.6	9.2	9.1	9.2	9.3	9.3
Finland	12.8	10.8	11.0	9.9	10.7	10.9	11.4	10.6	11.0	10.6	10.6
France	109.9	84.3	89.4	89.0	94.9	92.9	93.1	94.0	93.1	92.9	91.3
Germany	147.3	126.3	127.3	135.1	129.8	127.4	125.1	124.0	122.4	123.6	112.5
Gibraltar											
Greece	12.4	12.0	15.7	17.6	19.9	20.2	19.6	21.4	21.2	22.1	21.6
Iceland	0.6	0.5	0.6	0.8	0.9	0.9	0.9	1.0	1.0	1.0	1.0
Ireland	5.7	3.9	4.4	5.7	8.2	8.8	8.5	8.9	9.4	9.3	9.4
Italy	97.9	84.4	93.6	95.5	93.5	92.9	92.1	89.6	86.7	86.7	83.3
Liechtenstein											
Luxembourg											
Malta											
Monaco											
Netherlands	38.6	29.2	35.0	38.0	41.7	43.8	44.1	46.2	49.6	49.0	48.5
Norway	9.3	9.0	9.2	9.6	9.4	9.4	9.9	9.6	9.7	10.0	10.1
Portugal	8.5	8.8	11.1	13.0	15.5	16.2	15.2	15.4	16.0	14.4	14.4
Spain	52.2	42.9	48.7	56.3	70.0	73.8	75.5	77.6	78.8	78.1	78.7
Sweden	24.8	18.4	16.4	16.1	15.2	15.2	15.9	15.3	15.1	16.6	16.8
Switzerland	12.8	12.0	12.8	11.8	12.2	12.4	12.1	12.0	12.2	12.6	11.3
Turkey	14.8	16.8	22.1	28.4	31.1	30.6	31.2	32.0	30.0	30.7	31.1
United Kingdom	80.8	77.4	82.9	81.9	78.6	78.0	79.0	81.7	83.0	82.3	78.2
Eastern Europe											
Albania											
Belarus		25.2	24.8	10.4	7.0	7.1	7.4	7.5	6.9	6.8	7.0
Bosnia-Herzegovina											
Bulgaria	14.0	10.4	8.8	5.6	3.9	4.5	5.2	4.7	4.9	5.4	5.4
Croatia											
Czech Republic	11.6	10.6	8.4	8.0	7.9	8.2	8.7	9.5	9.9	9.8	9.9
Estonia											
Georgia											
Hungary	11.3	10.3	9.3	7.7	6.8	6.4	6.3	6.5	7.5	7.8	7.6
Latvia											
Lithuania		8.6	7.5	3.2	2.4	2.5	2.4	2.6	2.8	2.8	2.9
Macedonia											
Moldova											
Poland	17.1	16.4	15.8	14.9	20.0	19.4	19.9	21.1	21.9	23.3	24.3
Romania	18.6	15.0	18.7	13.5	10.0	10.6	9.4	10.9	10.5	10.3	10.8
Russia		244.5	249.7	146.1	123.5	123.5	123.4	123.3	121.9	127.1	125.9
Serbia and Montenegro											
Slovakia	6.7	6.2	5.0	3.2	3.4	3.5	3.3	3.2	3.8	3.4	3.8
Slovenia											
Ukraine		63.0	63.0	18.9	12.0	13.1	13.5	13.9	13.9	15.0	15.3

Source: BP Amoco, BP Statistical Review of World Energy

Table 11.18

Consumption of Natural Gas 1980-2007

Million tonnes of oil equivalent

	1980	1985	1990	1995	2000	2002	2003	2004	2005	2006	2007
Western Europe											
Austria	4.5	5.0	5.8	7.1	7.3	7.7	8.5	8.5	9.0	8.5	8.0
Belgium	10.3	8.4	9.5	10.6	13.4	13.4	14.4	14.9	14.9	15.3	15.2
Cyprus	-										
Denmark		0.6	1.8	3.1	4.4	4.6	4.7	4.7	4.5	4.6	4.1
Finland	0.8	0.8	2.3	2.9	3.4	3.6	4.0	3.9	3.6	3.8	3.7
France	23.6	23.3	26.4	29.6	35.7	37.5	39.0	40.1	41.3	39.7	37.7
Germany	51.7	49.2	53.9	67.0	71.5	74.3	77.0	77.3	77.6	78.5	74.5
Gibraltar											
Greece		0.1	0.1	0.1	1.8	1.9	2.2	2.4	2.5	2.9	3.6
Iceland											
Ireland	0.8	2.0	1.9	2.3	3.4	3.7	3.7	3.6	3.5	4.0	4.3
Italy	22.9	27.2	39.1	44.9	58.4	58.1	64.1	66.5	71.2	69.7	70.0
Liechtenstein											
Luxembourg											
Malta											
Monaco											
Netherlands	30.3	32.5	31.0	34.0	35.3	35.4	36.2	37.0	35.5	34.4	33.4
Norway	0.7	1.1	1.9	2.7	3.6	3.6	3.9	4.1	4.0	4.0	3.8
Portugal					2.1	2.5	2.7	3.4	3.8	3.7	3.9
Spain	1.8	2.1	5.0	7.5	15.2	18.8	21.3	24.7	29.1	30.3	31.6
Sweden		0.1	0.6	0.7	0.7	0.7	0.7	0.7	0.7	0.9	0.9
Switzerland	0.9	1.3	1.6	2.2	2.4	2.5	2.6	2.7	2.8	2.7	2.6
Turkey			3.0	6.1	13.1	15.6	18.8	19.9	24.2	27.4	31.6
United Kingdom	40.3	46.6	47.2	63.5	87.2	85.6	85.8	87.7	85.4	81.0	82.3
Eastern Europe											
Albania											
Belarus		8.3	12.4	11.1	14.6	14.9	15.4	16.6	17.0	17.6	17.5
Bosnia-Herzegovina											
Bulgaria	3.2	4.6	5.3	4.5	2.9	2.4	2.3	2.5	2.7	2.7	2.8
Croatia											
Czech Republic	3.3	3.7	4.9	6.5	7.5	7.8	7.8	8.2	8.6	8.9	8.0
Estonia											
Georgia											
Hungary	7.0	8.6	8.7	9.2	9.7	10.6	11.6	11.5	11.9	11.3	10.6
Latvia											
Lithuania		3.8	5.0	2.1	2.5	2.6	2.8	2.8	2.9	2.9	3.4
Macedonia											
Moldova											
Poland	8.8	8.9	8.9	8.9	10.0	10.1	10.1	11.8	12.3	12.3	12.3
Romania	32.4	31.9	27.7	21.6	15.4	15.5	16.5	15.7	15.8	16.4	14.7
Russia		325.1	378.1	340.0	339.5	350.0	353.6	361.7	364.6	388.9	394.9
Serbia and Montenegro											
Slovakia	3.3	4.2	5.3	5.1	5.8	5.8	5.7	5.5	5.9	5.7	5.3
Slovenia											
Ukraine		80.8	115.0	68.6	65.8	62.8	61.0	65.9	65.7	60.4	58.2

Source: *BP Amoco, BP Statistical Review of World Energy*
Notes: *Million tonnes of oil equivalent = the amount of oil required to fuel an oil-fired plant in order to generate the same amount of electricity*

Primary Energy Consumption

Table 11.19

Consumption of Nuclear Energy 1980-2007

Million tonnes of oil equivalent

	1980	1985	1990	1995	2000	2002	2003	2004	2005	2006	2007
Western Europe											
Austria											
Belgium	2.8	7.8	9.7	9.4	10.9	10.7	10.7	10.7	10.8	10.5	10.9
Cyprus											
Denmark											
Finland	1.6	4.3	4.3	4.3	5.1	5.4	5.5	5.5	5.5	5.4	5.4
France	13.9	50.7	71.1	85.4	94.0	98.8	99.8	101.7	102.4	102.1	99.7
Germany	12.6	31.4	34.5	34.9	38.4	37.3	37.4	37.8	36.9	37.9	31.8
Gibraltar											
Greece											
Iceland											
Ireland											
Italy	1.1	1.6									
Liechtenstein											
Luxembourg											
Malta											
Monaco											
Netherlands	0.9	0.9	0.8	0.9	0.9	0.9	0.9	0.9	0.9	0.8	1.0
Norway											
Portugal											
Spain	1.2	6.3	12.3	12.5	14.1	14.3	14.0	14.4	13.0	13.6	12.5
Sweden	6.0	13.3	15.4	15.8	13.0	15.4	15.3	17.3	16.4	15.2	15.3
Switzerland	3.1	5.1	5.3	5.6	6.0	6.1	6.2	6.1	5.2	6.3	6.3
Turkey											
United Kingdom	8.4	13.8	14.9	20.1	19.3	19.9	20.1	18.1	18.5	17.1	14.1
Eastern Europe											
Albania											
Belarus											
Bosnia-Herzegovina											
Bulgaria	1.4	3.0	3.3	3.9	4.1	4.6	4.5	4.4	4.2	4.4	3.3
Croatia											
Czech Republic		0.5	2.8	2.8	3.1	4.2	5.9	6.0	5.6	5.9	5.9
Estonia											
Georgia											
Hungary		1.5	3.1	3.2	3.2	3.2	2.5	2.7	3.1	3.0	3.3
Latvia											
Lithuania		2.1	3.9	2.7	1.9	3.2	3.5	3.4	2.3	2.0	2.2
Macedonia											
Moldova											
Poland											
Romania					1.2	1.2	1.1	1.3	1.3	1.3	1.6
Russia		22.5	26.8	22.5	29.5	32.1	33.6	32.7	33.4	35.4	36.2
Serbia and Montenegro											
Slovakia	1.0	2.1	2.7	2.6	3.7	4.1	4.0	3.9	4.0	4.1	3.5
Slovenia											
Ukraine		12.1	17.2	16.0	17.5	17.6	18.4	19.7	20.1	20.4	20.9

Source: *BP Amoco, BP Statistical Review of World Energy*
Notes: *Million tonnes of oil equivalent = the amount of oil required to fuel an oil-fired plant in order to generate the same amount of electricity*

Table 11.20

Residential Consumption of Electricity 1980-2007

'000 GWh

	1980	1985	1990	1995	2000	2002	2003	2004	2005	2006	2007
Western Europe											
Austria	8.8	8.3	11.9	13.6	13.0	14.2	14.4	13.4	13.6	13.5	13.3
Belgium	13.1	15.5	18.4	22.1	23.7	25.9	26.0	26.5	26.0	26.0	26.0
Cyprus	0.2	0.3	0.4	0.8	1.1	1.2	1.3	1.3	1.4	1.5	1.5
Denmark	7.4	9.1	9.7	10.3	10.2	10.2	10.3	10.3	10.4	10.5	10.6
Finland	8.1	12.2	14.6	16.3	18.1	19.9	20.4	20.4	20.6	20.7	20.8
France	61.5	85.8	96.9	108.8	128.7	133.0	141.6	147.7	149.8	153.5	156.2
Germany	115.0	132.6	137.1	127.2	128.9	131.2	139.5	140.4	141.8	144.2	145.2
Gibraltar											
Greece	5.7	7.7	9.1	11.5	14.2	15.8	16.4	16.9	16.9	17.1	17.3
Iceland	0.6	0.5	0.6	0.6	0.6	0.6	0.6	0.7	0.7	0.7	0.7
Ireland	3.6	4.0	4.1	5.0	6.4	6.6	7.0	7.3	7.5	7.7	7.9
Italy	37.8	44.5	52.7	57.2	61.1	63.0	65.0	66.6	67.0	67.8	68.5
Liechtenstein											
Luxembourg	0.5	0.6	0.6	0.7	0.7	0.7	0.7	0.7	0.7	0.7	0.8
Malta		0.2	0.3	0.4	0.6	0.6	0.6	0.6	0.6	0.6	0.6
Monaco											
Netherlands	15.1	16.0	16.5	19.7	21.8	22.8	23.3	23.5	24.2	24.6	24.8
Norway	22.5	28.9	30.3	34.6	34.6	34.6	32.0	32.4	33.5	34.0	34.5
Portugal	3.3	4.5	5.9	7.9	10.1	11.4	11.8	12.4	13.2	13.7	14.1
Spain	19.6	23.3	30.2	36.0	43.6	50.6	54.2	58.0	62.6	65.2	67.7
Sweden	25.7	39.7	38.1	42.4	42.0	41.5	42.0	41.4	42.7	42.9	43.1
Switzerland	10.1	12.0	13.6	15.2	15.7	16.2	16.7	17.1	17.6	17.9	18.2
Turkey	3.5	5.0	9.1	14.5	23.9	23.6	25.2	27.6	30.9	32.2	33.3
United Kingdom	86.1	88.2	93.8	102.2	111.8	114.5	115.8	115.5	116.8	117.3	117.7
Eastern Europe											
Albania			0.7	0.9	2.5	3.1	3.0	2.8	2.7	2.7	2.6
Belarus			3.5	4.9	5.6	5.8	6.1	6.1	6.0	6.0	6.0
Bosnia-Herzegovina			3.0	2.5	3.7	3.8	3.8	3.8	4.1	4.2	4.2
Bulgaria	6.8	9.6	10.5	11.0	9.9	9.3	9.3	8.8	9.0	9.0	8.9
Croatia			4.5	4.6	5.7	6.0	5.7	6.1	6.3	6.4	6.6
Czech Republic	6.2	8.0	9.6	14.8	13.8	14.1	14.5	14.5	14.7	14.9	14.9
Estonia			0.9	1.1	1.5	1.6	1.6	1.6	1.6	1.6	1.6
Georgia			2.9	4.6	2.7	2.5	2.7	2.8	3.0	3.1	3.2
Hungary	5.0	7.4	9.2	9.8	9.8	10.4	11.1	11.0	11.1	11.3	11.3
Latvia			1.3	1.2	1.2	1.3	1.4	1.5	1.6	1.6	1.7
Lithuania			1.8	1.5	1.8	1.8	1.9	2.1	2.1	2.2	2.3
Macedonia			1.7	2.4	2.7	2.7	2.9	2.9	3.0	3.1	3.1
Moldova			1.7	1.9	1.2	1.2	1.4	1.6	1.7	1.8	1.9
Poland	10.7	14.9	20.2	18.1	21.0	21.7	24.9	25.5	25.1	25.8	26.0
Romania	4.9	4.8	5.4	7.1	7.7	7.8	8.2	8.0	9.2	9.5	9.7
Russia			106.9	126.1	140.7	142.7	142.3	143.3	108.9	106.1	103.1
Serbia and Montenegro			10.7	16.1	16.3	16.3	16.3	13.6	14.2	13.8	13.4
Slovakia	2.4	2.9	3.7	5.0	5.4	5.2	5.0	4.8	4.7	4.6	4.5
Slovenia			2.2	2.6	2.6	2.7	3.0	3.0	3.0	3.0	3.0
Ukraine			17.2	36.0	30.1	21.8	23.1	24.2	26.1	27.0	27.9

Source: Euromonitor International from OECD

Residential Consumption of Gas

Table 11.21

Residential Consumption of Gas 1990-2007

'000 TJ

	1990	1995	2000	2002	2003	2004	2005	2006	2007
Western Europe									
Austria	36.2	47.5	54.4	59.8	64.5	61.7	67.0	71.6	74.2
Belgium	115.5	145.5	153.2	160.8	167.4	175.2	173.3	177.3	180.7
Cyprus									
Denmark	19.3	29.9	30.6	31.2	33.4	33.2	32.8	33.1	33.7
Finland	1.3	0.8	1.0	1.2	1.2	1.3	1.4	1.5	1.6
France	306.5	365.0	589.0	615.3	611.9	686.8	672.3	677.3	693.2
Germany	671.9	978.4	1,090.5	1,150.3	1,251.5	1,320.4	1,350.4	1,376.2	1,420.0
Gibraltar									
Greece	0.1	0.1	0.2	0.4	0.9	1.6	3.4	4.9	6.6
Iceland									
Ireland	5.4	11.7	20.4	22.1	25.0	27.5	24.2	26.9	27.6
Italy	534.9	636.8	696.6	711.8	803.5	836.6	874.1	882.2	909.8
Liechtenstein									
Luxembourg	6.5	8.5	9.8	10.6	11.0	11.8	10.9	11.5	11.6
Malta									
Monaco									
Netherlands	365.8	400.9	370.7	364.0	372.8	367.5	349.9	346.1	340.9
Norway		0.0	0.1	0.1	0.1	0.1	0.2	0.3	0.3
Portugal	1.9	1.9	4.6	6.8	7.4	8.4	9.3	9.8	10.8
Spain	29.6	46.6	94.0	117.9	137.8	141.2	148.3	149.9	154.2
Sweden	2.4	4.1	4.8	3.6	3.2	3.2	3.3	3.4	3.5
Switzerland	28.3	37.5	40.2	41.8	44.6	46.1	47.4	48.4	49.8
Turkey	2.4	52.2	125.4	145.0	173.4	181.3	222.6	240.5	268.5
United Kingdom	1,081.4	1,173.6	1,331.7	1,354.9	1,391.3	1,427.1	1,374.8	1,397.7	1,399.9
Eastern Europe									
Albania	0.4	0.2							
Belarus	35.0	42.6	46.7	52.8	52.1	52.1	54.2	58.7	61.1
Bosnia-Herzegovina	1.4	1.1	3.8	4.2	4.3	5.1	6.0	6.4	6.5
Bulgaria			0.0	0.1	0.1	0.3	0.7	1.0	1.3
Croatia	8.4	14.7	19.1	21.1	24.3	24.2	26.4	29.4	31.4
Czech Republic	50.0	76.2	95.3	103.7	111.7	109.4	107.5	115.3	116.5
Estonia	2.6	2.2	2.0	1.7	1.7	1.8	2.1	2.1	2.2
Georgia	52.0	2.7	11.2	5.2	5.9	6.9	8.2	9.3	10.8
Hungary	76.4	134.5	140.7	158.8	183.6	166.0	182.7	186.8	187.9
Latvia	4.4	4.6	3.0	3.7	4.1	4.4	4.7	5.0	5.4
Lithuania	10.3	8.6	4.8	5.1	5.5	5.9	6.3	6.8	7.2
Macedonia									
Moldova	10.2	12.8	8.9	9.6	10.1	12.4	13.3	14.0	15.6
Poland	139.2	177.6	142.0	141.4	142.0	140.5	150.2	145.7	147.0
Romania	105.0	83.3	103.1	109.4	119.1	118.3	107.0	104.4	99.9
Russia	2,192.7	2,011.8	2,006.1	1,962.4	2,116.2	1,987.3	1,774.4	1,703.8	1,656.2
Serbia and Montenegro		6.7	8.7	8.7	9.1	11.6	9.7	10.1	10.5
Slovakia	50.8	47.5	76.4	74.6	74.9	69.2	65.9	66.7	67.9
Slovenia	1.3	2.5	2.7	3.2	4.0	4.6	4.6	4.9	5.2
Ukraine	406.4	524.6	596.3	592.4	623.8	619.9	667.5	707.8	738.9

Source: *Euromonitor International from OECD*

Environmental Data

Air and Water Pollution

Table 12.1

Carbon Dioxide Emissions 2007
'000 metric tonnes

	Fossil Fuels	Natural Gases	Coal	Petroleum
Western Europe				
Austria	82,135.5	20,677.2	17,100.2	44,358.1
Belgium	127,839.7	35,789.5	17,114.8	74,935.4
Cyprus	9,267.0		159.3	9,107.7
Denmark	49,343.3	10,043.3	12,380.0	26,920.0
Finland	48,507.9	8,063.1	9,374.8	31,070.0
France	424,337.9	108,804.8	48,800.0	266,733.1
Germany	840,955.3	193,629.5	313,903.6	333,422.2
Gibraltar	4,581.3			4,581.3
Greece	103,297.3	6,304.0	34,593.3	62,400.0
Iceland	3,208.0		402.6	2,805.3
Ireland	45,363.9	7,768.6	8,115.1	29,480.2
Italy	476,671.3	183,270.3	66,916.8	226,484.2
Liechtenstein				
Luxembourg	14,049.6	2,963.2	280.6	10,805.8
Malta	3,114.3			3,114.3
Monaco				
Netherlands	279,300.3	81,748.2	45,377.5	152,174.6
Norway	55,732.1	11,200.0	15,580.9	28,951.2
Portugal	66,436.0	10,277.4	12,610.0	43,548.6
Spain	408,848.6	78,055.2	86,600.0	244,193.5
Sweden	60,279.5	2,027.6	8,645.6	49,606.4
Switzerland	46,928.9	6,904.3	283.9	39,740.7
Turkey	250,278.9	62,422.9	105,698.0	82,158.0
United Kingdom	586,370.4	191,564.9	144,900.0	249,905.5
Eastern Europe				
Albania	4,688.8	58.4	109.3	4,521.1
Belarus	68,344.5	43,641.2	361.5	24,341.8
Bosnia-Herzegovina	19,246.9	1,017.0	13,667.4	4,562.5
Bulgaria	50,904.7	10,447.3	26,230.0	14,227.3
Croatia	21,306.1	5,213.0	2,100.0	13,993.1
Czech Republic	116,373.7	17,753.0	68,320.0	30,300.7
Estonia	19,104.3	3,054.3	11,300.0	4,750.0
Georgia	5,192.8	3,250.0	85.0	1,857.8
Hungary	61,011.6	29,772.7	11,968.9	19,270.1
Latvia	9,062.1	3,910.5	266.4	4,885.2
Lithuania	14,289.3	5,850.2	815.7	7,623.3
Macedonia	7,973.8	215.9	5,128.4	2,629.6
Moldova	7,527.5	5,126.6	305.9	2,095.0
Poland	285,980.2	31,480.2	195,300.0	59,200.0
Romania	98,530.0	34,160.0	31,200.0	33,170.0
Russia	1,768,894.8	928,643.3	450,449.4	389,802.1
Serbia and Montenegro	54,960.0	4,910.2	38,139.7	11,910.0
Slovakia	37,342.7	11,507.1	16,463.7	9,371.9
Slovenia	16,931.5	2,348.8	6,807.0	7,775.8
Ukraine	352,583.7	178,625.2	124,800.0	49,158.5

Source: *Energy Information Administration of the US Government, International Energy Annual*

Table 12.2

Emissions of Air and Water Pollutants 2007

'000 metric tonnes / as stated

	Carbon Monoxide	Nitrogen Oxide	Daily Organic Water Pollutants (kg)	Particulate Matter	Sulphur Oxide
Western Europe					
Austria	790	252	101,003	27	35
Belgium	780	281	100,467	31	139
Cyprus	86	23	6,852		40
Denmark	567	214	83,223	14	38
Finland	554	211	67,594	44	124
France	5,177	1,061	279,914	218	406
Germany	3,521	1,238	787,457	171	587
Gibraltar					
Greece	889	310	58,182		527
Iceland	40	28	8,998		27
Ireland	198	110	83,522	9	32
Italy	3,858	1,170	519,129		538
Liechtenstein					
Luxembourg	48	18	6,630		2
Malta			4,096		
Monaco					
Netherlands	528	338	121,570	23	53
Norway	450	218	51,951	54	19
Portugal	688	288	133,059	0	261
Spain	2,170	1,566	407,166	154	1,172
Sweden	609	195	117,465	45	56
Switzerland	335	79	97,406		17
Turkey	3,778	951	185,974		1,443
United Kingdom	1,396	1,438	616,041	75	794
Eastern Europe					
Albania			16,600		
Belarus	107	45		38	122
Bosnia-Herzegovina			22,682		
Bulgaria	767	235	93,260	166	1,013
Croatia	250	65	39,441		75
Czech Republic	522	325	159,973	14	193
Estonia	177	36		48	114
Georgia					
Hungary	579	174	175,184	23	246
Latvia	271	39	29,971		2
Lithuania	193	55	37,780	7	38
Macedonia			14,110		
Moldova			19,654		
Poland	3,563	788	483,105		1,442
Romania	1,170	382	330,080		890
Russia	15,693	2,674	1,539,164	1,243	3,207
Serbia and Montenegro			98,105		
Slovakia	302	85	24,826		85
Slovenia	80	52	38,410		45
Ukraine	1,107	226	422,309	791	873

Source: *Euromonitor International from national statistics/World Resources Institute/World Bank*

Conservation

Table 12.3

Threatened Species 2007

Number

	Amphibians	Birds	Fish	Mammals	Reptiles	Vascular Plants
Western Europe						
Austria	0	5	7	6	1	4
Belgium	0	1	8	8	0	1
Cyprus	0	4	11	4	4	7
Denmark	0	3	11	3	0	3
Finland	0	3	2	4	0	1
France	2	5	27	15	5	7
Germany	0	4	16	9	0	12
Gibraltar	0	3	9	1	0	0
Greece	5	10	50	11	5	11
Iceland	0		11	6	0	
Ireland	0	1	8	3	0	1
Italy	6	7	31	12	5	19
Liechtenstein	0		0	2	0	0
Luxembourg	0		0	3	0	0
Malta	0	3	13	1	0	3
Monaco	0	0	10	0	0	0
Netherlands	0	1	9	10	0	0
Norway	0	2	11	10	0	2
Portugal		8	39	15	2	16
Spain	5	15	51	20	17	49
Sweden	0	3	9	5	0	3
Switzerland	1	2	8	4	0	3
Turkey	9	15	54	18	13	3
United Kingdom	0	3	16	9	0	13
Eastern Europe						
Albania	2	6	27	2	4	0
Belarus	0	3	0	6	0	0
Bosnia-Herzegovina	1	6	28	8	2	1
Bulgaria	0	12	13	13	2	0
Croatia	2	11	42	7	2	1
Czech Republic	0	5	9	7	0	4
Estonia	0	3	2	5	0	0
Georgia	1	8	8	13	7	0
Hungary	0	9	10	9	1	1
Latvia	0	4	4	5	0	0
Lithuania	0	4	4	6	0	0
Macedonia	0	10	8	9	2	0
Moldova	0	9	9	5	1	
Poland	0	5	4	13	0	4
Romania	0	12	13	15	2	1
Russia	0	51	22	45	6	7
Serbia and Montenegro		10	8	8		1
Slovakia	0	7	9	8	1	2
Slovenia	2	3	25	7	1	0
Ukraine	0	12	14	16	2	1

Source: *Euromonitor International from national statistics/World Resources Institute*

Table 12.4

Protection of Natural Areas 2007

Number

	National Systems, Sites	Biosphere Reserves, Sites	Wetlands, Sites
Western Europe			
Austria	294	7	33
Belgium	21		9
Cyprus	10		1
Denmark	85	1	17
Finland	285	2	49
France	1,452	10	21
Germany	7,428	14	32
Gibraltar	1		
Greece	89	2	10
Iceland	79		3
Ireland	71	2	45
Italy	409	10	50
Liechtenstein	10		1
Luxembourg	138		1
Malta	8		2
Monaco	2		1
Netherlands	52	1	43
Norway	180	1	32
Portugal	56	1	17
Spain	312	40	49
Sweden	1,651	2	51
Switzerland	209	2	11
Turkey	82	1	13
United Kingdom	518	9	145
Eastern Europe			
Albania	67		3
Belarus	84	3	8
Bosnia-Herzegovina	21		2
Bulgaria	112	16	10
Croatia	211	1	4
Czech Republic	1,765	5	11
Estonia	217	1	11
Georgia	18		2
Hungary	186	5	26
Latvia	209	1	6
Lithuania	122		5
Macedonia	26		1
Moldova	64		2
Poland	154	11	13
Romania	106	3	5
Russia	264	39	35
Serbia and Montenegro	115	2	5
Slovakia		2	14
Slovenia	33	3	3
Ukraine	5,374	4	33

Source: *Euromonitor International from national statistics/World Resources Institute/UNEP/UNESCO*

Conservation

Table 12.5

Sea, Lakes and Coastlines 2007

As stated

	Length of Marine Coastline (km)	Extent of Territorial Sea (nautical miles)	Fresh Water Resources (cu m per capita)
Western Europe			
Austria			9,560
Belgium	67	12	1,764
Cyprus	648	12	950
Denmark	7,314	12	1,113
Finland	1,250	12	21,019
France	3,427	12	3,343
Germany	2,389	12	1,861
Gibraltar	12	3	
Greece	13,676	6	6,763
Iceland	4,988	12	577,263
Ireland	1,448	12	12,840
Italy	7,600	12	3,346
Liechtenstein			
Luxembourg			6,589
Malta	197	12	127
Monaco	4	12	
Netherlands	451	12	5,563
Norway	21,925	12	83,334
Portugal	1,793	12	6,801
Spain	4,964	12	2,705
Sweden	3,218	12	19,525
Switzerland			7,477
Turkey	7,200	12	2,884
United Kingdom	12,429	12	2,453
Eastern Europe			
Albania	362	12	12,833
Belarus			5,924
Bosnia-Herzegovina	20		8,893
Bulgaria	354	12	2,757
Croatia	5,835	12	24,100
Czech Republic			1,288
Estonia	3,794	12	1,390
Georgia	310		12,734
Hungary			10,650
Latvia	531	12	15,800
Lithuania	99	12	7,379
Macedonia			3,077
Moldova			2,736
Poland	491	12	1,600
Romania	225	12	9,573
Russia	37,653	12	32,009
Serbia and Montenegro	199		19,835
Slovakia			9,246
Slovenia	47		16,109
Ukraine	2,782	12	2,929

Source: Euromonitor International from industry sources/national statistics

Table 12.6

World Forest Statistics 2007

'000 hectares, unless otherwise stated

	Total Land Area 2007	Total Forest Land 1995	Total Forest Land 2007	Total % Increase/ Decrease 1995-2007	Annual Average % Increase/ Decrease 1995-2007	Forest as % of Land Area 2007
Western Europe						
Austria	8,245	3,807	3,870	1.7	0.3	46.9
Belgium	3,023		667			22.1
Cyprus	924	167	175	4.8	1.0	18.9
Denmark	4,243	466	505	8.4	1.7	11.9
Finland	30,459	22,335	22,509	0.8	0.2	73.9
France	55,010	14,945	15,623	4.5	0.9	28.4
Germany	34,877	10,909	11,076	1.5	0.3	31.8
Gibraltar	1					
Greece	12,890	3,450	3,803	10.2	2.0	29.5
Iceland	10,025	32	49	54.7	10.9	0.5
Ireland	6,889	525	689	31.3	6.3	10.0
Italy	29,411	8,915	10,160	14.0	2.8	34.5
Liechtenstein	16	7	7	3.0	0.6	43.1
Luxembourg	259		87			33.5
Malta	32	0	0	0.0	0.0	0.9
Monaco						
Netherlands	3,388	353	367	4.0	0.8	10.8
Norway	30,428	9,216	9,416	2.2	0.4	30.9
Portugal	9,150	3,341	3,851	15.3	3.1	42.1
Spain	49,944	14,958	18,418	23.1	4.6	36.9
Sweden	41,033	27,421	27,546	0.5	0.1	67.1
Switzerland	4,000	1,177	1,228	4.4	0.9	30.7
Turkey	76,963	9,866	10,217	3.6	0.7	13.3
United Kingdom	24,193	2,702	2,863	5.9	1.2	11.8
Eastern Europe						
Albania	2,740	779	803	3.0	0.6	29.3
Belarus	20,748	7,612	7,910	3.9	0.8	38.1
Bosnia-Herzegovina	5,120	2,198	2,185	-0.6	-0.1	42.7
Bulgaria	10,797	3,351	3,710	10.7	2.1	34.4
Croatia	5,592	2,123	2,137	0.7	0.1	38.2
Czech Republic	7,726	2,634	2,652	0.7	0.1	34.3
Estonia	4,239	2,203	2,298	4.3	0.9	54.2
Georgia	6,949	2,760	2,760	0.0	0.0	39.7
Hungary	8,961	1,854	1,999	7.8	1.6	22.3
Latvia	6,229	2,830	2,960	4.6	0.9	47.5
Lithuania	6,268	1,983	2,126	7.2	1.4	33.9
Macedonia	2,543	906	906	0.0	0.0	35.6
Moldova	3,287	323	330	2.3	0.5	10.0
Poland	30,697	8,970	9,237	3.0	0.6	30.1
Romania	23,009	6,369	6,371	0.0	0.0	27.7
Russia	1,638,151	809,109	808,627	-0.1	0.0	49.4
Serbia and Montenegro	10,200	2,604	2,712	4.1	0.8	26.6
Slovakia	4,810	1,922	1,932	0.5	0.1	40.2
Slovenia	2,014	1,214	1,273	4.9	1.0	63.2
Ukraine	57,939	9,392	9,597	2.2	0.4	16.6

Source: *UN Food and Agriculture Organisation*

Total Consumption of Pesticides

Table 12.7

Consumption of Pesticides 2007
Tonnes

	Fungicides	Herbicides	Insecticides	Others	Total
Western Europe					
Austria	1,242	1,063	113	7	2,425
Belgium	2,975	5,555	650	131	9,312
Cyprus					
Denmark	284	1,692	113	560	2,648
Finland	225	1,458	16	91	1,790
France	60,321	39,314	873	16,245	116,754
Germany	6,645	12,611	993	4,225	24,474
Gibraltar					
Greece	5,933	3,209	2,880	55	12,077
Iceland					
Ireland	323	1,721	42	197	2,282
Italy	37,978	7,193	5,467	527	51,164
Liechtenstein					
Luxembourg					
Malta	37	26	13		76
Monaco					
Netherlands	3,016	2,602	165	178	5,961
Norway	62	172	5	3	242
Portugal	12,125	2,794	497	275	15,691
Spain	5,152	14,929	14,056	5,258	39,394
Sweden	358	1,677	10	58	2,104
Switzerland	639	609	33	28	1,309
Turkey	2,416	4,496	12,127	963	20,002
United Kingdom	4,457	20,782	1,517	3,307	30,063
Eastern Europe					
Albania					
Belarus					
Bosnia-Herzegovina					
Bulgaria	35	451	2	2	489
Croatia	1,873	551	41		2,465
Czech Republic	1,386	2,836	323	726	5,272
Estonia	9	364	4	12	390
Georgia					
Hungary	1,148	1,677	141	36	3,003
Latvia	32	369	3	54	457
Lithuania	88	334	12	65	500
Macedonia					
Moldova					
Poland	3,407	5,432	1,028		9,867
Romania	981	2,168	371		3,520
Russia	5,020	9,573	1,499	13	16,105
Serbia and Montenegro	522	1,782	501		2,805
Slovakia	1,522	2,301	539	187	4,549
Slovenia	1,079	483	151	77	1,791
Ukraine	3,428	15,678	8,360		27,466

Source: Euromonitor International from FAO

Table 12.8

Amounts of Waste Generated 2007

'000 tonnes / Kg per capita

	Municipal Waste	Municipal Waste per capita	Nuclear Waste: Spent Fuel Arising	Nuclear Waste per capita	Hazardous Industrial Waste	Hazardous Industrial Waste per capita
Western Europe						
Austria	4,621	556			1,121	135
Belgium	4,510	427	0.13	0.01		
Cyprus	572	669				
Denmark	3,719	683			422	77
Finland	2,258	428	0.07	0.01	1,866	354
France	35,833	584	1.09	0.02		
Germany	54,672	664	0.41	0.00	25,444	309
Gibraltar						
Greece	5,038	451			520	47
Iceland	329	1,094			7	23
Ireland	3,109	723			531	124
Italy	32,956	560			5,450	93
Liechtenstein						
Luxembourg	297	636			250	535
Malta						
Monaco						
Netherlands	9,852	602	0.01	0.00	2,374	145
Norway	3,564	763			958	205
Portugal	4,834	456			71	7
Spain	26,729	601	0.16	0.00		
Sweden	4,570	501	0.24	0.03	264	29
Switzerland	5,266	702	0.06	0.01	1,326	177
Turkey	35,149	479				
United Kingdom	39,695	654	1.25	0.02	5,612	92
Eastern Europe						
Albania						
Belarus						
Bosnia-Herzegovina						
Bulgaria	3,702	486			504	66
Croatia						
Czech Republic	2,939	286	0.04	0.00	851	83
Estonia	632	472			9,349	6,978
Georgia						
Hungary	4,789	476	0.04	0.00		
Latvia	1,000	438			13	6
Lithuania	724	214				
Macedonia						
Moldova						
Poland	8,440	222			845	22
Romania	9,737	452			3,083	143
Russia					139,310	981
Serbia and Montenegro						
Slovakia	1,416	263	0.05	0.01	1,476	274
Slovenia	902	449			211	105
Ukraine						

Source: *Euromonitor International from OECD/national statistics*

Waste and Waste Management

Table 12.9

Levels of Recycling of Packaging Waste 2007
% of total consumption

	Aluminium	Glass	Paper and Cardboard
Western Europe			
Austria	55	89	58
Belgium	25	110	45
Cyprus			
Denmark		92	62
Finland	99	99	86
France	19	55	61
Germany	100	101	79
Gibraltar			
Greece	35	29	40
Iceland		85	
Ireland	24	60	37
Italy	69	56	53
Liechtenstein			
Luxembourg			
Malta			
Monaco			
Netherlands	67	81	74
Norway		94	75
Portugal	17	37	47
Spain	30	41	59
Sweden	99	94	72
Switzerland	98	98	74
Turkey	56	37	55
United Kingdom	25	30	54
Eastern Europe			
Albania			
Belarus			
Bosnia-Herzegovina			
Bulgaria			
Croatia			
Czech Republic			50
Estonia			
Georgia			
Hungary			48
Latvia			
Lithuania			
Macedonia			
Moldova			
Poland		16	34
Romania			
Russia			
Serbia and Montenegro			
Slovakia		42	43
Slovenia			
Ukraine			

Source: *Euromonitor International from national statistics/World Resources Institute*

Section Thirteen

Foreign Trade

Imports

Table 13.1

Total Imports (cif) 1980-2007

US$ million

	1980	1985	1990	1995	1996	1997	1998	1999
Western Europe								
Austria	24,444	20,986	49,088	66,386	67,331	64,776	68,183	69,555
Belgium				159,683	163,604	157,260	164,669	164,607
Cyprus	1,202	1,247	2,568	3,694	3,983	3,698	3,685	3,618
Denmark	19,340	18,245	33,248	45,728	45,004	44,406	46,330	44,519
Finland	15,635	13,232	27,001	28,114	29,264	29,784	32,301	31,617
France	134,889	108,337	234,447	281,440	281,750	271,914	290,241	294,921
Germany	188,002	158,488	346,153	464,271	458,783	445,616	471,418	473,539
Gibraltar	146	145						
Greece	10,548	10,134	19,777	26,795	29,672	27,899	29,388	28,720
Iceland	999	905	1,680	1,756	2,032	1,992	2,489	2,503
Ireland	11,153	10,015	20,682	33,064	35,897	39,225	44,631	47,194
Italy	100,741	87,692	181,968	206,040	208,092	210,268	218,445	220,323
Liechtenstein								
Luxembourg	3,612	3,144	7,596	9,748	9,667	9,379	10,237	11,045
Malta	938	759	1,961	2,943	2,795	2,552	2,668	2,846
Monaco								
Netherlands	88,419	73,123	126,475	176,874	180,639	178,130	187,747	190,279
Norway	16,926	15,556	27,221	32,968	35,615	35,709	37,473	34,167
Portugal	9,309	7,652	25,264	33,306	35,177	35,064	38,536	39,825
Spain	34,078	29,963	87,554	113,319	121,782	122,711	133,149	144,436
Sweden	33,438	28,548	54,245	64,741	66,925	65,676	68,590	68,755
Switzerland	36,342	30,696	69,681	76,985	74,462	71,064	73,877	75,438
Turkey	7,910	11,344	22,302	35,709	43,627	48,559	45,921	40,671
United Kingdom	115,545	109,505	224,412	265,297	287,426	306,585	314,031	317,959
Eastern Europe								
Albania				714	937	646	842	1,154
Belarus				5,564	6,939	8,689	8,549	6,674
Bosnia-Herzegovina				524	1,204	1,555	2,120	2,431
Bulgaria		13,657	4,710	5,661	6,861	5,224	4,949	5,453
Croatia			5,188	7,352	7,784	9,101	8,276	7,799
Czech Republic				26,385	29,366	28,837	30,338	29,482
Estonia				2,400	2,896	3,518	3,925	3,427
Georgia				489	751	995	882	690
Hungary	9,245	8,224	8,671	15,380	18,058	21,115	25,679	27,923
Latvia				1,818	2,320	2,721	3,191	2,945
Lithuania				3,013	3,883	5,025	5,364	4,627
Macedonia				1,719	1,627	1,779	1,915	1,776
Moldova				841	1,072	1,171	1,024	586
Poland	16,690	11,855	8,413	29,050	37,137	42,308	46,495	45,903
Romania	13,843	11,267	9,843	10,278	11,435	11,280	11,821	10,392
Russia				68,863	74,879	79,076	63,817	43,588
Serbia and Montenegro								
Slovakia				9,225	11,432	10,774	13,725	11,888
Slovenia			4,727	9,492	9,423	9,357	10,110	10,083
Ukraine				15,484	17,603	17,128	14,676	11,846

Source: *Euromonitor International from International Monetary Fund (IMF), International Financial Statistics*
Notes: *US$ totals in this table may differ from the totals given for Imports (cif) by Origin and Imports (cif) by Commodity*

Total Imports (cif) 1980-2007 *(continued)*
US$ million

	2000	2001	2002	2003	2004	2005	2006	2007
Western Europe								
Austria	68,972	70,479	72,765	91,578	113,307	119,939	130,939	156,117
Belgium	176,957	178,683	198,036	234,902	285,506	318,738	351,893	413,975
Cyprus	3,846	3,923	3,863	4,288	5,659	6,282	6,951	8,687
Denmark	44,356	44,124	48,887	56,217	66,886	74,259	85,100	98,825
Finland	33,893	32,108	33,627	41,592	50,661	58,469	69,445	81,757
France	310,936	301,962	312,024	370,494	442,918	484,487	536,230	616,148
Germany	495,351	485,969	489,949	604,613	718,045	780,444	922,338	1,059,640
Gibraltar								
Greece	29,221	29,928	31,164	44,375	51,559	49,817	59,121	75,100
Iceland	2,591	2,253	2,274	2,789	3,553	4,557	5,083	6,105
Ireland	51,464	51,295	51,460	53,304	61,395	69,163	83,670	85,619
Italy	238,023	236,086	246,496	297,348	355,158	384,802	440,751	509,898
Liechtenstein								
Luxembourg	10,716	11,151	11,597	13,691	16,826	17,564	19,433	22,090
Malta	3,400	2,726	2,839	3,398	3,824	3,807	4,079	4,508
Monaco								
Netherlands	198,886	195,533	194,044	233,969	283,929	310,571	358,495	421,381
Norway	34,392	32,955	34,890	39,486	48,085	54,792	63,366	79,762
Portugal	38,185	39,415	38,308	40,835	49,210	53,380	65,592	76,372
Spain	152,870	153,607	163,501	208,512	257,591	287,617	326,033	384,955
Sweden	73,317	64,326	67,644	84,199	100,782	111,581	127,652	151,351
Switzerland	76,092	77,071	82,377	95,581	110,321	119,770	132,021	153,171
Turkey	54,503	41,399	49,663	65,637	96,368	98,998	133,584	168,527
United Kingdom	334,396	320,973	335,438	380,712	451,680	483,017	547,476	620,709
Eastern Europe								
Albania	1,090	1,327	1,503	1,864	2,309	2,618	3,058	4,196
Belarus	8,646	8,286	9,092	11,558	16,491	16,708	22,351	28,693
Bosnia-Herzegovina	2,290	2,340	2,781	3,276	3,957	4,660	4,908	5,800
Bulgaria	6,505	7,263	7,987	10,902	14,467	18,163	23,270	30,086
Croatia	7,887	9,147	10,722	14,209	16,589	18,560	21,488	25,830
Czech Republic	33,852	38,307	42,773	53,801	71,619	76,340	93,433	118,362
Estonia	4,236	4,300	4,810	6,480	8,334	10,187	11,884	15,061
Georgia	709	753	796	1,141	1,846	2,490	3,678	5,217
Hungary	31,955	33,725	37,788	47,602	59,637	65,783	77,206	94,397
Latvia	3,184	3,504	4,053	5,242	7,048	8,592	11,430	15,177
Lithuania	5,219	6,060	7,526	9,668	12,386	15,511	19,413	24,445
Macedonia	2,094	1,694	1,995	2,306	2,932	3,228	3,752	5,177
Moldova	776	893	1,039	1,403	1,773	2,293	2,693	3,690
Poland	48,940	50,275	55,113	68,004	87,909	100,903	124,647	159,541
Romania	13,055	15,561	17,862	24,003	32,664	40,463	51,106	69,602
Russia	49,125	59,140	67,063	83,677	107,120	137,977	181,161	245,364
Serbia and Montenegro								
Slovakia	13,412	15,501	17,460	23,760	30,469	36,168	47,309	62,139
Slovenia	10,116	10,148	10,933	13,853	17,571	19,626	23,014	29,481
Ukraine	13,956	15,775	16,977	23,020	28,997	36,136	45,039	60,618

Source: *Euromonitor International from International Monetary Fund (IMF), International Financial Statistics*
Notes: *US$ totals in this table may differ from the totals given for Imports (cif) by Origin and Imports (cif) by Commodity*

Imports

Table 13.2

Total Imports by Quarter 2006-2008

US$ million

	2006 1st Quarter	2006 2nd Quarter	2006 3rd Quarter	2006 4th Quarter	2007 1st Quarter	2007 2nd Quarter	2007 3rd Quarter	2007 4th Quarter	2008 1st Quarter	2008 2nd Quarter
Western Europe										
Austria	30,067.2	32,456.4	33,025.6	35,389.9	36,942.7	37,461.3	38,771.4	42,941.5	44,195.3	
Belgium	85,884.3	86,921.4	86,217.3	92,870.0	97,136.5	98,999.2	102,409.9	115,429.5	120,861.1	
Cyprus	1,587.8	1,794.9	1,763.3	1,804.6	1,812.0	2,178.5	2,224.5	2,471.8		
Denmark	20,067.9	21,240.5	20,662.9	23,128.5	23,147.5	23,447.5	24,134.2	28,095.5	28,259.1	30,316.2
Finland	15,857.5	17,181.4	17,616.5	18,789.2	19,198.5	20,307.2	19,916.0	22,335.6	23,046.9	25,038.4
France	128,858.9	137,184.8	128,151.7	142,034.5	144,097.2	152,024.2	148,680.2	171,346.3	178,855.3	188,189.3
Germany	211,969.5	224,836.4	232,399.8	253,132.3	249,046.3	257,103.3	262,036.3	291,454.2	302,761.1	
Gibraltar										
Greece	13,489.7	15,607.0	13,526.4	16,497.6	18,368.8	18,199.9	18,484.2	20,047.2	19,355.1	
Iceland	1,061.8	1,362.7	1,303.1	1,355.4	1,411.5	1,565.6	1,438.8	1,689.6	1,526.2	1,626.3
Ireland	18,422.5	18,175.1	17,976.4	29,096.0	21,517.6	19,785.3	20,474.4	23,841.3	23,151.9	
Italy	104,490.0	112,399.0	105,687.0	118,175.0	122,702.3	127,419.3	121,649.3	138,127.2	142,104.2	
Liechtenstein										
Luxembourg	4,554.3	5,011.7	4,657.1	5,209.1	5,240.9	5,694.4	5,371.0	5,784.1	6,063.6	
Malta	947.4	989.1	1,039.6	1,102.2	991.2	1,089.8	1,148.5	1,278.2		
Monaco										
Netherlands	82,893.7	88,918.0	90,043.4	96,639.9	97,050.4	102,273.9	103,871.9	118,184.9	124,834.9	
Norway	14,314.6	15,371.3	15,636.1	18,043.9	18,177.9	19,092.9	19,164.3	23,326.4	22,172.9	24,496.5
Portugal	15,390.9	16,423.7	16,231.8	17,545.7	17,264.7	18,891.5	18,656.6	21,559.6	22,538.7	24,518.5
Spain	76,088.9	82,900.5	78,795.8	88,247.8	88,418.3	94,937.5	92,454.0	109,145.1	111,416.1	
Sweden	28,963.7	31,525.3	31,223.1	35,939.9	34,797.6	36,203.5	37,283.8	43,066.1	43,302.0	48,695.6
Switzerland	31,399.0	32,923.2	31,875.0	35,823.7	36,447.2	37,500.7	37,299.0	41,924.0	43,385.7	47,386.0
Turkey	27,366.3	35,676.3	34,991.4	35,550.1	33,934.0	42,122.0	44,199.0	48,272.0	49,123.0	56,645.0
United Kingdom	128,429.7	140,041.8	136,369.7	142,634.8	145,939.0	152,626.5	157,284.6	164,858.9	160,809.8	
Eastern Europe										
Albania	650.2	764.2	761.6	882.5	863.9	1,006.5	1,051.3	1,274.6	1,157.8	1,379.0
Belarus	4,634.8	5,582.3	5,929.5	6,204.6	5,607.4	6,906.1	7,349.5	8,830.1	8,762.7	
Bosnia-Herzegovina										
Bulgaria	4,732.3	5,563.2	6,160.2	6,813.9	6,144.2	7,019.2	7,780.5	9,142.6	8,579.9	10,811.9
Croatia	4,756.8	5,542.5	5,444.9	5,744.1	5,596.6	6,583.0	6,459.0	7,191.0	7,283.9	8,817.7
Czech Republic	20,539.6	23,028.4	23,024.0	26,841.1	26,315.0	28,433.7	29,102.6	34,510.7	35,422.0	38,497.7
Estonia	2,540.3	3,015.6	3,101.1	3,227.1	3,439.6	3,867.2	3,613.0	4,141.4	3,914.0	
Georgia					1,045.1	1,179.3	1,317.7	1,674.6	1,410.3	
Hungary	17,313.8	18,876.1	19,502.6	21,513.6	21,521.4	22,737.7	23,713.2	26,424.7	27,067.1	
Latvia	2,255.5	2,739.1	3,024.8	3,411.0	3,340.4	3,764.8	3,968.5	4,103.0	3,949.7	4,207.7
Lithuania	4,141.5	4,875.3	5,161.7	5,234.1	5,209.0	6,194.1	6,349.4	6,692.7	7,705.2	8,688.4
Macedonia	719.2	985.4	967.8	1,079.7	1,013.2	1,176.3	1,267.2	1,720.4	1,572.2	
Moldova	496.9	645.0	673.8	769.3	759.0	855.4	915.6	1,159.8	1,045.8	
Poland	27,595.5	30,489.6	31,653.9	34,908.1	35,883.8	38,623.1	39,629.8	45,404.3	47,868.9	
Romania	10,307.7	12,532.9	12,903.4	15,362.1	14,973.7	16,764.3	17,294.4	20,569.3	19,271.6	22,804.6
Russia	34,937.2	42,202.8	47,329.1	56,691.9	47,408.7	57,640.9	63,767.9	76,546.5	65,793.0	82,232.4
Serbia and Montenegro										
Slovakia	10,713.7	11,812.6	11,293.3	13,489.4	13,602.7	15,216.0	15,026.4	18,293.8	17,670.3	20,841.2
Slovenia	5,141.3	5,585.5	5,675.6	6,611.7	6,614.8	7,270.2	7,305.1	8,290.4	8,404.9	9,399.9
Ukraine	9,793.4	10,612.2	11,801.3	12,831.7	12,964.5	14,338.1	15,053.1	18,262.2	18,805.9	

Source: *Euromonitor International from International Monetary Fund (IMF), International Financial Statistics*
Notes: *US$ totals in this table may differ from the totals given for Imports (cif) by Origin and Imports (cif) by Commodity*

Total Imports by Month 2007

US$ million

	January	February	March	April	May	June	July	August	September	October	November	December
Western Europe												
Austria	11,591.2	11,829.0	13,522.6	12,202.7	12,656.5	12,602.1	12,913.6	11,997.5	13,860.3	14,735.1	15,255.1	12,951.3
Belgium	31,429.0	30,491.7	35,289.2	31,454.6	33,342.9	34,276.4	34,146.0	32,519.1	35,822.1	40,131.0	40,308.0	34,764.8
Cyprus	596.2	550.2	665.6	712.1	707.0	759.4	751.7	723.4	749.4	852.2	867.5	752.2
Denmark	7,418.4	7,306.0	8,422.9	7,513.3	7,896.1	8,037.9	7,632.4	8,085.9	8,415.7	9,758.0	9,797.5	8,540.5
Finland	6,095.9	6,155.6	6,999.0	6,387.8	7,132.0	6,823.1	6,723.5	6,674.5	6,534.5	7,688.1	7,573.8	6,969.5
France	46,622.3	46,917.0	50,717.8	49,436.9	50,334.6	52,437.3	52,990.5	43,891.4	51,900.1	59,181.1	59,732.8	51,986.2
Germany	79,573.5	82,974.0	86,498.9	86,252.0	83,237.9	87,613.5	86,962.0	86,624.6	88,449.6	99,567.2	100,488.7	91,398.2
Gibraltar												
Greece	5,682.1	6,135.5	6,551.2	5,436.7	6,587.0	6,176.2	6,700.8	5,457.6	6,325.9	7,158.5	6,896.1	5,992.6
Iceland	428.7	448.8	529.7	504.7	536.1	521.5	518.9	456.8	461.6	648.1	514.4	523.3
Ireland	7,276.7	6,891.4	7,348.6	6,333.8	7,062.1	6,388.9	7,033.0	6,570.9	6,869.9	7,921.8	8,642.8	7,278.6
Italy	38,140.4	41,344.3	43,231.2	40,571.6	43,170.8	43,672.4	44,943.1	33,507.2	43,194.7	48,875.6	46,898.6	42,348.1
Liechtenstein												
Luxembourg	1,587.8	1,695.5	1,957.3	1,821.4	2,031.7	1,841.1	1,859.9	1,762.9	1,748.0	1,929.8	1,983.0	1,871.2
Malta	304.7	316.8	369.7	347.2	362.1	380.5	450.5	348.3	349.7	440.8	419.3	418.0
Monaco												
Netherlands	31,626.7	30,809.0	34,614.8	32,844.6	34,945.7	34,483.6	34,407.4	33,913.5	35,551.0	39,556.2	41,588.5	37,040.3
Norway	5,878.1	5,496.5	6,803.4	6,094.4	6,591.2	6,407.1	6,197.6	6,391.0	6,575.7	8,951.0	7,732.2	6,643.3
Portugal	5,598.2	5,381.0	6,285.5	5,990.2	6,589.9	6,311.3	6,520.0	5,641.2	6,495.4	7,386.6	7,618.9	6,554.1
Spain	28,065.4	28,433.5	31,919.4	29,813.5	32,349.2	32,774.8	32,893.1	27,169.5	32,391.5	37,013.9	37,097.9	35,033.3
Sweden	11,043.6	11,073.6	12,680.3	11,645.8	12,639.6	11,917.9	11,490.2	12,422.6	13,370.9	14,982.0	15,542.7	12,541.8
Switzerland	11,564.4	11,389.3	13,546.6	11,940.2	13,011.1	12,599.1	13,271.8	11,678.0	12,401.2	14,715.5	14,802.4	12,251.4
Turkey	10,177.6	10,989.7	12,766.7	12,923.3	14,935.3	14,263.4	15,112.0	14,678.0	14,409.0	15,600.0	16,625.0	16,047.0
United Kingdom	47,289.2	46,229.4	52,420.9	48,736.0	50,716.0	53,175.1	54,185.3	49,499.8	53,598.9	56,708.2	58,932.7	49,217.5
Eastern Europe												
Albania	253.1	280.7	330.1	326.5	344.7	335.3	344.2	325.6	381.5	392.7	464.5	417.4
Belarus	1,753.8	1,800.3	2,050.1	2,130.7	2,407.2	2,367.7	2,420.0	2,557.3	2,366.3	2,736.0	2,868.7	3,235.0
Bosnia-Herzegovina												
Bulgaria	1,983.5	1,886.6	2,282.6	2,198.1	2,407.6	2,451.4	2,654.7	2,484.3	2,635.9	2,996.1	3,177.3	2,928.3
Croatia	1,552.6	1,881.3	2,164.6	2,148.8	2,353.5	2,083.1	2,351.3	2,015.3	2,094.9	2,594.3	2,412.0	2,177.8
Czech Republic	8,384.3	8,340.8	9,624.0	9,293.5	9,578.5	9,604.5	9,614.9	9,500.8	10,030.7	12,195.8	12,272.7	9,921.5
Estonia	1,111.2	1,053.5	1,274.9	1,291.7	1,336.7	1,238.7	1,173.3	1,209.3	1,230.5	1,445.1	1,460.3	1,236.0
Georgia	328.5	334.8	381.9	364.7	438.5	376.1	430.1	463.6	424.0	523.1	446.1	705.4
Hungary	6,901.2	6,938.0	7,682.2	7,293.9	7,672.4	7,771.4	7,913.2	7,536.9	8,263.1	9,196.5	9,344.7	7,883.5
Latvia	1,046.8	1,077.8	1,254.0	1,213.5	1,317.9	1,276.4	1,432.2	1,283.4	1,281.8	1,392.1	1,361.7	1,239.1
Lithuania	1,640.0	1,705.1	1,874.2	1,988.5	2,157.9	2,045.8	2,149.2	2,110.8	2,110.5	2,194.0	2,323.8	2,145.5
Macedonia	322.5	328.4	362.3	397.1	376.3	402.9	449.7	394.5	423.1	617.1	538.1	565.3
Moldova	197.1	271.7	290.2	264.8	294.4	296.2	300.0	300.4	315.3	369.4	377.8	412.6
Poland	11,602.1	10,946.7	13,335.1	12,165.7	13,157.5	13,299.9	13,331.8	12,716.9	13,581.1	15,786.5	15,655.4	13,962.4
Romania	4,513.5	4,850.0	5,610.2	5,145.7	5,867.4	5,751.2	6,067.1	5,486.8	5,740.5	7,066.9	7,211.3	6,291.1
Russia	12,932.8	15,669.2	18,806.8	18,261.7	19,080.0	20,299.2	21,250.1	21,982.4	20,535.3	24,456.8	24,807.6	27,282.0
Serbia and Montenegro												
Slovakia	4,140.8	4,370.8	5,091.1	4,749.6	5,331.9	5,134.5	4,966.3	4,842.6	5,217.6	6,239.6	6,573.3	5,480.8
Slovenia	2,039.8	2,089.0	2,496.9	2,323.4	2,544.1	2,414.3	2,492.7	2,171.7	2,629.0	2,891.1	2,883.7	2,504.8
Ukraine	3,704.2	4,292.1	4,956.3	4,818.2	4,836.0	4,671.6	5,195.1	4,997.7	4,840.6	5,887.3	5,832.7	6,586.2

Source: Euromonitor International from International Monetary Fund (IMF), International Financial Statistics
Notes: US$ totals in this table may differ from the totals given for Imports (cif) by Origin and Imports (cif) by Commodity

Imports

Table 13.4

Imports (cif) by Origin 2007
US$ million

	France	Germany	Italy	Nether-lands	Sweden	UK	Total EU	Norway	Switzerland	Russia	Poland
Western Europe											
Austria	5,099	74,296	11,574	7,056	2,087	3,075	129,466	530	8,151	2,281	2,173
Belgium	46,285	73,395	15,534	73,028	8,890	25,695	293,597	4,169	3,349	6,685	3,610
Cyprus	467	809	883	352	84	830	5,944	9	65	51	35
Denmark	4,054	21,694	4,077	7,083	14,399	5,243	73,452	5,974	850	1,229	2,450
Finland	2,811	12,886	2,578	5,531	11,241	4,036	52,366	1,560	499	11,410	946
France		116,530	51,718	42,828	8,150	34,705	425,126	7,445	15,293	14,393	7,884
Germany	91,193		60,942	126,881	19,144	59,472	692,246	21,829	40,123	37,961	33,504
Gibraltar											
Greece	4,240	9,815	8,916	3,808	759	2,751	44,157	173	1,445	4,295	490
Iceland	191	809	229	375	674	359	4,023	306	132	78	115
Ireland	3,445	8,027	1,797	4,141	688	31,698	56,204	1,705	679	101	329
Italy	45,511	85,398		27,709	5,650	16,687	287,673	3,558	15,357	19,682	8,751
Liechtenstein											
Luxembourg	2,524	6,541	541	1,361	157	461	20,160	6	211	236	144
Malta	414	383	1,139	133	11	656	3,199	3	83	1	17
Monaco											
Netherlands	21,586	87,353	10,704		8,233	28,467	246,795	11,338	3,180	25,107	4,926
Norway	2,928	10,899	2,638	2,974	11,778	5,530	55,284		864	1,968	1,675
Portugal	6,571	10,082	4,102	3,564	848	2,698	56,894	951	546	774	331
Spain	47,305	58,610	31,351	17,228	4,476	17,734	228,552	2,680	4,192	10,547	3,735
Sweden	7,502	27,854	5,377	8,736		10,355	107,356	12,535	1,298	4,642	4,395
Switzerland	15,270	52,414	17,367	7,357	1,413	6,704	127,926	339		1,292	885
Turkey	7,832	17,548	9,967	2,655	1,716	5,471	68,590	496	5,269	23,506	1,645
United Kingdom	43,329	88,375	26,355	45,529	10,478		335,392	29,059	7,167	10,415	7,375
Eastern Europe											
Albania	33	214	1,233	47	10	40	2,727	2	29	68	18
Belarus	350	2,171	638	250	135	189	6,247	86	140	17,187	820
Bosnia-Herzegovina	98	982	779	129	34	40	4,726	3	69	116	100
Bulgaria	1,044	3,714	2,621	769	284	496	17,605	14	399	3,716	595
Croatia	925	3,694	4,126	436	263	463	16,294	86	400	2,597	504
Czech Republic	4,818	37,745	5,243	7,990	1,377	3,213	94,800	79	1,029	5,251	7,409
Estonia	322	1,986	438	530	1,573	485	12,194	85	51	1,559	700
Georgia	107	362	167	83	38	57	1,624	3	27	696	67
Hungary	4,146	25,454	4,318	4,114	1,302	2,381	66,440	51	678	6,578	3,765
Latvia	353	2,312	562	491	745	249	11,887	160	164	1,337	1,067
Lithuania	857	3,664	976	1,045	916	688	16,718	118	115	4,403	2,600
Macedonia	67	601	285	128	39	39	3,155	3	42	578	142
Moldova	92	408	266	88	15	28	2,264	5	25	932	193
Poland	8,494	48,221	10,909	9,452	4,419	4,985	121,699	1,325	1,096	14,398	
Romania	4,376	12,032	8,947	2,537	728	1,352	49,874	133	496	4,445	2,381
Russia	8,077	38,850	13,162	9,004	3,507	6,086	123,620	1,011	2,330		6,614
Serbia and Montenegro	0	0	0	0	0		0	0	0	706	0
Slovakia	2,375	13,324	2,367	1,337	488	719	44,791	60	343	5,535	2,980
Slovenia	1,582	5,734	5,400	1,047	227	477	23,318	17	291	672	488
Ukraine	1,350	8,932	2,984	2,182	780	950	33,859	253	491	19,073	6,137

Source: *International Monetary Fund (IMF), Direction of Trade Statistics*

Imports (cif) by Origin 2007 *(continued)*
US$ million

	Africa & Middle East	Asia/ Pacific	of which: Japan	China	Australasia	Latin America	of which: Brazil	USA	Canada	Total, including Others
Western Europe										
Austria	3,516	9,337	1,398	4,025	138	834	229	3,625	526	215,295
Belgium	17,378	45,489	10,382	17,171	2,283	10,133	4,047	22,425	2,479	447,240
Cyprus	908	991	221	457	29	286	233	105	13	9,377
Denmark	810	9,272	716	5,326	309	1,527	391	3,173	517	117,122
Finland	523	8,393	1,340	4,518	1,288	1,829	563	1,830	771	95,241
France	39,298	57,862	8,316	24,687	1,501	10,108	4,114	26,912	3,019	687,005
Germany	24,619	139,898	24,943	65,725	2,058	22,282	8,490	47,637	3,615	1,419,255
Gibraltar										4,600
Greece	6,958	11,149	1,694	3,828	147	1,302	328	1,727	211	88,619
Iceland	50	766	245	339	54	87	8	906	118	7,893
Ireland	727	7,845	1,347	2,779	255	650	240	9,376	443	82,599
Italy	61,239	62,857	7,332	29,802	2,107	14,522	5,192	15,199	2,346	601,463
Liechtenstein										
Luxembourg	68	5,193	143	4,701	3	128	26	968	217	28,386
Malta	52	669	88	127	12	37	24	174	7	4,527
Monaco										
Netherlands	29,398	101,946	15,282	51,936	2,273	21,708	8,291	36,016	3,700	531,145
Norway	946	9,403	1,772	4,857	193	2,000	853	3,875	3,415	93,390
Portugal	6,854	4,424	784	1,460	78	3,090	1,891	1,300	158	79,816
Spain	38,693	44,999	6,467	21,587	1,232	18,759	4,093	11,380	1,176	405,118
Sweden	1,290	14,194	3,002	6,453	463	2,189	712	4,719	523	183,019
Switzerland	4,656	12,243	2,919	3,984	240	2,120	831	9,345	951	173,299
Turkey	18,707	32,090	3,703	13,224	672	3,112	1,173	8,145	866	198,468
United Kingdom	25,615	104,658	15,404	45,665	5,666	12,733	4,300	53,916	11,171	687,170
Eastern Europe										
Albania	46	160	2	97	3	42	35	37	13	4,593
Belarus	114	1,656	208	816	8	246	106	388	49	33,187
Bosnia-Herzegovina	10	87	5	59	1	28	19	22	6	13,231
Bulgaria	275	1,442	119	837	40	1,019	256	325	32	42,183
Croatia	246	2,648	416	1,589	21	311	223	473	42	36,868
Czech Republic	561	12,076	2,489	5,992	24	303	117	1,462	229	177,360
Estonia	26	805	125	411	3	37	19	184	25	25,438
Georgia	297	1,044	98	204	13	86	76	267	16	7,006
Hungary	367	14,962	2,500	7,427	19	320	139	1,312	127	133,388
Latvia	40	663	55	354	7	30	13	174	25	30,751
Lithuania	115	1,150	88	685	8	123	29	539	23	41,428
Macedonia	29	218	6	82	3	84	49	37	16	8,558
Moldova	22	203	4	55	3	74	71	58	2	8,179
Poland	1,249	14,389	1,558	6,945	139	1,873	356	2,129	224	213,098
Romania	1,293	6,048	429	2,299	161	868	534	944	157	104,234
Russia	2,517	63,753	11,620	30,474	702	7,512	3,953	8,245	1,126	301,641
Serbia and Montenegro	597	430	0	355	3	43	31		13	2,530
Slovakia	100	6,486	655	2,169	14	70	40	538	79	114,210
Slovenia	393	2,111	128	614	18	434	199	385	87	40,188
Ukraine	848	15,330	1,193	6,453	86	460	301	1,476	131	113,724

Source: International Monetary Fund (IMF), Direction of Trade Statistics
Notes: US$ totals in this table may differ from the totals given for Imports (cif) by Commodity and Total Imports (cif)

Imports

Table 13.5

Imports (cif) by Origin 2007 (% Analysis)
% of total imports

	France	Germany	Italy	Nether-lands	Sweden	UK	Total EU	Norway	Switzerland	Russia	Poland
Western Europe											
Austria	2.37	34.51	5.38	3.28	0.97	1.43	60.13	0.25	3.79	1.06	1.01
Belgium	10.35	16.41	3.47	16.33	1.99	5.75	65.65	0.93	0.75	1.49	0.81
Cyprus	4.98	8.63	9.41	3.75	0.90	8.86	63.39	0.10	0.69	0.54	0.37
Denmark	3.46	18.52	3.48	6.05	12.29	4.48	62.71	5.10	0.73	1.05	2.09
Finland	2.95	13.53	2.71	5.81	11.80	4.24	54.98	1.64	0.52	11.98	0.99
France		16.96	7.53	6.23	1.19	5.05	61.88	1.08	2.23	2.10	1.15
Germany	6.43		4.29	8.94	1.35	4.19	48.78	1.54	2.83	2.67	2.36
Gibraltar											
Greece	4.78	11.08	10.06	4.30	0.86	3.10	49.83	0.19	1.63	4.85	0.55
Iceland	2.42	10.25	2.90	4.75	8.54	4.55	50.97	3.88	1.67	0.99	1.45
Ireland	4.17	9.72	2.18	5.01	0.83	38.38	68.04	2.06	0.82	0.12	0.40
Italy	7.57	14.20		4.61	0.94	2.77	47.83	0.59	2.55	3.27	1.45
Liechtenstein											
Luxembourg	8.89	23.04	1.91	4.80	0.55	1.62	71.02	0.02	0.74	0.83	0.51
Malta	9.15	8.47	25.16	2.93	0.25	14.49	70.66	0.07	1.84	0.02	0.38
Monaco											
Netherlands	4.06	16.45	2.02		1.55	5.36	46.46	2.13	0.60	4.73	0.93
Norway	3.14	11.67	2.82	3.18	12.61	5.92	59.20		0.92	2.11	1.79
Portugal	8.23	12.63	5.14	4.47	1.06	3.38	71.28	1.19	0.68	0.97	0.41
Spain	11.68	14.47	7.74	4.25	1.10	4.38	56.42	0.66	1.03	2.60	0.92
Sweden	4.10	15.22	2.94	4.77		5.66	58.66	6.85	0.71	2.54	2.40
Switzerland	8.81	30.24	10.02	4.25	0.82	3.87	73.82	0.20		0.75	0.51
Turkey	3.95	8.84	5.02	1.34	0.86	2.76	34.56	0.25	2.65	11.84	0.83
United Kingdom	6.31	12.86	3.84	6.63	1.52		48.81	4.23	1.04	1.52	1.07
Eastern Europe											
Albania	0.72	4.66	26.85	1.03	0.22	0.87	59.38	0.05	0.63	1.49	0.39
Belarus	1.05	6.54	1.92	0.75	0.41	0.57	18.82	0.26	0.42	51.79	2.47
Bosnia-Herzegovina	0.74	7.42	5.89	0.97	0.26	0.30	35.72	0.02	0.53	0.88	0.75
Bulgaria	2.47	8.80	6.21	1.82	0.67	1.18	41.74	0.03	0.95	8.81	1.41
Croatia	2.51	10.02	11.19	1.18	0.71	1.26	44.20	0.23	1.08	7.05	1.37
Czech Republic	2.72	21.28	2.96	4.51	0.78	1.81	53.45	0.04	0.58	2.96	4.18
Estonia	1.26	7.81	1.72	2.08	6.18	1.91	47.94	0.34	0.20	6.13	2.75
Georgia	1.52	5.16	2.39	1.18	0.54	0.81	23.18	0.04	0.39	9.93	0.95
Hungary	3.11	19.08	3.24	3.08	0.98	1.78	49.81	0.04	0.51	4.93	2.82
Latvia	1.15	7.52	1.83	1.60	2.42	0.81	38.66	0.52	0.53	4.35	3.47
Lithuania	2.07	8.84	2.36	2.52	2.21	1.66	40.35	0.28	0.28	10.63	6.27
Macedonia	0.78	7.02	3.33	1.50	0.46	0.45	36.87	0.03	0.49	6.75	1.66
Moldova	1.13	4.99	3.25	1.08	0.18	0.34	27.68	0.06	0.31	11.40	2.36
Poland	3.99	22.63	5.12	4.44	2.07	2.34	57.11	0.62	0.51	6.76	
Romania	4.20	11.54	8.58	2.43	0.70	1.30	47.85	0.13	0.48	4.26	2.28
Russia	2.68	12.88	4.36	2.98	1.16	2.02	40.98	0.34	0.77		2.19
Serbia and Montenegro	0.00	0.00	0.00	0.00	0.00		0.00	0.00	0.00	27.89	0.00
Slovakia	2.08	11.67	2.07	1.17	0.43	0.63	39.22	0.05	0.30	4.85	2.61
Slovenia	3.94	14.27	13.44	2.60	0.57	1.19	58.02	0.04	0.72	1.67	1.21
Ukraine	1.19	7.85	2.62	1.92	0.69	0.84	29.77	0.22	0.43	16.77	5.40

Source: International Monetary Fund (IMF), Direction of Trade Statistics

Imports (cif) by Origin 2007 (% Analysis) *(continued)*
% of total imports

	Africa & Middle East	Asia/ Pacific	of which: Japan	China	Australasia	Latin America	of which: Brazil	USA	Canada	Total, including Others
Western Europe										
Austria	1.63	4.34	0.65	1.87	0.06	0.39	0.11	1.68	0.24	100.00
Belgium	3.89	10.17	2.32	3.84	0.51	2.27	0.90	5.01	0.55	100.00
Cyprus	9.68	10.56	2.36	4.87	0.30	3.05	2.49	1.12	0.13	100.00
Denmark	0.69	7.92	0.61	4.55	0.26	1.30	0.33	2.71	0.44	100.00
Finland	0.55	8.81	1.41	4.74	1.35	1.92	0.59	1.92	0.81	100.00
France	5.72	8.42	1.21	3.59	0.22	1.47	0.60	3.92	0.44	100.00
Germany	1.73	9.86	1.76	4.63	0.14	1.57	0.60	3.36	0.25	100.00
Gibraltar										100.00
Greece	7.85	12.58	1.91	4.32	0.17	1.47	0.37	1.95	0.24	100.00
Iceland	0.63	9.71	3.11	4.29	0.68	1.11	0.10	11.47	1.49	100.00
Ireland	0.88	9.50	1.63	3.36	0.31	0.79	0.29	11.35	0.54	100.00
Italy	10.18	10.45	1.22	4.95	0.35	2.41	0.86	2.53	0.39	100.00
Liechtenstein										
Luxembourg	0.24	18.29	0.50	16.56	0.01	0.45	0.09	3.41	0.76	100.00
Malta	1.15	14.77	1.95	2.80	0.26	0.83	0.53	3.85	0.17	100.00
Monaco										
Netherlands	5.53	19.19	2.88	9.78	0.43	4.09	1.56	6.78	0.70	100.00
Norway	1.01	10.07	1.90	5.20	0.21	2.14	0.91	4.15	3.66	100.00
Portugal	8.59	5.54	0.98	1.83	0.10	3.87	2.37	1.63	0.20	100.00
Spain	9.55	11.11	1.60	5.33	0.30	4.63	1.01	2.81	0.29	100.00
Sweden	0.70	7.76	1.64	3.53	0.25	1.20	0.39	2.58	0.29	100.00
Switzerland	2.69	7.06	1.68	2.30	0.14	1.22	0.48	5.39	0.55	100.00
Turkey	9.43	16.17	1.87	6.66	0.34	1.57	0.59	4.10	0.44	100.00
United Kingdom	3.73	15.23	2.24	6.65	0.82	1.85	0.63	7.85	1.63	100.00
Eastern Europe										
Albania	1.00	3.48	0.04	2.12	0.07	0.92	0.77	0.81	0.28	100.00
Belarus	0.34	4.99	0.63	2.46	0.02	0.74	0.32	1.17	0.15	100.00
Bosnia-Herzegovina	0.08	0.66	0.04	0.45	0.01	0.21	0.15	0.17	0.04	100.00
Bulgaria	0.65	3.42	0.28	1.98	0.10	2.41	0.61	0.77	0.08	100.00
Croatia	0.67	7.18	1.13	4.31	0.06	0.84	0.60	1.28	0.11	100.00
Czech Republic	0.32	6.81	1.40	3.38	0.01	0.17	0.07	0.82	0.13	100.00
Estonia	0.10	3.17	0.49	1.62	0.01	0.14	0.07	0.72	0.10	100.00
Georgia	4.25	14.91	1.39	2.91	0.18	1.23	1.09	3.81	0.22	100.00
Hungary	0.27	11.22	1.87	5.57	0.01	0.24	0.10	0.98	0.09	100.00
Latvia	0.13	2.16	0.18	1.15	0.02	0.10	0.04	0.57	0.08	100.00
Lithuania	0.28	2.78	0.21	1.65	0.02	0.30	0.07	1.30	0.06	100.00
Macedonia	0.34	2.54	0.07	0.96	0.03	0.99	0.57	0.43	0.19	100.00
Moldova	0.27	2.48	0.05	0.67	0.04	0.91	0.87	0.71	0.02	100.00
Poland	0.59	6.75	0.73	3.26	0.07	0.88	0.17	1.00	0.11	100.00
Romania	1.24	5.80	0.41	2.21	0.15	0.83	0.51	0.91	0.15	100.00
Russia	0.83	21.14	3.85	10.10	0.23	2.49	1.31	2.73	0.37	100.00
Serbia and Montenegro	23.58	16.98	0.00	14.04	0.13	1.68	1.21		0.53	100.00
Slovakia	0.09	5.68	0.57	1.90	0.01	0.06	0.04	0.47	0.07	100.00
Slovenia	0.98	5.25	0.32	1.53	0.04	1.08	0.49	0.96	0.22	100.00
Ukraine	0.75	13.48	1.05	5.67	0.08	0.40	0.26	1.30	0.12	100.00

Source: *International Monetary Fund (IMF), Direction of Trade Statistics*

Imports   **Table 13.6**

Imports (cif) by Commodity: SITC Classification 2007

US$ million

	Food and live animals	Beverages and tobacco	Crude materials excluding fuels	Mineral fuels etc	Oils and fats
Western Europe					
Austria	7,237	704	6,125	21,430	314
Belgium	22,414	3,315	15,343	54,453	1,417
Cyprus	693	245	99	1,436	23
Denmark	8,400	1,113	2,685	5,260	551
Finland	2,800	587	7,320	12,040	63
France	33,876	5,040	13,450	86,540	1,912
Germany	47,403	6,553	34,612	129,125	3,608
Gibraltar					
Greece	5,860	942	1,630	13,615	216
Iceland	357	61	368	580	13
Ireland	5,549	1,091	1,454	6,490	221
Italy	29,250	4,100	20,540	61,332	3,303
Liechtenstein					
Luxembourg	1,416	478	1,794	2,122	18
Malta	446	46	43	415	9
Monaco					
Netherlands	24,427	3,498	13,956	69,201	2,560
Norway	3,540	568	5,461	3,046	361
Portugal	6,711	514	1,809	11,084	421
Spain	23,413	5,120	11,735	37,309	1,087
Sweden	8,572	991	4,390	17,423	488
Switzerland	5,911	1,515	2,517	12,860	272
Turkey	911	92	7,408	7,112	967
United Kingdom	40,126	7,954	14,981	63,685	1,658
Eastern Europe					
Albania	447	105	64	373	41
Belarus	1,729	290	928	8,518	135
Bosnia-Herzegovina	935	296	211	1,298	50
Bulgaria	1,038	88	1,783	1,572	72
Croatia	1,800	147	404	3,876	63
Czech Republic	4,270	630	2,810	9,930	187
Estonia	704	191	438	2,540	29
Georgia	578	95	40	876	31
Hungary	2,814	395	1,164	6,480	89
Latvia	960	332	420	1,620	53
Lithuania	1,606	284	688	4,945	98
Macedonia	385	34	149	880	32
Moldova	218	104	61	769	8
Poland	7,035	754	4,062	14,804	485
Romania	2,630	507	1,415	8,230	122
Russia	19,306	2,622	4,843	1,945	813
Serbia and Montenegro	972	191	521	2,230	21
Slovakia	2,507	468	1,861	7,351	94
Slovenia	1,277	162	1,428	2,991	66
Ukraine	2,663	567	1,492	14,462	159

Source: United Nations, UN Trade Statistics

Imports (cif) by Commodity: SITC Classification 2007 *(continued)*

US$ million

	Chemicals	Basic manufactures	Machinery and transport equipment	Miscellaneous manufactured goods	Others	Total
Western Europe						
Austria	15,854	24,462	49,354	18,850	1,276	145,606
Belgium	94,525	63,325	90,333	34,022	4,161	383,308
Cyprus	690	1,069	2,067	1,109	100	7,531
Denmark	9,980	15,490	34,400	13,750	1,288	92,918
Finland	8,213	9,181	28,114	6,802	1,723	76,843
France	71,118	81,304	201,211	75,305	500	570,258
Germany	110,126	133,862	346,018	97,977	97,039	1,006,322
Gibraltar						
Greece	9,462	10,281	19,253	7,807	241	69,308
Iceland	455	975	3,210	835	7	6,860
Ireland	10,929	7,493	33,465	9,812	4,893	81,396
Italy	57,387	78,615	128,461	49,181	39,967	472,136
Liechtenstein						
Luxembourg	2,020	4,243	6,081	2,084	1,113	21,367
Malta	390	435	2,137	567	48	4,537
Monaco						
Netherlands	46,705	41,507	124,005	38,301	713	364,872
Norway	6,493	12,221	28,578	10,464	260	70,993
Portugal	8,022	11,633	20,814	6,961	3,500	71,468
Spain	39,400	43,567	130,909	35,513	2,436	330,489
Sweden	14,076	20,510	52,004	14,875	4,218	137,549
Switzerland	32,506	27,400	41,012	27,061	1,777	152,831
Turkey	13,133	17,912	26,481	6,181	75,617	155,815
United Kingdom	62,125	75,512	216,663	90,538	84,286	657,529
Eastern Europe						
Albania	335	962	632	452	0	3,412
Belarus	2,535	4,113	5,329	1,004	1,345	25,927
Bosnia-Herzegovina	934	1,750	1,633	712	0	7,819
Bulgaria	2,538	5,513	8,439	1,974	4,553	27,571
Croatia	2,616	4,686	7,497	2,663	8	23,758
Czech Republic	10,700	21,300	43,058	10,460	1,590	104,934
Estonia	1,226	2,290	5,330	1,176	912	14,836
Georgia	399	587	1,360	448	83	4,497
Hungary	7,720	11,770	39,400	5,241	8,840	83,913
Latvia	1,308	2,280	4,130	1,427	423	12,953
Lithuania	2,540	3,267	7,015	1,567	135	22,145
Macedonia	393	1,289	766	275	3	4,206
Moldova	348	650	614	306	1	3,079
Poland	18,436	28,935	48,242	10,910	5,455	139,120
Romania	6,250	13,312	21,224	5,333	11	59,036
Russia	20,413	20,746	74,133	12,632	8,535	165,989
Serbia and Montenegro	2,010	3,130	5,340	1,570	64	16,049
Slovakia	4,811	9,063	19,107	5,661	382	51,305
Slovenia	3,074	5,966	8,073	2,272	96	25,404
Ukraine	6,558	8,090	15,705	2,870	510	53,079

Source: United Nations, UN Trade Statistics
Notes: US$ totals in this table may differ from the totals given for Imports (cif) by Origin and Total Imports (cif)

Imports

Table 13.7

Imports (cif) by Commodity: SITC Classification 2007 (% Analysis)
% of total imports

	Food and live animals	Beverages and tobacco	Crude materials excluding fuels	Mineral fuels etc	Oils and fats
Western Europe					
Austria	4.97	0.48	4.21	14.72	0.22
Belgium	5.85	0.86	4.00	14.21	0.37
Cyprus	9.20	3.25	1.32	19.07	0.30
Denmark	9.04	1.20	2.89	5.66	0.59
Finland	3.64	0.76	9.53	15.67	0.08
France	5.94	0.88	2.36	15.18	0.34
Germany	4.71	0.65	3.44	12.83	0.36
Gibraltar					
Greece	8.46	1.36	2.35	19.64	0.31
Iceland	5.20	0.89	5.36	8.45	0.18
Ireland	6.82	1.34	1.79	7.97	0.27
Italy	6.20	0.87	4.35	12.99	0.70
Liechtenstein					
Luxembourg	6.63	2.24	8.40	9.93	0.08
Malta	9.83	1.01	0.96	9.15	0.21
Monaco					
Netherlands	6.69	0.96	3.82	18.97	0.70
Norway	4.99	0.80	7.69	4.29	0.51
Portugal	9.39	0.72	2.53	15.51	0.59
Spain	7.08	1.55	3.55	11.29	0.33
Sweden	6.23	0.72	3.19	12.67	0.35
Switzerland	3.87	0.99	1.65	8.41	0.18
Turkey	0.58	0.06	4.75	4.56	0.62
United Kingdom	6.10	1.21	2.28	9.69	0.25
Eastern Europe					
Albania	13.12	3.07	1.88	10.92	1.21
Belarus	6.67	1.12	3.58	32.86	0.52
Bosnia-Herzegovina	11.95	3.78	2.70	16.60	0.64
Bulgaria	3.77	0.32	6.47	5.70	0.26
Croatia	7.58	0.62	1.70	16.31	0.26
Czech Republic	4.07	0.60	2.68	9.46	0.18
Estonia	4.75	1.29	2.95	17.12	0.20
Georgia	12.85	2.10	0.90	19.48	0.69
Hungary	3.35	0.47	1.39	7.72	0.11
Latvia	7.41	2.56	3.24	12.51	0.41
Lithuania	7.25	1.28	3.11	22.33	0.44
Macedonia	9.15	0.80	3.55	20.92	0.76
Moldova	7.08	3.38	1.99	24.98	0.27
Poland	5.06	0.54	2.92	10.64	0.35
Romania	4.45	0.86	2.40	13.94	0.21
Russia	11.63	1.58	2.92	1.17	0.49
Serbia and Montenegro	6.05	1.19	3.25	13.90	0.13
Slovakia	4.89	0.91	3.63	14.33	0.18
Slovenia	5.03	0.64	5.62	11.78	0.26
Ukraine	5.02	1.07	2.81	27.25	0.30

Source: United Nations, UN Trade Statistics

Imports (cif) by Commodity: SITC Classification 2007 (% Analysis) *(continued)*
% of total imports

	Chemicals	Basic manufactures	Machinery and transport equipment	Miscellaneous manufactured goods	Others	Total
Western Europe						
Austria	10.89	16.80	33.90	12.95	0.88	100.00
Belgium	24.66	16.52	23.57	8.88	1.09	100.00
Cyprus	9.16	14.19	27.45	14.73	1.32	100.00
Denmark	10.74	16.67	37.02	14.80	1.39	100.00
Finland	10.69	11.95	36.59	8.85	2.24	100.00
France	12.47	14.26	35.28	13.21	0.09	100.00
Germany	10.94	13.30	34.38	9.74	9.64	100.00
Gibraltar						
Greece	13.65	14.83	27.78	11.26	0.35	100.00
Iceland	6.63	14.21	46.79	12.17	0.10	100.00
Ireland	13.43	9.21	41.11	12.06	6.01	100.00
Italy	12.15	16.65	27.21	10.42	8.47	100.00
Liechtenstein						
Luxembourg	9.45	19.86	28.46	9.75	5.21	100.00
Malta	8.60	9.59	47.11	12.50	1.05	100.00
Monaco						
Netherlands	12.80	11.38	33.99	10.50	0.20	100.00
Norway	9.15	17.21	40.25	14.74	0.37	100.00
Portugal	11.22	16.28	29.12	9.74	4.90	100.00
Spain	11.92	13.18	39.61	10.75	0.74	100.00
Sweden	10.23	14.91	37.81	10.81	3.07	100.00
Switzerland	21.27	17.93	26.83	17.71	1.16	100.00
Turkey	8.43	11.50	17.00	3.97	48.53	100.00
United Kingdom	9.45	11.48	32.95	13.77	12.82	100.00
Eastern Europe						
Albania	9.83	28.19	18.53	13.24	0.00	100.00
Belarus	9.78	15.86	20.56	3.87	5.19	100.00
Bosnia-Herzegovina	11.94	22.38	20.89	9.11	0.00	100.00
Bulgaria	9.20	20.00	30.61	7.16	16.52	100.00
Croatia	11.01	19.72	31.55	11.21	0.03	100.00
Czech Republic	10.20	20.30	41.03	9.97	1.52	100.00
Estonia	8.26	15.43	35.93	7.93	6.15	100.00
Georgia	8.87	13.05	30.24	9.96	1.85	100.00
Hungary	9.20	14.03	46.95	6.25	10.53	100.00
Latvia	10.10	17.60	31.88	11.02	3.27	100.00
Lithuania	11.47	14.75	31.68	7.08	0.61	100.00
Macedonia	9.34	30.65	18.22	6.54	0.07	100.00
Moldova	11.30	21.10	19.93	9.92	0.05	100.00
Poland	13.25	20.80	34.68	7.84	3.92	100.00
Romania	10.59	22.55	35.95	9.03	0.02	100.00
Russia	12.30	12.50	44.66	7.61	5.14	100.00
Serbia and Montenegro	12.52	19.50	33.27	9.78	0.40	100.00
Slovakia	9.38	17.67	37.24	11.03	0.75	100.00
Slovenia	12.10	23.48	31.78	8.95	0.38	100.00
Ukraine	12.36	15.24	29.59	5.41	0.96	100.00

Source: United Nations, UN Trade Statistics

Exports

Table 13.8

Total Exports (fob) 1980-2007

US$ million

	1980	1985	1990	1995	1996	1997	1998	1999
Western Europe								
Austria	17,489	17,239	41,135	57,643	57,818	58,590	62,742	64,124
Belgium				175,849	175,356	171,881	179,078	178,972
Cyprus	532	476	957	1,229	1,395	1,101	1,061	995
Denmark	16,749	17,090	37,037	51,478	51,480	49,119	48,839	50,399
Finland	14,150	13,617	26,571	39,573	38,435	39,316	42,963	41,841
France	116,030	101,671	216,591	286,738	287,667	289,736	305,641	302,493
Germany	192,860	183,933	410,104	523,802	524,198	512,427	543,397	542,870
Gibraltar	40	62						
Greece	5,153	4,539	8,105	10,961	11,948	11,128	10,732	10,475
Iceland	918	815	1,592	1,804	1,639	1,852	2,050	2,005
Ireland	8,398	10,357	23,747	44,635	48,668	53,512	64,477	71,219
Italy	78,104	76,717	170,486	233,998	252,039	240,404	245,700	235,175
Liechtenstein								
Luxembourg	3,005	2,831	6,305	7,750	7,210	6,999	7,922	7,895
Malta	483	400	1,130	1,914	1,731	1,630	1,834	1,983
Monaco								
Netherlands	84,948	77,873	131,775	196,276	197,417	194,905	201,374	200,778
Norway	18,543	19,985	34,049	41,992	49,645	48,542	40,399	45,455
Portugal	4,640	5,685	16,422	23,207	24,605	23,973	24,814	25,227
Spain	20,720	24,247	55,521	91,046	101,996	104,359	109,228	109,964
Sweden	30,906	30,461	57,538	79,801	84,896	82,946	84,969	84,812
Switzerland	29,632	27,433	63,784	78,040	76,196	72,493	75,431	76,122
Turkey	2,910	7,958	12,959	21,637	23,225	26,261	26,974	26,587
United Kingdom	110,137	101,355	185,268	242,006	262,096	281,061	271,844	268,193
Eastern Europe								
Albania				202	211	139	208	351
Belarus				4,803	5,652	7,301	7,070	5,909
Bosnia-Herzegovina				24	58	193	352	518
Bulgaria		13,339	4,822	5,359	6,602	5,323	4,195	3,964
Croatia			4,020	4,517	4,643	3,981	4,517	4,303
Czech Republic				21,686	21,916	22,747	26,418	26,241
Estonia				1,663	1,766	2,127	2,509	2,381
Georgia				155	203	244	191	238
Hungary	8,671	8,538	9,598	12,801	15,631	18,990	22,992	24,950
Latvia				1,305	1,443	1,672	1,811	1,723
Lithuania				2,039	2,656	3,200	3,235	2,754
Macedonia				1,204	1,147	1,237	1,311	1,191
Moldova				739	823	890	644	474
Poland	14,191	11,489	13,627	22,895	24,440	25,751	27,191	27,397
Romania	11,209	12,167	5,775	7,910	8,085	8,431	8,300	8,505
Russia				82,913	90,563	89,008	74,884	75,665
Serbia and Montenegro								
Slovakia				8,595	8,823	8,254	10,721	10,226
Slovenia			4,118	8,316	8,312	8,372	9,048	8,546
Ukraine				13,128	14,401	14,232	12,637	11,582

Source: *Euromonitor International from International Monetary Fund (IMF), International Financial Statistics*
Notes: *US$ totals in this table may differ from the totals given for Exports (fob) by Destination and Exports (fob) by Commodity*

Total Exports (fob) 1980-2007 *(continued)*

US$ million

	2000	2001	2002	2003	2004	2005	2006	2007
Western Europe								
Austria	64,155	66,481	73,081	89,240	111,686	117,711	130,370	156,658
Belgium	187,838	190,327	215,779	255,549	306,721	335,837	366,923	432,315
Cyprus	951	976	770	834	1,081	1,303	1,153	1,254
Denmark	50,380	51,068	56,304	65,267	75,620	83,562	91,713	102,845
Finland	45,473	42,794	44,650	52,504	60,895	65,234	77,284	90,091
France	300,024	297,171	311,872	365,714	424,761	439,005	483,008	541,768
Germany	550,112	571,357	615,446	751,679	911,582	977,881	1,122,070	1,329,050
Gibraltar								
Greece	10,747	9,483	10,315	13,195	14,996	15,511	20,180	23,472
Iceland	1,892	2,022	2,227	2,385	2,896	2,942	3,239	4,350
Ireland	77,081	83,004	87,418	92,411	104,180	109,604	104,866	122,630
Italy	239,886	244,210	254,097	299,412	353,434	372,928	416,127	499,909
Liechtenstein								
Luxembourg	7,946	8,238	8,495	9,979	12,175	12,696	14,174	16,053
Malta	2,443	1,958	2,225	2,467	2,627	2,376	2,707	2,983
Monaco								
Netherlands	213,382	216,141	219,758	264,798	317,966	349,812	399,569	476,820
Norway	60,058	59,191	59,702	67,479	81,750	101,938	120,464	137,998
Portugal	23,274	24,445	25,523	30,591	33,014	32,156	42,881	50,243
Spain	113,325	115,155	123,507	155,995	182,107	190,982	213,341	248,917
Sweden	87,724	78,208	82,919	102,407	123,295	130,885	147,904	169,153
Switzerland	74,856	78,066	87,359	100,724	117,816	126,083	141,669	164,797
Turkey	27,775	31,334	34,561	46,576	61,683	71,928	81,912	106,851
United Kingdom	281,564	267,349	276,299	304,185	341,596	371,370	428,359	434,904
Eastern Europe								
Albania	258	307	340	448	605	658	798	1,073
Belarus	7,326	7,451	8,021	9,946	13,774	15,979	19,734	24,275
Bosnia-Herzegovina	675	799	887	1,230	1,769	3,173	4,227	4,686
Bulgaria	4,809	5,115	5,749	7,540	9,931	11,739	15,102	18,575
Croatia	4,432	4,666	4,904	6,187	8,024	8,773	10,376	12,364
Czech Republic	28,996	33,399	38,486	48,709	67,194	77,985	95,140	122,613
Estonia	3,166	3,314	3,448	4,539	5,934	7,675	8,755	10,958
Georgia	323	318	346	461	647	865	993	1,240
Hungary	28,016	30,530	34,512	42,532	54,892	62,179	74,216	93,985
Latvia	1,865	2,001	2,284	2,893	3,982	5,108	5,896	7,890
Lithuania	3,548	4,279	5,232	6,970	9,307	11,782	14,153	17,162
Macedonia	1,323	1,158	1,116	1,367	1,676	2,041	2,398	3,302
Moldova	472	568	644	789	980	1,091	1,052	1,342
Poland	31,651	36,092	41,010	53,537	73,792	89,347	109,584	136,360
Romania	10,367	11,391	13,876	17,619	23,485	27,730	32,336	40,042
Russia	105,565	101,884	107,301	135,929	183,207	243,798	303,926	355,175
Serbia and Montenegro								
Slovakia	11,889	12,641	14,478	21,966	27,605	31,998	41,939	57,770
Slovenia	8,732	9,252	10,357	12,767	15,879	17,896	20,985	26,553
Ukraine	14,573	16,265	17,957	23,067	32,666	34,228	38,368	49,296

Source: Euromonitor International from International Monetary Fund (IMF), International Financial Statistics
Notes: US$ totals in this table may differ from the totals given for Exports (fob) by Destination and Exports (fob) by Commodity

Exports

Table 13.9

Total Exports by Quarter 2006-2008
US$ million

	2006 1st Quarter	2006 2nd Quarter	2006 3rd Quarter	2006 4th Quarter	2007 1st Quarter	2007 2nd Quarter	2007 3rd Quarter	2007 4th Quarter	2008 1st Quarter	2008 2nd Quarter
Western Europe										
Austria	29,987.1	32,242.0	32,268.3	35,872.6	36,917.6	38,503.1	37,566.8	43,670.6	44,608.0	
Belgium	87,706.0	92,573.8	90,345.4	96,297.9	103,698.1	104,706.5	107,348.4	116,562.0	121,427.4	
Cyprus	335.0	278.8	236.0	303.0	333.5	343.0	256.1	321.8		
Denmark	21,668.0	22,855.0	22,703.5	24,486.0	24,048.7	24,497.8	25,397.5	28,901.0	29,320.3	31,854.5
Finland	16,912.5	20,043.4	19,220.4	21,107.6	20,558.5	23,370.1	21,983.6	24,179.0	24,560.8	28,061.6
France	115,897.0	124,274.2	114,284.5	128,552.3	129,876.0	134,646.0	129,177.0	148,069.0	156,819.0	162,133.0
Germany	258,305.0	270,377.5	281,702.5	311,685.0	313,067.3	322,909.3	330,909.3	362,164.2	378,588.1	
Gibraltar										
Greece	4,269.4	5,119.3	5,303.6	5,487.9	5,764.1	5,549.4	5,796.5	6,361.7	5,914.1	
Iceland	734.5	866.9	769.8	867.5	1,166.8	937.1	856.1	1,389.6	1,150.3	1,504.5
Ireland	26,901.2	28,539.7	28,465.9	20,959.2	29,782.9	30,560.5	30,829.2	31,457.4	32,057.8	
Italy	94,342.6	106,999.1	100,341.1	114,444.1	116,459.8	126,608.7	121,113.8	135,726.7	134,447.7	
Liechtenstein										
Luxembourg	3,392.5	3,564.2	3,386.7	3,828.6	3,915.1	4,103.8	3,819.5	4,214.7	4,649.9	
Malta	609.2	685.2	655.1	757.8	678.8	740.6	750.1	813.0		
Monaco										
Netherlands	93,697.8	98,775.1	98,289.1	108,807.0	110,787.5	113,930.6	116,611.7	135,490.3	140,102.4	
Norway	28,816.0	31,301.0	29,832.4	30,514.5	31,389.9	32,838.2	33,126.1	40,643.8	42,967.6	47,053.9
Portugal	9,855.6	10,819.6	10,671.1	11,534.3	12,168.1	12,517.7	12,149.0	13,408.5	14,877.6	15,489.3
Spain	50,707.4	55,120.6	49,612.1	57,900.9	59,169.2	62,720.4	58,237.5	68,789.8	71,134.1	
Sweden	34,499.8	37,173.7	35,126.7	41,103.7	40,328.2	40,954.7	39,953.9	47,916.2	49,615.4	53,432.7
Switzerland	33,052.8	35,173.7	34,950.3	38,492.1	39,104.4	40,283.7	40,599.6	44,809.4	47,040.8	53,053.9
Turkey	16,173.5	20,950.5	20,943.0	23,845.0	23,039.0	26,333.0	26,614.0	30,865.0	33,110.0	35,639.0
United Kingdom	101,344.0	123,571.5	99,463.4	103,980.1	102,675.8	107,819.7	107,082.8	117,325.7	114,600.3	
Eastern Europe										
Albania	173.8	208.3	195.0	215.6	238.0	278.1	270.7	285.8	308.0	407.4
Belarus	4,463.7	4,825.5	5,460.4	4,984.1	4,748.1	5,927.6	6,446.7	7,152.9	8,032.6	
Bosnia-Herzegovina										
Bulgaria	3,213.2	3,834.0	4,073.3	3,981.1	3,802.4	4,505.7	4,932.9	5,334.1	5,474.0	6,383.8
Croatia	2,371.3	2,428.8	2,582.4	2,993.8	2,633.4	3,053.4	3,164.0	3,513.5	3,259.9	3,792.7
Czech Republic	21,574.1	23,363.1	23,167.9	27,035.0	28,135.7	29,304.4	29,706.0	35,467.0	37,349.5	40,479.7
Estonia	1,918.2	2,245.2	2,238.4	2,353.5	2,459.7	2,811.9	2,636.2	3,049.7	2,994.7	
Georgia					223.7	320.3	330.5	365.7	330.6	
Hungary	16,417.3	18,281.8	18,505.6	21,011.7	21,325.5	22,744.5	23,584.2	26,330.7	27,498.7	
Latvia	1,248.9	1,482.5	1,535.7	1,628.7	1,696.6	1,951.7	2,000.0	2,241.5	2,312.2	2,508.2
Lithuania	3,161.2	3,688.6	3,700.6	3,602.9	3,667.6	4,270.8	4,597.3	4,626.6	5,474.5	6,749.7
Macedonia	450.5	585.2	699.1	662.6	680.3	865.9	832.7	923.2	919.1	
Moldova	234.8	249.3	256.9	292.3	274.4	325.7	322.4	419.3	346.9	
Poland	24,706.7	26,974.9	27,788.3	30,114.2	31,209.8	32,762.3	34,070.1	38,317.9	41,113.7	
Romania	7,478.4	8,129.2	8,217.4	8,511.0	9,160.6	9,618.6	10,044.3	11,218.2	11,932.4	13,624.2
Russia	67,232.4	76,471.3	79,813.7	80,408.6	72,040.4	84,181.5	89,517.2	109,436.0	109,577.8	127,499.3
Serbia and Montenegro										
Slovakia	8,693.8	10,051.2	10,690.8	12,503.3	12,839.1	13,988.7	14,100.2	16,841.8	17,316.6	19,636.3
Slovenia	4,773.6	5,279.9	5,180.4	5,750.8	6,173.5	6,636.0	6,594.1	7,149.0	7,465.9	8,233.2
Ukraine	8,065.3	9,329.8	10,538.4	10,434.5	10,732.7	12,398.4	12,560.0	13,605.0	13,790.7	

Source: *Euromonitor International from International Monetary Fund (IMF), International Financial Statistics*
Notes: *US$ totals in this table may differ from the totals given for Exports (fob) by Destination and Exports (fob) by Commodity*

Table 13.10

Total Exports by Month 2007

US$ million

	January	February	March	April	May	June	July	August	September	October	November	December
Western Europe												
Austria	11,567.0	11,808.1	13,542.5	12,508.7	12,990.3	13,004.1	12,981.6	11,417.6	13,167.6	15,825.0	15,638.4	12,207.2
Belgium	33,032.6	32,858.1	38,147.6	32,939.4	34,945.8	37,164.9	36,358.1	33,150.3	38,192.2	41,010.4	41,045.6	33,470.0
Cyprus	136.7	87.7	109.1	107.4	117.5	118.0	92.2	75.3	88.6	114.2	112.4	95.2
Denmark	7,837.8	7,194.4	9,016.5	7,601.3	8,080.0	8,816.5	8,079.9	8,343.8	8,973.8	9,860.4	10,524.9	8,515.6
Finland	6,398.4	6,415.6	7,801.0	8,204.4	7,848.8	7,389.2	7,161.1	7,269.6	7,568.3	8,186.1	8,688.5	7,160.3
France	40,381.9	41,615.4	48,003.6	43,734.1	43,519.1	47,496.4	46,508.7	36,910.5	45,820.7	52,948.8	50,219.6	44,609.1
Germany	100,597.8	101,476.8	110,992.7	106,514.1	106,600.1	109,795.1	111,571.1	105,801.1	113,537.1	126,384.7	128,840.7	106,938.8
Gibraltar												
Greece	1,739.2	1,759.5	2,265.4	1,825.3	1,773.5	1,950.5	1,939.4	1,687.2	2,169.9	2,141.4	2,314.8	1,905.5
Iceland	363.5	348.6	449.8	287.3	330.8	317.0	317.6	243.1	291.9	491.7	528.5	365.5
Ireland	9,490.8	9,109.6	11,182.3	10,101.1	10,029.6	10,430.2	10,577.3	9,578.7	10,672.6	10,874.2	11,746.5	8,837.1
Italy	33,912.3	39,093.1	43,472.8	39,039.3	42,822.6	44,740.8	48,132.6	31,802.5	41,172.8	49,427.0	46,820.3	39,472.9
Liechtenstein												
Luxembourg	1,268.0	1,230.1	1,416.7	1,355.1	1,351.3	1,396.9	1,370.4	1,149.6	1,299.1	1,480.6	1,463.5	1,270.3
Malta	227.8	192.4	258.6	225.8	272.5	242.3	270.6	225.7	253.9	272.4	280.9	259.8
Monaco												
Netherlands	35,409.4	34,908.1	40,470.0	36,148.0	38,323.2	39,459.4	38,286.3	37,593.6	40,731.8	45,386.2	48,225.6	41,878.4
Norway	10,583.6	9,580.7	11,225.8	10,942.7	10,959.2	10,935.6	10,512.0	11,023.8	11,590.9	13,395.7	13,423.4	13,824.5
Portugal	3,952.2	3,796.9	4,419.1	3,881.2	4,266.5	4,370.0	4,599.8	3,270.4	4,278.8	4,752.9	4,846.4	3,809.3
Spain	18,156.3	19,427.0	21,585.8	19,460.8	21,643.2	21,616.3	21,014.1	16,517.2	20,706.3	23,768.2	24,326.1	20,695.4
Sweden	12,878.0	12,755.8	14,694.5	13,162.2	14,135.9	13,656.6	12,501.4	13,027.8	14,424.8	16,674.5	16,995.4	14,246.1
Switzerland	12,626.6	12,408.8	14,106.4	12,461.6	13,848.6	13,977.1	14,555.6	12,212.6	13,855.4	15,934.3	16,418.1	12,392.0
Turkey	6,525.6	7,610.7	8,902.7	8,283.0	9,113.6	8,936.4	8,913.8	8,708.7	8,991.5	9,887.0	11,302.0	9,676.0
United Kingdom	32,463.9	32,783.8	37,429.6	35,067.8	36,070.4	36,679.1	36,609.1	34,492.2	35,982.1	39,698.6	41,436.7	36,191.0
Eastern Europe												
Albania	69.7	80.8	87.5	84.9	92.2	101.1	104.3	73.1	93.2	95.6	110.0	80.3
Belarus	1,386.3	1,497.3	1,848.4	1,823.2	2,073.4	2,014.2	2,163.8	2,195.5	2,095.7	2,252.4	2,442.4	2,482.7
Bosnia-Herzegovina												
Bulgaria	1,131.4	1,187.5	1,493.1	1,393.0	1,491.9	1,583.6	1,709.0	1,565.2	1,673.7	1,860.8	1,865.9	1,619.9
Croatia	761.9	908.1	964.2	980.6	1,040.4	1,033.1	1,211.2	912.0	1,042.2	1,291.4	1,150.3	1,068.9
Czech Republic	8,838.1	9,004.5	10,313.2	9,534.1	9,836.5	9,993.4	9,530.6	9,468.8	10,719.7	12,650.8	12,922.8	9,800.6
Estonia	788.8	800.8	870.1	892.4	1,004.2	915.2	867.7	895.1	873.4	1,072.1	1,112.1	865.6
Georgia	69.5	67.5	86.7	99.6	112.6	108.1	118.9	114.4	97.2	130.2	111.1	124.4
Hungary	6,619.9	6,871.3	7,834.3	7,079.9	7,705.7	7,958.9	7,726.4	7,289.0	8,568.8	9,257.3	9,444.9	7,628.5
Latvia	520.5	537.1	649.0	623.0	676.4	663.9	662.5	674.5	670.5	759.2	770.6	682.5
Lithuania	1,173.2	1,105.9	1,381.7	1,328.9	1,459.7	1,477.5	1,550.0	1,552.9	1,496.0	1,585.6	1,505.6	1,545.7
Macedonia	193.6	213.1	273.6	272.0	286.6	307.3	269.4	293.2	270.1	307.1	305.8	310.3
Moldova	73.7	90.7	110.0	101.4	109.2	115.1	106.7	106.5	109.2	143.3	148.7	127.3
Poland	10,056.6	9,785.1	11,368.1	10,331.9	11,250.3	11,180.1	10,976.9	11,414.0	11,679.2	13,804.6	13,671.4	10,841.9
Romania	2,695.8	3,004.1	3,460.8	2,934.5	3,333.2	3,350.9	3,599.0	3,031.6	3,413.8	3,958.6	3,989.2	3,270.4
Russia	21,611.9	23,738.1	26,690.3	27,335.6	29,850.0	26,995.8	29,938.1	31,090.5	28,488.6	34,743.2	36,125.5	38,567.2
Serbia and Montenegro												
Slovakia	4,105.0	4,051.4	4,682.8	4,472.0	4,875.5	4,641.2	4,689.3	4,358.4	5,052.5	6,117.6	5,985.8	4,738.5
Slovenia	1,892.9	1,943.2	2,342.2	2,088.2	2,276.4	2,247.9	2,323.6	1,970.5	2,307.0	2,576.5	2,542.8	2,041.2
Ukraine	3,212.2	3,410.9	4,108.6	4,062.4	4,092.6	4,242.4	4,260.6	4,174.8	4,120.7	4,349.2	4,455.3	4,806.4

Source: Euromonitor International from International Monetary Fund (IMF), International Financial Statistics
Notes: US$ totals in this table may differ from the totals given for Exports (fob) by Destination and Exports (fob) by Commodity

Exports

Table 13.11

Exports (fob) by Destination 2007

US$ million

	France	Germany	Italy	Nether-lands	Sweden	UK	Total EU	Norway	Switzerland	Russia	Poland
Western Europe											
Austria	5,877.1	48,816.3	14,478.4	2,941.1	1,803.2	5,839.9	118,849.4	794.7	7,092.6	3,996.9	4,421.4
Belgium	72,020.3	84,406.0	22,447.2	51,575.8	6,475.6	32,925.2	330,000.4	1,826.7	7,556.4	4,494.2	6,190.4
Cyprus	11.9	91.6	40.4	22.6	10.3	198.9	824.2	3.4	6.0	26.6	3.6
Denmark	4,996.9	17,996.0	3,595.9	4,965.6	15,067.9	8,282.1	72,686.4	5,895.2	867.3	1,872.7	2,372.5
Finland	3,220.4	9,810.3	2,531.8	5,004.1	9,644.6	5,237.1	51,143.8	2,809.5	848.9	9,250.4	2,127.9
France		82,319.7	49,348.4	22,609.3	7,336.8	45,071.0	357,276.9	2,252.4	14,239.6	7,691.9	8,661.4
Germany	128,610.0		89,213.0	85,178.3	29,703.2	97,127.8	858,853.5	10,331.6	50,111.9	38,635.2	49,545.9
Gibraltar											
Greece	987.3	2,718.2	2,540.9	477.5	243.0	1,284.2	15,359.3	45.9	172.8	494.4	320.7
Iceland	123.0	638.1	31.6	1,016.6	34.2	632.5	3,570.1	182.8	60.5	65.1	29.8
Ireland	7,063.1	8,926.3	4,319.8	4,764.7	1,365.6	22,693.2	76,778.7	798.1	4,447.8	425.6	812.2
Italy	56,233.5	63,266.1		11,570.5	5,435.6	28,526.9	295,284.9	2,163.8	18,450.1	13,187.2	11,931.4
Liechtenstein											
Luxembourg	3,659.0	4,743.6	1,666.1	1,202.2	728.1	1,596.5	19,669.5	81.5	202.9	202.2	421.2
Malta	368.4	400.5	117.2	16.2	10.6	292.1	1,423.1	5.4	10.7	2.9	20.7
Monaco											
Netherlands	46,693.7	134,704.0	27,865.5		9,744.4	50,442.6	430,162.1	4,370.0	6,861.1	9,543.3	9,825.6
Norway	10,947.6	16,793.3	3,740.8	13,971.1	8,917.6	35,842.6	110,196.4		920.5	935.9	1,611.0
Portugal	6,312.6	6,629.9	2,084.0	1,708.3	615.0	3,037.0	38,301.6	140.3	363.1	197.1	358.8
Spain	45,094.7	25,902.6	20,450.1	7,830.9	2,280.6	18,110.9	166,816.9	1,390.0	3,268.3	2,821.0	3,141.3
Sweden	8,510.9	17,644.0	5,339.1	8,565.7		12,053.4	103,131.8	15,880.7	1,527.3	3,372.8	4,155.0
Switzerland	14,379.8	34,922.6	14,984.3	5,186.9	1,583.9	8,771.6	106,516.4	697.3		2,437.9	1,804.4
Turkey	5,975.1	11,993.6	7,478.7	3,018.4	882.8	8,626.3	60,406.2	375.2	935.1	4,727.2	1,437.4
United Kingdom	35,921.5	48,995.0	18,232.5	29,986.2	9,723.7		253,551.6	5,480.1	7,794.8	5,623.4	4,704.5
Eastern Europe											
Albania	5.8	27.4	573.8	33.1	21.5	6.0	783.0	0.7	1.1	4.1	1.1
Belarus	77.0	730.6	181.4	4,331.8	77.1	1,527.8	10,667.1	76.4	9.2	8,886.6	1,224.1
Bosnia-Herzegovina	64.3	419.6	507.4	27.3	25.6	15.9	2,278.1	7.0	15.5	4.6	39.3
Bulgaria	736.9	1,899.6	1,883.0	220.4	110.2	461.9	11,206.5	24.8	112.4	452.0	301.4
Croatia	275.1	1,231.8	2,342.9	126.3	147.3	240.4	7,303.5	13.3	132.3	156.6	118.6
Czech Republic	6,565.4	37,863.8	5,960.9	4,421.4	2,151.8	6,130.8	104,529.4	641.4	1,800.4	2,869.8	7,383.5
Estonia	149.3	577.0	117.5	296.3	1,456.9	309.5	7,698.7	372.7	36.9	976.2	159.3
Georgia	40.0	57.6	54.4	11.6	0.1	83.2	521.3	0.2	1.0	74.6	3.7
Hungary	4,504.1	26,886.4	5,394.7	2,768.9	1,051.4	4,280.5	75,427.2	257.9	1,070.4	3,072.1	3,982.1
Latvia	123.9	692.3	121.1	167.1	615.2	541.2	6,027.2	203.6	55.0	1,074.7	285.5
Lithuania	626.0	1,798.4	390.3	511.5	652.4	782.5	11,106.7	394.5	47.6	2,581.1	1,075.3
Macedonia	20.5	523.6	364.7	63.5	16.4	62.7	2,322.9	3.3	12.6	34.8	7.4
Moldova	29.3	149.2	176.0	16.3	12.6	28.0	908.2	1.4	2.8	343.0	110.0
Poland	8,548.0	36,316.8	9,293.6	5,362.9	4,515.9	8,339.1	110,692.6	2,514.7	1,002.7	6,505.7	
Romania	3,117.7	6,829.0	6,924.2	831.9	259.4	1,661.1	29,065.7	414.0	307.4	587.0	870.3
Russia	12,253.0	32,749.9	19,255.9	26,086.3	3,961.4	9,657.1	179,821.2	1,437.0	3,824.8		13,097.0
Serbia and Montenegro	0.0	0.0	0.0	0.0	0.0		0.0	0.0	0.0	64.8	0.0
Slovakia	3,924.5	12,460.6	3,711.6	2,078.2	878.7	2,795.8	50,542.5	153.6	484.3	1,322.3	3,627.0
Slovenia	1,781.3	5,620.0	3,754.8	460.8	249.7	728.4	20,898.9	67.2	265.5	1,329.9	988.8
Ukraine	483.1	1,674.3	2,988.5	608.9	75.6	195.0	15,442.5	84.3	90.4	11,074.2	1,530.6

Source: *International Monetary Fund (IMF), Direction of Trade Statistics*

Exports (fob) by Destination 2007 *(continued)*

US$ million

	Africa & Middle East	Asia/ Pacific	of which: Japan	China	Australasia	Latin America	of which: Brazil	USA	Canada	Total, including Others
Western Europe										
Austria	5,011.1	8,525.8	1,552.6	2,295.3	1,047.2	2,046.7	698.1	8,018.4	1,237.1	245,770.2
Belgium	18,626.2	23,853.2	3,354.6	4,583.3	1,930.1	5,377.8	2,077.4	24,731.6	2,945.8	479,497.9
Cyprus	166.8	77.0	20.0	10.4	5.8	1.4		8.6	3.4	1,409.9
Denmark	2,553.5	6,896.5	1,900.8	1,761.7	871.7	1,427.1	359.9	6,278.1	967.9	121,189.9
Finland	5,995.5	8,484.5	1,609.2	2,961.6	742.8	1,773.2	656.2	5,731.0	695.8	111,670.7
France	45,626.5	46,436.3	7,908.9	12,416.8	3,544.4	12,527.6	4,236.2	34,010.9	3,601.7	621,946.4
Germany	54,970.5	114,722.4	17,871.6	41,044.7	8,973.7	28,529.0	9,370.8	100,128.0	8,652.9	1,760,233.3
Gibraltar										370.0
Greece	1,630.6	724.7	173.4	152.0	104.8	274.2	48.8	980.2	101.6	37,944.1
Iceland	140.9	284.2	206.3	37.4	6.9	14.0	4.2	346.8	23.1	5,000.4
Ireland	2,974.7	9,036.1	2,378.2	1,771.1	1,233.9	1,597.0	222.6	21,673.8	535.1	127,020.0
Italy	42,474.7	35,943.3	5,939.0	8,672.4	4,357.9	15,980.4	3,540.4	33,460.5	3,797.6	615,685.4
Liechtenstein										
Luxembourg	266.1	562.4	46.6	266.5	40.6	166.9	47.6	407.8	85.1	26,121.0
Malta	201.7	843.0	142.1	37.3	7.7	30.7	8.0	330.9	15.4	3,086.5
Monaco										
Netherlands	22,237.5	24,071.2	3,612.5	5,115.5	1,927.9	7,840.0	1,727.0	23,986.4	2,099.4	634,125.2
Norway	1,589.3	6,945.8	1,318.6	1,609.5	313.3	1,377.3	475.8	8,388.8	3,989.9	146,093.3
Portugal	3,998.2	2,457.8	403.8	247.2	98.4	944.0	356.4	2,443.1	197.7	53,145.2
Spain	15,956.4	9,303.6	1,749.2	2,725.6	1,575.7	12,452.2	1,758.2	10,150.7	991.4	262,491.0
Sweden	7,528.1	12,469.5	2,061.2	3,292.7	2,128.8	3,622.4	1,175.7	12,797.4	1,632.4	199,601.4
Switzerland	8,773.8	22,764.3	5,606.3	4,514.8	1,838.8	4,660.0	1,555.2	16,747.9	2,412.9	189,664.2
Turkey	19,196.4	6,179.0	246.8	1,039.0	342.8	982.5	229.9	4,217.4	369.8	133,222.4
United Kingdom	30,909.1	43,428.6	7,562.5	7,552.4	5,715.6	7,355.7	2,153.1	62,600.2	6,563.9	480,967.9
Eastern Europe										
Albania	3.5	66.5	0.8	61.2	0.2	8.9	2.3	9.2	2.0	1,030.9
Belarus	289.2	1,642.2	38.4	484.6	12.6	482.8	372.8	348.5	10.5	34,701.6
Bosnia-Herzegovina	46.2	32.6	3.4	24.8	2.6	1.3	0.1	24.1	5.0	5,700.3
Bulgaria	766.8	781.5	36.1	95.5	14.7	233.9	32.1	428.2	75.7	23,983.1
Croatia	316.4	215.3	68.3	19.8	15.2	100.8	8.1	347.1	23.7	16,641.4
Czech Republic	2,332.5	3,283.8	500.7	694.1	273.7	740.0	226.5	2,367.0	156.3	199,595.1
Estonia	514.5	295.3	57.4	88.3	5.1	46.6	27.5	455.2	93.4	17,464.0
Georgia	60.7	336.2	0.5	13.2	3.4	27.1	11.1	172.0	61.5	1,931.1
Hungary	2,942.7	2,883.1	403.3	1,030.5	154.6	419.3	90.6	2,232.5	177.8	149,801.8
Latvia	128.9	201.9	39.4	22.9	5.1	41.7	1.7	112.1	22.4	16,811.8
Lithuania	257.4	666.7	17.0	21.0	11.2	60.2	3.2	439.6	76.0	31,093.5
Macedonia	16.1	21.3	5.8	8.9	3.6	0.1		69.7	8.1	5,034.6
Moldova	28.2	45.6	3.3	1.3	0.5	7.2	1.6	22.5	2.3	2,938.6
Poland	2,374.1	3,146.1	297.8	996.3	220.0	1,208.6	277.6	2,079.4	519.6	206,887.0
Romania	2,049.1	1,216.0	116.9	214.9	19.9	408.3	70.0	814.0	56.3	57,110.0
Russia	10,946.6	54,062.8	8,946.7	17,396.2	65.6	3,061.9	853.9	16,597.7	1,187.3	460,398.1
Serbia and Montenegro	167.9	13.1		6.1	4.1	3.2	0.7		12.8	378.1
Slovakia	532.7	1,044.0	128.6	444.3	109.8	248.4	65.2	1,447.1	118.8	107,653.7
Slovenia	713.5	466.1	33.5	94.8	48.1	113.6	30.1	460.6	59.7	42,604.1
Ukraine	7,699.4	6,325.5	142.6	605.4	25.7	1,086.8	187.5	1,199.5	109.7	72,150.4

Source: International Monetary Fund (IMF), Direction of Trade Statistics
Notes: US$ totals in this table may differ from the totals given for Exports (fob) by Commodity and Total Exports (fob)

Exports

Table 13.12

Exports (fob) by Destination 2007 (% Analysis)
% of total exports

	France	Germany	Italy	Nether-lands	Sweden	UK	Total EU	Norway	Switzerland	Russia	Poland
Western Europe											
Austria	2.39	19.86	5.89	1.20	0.73	2.38	48.36	0.32	2.89	1.63	1.80
Belgium	15.02	17.60	4.68	10.76	1.35	6.87	68.82	0.38	1.58	0.94	1.29
Cyprus	0.84	6.50	2.86	1.60	0.73	14.11	58.46	0.24	0.43	1.88	0.26
Denmark	4.12	14.85	2.97	4.10	12.43	6.83	59.98	4.86	0.72	1.55	1.96
Finland	2.88	8.79	2.27	4.48	8.64	4.69	45.80	2.52	0.76	8.28	1.91
France		13.24	7.93	3.64	1.18	7.25	57.44	0.36	2.29	1.24	1.39
Germany	7.31		5.07	4.84	1.69	5.52	48.79	0.59	2.85	2.19	2.81
Gibraltar											
Greece	2.60	7.16	6.70	1.26	0.64	3.38	40.48	0.12	0.46	1.30	0.85
Iceland	2.46	12.76	0.63	20.33	0.68	12.65	71.40	3.66	1.21	1.30	0.60
Ireland	5.56	7.03	3.40	3.75	1.08	17.87	60.45	0.63	3.50	0.34	0.64
Italy	9.13	10.28		1.88	0.88	4.63	47.96	0.35	3.00	2.14	1.94
Liechtenstein											
Luxembourg	14.01	18.16	6.38	4.60	2.79	6.11	75.30	0.31	0.78	0.77	1.61
Malta	11.94	12.98	3.80	0.52	0.34	9.46	46.11	0.18	0.35	0.10	0.67
Monaco											
Netherlands	7.36	21.24	4.39		1.54	7.95	67.84	0.69	1.08	1.50	1.55
Norway	7.49	11.49	2.56	9.56	6.10	24.53	75.43		0.63	0.64	1.10
Portugal	11.88	12.47	3.92	3.21	1.16	5.71	72.07	0.26	0.68	0.37	0.68
Spain	17.18	9.87	7.79	2.98	0.87	6.90	63.55	0.53	1.25	1.07	1.20
Sweden	4.26	8.84	2.67	4.29		6.04	51.67	7.96	0.77	1.69	2.08
Switzerland	7.58	18.41	7.90	2.73	0.84	4.62	56.16	0.37		1.29	0.95
Turkey	4.49	9.00	5.61	2.27	0.66	6.48	45.34	0.28	0.70	3.55	1.08
United Kingdom	7.47	10.19	3.79	6.23	2.02		52.72	1.14	1.62	1.17	0.98
Eastern Europe											
Albania	0.56	2.66	55.66	3.21	2.08	0.58	75.95	0.07	0.10	0.40	0.11
Belarus	0.22	2.11	0.52	12.48	0.22	4.40	30.74	0.22	0.03	25.61	3.53
Bosnia-Herzegovina	1.13	7.36	8.90	0.48	0.45	0.28	39.97	0.12	0.27	0.08	0.69
Bulgaria	3.07	7.92	7.85	0.92	0.46	1.93	46.73	0.10	0.47	1.88	1.26
Croatia	1.65	7.40	14.08	0.76	0.88	1.44	43.89	0.08	0.79	0.94	0.71
Czech Republic	3.29	18.97	2.99	2.22	1.08	3.07	52.37	0.32	0.90	1.44	3.70
Estonia	0.86	3.30	0.67	1.70	8.34	1.77	44.08	2.13	0.21	5.59	0.91
Georgia	2.07	2.98	2.82	0.60	0.01	4.31	27.00	0.01	0.05	3.86	0.19
Hungary	3.01	17.95	3.60	1.85	0.70	2.86	50.35	0.17	0.71	2.05	2.66
Latvia	0.74	4.12	0.72	0.99	3.66	3.22	35.85	1.21	0.33	6.39	1.70
Lithuania	2.01	5.78	1.26	1.64	2.10	2.52	35.72	1.27	0.15	8.30	3.46
Macedonia	0.41	10.40	7.24	1.26	0.33	1.25	46.14	0.07	0.25	0.69	0.15
Moldova	1.00	5.08	5.99	0.56	0.43	0.95	30.91	0.05	0.09	11.67	3.74
Poland	4.13	17.55	4.49	2.59	2.18	4.03	53.50	1.22	0.48	3.14	
Romania	5.46	11.96	12.12	1.46	0.45	2.91	50.89	0.72	0.54	1.03	1.52
Russia	2.66	7.11	4.18	5.67	0.86	2.10	39.06	0.31	0.83		2.84
Serbia and Montenegro	0.00	0.00	0.00	0.00	0.00		0.00	0.00	0.00	17.13	0.00
Slovakia	3.65	11.57	3.45	1.93	0.82	2.60	46.95	0.14	0.45	1.23	3.37
Slovenia	4.18	13.19	8.81	1.08	0.59	1.71	49.05	0.16	0.62	3.12	2.32
Ukraine	0.67	2.32	4.14	0.84	0.10	0.27	21.40	0.12	0.13	15.35	2.12

Source: International Monetary Fund (IMF), Direction of Trade Statistics

Exports (fob) by Destination 2007 (% Analysis) *(continued)*

% of total exports

	Africa & Middle East	Asia/ Pacific	of which: Japan	China	Australasia	Latin America	of which: Brazil	USA	Canada	Total, including Others
Western Europe										
Austria	2.04	3.47	0.63	0.93	0.43	0.83	0.28	3.26	0.50	100.00
Belgium	3.88	4.97	0.70	0.96	0.40	1.12	0.43	5.16	0.61	100.00
Cyprus	11.83	5.46	1.42	0.74	0.41	0.10	0.00	0.61	0.24	100.00
Denmark	2.11	5.69	1.57	1.45	0.72	1.18	0.30	5.18	0.80	100.00
Finland	5.37	7.60	1.44	2.65	0.67	1.59	0.59	5.13	0.62	100.00
France	7.34	7.47	1.27	2.00	0.57	2.01	0.68	5.47	0.58	100.00
Germany	3.12	6.52	1.02	2.33	0.51	1.62	0.53	5.69	0.49	100.00
Gibraltar										100.00
Greece	4.30	1.91	0.46	0.40	0.28	0.72	0.13	2.58	0.27	100.00
Iceland	2.82	5.68	4.13	0.75	0.14	0.28	0.08	6.94	0.46	100.00
Ireland	2.34	7.11	1.87	1.39	0.97	1.26	0.18	17.06	0.42	100.00
Italy	6.90	5.84	0.96	1.41	0.71	2.60	0.58	5.43	0.62	100.00
Liechtenstein										
Luxembourg	1.02	2.15	0.18	1.02	0.16	0.64	0.18	1.56	0.33	100.00
Malta	6.53	27.31	4.60	1.21	0.25	0.99	0.26	10.72	0.50	100.00
Monaco										
Netherlands	3.51	3.80	0.57	0.81	0.30	1.24	0.27	3.78	0.33	100.00
Norway	1.09	4.75	0.90	1.10	0.21	0.94	0.33	5.74	2.73	100.00
Portugal	7.52	4.62	0.76	0.47	0.19	1.78	0.67	4.60	0.37	100.00
Spain	6.08	3.54	0.67	1.04	0.60	4.74	0.67	3.87	0.38	100.00
Sweden	3.77	6.25	1.03	1.65	1.07	1.81	0.59	6.41	0.82	100.00
Switzerland	4.63	12.00	2.96	2.38	0.97	2.46	0.82	8.83	1.27	100.00
Turkey	14.41	4.64	0.19	0.78	0.26	0.74	0.17	3.17	0.28	100.00
United Kingdom	6.43	9.03	1.57	1.57	1.19	1.53	0.45	13.02	1.36	100.00
Eastern Europe										
Albania	0.34	6.45	0.08	5.94	0.02	0.86	0.22	0.89	0.19	100.00
Belarus	0.83	4.73	0.11	1.40	0.04	1.39	1.07	1.00	0.03	100.00
Bosnia-Herzegovina	0.81	0.57	0.06	0.44	0.05	0.02	0.00	0.42	0.09	100.00
Bulgaria	3.20	3.26	0.15	0.40	0.06	0.98	0.13	1.79	0.32	100.00
Croatia	1.90	1.29	0.41	0.12	0.09	0.61	0.05	2.09	0.14	100.00
Czech Republic	1.17	1.65	0.25	0.35	0.14	0.37	0.11	1.19	0.08	100.00
Estonia	2.95	1.69	0.33	0.51	0.03	0.27	0.16	2.61	0.53	100.00
Georgia	3.15	17.41	0.03	0.68	0.17	1.40	0.57	8.91	3.18	100.00
Hungary	1.96	1.92	0.27	0.69	0.10	0.28	0.06	1.49	0.12	100.00
Latvia	0.77	1.20	0.23	0.14	0.03	0.25	0.01	0.67	0.13	100.00
Lithuania	0.83	2.14	0.05	0.07	0.04	0.19	0.01	1.41	0.24	100.00
Macedonia	0.32	0.42	0.12	0.18	0.07	0.00	0.00	1.38	0.16	100.00
Moldova	0.96	1.55	0.11	0.04	0.02	0.25	0.06	0.77	0.08	100.00
Poland	1.15	1.52	0.14	0.48	0.11	0.58	0.13	1.01	0.25	100.00
Romania	3.59	2.13	0.20	0.38	0.03	0.71	0.12	1.43	0.10	100.00
Russia	2.38	11.74	1.94	3.78	0.01	0.67	0.19	3.61	0.26	100.00
Serbia and Montenegro	44.41	3.46	0.00	1.62	1.09	0.84	0.19		3.37	100.00
Slovakia	0.49	0.97	0.12	0.41	0.10	0.23	0.06	1.34	0.11	100.00
Slovenia	1.67	1.09	0.08	0.22	0.11	0.27	0.07	1.08	0.14	100.00
Ukraine	10.67	8.77	0.20	0.84	0.04	1.51	0.26	1.66	0.15	100.00

Source: *International Monetary Fund (IMF), Direction of Trade Statistics*

Exports

Table 13.13

Exports (fob) by Commodity: SITC Classification 2007

US$ million

	Food and live animals	Beverages and tobacco	Crude materials excluding fuels	Mineral fuels etc	Oils and fats
Western Europe					
Austria	6,042.3	2,610.1	3,802.6	8,577.4	110.1
Belgium	27,126.6	2,550.9	10,759.3	33,370.9	1,088.7
Cyprus	223.9	61.9	76.5	278.6	1.7
Denmark	15,013.0	989.3	3,569.5	10,563.7	521.1
Finland	1,262.0	153.8	4,941.0	4,525.0	101.4
France	35,513.2	14,472.2	11,619.4	22,530.1	1,175.9
Germany	37,680.8	7,845.0	20,583.6	30,288.7	1,625.0
Gibraltar					
Greece	3,217.4	662.1	1,395.3	3,043.5	669.1
Iceland	1,804.2	5.6	49.9	93.0	40.1
Ireland	9,070.7	1,775.6	1,947.0	791.8	23.9
Italy	19,436.4	6,052.8	4,822.2	15,483.1	2,224.7
Liechtenstein					
Luxembourg	699.9	231.7	300.0	127.2	1.1
Malta	163.1	14.6	12.7	48.1	
Monaco					
Netherlands	40,382.0	7,814.5	19,940.8	56,400.0	2,873.7
Norway	6,362.0	86.7	1,319.2	90,799.0	131.1
Portugal	2,149.9	1,393.0	1,851.8	2,709.6	223.1
Spain	26,815.2	3,576.1	4,792.5	10,182.5	2,825.6
Sweden	4,580.0	833.0	9,263.4	9,523.6	192.7
Switzerland	3,202.3	1,125.8	1,751.0	4,074.6	24.6
Turkey	5,075.7	542.5	965.7	151.9	388.6
United Kingdom	12,733.1	8,030.5	8,525.1	48,234.5	539.3
Eastern Europe					
Albania	36.5	11.2	135.4	39.0	0.6
Belarus	1,518.4	84.4	468.6	9,174.5	33.4
Bosnia-Herzegovina	147.8	23.7	500.3	307.5	15.1
Bulgaria	1,169.2	319.7	1,157.5	1,947.6	54.1
Croatia	1,123.5	195.2	699.0	1,910.2	19.2
Czech Republic	2,870.7	499.5	2,569.3	2,926.3	91.3
Estonia	511.0	163.9	867.0	1,822.5	31.3
Georgia	115.9	125.2	243.5	30.7	0.0
Hungary	3,963.8	191.7	1,177.0	1,797.1	142.8
Latvia	636.1	168.0	1,110.9	292.1	13.7
Lithuania	1,880.1	274.0	655.1	3,449.9	34.4
Macedonia	209.0	216.1	125.0	264.0	2.2
Moldova	220.0	195.9	62.6	3.9	34.6
Poland	10,350.0	910.0	2,695.1	5,229.9	224.0
Romania	776.4	65.3	2,037.9	3,576.1	71.9
Russia	4,228.8	614.0	12,530.1	168,597.0	496.9
Serbia and Montenegro	833.0	101.3	281.9	111.1	90.5
Slovakia	1,907.7	71.9	1,287.4	3,553.3	78.8
Slovenia	550.9	78.6	586.0	651.0	10.3
Ukraine	3,116.7	526.0	2,819.0	2,450.9	1,051.0

Source: United Nations, UN Trade Statistics

Exports (fob) by Commodity: SITC Classification 2007 *(continued)*

US$ million

	Chemicals	Basic manufactures	Machinery and transport equipment	Miscellaneous manufactured goods	Others	Total
Western Europe						
Austria	13,893.6	31,402.9	59,745.5	16,030.1	4,712.3	146,926.8
Belgium	112,288.8	78,905.2	90,492.3	33,319.8	10,193.0	400,095.5
Cyprus	198.7	61.3	456.7	128.8	0.3	1,488.5
Denmark	11,093.1	9,769.6	26,412.9	14,449.5	2,840.9	95,222.7
Finland	6,283.7	26,240.1	35,397.3	3,990.2	1,095.4	83,989.9
France	79,436.0	71,014.3	210,955.9	53,903.0	11,193.1	511,813.1
Germany	166,005.5	166,806.3	581,432.9	113,703.3	80,756.5	1,206,727.7
Gibraltar						
Greece	2,845.2	4,443.1	2,778.1	2,508.2	627.4	22,189.4
Iceland	92.7	985.7	385.9	117.7	26.9	3,601.6
Ireland	54,745.9	2,093.8	29,370.3	10,977.8	3,940.8	114,737.8
Italy	45,778.1	92,448.5	162,649.5	76,990.0	11,077.0	436,962.4
Liechtenstein						
Luxembourg	963.9	7,400.1	3,866.1	1,368.1	677.0	15,635.1
Malta	193.0	148.5	1,821.0	475.5	22.4	2,898.8
Monaco						
Netherlands	69,336.0	39,734.4	124,000.0	39,351.1	1,750.0	401,582.7
Norway	3,019.9	12,710.1	10,529.9	2,860.0	4,419.3	132,237.2
Portugal	3,060.0	9,699.9	14,778.0	6,981.2	3,416.0	46,262.6
Spain	25,890.6	37,237.3	89,611.3	21,216.0	3,339.9	225,487.1
Sweden	17,560.7	30,214.6	65,121.6	12,753.9	9,337.5	159,381.0
Switzerland	56,756.0	17,818.5	38,414.2	34,582.9	201.0	157,951.0
Turkey	1,551.4	14,315.3	8,054.9	15,891.4	44,311.3	91,248.6
United Kingdom	69,416.3	52,827.7	204,231.6	50,397.3	21,964.8	476,900.1
Eastern Europe						
Albania	2.6	109.1	33.8	485.0		853.0
Belarus	2,027.9	3,722.5	4,354.4	1,291.3	325.1	23,000.3
Bosnia-Herzegovina	380.1	1,312.2	533.2	734.9	0.2	3,955.0
Bulgaria	1,332.2	4,868.1	2,616.2	3,721.6	535.9	17,722.1
Croatia	1,016.0	1,692.5	3,317.2	1,610.0	1.6	11,584.3
Czech Republic	6,239.5	21,592.8	55,437.1	11,058.5	1,844.2	105,129.1
Estonia	500.3	1,653.6	3,221.9	1,424.3	491.8	10,687.4
Georgia	93.3	160.3	221.9	38.8	57.3	1,086.9
Hungary	6,404.8	7,715.3	49,003.7	6,295.3	4,581.3	81,272.8
Latvia	495.0	1,623.0	1,028.4	780.1	241.0	6,388.2
Lithuania	1,423.0	1,727.9	3,540.1	2,440.0	105.5	15,529.9
Macedonia	107.8	955.1	125.3	621.9	4.1	2,630.6
Moldova	26.5	167.5	62.6	330.0	0.0	1,103.7
Poland	8,880.0	28,784.2	50,562.1	15,450.1	1,470.0	124,555.2
Romania	2,072.7	7,141.0	11,897.0	8,670.0	16.7	36,324.9
Russia	12,905.0	49,647.2	14,020.1	2,125.9	82,293.6	347,458.6
Serbia and Montenegro	568.0	1,859.9	553.1	622.0	28.9	5,049.8
Slovakia	2,783.2	12,196.6	21,651.7	4,886.6	81.5	48,498.7
Slovenia	3,150.0	5,955.4	8,460.0	2,912.0	51.2	22,405.3
Ukraine	3,982.9	20,449.0	6,208.3	1,652.3	450.4	42,706.6

Source: United Nations, UN Trade Statistics
Notes: US$ totals in this table may differ from the totals given for Exports (fob) by Destination and Total Exports (fob)

Exports

Table 13.14

Exports (fob) by Commodity: SITC Classification 2007 (% Analysis)
% of total exports

	Food and live animals	Beverages and tobacco	Crude materials excluding fuels	Mineral fuels etc	Oils and fats
Western Europe					
Austria	4.11	1.78	2.59	5.84	0.07
Belgium	6.78	0.64	2.69	8.34	0.27
Cyprus	15.04	4.16	5.14	18.72	0.12
Denmark	15.77	1.04	3.75	11.09	0.55
Finland	1.50	0.18	5.88	5.39	0.12
France	6.94	2.83	2.27	4.40	0.23
Germany	3.12	0.65	1.71	2.51	0.13
Gibraltar					
Greece	14.50	2.98	6.29	13.72	3.02
Iceland	50.09	0.15	1.38	2.58	1.11
Ireland	7.91	1.55	1.70	0.69	0.02
Italy	4.45	1.39	1.10	3.54	0.51
Liechtenstein					
Luxembourg	4.48	1.48	1.92	0.81	0.01
Malta	5.63	0.50	0.44	1.66	
Monaco					
Netherlands	10.06	1.95	4.97	14.04	0.72
Norway	4.81	0.07	1.00	68.66	0.10
Portugal	4.65	3.01	4.00	5.86	0.48
Spain	11.89	1.59	2.13	4.52	1.25
Sweden	2.87	0.52	5.81	5.98	0.12
Switzerland	2.03	0.71	1.11	2.58	0.02
Turkey	5.56	0.59	1.06	0.17	0.43
United Kingdom	2.67	1.68	1.79	10.11	0.11
Eastern Europe					
Albania	4.28	1.31	15.87	4.57	0.07
Belarus	6.60	0.37	2.04	39.89	0.15
Bosnia-Herzegovina	3.74	0.60	12.65	7.78	0.38
Bulgaria	6.60	1.80	6.53	10.99	0.31
Croatia	9.70	1.68	6.03	16.49	0.17
Czech Republic	2.73	0.48	2.44	2.78	0.09
Estonia	4.78	1.53	8.11	17.05	0.29
Georgia	10.66	11.51	22.40	2.82	0.00
Hungary	4.88	0.24	1.45	2.21	0.18
Latvia	9.96	2.63	17.39	4.57	0.21
Lithuania	12.11	1.76	4.22	22.21	0.22
Macedonia	7.95	8.22	4.75	10.04	0.08
Moldova	19.94	17.75	5.67	0.35	3.13
Poland	8.31	0.73	2.16	4.20	0.18
Romania	2.14	0.18	5.61	9.84	0.20
Russia	1.22	0.18	3.61	48.52	0.14
Serbia and Montenegro	16.50	2.01	5.58	2.20	1.79
Slovakia	3.93	0.15	2.65	7.33	0.16
Slovenia	2.46	0.35	2.62	2.91	0.05
Ukraine	7.30	1.23	6.60	5.74	2.46

Source: *United Nations, UN Trade Statistics*

Exports (fob) by Commodity: SITC Classification 2007 (% Analysis) *(continued)*

% of total exports

	Chemicals	Basic manufactures	Machinery and transport equipment	Miscellaneous manufactured goods	Others	Total
Western Europe						
Austria	9.46	21.37	40.66	10.91	3.21	100.00
Belgium	28.07	19.72	22.62	8.33	2.55	100.00
Cyprus	13.35	4.12	30.69	8.66	0.02	100.00
Denmark	11.65	10.26	27.74	15.17	2.98	100.00
Finland	7.48	31.24	42.14	4.75	1.30	100.00
France	15.52	13.88	41.22	10.53	2.19	100.00
Germany	13.76	13.82	48.18	9.42	6.69	100.00
Gibraltar						
Greece	12.82	20.02	12.52	11.30	2.83	100.00
Iceland	2.57	27.37	10.72	3.27	0.75	100.00
Ireland	47.71	1.82	25.60	9.57	3.43	100.00
Italy	10.48	21.16	37.22	17.62	2.53	100.00
Liechtenstein						
Luxembourg	6.17	47.33	24.73	8.75	4.33	100.00
Malta	6.66	5.12	62.82	16.40	0.77	100.00
Monaco						
Netherlands	17.27	9.89	30.88	9.80	0.44	100.00
Norway	2.28	9.61	7.96	2.16	3.34	100.00
Portugal	6.61	20.97	31.94	15.09	7.38	100.00
Spain	11.48	16.51	39.74	9.41	1.48	100.00
Sweden	11.02	18.96	40.86	8.00	5.86	100.00
Switzerland	35.93	11.28	24.32	21.89	0.13	100.00
Turkey	1.70	15.69	8.83	17.42	48.56	100.00
United Kingdom	14.56	11.08	42.82	10.57	4.61	100.00
Eastern Europe						
Albania	0.30	12.79	3.96	56.85		100.00
Belarus	8.82	16.18	18.93	5.61	1.41	100.00
Bosnia-Herzegovina	9.61	33.18	13.48	18.58	0.01	100.00
Bulgaria	7.52	27.47	14.76	21.00	3.02	100.00
Croatia	8.77	14.61	28.64	13.90	0.01	100.00
Czech Republic	5.94	20.54	52.73	10.52	1.75	100.00
Estonia	4.68	15.47	30.15	13.33	4.60	100.00
Georgia	8.59	14.75	20.42	3.57	5.27	100.00
Hungary	7.88	9.49	60.30	7.75	5.64	100.00
Latvia	7.75	25.41	16.10	12.21	3.77	100.00
Lithuania	9.16	11.13	22.80	15.71	0.68	100.00
Macedonia	4.10	36.31	4.76	23.64	0.16	100.00
Moldova	2.40	15.18	5.67	29.90	0.00	100.00
Poland	7.13	23.11	40.59	12.40	1.18	100.00
Romania	5.71	19.66	32.75	23.87	0.05	100.00
Russia	3.71	14.29	4.04	0.61	23.68	100.00
Serbia and Montenegro	11.25	36.83	10.95	12.32	0.57	100.00
Slovakia	5.74	25.15	44.64	10.08	0.17	100.00
Slovenia	14.06	26.58	37.76	13.00	0.23	100.00
Ukraine	9.33	47.88	14.54	3.87	1.05	100.00

Source: United Nations, UN Trade Statistics

Trade Balance

Table 13.15

Trade Balance 1980-2007 (US$)

US$ million

	1980	1985	1990	1995	1996	1997	1998	1999
Western Europe								
Austria	-6,955	-3,747	-7,953	-8,743	-9,513	-6,186	-5,440	-5,431
Belgium				16,166	11,752	14,621	14,409	14,365
Cyprus	-671	-771	-1,611	-2,465	-2,587	-2,597	-2,624	-2,623
Denmark	-2,591	-1,155	3,789	5,750	6,476	4,712	2,509	5,880
Finland	-1,484	385	-430	11,459	9,170	9,532	10,662	10,224
France	-18,859	-6,666	-17,856	5,298	5,917	17,822	15,400	7,572
Germany	4,858	25,445	63,951	59,531	65,415	66,811	71,979	69,331
Gibraltar	-107	-83						
Greece	-5,395	-5,596	-11,672	-15,834	-17,724	-16,771	-18,656	-18,244
Iceland	-81	-90	-89	48	-393	-140	-438	-499
Ireland	-2,755	342	3,065	11,571	12,771	14,287	19,846	24,025
Italy	-22,637	-10,976	-11,482	27,958	43,947	30,136	27,255	14,852
Liechtenstein								
Luxembourg	-607	-314	-1,291	-1,998	-2,456	-2,379	-2,315	-3,150
Malta	-455	-359	-831	-1,029	-1,064	-922	-834	-863
Monaco								
Netherlands	-3,472	4,750	5,300	19,402	16,778	16,775	13,627	10,499
Norway	1,616	4,430	6,828	9,024	14,030	12,833	2,926	11,289
Portugal	-4,670	-1,967	-8,843	-10,100	-10,572	-11,091	-13,722	-14,598
Spain	-13,358	-5,716	-32,033	-22,273	-19,786	-18,352	-23,921	-34,472
Sweden	-2,533	1,913	3,293	15,061	17,972	17,271	16,379	16,057
Switzerland	-6,709	-3,264	-5,897	1,055	1,735	1,429	1,554	684
Turkey	-4,999	-3,386	-9,343	-14,072	-20,402	-22,298	-18,947	-14,084
United Kingdom	-5,408	-8,150	-39,144	-23,291	-25,330	-25,524	-42,187	-49,766
Eastern Europe								
Albania				-511	-726	-507	-634	-803
Belarus				-760	-1,288	-1,388	-1,480	-765
Bosnia-Herzegovina				-500	-1,146	-1,362	-1,768	-1,913
Bulgaria		-318	112	-302	-259	100	-755	-1,490
Croatia			-1,168	-2,834	-3,140	-5,120	-3,758	-3,496
Czech Republic				-4,699	-7,451	-6,091	-3,919	-3,241
Estonia				-737	-1,130	-1,390	-1,415	-1,046
Georgia				-333	-548	-751	-691	-452
Hungary	-573	314	927	-2,578	-2,427	-2,126	-2,687	-2,973
Latvia				-513	-876	-1,049	-1,380	-1,222
Lithuania				-974	-1,228	-1,824	-2,129	-1,873
Macedonia				-515	-479	-542	-604	-585
Moldova				-102	-249	-282	-380	-112
Poland	-2,499	-366	5,214	-6,155	-12,697	-16,556	-19,303	-18,506
Romania	-2,634	900	-4,068	-2,368	-3,351	-2,849	-3,521	-1,887
Russia				14,050	15,684	9,932	11,068	32,078
Serbia and Montenegro								
Slovakia				-630	-2,609	-2,520	-3,004	-1,662
Slovenia			-609	-1,175	-1,111	-985	-1,062	-1,537
Ukraine				-2,356	-3,202	-2,896	-2,039	-264

Source: *Euromonitor International from International Monetary Fund (IMF), International Financial Statistics*

Trade Balance 1980-2007 (US$) *(continued)*

US$ million

	2000	2001	2002	2003	2004	2005	2006	2007
Western Europe								
Austria	-4,818	-3,998	316	-2,338	-1,621	-2,228	-569	541
Belgium	10,881	11,644	17,743	20,647	21,215	17,099	15,030	18,340
Cyprus	-2,895	-2,947	-3,094	-3,455	-4,577	-4,979	-5,798	-7,432
Denmark	6,024	6,944	7,417	9,051	8,734	9,303	6,613	4,020
Finland	11,580	10,686	11,023	10,911	10,234	6,765	7,839	8,334
France	-10,912	-4,791	-152	-4,780	-18,157	-45,482	-53,222	-74,380
Germany	54,761	85,388	125,497	147,066	193,537	197,437	199,732	269,410
Gibraltar								
Greece	-18,474	-20,444	-20,849	-31,180	-36,564	-34,306	-38,940	-51,628
Iceland	-699	-232	-46	-404	-657	-1,614	-1,844	-1,756
Ireland	25,617	31,709	35,958	39,107	42,785	40,441	21,196	37,011
Italy	1,863	8,124	7,601	2,064	-1,724	-11,874	-24,624	-9,989
Liechtenstein								
Luxembourg	-2,769	-2,913	-3,102	-3,712	-4,651	-4,868	-5,259	-6,037
Malta	-957	-768	-614	-931	-1,197	-1,432	-1,371	-1,525
Monaco								
Netherlands	14,496	20,608	25,714	30,829	34,037	39,241	41,074	55,439
Norway	25,666	26,236	24,812	27,994	33,665	47,146	57,098	58,237
Portugal	-14,910	-14,970	-12,785	-10,244	-16,196	-21,224	-22,712	-26,129
Spain	-39,545	-38,452	-39,994	-52,517	-75,484	-96,635	-112,692	-136,038
Sweden	14,407	13,882	15,275	18,208	22,513	19,304	20,252	17,802
Switzerland	-1,236	996	4,982	5,143	7,495	6,313	9,648	11,626
Turkey	-26,728	-10,065	-15,101	-19,061	-34,685	-27,070	-51,672	-61,676
United Kingdom	-52,832	-53,624	-59,139	-76,527	-110,084	-111,647	-119,117	-185,805
Eastern Europe								
Albania	-832	-1,020	-1,164	-1,416	-1,703	-1,960	-2,261	-3,124
Belarus	-1,320	-836	-1,071	-1,612	-2,717	-729	-2,618	-4,418
Bosnia-Herzegovina	-1,615	-1,541	-1,893	-2,046	-2,188	-1,487	-681	-1,114
Bulgaria	-1,696	-2,148	-2,238	-3,361	-4,536	-6,423	-8,168	-11,511
Croatia	-3,455	-4,481	-5,818	-8,022	-8,565	-9,788	-11,112	-13,465
Czech Republic	-4,857	-4,908	-4,287	-5,092	-4,426	1,645	1,707	4,251
Estonia	-1,069	-986	-1,363	-1,942	-2,400	-2,512	-3,129	-4,104
Georgia	-387	-436	-450	-680	-1,199	-1,624	-2,685	-3,977
Hungary	-3,939	-3,195	-3,276	-5,070	-4,744	-3,605	-2,990	-412
Latvia	-1,319	-1,504	-1,769	-2,350	-3,066	-3,483	-5,535	-7,287
Lithuania	-1,671	-1,781	-2,294	-2,698	-3,079	-3,729	-5,259	-7,283
Macedonia	-771	-536	-880	-939	-1,256	-1,187	-1,355	-1,875
Moldova	-305	-325	-395	-614	-793	-1,202	-1,642	-2,348
Poland	-17,289	-14,183	-14,103	-14,467	-14,117	-11,556	-15,063	-23,181
Romania	-2,688	-4,170	-3,986	-6,384	-9,179	-12,733	-18,770	-29,560
Russia	56,440	42,744	40,238	52,252	76,087	105,821	122,765	109,811
Serbia and Montenegro								
Slovakia	-1,523	-2,860	-2,983	-1,794	-2,864	-4,171	-5,370	-4,369
Slovenia	-1,384	-895	-576	-1,086	-1,692	-1,730	-2,029	-2,928
Ukraine	617	490	980	47	3,669	-1,908	-6,671	-11,322

Source: Euromonitor International from International Monetary Fund (IMF), International Financial Statistics

Trade Balance

Table 13.16

Trade Balance by Quarter 2006-2008
US$ million

	2006 1st Quarter	2006 2nd Quarter	2006 3rd Quarter	2006 4th Quarter	2007 1st Quarter	2007 2nd Quarter	2007 3rd Quarter	2007 4th Quarter	2008 1st Quarter	2008 2nd Quarter
Western Europe										
Austria	-80.0	-214.4	-757.3	482.7	-25.1	1,041.7	-1,204.6	729.0	412.6	
Belgium	1,821.7	5,652.4	4,128.1	3,427.9	6,561.6	5,707.4	4,938.5	1,132.5	566.3	
Cyprus	-1,252.8	-1,516.1	-1,527.3	-1,501.6	-1,478.4	-1,835.5	-1,968.5	-2,150.1		
Denmark	1,600.2	1,614.5	2,040.6	1,357.5	901.1	1,050.3	1,263.3	805.6	1,061.2	1,538.2
Finland	1,055.0	2,862.0	1,603.9	2,318.4	1,360.0	3,062.9	2,067.6	1,843.4	1,513.9	3,023.2
France	-12,961.9	-12,910.6	-13,867.2	-13,482.2	-14,221.2	-17,378.2	-19,503.2	-23,277.3	-22,036.3	-26,056.3
Germany	46,335.5	45,541.1	49,302.7	58,552.7	64,021.0	65,806.0	68,873.0	70,710.0	75,827.0	
Gibraltar										
Greece	-9,220.3	-10,487.7	-8,222.8	-11,009.7	-12,604.7	-12,650.5	-12,687.7	-13,685.5	-13,441.0	
Iceland	-327.3	-495.8	-533.4	-487.9	-244.7	-628.6	-582.6	-300.0	-375.9	-121.7
Ireland	8,478.7	10,364.5	10,489.5	-8,136.7	8,265.3	10,775.2	10,354.8	7,616.1	8,905.9	
Italy	-10,147.4	-5,399.9	-5,345.9	-3,730.9	-6,242.5	-810.5	-535.5	-2,400.5	-7,656.4	
Liechtenstein										
Luxembourg	-1,161.8	-1,447.5	-1,270.3	-1,380.5	-1,325.7	-1,590.6	-1,551.5	-1,569.3	-1,413.7	
Malta	-338.2	-303.8	-384.5	-344.4	-312.4	-349.2	-398.4	-465.2		
Monaco										
Netherlands	10,804.2	9,857.1	8,245.6	12,167.1	13,737.1	11,656.7	12,739.8	17,305.4	15,267.6	
Norway	14,501.5	15,929.8	14,196.3	12,470.6	13,212.0	13,745.3	13,961.8	17,317.4	20,794.7	22,557.4
Portugal	-5,535.3	-5,604.1	-5,560.7	-6,011.4	-5,096.5	-6,373.7	-6,507.6	-8,151.1	-7,661.1	-9,029.2
Spain	-25,381.6	-27,779.8	-29,183.8	-30,346.8	-29,249.1	-32,217.1	-34,216.5	-40,355.2	-40,281.9	
Sweden	5,536.1	5,648.4	3,903.6	5,163.9	5,530.6	4,751.2	2,670.1	4,850.1	6,313.4	4,737.1
Switzerland	1,653.8	2,250.5	3,075.3	2,668.3	2,657.1	2,782.9	3,300.5	2,885.4	3,655.2	5,668.0
Turkey	-11,192.9	-14,725.8	-14,048.4	-11,705.1	-10,895.0	-15,789.0	-17,585.0	-17,407.0	-16,013.0	-21,006.0
United Kingdom	-27,085.7	-16,470.3	-36,906.3	-38,654.6	-43,263.2	-44,806.9	-50,201.7	-47,533.2	-46,209.5	
Eastern Europe										
Albania	-476.5	-555.9	-566.6	-666.9	-625.9	-728.4	-780.6	-988.7	-849.8	-971.6
Belarus	-171.1	-756.8	-469.1	-1,220.5	-859.3	-978.5	-902.8	-1,677.2	-730.1	
Bosnia-Herzegovina										
Bulgaria	-1,519.1	-1,729.2	-2,087.0	-2,832.8	-2,341.7	-2,513.5	-2,847.5	-3,808.5	-3,105.9	-4,428.1
Croatia	-2,385.5	-3,113.7	-2,862.4	-2,750.4	-2,963.1	-3,529.6	-3,295.1	-3,677.4	-4,024.0	-5,025.0
Czech Republic	1,034.5	334.7	143.9	193.8	1,820.7	870.7	603.4	956.3	1,927.5	1,982.0
Estonia	-622.1	-770.4	-862.7	-873.7	-979.9	-1,055.3	-976.8	-1,091.7	-919.3	
Georgia					-821.4	-859.0	-987.2	-1,308.9	-1,079.8	
Hungary	-896.5	-594.3	-997.0	-501.9	-195.9	6.8	-129.0	-94.0	431.6	
Latvia	-1,006.6	-1,256.5	-1,489.1	-1,782.3	-1,643.8	-1,813.1	-1,968.5	-1,861.6	-1,637.5	-1,699.4
Lithuania	-980.4	-1,186.6	-1,461.1	-1,631.2	-1,541.4	-1,923.2	-1,752.1	-2,066.1	-2,230.7	-1,938.7
Macedonia	-268.7	-400.2	-268.6	-417.0	-332.9	-310.3	-434.5	-797.2	-653.1	
Moldova	-262.1	-395.6	-416.9	-477.0	-484.6	-529.7	-593.2	-740.5	-698.9	
Poland	-2,888.8	-3,514.7	-3,865.6	-4,793.9	-4,674.1	-5,860.8	-5,559.7	-7,086.4	-6,755.3	
Romania	-2,829.3	-4,403.7	-4,686.0	-6,851.1	-5,813.1	-7,145.7	-7,250.1	-9,351.1	-7,339.2	-9,180.4
Russia	32,295.2	34,268.5	32,484.6	23,716.7	24,631.7	26,540.6	25,749.3	32,889.4	43,784.9	45,266.9
Serbia and Montenegro										
Slovakia	-2,020.0	-1,761.4	-602.4	-986.1	-763.5	-1,227.3	-926.2	-1,452.0	-353.7	-1,204.9
Slovenia	-367.8	-305.5	-495.2	-860.9	-441.3	-634.2	-711.0	-1,141.5	-939.0	-1,166.7
Ukraine	-1,728.1	-1,282.4	-1,262.9	-2,397.2	-2,231.8	-1,939.7	-2,493.1	-4,657.2	-5,015.2	

Source: *Euromonitor International from International Monetary Fund (IMF), International Financial Statistics*

Trade Balance by Month 2007

US$ million

	January	February	March	April	May	June	July	August	September	October	November	December
Western Europe												
Austria	-24.2	-20.8	19.9	306.0	333.8	402.0	68.0	-580.0	-692.6	1,089.9	383.2	-744.1
Belgium	1,603.6	2,366.4	2,858.4	1,484.7	1,602.9	2,888.5	2,212.1	631.1	2,370.1	879.4	737.6	-1,294.9
Cyprus	-459.5	-462.4	-556.5	-604.7	-589.5	-641.3	-659.5	-648.2	-660.8	-737.9	-755.2	-657.0
Denmark	419.4	-111.6	593.6	88.1	183.8	778.7	447.5	257.9	558.1	102.4	727.3	-24.9
Finland	302.4	260.0	802.0	1,816.6	716.9	566.1	437.5	595.1	1,033.8	497.9	1,114.7	190.9
France	-6,240.4	-5,301.6	-2,714.1	-5,702.7	-6,815.6	-4,940.9	-6,481.7	-6,981.0	-6,079.4	-6,232.3	-9,513.1	-7,377.1
Germany	21,024.3	18,502.8	24,493.9	20,262.1	23,362.2	22,181.6	24,609.1	19,176.5	25,087.5	26,817.5	28,352.0	15,540.5
Gibraltar												
Greece	-3,942.9	-4,376.0	-4,285.9	-3,611.3	-4,813.5	-4,225.7	-4,761.4	-3,770.4	-4,155.9	-5,017.1	-4,581.3	-4,087.1
Iceland	-65.2	-100.2	-79.8	-217.4	-205.4	-204.4	-201.3	-213.7	-169.7	-156.3	14.1	-157.8
Ireland	2,214.1	2,218.2	3,833.6	3,767.3	2,967.5	4,041.3	3,544.2	3,007.8	3,802.7	2,952.3	3,103.7	1,558.6
Italy	-4,228.1	-2,251.2	241.6	-1,532.3	-348.2	1,068.4	3,189.5	-1,704.7	-2,021.9	551.4	-78.3	-2,875.2
Liechtenstein												
Luxembourg	-319.7	-465.4	-540.7	-466.3	-680.3	-444.2	-489.5	-613.3	-448.9	-449.2	-519.4	-600.9
Malta	-76.9	-124.4	-111.1	-121.4	-89.6	-138.2	-179.9	-122.6	-95.8	-168.4	-138.5	-158.3
Monaco												
Netherlands	3,782.7	4,099.1	5,855.2	3,303.4	3,377.5	4,975.9	3,878.9	3,680.2	5,180.8	5,830.1	6,637.2	4,838.2
Norway	4,705.5	4,084.2	4,422.4	4,848.3	4,368.0	4,528.5	4,314.4	4,632.8	5,015.2	4,444.8	5,691.2	7,181.2
Portugal	-1,646.1	-1,584.1	-1,866.4	-2,109.0	-2,323.4	-1,941.3	-1,920.2	-2,370.8	-2,216.6	-2,633.8	-2,772.5	-2,744.8
Spain	-9,909.1	-9,006.5	-10,333.6	-10,352.7	-10,706.0	-11,158.5	-11,879.0	-10,652.3	-11,685.2	-13,245.6	-12,771.7	-14,337.8
Sweden	1,834.4	1,682.2	2,014.2	1,516.4	1,496.3	1,738.7	1,011.2	605.2	1,053.9	1,692.5	1,452.7	1,704.3
Switzerland	1,062.1	1,019.5	559.8	521.5	837.5	1,378.0	1,283.8	534.6	1,454.2	1,218.8	1,615.6	140.7
Turkey	-3,652.0	-3,379.0	-3,864.0	-4,640.3	-5,821.7	-5,327.0	-6,198.2	-5,969.4	-5,417.5	-5,713.0	-5,323.0	-6,371.0
United Kingdom	-14,825.3	-13,445.6	-14,991.3	-13,668.2	-14,645.6	-16,496.1	-17,576.2	-15,007.6	-17,616.8	-17,009.6	-17,496.0	-13,026.5
Eastern Europe												
Albania	-183.4	-199.9	-242.6	-241.6	-252.5	-234.2	-239.8	-252.4	-288.3	-297.1	-354.5	-337.1
Belarus	-367.5	-303.0	-201.7	-307.5	-333.7	-353.6	-256.2	-361.8	-270.6	-483.5	-426.3	-752.3
Bosnia-Herzegovina												
Bulgaria	-852.1	-699.0	-789.6	-805.0	-915.7	-867.7	-945.7	-919.1	-962.2	-1,135.3	-1,311.5	-1,308.4
Croatia	-790.7	-973.2	-1,200.4	-1,168.2	-1,313.1	-1,050.0	-1,140.1	-1,103.4	-1,052.7	-1,302.9	-1,261.7	-1,108.9
Czech Republic	453.8	663.7	689.2	240.5	258.0	388.9	-84.3	-31.9	689.0	455.0	650.2	-120.9
Estonia	-322.3	-252.7	-404.8	-399.3	-332.5	-323.5	-305.6	-314.2	-357.1	-373.0	-348.2	-370.5
Georgia	-259.0	-267.2	-295.2	-265.1	-325.9	-268.0	-311.2	-349.2	-326.8	-392.9	-335.0	-581.0
Hungary	-281.3	-66.7	152.1	-214.0	33.3	187.5	-186.8	-247.9	305.7	60.8	100.2	-255.0
Latvia	-526.2	-540.7	-604.9	-590.5	-641.5	-612.5	-769.7	-609.0	-611.4	-632.9	-591.1	-556.6
Lithuania	-466.8	-599.2	-492.5	-659.6	-698.2	-568.4	-599.2	-558.0	-614.6	-608.4	-818.2	-599.8
Macedonia	-128.9	-115.2	-88.8	-125.1	-89.6	-95.6	-180.3	-101.2	-153.0	-310.0	-232.2	-255.0
Moldova	-123.4	-181.0	-180.2	-163.4	-185.2	-181.1	-193.3	-193.9	-206.1	-226.1	-229.1	-285.3
Poland	-1,545.5	-1,161.6	-1,967.0	-1,833.8	-1,907.2	-2,119.8	-2,354.9	-1,302.9	-1,901.9	-1,981.9	-1,984.0	-3,120.6
Romania	-1,817.7	-1,846.0	-2,149.4	-2,211.3	-2,534.2	-2,400.3	-2,468.2	-2,455.2	-2,326.7	-3,108.3	-3,222.1	-3,020.7
Russia	8,679.1	8,069.0	7,883.6	9,073.9	10,770.1	6,696.6	8,688.0	9,108.1	7,953.2	10,286.4	11,317.9	11,285.2
Serbia and Montenegro												
Slovakia	-35.8	-319.4	-408.3	-277.6	-456.4	-493.3	-277.0	-484.1	-165.1	-122.0	-587.6	-742.4
Slovenia	-146.9	-145.8	-154.7	-235.2	-267.7	-166.4	-169.1	-201.1	-321.9	-314.6	-340.9	-463.6
Ukraine	-492.0	-881.2	-847.7	-755.8	-743.4	-429.2	-934.6	-822.9	-719.9	-1,538.1	-1,377.4	-1,779.8

Source: Euromonitor International from International Monetary Fund (IMF), International Financial Statistics

Health

Medical Services

Table 14.1

Hospitals and Beds 2007

As stated

	In-patient Beds ('000)	Hospitals and Clinics	Beds per '000 inhabitants
Western Europe			
Austria	61	259	7.4
Belgium	55	218	5.2
Cyprus	3	94	3.1
Denmark	19	63	3.5
Finland	36	356	6.9
France	435	2,584	7.1
Germany	687	3,369	8.3
Gibraltar			
Greece	52	305	4.6
Iceland	2	20	7.1
Ireland	23	175	5.4
Italy	225	1,299	3.8
Liechtenstein			
Luxembourg	3		5.8
Malta	3	9	8.1
Monaco			
Netherlands	79	192	4.8
Norway	19		4.0
Portugal	38	217	3.6
Spain	141	719	3.2
Sweden	26	79	2.9
Switzerland	40	327	5.3
Turkey	197	1,190	2.7
United Kingdom	230		3.8
Eastern Europe			
Albania	9	49	2.8
Belarus	106	711	10.9
Bosnia-Herzegovina	12	39	3.0
Bulgaria	47	319	6.2
Croatia	24	77	5.3
Czech Republic	84	351	8.2
Estonia	7	51	5.5
Georgia	16	261	3.7
Hungary	79	184	7.9
Latvia	17	102	7.6
Lithuania	26	165	7.7
Macedonia	9	54	4.7
Moldova	22	80	5.9
Poland	207	884	5.4
Romania	143	423	6.6
Russia	1,303	8,263	9.2
Serbia and Montenegro	12	114	1.1
Slovakia	37	156	6.9
Slovenia	10	30	4.9
Ukraine	402	2,589	8.7

Source: *Euromonitor International from OECD/World Health Organisation/National Statistics*

Table 14.2

Health Personnel 2007
Number

	Active Pharmacists	Dentists	Doctors	Midwives	Nurses
Western Europe					
Austria	5,237	4,175	30,811	2,229	77,638
Belgium	12,873	8,951	43,012		155,751
Cyprus	- 186				
Denmark	3,707	4,478	17,189		40,351
Finland	8,679	4,541	13,511	1,920	46,582
France	72,335	41,484	210,862	17,659	500,070
Germany	48,217	65,774	312,659	17,313	767,000
Gibraltar					
Greece	9,546	14,017	59,364		48,024
Iceland	318	305	1,027	247	4,045
Ireland	3,965	2,518	13,011		70,566
Italy	40,314	41,300	207,667		326,087
Liechtenstein					
Luxembourg	379	419	1,387		6,946
Malta	937	175	1,678		
Monaco					
Netherlands	2,836	8,812	65,686	2,226	244,909
Norway	3,037	4,647	18,908	6,603	75,425
Portugal	10,946	6,215	38,335		50,154
Spain	43,898	25,570	142,766	7,473	331,173
Sweden	6,329	7,192	42,388		106,979
Switzerland	4,508	3,932	29,212		79,546
Turkey	26,205	18,407	111,707	46,655	130,159
United Kingdom	34,055	29,593	175,929		569,880
Eastern Europe					
Albania	1,130	972	6,022		
Belarus	2,940	8,096	45,169	4,111	77,714
Bosnia-Herzegovina	270	820	7,324		
Bulgaria	792	6,524	32,828	3,970	31,500
Croatia	2,597	510	8,061		37,297
Czech Republic	5,984	6,965	36,069	4,508	88,996
Estonia	883	1,196	4,330	318	9,124
Georgia	225	1,045	19,791		11,200
Hungary	5,433	5,961	39,190	1,921	91,879
Latvia		1,299	7,902		13,400
Lithuania	2,440	3,322	13,640	917	25,051
Macedonia	891	1,229	6,376	2,475	10,278
Moldova	3,460	1,615	8,428		
Poland	23,919	15,534	64,600	19,850	174,201
Romania	832	11,236	49,657		71,029
Russia	11,560	64,356	633,601	86,656	1,147,112
Serbia and Montenegro	2,004	3,529	22,752		
Slovakia	2,677	3,146	16,571	1,592	31,257
Slovenia	896	1,285	4,902	774	15,489
Ukraine	21,643	19,161	235,837		582,129

Source: Euromonitor International from OECD/World Health Organisation

Causes of Death

Table 14.3

Causes of Death: Male 2007

Per 100,000 inhabitants

	Tuberculosis	HIV	Cancer	Diabetes	Mental and Behaviour Disorders	Diseases of Circulatory System	Diseases of Respiratory System	Diseases of Digestive System
Western Europe								
Austria	0.8	1.7	249.3	36.9	12.3	333.1	61.2	45.6
Belgium	0.8	0.9	324.4	12.0	19.6	327.9	127.7	43.7
Cyprus								
Denmark	0.8	1.1	294.3	26.9	34.4	392.6	100.4	45.5
Finland	0.7	0.1	214.0	9.8	30.8	362.4	52.9	56.7
France	1.0	2.6	305.3	20.2	27.9	254.8	67.0	47.0
Germany	0.7	1.0	278.6	23.7	13.9	367.6	65.6	53.5
Gibraltar								
Greece	0.8	0.2	291.2	9.9	1.2	443.3	73.4	24.5
Iceland								
Ireland	0.5	0.1	187.1	11.9	11.8	236.7	85.0	23.0
Italy	1.0	2.5	320.2	26.2	12.3	378.2	77.2	43.7
Liechtenstein								
Luxembourg								
Malta								
Monaco								
Netherlands	0.5	0.8	264.2	19.6	23.7	247.2	90.8	28.7
Norway	0.5	0.9	243.1	12.0	17.2	293.7	65.5	28.2
Portugal	4.7	0.2	395.4	19.9	11.2	635.6	58.9	117.5
Spain	1.4	5.8	289.1	18.6	19.1	263.0	105.7	49.1
Sweden	0.2	0.5	265.8	21.8	29.0	423.8	67.6	32.6
Switzerland	0.3	1.5	235.8	17.3	26.8	259.0	55.8	28.1
Turkey								
United Kingdom	0.7	0.4	271.8	10.6	19.2	338.5	118.7	46.1
Eastern Europe								
Albania	0.8	0.0	117.9	5.7	3.7	294.8	33.6	13.0
Belarus	16.7		246.9	4.2	10.7	816.2	100.8	43.9
Bosnia-Herzegovina								
Bulgaria	5.2	0.0	261.3	22.6	3.6	992.4	52.3	54.7
Croatia	4.4	0.1	336.9	17.3	16.4	472.9	87.8	70.4
Czech Republic	0.7	0.0	324.2	10.9	3.3	486.6	52.2	51.3
Estonia	5.9	3.5	318.4	11.5	22.9	645.4	49.9	64.6
Georgia	8.3	0.0	92.9	13.9	0.7	581.0	23.7	36.5
Hungary	4.7	0.2	395.4	19.9	11.2	635.6	58.9	117.5
Latvia	17.1	0.8	294.1	7.5	2.6	742.6	58.8	54.8
Lithuania	19.6	0.2	281.6	9.5	2.8	694.1	79.7	72.7
Macedonia								
Moldova								
Poland	3.6	0.5	280.5	11.1	8.7	431.0	54.0	49.6
Romania	17.1	1.1	242.0	9.9	7.8	736.7	80.8	89.8
Russia	43.2	0.5	238.1	4.9	9.8	987.2	114.8	77.3
Serbia and Montenegro								
Slovakia	1.5	0.1	271.9	9.6	0.2	510.9	55.0	61.2
Slovenia	0.3	0.2	288.1	21.8	7.1	317.3	76.6	73.9
Ukraine	39.5		241.6	5.3	9.1	938.6	99.6	70.4

Source: World Health Organisation/Euromonitor International

Table 14.4

Causes of Death: Female 2007

Per 100,000 inhabitants

	Tuberculosis	HIV	Cancer	Diabetes	Mental and Behaviour Disorders	Diseases of Circulatory System	Diseases of Respiratory System	Diseases of Digestive System
Western Europe								
Austria	0.6	0.2	215.1	49.0	3.8	480.6	57.3	34.2
Belgium	0.2	0.3	228.0	22.5	30.7	388.4	93.3	48.8
Cyprus								
Denmark	1.0	0.4	288.2	31.2	44.5	409.4	106.8	51.2
Finland	0.5	0.1	184.5	10.4	66.6	358.4	39.0	40.8
France	0.7	0.8	192.3	22.9	39.1	282.8	59.1	37.6
Germany	0.3	0.2	235.6	35.1	11.3	492.4	57.4	50.3
Gibraltar								
Greece	0.3	0.1	177.8	10.8	1.8	468.8	66.8	16.9
Iceland								
Ireland	0.5	0.2	176.0	10.8	14.0	225.4	99.1	25.8
Italy	0.5	0.7	221.8	36.2	22.1	442.4	54.0	41.3
Liechtenstein								
Luxembourg								
Malta								
Monaco								
Netherlands	0.1	0.2	221.9	25.2	54.2	263.2	86.4	35.5
Norway	0.1	0.3	208.6	12.9	33.8	350.8	63.8	33.1
Portugal	1.3	0.1	278.8	25.1	4.4	678.2	40.8	61.8
Spain	0.6	1.1	164.6	27.5	34.9	304.4	70.0	40.7
Sweden	0.0	0.2	227.5	22.0	54.0	452.9	65.8	34.6
Switzerland	0.2	0.3	185.7	22.8	45.4	317.9	45.4	29.8
Turkey								
United Kingdom	0.5	0.3	238.9	11.2	37.4	354.0	134.0	51.6
Eastern Europe								
Albania	0.5	0.0	70.9	5.7	4.0	261.6	23.7	8.0
Belarus	2.6		153.6	7.6	3.9	812.5	39.5	24.7
Bosnia-Herzegovina								
Bulgaria	1.5	0.0	167.4	27.5	1.5	899.8	27.4	23.3
Croatia	2.5	0.0	215.1	23.5	13.5	575.2	60.7	40.9
Czech Republic	0.5	0.0	245.4	14.5	1.0	553.7	36.5	36.7
Estonia	1.1	0.9	213.3	18.2	8.2	688.2	18.8	41.7
Georgia	1.9	0.0	85.1	13.7	0.1	609.1	16.5	15.3
Hungary	1.3	0.1	278.8	25.1	4.4	678.2	40.8	61.8
Latvia	5.8	0.4	216.4	16.6	1.2	840.4	20.6	41.3
Lithuania	3.5	0.0	201.6	11.3	1.0	736.5	28.4	46.8
Macedonia								
Moldova								
Poland	0.8	0.1	196.9	15.1	1.5	447.9	32.9	34.7
Romania	3.5	0.8	163.5	11.0	2.2	759.3	45.5	52.5
Russia	7.1	0.2	171.0	10.0	3.6	997.6	38.0	48.7
Serbia and Montenegro								
Slovakia	1.0	0.1	176.1	11.3	0.0	545.1	38.5	32.0
Slovenia	0.1	0.0	224.6	33.3	5.5	379.6	61.9	51.5
Ukraine	5.5		158.8	6.7	2.4	1,031.7	31.8	33.8

Source: World Health Organisation/Euromonitor International

Illness | | | | | | | | | Table 14.5

Reported AIDS Cases by Date of Report 1985-2007
Number

	1985	1990	1995	2000	2002	2003	2004	2005	2006	2007
Western Europe										
Austria	28	164	209	85	94	50	72	58	58	57
Belgium	69	206	254	145	133	126	122	150	100	91
Cyprus		6	6	11	4	5	2	3	3	3
Denmark	38	197	213	58	44	39	59	44	50	49
Finland	4	16	41	17	20	25	19	26	44	48
France	584	4,323	5,314	1,735	1,639	1,465	1,375	1,314	1,018	869
Germany	313	1,555	1,920	780	652	648	668	626	366	319
Gibraltar										
Greece	14	143	216	131	99	94	86	100	91	90
Iceland	1	3	4	1		1	3	1	3	2
Ireland	7	68	53	13	35	39	44	48	24	22
Italy	198	3,135	5,653	1,948	1,756	1,718	1,616	1,499	1,126	994
Liechtenstein										
Luxembourg	2	9	15	10	1	8	12	8	9	9
Malta		1	4	3	4	2	1	3	4	4
Monaco	1	2	3							
Netherlands	65	419	534	250	295	281	281	314	189	164
Norway	14	60	68	38	38	50	36	32	25	20
Portugal	29	261	821	1,011	1,004	894	788	761	695	629
Spain	176	3,945	7,179	2,849	2,266	2,226	2,029	1,752	1,518	1,361
Sweden	34	132	196	61	61	53	65	46	57	58
Switzerland	120	612	620	210	205	215	220	185	154	140
Turkey	2	14	27	48	44	44	55	30	31	29
United Kingdom	246	1,242	1,770	833	889	928	881	833	858	877
Eastern Europe										
Albania			3	3	10	5	6	9	15	18
Belarus			3		21	33	90	162	269	314
Bosnia-Herzegovina			7	4	5	6	5	6	4	3
Bulgaria		4	1	16	13	15	20	19	16	16
Croatia		9	15	19	19	10	13	17	20	23
Czech Republic		5	13	14	8	8	13	11	12	13
Estonia			4	3	6	10	29	29	32	37
Georgia		2	4	15	48	46	112	120	133	148
Hungary		19	31	27	26	26	23	33	22	21
Latvia		2	3	23	56	75	76	75	61	58
Lithuania		1	1	7	9	9	21	10	27	32
Macedonia		1	5	4	5		3	12	6	7
Moldova			2	4	19	46	58	60	103	118
Poland		21	115	124	124	143	175	149	114	104
Romania	5	1,202	767	662	343	363	308	306	211	191
Russia		50	46	157	213	314	396	548	842	959
Serbia and Montenegro	2	53	98	75	73	64	58	54	62	64
Slovakia	1	1	2	5	2	2	2	3	4	5
Slovenia		3	15	7	3	6	10	10	5	5
Ukraine		1	42	650	1,340	1,865	2,683	4,025	4,535	4,891

Source: UNAIDS/World Health Organisation

Table 14.6

Food Supply: Average Consumption of Calories, Protein and Fat 2007

Daily averages, calories / grams per inhabitant

	Calories (number)	Protein (grams)	Fat (grams)
Western Europe			
Austria	3,945	110.1	158.9
Belgium	3,772	107.5	172.3
Cyprus			
Denmark	3,538	121.5	149.8
Finland	3,283	106.9	122.7
France	3,680	122.2	170.9
Germany	3,638	100.0	159.6
Gibraltar			
Greece	3,742	115.9	155.3
Iceland			
Ireland	3,700	112.9	131.5
Italy	3,697	114.7	162.9
Liechtenstein			
Luxembourg			
Malta			
Monaco			
Netherlands	3,446	119.8	144.3
Norway	3,510	109.2	139.3
Portugal	3,899	128.4	141.8
Spain	3,554	118.9	158.1
Sweden	3,255	109.7	128.9
Switzerland	3,548	94.1	157.8
Turkey	3,345	96.0	89.5
United Kingdom	3,403	104.1	144.2
Eastern Europe			
Albania			
Belarus	2,998	78.9	91.6
Bosnia-Herzegovina			
Bulgaria	2,984	91.1	106.7
Croatia	2,954	78.7	92.5
Czech Republic	3,046	85.1	122.7
Estonia	3,253	92.1	104.3
Georgia			
Hungary	3,675	106.2	153.9
Latvia	2,735	79.0	108.1
Lithuania	3,544	100.7	103.6
Macedonia			
Moldova			
Poland	3,520	98.0	118.0
Romania	3,516	108.1	97.4
Russia	3,114	88.1	82.1
Serbia and Montenegro			
Slovakia	2,743	71.4	116.2
Slovenia	3,199	110.3	111.4
Ukraine	3,178	80.1	78.6

Source: Euromonitor International from FAO/National Statistics

Health Expenditure

Table 14.7

Government Health Expenditure Statistics 2007
As stated

	Total Health Expenditure as % of GDP	Per Capita Health Expenditure (US$)	Government Expenditure on Drugs (US$ million)
Western Europe			
Austria	10.3	3,799	3,003.4
Belgium	10.5	3,577	4,243.4
Cyprus	6.2	1,371	
Denmark	9.1	3,457	1,380.0
Finland	7.7	2,582	1,692.0
France	11.3	3,763	33,107.6
Germany	10.9	3,602	40,224.9
Gibraltar			
Greece	10.9	3,515	3,838.6
Iceland	9.6	3,755	127.0
Ireland	7.7	3,313	1,767.7
Italy	9.1	2,717	18,988.0
Liechtenstein			
Luxembourg	8.9	6,358	232.3
Malta	10.5	1,562	
Monaco	9.9	6,089	
Netherlands	9.5	3,638	4,407.2
Norway	8.6	4,999	1,590.1
Portugal	11.0	2,317	3,059.1
Spain	8.1	2,588	19,326.2
Sweden	9.1	3,149	3,059.1
Switzerland	11.8	4,437	3,327.0
Turkey	7.7	647	4,760.0
United Kingdom	8.7	3,105	15,372.0
Eastern Europe			
Albania	6.8	195	
Belarus	6.6	286	
Bosnia-Herzegovina	8.0	232	
Bulgaria	8.9	347	
Croatia	8.9	852	
Czech Republic	7.3	1,653	2,201.6
Estonia	5.3	640	
Georgia	6.1	115	
Hungary	9.2	1,749	2,457.5
Latvia	7.4	618	
Lithuania	6.2	571	
Macedonia	8.0	249	
Moldova	8.5	67	
Poland	6.2	968	2,594.1
Romania	5.5	356	
Russia	6.9	540	
Serbia and Montenegro	9.4	324	
Slovakia	7.5	1,320	1,115.8
Slovenia	8.8	1,694	
Ukraine	8.4	210	

Source: Euromonitor International from IMF

Section Fifteen

Household Profiles

Average Number of Occupants per Household

Table 15.1

Average Number of Occupants per Household at Jan 1st 1985-2007
Persons

	1985	1990	1995	2000	2001	2002	2003	2004	2005	2006	2007
Western Europe											
Austria	2.65	2.57	2.52	2.42	2.40	2.39	2.38	2.37	2.36	2.36	2.35
Belgium	2.56	2.51	2.47	2.42	2.40	2.39	2.37	2.36	2.36	2.35	2.35
Cyprus	3.05	2.97	2.94	2.98	3.01	3.04	3.07	3.07	3.10	3.11	3.17
Denmark	2.37	2.27	2.21	2.19	2.19	2.19	2.18	2.18	2.18	2.18	2.19
Finland	2.39	2.29	2.23	2.17	2.18	2.17	2.17	2.16	2.16	2.16	2.16
France	2.71	2.63	2.53	2.44	2.43	2.43	2.42	2.41	2.40	2.39	2.38
Germany [a]	2.36	2.27	2.21	2.16	2.14	2.13	2.12	2.11	2.10	2.09	2.08
Gibraltar	4.14	4.14	3.92	3.76	3.71	3.67	3.64	3.62	3.62	3.62	3.62
Greece	3.22	3.19	3.10	3.01	2.98	2.96	2.94	2.92	2.90	2.88	2.86
Iceland	2.39	2.38	2.39	2.34	2.34	2.34	2.33	2.34	2.35	2.34	2.36
Ireland	3.72	3.47	3.32	3.08	3.05	3.03	3.01	3.00	3.00	3.02	3.02
Italy	2.99	2.88	2.73	2.63	2.61	2.59	2.59	2.60	2.61	2.60	2.59
Liechtenstein	2.44	2.49	2.55	2.54	2.54	2.55	2.55	2.55	2.59	2.63	2.63
Luxembourg	2.76	2.69	2.63	2.58	2.57	2.55	2.54	2.53	2.53	2.52	2.92
Malta	3.22	3.24	3.28	3.23	3.28	3.33	3.42	3.43	3.44	3.43	3.47
Monaco	2.25	2.50	2.22	2.23	2.33	2.43	2.51	2.50	2.50	2.50	2.50
Netherlands	2.58	2.46	2.38	2.33	2.33	2.32	2.31	2.30	2.29	2.28	2.27
Norway	2.54	2.42	2.36	2.30	2.30	2.29	2.28	2.27	2.27	2.26	2.26
Portugal	3.27	3.17	3.00	2.84	2.81	2.79	2.77	2.75	2.73	2.71	2.70
Spain	3.67	3.34	3.07	2.86	2.84	2.82	2.83	2.83	2.84	2.85	2.87
Sweden	2.27	2.23	2.19	2.16	2.15	2.15	2.14	2.14	2.13	2.13	2.13
Switzerland	2.45	2.35	2.30	2.25	2.25	2.24	2.24	2.24	2.24	2.24	2.24
Turkey	5.10	4.96	4.85	4.77	4.75	4.72	4.69	4.67	4.65	4.63	4.61
United Kingdom	2.56	2.46	2.39	2.33	2.32	2.32	2.31	2.30	2.30	2.30	2.30
Eastern Europe											
Albania	3.29	3.51	3.04	3.08	3.10	3.12	2.85	2.84	2.85	2.84	2.88
Belarus	2.94	2.84	2.73	2.57	2.56	2.53	2.51	2.50	2.48	2.47	2.45
Bosnia-Herzegovina	3.71	3.61	3.12	4.08	3.84	3.59	3.23	3.09	2.92	2.77	2.67
Bulgaria	3.00	2.95	2.81	2.73	2.71	2.70	2.69	2.67	2.65	2.64	2.63
Croatia	2.98	3.08	3.08	3.00	3.00	3.02	3.03	3.04	3.05	3.06	3.06
Czech Republic	2.55	2.58	2.63	2.67	2.67	2.67	2.68	2.69	2.70	2.72	2.73
Estonia	3.91	3.31	2.80	2.36	2.36	2.35	2.35	2.35	2.35	2.36	2.36
Georgia				3.77	3.62	3.47	3.32	3.20	3.09	2.99	2.91
Hungary	2.76	2.75	2.75	2.70	2.74	2.74	2.73	2.74	2.74	2.74	2.74
Latvia	3.63	3.32	3.11	2.97	2.96	2.95	2.95	2.94	2.93	2.93	2.92
Lithuania	2.96	2.86	2.75	2.60	2.57	2.56	2.54	2.53	2.51	2.49	2.48
Macedonia				3.68	3.63	3.58	3.53	3.48	3.43	3.38	3.32
Moldova			4.03	3.83	3.91	3.96	4.11	4.03	4.00	3.91	3.93
Poland	3.17	3.13	3.06	2.92	2.89	2.87	2.85	2.83	2.81	2.80	2.78
Romania	3.88	3.66	3.34	3.08	3.03	2.98	2.92	2.87	2.85	2.83	2.79
Russia	4.25	3.49	3.04	2.81	2.79	2.76	2.74	2.72	2.71	2.69	2.68
Serbia and Montenegro	1.36	1.37	3.47	3.43	3.37	3.29	3.23	3.18	3.13	3.10	3.08
Slovakia	2.97	2.91	2.78	2.63	2.60	2.57	2.55	2.53	2.51	2.50	2.48
Slovenia	3.20	3.18	3.06	2.96	2.94	2.91	2.89	2.88	2.86	2.86	2.85
Ukraine	3.01	2.93	2.72	2.50	2.46	2.45	2.42	2.40	2.37	2.36	2.34

Source: *National statistics/UN//Euromonitor International*
Notes: *(a) Data prior to 1991 refer to former East and West Germany*

Table 15.2

Household Facilities: Latest Year

% of total households

	Year	Bath or Shower	Flush Toilet	Kitchen	Central Heating	Electric Lighting	Water Supply
Western Europe							
Austria	2007	98.7	99.9	100.0	69.4		100.0
Belgium	2007	97.1	97.3	91.6	75.7		99.8
Denmark	1993	90.9	97.7	98.0	95.1		100.0
Finland	2007	98.9	96.3		93.5	99.4	98.2
France	1992	94.8	95.8	93.7	79.3		99.9
Germany	2007				70.9	100.0	100.0
Greece	2007	92.6	96.2	99.5	64.3	99.6	99.2
Ireland	2007	99.7	99.7		90.7		99.8
Italy	2001	98.8	99.8	90.7	94.4		99.0
Netherlands	2007	100.0	100.0	100.0	91.5		100.0
Norway	2007	98.1	98.8	98.5	11.6	100.0	
Portugal	2001	94.0	92.0	99.7	5.4	99.3	98.1
Spain	2007	99.3			52.7		99.6
Sweden	1993	99.1		100.0	100.0		100.0
Switzerland	2000			99.6	90.3		
Turkey	2007	60.5	58.9	58.0	15.9	53.0	49.0
United Kingdom	1996				88.0		99.1
Eastern Europe							
Belarus	2007	69.3	75.6		79.3		78.6
Bulgaria	2007	54.2	60.6	98.9	16.4	96.5	95.1
Croatia	2007	85.6	87.2		33.9	98.6	91.3
Czech Republic	2007	95.6	98.7	98.3	85.2		99.7
Estonia	2007	80.9	91.2	99.0	83.0		92.0
Hungary	2007	91.0	93.0	99.8	59.8		95.0
Latvia	2007	71.1	76.3	97.8	65.1	99.6	85.4
Lithuania	2007	76.0	74.0	97.0	78.0	100.0	86.0
Poland	2001	82.2	82.2	99.4	72.9		93.4
Romania	2002	51.9	51.9	91.1	37.6	98.0	72.4
Russia	2007	81.9	77.2		92.3		89.1
Slovakia	2001	92.8	87.9	99.4	76.3		94.7
Slovenia	2007	97.9	98.3	98.7	85.4	99.8	99.8
Ukraine	2007	51.3	54.6		57.3		56.8

Source: Euromonitor International from national statistics/trade sources

Households

Table 15.3

Number of Households 1985-2007

'000

	1985	1990	1995	1996	1997	1998	1999	2000
Western Europe								
Austria	2,858	2,977	3,150	3,183	3,201	3,228	3,269	3,302
Belgium	3,857	3,959	4,095	4,116	4,147	4,179	4,209	4,238
Cyprus	212	229	249	253	259	260	263	264
Denmark	2,160	2,265	2,358	2,374	2,392	2,407	2,423	2,434
Finland	2,045	2,171	2,290	2,310	2,333	2,355	2,365	2,382
France	20,331	21,542	22,790	23,044	23,299	23,554	23,810	24,063
Germany	32,967	34,775	36,938	37,281	37,457	37,532	37,795	38,124
Gibraltar	7	7	7	7	7	7	7	7
Greece	3,076	3,178	3,417	3,456	3,498	3,541	3,579	3,628
Iceland	101	107	112	115	117	118	118	120
Ireland	954	1,012	1,085	1,123	1,146	1,172	1,199	1,226
Italy	18,916	19,694	20,822	21,011	21,179	21,336	21,488	21,645
Liechtenstein				12	12	13	13	13
Luxembourg	133	142	156	158	161	164	166	169
Malta	107	111	115	117	118	123	121	120
Monaco	12	12	14	14	15	15	15	15
Netherlands	5,613	6,061	6,469	6,518	6,581	6,656	6,745	6,801
Norway	1,633	1,751	1,843	1,862	1,880	1,901	1,923	1,946
Portugal	3,064	3,150	3,335	3,381	3,431	3,481	3,534	3,592
Spain	10,439	11,615	12,810	13,052	13,294	13,537	13,781	14,025
Sweden	3,670	3,830	4,030	4,049	4,065	4,077	4,093	4,105
Switzerland	2,640	2,842	3,052	3,086	3,107	3,127	3,152	3,182
Turkey	9,730	11,189	12,609	12,900	13,190	13,477	13,761	14,035
United Kingdom	22,087	23,236	24,278	24,474	24,665	24,852	25,035	25,214
Eastern Europe								
Albania	900	937	1,037	1,087	1,023	1,010	999	1,001
Belarus	3,381	3,586	3,734	3,768	3,803	3,830	3,855	3,899
Bosnia-Herzegovina	1,124	1,236	1,017	1,016	1,039	1,078	1,118	1,150
Bulgaria	2,985	2,970	2,952	2,946	2,941	2,935	2,930	2,925
Croatia	1,578	1,551	1,516	1,510	1,503	1,497	1,490	1,482
Czech Republic	4,045	3,997	3,918	3,904	3,887	3,870	3,851	3,837
Estonia	389	475	517	527	537	551	564	582
Georgia						1,199	1,225	1,252
Hungary	3,858	3,775	3,757	3,748	3,741	3,735	3,729	3,783
Latvia	707	803	803	803	803	803	803	803
Lithuania	1,191	1,290	1,323	1,322	1,328	1,336	1,342	1,349
Macedonia	430	470	510	518	526	534	542	549
Moldova			1,088	1,126	1,126	1,144	1,115	1,083
Poland	11,681	12,142	12,501	12,628	12,750	12,886	13,007	13,123
Romania	5,843	6,346	6,663	6,779	6,892	6,951	7,036	7,131
Russia	33,553	42,280	48,872	49,784	50,569	51,231	51,772	52,197
Serbia and Montenegro	2,765	2,837	3,024	3,042	3,050	3,049	3,043	3,033
Slovakia	1,732	1,811	1,924	1,947	1,969	1,994	2,020	2,045
Slovenia	609	627	649	654	659	663	667	672
Ukraine	16,843	17,595	18,856	19,110	19,263	19,412	19,547	19,640

Source: *National statistical offices/Euromonitor International*

Households

Number of Households 1985-2007 *(continued)*
'000

	2001	2002	2003	2004	2005	2006	2007
Western Europe							
Austria	3,340	3,373	3,407	3,441	3,475	3,509	3,543
Belgium	4,278	4,319	4,362	4,398	4,433	4,464	4,494
Cyprus	264	266	266	269	269	272	270
Denmark	2,445	2,456	2,467	2,473	2,481	2,487	2,491
Finland	2,382	2,396	2,404	2,413	2,421	2,431	2,438
France	24,314	24,562	24,807	25,051	25,291	25,530	25,766
Germany	38,456	38,720	38,944	39,122	39,274	39,402	39,514
Gibraltar	7	7	7	7	7	7	8
Greece	3,664	3,707	3,746	3,786	3,825	3,863	3,900
Iceland	122	123	124	125	126	127	127
Ireland	1,256	1,288	1,317	1,343	1,370	1,396	1,422
Italy	21,811	21,975	22,136	22,292	22,442	22,585	22,721
Liechtenstein	13	13	14	14	14	14	14
Luxembourg	172	175	177	179	181	183	160
Malta	119	119	116	117	117	118	117
Monaco	15	14	14	14	15	15	15
Netherlands	6,867	6,934	7,002	7,058	7,114	7,161	7,200
Norway	1,962	1,979	1,998	2,016	2,032	2,049	2,066
Portugal	3,651	3,708	3,758	3,809	3,856	3,898	3,933
Spain	14,271	14,511	14,743	14,961	15,163	15,347	15,514
Sweden	4,128	4,153	4,175	4,197	4,223	4,248	4,272
Switzerland	3,208	3,246	3,270	3,289	3,309	3,326	3,344
Turkey	14,304	14,583	14,862	15,134	15,409	15,671	15,922
United Kingdom	25,388	25,560	25,731	25,900	26,068	26,233	26,398
Eastern Europe							
Albania	995	994	1,094	1,105	1,107	1,118	1,109
Belarus	3,909	3,931	3,940	3,951	3,959	3,967	3,975
Bosnia-Herzegovina	1,171	1,185	1,193	1,199	1,205	1,211	1,217
Bulgaria	2,922	2,918	2,915	2,912	2,911	2,907	2,901
Croatia	1,477	1,472	1,466	1,461	1,458	1,454	1,451
Czech Republic	3,828	3,817	3,804	3,792	3,785	3,774	3,766
Estonia	580	578	576	575	573	570	568
Georgia	1,290	1,330	1,373	1,410	1,446	1,480	1,512
Hungary	3,721	3,714	3,711	3,697	3,686	3,678	3,669
Latvia	799	794	791	789	786	783	780
Lithuania	1,357	1,357	1,362	1,364	1,365	1,366	1,366
Macedonia	557	564	571	578	585	591	598
Moldova	1,046	1,018	969	973	970	980	965
Poland	13,239	13,337	13,426	13,511	13,582	13,650	13,715
Romania	7,223	7,320	7,459	7,554	7,611	7,643	7,713
Russia	52,509	52,711	52,855	52,949	53,003	53,013	52,992
Serbia and Montenegro	3,019	3,002	2,983	2,968	2,959	2,957	2,961
Slovakia	2,072	2,092	2,111	2,129	2,143	2,158	2,171
Slovenia	676	685	690	694	698	701	705
Ukraine	19,751	19,668	19,731	19,764	19,834	19,846	19,889

Source: National statistical offices/Euromonitor International

Households

Table 15.4

Households by Number of Persons 2007

% of total households

	One Person	Two Persons	Three Persons	Four Persons	Five or More Persons
Western Europe					
Austria	30.7	34.0	15.1	14.9	5.3
Belgium	33.0	32.4	15.2	12.7	6.7
Cyprus					
Denmark	40.1	34.0	12.4	10.1	3.5
Finland	38.7	34.2	12.9	9.6	4.5
France	34.1	32.4	14.9	12.2	6.3
Germany	37.7	34.5	13.5	10.4	3.9
Gibraltar					
Greece	18.0	33.4	22.5	18.7	7.3
Iceland					
Ireland	21.2	28.8	19.3	17.3	13.4
Italy	27.4	30.3	20.1	15.0	7.2
Liechtenstein					
Luxembourg					
Malta					
Monaco					
Netherlands	35.2	32.5	12.5	13.6	6.2
Norway	41.5	30.2	12.4	10.6	5.3
Portugal	19.4	29.8	25.6	18.3	6.9
Spain	23.0	25.6	21.0	20.4	9.8
Sweden	44.7	32.9	9.7	8.4	4.2
Switzerland	38.6	31.5	11.6	12.2	6.1
Turkey	1.5	17.8	22.5	27.0	31.1
United Kingdom	28.0	37.6	15.2	13.0	6.2
Eastern Europe					
Albania					
Belarus	22.3	28.4	27.5	16.0	5.8
Bosnia-Herzegovina					
Bulgaria	20.4	27.2	10.4	22.9	19.1
Croatia	34.8	25.7	12.0	15.1	12.4
Czech Republic	25.2	35.2	20.8	13.8	5.0
Estonia	44.4	22.3	14.7	10.6	7.9
Georgia					
Hungary	26.4	34.4	7.3	23.0	8.9
Latvia	34.2	31.0	17.9	11.6	5.3
Lithuania	24.5	29.5	22.7	18.6	4.7
Macedonia					
Moldova					
Poland	24.1	27.1	23.3	16.1	9.3
Romania	23.5	34.5	15.3	13.9	12.9
Russia	24.0	28.3	24.4	15.0	8.2
Serbia and Montenegro					
Slovakia	30.1	33.6	18.3	13.7	4.3
Slovenia	20.5	26.0	27.9	21.3	4.3
Ukraine	21.7	31.9	12.4	24.8	9.2

Source: National statistical offices/Euromonitor International

Table 15.5

Households by Number of Rooms 2007

% of total households

	One Room	Two Rooms	Three Rooms	Four Rooms	Five or More Rooms
Western Europe					
Austria	8.8	19.8	31.7	20.0	19.7
Belgium	6.3	14.3	19.4	22.2	37.8
Cyprus					
Denmark	6.6	21.1	23.1	20.0	29.3
Finland	13.7	31.7	20.9	19.7	13.9
France	6.7	12.5	21.4	26.3	33.1
Germany	2.2	6.3	21.8	29.5	40.3
Gibraltar					
Greece	3.2	15.7	27.4	38.1	15.5
Iceland					
Ireland	0.5	2.5	6.3	15.2	75.5
Italy	0.7	8.6	24.8	34.8	31.1
Liechtenstein					
Luxembourg					
Malta					
Monaco					
Netherlands	2.8	7.1	21.4	33.8	34.9
Norway	4.5	11.6	18.8	17.2	47.8
Portugal	0.8	2.1	12.7	29.6	54.8
Spain	0.6	2.4	8.9	17.6	70.5
Sweden	8.2	22.4	25.4	21.3	22.6
Switzerland	4.1	11.5	26.4	29.2	28.9
Turkey	4.0	15.2	26.6	37.6	16.5
United Kingdom	0.2	2.3	7.6	18.1	71.8
Eastern Europe					
Albania					
Belarus	18.0	39.0	32.2	8.7	2.1
Bosnia-Herzegovina					
Bulgaria	9.4	37.0	38.3	10.7	4.5
Croatia	24.2	48.1	20.8	4.3	2.7
Czech Republic	13.8	38.4	27.1	10.5	10.2
Estonia	18.8	49.4	28.9	1.8	1.1
Georgia					
Hungary	17.2	41.3	28.1	7.3	6.0
Latvia	17.7	47.9	23.4	6.4	4.6
Lithuania	15.2	44.6	31.2	6.4	2.6
Macedonia					
Moldova					
Poland	1.9	13.4	30.6	43.6	10.5
Romania	10.1	35.4	37.6	11.5	5.4
Russia	14.6	39.8	25.9	13.3	6.4
Serbia and Montenegro					
Slovakia	15.8	40.6	29.2	8.5	5.8
Slovenia	14.4	29.6	26.5	15.3	14.2
Ukraine	11.2	29.7	31.3	19.8	8.0

Source: National statistical offices/Euromonitor International

Housing Stock

Table 15.6

Total Housing Stock 1980-2007

'000 units

	1980	1985	1990	1995	2000	2002	2003	2004	2005	2006	2007
Western Europe											
Austria	3,038	3,141	3,347	3,590	3,827	3,896	3,921	3,940	3,956	3,969	3,981
Belgium	3,811	3,997	3,882	3,931	4,186	4,320	4,387	4,454	4,510	4,563	4,611
Cyprus	151	187	222	251							
Denmark	2,109	2,228	2,353	2,427	2,489	2,523	2,541	2,561	2,579	2,595	2,612
Finland	1,838	2,015	2,210	2,374	2,512	2,574	2,604	2,632	2,660	2,687	2,711
France	23,432	25,132	26,792	28,283	29,699	30,337	30,669	30,984	31,306	31,622	31,921
Germany	30,956	32,645	33,856	35,954	38,384	38,925	39,142	39,363	39,589	39,799	39,991
Gibraltar											
Greece	3,940	4,262	4,588	4,946	5,387	5,584	5,712	5,839	5,938	6,044	6,143
Iceland											
Ireland	879	961	1,026	1,115	1,293	1,387	1,441	1,505	1,577	1,652	1,740
Italy	21,585	23,282	24,768	26,039	27,107	27,487	27,664	27,843	28,011	28,188	28,348
Liechtenstein											
Luxembourg											
Malta											
Monaco											
Netherlands	4,918	5,415	5,802	6,192	6,590	6,710	6,764	6,810	6,858	6,909	6,952
Norway	1,544	1,651	1,751	1,844	1,940	1,985	2,004	2,024	2,042	2,061	2,080
Portugal	3,756	3,906	4,130	4,508	5,002	5,225	5,309	5,387	5,463	5,531	5,582
Spain	13,356	15,062	16,854	18,707	20,572	21,311	21,672	22,020	22,357	22,671	22,978
Sweden	3,627	3,835	4,045	4,234	4,294	4,329	4,351	4,380	4,404	4,430	4,456
Switzerland	2,703	2,925	3,140	3,390	3,575	3,638	3,672	3,700	3,728	3,759	3,782
Turkey	10,359	11,306	12,331	13,651	15,405	16,176	16,565	16,941	17,326	17,702	18,071
United Kingdom	21,448	22,383	23,510	24,341	25,283	25,617	25,787	25,947	26,108	26,265	26,421
Eastern Europe											
Albania											
Belarus	2,665	2,936	3,285	3,621	3,819	3,871	3,894	3,907	3,921	3,929	3,938
Bosnia-Herzegovina											
Bulgaria	2,839	3,162	3,387	3,474	3,669	3,692	3,697	3,705	3,709	3,716	3,722
Croatia	1,356	1,502	1,589	1,607	1,653	1,674	1,683	1,692	1,701	1,710	1,718
Czech Republic	3,495	3,618	3,696	3,709	3,788	3,856	3,887	3,914	3,943	3,973	4,001
Estonia	465	533	596	617	621	623	624	626	630	633	636
Georgia											
Hungary	3,542	3,826	3,853	3,989	4,065	4,104	4,134	4,173	4,202	4,223	4,243
Latvia	854	902	953	952	941	958	967	987	991	994	995
Lithuania	999	1,077	1,159	1,247	1,309	1,295	1,292	1,300	1,306	1,311	1,317
Macedonia											
Moldova											
Poland	9,794	10,666	11,022	11,304	11,621	11,764	11,828	11,894	11,952	12,018	12,071
Romania	6,999	7,645	7,896	7,985	8,084	8,128	8,146	8,166	8,187	8,203	8,221
Russia	23,731	29,922	38,679	45,245	48,561	49,073	49,265	49,462	49,669	49,796	49,988
Serbia and Montenegro											
Slovakia	1,441	1,508	1,597	1,666	1,702	1,725	1,736	1,748	1,759	1,771	1,783
Slovenia	578	632	690	737	771	785	791	798	804	809	814
Ukraine	16,557	17,146	17,656	18,303	18,921	19,023	19,049	19,072	19,120	19,159	19,188

Source: National statistical offices/Euromonitor International

Table 15.7

New Dwellings Completed 1980-2007

'000 units

	1980	1985	1990	1995	2000	2002	2003	2004	2005	2006	2007
Western Europe											
Austria	51.0	41.2	36.6	53.4	53.8	41.9	40.2	36.2	34.0	33.2	32.6
Belgium	48.6	30.3	43.1	41.6	39.7	36.5	34.9	32.5	30.4	28.2	26.5
Cyprus	9.0	7.5	8.1	8.8							
Denmark	30.3	22.7	27.2	13.5	16.3	18.4	23.8	25.1	26.1	27.0	27.7
Finland	49.6	50.3	65.4	25.0	32.7	27.2	28.1	25.9	25.0	24.5	23.3
France	341.6	327.7	317.7	288.1	316.7	334.0	320.0	317.4	305.2	303.0	299.0
Germany	379.3	280.9	256.5	602.8	423.1	289.6	268.1	278.0	259.2	254.1	249.6
Gibraltar											
Greece	136.0	88.5	120.2	70.9	89.3	128.2	127.0	120.1	110.3	102.7	95.4
Iceland											
Ireland	27.8	23.9	19.5	30.6	49.8	57.7	68.8	77.0	81.0	93.4	103.4
Italy	287.0	180.7	194.9	145.3	142.4	145.8	142.4	138.9	134.2	130.8	126.2
Liechtenstein											
Luxembourg											
Malta											
Monaco											
Netherlands	116.4	98.1	97.4	93.8	70.7	66.7	59.6	55.1	51.2	48.4	46.4
Norway	38.1	26.1	27.1	19.2	19.5	21.7	20.5	19.4	18.9	18.6	18.2
Portugal	40.9	39.1	46.8	68.0	110.1	118.0	115.5	112.5	108.2	103.3	98.1
Spain	262.9	188.7	281.2	221.3	415.8	519.7	506.3	492.2	481.6	469.5	462.1
Sweden	51.4	32.9	58.4	12.7	13.0	19.9	20.0	25.3	25.7	26.1	26.5
Switzerland	40.9	44.2	40.0	46.2	32.2	28.6	32.1	29.2	27.8	26.3	25.1
Turkey	139.2	121.0	232.0	248.9	245.2	161.5	156.4	151.4	147.2	139.8	133.7
United Kingdom	242.0	207.5	203.4	199.7	178.9	183.1	173.2	169.2	168.4	166.8	164.4
Eastern Europe											
Albania											
Belarus	80.4	88.5	86.1	52.8	39.4	28.8	24.3	21.1	19.0	16.8	15.1
Bosnia-Herzegovina											
Bulgaria	74.3	64.9	26.0	6.8	8.8	6.2	6.3	6.4	6.5	6.7	6.9
Croatia	31.0	22.8	18.6	7.4	16.0	18.0	18.5	18.8	19.1	19.4	19.6
Czech Republic	80.7	66.7	44.6	12.7	25.2	27.3	27.1	32.3	33.9	35.1	36.0
Estonia	14.4	13.5	7.6	1.1	0.7	1.1	2.4	3.1	2.7	2.7	2.6
Georgia											
Hungary	89.1	72.5	43.8	24.7	21.6	31.5	35.5	43.9	46.5	48.4	49.9
Latvia	19.9	19.9	13.3	1.8	0.9	0.8	0.8	2.8	2.7	2.6	2.5
Lithuania	28.3	28.8	22.1	5.6	4.5	4.6	4.6	6.8	6.7	6.6	6.4
Macedonia											
Moldova											
Poland	217.1	189.6	134.2	67.1	87.8	97.6	162.7	108.1	102.2	96.2	91.9
Romania	197.8	105.6	48.6	35.8	26.4	27.7	28.3	28.7	29.3	29.7	30.2
Russia	436.8	671.8	800.0	602.0	351.7	329.4	312.4	293.1	282.9	274.8	263.3
Serbia and Montenegro											
Slovakia	48.2	38.0	24.7	6.2	12.9	14.2	13.3	12.5	12.0	11.3	10.7
Slovenia	13.6	10.8	8.1	6.1	6.8	7.3	6.6	7.0	6.6	6.1	5.7
Ukraine	329.0	341.0	289.0	118.0	62.9	60.4	59.3	58.4	57.6	56.8	56.2

Source: National statistical offices/Euromonitor International

Possession of Household Durables

Table 15.8

Possession of Household Durables 2007
% of total households

	Air Cond-itioner	Bicycle	Black/White TV	Camera	CD Player	Colour TV	Dish-washer	Freezer
Western Europe								
Austria	5.3	80.2	1.0	97.9	68.8	98.8	77.2	86.2
Belgium	6.1	71.6	2.3	81.2	65.4	98.9	48.2	61.1
Cyprus								
Denmark	4.1	61.2	1.5	99.2	87.4	98.1	65.0	98.5
Finland	2.6	85.0	1.7	85.9	62.8	97.1	60.2	90.5
France	6.8	74.3	1.1	76.8	23.8	95.4	45.3	53.9
Germany	6.0	81.3	0.7	81.1	83.4	97.9	63.5	72.2
Gibraltar								
Greece	15.1	43.1	2.0	88.4	19.1	99.6	31.9	22.2
Iceland								
Ireland	6.8	61.0	0.4	86.9	40.5	99.6	56.5	37.5
Italy	26.2	57.5	2.0	63.8	12.6	96.4	38.6	48.2
Liechtenstein								
Luxembourg								
Malta								
Monaco								
Netherlands	5.8	91.4	3.9	90.2	86.8	98.5	53.0	83.6
Norway	2.5	80.7	1.7	89.5	87.8	98.3	69.5	91.0
Portugal	3.4	32.7	3.8	40.8	43.2	98.9	22.9	55.4
Spain	17.1	37.7	2.0	67.9	41.4	99.5	36.7	31.1
Sweden	2.7	84.5	1.7	90.3	82.1	97.5	65.2	98.7
Switzerland	8.7	85.8	1.8	98.8	58.4	98.4	69.0	69.1
Turkey	8.1	16.3	9.3	29.8	7.4	92.4	27.9	2.9
United Kingdom	7.0	63.1	0.3	83.1	88.1	99.6	40.2	97.5
Eastern Europe								
Albania								
Belarus	1.4	30.4	8.0	27.0	6.2	94.8	3.9	16.0
Bosnia-Herzegovina								
Bulgaria	1.8	40.4	9.1	40.8	7.1	91.5	5.1	27.3
Croatia	19.8	40.7	4.4	59.5	21.9	96.2	20.2	69.7
Czech Republic	3.8	46.4	3.8	57.2	24.9	97.9	19.6	35.8
Estonia	3.0	74.5	3.4	49.3	14.1	96.4	4.6	39.9
Georgia								
Hungary	3.4	75.4	2.4	70.5	28.6	97.9	8.3	48.0
Latvia	3.0	26.0	4.4	30.8	8.3	95.3	2.0	15.7
Lithuania	2.9	28.1	5.0	33.9	7.8	97.0	2.4	19.0
Macedonia								
Moldova								
Poland	3.2	65.5	0.8	57.3	16.1	98.7	7.3	31.4
Romania	1.8	11.0	3.8	40.3	3.1	88.3	4.5	22.2
Russia	2.8	36.0	9.7	43.1	11.3	95.1	4.9	26.1
Serbia and Montenegro								
Slovakia	3.1	43.4	2.8	46.3	11.3	98.3	7.5	46.6
Slovenia	13.1	41.2	1.2	66.1	27.1	97.0	45.7	82.0
Ukraine	1.9	9.0	9.9	22.2	9.2	96.9	4.4	18.1

Source: National statistical offices/Euromonitor International

Possession of Household Durables

Possession of Household Durables 2007 *(continued)*
% of total households

	Hi-fi Stereo	Microwave Oven	Motor-cycle	Passenger Car	Personal Computer	Piano	Refrig-erator	Sewing Machine
Western Europe								
Austria	84.5	71.7	29.1	88.0	77.6	7.7	98.8	45.0
Belgium	79.8	80.4	14.8	88.2	62.3	1.8	99.1	41.3
Cyprus								
Denmark	90.2	73.8	21.0	72.7	86.6	5.5	99.1	43.5
Finland	89.9	91.3	12.6	80.8	69.8	6.3	97.4	51.7
France	65.1	79.2	18.5	83.0	61.8	4.2	97.1	54.2
Germany	74.0	69.7	24.4	77.3	75.0	5.6	99.2	57.3
Gibraltar								
Greece	60.6	36.3	11.4	72.4	40.0	1.6	95.1	33.1
Iceland								
Ireland	72.3	89.6	5.9	81.7	66.3	3.5	99.6	61.2
Italy	58.9	33.7	17.5	80.1	60.5	7.3	97.8	56.3
Liechtenstein								
Luxembourg								
Malta								
Monaco								
Netherlands	91.3	90.9	11.4	77.1	87.1	5.9	98.5	50.6
Norway	90.8	81.3	11.1	78.6	79.8	4.4	99.0	52.7
Portugal	46.9	58.9	19.2	66.4	50.2	3.5	98.2	35.7
Spain	62.2	76.5	21.2	77.1	58.3	2.8	100.0	49.1
Sweden	87.9	78.7	4.0	85.2	80.4	7.4	99.1	39.6
Switzerland	90.0	62.9	32.7	88.1	76.0	7.0	99.9	49.1
Turkey	41.8	5.5	12.0	37.6	21.8	1.5	98.2	43.6
United Kingdom	75.4	91.8	9.4	77.3	69.9	3.0	99.3	38.2
Eastern Europe								
Albania								
Belarus	24.8	20.1	4.3	28.2	19.5	2.9	96.8	45.8
Bosnia-Herzegovina								
Bulgaria	27.3	28.0	5.5	45.7	31.0	0.7	87.3	9.0
Croatia	35.0	27.1	20.1	58.4	34.5	3.5	93.3	7.0
Czech Republic	46.2	77.8	26.2	72.1	53.1	3.7	74.1	59.1
Estonia	51.5	54.7	2.4	50.0	48.5	1.9	94.9	25.1
Georgia								
Hungary	35.4	76.0	14.0	49.3	55.5	1.9	71.7	39.6
Latvia	48.3	32.0	0.7	47.9	44.5	7.1	93.8	37.3
Lithuania	41.0	49.0	2.5	52.0	48.2	2.0	98.0	26.1
Macedonia								
Moldova								
Poland	44.9	41.7	3.4	51.3	48.2	2.1	98.9	40.2
Romania	14.0	29.3	1.2	25.6	26.5	0.1	86.0	18.2
Russia	39.0	38.2	17.3	38.3	38.0	0.6	96.1	42.8
Serbia and Montenegro								
Slovakia	41.8	71.6	6.8	54.1	46.4	3.3	96.2	22.0
Slovenia	53.9	45.5	3.0	80.5	67.8	6.4	99.1	47.4
Ukraine	25.9	28.7	2.2	32.4	23.0	0.8	91.3	17.0

Source: National statistical offices/Euromonitor International

Possession of Household Durables

Possession of Household Durables 2007 *(continued)*
% of total households

	Shower	Telephone	Tumble Drier	Vacuum Cleaner	Video Camera	Videotape Recorder	Washing Machine
Western Europe							
Austria	93.0	72.5	22.1	98.1	22.0	66.0	96.3
Belgium	88.8	54.5	50.5	96.1	32.1	76.9	89.0
Cyprus							
Denmark	99.1	78.9	51.7	96.3	21.8	84.7	80.9
Finland	99.9	57.7	54.6	96.8	22.7	75.6	91.7
France	90.0	98.0	42.0	90.0	8.4	62.3	93.0
Germany	99.1	99.7	43.4	95.2	12.1	48.4	96.6
Gibraltar							
Greece	97.0	96.4	12.2	70.0	6.0	46.7	92.2
Iceland							
Ireland	97.2	82.7	26.4	95.8	13.3	82.0	96.6
Italy	80.7	70.7	17.2	79.5	26.1	71.1	96.8
Liechtenstein							
Luxembourg							
Malta							
Monaco							
Netherlands	98.3	99.7	60.9	97.1	29.7	80.5	97.0
Norway	99.5	90.3	42.5	95.6	23.8	43.3	89.8
Portugal	95.1	76.8	12.8	80.5	16.1	48.1	87.6
Spain	98.0	98.4	16.2	83.1	9.2	67.4	98.9
Sweden	98.2	99.0	45.2	96.4	27.3	79.2	74.9
Switzerland	99.6	88.5	40.7	99.0	52.3	67.6	99.3
Turkey	78.7	85.2	1.5	80.8	3.5	14.0	89.6
United Kingdom	92.0	90.3	58.1	95.6	11.6	84.9	96.4
Eastern Europe							
Albania							
Belarus	72.4	55.0	1.5	66.6	0.7	25.4	73.4
Bosnia-Herzegovina							
Bulgaria	60.8	71.4	3.8	82.4	0.2	40.1	69.3
Croatia	77.7	84.0	8.3	82.0	6.4	40.1	87.4
Czech Republic	78.1	35.3	2.3	89.4	7.1	62.1	93.2
Estonia	76.6	52.9	5.8	84.1	8.2	36.1	83.8
Georgia							
Hungary	74.4	46.7	2.0	93.1	12.1	63.1	86.5
Latvia	66.0	49.2	3.4	78.6	5.9	36.0	86.4
Lithuania	69.4	38.2	3.7	75.0	8.1	25.0	86.4
Macedonia							
Moldova							
Poland	77.3	62.4	1.2	94.5	5.8	77.9	85.2
Romania	44.7	38.2	0.5	55.8	0.9	5.2	67.2
Russia	62.5	58.8	1.0	84.7	6.9	17.0	96.1
Serbia and Montenegro							
Slovakia	78.7	41.4	1.5	88.4	5.6	52.1	75.0
Slovenia	77.7	80.0	9.1	93.8	5.3	52.2	96.8
Ukraine	71.0	54.5	1.5	65.9	3.8	10.0	78.5

Source: National statistical offices/Euromonitor International

Section Sixteen

Income and Deductions

Annual Gross Income

Table 16.1

Annual Gross Income 1990-2007
Billion units of national currency / as stated

	1990	1995	2000	2002	2003	2004	2005	2006	2007	US$ per capita 2007
Western Europe										
Austria	129.4	171.0	201.6	211.8	217.4	225.1	234.5	244.0	254.1	41,881
Belgium	130.8	168.0	195.8	208.0	208.9	213.7	221.5	230.5	239.7	31,087
Denmark	720.6	891.3	1,075.3	1,154.8	1,195.6	1,243.9	1,294.3	1,370.0	1,428.1	48,163
Finland	76.1	84.3	105.8	115.9	119.8	124.7	129.0	133.9	140.0	36,356
France	992.3	1,176.3	1,391.8	1,518.3	1,563.6	1,625.5	1,686.0	1,754.2	1,812.4	40,452
Germany	1,262.0	1,844.2	2,058.5	2,136.7	2,158.0	2,196.4	2,236.1	2,295.4	2,334.2	38,868
Greece	41.1	83.6	120.6	135.9	146.2	157.0	168.9	182.0	193.6	23,763
Ireland	30.5	38.7	60.4	69.8	74.3	79.2	86.8	95.5	105.5	33,630
Italy	582.9	755.9	874.7	948.4	969.3	1,002.7	1,029.5	1,068.8	1,105.0	25,719
Netherlands	177.4	215.7	277.4	309.2	325.2	331.2	339.7	354.1	370.3	31,025
Norway	559.2	720.7	1,012.1	1,134.5	1,194.8	1,259.6	1,311.9	1,396.3	1,488.6	54,367
Portugal	47.3	80.0	110.3	121.8	126.3	131.3	137.7	143.8	151.0	19,512
Spain	305.0	425.9	567.3	644.8	681.1	759.1	818.0	880.0	935.4	28,820
Sweden	1,225.0	1,564.9	1,853.1	1,989.9	2,063.0	2,139.9	2,220.5	2,310.7	2,421.7	39,316
Switzerland	259.3	304.5	342.4	351.4	345.9	351.2	363.0	377.8	392.3	43,588
Turkey	0.4	7.5	141.9	300.9	412.4	508.3	581.4	676.5	767.0	8,013
United Kingdom	530.6	711.2	911.1	1,000.6	1,049.0	1,100.8	1,168.0	1,213.9	1,286.8	42,413
Eastern Europe										
Belarus	0.0	83.6	6,463.0	19,026.9	25,346.0	32,181.7	40,708.2	49,178.3	61,794.5	2,953
Bulgaria	0.0	0.7	23.5	29.1	30.8	34.2	38.2	43.3	49.5	4,540
Croatia	0.2	69.5	109.3	130.3	139.1	148.7	159.7	170.9	186.1	7,815
Czech Republic	595.1	1,189.4	1,732.1	1,927.3	2,038.1	2,172.1	2,268.1	2,435.5	2,646.5	12,677
Estonia	7.0	34.9	71.3	90.2	98.1	106.9	122.2	141.8	162.4	10,602
Hungary	1,699.2	4,900.0	10,952.7	13,869.2	15,209.5	16,791.5	18,048.8	19,424.1	20,612.9	11,161
Latvia	0.1	2.1	4.0	4.7	5.3	6.2	7.3	9.0	11.0	9,402
Lithuania	0.1	21.7	40.0	43.8	46.6	51.5	58.6	67.3	79.5	9,304
Poland	45.7	315.8	680.5	752.3	763.3	808.9	850.3	907.9	986.1	9,350
Romania	0.1	6.2	69.2	130.3	169.9	215.1	250.8	298.3	352.3	6,704
Russia	0.6	900.2	4,384.5	7,748.5	9,466.9	11,875.6	14,479.0	17,284.2	20,757.6	5,712
Slovakia	153.0	457.8	781.8	931.3	988.8	1,076.7	1,186.8	1,301.4	1,427.9	10,725
Slovenia	3.8	11.9	16.3	20.4	21.8	23.4	24.7	26.4	28.8	19,638
Ukraine	0.0	31.3	128.3	171.7	209.2	273.0	382.1	464.0	607.7	2,590

Source: *Euromonitor International from national statistics*

Table 16.2

Gross Income by Source 2007

% of gross income

	Benefits	Employment	Investments	Other Sources	Total
Western Europe					
Austria	10.62	82.94	5.77	0.67	100.00
Belgium	26.17	57.76	15.43	0.64	100.00
Denmark	19.02	67.07	7.56	6.35	100.00
Finland	16.80	68.55	12.57	2.08	100.00
France	29.15	62.71	7.70	0.43	100.00
Germany	20.07	62.86	13.90	3.17	100.00
Greece	20.60	55.45	20.16	3.80	100.00
Ireland	13.34	67.06	14.48	5.12	100.00
Italy	19.53	60.05	17.93	2.49	100.00
Netherlands	23.31	62.82	13.16	0.72	100.00
Norway	21.94	71.75	6.03	0.27	100.00
Portugal	16.10	73.62	4.00	6.29	100.00
Spain	12.38	74.99	8.52	4.10	100.00
Sweden	19.90	70.55	6.06	3.49	100.00
Switzerland	22.52	72.96	2.89	1.63	100.00
Turkey	7.16	70.73	19.03	3.08	100.00
United Kingdom	19.09	68.14	7.96	4.81	100.00
Eastern Europe					
Belarus	23.85	69.71	0.83	5.61	100.00
Bulgaria	20.07	47.98	20.42	11.52	100.00
Croatia	23.45	66.06	6.16	4.33	100.00
Czech Republic	12.39	65.53	17.19	4.89	100.00
Estonia	29.92	62.92	1.15	6.02	100.00
Hungary	19.03	57.66	12.71	10.60	100.00
Latvia	17.80	63.33	18.31	0.57	100.00
Lithuania	21.17	64.42	6.06	8.35	100.00
Poland	25.37	60.19	2.56	11.88	100.00
Romania	13.36	73.01	9.49	4.15	100.00
Russia	14.20	77.93	6.26	1.62	100.00
Slovakia	18.47	77.65	1.26	2.62	100.00
Slovenia	23.30	63.15	4.09	9.46	100.00
Ukraine	13.53	82.67	0.98	2.82	100.00

Source: *Euromonitor International from national statistics*

Income and Deductions

Table 16.3

Annual Disposable Income 1990-2007

Billion units of national currency / as stated

	1990	1995	2000	2002	2003	2004	2005	2006	2007	US$ per capita 2007
Western Europe										
Austria	81.2	117.7	136.3	141.2	145.6	151.3	158.0	164.8	172.1	28,368
Belgium	107.8	137.2	156.4	165.9	167.1	170.9	177.3	184.9	192.7	24,990
Denmark	433.5	530.4	595.5	649.1	665.3	689.1	710.4	752.3	786.2	26,514
Finland	48.6	53.6	66.3	74.0	77.8	81.7	83.4	86.4	89.9	23,346
France	665.0	786.7	923.0	1,015.5	1,042.7	1,089.4	1,127.1	1,175.3	1,214.4	27,105
Germany	887.7	1,245.1	1,383.5	1,447.3	1,475.2	1,502.0	1,528.7	1,562.4	1,586.1	26,412
Greece	34.3	69.4	93.3	104.0	112.3	121.3	130.6	140.7	149.7	18,375
Ireland	26.4	33.8	54.5	64.0	67.5	70.1	78.0	86.4	95.2	30,338
Italy	535.3	701.4	819.7	901.1	927.5	959.1	983.4	1,012.3	1,045.0	24,324
Netherlands	139.4	165.2	207.9	238.6	246.9	251.4	254.7	261.3	272.6	22,843
Norway	366.3	480.6	655.2	732.7	786.7	838.8	883.0	946.2	1,011.7	36,951
Portugal	39.1	61.7	83.2	91.9	95.1	98.7	102.4	106.8	112.3	14,514
Spain	217.3	300.6	396.3	447.6	474.3	540.4	580.9	619.4	657.1	20,246
Sweden	765.4	935.8	1,079.5	1,172.9	1,223.7	1,277.3	1,331.9	1,385.7	1,452.2	23,577
Switzerland	204.2	244.8	276.4	285.0	284.1	292.2	298.3	306.9	316.2	35,139
Turkey	0.3	5.5	119.7	250.4	342.7	422.7	482.7	561.5	635.9	6,643
United Kingdom	358.4	495.7	632.5	697.5	729.4	757.9	792.3	819.9	866.3	28,552
Eastern Europe										
Belarus	0.0	68.3	5,061.9	15,289.5	20,648.7	26,503.7	33,383.2	40,225.6	49,719.0	2,376
Bulgaria	0.0	0.7	19.9	24.6	25.9	28.7	32.1	36.4	41.6	3,815
Croatia	0.2	65.8	93.9	112.5	119.7	127.9	137.1	146.3	159.7	6,704
Czech Republic	321.2	861.5	1,231.1	1,348.4	1,408.8	1,460.6	1,522.0	1,624.7	1,765.4	8,457
Estonia	5.2	25.4	53.5	66.9	71.6	78.0	88.6	105.9	122.7	8,008
Hungary	1,192.5	3,437.5	7,712.5	9,849.1	10,909.3	12,122.8	12,969.1	13,643.0	14,274.9	7,729
Latvia	0.0	1.6	3.1	3.6	4.1	4.7	5.6	7.1	9.0	7,668
Lithuania	0.1	17.8	32.0	35.5	37.8	41.4	46.7	53.1	62.7	7,341
Poland	38.6	241.3	524.1	577.9	588.9	627.8	651.5	688.9	742.6	7,042
Romania	0.1	5.0	56.4	103.7	129.3	168.3	197.4	235.9	280.8	5,343
Russia	0.5	759.0	3,530.1	6,278.8	7,657.2	9,614.9	11,967.8	14,438.8	17,552.9	4,830
Slovakia	123.5	331.2	588.7	692.5	734.2	811.8	890.8	969.5	1,063.7	7,990
Slovenia	2.9	9.3	11.9	14.7	15.6	16.8	17.8	18.9	20.5	13,991
Ukraine	0.0	24.5	100.1	134.0	163.1	212.6	298.8	364.1	478.4	2,039

Source: *Euromonitor International from national statistics*

Income and Deductions

Table 16.4

Tax and Social Security Contributions 1990-2007

Billion units of national currency / as stated

	1990	1995	2000	2002	2003	2004	2005	2006	2007	US$ per capita 2007
Western Europe										
Austria	48.3	53.3	65.3	70.6	71.8	73.8	76.4	79.2	82.0	13,513
Belgium	23.0	30.7	39.4	42.1	41.8	42.9	44.2	45.6	47.0	6,097
Denmark	287.1	360.9	479.8	505.7	530.3	554.8	583.9	617.6	641.9	21,649
Finland	27.6	30.7	39.5	42.0	42.0	43.0	45.6	47.6	50.1	13,010
France	327.3	389.6	468.8	502.8	521.0	536.0	558.9	578.9	598.0	13,348
Germany	374.3	599.2	675.0	689.4	682.8	694.4	707.5	732.9	748.0	12,456
Greece	6.9	14.2	27.4	31.9	34.0	35.7	38.3	41.3	43.9	5,388
Ireland	4.1	4.9	5.9	5.8	6.8	9.1	8.8	9.1	10.3	3,292
Italy	47.6	54.6	55.0	47.3	41.8	43.6	46.1	56.6	59.9	1,395
Netherlands	37.9	50.5	69.5	70.5	78.3	79.8	84.9	92.8	97.6	8,182
Norway	192.9	240.1	356.9	401.8	408.1	420.8	428.8	450.1	476.9	17,417
Portugal	8.2	18.3	27.1	29.9	31.2	32.6	35.3	37.0	38.7	4,998
Spain	87.7	125.4	171.0	197.2	206.9	218.7	237.2	260.6	278.3	8,575
Sweden	459.6	629.1	773.6	817.0	839.3	862.6	888.6	925.0	969.4	15,739
Switzerland	55.2	59.8	66.0	66.5	61.8	59.0	64.6	70.8	76.0	8,450
Turkey	0.1	2.1	22.2	50.5	69.7	85.6	98.7	115.0	131.1	1,370
United Kingdom	172.2	215.6	278.6	303.1	319.6	342.9	375.8	394.0	420.5	13,861
Eastern Europe										
Belarus	0.0	15.3	1,401.1	3,737.4	4,697.3	5,678.0	7,325.0	8,952.7	12,075.5	577
Bulgaria	0.0	0.0	3.6	4.6	4.9	5.4	6.1	6.9	7.9	725
Croatia	0.0	3.7	15.3	17.9	19.4	20.7	22.7	24.5	26.5	1,111
Czech Republic	273.9	327.9	501.1	578.8	629.3	711.5	746.0	810.8	881.0	4,220
Estonia	1.8	9.5	17.7	23.3	26.4	28.9	33.6	35.9	39.7	2,595
Hungary	506.7	1,462.5	3,240.2	4,020.1	4,300.1	4,668.7	5,079.7	5,781.0	6,338.0	3,432
Latvia	0.0	0.5	0.9	1.1	1.2	1.5	1.7	1.8	2.0	1,734
Lithuania	0.0	3.9	8.0	8.3	8.8	10.1	11.9	14.2	16.8	1,964
Poland	7.2	74.4	156.4	174.4	174.4	181.1	198.7	219.0	243.5	2,309
Romania	0.0	1.2	12.8	26.6	40.6	46.8	53.3	62.4	71.5	1,361
Russia	0.1	141.2	854.4	1,469.7	1,809.7	2,260.7	2,511.1	2,845.4	3,204.7	882
Slovakia	29.5	126.7	193.1	238.8	254.6	265.0	296.0	331.9	364.1	2,735
Slovenia	0.9	2.6	4.4	5.7	6.2	6.7	6.9	7.5	8.3	5,647
Ukraine	0.0	6.8	28.2	37.6	46.1	60.4	83.2	100.0	129.3	551

Source: *Euromonitor International from national statistics*

Industrial Markets

Industrial Output

Table 17.1

Indices of General Industrial Production 1980-2007

1995 = 100

	1980	1985	1990	1995	2000	2002	2003	2004	2005	2006	2007
Western Europe											
Austria	68.1	74.2	89.0	100.0	134.1	139.3	142.0	151.1	157.3	170.2	176.0
Belgium	80.9	84.1	99.4	100.0	115.5	116.6	117.5	121.5	121.0	127.0	130.3
Cyprus	63.0	73.3	97.2	100.0	105.4	105.2	113.6	115.8	116.7	117.6	117.7
Denmark	66.3	80.2	86.2	100.0	115.5	119.1	119.2	118.6	121.1	125.4	127.1
Finland	65.7	76.2	87.3	100.0	144.5	147.7	149.4	157.5	157.6	169.9	160.4
France	87.9	86.1	100.4	100.0	114.4	114.4	114.0	116.6	116.7	117.0	122.3
Germany			100.0	100.0	114.5	113.6	114.0	117.4	121.3	128.5	134.1
Gibraltar											
Greece	91.9	98.4	101.8	100.0	122.5	121.3	121.6	123.1	121.8	122.7	122.0
Iceland											
Ireland	34.4	44.0	63.1	100.0	201.6	237.9	249.0	249.8	257.3	270.4	294.7
Italy	82.0	79.5	93.5	100.0	107.7	105.4	104.2	105.3	103.0	105.4	110.4
Liechtenstein											
Luxembourg	68.1	82.4	98.0	100.0	122.1	129.5	134.1	139.5	140.3	142.6	149.7
Malta											
Monaco											
Netherlands	79.1	83.9	92.2	100.0	110.0	111.7	110.2	114.6	113.8	115.2	116.8
Norway	49.7	60.1	78.6	100.0	110.7	110.0	105.8	108.1	106.9	104.7	107.5
Portugal	62.3	73.5	100.6	100.0	118.1	121.2	121.3	118.1	118.5	121.8	127.5
Spain	81.0	83.4	97.2	100.0	119.3	118.0	119.9	122.0	122.1	126.7	133.3
Sweden	73.6	81.0	89.2	100.0	119.9	118.6	120.2	126.5	129.9	133.7	142.8
Switzerland	79.9	82.3	97.0	100.0	121.7	114.6	114.6	119.7	122.9	132.5	135.3
Turkey		60.0	85.5	100.0	121.2	121.1	131.8	144.5	152.4	161.4	167.7
United Kingdom	76.5	82.6	94.1	100.0	107.2	103.6	103.3	104.2	102.2	102.3	103.7
Eastern Europe											
Albania				100.0	121.3	75.6	70.5	67.2	60.2	55.1	51.0
Belarus			169.2	100.0	164.3	181.9	194.8	225.7	249.4	277.9	314.0
Bosnia-Herzegovina											
Bulgaria	143.4	177.8	166.1	100.0	78.2	83.6	95.4	111.7	119.1	126.1	127.7
Croatia			178.3	100.0	114.5	128.0	133.3	138.1	145.1	159.0	156.0
Czech Republic			131.8	100.0	105.7	114.8	121.2	132.8	141.6	157.5	174.5
Estonia			207.0	100.0	135.9	160.1	177.6	196.2	217.8	233.7	246.7
Georgia											
Hungary	111.7	122.9	113.8	100.0	168.4	180.7	192.7	206.9	222.3	244.4	260.0
Latvia			260.4	100.0	104.9	118.6	126.4	134.0	141.5	148.3	151.8
Lithuania			197.2	100.0	110.1	131.4	152.9	169.4	181.4	195.3	202.5
Macedonia			207.5	100.0	110.4	93.9	98.3	96.1	102.9	106.6	105.7
Moldova											
Poland	99.9	98.9	80.8	100.0	143.5	146.1	158.9	179.1	186.4	208.8	219.4
Romania	148.6	183.5	152.7	100.0	83.2	94.5	97.5	101.9	104.2	111.9	115.5
Russia			202.4	100.0	105.2	111.8	121.6	131.7	137.4	142.8	148.0
Serbia and Montenegro				100.0	102.1	104.1	101.3	109.2	109.6	114.8	113.6
Slovakia			125.3	100.0	115.2	130.8	137.4	143.4	148.4	163.4	177.8
Slovenia			124.7	100.0	111.8	117.9	119.6	126.2	130.1	138.8	144.5
Ukraine			190.8	100.0	109.0	131.3	152.1	170.2	174.9	185.0	190.7

Source: *United Nations/Euromonitor International*
Notes: *Indices based on value of production (or contribution to GDP) at constant prices*

Table 17.2

Indices of General Industrial Production by Quarter 2006-2008
1995 = 100

	2006 1st Quarter	2006 2nd Quarter	2006 3rd Quarter	2006 4th Quarter	2007 1st Quarter	2007 2nd Quarter	2007 3rd Quarter	2007 4th Quarter	2008 1st Quarter	2008 2nd Quarter
Western Europe										
Austria	156.7	168.6	169.4	180.6	168.9	175.3	174.8	189.5	177.2	
Belgium	127.8	127.8	120.8	131.6	131.8	131.5	125.0	133.7	133.9	
Cyprus	111.8	119.4	118.8	121.3	112.2	121.6	124.1	127.3	116.3	
Denmark	123.7	124.2	120.0	133.6	128.8	121.7	119.7	133.6	127.4	
Finland	157.2	179.6	175.4	178.0	163.7	183.9	179.7	193.5	166.5	
France	121.5	119.6	107.1	122.2	120.2	117.5	108.4	130.2	121.5	
Germany	124.5	126.9	128.4	134.2	132.2	134.7	136.7	142.2	138.8	
Gibraltar										
Greece	118.7	126.8	124.0	121.2	121.6	127.7	127.5	124.5	118.0	
Iceland										
Ireland	269.6	295.1	249.7	267.3	293.8	292.2	274.1	300.1	303.2	
Italy	105.9	110.5	97.0	108.1	110.4	109.8	96.2	107.3	108.6	
Liechtenstein										
Luxembourg	160.2	144.0	127.1	141.1	151.6	146.4	129.1	146.9	151.1	
Malta										
Monaco										
Netherlands	125.7	113.3	105.4	124.2	120.3	113.5	111.4	134.4	126.9	
Norway	110.9	102.2	98.5	106.6	107.3	99.3	99.6	108.5	108.7	
Portugal	122.0	122.0	118.1	125.1	126.6	123.9	119.9	125.4	122.9	
Spain	127.8	130.5	119.2	129.2	133.3	133.6	120.8	130.7	128.1	
Sweden	135.6	135.0	120.5	145.6	143.5	141.0	123.7	146.1	143.6	
Switzerland	126.1	131.4	130.8	141.9	135.1	144.6	144.9	155.6	141.1	
Turkey	144.8	167.1	167.6	166.0	158.2	173.3	174.5	173.8	169.1	
United Kingdom	103.5	100.8	98.2	103.9	101.7	101.2	98.8	106.1	101.5	
Eastern Europe										
Albania										
Belarus	233.3	275.4	282.9	320.0	249.0	303.3	307.1	349.6		
Bosnia-Herzegovina										
Bulgaria	119.0	122.9	126.8	135.9	129.6	133.8	140.2	147.4	134.6	
Croatia	138.6	173.3	156.4	167.6	149.6	162.1	163.3	165.1		
Czech Republic	152.5	158.7	150.8	167.8	169.8	173.6	161.5	181.3	179.5	
Estonia	224.4	242.8	236.6	254.1	247.3	260.4	247.6	266.2	246.7	
Georgia										
Hungary	231.5	238.0	240.0	267.9	252.2	256.3	262.6	286.6	269.3	
Latvia	150.7	142.8	143.5	156.5	151.8	144.6	145.2	154.7	147.8	
Lithuania	196.6	196.5	189.8	196.1	194.3	202.3	205.9	207.5	208.6	
Macedonia	91.4	109.8	112.5	113.5	99.9	107.2	114.3	121.1	105.8	
Moldova										
Poland	194.2	205.8	210.4	224.9	219.6	223.6	227.6	244.5	238.5	
Romania	106.8	115.5	111.0	116.0	112.9	118.7	119.1	120.8	118.8	
Russia	134.5	139.3	142.6	153.0	150.3	153.9	157.4	167.6	159.6	
Serbia and Montenegro	104.5	112.0	113.5	129.2	109.8	118.2	117.9	130.1	115.7	
Slovakia	154.4	160.9	160.2	174.7	176.8	183.5	178.3	194.1	189.6	
Slovenia	131.2	138.9	136.6	146.5	143.2	148.7	144.9	152.1	145.5	
Ukraine	166.9	180.5	190.3	202.1	186.4	198.4	212.1	218.8	200.3	

Source: *United Nations/Euromonitor International*
Notes: *Indices based on value of production (or contribution to GDP) at constant prices*

Industrial Output

Table 17.3

Indices of General Industrial Production by Month 2007

1995 = 100

	January	February	March	April	May	June	July	August	September	October	November	December
Western Europe												
Austria	152.6	162.4	191.8	171.2	172.5	182.2	176.6	159.8	188.2	193.8	190.5	184.2
Belgium	128.9	125.8	140.8	126.7	129.7	138.3	120.3	121.7	132.9	141.7	135.0	124.3
Cyprus	108.5	105.4	122.7	113.0	121.8	129.8	139.3	100.4	132.6	132.8	123.3	125.9
Denmark	131.3	121.4	133.6	113.3	122.7	129.0	103.1	127.4	128.4	144.1	138.5	118.2
Finland	153.8	156.1	181.0	172.2	189.0	190.4	171.7	179.6	187.8	204.0	206.4	170.1
France	118.1	114.3	128.3	114.7	112.8	124.9	117.7	89.1	118.5	132.9	124.9	132.9
Germany	125.0	128.5	143.0	132.6	133.1	138.5	137.7	127.2	145.2	146.4	147.2	133.0
Gibraltar												
Greece	114.9	124.0	125.9	119.3	130.4	133.3	136.7	114.9	131.0	125.8	126.1	121.5
Iceland												
Ireland	280.0	292.6	308.8	292.4	288.2	296.0	270.6	275.0	276.7	302.3	295.6	302.4
Italy	105.4	107.2	118.5	100.4	116.9	112.0	116.4	64.6	107.6	118.2	111.0	92.7
Liechtenstein												
Luxembourg	153.6	143.5	157.8	144.5	146.8	147.8	137.6	112.3	137.2	147.7	150.4	142.5
Malta												
Monaco												
Netherlands	118.0	118.4	124.6	111.6	111.6	117.4	108.9	104.1	121.3	129.2	136.6	137.3
Norway	110.7	103.5	107.6	105.0	100.7	92.3	95.1	102.6	101.1	110.6	110.2	104.6
Portugal	127.4	118.6	133.7	117.1	128.5	125.9	129.6	101.8	128.2	130.3	127.5	118.5
Spain	130.8	127.1	142.0	122.6	140.8	137.4	137.1	96.8	128.5	140.3	135.9	115.8
Sweden	138.7	136.1	155.6	136.6	145.1	141.5	104.4	128.7	138.1	149.2	152.6	136.6
Switzerland												
Turkey	150.6	151.8	172.2	164.8	178.2	177.0	173.8	172.4	177.1	173.2	183.7	164.5
United Kingdom	99.5	96.8	108.7	97.9	103.7	102.1	98.7	97.6	100.1	110.4	110.0	97.9
Eastern Europe												
Albania												
Belarus	241.1	244.2	261.6	275.7	310.8	323.4	296.7	307.6	317.2	313.7	349.8	385.2
Bosnia-Herzegovina												
Bulgaria	118.1	127.1	143.6	129.7	132.3	139.4	143.6	138.9	138.3	145.3	148.0	149.0
Croatia	139.3	144.4	165.0	156.7	170.5	159.1	172.0	157.5	160.3	170.2	167.4	157.6
Czech Republic	164.6	159.9	184.9	168.5	175.6	176.8	160.3	156.7	167.4	188.1	197.5	158.2
Estonia	234.9	238.6	268.5	250.0	270.3	261.0	228.7	255.8	258.3	284.2	276.0	238.5
Georgia												
Hungary	246.4	242.7	267.5	247.3	251.3	270.2	260.9	245.2	281.6	300.4	303.9	255.4
Latvia	142.9	149.2	163.4	138.8	147.6	147.2	139.6	152.7	143.4	156.7	159.0	148.5
Lithuania	191.5	187.2	204.3	194.6	205.8	206.6	206.1	212.2	199.4	208.0	208.4	205.9
Macedonia	88.4	100.4	111.1	107.8	103.4	110.2	111.0	112.2	119.6	127.7	117.8	118.0
Moldova												
Poland	210.9	208.9	239.1	219.0	225.6	226.2	221.9	224.1	236.8	259.7	247.3	226.4
Romania	105.4	111.0	122.2	109.7	125.2	121.1	120.0	114.1	123.4	126.7	123.9	111.7
Russia	144.0	144.2	162.5	151.3	151.9	158.5	160.1	156.1	155.9	160.2	166.6	175.9
Serbia and Montenegro	104.7	104.2	120.4	115.0	119.4	120.3	116.8	118.6	118.4	133.9	125.4	131.1
Slovakia	172.9	167.1	190.3	176.4	190.5	183.5	179.7	166.3	188.8	203.8	203.5	175.1
Slovenia	139.1	135.2	155.3	143.3	150.4	152.4	152.1	131.5	151.3	166.4	159.1	130.9
Ukraine	179.2	178.4	201.6	195.7	199.4	200.2	205.0	226.2	205.0	226.2	215.5	214.8

Source: United Nations/Euromonitor International
Notes: Indices based on value of production (or contribution to GDP) at constant prices

Table 17.4

Indices of Manufacturing Production 1980-2007

1995 = 100

	1980	1985	1990	1995	2000	2002	2003	2004	2005	2006	2007
Western Europe											
Austria	66.5	72.5	88.7	100.0	137.3	139.9	142.9	153.6	160.1	173.4	183.2
Belgium	74.4	77.4	94.0	100.0	116.2	117.1	117.7	122.7	120.3	126.1	129.6
Cyprus		79.7	103.3	100.0	100.1	95.8	103.8	105.7	104.9	104.3	103.6
Denmark	64.8	79.1	86.2	100.0	115.6	119.1	118.3	118.0	120.0	125.0	129.0
Finland	66.1	76.7	87.0	100.0	147.9	150.2	150.1	150.7	161.7	172.7	170.7
France	93.7	91.9	102.2	100.0	116.3	115.7	114.9	117.9	118.1	119.1	122.4
Germany			100.0	100.0	116.3	115.3	115.7	119.4	123.8	131.7	137.1
Gibraltar											
Greece	99.4	100.3	102.2	100.0	114.8	111.8	111.3	112.7	111.8	112.7	113.3
Iceland											
Ireland	31.6	41.4	61.6	100.0	208.8	247.8	259.1	259.5	267.6	281.8	297.0
Italy	83.1	79.8	93.9	100.0	106.7	104.1	101.9	102.6	99.8	102.1	107.1
Liechtenstein											
Luxembourg	69.4	84.7	99.0	100.0	123.6	128.9	134.1	140.3	142.7	145.9	151.6
Malta											
Monaco											
Netherlands	73.3	79.9	92.9	100.0	113.8	113.4	112.2	116.1	116.3	118.9	122.2
Norway	80.8	88.9	89.7	100.0	103.0	101.2	96.8	98.6	100.8	105.6	112.3
Portugal	69.5	81.3	104.3	100.0	114.8	117.9	117.3	116.4	114.6	117.2	118.8
Spain	81.3	82.2	96.8	100.0	119.7	117.8	119.6	121.0	120.6	125.6	132.5
Sweden	73.7	81.0	89.1	100.0	121.8	121.7	124.6	130.2	133.4	139.5	146.0
Switzerland	79.2	81.6	97.0	100.0	123.2	115.4	115.3	120.8	124.6	135.2	144.0
Turkey		65.2	90.5	100.0	121.3	121.7	133.0	146.8	153.8	162.5	167.1
United Kingdom	80.7	83.9	97.7	100.0	106.6	102.3	102.7	104.8	103.5	105.3	106.2
Eastern Europe											
Albania				100.0	116.0	53.6	54.7	51.4	44.5	39.4	34.3
Belarus			170.9	100.0	167.0	184.3	197.2	229.4	253.5	282.9	294.0
Bosnia-Herzegovina											
Bulgaria				100.0	74.7	81.3	96.5	117.1	126.6	135.8	140.0
Croatia			188.0	100.0	108.5	120.5	126.7	131.8	140.5	151.0	158.0
Czech Republic			162.9	100.0	108.2	118.6	125.0	138.4	148.9	166.9	186.1
Estonia			215.5	100.0	145.3	174.2	192.8	216.3	241.9	262.6	275.7
Georgia											
Hungary	115.4	126.9	116.4	100.0	186.8	201.5	215.8	234.1	252.6	278.4	295.0
Latvia			261.8	100.0	108.4	123.8	133.6	141.7	151.0	158.3	164.0
Lithuania			216.0	100.0	111.9	133.6	152.1	170.1	184.8	200.7	211.1
Macedonia											
Moldova											
Poland	93.8	90.9	75.7	100.0	153.7	156.3	172.7	198.0	207.1	235.3	260.0
Romania			159.7	100.0	85.1	99.9	103.8	109.4	112.4	121.8	128.0
Russia			230.4	100.0	107.5	110.8	122.2	135.0	142.2	149.3	152.9
Serbia and Montenegro	265.7	302.9	281.7	100.0	108.4	112.6	107.6	118.2	117.3	123.6	123.9
Slovakia			127.9	100.0	116.6	138.7	148.9	156.3	164.4	184.7	203.6
Slovenia			126.1	100.0	112.7	118.2	120.0	125.9	130.4	139.3	145.9
Ukraine			201.2	100.0	113.2	144.5	170.8	195.7	201.6	214.3	217.3

Source: *United Nations/Euromonitor International*
Notes: *Indices based on value of production (or contribution to GDP) at constant prices*

Industrial Output

Table 17.5

Indices of Manufacturing Production by Quarter 2006-2008
1995 = 100

	2006 1st Quarter	2006 2nd Quarter	2006 3rd Quarter	2006 4th Quarter	2007 1st Quarter	2007 2nd Quarter	2007 3rd Quarter	2007 4th Quarter	2008 1st Quarter	2008 2nd Quarter
Western Europe										
Austria	156.0	172.1	174.7	184.2	170.6	181.2	180.8	192.2	178.2	
Belgium	126.9	127.5	119.1	130.3	131.2	131.5	123.7	132.7	133.5	
Cyprus	98.3	108.7	100.2	111.1	98.4	110.5	104.9	117.3	101.4	
Denmark	122.3	123.6	121.2	132.8	130.9	127.7	124.0	136.7	130.1	
Finland	157.6	182.7	175.5	187.0	166.3	190.0	184.9	199.5	168.1	
France	120.4	123.1	109.5	123.4	121.9	122.7	112.3	126.8	122.6	
Germany	126.3	130.6	132.5	137.7	135.8	139.4	141.7	146.5	143.0	
Gibraltar										
Greece	108.5	118.6	111.8	112.0	111.3	118.7	114.3	114.4	108.3	
Iceland										
Ireland	278.8	310.0	261.2	277.4	306.0	306.3	286.4	313.1	315.9	
Italy	104.3	106.6	91.8	106.1	107.1	108.1	92.9	103.4	104.4	
Liechtenstein										
Luxembourg	145.4	147.5	140.1	148.9	151.0	154.4	135.8	146.1	146.3	
Malta										
Monaco										
Netherlands	118.5	121.9	117.7	129.4	125.8	126.8	121.3	129.1	126.6	
Norway	107.3	103.5	98.8	112.6	112.2	109.7	103.0	114.7	114.8	
Portugal	116.0	118.4	114.9	119.4	121.3	122.3	117.3	123.0	120.5	
Spain	125.7	131.1	117.3	128.4	132.3	134.0	119.1	129.0	126.0	
Sweden	137.8	141.8	128.7	152.0	146.8	147.9	130.7	152.9	147.0	
Switzerland	127.0	134.6	133.9	145.2	137.8	148.6	148.9	159.1	143.7	
Turkey	146.0	170.0	167.2	166.9	158.4	175.0	172.7	175.2	168.3	
United Kingdom	100.3	104.4	104.6	107.2	102.3	104.9	103.7	108.5	102.4	
Eastern Europe										
Albania										
Belarus										
Bosnia-Herzegovina										
Bulgaria	119.7	135.3	139.7	148.3	134.9	145.7	151.6	155.5	141.6	
Croatia	130.5	160.1	152.9	160.5	143.9	161.1	160.6	160.2	121.0	
Czech Republic	159.1	169.8	160.9	177.8	180.0	186.9	173.2	192.8	190.6	
Estonia	238.7	279.8	270.0	283.8	268.1	295.7	275.7	287.5	269.0	
Georgia										
Hungary	258.7	273.0	278.1	307.3	285.9	295.5	305.2	328.3	306.2	
Latvia	144.8	159.7	164.3	164.2	148.3	159.5	163.8	155.0	142.1	
Lithuania	190.7	208.8	203.9	199.7	191.1	215.8	221.6	208.9	209.0	
Macedonia										
Moldova										
Poland	213.7	233.9	239.9	253.8	248.2	256.6	261.7	276.0	269.6	
Romania	112.4	125.0	123.5	128.2	123.2	131.0	131.2	132.2	130.0	
Russia	130.0	150.3	154.9	160.7	154.5	172.8	179.3	184.3	167.3	
Serbia and Montenegro	105.7	124.7	125.3	138.8	114.9	131.3	130.1	139.0	119.5	
Slovakia	167.9	183.4	183.8	199.5	201.2	214.3	204.7	225.4	217.6	
Slovenia	132.0	140.4	138.6	146.3	149.8	151.8	148.0	154.7	149.8	
Ukraine										

Source: *United Nations/Euromonitor International*
Notes: *Indices based on value of production (or contribution to GDP) at constant prices*

Table 17.6

Indices of Manufacturing Production by Month 2007

1995 = 100

	January	February	March	April	May	June	July	August	September	October	November	December
Western Europe												
Austria	152.0	164.1	195.8	176.4	179.1	188.3	182.7	164.4	195.3	199.8	193.4	183.4
Belgium	127.5	124.6	141.4	126.1	129.6	138.9	118.7	119.8	132.6	142.1	134.0	122.2
Cyprus	91.8	92.6	110.7	102.5	112.5	116.6	121.9	79.0	113.8	117.5	116.6	117.7
Denmark	130.6	122.0	140.2	117.9	128.0	137.2	106.1	131.7	134.1	150.2	142.7	117.0
Finland	154.9	157.7	186.3	177.7	197.2	195.2	173.9	186.1	194.8	210.5	213.4	174.5
France	118.4	116.0	131.4	118.9	117.6	131.7	122.7	90.0	124.1	138.5	127.3	114.6
Germany	127.4	132.1	147.8	136.4	137.8	143.9	142.8	131.3	151.0	151.4	152.1	136.1
Gibraltar												
Greece	102.4	113.7	117.9	111.0	122.5	122.6	122.2	100.3	120.5	116.8	116.5	109.8
Iceland												
Ireland	290.1	304.8	323.1	306.9	302.2	309.9	282.4	288.1	288.5	316.2	308.5	314.5
Italy	100.6	104.2	116.4	98.4	115.6	110.2	114.2	59.0	105.6	116.4	107.2	86.5
Liechtenstein												
Luxembourg	153.2	140.0	160.0	151.4	154.6	157.3	145.1	117.2	145.1	153.2	150.5	134.5
Malta												
Monaco												
Netherlands	119.7	123.6	134.0	125.0	125.4	130.1	121.3	113.0	129.5	128.4	133.3	125.7
Norway	113.8	108.8	113.9	102.9	110.2	115.9	78.3	112.3	118.4	125.5	121.0	97.8
Portugal	119.5	114.0	130.4	115.3	126.9	124.8	126.7	97.8	127.4	130.1	125.7	113.2
Spain	128.3	126.4	142.3	122.0	141.8	138.1	136.5	92.8	128.0	140.5	134.8	111.7
Sweden	139.7	139.7	161.2	140.1	152.1	151.5	106.9	136.2	148.9	158.8	160.9	139.0
Switzerland												
Turkey	148.9	152.3	174.0	165.8	180.4	178.7	171.5	169.3	177.2	175.0	186.6	163.8
United Kingdom	99.2	96.8	111.1	100.1	107.3	107.5	103.1	103.2	105.0	115.1	113.4	97.1
Eastern Europe												
Albania												
Belarus												
Bosnia-Herzegovina												
Bulgaria	118.4	131.2	155.1	137.8	146.1	153.1	157.2	149.3	148.4	156.3	157.7	152.6
Croatia	130.1	139.7	162.0	153.9	171.2	158.1	171.3	153.3	157.2	167.0	163.7	149.9
Czech Republic	173.3	169.6	197.0	179.7	189.1	191.7	172.8	166.9	179.8	201.5	211.2	165.7
Estonia	253.0	253.5	297.9	279.7	308.5	299.0	252.5	287.1	287.5	313.7	298.9	249.8
Georgia												
Hungary	277.4	275.5	304.8	284.8	288.6	313.3	302.6	283.2	329.6	348.4	346.9	289.4
Latvia	135.3	140.3	169.3	146.2	164.2	168.1	157.5	174.3	159.6	165.5	157.9	141.6
Lithuania	187.3	179.5	206.6	202.9	221.1	223.5	223.9	228.9	212.1	216.7	207.7	202.4
Macedonia												
Moldova												
Poland	238.1	233.8	272.7	249.3	259.6	261.0	254.4	257.9	272.9	296.6	279.6	251.8
Romania	113.8	121.4	134.4	120.6	139.4	133.0	131.8	124.5	137.4	140.7	135.7	120.3
Russia	141.4	147.2	174.9	164.5	169.3	184.6	183.5	176.9	177.6	178.9	182.4	191.5
Serbia and Montenegro	103.1	110.1	131.6	126.9	133.5	133.5	128.1	131.4	130.9	145.6	133.8	137.7
Slovakia	195.7	190.4	217.5	204.8	222.5	215.6	197.7	193.4	223.0	240.1	238.2	198.0
Slovenia	139.6	136.7	157.5	145.4	153.6	156.4	156.2	132.5	155.2	170.4	161.6	132.1
Ukraine												

Source: *United Nations/Euromonitor International*
Notes: *Indices based on value of production (or contribution to GDP) at constant prices*

Industrial Output

Table 17.7

Indices of Mining Production 1980-2007
1995 = 100

	1980	1985	1990	1995	2000	2002	2003	2004	2005	2006	2007
Western Europe											
Austria	107.0	117.7	111.5	100.0	112.3	113.1	112.5	106.2	107.8	114.9	109.4
Belgium			69.0	100.0	138.1	182.2	173.9	176.0	186.7	195.5	207.9
Cyprus			82.2	100.0	135.3	143.6	149.0	156.0	156.8	157.2	164.0
Denmark			103.1	100.0	93.8	88.2	95.8	100.7	105.0	99.3	87.5
Finland			94.9	100.0	99.4	131.1	131.7	115.5	151.1	187.6	145.2
France			116.0	100.0	88.4	83.0	81.9	81.3	79.2	81.9	82.4
Germany	57.2	104.7	100.0	100.0	79.6	73.1	72.5	70.3	69.3	67.0	65.3
Gibraltar											
Greece	155.3	153.7	120.9	100.0	109.3	122.7	116.4	116.5	110.3	107.1	104.0
Iceland											
Ireland	65.6	65.6	85.7	100.0	114.7	109.0	132.6	129.8	129.3	141.1	145.0
Italy			87.6	100.0	98.4	106.1	108.3	105.9	114.2	110.7	113.3
Liechtenstein											
Luxembourg			103.4	100.0	108.8	99.8	88.4	87.1	85.4	67.4	61.4
Malta											
Monaco											
Netherlands			89.1	100.0	97.2	104.5	101.3	112.3	102.4	98.7	101.7
Norway			94.1	100.0	115.7	117.3	115.7	114.2	110.2	105.1	104.0
Portugal			114.3	100.0	103.8	100.2	90.8	94.5	92.5	83.4	92.3
Spain			101.9	100.0	91.1	87.7	87.7	83.5	80.1	82.2	83.8
Sweden			95.0	100.0	97.8	99.4	96.2	105.7	111.9	113.3	119.4
Switzerland				100.0	94.2	93.3	92.6	96.5	91.5	100.5	98.2
Turkey			95.5	100.0	106.6	89.9	86.8	90.4	102.9	107.3	110.3
United Kingdom			73.3	100.0	105.1	99.7	94.6	87.1	79.8	73.4	75.1
Eastern Europe											
Albania				100.0	36.4	31.8	28.7	26.4	24.3	22.1	19.9
Belarus				100.0	117.5	134.7	147.4	160.8	173.5	178.0	182.0
Bosnia-Herzegovina											
Bulgaria				100.0	80.7	73.3	78.4	94.8	95.0	96.7	95.3
Croatia			132.1	100.0	97.8	116.7	119.3	115.5	112.0	122.7	128.0
Czech Republic	125.0	137.5	144.7	100.0	88.2	89.7	90.0	89.4	89.9	90.9	89.7
Estonia	268.8	236.5	195.7	100.0	91.7	109.7	115.4	105.2	117.1	125.4	129.5
Georgia											
Hungary			192.3	100.0	68.2	71.9	69.4	76.3	73.6	85.8	68.0
Latvia	579.9	168.2	257.7	100.0	134.9	154.2	162.4	180.2	226.2	247.2	273.0
Lithuania				100.0	198.1	248.9	271.8	251.2	231.4	228.8	227.1
Macedonia											
Moldova											
Poland			108.8	100.0	82.1	75.5	74.1	76.3	74.3	75.3	73.2
Romania			120.5	100.0	79.8	79.8	79.2	81.4	80.2	83.1	80.9
Russia			141.2	100.0	105.0	118.8	129.2	137.8	139.8	143.1	145.0
Serbia and Montenegro			129.7	100.0	93.8	83.6	84.6	83.6	85.3	88.3	85.3
Slovakia			233.6	100.0	101.4	113.4	106.9	95.2	92.1	83.2	80.0
Slovenia			132.3	100.0	95.2	94.5	99.9	92.9	99.3	109.5	115.1
Ukraine			201.2	100.0	104.6	110.5	116.6	121.4	126.7	134.1	138.6

Source: United Nations/Euromonitor International
Notes: Indices based on value of production (or contribution to GDP) at constant prices

Table 17.8

Indices of Mining Production by Quarter 2006-2008
1995 = 100

	2006 1st Quarter	2006 2nd Quarter	2006 3rd Quarter	2006 4th Quarter	2007 1st Quarter	2007 2nd Quarter	2007 3rd Quarter	2007 4th Quarter	2008 1st Quarter	2008 2nd Quarter
Western Europe										
Austria	92.8	122.2	118.9	128.8	100.2	113.8	118.1	127.4	100.1	
Belgium	159.2	205.9	179.4	237.7	185.0	219.0	199.1	192.3	207.4	
Cyprus	156.1	158.3	146.0	180.4	154.3	163.9	146.0	174.4	176.7	
Denmark	106.1	102.4	85.5	102.7	92.0	78.2	87.3	99.6	95.3	
Finland	77.6	205.9	362.9	116.6	84.9	172.5	214.5	127.3	97.2	
France	75.3	85.8	78.3	85.5	77.5	86.3	83.1	81.8	78.4	
Germany	60.0	67.6	68.7	71.7	61.6	66.4	70.8	67.7	58.9	
Gibraltar										
Greece	97.1	111.6	118.3	101.5	104.2	106.2	114.3	99.9	91.2	
Iceland										
Ireland	154.7	128.6	120.2	160.9	147.0	160.4	165.7	131.3	129.5	
Italy	110.6	111.5	107.8	112.7	111.7	116.7	111.9	106.0	105.5	
Liechtenstein										
Luxembourg	52.9	78.8	65.9	70.9	58.1	77.1	66.1	71.6	62.0	
Malta										
Monaco										
Netherlands	142.9	69.7	44.4	96.8	102.9	57.3	57.3	140.2	129.8	
Norway	109.5	103.4	101.7	104.7	104.1	94.8	97.4	104.5	103.7	
Portugal	83.7	89.0	80.2	80.5	91.4	94.6	87.7	94.3	94.2	
Spain	81.2	87.9	77.1	82.5	76.3	87.3	82.1	78.7	72.9	
Sweden	106.2	114.4	107.2	118.5	119.1	110.7	118.7	124.9	108.5	
Switzerland	63.5	111.3	115.4	111.6	78.8	118.1	117.5	111.9	76.7	
Turkey	91.7	105.7	124.6	107.3	99.1	118.8	140.9	111.9	109.9	
United Kingdom	80.8	73.9	65.6	73.5	75.3	73.3	65.6	74.5	71.6	
Eastern Europe										
Albania										
Belarus										
Bosnia-Herzegovina										
Bulgaria	91.5	93.1	101.7	100.5	88.3	84.4	89.3	95.3	88.9	
Croatia	108.3	122.0	130.8	129.8	124.1	128.7	128.9	126.7	102.4	
Czech Republic	86.6	89.3	92.6	100.0	87.7	90.0	89.0	95.7	89.7	
Estonia	101.9	126.3	160.0	122.1	107.2	113.3	166.8	141.3	114.0	
Georgia										
Hungary	54.2	95.8	101.8	91.0	57.5	81.1	74.8	70.8	64.3	
Latvia	169.4	291.2	306.5	221.7	281.0	336.9	313.4	255.2	281.0	
Lithuania	159.5	264.2	246.4	245.2	169.8	254.8	254.4	245.5	170.3	
Macedonia										
Moldova										
Poland	73.1	72.6	78.1	77.3	71.1	72.3	74.0	75.4	70.2	
Romania	79.7	81.5	83.4	86.5	78.3	83.8	84.8	83.3	76.1	
Russia	135.6	141.3	149.3	145.0	141.3	144.4	150.5	146.4	142.1	
Serbia and Montenegro	83.6	80.7	90.8	98.1	85.4	81.7	90.1	93.7	90.2	
Slovakia	76.2	83.9	85.3	87.2	75.1	87.7	89.3	85.9	75.5	
Slovenia	98.9	109.6	101.4	128.0	107.8	123.5	101.6	118.9	113.8	
Ukraine										

Source: *United Nations/Euromonitor International*
Notes: *Indices based on value of production (or contribution to GDP) at constant prices*

Industrial Output

Table 17.9

Indices of Mining Production by Month 2007

1995 = 100

	January	February	March	April	May	June	July	August	September	October	November	December
Western Europe												
Austria	90.7	93.1	116.8	111.7	114.0	115.6	116.7	115.8	122.0	136.5	124.3	121.4
Belgium	160.3	178.4	216.4	216.2	218.2	222.6	161.0	221.9	214.5	223.7	200.2	152.9
Cyprus	140.3	145.6	177.1	145.1	172.8	173.8	186.4	90.8	160.7	186.3	197.8	139.2
Denmark	102.1	94.0	80.0	73.8	82.0	78.7	77.6	96.8	87.6	100.6	97.2	101.1
Finland	92.8	69.7	92.2	102.7	120.9	294.1	258.2	191.2	194.0	186.0	131.1	64.7
France	70.7	75.5	86.2	82.2	83.4	93.4	94.7	68.9	85.7	100.8	83.1	61.4
Germany	59.9	59.3	65.6	65.9	66.0	67.2	71.0	70.4	71.0	73.9	67.8	61.5
Gibraltar												
Greece	101.2	105.2	106.3	102.8	104.3	111.6	116.9	100.5	125.6	106.9	99.9	92.9
Iceland												
Ireland	129.8	129.3	133.3	128.3	156.2	196.8	195.8	123.9	177.4	140.3	129.5	124.1
Italy	103.4	115.1	116.7	114.3	120.7	115.1	112.6	111.7	111.4	113.8	104.7	99.6
Liechtenstein												
Luxembourg	43.5	60.8	70.1	75.9	78.7	76.6	71.4	51.7	75.4	80.6	70.9	63.3
Malta												
Monaco												
Netherlands	110.1	104.1	94.6	62.6	50.3	59.0	49.3	55.2	67.3	111.4	140.4	168.8
Norway	108.5	98.2	105.6	106.1	96.6	81.7	102.4	97.8	92.0	104.1	104.5	104.9
Portugal	88.5	81.9	103.7	88.6	103.8	91.2	93.4	79.0	90.8	100.6	98.4	83.9
Spain	72.4	72.4	83.9	78.3	92.3	91.5	91.0	69.9	85.5	89.4	85.8	60.9
Sweden	117.3	115.2	124.8	114.6	105.5	112.0	113.4	123.3	119.3	124.6	120.6	129.4
Switzerland												
Turkey	100.4	93.9	103.0	113.7	124.2	118.4	135.8	142.4	144.5	123.0	110.3	102.4
United Kingdom	74.7	71.7	79.4	74.4	77.2	68.3	70.3	61.4	65.2	75.4	73.4	74.8
Eastern Europe												
Albania												
Belarus												
Bosnia-Herzegovina												
Bulgaria	92.2	86.7	86.0	88.9	77.7	86.6	90.7	86.1	90.9	99.6	87.2	99.2
Croatia	122.8	117.8	131.6	130.0	134.0	122.1	121.0	127.6	138.1	132.2	127.7	120.1
Czech Republic	82.5	83.1	97.4	91.7	90.2	88.2	82.5	94.8	89.6	103.8	98.8	84.5
Estonia	106.2	93.6	121.9	12.3	151.9	175.7	180.9	169.7	149.7	164.6	139.2	120.0
Georgia												
Hungary	52.1	54.3	66.2	72.1	88.3	83.0	82.2	74.4	67.9	83.8	69.5	59.0
Latvia	188.8	192.4	273.8	299.4	366.7	344.7	305.1	335.9	299.1	297.6	269.7	198.2
Lithuania	169.6	144.8	195.1	232.6	283.3	248.6	235.7	282.3	245.2	294.6	233.6	208.4
Macedonia												
Moldova												
Poland	70.8	67.7	74.9	72.7	73.2	71.1	72.4	73.2	76.5	85.0	76.4	64.9
Romania	76.0	75.8	83.2	78.4	86.1	86.9	82.6	87.8	83.9	83.6	84.7	81.6
Russia	144.5	133.0	146.4	140.6	146.3	146.3	153.6	152.1	145.8	147.9	143.4	147.8
Serbia and Montenegro	89.0	79.2	87.9	83.9	79.1	82.2	91.6	87.8	90.7	96.5	91.4	93.3
Slovakia	73.5	67.6	84.3	82.2	89.9	90.9	91.0	89.0	87.8	92.0	87.0	78.7
Slovenia	89.1	102.3	131.9	127.1	128.5	114.8	87.5	115.4	102.0	126.0	137.9	92.7
Ukraine												

Source: *United Nations/Euromonitor International*
Notes: *Indices based on value of production (or contribution to GDP) at constant prices*

Metal Production **Table 17.10**

Production of Selected Metals 2007
'000 tonnes

	Alumin-ium	Crude Steel	Pig Iron	Refined Copper	Refined Lead	Refined Tin	Slab Zinc	Smelter Copper
Western Europe								
Austria		7,578.0	5,319.0	72.9	22.0			
Belgium		10,745.0	6,489.0	382.7	66.0		214.2	
Cyprus				0.8				
Denmark		137.9						
Finland		4,428.0	2,916.0	88.0			278.0	191.0
France	438.0	19,248.0	12,432.0		1.5		194.0	
Germany	639.9	48,552.0	31,152.0	236.0	122.5	0.1	326.0	225.0
Gibraltar								
Greece	163.5	2,676.0			4.0			
Iceland	333.0							
Ireland		89.7			20.7			
Italy	195.5	31,932.0	11,100.0	39.7	32.0		100.0	
Liechtenstein								
Luxembourg		2,892.0						
Malta								
Monaco								
Netherlands	296.0	7,308.0	6,372.0		17.0		239.8	
Norway	1,480.0	708.0	98.0	41.4			124.0	36.5
Portugal		1,505.4			3.0	0.2	11.2	
Spain	460.0	18,876.0	3,672.0	375.0	115.0		460.0	355.0
Sweden	104.4	5,664.0	3,672.5	185.0	29.6			170.0
Switzerland	11.0	1,304.5	80.0		9.0			
Turkey	60.0	25,380.0	4,332.0	110.0	9.0			8.0
United Kingdom	377.0	14,472.0	10,980.0		110.0			
Eastern Europe								
Albania		156.9						
Belarus		2,408.0						
Bosnia-Herzegovina	148.0	555.8	60.0					
Bulgaria		2,160.0	1,066.7	69.5	87.3	0.0	91.0	258.0
Croatia	4.2	92.9						
Czech Republic	15.0	7,056.0	5,292.0	14.0	24.4			
Estonia								
Georgia								
Hungary	30.8	2,232.0	1,380.0	10.0				
Latvia		551.3						
Lithuania								
Macedonia		332.3						
Moldova		960.0						
Poland	48.9	10,584.0	5,904.0	591.0	46.7		171.0	570.0
Romania	284.0	6,312.0	3,936.0	16.0	33.5		46.0	0.1
Russia	3,750.0	72,396.0	51,528.0	668.0	61.0	5.7	205.0	720.0
Serbia and Montenegro	129.0	2,131.0	2,038.8	28.0	1.2		27.2	22.5
Slovakia	162.2	4,848.0	4,008.0					
Slovenia	173.1	636.0			15.4			
Ukraine	115.6	28,956.0	36,096.0	16.7	5.5			

Source: Euromonitor International from industry sources/national statistics

Mineral Production **Table 17.11**

Production of Selected Minerals 2007
'000 tonnes

	Bauxite	Copper Ore	Gold (tonnes)	Iron Ore	Lead Ore	Silver (tonnes)	Tin Ore	Zinc Ore
Western Europe								
Austria				2,131.0				
Belgium								
Cyprus		0.6						
Denmark								
Finland		12.5	5.0			52.1		77.5
France	162.4			11.6		0.4		
Germany		5.0		413.0				
Gibraltar								
Greece	2,106.1			1,500.0	13.0	78.8		38.4
Iceland								
Ireland					60.1	15.1		464.5
Italy	300.0		0.1		0.6	5.1		
Liechtenstein								
Luxembourg								
Malta								
Monaco								
Netherlands								
Norway				652.5				
Portugal		73.0		14.0		18.6	0.0	
Spain		9.4	1.2			5.7		
Sweden		89.2	7.0	22,800.0	59.3	284.6		229.8
Switzerland								
Turkey	838.9	26.3	1.9	4,116.0	19.0	235.7		65.2
United Kingdom				0.3	0.5			
Eastern Europe								
Albania	5.0	0.6						
Belarus								
Bosnia-Herzegovina	947.5			133.4				
Bulgaria		102.6	3.7	146.6	15.5	49.8		10.2
Croatia								
Czech Republic			0.5	16.4		25.0		
Estonia								
Georgia		16.9	1.4		0.5	32.7		0.6
Hungary	499.0							
Latvia								
Lithuania								
Macedonia		8.4		15.0	21.3	10.0		24.5
Moldova								
Poland		496.1	1.9		47.7	1,266.6		120.6
Romania	127.0	11.0	0.5	313.0	6.1	18.0		8.0
Russia	6,590.0	687.1	156.0	104,664.0	36.7	1,116.8	4.9	193.2
Serbia and Montenegro	670.4	9.3	0.3		1.0	2.5		10.2
Slovakia		0.0	0.1	231.0				
Slovenia								
Ukraine			0.1	77,952.0				

Source: *Euromonitor International from industry sources/national statistics*

IT and Telecommunications

Internet   **Table 18.1**

Internet Users 1995-2007
'000

	1995	1996	1997	1998	1999	2000	2001	2002	2003	2004	2005	2006	2007
Western Europe													
Austria	150	550	760	1,230	1,840	2,700	3,150	3,340	3,730	3,900	4,000	4,200	4,457
Belgium	100	300	500	800	1,400	3,000	3,200	3,400	4,000	4,200	4,800	5,371	5,824
Cyprus	3	5	33	68	88	120	150	210	250	298	326	357	398
Denmark	200	300	600	1,200	1,626	2,090	2,300	2,391	2,481	2,725	2,854	3,171	3,437
Finland	710	860	1,000	1,311	1,667	1,927	2,235	2,529	2,560	2,680	2,800	2,925	3,066
France	950	1,504	2,485	3,704	5,370	8,460	15,653	18,057	21,765	23,732	26,154	30,100	33,653
Germany	1,500	2,500	5,500	8,100	17,100	24,800	26,000	28,000	33,000	35,200	35,700	38,600	41,650
Gibraltar			1	1	2	6	6	6	6	6	6	6	7
Greece	80	150	200	350	750	1,000	915	1,485	1,718	1,955	2,001	2,048	2,312
Iceland	30	40	75	100	115	125	140	150	166	168	183	194	210
Ireland	40	80	150	300	410	679	895	1,102	1,260	1,198	1,400	1,437	1,595
Italy	300	585	1,300	2,600	8,200	13,200	15,600	19,800	22,880	27,170	28,000	28,855	30,150
Liechtenstein						12	15	20	20	22	22	22	22
Luxembourg	7	23	30	50	75	100	160	165	170	271	315	339	367
Malta	1	4	15	25	30	51	70	80	96	112	127	149	176
Monaco													
Netherlands	1,000	1,500	2,200	3,500	6,200	7,000	7,900	8,200	8,500	10,000	12,060	14,544	15,246
Norway	280	800	900	1,000	1,100	1,200	1,319	1,399	1,583	1,792	2,702	4,074	4,321
Portugal	150	300	500	1,000	1,500	1,680	1,860	2,267	2,674	2,576	2,856	3,213	3,565
Spain	150	526	1,110	1,733	2,830	5,486	7,388	7,856	15,300	15,140	17,233	18,578	20,329
Sweden	450	800	2,100	2,961	3,666	4,048	4,600	5,125	5,655	6,800	6,890	6,981	7,250
Switzerland	250	322	548	939	1,473	2,096	2,800	3,000	3,300	3,500	3,800	4,360	4,836
Turkey	50	120	300	450	1,500	2,500	3,500	4,300	6,000	10,220	11,204	12,283	13,660
United Kingdom	1,100	2,400	4,310	8,000	12,500	15,800	19,800	25,000	26,025	28,094	32,076	33,534	35,607
Eastern Europe													
Albania	0	1	2	2	3	4	10	12	30	75	188	471	722
Belarus	0	3	5	8	50	187	430	891	1,607	2,461	3,394	5,478	6,491
Bosnia-Herzegovina		1	2	5	7	40	45	100	150	585	806	950	1,179
Bulgaria	10	60	100	150	235	430	605	630	932	1,234	1,592	1,870	2,171
Croatia	24	40	80	150	200	299	518	789	1,014	1,375	1,472	1,576	1,696
Czech Republic	150	200	300	400	700	1,000	1,500	2,600	2,395	2,576	2,758	3,541	4,238
Estonia	40	50	80	150	200	392	430	444	600	670	690	760	805
Georgia	1	2	3	5	20	23	47	74	117	176	271	332	442
Hungary	70	100	200	400	600	715	1,480	1,600	2,400	2,700	3,000	3,500	3,983
Latvia		20	50	80	105	150	170	310	560	810	1,030	1,071	1,154
Lithuania	3	10	35	70	103	225	250	500	696	767	883	1,083	1,244
Macedonia	1	2	10	20	29	39	49	59	68	78	88	98	117
Moldova	0	0	1	11	25	53	60	150	288	406	550	728	954
Poland	250	500	800	1,581	2,100	2,800	3,800	8,880	8,970	9,000	10,000	11,000	12,154
Romania	17	50	100	500	600	800	1,000	2,200	4,000	4,500	4,773	7,000	8,249
Russia	220	400	700	1,200	1,500	2,900	4,300	6,000	12,000	18,500	21,800	25,689	29,689
Serbia and Montenegro		20	50	65	80	400	600	640	787	904	1,070	1,249	1,601
Slovakia	28	42	63	145	292	507	674	863	1,376	1,652	1,905	2,256	2,534
Slovenia	57	100	150	200	250	300	600	750	800	950	1,090	1,251	1,359
Ukraine	22	50	100	150	200	350	600	900	2,500	3,750	4,560	5,545	6,447

Source: International Telecommunications Union/World Bank/Trade Sources/Euromonitor International

Table 18.2

Dial-up Internet Subscribers 1995-2007

'000

	1995	1996	1997	1998	1999	2000	2001	2002	2003	2004	2005	2006	2007
Western Europe													
Austria	27	31	35	215	574	860	779	749	879	714	598	486	383
Belgium	5	25	76	196	488	1,024	966	879	666	416	284	200	133
Cyprus	0	1	15	25	40	52	63	73	66	64	59	37	24
Denmark	20	130	270	580	1,125	1,231	1,233	1,120	964	744	460	293	116
Finland	10	58	160	290	461	596	889	820	846	615	403	292	188
France	40	170	540	1,280	3,010	5,263	6,385	7,469	7,048	5,378	3,746	2,553	1,546
Germany	630	1,200	2,670	3,750	7,980	12,735	11,900	11,795	12,530	12,100	9,300	7,330	5,940
Gibraltar													
Greece	6	15	42	100	193	271	288	392	520	649	647	619	489
Iceland	0	2	4	9	13	45	40	27	10	10	9	11	9
Ireland	5	25	57	120	240	550	600	648	683	664	603	519	440
Italy	47	131	360	1,140	2,870	5,685	11,610	12,150	14,550	12,426	10,803	9,602	8,202
Liechtenstein													
Luxembourg	2	3	3	6	11	25	41	64	92	77	49	37	30
Malta													
Monaco													
Netherlands	4	66	421	992	2,667	3,408	4,034	3,431	3,012	3,794	3,556	3,494	3,382
Norway	7	160	236	370	702	1,153	1,147	1,198	889	747	429	241	141
Portugal	14	42	89	173	255	313	370	404	402	375	246	261	239
Spain	35	90	220	667	2,240	3,146	3,244	2,677	2,559	1,852	1,199	532	386
Sweden	54	236	653	1,450	1,873	2,160	2,465	2,454	2,262	1,990	1,459	1,125	933
Switzerland	1	24	171	425	992	1,609	2,060	1,882	1,947	968	860	750	657
Turkey	28	68	113	194	312	460	669	919	996	931	663	406	247
United Kingdom	80	420	1,230	3,750	7,400	8,368	11,029	10,929	11,328	8,231	5,539	3,981	3,068
Eastern Europe													
Albania													
Belarus	0	1	1	2	4	5	8	18	23	30	36	40	42
Bosnia-Herzegovina													
Bulgaria	0	0	0	1	2	6	7	9	11	21	41	64	82
Croatia	0	4	11	30	75	187	331	538	567	832	838	821	738
Czech Republic	2	5	10	18	200	416	1,250	1,629	2,114	1,893	1,702	1,426	1,180
Estonia	0	6	16	35	60	80	69	75	47	33	18	12	9
Georgia													
Hungary	3	12	30	73	136	217	293	362	391	331	337	315	279
Latvia	0	0	1	2	21	33	40	28	27	18	12	6	4
Lithuania	0	2	7	16	31	53	56	59	47	45	39	31	24
Macedonia													
Moldova													
Poland	23	105	232	421	750	930	1,128	1,484	2,532	1,699	1,741	1,203	834
Romania	1	6	15	27	50	100	300	350	449	824	1,328	1,525	1,250
Russia	10	35	120	260	400	492	1,027	1,880	2,957	4,725	6,811	8,500	9,433
Serbia and Montenegro													
Slovakia	4	7	21	35	47	68	100	130	160	152	113	78	60
Slovenia	1	3	11	43	72	139	172	184	186	232	201	181	137
Ukraine	2	5	14	28	45	67	120	229	486	862	1,440	2,042	2,270

Source: *Euromonitor International from trade sources/national statistics*

Internet

Table 18.3

Broadband Internet Subscribers 1998-2007
'000

	1998	1999	2000	2001	2002	2003	2004	2005	2006	2007
Western Europe										
Austria	0.0	50.9	190.5	320.6	451.0	618.6	870.0	1,174.0	1,428.0	1,543.5
Belgium	10.9	71.0	126.6	458.8	815.4	1,242.9	1,617.2	1,902.7	2,242.6	2,512.9
Cyprus	0.0	0.0	0.0	2.5	5.9	10.0	17.1	31.9	49.6	66.7
Denmark	0.0	10.0	56.6	223.3	451.3	718.3	1,017.6	1,349.0	1,590.7	1,866.3
Finland	0.0	5.0	20.3	61.5	237.5	472.1	785.5	1,210.6	1,427.2	1,732.6
France	0.0	20.0	181.6	601.5	1,591.0	3,569.4	6,561.0	9,471.0	12,699.0	14,250.0
Germany	0.0	20.0	265.0	2,100.0	3,205.0	4,470.0	6,900.0	10,700.0	14,085.2	17,472.0
Gibraltar										
Greece	0.0	0.0	0.0	0.0	2.0	10.5	51.5	155.4	298.2	787.0
Iceland	0.0	0.1	2.4	10.4	24.3	41.6	55.8	78.0	87.7	90.6
Ireland	0.0	0.0	0.0	0.0	10.6	41.8	152.1	322.5	517.3	653.0
Italy	0.0	30.0	115.0	390.0	850.0	2,250.0	4,724.5	6,896.7	8,638.9	10,477.7
Liechtenstein										
Luxembourg	0.0	0.0	0.0	1.2	5.7	15.4	36.5	70.1	93.2	105.1
Malta										
Monaco										
Netherlands	75.5	167.8	260.0	466.2	1,069.0	1,988.0	3,084.6	4,113.6	4,705.8	5,470.0
Norway	0.0	2.3	22.4	88.4	205.3	398.8	671.7	991.3	1,278.3	1,388.0
Portugal	0.0	0.3	25.2	96.3	262.8	503.1	858.4	1,212.0	1,355.6	1,555.6
Spain	0.0	1.0	76.4	430.1	1,247.5	2,121.9	3,401.4	5,035.2	6,654.9	7,483.8
Sweden	0.0	7.0	82.5	354.0	578.4	981.1	1,302.9	1,830.0	2,346.3	2,596.0
Switzerland	0.0	0.1	56.4	140.0	455.2	783.9	1,282.0	1,725.4	2,140.3	2,322.6
Turkey	0.0	0.0	0.0	10.9	21.2	199.3	577.9	1,589.8	2,773.7	3,767.9
United Kingdom	0.0	0.0	52.9	331.0	1,356.5	3,113.7	6,834.9	10,034.5	12,594.1	14,361.8
Eastern Europe										
Albania										
Belarus	0.0	0.0	0.0	0.0	0.0	0.1	0.8	1.6	1.1	3.0
Bosnia-Herzegovina										
Bulgaria	0.0	0.0	0.0	0.0	0.0	0.0	35.5	165.5	384.3	606.4
Croatia	0.0	0.0	0.0	0.0	0.0	3.4	23.0	116.0	251.8	435.1
Czech Republic	0.0	0.0	2.5	6.2	15.3	34.7	236.0	650.0	962.0	1,252.3
Estonia	0.0	0.0	3.0	17.3	45.7	90.3	138.7	179.2	228.1	266.3
Georgia										
Hungary	0.0	1.1	3.4	28.3	83.8	264.3	450.1	639.5	976.7	1,170.3
Latvia	0.0	0.0	0.3	3.2	10.0	19.5	49.1	60.8	109.7	151.8
Lithuania	0.0	0.1	0.1	2.8	40.3	114.1	129.1	218.8	386.4	519.1
Macedonia										
Moldova										
Poland	0.0	0.0	0.0	12.0	121.7	195.8	811.8	945.2	2,032.7	3,040.0
Romania	0.0	0.0	1.0	6.0	15.8	196.1	382.8	751.1	1,769.3	2,591.6
Russia	0.0	0.0	0.0	0.0	11.0	343.0	675.0	1,589.0	2,900.0	6,200.1
Serbia and Montenegro										
Slovakia	0.0	0.0	0.0	0.0	4.1	22.5	78.8	181.5	317.0	368.5
Slovenia	0.0	0.0	1.5	5.5	24.0	58.0	115.1	196.7	263.7	347.8
Ukraine	0.0	0.0	0.0	0.0	0.5	13.6	58.2	160.0	348.0	800.0

Source: *Euromonitor International from trade sources/national statistics*

Table 18.4

Availability of Digital Main Lines 1990-2007

% of lines connected to digital exchanges

	1990	1995	2000	2002	2003	2004	2005	2006	2007
Western Europe									
Austria	11.0	61.0	100.0	100.0	100.0	100.0	100.0	100.0	100.0
Belgium	37.2	66.8	100.0	100.0	100.0	100.0	100.0	100.0	100.0
Cyprus	51.0	68.5	100.0	100.0	100.0	100.0	100.0	100.0	100.0
Denmark	28.0	61.0	100.0	100.0	100.0	100.0	100.0	100.0	100.0
Finland	35.1	89.8	100.0	100.0	100.0	100.0	100.0	100.0	100.0
France	75.0	90.0	100.0	100.0	100.0	100.0	100.0	100.0	100.0
Germany	12.0	56.3	100.0	100.0	100.0	100.0	100.0	100.0	100.0
Gibraltar		100.0	100.0	100.0	100.0	100.0	100.0	100.0	100.0
Greece	0.5	37.1	93.4	96.5	99.6	100.0	100.0	100.0	100.0
Iceland	41.0	100.0	100.0	100.0	100.0	100.0	100.0	100.0	100.0
Ireland	55.0	79.0	100.0	100.0	100.0	100.0	100.0	100.0	100.0
Italy	33.0	76.6	99.7	99.9	99.9	100.0	100.0	100.0	100.0
Liechtenstein	27.0	75.0	100.0	100.0	100.0	100.0	100.0	100.0	100.0
Luxembourg	33.0	100.0	100.0	100.0	100.0	100.0	100.0	100.0	100.0
Malta	48.0	100.0	100.0	100.0	100.0	100.0	100.0	100.0	100.0
Monaco		100.0	100.0	100.0	100.0	100.0	100.0	100.0	100.0
Netherlands	69.0	69.0	97.0	99.5	100.0	100.0	100.0	100.0	100.0
Norway	38.0	82.0	100.0	100.0	100.0	100.0	100.0	100.0	100.0
Portugal	30.0	70.0	100.0	100.0	100.0	100.0	100.0	100.0	100.0
Spain	28.4	56.7	86.6	99.8	100.0	100.0	100.0	100.0	100.0
Sweden	38.0	91.0	100.0	100.0	100.0	100.0	100.0	100.0	100.0
Switzerland	29.0	75.0	100.0	100.0	100.0	100.0	100.0	100.0	100.0
Turkey	48.0	77.0	87.3	90.0	90.1	90.8	97.8	100.0	100.0
United Kingdom	46.9	87.7	100.0	100.0	100.0	100.0	100.0	100.0	100.0
Eastern Europe									
Albania	10.0	12.8	78.9	97.0	97.8	97.8	98.6	99.1	99.4
Belarus	2.9	15.4	35.8	43.7	48.6	54.5	58.5	62.6	66.0
Bosnia-Herzegovina		30.0	41.6	77.4	81.9	89.6	94.0	96.3	100.0
Bulgaria	1.0	2.0	12.0	19.0	26.0	34.0	47.0	59.1	70.0
Croatia	15.5	51.5	77.7	100.0	100.0	100.0	100.0	100.0	100.0
Czech Republic	2.0	23.0	85.7	100.0	100.0	100.0	100.0	100.0	100.0
Estonia		20.0	71.2	78.4	79.4	81.0	81.0	81.9	82.7
Georgia	11.1	10.8	18.4	36.1	36.1	39.9	44.0	52.4	55.6
Hungary	5.0	54.4	85.8	90.0	90.0	93.5	100.0	100.0	100.0
Latvia	1.5	13.1	52.2	83.2	88.7	91.1	92.6	96.0	98.5
Lithuania		6.4	46.5	87.6	90.7	92.6	93.1	95.0	96.5
Macedonia	10.0	17.7	80.1	92.7	96.6	99.0	100.0	100.0	100.0
Moldova	4.3	6.8	34.0	54.5	52.4	59.3	65.5	69.8	76.0
Poland	1.0	48.0	77.6	89.2	95.7	100.0	100.0	100.0	100.0
Romania	0.4	15.7	54.8	71.9	74.3	77.2	89.1	94.2	99.2
Russia	5.0	15.5	31.2	38.8	40.9	44.2	46.9	49.5	51.9
Serbia and Montenegro	12.0	20.0	53.0	89.0	92.0	92.1	100.0	100.0	100.0
Slovakia		25.7	70.4	78.2	84.3	100.0	100.0	100.0	100.0
Slovenia	14.6	53.2	99.2	100.0	100.0	100.0	100.0	100.0	100.0
Ukraine	1.7	3.4	53.3	68.2	70.1	71.5	72.9	74.6	76.1

Source: Euromonitor International from International Telecommunications Union/national statistics

Telecommunications

Table 18.5

Capital Investment in Telecommunications 1990-2007

Million units of national currency / as stated

	1990	1995	2000	2002	2003	2004	2005	2006	2007	US$ million 2007
Western Europe										
Austria	1,163	1,170	918	959	772	747	650	630	608	833.0
Belgium	629	993	1,574	1,258	1,051	1,002	1,062	1,008	996	1,365.1
Cyprus	28	38	118	105	98	75	80	82	92	125.8
Denmark	3,254	3,078	9,015	7,652	5,607	5,722	6,843	6,727	7,174	1,317.9
Finland	499	616	888	774	762	726	675	658	639	875.9
France	3,987	4,772	7,841	5,800	5,226	5,495	6,305	7,115	7,324	10,039.1
Germany	9,832	7,921	9,650	7,100	5,500	5,700	5,537	5,135	5,024	6,886.3
Gibraltar	2	2	3	3	2	2	3	3	3	5.3
Greece	175	458	2,114	1,368	1,196	1,043	949	935	904	1,238.5
Iceland	838	1,958	5,459	3,063	3,139	3,897	5,689	6,434	7,185	112.2
Ireland	223	246	410	298	257	242	243	256	262	358.6
Italy	5,113	3,966	7,113	9,472	7,887	8,269	8,661	8,454	8,657	11,865.1
Liechtenstein	12	16	18	18	19	19	19	20	21	17.1
Luxembourg	51	57	63	73	129	92	82	92	84	115.2
Malta	21	13	27	64	58	50	50	51	60	82.2
Monaco	1	1	1	1	1	1	1	1	1	1.7
Netherlands	1,108	1,250	3,353	3,182	3,313	3,312	3,445	3,360	3,412	4,676.0
Norway	2,747	5,129	18,718	20,659	21,033	21,869	22,738	24,182	25,081	4,278.9
Portugal	507	927	2,212	2,192	848	1,016	934	998	1,017	1,394.5
Spain	4,335	2,334	7,332	5,556	4,542	4,666	5,581	5,830	6,104	8,366.3
Sweden	6,286	7,783	22,621	10,869	11,746	11,592	8,832	6,072	6,715	993.5
Switzerland	3,077	2,156	3,794	2,579	2,133	2,060	2,030	2,012	1,973	1,643.5
Turkey	2	20	393	299	345	1,447	1,862	2,141	2,509	1,925.1
United Kingdom	2,758	4,557	10,971	9,000	8,411	7,629	7,442	7,408	7,248	14,502.6
Eastern Europe										
Albania	30	476	2,640	4,510	7,849	6,277	5,733	5,448	5,288	58.5
Belarus		482	39,390	111,829	215,101	288,841	343,441	382,535	418,380	195.0
Bosnia-Herzegovina		20	111	167	194	404	474	524	571	399.8
Bulgaria		3	115	847	606	580	922	1,003	1,093	764.8
Croatia	2	2,079	2,718	1,431	1,313	1,718	1,884	2,045	2,332	434.7
Czech Republic		20,000	46,430	26,542	42,525	12,206	13,736	14,631	15,708	774.0
Estonia		554	863	914	860	782	802	846	877	76.7
Georgia	18	5	163	151	142	149	156	168	181	108.6
Hungary	13,334	85,651	152,784	176,977	109,020	91,405	93,107	92,104	96,122	523.5
Latvia		62	44	57	23	15	29	29	34	67.1
Lithuania	35	120	517	339	310	273	394	425	449	177.8
Macedonia		1,604	3,033	2,530	2,137	1,878	1,619	1,268	1,009	22.5
Moldova		64	425	978	618	840	1,230	1,374	1,588	130.8
Poland	160	2,149	5,953	5,830	5,863	5,959	5,966	6,090	6,184	2,234.1
Romania	0	48	1,273	997	975	1,112	1,177	1,246	1,353	555.0
Russia	3	4,491	16,698	31,737	31,194	35,325	41,054	47,711	53,868	2,105.8
Serbia and Montenegro		294	3,554	13,627	11,661	21,662	79,000	95,324	106,891	1,541.1
Slovakia		5,607	8,187	29,070	12,698	13,700	13,042	12,873	12,950	524.4
Slovenia	29	48	319	150	147	167	182	196	208	285.0
Ukraine		270	1,458	2,486	4,121	5,781	8,110	10,256	12,385	2,452.4

Source: *Euromonitor International from International Telecommunications Union/national statistics*

Table 18.6

Mobile Telecommunications Revenues 1995-2007

% of telecom revenue

	1995	1996	1997	1998	1999	2000	2001	2002	2003	2004	2005	2006	2007
Western Europe													
Austria		12	25	34	43	47	47	55	60	63	61	63	65
Belgium	10	15	21	23	34	48	57	61	64	66	69	71	73
Cyprus		11	17	21	27	32	38	42	46	49	47	47	46
Denmark	14	21	22	22	20	24	24	29	32	34	37	39	41
Finland	20	25	29	36	39	36	43	49	50	50	50	51	51
France	7	11	14	17	21	26	31	35	35	38	40	42	44
Germany	10	18	21	11	27	31	32	32	33	34	35	36	37
Gibraltar													
Greece	11	16	21	27	35	34	30	27	47	52	54	55	57
Iceland	10	17	20	21	25	27	35	39	40	42	43	44	46
Ireland			18	22	28	42	44	49	53	58	45	47	50
Italy		23	27	28	33	38	46	48	49	40	40	40	41
Liechtenstein													
Luxembourg	5	8	11	13	14	18	33	40	42	47	51	53	56
Malta	5	6	7	11	14	44	25	43	49	45	47	48	51
Monaco													
Netherlands	10	14	19	24	26	26	32	35	37	41	43	44	47
Norway	15	21	22	12	15	18	22	25	22	25	28	29	32
Portugal	14	19	25	29	33	41	45	37	33	36	38	38	39
Spain	5	17	23	29	35	41	43	39	41	28	30	33	35
Sweden	25	21	16	19	22	21	21	22	22	22	22	23	23
Switzerland	6	8	14	16	19	23	26	28	29	30	30	31	31
Turkey	7	9	15	8	48	65	54	37	37	44	52	58	65
United Kingdom	13	15	13	15	18	18	20	20	24	27	28	29	31
Eastern Europe													
Albania		30	30	25	19	27	40	60	70	77	81	82	83
Belarus		0	0	0	0	0	0	0	0	0	0	0	0
Bosnia-Herzegovina		2	8	14	21	26	30	34	39	40	43	46	49
Bulgaria							38	41	45	49	55	60	66
Croatia	4	6	10	14	21	28	35	44	52	53	53	54	54
Czech Republic	7	13	23	37	42	45	54	50	52	58	60	64	69
Estonia	29	31	45	49	49	47	53	57	57	48	50	51	52
Georgia			5	18	16	51	52	56	58	59	59	61	62
Hungary	33	34	38	42	44	30	29	35	33	34	34	34	35
Latvia	6	4	25	47	66	81	89	92	93	92	93	93	93
Lithuania	0	0	0					49	49	51	47	46	47
Macedonia		1	8	18	28	32	32	32	32	35	34	34	35
Moldova							26	30	31	37	37	39	40
Poland	8	11	29	22	23	24	32	44	49	44	46	49	50
Romania								39	45	46	50	54	58
Russia		3	4	2	4	26	33	35	38	44	46	49	51
Serbia and Montenegro			2	1	2	5	9	12	17	23	44	51	57
Slovakia	12	31	20	26	57	35	45	42	53	59	60	65	68
Slovenia				39	54	66	42	44	56	49	53	57	57
Ukraine			1	0	9	20	25	27	38	42	46	49	51

Source: *Euromonitor International from International Telecommunications Union*

Telecommunications

Table 18.7

Mobile Telephone Calls 1995-2007
million minutes

	1995	1996	1997	1998	1999	2000	2001	2002	2003	2004	2005	2006	2007
Western Europe													
Austria				2,400	4,400	6,000	8,100	9,000	9,147	9,261	9,367	9,475	9,585
Belgium													
Cyprus													
Denmark	564	979	1,301	1,621	2,117	2,695	2,929	3,546	3,748	3,996	4,192	4,345	4,463
Finland	316	919	2,246	3,435	4,611	5,294	6,520	7,276	7,655	7,945	8,162	8,327	8,455
France				10,065	20,695	35,524	44,273	51,747	54,929	56,283	57,191	57,913	58,560
Germany			7,500	10,600	17,900	24,347	28,292	30,230	33,607	34,678	35,269	35,643	35,921
Gibraltar			1	2	3	5	6	7	7	8	9	9	10
Greece						5,700	7,400	8,654	9,056	9,327	9,476	9,571	9,644
Iceland					156	194	224	235	243	248	252	255	259
Ireland													
Italy				366		58,000	72,000	74,469	75,839	76,661	77,279	77,821	78,320
Liechtenstein													
Luxembourg						170	230	266	271	275	279	284	288
Malta			9	22	38	33	57	62	66	68	69	70	71
Monaco													
Netherlands						6,200	8,200	8,006	9,178	9,438	9,606	9,731	9,838
Norway					2,623	2,994	3,583	4,165	4,540	4,773	4,957	5,105	5,220
Portugal	436	787	1,038	2,126	4,134	6,187	8,691	9,409	9,904	10,155	10,317	10,439	10,540
Spain				5,216	10,427	17,026	22,942	25,940	27,788	28,648	29,148	29,486	29,749
Sweden			2,553		3,867	4,742	5,466	6,276	6,446	6,771	7,026	7,222	7,367
Switzerland					2,623	4,148	4,757	4,941	5,229	5,364	5,450	5,511	5,562
Turkey								7,444	8,712	9,606	10,231	10,682	11,046
United Kingdom	5,059	6,806	9,572	14,631	25,539	38,206	46,292	53,827	57,519	58,791	59,616	60,261	60,835
Eastern Europe													
Albania													
Belarus	6		13	17	30			323	867	1,713	2,403	2,735	2,860
Bosnia-Herzegovina													
Bulgaria													
Croatia								1,291	1,665	1,867	1,973	2,027	2,058
Czech Republic				1				2,006	2,245	2,344	2,389	2,412	2,428
Estonia													
Georgia													
Hungary													
Latvia													
Lithuania				85	180	284	552	893	1,105	1,227	1,288	1,319	1,337
Macedonia													
Moldova													
Poland													
Romania				68	254	703		1,556	2,075	2,522	2,856	3,073	3,205
Russia													
Serbia and Montenegro								343	456	546	608	646	669
Slovakia				176	483	662	1,133	2,192	2,984	3,512	3,802	3,957	4,050	4,115
Slovenia								1,826	1,869	1,894	1,913	1,929	1,944
Ukraine													

Source: *Euromonitor International from International Telecommunications Union*

Table 18.8

Mobile Telephone Users 1990-2007

'000

	1990	1995	2000	2002	2003	2004	2005	2006	2007
Western Europe									
Austria	73.7	383.5	6,117.0	6,736.0	7,274.0	7,992.0	8,650.0	9,255.0	9,669.7
Belgium	42.9	235.3	5,629.0	8,101.8	8,605.8	9,131.7	9,460.0	9,659.8	9,851.7
Cyprus	- 3.2	44.5	218.3	418.0	551.8	640.5	718.8	777.5	806.5
Denmark	148.2	822.3	3,363.6	4,477.8	4,767.1	5,166.9	5,449.2	5,840.9	6,056.3
Finland	257.9	1,039.1	3,728.6	4,516.8	4,747.1	4,988.0	5,270.0	5,670.0	5,941.9
France	283.2	1,302.5	29,052.4	38,585.3	41,702.0	44,544.0	48,088.0	51,662.0	54,716.2
Germany	272.6	3,725.0	48,202.0	59,128.0	64,800.0	71,300.0	79,200.0	84,300.0	87,580.4
Gibraltar		0.7	5.6	12.2	15.9	18.4	20.7	22.4	23.8
Greece		273.0	5,932.4	9,314.3	8,936.2	9,324.3	10,260.4	11,097.5	11,589.6
Iceland	10.0	30.9	214.9	261.0	279.7	290.1	304.0	328.5	338.0
Ireland	25.0	158.0	2,461.0	3,000.0	3,500.0	3,860.0	4,270.0	4,690.0	4,995.1
Italy	266.0	3,923.0	42,246.0	54,200.0	56,770.0	62,750.0	71,500.0	76,083.5	78,438.3
Liechtenstein	0.6	9.5	14.7	21.8	25.0	25.5	27.5	28.8	30.1
Luxembourg	0.8	26.8	303.3	473.0	539.0	646.0	720.0	713.8	735.8
Malta	1.1	10.8	114.4	276.9	290.0	306.1	324.0	346.8	360.8
Monaco	0.4	3.0	18.7	23.5	24.4	24.8	24.9	24.8	24.6
Netherlands	79.0	539.0	10,755.0	12,100.0	13,200.0	14,800.0	15,834.0	16,556.7	17,082.9
Norway	196.8	981.3	3,224.0	3,790.0	4,060.8	4,524.8	4,754.5	5,040.6	5,241.0
Portugal	6.5	340.8	6,665.0	8,670.0	10,030.5	10,362.1	11,447.3	12,226.4	12,889.9
Spain	54.7	945.0	24,265.1	33,531.0	37,219.8	38,622.6	42,694.1	46,152.0	48,310.0
Sweden	461.2	2,008.0	6,372.3	7,949.0	8,801.0	8,785.0	9,104.0	9,607.0	9,930.5
Switzerland	125.0	447.2	4,638.5	5,736.3	6,189.0	6,275.0	6,834.0	7,418.0	7,834.5
Turkey	31.8	437.1	16,133.4	23,323.1	27,887.5	34,707.5	43,609.0	52,662.7	59,855.9
United Kingdom	1,114.0	5,735.8	43,452.0	49,228.0	54,256.2	59,687.9	65,471.7	69,656.6	73,408.3
Eastern Europe									
Albania		1.8	29.8	851.0	1,100.0	1,259.6	1,530.2	1,748.7	1,996.8
Belarus		5.9	49.4	462.6	1,118.0	2,239.3	4,099.5	5,960.0	7,575.7
Bosnia-Herzegovina		0.8	93.4	748.8	1,074.8	1,407.4	1,594.4	1,887.8	2,188.0
Bulgaria		20.9	738.0	2,597.5	3,500.9	4,729.7	6,244.9	8,253.4	9,308.6
Croatia	0.2	33.7	1,033.0	2,340.0	2,537.3	2,835.5	3,649.7	4,469.7	4,906.1
Czech Republic		48.9	4,346.0	8,610.2	9,708.7	10,782.6	11,775.9	12,149.9	12,422.1
Estonia		30.5	557.0	881.0	1,050.2	1,255.7	1,445.3	1,658.7	1,795.3
Georgia		0.1	195.0	503.6	711.2	840.6	1,174.3	1,703.9	2,125.2
Hungary	2.6	265.0	3,076.3	6,886.1	7,944.6	8,727.2	9,320.0	9,965.0	10,334.5
Latvia		15.0	401.3	917.2	1,219.6	1,536.7	1,871.6	2,183.7	2,346.7
Lithuania		14.8	524.0	1,645.6	2,169.9	3,051.2	4,353.4	4,718.2	4,965.5
Macedonia		0.8	115.7	365.3	776.0	985.6	1,261.3	1,417.0	1,561.5
Moldova		0.0	139.0	339.0	475.9	787.0	1,089.8	1,358.2	1,761.2
Poland		75.0	6,747.0	13,898.5	17,401.2	23,096.1	29,166.4	36,745.5	41,530.9
Romania		9.1	2,499.0	5,110.6	7,039.9	10,215.4	13,354.1	17,400.0	20,132.9
Russia		88.5	3,263.2	17,608.8	36,135.1	73,722.2	120,000.0	144,038.3	154,412.4
Serbia and Montenegro			1,304.0	2,750.0					
Slovakia		12.3	1,243.7	2,923.4	3,678.8	4,275.2	4,540.4	4,893.2	5,149.0
Slovenia		27.3	1,215.6	1,667.2	1,739.1	1,848.6	1,759.2	1,819.6	1,887.6
Ukraine		14.0	818.5	3,692.7	6,498.4	13,735.0	29,999.9	49,076.2	54,663.2

Source: International Telecommunications Union/World Bank/Trade Sources/Euromonitor International

Telecommunications

Table 18.9

Telephone Lines in Use 1990-2007
'000

	1990	1995	2000	2002	2003	2004	2005	2006	2007
Western Europe									
Austria	3,223	3,797	3,997	3,883	3,877	3,821	3,739	3,703	3,647
Belgium	3,913	4,682	5,036	4,932	4,875	4,801	4,767	4,713	4,661
Cyprus	246	347	440	427	424	418	420	418	415
Denmark	2,911	3,193	3,835	3,701	3,614	3,491	3,349	3,239	3,123
Finland	2,670	2,810	2,849	2,726	2,568	2,368	2,120	1,989	1,900
France	28,085	32,400	33,987	34,124	33,913	33,703	33,707	33,569	33,456
Germany	31,887	42,000	50,220	53,670	54,233	54,574	54,700	55,048	55,322
Gibraltar	11	17	24	25	25	25	26	26	26
Greece	3,949	5,163	5,659	6,294	6,300	6,352	6,312	6,331	6,341
Iceland	130	149	196	188	193	190	194	196	197
Ireland	983	1,310	1,832	1,975	1,955	2,015	2,052	2,079	2,122
Italy	22,350	24,845	27,153	27,142	26,596	25,957	25,049	24,632	24,251
Liechtenstein	17	20	20	20	20	20	20	20	20
Luxembourg	184	229	249	249	245	245	245	243	243
Malta	128	171	204	207	208	207	202	200	198
Monaco	24	31	30	30	30	31	31	31	31
Netherlands	6,940	8,124	9,889	8,026	7,846	7,861	7,600	7,688	7,866
Norway	2,132	2,444	2,401	2,317	2,236	2,180	2,129	2,132	2,119
Portugal	2,379	3,643	4,321	4,310	4,281	4,238	4,234	4,209	4,186
Spain	12,603	15,095	17,104	17,641	17,759	17,934	18,004	18,127	18,251
Sweden	5,849	6,013	6,728	6,579	6,543	6,447	6,379	6,314	6,239
Switzerland	3,943	4,480	5,236	5,388	5,323	5,253	5,150	5,073	4,992
Turkey	6,861	13,127	18,395	18,890	18,917	19,125	18,978	19,008	19,039
United Kingdom	25,368	29,411	35,228	34,738	34,550	34,570	33,822	34,194	34,079
Eastern Europe									
Albania	40	42	153	220	255	275	354	394	427
Belarus	1,574	1,968	2,752	2,967	3,071	3,176	3,284	3,397	3,514
Bosnia-Herzegovina		238	780	903	938	952	969	992	1,011
Bulgaria	2,175	2,563	2,882	2,872	2,818	2,727	2,490	2,376	2,290
Croatia	823	1,287	1,721	1,825	1,871	1,888	1,883	1,902	1,913
Czech Republic	1,624	2,444	3,872	3,675	3,626	3,428	3,217	3,078	2,915
Estonia	320	412	523	475	461	444	442	440	442
Georgia	540	554	509	640	667	683	570	579	604
Hungary	996	2,157	3,798	3,669	3,603	3,564	3,356	3,324	3,301
Latvia	620	705	735	701	654	650	731	743	762
Lithuania	781	941	1,188	936	824	820	756	734	727
Macedonia	286	351	507	560	525	537	533	525	525
Moldova	462	566	584	719	791	863	929	982	1,045
Poland	3,293	5,728	10,946	11,860	12,292	12,553	11,836	11,839	11,698
Romania	2,366	2,968	3,899	4,215	4,332	4,389	4,386	4,401	4,424
Russia	20,700	25,019	32,070	35,500	36,100	38,500	40,100	41,663	42,825
Serbia and Montenegro	1,682	2,017	2,406	2,493	2,612	2,685	2,666	2,727	2,767
Slovakia	711	1,118	1,698	1,403	1,295	1,250	1,197	1,192	1,184
Slovenia	422	615	785	808	812	811	816	819	822
Ukraine	7,028	8,311	10,417	10,833	11,110	12,142	11,667	11,975	12,295

Source: *Euromonitor International from International Telecommunications Union/national statistics*

Table 18.10

International Outgoing Telephone Calls 1990-2007
Million minutes

	1990	1995	2000	2002	2003	2004	2005	2006	2007
Western Europe									
Austria	559	901	1,087	1,367	1,207	1,181	1,230	1,190	1,185
Belgium	731	1,106	1,543	1,351	1,558	1,728	1,776	1,869	1,988
Cyprus	57	117	193	256	344	416	467	509	550
Denmark	368	529	707	795	641	610	631	658	664
Finland	186	314	468	469	231	215	213	223	221
France	2,126	2,850	4,952	4,703	4,907	4,281	4,116	4,145	4,121
Germany	3,146	5,238	9,223	9,474	9,544	10,091	10,000	10,186	10,413
Gibraltar		12	18	18	18	19	19	20	20
Greece	213	463	793	807	798	936	968	1,010	1,040
Iceland	19	29	60	44	43	33	32	32	33
Ireland	261	407	1,250	1,395	862	1,176	1,149	1,168	1,202
Italy	1,043	1,839	4,138	5,478	5,986	3,633	3,596	3,739	3,812
Liechtenstein	11	16	55	43	42	44	43	44	44
Luxembourg	151	232	326	440	433	435	427	423	419
Malta	13	29	43	44	22	17	24	28	30
Monaco									
Netherlands	905	1,459	2,550	2,220	2,072	2,055	2,094	2,157	2,209
Norway	281	437	559	574	558	516	562	560	562
Portugal	156	300	505	511	485	508	591	611	647
Spain	611	1,063	2,956	2,773	3,256	3,689	4,705	5,057	5,579
Sweden	631	875	1,086	1,153	1,162	1,184	1,161	1,187	1,196
Switzerland	1,332	1,733	2,624	2,403	2,472	2,685	2,489	2,524	2,547
Turkey	159	374	732	650	939	715	721	750	744
United Kingdom	2,530	4,068	7,981	6,105	6,259	6,021	5,741	5,628	5,541
Eastern Europe									
Albania	20	23	72	62	62	60	61	61	62
Belarus		132	179	241	268	299	314	333	350
Bosnia-Herzegovina		10	93	141	191	204	247	276	303
Bulgaria	62	84	110	137	88	110	154	169	181
Croatia	69	211	222	361	343	320	377	384	401
Czech Republic	83	259	360	392	345	289	422	447	475
Estonia		53	78	103	88	76	73	72	70
Georgia	5	13	60	70	85	70	63	71	77
Hungary	122	247	211	240	309	335	449	483	508
Latvia		44	58	63	50	44	40	38	35
Lithuania	2	55	39	34	35	45	54	61	70
Macedonia		45	73	65	62	21	16	14	13
Moldova		66	43	53	62	81	88	102	111
Poland	81	381	676	621	863	445	451	465	464
Romania	25	88	169	212	184	252	248	267	290
Russia	72	898	944	1,219	1,290	1,258	1,171	1,130	1,114
Serbia and Montenegro	100	212	287	306	315	375	158	153	162
Slovakia	4	59	162	167	140	133	168	166	172
Slovenia		101	102	107	107	166	183	205	219
Ukraine		422	383	446	462	439	389	367	342

Source: Euromonitor International from International Telecommunications Union/national statistics

Telecommunications

Table 18.11

National Telephone Calls 1995-2007

Million minutes

	1995	1996	1997	1998	1999	2000	2001	2002	2003	2004	2005	2006	2007
Western Europe													
Austria	13,760	14,340	14,362	12,850	10,969	8,176	5,988	8,618	13,643	11,800	7,117	5,598	4,419
Belgium					20,805	22,000	21,694	20,295	18,351	16,225	14,673	13,697	12,676
Cyprus	1,783	2,008	2,219	3,150	4,179	3,480	3,693	4,260	4,571	4,656	4,831	5,039	5,206
Denmark	12,657	13,037	13,819	15,000	16,500	22,438	22,830	30,318	36,860	32,280	34,349	36,798	38,791
Finland	13,982	14,908	15,627	16,757	17,866	17,983	18,244	18,677	19,792	20,466	21,163	22,065	22,880
France	104,400	108,500	114,100	119,100	132,833	121,949	118,481	112,456	107,776	106,840	105,302	105,092	104,214
Germany	167,762	157,239	178,100	190,476	230,115	273,085	325,023	190,723	194,898	192,712	185,100	183,321	179,635
Gibraltar	144	160	171	188	211	151	161	172	169	178	186	183	195
Greece							31,500	19,817	18,972	18,804	18,408	18,323	18,111
Iceland				1,524	1,702	1,915	1,696	1,769	1,844	1,827	1,809	1,823	1,816
Ireland	6,779	7,212	7,755	8,447	8,987	9,480	9,673	9,110	5,805	5,798	5,679	5,694	5,658
Italy	99,464	103,832	112,018	115,635	111,913	125,510	126,611	131,908	91,288	121,505	127,426	136,712	139,388
Liechtenstein	57	58	52	64	67	71	77	74	73	74	79	80	81
Luxembourg	1,302	1,470	1,511	1,751	2,144	2,162	2,250	2,238	2,200	2,096	1,752	1,643	1,588
Malta	812	837	852	885	894	998	1,041	1,180	1,185	1,231	1,278	1,277	1,334
Monaco	1,256	1,282	1,263	1,223	1,206	1,214	1,210	1,227	1,235	1,243	1,251	1,259	1,267
Netherlands				34,900	34,900	34,400	32,300	31,803	31,150	30,143	29,752	29,099	29,015
Norway	11,625	13,211	14,299	17,030	21,294	24,758	23,642	23,430	22,530	23,141	23,004	23,713	23,799
Portugal				11,502	12,580	14,606	15,255	21,926	19,302	19,950	21,572	21,538	22,351
Spain	45,587	49,640	54,500	58,359	65,184	51,345	59,632	61,418	58,223	53,787	52,790	55,229	56,508
Sweden	32,600	34,500	33,389	37,179	38,607	55,421	56,719	51,943	48,535	45,769	43,671	43,280	43,333
Switzerland	14,831	15,333	16,780	16,860	18,495	17,213	16,910	16,214	14,639	13,968	13,607	13,483	13,383
Turkey	37,384	34,584	31,382	29,132	27,366	26,859	56,779	58,954	53,312	54,884	52,897	52,623	52,415
United Kingdom	116,632	126,019	133,646	138,533	135,513	135,911	129,429	123,339	120,328	114,283	109,487	107,336	104,367
Eastern Europe													
Albania	123	175	248	196	235	235	88	1,055	765	436	567	663	745
Belarus	1,287	1,502	1,617	1,826	1,881	2,046	2,281	2,457	2,643	2,764	2,859	2,947	3,025
Bosnia-Herzegovina													
Bulgaria					27,323	12,798	6,873	7,251	5,536	5,204	2,599	1,908	1,383
Croatia								4,928	4,887	4,854	4,670	4,634	4,617
Czech Republic					9,337	10,629	11,979	6,254	5,571	4,591	3,762	3,178	2,636
Estonia	114	162	1,520	1,857	1,891	2,304	1,815	1,954	1,901	1,948	1,975	1,982	2,010
Georgia						2,440	2,232	2,617	2,768	2,829	2,891	2,989	3,067
Hungary	6,450	8,391	8,938	9,383	10,708	11,650	11,898	8,176	7,408	7,158	7,342	7,093	6,994
Latvia			859	1,618	1,742	1,719	1,655	1,638	1,447	1,355	1,205	1,121	1,060
Lithuania		2,493	3,147	3,865	4,537	4,138	2,958	1,655	1,381	1,557	1,574	1,559	1,626
Macedonia	2,274	2,773	1,867	2,164	2,337	2,277	2,105	1,843	1,514	1,140	744	557	457
Moldova	229	480	1,159	1,593	1,820	2,049	2,309	2,287	2,189	2,816	3,261	3,624	4,081
Poland	23,110	30,042	36,351	49,438	63,775	36,352	36,352	26,037	24,345	25,474	26,162	26,236	26,902
Romania	7,173	6,703	6,265	5,915	5,692	5,460	5,172	7,197	7,960	7,658	7,433	7,314	6,898
Russia	32,952	34,132	37,207	38,236	40,762	42,239	43,830	46,756	48,723	52,177	54,824	57,605	59,691
Serbia and Montenegro	12,207	14,118	17,490										
Slovakia	2,295	2,735	3,424	3,490	3,626	3,193	2,131	1,664	3,170	2,741	3,245	3,678	4,017
Slovenia	3,392	3,311	4,511	4,261	3,918	3,690	4,189	4,298	4,299	4,421	4,495	4,563	4,655
Ukraine	20,670	22,983	23,404	24,120	25,055	25,908	26,537	29,822	30,727	33,095	35,645	36,702	38,172

Source: *Euromonitor International from International Telecommunications Union/national statistics*

Labour

Total Employment

Table 19.1

General Level of Employment 1980-2007

'000

	1980	1985	1990	1995	2000	2002	2003	2004	2005	2006	2007
Western Europe											
Austria	3,023	3,234	3,421	3,735	3,777	3,833	3,798	3,744	3,824	3,928	3,972
Belgium	3,699	3,505	3,623	3,793	4,102	4,021	4,027	4,092	4,237	4,302	4,366
Cyprus	193	241	272	295	294	315	327	336	348	357	378
Denmark	2,402	2,501	2,670	2,603	2,722	2,715	2,692	2,720	2,733	2,787	2,811
Finland	2,194	2,434	2,493	2,137	2,355	2,394	2,384	2,385	2,401	2,444	2,492
France	21,478	21,566	23,137	23,184	23,636	24,312	24,473	24,720	24,919	25,302	25,848
Germany				36,049	36,603	36,535	36,171	35,660	36,568	37,323	38,189
Gibraltar	12	12	14	11	12	12	12	13	13	13	13
Greece	3,504	3,597	3,706	3,823	3,992	4,016	4,117	4,164	4,429	4,453	4,551
Iceland	119	121	135	142	156	157	157	156	161	165	167
Ireland	1,048	1,077	1,133	1,265	1,662	1,765	1,793	1,836	1,929	1,987	2,026
Italy	20,239	20,770	21,434	20,093	21,227	21,921	22,131	22,381	22,566	22,903	22,971
Liechtenstein			20	22	27	29	29	30	30	31	31
Luxembourg	153	158	158	164	181	188	187	188	194	195	203
Malta	120	113	127	133	143	149	149	146	148	151	155
Monaco											
Netherlands	5,344	5,561	6,357	6,831	7,732	7,913	8,013	7,967	7,880	8,008	8,119
Norway	1,864	2,007	2,027	2,080	2,270	2,285	2,267	2,275	2,291	2,297	2,302
Portugal	3,960	4,234	4,662	4,442	4,920	5,117	5,128	5,127	5,122	5,159	5,170
Spain	11,557	10,641	12,579	12,512	15,506	16,630	17,296	17,971	18,973	19,748	20,389
Sweden	4,098	4,269	4,501	3,984	4,159	4,242	4,235	4,211	4,264	4,350	4,409
Switzerland				3,748	3,879	3,965	3,963	3,959	3,975	4,023	4,041
Turkey		19,802	19,623	20,679	21,148	21,355	21,148	21,791	22,046	22,315	22,516
United Kingdom	25,215	24,555	26,923	25,732	27,434	27,866	28,166	28,411	28,674	28,895	29,075
Eastern Europe											
Albania				1,077	989	1,028	1,053	1,081	1,113	1,153	1,188
Belarus				4,410	4,609	4,365	4,341	4,341	4,357	4,338	4,319
Bosnia-Herzegovina						394	387	388	388	387	386
Bulgaria				3,216	2,934	2,801	2,834	2,922	2,980	2,946	2,950
Croatia		1,935	1,947	1,712	1,577	1,672	1,538	1,563	1,573	1,571	1,554
Czech Republic			5,225	5,001	4,723	4,764	4,733	4,706	4,766	4,829	4,939
Estonia			790	662	615	586	594	596	608	646	662
Georgia					1,749	1,839	1,814	1,783	1,745	1,710	1,677
Hungary	4,654	4,504	4,105	3,679	3,849	3,870	3,922	3,900	3,902	3,930	3,945
Latvia			1,061	898	973	989	1,007	1,018	1,036	1,089	1,116
Lithuania			1,622	1,529	1,398	1,406	1,438	1,436	1,474	1,499	1,503
Macedonia				555	551	561	545	523	545	542	538
Moldova					1,515	1,505	1,357	1,316	1,319	1,292	1,258
Poland			17,149	14,727	14,526	13,782	13,616	13,795	14,115	14,618	15,218
Romania			11,113	11,152	10,764	9,234	9,222	9,158	9,149	9,316	9,383
Russia				62,757	62,845	65,766	66,496	67,134	67,824	68,233	68,422
Serbia and Montenegro				3,947	3,324	3,221	3,130	3,087	3,036	2,986	2,945
Slovakia			2,430	2,157	2,109	2,137	2,170	2,178	2,218	2,305	2,349
Slovenia				882	894	923	896	946	949	961	985
Ukraine				24,091	20,472	20,561	20,606	20,296	20,680	20,732	20,769

Source: *International Labour Organisation/Euromonitor International*

Table 19.2

Employment by Activity 2007

% of total employed population

	Agriculture, Forestry & Fishing	Community, Social & Personal Services	Construction	Electricity, Gas & Water	Finance, Insurance, Real Estate & Business	Manufact- uring
Western Europe						
Austria	5.7	25.5	8.3	0.8	12.2	19.0
Belgium	1.9	35.1	7.0	0.8	13.3	16.5
Cyprus	4.0	26.2	11.0	0.8	13.0	9.9
Denmark	2.9	36.4	7.4	0.6	13.8	15.1
Finland	4.5	33.0	6.7	0.6	13.7	17.9
France	3.7	33.4	6.9	0.8	13.6	16.0
Germany	2.2	30.4	6.5	0.8	13.8	21.8
Gibraltar						
Greece	11.7	24.6	8.2	0.9	9.1	12.4
Iceland	6.1	34.5	9.2	0.9	13.0	11.1
Ireland	5.5	27.0	14.0	0.5	13.4	12.3
Italy	4.2	25.2	8.3	0.7	13.6	20.7
Liechtenstein						
Luxembourg	1.2	20.5	9.9	0.6	29.7	9.9
Malta	1.6	29.0	8.5	2.3	11.0	16.7
Monaco						
Netherlands	3.2	33.4	6.0	0.5	15.6	12.4
Norway	3.2	38.4	7.1	0.7	13.2	11.2
Portugal	11.6	22.8	10.7	0.5	7.5	19.1
Spain	4.5	22.0	13.0	0.6	12.2	15.2
Sweden	1.9	38.1	6.5	0.6	16.1	14.7
Switzerland	3.7	26.7	7.0	0.6	17.4	16.1
Turkey	25.7	12.2	5.9	0.4	4.8	19.1
United Kingdom	1.4	34.7	8.2	0.6	15.9	12.6
Eastern Europe						
Albania	58.6	18.4	5.2	1.1		6.6
Belarus	16.4	23.8	4.1	2.4	2.7	22.2
Bosnia-Herzegovina						
Bulgaria	23.3	17.7	5.9	1.6	6.6	19.9
Croatia	15.7	21.2	8.5	1.3	7.8	17.9
Czech Republic	3.7	23.6	9.0	1.6	8.7	28.4
Estonia	4.8	26.0	10.2	1.8	9.1	20.1
Georgia	54.6	17.6	2.6	1.5	2.2	5.2
Hungary	4.7	27.0	8.3	1.7	9.4	21.8
Latvia	10.6	26.0	9.9	2.0	8.4	14.6
Lithuania	11.8	24.6	10.6	1.7	6.7	17.8
Macedonia	21.0	21.1	7.7	2.9	3.7	21.4
Moldova	31.0	24.2	5.5	2.0	3.8	11.2
Poland	14.9	24.0	6.6	1.5	8.1	20.7
Romania	29.8	16.9	6.3	2.1	4.2	20.9
Russia	9.8	26.7	6.7	3.0	7.5	18.0
Serbia and Montenegro						
Slovakia	4.1	24.4	10.0	1.7	8.1	26.3
Slovenia	9.5	24.6	5.8	1.0	9.2	26.9
Ukraine	16.8	23.4	4.8		6.8	19.3

Source: International Labour Organisation/Euromonitor International

Total Employment

Employment by Activity 2007 *(continued)*

% of total employed population

	Mining & Quarrying	Transport, Storage & Commun- ications	Wholesale & Retail Trade, Restaurants & Hotels	Undefined Sectors	Total
Western Europe					
Austria	0.3	6.1	21.7	0.4	100.0
Belgium	0.2	7.5	16.2	1.3	100.0
Cyprus	0.2	5.8	24.0	5.0	100.0
Denmark	0.2	6.1	17.5		100.0
Finland	0.2	7.4	15.4	0.5	100.0
France	0.2	6.4	16.5	2.5	100.0
Germany	0.3	5.6	17.9	0.6	100.0
Gibraltar					
Greece	0.4	6.4	24.7	1.7	100.0
Iceland	0.1	7.4	17.7	0.2	100.0
Ireland	0.6	5.9	19.9	0.9	100.0
Italy	0.2	5.2	20.3	1.6	100.0
Liechtenstein					
Luxembourg	0.1	7.2	18.1	2.7	100.0
Malta		7.6	23.5		100.0
Monaco					
Netherlands	0.1	6.1	18.6	4.1	100.0
Norway	1.5	6.5	18.1	0.1	100.0
Portugal	0.3	4.8	19.8	2.9	100.0
Spain	0.3	5.8	22.2	4.1	100.0
Sweden	0.2	6.3	15.3	0.2	100.0
Switzerland	0.1	6.5	20.8	1.2	100.0
Turkey	0.6	5.2	21.8	4.4	100.0
United Kingdom	0.4	6.8	18.7	0.7	100.0
Eastern Europe					
Albania	0.6	1.2	8.3		100.0
Belarus	1.3	6.6	17.4	3.2	100.0
Bosnia-Herzegovina					
Bulgaria	0.8	6.4	17.9		100.0
Croatia	0.4	6.5	20.3	0.3	100.0
Czech Republic	1.1	7.4	16.5	0.0	100.0
Estonia	0.7	9.6	17.5		100.0
Georgia	0.4	3.8	11.4	0.7	100.0
Hungary	0.4	7.6	19.2	0.0	100.0
Latvia	0.3	9.0	18.6	0.4	100.0
Lithuania	0.3	6.5	19.7	0.2	100.0
Macedonia	0.7	5.3	15.9	0.2	100.0
Moldova	0.3	5.2	16.4	0.4	100.0
Poland	1.6	6.6	15.9	0.1	100.0
Romania	1.2	5.3	13.3		100.0
Russia	1.7	9.1	17.5	0.1	100.0
Serbia and Montenegro					
Slovakia	0.7	6.9	17.5	0.2	100.0
Slovenia	0.6	5.5	16.5	0.4	100.0
Ukraine		6.9	22.0		100.0

Source: International Labour Organisation/Euromonitor International

Table 19.3

Employed Population by Quarter 2006-2008

'000

	2006 1st Quarter	2006 2nd Quarter	2006 3rd Quarter	2006 4th Quarter	2007 1st Quarter	2007 2nd Quarter	2007 3rd Quarter	2007 4th Quarter	2008 1st Quarter	2008 2nd Quarter
Western Europe										
Austria	3,818.3	3,917.1	4,025.5	3,952.5	3,893.6	3,978.6	4,038.2	3,976.8	3,960.2	
Belgium	4,244.6	4,253.7	4,315.5	4,394.7	4,333.9	4,330.8	4,371.3	4,429.1	4,435.3	
Cyprus	350.6	356.3	359.9	362.0	369.2	377.8	379.7	384.8	379.7	
Denmark	2,749.8	2,771.8	2,813.8	2,810.8	2,796.1	2,824.4	2,814.3	2,809.2	2,824.4	
Finland	2,356.9	2,534.8	2,469.4	2,413.3	2,415.3	2,524.6	2,541.6	2,485.6	2,475.1	2,576.2
France	25,084.7	25,245.5	25,510.2	25,368.7	25,467.6	25,819.8	26,088.8	26,014.5	26,037.7	
Germany	36,737.2	37,187.1	37,466.1	37,901.6	37,648.2	38,047.2	38,275.2	38,784.3	38,310.2	
Gibraltar										
Greece	4,400.3	4,453.1	4,494.5	4,462.4	4,501.7	4,561.1	4,580.7	4,560.3	4,552.7	
Iceland	158.9	166.7	168.4	165.1	162.5	168.4	170.1	165.8	163.6	
Ireland	1,947.2	1,965.6	2,020.5	2,013.5	1,989.9	2,009.5	2,053.2	2,051.2		
Italy	22,662.5	23,100.7	22,915.4	22,932.8	22,599.9	23,046.6	23,164.5	23,074.1	22,920.5	
Liechtenstein										
Luxembourg	194.4	194.4	196.2	196.2	198.8	199.2	202.4	211.1	204.9	
Malta	150.1	150.9	152.8	151.8	153.1	154.9	156.3	155.3	157.1	
Monaco										
Netherlands	7,914.7	7,988.6	8,040.8	8,087.8	8,021.0	8,123.8	8,165.9	8,164.8	8,155.3	
Norway	2,261.4	2,288.6	2,314.9	2,322.6	2,257.7	2,292.6	2,316.1	2,339.7	2,351.9	
Portugal	5,126.5	5,180.4	5,186.9	5,142.4	5,135.7	5,154.6	5,200.3	5,188.2	5,191.0	
Spain	19,400.2	19,693.2	19,895.7	20,001.9	20,102.2	20,400.8	20,544.3	20,510.6	20,824.7	20,847.9
Sweden	4,242.0	4,332.2	4,451.2	4,376.3	4,301.9	4,404.0	4,513.4	4,416.2	4,396.4	4,493.0
Switzerland	3,975.8	4,003.5	4,054.1	4,059.7	3,990.0	4,028.4	4,068.1	4,076.9		
Turkey	20,871.8	22,709.7	23,186.3	22,493.0	21,565.1	23,008.9	23,374.8	22,113.8	21,550.9	
United Kingdom	28,749.1	28,790.0	29,038.4	29,002.5	28,814.5	28,939.9	29,219.5	29,326.0		
Eastern Europe										
Albania	1,150.6	1,151.0	1,154.9	1,155.7	1,186.2	1,186.5	1,190.0			
Belarus										
Bosnia-Herzegovina										
Bulgaria	2,785.7	2,973.9	3,032.3	2,993.3	2,843.7	2,950.4	3,007.0	2,998.8	2,983.8	
Croatia					1,504.3	1,549.2	1,599.0	1,563.8		
Czech Republic	4,786.1	4,826.9	4,840.3	4,862.6	4,881.3	4,930.4	4,958.5	4,983.9	4,975.0	
Estonia	634.7	650.0	649.6	650.7	654.0	665.7	669.3	660.9	663.6	
Georgia										
Hungary	3,885.0	3,933.8	3,948.1	3,952.9	3,924.4	3,961.6	3,966.5	3,928.3	3,862.8	
Latvia	1,058.6	1,073.7	1,120.9	1,103.4	1,082.3	1,105.9	1,128.7	1,146.6	1,135.6	
Lithuania	1,484.2	1,501.9	1,511.4	1,498.1	1,477.1	1,512.5	1,528.5	1,494.0	1,479.6	
Macedonia	531.3	537.6	547.6	549.5	528.0	537.1	545.3	541.5		
Moldova					1,195.9	1,337.5	1,305.0	1,193.1		
Poland	14,191.2	14,461.2	14,908.3	14,913.3	14,816.8	15,129.4	15,409.2	15,514.8	15,491.8	
Romania	9,031.1	9,475.9	9,658.8	9,097.5	9,135.3	9,473.3	9,722.0	9,203.5	9,148.0	
Russia	67,842.9	67,661.2	69,121.3	68,304.9	67,083.5	68,511.6	69,437.5	68,655.1		
Serbia and Montenegro										
Slovakia	2,261.2	2,297.7	2,323.9	2,335.8	2,318.9	2,329.2	2,357.9	2,389.6	2,382.4	
Slovenia	946.1	969.5	973.7	956.0	957.3	993.3	1,005.9	983.1	970.3	
Ukraine										

Source: International Labour Organisation/Euromonitor International

Total Employment

Table 19.4

Level of Paid Employment in Manufacturing 1980-2007
'000

	1980	1985	1990	1995	2000	2002	2003	2004	2005	2006	2007
Western Europe											
Austria	1,259	1,153	1,098	862	726	712	698	656	668	701	706
Belgium	1,008	873	856	747	714	697	672	677	682	667	667
Cyprus	30	34	37	34	27	31	29	29	31	30	30
Denmark	374	398	401	496	488	441	422	419	424	411	407
Finland	567	528	495	403	437	436	418	411	414	417	420
France	5,182	4,584	4,410	3,909	3,900	3,807	3,712	3,618	3,524	3,495	3,477
Germany	8,717	8,064	8,876	8,499	8,141	8,080	7,839	7,723	7,613	7,741	7,800
Gibraltar	3	3	1	1	1	0	1	1	0	1	1
Greece	496	462	457	398	409	430	413	419	413	409	408
Iceland	25	27	23	21	21	20	19	20	19	18	18
Ireland	243	201	210	229	270	261	263	258	251	245	239
Italy	4,745	4,101	4,081	4,027	4,060	4,103	4,126	4,067	4,086	4,075	4,050
Liechtenstein											
Luxembourg	38	35	34	32	33	33	32	32	32	32	32
Malta	40	34	36	31	31	28	27	27	26	25	24
Monaco											
Netherlands	1,121	1,042	1,145	1,029	1,042	1,015	980	993	965	957	947
Norway	371	337	301	300	284	281	268	255	256	262	264
Portugal	921	926	1,037	858	961	918	884	872	853	867	872
Spain	2,723	2,199	2,557	2,045	2,578	2,688	2,680	2,709	2,720	2,716	2,714
Sweden	1,002	935	903	716	721	676	656	641	616	614	608
Switzerland	692	665	728	738	698	689	667	654	656	668	674
Turkey	1,986	2,129	2,582	2,525	2,845	3,034	3,026	3,121	3,366	3,478	3,530
United Kingdom	6,935	5,567	4,756	4,072	3,941	3,580	3,446	3,253	3,131	3,041	2,970
Eastern Europe											
Albania					32	35	37	38	40	42	43
Belarus		1,430	1,437	1,216	1,208	1,146	1,123	1,121	1,111	1,101	1,095
Bosnia-Herzegovina								89	83	83	83
Bulgaria	1,308	1,512	1,588	787	562	574	598	607	607	611	616
Croatia		537	546	338	278	274	277	277	274	280	272
Czech Republic	1,540	1,646	1,543	1,332	1,192	1,216	1,189	1,175	1,197	1,254	1,277
Estonia		215	206	158	133	123	129	134	133	131	135
Georgia					86	65	68	65	65	65	64
Hungary	1,386	1,278	1,118	652	753	746	734	715	689	692	693
Latvia			236	165	149	154	157	163	158	160	155
Lithuania		670	652	318	243	252	254	246	255	255	255
Macedonia		178	187	120	99	91	89	84	82	78	75
Moldova		387	365	156	98	104	104	108	106	104	104
Poland	4,126	3,702	3,014	2,616	2,467	2,221	2,206	2,244	2,259	2,311	2,334
Romania	3,031	3,266	3,452	2,192	1,560	1,593	1,582	1,492	1,425	1,442	1,451
Russia	23,812	23,490	18,884	13,181	12,335	13,185	12,536	12,448	12,278	12,233	12,097
Serbia and Montenegro				801	668	594	553	523	490	462	437
Slovakia				556	516	549	539	547	557	574	599
Slovenia		383	373	297	253	269	252	254	261	248	241
Ukraine			5,975	4,159	2,916	2,500	2,356	2,351	2,371	2,329	2,310

Source: *International Labour Organisation/Euromonitor International*

Table 19.5

Total Unemployed 1980-2007
'000

	1980	1985	1990	1995	2000	2002	2003	2004	2005	2006	2007
Western Europe											
Austria	62	121	115	144	139	161	169	194	208	196	186
Belgium	453	455	285	390	308	333	364	381	389	384	369
Cyprus	4	8	5	8	15	11	14	15	19	17	15
Denmark	245	252	242	196	131	134	158	163	143	118	108
Finland	114	144	82	383	254	238	235	229	219	204	183
France	1,492	2,474	2,205	2,899	2,590	2,341	2,656	2,727	2,716	2,564	2,340
Germany				4,035	3,128	3,484	4,024	4,386	4,582	4,279	3,481
Gibraltar	0	0	0	2	0	0	0	0	0	1	1
Greece	215	296	282	425	491	428	403	447	420	427	407
Iceland	1	1	2	7	4	5	6	5	4	4	3
Ireland	204	225	172	178	75	77	82	84	86	91	94
Italy	2,198	2,345	2,489	2,639	2,495	2,164	2,098	2,013	1,944	1,724	1,756
Liechtenstein			0	0	0	0	1	1	1	1	1
Luxembourg	1	3	2	5	4	5	7	10	9	10	9
Malta	4	10	5	5	10	11	12	12	12	12	11
Monaco											
Netherlands	382	623	514	527	264	260	355	418	428	357	296
Norway	67	53	113	107	81	93	106	107	109	113	116
Portugal	401	451	256	338	206	271	342	365	423	428	448
Spain	1,488	2,939	2,441	3,716	2,496	2,155	2,242	2,214	1,912	1,837	1,797
Sweden	103	110	75	334	201	178	216	247	269	251	261
Switzerland				129	106	119	170	178	185	168	177
Turkey		1,730	1,523	1,608	1,933	2,464	2,493	2,498	2,518	2,452	2,446
United Kingdom	1,649	3,155	2,003	2,470	1,637	1,533	1,479	1,428	1,426	1,657	1,660
Eastern Europe											
Albania				232	294	290	270	254	219	192	173
Belarus				134	98	133	139	87	70	65	61
Bosnia-Herzegovina						282	297	316	338	341	343
Bulgaria				565	559	599	449	400	334	291	257
Croatia		165	160	163	295	265	256	250	229	196	173
Czech Republic			227	207	457	374	399	427	409	371	280
Estonia			5	68	90	67	66	64	52	40	36
Georgia					212	265	236	258	279	293	301
Hungary	418	396	420	417	263	239	245	253	304	317	334
Latvia			321	258	159	135	119	119	99	78	69
Lithuania			273	266	274	224	204	184	133	89	75
Macedonia		136	159	229	262	263	316	309	324	339	353
Moldova					140	110	117	117	104	100	98
Poland				2,277	2,785	3,431	3,329	3,230	3,047	2,341	1,823
Romania			566	968	821	845	692	800	702	726	705
Russia				6,712	7,138	6,153	5,716	5,775	5,608	5,449	5,288
Serbia and Montenegro				609	481	517	562	581	601	619	641
Slovakia			202	324	485	487	459	481	428	356	330
Slovenia				70	66	58	62	60	66	60	50
Ukraine				1,426	2,656	2,141	2,008	1,907	1,601	1,455	1,336

Source: International Labour Organisation/Euromonitor International

Total Unemployed Population

Table 19.6

Unemployed Population by Quarter 2006-2008

'000

	2006 1st Quarter	2006 2nd Quarter	2006 3rd Quarter	2006 4th Quarter	2007 1st Quarter	2007 2nd Quarter	2007 3rd Quarter	2007 4th Quarter	2008 1st Quarter	2008 2nd Quarter
Western Europe										
Austria	247.9	174.6	161.8	197.6	225.5	167.3	156.7	193.2	146.4	
Belgium	384.0	374.5	406.2	372.5	379.5	355.1	384.2	358.7	355.4	
Cyprus	19.5	15.6	16.3	16.2	18.1	13.9	14.3	14.6	15.6	12.1
Denmark	143.4	116.5	113.9	97.8	134.9	110.2	102.2	82.8	120.0	
Finland	218.5	241.4	180.8	176.5	198.2	210.5	163.6	160.9	157.1	180.2
France	2,740.0	2,438.5	2,571.8	2,504.3	2,510.2	2,230.5	2,301.1	2,316.4	2,375.0	2,204.1
Germany	4,740.1	4,283.2	4,366.2	3,726.5	3,778.6	3,437.2	3,404.9	3,305.1	3,353.4	
Gibraltar										
Greece	465.4	420.4	401.7	422.1	445.2	397.6	387.1	396.1	406.1	
Iceland	3.0	5.4	3.4	3.2	2.9	4.8	3.2	2.9	3.5	
Ireland	86.1	89.2	102.3	86.6	85.2	93.0	101.3	96.0		
Italy	1,931.5	1,670.4	1,533.6	1,760.0	1,813.8	1,646.4	1,632.7	1,929.5	2,053.2	
Liechtenstein										
Luxembourg	10.3	9.0	9.2	10.3	9.3	8.2	8.1	8.7	8.9	
Malta	12.3	11.8	12.1	12.6	11.5	10.5	10.4	10.4	9.0	8.9
Monaco										
Netherlands	413.7	379.3	335.8	300.5	345.5	302.7	277.8	257.2	255.6	
Norway	131.9	113.4	114.8	91.9	133.0	112.8	120.8	99.1	125.3	110.7
Portugal	449.8	426.2	410.1	426.7	491.6	439.9	429.6	432.0	462.9	449.4
Spain	1,948.4	1,813.5	1,772.9	1,813.1	1,826.6	1,751.6	1,767.4	1,842.8	1,823.8	1,997.7
Sweden	266.6	260.1	266.6	211.7	281.4	257.9	275.3	230.7	267.7	295.5
Switzerland	190.1	165.1	155.8	159.5	203.0	172.4	162.4	170.8	208.2	184.7
Turkey	2,739.5	2,302.1	2,306.8	2,459.4	2,640.4	2,310.5	2,337.5	2,496.7	2,713.9	
United Kingdom	1,582.6	1,637.4	1,759.7	1,648.3	1,702.4	1,628.1	1,738.5	1,570.9		
Eastern Europe										
Albania	194.0	191.8	191.7	191.1	176.0	172.9	169.4			
Belarus										
Bosnia-Herzegovina										
Bulgaria	300.4	294.4	295.8	274.9	291.2	253.9	251.0	229.9	244.3	
Croatia	210.6	193.8	184.1	196.3	193.6	172.2	160.0	164.9	180.3	162.5
Czech Republic	412.3	366.7	359.1	345.9	323.7	277.1	267.1	250.5	258.7	
Estonia	54.1	41.8	34.3	31.7	37.3	35.0	34.4	36.8	30.9	31.4
Georgia										
Hungary	350.0	300.5	304.0	312.5	352.0	325.4	324.5	332.9	357.0	330.1
Latvia					78.1	72.2	65.8	59.4	60.6	
Lithuania	103.9	82.1	82.6	88.6	90.5	72.2	66.7	70.8	85.1	
Macedonia	335.5	336.8	340.6	342.5	359.9	352.8	346.3	352.0		
Moldova					105.3	84.7	103.1	98.6		
Poland	2,631.2	2,390.9	2,220.1	2,121.6	2,145.6	1,852.6	1,689.3	1,606.0	1,822.1	1,578.6
Romania	822.7	730.8	665.5	683.7	832.2	683.6	631.2	672.9	733.1	662.2
Russia	6,022.6	5,657.7	5,006.7	5,108.9	6,214.5	5,139.5	4,918.0	4,881.1		
Serbia and Montenegro										
Slovakia	399.6	362.3	338.0	322.1	358.0	327.3	321.2	312.9	367.8	
Slovenia	65.8	61.5	58.4	55.9	54.1	49.6	47.9	48.1	44.2	40.9
Ukraine										

Source: International Labour Organisation/Euromonitor International

Table 19.7

Unemployment Rate 1980-2007

% of economically active population

	1980	1985	1990	1995	2000	2002	2003	2004	2005	2006	2007
Western Europe											
Austria	2.0	3.6	3.2	3.7	3.5	4.0	4.3	4.9	5.2	4.7	4.5
Belgium	10.9	11.5	7.3	9.3	7.0	7.6	8.3	8.5	8.4	8.2	7.8
Cyprus	2.2	3.3	1.8	2.6	4.9	3.3	4.2	4.3	5.3	4.5	3.9
Denmark	9.3	9.1	8.3	7.0	4.6	4.7	5.5	5.6	5.0	4.1	3.7
Finland	4.9	5.6	3.2	15.2	9.7	9.0	9.0	8.8	8.4	7.7	6.9
France	6.5	10.3	8.7	11.1	9.9	8.8	9.8	9.9	9.8	9.2	8.3
Germany				10.1	7.9	8.7	10.0	11.0	11.1	10.3	8.4
Gibraltar	1.7	3.7	2.7	16.6	3.2	3.6	3.8	3.4	3.7	3.8	3.9
Greece	5.8	7.6	7.1	10.0	10.9	9.6	8.9	9.7	8.7	8.8	8.2
Iceland	0.4	0.9	1.8	4.9	2.4	3.3	3.4	3.0	2.6	2.2	2.0
Ireland	16.3	17.3	13.2	12.3	4.3	4.2	4.4	4.4	4.3	4.4	4.4
Italy	9.8	10.1	10.4	11.6	10.5	9.0	8.7	8.3	7.9	7.0	7.1
Liechtenstein			0.1	0.9	1.1	1.4	2.2	2.4	2.5	2.6	2.7
Luxembourg	0.7	1.7	1.2	3.0	2.3	2.6	3.7	5.1	4.5	4.7	4.1
Malta	3.3	8.1	3.9	3.8	6.3	6.8	7.5	7.3	7.3	7.5	6.5
Monaco											
Netherlands	6.7	10.1	7.5	7.2	3.3	3.2	4.2	5.0	5.2	4.3	3.5
Norway	3.5	2.6	5.3	4.9	3.4	3.9	4.5	4.5	4.5	4.7	4.8
Portugal	9.2	9.6	5.2	7.1	4.0	5.0	6.3	6.6	7.6	7.7	8.0
Spain	11.4	21.6	16.3	22.9	13.9	11.5	11.5	11.0	9.2	8.5	8.1
Sweden	2.4	2.5	1.6	7.7	4.6	4.0	4.9	5.5	5.9	5.5	5.6
Switzerland			1.3	3.3	2.7	2.9	4.1	4.3	4.4	4.0	4.2
Turkey		8.0	7.2	7.2	8.4	10.3	10.5	10.3	10.3	9.9	9.8
United Kingdom	6.1	11.4	6.9	8.8	5.6	5.2	5.0	4.8	4.7	5.4	5.4
Eastern Europe											
Albania				17.7	22.9	22.0	20.4	19.1	16.4	14.3	12.7
Belarus				3.0	2.1	3.0	3.1	2.0	1.6	1.5	1.4
Bosnia-Herzegovina						41.7	43.4	44.9	46.5	46.9	47.0
Bulgaria				14.9	16.0	17.6	13.7	12.0	10.1	9.0	8.0
Croatia		7.9	7.6	8.7	15.8	13.7	14.3	13.8	12.7	11.1	10.0
Czech Republic			4.2	4.0	8.8	7.3	7.8	8.3	7.9	7.1	5.4
Estonia			0.7	9.3	12.7	10.3	10.0	9.6	7.9	5.9	5.1
Georgia					10.8	12.6	11.5	12.6	13.8	14.6	15.2
Hungary	8.2	8.1	9.3	10.2	6.4	5.8	5.9	6.1	7.2	7.5	7.8
Latvia			23.2	22.3	14.0	12.0	10.6	10.4	8.7	6.7	5.8
Lithuania			14.4	14.8	16.4	13.8	12.4	11.4	8.3	5.6	4.8
Macedonia		21.6	23.6	29.2	32.2	31.9	36.7	37.2	37.3	38.5	39.6
Moldova					8.5	6.8	7.9	8.1	7.3	7.2	7.2
Poland				13.4	16.1	19.9	19.6	19.0	17.8	13.8	10.7
Romania			4.8	8.0	7.1	8.4	7.0	8.0	7.1	7.2	7.0
Russia				9.7	10.2	8.6	7.9	7.9	7.6	7.4	7.1
Serbia and Montenegro				13.4	12.6	13.8	15.2	15.8	16.5	17.2	17.9
Slovakia			7.7	13.0	18.7	18.6	17.5	18.1	16.2	13.4	12.3
Slovenia				7.4	6.9	5.9	6.5	6.0	6.5	5.9	4.8
Ukraine				5.6	11.5	9.4	8.9	8.6	7.2	6.6	6.0

Source: International Labour Organisation/Euromonitor International

447

Trends in Unemployment Rate | **Table 19.8**

Unemployment Rate by Quarter 2006-2008
% of economically active population

	2006 1st Quarter	2006 2nd Quarter	2006 3rd Quarter	2006 4th Quarter	2007 1st Quarter	2007 2nd Quarter	2007 3rd Quarter	2007 4th Quarter	2008 1st Quarter	2008 2nd Quarter
Western Europe										
Austria	5.9	4.3	3.9	4.8	5.3	4.1	3.8	4.7	4.8	3.8
Belgium	8.6	8.3	8.1	7.9	8.3	7.9	7.6	7.4	7.4	6.9
Cyprus	7.0	6.5	6.4	6.6	5.1	4.9	4.8	4.9		
Denmark	6.2	5.5	5.6	5.4	5.6	5.2	4.5	4.5	4.4	4.3
Finland	9.1	9.4	9.3	9.1	8.2	8.0	8.0	7.8		
France	10.2	9.2	8.9	8.6	7.9	7.6	7.9	8.1		
Germany	8.2	8.7	8.7	8.7	7.8	8.0	8.0	8.0		
Gibraltar										
Greece	7.1	7.0	7.4	7.5	7.4	7.2	7.6	7.6	7.8	7.6
Iceland	4.2	4.1	4.1	4.2	4.5	4.4	4.5	4.1		
Ireland	6.7	6.7	6.3	6.3	6.6	6.6	6.6	6.6		
Italy	4.2	4.2	3.9	3.7	4.0	4.0	3.7	3.5		
Liechtenstein										
Luxembourg	7.3	7.3	7.5	7.3	6.5	6.6	6.5	5.9		
Malta	10.6	8.3	10.9	11.9	10.4	9.7	10.3	10.1		
Monaco										
Netherlands	5.3	5.1	4.9	4.5	5.1	5.1	5.1	4.9	5.1	5.3
Norway	11.8	12.2	12.5	11.4	10.0	11.1	11.4	11.3	10.7	11.1
Portugal	7.0	7.2	7.2	7.2	6.6	6.7	6.7	6.7		
Spain	4.7	4.7	4.6	4.7	5.1	5.2	4.8	5.1		
Sweden	3.7	3.7	3.7	4.0	3.8	3.9	4.1	4.2		
Switzerland	4.0	3.9	3.9	3.8	3.8	3.7	3.7	3.6		
Turkey	5.6	5.4	5.3	5.3	5.5	5.3	5.0	5.0		
United Kingdom	4.4	4.1	4.3	4.3	4.5	4.4	4.5	4.8		
Eastern Europe										
Albania	14.4	14.3	14.2	14.3	14.0	13.9	13.6			
Belarus										
Bosnia-Herzegovina										
Bulgaria	9.7	9.0	8.9	8.4	10.5	8.9	8.7	8.0	8.5	7.1
Croatia	2.9	2.7	3.2	3.3	3.2	3.1	3.7	4.0		
Czech Republic	3.5	3.7	3.6	3.6	3.7	3.1	3.0	3.0		
Estonia	6.8	7.2	6.7	6.4	6.4	6.2	6.1	6.0		
Georgia										
Hungary	4.3	4.7	4.8	4.9	4.4	4.5	4.7	4.7	5.2	5.7
Latvia	5.9	4.6	4.7	5.3	4.3	4.3	4.6	5.1		
Lithuania	4.7	4.8	4.9	4.9	3.9	4.0	4.0	4.0		
Macedonia										
Moldova	4.2	4.1	3.8	4.1	3.5	3.4	3.2	3.3	3.2	2.8
Poland	7.8	8.0	8.3	8.3	8.0	7.9	7.9	7.7		
Romania	13.4	13.2	13.1	12.7	12.2	12.2	12.6	12.4	11.5	11.5
Russia	12.8	12.1	12.0	12.2	12.6	11.6	11.4	11.6		
Serbia and Montenegro										
Slovakia	5.3	5.7	5.6	5.4	4.3	4.8	4.7	4.7		
Slovenia	3.2	3.4	3.4	3.4	3.3	3.3	3.3	3.2		
Ukraine										

Source: *International Labour Organisation/Euromonitor International*

Table 19.9

Unemployment Rate by Month 2007-2008

% of economically active population

	July 2007	August 2007	September 2007	October 2007	November 2007	December 2007	January 2008	February 2008	March 2008	April 2008	May 2008	June 2008
Western Europe												
Austria	3.7	4.0	3.8	4.3	4.6	5.2	5.3	4.8	4.3	4.2	3.7	3.5
Belgium	7.6	7.7	7.4	7.5	7.3	7.3	7.5	7.4	7.2	7.1	6.8	6.9
Cyprus	5.8	5.5	5.3	5.1	5.2	5.1	4.1	3.2	3.6		4.9	4.7
Denmark	12.1	12.4	5.7	5.8	6.1	5.8	3.3	2.4	2.1		12.2	
Finland	8.7	8.3	8.1	7.9	7.9	8.4	6.7	7.3	5.4		8.0	7.8
France	8.9	8.5	8.3	8.1	8.3	8.3	7.8	7.2	7.1		8.0	8.0
Germany	9.0	8.0	8.0	8.0	7.8	7.8	8.0	7.5	7.0		8.2	8.2
Gibraltar												
Greece			7.7	8.1	7.9	7.7	8.2					
Iceland												
Ireland	8.3	7.6	7.4	7.4	7.4	6.6	4.7	5.3	6.1		6.4	
Italy	4.2	4.0	3.8	3.6	3.5	3.7	8.3				3.9	4.1
Liechtenstein												
Luxembourg	6.9	6.4	6.3	6.1	6.2	6.5		4.0	3.9		6.3	6.2
Malta	4.2	3.8	5.7	4.2	5.1	5.4	6.1	5.5	5.4		4.2	
Monaco												
Netherlands	2.9	2.8	5.1	5.3	5.1	5.1	3.5	3.1	2.6			
Norway	8.3	6.7	9.3	10.0	9.4	9.1	4.6	5.0			7.9	
Portugal	7.6	7.1	7.1	7.1	6.6	6.6	7.6	7.3	7.2		6.9	6.9
Spain	6.3	5.9	5.6	7.1	4.9	4.8	9.4	10.3	10.5		5.9	5.6
Sweden	4.5	4.4	4.1	3.8	3.8	3.9	5.7	6.1	5.0		4.2	4.1
Switzerland	3.7	3.6	3.7	3.8	3.8	3.9	4.1	3.7	3.5		3.6	3.7
Turkey	5.5	5.3	5.3	5.4	5.6	5.6	11.8				5.1	5.3
United Kingdom	4.5	4.3	4.3	4.7	4.9	4.6	5.2	5.3			5.4	5.2
Eastern Europe												
Albania												
Belarus												
Bosnia-Herzegovina												
Bulgaria	9.0	8.6	8.4	8.0	7.8	8.1	8.8	8.6	8.1	7.5	7.1	6.8
Croatia	4.2	3.6	3.6	3.5	3.9	3.8	10.3	8.5			4.3	4.2
Czech Republic	4.2	3.8	3.5	3.3	3.9	3.9	4.7	4.2	4.2		3.5	3.3
Estonia	7.7	7.2	8.5	7.4	5.9	5.9	4.6	4.4	4.5		6.8	6.4
Georgia												
Hungary	1.9	1.7	4.2	4.2	4.5	4.4	8.4	7.9	7.9		2.0	
Latvia	5.4	5.1	4.4	4.1	4.3	4.3	6.3	5.4	5.4		5.4	5.4
Lithuania	4.3	4.1	3.9	3.8	3.7	3.8	5.4	4.9	5.1		4.3	4.3
Macedonia												
Moldova												
Poland	8.3	8.1	7.8	7.8	7.9	7.9	9.0	8.1	7.4		7.7	7.7
Romania	6.5	6.5	13.1	12.9	12.6	12.6	6.9					
Russia												
Serbia and Montenegro												
Slovakia	5.4	4.7	4.6	4.5	4.6	4.4	11.5	11.5	11.6		5.3	5.1
Slovenia			3.8	3.9	3.7	3.6	5.0	4.0	4.0			
Ukraine												

Source: International Labour Organisation/Euromonitor International

Hours of Work

Table 19.10

Average Working Week in Non-Agricultural Activities 1980-2007
Hours

	1980	1985	1990	1995	2000	2002	2003	2004	2005	2006	2007
Western Europe											
Austria			34.6	35.4	35.4	35.4	35.8	34.2	33.5	33.0	32.6
Belgium	33.8	33.3	33.7	36.2	33.0	32.9	32.9	32.8	32.7	32.7	32.6
Cyprus	42.0	41.0	42.0	40.0	40.0	39.8	39.7	39.8	39.9	39.9	40.0
Denmark	32.6	32.1	31.5	31.5	31.6	31.7	31.7	31.7	31.7	31.8	31.8
Finland		36.4	35.5	36.5	36.3	36.0	35.9	36.0	35.9	35.8	35.8
France	40.8	38.9	39.0	38.9	36.9	35.7	35.6	35.6	35.7	35.8	35.9
Germany	41.6	40.7	39.7	38.5	38.2	37.9	38.0	38.0	37.9	37.8	37.7
Gibraltar	43.2	44.5	45.1	43.6	43.0	43.2	42.0	41.7	41.6	41.2	41.0
Greece				41.0	41.0	41.0	41.0	42.9	41.1	41.1	41.2
Iceland	49.3	48.6	46.4	46.0	42.8	41.6	41.0	40.4	39.8	39.2	38.7
Ireland			35.4	38.6	37.1	36.8	36.5	36.3	36.2	36.0	35.9
Italy	39.0	38.7	38.8	39.4	39.1	38.2	38.1	39.1	39.0	38.9	38.9
Liechtenstein											
Luxembourg	40.2	40.6	40.3	40.8	40.7	40.6	40.6	40.6	40.6	40.5	40.5
Malta	40.0	40.0	39.3	38.8	38.0	38.3	38.2	38.4	38.5	38.6	38.7
Monaco											
Netherlands	40.6	40.3	40.1	39.3	38.4	38.4	38.3	38.4	38.4	38.4	38.4
Norway	35.5	35.5	35.3	34.9	34.7	34.5	34.3	34.2	34.2	34.1	34.0
Portugal	38.4	41.0	41.1	38.1	37.3	37.0	36.5	35.4	35.7	35.9	36.1
Spain	40.1	37.5	36.6	36.0	35.8	35.3	35.1	34.9	34.6	34.4	34.2
Sweden	35.6	36.3	37.5	36.6	36.9	36.4	36.0	35.9	36.4	36.4	36.5
Switzerland	44.3	43.4	42.2	41.9	36.4	35.6	35.6	36.1	36.0	36.1	36.2
Turkey			50.1	51.3	51.6	51.8	51.9	52.5	54.0	54.6	55.3
United Kingdom			40.5	40.3	39.8	39.6	39.6	39.6	39.5	39.5	39.4
Eastern Europe											
Albania											
Belarus				35.5	38.3	38.0	38.3	39.0	39.2	39.4	39.7
Bosnia-Herzegovina											
Bulgaria					33.0	33.0	33.0	34.0	34.4	35.0	35.3
Croatia		45.5	44.5	44.5	41.8	41.5	41.5	41.5	41.3	41.2	41.1
Czech Republic				40.4	40.5	40.6	40.6	40.5	40.5	40.5	40.5
Estonia				34.0	34.7	34.8	34.4	34.7	34.9	35.0	35.0
Georgia					38.6	39.0	39.2	39.4	39.7	39.9	40.1
Hungary				36.6	37.3	36.8	37.0	37.6	37.7	37.9	38.1
Latvia				40.8	41.3	40.2	39.8	39.4	39.8	40.0	40.1
Lithuania				37.2	37.9	37.5	37.8	38.1	38.1	38.1	38.2
Macedonia											
Moldova				28.8	29.7	31.7	32.2	32.4	32.2	32.3	32.4
Poland	37.5	39.8	37.0	40.4	40.0	39.7	39.8	39.8	39.6	39.6	39.5
Romania				39.0	37.4	37.0	37.0	37.0	37.0	37.0	37.0
Russia				32.6	32.9	33.2	33.3	33.5	33.6	33.7	33.8
Serbia and Montenegro											
Slovakia				37.0	36.5	35.5	34.5	35.3	35.0	34.6	34.6
Slovenia		37.4	37.7	40.7	40.5	36.3	36.7	36.0	36.3	36.3	36.2
Ukraine					32.0	33.8	34.3	34.8	34.8	35.0	35.2

Source: *International Labour Organisation/Euromonitor International*
Notes: *Hours actually worked by wage earners, unless otherwise stated*

Table 19.11

Average Working Week in Manufacturing 1980-2007

Hours

	1980	1985	1990	1995	2000	2002	2003	2004	2005	2006	2007
Western Europe											
Austria	36.5	36.2	34.9	34.7	35.1	34.7	34.8	35.1	34.8	34.7	34.7
Belgium	33.4	33.1	33.4	32.9	32.9	32.9	32.9	32.9	32.9	32.9	32.8
Cyprus	41.0	41.0	41.0	40.0	40.2	40.0	40.1	40.0	39.9	39.9	39.8
Denmark	32.6	32.1	31.5	31.5	31.6	31.7	31.7	31.7	31.7	31.8	31.8
Finland	33.2	32.3	38.2	38.0	38.0	37.6	37.5	37.5	37.4	37.3	37.2
France	40.6	38.6	38.7	38.7	36.6	36.0	36.1	36.7	36.9	37.3	37.6
Germany	41.6	40.7	37.8	38.6	37.9	37.6	37.7	37.6	37.5	37.5	37.4
Gibraltar	45.8	48.7	46.9	46.8	45.1	46.9	44.8	50.0	49.1	50.2	50.2
Greece	40.7	39.3	41.1	41.1	43.0	42.0	42.0	42.3	42.3	42.4	42.5
Iceland				42.9	43.5	42.3	42.5	42.5	42.3	42.0	41.8
Ireland	41.1	41.1	41.5	40.8	40.7	39.3	39.7	39.9	40.0	39.8	39.9
Italy	38.5	39.0	39.0	40.7	40.5	39.4	39.2	39.4	39.8	39.9	40.1
Liechtenstein											
Luxembourg	40.0	40.2	39.8	40.2	40.0	39.7	39.7	39.6	39.5	39.4	39.3
Malta	40.0	40.0	39.9	39.9	41.0	40.0	38.7	39.4	39.6	39.8	39.8
Monaco											
Netherlands	40.8	40.3	39.9	39.0	38.6	38.5	38.5	38.5	38.5	38.5	38.5
Norway	38.1	38.2	37.0	36.7	36.5	36.7	36.3	36.3	36.3	36.2	36.2
Portugal	39.0	40.8	40.7	38.2	39.5	38.5	37.9	39.5	39.9	40.1	40.3
Spain	38.8	36.5	36.7	36.8	36.1	36.2	36.0	35.8	36.2	36.2	36.3
Sweden	37.7	38.4	38.5	37.6	38.2	37.9	37.5	37.5	37.9	38.1	38.2
Switzerland	43.8	43.0	41.6	41.4	41.1	39.4	39.6	39.9	40.3	40.5	40.8
Turkey			48.8	50.9	51.3	51.9	52.2	52.1	53.7	54.2	54.7
United Kingdom		41.8	42.4	42.2	41.4	41.0	41.0	40.9	40.8	40.6	40.5
Eastern Europe											
Albania											
Belarus											
Bosnia-Herzegovina											
Bulgaria					33.0	33.0	33.0	34.0	34.4	35.0	35.3
Croatia		46.2	45.1	44.3	41.5	41.3	41.3	41.4	41.0	40.9	40.7
Czech Republic	43.5	43.1	40.1	40.4	40.7	40.7	40.7	40.6	40.6	40.5	40.5
Estonia				33.1	33.9	34.0	33.7	34.0	34.0	34.1	34.2
Georgia					38.0	39.3	40.1	40.7	41.4	42.1	42.6
Hungary	40.2	36.3	35.9	36.8	37.4	36.8	37.0	37.6	37.7	37.9	38.2
Latvia				38.8	41.0	40.4	40.4	40.6	40.9	41.0	41.2
Lithuania					38.6	38.6	38.8	38.9	38.9	39.0	39.1
Macedonia											
Moldova		34.9	34.5	22.3	24.4	27.7	29.7	30.3	30.4	31.1	31.5
Poland	39.8	38.3	35.8	41.7	41.3	41.0	41.1	41.2	41.2	41.2	41.3
Romania		39.5	39.0	38.2	39.5	40.9	40.9	40.8	40.6	41.0	41.0
Russia				28.9	29.1	28.9	28.8	28.6	28.5	28.4	28.3
Serbia and Montenegro											
Slovakia				35.3	35.5	34.5	34.3	35.5	35.5	35.5	35.5
Slovenia		37.1	37.5	40.7	40.3	36.0	36.7	36.1	37.1	37.4	37.6
Ukraine					29.5	33.0	34.0	35.5	35.5	36.2	36.7

Source: *International Labour Organisation/Euromonitor International*
Notes: *Hours actually worked by wage earners, unless otherwise stated*

Economically Active Population by Age Group 2007

'000

	Under 15	15-19	20-24	25-29	30-34	35-39	40-44
Western Europe							
Austria		208.5	408.5	431.1	469.9	607.0	660.1
Belgium		64.4	386.8	583.5	611.8	666.5	717.7
Cyprus		4.1	34.8	56.6	52.9	48.2	50.2
Denmark		223.0	225.0	269.5	343.5	368.4	384.4
Finland		107.3	233.6	279.8	277.9	294.9	341.3
France		726.8	2,574.8	3,153.4	3,724.2	3,807.8	3,962.1
Germany		1,522.1	3,452.6	4,113.5	3,939.8	5,532.0	6,669.6
Gibraltar							
Greece		49.0	329.8	701.1	757.5	774.3	677.6
Iceland		2.7	12.1	19.2	19.6	21.3	18.3
Ireland		68.2	250.8	311.6	302.1	259.6	244.0
Italy		338.6	1,596.7	2,685.9	3,722.5	3,975.9	3,845.9
Liechtenstein							
Luxembourg		2.4	11.8	26.6	31.8	34.8	33.6
Malta		10.1	23.4	22.3	20.1	17.6	19.6
Monaco							
Netherlands		550.7	769.5	836.2	953.2	1,117.0	1,129.8
Norway		108.7	195.3	230.2	285.9	314.1	300.8
Portugal	1.1	76.3	411.8	740.3	774.5	716.1	712.2
Spain		554.4	1,966.9	3,249.2	3,408.7	3,144.7	2,940.1
Sweden		143.2	361.3	461.9	553.1	599.9	594.0
Switzerland			583.2			1,421.1	
Turkey		1,550.7	2,907.3	4,324.5	4,082.1	3,400.4	2,898.2
United Kingdom		1,801.5	2,812.0		6,382.3		
Eastern Europe							
Albania							
Belarus		135.1		1,022.6		1,220.4	
Bosnia-Herzegovina							
Bulgaria		40.3	221.1	340.3	413.2	456.0	460.0
Croatia		34.5	156.7	184.9	174.8	189.3	244.3
Czech Republic		52.8	372.3	654.7	777.6	640.8	670.7
Estonia		9.8	65.0	80.1	85.1	78.7	87.8
Georgia		56.0	141.4	176.8	185.8	204.2	231.8
Hungary		26.0	267.7	638.8	612.7	622.4	450.6
Latvia		26.3	116.8	130.8	139.6	134.7	148.2
Lithuania		10.0	131.6	195.3	198.3	215.6	225.7
Macedonia		21.1	81.4	121.5	119.1	121.1	119.1
Moldova		34.2	96.8	109.8	144.5	135.7	191.6
Poland		138.4	1,618.7	2,574.2	2,440.3	2,014.9	1,993.6
Romania		237.9	756.3	1,485.5	1,321.6	1,703.5	968.5
Russia		1,928.7	7,583.2	9,495.2	9,084.3	7,855.6	9,650.4
Serbia and Montenegro							
Slovakia		23.5	268.8	393.9	367.6	325.3	353.2
Slovenia		22.5	84.4	133.4	142.3	136.6	135.9
Ukraine		676.1	2,418.2	2,687.8	2,715.6	2,446.6	3,003.0

Source: International Labour Organisation/Euromonitor International

Economically Active Population by Age Group 2007 *(continued)*

'000

	45-49	50-54	55-59	60-64	Over 65	Total
Western Europe						
Austria	577.5	404.3	268.6	73.6	48.4	4,157.5
Belgium	671.0	542.8	354.8	94.0	42.3	4,735.6
Cyprus	48.5	40.1	30.9	16.8	10.0	393.1
Denmark	332.7	296.8	335.2	121.7	18.2	2,918.5
Finland	338.0	335.8	298.4	134.9	33.2	2,675.1
France	3,756.5	3,452.7	2,534.3	383.8	110.9	28,187.2
Germany	5,612.2	4,834.9	3,940.8	1,479.0	573.7	41,670.2
Gibraltar						
Greece	596.1	508.1	342.1	152.4	69.3	4,957.5
Iceland	21.9	20.0	16.9	10.1	8.1	170.2
Ireland	222.5	186.0	147.9	87.0	40.2	2,119.8
Italy	3,215.9	2,570.1	1,847.3	572.3	355.7	24,726.9
Liechtenstein						
Luxembourg	29.9	24.0	13.3	2.4	0.9	211.5
Malta	20.8	19.5	9.7	2.5		165.6
Monaco						
Netherlands	1,045.6	858.6	800.6	353.4		8,414.7
Norway	278.7	261.1	241.5	150.2	51.3	2,417.9
Portugal	646.4	540.7	437.7	230.1	330.7	5,618.0
Spain	2,551.1	1,938.3	1,481.4	786.0	165.5	22,186.6
Sweden	538.2	498.1	546.3	374.0		4,670.2
Switzerland		1,511.7		620.3	81.7	4,218.0
Turkey	2,282.5	1,548.2	876.6	499.2	592.2	24,961.9
United Kingdom	11,525.8	8,213.4				30,735.0
Eastern Europe						
Albania						
Belarus	1,348.1		552.1	72.7	28.8	4,379.9
Bosnia-Herzegovina						
Bulgaria	499.4	361.1	301.0	89.6	24.6	3,206.5
Croatia	246.7	228.2	145.3	58.0	64.1	1,726.8
Czech Republic	599.6	685.3	544.6	158.1	61.5	5,218.1
Estonia	91.5	80.5	60.5	34.5	24.8	698.3
Georgia	227.5	188.7	182.0	74.5	309.0	1,977.7
Hungary	538.9	622.3	368.8	103.6	27.1	4,278.9
Latvia	156.7	128.2	102.2	54.2	38.3	1,176.0
Lithuania	220.5	167.5	137.1	51.7	24.9	1,578.1
Macedonia	117.9	101.1	58.5	21.4	8.5	890.7
Moldova	253.3	158.9	134.3	41.5	55.3	1,355.8
Poland	2,431.5	2,122.1	1,145.0	279.7	282.7	17,040.9
Romania	1,167.9	1,115.9	675.1	269.0	387.3	10,088.5
Russia	10,538.8	9,717.2	5,029.2	1,397.2	1,430.4	73,710.2
Serbia and Montenegro						
Slovakia	367.1	353.0	174.1	41.0	11.3	2,678.7
Slovenia	148.7	118.9	66.5	17.5	28.1	1,034.8
Ukraine	2,986.6	2,516.4	1,366.0	586.1	702.3	22,104.6

Source: International Labour Organisation/Euromonitor International

Economically Active Population   **Table 19.13**

Economically Active Population by Age Group 2007 (% Analysis)
% of total EAP

	Under 15	15-19	20-24	25-29	30-34	35-39	40-44
Western Europe							
Austria	5.0	9.8	10.4	11.3	14.6		15.9
Belgium	1.4	8.2	12.3	12.9	14.1		15.2
Cyprus	1.0	8.9	14.4	13.5	12.3		12.8
Denmark	7.6	7.7	9.2	11.8	12.6		13.2
Finland	4.0	8.7	10.5	10.4	11.0		12.8
France	2.6	9.1	11.2	13.2	13.5		14.1
Germany	3.7	8.3	9.9	9.5	13.3		16.0
Gibraltar							
Greece	1.0	6.7	14.1	15.3	15.6		13.7
Iceland	1.6	7.1	11.3	11.5	12.5		10.7
Ireland	3.2	11.8	14.7	14.3	12.2		11.5
Italy	1.4	6.5	10.9	15.1	16.1		15.6
Liechtenstein							
Luxembourg	1.1	5.6	12.6	15.0	16.5		15.9
Malta	6.1	14.1	13.5	12.1	10.6		11.8
Monaco							
Netherlands	6.5	9.1	9.9	11.3	13.3		13.4
Norway	4.5	8.1	9.5	11.8	13.0		12.4
Portugal	1.4	7.3	13.2	13.8	12.7		12.7
Spain	2.5	8.9	14.6	15.4	14.2		13.3
Sweden	3.1	7.7	9.9	11.8	12.8		12.7
Switzerland		13.8			33.7		
Turkey	6.2	11.6	17.3	16.4	13.6		11.6
United Kingdom	5.9	9.1		20.8			
Eastern Europe							
Albania							
Belarus	3.1		23.3		27.9		
Bosnia-Herzegovina							
Bulgaria	1.3	6.9	10.6	12.9	14.2		14.3
Croatia	2.0	9.1	10.7	10.1	11.0		14.1
Czech Republic	1.0	7.1	12.5	14.9	12.3		12.9
Estonia	1.4	9.3	11.5	12.2	11.3		12.6
Georgia	2.8	7.1	8.9	9.4	10.3		11.7
Hungary	0.6	6.3	14.9	14.3	14.5		10.5
Latvia	2.2	9.9	11.1	11.9	11.5		12.6
Lithuania	0.6	8.3	12.4	12.6	13.7		14.3
Macedonia	2.4	9.1	13.6	13.4	13.6		13.4
Moldova	2.5	7.1	8.1	10.7	10.0		14.1
Poland	0.8	9.5	15.1	14.3	11.8		11.7
Romania	2.4	7.5	14.7	13.1	16.9		9.6
Russia	2.6	10.3	12.9	12.3	10.7		13.1
Serbia and Montenegro							
Slovakia	0.9	10.0	14.7	13.7	12.1		13.2
Slovenia	2.2	8.2	12.9	13.8	13.2		13.1
Ukraine	3.1	10.9	12.2	12.3	11.1		13.6

Source: International Labour Organisation/Euromonitor International

Economically Active Population by Age Group 2007 (% Analysis) *(continued)*

% of total EAP

	45-49	50-54	55-59	60-64	Over 65	Total
Western Europe						
Austria	13.9	9.7	6.5	1.8	1.2	100.0
Belgium	14.2	11.5	7.5	2.0	0.9	100.0
Cyprus	12.3	10.2	7.9	4.3	2.5	100.0
Denmark	11.4	10.2	11.5	4.2	0.6	100.0
Finland	12.6	12.6	11.2	5.0	1.2	100.0
France	13.3	12.2	9.0	1.4	0.4	100.0
Germany	13.5	11.6	9.5	3.5	1.4	100.0
Gibraltar						
Greece	12.0	10.2	6.9	3.1	1.4	100.0
Iceland	12.8	11.8	10.0	5.9	4.7	100.0
Ireland	10.5	8.8	7.0	4.1	1.9	100.0
Italy	13.0	10.4	7.5	2.3	1.4	100.0
Liechtenstein						
Luxembourg	14.1	11.3	6.3	1.1	0.4	100.0
Malta	12.6	11.8	5.9	1.5		100.0
Monaco						
Netherlands	12.4	10.2	9.5	4.2		100.0
Norway	11.5	10.8	10.0	6.2	2.1	100.0
Portugal	11.5	9.6	7.8	4.1	5.9	100.0
Spain	11.5	8.7	6.7	3.5	0.7	100.0
Sweden	11.5	10.7	11.7	8.0		100.0
Switzerland		35.8		14.7	1.9	100.0
Turkey	9.1	6.2	3.5	2.0	2.4	100.0
United Kingdom	37.5	26.7				100.0
Eastern Europe						
Albania						
Belarus	30.8		12.6	1.7	0.7	100.0
Bosnia-Herzegovina						
Bulgaria	15.6	11.3	9.4	2.8	0.8	100.0
Croatia	14.3	13.2	8.4	3.4	3.7	100.0
Czech Republic	11.5	13.1	10.4	3.0	1.2	100.0
Estonia	13.1	11.5	8.7	4.9	3.5	100.0
Georgia	11.5	9.5	9.2	3.8	15.6	100.0
Hungary	12.6	14.5	8.6	2.4	0.6	100.0
Latvia	13.3	10.9	8.7	4.6	3.3	100.0
Lithuania	14.0	10.6	8.7	3.3	1.6	100.0
Macedonia	13.2	11.4	6.6	2.4	1.0	100.0
Moldova	18.7	11.7	9.9	3.1	4.1	100.0
Poland	14.3	12.5	6.7	1.6	1.7	100.0
Romania	11.6	11.1	6.7	2.7	3.8	100.0
Russia	14.3	13.2	6.8	1.9	1.9	100.0
Serbia and Montenegro						
Slovakia	13.7	13.2	6.5	1.5	0.4	100.0
Slovenia	14.4	11.5	6.4	1.7	2.7	100.0
Ukraine	13.5	11.4	6.2	2.7	3.2	100.0

Source: International Labour Organisation/Euromonitor International

Economically Active Population

Table 19.14

Economically Active Population by Sex 2007
As stated

	Total ('000)	EAP as % Total Population	Males ('000)	Males as % Total EAP	Females ('000)	Females as % Total EAP
Western Europe						
Austria	4,157	50.0	2,254	54.2	1,903	45.8
Belgium	4,736	44.8	2,604	55.0	2,132	45.0
Cyprus	393	46.0	217	55.1	176	44.9
Denmark	2,919	53.6	1,538	52.7	1,381	47.3
Finland	2,675	50.7	1,380	51.6	1,295	48.4
France	28,187	45.9	15,036	53.3	13,152	46.7
Germany	41,670	50.6	22,820	54.8	18,850	45.2
Gibraltar	13	45.0	8	57.6	6	42.4
Greece	4,957	44.4	2,925	59.0	2,032	41.0
Iceland	170	56.5	91	53.3	80	46.7
Ireland	2,120	49.3	1,209	57.0	911	43.0
Italy	24,727	42.0	14,784	59.8	9,943	40.2
Liechtenstein	32	89.6				
Luxembourg	212	45.3	118	55.7	94	44.3
Malta	166	40.7	110	66.7	55	33.3
Monaco						
Netherlands	8,415	51.4	4,552	54.1	3,863	45.9
Norway	2,418	51.8	1,280	52.9	1,138	47.1
Portugal	5,618	53.0	2,999	53.4	2,619	46.6
Spain	22,187	49.9	12,753	57.5	9,433	42.5
Sweden	4,670	51.2	2,450	52.5	2,221	47.5
Switzerland	4,218	56.3	2,276	54.0	1,942	46.0
Turkey	24,962	34.0	18,645	74.7	6,317	25.3
United Kingdom	30,735	50.6	16,689	54.3	14,046	45.7
Eastern Europe						
Albania	1,360	42.6	673	49.5	688	50.5
Belarus	4,380	44.9	2,051	46.8	2,329	53.2
Bosnia-Herzegovina	729	18.5				
Bulgaria	3,207	42.1	1,711	53.4	1,496	46.6
Croatia	1,727	38.9	930	53.9	797	46.1
Czech Republic	5,218	50.7	2,918	55.9	2,300	44.1
Estonia	698	52.1	348	49.9	350	50.1
Georgia	1,978	45.0	1,060	53.6	918	46.4
Hungary	4,279	42.5	2,312	54.0	1,967	46.0
Latvia	1,176	51.6	610	51.9	566	48.1
Lithuania	1,578	46.6	797	50.5	781	49.5
Macedonia	891	43.7	536	60.2	354	39.8
Moldova	1,356	35.7	645	47.6	711	52.4
Poland	17,041	44.7	9,390	55.1	7,651	44.9
Romania	10,088	46.8	5,519	54.7	4,570	45.3
Russia	73,710	51.9	37,247	50.5	36,463	49.5
Serbia and Montenegro	3,586	34.3	2,114	59.0	1,472	41.0
Slovakia	2,679	49.7	1,492	55.7	1,187	44.3
Slovenia	1,035	51.5	562	54.3	473	45.7
Ukraine	22,105	47.6	11,403	51.6	10,701	48.4

Source: *International Labour Organisation/Euromonitor International*

Table 19.15

Employed Male Population by Quarter 2006-2008

'000

	2006 1st Quarter	2006 2nd Quarter	2006 3rd Quarter	2006 4th Quarter	2007 1st Quarter	2007 2nd Quarter	2007 3rd Quarter	2007 4th Quarter	2008 1st Quarter	2008 2nd Quarter
Western Europe										
Austria	2,071.0	2,149.4	2,208.4	2,161.6	2,111.5	2,178.2	2,203.6	2,167.8	2,130.3	
Belgium	2,367.9	2,365.8	2,406.1	2,462.0	2,416.2	2,396.4	2,419.3	2,426.6	2,431.8	
Cyprus	196.4	201.1	201.8	201.8	204.6	209.3	210.8	212.9	209.5	
Denmark	1,458.0	1,473.0	1,499.0	1,499.0	1,491.0	1,498.1	1,491.0	1,480.9	1,492.0	
Finland	1,224.5	1,271.2	1,305.2	1,263.5	1,236.3	1,310.3	1,327.3	1,284.0	1,274.7	1,336.7
France	13,661.7	13,740.8	13,916.0	13,731.7	13,790.5	13,979.9	14,132.8	14,032.7	14,043.3	
Germany										
Gibraltar										
Greece	2,702.9	2,723.4	2,741.8	2,732.3	2,739.3	2,762.3	2,777.7	2,764.5	2,758.9	
Iceland	83.1	88.6	90.6	88.5	86.0	89.2	91.1	89.0	87.1	
Ireland	1,113.7	1,125.5	1,153.9	1,149.0	1,135.3	1,143.0	1,164.2	1,160.4		
Italy	13,785.6	14,050.0	13,965.2	13,874.6	13,718.8	14,004.4	14,080.0	13,959.4	13,800.5	
Liechtenstein										
Luxembourg	111.8	111.8	110.3	110.3	112.2	114.2	114.8	113.5	112.8	
Malta	104.5	103.2	103.0	103.3	104.0	103.9	104.3	102.9	106.0	
Monaco										
Netherlands	4,345.0	4,387.9	4,419.6	4,437.4	4,376.4	4,420.9	4,447.9	4,429.9	4,416.3	
Norway	1,194.5	1,207.1	1,223.6	1,226.5	1,190.9	1,210.7	1,223.9	1,233.3	1,237.0	
Portugal	2,778.2	2,796.0	2,803.4	2,779.5	2,779.6	2,786.4	2,804.8	2,805.8	2,807.6	
Spain	11,575.8	11,704.2	11,859.6	11,831.5	11,846.6	11,999.6	12,081.5	11,989.0	12,205.8	12,139.8
Sweden	2,396.1	2,454.9	2,514.1	1,738.5	2,256.2	2,308.1	2,368.7	2,316.0	2,313.9	2,363.4
Switzerland	2,159.2	2,176.9	2,203.6	2,207.9	2,163.6	2,187.2	2,205.4	2,205.3		
Turkey	15,814.3	16,755.0	17,132.6	16,800.9	16,190.9	17,014.2	17,388.2	16,776.5	16,299.3	
United Kingdom	15,426.9	15,479.7	15,693.1	15,648.2	15,575.4	15,666.0	15,840.3	15,854.3		
Eastern Europe										
Albania										
Belarus										
Bosnia-Herzegovina										
Bulgaria	1,482.8	1,581.2	1,607.6	1,599.4	1,510.0	1,561.1	1,598.5	1,602.8	1,584.0	
Croatia					816.4	841.2	867.9	844.7		
Czech Republic	2,711.4	2,736.6	2,751.4	2,764.7	2,753.8	2,778.8	2,810.3	2,826.7	2,821.4	
Estonia	314.8	323.4	326.6	326.9	325.2	329.3	333.1	331.0	335.7	
Georgia										
Hungary	2,099.1	2,143.3	2,151.0	2,155.8	2,126.1	2,155.8	2,162.6	2,130.1	2,093.0	
Latvia	547.8	537.0	582.5	565.4	552.9	565.7	582.2	589.1	581.1	
Lithuania	749.7	756.3	758.9	758.4	741.1	760.3	773.7	756.1	746.2	
Macedonia	323.1	335.3	332.6	333.8	319.0	329.2	335.5	329.2		
Moldova					573.2	620.3	605.7	558.9		
Poland	7,883.0	8,000.0	8,252.0	8,288.0	8,275.4	8,411.2	8,525.5	8,605.4	8,619.5	
Romania	4,924.3	5,132.9	5,233.2	5,012.8	4,974.7	5,108.4	5,227.0	4,990.1	5,013.2	
Russia										
Serbia and Montenegro										
Slovakia	1,272.4	1,293.3	1,303.9	1,307.8	1,301.3	1,313.4	1,340.5	1,353.7	1,344.1	
Slovenia	516.8	521.3	532.7	524.1	524.0	542.0	551.3	540.7	529.7	
Ukraine										

Source: International Labour Organisation/Euromonitor International

Total Employment

Table 19.16

Employed Female Population by Quarter 2006-2008
'000

	2006 1st Quarter	2006 2nd Quarter	2006 3rd Quarter	2006 4th Quarter	2007 1st Quarter	2007 2nd Quarter	2007 3rd Quarter	2007 4th Quarter	2008 1st Quarter	2008 2nd Quarter
Western Europe										
Austria	1,747.3	1,767.6	1,817.0	1,790.8	1,782.3	1,800.3	1,834.5	1,809.0	1,830.2	
Belgium	1,876.7	1,888.0	1,909.4	1,932.6	1,917.3	1,934.4	1,951.9	2,002.8	2,003.8	
Cyprus	154.2	155.2	158.1	160.2	164.7	168.6	168.9	171.8	170.2	
Denmark	1,291.8	1,298.8	1,314.8	1,311.8	1,305.0	1,326.3	1,323.3	1,328.3	1,332.4	
Finland	1,156.2	1,189.8	1,189.5	1,174.5	1,179.0	1,214.1	1,214.4	1,201.7	1,200.5	1,239.4
France	11,423.5	11,504.9	11,595.3	11,635.1	11,677.6	11,840.3	11,956.7	11,980.2	11,992.6	
Germany										
Gibraltar										
Greece	1,697.5	1,729.7	1,752.7	1,730.1	1,762.2	1,798.8	1,803.0	1,795.8	1,793.9	
Iceland	76.0	78.1	77.6	76.6	76.7	79.3	79.0	76.8	76.5	
Ireland	833.5	840.1	866.5	864.5	854.5	866.4	889.1	890.9		
Italy	8,876.9	9,050.8	8,950.5	9,057.9	8,881.0	9,042.3	9,084.6	9,114.5	9,119.3	
Liechtenstein										
Luxembourg	82.6	82.6	85.9	85.9	86.6	84.9	87.5	97.8	92.2	
Malta	45.7	47.8	49.8	48.5	49.0	51.0	52.0	52.4	51.2	
Monaco										
Netherlands	3,569.7	3,600.7	3,621.2	3,650.5	3,644.6	3,702.8	3,717.9	3,735.1	3,739.3	
Norway	1,066.8	1,081.5	1,091.2	1,096.1	1,066.1	1,082.1	1,092.5	1,106.6	1,114.1	
Portugal	2,348.3	2,384.5	2,383.5	2,362.9	2,356.2	2,368.3	2,395.4	2,382.4	2,383.5	
Spain	7,824.4	7,989.0	8,036.1	8,170.4	8,255.4	8,401.1	8,462.8	8,521.9	8,619.0	8,707.9
Sweden	2,025.4	2,061.1	2,128.0	2,083.5	2,045.7	2,095.5	2,145.4	2,099.8	2,082.7	2,129.4
Switzerland	1,816.6	1,826.6	1,850.6	1,851.7	1,826.5	1,841.0	1,862.8	1,871.9		
Turkey	5,065.1	5,949.7	6,050.0	5,693.4	5,377.2	5,985.6	5,981.8	5,348.2	5,259.9	
United Kingdom	13,321.3	13,311.3	13,345.2	13,354.2	13,238.6	13,273.4	13,379.8	13,472.2		
Eastern Europe										
Albania										
Belarus										
Bosnia-Herzegovina										
Bulgaria	1,302.9	1,392.6	1,424.7	1,393.9	1,333.6	1,389.3	1,408.5	1,396.1	1,399.7	
Croatia					687.9	707.9	731.0	719.3		
Czech Republic	2,073.7	2,089.3	2,088.1	2,097.0	2,127.7	2,151.8	2,147.9	2,157.1	2,153.5	
Estonia	319.9	326.6	323.0	323.8	328.8	336.5	336.2	329.8	327.8	
Georgia										
Hungary	1,785.9	1,790.6	1,797.1	1,797.1	1,798.3	1,805.7	1,803.8	1,798.2	1,769.8	
Latvia	510.7	536.7	538.4	538.0	529.5	540.1	546.4	557.5	554.5	
Lithuania	734.6	745.5	752.5	739.8	736.0	752.3	754.8	737.8	733.5	
Macedonia	208.3	202.2	215.1	215.7	208.9	207.9	209.9	212.3		
Moldova					621.4	717.2	700.3	634.5		
Poland	6,314.7	6,458.7	6,653.7	6,623.7	6,542.1	6,718.2	6,883.1	6,909.1	6,872.5	
Romania	4,106.8	4,343.1	4,425.6	4,084.7	4,159.8	4,365.3	4,495.6	4,213.1	4,133.2	
Russia										
Serbia and Montenegro										
Slovakia	988.8	1,004.4	1,020.0	1,028.1	1,017.5	1,015.7	1,017.6	1,035.9	1,038.3	
Slovenia	429.3	448.2	441.0	431.9	433.3	451.3	454.6	442.3	440.7	
Ukraine										

Source: *International Labour Organisation/Euromonitor International*

Table 19.17

Unemployed Male Population by Quarter 2006-2008

'000

	2006 1st Quarter	2006 2nd Quarter	2006 3rd Quarter	2006 4th Quarter	2007 1st Quarter	2007 2nd Quarter	2007 3rd Quarter	2007 4th Quarter	2008 1st Quarter	2008 2nd Quarter
Western Europe										
Austria	139.7	81.0	71.7	95.6	120.0	74.8	67.9	92.1	66.8	
Belgium	196.5	192.6	204.8	191.1	196.2	182.8	192.6	184.4	184.2	
Cyprus	10.9	6.9	6.2	7.7	8.9	6.9	6.9	6.6	9.1	
Denmark	69.7	53.0	48.5	42.5	61.0	48.6	43.6	37.5	60.3	
Finland	111.9	121.9	84.3	84.6	100.7	104.4	76.4	80.1	76.4	88.6
France	1,296.6	1,067.3	1,147.2	1,131.9	1,145.1	1,005.1	1,017.7	1,038.8	1,057.3	980.4
Germany					2,154.0	1,874.1	1,854.3	1,785.1	1,900.4	
Gibraltar										
Greece	180.8	159.4	146.2	157.2	181.0	156.2	154.4	164.3	175.6	
Iceland	1.5	2.9	1.7	1.9	1.5	2.8	1.3	1.7	1.9	
Ireland	47.8	48.7	57.6	73.1	53.3	56.9	61.8	61.5		
Italy	919.2	798.0	729.4	849.1	902.0	788.1	770.4	910.9	987.7	
Liechtenstein										
Luxembourg	4.0	4.0	4.0	4.0	4.6	4.8	3.5	3.7	2.7	
Malta	7.4	7.1	7.2	7.5	7.1	6.6	6.3	6.3	6.0	6.0
Monaco										
Netherlands	192.4	174.1	147.3	133.8	160.3	135.6	123.2	113.2	120.3	
Norway	77.7	64.0	60.6	52.0	77.5	63.1	63.4	57.1	70.2	61.5
Portugal	209.4	196.1	184.1	190.6	231.7	203.2	191.6	193.4	210.2	203.9
Spain	853.8	770.7	756.7	784.5	777.1	734.1	763.4	821.9	759.7	882.2
Sweden	146.8	137.3	134.9	117.9	155.6	135.8	137.9	120.3	136.9	151.4
Switzerland	97.5	80.4	72.9	73.9	101.6	82.5	75.1	82.8	104.7	88.6
Turkey	2,097.4	1,729.2	1,644.9	1,764.8	2,003.5	1,701.2	1,656.5	1,848.9	2,053.8	
United Kingdom	945.3	964.4	1,021.9	952.4	992.4	942.9	989.4	895.3		
Eastern Europe										
Albania										
Belarus										
Bosnia-Herzegovina										
Bulgaria	167.3	161.8	156.2	150.1	163.6	148.0	134.1	124.6	140.6	
Croatia	108.1	97.3	91.6	97.3	94.8	99.6	76.5	78.6	92.5	81.5
Czech Republic	192.1	165.4	164.5	154.1	141.7	127.8	121.6	110.8	111.0	
Estonia	25.1	21.0	17.5	21.5	23.2	20.0	16.4	15.3	12.4	
Georgia										
Hungary	173.3	157.9	161.1	166.2	175.5	162.7	159.2	176.7	177.9	
Latvia	46.0	45.1	43.4	42.9	45.9	41.6	36.9	33.3	35.9	
Lithuania	58.1	42.4	40.9	45.4	48.9	38.2	34.0	37.2	48.7	
Macedonia	204.5	196.6	201.1	201.3	213.3	209.7	203.0	206.6		
Moldova					59.5	47.0	57.0	59.1		
Poland	1,422.0	1,247.8	1,099.5	1,044.6	1,151.2	954.5	833.7	802.1	941.4	794.6
Romania	497.8	443.3	425.0	436.1	603.8	446.7	348.9	376.1	459.0	422.9
Russia										
Serbia and Montenegro										
Slovakia	207.7	181.5	173.5	160.8	178.0	164.8	166.5	150.8	153.2	
Slovenia	29.7	27.0	25.1	24.6	24.4	21.9	21.1	21.8	21.2	19.5
Ukraine										

Source: International Labour Organisation/Euromonitor International

Total Unemployed Population

Table 19.18

Unemployed Female Population by Quarter 2006-2008

'000

	2006 1st Quarter	2006 2nd Quarter	2006 3rd Quarter	2006 4th Quarter	2007 1st Quarter	2007 2nd Quarter	2007 3rd Quarter	2007 4th Quarter	2008 1st Quarter	2008 2nd Quarter
Western Europe										
Austria	102.7	95.5	92.9	102.9	100.7	94.5	91.5	101.1	80.8	
Belgium	187.5	182.1	201.0	181.6	183.6	172.4	191.1	174.4	171.5	
Cyprus	11.0	8.1	8.5	8.3	9.7	6.2	8.5	7.2	8.8	
Denmark	74.0	63.5	65.3	55.2	73.9	61.6	58.5	45.4	60.0	
Finland	106.2	119.9	96.5	91.8	97.0	105.6	87.1	81.9	80.4	92.0
France	1,428.1	1,381.0	1,429.8	1,372.8	1,360.4	1,224.7	1,288.1	1,278.2	1,317.6	1,223.8
Germany					1,630.4	1,561.4	1,552.0	1,514.4	1,454.8	
Gibraltar										
Greece	299.5	274.7	213.1	278.7	264.3	240.8	232.6	232.4	232.1	
Iceland	1.4	2.4	1.7	1.4	1.4	2.1	1.9	1.2	1.5	
Ireland	35.3	36.9	41.6	23.1	31.9	36.1	39.5	34.6		
Italy	1,012.3	872.3	804.2	910.9	911.9	858.3	862.3	1,018.5	1,065.4	
Liechtenstein										
Luxembourg	5.3	5.3	6.0	6.0	5.0	2.9	5.2	4.4	6.2	
Malta	4.9	4.6	5.0	5.1	4.3	3.7	4.2	4.2	3.1	2.8
Monaco										
Netherlands	219.7	204.9	190.0	167.1	183.6	167.2	155.0	145.2	133.0	
Norway	53.8	48.6	52.8	42.5	55.9	49.7	56.7	42.2	55.0	49.2
Portugal	245.2	230.2	223.7	233.5	261.3	236.8	237.2	238.0	252.6	245.4
Spain	1,097.0	1,041.0	1,015.0	1,029.2	1,047.9	1,014.2	1,004.4	1,025.4	1,069.9	1,109.7
Sweden	119.9	122.6	131.8	93.7	126.2	121.8	137.2	110.4	125.4	137.9
Switzerland	92.0	84.7	83.2	86.0	100.9	90.1	87.7	88.0	102.9	96.2
Turkey	645.3	574.8	659.5	691.8	639.8	609.0	677.9	648.4	662.8	
United Kingdom	637.7	672.8	738.2	695.3	710.2	685.4	749.0	675.4		
Eastern Europe										
Albania										
Belarus										
Bosnia-Herzegovina										
Bulgaria	133.7	132.8	139.1	124.8	127.9	107.3	115.9	104.7	104.8	
Croatia	103.3	96.5	92.2	98.5	94.7	85.2	79.4	82.0	88.2	80.6
Czech Republic	222.6	202.0	201.5	185.9	173.7	149.8	148.1	144.8	136.2	
Estonia	18.6	21.7	19.4	17.1	16.7	19.2	16.0	16.6	21.1	
Georgia										
Hungary	150.3	147.7	157.2	153.3	162.4	154.7	169.7	173.9	178.1	
Latvia	33.9	33.6	33.3	33.2	32.8	30.8	28.5	25.6	25.3	
Lithuania	47.5	39.5	40.7	42.8	42.0	34.0	32.1	33.5	38.0	
Macedonia	130.9	140.2	139.5	141.2	146.5	143.1	143.4	145.4		
Moldova					46.0	38.1	46.5	38.6		
Poland	1,225.0	1,147.3	1,111.1	1,066.5	1,009.8	899.4	845.5	797.2	884.0	780.7
Romania	317.4	281.5	247.3	254.3	258.6	243.1	264.0	278.8	271.7	241.6
Russia										
Serbia and Montenegro										
Slovakia	190.2	177.6	170.3	160.7	164.8	163.9	170.2	160.3	158.7	
Slovenia	36.1	34.4	33.3	31.4	29.6	27.7	26.8	26.3	23.1	21.4
Ukraine										

Source: International Labour Organisation/Euromonitor International

Education

Table 20.1

Pre-primary Education: Schools, Staff and Pupils: 2007
As stated

	Pre-Primary Schools	Staff ('000)	Pupils ('000)	Pupil to Staff Ratio
Western Europe				
Austria	5,155	16.3	210.8	12.9
Belgium	4,920	29.8	395.7	13.3
Cyprus		1.2		
Denmark	2,014	43.0	250.9	5.8
Finland	2,930	11.8	140.4	11.9
France	17,395	142.4	2,549.3	17.9
Germany	1,484	214.2	2,094.7	9.8
Gibraltar		0.0		
Greece	5,713	11.8	135.1	11.4
Iceland		1.9		
Ireland		5.0	112.5	22.4
Italy	24,414	134.4	1,676.0	12.5
Liechtenstein		0.1		
Luxembourg		1.3		
Malta		1.5		
Monaco		0.1		
Netherlands	7,421		360.9	
Norway	6,557		163.2	
Portugal	7,054	18.5	260.9	14.1
Spain		118.5	1,548.2	13.1
Sweden	7,036	34.8	344.6	9.9
Switzerland		11.0	149.2	13.5
Turkey	21,761	20.4	434.1	21.3
United Kingdom	3,998	42.6	526.5	12.4
Eastern Europe				
Albania		4.0		
Belarus	4,298	44.2	281.5	6.4
Bosnia-Herzegovina				
Bulgaria	3,358	18.3	200.4	11.0
Croatia	1,130	6.2	91.8	14.8
Czech Republic	4,530	25.0	293.6	11.7
Estonia	620	5.7	57.9	10.3
Georgia	1,172			
Hungary	4,524	30.2	316.2	10.5
Latvia	564	6.4	65.7	10.3
Lithuania	661	11.0	84.8	7.7
Macedonia		2.8		
Moldova		10.4		
Poland	17,280	46.7	811.5	17.4
Romania	3,604	36.3	661.4	18.2
Russia	45,043	637.3	4,538.5	7.1
Serbia and Montenegro		10.3		
Slovakia	2,910	10.0	154.8	15.5
Slovenia	782	2.3	30.1	13.1
Ukraine	15,200	126.7	983.5	7.8

Source: Euromonitor International from UNESCO

Table 20.2

Primary Education: Schools, Staff and Pupils: 2007

As stated

	Primary Schools	Staff ('000)	Pupils ('000)	Pupil to Staff Ratio
Western Europe				
Austria			365.3	
Belgium			728.6	
Cyprus				
Denmark	2,400	69.3	423.1	6.1
Finland	3,539	23.7	382.9	16.1
France	37,734	201.2	3,760.6	18.7
Germany			3,310.7	
Gibraltar				
Greece	5,712	66.5	666.3	10.0
Iceland				
Ireland			460.1	
Italy	17,613	267.7	2,734.9	10.2
Liechtenstein				
Luxembourg				
Malta				
Monaco				
Netherlands			1,267.8	
Norway	1,875	39.5	432.0	10.9
Portugal			729.6	
Spain		182.2	2,517.8	13.8
Sweden	4,882	67.7	601.7	8.9
Switzerland			525.1	
Turkey	34,956	385.5	7,734.3	20.1
United Kingdom	22,170	254.8	4,981.2	19.6
Eastern Europe				
Albania				
Belarus	553	21.5	297.5	13.8
Bosnia-Herzegovina				
Bulgaria	2,131	16.7	268.9	16.1
Croatia			184.7	
Czech Republic	3,658	24.6	456.6	18.6
Estonia			72.2	
Georgia				
Hungary	3,571	29.6	409.1	13.8
Latvia	53	6.1	70.5	11.5
Lithuania	123	10.3	138.9	13.4
Macedonia				
Moldova				
Poland	14,147	181.1	2,555.7	14.1
Romania	6,272	59.7	1,042.9	17.5
Russia	20,724	309.6	5,031.0	16.3
Serbia and Montenegro				
Slovakia			219.4	
Slovenia			102.2	
Ukraine	26,301	93.5	1,648.1	17.6

Source: Euromonitor International from UNESCO

Secondary Education

Table 20.3

Secondary Education: Staff and Pupils: 2007

As stated

	Staff ('000)	Total Pupils ('000)	Pupils in Training Colleges ('000)	Pupils in Technical Colleges ('000)	Pupil to Staff Ratio
Western Europe					
Austria		778.2			
Belgium		628.5			
Cyprus					
Denmark	69.4	455.6	122.7	129.6	6.6
Finland	20.3	367.7	136.0	275.9	18.1
France	513.5	5,765.8	725.4	1,513.6	11.2
Germany		8,151.6			
Gibraltar					
Greece	86.3	666.5	115.5	113.7	7.7
Iceland					
Ireland		320.3			
Italy	392.5	4,477.0	742.2	1,981.5	11.4
Liechtenstein					
Luxembourg					
Malta					
Monaco					
Netherlands		1,337.6			
Norway	47.8	432.9	144.0	4.5	9.1
Portugal		530.4			
Spain	282.8	2,953.3	438.4		10.4
Sweden	83.3	530.3	143.3	61.5	6.4
Switzerland		576.7			
Turkey	146.7	4,897.1	1,433.2	1,229.6	33.4
United Kingdom	296.6	3,841.9	3,247.5	1,630.0	13.0
Eastern Europe					
Albania					
Belarus	103.7	926.8	168.4	158.0	8.9
Bosnia-Herzegovina					
Bulgaria	58.0	695.5	1.3	234.0	12.0
Croatia		388.7			
Czech Republic	78.8	960.0	190.0	238.8	12.2
Estonia		126.3			
Georgia					
Hungary	105.0	919.4		135.3	8.8
Latvia	25.6	271.9	21.9	17.9	10.6
Lithuania	44.8	416.9	0.4	47.1	9.3
Macedonia					
Moldova					
Poland	182.8	3,027.2	0.1	62.4	16.6
Romania	142.4	2,052.6	314.6	131.3	14.4
Russia	1,278.5	10,503.6	1,550.6	2,524.9	8.2
Serbia and Montenegro					
Slovakia		683.4			
Slovenia		153.3			
Ukraine	344.2	3,842.6	490.1	2,174.1	11.2

Source: *Euromonitor International from UNESCO*

Table 20.4

Higher and University Education: Establishments, Staff and Students: 2007

As stated

	Establish-ments	Teaching Staff ('000)	Students ('000)	Student to Staff Ratio	University Teachers ('000)	University Teachers (% of total)	University Students ('000)	University Students (% of total)	University Students to Staff Ratio
Western Europe									
Austria			255.7						
Belgium	-		414.5						
Cyprus									
Denmark	171	20.4	245.2	12.0			185.2	75.5	
Finland	21	19.9	319.7	16.0	8.2	41.1	181.8	56.9	22.2
France	272	138.5	2,300.4	16.6	75.2	54.3	1,282.2	55.7	17.0
Germany			2,339.3						
Gibraltar									
Greece	21	28.5	703.2	24.7	12.1	42.4	431.3	61.3	35.7
Iceland									
Ireland			209.2						
Italy		102.1	2,176.5	21.3	102.2	100.1	2,158.4	99.2	21.1
Liechtenstein									
Luxembourg									
Malta									
Monaco									
Netherlands			584.3						
Norway	69	21.7	222.0	10.2	11.2	51.7	93.3	42.0	8.3
Portugal			389.3						
Spain	3,153	158.9	1,833.9	11.5	111.1	69.9	1,481.8	80.8	13.3
Sweden		45.0	470.4	10.5	37.2	82.7	430.4	91.5	11.6
Switzerland			223.1						
Turkey	1,282	88.6	2,132.7	24.1	88.4	99.8	2,138.9	100.3	24.2
United Kingdom	145	131.0	2,186.5	16.7	44.3	33.9	2,085.7	95.4	47.0
Eastern Europe									
Albania									
Belarus	56	44.4	580.2	13.1	24.8	56.0	405.4	69.9	16.3
Bosnia-Herzegovina									
Bulgaria	53	22.0	224.3	10.2	22.2	101.0	220.8	98.5	9.9
Croatia			161.9						
Czech Republic	249	28.7	380.3	13.2	18.8	65.3	327.1	86.0	17.4
Estonia			71.5						
Georgia									
Hungary	72	23.2	530.5	22.9	23.2	100.0	141.0	26.6	6.1
Latvia	60	6.2	134.9	21.6	5.2	83.7	134.9	100.0	25.8
Lithuania	49	13.2	237.8	18.0	8.8	66.8	146.7	61.7	16.6
Macedonia									
Moldova									
Poland	450	83.2	2,283.1	27.4	23.0	27.7	568.7	24.9	24.7
Romania	111	32.1	692.2	21.5	32.1	99.9	693.5	100.2	21.6
Russia	1,075	661.3	9,730.6	14.7			7,837.5	80.5	
Serbia and Montenegro									
Slovakia			184.3						
Slovenia			115.1						
Ukraine	349	217.5	2,997.3	13.8			2,326.9	77.6	

Source: Euromonitor International from UNESCO

Population

Total Population: National Estimates at Mid-Year

Table 21.1

Total Population 1980-2008: National Estimates at Mid-Year
'000

	1980	1985	1990	1995	1998	1999	2000	2001
Western Europe								
Austria	7,549	7,565	7,678	7,948	7,977	7,992	8,012	8,043
Belgium	9,859	9,858	9,967	10,137	10,203	10,226	10,251	10,287
Cyprus	614	651	685	737	770	781	792	802
Denmark	5,123	5,114	5,141	5,233	5,304	5,322	5,340	5,359
Finland	4,780	4,902	4,986	5,108	5,153	5,165	5,176	5,188
France	53,880	55,284	56,709	57,844	58,398	58,661	59,013	59,393
Germany	78,289	77,685	79,433	81,678	82,047	82,100	82,212	82,350
Gibraltar	27	27	27	27	27	27	28	28
Greece	9,643	9,934	10,157	10,634	10,835	10,883	10,917	10,950
Iceland	229	243	256	269	277	280	283	285
Ireland	3,413	3,546	3,514	3,609	3,713	3,755	3,805	3,866
Italy	56,434	56,593	56,719	56,846	56,911	56,922	56,949	56,981
Liechtenstein	26	27	29	31	32	32	33	33
Luxembourg	364	368	384	411	429	434	439	443
Malta	326	346	362	379	386	388	390	393
Monaco	26	29	30	32	32	32	32	32
Netherlands	14,150	14,492	14,952	15,459	15,707	15,812	15,926	16,046
Norway	4,086	4,153	4,241	4,359	4,431	4,462	4,491	4,514
Portugal	9,766	10,024	9,983	10,030	10,129	10,172	10,226	10,293
Spain	37,439	38,419	38,850	39,387	39,721	39,926	40,263	40,720
Sweden	8,310	8,350	8,559	8,827	8,851	8,858	8,872	8,896
Switzerland	6,319	6,470	6,716	7,041	7,110	7,144	7,184	7,230
Turkey	44,585	50,230	56,104	61,771	65,214	66,338	67,393	68,367
United Kingdom	56,314	56,550	57,248	58,019	58,487	58,682	58,893	59,109
Eastern Europe								
Albania	2,698	2,995	3,291	3,136	3,085	3,081	3,083	3,091
Belarus	9,627	9,958	10,189	10,194	10,072	10,035	10,005	9,971
Bosnia-Herzegovina	3,932	4,157	4,240	3,411	3,635	3,741	3,817	3,864
Bulgaria	8,851	8,952	8,718	8,264	8,062	8,006	7,954	7,903
Croatia	4,600	4,712	4,781	4,581	4,527	4,498	4,440	4,441
Czech Republic	10,285	10,302	10,303	10,308	10,260	10,245	10,228	10,213
Estonia	1,477	1,529	1,569	1,437	1,386	1,376	1,370	1,364
Georgia	5,092	5,314	5,436	4,993	4,801	4,747	4,693	4,640
Hungary	10,713	10,628	10,374	10,329	10,267	10,238	10,211	10,188
Latvia	2,512	2,579	2,663	2,485	2,410	2,390	2,373	2,355
Lithuania	3,413	3,545	3,698	3,629	3,549	3,524	3,500	3,481
Macedonia	1,801	1,834	1,916	1,968	1,997	2,005	2,013	2,019
Moldova	4,031	4,252	4,396	4,363	4,228	4,173	4,117	4,061
Poland	35,574	37,202	38,031	38,275	38,284	38,270	38,258	38,248
Romania	22,207	22,733	23,202	22,239	22,001	21,953	21,908	21,860
Russia	138,483	143,033	147,969	148,376	147,671	147,215	146,597	145,976
Serbia and Montenegro	9,560	9,874	10,218	10,847	10,866	10,825	10,770	10,700
Slovakia	4,980	5,156	5,278	5,353	5,374	5,377	5,379	5,379
Slovenia	1,901	1,942	1,998	1,990	1,982	1,983	1,989	1,992
Ukraine	49,866	50,752	51,590	51,087	49,759	49,330	48,889	48,452

Source: National statistical offices/UN/Euromonitor International

Total Population 1980-2008: National Estimates at Mid-Year *(continued)*

'000

	2002	2003	2004	2005	2006	2007	2008	% Growth 1980-2008
Western Europe								
Austria	8,084	8,121	8,173	8,236	8,290	8,333	8,367	10.8
Belgium	10,333	10,376	10,421	10,479	10,541	10,594	10,639	7.9
Cyprus	812	822	832	841	850	859	868	41.5
Denmark	5,376	5,391	5,405	5,419	5,437	5,454	5,468	6.7
Finland	5,201	5,213	5,228	5,246	5,266	5,287	5,306	11.0
France	59,778	60,155	60,523	60,877	61,229	61,588	61,943	15.0
Germany	82,488	82,534	82,516	82,469	82,375	82,264	82,172	5.0
Gibraltar	28	29	29	29	29	29	29	10.1
Greece	10,988	11,024	11,062	11,104	11,147	11,190	11,232	16.5
Iceland	288	291	294	297	300	302	305	32.9
Ireland	3,932	3,996	4,068	4,159	4,254	4,339	4,413	29.3
Italy	57,157	57,605	58,175	58,607	58,820	58,932	59,014	4.6
Liechtenstein	34	34	34	35	35	35	36	39.7
Luxembourg	447	451	455	459	464	469	475	30.4
Malta	396	399	401	404	406	407	409	25.3
Monaco	32	32	32	33	33	33	33	25.2
Netherlands	16,149	16,225	16,282	16,320	16,346	16,371	16,397	15.9
Norway	4,538	4,565	4,592	4,623	4,656	4,686	4,716	15.4
Portugal	10,368	10,441	10,502	10,549	10,589	10,626	10,656	9.1
Spain	41,314	42,005	42,692	43,398	44,121	44,770	45,289	21.0
Sweden	8,925	8,958	8,994	9,030	9,081	9,135	9,179	10.5
Switzerland	7,285	7,339	7,390	7,437	7,478	7,514	7,545	19.4
Turkey	69,304	70,231	71,151	72,067	72,984	73,900	74,810	67.8
United Kingdom	59,328	59,569	59,880	60,227	60,550	60,861	61,167	8.6
Eastern Europe								
Albania	3,106	3,125	3,144	3,163	3,181	3,199	3,217	19.2
Belarus	9,925	9,878	9,839	9,802	9,767	9,735	9,704	0.8
Bosnia-Herzegovina	3,889	3,901	3,910	3,921	3,931	3,938	3,942	0.3
Bulgaria	7,852	7,803	7,753	7,702	7,650	7,598	7,545	-14.7
Croatia	4,443	4,442	4,443	4,443	4,441	4,437	4,432	-3.7
Czech Republic	10,205	10,207	10,216	10,236	10,269	10,302	10,327	0.4
Estonia	1,359	1,354	1,349	1,346	1,342	1,337	1,333	-9.8
Georgia	4,589	4,540	4,495	4,453	4,414	4,378	4,345	-14.7
Hungary	10,159	10,130	10,107	10,087	10,067	10,048	10,029	-6.4
Latvia	2,339	2,325	2,313	2,301	2,288	2,274	2,260	-10.0
Lithuania	3,469	3,454	3,436	3,414	3,394	3,376	3,357	-1.6
Macedonia	2,024	2,028	2,032	2,035	2,037	2,039	2,040	13.3
Moldova	4,005	3,951	3,901	3,855	3,813	3,777	3,745	-7.1
Poland	38,230	38,205	38,182	38,165	38,129	38,074	38,018	6.9
Romania	21,803	21,742	21,685	21,634	21,583	21,526	21,466	-3.3
Russia	145,306	144,566	143,821	143,114	142,404	141,720	141,074	1.9
Serbia and Montenegro	10,623	10,550	10,494	10,461	10,454	10,467	10,490	9.7
Slovakia	5,379	5,380	5,382	5,387	5,390	5,393	5,394	8.3
Slovenia	1,995	1,996	1,997	2,000	2,007	2,013	2,020	6.2
Ukraine	48,032	47,633	47,271	46,925	46,607	46,329	46,056	-7.6

Source: National statistical offices/UN/Euromonitor International

Total Population: National Estimates at January 1st   **Table 21.2**

Total Population 1980-2008: National Estimates at January 1st
'000

	1980	1985	1990	1995	1998	1999	2000	2001
Western Europe								
Austria	7,546	7,563	7,645	7,943	7,971	7,982	8,002	8,021
Belgium	9,855	9,858	9,948	10,131	10,192	10,214	10,239	10,263
Cyprus	611	647	681	731	764	776	786	797
Denmark	5,122	5,111	5,135	5,216	5,295	5,314	5,330	5,349
Finland	4,771	4,894	4,974	5,099	5,147	5,160	5,171	5,181
France	53,731	55,157	56,577	57,753	58,299	58,497	58,825	59,200
Germany	78,180	77,709	79,113	81,539	82,057	82,037	82,163	82,260
Gibraltar	27	27	27	27	27	27	27	28
Greece	9,584	9,919	10,121	10,595	10,808	10,861	10,904	10,931
Iceland	228	241	255	267	275	278	281	284
Ireland	3,393	3,544	3,507	3,598	3,694	3,732	3,778	3,833
Italy	56,388	56,588	56,694	56,846	56,908	56,914	56,929	56,968
Liechtenstein	26	27	28	31	31	32	32	33
Luxembourg	364	367	382	408	426	432	437	441
Malta	324	344	360	378	385	387	389	392
Monaco	26	28	30	32	32	32	32	32
Netherlands	14,091	14,454	14,893	15,424	15,654	15,760	15,864	15,987
Norway	4,079	4,146	4,233	4,348	4,418	4,445	4,478	4,503
Portugal	9,714	10,017	9,996	10,018	10,110	10,149	10,195	10,257
Spain	37,242	38,353	38,826	39,343	39,639	39,803	40,050	40,477
Sweden	8,303	8,343	8,527	8,816	8,848	8,854	8,861	8,883
Switzerland	6,304	6,456	6,674	7,019	7,096	7,124	7,164	7,204
Turkey	44,021	49,663	55,495	61,204	64,642	65,787	66,889	67,896
United Kingdom	56,285	56,482	57,157	57,943	58,395	58,580	58,785	59,000
Eastern Europe								
Albania	2,671	2,957	3,289	3,150	3,088	3,081	3,080	3,085
Belarus	9,592	9,929	10,189	10,210	10,093	10,051	10,019	9,990
Bosnia-Herzegovina	3,914	4,122	4,308	3,421	3,575	3,694	3,787	3,846
Bulgaria	8,835	8,954	8,767	8,303	8,091	8,033	7,978	7,929
Croatia	4,598	4,702	4,778	4,669	4,501	4,554	4,442	4,437
Czech Republic	10,277	10,302	10,301	10,317	10,268	10,253	10,236	10,220
Estonia	1,472	1,523	1,571	1,448	1,393	1,379	1,372	1,367
Georgia	5,073	5,287	5,460	5,033	4,829	4,774	4,720	4,666
Hungary	10,709	10,657	10,375	10,337	10,280	10,253	10,222	10,200
Latvia	2,509	2,570	2,668	2,501	2,421	2,399	2,382	2,364
Lithuania	3,404	3,529	3,694	3,643	3,562	3,536	3,512	3,487
Macedonia	1,795	1,828	1,909	1,963	1,993	2,002	2,009	2,016
Moldova	4,010	4,232	4,389	4,379	4,255	4,201	4,145	4,089
Poland	35,413	37,063	37,988	38,265	38,290	38,277	38,263	38,254
Romania	22,133	22,687	23,211	22,285	22,026	21,976	21,929	21,887
Russia	138,127	142,539	147,665	148,460	147,802	147,539	146,890	146,304
Serbia and Montenegro	9,522	9,848	10,156	10,819	10,883	10,849	10,801	10,738
Slovakia	4,963	5,140	5,270	5,349	5,373	5,376	5,379	5,379
Slovenia	1,893	1,937	1,996	1,989	1,985	1,978	1,988	1,990
Ukraine	49,781	50,648	51,557	51,300	49,973	49,545	49,115	48,664

Source: *Euromonitor International from national statistics/UN*

Total Population 1980-2008: National Estimates at January 1st *(continued)*

'000

	2002	2003	2004	2005	2006	2007	2008	% Growth 1980-2008
Western Europe								
Austria	8,065	8,102	8,140	8,207	8,266	8,314	8,352	10.7
Belgium	10,310	10,356	10,396	10,446	10,511	10,570	10,618	7.7
Cyprus	807	817	827	836	846	855	864	41.4
Denmark	5,368	5,384	5,398	5,411	5,427	5,447	5,462	6.6
Finland	5,195	5,206	5,220	5,237	5,256	5,277	5,297	11.0
France	59,586	59,970	60,340	60,706	61,048	61,410	61,767	15.0
Germany	82,440	82,537	82,532	82,501	82,438	82,312	82,216	5.2
Gibraltar	28	28	29	29	29	29	29	10.3
Greece	10,969	11,006	11,041	11,083	11,125	11,169	11,211	17.0
Iceland	287	290	293	296	298	301	303	33.0
Ireland	3,900	3,964	4,028	4,109	4,209	4,299	4,378	29.0
Italy	56,994	57,321	57,888	58,462	58,752	58,888	58,976	4.6
Liechtenstein	34	34	34	35	35	35	35	37.5
Luxembourg	445	449	452	457	461	467	472	29.6
Malta	394	397	400	403	405	407	408	25.9
Monaco	32	32	32	33	33	33	33	25.9
Netherlands	16,105	16,193	16,258	16,306	16,334	16,358	16,383	16.3
Norway	4,524	4,552	4,577	4,606	4,640	4,671	4,701	15.3
Portugal	10,329	10,407	10,475	10,529	10,570	10,609	10,643	9.6
Spain	40,964	41,664	42,345	43,038	43,758	44,484	45,056	21.0
Sweden	8,909	8,941	8,976	9,011	9,048	9,113	9,157	10.3
Switzerland	7,256	7,314	7,364	7,415	7,459	7,497	7,530	19.5
Turkey	68,838	69,770	70,692	71,610	72,524	73,443	74,358	68.9
United Kingdom	59,218	59,438	59,700	60,060	60,393	60,707	61,015	8.4
Eastern Europe								
Albania	3,098	3,115	3,134	3,154	3,172	3,190	3,208	20.1
Belarus	9,951	9,899	9,858	9,820	9,784	9,750	9,719	1.3
Bosnia-Herzegovina	3,881	3,897	3,905	3,915	3,926	3,935	3,940	0.7
Bulgaria	7,877	7,827	7,778	7,728	7,676	7,624	7,571	-14.3
Croatia	4,444	4,442	4,442	4,444	4,443	4,440	4,435	-3.5
Czech Republic	10,206	10,203	10,211	10,221	10,251	10,287	10,317	0.4
Estonia	1,361	1,356	1,351	1,348	1,345	1,340	1,335	-9.3
Georgia	4,614	4,564	4,517	4,473	4,433	4,395	4,361	-14.0
Hungary	10,175	10,142	10,117	10,098	10,077	10,058	10,039	-6.3
Latvia	2,346	2,331	2,319	2,306	2,295	2,280	2,267	-9.6
Lithuania	3,476	3,463	3,446	3,425	3,403	3,385	3,366	-1.1
Macedonia	2,022	2,026	2,030	2,034	2,036	2,038	2,040	13.7
Moldova	4,033	3,978	3,925	3,877	3,833	3,794	3,760	-6.2
Poland	38,242	38,219	38,191	38,174	38,157	38,102	38,046	7.4
Romania	21,833	21,773	21,711	21,659	21,610	21,556	21,497	-2.9
Russia	145,649	144,964	144,168	143,474	142,754	142,054	141,386	2.4
Serbia and Montenegro	10,662	10,584	10,517	10,471	10,452	10,456	10,477	10.0
Slovakia	5,379	5,379	5,380	5,385	5,389	5,392	5,394	8.7
Slovenia	1,994	1,995	1,996	1,998	2,003	2,010	2,016	6.5
Ukraine	48,241	47,823	47,442	47,100	46,749	46,466	46,192	-7.2

***Source:** Euromonitor International from national statistics/UN*

Total Population: National Estimates at January 1st | **Table 21.3**

Population by Sex and Age at January 1st 2008
'000

	Total	Male	Female	0-14	15-64	65+
Western Europe						
Austria	8,352	4,065	4,287	1,287	5,634	1,431
Belgium	10,618	5,199	5,419	1,795	7,006	1,817
Cyprus	864	420	443	160	595	109
Denmark	5,462	2,704	2,758	1,009	3,602	850
Finland	5,297	2,595	2,702	895	3,528	874
France	61,767	30,023	31,744	11,327	40,285	10,154
Germany	82,216	40,274	41,942	11,270	54,468	16,478
Gibraltar	29	15	15	5	19	5
Greece	11,211	5,549	5,663	1,596	7,531	2,084
Iceland	303	153	151	64	202	37
Ireland	4,378	2,187	2,191	893	2,994	492
Italy	58,976	28,657	30,318	8,246	38,867	11,863
Liechtenstein	35	17	18	6	25	4
Luxembourg	472	233	239	85	320	67
Malta	408	203	205	66	285	57
Monaco	33	16	17	5	21	7
Netherlands	16,383	8,103	8,281	2,934	11,042	2,406
Norway	4,701	2,335	2,366	900	3,111	690
Portugal	10,643	5,154	5,489	1,644	7,152	1,847
Spain	45,056	22,222	22,835	6,610	30,864	7,583
Sweden	9,157	4,544	4,613	1,529	6,017	1,611
Switzerland	7,530	3,683	3,848	1,167	5,125	1,239
Turkey	74,358	37,478	36,880	20,467	49,479	4,412
United Kingdom	61,015	29,927	31,088	10,685	40,500	9,830
Eastern Europe						
Albania	3,208	1,595	1,613	784	2,127	297
Belarus	9,719	4,547	5,172	1,395	6,919	1,404
Bosnia-Herzegovina	3,940	1,915	2,025	654	2,705	581
Bulgaria	7,571	3,669	3,903	1,000	5,253	1,318
Croatia	4,435	2,136	2,299	687	2,980	767
Czech Republic	10,317	5,037	5,280	1,470	7,338	1,509
Estonia	1,335	614	721	197	909	229
Georgia	4,361	2,056	2,304	757	2,984	620
Hungary	10,039	4,764	5,275	1,510	6,912	1,618
Latvia	2,267	1,044	1,222	310	1,566	391
Lithuania	3,366	1,567	1,799	516	2,317	534
Macedonia	2,040	1,017	1,023	373	1,431	237
Moldova	3,760	1,799	1,961	690	2,651	418
Poland	38,046	18,390	19,655	5,865	27,082	5,098
Romania	21,497	10,467	11,030	3,285	15,025	3,186
Russia	141,386	65,365	76,022	20,686	101,268	19,432
Serbia and Montenegro	10,477	5,177	5,301	1,912	7,051	1,514
Slovakia	5,394	2,619	2,774	851	3,897	645
Slovenia	2,016	990	1,026	280	1,411	325
Ukraine	46,192	21,294	24,898	6,486	32,190	7,517

Source: Euromonitor International from national statistics/UN

Table 21.4

Population by Sex and Age (%) at January 1st 2008
% of total population

	Total	Male	Female	0-14	15-64	65+
Western Europe						
Austria	100.00	48.68	51.32	15.40	67.46	17.13
Belgium	100.00	48.96	51.04	16.91	65.98	17.11
Cyprus	100.00	48.66	51.34	18.48	68.87	12.65
Denmark	100.00	49.51	50.49	18.48	65.95	15.57
Finland	100.00	48.99	51.01	16.90	66.61	16.49
France	100.00	48.61	51.39	18.34	65.22	16.44
Germany	100.00	48.99	51.01	13.71	66.25	20.04
Gibraltar	100.00	50.12	49.88	17.80	65.45	16.75
Greece	100.00	49.49	50.51	14.24	67.17	18.59
Iceland	100.00	50.26	49.74	21.22	66.64	12.14
Ireland	100.00	49.96	50.04	20.39	68.38	11.23
Italy	100.00	48.59	51.41	13.98	65.90	20.12
Liechtenstein	100.00	49.32	50.68	16.86	71.04	12.10
Luxembourg	100.00	49.41	50.59	18.09	67.81	14.11
Malta	100.00	49.75	50.25	16.20	69.85	13.94
Monaco	100.00	47.48	52.52	13.73	63.72	22.55
Netherlands	100.00	49.46	50.54	17.91	67.40	14.69
Norway	100.00	49.67	50.33	19.15	66.17	14.68
Portugal	100.00	48.42	51.58	15.44	67.20	17.35
Spain	100.00	49.32	50.68	14.67	68.50	16.83
Sweden	100.00	49.63	50.37	16.70	65.70	17.60
Switzerland	100.00	48.90	51.10	15.49	68.06	16.45
Turkey	100.00	50.40	49.60	27.52	66.54	5.93
United Kingdom	100.00	49.05	50.95	17.51	66.38	16.11
Eastern Europe						
Albania	100.00	49.72	50.28	24.43	66.31	9.27
Belarus	100.00	46.79	53.21	14.36	71.19	14.45
Bosnia-Herzegovina	100.00	48.61	51.39	16.60	68.65	14.75
Bulgaria	100.00	48.45	51.55	13.21	69.38	17.41
Croatia	100.00	48.16	51.84	15.50	67.20	17.30
Czech Republic	100.00	48.82	51.18	14.25	71.13	14.62
Estonia	100.00	46.02	53.98	14.77	68.11	17.12
Georgia	100.00	47.16	52.84	17.36	68.42	14.22
Hungary	100.00	47.46	52.54	15.04	68.85	16.11
Latvia	100.00	46.07	53.93	13.66	69.08	17.26
Lithuania	100.00	46.56	53.44	15.33	68.82	15.85
Macedonia	100.00	49.87	50.13	18.27	70.14	11.60
Moldova	100.00	47.85	52.15	18.36	70.52	11.12
Poland	100.00	48.34	51.66	15.42	71.18	13.40
Romania	100.00	48.69	51.31	15.28	69.90	14.82
Russia	100.00	46.23	53.77	14.63	71.62	13.74
Serbia and Montenegro	100.00	49.41	50.59	18.25	67.30	14.45
Slovakia	100.00	48.56	51.44	15.77	72.26	11.97
Slovenia	100.00	49.10	50.90	13.89	69.97	16.13
Ukraine	100.00	46.10	53.90	14.04	69.69	16.27

Source: Euromonitor International from national statistics/UN

Births

Table 21.5

Number of Live Births 1980-2007
'000

	1980	1985	1990	1995	2000	2002	2003	2004	2005	2006	2007
Western Europe											
Austria	90.9	87.4	90.5	88.7	78.3	78.4	76.9	79.0	78.2	77.6	77.2
Belgium	124.8	114.3	123.6	114.2	114.9	111.2	112.1	115.6	118.0	120.8	122.0
Cyprus	12.4	13.2	12.8	11.5	10.1	9.9	9.9	9.9	10.0	10.2	10.3
Denmark	57.3	53.7	63.4	69.8	67.1	64.1	64.7	64.6	64.3	65.0	63.9
Finland	63.1	62.8	65.5	63.1	56.7	55.6	56.6	57.8	57.7	58.8	59.0
France	800.4	768.4	762.4	729.6	774.8	761.6	761.5	767.8	774.4	786.7	784.0
Germany	865.8	813.8	905.7	765.2	767.0	719.3	706.7	705.6	685.8	672.6	663.0
Gibraltar			0.5	0.4	0.4	0.4	0.4	0.4	0.4	0.4	0.4
Greece	148.1	116.5	102.2	101.5	101.0	99.6	99.2	97.5	97.0	96.7	96.4
Iceland	4.3	4.3	4.5	4.4	4.2	4.2	4.2	4.2	4.2	4.3	4.3
Ireland	74.1	62.4	53.0	48.8	54.2	58.8	60.9	62.5	63.4	64.3	65.3
Italy	640.4	577.3	569.3	525.6	543.0	538.6	541.0	541.1	538.9	535.3	530.4
Liechtenstein			0.4	0.4	0.4	0.4	0.3	0.4	0.4	0.4	0.4
Luxembourg	4.1	4.3	4.8	5.4	5.5	5.4	5.4	5.4	5.3	5.4	5.4
Malta	5.7	5.6	5.4	5.0	4.3	4.1	4.0	3.9	3.9	3.9	4.0
Monaco			0.8	0.8	0.8	0.8	0.8	0.8	0.9	0.9	1.0
Netherlands	181.3	178.1	198.0	190.5	206.6	202.1	200.3	194.0	187.9	185.1	182.4
Norway	51.0	51.1	60.9	60.3	59.2	55.4	56.5	57.0	56.8	55.9	55.2
Portugal	158.4	130.5	116.4	107.1	120.0	114.5	116.7	118.3	118.9	119.4	119.5
Spain	571.0	456.3	401.4	363.5	397.6	418.8	441.9	454.6	465.6	471.1	476.6
Sweden	97.1	98.5	123.9	103.4	90.4	95.8	99.2	100.9	101.3	105.9	106.4
Switzerland	73.7	74.7	83.9	82.2	78.5	72.3	71.8	73.1	72.9	72.4	72.1
Turkey	1,448.1	1,437.4	1,395.0	1,468.0	1,494.0	1,460.0	1,410.0	1,360.0	1,361.0	1,360.0	1,360.1
United Kingdom	753.7	750.7	798.6	732.0	679.3	668.8	695.5	716.0	722.5	740.5	738.6
Eastern Europe											
Albania	73.3	78.1	77.8	67.1	56.3	54.1	53.3	52.8	52.4	52.1	51.9
Belarus	154.4	165.0	142.2	101.1	93.7	88.4	85.6	84.9	84.3	83.6	82.8
Bosnia-Herzegovina	74.1	74.0	61.2	45.3	39.2	36.9	36.0	35.4	34.9	34.6	34.4
Bulgaria	128.2	119.0	105.2	72.0	73.7	66.5	67.4	69.9	71.1	72.4	71.9
Croatia	68.2	62.7	55.4	50.2	43.7	40.1	39.7	40.3	42.5	42.4	42.6
Czech Republic	153.8	135.9	130.6	96.1	90.9	92.8	93.7	97.7	102.2	105.8	103.9
Estonia	22.2	23.6	22.3	13.5	13.1	13.0	13.0	14.0	14.4	14.7	14.8
Georgia	91.5	95.3	87.5	66.8	53.0	51.0	50.2	49.6	48.9	48.2	47.6
Hungary	148.7	130.2	125.7	112.1	97.6	96.8	94.6	95.1	97.5	99.4	99.0
Latvia	35.5	39.8	37.9	21.6	20.2	20.0	21.0	20.3	21.5	21.7	22.1
Lithuania	51.8	58.5	56.9	41.2	34.1	30.0	30.6	30.4	30.5	31.1	31.2
Macedonia	37.2	35.3	33.0	29.2	25.2	24.3	23.9	23.5	23.1	22.7	22.4
Moldova	83.9	93.7	82.4	60.8	48.8	46.1	45.2	44.4	43.9	43.5	43.4
Poland	695.8	680.1	547.7	433.1	378.3	353.8	351.1	356.1	364.4	368.3	369.2
Romania	398.9	358.8	314.7	236.6	234.5	210.5	212.5	216.3	221.0	221.7	221.7
Russia	2,202.8	2,375.1	1,988.9	1,363.8	1,266.8	1,397.0	1,477.3	1,502.5	1,457.4	1,474.5	1,492.5
Serbia and Montenegro	160.8	155.7	143.2	128.6	123.4	124.0	124.5	125.1	125.7	126.2	126.7
Slovakia	95.1	90.2	80.0	61.4	55.2	50.8	51.7	53.7	54.4	52.6	52.4
Slovenia	29.9	25.9	22.4	19.0	18.2	17.5	17.3	18.0	18.2	18.2	18.4
Ukraine	742.5	762.8	657.2	492.9	385.1	390.7	408.6	427.3	426.1	460.4	472.7

Source: National statistical offices/UN/Euromonitor International

Table 21.6

Number of Deaths 1980-2007

'000

	1980	1985	1990	1995	2000	2002	2003	2004	2005	2006	2007
Western Europe											
Austria	92.4	89.6	83.0	81.2	76.8	76.1	77.2	74.3	75.2	75.3	75.4
Belgium	114.4	112.7	104.5	104.6	104.9	105.6	107.0	101.9	103.3	102.4	103.6
Cyprus	5.3	5.7	5.7	5.3	5.4	5.6	5.7	5.9	6.0	6.2	6.3
Denmark	55.9	58.4	60.9	63.1	58.0	58.6	57.6	55.8	55.0	55.5	54.8
Finland	44.4	48.2	50.1	49.3	49.3	49.4	49.0	47.6	47.9	48.1	48.3
France	547.1	552.5	526.2	531.6	530.9	535.1	552.3	509.4	527.5	520.3	524.1
Germany	952.4	929.6	921.4	884.6	838.8	841.7	853.9	818.3	830.2	839.2	834.0
Gibraltar			0.3	0.2	0.3	0.2	0.2	0.2	0.2	0.2	0.2
Greece	87.3	92.9	94.2	100.2	103.0	100.1	99.3	97.3	96.6	96.2	95.9
Iceland	1.5	1.7	1.7	1.8	1.8	1.8	1.8	1.8	1.8	1.8	1.9
Ireland	33.5	33.2	31.4	32.3	31.1	32.0	33.9	34.3	33.9	33.7	33.7
Italy	554.5	547.4	543.7	556.7	560.0	550.1	549.1	546.6	542.3	537.2	531.2
Liechtenstein			0.2	0.2	0.2	0.2	0.2	0.2	0.2	0.2	0.2
Luxembourg	4.2	4.0	4.0	4.0	3.9	3.9	4.0	4.0	4.0	4.0	4.1
Malta	3.0	3.0	2.7	2.9	3.0	3.0	3.1	3.1	3.1	3.2	3.2
Monaco			0.6	0.6	0.5	0.6	0.6	0.5	0.6	0.6	0.6
Netherlands	114.3	122.7	128.8	135.7	140.5	142.4	141.9	136.6	136.4	135.8	137.4
Norway	41.3	44.4	46.0	45.2	44.0	44.5	42.5	41.2	41.2	41.2	41.2
Portugal	95.0	97.3	103.1	103.5	105.4	108.1	110.7	112.7	113.9	114.9	115.5
Spain	289.3	312.5	333.1	346.2	360.4	368.6	384.8	371.9	387.0	381.0	385.8
Sweden	91.8	94.0	95.2	94.0	93.5	95.0	93.0	90.5	91.7	91.2	91.1
Switzerland	59.1	59.6	63.7	63.4	62.5	61.2	63.1	60.2	61.1	61.4	61.8
Turkey	427.2	422.5	404.0	436.0	477.0	469.0	446.0	443.0	450.0	450.0	460.5
United Kingdom	659.9	670.7	641.8	645.5	608.4	606.2	611.2	583.1	583.0	586.0	584.9
Eastern Europe											
Albania	16.7	17.2	18.7	19.5	17.7	17.3	17.3	17.4	17.6	18.0	18.4
Belarus	95.5	105.7	109.6	133.8	134.9	146.5	132.9	130.1	126.6	122.9	119.8
Bosnia-Herzegovina	25.8	28.8	28.4	27.3	31.0	32.9	33.8	34.6	35.4	36.2	37.0
Bulgaria	98.0	107.5	108.6	114.7	115.1	112.6	111.9	110.1	113.4	113.2	112.6
Croatia	50.1	52.1	52.2	50.5	50.2	50.6	52.6	49.8	51.8	51.2	51.7
Czech Republic	135.5	131.6	129.2	117.9	109.0	108.2	111.3	107.2	107.9	104.4	105.1
Estonia	18.2	19.3	19.5	20.8	18.4	18.4	18.2	17.7	17.3	17.6	17.6
Georgia	43.6	46.6	49.1	50.8	50.2	50.7	50.9	51.2	51.4	51.6	51.8
Hungary	145.4	147.6	145.7	145.4	135.6	132.8	135.8	132.5	135.7	132.3	132.2
Latvia	32.1	34.2	34.8	38.9	32.2	32.5	32.4	32.0	32.8	33.4	33.4
Lithuania	35.9	39.2	39.8	45.3	38.9	41.1	41.0	41.3	43.8	44.7	44.9
Macedonia	12.2	13.7	15.1	15.9	16.8	17.3	17.5	17.7	18.0	18.3	18.5
Moldova	43.9	44.1	44.9	49.5	50.5	49.8	49.4	48.9	48.4	48.0	47.6
Poland	350.2	384.0	390.3	386.1	368.0	359.5	365.2	363.5	368.3	376.0	377.6
Romania	231.9	246.7	247.1	271.7	255.8	269.7	266.6	258.9	262.1	264.6	267.0
Russia	1,525.8	1,625.3	1,656.0	2,203.8	2,225.3	2,332.3	2,365.8	2,295.4	2,303.9	2,309.5	2,309.9
Serbia and Montenegro	85.7	94.7	98.4	103.9	109.3	110.4	111.0	111.6	112.4	113.2	114.0
Slovakia	50.6	52.5	54.6	52.7	52.7	51.5	52.2	51.9	53.5	52.8	53.0
Slovenia	18.8	19.9	18.6	19.0	18.6	18.7	19.5	18.5	18.8	18.5	18.7
Ukraine	568.2	617.5	629.6	792.6	758.1	754.9	765.4	761.3	782.0	758.1	762.9

Source: National statistical offices/UN/Euromonitor International

Births

Table 21.7

Birth Rates 1980-2007
Per '000 inhabitants

	1980	1985	1990	1995	2000	2002	2003	2004	2005	2006	2007
Western Europe											
Austria	12.0	11.6	11.8	11.2	9.8	9.7	9.5	9.7	9.5	9.4	9.3
Belgium	12.7	11.6	12.4	11.3	11.2	10.8	10.8	11.1	11.3	11.5	11.5
Cyprus	20.1	20.5	18.6	15.7	12.8	12.3	12.1	12.0	12.0	12.0	12.1
Denmark	11.2	10.5	12.3	13.3	12.6	11.9	12.0	12.0	11.9	12.0	11.7
Finland	13.2	12.8	13.1	12.3	11.0	10.7	10.9	11.0	11.0	11.2	11.2
France	14.9	13.9	13.4	12.6	13.1	12.7	12.7	12.7	12.7	12.8	12.7
Germany	11.1	10.5	11.4	9.4	9.3	8.7	8.6	8.6	8.3	8.2	8.1
Gibraltar			19.7	15.9	14.8	13.2	13.0	14.5	14.4	14.7	15.1
Greece	15.4	11.7	10.1	9.5	9.5	9.4	9.5	9.6	9.7	9.7	9.7
Iceland	18.6	17.7	17.5	16.5	14.8	14.5	14.4	14.3	14.3	14.3	14.3
Ireland	21.7	17.6	15.1	13.5	14.4	15.4	15.4	15.2	14.7	14.4	14.2
Italy	11.3	10.2	10.0	9.2	9.5	9.4	9.4	9.7	9.5	9.4	9.2
Liechtenstein			13.2	13.8	12.9	11.7	10.2	10.8	10.9	10.3	9.9
Luxembourg	11.3	11.8	12.6	13.3	12.6	12.2	12.0	11.8	11.7	11.6	11.5
Malta	17.6	16.4	15.0	13.3	11.0	10.3	10.0	9.8	9.7	9.7	9.7
Monaco			26.1	26.2	23.8	23.9	26.1	25.5	27.4	28.4	29.4
Netherlands	12.8	12.3	13.2	12.3	13.0	12.5	12.3	11.9	11.5	11.3	11.1
Norway	12.5	12.3	14.4	13.8	13.2	12.2	12.4	12.4	12.3	12.0	11.8
Portugal	16.2	13.0	11.7	10.7	11.7	11.0	10.8	10.4	10.4	10.4	10.4
Spain	15.3	11.9	10.3	9.2	9.9	10.1	10.5	10.6	10.7	10.7	10.5
Sweden	11.7	11.8	14.5	11.7	10.2	10.7	11.1	11.2	11.2	11.7	11.6
Switzerland	11.7	11.5	12.5	11.7	10.9	9.9	9.8	9.9	9.8	9.7	9.6
Turkey	32.5	28.6	24.9	23.8	22.2	21.1	20.1	19.1	18.9	18.6	18.4
United Kingdom	13.4	13.3	14.0	12.6	11.5	11.3	11.7	12.0	12.0	12.2	12.1
Eastern Europe											
Albania	27.4	26.2	24.3	21.1	18.1	17.4	17.1	16.8	16.6	16.4	16.3
Belarus	16.3	16.6	14.1	10.5	9.1	9.2	9.2	9.3	9.3	9.3	9.4
Bosnia-Herzegovina	18.9	17.8	14.9	12.3	10.6	9.7	9.4	9.1	8.9	8.8	8.7
Bulgaria	14.5	13.3	12.1	8.7	9.3	8.5	8.6	9.0	9.2	9.5	9.5
Croatia	14.8	13.3	11.6	11.0	9.9	9.0	8.9	9.1	9.6	9.5	9.6
Czech Republic	15.0	13.2	12.7	9.3	8.9	9.1	9.2	9.6	10.0	10.3	10.1
Estonia	15.0	15.5	14.2	9.4	9.5	9.6	9.6	10.4	10.7	11.0	11.1
Georgia	18.0	18.0	16.4	13.1	11.2	11.1	11.0	11.0	10.9	10.9	10.8
Hungary	13.9	12.3	12.1	10.8	9.6	9.5	9.3	9.4	9.7	9.9	9.9
Latvia	14.1	15.4	14.2	8.7	8.5	8.6	9.0	8.8	9.3	9.5	9.7
Lithuania	15.2	16.5	15.4	11.4	9.8	8.7	8.9	8.9	8.9	9.2	9.3
Macedonia	20.9	19.1	17.3	14.9	12.5	12.0	11.8	11.6	11.4	11.2	11.0
Moldova	20.8	22.2	18.9	14.0	11.8	11.4	11.3	11.3	11.3	11.3	11.4
Poland	19.6	18.3	14.4	11.3	9.9	9.3	9.2	9.3	9.5	9.7	9.7
Romania	18.0	15.8	13.6	10.6	10.7	9.7	9.8	10.0	10.2	10.3	10.3
Russia	15.9	16.6	13.4	9.2	8.6	9.6	10.2	10.4	10.2	10.4	10.5
Serbia and Montenegro	17.4	16.3	14.7	12.7	12.2	12.4	12.6	12.7	12.8	12.9	12.9
Slovakia	19.1	17.5	15.2	11.5	10.3	9.5	9.6	10.0	10.1	9.8	9.7
Slovenia	15.7	13.4	11.2	9.5	9.1	8.8	8.7	9.0	9.1	9.1	9.1
Ukraine	14.9	15.0	12.7	9.6	7.9	8.1	8.6	9.0	9.1	9.9	10.2

Source: National statistical offices/UN/Euromonitor International

Table 21.8

Birth Rates by Quarter 2006-2008

Per '000 inhabitants

	2006 1st Quarter	2006 2nd Quarter	2006 3rd Quarter	2006 4th Quarter	2007 1st Quarter	2007 2nd Quarter	2007 3rd Quarter	2007 4th Quarter	2008 1st Quarter	2008 2nd Quarter
Western Europe										
Austria	8.7	9.4	10.0	9.4	8.6	9.3	9.9	9.2	8.9	9.4
Belgium										
Cyprus	11.4	11.1	13.0	12.6						
Denmark										
Finland	11.1	11.1	11.1	11.3	11.1	11.4	11.6	10.6	11.4	11.4
France										
Germany	8.0	8.1	8.7	7.9	7.9	7.8	8.6	7.9	7.6	8.9
Gibraltar										
Greece	8.8	9.4								
Iceland										
Ireland	14.2	14.2	15.0	14.3	15.3	14.7	15.9			
Italy	9.2	8.9	9.8	9.5	9.1	8.9	9.5	9.5		
Liechtenstein										
Luxembourg					11.2	11.2	11.8	11.7		
Malta										
Monaco										
Netherlands	11.3	11.1	11.7	11.2	11.0	10.8	11.8	10.9	10.9	11.3
Norway	12.1	12.5	12.5	10.9	11.8	12.3	12.2	10.8	11.9	
Portugal	10.3	10.1	10.8	10.5						
Spain					11.0					
Sweden	11.9	12.3	12.0	10.4	11.7	12.3	12.0	10.6	11.8	12.6
Switzerland		9.6		9.4	9.3	9.6	10.1	9.3	9.5	9.8
Turkey										
United Kingdom	12.0	12.3	12.4	12.3	12.1	12.7	13.3			
Eastern Europe										
Albania										
Belarus	9.3	9.0	9.8	9.5	9.5		10.7	10.1		
Bosnia-Herzegovina										
Bulgaria										
Croatia										
Czech Republic	9.8	10.8	10.7	10.0						
Estonia		11.3	11.4	10.3	11.1	11.8	11.9	11.3	11.8	12.2
Georgia										
Hungary	9.6	9.6	10.4	9.8	9.7	9.4	10.5	9.8	9.8	10.5
Latvia	9.0	9.7	9.9	9.6	9.5	9.6	10.4	9.4	10.6	10.3
Lithuania	8.4	9.1	10.1	8.9	8.7	8.9	10.3	9.1	9.2	10.0
Macedonia	10.6	10.7	12.2	11.2	10.8	10.9	11.4	10.9	11.2	10.4
Moldova	11.2	10.9	12.3	10.9	11.1	11.0	12.1	11.4	11.4	11.6
Poland					9.1					
Romania	10.1	10.2	10.9	9.9	10.3	9.8	10.9	10.1	10.8	9.9
Russia	9.8	10.3	10.6	10.7	10.2	10.3	10.7	11.0	11.3	11.2
Serbia and Montenegro				15.9	11.3	11.9	13.8	14.6	11.5	12.1
Slovakia	9.7	10.4	11.2	7.7	9.2	9.7	10.4	9.6	9.7	9.8
Slovenia	8.6	9.0	9.5	9.1	9.2	9.4	9.9			
Ukraine	9.3	9.5	10.6	10.1	9.8	9.7	10.1			

Source: National statistical offices/UN/Euromonitor International

Births

Table 21.9

Birth Rates by Month 2007-2008
Per '000 inhabitants

	July 2007	August 2007	September 2007	October 2007	November 2007	December 2007	January 2008	February 2008	March 2008	April 2008	May 2008	June 2008
Western Europe												
Austria	10.0	10.0	9.5	10.2	9.1	8.4	8.4	9.2	9.0	9.7	9.2	
Belgium												
Cyprus												
Denmark												
Finland												
France												
Germany	8.8	8.9	8.3	9.0	8.0	6.7	8.3	7.5	7.1	8.2	9.0	
Gibraltar												
Greece												
Iceland												
Ireland												
Italy	9.4	9.3	9.6	10.4	9.3	8.7						
Liechtenstein												
Luxembourg	12.6	11.4	11.4	12.4	10.8	12.0						
Malta												
Monaco												
Netherlands	11.6	11.8	12.0	11.4	10.9	10.5	10.9	11.0	10.7	11.1	11.3	
Norway												
Portugal												
Spain												
Sweden	12.4	12.0	11.7	11.4	10.6	9.9	11.6	12.1	11.9	12.8	12.4	
Switzerland	10.2	10.2	10.1	9.7	9.2	9.1	9.8	9.7	9.2	9.8	9.8	
Turkey												
United Kingdom												
Eastern Europe												
Albania												
Belarus	10.2	10.6	11.4	9.8	10.7	9.9						
Bosnia-Herzegovina												
Bulgaria												
Croatia												
Czech Republic												
Estonia	13.0	11.0		12.6	10.9	10.4	13.2	11.0	11.3	12.1	12.0	12.3
Georgia												
Hungary	10.5	10.5	10.6	9.9	9.9	9.7	10.2	9.9	9.3	9.6	10.8	
Latvia	10.8	11.1	9.2	10.8	9.2	8.3	11.7	10.0	10.1	10.4		10.2
Lithuania	10.6	11.0	9.3	10.1	8.9	8.3	10.6	8.5	8.4	10.2	10.2	9.5
Macedonia	11.9	12.0	10.2	11.2	11.4	9.9	11.9	11.3	10.4	10.1	10.6	
Moldova	12.0	11.9	12.2	12.5	12.1	9.6	11.7	12.3	10.2	10.3	11.2	13.2
Poland												
Romania	11.2	11.2	10.3	11.5	10.3	8.5	11.4	10.8	10.0	9.9	10.1	
Russia	10.6	10.8	10.8	11.0	11.0	11.0	11.3	11.4	11.1	11.3	11.1	
Serbia and Montenegro	13.6	14.9	12.9	15.2	13.5	15.3	10.2	12.5	11.9	10.9	12.6	
Slovakia	10.3	10.2	10.5	9.3	9.1	10.5	9.8	9.7	9.6	10.0	9.7	
Slovenia												
Ukraine	10.0	10.1	10.2									

Source: *National statistical offices/UN/Euromonitor International*

Table 21.10

Death Rates 1980-2007

Per '000 inhabitants

	1980	1985	1990	1995	2000	2002	2003	2004	2005	2006	2007
Western Europe											
Austria	12.2	11.8	10.8	10.2	9.6	9.4	9.5	9.1	9.1	9.1	9.1
Belgium	11.6	11.4	10.5	10.3	10.2	10.2	10.3	9.8	9.9	9.7	9.8
Cyprus	8.6	8.8	8.3	7.3	6.9	7.0	7.0	7.1	7.2	7.3	7.4
Denmark	10.9	11.4	11.9	12.1	10.9	10.9	10.7	10.3	10.1	10.2	10.0
Finland	9.3	9.8	10.0	9.6	9.5	9.5	9.4	9.1	9.1	9.1	9.1
France	10.2	10.0	9.3	9.2	9.0	9.0	9.2	8.4	8.7	8.5	8.5
Germany	12.2	12.0	11.6	10.8	10.2	10.2	10.3	9.9	10.1	10.2	10.1
Gibraltar			10.4	7.5	9.5	8.6	8.2	8.3	8.5	8.3	8.2
Greece	9.1	9.4	9.3	9.4	9.6	9.5	9.6	9.5	9.5	9.4	9.6
Iceland	6.6	6.9	6.8	6.8	6.4	6.2	6.1	6.1	6.1	6.1	6.2
Ireland	9.8	9.4	8.9	8.9	8.2	7.5	7.2	6.9	6.6	6.5	6.4
Italy	9.8	9.7	9.6	9.8	9.8	9.8	10.2	9.4	9.7	9.7	9.8
Liechtenstein			6.8	7.3	7.3	6.4	6.4	5.8	6.2	6.3	6.4
Luxembourg	11.4	10.9	10.5	9.8	9.0	8.9	8.8	8.8	8.7	8.7	8.7
Malta	9.1	8.6	7.6	7.6	7.7	7.7	7.7	7.7	7.8	7.8	7.9
Monaco			19.4	17.7	17.1	17.5	19.1	16.2	18.4	18.1	18.7
Netherlands	8.1	8.5	8.6	8.8	8.8	8.8	8.7	8.4	8.4	8.3	8.4
Norway	10.1	10.7	10.9	10.4	9.8	9.8	9.3	9.0	8.9	8.9	8.8
Portugal	9.7	9.7	10.3	10.4	10.3	10.2	10.4	9.7	10.2	9.7	9.7
Spain	7.7	8.1	8.6	8.8	9.0	8.9	9.2	8.7	8.9	8.6	8.5
Sweden	11.0	11.3	11.1	10.6	10.5	10.6	10.4	10.1	10.2	10.0	10.0
Switzerland	9.4	9.2	9.5	9.0	8.7	8.4	8.6	8.1	8.2	8.2	8.2
Turkey	9.6	8.4	7.2	7.1	7.1	6.8	6.4	6.2	6.2	6.2	6.2
United Kingdom	11.7	11.9	11.2	11.1	10.3	10.2	10.3	9.7	9.7	9.7	9.6
Eastern Europe											
Albania	6.2	5.8	5.8	6.1	5.7	5.6	5.5	5.5	5.6	5.7	5.8
Belarus	9.6	10.0	10.9	12.9	14.2	14.4	14.5	14.6	14.6	14.7	14.7
Bosnia-Herzegovina	6.6	6.9	7.0	7.4	8.4	8.7	8.8	8.9	9.1	9.2	9.4
Bulgaria	11.1	12.0	12.5	13.9	14.5	14.3	14.3	14.2	14.7	14.8	14.8
Croatia	10.9	11.1	10.9	11.0	11.3	11.4	11.8	11.2	11.7	11.5	11.7
Czech Republic	13.2	12.8	12.5	11.4	10.7	10.6	10.9	10.5	10.5	10.2	10.2
Estonia	12.3	12.7	12.4	14.5	13.4	13.5	13.4	13.1	12.9	13.1	13.2
Georgia	8.6	8.8	9.2	10.0	10.6	11.0	11.1	11.3	11.5	11.6	11.8
Hungary	13.6	13.9	14.0	14.1	13.3	13.1	13.4	13.1	13.5	13.1	13.2
Latvia	12.8	13.2	13.1	15.7	13.6	13.9	13.9	13.8	14.2	14.6	14.7
Lithuania	10.5	11.1	10.8	12.5	11.1	11.8	11.9	12.0	12.8	13.2	13.3
Macedonia	6.9	7.5	7.9	8.1	8.4	8.6	8.6	8.7	8.9	9.0	9.1
Moldova	10.9	10.5	10.3	11.4	12.2	12.3	12.4	12.4	12.4	12.5	12.5
Poland	9.8	10.3	10.3	10.1	9.6	9.4	9.6	9.5	9.6	9.9	9.9
Romania	10.4	10.9	10.6	12.2	11.7	12.4	12.3	11.9	12.1	12.3	12.4
Russia	11.0	11.4	11.2	14.9	15.2	16.1	16.4	16.0	16.1	16.2	16.3
Serbia and Montenegro	9.2	9.8	10.0	10.0	10.6	10.8	11.0	11.1	11.3	11.4	11.5
Slovakia	10.2	10.2	10.3	9.8	9.8	9.6	9.7	9.6	9.9	9.8	9.8
Slovenia	9.9	10.2	9.3	9.5	9.3	9.4	9.7	9.3	9.4	9.2	9.3
Ukraine	11.4	12.2	12.2	15.5	15.5	15.7	16.1	16.1	16.7	16.3	16.5

Source: National statistical offices/UN/Euromonitor International

Deaths

Table 21.11

Death Rates by Quarter 2006-2008

Per '000 inhabitants

	2006 1st Quarter	2006 2nd Quarter	2006 3rd Quarter	2006 4th Quarter	2007 1st Quarter	2007 2nd Quarter	2007 3rd Quarter	2007 4th Quarter	2008 1st Quarter	2008 2nd Quarter
Western Europe										
Austria	9.3	9.1	8.6	9.2	9.4	8.9	8.6	9.3	9.5	8.8
Belgium										
Cyprus	8.3	7.2	6.7	7.4						
Denmark										
Finland	9.5	9.2	8.5	9.2	10.1	9.0	8.7	8.8	9.8	9.1
France										
Germany	10.9	10.1	9.9	9.8	10.9	10.0	9.4	10.3	11.3	
Gibraltar										
Greece	9.7	9.3								
Iceland										
Ireland	6.9	6.6	6.3	6.1	7.4	6.3	5.9			
Italy	10.8	9.4	9.1	9.5	10.7	9.4	9.0	9.9		
Liechtenstein										
Luxembourg					9.2	8.6	8.1	8.9		
Malta										
Monaco										
Netherlands	9.0	8.2	8.0	8.0	9.0	8.2	7.7	8.7	9.2	8.4
Norway	9.3	8.5	8.5	9.1	9.8	8.4	8.2	8.8	9.3	
Portugal	11.0	8.9	9.0	9.6						
Spain				8.6						
Sweden	10.8	9.7	9.6	10.1	11.0	9.7	9.2	10.0	10.5	9.7
Switzerland		7.9		8.1	9.0	7.8	7.6	8.5	8.9	7.7
Turkey										
United Kingdom	10.9	9.6	8.8	9.4	10.8	9.7	8.5			
Eastern Europe										
Albania										
Belarus	15.6	14.7	13.1	14.7	15.1		13.0	13.8		
Bosnia-Herzegovina										
Bulgaria										
Croatia										
Czech Republic	10.8	10.1	9.5	10.2						
Estonia		13.2	11.7	12.9	14.6	12.7	12.5	13.5	14.0	12.6
Georgia										
Hungary	13.8	13.1	12.4	13.3	14.1	12.8	12.5	13.2	13.8	12.5
Latvia	16.1	14.4	13.0	14.4	16.6	14.1	13.4	14.6	14.9	13.8
Lithuania	13.3	13.2	12.0	13.3	14.7	13.0	11.9	13.6	13.8	12.5
Macedonia	9.9	8.7	8.2	9.1	10.5	8.7	8.2	8.9	9.8	8.7
Moldova	14.8	12.6	10.4	12.0	13.9	12.0	10.8	13.2	13.9	12.5
Poland				9.8						
Romania	13.4	12.3	10.7	12.6	13.5	12.0	11.1	12.9	13.5	12.3
Russia	17.2	16.4	15.8	15.5	16.8	16.4	16.0	15.9	17.3	16.6
Serbia and Montenegro				12.2	11.5	11.2	10.6	12.5	11.7	11.3
Slovakia	10.0	9.6	9.6	9.9	10.3	9.5	9.6	10.0	10.0	9.7
Slovenia	9.8	9.4	8.5	9.2	10.4	9.3	9.0			
Ukraine	18.2	16.2	14.4	16.3	17.7	15.9	16.4			

Source: *National statistical offices/UN/Euromonitor International*

Table 21.12

Death Rates by Month 2007-2008

Per '000 inhabitants

	July 2007	August 2007	September 2007	October 2007	November 2007	December 2007	January 2008	February 2008	March 2008	April 2008	May 2008	June 2008
Western Europe												
Austria	9.3	8.5	7.9	9.2	9.6	9.3	9.5	9.8	9.3	9.6	8.7	
Belgium												
Cyprus												
Denmark												
Finland												
France												
Germany	9.9	9.4	8.8	10.5	10.6	9.8	12.5	10.8	10.7	11.3		
Gibraltar												
Greece												
Iceland												
Ireland												
Italy	9.3	9.2	8.5	9.7	10.1	9.8						
Liechtenstein												
Luxembourg	7.7	8.1	8.4	8.8	8.5	9.4						
Malta												
Monaco												
Netherlands	7.7	7.7	7.6	8.2	8.7	9.3	9.6	9.1	9.0	8.7	8.4	
Norway												
Portugal												
Spain												
Sweden	9.2	9.0	9.5	9.6	9.9	10.6	10.7	10.3	10.7	10.4	9.5	9.3
Switzerland	7.4	7.5	7.9	7.9	8.5	9.1	9.3	8.8	8.6	8.3	7.7	
Turkey												
United Kingdom												
Eastern Europe												
Albania												
Belarus	13.1	13.1	12.8	12.6	14.6	14.4						
Bosnia-Herzegovina												
Bulgaria												
Croatia												
Czech Republic												
Estonia	12.6	12.0		13.6	13.4	13.5	14.4	13.9	13.7	12.9	12.7	12.3
Georgia												
Hungary	13.4	12.0	12.2	12.7	13.2	13.6	14.0	13.7	13.6	13.3	12.3	
Latvia	14.0	13.5	12.7	15.4	14.4	14.2	16.4	13.8	14.6	14.4	13.6	13.5
Lithuania	11.9	12.3	11.5	14.0	13.4	13.6	16.1	12.8	12.5	12.7	12.7	12.2
Macedonia	8.3	8.5	7.8	8.9	9.2	8.8	10.6	9.5	9.2	8.7	8.9	
Moldova	11.4	10.5	10.6	12.7	14.0	12.9	16.0	13.7	12.0	11.8	13.0	
Poland												
Romania	12.2	10.7	10.5	12.4	13.0	13.3	14.2	13.5	12.8	12.8	12.1	12.0
Russia	16.2	16.0	15.9	15.9	15.9	15.9	18.1	17.1	16.8	16.8	16.6	
Serbia and Montenegro	11.5	10.9	9.6	11.9	11.9	13.7	11.4	11.9	11.9	11.1	11.5	
Slovakia	10.0	9.4	9.5	9.5	9.2	11.2	10.1	10.2	9.8	9.9	9.7	
Slovenia												
Ukraine	16.6	16.4	16.2									

Source: National statistical offices/UN/Euromonitor International

Deaths

Table 21.13

Infant Mortality Rates 1980-2007
Deaths per '000 live births

	1980	1985	1990	1995	2000	2002	2003	2004	2005	2006	2007
Western Europe											
Austria	14.3	11.2	7.8	5.4	4.8	4.1	4.5	4.0	3.9	3.8	3.7
Belgium	12.1	9.8	6.5	5.8	4.8	4.3	4.2	4.1	4.0	3.9	3.8
Cyprus	18.0	14.4	11.0	8.5	5.6	4.7	4.1	3.5	4.6	4.5	4.4
Denmark	8.4	7.9	7.5	5.1	5.3	4.3	4.4	4.4	4.3	4.2	4.1
Finland	7.6	6.3	5.6	3.9	3.6	3.0	3.2	3.0	2.9	2.7	2.7
France	10.0	8.3	7.3	4.9	4.4	4.1	4.1	4.0	4.0	3.8	3.7
Germany	12.4	9.1	7.0	5.3	4.4	4.1	4.1	4.0	3.9	3.9	3.7
Gibraltar				7.0	6.4	6.2	6.1	5.9	5.8	5.7	5.6
Greece	17.9	14.1	9.7	8.1	6.0	5.1	4.8	4.6	4.4	4.1	4.0
Iceland	7.7	5.7	5.9	6.1	3.0	2.2	2.4	2.8	2.3	1.4	1.4
Ireland	11.1	8.8	8.2	6.4	6.2	5.2	5.1	5.0	4.9	4.8	4.7
Italy	14.6	10.5	8.2	6.2	4.5	4.5	4.3	4.1	4.0	3.9	3.8
Liechtenstein				3.6	3.4	3.2	3.2	3.1	3.0	2.9	2.9
Luxembourg	12.0	9.5	7.0	6.0	5.0	5.0	5.0	5.0	4.0	4.0	3.9
Malta	14.0	11.4	9.0	8.9	6.1	6.0	5.9	5.9	6.0	5.9	5.8
Monaco			7.0	6.0	5.0	4.4	4.0	3.0	3.0	3.0	2.9
Netherlands	8.6	8.0	7.1	5.5	5.1	4.9	4.7	4.6	4.6	4.5	4.3
Norway [a]	8.1	8.5	6.9	4.0	3.8	3.4	3.4	3.3	3.2	3.1	2.9
Portugal [b]	24.2	17.8	11.0	7.5	5.5	5.0	3.9	3.7	3.4	3.2	3.1
Spain	12.3	8.9	7.6	5.5	3.9	3.7	3.4	3.1	3.0	2.9	2.8
Sweden	6.9	6.8	6.0	4.1	3.4	3.4	3.0	2.9	2.8	2.7	2.6
Switzerland	9.1	6.9	6.8	5.0	4.9	4.5	4.3	4.2	4.1	4.0	3.9
Turkey	93.4	93.6	54.0	44.6	40.2	39.5	38.3	37.5	36.6	36.5	35.6
United Kingdom	13.9	10.7	8.9	7.0	6.3	5.9	6.0	5.8	5.6	5.6	5.4
Eastern Europe											
Albania	47.0	41.7	37.0	29.0	22.0	19.4	18.0	17.0	16.0	15.2	14.6
Belarus	16.2	14.6	12.1	13.5	9.3	7.9	7.5	7.1	6.7	6.4	6.2
Bosnia-Herzegovina	31.0	24.3	18.0	16.0	15.0	15.0	14.0	13.0	13.0	12.8	12.7
Bulgaria [c]	20.2	15.4	14.8	14.8	13.3	13.3	13.0	12.6	12.2	12.1	11.8
Croatia	20.6	16.6	10.7	8.9	7.4	6.9	6.7	6.5	6.3	6.2	6.0
Czech Republic	16.9	12.5	10.8	7.7	4.1	4.1	4.0	3.8	3.6	3.5	3.5
Estonia	17.1	14.1	12.3	14.8	8.4	5.7	6.8	6.6	6.2	5.9	5.5
Georgia	49.1	46.5	43.0	41.0	41.0	41.0	41.0	41.0	41.0	40.6	40.2
Hungary	23.2	20.4	14.8	10.7	9.2	7.2	7.3	6.9	6.8	6.3	6.0
Latvia	15.3	13.0	13.7	18.8	10.4	9.8	10.0	9.3	9.0	8.7	8.3
Lithuania	14.5	14.2	10.2	12.5	8.6	7.9	7.0	6.7	6.5	6.1	5.9
Macedonia	53.0	43.3	34.0	24.0	22.0	22.0	20.3	17.6	15.0	13.8	12.8
Moldova	35.0	30.9	19.0	21.2	18.3	14.7	14.4	12.2	12.4	11.8	11.2
Poland	25.4	22.2	19.4	13.6	8.1	7.4	6.9	6.6	6.3	5.9	5.8
Romania	29.3	25.6	26.9	21.2	18.6	16.1	15.7	15.0	14.5	13.7	13.2
Russia	22.0	20.8	17.6	18.2	15.2	13.2	12.3	11.5	11.0	10.6	10.2
Serbia and Montenegro	36.0	30.0	23.0	17.0	13.4	9.6	9.1	8.5	8.0	7.6	7.3
Slovakia	20.9	16.3	12.0	11.0	8.6	7.7	8.2	7.3	7.1	6.7	6.3
Slovenia	15.3	13.0	8.4	5.5	4.9	3.9	4.1	4.0	3.9	3.7	3.7
Ukraine	16.6	15.9	13.0	14.8	12.0	10.3	9.8	9.5	9.1	8.7	8.4

Source: *Euromonitor International from UN/national statistical offices/Eurostat*
Notes: *Rates refer to deaths of infants under one year*
(a) Rates from 1977 to 1990 are annual averages for five-year periods, (b) NUTS Nomenclature of Territorial Units of Statistics; Note: 1998 data new methodology, (c) The crude death rates are calculated per thousands of the average annual population

Table 21.14

Marriage Rates 1980-2007

Per '000 inhabitants

	1980	1985	1990	1995	2000	2002	2003	2004	2005	2006	2007
Western Europe											
Austria	6.2	5.9	5.9	5.4	4.9	4.5	4.6	4.7	4.8	4.8	4.9
Belgium	6.7	5.8	6.5	5.1	4.4	3.9	4.0	4.2	4.2	4.2	4.2
Cyprus	8.3	8.7	8.2	9.1	11.8	12.7	13.2	13.3	13.4	13.3	13.3
Denmark	5.2	5.7	6.1	6.7	7.2	6.9	6.5	7.0	7.1	7.1	7.1
Finland	6.2	5.3	5.0	4.7	5.1	5.2	5.0	5.6	5.7	5.7	5.7
France	6.2	4.9	5.1	4.4	5.1	4.7	4.6	4.3	4.2	4.1	4.0
Germany	6.4	6.4	6.5	5.3	5.1	4.8	4.6	4.8	4.8	4.8	4.9
Gibraltar					5.4	5.9	6.3	5.5	5.6	5.7	5.8
Greece	6.5	6.4	5.8	6.0	4.5	5.3	5.5	5.5	5.4	5.4	5.3
Iceland	5.7	5.2	4.5	4.6	6.3	5.8	5.1	5.2	5.4	5.5	5.5
Ireland	6.4	5.3	5.1	4.3	5.1	5.1	5.1	5.1	5.0	5.0	4.9
Italy	5.7	5.3	5.6	5.1	5.0	4.7	4.6	4.5	4.5	4.4	4.4
Liechtenstein	13.5	12.7	11.5	13.4	7.3	5.2	4.4	4.8	5.4	5.6	5.5
Luxembourg	5.9	5.4	6.1	5.1	4.9	4.5	4.5	4.4	4.5	4.5	4.5
Malta	8.9	7.4	6.9	6.1	6.5	5.7	5.9	6.0	5.9	6.0	6.1
Monaco	6.5			6.0	5.0	5.4	5.7	5.3	5.0	4.9	4.9
Netherlands	6.4	5.7	6.4	5.3	5.6	5.2	5.0	4.5	4.4	4.3	4.2
Norway	5.4	4.9	5.2	5.0	5.7	5.3	4.9	4.9	4.8	4.8	4.8
Portugal	7.4	6.8	7.2	6.6	6.3	5.5	5.2	5.0	5.0	5.0	4.9
Spain	5.9	5.2	5.7	5.1	5.4	5.2	5.1	5.1	5.0	5.0	4.9
Sweden	4.5	4.6	4.7	3.8	4.5	4.3	4.4	4.8	4.8	4.9	4.9
Switzerland	5.7	6.0	7.0	5.8	5.5	5.5	5.5	5.4	5.3	5.2	5.2
Turkey	8.3	7.4	8.3	7.6	6.9	6.5	6.8	6.7	6.7	6.6	6.5
United Kingdom	7.4	7.0	6.6	5.6	5.2	4.9	5.2	5.2	5.2	5.1	5.1
Eastern Europe											
Albania	8.1	8.5	8.8	7.9	8.4	8.5	8.8	6.7	6.9	6.9	7.0
Belarus	10.2	9.9	9.7	7.5	6.2	6.7	7.1	7.2	7.2	7.3	7.4
Bosnia-Herzegovina			7.0	6.4	5.8	5.2	5.3	5.7	5.5	5.6	5.6
Bulgaria	7.9	7.4	6.8	4.4	4.4	3.7	3.9	4.0	4.0	4.0	4.0
Croatia	7.2	6.6	5.8	5.2	5.0	5.1	5.0	5.1	5.1	5.1	5.2
Czech Republic	7.6	7.8	8.8	5.3	5.4	5.2	4.8	5.0	5.1	5.1	5.1
Estonia	8.8	8.4	7.5	4.8	4.0	4.3	4.2	4.5	4.5	4.6	4.6
Georgia	10.0	8.4	6.4	4.3	2.7	2.7	2.8	3.3	4.0	4.9	5.1
Hungary	7.5	6.9	6.4	5.2	4.7	4.5	4.5	4.3	4.3	4.3	4.3
Latvia	9.8	9.4	8.9	4.4	3.9	4.2	4.3	4.5	4.6	4.7	4.8
Lithuania	9.3	9.7	9.8	6.1	4.8	4.6	4.9	5.6	5.8	6.0	6.3
Macedonia			8.2	8.1	7.1	7.2	7.1	6.9	7.1	7.1	7.2
Moldova	11.5	9.7	9.3	7.5	5.2	5.4	6.3	6.4	6.5	6.4	6.5
Poland	8.7	7.2	6.7	5.4	5.5	5.0	5.1	5.1	5.2	5.2	5.2
Romania	8.3	7.1	8.3	6.9	6.2	5.9	6.2	6.2	6.3	6.3	6.4
Russia	10.6	9.7	8.9	7.2	6.1	7.0	7.5	6.8	7.4	7.6	7.7
Serbia and Montenegro	7.8	7.1	6.4	5.6	5.4	4.3	4.3	4.4	4.4	4.4	4.3
Slovakia	8.0	7.6	7.7	5.1	4.8	4.7	4.8	4.9	4.9	5.0	5.0
Slovenia	6.5	5.5	4.3	4.1	3.6	3.5	3.4	3.3	3.3	3.2	3.2
Ukraine	9.3	9.7	9.4	8.4	5.6	6.6	7.8	5.9	5.8	5.8	5.8

Source: *National statistical offices/Council of Europe/UN/Euromonitor International*
Notes: *Rates refer to legal marriages (recognised marriages performed and registered)*

Divorce Rates

Table 21.15

Divorce Rates 1980-2007

Per '000 inhabitants

	1980	1985	1990	1995	2000	2002	2003	2004	2005	2006	2007
Western Europe											
Austria	1.8	2.0	2.1	2.3	2.4	2.4	2.3	2.3	2.3	2.2	2.2
Belgium	1.5	1.9	2.0	3.5	2.6	3.0	3.0	3.0	3.0	3.0	3.0
Cyprus	0.3	0.4	0.5	1.0	1.5	1.6	1.8	2.0	1.8	1.9	1.9
Denmark	2.7	2.8	2.7	2.5	2.7	2.9	2.9	2.9	3.0	3.0	3.0
Finland	2.0	1.9	2.6	2.8	2.7	2.6	2.6	2.5	2.5	2.5	2.5
France	1.5	1.9	1.9	2.1	1.9	2.1	2.1	2.1	2.2	2.2	2.2
Germany	1.8	2.3	2.0	2.1	2.4	2.5	2.6	2.7	2.7	2.8	2.8
Gibraltar					3.5	5.4	5.6	4.1	3.3	3.3	3.2
Greece	0.7	0.8	0.6	1.0	1.0	1.0	1.1	1.1	1.1	1.2	1.2
Iceland	1.9	2.2	1.9	1.8	1.9	1.8	1.8	1.9	1.9	1.9	1.9
Ireland					0.7	0.7	0.7	0.7	0.7	0.7	0.7
Italy	0.2	0.3	0.5	0.5	0.7	0.7	0.8	0.8	0.8	0.8	0.8
Liechtenstein			1.0	1.2	3.9	3.0	2.5	2.9	2.7	2.8	2.9
Luxembourg	1.6	1.8	2.0	1.8	2.4	2.5	2.3	2.3	2.3	2.3	2.4
Malta											
Monaco	1.8			2.5	2.6	2.1	2.3	2.5	2.1	2.1	2.2
Netherlands	1.8	2.4	1.9	2.2	2.2	2.1	1.9	1.9	1.8	1.8	1.8
Norway	1.6	2.0	2.4	2.4	2.2	2.3	2.4	2.4	2.4	2.5	2.5
Portugal	0.6	0.9	0.9	1.2	1.9	2.7	2.1	2.2	2.3	2.4	2.4
Spain		0.5	0.6	0.8	1.0	1.0	1.0	1.0	1.1	1.1	1.1
Sweden	2.4	2.4	2.3	2.6	2.4	2.4	2.4	2.2	2.2	2.2	2.2
Switzerland	1.7	1.8	2.0	2.2	1.5	2.3	2.3	2.4	2.5	2.6	2.6
Turkey	0.4	0.4	0.5	0.5	0.5	0.7	0.7	0.8	0.8	0.8	0.8
United Kingdom	2.8	3.1	2.9	2.9	2.6	2.7	2.8	2.8	2.9	2.9	2.9
Eastern Europe											
Albania	0.8	0.8	0.8	0.7	0.7	1.1	1.2	0.9	1.2	1.4	1.4
Belarus	3.3	3.1	3.4	4.1	4.3	3.8	3.2	3.1	2.9	2.8	2.7
Bosnia-Herzegovina			0.4	0.5	0.5	0.6	0.5	0.4	0.5	0.4	0.4
Bulgaria	1.5	1.6	1.3	1.3	1.3	1.3	1.5	1.9	2.0	2.2	2.4
Croatia	1.2	1.1	1.1	0.9	1.0	1.0	1.1	1.1	1.2	1.2	1.2
Czech Republic	2.6	3.0	3.1	3.0	2.9	3.1	3.2	3.2	3.3	3.3	3.3
Estonia	4.2	4.0	3.7	5.1	3.1	3.0	2.9	3.1	3.1	3.1	3.1
Georgia	1.3	1.2	1.3	0.5	0.4	0.4	0.4	0.4	0.4	0.5	0.5
Hungary	2.6	2.8	2.4	2.4	2.3	2.5	2.5	2.4	2.4	2.4	2.4
Latvia	5.0	4.5	4.0	3.1	2.6	2.5	2.1	2.3	2.3	2.3	2.4
Lithuania	3.2	3.2	3.5	2.8	3.1	3.0	3.1	3.2	3.2	3.3	3.4
Macedonia			0.4	0.4	0.7	0.6	0.7	0.8	0.8	0.8	0.8
Moldova	2.8	2.6	3.0	3.3	2.3	3.1	3.7	3.8	3.9	3.9	4.0
Poland	1.1	1.3	1.1	1.0	1.1	1.2	1.3	1.5	1.5	1.5	1.6
Romania	1.5	1.4	1.4	1.6	1.4	1.5	1.5	1.6	1.7	1.7	1.8
Russia	4.2	4.0	3.8	4.5	4.3	5.9	5.5	4.4	4.2	4.1	4.0
Serbia and Montenegro	1.2	1.2	1.1	0.7	0.8	1.0	0.8	0.9	0.9	0.9	0.9
Slovakia	1.3	1.5	1.7	1.7	1.7	2.0	2.0	2.0	2.1	2.2	2.2
Slovenia	1.2	1.3	0.9	0.8	1.1	1.2	1.2	1.2	1.2	1.2	1.2
Ukraine	3.7	3.6	3.7	3.9	4.0	3.8	3.7	3.6	3.6	3.6	3.5

Source: *National statistical offices/Council of Europe/UN/Euromonitor International*
Notes: *Rates refer to final divorce decrees granted under civil law*

Table 21.16

Fertility Rates 1980-2007

Children born per female

	1980	1985	1990	1995	2000	2002	2003	2004	2005	2006	2007
Western Europe											
Austria	1.7	1.5	1.5	1.4	1.4	1.4	1.4	1.4	1.4	1.4	1.4
Belgium	1.7	1.5	1.6	1.6	1.6	1.6	1.6	1.7	1.7	1.7	1.7
Cyprus	2.4	2.4	2.4	2.1	1.6	1.5	1.5	1.5	1.4	1.4	1.4
Denmark	1.6	1.5	1.7	1.8	1.8	1.7	1.8	1.8	1.8	1.8	1.8
Finland	1.6	1.6	1.8	1.8	1.7	1.7	1.8	1.8	1.8	1.8	1.8
France	2.0	1.8	1.8	1.7	1.9	1.9	1.9	1.9	1.9	1.9	2.0
Germany	1.6	1.4	1.5	1.3	1.4	1.3	1.3	1.4	1.3	1.4	1.4
Gibraltar											
Greece	2.2	1.7	1.4	1.3	1.3	1.3	1.3	1.3	1.2	1.2	1.2
Iceland	2.5	1.9	2.3	2.1	2.1	1.9	2.0	2.0	2.1	2.1	2.1
Ireland	3.2	2.5	2.1	1.8	1.9	2.0	2.0	2.0	2.0	2.1	2.1
Italy	1.6	1.4	1.3	1.2	1.2	1.3	1.3	1.3	1.3	1.3	1.3
Liechtenstein											
Luxembourg	1.5	1.4	1.6	1.7	1.8	1.6	1.6	1.7	1.7	1.7	1.7
Malta	2.0	2.0	2.1	1.8	1.7	1.5	1.5	1.4	1.4	1.4	1.3
Monaco											
Netherlands	1.6	1.5	1.6	1.5	1.7	1.7	1.8	1.7	1.7	1.8	1.8
Norway	1.7	1.7	1.9	1.9	1.9	1.8	1.8	1.8	1.8	1.9	1.9
Portugal	2.3	1.7	1.6	1.4	1.6	1.5	1.5	1.5	1.5	1.5	1.5
Spain	2.2	1.6	1.4	1.2	1.3	1.3	1.3	1.3	1.3	1.3	1.4
Sweden	1.7	1.7	2.1	1.7	1.6	1.7	1.7	1.8	1.8	1.8	1.8
Switzerland	1.6	1.5	1.6	1.5	1.5	1.4	1.4	1.4	1.4	1.4	1.4
Turkey	4.4	3.6	3.1	2.8	2.3	2.2	2.2	2.2	2.2	2.2	2.2
United Kingdom	1.9	1.8	1.8	1.7	1.6	1.6	1.7	1.8	1.8	1.8	1.8
Eastern Europe											
Albania	3.8	3.2	2.9	2.6	2.4	2.3	2.2	2.2	2.1	2.1	2.1
Belarus	2.0	2.1	1.9	1.4	1.3	1.2	1.2	1.2	1.2	1.2	1.2
Bosnia-Herzegovina	2.1	2.0	1.7	1.5	1.4	1.3	1.3	1.3	1.2	1.2	1.2
Bulgaria	2.1	2.0	1.8	1.2	1.3	1.2	1.2	1.3	1.3	1.3	1.3
Croatia	1.9	1.8	1.7	1.6	1.4	1.3	1.3	1.4	1.4	1.4	1.4
Czech Republic	2.1	2.0	1.9	1.3	1.1	1.2	1.2	1.2	1.3	1.3	1.3
Estonia	2.0	2.1	2.0	1.3	1.4	1.4	1.4	1.5	1.5	1.5	1.5
Georgia	2.3	2.3	2.1	1.8	1.5	1.5	1.5	1.4	1.4	1.4	1.4
Hungary	1.9	1.9	1.9	1.6	1.3	1.3	1.3	1.3	1.3	1.3	1.3
Latvia	1.9	2.1	2.0	1.3	1.2	1.2	1.3	1.2	1.3	1.3	1.3
Lithuania	2.0	2.1	2.0	1.6	1.4	1.2	1.3	1.3	1.3	1.3	1.3
Macedonia	2.5	2.3	2.1	2.0	1.8	1.8	1.8	1.7	1.6	1.6	1.5
Moldova	2.7	2.8	2.4	1.9	1.3	1.3	1.3	1.3	1.3	1.3	1.2
Poland	2.3	2.3	2.0	1.6	1.4	1.2	1.2	1.2	1.2	1.3	1.3
Romania	2.4	2.3	1.8	1.3	1.3	1.3	1.3	1.3	1.3	1.3	1.3
Russia	1.9	2.1	1.9	1.3	1.2	1.3	1.3	1.3	1.3	1.3	1.3
Serbia and Montenegro	2.3	2.2	2.1	1.9	1.7	1.7	1.7	1.6	1.6		
Slovakia	2.3	2.3	2.1	1.5	1.3	1.2	1.2	1.2	1.3	1.3	1.3
Slovenia	2.1	1.7	1.5	1.3	1.3	1.2	1.2	1.3	1.3	1.3	1.3
Ukraine	2.0	2.0	1.8	1.4	1.1	1.1	1.2	1.2	1.2	1.3	1.3

Source: National statistical offices/UN/Euromonitor International

Life Expectancy at Birth: Total Population

Table 21.17

Life Expectancy at Birth: Males and Females 2008
Years

	Male	Female
Western Europe		
Austria	77.0	82.8
Belgium	76.4	82.5
Cyprus	77.1	81.4
Denmark	76.5	80.9
Finland	76.3	83.0
France	77.5	84.3
Germany	76.8	82.4
Gibraltar	74.4	79.5
Greece	77.2	82.0
Iceland	80.0	83.8
Ireland	78.0	82.2
Italy	78.1	83.8
Liechtenstein	77.1	83.5
Luxembourg	77.3	82.7
Malta	78.3	81.9
Monaco	76.9	84.3
Netherlands	77.7	82.0
Norway	78.3	82.9
Portugal	75.0	81.8
Spain	77.3	84.1
Sweden	79.0	83.3
Switzerland	79.2	84.4
Turkey	69.4	74.3
United Kingdom	77.2	81.7
Eastern Europe		
Albania	73.0	78.8
Belarus	63.3	74.8
Bosnia-Herzegovina	72.2	77.5
Bulgaria	70.2	76.8
Croatia	72.8	79.5
Czech Republic	73.2	79.5
Estonia	66.8	77.7
Georgia	68.3	75.2
Hungary	69.6	77.6
Latvia	65.4	76.7
Lithuania	65.1	77.3
Macedonia	71.9	76.0
Moldova	65.2	72.8
Poland	71.6	79.9
Romania	69.3	76.1
Russia	59.1	72.8
Serbia and Montenegro	70.6	75.9
Slovakia	70.5	78.4
Slovenia	74.5	81.5
Ukraine	62.4	74.2

Source: *Euromonitor International from World Bank*

Table 21.18

Population Density 1980-2008

Persons per sq km

	1980	1985	1990	1995	2000	2003	2004	2005	2006	2007	2008
Western Europe											
Austria	91.5	91.7	92.7	96.3	97.1	98.3	98.7	99.5	100.3	100.8	101.3
Belgium	326.0	326.0	329.0	335.1	338.7	342.6	343.9	345.5	347.7	349.7	351.3
Cyprus	66.1	70.1	73.7	79.1	85.1	88.4	89.5	90.5	91.5	92.5	93.5
Denmark	120.9	120.6	121.1	122.9	125.6	126.9	127.2	127.5	127.9	128.4	128.7
Finland	15.7	16.1	16.3	16.7	17.0	17.1	17.1	17.2	17.3	17.3	17.4
France	97.7	100.3	102.8	105.0	106.9	109.0	109.7	110.4	111.0	111.6	112.3
Germany	224.2	222.8	226.8	233.8	235.6	236.7	236.6	236.5	236.4	236.0	235.7
Gibraltar	2,654.8	2,660.1	2,684.4	2,730.6	2,737.9	2,844.2	2,882.2	2,910.0	2,925.4	2,930.6	2,928.6
Greece	74.4	77.0	78.5	82.2	84.6	85.4	85.7	86.0	86.3	86.6	87.0
Iceland	2.3	2.4	2.5	2.7	2.8	2.9	2.9	2.9	3.0	3.0	3.0
Ireland	49.2	51.4	50.9	52.2	54.8	57.5	58.5	59.6	61.1	62.4	63.6
Italy	191.7	192.4	192.8	193.3	193.6	194.9	196.8	198.8	199.8	200.2	200.5
Liechtenstein	161.3	166.8	177.8	191.4	202.7	211.6	214.3	216.3	218.2	219.8	221.8
Luxembourg											
Malta	1,012.9	1,076.1	1,125.4	1,180.6	1,215.3	1,241.6	1,250.4	1,258.2	1,264.8	1,270.6	1,275.7
Monaco											
Netherlands	415.9	426.6	439.6	455.3	468.2	477.9	479.9	481.3	482.1	482.8	483.6
Norway	13.4	13.6	13.9	14.3	14.7	15.0	15.0	15.1	15.2	15.4	15.5
Portugal	106.2	109.5	109.2	109.5	111.4	113.7	114.5	115.1	115.5	115.9	116.3
Spain	74.6	76.8	77.7	78.8	80.3	83.5	84.8	86.2	87.6	89.1	90.2
Sweden	20.2	20.3	20.8	21.5	21.6	21.8	21.9	22.0	22.0	22.2	22.3
Switzerland	157.6	161.4	166.8	175.5	179.1	182.8	184.1	185.4	186.5	187.4	188.3
Turkey	57.2	64.5	72.1	79.5	86.9	90.7	91.9	93.0	94.2	95.4	96.6
United Kingdom	232.6	233.5	236.3	239.5	243.0	245.7	246.8	248.3	249.6	250.9	252.2
Eastern Europe											
Albania	97.5	107.9	120.1	115.0	112.4	113.7	114.4	115.1	115.8	116.4	117.1
Belarus	46.2	47.9	49.1	49.2	48.3	47.7	47.5	47.3	47.2	47.0	46.8
Bosnia-Herzegovina				66.8	74.0	76.1	76.3	76.5	76.7	76.9	77.0
Bulgaria	79.9	80.9	79.2	75.1	72.1	70.8	71.5	71.1	71.0	70.6	70.1
Croatia	82.2	84.1	85.4	83.5	79.4	79.4	79.4	79.5	79.4	79.4	79.3
Czech Republic	133.0	133.3	133.3	133.5	132.5	132.0	132.2	132.3	132.7	133.2	133.5
Estonia	34.8	36.0	37.2	34.2	32.4	32.0	31.9	31.8	31.7	31.6	31.5
Georgia				72.4	67.9	65.7	65.0	64.4	63.8	63.3	62.8
Hungary	119.1	118.6	115.4	115.0	114.1	113.2	112.9	112.7	112.5	112.2	112.0
Latvia	40.4	41.4	43.0	40.3	38.4	37.4	37.2	37.0	36.8	36.6	36.4
Lithuania	52.5	54.5	57.0	58.1	56.0	55.2	55.0	54.6	54.3	54.0	53.7
Macedonia				77.2	79.0	79.7	79.8	80.0	80.1	80.2	80.2
Moldova				133.0	126.1	121.0	119.4	117.9	116.6	115.4	114.4
Poland	116.3	121.7	124.8	125.7	125.7	124.8	125.5	124.6	124.4	124.1	123.9
Romania	96.1	98.5	101.2	97.1	95.5	94.7	94.4	94.2	93.9	93.7	93.4
Russia	8.2	8.4	8.7	9.1	9.0	8.8	8.8	8.8	8.7	8.7	8.6
Serbia and Montenegro				106.1	105.9	103.8	103.1	102.7	102.5	102.5	102.7
Slovakia	103.2	106.9	109.6	111.2	111.8	111.8	111.9	112.0	112.0	112.1	112.1
Slovenia	94.1	96.3	99.2	98.8	98.7	99.1	99.1	99.2	99.5	99.8	100.1
Ukraine	85.9	87.4	89.0	88.5	84.8	82.5	81.9	81.3	80.7	80.2	79.7

Source: National statistical offices/UN/Euromonitor International

Urban Population

Table 21.19

Urban Population 1980-2007
% of total population

	1980	1985	1990	1995	2000	2002	2003	2004	2005	2006	2007
Western Europe											
Austria	54.4	58.8	63.5	65.7	66.5	66.8	66.8	66.9	67.0	67.1	67.2
Belgium	95.4	95.9	96.4	96.8	97.1	97.2	97.2	97.3	97.3	97.3	97.3
Cyprus	58.6	64.7	66.8	68.0	68.6	68.9	69.0	69.2	69.3	69.5	69.7
Denmark	83.9	84.3	84.8	85.1	85.1	85.2	85.3	85.4	85.5	85.6	85.7
Finland	56.5	56.6	56.8	57.8	60.4	61.4	62.0	62.1	62.2	62.3	62.4
France	73.3	73.7	74.1	74.9	75.7	76.1	76.3	76.5	76.7	76.9	77.1
Germany	82.6	84.0	85.3	86.5	87.5	87.9	88.1	88.3	88.5	88.7	88.8
Gibraltar	100.0	100.0	100.0	100.0	100.0	100.0	100.0	100.0	100.0	100.0	100.0
Greece	57.7	58.4	58.8	59.3	60.1	60.6	60.9	61.1	61.5	61.8	62.1
Iceland	88.3	89.6	90.8	91.6	92.3	92.5	92.6	92.7	92.8	92.9	93.0
Ireland	55.3	56.3	56.9	57.9	59.1	59.6	59.9	60.1	60.4	60.7	61.0
Italy	66.6	66.8	66.7	66.9	67.2	67.3	67.4	67.5	67.6	67.7	67.8
Liechtenstein	18.3	17.6	16.9	16.5	15.1	14.8	14.7	14.6	14.6	14.5	14.5
Luxembourg	80.0	80.7	80.9	82.9	83.8	83.4	83.2	83.0	82.8	82.7	82.5
Malta	89.8	89.8	90.4	90.9	93.4	94.2	94.6	95.0	95.3	95.6	95.8
Monaco	100.0	100.0	100.0	100.0	100.0	100.0	100.0	100.0	100.0	100.0	100.0
Netherlands	58.3	59.2	60.0	60.9	63.0	63.9	64.3	64.8	65.3	65.7	66.2
Norway	70.5	71.3	72.1	73.4	76.1	77.7	78.6	79.5	80.4	81.1	81.9
Portugal	29.4	37.5	46.3	50.3	53.1	54.1	54.6	55.1	55.7	56.2	56.8
Spain	72.8	74.2	75.3	75.9	76.3	76.5	76.5	76.6	76.7	76.8	76.9
Sweden	83.1	83.1	83.1	83.2	83.3	83.3	83.4	83.4	83.4	83.5	83.5
Switzerland	62.1	66.4	68.0	67.7	67.6	67.8	67.9	67.9	68.0	68.1	68.2
Turkey	49.4	55.9	59.6	62.1	64.8	65.9	66.4	66.9	67.4	67.9	68.4
United Kingdom	87.9	88.5	88.7	88.7	88.9	89.0	89.1	89.1	89.2	89.3	89.4
Eastern Europe											
Albania	33.7	34.9	36.4	39.1	41.8	43.1	43.9	44.6	45.4	46.1	46.9
Belarus	58.4	64.2	66.8	68.1	70.2	71.1	71.5	71.9	72.3	72.7	73.0
Bosnia-Herzegovina	35.5	37.6	39.2	41.1	43.2	44.2	44.7	45.2	45.7	46.3	46.9
Bulgaria	63.7	65.8	67.1	67.8	68.4	69.6	69.9	70.3	70.7	71.1	71.5
Croatia	50.1	52.2	54.0	55.8	57.7	58.6	59.0	59.5	59.9	60.3	60.8
Czech Republic	74.6	75.2	75.0	74.5	74.1	74.0	74.1	74.3	74.5	74.7	74.8
Estonia	69.8	71.0	71.5	70.0	69.2	69.2	69.2	69.3	69.3	69.3	69.4
Georgia	51.6	53.9	55.2	54.0	52.7	52.3	52.2	52.2	52.2	52.3	52.3
Hungary	57.6	62.8	65.4	65.2	64.5	65.4	65.6	66.0	66.2	66.5	66.8
Latvia	66.9	68.5	69.0	68.7	68.1	67.9	67.8	67.9	68.0	68.1	68.2
Lithuania	60.9	65.1	68.1	67.5	67.1	66.9	66.9	67.0	67.1	67.1	67.2
Macedonia	53.5	55.7	57.8	60.7	64.9	66.5	67.3	68.1	68.9	69.6	70.3
Moldova	40.4	44.2	46.8	46.3	46.1	46.3	46.4	46.5	46.7	46.9	47.1
Poland	59.7	61.2	61.8	61.8	61.8	61.7	61.7	61.8	61.8	61.8	61.8
Romania	49.2	53.0	54.3	54.9	54.6	54.8	54.8	54.8	54.9	54.9	54.9
Russia	70.6	72.6	73.7	72.9	72.9	73.3	73.4	73.5	73.6	73.7	73.9
Serbia and Montenegro											
Slovakia	51.9	55.6	56.9	56.3	55.5	55.5	55.6	55.8	55.9	56.2	56.3
Slovenia	49.3	50.4	50.8	50.8	50.8	50.8	50.8	50.8	50.8	50.9	51.0
Ukraine	64.6	66.4	67.5	67.8	67.4	67.3	67.4	67.5	67.6	67.7	67.8

Source: National statistical offices/UN/Euromonitor International

Table 21.20

Rural Population 1980-2007

% of total population

	1980	1985	1990	1995	2000	2002	2003	2004	2005	2006	2007
Western Europe											
Austria	45.6	41.2	36.5	34.3	33.5	33.2	33.2	33.1	33.0	32.9	32.8
Belgium	4.6	4.1	3.6	3.2	2.9	2.8	2.8	2.7	2.7	2.7	2.7
Cyprus	41.4	35.3	33.2	32.0	31.4	31.1	31.0	30.8	30.7	30.5	30.3
Denmark	16.1	15.7	15.2	14.9	14.9	14.8	14.7	14.6	14.5	14.4	14.3
Finland	43.5	43.4	43.2	42.2	39.6	38.6	38.0	37.9	37.8	37.7	37.6
France	26.7	26.3	25.9	25.1	24.3	23.9	23.7	23.5	23.3	23.1	22.9
Germany	17.4	16.0	14.7	13.5	12.5	12.1	11.9	11.7	11.5	11.3	11.2
Gibraltar											
Greece	42.3	41.6	41.2	40.7	39.9	39.4	39.1	38.9	38.5	38.2	37.9
Iceland	11.7	10.4	9.2	8.4	7.7	7.5	7.4	7.3	7.2	7.1	7.0
Ireland	44.7	43.7	43.1	42.1	40.9	40.4	40.1	39.9	39.6	39.3	39.0
Italy	33.4	33.2	33.3	33.1	32.8	32.7	32.6	32.5	32.4	32.3	32.2
Liechtenstein	81.7	82.4	83.1	83.5	84.9	85.2	85.3	85.4	85.4	85.5	85.5
Luxembourg	20.0	19.3	19.1	17.1	16.2	16.6	16.8	17.0	17.2	17.3	17.5
Malta	10.2	10.2	9.6	9.1	6.6	5.8	5.4	5.0	4.7	4.4	4.2
Monaco											
Netherlands	41.7	40.8	40.0	39.1	37.0	36.1	35.7	35.2	34.7	34.3	33.8
Norway	29.5	28.7	27.9	26.6	23.9	22.3	21.4	20.5	19.6	18.9	18.1
Portugal	70.6	62.5	53.7	49.7	46.9	45.9	45.4	44.9	44.3	43.8	43.2
Spain	27.2	25.8	24.7	24.1	23.7	23.5	23.5	23.4	23.3	23.2	23.1
Sweden	16.9	16.9	16.9	16.8	16.7	16.7	16.6	16.6	16.6	16.5	16.5
Switzerland	37.9	33.6	32.0	32.3	32.4	32.2	32.1	32.1	32.0	31.9	31.8
Turkey	50.6	44.1	40.4	37.9	35.2	34.1	33.6	33.1	32.6	32.1	31.6
United Kingdom	12.1	11.5	11.3	11.3	11.1	11.0	10.9	10.9	10.8	10.7	10.6
Eastern Europe											
Albania	66.3	65.1	63.6	60.9	58.2	56.9	56.1	55.4	54.6	53.9	53.1
Belarus	41.6	35.8	33.2	31.9	29.8	28.9	28.5	28.1	27.7	27.3	27.0
Bosnia-Herzegovina	64.5	62.4	60.8	58.9	56.8	55.8	55.3	54.8	54.3	53.7	53.1
Bulgaria	36.3	34.2	32.9	32.2	31.6	30.4	30.1	29.7	29.3	28.9	28.5
Croatia	49.9	47.8	46.0	44.2	42.3	41.4	41.0	40.5	40.1	39.7	39.2
Czech Republic	25.4	24.8	25.0	25.5	25.9	26.0	25.9	25.7	25.5	25.3	25.2
Estonia	30.2	29.0	28.5	30.0	30.8	30.8	30.8	30.7	30.7	30.7	30.6
Georgia	48.4	46.1	44.8	46.0	47.3	47.7	47.8	47.8	47.8	47.7	47.7
Hungary	42.4	37.2	34.6	34.8	35.5	34.6	34.4	34.0	33.8	33.5	33.2
Latvia	33.1	31.5	31.0	31.3	31.9	32.1	32.2	32.1	32.0	31.9	31.8
Lithuania	39.1	34.9	31.9	32.5	32.9	33.1	33.1	33.0	32.9	32.9	32.8
Macedonia	46.5	44.3	42.2	39.3	35.1	33.5	32.7	31.9	31.1	30.4	29.7
Moldova	59.6	55.8	53.2	53.7	53.9	53.7	53.6	53.5	53.3	53.1	52.9
Poland	40.3	38.8	38.2	38.2	38.2	38.3	38.3	38.2	38.2	38.2	38.2
Romania	50.8	47.0	45.7	45.1	45.4	45.2	45.2	45.2	45.1	45.1	45.1
Russia	29.4	27.4	26.3	27.1	27.1	26.7	26.6	26.5	26.4	26.3	26.1
Serbia and Montenegro											
Slovakia	48.1	44.4	43.1	43.7	44.5	44.5	44.4	44.2	44.1	43.8	43.7
Slovenia	50.7	49.6	49.2	49.2	49.2	49.2	49.2	49.2	49.2	49.1	49.0
Ukraine	35.4	33.6	32.5	32.2	32.6	32.7	32.6	32.5	32.4	32.3	32.2

Source: National statistical offices/UN/Euromonitor International

Total Population: National Estimates at January 1st

Table 21.21

Males and Females by Age at January 1st 2008
'000

	Males				**Females**		
	0-14	**15-64**	**65+**	**0-14**	**15-64**	**65+**
Western Europe						
Austria	659	2,822	584	628	2,812	847
Belgium	919	3,523	757	877	3,483	1,059
Cyprus	82	290	49	78	305	61
Denmark	516	1,817	370	493	1,785	480
Finland	457	1,783	355	438	1,745	519
France	5,799	20,034	4,191	5,528	20,252	5,964
Germany	5,782	27,575	6,917	5,488	26,893	9,561
Gibraltar						
Greece	822	3,807	920	774	3,725	1,164
Iceland	33	103	17	31	99	20
Ireland	458	1,511	219	435	1,483	273
Italy	4,239	19,463	4,955	4,007	19,403	6,908
Liechtenstein						
Luxembourg	44	162	28	41	158	39
Malta	34	145	24	32	140	33
Monaco						
Netherlands	1,502	5,565	1,036	1,433	5,478	1,370
Norway	461	1,578	296	439	1,533	394
Portugal	845	3,537	772	799	3,615	1,075
Spain	3,397	15,610	3,214	3,212	15,254	4,368
Sweden	784	3,054	707	746	2,963	904
Switzerland	598	2,563	521	568	2,562	718
Turkey	10,433	25,056	1,989	10,034	24,423	2,423
United Kingdom	5,475	20,188	4,264	5,211	20,312	5,565
Eastern Europe						
Albania	404	1,052	139	379	1,075	159
Belarus	716	3,358	473	679	3,561	931
Bosnia-Herzegovina	337	1,336	242	317	1,369	339
Bulgaria	514	2,614	541	487	2,639	777
Croatia	352	1,486	298	335	1,495	469
Czech Republic	755	3,686	596	715	3,652	912
Estonia	101	437	76	96	472	153
Georgia	395	1,420	241	361	1,564	379
Hungary	774	3,399	591	735	3,512	1,027
Latvia	158	758	128	151	808	263
Lithuania	265	1,120	183	251	1,197	351
Macedonia	193	723	102	179	708	135
Moldova	355	1,292	152	335	1,359	266
Poland	3,009	13,453	1,928	2,856	13,628	3,171
Romania	1,685	7,484	1,298	1,600	7,541	1,889
Russia	10,592	48,584	6,188	10,094	52,684	13,244
Serbia and Montenegro	991	3,536	650	921	3,515	864
Slovakia	436	1,942	241	414	1,955	405
Slovenia	144	720	126	136	691	199
Ukraine	3,328	15,436	2,530	3,158	16,754	4,987

Source: *Euromonitor International from national statistics/UN*

Table 21.22

Number of Males, 1990-2008 at January 1st
'000

	1990	1995	2000	2002	2003	2004	2005	2006	2007	2008
Western Europe										
Austria	3,655	3,831	3,868	3,907	3,929	3,950	3,986	4,019	4,045	4,065
Belgium	4,860	4,955	5,006	5,042	5,067	5,087	5,111	5,144	5,174	5,199
Cyprus	339	365	387	395	399	403	407	411	416	420
Denmark	2,531	2,573	2,634	2,654	2,662	2,670	2,677	2,686	2,696	2,704
Finland	2,413	2,482	2,523	2,538	2,545	2,553	2,562	2,572	2,584	2,595
France	27,544	28,078	28,568	28,943	29,133	29,318	29,495	29,661	29,843	30,023
Germany	38,110	39,645	40,091	40,275	40,345	40,356	40,354	40,340	40,300	40,274
Gibraltar	14	14	14	14	14	14	15	15	15	15
Greece	4,982	5,243	5,400	5,430	5,449	5,464	5,487	5,508	5,529	5,549
Iceland	128	134	141	144	145	147	148	150	151	153
Ireland	1,743	1,787	1,877	1,938	1,970	2,003	2,047	2,102	2,147	2,187
Italy	27,528	27,570	27,566	27,587	27,766	28,069	28,377	28,527	28,604	28,657
Liechtenstein	14	15	16	16	17	17	17	17	17	17
Luxembourg	187	200	215	219	221	223	225	228	230	233
Malta	178	187	193	196	197	199	200	201	202	203
Monaco	14	15	15	15	15	15	15	15	16	16
Netherlands	7,358	7,627	7,846	7,972	8,015	8,046	8,066	8,077	8,089	8,103
Norway	2,093	2,150	2,217	2,242	2,256	2,269	2,284	2,302	2,319	2,335
Portugal	4,819	4,827	4,918	4,989	5,030	5,066	5,094	5,116	5,136	5,154
Spain	19,025	19,269	19,607	20,082	20,450	20,802	21,173	21,561	21,930	22,222
Sweden	4,212	4,356	4,380	4,408	4,427	4,447	4,466	4,487	4,521	4,544
Switzerland	3,258	3,428	3,501	3,544	3,575	3,602	3,629	3,653	3,669	3,683
Turkey	28,113	30,962	33,789	34,752	35,211	35,667	36,124	36,575	37,027	37,478
United Kingdom	27,774	28,156	28,634	28,898	29,036	29,193	29,395	29,578	29,755	29,927
Eastern Europe										
Albania	1,687	1,588	1,533	1,541	1,551	1,561	1,571	1,580	1,588	1,595
Belarus	4,777	4,780	4,703	4,666	4,638	4,617	4,597	4,579	4,562	4,547
Bosnia-Herzegovina	2,129	1,692	1,851	1,892	1,898	1,901	1,904	1,909	1,913	1,915
Bulgaria	4,324	4,069	3,888	3,834	3,807	3,780	3,752	3,723	3,695	3,669
Croatia	2,315	2,244	2,138	2,139	2,138	2,138	2,139	2,139	2,138	2,136
Czech Republic	4,998	5,013	4,981	4,968	4,967	4,975	4,981	5,003	5,021	5,037
Estonia	735	671	633	628	625	622	621	619	617	614
Georgia	2,595	2,391	2,238	2,185	2,159	2,136	2,114	2,093	2,074	2,056
Hungary	4,985	4,942	4,865	4,837	4,818	4,804	4,793	4,785	4,774	4,764
Latvia	1,241	1,154	1,097	1,080	1,073	1,068	1,063	1,057	1,051	1,044
Lithuania	1,747	1,717	1,644	1,624	1,617	1,609	1,598	1,587	1,577	1,567
Macedonia	958	983	1,004	1,010	1,012	1,014	1,015	1,016	1,017	1,017
Moldova	2,098	2,098	1,985	1,930	1,903	1,878	1,855	1,834	1,815	1,799
Poland	18,516	18,602	18,550	18,525	18,507	18,486	18,470	18,454	18,422	18,390
Romania	11,451	10,938	10,724	10,664	10,628	10,592	10,562	10,535	10,499	10,467
Russia	69,115	69,659	68,698	67,922	67,491	67,024	66,603	66,164	65,758	65,365
Serbia and Montenegro	5,044	5,372	5,360	5,283	5,238	5,200	5,174	5,163	5,165	5,177
Slovakia	2,578	2,605	2,614	2,612	2,611	2,611	2,613	2,616	2,618	2,619
Slovenia	968	964	971	975	976	977	977	981	986	990
Ukraine	23,826	23,792	22,755	22,316	22,113	21,927	21,754	21,575	21,435	21,294

Source: *Euromonitor International from national statistics/UN*

Total Population: National Estimates at January 1st | **Table 21.23**

Number of Females, 1990-2008 at January 1st
'000

	1990	1995	2000	2002	2003	2004	2005	2006	2007	2008
Western Europe										
Austria	3,990	4,112	4,134	4,158	4,173	4,190	4,220	4,247	4,269	4,287
Belgium	5,088	5,176	5,233	5,267	5,289	5,309	5,335	5,368	5,396	5,419
Cyprus	341	366	399	412	418	424	429	434	439	443
Denmark	2,605	2,642	2,696	2,714	2,721	2,728	2,734	2,742	2,751	2,758
Finland	2,562	2,617	2,648	2,657	2,661	2,667	2,675	2,683	2,693	2,702
France	29,033	29,674	30,257	30,643	30,836	31,022	31,211	31,387	31,567	31,744
Germany	41,003	41,894	42,073	42,166	42,192	42,176	42,147	42,098	42,012	41,942
Gibraltar	13	14	14	14	14	14	15	15	15	15
Greece	5,139	5,352	5,504	5,539	5,558	5,576	5,596	5,617	5,640	5,663
Iceland	127	133	140	143	145	146	147	149	150	151
Ireland	1,764	1,810	1,901	1,962	1,994	2,025	2,062	2,107	2,152	2,191
Italy	29,167	29,276	29,363	29,407	29,555	29,820	30,086	30,225	30,284	30,318
Liechtenstein	15	16	17	17	17	17	18	18	18	18
Luxembourg	195	208	222	226	227	229	231	234	236	239
Malta	182	191	196	199	200	201	203	204	204	205
Monaco	16	17	17	17	17	17	17	17	17	17
Netherlands	7,534	7,797	8,018	8,133	8,177	8,212	8,240	8,257	8,269	8,281
Norway	2,140	2,198	2,261	2,282	2,296	2,308	2,322	2,338	2,352	2,366
Portugal	5,177	5,191	5,277	5,340	5,377	5,408	5,435	5,454	5,473	5,489
Spain	19,802	20,075	20,443	20,883	21,213	21,543	21,865	22,197	22,555	22,835
Sweden	4,315	4,460	4,481	4,501	4,514	4,529	4,545	4,561	4,592	4,613
Switzerland	3,416	3,591	3,664	3,711	3,739	3,763	3,786	3,807	3,828	3,848
Turkey	27,382	30,242	33,100	34,086	34,559	35,025	35,486	35,950	36,416	36,880
United Kingdom	29,383	29,787	30,151	30,320	30,402	30,507	30,665	30,815	30,952	31,088
Eastern Europe										
Albania	1,602	1,562	1,547	1,557	1,564	1,573	1,583	1,592	1,602	1,613
Belarus	5,411	5,431	5,316	5,284	5,261	5,242	5,223	5,205	5,188	5,172
Bosnia-Herzegovina	2,179	1,730	1,936	1,989	1,999	2,005	2,011	2,017	2,022	2,025
Bulgaria	4,444	4,234	4,091	4,043	4,020	3,999	3,976	3,953	3,928	3,903
Croatia	2,463	2,425	2,304	2,305	2,304	2,304	2,305	2,303	2,302	2,299
Czech Republic	5,302	5,304	5,256	5,238	5,237	5,237	5,240	5,248	5,266	5,280
Estonia	836	777	739	734	731	729	727	725	723	721
Georgia	2,865	2,642	2,482	2,429	2,404	2,381	2,360	2,340	2,321	2,304
Hungary	5,390	5,395	5,356	5,338	5,324	5,313	5,304	5,292	5,284	5,275
Latvia	1,428	1,346	1,285	1,266	1,258	1,251	1,244	1,237	1,230	1,222
Lithuania	1,946	1,926	1,868	1,851	1,845	1,837	1,827	1,817	1,808	1,799
Macedonia	951	981	1,005	1,012	1,015	1,017	1,019	1,020	1,022	1,023
Moldova	2,291	2,281	2,161	2,103	2,074	2,047	2,022	1,999	1,979	1,961
Poland	19,472	19,663	19,713	19,717	19,712	19,704	19,704	19,703	19,680	19,655
Romania	11,761	11,347	11,205	11,169	11,145	11,119	11,097	11,075	11,056	11,030
Russia	78,550	78,801	78,192	77,727	77,473	77,144	76,871	76,590	76,296	76,022
Serbia and Montenegro	5,112	5,447	5,441	5,380	5,346	5,317	5,297	5,289	5,291	5,301
Slovakia	2,692	2,743	2,764	2,767	2,768	2,769	2,771	2,773	2,774	2,774
Slovenia	1,028	1,025	1,017	1,019	1,019	1,020	1,021	1,022	1,024	1,026
Ukraine	27,730	27,508	26,360	25,925	25,711	25,515	25,346	25,175	25,031	24,898

Source: *Euromonitor International from national statistics/UN*

Table 21.24

Number of Children Aged 0-14 Years, 1990-2008 at January 1st
'000

	1990	1995	2000	2002	2003	2004	2005	2006	2007	2008
Western Europe										
Austria	1,340	1,417	1,372	1,346	1,339	1,329	1,323	1,313	1,300	1,287
Belgium	1,801	1,827	1,805	1,805	1,803	1,797	1,795	1,796	1,795	1,795
Cyprus	176	184	178	173	171	169	166	164	162	160
Denmark	881	901	981	1,005	1,013	1,018	1,018	1,016	1,015	1,009
Finland	962	972	943	932	927	920	915	907	901	895
France	11,389	11,330	11,096	11,152	11,171	11,189	11,204	11,228	11,272	11,327
Germany	12,639	13,294	12,897	12,619	12,416	12,162	11,925	11,650	11,448	11,270
Gibraltar	5	5	5	5	5	5	5	5	5	5
Greece	1,984	1,850	1,682	1,626	1,610	1,599	1,598	1,594	1,594	1,596
Iceland	64	65	65	66	66	65	65	65	65	64
Ireland	959	883	829	827	832	841	851	862	878	893
Italy	9,522	8,402	8,151	8,109	8,147	8,190	8,256	8,284	8,272	8,246
Liechtenstein	6	6	6	6	6	6	6	6	6	6
Luxembourg	66	74	82	84	84	84	85	85	85	85
Malta	85	83	78	75	73	72	70	69	67	66
Monaco	4	4	4	4	4	4	4	4	4	5
Netherlands	2,715	2,838	2,946	2,998	3,010	3,016	3,009	2,985	2,959	2,934
Norway	801	845	895	906	910	911	909	907	904	900
Portugal	2,081	1,796	1,655	1,640	1,646	1,649	1,647	1,644	1,643	1,644
Spain	7,856	6,657	5,965	5,960	6,049	6,151	6,241	6,342	6,481	6,610
Sweden	1,522	1,663	1,640	1,620	1,612	1,599	1,584	1,561	1,546	1,529
Switzerland	1,137	1,237	1,249	1,225	1,222	1,214	1,205	1,194	1,181	1,167
Turkey	19,417	19,664	20,131	20,370	20,447	20,492	20,503	20,530	20,515	20,467
United Kingdom	10,833	11,292	11,244	11,061	10,970	10,892	10,848	10,766	10,718	10,685
Eastern Europe										
Albania	1,078	1,025	970	916	884	854	829	809	794	784
Belarus	2,351	2,252	1,898	1,745	1,670	1,595	1,530	1,476	1,433	1,395
Bosnia-Herzegovina	1,042	744	690	692	693	692	688	680	669	654
Bulgaria	1,801	1,506	1,267	1,179	1,141	1,102	1,069	1,041	1,018	1,000
Croatia	952	858	760	748	736	723	712	703	693	687
Czech Republic	2,239	1,945	1,700	1,622	1,590	1,554	1,527	1,501	1,483	1,470
Estonia	350	302	251	234	225	216	208	202	199	197
Georgia	1,343	1,187	1,019	948	912	878	845	814	784	757
Hungary	2,131	1,892	1,729	1,660	1,634	1,606	1,580	1,553	1,529	1,510
Latvia	572	522	428	390	373	357	341	329	318	310
Lithuania	834	798	710	660	633	609	585	560	538	516
Macedonia	499	483	444	427	419	410	401	392	382	373
Moldova	1,240	1,192	1,006	910	862	816	776	742	713	690
Poland	9,600	8,849	7,480	7,039	6,804	6,580	6,377	6,189	6,012	5,865
Romania	5,508	4,694	4,126	3,857	3,708	3,566	3,437	3,360	3,319	3,285
Russia	34,031	32,050	27,066	24,702	23,554	22,613	21,871	21,244	20,869	20,686
Serbia and Montenegro	2,377	2,373	2,165	2,064	2,017	1,976	1,945	1,925	1,914	1,912
Slovakia	1,341	1,224	1,065	1,007	975	944	919	894	871	851
Slovenia	418	369	320	307	299	292	287	283	281	280
Ukraine	11,084	10,529	8,781	7,953	7,569	7,246	6,990	6,765	6,606	6,486

Source: Euromonitor International from national statistics/UN

Total Population: National Estimates at January 1st

Table 21.25

Number of Persons of Working Age (15-64 Years), 1990-2008 at January 1st
'000

	1990	1995	2000	2002	2003	2004	2005	2006	2007	2008
Western Europe										
Austria	5,165	5,330	5,397	5,469	5,510	5,547	5,572	5,591	5,610	5,634
Belgium	6,673	6,707	6,719	6,758	6,791	6,819	6,851	6,906	6,965	7,006
Cyprus	431	468	519	540	550	559	569	578	587	595
Denmark	3,454	3,516	3,558	3,569	3,572	3,575	3,581	3,589	3,598	3,602
Finland	3,350	3,407	3,461	3,476	3,481	3,486	3,491	3,508	3,507	3,528
France	37,317	37,736	38,311	38,779	39,037	39,301	39,533	39,785	40,066	40,285
Germany	54,680	55,702	55,915	55,756	55,682	55,510	55,209	54,918	54,602	54,468
Gibraltar	18	18	18	18	19	19	19	19	19	19
Greece	6,781	7,197	7,432	7,456	7,468	7,471	7,478	7,472	7,506	7,531
Iceland	164	172	183	188	191	193	196	198	200	202
Ireland	2,148	2,304	2,525	2,638	2,690	2,738	2,800	2,880	2,942	2,994
Italy	38,820	39,073	38,466	38,230	38,273	38,569	38,827	38,875	38,878	38,867
Liechtenstein	20	21	23	24	24	24	25	25	25	25
Luxembourg	264	277	293	298	301	304	307	311	316	320
Malta	238	251	263	270	273	276	279	282	284	285
Monaco	20	20	21	21	21	21	21	21	21	21
Netherlands	10,272	10,552	10,766	10,908	10,962	10,991	11,008	11,019	11,031	11,042
Norway	2,741	2,809	2,901	2,942	2,968	2,993	3,019	3,051	3,084	3,111
Portugal	6,593	6,747	6,905	6,981	7,026	7,064	7,091	7,115	7,140	7,152
Spain	25,755	26,740	27,379	28,053	28,571	29,050	29,569	30,108	30,558	30,864
Sweden	5,488	5,614	5,689	5,757	5,795	5,835	5,873	5,922	5,984	6,017
Switzerland	4,565	4,750	4,821	4,900	4,950	4,994	5,035	5,073	5,103	5,125
Turkey	33,565	38,532	43,177	44,704	45,445	46,189	46,940	47,746	48,603	49,479
United Kingdom	37,340	37,477	38,248	38,750	38,993	39,280	39,595	39,969	40,267	40,500
Eastern Europe										
Albania	2,036	1,928	1,884	1,942	1,983	2,025	2,060	2,088	2,110	2,127
Belarus	6,764	6,712	6,790	6,835	6,840	6,849	6,860	6,873	6,886	6,919
Bosnia-Herzegovina	3,003	2,405	2,644	2,691	2,692	2,689	2,690	2,695	2,700	2,705
Bulgaria	5,830	5,564	5,421	5,364	5,353	5,346	5,334	5,314	5,287	5,253
Croatia	3,276	3,175	2,984	2,985	2,984	2,986	2,988	2,987	2,988	2,980
Czech Republic	6,777	7,018	7,124	7,170	7,196	7,234	7,259	7,293	7,323	7,338
Estonia	1,039	953	916	917	916	917	917	917	912	909
Georgia	3,607	3,275	3,112	3,054	3,026	3,004	2,988	2,981	2,981	2,984
Hungary	6,870	6,987	6,961	6,963	6,949	6,944	6,940	6,932	6,928	6,912
Latvia	1,781	1,642	1,600	1,591	1,589	1,587	1,584	1,580	1,573	1,566
Lithuania	2,461	2,402	2,319	2,314	2,320	2,319	2,323	2,321	2,319	2,317
Macedonia	1,268	1,309	1,363	1,382	1,390	1,399	1,407	1,415	1,423	1,431
Moldova	2,785	2,786	2,727	2,703	2,692	2,681	2,672	2,664	2,658	2,651
Poland	24,607	25,230	26,164	26,392	26,527	26,659	26,778	26,892	26,992	27,082
Romania	15,319	14,912	14,873	14,933	14,975	15,012	15,047	15,053	15,038	15,025
Russia	99,056	99,008	101,761	102,551	102,532	102,264	101,916	101,637	101,295	101,268
Serbia and Montenegro	6,810	7,209	7,193	7,102	7,051	7,012	6,991	6,994	7,017	7,051
Slovakia	3,387	3,547	3,700	3,759	3,788	3,815	3,840	3,862	3,882	3,897
Slovenia	1,367	1,381	1,392	1,399	1,401	1,405	1,404	1,407	1,411	1,411
Ukraine	34,298	33,811	33,515	33,326	33,060	32,826	32,603	32,417	32,256	32,190

Source: *Euromonitor International from national statistics/UN*

Table 21.26

Total Population: National Estimates at January 1st

Number of Persons Aged 65 Years and Over, 1990-2008 at January 1st

'000

	1990	1995	2000	2002	2003	2004	2005	2006	2007	2008
Western Europe										
Austria	1,140	1,197	1,234	1,250	1,253	1,264	1,312	1,362	1,404	1,431
Belgium	1,474	1,597	1,715	1,746	1,762	1,780	1,800	1,809	1,810	1,817
Cyprus	74	79	89	94	96	99	101	104	107	109
Denmark	800	799	790	795	798	805	813	823	834	850
Finland	662	720	767	787	799	813	831	841	869	874
France	7,872	8,686	9,419	9,655	9,762	9,850	9,969	10,035	10,072	10,154
Germany	11,794	12,542	13,351	14,066	14,439	14,860	15,367	15,870	16,262	16,478
Gibraltar	3	4	4	4	5	5	5	5	5	5
Greece	1,356	1,548	1,790	1,887	1,929	1,971	2,007	2,060	2,069	2,084
Iceland	27	30	33	33	34	34	35	35	36	37
Ireland	399	411	424	435	441	449	458	467	479	492
Italy	8,352	9,371	10,313	10,655	10,901	11,128	11,379	11,592	11,737	11,863
Liechtenstein	3	3	3	4	4	4	4	4	4	4
Luxembourg	51	57	62	63	64	64	65	65	66	67
Malta	38	43	48	50	51	52	53	54	56	57
Monaco	7	7	7	7	7	7	7	7	7	7
Netherlands	1,906	2,034	2,152	2,199	2,220	2,251	2,289	2,330	2,368	2,406
Norway	691	695	683	676	674	674	678	682	684	690
Portugal	1,322	1,475	1,635	1,709	1,736	1,761	1,791	1,810	1,826	1,847
Spain	5,215	5,946	6,706	6,951	7,044	7,144	7,228	7,308	7,445	7,583
Sweden	1,518	1,540	1,533	1,532	1,534	1,541	1,554	1,565	1,583	1,611
Switzerland	972	1,032	1,094	1,131	1,142	1,157	1,174	1,192	1,213	1,239
Turkey	2,513	3,008	3,581	3,764	3,878	4,011	4,167	4,248	4,325	4,412
United Kingdom	8,984	9,175	9,293	9,407	9,475	9,528	9,617	9,658	9,722	9,830
Eastern Europe										
Albania	175	197	226	240	247	256	265	275	286	297
Belarus	1,074	1,247	1,332	1,370	1,388	1,414	1,430	1,435	1,431	1,404
Bosnia-Herzegovina	263	272	453	498	512	524	537	552	567	581
Bulgaria	1,136	1,233	1,290	1,333	1,333	1,330	1,325	1,321	1,318	1,318
Croatia	550	636	697	710	722	733	745	753	759	767
Czech Republic	1,285	1,354	1,412	1,415	1,418	1,423	1,435	1,456	1,481	1,509
Estonia	182	193	205	211	215	219	222	225	228	229
Georgia	509	570	589	612	625	636	640	638	631	620
Hungary	1,374	1,458	1,531	1,552	1,559	1,567	1,578	1,591	1,601	1,618
Latvia	315	336	353	364	370	375	381	386	390	391
Lithuania	399	443	483	502	510	518	517	522	528	534
Macedonia	142	171	202	212	217	222	226	229	233	237
Moldova	364	401	412	420	424	428	428	427	423	418
Poland	3,781	4,186	4,619	4,811	4,888	4,951	5,018	5,076	5,099	5,098
Romania	2,383	2,679	2,930	3,043	3,090	3,133	3,175	3,197	3,198	3,186
Russia	14,578	17,402	18,063	18,397	18,878	19,291	19,687	19,873	19,890	19,432
Serbia and Montenegro	969	1,237	1,442	1,496	1,516	1,528	1,534	1,533	1,525	1,514
Slovakia	541	578	613	613	616	620	626	633	639	645
Slovenia	212	240	275	289	295	300	306	313	319	325
Ukraine	6,175	6,961	6,819	6,962	7,193	7,369	7,507	7,567	7,603	7,517

Source: Euromonitor International from national statistics/UN

Total Population: National Estimates at January 1st   **Table 21.27**

Population by Age Group at January 1st 2008
'000

	0-4	5-9	10-14	15-19	20-24	25-29	30-34	35-39
Western Europe								
Austria	400.4	414.3	471.9	503.1	519.0	542.6	544.8	656.4
Belgium	598.9	588.9	607.4	650.2	634.4	676.3	677.3	754.6
Cyprus	50.8	50.5	58.2	65.7	67.1	67.0	61.7	59.4
Denmark	322.2	334.1	353.1	334.3	295.7	316.2	366.4	386.4
Finland	291.9	286.4	317.0	331.7	325.7	333.3	323.6	323.9
France	3,856.2	3,824.2	3,646.7	3,878.2	3,879.7	3,976.0	3,981.5	4,369.6
Germany	3,436.0	3,817.1	4,017.1	4,651.3	4,843.4	4,985.4	4,713.3	6,045.7
Gibraltar								
Greece	537.6	514.5	544.0	585.6	669.9	822.0	870.7	881.8
Iceland	21.2	20.9	22.3	22.7	21.5	21.5	21.4	20.9
Ireland	315.5	298.4	278.8	287.5	327.8	400.4	361.9	335.4
Italy	2,746.9	2,747.6	2,751.4	2,944.4	3,029.2	3,546.2	4,395.9	4,762.9
Liechtenstein								
Luxembourg	27.2	28.6	29.6	28.9	28.6	30.4	33.9	38.2
Malta	19.7	21.4	25.0	27.6	30.1	31.7	31.0	26.6
Monaco								
Netherlands	945.6	1,010.6	978.2	1,003.5	974.8	986.0	1,022.1	1,273.0
Norway	287.3	298.6	314.3	315.9	282.0	289.8	316.8	358.2
Portugal	547.2	555.4	540.9	580.0	650.3	776.0	853.4	803.2
Spain	2,371.0	2,163.8	2,074.7	2,259.3	2,708.0	3,568.9	3,990.0	3,794.6
Sweden	514.4	475.0	539.8	635.7	551.0	547.0	590.0	624.6
Switzerland	364.8	381.6	420.2	452.6	447.1	474.7	503.9	580.0
Turkey	6,463.1	6,963.7	7,040.2	6,465.1	6,385.1	6,768.9	6,592.8	5,723.4
United Kingdom	3,589.8	3,409.2	3,686.1	3,993.7	4,106.4	3,993.2	3,841.5	4,491.6
Eastern Europe								
Albania	250.7	251.9	281.0	314.0	293.6	239.1	208.8	198.4
Belarus	430.4	457.7	507.4	715.8	840.7	759.6	692.7	678.6
Bosnia-Herzegovina	181.9	224.7	247.5	255.2	278.2	282.7	308.2	297.5
Bulgaria	334.6	325.4	340.3	466.0	518.3	549.3	580.6	549.4
Croatia	208.5	223.6	255.3	264.7	295.5	315.0	302.6	293.8
Czech Republic	503.6	457.3	508.9	646.4	681.1	793.1	924.1	736.4
Estonia	70.2	62.0	65.0	97.2	106.0	97.2	92.0	92.5
Georgia	229.3	239.8	287.9	362.4	362.8	317.3	296.0	279.9
Hungary	484.8	481.9	542.8	619.1	654.6	759.3	847.2	722.7
Latvia	107.0	96.1	106.5	167.3	185.3	162.9	158.0	159.2
Lithuania	151.4	164.6	199.9	261.4	272.1	230.1	223.1	246.1
Macedonia	112.6	121.6	138.5	156.7	161.2	163.6	156.0	148.6
Moldova	208.8	218.2	263.2	351.2	385.8	301.7	237.4	213.3
Poland	1,788.6	1,860.0	2,216.8	2,710.4	3,204.0	3,167.2	2,914.8	2,476.9
Romania	1,074.9	1,085.8	1,124.5	1,485.0	1,660.7	1,710.3	1,731.6	1,811.9
Russia	7,321.0	6,479.6	6,885.7	10,195.4	12,743.6	11,446.0	10,470.2	9,673.8
Serbia and Montenegro	654.8	621.9	635.4	718.1	778.0	785.4	762.2	722.9
Slovakia	266.6	267.3	317.0	390.7	434.4	463.6	458.8	376.1
Slovenia	91.5	91.1	97.5	114.3	133.3	152.5	151.7	145.1
Ukraine	2,156.8	1,931.3	2,397.8	3,217.5	3,883.5	3,513.1	3,326.6	3,183.2

Source: *Euromonitor International from national statistics/UN*

Population by Age Group at January 1st 2008 *(continued)*

'000

	40-44	45-49	50-54	55-59	60-64	65-69	70-74	75-79	80+
Western Europe									
Austria	718.4	661.3	552.7	495.2	441.0	471.1	298.6	278.4	382.6
Belgium	807.4	799.7	738.6	677.2	590.7	462.0	450.5	406.0	498.5
Cyprus	61.9	62.1	57.5	49.1	43.3	35.3	27.9	21.7	24.4
Denmark	428.8	379.2	363.3	356.0	375.3	266.2	203.3	156.9	224.0
Finland	373.5	374.3	387.4	404.3	350.6	253.7	209.2	183.1	227.6
France	4,391.1	4,260.8	4,133.0	4,124.3	3,291.0	2,465.8	2,414.3	2,205.1	3,069.2
Germany	7,184.0	6,710.9	5,797.6	5,276.5	4,260.2	5,327.5	4,214.2	3,046.9	3,889.1
Gibraltar									
Greece	843.5	797.8	745.4	679.9	634.4	566.1	584.5	480.7	452.9
Iceland	21.0	21.7	20.1	17.4	14.1	10.4	8.5	7.8	10.1
Ireland	307.7	284.5	256.0	232.7	200.1	151.9	123.8	96.1	119.8
Italy	4,869.7	4,305.2	3,854.0	3,747.6	3,411.4	3,295.0	2,878.7	2,460.8	3,228.6
Liechtenstein									
Luxembourg	40.4	37.3	32.1	27.6	22.7	18.7	16.8	14.3	16.7
Malta	24.9	28.9	29.3	28.9	26.3	17.8	14.7	11.3	13.0
Monaco									
Netherlands	1,302.2	1,252.7	1,141.7	1,089.8	996.7	725.8	588.5	484.6	607.5
Norway	348.0	321.7	310.0	291.6	276.7	188.1	148.6	136.8	216.8
Portugal	789.6	758.6	695.8	662.2	583.2	515.8	490.9	398.0	442.2
Spain	3,596.6	3,275.6	2,824.6	2,525.4	2,321.2	1,902.8	1,887.1	1,672.0	2,120.8
Sweden	671.1	588.3	584.0	599.9	625.0	456.0	354.6	310.0	490.8
Switzerland	641.3	588.8	516.6	475.2	444.6	349.9	291.6	246.0	351.1
Turkey	4,825.0	4,239.9	3,613.8	2,790.7	2,073.8	1,670.8	1,330.9	749.9	660.7
United Kingdom	4,714.7	4,308.3	3,772.9	3,699.3	3,578.6	2,732.2	2,382.1	1,973.3	2,742.1
Eastern Europe									
Albania	212.2	217.5	183.9	140.1	119.3	111.0	82.5	54.9	49.0
Belarus	711.9	827.3	725.6	614.1	352.9	434.0	394.7	360.3	215.1
Bosnia-Herzegovina	293.7	291.5	263.7	233.3	200.9	211.3	190.3	111.3	68.3
Bulgaria	498.8	527.0	539.3	548.5	475.9	385.8	369.1	291.6	271.6
Croatia	316.5	328.7	335.4	302.7	225.5	232.9	218.1	169.1	147.1
Czech Republic	708.5	638.4	750.5	772.2	687.5	475.0	363.0	326.1	344.5
Estonia	86.9	95.9	91.5	85.9	64.4	71.4	59.2	49.5	48.5
Georgia	302.7	338.9	299.8	247.7	176.5	181.2	193.4	128.9	116.5
Hungary	626.9	629.7	790.5	691.9	570.0	498.5	407.0	340.4	371.5
Latvia	156.8	172.4	152.9	139.2	111.7	127.4	100.7	82.4	80.7
Lithuania	251.0	267.1	214.7	192.7	158.3	164.8	142.8	116.4	109.8
Macedonia	146.3	143.1	138.9	121.6	94.8	80.3	68.4	48.5	39.3
Moldova	228.7	275.5	269.2	230.5	158.0	138.1	125.4	83.1	71.4
Poland	2,382.2	2,761.9	3,024.2	2,693.5	1,746.8	1,449.7	1,369.7	1,148.5	1,130.5
Romania	1,354.1	1,352.5	1,542.0	1,388.7	988.6	981.9	913.6	695.4	595.4
Russia	9,770.7	11,902.0	10,890.8	9,295.8	4,879.4	6,555.2	5,165.6	4,178.0	3,533.2
Serbia and Montenegro	686.1	679.3	730.7	697.3	491.4	421.3	442.0	353.1	297.6
Slovakia	374.4	382.1	404.0	357.9	255.3	205.7	162.8	137.5	139.5
Slovenia	157.1	154.4	158.1	141.4	103.1	98.6	85.1	70.4	71.2
Ukraine	3,182.7	3,653.7	3,293.4	3,058.3	1,877.6	2,586.9	1,979.1	1,535.0	1,415.8

Source: Euromonitor International from national statistics/UN

Total Population: National Estimates at January 1st

Table 21.28

Population by Age Group (%) at January 1st 2008
% of total

	0-4	5-9	10-14	15-19	20-24	25-29	30-34	35-39
Western Europe								
Austria	4.79	4.96	5.65	6.02	6.21	6.50	6.52	7.86
Belgium	5.64	5.55	5.72	6.12	5.97	6.37	6.38	7.11
Cyprus	5.89	5.85	6.74	7.60	7.77	7.76	7.14	6.88
Denmark	5.90	6.12	6.47	6.12	5.41	5.79	6.71	7.08
Finland	5.51	5.41	5.98	6.26	6.15	6.29	6.11	6.11
France	6.24	6.19	5.90	6.28	6.28	6.44	6.45	7.07
Germany	4.18	4.64	4.89	5.66	5.89	6.06	5.73	7.35
Gibraltar								
Greece	4.80	4.59	4.85	5.22	5.98	7.33	7.77	7.87
Iceland	6.99	6.90	7.34	7.48	7.08	7.09	7.04	6.88
Ireland	7.21	6.82	6.37	6.57	7.49	9.14	8.27	7.66
Italy	4.66	4.66	4.67	4.99	5.14	6.01	7.45	8.08
Liechtenstein								
Luxembourg	5.77	6.05	6.27	6.13	6.05	6.44	7.17	8.09
Malta	4.83	5.25	6.13	6.75	7.36	7.75	7.59	6.52
Monaco								
Netherlands	5.77	6.17	5.97	6.13	5.95	6.02	6.24	7.77
Norway	6.11	6.35	6.69	6.72	6.00	6.16	6.74	7.62
Portugal	5.14	5.22	5.08	5.45	6.11	7.29	8.02	7.55
Spain	5.26	4.80	4.60	5.01	6.01	7.92	8.86	8.42
Sweden	5.62	5.19	5.89	6.94	6.02	5.97	6.44	6.82
Switzerland	4.84	5.07	5.58	6.01	5.94	6.30	6.69	7.70
Turkey	8.69	9.37	9.47	8.69	8.59	9.10	8.87	7.70
United Kingdom	5.88	5.59	6.04	6.55	6.73	6.54	6.30	7.36
Eastern Europe								
Albania	7.82	7.85	8.76	9.79	9.15	7.45	6.51	6.18
Belarus	4.43	4.71	5.22	7.37	8.65	7.82	7.13	6.98
Bosnia-Herzegovina	4.62	5.70	6.28	6.48	7.06	7.17	7.82	7.55
Bulgaria	4.42	4.30	4.49	6.15	6.85	7.25	7.67	7.26
Croatia	4.70	5.04	5.76	5.97	6.66	7.10	6.82	6.63
Czech Republic	4.88	4.43	4.93	6.27	6.60	7.69	8.96	7.14
Estonia	5.26	4.65	4.87	7.28	7.94	7.28	6.89	6.93
Georgia	5.26	5.50	6.60	8.31	8.32	7.28	6.79	6.42
Hungary	4.83	4.80	5.41	6.17	6.52	7.56	8.44	7.20
Latvia	4.72	4.24	4.70	7.38	8.18	7.18	6.97	7.03
Lithuania	4.50	4.89	5.94	7.76	8.08	6.83	6.63	7.31
Macedonia	5.52	5.96	6.79	7.68	7.90	8.02	7.65	7.29
Moldova	5.55	5.80	7.00	9.34	10.26	8.02	6.31	5.67
Poland	4.70	4.89	5.83	7.12	8.42	8.32	7.66	6.51
Romania	5.00	5.05	5.23	6.91	7.73	7.96	8.06	8.43
Russia	5.18	4.58	4.87	7.21	9.01	8.10	7.41	6.84
Serbia and Montenegro	6.25	5.94	6.06	6.85	7.43	7.50	7.27	6.90
Slovakia	4.94	4.96	5.88	7.24	8.05	8.60	8.51	6.97
Slovenia	4.54	4.52	4.84	5.67	6.61	7.56	7.52	7.20
Ukraine	4.67	4.18	5.19	6.97	8.41	7.61	7.20	6.89

Source: *Euromonitor International from national statistics/UN*

Total Population: National Estimates at January 1st

Population by Age Group (%) at January 1st 2008 *(continued)*
% of total

	40-44	45-49	50-54	55-59	60-64	65-69	70-74	75-79	80+
Western Europe									
Austria	8.60	7.92	6.62	5.93	5.28	5.64	3.58	3.33	4.58
Belgium	7.60	7.53	6.96	6.38	5.56	4.35	4.24	3.82	4.69
Cyprus	7.17	7.19	6.66	5.68	5.02	4.09	3.23	2.52	2.82
Denmark	7.85	6.94	6.65	6.52	6.87	4.87	3.72	2.87	4.10
Finland	7.05	7.07	7.31	7.63	6.62	4.79	3.95	3.46	4.30
France	7.11	6.90	6.69	6.68	5.33	3.99	3.91	3.57	4.97
Germany	8.74	8.16	7.05	6.42	5.18	6.48	5.13	3.71	4.73
Gibraltar									
Greece	7.52	7.12	6.65	6.06	5.66	5.05	5.21	4.29	4.04
Iceland	6.93	7.16	6.62	5.72	4.64	3.43	2.82	2.56	3.34
Ireland	7.03	6.50	5.85	5.32	4.57	3.47	2.83	2.20	2.74
Italy	8.26	7.30	6.53	6.35	5.78	5.59	4.88	4.17	5.47
Liechtenstein									
Luxembourg	8.57	7.90	6.79	5.85	4.82	3.97	3.57	3.03	3.54
Malta	6.11	7.07	7.17	7.08	6.45	4.37	3.61	2.77	3.19
Monaco									
Netherlands	7.95	7.65	6.97	6.65	6.08	4.43	3.59	2.96	3.71
Norway	7.40	6.84	6.59	6.20	5.89	4.00	3.16	2.91	4.61
Portugal	7.42	7.13	6.54	6.22	5.48	4.85	4.61	3.74	4.15
Spain	7.98	7.27	6.27	5.61	5.15	4.22	4.19	3.71	4.71
Sweden	7.33	6.42	6.38	6.55	6.83	4.98	3.87	3.39	5.36
Switzerland	8.52	7.82	6.86	6.31	5.90	4.65	3.87	3.27	4.66
Turkey	6.49	5.70	4.86	3.75	2.79	2.25	1.79	1.01	0.89
United Kingdom	7.73	7.06	6.18	6.06	5.87	4.48	3.90	3.23	4.49
Eastern Europe									
Albania	6.62	6.78	5.73	4.37	3.72	3.46	2.57	1.71	1.53
Belarus	7.32	8.51	7.47	6.32	3.63	4.47	4.06	3.71	2.21
Bosnia-Herzegovina	7.45	7.40	6.69	5.92	5.10	5.36	4.83	2.83	1.73
Bulgaria	6.59	6.96	7.12	7.24	6.29	5.10	4.87	3.85	3.59
Croatia	7.14	7.41	7.56	6.83	5.08	5.25	4.92	3.81	3.32
Czech Republic	6.87	6.19	7.27	7.48	6.66	4.60	3.52	3.16	3.34
Estonia	6.51	7.19	6.85	6.43	4.82	5.35	4.43	3.71	3.63
Georgia	6.94	7.77	6.87	5.68	4.05	4.16	4.44	2.96	2.67
Hungary	6.24	6.27	7.87	6.89	5.68	4.97	4.05	3.39	3.70
Latvia	6.92	7.61	6.75	6.14	4.93	5.62	4.44	3.63	3.56
Lithuania	7.46	7.93	6.38	5.73	4.70	4.90	4.24	3.46	3.26
Macedonia	7.17	7.01	6.81	5.96	4.65	3.94	3.35	2.38	1.93
Moldova	6.08	7.33	7.16	6.13	4.20	3.67	3.34	2.21	1.90
Poland	6.26	7.26	7.95	7.08	4.59	3.81	3.60	3.02	2.97
Romania	6.30	6.29	7.17	6.46	4.60	4.57	4.25	3.23	2.77
Russia	6.91	8.42	7.70	6.57	3.45	4.64	3.65	2.96	2.50
Serbia and Montenegro	6.55	6.48	6.97	6.66	4.69	4.02	4.22	3.37	2.84
Slovakia	6.94	7.08	7.49	6.64	4.73	3.81	3.02	2.55	2.59
Slovenia	7.79	7.66	7.84	7.01	5.11	4.89	4.22	3.49	3.53
Ukraine	6.89	7.91	7.13	6.62	4.06	5.60	4.28	3.32	3.07

Source: *Euromonitor International from national statistics/UN*

Total Population: National Estimates at January 1st

Table 21.29

Total Population 2009-2018 at January 1st
'000

	2009	2010	2011	2012	2013	2014	2015	2016	2017	2018
Western Europe										
Austria	8,383	8,409	8,434	8,459	8,484	8,507	8,530	8,553	8,574	8,595
Belgium	10,661	10,699	10,736	10,773	10,809	10,844	10,879	10,913	10,947	10,980
Cyprus	873	882	891	900	910	919	929	938	947	957
Denmark	5,475	5,488	5,501	5,512	5,523	5,534	5,545	5,555	5,566	5,577
Finland	5,315	5,332	5,349	5,366	5,382	5,399	5,415	5,431	5,446	5,461
France	62,119	62,465	62,806	63,140	63,468	63,788	64,101	64,407	64,707	65,000
Germany	82,128	82,024	81,906	81,774	81,629	81,472	81,302	81,121	80,928	80,726
Gibraltar	29	29	29	29	29	29	29	29	29	29
Greece	11,252	11,290	11,325	11,357	11,387	11,414	11,437	11,457	11,473	11,486
Iceland	306	308	311	313	316	318	320	322	324	326
Ireland	4,448	4,507	4,560	4,613	4,665	4,716	4,766	4,815	4,862	4,908
Italy	59,052	59,115	59,164	59,198	59,219	59,224	59,216	59,195	59,160	59,114
Liechtenstein	36	36	36	37	37	37	38	38	38	38
Luxembourg	478	483	489	494	499	504	510	515	521	527
Malta	410	411	413	415	416	418	420	421	422	424
Monaco	33	33	33	33	33	34	34	34	34	34
Netherlands	16,410	16,439	16,470	16,501	16,531	16,561	16,590	16,619	16,646	16,673
Norway	4,731	4,760	4,790	4,820	4,850	4,880	4,911	4,943	4,976	5,009
Portugal	10,670	10,694	10,716	10,736	10,752	10,767	10,779	10,788	10,794	10,798
Spain	45,521	45,928	46,305	46,673	47,035	47,388	47,732	48,067	48,391	48,700
Sweden	9,201	9,244	9,288	9,332	9,376	9,421	9,466	9,513	9,561	9,609
Switzerland	7,560	7,589	7,618	7,647	7,675	7,704	7,732	7,761	7,790	7,819
Turkey	75,263	76,157	77,039	77,910	78,766	79,607	80,432	81,239	82,030	82,804
United Kingdom	61,319	61,621	61,921	62,221	62,521	62,822	63,122	63,422	63,720	64,018
Eastern Europe										
Albania	3,226	3,245	3,265	3,286	3,306	3,327	3,346	3,365	3,382	3,399
Belarus	9,688	9,658	9,627	9,596	9,566	9,536	9,506	9,475	9,445	9,414
Bosnia-Herzegovina	3,943	3,942	3,937	3,930	3,921	3,910	3,899	3,887	3,875	3,862
Bulgaria	7,519	7,467	7,415	7,362	7,306	7,250	7,191	7,131	7,070	7,009
Croatia	4,429	4,421	4,413	4,404	4,394	4,384	4,374	4,363	4,351	4,340
Czech Republic	10,338	10,353	10,365	10,368	10,367	10,364	10,361	10,358	10,357	10,357
Estonia	1,331	1,326	1,322	1,317	1,312	1,307	1,302	1,298	1,293	1,289
Georgia	4,329	4,301	4,275	4,252	4,231	4,210	4,188	4,164	4,139	4,113
Hungary	10,020	10,000	9,980	9,954	9,926	9,898	9,871	9,844	9,818	9,793
Latvia	2,253	2,240	2,228	2,214	2,199	2,185	2,172	2,159	2,146	2,133
Lithuania	3,348	3,329	3,311	3,292	3,272	3,253	3,234	3,216	3,198	3,181
Macedonia	2,041	2,041	2,041	2,041	2,040	2,039	2,037	2,035	2,033	2,031
Moldova	3,731	3,707	3,688	3,675	3,664	3,655	3,645	3,634	3,622	3,609
Poland	37,990	37,929	37,871	37,813	37,751	37,689	37,631	37,575	37,522	37,473
Romania	21,435	21,370	21,302	21,232	21,145	21,056	20,953	20,844	20,733	20,621
Russia	140,762	140,181	139,640	139,139	138,679	138,261	137,865	137,489	137,137	136,795
Serbia and Montenegro	10,503	10,525	10,540	10,552	10,560	10,568	10,575	10,581	10,586	10,590
Slovakia	5,395	5,397	5,398	5,398	5,398	5,398	5,398	5,397	5,396	5,395
Slovenia	2,023	2,029	2,035	2,039	2,042	2,045	2,048	2,051	2,053	2,056
Ukraine	45,919	45,641	45,356	45,067	44,774	44,481	44,187	43,892	43,596	43,298

Source: Euromonitor International from national statistics/UN

Table 21.30

Number of Children Aged 0-14 Years, 2009-2018 at January 1st
'000

	2009	2010	2011	2012	2013	2014	2015	2016	2017	2018
Western Europe										
Austria	1,272	1,259	1,249	1,238	1,232	1,228	1,228	1,227	1,228	1,227
Belgium	1,800	1,808	1,818	1,826	1,834	1,843	1,852	1,860	1,868	1,878
Cyprus	158	157	157	157	158	159	161	163	165	167
Denmark	1,003	993	983	974	965	957	949	940	933	928
Finland	891	887	884	885	886	890	894	898	903	908
France	11,413	11,493	11,556	11,610	11,673	11,721	11,749	11,746	11,746	11,755
Germany	11,116	10,990	10,867	10,724	10,564	10,421	10,302	10,181	10,089	10,020
Gibraltar	5	5	5	5	5	5	5	5	5	5
Greece	1,602	1,606	1,609	1,615	1,621	1,630	1,637	1,640	1,640	1,638
Iceland	64	64	64	64	64	64	64	64	64	64
Ireland	907	918	928	935	940	943	945	946	947	942
Italy	8,233	8,223	8,209	8,184	8,150	8,104	8,046	7,968	7,888	7,800
Liechtenstein	6	6	6	6	6	6	6	6	6	6
Luxembourg	86	86	86	86	86	86	87	87	88	89
Malta	65	64	63	62	62	62	61	61	62	62
Monaco	5	5	5	5	5	5	5	5	5	5
Netherlands	2,911	2,886	2,867	2,847	2,826	2,799	2,771	2,738	2,711	2,686
Norway	897	893	889	884	880	879	877	876	877	880
Portugal	1,645	1,649	1,650	1,650	1,650	1,647	1,636	1,626	1,613	1,596
Spain	6,731	6,851	6,972	7,091	7,207	7,313	7,401	7,468	7,515	7,550
Sweden	1,519	1,513	1,516	1,527	1,542	1,559	1,577	1,594	1,611	1,624
Switzerland	1,156	1,145	1,137	1,128	1,122	1,117	1,115	1,118	1,122	1,128
Turkey	20,383	20,265	20,145	20,009	19,861	19,704	19,555	19,414	19,342	19,292
United Kingdom	10,668	10,664	10,671	10,676	10,690	10,722	10,772	10,842	10,923	10,996
Eastern Europe										
Albania	775	768	761	756	752	749	747	745	744	743
Belarus	1,369	1,349	1,336	1,329	1,324	1,317	1,306	1,293	1,284	1,279
Bosnia-Herzegovina	638	622	605	587	570	555	541	529	520	513
Bulgaria	986	977	973	970	971	970	961	951	939	927
Croatia	680	674	668	659	652	647	644	642	644	646
Czech Republic	1,457	1,456	1,466	1,481	1,494	1,507	1,522	1,534	1,544	1,552
Estonia	198	199	202	204	207	211	214	216	219	221
Georgia	733	714	699	688	680	673	667	660	654	647
Hungary	1,494	1,481	1,469	1,462	1,460	1,459	1,461	1,458	1,457	1,455
Latvia	307	306	308	312	317	322	326	329	332	335
Lithuania	501	491	482	475	470	465	462	460	461	463
Macedonia	364	356	349	343	338	334	329	325	322	318
Moldova	672	657	646	638	633	631	629	628	627	626
Poland	5,744	5,645	5,576	5,526	5,499	5,489	5,493	5,501	5,524	5,556
Romania	3,267	3,250	3,241	3,234	3,223	3,204	3,183	3,160	3,143	3,128
Russia	20,763	20,867	21,055	21,332	21,681	22,027	22,428	22,808	23,175	23,429
Serbia and Montenegro	1,915	1,921	1,929	1,939	1,950	1,961	1,969	1,975	1,977	1,977
Slovakia	832	820	813	807	803	801	799	799	801	804
Slovenia	280	280	281	282	283	285	287	289	291	292
Ukraine	6,402	6,340	6,289	6,241	6,212	6,183	6,169	6,155	6,148	6,131

Source: *Euromonitor International from national statistics/UN*

Total Population: National Estimates at January 1st

Table 21.31

Number of Persons of Working Age (15-64 Years), 2009-2018 at January 1st
'000

	2009	2010	2011	2012	2013	2014	2015	2016	2017	2018
Western Europe										
Austria	5,655	5,669	5,700	5,718	5,716	5,713	5,711	5,709	5,708	5,706
Belgium	7,027	7,035	7,042	7,030	7,019	7,007	6,996	6,986	6,976	6,960
Cyprus	602	610	616	622	627	631	636	640	643	647
Denmark	3,601	3,598	3,592	3,581	3,573	3,568	3,568	3,568	3,568	3,567
Finland	3,536	3,540	3,529	3,507	3,483	3,456	3,433	3,411	3,393	3,372
France	40,438	40,583	40,742	40,731	40,677	40,629	40,602	40,600	40,626	40,634
Germany	54,314	54,152	54,212	54,206	54,121	53,961	53,704	53,421	53,117	52,778
Gibraltar	19	19	19	19	19	19	19	19	19	19
Greece	7,557	7,562	7,559	7,541	7,527	7,519	7,518	7,497	7,484	7,471
Iceland	204	206	207	208	209	210	211	211	212	212
Ireland	3,036	3,071	3,100	3,128	3,158	3,187	3,217	3,246	3,274	3,305
Italy	38,836	38,807	38,794	38,617	38,449	38,274	38,141	38,025	37,934	37,847
Liechtenstein	25	26	26	26	26	26	27	27	27	27
Luxembourg	325	329	333	337	341	345	349	352	356	359
Malta	286	287	287	286	286	285	284	283	282	281
Monaco	21	21	21	21	21	21	21	21	22	22
Netherlands	11,043	11,039	11,040	10,974	10,919	10,882	10,854	10,836	10,816	10,786
Norway	3,133	3,151	3,167	3,178	3,191	3,204	3,218	3,233	3,248	3,259
Portugal	7,154	7,148	7,139	7,135	7,125	7,106	7,097	7,081	7,067	7,053
Spain	31,081	31,234	31,344	31,440	31,530	31,626	31,730	31,841	31,965	32,086
Sweden	6,036	6,040	6,036	6,023	6,008	5,993	5,981	5,976	5,977	5,980
Switzerland	5,139	5,149	5,158	5,163	5,167	5,167	5,169	5,167	5,167	5,163
Turkey	50,363	51,241	52,133	53,030	53,923	54,800	55,643	56,419	57,093	57,714
United Kingdom	40,672	40,812	40,928	40,962	40,936	40,942	40,969	40,999	41,030	41,068
Eastern Europe										
Albania	2,143	2,159	2,178	2,196	2,214	2,230	2,244	2,255	2,263	2,270
Belarus	6,964	7,002	7,035	7,046	7,023	7,006	6,958	6,918	6,884	6,852
Bosnia-Herzegovina	2,710	2,715	2,719	2,723	2,725	2,726	2,722	2,715	2,704	2,690
Bulgaria	5,215	5,171	5,115	5,048	4,976	4,903	4,832	4,757	4,696	4,632
Croatia	2,980	2,982	2,991	2,990	2,983	2,972	2,955	2,935	2,915	2,890
Czech Republic	7,333	7,308	7,276	7,205	7,128	7,057	6,992	6,925	6,862	6,804
Estonia	907	902	898	890	881	871	860	852	843	835
Georgia	2,986	2,985	2,979	2,969	2,955	2,938	2,919	2,897	2,872	2,844
Hungary	6,896	6,870	6,858	6,834	6,789	6,736	6,680	6,623	6,569	6,519
Latvia	1,557	1,547	1,536	1,522	1,505	1,486	1,467	1,451	1,435	1,419
Lithuania	2,311	2,305	2,294	2,284	2,271	2,256	2,238	2,218	2,197	2,175
Macedonia	1,437	1,442	1,445	1,446	1,446	1,445	1,442	1,438	1,432	1,426
Moldova	2,645	2,639	2,632	2,624	2,615	2,603	2,588	2,568	2,544	2,519
Poland	27,147	27,179	27,181	27,060	26,878	26,653	26,412	26,149	25,862	25,565
Romania	15,005	14,963	14,938	14,871	14,797	14,710	14,570	14,429	14,291	14,143
Russia	101,337	101,356	101,147	100,400	99,491	98,633	97,473	96,419	95,402	94,431
Serbia and Montenegro	7,084	7,105	7,112	7,108	7,095	7,075	7,051	7,022	6,989	6,955
Slovakia	3,912	3,916	3,919	3,916	3,903	3,885	3,865	3,837	3,802	3,765
Slovenia	1,411	1,414	1,419	1,417	1,412	1,405	1,398	1,389	1,380	1,369
Ukraine	32,191	32,126	32,122	31,926	31,685	31,335	30,875	30,465	30,062	29,719

Source: Euromonitor International from national statistics/UN

Table 21.32

Number of Persons Aged 65 Years and Over, 2009-2018 at January 1st

'000

	2009	2010	2011	2012	2013	2014	2015	2016	2017	2018
Western Europe										
Austria	1,456	1,481	1,485	1,502	1,535	1,566	1,592	1,616	1,637	1,662
Belgium	1,834	1,856	1,877	1,917	1,955	1,994	2,031	2,067	2,102	2,142
Cyprus	112	115	118	121	125	129	132	136	139	143
Denmark	871	897	926	957	986	1,009	1,028	1,048	1,064	1,082
Finland	889	906	936	974	1,013	1,052	1,088	1,121	1,151	1,182
France	10,268	10,390	10,508	10,799	11,118	11,439	11,751	12,061	12,334	12,611
Germany	16,698	16,881	16,826	16,845	16,944	17,090	17,296	17,519	17,722	17,929
Gibraltar	5	5	5	5	5	5	5	5	5	5
Greece	2,093	2,122	2,156	2,201	2,239	2,265	2,282	2,320	2,349	2,377
Iceland	38	39	40	41	42	44	45	47	48	50
Ireland	505	518	533	550	567	586	605	623	642	662
Italy	11,983	12,085	12,161	12,397	12,619	12,847	13,030	13,201	13,338	13,467
Liechtenstein	4	5	5	5	5	5	5	5	5	5
Luxembourg	67	68	69	70	72	73	74	76	77	79
Malta	59	61	63	66	69	72	74	77	79	81
Monaco	7	7	7	8	8	8	8	8	8	8
Netherlands	2,456	2,514	2,563	2,679	2,787	2,881	2,965	3,045	3,120	3,201
Norway	700	716	734	757	778	798	816	834	851	870
Portugal	1,871	1,897	1,927	1,950	1,977	2,014	2,046	2,081	2,115	2,150
Spain	7,709	7,843	7,989	8,142	8,298	8,449	8,601	8,758	8,911	9,065
Sweden	1,646	1,691	1,736	1,782	1,825	1,868	1,908	1,943	1,973	2,004
Switzerland	1,265	1,294	1,323	1,355	1,387	1,419	1,448	1,476	1,501	1,529
Turkey	4,517	4,651	4,762	4,871	4,981	5,103	5,234	5,406	5,595	5,798
United Kingdom	9,979	10,145	10,323	10,583	10,895	11,157	11,380	11,581	11,768	11,954
Eastern Europe										
Albania	308	318	326	333	340	347	355	365	375	386
Belarus	1,356	1,306	1,256	1,221	1,219	1,213	1,242	1,263	1,277	1,284
Bosnia-Herzegovina	594	605	613	620	625	630	636	643	650	659
Bulgaria	1,319	1,319	1,327	1,345	1,358	1,376	1,398	1,423	1,435	1,449
Croatia	769	765	754	755	760	765	775	785	792	803
Czech Republic	1,548	1,589	1,623	1,682	1,745	1,800	1,848	1,899	1,951	2,001
Estonia	226	224	222	223	224	225	228	230	232	234
Georgia	610	602	597	595	596	599	602	607	614	621
Hungary	1,629	1,649	1,653	1,658	1,678	1,703	1,729	1,763	1,792	1,820
Latvia	390	387	383	379	378	378	379	378	379	379
Lithuania	537	534	535	533	531	532	535	538	541	544
Macedonia	240	244	247	251	255	260	266	272	279	287
Moldova	414	412	411	413	416	421	429	439	451	464
Poland	5,099	5,105	5,113	5,227	5,375	5,547	5,726	5,924	6,136	6,351
Romania	3,163	3,156	3,123	3,127	3,125	3,142	3,200	3,255	3,299	3,350
Russia	18,663	17,959	17,439	17,407	17,506	17,601	17,964	18,262	18,560	18,934
Serbia and Montenegro	1,504	1,499	1,499	1,505	1,515	1,532	1,555	1,584	1,619	1,658
Slovakia	651	660	666	675	692	712	734	761	792	825
Slovenia	332	335	335	340	347	355	363	373	383	394
Ukraine	7,326	7,175	6,945	6,900	6,877	6,963	7,143	7,272	7,385	7,448

Source: Euromonitor International from national statistics/UN

Retailing

Retail Industry
Table 22.1

Total Retail Sales 2000-2007
US$ billion

	2000	2001	2002	2003	2004	2005	2006	2007
Western Europe								
Austria	45.3	44.7	47.2	57.0	63.5	64.5	66.0	67.3
Belgium	51.4	50.7	55.0	68.5	78.2	80.5	83.4	85.8
Denmark	22.8	22.8	24.6	31.3	35.6	37.2	40.1	41.2
Finland	21.9	22.6	25.0	31.2	35.6	37.4	40.0	42.3
France	309.2	311.5	336.5	413.4	461.5	466.4	480.2	493.0
Germany	323.5	318.4	333.5	408.1	455.3	464.0	479.7	489.6
Greece	24.3	25.0	27.7	35.6	41.7	43.8	45.9	47.4
Ireland	22.0	22.4	24.3	29.9	34.2	36.1	38.0	40.0
Italy	213.9	213.5	230.3	283.1	318.5	325.3	332.0	339.6
Netherlands	65.8	67.6	73.8	88.1	95.8	94.3	99.0	103.7
Norway	25.2	25.3	29.9	35.2	38.3	41.9	44.2	47.6
Portugal	25.5	25.1	28.0	34.6	38.3	40.0	41.5	42.9
Spain	142.4	143.0	164.0	206.1	237.0	247.8	259.7	266.3
Sweden	40.0	37.0	40.6	50.9	57.4	58.2	62.2	61.1
Switzerland	53.1	53.1	58.5	67.7	73.3	73.9	74.9	75.0
Turkey	77.8	79.7	84.2	91.0	100.8	111.2	113.8	134.8
United Kingdom	331.2	325.8	354.9	408.6	487.3	497.6	523.3	527.3
Eastern Europe								
Bulgaria	3.9	4.2	5.2	6.7	7.9	8.4	9.1	9.3
Czech Republic	13.7	14.7	17.6	21.1	23.8	26.4	28.9	30.1
Hungary	13.2	14.0	16.7	20.8	24.8	26.5	26.7	26.8
Poland	52.1	57.8	61.0	66.6	72.4	83.8	89.2	93.8
Romania	9.4	8.8	8.9	10.1	11.9	15.4	18.7	23.7
Russia	56.4	68.8	78.8	98.4	127.3	158.0	198.9	241.4
Slovakia	6.0	5.9	6.2	8.1	9.7	11.1	12.9	13.4
Ukraine	14.3	15.8	18.0	20.6	23.3	27.3	31.4	36.8

Source: Euromonitor International from national sources

Table 22.2

Store-based Retailer Sales by Type 2007
US$ billion

	Grocery Retailers	Non-Grocery Retailers	Total
Western Europe			
Austria	26.5	38.5	65.0
Belgium	41.3	42.6	84.0
Denmark	20.7	20.0	40.7
Finland	18.2	22.6	40.8
France	264.4	209.0	473.4
Germany	216.2	227.4	443.7
Greece	18.9	28.2	47.2
Ireland	17.9	21.1	39.0
Italy	136.3	195.8	332.2
Netherlands	41.3	58.5	99.8
Norway	23.3	22.4	45.7
Portugal	22.2	19.7	41.9
Spain	119.5	140.8	260.2
Sweden	29.6	29.8	59.4
Switzerland	35.3	36.6	71.9
Turkey	63.9	69.4	133.3
United Kingdom	242.4	244.1	486.5
Eastern Europe			
Bulgaria	3.7	5.5	9.2
Czech Republic	13.1	15.8	28.9
Hungary	14.2	12.0	26.3
Poland	44.2	47.9	92.1
Romania	12.9	10.4	23.3
Russia	126.9	107.0	233.9
Slovakia	6.7	6.4	13.1
Ukraine	20.2	15.3	35.5

Source: Euromonitor International from national sources

Table 22.3

Number of Store-based Retailers by Type 2007
No of outlets

	Grocery Retailers	Non-Grocery Retailers	Total
Western Europe			
Austria	16,908	35,255	52,163
Belgium	25,301	49,733	75,034
Denmark	9,666	14,634	24,299
Finland	6,943	22,058	29,001
France	138,718	267,780	406,498
Germany	111,780	170,058	281,838
Greece	40,114	106,910	147,024
Ireland	8,866	14,775	23,641
Italy	268,555	661,987	930,542
Netherlands	34,049	70,542	104,591
Norway	9,793	22,004	31,797
Portugal	41,230	46,567	87,797
Spain	160,989	395,161	556,150
Sweden	13,417	35,142	48,559
Switzerland	17,384	31,384	48,768
Turkey	257,077	250,262	507,339
United Kingdom	97,499	197,625	295,124
Eastern Europe			
Bulgaria	37,129	47,573	84,702
Czech Republic	20,390	66,835	87,225
Hungary	31,947	101,149	133,096
Poland	167,736	165,641	333,377
Romania	75,434	61,977	137,411
Russia	322,467	163,970	486,437
Slovakia	27,559	16,585	44,144
Ukraine	59,760	61,683	121,443

Source: *Euromonitor International from national sources*

Table 22.4

Sales of Grocery Retailers by Type (% Analysis) 2007

% of total

	Hypermarkets	Supermarkets	Discounters	Small grocery retailers	Food/drink tobacco specialists	Other grocery retailers	Total
Western Europe							
Austria	5.86	38.45	20.38	15.25	11.12	8.94	100.00
Belgium	9.62	48.21	11.34	16.18	13.58	1.07	100.00
Denmark	30.05	29.13	23.37	11.23	5.80	0.43	100.00
Finland	27.42	31.28	3.08	28.66	6.80	2.77	100.00
France	41.06	30.97	5.53	5.49	16.13	0.83	100.00
Germany	18.53	26.67	35.20	11.55	6.83	1.24	100.00
Greece	5.44	50.47	5.65	22.99	12.40	3.05	100.00
Ireland	0.64	45.61	3.76	41.18	8.24	0.57	100.00
Italy	19.09	32.83	7.57	24.46	15.68	0.36	100.00
Netherlands	2.32	61.59	12.65	9.98	9.10	4.35	100.00
Norway	8.77	31.01	38.17	12.36	8.63	1.07	100.00
Portugal	29.60	27.83	11.42	8.23	18.75	4.18	100.00
Spain	17.02	46.48	6.75	4.61	22.62	2.52	100.00
Sweden	17.37	45.95	10.28	10.96	14.56	0.88	100.00
Switzerland	16.38	53.69	7.81	10.82	11.16	0.14	100.00
Turkey	5.04	26.49	8.36	39.02	21.09		100.00
United Kingdom	33.58	34.68	2.82	19.28	8.13	1.51	100.00
Eastern Europe							
Bulgaria	10.85	17.32		51.81	15.89	4.14	100.00
Czech Republic	36.30	12.53	15.24	3.79	10.07	22.07	100.00
Hungary	27.37	7.79	11.70	40.83	11.82	0.50	100.00
Poland	15.20	13.02	10.56	48.53	7.09	5.60	100.00
Romania	12.03	11.86	7.16	26.09	9.21	33.65	100.00
Russia	6.74	31.62	9.51	31.93	2.24	17.96	100.00
Slovakia	22.75	23.80	4.42	23.92	3.51	21.60	100.00
Ukraine	11.93	46.10	2.00	4.74	3.24	31.99	100.00

Source: Euromonitor International from national sources

Retailers

Table 22.5

Sales of Non-Grocery Retailers by Type (% Analysis) 2007

% of total

	Department stores	Variety stores	Mass merchandisers	Health and beauty retailers
Western Europe				
Austria		0.76		14.73
Belgium	3.01	2.06		19.64
Denmark	3.58	2.31		12.50
Finland	7.41	5.20	0.83	14.64
France	2.40	2.34		24.91
Germany	5.38	2.42		28.20
Greece	1.56	5.44		19.19
Ireland	9.60	17.22		13.54
Italy	1.45	1.01		17.25
Netherlands	5.86	3.42		19.19
Norway	0.34	2.51		12.69
Portugal	2.05			24.88
Spain	8.53			21.24
Sweden	2.97	0.12	3.74	16.18
Switzerland	11.68	1.22		16.34
Turkey	1.90	0.01		10.54
United Kingdom	11.78	5.52	1.30	9.54
Eastern Europe				
Bulgaria		0.11		17.47
Czech Republic	3.71	7.67		15.30
Hungary	1.31	8.69		15.72
Poland	4.68	0.85		17.65
Romania	1.89			18.70
Russia	7.98			13.31
Slovakia	3.26	6.31		31.81
Ukraine		1.69		20.80

Source: *Euromonitor International from national sources*

Sales of Non-Grocery Retailers by Type (% Analysis) 2007 *(continued)*

% of total

	Clothing and footwear retailers	Home furniture and household goods retailers	Durable goods retailers	Leisure and personal goods retailers	Other non-grocery retailers	Total
Western Europe						
Austria	14.63	27.93	12.89	14.87	14.19	100.00
Belgium	18.62	23.83	11.07	16.21	5.54	100.00
Denmark	22.20	28.52	12.01	16.78	2.09	100.00
Finland	8.83	29.03	16.72	10.20	7.16	100.00
France	14.56	20.89	11.21	17.31	6.39	100.00
Germany	16.93	21.86	10.37	13.69	1.15	100.00
Greece	9.03	17.40	17.24	18.48	11.65	100.00
Ireland	18.57	21.36	2.90	14.34	2.47	100.00
Italy	26.39	17.86	7.11	11.16	17.77	100.00
Netherlands	17.97	24.09	9.03	15.69	4.75	100.00
Norway	21.40	31.83	13.85	16.14	1.24	100.00
Portugal	22.11	19.90	11.44	18.59	1.03	100.00
Spain	16.44	17.53	6.12	26.95	3.18	100.00
Sweden	18.74	26.84	10.89	14.82	5.69	100.00
Switzerland	20.01	12.52	8.23	14.49	15.52	100.00
Turkey	20.63	18.67	18.98	29.27		100.00
United Kingdom	23.53	17.54	8.80	18.21	3.78	100.00
Eastern Europe						
Bulgaria	26.62	29.02	11.03	12.25	3.50	100.00
Czech Republic	15.65	16.68	10.11	10.13	20.76	100.00
Hungary	12.22	21.51	11.15	19.46	9.93	100.00
Poland	11.56	35.25	11.68	14.14	4.20	100.00
Romania	5.62	17.49	19.39	19.93	16.97	100.00
Russia	12.05	16.04	29.39	12.70	8.52	100.00
Slovakia	18.09	17.48	5.43	17.29	0.32	100.00
Ukraine	33.20	11.19	14.27	10.00	8.85	100.00

Source: Euromonitor International from national sources

Retailers

Table 22.6

Non-Store Retail Sales by Type 2007
US$ billion

	Vending	Home shopping	Internet retailing	Direct selling	Total
Western Europe					
Austria	0.13	1.09	0.61	0.43	2.27
Belgium	0.58	0.31	0.77	0.13	1.80
Denmark	0.07	0.15	0.19	0.07	0.47
Finland	0.13	0.56	0.66	0.14	1.49
France	0.69	7.00	10.27	1.67	19.63
Germany	4.46	22.43	15.24	3.77	45.90
Greece	0.01	0.02	0.01	0.15	0.18
Ireland	0.24	0.20	0.44	0.06	0.94
Italy	1.88	1.03	1.83	2.74	7.48
Netherlands	0.51	1.00	2.18	0.17	3.86
Norway	0.05	1.00	0.69	0.16	1.90
Portugal	0.35	0.29	0.15	0.14	0.93
Spain	2.69	0.53	2.19	0.64	6.05
Sweden	0.05	0.79	0.70	0.15	1.70
Switzerland	0.60	1.16	1.08	0.21	3.05
Turkey	0.02		0.84	0.70	1.56
United Kingdom	2.48	12.62	24.17	1.46	40.72
Eastern Europe					
Bulgaria	0.01	0.00	0.02	0.09	0.11
Czech Republic	0.05	0.23	0.63	0.29	1.21
Hungary	0.03	0.11	0.13	0.24	0.52
Poland	0.06	0.13	0.96	0.60	1.75
Romania	0.00	0.03	0.01	0.32	0.36
Russia	0.35	2.05	1.99	3.07	7.47
Slovakia	0.03	0.12	0.04	0.11	0.30
Ukraine	0.01	0.03	0.76	0.53	1.32

Source: *Euromonitor International from national sources*

Table 22.7

Non-Store Retail Sales by Type (% Analysis) 2007

% of total

	Vending	Home shopping	Internet retailing	Direct selling	Total
Western Europe					
Austria	5.9	48.1	27.1	18.9	100.0
Belgium	32.5	17.3	42.9	7.3	100.0
Denmark	14.1	30.9	40.4	14.5	100.0
Finland	8.7	37.3	44.6	9.4	100.0
France	3.5	35.7	52.3	8.5	100.0
Germany	9.7	48.9	33.2	8.2	100.0
Greece	4.3	10.3	3.8	81.5	100.0
Ireland	25.7	21.3	46.7	6.2	100.0
Italy	25.1	13.8	24.5	36.6	100.0
Netherlands	13.1	26.0	56.4	4.5	100.0
Norway	2.7	52.7	36.1	8.5	100.0
Portugal	37.7	31.2	16.2	14.9	100.0
Spain	44.5	8.7	36.2	10.6	100.0
Sweden	3.0	46.7	41.2	9.0	100.0
Switzerland	19.6	38.0	35.5	6.9	100.0
Turkey	1.3		53.8	44.8	100.0
United Kingdom	6.1	31.0	59.4	3.6	100.0
Eastern Europe					
Bulgaria	9.1	2.3	13.4	75.2	100.0
Czech Republic	4.6	19.0	52.3	24.1	100.0
Hungary	6.7	20.4	25.5	47.4	100.0
Poland	3.3	7.5	54.8	34.3	100.0
Romania	0.2	7.6	4.0	88.2	100.0
Russia	4.7	27.5	26.7	41.1	100.0
Slovakia	11.1	39.4	14.1	35.4	100.0
Ukraine	0.6	2.0	57.4	40.0	100.0

Source: Euromonitor International from national sources

Travel and Tourism

Length of Tourist Stay

Table 23.1

Average Tourist Stay in Accommodation Establishments 1990-2007

Nights

	1990	1995	2000	2001	2002	2003	2004	2005	2006	2007
Western Europe										
Austria	4.90	4.80	4.00	3.80	3.86	3.81	3.72	3.69	3.60	3.54
Belgium										
Cyprus	12.80	11.02	11.00	6.80	6.70	6.48	6.73	6.79	6.32	6.30
Denmark										
Finland		1.84	1.90	1.88	1.90	1.89	1.83	1.84	1.82	1.81
France			1.88	1.89	1.90	1.87	1.82	1.81	1.82	1.83
Germany	2.20	2.39	2.32	2.33	2.31	2.29	2.25	2.22	2.19	2.17
Gibraltar										
Greece										
Iceland			1.86	1.85	1.80	1.80	1.80	1.80	1.80	1.80
Ireland										
Italy	4.27	4.29	4.23	4.28	4.21	4.16	4.02	4.02	3.94	3.90
Liechtenstein			2.12	2.13	2.18	2.10	2.10	2.20	2.10	2.10
Luxembourg		3.29	3.00	2.10	2.00	2.00	2.00	2.00	1.90	1.90
Malta			8.30	9.00	8.80	9.00	9.50	8.40	8.40	8.40
Monaco	2.96	2.84	2.87	2.96	2.91	2.87	2.78	2.81	2.92	2.96
Netherlands	3.72	3.00	3.19	3.20	1.90	1.90	1.80	1.80	1.80	1.80
Norway	1.73	1.61	1.67	1.67	1.69	1.66	1.66	1.65	1.62	1.61
Portugal	4.60	4.09	3.60	3.60	3.50	3.30	3.10	3.10	3.00	2.95
Spain	5.57	4.26	3.83	3.82	3.72	3.65	3.51	3.48	3.25	3.14
Sweden										
Switzerland	3.50	3.01	2.50	2.60	2.40	2.50	2.45	2.40	2.40	2.40
Turkey	3.43	4.00	4.20	3.10	3.29	3.28	3.29	3.20	2.90	2.80
United Kingdom										
Eastern Europe										
Albania		2.20	1.70	2.20	2.10	2.10	2.70	2.70	3.00	3.20
Belarus					2.78	2.70	2.77	2.93	3.00	3.05
Bosnia-Herzegovina			2.30	2.30	2.23	2.19	2.14	2.11	2.09	2.07
Bulgaria		3.50	3.90	4.30	4.20	4.30	4.30	4.30	4.10	4.15
Croatia		5.29	5.49	5.50	5.06	5.25	5.08	4.48	4.33	4.22
Czech Republic	2.40	3.10	3.30	3.60	3.80	3.70	3.40	2.80	2.80	2.80
Estonia		1.81	1.53	1.59	1.99	2.04	1.95	1.98	2.01	2.04
Georgia										
Hungary	3.70	3.18	2.86	2.85	2.81	2.79	2.71	2.66	2.63	2.61
Latvia		2.85	2.90	2.80	2.50	2.48	2.32	2.23	2.23	2.23
Lithuania		6.40	4.70	2.18	2.13	1.98	2.10	2.15	2.06	2.04
Macedonia	3.20	3.60	3.90	3.80	4.20	4.20	4.00	3.90	3.80	3.72
Moldova							2.40	2.60	2.90	3.09
Poland	2.30	2.40	3.35	1.94	1.88	1.89	1.91	1.93	1.93	1.93
Romania	2.96	3.40	3.20	3.70	3.60	3.50	3.25	3.20	3.18	3.17
Russia							5.00	4.81	5.30	5.30
Serbia and Montenegro	4.10	4.04	4.20	4.20	4.00	4.10	4.19	4.17	4.17	4.17
Slovakia	3.20	3.40	3.10	3.00	3.20	3.20	2.90	2.80	2.80	2.80
Slovenia		3.73	3.31	3.28	3.24	3.23	3.12	3.01	2.97	2.95
Ukraine			2.70	2.60	2.60	2.60	2.60	2.60	2.60	2.60

Source: *Euromonitor International from World Tourism Organisation*

Table 23.2

Average Tourist Stay in the Country 1990-2007
Nights

	1990	1995	2000	2001	2002	2003	2004	2005	2006	2007
Western Europe										
Austria			4.60	4.60	4.60	4.53	4.40	4.40	4.30	4.30
Belgium										
Cyprus	14.80	11.51	11.00	7.75	7.52	7.42	7.91	7.94	7.52	7.55
Denmark								5.00	5.00	5.00
Finland			2.06	2.09	2.10	2.12	2.10	2.16	2.16	2.17
France	6.90	8.17	7.48	7.31	7.64	7.56	7.47	6.47	6.28	6.17
Germany				2.30	2.30	2.30	2.30	2.20	2.20	2.20
Gibraltar	3.00	4.00	4.30	4.40	4.40	4.40	4.50	4.55	4.59	4.63
Greece				5.90	5.98	5.97	6.00	5.54	5.56	5.58
Iceland			1.80	1.80	1.80	1.80	1.80	1.80	1.80	1.80
Ireland	11.00	8.42	7.40	7.85	7.86	7.71	7.42	7.49	7.60	7.68
Italy						3.99	3.84	3.89	3.81	3.78
Liechtenstein	1.91	2.10	2.10	2.13	2.17	2.10	2.10	2.20	2.10	2.10
Luxembourg		3.00	2.80	2.90	2.80	2.90	2.80	2.70	2.70	2.70
Malta	9.26	9.80	8.40	9.40	9.30	10.20	9.70	9.50	9.50	9.50
Monaco										
Netherlands			2.70	2.66	2.70	2.80	2.60	2.50	2.50	2.50
Norway										
Portugal	7.40	7.00	6.70	6.70	4.70	4.60	4.34	4.39	3.85	3.80
Spain	11.41	12.30	13.41	5.31	5.10	5.02	4.88	4.78	5.20	5.41
Sweden				2.22	2.28	2.28	2.08	2.06	2.33	2.33
Switzerland									2.50	2.50
Turkey	8.33	9.00	4.19	4.14	4.39	4.54	4.53	4.33	3.92	3.69
United Kingdom	10.90	9.40	8.08	8.30	8.20	8.20	8.20	8.30	8.40	8.40
Eastern Europe										
Albania			3.10	2.70	3.97	3.34	2.70	2.30	2.20	2.15
Belarus										
Bosnia-Herzegovina										
Bulgaria	6.00	6.60	8.35	8.35	8.50	8.60	4.20	4.20	4.10	4.15
Croatia				5.87	5.71	5.58	5.39	5.43	5.43	5.43
Czech Republic	3.32	3.13	3.50	3.20	3.30	3.30	3.10	3.10	3.10	3.10
Estonia		1.90	1.90	1.94	1.99	2.04	2.00	2.05	2.15	2.21
Georgia			7.10	7.80	7.80	7.90	7.90	8.12	8.25	8.32
Hungary	6.58	6.39	3.51	3.55	3.44	3.41	3.21	3.13	3.04	2.97
Latvia			2.60	2.62	2.41	2.37	2.20	2.21	2.29	2.35
Lithuania		8.80	6.00	3.00	2.90	2.70	2.59	2.59	2.52	2.47
Macedonia					2.20	2.20	2.20	2.30	2.20	2.20
Moldova							2.50	2.80	3.40	3.64
Poland		4.70	4.80	4.50	3.90	4.10	4.60	4.40	3.40	3.40
Romania			2.48	2.61	2.50	2.50	2.50	2.40	2.30	2.30
Russia							4.38	4.63	5.20	5.30
Serbia and Montenegro										
Slovakia			3.90	3.60	3.60	3.60	3.30	3.20	3.20	3.20
Slovenia	3.10	3.12	3.12	3.13	3.09	3.04	2.91	2.80	2.78	2.77
Ukraine			5.30	4.80	5.00	4.80	4.00	3.80	4.37	4.35

Source: *Euromonitor International from World Tourism Organisation*

Length of Tourist Stay

Table 23.3

Domestic Tourist Nights 1990-2007
'000 nights

	1990	1995	2000	2001	2002	2003	2004	2005	2006	2007
Western Europe										
Austria	15,620	16,302	18,897	19,329	19,302	19,634	19,800	20,329	21,184	21,754
Belgium		3,054	4,045	4,057	4,091	4,061	4,090	4,313	4,737	5,040
Cyprus	178	374	597	729	868	957	1,069	1,040	1,114	1,188
Denmark	16,835	18,727	19,602	20,103	20,953	21,678	21,534	21,914	24,000	25,159
Finland		8,464	9,786	9,882	9,552	9,671	10,032	10,388	10,676	10,964
France	72,556	90,349	114,059	115,576	114,454	115,536	118,134	120,326	123,105	125,421
Germany	234,579	149,628	170,947	171,674	164,383	163,554	165,655	168,843	172,428	175,416
Gibraltar										
Greece	11,346	12,523	14,628	13,290	13,128	13,716	13,280	13,942	14,249	14,441
Iceland		246	296	275	290	299	323	361	387	413
Ireland		6,698	6,786	7,533	7,395	7,829	7,799	8,174	7,978	8,228
Italy	123,975	123,467	136,392	138,559	133,295	135,217	136,845	138,123	140,397	141,660
Liechtenstein		1	3	3	3	3	3	3	3	3
Luxembourg		81	68	72	78	80	85	85	77	78
Malta										
Monaco										
Netherlands	7,102	8,799	14,027	13,608	13,593	13,384	13,761	14,375	15,783	16,663
Norway	8,665	9,862	11,398	11,599	11,482	11,262	11,764	12,349	12,859	13,223
Portugal	7,295	7,580	9,693	9,985	10,336	10,404	10,901	11,370	12,350	12,894
Spain	50,869	58,281	83,382	85,261	86,718	91,295	100,044	106,875	115,088	120,954
Sweden	12,528	14,771	16,586	16,737	16,143	16,235	16,465	17,517	18,606	19,211
Switzerland	13,152	12,316	14,013	14,313	14,196	14,236	13,837	14,622	15,204	15,495
Turkey	6,878	9,624	16,351	14,147	15,152	16,199	18,341	18,807	21,476	23,382
United Kingdom		450,000	576,370	529,600	531,940	490,540	408,950	442,300	400,100	386,033
Eastern Europe										
Albania		122	228	303	390	410	175	244	370	454
Belarus					2,491	2,753	2,926	3,306	3,649	3,913
Bosnia-Herzegovina			248	452	496	494	511	533	583	619
Bulgaria		3,648	3,024	2,842	2,982	3,058	3,423	3,957	4,342	4,663
Croatia		4,370	2,949	2,919	2,691	2,839	2,900	2,862	2,886	2,910
Czech Republic	25,390	10,142	12,358	9,071	10,476	9,779	9,051	8,601	8,854	9,012
Estonia		293	459	489	450	558	691	751	989	1,138
Georgia			2,115	2,179	2,277	2,398	2,476	2,576	2,647	2,715
Hungary	8,768	6,342	7,855	7,754	8,089	8,571	8,391	8,958	9,606	10,104
Latvia		735	669	638	674	669	717	796	855	909
Lithuania		326	293	281	331	342	511	728	934	1,121
Macedonia	738	464	443	266	366	347	289	275	267	260
Moldova			212	253	316	400	1,313	1,432	1,539	1,628
Poland	5,744	3,903	9,352	8,297	8,382	8,813	11,572	12,464	13,910	14,814
Romania		17,957	13,862	14,071	13,369	13,867	13,980	14,094	14,929	15,227
Russia				37,143	35,343	35,499	35,549	40,730	82,630	86,331
Serbia and Montenegro		6,834	5,513	5,297	5,118	4,650	4,915	4,707	4,320	4,191
Slovakia	8,320	2,179	3,768	3,837	4,917	4,789	4,148	3,978	3,936	3,913
Slovenia	1,986	2,066	1,860	1,715	1,714	1,725	1,707	1,653	1,746	1,741
Ukraine			7,986	8,299	8,398	8,411	8,486	8,554	8,611	8,658

Source: *Euromonitor International from World Tourism Organisation*

Table 23.4

International Tourist Nights 1990-2007
'000 nights

	1990	1995	2000	2001	2002	2003	2004	2005	2006	2007
Western Europe										
Austria	94,788	56,198	58,029	58,737	60,249	60,622	60,746	62,396	62,789	63,051
Belgium	7,032	7,895	10,184	10,011	10,410	10,280	10,315	10,297	10,634	10,718
Cyprus	9,426	14,222	16,790	18,070	15,235	13,424	13,554	13,899	13,227	13,131
Denmark	24,330	28,113	26,280	25,456	25,663	26,152	24,925	23,012	23,371	23,627
Finland	2,830	2,926	3,562	3,675	3,721	3,758	3,758	3,887	4,354	4,613
France	38,720	54,339	77,014	75,652	77,602	69,323	70,391	72,054	68,821	69,745
Germany	39,146	28,659	36,354	34,660	34,553	35,172	38,491	40,839	44,921	48,323
Gibraltar		144	138	137	136	136	135	134	134	133
Greece	35,012	38,772	46,212	41,815	40,350	39,760	38,310	40,075	42,459	44,224
Iceland		598	890	908	970	1,070	1,146	1,208	1,341	1,436
Ireland	8,208	12,452	16,903	17,982	17,714	18,039	17,934	17,446	19,080	19,734
Italy	60,301	84,566	97,221	100,322	97,837	93,935	97,175	102,312	107,859	112,482
Liechtenstein		127	131	120	106	105	101	108	115	119
Luxembourg		1,051	1,169	1,174	1,167	1,144	1,195	1,273	1,284	1,293
Malta	9,604	7,632	6,978	7,475	7,021	7,712	7,725	7,603	7,377	7,236
Monaco		626	861	798	765	674	695	803	916	1,010
Netherlands	6,613	9,581	15,695	14,955	14,922	13,798	14,616	15,143	15,976	16,466
Norway	3,802	4,985	4,967	4,815	4,706	4,375	4,596	4,761	4,914	5,023
Portugal	19,349	20,357	24,102	23,578	25,119	23,215	23,002	23,873	25,216	25,384
Spain	68,630	101,182	143,762	143,421	135,836	136,865	134,654	138,762	151,940	158,529
Sweden	3,053	3,696	4,679	4,927	4,868	4,833	5,061	5,382	5,606	5,766
Switzerland	19,957	18,386	19,914	19,273	17,768	16,964	17,247	18,321	19,644	20,422
Turkey	13,271	18,438	28,377	36,307	43,225	40,819	49,614	55,996	46,588	49,779
United Kingdom	196,100	220,300	203,759	189,516	199,285	203,432	227,406	247,587	273,417	289,561
Eastern Europe										
Albania		89	98	91	143	137	85	110	129	142
Belarus					496	538	575	597	688	758
Bosnia-Herzegovina			263	330	392	419	460	485	594	655
Bulgaria		5,279	5,101	6,118	6,985	8,987	10,139	11,471	11,960	12,449
Croatia		4,574	15,125	16,989	16,905	16,830	17,072	18,415	17,807	17,980
Czech Republic	9,350	9,768	12,811	14,703	13,327	13,688	15,881	16,607	17,035	17,392
Estonia		615	1,253	1,341	1,887	2,086	2,602	2,791	2,772	2,828
Georgia			2,730	2,417	2,387	2,314	2,275	2,176	2,135	2,096
Hungary	13,618	9,998	10,514	10,894	10,361	10,040	10,508	10,779	10,046	10,227
Latvia		668	691	837	853	963	1,158	1,507	1,745	1,983
Lithuania		415	570	656	719	766	1,131	1,334	1,451	1,549
Macedonia	474	243	439	197	249	321	329	391	392	413
Moldova		99	85	64	76	84	153	170	202	222
Poland	5,350	3,064	4,944	4,918	4,999	5,450	6,876	7,869	7,911	7,946
Romania	4,238	2,208	2,085	2,301	2,471	2,688	3,211	3,377	3,169	3,280
Russia				10,200	10,564	10,036	10,687	10,696	12,637	12,643
Serbia and Montenegro		673	716	1,047	1,404	1,425	1,715	1,966	2,401	2,568
Slovakia	1,936	2,340	3,138	3,550	4,050	3,989	3,820	4,055	4,362	4,581
Slovenia	1,573	2,059	2,758	2,879	3,049	3,166	3,258	3,322	3,401	3,457
Ukraine			948	1,070	1,453	1,420	1,380	1,395	1,408	1,418

Source: *Euromonitor International from World Tourism Organisation*

Tourism Expenditure | **Table 23.5**

Tourist Expenditure 1980-2007
US$ million

	1980	1985	1990	1995	2000	2002	2003	2004	2005	2006	2007
Western Europe											
Austria	2,847	2,723	7,723	11,657	8,463	9,460	11,757	11,834	10,994	9,348	8,525
Belgium	3,272	2,050	5,471	9,215	9,429	10,185	12,210	13,956	14,814	15,482	15,996
Cyprus	56	78	111	293	413	516	611	810	932	982	1,032
Denmark	1,560	1,410	3,676	4,280	4,669	5,828	6,658	7,269	6,850	7,428	7,841
Finland	544	777	2,740	2,319	1,852	2,006	2,433	2,821	3,057	3,424	3,730
France	6,027	4,557	12,424	16,328	17,906	19,518	23,392	28,703	30,458	31,264	31,936
Germany			29,509	52,194	52,824	53,006	65,234	71,187	74,189	74,123	74,068
Gibraltar											
Greece	190	368	1,090	1,322	4,558	2,436	2,431	2,872	3,039	2,997	3,090
Iceland	42	94	278	282	471	370	521	693	980	1,076	1,172
Ireland	535	429	1,159	2,030	2,600	3,755	4,736	5,177	6,074	6,862	7,519
Italy	1,907	1,880	14,045	12,420	15,685	16,924	20,589	20,460	22,370	23,152	23,804
Liechtenstein	3										
Luxembourg					1,318	1,942	2,423	2,911	2,976	3,136	3,269
Malta	41	50	134	200	200	154	215	256	268	321	359
Monaco	6										
Netherlands	4,664	3,416	7,376	11,455	12,191	12,976	14,593	16,346	16,082	17,087	17,645
Norway	1,310	1,722	3,679	4,221	4,558	5,189	6,716	8,489	10,182	11,586	12,862
Portugal	290	235	867	2,141	2,228	2,125	2,409	2,763	3,050	3,298	3,453
Spain	1,229	1,010	4,254	4,461	5,572	7,295	9,071	12,153	15,046	16,697	17,876
Sweden	2,235	1,967	6,134	5,621	8,048	7,301	8,296	10,130	10,771	11,543	12,186
Switzerland	2,357	2,399	5,817	7,346	6,335	5,537	6,883	8,104	8,837	9,919	10,640
Turkey	115	324	520	912	1,713	1,881	2,113	2,524	2,872	2,743	2,917
United Kingdom	6,410	6,369	19,063	24,268	38,262	41,744	47,853	56,444	59,532	63,319	66,024
Eastern Europe											
Albania				5	272	366	489	642	786	965	1,128
Belarus				87	243	559	473	538	604	735	836
Bosnia-Herzegovina					78	85	106	117	122	158	181
Bulgaria	37	74	257	195	538	717	1,033	1,363	1,309	1,474	1,601
Croatia				421	568	781	672	848	754	737	746
Czech Republic				1,633	1,276	1,597	1,934	2,280	2,405	2,670	2,891
Estonia				91	204	231	319	400	448	592	682
Georgia					110	149	130	147	169	167	170
Hungary	196	208	477	1,070	1,651	2,133	2,594	2,848	2,382	2,126	1,984
Latvia				24	247	230	328	378	584	702	793
Lithuania				108	253	326	471	636	744	909	1,047
Macedonia				27	34	45	48	54	60	71	79
Moldova				56	73	95	99	113	141	187	216
Poland	380	184	423	5,500	3,313	3,202	2,801	3,841	4,341	5,760	6,405
Romania			103	697	425	396	479	539	925	1,310	1,448
Russia				11,599	8,848	11,284	12,880	15,285	17,434	18,235	18,903
Serbia and Montenegro											
Slovakia				330	296	442	573	745	846	1,055	1,186
Slovenia				524	511	608	753	868	950	974	991
Ukraine					576	657	789	2,463	2,805	2,834	2,858

Source: Euromonitor International from World Tourism Organisation

Table 23.6

Tourism Receipts 1980-2007

US$ million

	1980	1985	1990	1995	2000	2002	2003	2004	2005	2006	2007
Western Europe											
Austria	6,442	5,084	13,410	14,593	9,998	11,136	13,842	15,290	15,589	16,510	17,168
Belgium	1,810	1,663	3,718	5,719	6,592	6,935	8,193	9,209	9,842	10,242	10,550
Cyprus	203	380	1,258	1,783	1,941	1,927	2,097	2,239	2,318	2,420	2,505
Denmark	1,337	1,326	3,322	3,672	3,671	4,791	5,271	5,652	5,293	5,587	5,832
Finland	677	501	1,170	1,676	1,406	1,578	1,870	2,067	2,180	2,380	2,547
France	8,197	7,942	20,185	27,527	30,981	32,437	36,619	44,895	43,942	46,499	48,630
Germany	6,715	5,018	10,493	18,028	18,611	19,278	23,125	27,613	29,121	32,846	35,950
Gibraltar	6	15	112	87	82	80	79	78	77	77	77
Greece	1,734	1,428	2,587	4,136	9,219	9,909	10,766	12,715	13,578	14,402	15,089
Iceland	23	41	139	167	227	256	319	370	408	439	465
Ireland	574	531	1,447	2,688	3,387	3,765	3,862	4,375	4,782	5,369	5,858
Italy	8,213	8,758	20,016	27,723	27,493	26,873	31,247	35,378	35,319	38,257	40,356
Liechtenstein	16	20									
Luxembourg					1,686	2,406	2,994	3,653	3,614	3,626	3,636
Malta	329	149	496	660	610	614	722	770	754	770	781
Monaco	260	300									
Netherlands	1,662	1,661	3,636	5,762	7,197	7,710	9,164	10,311	10,383	11,381	11,935
Norway	751	755	1,570	2,386	2,050	2,179	2,500	2,980	3,332	3,613	3,868
Portugal	1,147	1,137	3,555	4,339	5,243	5,798	6,622	7,672	7,676	8,388	8,833
Spain	6,968	8,151	18,593	25,388	31,454	31,880	39,634	45,067	47,681	51,292	53,871
Sweden	962	1,190	2,916	3,462	4,064	4,710	5,304	6,163	7,361	9,133	10,610
Switzerland	3,149	3,145	6,789	9,365	7,576	7,260	8,617	9,600	10,095	10,640	11,094
Turkey	327	1,482	3,308	4,957	7,636	11,901	13,203	15,888	18,152	16,853	17,985
United Kingdom	6,922	7,120	14,003	18,554	21,769	20,549	22,668	28,202	30,577	33,888	36,253
Eastern Europe											
Albania				7	398	487	522	735	854	1,012	1,144
Belarus				23	93	234	267	270	253	272	285
Bosnia-Herzegovina				7	233	288	377	481	512	592	659
Bulgaria	260	343	320	473	1,074	1,096	1,621	2,202	2,412	2,610	2,762
Croatia				1,351	2,758	3,812	6,310	6,727	7,370	7,990	8,507
Czech Republic	338	307	470	2,875	2,973	2,964	3,566	4,187	4,623	5,026	5,362
Estonia				353	505	555	671	887	948	1,035	1,108
Georgia					97	126	147	177	241	313	373
Hungary	504	512	1,000	1,723	3,733	3,728	4,061	4,034	4,120	4,254	4,357
Latvia				20	131	161	222	267	341	480	579
Lithuania				124	391	505	638	776	921	1,038	1,155
Macedonia			45	19	38	39	57	72	84	129	144
Moldova				57	39	50	54	91	103	112	120
Poland	282	118	358	6,600	5,677	4,999	5,450	6,876	7,869	7,911	7,946
Romania	136	182	106	590	359	335	449	503	1,052	1,308	1,415
Russia	325	163	410	4,312	3,430	4,168	4,502	5,530	5,870	7,628	8,361
Serbia and Montenegro				42	30	97	201	253	292	299	308
Slovakia				620	433	736	865	901	1,210	1,513	1,702
Slovenia				1,082	961	1,086	1,342	1,625	1,795	1,797	1,799
Ukraine					736	788	935	2,560	3,125	3,485	3,725

Source: Euromonitor International from World Tourism Organisation

Table 23.7

Tourist Accommodation

Total Number of Rooms in Tourist Accommodation 1990-2007
'000

	1990	1995	2000	2001	2002	2003	2004	2005	2006	2007
Western Europe										
Austria	317.8	309.7	286.8	288.3	282.7	282.6	290.5	289.9	282.0	278.1
Belgium		59.7	61.9	61.8	62.7	63.2	64.0	66.6	67.8	68.7
Cyprus	24.5	35.0	43.4	43.3	44.5	44.9	45.5	45.2	44.4	43.9
Denmark	35.6	38.3	39.5	40.2	41.2	41.7	43.2	42.8	43.4	44.1
Finland	46.5	54.0	54.9	55.3	54.9	55.8	53.5	53.3	54.5	55.0
France	547.0	596.7	589.2	600.5	603.6	603.3	615.4	613.8	612.4	611.6
Germany		819.0	877.1	884.5	891.9	892.3	889.3	890.2	897.0	902.7
Gibraltar										
Greece	232.8	283.4	313.0	320.5	330.3	339.5	351.9	358.7	364.2	372.6
Iceland	3.3	4.9	6.0	6.2	6.8	7.3	7.5	8.0	8.0	8.1
Ireland	22.8	36.8	60.4	61.2	62.8	63.1	62.4	64.2	63.4	64.0
Italy	938.1	944.1	966.1	975.6	986.3	999.7	1,011.8	1,020.5	1,034.7	1,046.6
Liechtenstein			0.6	0.6	0.6	0.6	0.6	0.6	0.6	0.7
Luxembourg	7.9	8.2	7.7	7.7	7.6	7.5	7.4	7.5	7.5	7.5
Malta	34.2									
Monaco			2.2	2.2	2.2	2.2	2.2	2.6	2.6	2.6
Netherlands	60.7	71.3	82.0	84.1	86.2	88.1	93.0	94.4	94.5	94.6
Norway	54.0	60.0	65.2	66.4	66.7	67.1	66.4	67.5	69.5	70.1
Portugal	79.4	90.0	97.7	99.1	99.8	106.0	106.4	112.9	117.6	120.2
Spain	603.0	564.6	677.1	685.7	713.5	740.9	767.0	797.4	810.6	821.6
Sweden	82.0	100.0	96.1	99.3	95.1	96.4	98.9	100.2	101.7	102.9
Switzerland	146.9	143.5	140.8	140.6	139.9	140.0	133.6	127.4	127.5	127.6
Turkey	82.1	133.2	155.4	176.6	189.5	201.5	217.1	230.6	241.7	250.9
United Kingdom		440.0	463.0	465.8	591.3	599.9	606.9	518.0	593.1	600.1
Eastern Europe										
Albania		3.0	3.0	3.9	4.1	4.2	3.4	3.9	4.3	4.6
Belarus			2.0	2.0	12.5	12.7	12.9	12.9	13.3	13.5
Bosnia-Herzegovina		1.1	4.4	7.0	7.3	7.7	8.4	8.7	9.0	9.3
Bulgaria		57.0								
Croatia		85.4	81.3	74.1	77.3	77.1	79.2	80.7	76.0	77.3
Czech Republic	63.1	53.7	96.4	95.5	96.7	98.1	98.8	100.0	101.6	102.9
Estonia		4.4	7.6	8.5	10.8	12.4	15.0	16.6	17.8	19.0
Georgia			8.7	9.4	9.6	9.6	9.7	6.8	10.0	10.1
Hungary	34.0	47.8	57.9	59.9	62.4	64.1	64.3	66.1	66.9	67.7
Latvia		5.4	6.4	7.0	7.2	7.6	8.8	9.2	9.7	10.1
Lithuania		5.3	5.9	5.6	6.2	7.4	9.5	10.1	10.8	11.4
Macedonia	6.0	6.0	6.6	6.7	6.8	6.8	6.9	6.9	7.0	7.1
Moldova		2.6	3.0	2.9	2.8	2.6	2.6	2.5	2.5	2.4
Poland	43.4	48.2	60.9	60.7	65.7	68.6	83.0	84.9	88.4	90.0
Romania	87.1	95.5	95.4	95.2	95.1	97.3	101.6	105.8	111.8	116.1
Russia		214.1	183.4	179.3	178.3	177.2	178.6	199.0	208.3	213.5
Serbia and Montenegro	37.9	37.9	37.4	37.8	37.9	37.1	38.7	39.7	40.0	40.1
Slovakia	14.5	23.4	28.4	31.7	34.6	35.9	35.5	35.7	35.9	36.2
Slovenia		16.2	16.3	15.0	15.1	15.5	15.8	15.8	16.4	16.6
Ukraine			44.8	43.5	35.1	32.6	32.6	33.4	33.8	34.2

Source: Euromonitor International from World Tourism Organisation

Table 23.8

Hotel Bed Occupancy Rates 1990-2007

% of beds occupied

	1990	1995	2000	2001	2002	2003	2004	2005	2006	2007
Western Europe										
Austria	31.8	33.3	34.9	34.9	35.9	36.1	34.6	35.8	35.6	35.4
Belgium		31.3	30.5	30.1	30.3	30.5	30.6	30.6	30.6	30.7
Cyprus	62.3	58.6	65.1	73.9	63.0	57.5	57.6	61.6	59.9	60.0
Denmark	34.7	35.5	37.4	36.6	36.4	35.7	35.6	36.2	36.2	36.1
Finland	48.6	45.0	47.8	48.0	47.0	46.8	46.3	47.8	49.9	50.9
France	52.4	49.5	60.3	60.5	60.3	58.4	58.6	59.1	60.4	61.1
Germany	42.8	33.9	35.0	34.7	33.2	33.5	34.2	35.0	35.9	36.7
Gibraltar	40.8	39.2	37.8	37.8	37.8	38.2	38.4	38.6	38.7	38.8
Greece		56.6	65.0	63.4	61.8	60.7	55.6	58.6	58.4	58.2
Iceland	41.0	44.8	46.0	45.2	44.3	42.3	43.3	45.0	47.0	48.7
Ireland			65.0	61.0	59.0	60.0	60.0	62.0	64.0	65.0
Italy	41.5	40.0	42.7	43.2	39.6	39.6	39.8	40.1	40.8	41.2
Liechtenstein	33.4	28.4	30.9	29.2	26.7	25.3	24.2	25.6	25.6	25.6
Luxembourg		37.9	51.1	25.9	25.6	25.1	28.2	29.5	29.9	30.2
Malta	56.4	55.5	47.0	52.7	48.3	53.7	52.8	52.8	51.8	51.2
Monaco	55.7	49.5	71.5	65.9	63.8	59.0	58.0	58.4	58.8	59.1
Netherlands	38.5	35.3	48.5	46.2	45.5	42.8	42.1	42.1	45.3	45.3
Norway	35.4	36.7	37.5	37.0	36.3	35.5	37.0	38.1	37.3	37.5
Portugal	29.9	38.0	42.2	41.7	39.3	38.0	38.6	46.6	48.3	49.2
Spain	52.3	60.7	58.9	58.1	55.3	54.5	53.5	54.2	56.4	57.3
Sweden	31.0	32.0	35.0	34.4	35.2	34.3	34.3	35.0	36.1	36.3
Switzerland	44.0	38.5	42.3	41.8	40.1	38.7	39.2	39.7	41.7	42.4
Turkey	48.2	47.0	36.8	46.7	48.7	46.9	50.1	52.4	47.3	48.4
United Kingdom	57.0	44.0	43.0	42.0	44.0	44.0	45.0	44.0	47.0	47.5
Eastern Europe										
Albania		32.4	20.0	29.0	41.0	42.0	39.0	46.0	60.0	67.8
Belarus					35.4	38.2	40.5	45.5	49.3	52.5
Bosnia-Herzegovina			15.0	12.1	11.3	11.1	11.0	10.6	10.3	10.1
Bulgaria		36.5	28.3	29.0	30.7	34.8	35.9	37.6	35.8	36.8
Croatia	16.6	11.1	24.8	30.3	25.5	27.8	27.5	28.7	34.8	34.9
Czech Republic	46.0	28.8	46.0	45.1	39.7	35.4	37.0	35.8	35.8	35.8
Estonia		35.0	48.0	49.0	45.0	47.0	47.0	47.0	47.0	47.0
Georgia			34.0	71.0	71.0	72.0	72.0	72.3	73.4	74.7
Hungary	55.4	45.4	46.7	41.5	40.0	38.6	41.0	42.1	42.4	42.6
Latvia			32.0	32.0	31.1	31.7	31.5	36.4	35.6	35.6
Lithuania		23.0	28.4	31.7	35.2	32.5	36.7	40.8	42.1	43.2
Macedonia	10.9	10.6	15.0	7.8	10.2	11.2	10.3	11.1	10.8	10.8
Moldova		17.9	19.8	17.1	14.0	22.1	25.2	26.6	30.9	32.6
Poland	39.5	42.7	39.6	37.9	35.7	35.7	32.2	40.5	42.2	43.0
Romania		52.1	35.2	38.4	34.0	34.6	36.7	33.4	33.6	33.7
Russia		38.0	37.0	38.0	37.0	34.0	37.0	34.0	35.0	35.5
Serbia and Montenegro	37.8	24.6	21.7	21.8	22.5	21.5	21.9	21.3	21.3	21.1
Slovakia	48.7	31.9	29.2	33.2	40.0	38.7	34.7	35.0	35.7	36.1
Slovenia		33.4	39.4	46.4	47.4	47.6	48.0	47.6	47.6	47.6
Ukraine			24.0	25.0	26.0	30.0	31.0	33.0	34.1	35.0

Source: Euromonitor International from World Tourism Organisation

Tourist Accommodation

Table 23.9

Total Number of Bed Places in Tourist Accommodation 1990-2007
'000

	1990	1995	2000	2001	2002	2003	2004	2005	2006	2007
Western Europe										
Austria	650.6	646.1	642.6	642.8	628.7	631.1	637.1	639.4	643.7	647.4
Belgium		154.7	158.6	158.7	161.5	163.7	169.6	168.4	172.9	174.9
Cyprus	51.8	73.1	84.5	87.8	90.1	91.1	92.2	91.3	89.5	88.4
Denmark	88.5	99.0	102.1	103.1	105.2	106.1	109.1	108.1	108.9	109.6
Finland	97.4	113.0	117.3	118.5	117.9	120.1	120.1	115.2	118.2	119.5
France	1,082.1	1,193.3	1,178.3	1,201.0	1,207.2	1,206.6	1,230.8	1,227.6	1,224.8	1,223.1
Germany	1,110.0	1,490.9	1,649.2	1,659.7	1,671.1	1,672.2	1,667.9	1,678.3	1,690.9	1,701.5
Gibraltar										
Greece	438.4	535.8	594.0	608.1	626.9	644.9	668.3	682.1	693.3	702.6
Iceland	6.3	8.8	12.5	12.6	14.0	14.9	15.5	16.6	16.8	17.1
Ireland	45.2	79.8	140.2	141.4	145.6	146.9	145.3	149.6	148.8	151.0
Italy	1,703.5	1,738.0	1,854.1	1,891.3	1,929.5	1,969.5	1,999.7	2,028.5	2,087.0	2,135.8
Liechtenstein	1.2	1.2	1.2	1.2	1.1	1.2	1.2	1.2	1.3	1.3
Luxembourg			14.7	14.6	14.5	14.6	14.2	14.2	14.2	14.2
Malta	37.9	37.3	40.6	40.7	39.8	41.4	39.8	39.4	39.4	39.4
Monaco				3.5	3.5	3.2	3.7	5.3	5.3	5.3
Netherlands	111.3	142.5	173.0	174.0	177.4	180.2	189.8	192.2	192.1	192.0
Norway	112.7	131.2	140.6	143.8	143.6	143.8	141.1	143.6	151.3	153.8
Portugal	179.3	204.1	223.0	228.7	239.9	245.8	253.9	263.8	264.0	266.3
Spain	1,102.3	1,074.0	1,315.7	1,333.4	1,395.4	1,451.9	1,511.6	1,578.6	1,615.3	1,645.8
Sweden	161.9	222.5	188.3	194.8	180.8	184.8	190.0	197.5	201.3	204.5
Switzerland	269.8	265.0	259.7	260.1	259.0	258.7	251.3	239.2	240.4	241.2
Turkey	165.0	274.1	332.3	366.6	393.7	418.2	452.4	481.7	507.2	528.5
United Kingdom	993.5	879.7	1,111.0	1,130.0	1,188.0	1,062.0	1,223.0	1,062.0	1,201.7	1,211.4
Eastern Europe										
Albania		5.8	5.9	7.7	8.0	8.4	6.6	7.6	8.4	9.0
Belarus		1.0	14.4	18.8	23.1	23.6	23.6	23.5	24.1	24.4
Bosnia-Herzegovina		1.9	9.1	14.1	14.7	15.9	17.3	18.2	20.0	21.6
Bulgaria	114.3	114.2	120.2	116.0	132.0	144.0	171.0	221.1	252.3	274.6
Croatia		205.2	199.5	182.0	187.9	193.5	199.0	203.5	163.2	166.8
Czech Republic		131.2	236.5	218.6	223.4	226.8	229.7	232.2	236.1	239.3
Estonia		8.5	18.6	20.3	22.8	27.5	32.9	38.1	40.9	43.6
Georgia			17.2	18.3	17.6	17.7	18.1	14.0	20.5	20.9
Hungary	85.3	119.1	143.6	148.2	154.6	158.6	158.0	162.2	158.8	160.9
Latvia		14.0	11.9	13.1	13.7	15.0	17.9	19.2	19.7	20.0
Lithuania		10.5	11.1	10.7	12.0	14.3	18.6	19.9	21.5	22.8
Macedonia	15.1	15.0	16.1	16.3	16.5	16.3	16.5	16.4	16.8	16.9
Moldova		5.3	5.6	5.5	5.5	4.7	4.9	4.9	4.5	4.4
Poland	90.4	93.3	120.3	118.2	127.6	134.3	165.3	169.6	178.1	181.9
Romania	168.0	205.7	199.3	199.3	197.3	201.6	207.8	216.5	228.1	236.4
Russia		426.1	346.1	338.4	343.3	364.0	344.4	414.1	431.0	445.0
Serbia and Montenegro	83.7	85.6	78.6	79.6	79.5	77.5	83.0	85.7	86.2	86.5
Slovakia	33.6	53.9	73.0	82.2	87.6	90.8	90.0	90.1	91.0	91.6
Slovenia		33.9	33.5	30.5	30.7	32.0	32.7	33.2	34.4	35.1
Ukraine			102.9	100.7	90.3	86.2	84.3	86.8	88.2	89.4

Source: Euromonitor International from World Tourism Organisation

Table 23.10

International Tourist Arrivals 1990-2007

'000

	1990	1995	2000	2001	2002	2003	2004	2005	2006	2007
Western Europe										
Austria		17,173	17,982	18,180	18,611	19,078	19,373	19,952	20,261	20,570
Belgium		5,523	6,403	6,398	6,720	6,690	6,710	6,747	6,867	6,953
Cyprus	1,676	2,253	2,912	2,841	2,495	2,416	2,478	2,657	2,629	2,757
Denmark	4,180	3,417	3,445	3,684	3,436	3,474	4,421	4,699	4,716	4,733
Finland			3,789	4,252	4,687	4,527	4,854	5,038	5,345	5,601
France	52,497	60,033	77,190	75,202	77,012	75,048	75,121	75,908	79,083	80,671
Germany										
Gibraltar	4,373	5,505	6,786	6,962	7,127	7,305	7,430	7,600	7,771	7,926
Greece	9,310	10,130	13,095	14,057	14,180	13,969	13,313	14,276	16,039	17,018
Iceland	354	473	634	672	705	771	836	871	971	1,042
Ireland	3,666	4,821	6,646	6,353	6,476	6,764	6,953	7,333	8,001	8,446
Italy	60,301	55,706	62,702	60,960	63,561	63,026	58,480	59,230	66,353	67,540
Liechtenstein	72	59	62	57	49	49	49	50	55	58
Luxembourg	694	768	852	836	885	867	878	913	908	917
Malta	872	1,116	1,216	1,180	1,134	1,127	1,156	1,171	1,124	1,133
Monaco	246	233	300	270	263	235	250	286	313	330
Netherlands		6,574	10,003	9,500	9,595	9,181	9,646	10,012	10,739	11,143
Norway	1,955	2,880	3,104	3,073	3,111	3,269	3,629	3,824	3,945	4,038
Portugal	18,422	23,065	28,014	28,150	27,194	27,532	21,194	21,172	22,588	23,473
Spain		38,803	47,897	50,094	52,327	50,854	52,430	55,914	58,190	59,816
Sweden	5,227	7,378	7,351	7,436	7,458	7,627	7,720	7,815	7,937	8,031
Switzerland	8,015	6,946	7,821	7,455	6,866	6,530	6,397	7,229	7,863	8,259
Turkey	6,389	7,727	10,429	11,619	13,256	14,030	17,517	21,125	19,820	20,271
United Kingdom	18,255	23,537	25,209	22,835	24,180	24,715	27,755	29,971	32,713	33,768
Eastern Europe										
Albania		249	317	354	470	557	645	748	937	1,072
Belarus		161	60	61	63	64	67	91	89	91
Bosnia-Herzegovina		36	106	139	160	165	190	217	256	289
Bulgaria	10,330	8,005	4,922	5,104	5,563	6,241	6,982	7,282	7,499	7,696
Croatia		16,100	37,226	40,129	41,737	42,857	44,974	45,762	47,733	49,376
Czech Republic	46,607	98,060	104,246	103,070	97,606	94,985	95,897	93,942	93,431	92,843
Estonia		2,110	3,310	3,230	3,253	3,378	3,419	3,617	3,660	3,704
Georgia		85	387	302	298	313	368	560	983	1,265
Hungary	37,632	39,240	31,142	30,679	31,739	31,412	33,934	36,172	38,318	39,969
Latvia		1,633	1,882	2,061	2,297	2,524	3,127	3,791	4,649	5,185
Lithuania		609	1,240	1,271	1,428	1,492	1,801	2,000	2,180	2,309
Macedonia		2,628	2,864	1,730	2,079	2,183	2,594	3,246	3,369	3,446
Moldova		33	19	16	20	24	26	25	14	14
Poland	18,211	82,244	84,515	61,431	50,735	52,130	61,918	64,606	65,115	65,433
Romania	6,533	5,445	5,264	4,937	4,794	5,594	6,599	5,839	6,037	6,178
Russia	7,204	10,290	21,206	21,595	23,309	22,521	22,064	22,201	22,486	22,664
Serbia and Montenegro		223	228	351	448	481	580	725	847	908
Slovakia		12,532	12,217	11,865	11,631	11,475	12,610	13,880	14,518	14,837
Slovenia		732	1,090	1,219	1,302	1,373	1,499	1,555	1,617	1,661
Ukraine			6,425	9,167	12,793	12,514	15,629	17,630	18,900	19,958

Source: Euromonitor International from World Tourism Organisation

Tourist Arrivals

Table 23.11

Tourist Arrivals by Method 2007
'000

	Air	Rail	Road	Sea	Total
Western Europe					
Austria					20,570
Belgium	5,986			967	6,953
Denmark					4,733
Finland	2,217	79	1,667	1,639	5,601
France	18,904	5,062	48,710	7,995	80,671
Germany	68,725				
Greece	12,212	84	3,651	2,393	17,018
Ireland	6,655		774	1,018	8,446
Italy	21,905	1,934	41,766	1,935	67,540
Netherlands					11,143
Norway	1,762	85	1,481	710	4,038
Portugal	6,998		16,475		23,473
Spain	43,631	289	14,205	1,692	59,816
Sweden					8,031
Switzerland					8,259
Turkey	14,406	74	4,302	1,490	20,271
United Kingdom	25,381	3,372	3,365	5,015	33,768
Eastern Europe					
Belarus					91
Bulgaria	2,362	186	4,966	182	7,696
Croatia	2,084	318	45,895	1,079	49,376
Czech Republic	5,896	2,719	84,228		92,843
Estonia	222	34	1,084	2,364	3,704
Hungary	2,059	1,613	36,054	243	39,969
Latvia	715	173	4,040	258	5,185
Lithuania	424	477	1,228	180	2,309
Poland	2,761	1,717	60,614	340	65,433
Romania	1,148	323	4,493	214	6,178
Russia	4,461	7,245	9,842	1,116	22,664
Slovakia	17	63	14,753	3	14,837
Slovenia	320	49	1,291	2	1,661
Ukraine	1,117	7,079	11,502	260	19,958

Source: *Euromonitor International from World Tourism Organisation*

Table 23.12

Tourist Arrivals by Region 2007

'000

	Africa	Americas	East Asia /Pacific	Europe	Middle East	South Asia
Western Europe						
Austria	46	856	812	18,714	86	55
Belgium	67	419	310	6,103	22	33
Denmark		225	98	4,410		
Finland	14	171	259	5,145	4	8
France	1,237	5,674	3,405	69,967	388	
Germany	179	2,987	2,335	19,575	217	
Greece	32	544	335	16,026	80	1
Ireland	51	1,117	250	7,029		
Italy	259	3,645	1,211	36,250	252	194
Netherlands	96	1,375	750	8,921		
Norway		186	40	3,812		
Portugal		1,269	112	21,865		227
Spain	100	2,451	264	56,895	33	73
Sweden	66	490	429	7,046		
Switzerland	89	981	941	6,038	89	121
Turkey	160	480	492	17,520	660	960
United Kingdom	724	5,334	2,384	24,301	487	538
Eastern Europe						
Belarus		6	3	91	1	1
Bulgaria	3	93	41	7,530	15	14
Croatia		1,228	978	47,170		
Czech Republic	20	463	553	5,481		
Estonia	1	121	26	3,555		
Hungary	18	542	307	39,102		
Latvia	1	22	21	5,138	1	1
Lithuania	5	43	53	2,207		
Poland	16	487	213	64,692	8	16
Romania	9	176	63	5,887	26	16
Russia	29	488	1,404	21,017	35	73
Slovakia	28	359	635	13,807		9
Slovenia	1	69	53	1,537		1
Ukraine	12	149	43	19,700	23	15

Source: *Euromonitor International from World Tourism Organisation*

Index

K

L

M